ANCIENT MAN:

A HANDBOOK
OF PUZZLING ARTIFACTS

Compiled by

WILLIAM R. CORLISS

Illustrated by John C. Holden

Published and Distributed by

The Sourcebook Project   Glen Arm, Md. 21057

ISBN 0-915554-03-8

LC 77-99243

NOTICE

This handbook is one of a series published by the
Sourcebook Project, P. O. Box 107, Glen Arm,
MD 21057. The handbooks and closely related
loose-leaf sourcebooks may be purchased directly
from the Project. Write for details and prices.

First printing: March 1978

Printed in the United States of America

TABLE OF CONTENTS

Chapter 6. BIOLOGICAL EVIDENCE

Chapter 7. MYTHS AND LEGENDS

PREFACE

The primary objective of this handbook is to provide libraries and individuals with a wide selection of reliable descriptions of unusual artifacts of ancient man. To meet this goal, I have analyzed hundreds of volumes of archeological journals as well as the complete files of Nature and Science. The result of this research is an incomparable collection of information on the frontiers of archeology. From this assemblage, I have selected the most interesting and controversial for this book.

My criteria for selecting "puzzling" data were: (1) the information contradicted current archeological theories, or (2) the article raised personal questions not answered adequately to my knowledge. Usually both criteria were satisfied simultaneously. Much of the information printed herein will prove controversial, particularly that selected from amateur archeological and so-called Fortean publications. It will soon become obvious to the reader that secondary objectives are the posing of challenges to establishment science and the stimulation of useful controversy.

I make no claim to completeness because new and relevant material is being discovered constantly as my search of the literature continues. Indeed, the near-infinite mine of museum reports, university theses, and foreign journals has scarcely been touched. Even so, I have collected much more intriguing archeological information than I can conveniently publish here. However, the complete master file is being published in looseleaf "sourcebooks." The Sourcebook Project welcomes inquiries concerning these cumulative sourcebooks.

The looseleaf sourcebooks were, in fact, the first publications of the Sourcebook Project. Although thousands of these notebooks have been sold to libraries, feedback from librarians indicated that casebound books would be more acceptable. Such suggestions were a major factor in the decision to publish selections from our collection in a series of casebound handbooks.

My hope is that this handbook will become a standard reference work on the frontiers of archeology. To this end, I have utilized reports taken primarily from scientific journals. The screening provided by editors and referees of these publications helps to minimize hoaxes and errors. In expectation that establishment archeology is too conservative and too confined by dogmas, I have introduced a handful of articles from fringe periodicals and books that are doubtless considered offbeat and "wild" by most professional archeologists.

The book's organization is also unconventional. Rather than categorize data according to cultures, time periods, or similar pigeonholes, dictated in part by prevailing dogmas, I have simply arranged the information according to the nature of the artifact. Thus, all stone circles are described in the same section, regardless of geographical location, supposed time of construction, or assumed purpose. Many global similarities become apparent in this way.

Most of the 240 illustrations consist of line drawings by John C. Holden and are based on sketches and photos in the original articles. Since many of the articles are decades old, it was impossible to ferret out all original photos. Actually, in the older literature, line drawings predominate in any case.

Since the bulk of this handbook consists of direct quotations from original sources, I hasten to acknowledge the many writers of papers, letters-to-the-editor, and sundry publications who have contributed these descriptions of artifacts. When lengthy quotations are taken from publications still protected by copyright, permissions have been obtained.

Readers deeply interested in the subjects covered so fleetingly in this book should subscribe to some of the key publications quoted. To facilitate such contacts, I list below the addresses of the more important and interesting journals quoted in the main text:

AMERICAN ANTHROPOLOGIST, American Anthropological Association, 1703 New Hampshire Ave., NW, Washington, DC 20009
AMERICAN ANTIQUITY, Society for American Archeology, 1703 New Hampshire Ave., NW, Washington, DC 20009
ANTIQUITY, St. John's College, Cambridge CB2 1TP, ENGLAND
ARCHAEOLOGY, Archaeological Institute of America, 260 West Broadway, New York, NY 10013
CURRENT ANTHROPOLOGY, Editorial Office, University of British Columbia, Vancouver, B.C., V6T 1W5, CANADA
EARLY SITES RESEARCH SOCIETY, BULLETIN, RFD 2, Danielson, CT 06239
EPIGRAPHIC SOCIETY, OCCASIONAL PAPERS, 6 Woodland St., Arlington, MA 02174
INFO JOURNAL, International Fortean Organization, 7317 Baltimore Ave., College Park, MD 20740
MAN, Royal Anthropological Institute, 6 Burlington Gardens, London, W1X 2EX, ENGLAND
NATURE, 4 Little Essex St., London, WC2R 3LF, ENGLAND
NEARA JOURNAL, New England Antiquities Research Association, 4 Smith St., Milford, NH 03055
PURSUIT, Society for the Investigation of the Unexplained, Columbia, NJ 07832
SCIENCE, American Association for the Advancement of Science, 1515 Massachusetts Ave., NW, Washington, DC 20005

William R. Corliss

Glen Arm, Maryland
January 2, 1978

Chapter 1

THE
ENGINEERING STRUCTURES
OF ANCIENT MAN

INTRODUCTION

The Seven Wonders of the Ancient World were all massive, complex structures reared by able engineers. Pyramids, waterworks, great walls, road systems, and similar constructions convey forcefully the ability of a people to design and carry out large enterprises involving large labor forces and immense volumes of intractible materials. That the ancient Greeks and Romans could do these things is well known. Using the same yardsticks, we find that similar, even more impressive "wonders" were constructed all over the world long before classical antiquity.

The primary implication of an ancient engineering structure is usually that of precocious technology and/or impressive social infrastructure. But two other types of anomalies may exist: (1) the structures may indicate a geographical diffusion of ideas and techniques that does not square with current anthropological theory; and (2) the apparent purposes of the structures may be mysterious or they may infer unexpected scientific or religious objectives.

It is important to point out that, although this is the largest chapter in this handbook, only a fraction of the puzzling ancient structures are described. In addition, ancient man may have built even more impressive structures of materials less durable than stone. What will be left of the Wonders of the Modern World 5,000-10,000 years from now?

STANDING STONES AND DOLMENS

A universal and perpetual human urge is the erection of monoliths and other simple stone structures. From ancient man we have inherited many thousands of menhirs (single standing stones, dolmens (tabular stones supported by other stones), rocking stones, and similar stone structures. Not all standing stones and dolmens are incredibly ancient, for the practice of raising simple stonework has persisted down into historical times, especially in India. The main purposes of menhirs and dolmens have probably not changed down the millennia; namely, the commemoration of an individual or event, as a geographical marker or a religious symbol, etc.

These simple stones are anomalous when: (1) they seem to betoken a common, worldwide ancient culture; or (2) they possess hard-to-plumb purposes. The examples described below hint mainly at a global megalithic culture 3,000-5,000 years ago, although a good case could probably be made for the separate, independent origins for such elementary constructions.

For descriptions of the more complex stone circles and rows, the reader should consult later sections in this chapter.

• North America

A REMARKABLE STANDING-STONES SITE LOCATED
Anonymous; *NEARA Newsletter*, 6:40, 1971.

Thanks to some of our valued contacts in the Massachusetts Archaeological Society, NEARA has located a potentially very important standing-stones site on a mountaintop in the northern Berkshires. Due to the necessity of averting vandalization of the site pending a full and thorough investigation, it is not possible at this time to disclose the exact location. First visited by NEARA members Andrew E. Rothovius and William German in May, the site was surveyed by President Stone and Chief Archaeologist Whittall in July. It comprises a half-dozen standing stones, shaped and tapered to points---as in similar West European stones---and set up on the crest of the mountain in a pattern suggesting orientation on the celestial North Pole. In addition, there are about 15 stones that have fallen, including a giant menhir 17-1/2 feet long. It will be necessary to determine the pattern in which these fallen stones originally stood, and to excavate the thin topsoil of the mountaintop for any surviving artifacts, before any determination can be arrived at regarding the antiquity and purpose of the site.

THE HASSANEGHK DOLMEN
Whittall, James P., Jr.; *NEARA Newsletter*, 4:38–39, 1969.

In Westport, Massachusetts, on the coast of Buzzard's Bay, some five hundred yards from the sea, there is a stone structure very similar to the ancient structures in Europe known as dolmens. This consists of a large capstone resting on three legs. The granite capstone weighs approximately four tons and stands about two feet off the ground. It has been quarried elsewhere, by the fire and water method.

The history of this dolmen is obscured by time and Indian legend. Its original purpose is unknown, yet it is not unlike various megalithic graves in Western Europe, especially in the British isles. I have seen a matching structure in the Orkney Islands, origin unknown though presumably ancient.

This area was inhabited prior to the time of the English colonists, by the Coaxets Indians of the Wampanoag tribe. In 1652 a group of colonists from the Plymouth Plantation bought the area from the Indians, but no actual settlers moved in until about 1673. Further settlement was delayed by King Philip's War and remained sparse until the 1700's.

When the colonists arrived in the immediate area of the Dolmen, the place was called "Hassaneghk" by the Indians. This meant "stone house with stone roof", a non-Indian form of construction. Since there is no evidence of any stone house of any description then or now known within miles of the area, it is safe to consider the reference was to this structure. The word "Hassaneghk" has since been corrupted by the colonists to its present form of "Horseneck".

All references to this structure by owners of the property (three families) down to the present day, state that the Dolmen was an Indian relic, used as a threshing table for corn. It is an established fact that the Indians of this area did not do heavy stone work, much less move a four ton slab of granite onto leg piers for corn threshing!

There are several markings on the capstone, some illegible, others faintly discernible due to weathering. These are under further investigation. What can be read, though heavily weathered, is "1MC91", and a small triangle pointing North in one corner. Are these initials and a date ---1691 or 1791 or 1891, or something else?

One can speculate for hours as to who built this dolmen. I think the evidence on hand today points to a very ancient date, yet how ancient may never be exactly determined, without further evidence than we now possess. Presently, NEARA is attempting to obtain some of this evidence, with the hope that it will shed new light on the builders of this dolmen.

References
1. The Wampanoag Indian Federation, Milton A. Travers of the Algonquin Nation (1961)
2. History of New Bedford, Daniel Ricketson (1858)

ROCKING STONE

Anonymous; *American Journal of Science*, 1:5:252–253, 1822.

Moveable rocks, or masses of stone so nicely balanced as to be set in motion by a very small force, have excited the attention of both ancient and modern writers.   As far as my information extends, there is but one of these famous rocks, noticed as being found in the United States---this is in Morse's Geography.   When mentioning the curiosities in New Hampshire, the author makes the following statement: "In the town of Durham, is a rock computed to weigh sixty or seventy tons.   It lies so exactly poised on another rock as to be easily moved with one finger.   It is on the top of a hill and appears to be natural." Putnam's rock, mentioned in the last number of your Journal, seems also to have been of this description. This rocking stone which I visited last spring, is situated on the farm of Mrs. McCabbe in Phillips Town, Putnam County, New York.   The West-Chester and Dutchess turnpike road, which runs a northeast direction from the village of Peekskill to the town of Kent, lies about one mile to the east of this rock.   The person who wishes to visit it must travel eight miles on this road from the village of Peekskill, and then ascend a very high and steep hill on the left hand, near the top of which the rock may be seen.   The moveable stone is about thirty-one feet in circumference, and five feet through in the thickest part---it is of granite, the mica bed so stratified as to present somewhat the appearance of gneiss, and it stands or is supported on a base or pedestal of the same mineral.   A better idea will be formed of the figure and position of this rock from the rough sketch which accompanies this, than from any verbal description.   The under

Rocking stone near Peekskill, New York

rock or pedestal (R) is about one foot and a half high, and is almost flat on its upper surface. The rolling rock (C) rests on this plane. Although it cannot be shaken as easily as the wonderful rock in Asia mentioned by Pliny---or as the Gygonian stone, which trembled on being "struck with the stalk of an Asphodel;" it can however be rolled a little by the hand, and with a small lever it can be moved with great ease;---notwithstanding this, six men with crowbars have been unable to roll it down from its pedestal. Large masses of steatite are scattered around---good specimens of Asbestus, may also be obtained at a short distance. I found some very pretty specimens of blue quartz in the blocks of granite, which form the fence along the road. On the west of the rocking stone, about half a mile, there is a lake three miles long and half a mile wide---a sheet of water of much magnitude is not frequently met with on such an elevation.

THE QUISTA DOLMEN
Whittall, James P., Jr.; *NEARA Newsletter*, 6:16, 1971.

On the island of Martha's Vineyard, hidden from motorists travelling to Gay Head, there is a small knoll called Quista, on which stands an unusual structure that has given rise to much speculation since its discovery. Four large boulders are arranged in a rough circle with an opening on the downhill side. These stones are about two feet in height and form a remarkably tight wall. The two on either side of the opening were evidently selected for their smooth surface and give the doorway a symmetrical appearance. On top of these stones rests a huge quarried capstone, roughly circular in shape and weighing about two tons. A few quoins are placed beneath it, to chink up various openings. The chamber thus formed is about two and a half feet in height, and slightly more than three feet wide by about six feet long. The opening faces to the southwest.

To consider this structure as a functioning part of a colonial farmstead lacks for a logical purpose. It is highly improbable that an early settler would expend the energy necessary to erect such a structure which would seem to be of little service to him. There is no historical record of this stonework. The only justifiable use of this chamber would be a burial crypt. A plausible explanation is that it marks the last resting place of some early explorer who was of too great a consequence to be thrown overboard after death. The choice of this spot not far from Menemsha Pond would be logical in the prescribed manner of burial for the dead during the period 1660 B.C. to 2500 B.C. It is truly a fantastic old date to consider, but if we compare this structure to those in Western Europe, we find that we have a chamber that parallels very closely the portal graves or dolmens of the megalithic period, 3000 to 1000 B.C. This is the only stonework of this kind on the island, yet scattered throughout New England are others similarly unexplained. In fact, seven miles away, directly across the bay from this dolmen is the Hassaneghk Dolmen in Westport.

Suggestions have been made that this dolmen could be the grave of a Viking chieftain. Perhaps, but if we consider it Norse we must go back in time before the popular period of Viking contact in the New World around 1000 A. D. Norse burials of that period were generally conducted in a different manner than this structure suggests. There are in Sweden chambers similar to this one, notably north of Gothenburg, but of the period 3000-2500 B. C.

In 1934, Dr. Frederick Johnson of the Peabody Museum at Harvard University excavated the chamber. His only findings were artifacts of colonial origin which came from the topsoil. No other material was uncovered. Therefore he felt that because of the lack of evidence to the contrary, the structure had to be considered of colonial origin. "More serious considerations having to do with the dolmen are almost immediately frustrated by lack of any further evidence." Perhaps the structure itself had long before been cleaned out by some settler in search of treasure or Indians utilizing items found there. Then again, the ravages of time and New England soil conditions would over a great period of time destroy all evidence of any burial that might have taken place.

. . . .

ON THE CELTIC ANTIQUITIES OF AMERICA
Finch, John; *American Journal of Science*, 1:7:149–161, 1824.

4. Rocking Stones, are memorials raised by the same people, and the same race of men, who elevated the cromlechs; they consist of an enormous stone so equally poised upon its base, that a very small force is sufficient to move it; sometimes even the touch of a finger will cause it to vibrate.

There are several of these memorials of a former race, in the United States of America, but of the origin of the whole of them we cannot be certain, until an accurate account is published of their size, appearance, and situation, and it would be desirable if they were illustrated by correct drawings. In the State of New-York there are probably three or more. Professor Green has described one, in the American Journal of Science, vol. 5. page 252. It is situated near the top of a high hill, near the village of Peekskill, in Putnam county; the moveable stone is thirty-one feet in circumference; the rock is of granite, but the mica contained in it being schistose, gives it some resemblance to gneiss, and it is supported by a base of the same material. This rocking stone can be moved by the hand, although six men with iron bars were unable to throw it off its pedestal. From the drawing which accompanies the description in Silliman's Journal, this rock presents every appearance of an artificial monument, and may perhaps with safety be classed amongst the celtic antiquities of North-America. --- Putnam's rock, which was thrown from its elevation on one of the mountains in the Highlands during the revolutionary war, may have been a rock of this description.

There is also a rocking stone in Orange County, State of New-York, of which no account has yet been published.

In the State of Massachusetts, I have heard of some near Boston,

between Lynn and Salem, but do not vouch for the accuracy of the statement, until they undergo a careful examination.

There is one at Roxbury, near Boston, described in the Journal of
Science, edited in that city.

A small rocking stone occurs at Ashburnham, in the same State.

In New-Hampshire there are two; one at Andover, weighing fifteen or
twenty tons, and the other at Durham. This was a short time since a
very splendid rocking stone, weighing between fifty and sixty tons, and
so exactly poised, that the wind would move it, and its vibrations could
be plainly seen at some distance. But, two years ago, a party from
Portsmouth visited it, and after several hours of labor succeeded in
moving it from its position. A proper feeling on the part of the persons
who effected this mischief, would cause them to restore it to its original
place. The rock is forty five feet in circumference and seven in thickness. (pp. 157-158)

• South America

GIANT MONOLITHS OF QUIRAGUA MONUMENTAL OF A ONCE POWERFUL RACE

Anonymous; *Pan-American Magazine,* 37:458-460, 1924.

In the midst of dense woods, about 100 miles east of Guatemala City
there rise out of the encrouching jungle huge and superbly carved monoliths. Stones of immense size, covered with ornaments, glyphs, gods,
and mystic signs are scattered over the ground, almost invisible by ferns
and plants struggling for light; ruins of temples---gray shadows in the
green.---

75 Acres of this land contain these ruins of cities, temples and monuments which declare more vividly than printed words the tale of their
progress and achievements. A mighty race of people lived in these valleys
along the coastline through Honduras up to Yucatan, built these castles and
marvels of art in long centuries. But when?---No legend, no traditions,
no interpretation of their glyphs, ---dense mystery!---

But a master race they were, like the Brahmans of early India,
glorious in culture like old Egypt, in their powerful skill of building like
the ancient Greeks.

There are many theories about their origin, some very attractive,
like that one, that all these countries were submerged when Atlantis, the
Island and Motherland, flourishing in a high culture, was destroyed and
that, remaining under sea for a certain and unknown period, they rose once

more and were peopled from the Highlands. Or another, that before Atlantis disappeared, some of the inhabitants set out, warned by a Godsend, settling east and west, forming perhaps new races, as the Egyptian, or mixing with the Brahmans, hence the startling resemblance in some pieces with Egyptian, old Indian and even Chinese art. And while those, merging with asiatic races, or even giving them their origins, thrived, those having settled in the lands from Guatemala up to Yucatan, developing the high grade of culture and civilization we find today, someway vanished.---
Were they wiped out by fever, by catastrophic deseases, by races stronger than they? Did the disaster of Atlantis deprive them of support, leaving them degenerating without the life-blood of the mother country to perish under the murderous climate as a weak settlement unable to help itself? No answer,---dead, silent lie those grim stones, holding their secret.---

Dreamy coloured orchids catch the wandering eye, a gorgeous beauty, fit for this thicket of palms, tremendous ferns, arched forests, impossible to discribe. A tangled mass of green life struggling desperately for more light, or death.---

Through the arches of the palms suddenly appears a group of mounds, still overgrown with masses of foliage, and beyond these an avenue of great stones, carved monoliths leading to some---as yet---invisible altar or temple. From each pillar stares---impassive, gloomy or sullen---a gigantic face.---Each figure is crowned with a tall feather headdress, is belted with a short, embroidered skirt, naked with heavy ornaments at wrist and ankle, like Korean Eunuchs in the Heaven sacrifice. On the sides of the stones are columns of glyphs, until now undecipherable, but nearly all plain and well preserved, and, when the cue shall have been found, easily legible. The faces are well carved, of a heavy, full type, with thick lips, narrow eyes, and thin, carefully pointed egyptian beards, like the sargent Pharaoh in the Boston Library. Several show remarkably cruel strength, which lessens with each set of pillars to be a weak, purposeless, degenerate type, loose lipped, chinless, and imbecile.

· · · · · · · · · ·

THE MONOLITHS OF TAFI
Anonymous; *Science*, 5:724, 1897.

Tafi is the name of a broad valley in the province of Tucaman, Argentine Republic. The well-known scientist, Professor Ambrosetti, in a recent visit there, had his attention called to an extraordinary collocation of monolithic pillars and stone enclosures, erected in remote ages by the native inhabitants. He describes them in Globus, Bd. LXXI., No. 11. The monoliths are from six to ten feet in height above the soil, some plain, others decorated with conventional designs, others rudely chipped into the likeness of faces, etc. They extend over a considerable area and their purpose is problematical.

Ambrosetti is inclined to attribute them to the predecessors of the

Calchaqui Indians, who occupied this territory at the Conquest. He suggests that they are the work of the same people who erected the buildings of Tiahuanuco; a suggestion which I think is extremely probable, for some of the decoration shown in his cuts is strikingly like that on the stone pillars of Hatuncolla, two leagues from Lake Titicaca, portrayed in Squier's 'Peru,' pp. 385-6.

• Pacific Islands

MYSTERY MONUMENTS OF THE MARIANAS
Searles, P. J.; *Scientific Monthly*, 25:385-391, 1927.

Thousands of miles from civilization, hidden in tangled jungle growths, seldom described and photographed, as have been the pyramids of the Mayas, the ruins of Angkor Wat or the monstrosities of Easter Island, for hundreds perhaps thousands of years, have lain concealed the mystery monuments of the Marianas. Surpassing Stonehenge in extent, with single stones larger than any in the pyramids of Egypt, these Lat'te or "Casas de los Antiguos," as they were known to the Spanish, are the relics of a race whose origin is lost in the dim mists of antiquity and whose history and characteristics had even been forgotten over four hundred years ago. What are they, why were they erected, and by whom? These are puzzles still to be solved.
. . . .

Dotting the islands here and there are found those magnificent structures, the Lat'te, erected unknown centuries ago by a lost race whose name even is forgotten. Massive and imposing even when partially laid low by the hand of time working through earthquakes and typhoons, hid in the shadowy depths of the jungles, they convey an impression of high intelligence and skill on the part of their builders. Battling to the scientist as well as to the layman, they represent an ancient epoch as mythical as Atlantis. What are they?

A Lat'te is composed primarily of upright monoliths called "halege," surmounted by hemispherical capitals called "tasa." The upright stones are usually placed in two parallel rows of from four to six stones in each row, the long axis of the Lat'te always being parallel with the line of the sea shore or a river bed. In Guam are found several different detailed forms. The uprights are sometimes slab-like, sometimes cut square; in fact, many shapes are extant. The capitals also vary in shape and size. Lat'te range from small rude structures constructed of natural boulders capped with coral heads, to massive stone columns, square in shape, fifteen or more feet in height and six feet in diameter, headed with enormous blocks of stone.

The Island of Tinian presents two of these largest of monuments carved by prehistoric man, part of the "House of Taga." The only standing survivors of ten original monoliths, these two shafts still rear their lofty heads on the south-western side of the island, very near the beach. Three others are completely shattered as if by earthquake, two have lost their capitals, and three have fallen but still retain the "tasa" intact. They are all shaped like truncated pyramids, capped by hemispherical stones. The pillars are eighteen feet in circumference at the base and fifteen feet at the top. They are twelve feet high and support capitals five feet high and six feet in diameter. Each monolith weighs about thirty tons. The two parallel rows originally stood seven feet apart and form a ground plan about fifty-five feet long by eleven feet wide. They are cut from a rough metamorphosed coral known in the Marianas as "cascajo."

Don Felipe de la Corte de Calderon, Spanish governor of the Marianas from 1855 to 1866, in various manuscript reports to the Crown (not published), tells of the Lat'te.

It should also be noticed that not only Guam but Rota, Tinian, and Saipan also possess ruins of houses of an architecture which tends to demonstrate the existence of a people gifted with certain ideas which showed them to be above the stage of the mere savage. All these ruins consist of pyramids finished at the top with semispherical, carved stones, the semisphere in some instances being built of small stones cemented together.

In all the islands, at places formerly inhabited, are found certain monuments, which the natives call "latde" (sic), or "Houses

One of Guam's smaller lat'te

of the Old People." They consist invariably of a double row of rough stone pyramids or truncated cones supporting stone hemispheres, flat side up. These pyramids, similar in shape to the stone pillars called "Guarda Cantones," which are often placed along the edges of royal highways in Spain, stand in two rows, like the pillars of a house; and even though we have no exact data on the subject, this position together with their native name makes us believe that formerly they served as supports for stringers on which rested rafters that reached to the ground; but if this is correct, the house must have been very low. In early descriptions of the islands it is said that the natives buried their dead in the houses and even today the people have a superstitious fear of digging up or working the ground between these rows of stones....

In Guam, Rota, and Saipan, the latde pillars consist of only two rough hewn stones, one cone shaped and the other a half sphere placed on top of it, both of them together not being higher than five feet from the ground; while in Tinian close to the Deputy Governor's house stands a group of these pillars, called "House of Taga"--- a chieftain famous in local history---which is composed of twelve truncated pyramids four or five feet wide at the base and fifteen feet high, their squared tops measuring about two feet to a side. On them rest hemispheres from six to seven feet in diameter.

These pillars, crowned with their hemispherical caps and standing in two files, distant from each other about four varas from center to center, constitute a monument worthy of special attention, not so much for its size as because it resembles nothing to be seen elsewhere outside of the Marianas; moreover, it is not unique, but represents a type repeated over and over again in the other islands of the group. If we knew more about these latde we might determine the true origin of these natives of whom it may be confidently asserted that they are not the descendants of primitive savages. This is proved not only by the labor and skill required to dress the stones, but also by their unvarying pyramidal and hemispherical character. It seems strange that the history of the first missionaries makes no mention of them, since one would think such pillars could not fail to attract attention when discovered among the thatched huts of naked Indians.

....

How the Lat'te were built is unknown. Tools, chipped and polished from basaltic rock, were the only implements the primitive people had, yet they formed blocks of fifty tons or more. The cultural level of the Egyptians was vastly superior to that of the ancient Polynesians, the Egyptian workmen knowing the use of bronze cutters set with diamonds and corundum, yet their pyramidal stones were not so large. Mr. Hornbostel has advanced the interesting and plausible theory that the stones were shaped by the alternate use of fire and water, the fire to heat and the water crack, the process continuing until huge monolith was fashioned from the rocky earth, later to be more carefully carved by the stone implements. By whatever means secured and erected, the Lat'te remain magnificent monuments to an ancient race, comparable, in size, skill and industry required, to the remains at Stonehenge, Easter Island or the Maya cities.

Who built the Lat'te and when? This is a mystery which may never

be solved. It was almost certainly not the Chamorros found in the
Marianas by the Spanish discoverers and settlers. When the Spanish first
arrived, the Lat'te were already partly in ruins, and the natives dis-
claimed all knowledge of the builders except that they were "the people
who came before." Cannibalism was unknown and forgotten by the sixteenth century, yet remains of cannibal feasts are found in the Lat'te.
Perhaps they are relics of ancestors of the Chamorros, ancestors long
dead and forgotten. Perhaps they were erected by a race antedating the
Chamorros and which has disappeared in the mists of the past. Nothing
corresponding to the Lat'te is found in Polynesia, but archeologists hope
that in Micronesia and Melanesia further study may give a clue. Were
the Lat'te only part of dwellings (though this hardly seems possible),
were they temples to the sun or were they religious structures dedicated
to ancestral worship? Have they a relation to any Asiatic monuments or
to the astounding and unique figures of Easter Island? These questions
still remain to be answered. But there in the Marianas the Lat'te stand
or lie fallen in the tangled jungles, hidden by the dense growth of vegetation, far from the ways of man; monuments to a people of genius, lost in
antiquity, who perhaps with weird rites sacrificed to the blazing tropical
sun at a time when Rome ruled the world and Christ taught in Jerusalem.

MEGALITHIC MONUMENTS
Perry, W. J.; *The Megalithic Culture of Indonesia,* London, 1918,
pp. 10-19.

It has long been a matter of common knowledge that megalithic monuments are to be found in Assam. Unfortunately, Dutch ethnographers,
in their desire to record the less material elements of the cultures of
their subject peoples, have often overlooked, among other things, the
stone monuments which exist in certain parts of the East Indian Archipelago. Consequently, it is not generally known that stone structures,
which conform to the types enumerated, exist in certain places. These
structures are not always made of large stones, nor are these stones
always unworked, but they are unmistakably "megalithic monuments" in
size or form. The objection that, to be called "megalithic" a structure
must be made of large unworked stones, is quite just, if one submits to
the strict limitations of the meaning assigned to the term by archaeologists and ethnologists; but the adoption of such a rigid interpretation
would close the door upon all real investigation. The principle adopted
in this book is that of examining the facts without any reservations: so
the only criterion that will be adopted with regard to stone monuments
will be that of form. Any structures which are not of the types enumerated will be examined later.
    In the Timor region the presence of megalithic monuments is as yet
only definitely established in Sumba, although they are probably to be
found in the neighbouring islands. And the only account of these structures which is at all detailed is that of Dr. ten Kate, who describes some

which he saw in the course of a rapid journey through the island.

At Samparengo he saw dolmens of rough stones, examples of which were also seen by him at Laonatang, a village in the Kanata district. In this latter place he reports a dolmen consisting of a table-stone supported by four pillars. He saw some old megalithic monuments, most of them dolmens and "hunenbetter," in the bush about Lambanapu. He reproduces, in one of his articles, a drawing of a dolmen in front of the house of a chief of Lewa who lived at Lambanapu.

Ten Kate saw a dolmen in front of one of the houses at Watubela. He also reports dolmens at Kopa and "hunenbetter" at Labai. On a hill near the shore close to Landuwitu-Ratimbera, and near Peremadita he saw a number of dolmens, one of which was 5 feet high. He describes some trilithons at the latter place, and gives reproductions of dolmens at Wainbidi and Waijelu. Roos records dolmens at Kambera. Ten Kate found many dolmens on the island of Salura.

The villages of Sumba are often built in the form of a square, round which are to be found dolmens made of great stones, 10 to 12 feet high, 4 feet broad, and 18 inches thick, resting upon short piles.

In Keisar, Leti Moa and Lakor, and Timorlaut, there are stone structures which may possibly be related to dolmens. Each of these consists of a large flat stone which rests upon several smaller ones, the latter being of such a size that the large stone is only a few inches from the ground. The description suggests that they are dolmens of a modified type, but it would not be wise to assume that they are real dolmens. They will be considered later.

In the Kei Islands cromlechs are to be found, but no information is to hand as to the size of the stones of which they are made.

Dolmen at Waijelo, Sumba

The offering-places, in the villages of West Seran, consist either of a large stone resting upon three or four others, or of a large stone half-buried in the ground, the descriptions therefore suggesting, in the first case, a dolmen, and, in the second case, a menhir. Riedel also mentions a structure consisting of a large flat stone surrounded by smaller stones, the description suggesting a dolmen associated with a cromlech.

Cromlechs are reported by Bastian in Halmahera. No evidence is yet to hand of the presence of megalithic structures in the Philippines, or in Formosa.

In the Minahassa district of North Celebes the dead are sometimes placed in rock-cut tombs. The cousins Sarasin saw, in a hill near Kema, some of these tombs, the openings of which were closed with boards or hewn stones. Menhirs are sometimes erected in pairs near the large stone urns in which, in this district, the dead are generally placed. In each Minahassa village there is a stone structure, which consists of two, three, or sometimes still more stones. In the latter case a number of smaller stones surround one or more large stones, the description suggesting a cromlech associated with menhirs. Menhirs are reported among the Posso-Todjo of Central Celebes. At Bulili among the To Bada is a cromlech, and on the same hill are many large blocks of stone which may at some time have formed part of a stone structure. Among the To Lage a menhir is reported at Wawo Lage, and not far from the village of Pakambia some menhirs are to be found.

On the Paloppo river the Sarasin cousins saw the mausoleum of a chief, which was pyramidal in form. On the top of it was a porcelain pot. Many rock-cut tombs similar to those found in Minahassa are to be seen in the Simbuang-Mapak valley. They are called Liang, and are hewn out of the steep face of the rocky eminence on which is placed the village to which they belong. In the Rantepao valley alignments are to be found on some of the small hills.

The Dusun of British North Borneo erect cromlechs. They are only people of Borneo, who, so far as it has been possible to discover, erect stone structures of the megalithic type.

In South Nias menhirs are erected, and in East Nias each village has one such menhir. De Zwaan gives a photograph in his book of a menhir on the bank of the river Masio. A cromlech is reported by Modigliani on the island of Nacco to the west of Nias.

The Khasi of Assam have an elaborate system of megalithic structures, chiefly alignments and menhirs, dolmens being comparatively rare.

The Garo erect menhirs, which they call asong and kosi, according as they are placed near the village or in the forest. The Naga have several megalithic structures: there are two 'Stonehenges," one at Maram, which consists of an avenue of two alignments; and another at Uilong, which consists of two contiguous cromlechs, one oval and the other circular, with an alignment running from the edge of the former. Mr. Hodson reproduces a photograph of a menhir at Maikel which is surrounded by a cromlech; another of a huge menhir at Maram; and a third of a dolmen near the latter place. Each Marring Naga village has a cromlech. The Tangkhul Naga are closely associated with a menhir, and the Kabui Naga erect menhirs.

Several of the clans of the Old Kuki of Manipur erect megalithic monuments: The Amol erect menhirs; the Hrangchal have a large menhir at Vanlaiphai; a number of dolmens made of three rough slabs placed on edge, with a fourth for a roof, which are still to be seen on the Biate hill, are the work of the Biate; a menhir is erected on certain occasions by the Thado; and dolmen-shaped structures are reported among the Chawte.

Menhirs are erected by the Kohlen clan of the Lushei. Facing page 65 of his book, Colonel Shakespear reproduces a photograph of the posts which the Lushei erect to commemorate the slaying of a buffalo on the occasion of a feast. In a corner of this photograph is a dolmen, formed, apparently, of four stones placed on edge with a slab covering them.

Of the Chin tribes, the Sokte erect menhirs, and the Welaung, Chinbok, and Yindu erect dolmens, of which numbers, some made of enormous stones, are to be seen in the Chinbok and Yindu country.

The Mikir erect menhirs, alignments, and dolmens.

This survey demonstrates the widespread existence in Indonesia of unmistakable megalithic monuments. The accounts of these structures which are given by ethnographers and travellers are so meagre that no comparative study of their form and structure can be attempted. Without doubt the future consideration of these matters will enable students to draw therefrom important conclusions. (pp. 10-15)

• Asia

A CHINESE PUZZLE

C., O. G. S.; *Antiquity*, 26:207-208, 1952.

In July, 1940, the Editor received, through a correspondent, information about a megalithic structure in China which outwardly seemed to resemble those European monuments which used to be called 'dolmens'. The times were not favourable for further investigation, but we have now followed the matter up, with the following result.

The structure was discovered by the Rev. Robert S. Harrison, who was then residing at Lingling (Yungchow) in S. Hunan. It is situated at Hwang T'ien P'u in the Lingling district, and the approximate coordinates are Lat. 26° 15' N., Long. 111° 40' E. In his original letter of 1940 Mr. Harrison quite properly pointed out that the structure might be of natural origin. It consists of a huge block (or capstone), resting on three smaller uprights between 3 feet 3 inches and 3 feet 6 inches high. The capstone is a little over 5 feet thick and about 7 feet square. The N. E. and N. W. sides are more weathered than the others, and the top and sides have been eroded into grooves by the action of rain-water. A piece of one of the uprights had been chipped off by workmen in need of metal for road-repairing. Locally it is regarded as the work of fairies and of immemorial antiquity. It is not associated with any religious rites or regarded with any reverence. At Mr. Harrison's request the district magistrate, though regarding it without interest as being the work of prehistoric barbarians, promised to protect it.

. . . .

Possible Chinese dolmen

SOME POINTS OF INTEREST FROM HAN HUNG SU'S "STUDIES ON MEGALITHIC CULTURE OF KOREA"
Hoyt, James; *American Anthropologist,* 50:573–574, 1948.

Up to today very little research has been done on Korean megalithic culture. Some reports have been presented by Western travelers and missionaries but they are not very satisfactory. However, a number of interesting articles have been contributed by Japanese and Korean anthropologists, above all by Han Hung Su, formerly of the University of Praha and at present at the University of Vienna. He wrote, in the Korean language, Studies on Megalithic Culture of Korea, which appeared in the Chintan Hakpo (July 1935), a quarterly journal published in Seoul.

According to Mr. Han, megalithic monuments in Korea may be divided into three classes: Standing stones (menhirs), supported stones (dolmens), and stone piles and fences.

Standing stones are found in large numbers in the southwest, in the vicinity of Seoul, and near the famous Diamond Mountain. Many Korean menhirs retain their original form, while others were altered at a later time. During the period of predominance of Buddhism many menhirs were carved into statues of Bodhisattvas. They are common all over Korea and are called "miruk" by the Koreans. Han Hung Su reports numerous Buddhist statues which he believes to have originally been megalithic monuments. The dimensions of the figures lead him to believe that the stones were not originally designed for sculpture. The positions of the arms are often unnatural, the noses flat, the figure poorly proportioned. But the real proof of the megalithic origin of these statues lies in the fact that the Buddhist images are often found near numbers of menhirs which retain their original shape.   Furthermore, these menhirs also are called "miruk," though no trace of carving is visible.

One menhir of particular interest because of its "mushroom" shape has been found in northern Korea.   Women living in the neighborhood still have faith that the stone will bring them fertility.   Legends concerning menhirs are varied.   In some areas it is maintained that they were erected by ancient "strong men."   Some say that "witches" were turned into stone; others tell of monoliths springing up from the ground.   And many old women still approach them to beg for long life.

The second type of megalithic remains found in Korea is the dolmen. They are found in large numbers all over Korea.   These dolmens have been described as having two or three supporting stones.   But the observer is very often speaking of the dolmen as it exists today and not of the original.   Korean dolmens may be divided into two main groups according to geographical location.   The "Northern type" has a smoother cover and seems to have been more systematically constructed.   The "Southern type" is more often chamber-like.   Those with four supporting stones become rectangular chambers, and are of a more refined type.

Han Hung Su visited villages where broken pieces of stone were scattered and buried.   Upon interrogation, elderly villagers reported that dolmens had been intact during their life-times.   Reasons why the dolmens had been broken were given as follows: (1) Curiosity of the natives led them to break into the dolmens.   (2) There was a desire to loot what they believe to be old burial tombs.   (3) The dolmens were broken up to make mortars and other utilitarian objects.   Han Hung Su also notes that the southern dolmens are smaller in size and fewer in number.   In the north, covers are larger and not so easily broken; but

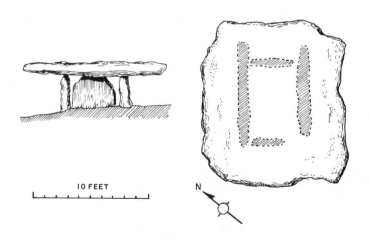

Korean dolmen

in the south fragments from dolmens may be found all around the sites. The northern dolmens are flat on top; southern ones are curved.

The outstanding megalithic monument consists of a group of forty dolmens located between two villages in Annak District. The dolmens are in a row five hundred meters long and all face the same direction. In between the dolmens there are from three to five regularly distanced stones of irregular shape.

The third class, stone mounds, contain megalithic elements, but are said to represent a later development. Many of them are found in mountain passes. One legend which seems to be common all over Korea is that they were piles of rock ammunition stored for use in warfare. It is also said that they are burial mounds for unfaithful wives, built that their infamy should be commemorated. In connection with these mounds there exists the unexplained custom of expectorating whenever one passes by.

Han Hung Su reports seven stones which deserve to be placed in a special category. They are located in an area where rocks are few. The stones are arranged in the form of the Big Dipper. One local tradition says that the stones dropped down from heaven. According to another version a "strong man" arranged them in ancient times. Women in the vicinity go to the rocks to ask that they may bear children. Granted this wish, they name the child "Dipper"; so there are many children in the vicinity with that name. The woman who desires a child will spread thread between the rocks, then face north and make her wish. Thread, it is interesting to note, is still used today to tie together the nuptial cups in the Korean wedding ceremony.

In the shell mounds near Kimhae, there are megalithic tombs which are very similar to what western anthropologists call the "Corridor Tomb." There are but few examples extant, and the subject requires further study. There is an interesting possibility of connection with Japanese megalithic tombs. Also worthy of further study are the royal graves of the Three Kingdom Period, which may be direct descendants of the dolmen.

MONOLITHS IN ASSAM

Anonymous; *Nature*, 126:71, 1930.

Mr. J. P. Mills, and Mr. J. H. Hutton in vol. 25, No. 1, of the Journal and Proceedings of the Asiatic Society of Bengal describe a series of five groups of remarkable monoliths in the Cachar Hills not previously recorded in print. The monoliths are pear-shaped, artificially dressed, and each contains a cavity in the bulbous end. They are now recumbent, though they appear at one time to have been erected on their narrow ends. They fall into two distinct types which may be regarded as male and female. The former constitute the whole of a large group at Kartong, and a smaller group between Kartong and Kobak. Most of the stones are incised with geometric designs and forms of men and animals, such as the pig and the mithun. While the monoliths may be interpreted as embodying the phallic principle, assisting the fertilising of Nature, the hollows seem

to have been meant for some specific purpose not easy to discern. It may
be that they were intended to hold water to promote rainfall, or they may
have been intended to contain offerings on the analogy of holes recently
scooped out in ancient monoliths at Kasomari. It is concluded that the
North Cachar hollowed monoliths must be regarded as a specialised development of a phallic ancestral cult typical of Assam. It is clear that
they were not erected by the Nagas and old Kukis who are the present inhabitants of the area. Local tradition assigns them to the Mikirs. This
may be the case, subsequent invasion having overwhelmed the Mikirs and
left them in isolated communities too weak to provide the labour requisite
to carry on the custom. It is more probable, however, that it is to be
associated with the Khasi Synteng group of tribes and that it has disappeared owing to their migration into an unsuitable environment.

THE STONE MONUMENTS OF THE KHASI HILLS
Clarke, C. B.; *Anthropological Institute, Journal*, 3:480–493, 1874.

Almost throughout Khasi-land, and in a less degree through the Jain-
tea country, monumental stones are common. They are numerous in
villages in the valleys, but are specially prominent, and sometimes of
gigantic size, scattered over the rounded hill-tops where they form a
feature in the landscape. In all modern treatises of Archaeology and
Anthropology the study of monumental stones forms an important chapter.
Monuments of a remarkable similarity in design are found alike in Europe,
Asia, and isolated islands in the Pacific Ocean, and these are in general
of such extreme antiquity that they are treated as belonging to the prehistoric age. The Khasi stone monuments have attracted already much
attention; first because of their great number and size; and, secondly and
chiefly, because on these hills the erection of these monuments is now in
full practice. It is reasonably supposed that a careful study of the Khasi
method of raising the stones, and of the traditions or customs in accordance with which they raise them, may throw some light upon more ancient
monuments of the same kind, even upon Stonehenge. It has been proposed
to send out a commission from England to survey these Khasi stone monuments. They are described by Dr. Hooker, in his work (Min. Journ. II.
276), also by Colonel Raban in the Calcutta Review, and some account has
been lately given by Major Godwin-Austen in the "Journal of the Anthropological Institute," No. 2, Oct. 1871. The present memoir was written
years ago, previous to some of these published accounts, but contains
several details not given by any of them.
   3. The Khasi stones are of three classes, viz:---
        a. The funeral pyres.
        b. The kists containing the pots of ashes.
        c. The monumental groups.
It is the last class (c.) which has, hitherto, nearly monopolised attention,
and to which the published notices almost exclusively refer.
. . . .

The Monumental Groups. There are two general types of monumental stones, viz., the upright slab and the horizontal slab.

The upright slabs are commonly grouped in threes or fives (sometimes they are seven or more); they are nearly always oblong and set up in a row with the tallest stone in the middle; annexed is a representation of a common type containing five stones.

Five-stone Khasi monument

A common height for the middle stone of such a monument will be six to ten feet, by 2-3 feet wide. The stones are sunk not very deep, say 1-2 feet, into the earth; great numbers of fallen stones are seen. Monuments of this character are often placed on the crest of the hills, and in many parts of Khasi-land the landscape appears dotted over with them.

The horizontal slabs are commonly grouped in pairs. The flat slabs may be 5-10 feet long, and are rarely so exactly quadrangular, and they generally have some of the corners irregularly rounded off, and thus pass into the oval or round horizontal slab, which is also a frequent type.

The upright and horizontal slabs are often combined to form a single monument, and perhaps the commonest of all the combinations is that in which five upright slabs have two horizontal before them. The combinations adopted are, however, endless in variety. In these combinations it must be understood that the whole group of stones forms one indivisible monument, which may be the monument of one individual, a household, or a family. Families retain a history of the monuments which belong to the family, and thus in a small degree of the names of their ancestors. Such family monuments may be repaired, added to, or rebuilt from time to time. They are not necessarily placed where the family ashes are kept in kists, or near such kists; but they are usually at no great distance from the village where the family dwells.

The putting up a large stone, say one that stands fifteen feet out of the ground, is a very costly matter, and the monuments of the first class in size in the Khasi country are not very numerous; in the monuments of small stones, the number of stones is often great, I have noticed twenty-one stones in a row, no stone exceeding two feet high.

The upright slabs are (particularly when unaccompanied by any horizontal slabs) usually placed in a straight line. But frequently, where the horizontal slab is round, the upright slabs stand in the arc of a circle, and sometimes the upright slabs are placed in a curved line apparently by accident, or because the nature of the steep ground suggested such an arrangement. Two such monuments occur on the main road to Lailankote.

Major Godwin-Austen states in his article on the subject that the upright slabs <u>always</u> stand in threes, fives, sevens, etc. This is a mistake; to have the number of stones unequal, with the central slab the tallest, is perhaps the plan adopted in forty-nine monuments out of fifty; but among the vast variety of monuments in these hills a dozen monuments on the binary type may soon be found in which there are two equal upright slabs in the middle, and the other stones placed symmetrically on each side of them.

. . . .

Megalithic monuments in the Khasi Hills, India

• Africa

TRIDENTS AND TRILITHS IN WEST AFRICA
Rodd, Francis; *Man*, 32:139–140, 1932.

My friend Mr. Palmer raises one or two very interesting points in his note on "Trident Sceptres in W. Africa." I agree that we must probably look for a pre-Moslem and, perhaps, definitely non-Semitic origin for the trident or tri-form ornament in northern equatorial Africa. I also agree that the tri-form ornament is traditional among the Tuareg though its occurrence is principally cruciform.   There are a number of examples of cruciform ornament referred to in my book (The People of the Veil, chap. ix) wherein the Tuareg bridle stick is also referred to.   "On these sticks are slung the bridles and ropes when a camel is unsaddled. They are planted outside a man's tent and sometimes indicate his high position or prosperity." The only two examples I saw had a cruciform top, but I heard of a trident topped stick which was described as being some-what like this:---

The triliths Mr. Palmer refers to exist in Air but are not very common in the form of two pillars with a stone on top. The ordinary form consists of three pillars set upright on the plan of an equilateral triangle, with the apex directed towards Mecca, and purporting to be Moslem places of prayer. On the other hand, the usual form of places of prayer is a rough semi-circle of small stones on the ground, directed east. I know of one large rectangular formal enclosure with two upright pillar stones in the eastern face. The horizontal slab stone might well have been one of many suitable pieces lying around.

. . . .

Group of triliths from Ahaggar

THE MENHIRS OF MADAGASCAR

Lewis, A. L.; *Royal Anthropological Institute, Journal,* 47:448–453, 1917.

There are, in that part of Madagascar known as the plateau of Emyrne, or Imerina, numerous menhirs, which, however, are of no great antiquity; according to tradition the first of them to be set up were for the commemoration of successes in war; afterwards the practice was extended to signalizing the foundation of new villages by the king, then the nobility began to erect stones as thank-offerings to the king for favours conferred by him upon them, and finally the people at large devoted them to the cult of the dead by placing a standing stone at the head of their tombs. From being merely commemorative of some particular act or occurrence these stones have become sacred objects and instruments of a cult which is practised even at the present time, especially by women desiring children, or an easy delivery during child-birth, and who, having rubbed the stone with grease, rub themselves against it. When either men or women desire the curing of an illness, or success in some undertaking they throw fine gravel at the greasy part of the stone, and, if it sticks there, hope for success, or they try to throw a stone so that it lodges on the narrow top of the menhir; if after this their wishes are gratified they bestow another coat of grease on the stone.

As I have already said, these particular menhirs are comparatively modern, the oldest of them having been set up in the sixteenth century by Ralambo, who is said to have been king of the Hovas from 1575 to 1610, or thereabouts, to commemorate the capture of a village from another king; Ralambo stood by it to thank the chief of the village who had betrayed it to him, and who placed the smaller stone by the side of it, in token of submission to and confidence in his new lord; after that the village was removed by the inhabitants to a more convenient situation, and another stone was set up by the king then reigning in commemoration of the new foundation. It will be observed that these stones are not only the oldest, but the smallest, of those described by M. Barthere, being only 2-1/2 feet high.

Another stone was set up by another king in the seventeenth century to perpetuate the remembrance of his coronation; on which occasion he sacrificed at the foot of the menhir seven oxen for the people, one of a specially marked kind for the nobility, and another of a notable description for the royal family, and he also instituted a market on the spot.

The first of the kings who aspired to the government of the whole of Madagascar set up a very peculiarly shaped stone, saying that the higher part was for him and the lower part for the people, but that they were united in the same block because he did not wish them to separate themselves from him. This is considered a very sacred stone, and animals are sacrificed there, and their blood sprinkled on both parts of the top of it. The sprinkling of blood on stones was also found by Colonel Forbes Leslie to be practised in India; this might be taken to show some direct connection between the two localities, but I do not think it does so; the idea of sacrificing animals or birds at places marked by special stones might quite well be evolved independently, and the further idea of smearing the stones with the blood of the sacrifices would follow quite naturally.

Near the same village (Ivato) are two other stones. M. Barthere thinks that the shape of one of them must have some peculiar signification, but has not been able to discover it; this stone, however, is never oiled, that honour being reserved for the other stone, which is 100 metres further north.

These menhirs are all thin slabs, and, out of nine, the orientation of which is given, the broad sides of five face nearly east and west, those of two about north-west and south-east, of one north and south, and of another north-east and south-west.

. . . .

Sketch of postage stamp showing lyre-shaped monoliths at Kaffrine, Senegal

• Middle East

PREHISTORIC GALILEE
Petre, F. Turville; *Antiquity*, 1:299–310, 1927.

An account of the prehistoric sites of Galilee would be incomplete without some reference to the numerous megalithic remains of the district. Since practically no excavations have been carried out at these sites, it is impossible with certainty to assign any date for the arrival of this culture in Palestine; in view, however, of the fact that dolmens and other megalithic constructions are most numerous east of Jordan, rather rarer in eastern and central Palestine, and practically unknown on the Mediterranean coast and in northern Syria, it would seem that they are the work of nomadic or semi-nomadic tribes from Arabia, and they may perhaps be tentatively ascribed to the period of the first Semitic migration during the late Neolithic and early Bronze Ages about the beginning of the third millennium B.C.

Three important groups of dolmens are so far known in northern Galilee. The northernmost of these groups is near the village of Beit Jahun on the northern plateau. North of the village on the slopes of the Wadi-es-Suwan Mader found twenty-one dolmens, seven of which were in a state of good preservation; south of the village he found three more. They do not form a definite necropolis, but are scattered at random about the hills. The dolmens stand on the natural surface of the ground, with no foundation terrace, or are sunk slightly into the earth; in both cases they are low, seldom rising more than a metre above the ground. The dolmen chamber is long and narrow, broader at the inner end than at the entrance, and frequently narrowing from the base upwards. It is built of thin, roughly hewn limestone slabs; sometimes two or even three slabs are used in each long side. The broader end is closed with a slab, the entrance with piled up stones and the whole is covered with a large trimmed capstone. The majority of the dolmens are orientated SW-NE with the entrance at the north-eastern end, so that the body would lie with the head at the south-west end looking north-east, but the opposite arrangement, as well as N-S and W-E orientation is also found. Many of the dolmens are surrounded by stone circles. The use of thin, regularly trimmed slabs and the invariable wedge-shaped ground plan of the chamber must indicate a comparatively developed stage of dolmen construction.

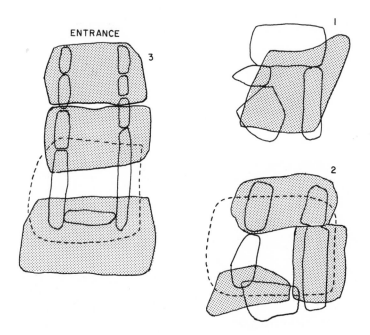

ENTRANCE

Dolmens in Galilee

Another group consisting of thirteen dolmens in all is to be found on the plateau between Safsaf and Meiron at the western foot of Jebel Jermuk. The majority of the dolmens resemble those from Beit Jahun in having a wedge-shaped ground plan and in being low and sometimes sunk into the ground. One dolmen stands on the top of an artificial heap of stones, and similar heaps on which dolmens probably formerly stood are to be seen in the vicinity. The orientation of the dolmens at this site is various, N-S, W-E and most frequently NW-SE with the entrance at the south-eastern end.

The third group was discovered by Karge in the desolate stretch of country strewn with basalt blocks which forms the eastern slopes of the Galilean highlands overlooking the northern end of the Sea of Galilee and the plain of the Ebteha. The dolmens are most numerous in the southern part of the necropolis immediately to the east of Kerazeh, the biblical Korazain, between this site and the Jordan valley, but they extend north-wards as far as Khirbet Hajar-ed-Damm and Khirbet abu Loze. All over this area of some three kilometres square small groups of dolmens are to be found.

The dolmen itself is built of local basalt blocks, occasionally roughly trimmed, but usually left in their natural state; the predominant orientation is W-E with a slight tendency towards SW-NE; the entrance is usually at the eastern end. Three distinct stages of dolmen construction are represented. The simplest form, which is rare, consists of four orthostatic blocks and a coverstone. In the next stage the dolmen chamber is built up of a lower course of orthostatic blocks, upon which a second course of blocks is laid flat, and upon these the coverstone rests; the western end is closed by an orthostatic block, the entrance at the eastern end is closed by smaller stones. Small stones are also used to fill in the gaps between the side blocks. Sometimes two courses of blocks lie between the orthostatic slabs below, and the coverstone above, and not infrequently a rough appearance of vaulting is produced by the upper blocks overlapping those below them.

The third type is a simple form of corridor tomb (allee couverte) in that the true dolmen chamber is extended eastwards to form a kind of corridor entrance. There is no definite division between the entrance passage and the true dolmen chamber such as is usual in Europe. The main chamber is distinguishable from the passage solely in being covered by the capstone, while the passage is roofed by a single course of blocks resting directly on the orthostatic slabs which form its sides.

In addition to this necropolis, the hills between Tell Hum and Safed are strewn with the remains of megalithic constructions; these include isolated dolmens, stone circles, cyclopean walls and small circular enclosures, the walls of which stand at present about one metre above the ground; they perhaps formed the foundations of ancient huts. Such remains are particularly numerous on the land called Shegerat-el-Mubarakat south-west of Kerazeh, which is possibly the site of a large megalithic village. Unfortunately none of these sites has yet been excavated or even exhaustively explored.

• Europe

ANTIQUITIES ON THE ISLAND OF MINORCA
Sanz, Hernandez; *American Antiquarian*, 8:124-126, 1886.

In spite of the destroying hand of time, there are still to be found in
Minorca (Balearic Isles), several megalithic monuments of past ages
scattered all over the eastern part of the island, which by the rudeness
of their construction show themselves to be the work of the early inhabitants. Even to-day the enormous heaps of stone called talayots cause
great astonishment; the great stone tables, the artificial caves or cellars,
rows of pillars and circles of menhirs, and those strange constructions
in the form of a ship, the only ones in the world. It would be a most difficult task to suggest a creditable account of their origin wrapped as is the
problem in the obscurity of history, difficult, if not impossible to solve.
We will content ourselves with a description of them as they are found to-
day when the lapse of ages and lack of care in their preservation cause a
sigh of regret for their state of decay.

1. Talayot with High Doorway at Torrello. Talayots are megalithic
monuments in form of a truncated cone whose base is circular, elliptic
or oval, and a few like a quadrangular truncated pyramid, formed by
greater or lesser number of rows of great stones mostly unhewn and with
no union whatever. From observation of the 130 or more which are to be
found to-day on the island, all do not seem to be of the same epoch, since
in some of them a certain grade of perfection in the cut of the stones is
seen which in others is lacking. As perfect types we may cite those in the
village of St. Augustine and Torrello which we will hereinafter describe.
The state of decay in which many of these monuments are to day will not
allow us to decide whether in their primitive state they were all hollow or
not allow us to decide whether in their primitive state they were all hollow
or not, although we are inclined to believe that some were solid on account
of being sloping on the outside and having no trace of an outer door. They
are commonly divided into two classes of talayots, those with high and low
doorways, according as their entrance is situated in the upper or lower
part of the monument. As a perfect model of the former we give that of
Torello (near Mahon) which exists in a pretty good state of preservation.
Its height is approximately 10 meters, it being impossible to ascertain its
exact measurement on account of the dense fields of brambles which surround it, and the modern buildings in its neighborhood. Its high or superior door which is reached by some projecting stepping-stones on the outside of the talayot, is 1.40 meters high by 1.00 meter wide; the upper
stone or lintel very well cut, measures 1.50 meters in length. Besides
this are remains of two other talayots completely in ruins, but which
must have been much smaller and some other monuments of the same
epoch.
. . . .

3. Dolmen and Talayot of Telaty de Dalt. By the name of dolmens,

sacrificial altars or tables in Minorca are known certain cyclopean monuments almost always composed of two great broad stones, situated, one vertically or on end, and the other, called the shelf, horizontally and in perfect equilibrium upon the former, forming a sort of table as the people have appropriately named it. Aside from these and departing from the general rule some few there are with two feet or supports, the second of which some archaeologists believe to be an extra prop to the shelf. If it be true that the altar of Torretrencada has a second foot which acts as a prop merely, the same cannot be said of that at Telaty de Dalt in spite of what has been said, since only an edge of the end which has the foot beams against the side of the shelf. Was this put there to form a second table? Some say this, but others say that doubtless they were thrown down in time and remained in the position in which they are now found, which is not very probable because the lower edge of the right foot is cut to a basil or bevel and rests upon a smooth stone, rather wide, showing that it could never have been placed in equilibrium. Of the sixteen altars still existing on the island, one of the best preserved is that of Telaty de Dalt. Its dimensions are as follows: Large altar (?). Right foot, height 2.89 m. width 2.50 m., thickness 0.37 m. Shelf, length 4.00 m., width 1.50 m., thickness 0.50 m. Small altar or prop (?). Foot, height, 2.83 m., width 0.35, thickness 0.20 m. Upper edge or shelf (?), length 0.75 m., width 0.50 m., thickness 0.30 m. These monuments are encircled by thirteen menhirs, some standing, some fallen, united or connected by large blocks forming an irregular circle open toward the north. The general height of the menhirs is 2 meters approximately, with the exception of one, which is 2.70 m.

4. Low Portal of the Talayot of Cornia. One of the most perfect and most characteristic types of talayots with the low entrance is situated in the estate of Cornia, (Mahon), the diameter of which is approximately 15 meters and not less than 11 meters in height. The low entrance or inferior door measures 0.80 m. in height and 0.60 m. in width. Within them are 10 or 12 steps, a stairway which once undoubtedly led to the upper part of the talayot, but the roof has fallen in and filled up the space entirely. Near this, which is the principal one of the group, are several remains of artificial caves or cellars, some menhirs and large monoliths.

....

GRAVES AND SMALL MOUNDS

Another natural human inclination is the commemoration of the dead with some sort of edifice. Ancient man did this, and so do we today. Ancient earthen burial mounds are found everywhere and are remarkable only if immense in size, profuse in number, or of perplexing construction. Since this is a book on the unusual artifact, the thousands of Indian mounds found by the first American settlers are passed by, as are similar structures in other parts of the world. Exceptions are made for burial mounds of peculiar or especially ambitious structure, particularly passage graves and mounds with pyramidal inclinations. Passage graves, with their long entrances, frequently have astronomical alignments. Pyramidal structures, of course, may be allied to the larger pyramids of Egypt and America with their astronomical, engineering, and occult significance.

• North America

THE EFFIGY MOUND; A COVERED CAIRN BURIAL SITE IN ANDOVER, MASS.
Glynn, Frank; *NEARA Newsletter*, 4:75-79, 1969.

The site is located on the brow of the hill on the 160-180' contour. Haggett's Pond's elevation is 116'. With leaves down, there is a fine prospect over the 220 acre pond and meadows to the east.

The site was reported by W. B. Goodwin in "Greater Ireland in New England," Meador Publishing Co., Boston, Mass., 1945; pages 100-108 and also the mislabeled photograph on p. 56, actually the site's northeast chamber.

His exploration entailed (1) photography, (2) a survey of the cairn by Blizzard & Carrington, (3) breaking out a concrete wall erected in the east chamber c 1900.

There are various neighborhood legends concerning the Nineteenth Century exploitation of the cairn in connection with a "Coney Island" at the pond. The most exasperating of these relates that a small wooden shed was erected to house "curios" from the site, with a separate admission charged. It is thought that some of these specimens are in the elusive Follansbee Collection. The presence today of such rare plants as the heather and mayflower rather confirm the story that the site was highly developed as an arboretum, with a tea house perched atop the east end of the cairn, etc., etc. Seven surfaced fragments of an orange flower pot, and a rusted corset stay two inches deep in the north east chamber, were the only modern evidence produced by the 1951 tests.

The Cairn. As the drawing indicates, the cairn is a large, man-made agglomeration of stone with architectural features. The stones range in size from cobbles to three tons. Beehive vaulting to a single large capstone is employed in the north east chamber. Rectangular slabs roof the east chamber.

Stone-quarrying techniques evident are splitting and a rude dressing of protrusions. Implements comparable to those found in pre-historic steatite quarries were excavated. Sizeable crevices between larger stones were chinked with smaller ones in the chambers.

19th century activities indicated are (1) carting away of stone nearest wood-road, (2) modification of the passage and (3) the east chamber.

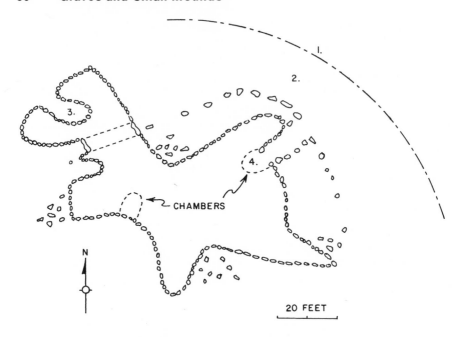

Massachusetts burial cairn?

TUMULI IN SOUTHWESTERN PENNSYLVANIA

Carpenter, Edmund S.; *American Antiquity*, 16:329–346, 1951.

Stone Graves. One of the most baffling riddles in Pennsylvania prehistory relates to the reported occurrence in this southwestern area of whole cemeteries of stone-covered and often stone-lined burial vaults, apparently unrelated to artificial mounds. Small of size, the vaults long excited the curiosity of all observers. Although actually a large number of the graves appear to have been either those of children or bundle burials, the early settlers both here and elsewhere had quite a different interpretation; they were the remains of a race of dwarfs. Both Smith and Farabee opened a number of these stone graves, and while Smith found only five perforated canine teeth, Farabee obtained utterly nothing and could only repeat the statements of farmers who alleged finding shell beads and copper pendants. Stone-covered graves opened by Engberg, appear to belong to the Monongahela aspect and may be unrelated to these large cemeteries. (p. 345)

THE STONE GRAVES OF TENNESSEE

Thompson, Alton Howard; *American Antiquarian*, 23:411-419, 1901.

The stone graves of Tennessee and the adjoining regions are unique in many respects and present features of peculiar interest to the archaeologist. Their structure is, of course the result of environment, the thin stone slabs being found abundantly in the locality, and being besides easy to procure the suggestion of their adaptability to the purposes of, sepulture was not unnatural. To a people possessed of such love and veneration for their dead as these tribes exhibited, the presence of such an excellent and accessible material was a great convenience.

The contents of these remarkable burial places are also of great interest in that these are peculiar and to a great extent characteristic. The pottery is very unusual in sculptural decoration, and is unique in some of its forms, having peculiarities of its own which are related in but a limited degree even to that of the mounds further north and west. The most of it is indigenous in pattern. Flints of wonderful construction have been found, and also carved shells, copper implements and ornaments, etc., which are in many respects peculiar to the stone graves and to the caves and mounds of this region. Some of these remains are, of course, related to those of the mounds north and west, but the finest of them are almost unique and are found no where else but in the stone grave region.

Concerning the method of burial in this region, Dr. Joseph Jones says, (Aboriginal Remains of Tennessee), "The ancient race of Tennessee buried their dead in rude stone coffins or, cists, constructed of flat pieces of limestone or slaty sandstone which abound in middle Tennessee. Extensive graveyards in which stone coffins lie close together are found in Tennessee and Kentucky, along the river courses, in the valleys and around the springs. A considerable portion of the city of Nashville has been built over an extensive graveyard which laid along the valley of Lick Branch. A large number of the graves have been destroyed in the building of North Nashville, numbers being exposed in digging the cellars. Around these graves were formerly scattered fragments of pottery, arrow heads, stone implements, etc. The graves, although generally considered as rude fabrics, nevertheless exhibit considerable skill in their construction. The manner of burial seems to have been as follows:---an excavation was made of the proper size and the bottom paved with flat stones. Then others were placed on edge along the sides and at the head and foot. These were twelve to eighteen inches wide. The body was then placed within this rude coffin and with it were arranged painted vases, ornaments of pearl, beads, various kinds of weapons, large seashells, stone hatchets, flint implements, copper tools and plates, etc. The top of the grave was then covered over with flat stones. The top slabs or many of them are now upon the level of the ground, but were probably originally covered with several inches of earth. Even yet in the most carefully constructed burial mounds the graves were covered with a foot or more of earth and to discover their location it is necessary to probe with an iron rod. In some localities the sides of the tombs stood up above the surface from four to eight inches, as in the instances described by Bartram. When a number of coffins were placed together, the side stones of the first frequently constituted the sides of the second and so on. Many of the stone graves are quite small and capable of containing only the body of a new born infant. These small graves were constructed with much care and they were made of much thinner and smoother slabs than those of adults. Many of the short, square graves were not over eighteen inches or two feet in length and contained the bones of adults pitched in promiscuously. This class of grave containing the bones of adults packed in a small space were constructed at the general burial festivals, or held the bones of warriors or others which had been transported from a distance."

It was formerly held that these small graves indicated that that the people were a race of pigmies, but this erroneous idea has been thoroughly refuted. Dr. Jones demonstrated that they "contained the bones of children who had died during the process of dentition," (as was easily proven by the jaws which contained the milk-teeth and some of the permanent ones in course of eruption), "or adult bones loosly thrown in, or the bones of small animals." Haywood, in his Natural and Aboriginal History of Tennessee was one of the first to promulgate the pigmy theory and is the most responsible for its early prevalence. He says, "A number of small skeletons were discovered near Sparta, White Co., Tennessee. An account of which is given by a Mr. Lane. These graves were about two feet in length, fourteen inches wide, and sixteen inches in depth. The graves contained the small skeletons of human beings much decayed, together with ornaments and pretty shells and the bones of small animals. One skeleton as it lay was found to be two feet and ten inches in length." "From the great numbers of small graves found here," says Mr. Lane, all of the same description, it seems to indicate that there were, in ancient times a race of people whose height was from two feet ten inches to three feet." The pigmy theory was very extensively quoted and received until exploded by Dr. Jones. He says, "I myself examined the bones from fifteen aboriginal cemeteries and have never discovered a single skeleton of an adult of unusually small stature. I have examined graves of all sizes, from those just large enough for the still-born infant to those containing a skeleton more than seven feet in length. It is true in many cases the small graves contained either the skeletons of children, or the bones of full grown adults, which had been deposited in the square stone coffins after they had been separated from the flesh and disjointed."

Dr. Troost, in his Ancient Remains of Tennesse, after examining six extensive burying places about Nashville says, "I have opened numbers of these small graves and found them filled with a parcel of moulded bones which belonged to common sized men. Indians have burying festivals when they collect the bones of those slain in battle and preserved against such an occasion: and thus, in my opinion, originated those small graves which were attributed formerly to pigmies." (pp. 411-413)

A STRANGE CAVERN
Anonymous; *American Antiquarian*, 13:180-181, 1891.

The residents of East Union, Ohio, several miles east of Wooster, are considerably worked up over the discovery of a cave near the village. J. M. Davis, Will S. Grady and Alexander Hunter, while out hunting, chased a rabbit into a burrow on a hill near the line of the Cleveland, Akron & Columbus railway. Determined to secure the game, they procured a mattock and shovel and proceeded to dig it out. After excavating the earth to a depth of about four feet they uncovered a curiously shaped stone, upon which were the evident marks of human workmanship. Examining it closely it proved to be a piece of rock resembling granite in color and nearly as hard, three feet square and covered on its upper side with rude engravings of human heads, arrows, hearts and fishes. Abandoning the rabbit, they called to their aid Peter Lawrence and Simon Buch, who were at work near by, and succeeded in raising the stone upon its edge. It proved to be about seven and a half inches in thickness, and on its under side was a rude picture of the sun, in the center of which are a tomahawk and pipe more deeply engraved. The stone itself closed the opening into a subterranean chamber, which, with the aid of a ladder and lantern, was found to be in the form of a cubical cistern (perfectly dry), ten feet high, ten feet wide and ten feet long, carved in solid sandstone, with exquisite precision, and containing a few arrow-heads, stone pestle and mortar, the remains of a fire, and in the northwest corner, sitting in an upright position, a human skeleton, in a good state of preservation, with circlets of copper about its neck, wrist and ankle bones. Its eyeless sockets were turned toward the entrance, and looked sad and ghastly.

. . . .

WHAT ARE THE BURNT ROCK MOUNDS OF TEXAS?
Kelley, J. Charles, and Campbell, T. N.; *American Antiquity*, 7:319-322, 1942.

In the Edwards Plateau and Trans-Pecos regions of southwestern Texas are a large number of archaeological sites which have been referred to as "burnt rock mounds." Although this name is now well established in the archaeological literature of Texas, one looks in vain for a satisfactory statement concerning the origin and nature of these rather unusual sites. Quite a number have been excavated, but as yet few detailed reports on individual sites have appeared. The authors of recent reports assume that the term "burnt rock mound" is well understood and, although implying that it represents a distinct culture trait, do not explain what it means. It is evident that many archaeologists do not understand its meaning, for at recent archaeological meetings outside of Texas the writers of this paper have frequently been asked, "Just what is a burnt rock mound?" In view of this, it seems advisable to put on record a brief summary of what is known at present about the formation of these sites.

Burnt rock mounds are low eminences or knolls which are made up of thousands of densely packed angular fragments of limestone or other available country rock. They also contain varying amounts of soil, charcoal and ash, snail and mussel shells, animal bones, artifacts, and occasionally human burials. In outline, these mounds are circular or oval and, in size, they vary from a few square yards up to several acres. The thickness of the deposit also varies greatly, but even in the larger mounds it rarely exceeds six or eight feet.

Some of the largest and best known of the burnt rock mounds are situated in the eastern part of the Edwards Plateau, notably along the Balcones escarpment. Here they occur in two different physiographic positions: (1) on bedrock or on residual soil near streams and springs, and (2) on the alluvial terraces of stream valleys.

Pearce, who excavated a number of these sites in the vicinity of Austin, published the first description of a burnt rock mound in 1919. Neither Pearce nor those who follow regard these sites as mounds in the sense of having been purposefully constructed by man. All agree that the mounds grew by accretion incident to occupation. Pearce states:

> The general contents of the mounds force the conclusion that they are largely kitchen-middens in origin. Limestone slabs were probably placed about fires to keep the fire together and for cooking and boiling water. After being heated a few times, a rain would cause them to break into small fragments that were no longer serviceable. These were then thrown back in a heap and new slabs placed in and about the fire. To the heap was also added the rejects and fragments from the making of flint implements.

The limestone referred to is derived from Cretaceous formations which crop out obtensively over the Edwards Plateau. The dark gray color of the limestone fragments from the mounds is due to contact with fire, and the angularity is a result of thermal fracturing. All of the evidence supports Pearce's conclusion that burnt rock mounds are accumulations of hearthstones. However, Pearce does not explain why hearths should continue to be built in the same places, so that burnt rock mounds would be formed. Wilson accounts for all burnt rock mounds in terms of their use in the preparation of sotol for food, but this hardly explains why the same places should be used continuously or repeatedly. Furthermore, sotol does not grow in the eastern part of the Edwards Plateau, where some of the largest burnt rock mounds occur.

. . . .

AN INDIAN CAIRN
Anonymous; *Scientific American*, 3:234, 1848.

On the road to Oregon about one hundred miles west of Fort Laramie there is a pile of stones about 200 feet high, and three hundred feet in circumference at the base. The stones vary in size from the size of ones thumb to that of a water pail, all placed as regular as masonry. This could not have been a freak of nature. They must have been piled up by men to commemorate some great event---but by whom and for what purpose who can tell?---A short distance from this pile are two large rocks about twenty feet apart and 50 feet high. The opposing surfaces show that they were once united, but thrown apart from some convulsion of nature.

Independence Rock, on the same route is an immense pile, covering 20 acres of ground and is 3000 feet high. On one side it is broken and falls off. From the top you can see hundreds of miles.

On the side of this rock next the road are ten thousand names of men or emigrants who were going to Oregon.

In the top of it is a large hole or reservoir, that will hold six or eight barrels of water. There are also holes in the side that form complete rooms. On the walls of these rooms are written a great many names. At the foot of the rock runs the Sweet Water river a beautiful clear stream.

DATA ON THE STRUCTURE OF PRECOLUMBIAN HUASTEC MOUNDS IN THE TAMPICO REGION, MEXICO
Muir, John M.; *Royal Anthropological Institute, Journal*, 56:231-238, 1926.

Large numbers of artificial mounds are scattered throughout the Tampico district of Mexico, extending from Xicotencatl, about 140 kilometres north-west of Tampico, in the State of Tamaulipas, and to the Tuxpam River some 150 kilometres southward in the State of Vera Cruz.

. . . .

These mounds belong to the Huastec civilization. They usually occur in groups among which the largest individual mounds reach a height of 5 or 6 metres with a diameter at the base of 9 to 11 metres. In the vicinity of the larger mounds lie several of an intermediate, and many of small size down to a metre or less in height.

With a view to finding out whether the mounds had any definite alignment or relation to one another it was decided to map two separate groups in different localities.

A prominent series of these Huastec mounds occurs in the Hacienda Santa Fe, near Topila, on the south bank of the Panuco River, about 23 kilometres south-west of Tampico. They were formerly mapped by the author and reproduced by Dr. Staub.

In 1925 it was decided to re-map them, the work being undertaken by Mr. Cecil Drake. The general trend of the mounds is N. 20°E. The group as a whole surrounds a centre court 85 metres long in a north to south direction, and 35 metres wide from east to west. The tallest mound, "22.1," in the north-east, has a height of 7 metres. A small trench cut in the northernmost of the two latter mounds shows the presence of horizontal cement flooring in the structure. Five floors in all, 2 cm. to 3 cm. thick, were seen, respectively, 20 cm., 30 cm., 105 cm., 160 cm., and 180 cm. from the top of the mound. The cement floors contained fragments of charcoal, and the material was evidently obtained from the sandy limestones, of Oligocene age, in the neighbouring hills. The mounds themselves have been built up from the soil of the immediate neighbourhood. To the east of the mounds, in the road, much broken pottery is visible, and small arrow-heads of flint and obsidian have been found.

. . . .

Section of a Huastec mound, Tampico, Mexico

The following generalizations can be made:---In building Huastec mounds any material conveniently available was used---shell, stone slabs, and, as previously mentioned, even asphalt from seepages. In the alluvial sections of the Panuco Valley, no other material being available, only soil entered into the construction of a mound. The present rounded or conical outline of the mounds is due to time and natural degradation.

The general aspect of Huastec mounds having been discussed, mention will be made of two interesting discoveries in Mound E.

On June 20th, 1925, the writer was advised by Mr. Charles McNair that, on a visit to the mounds in the Colonia Flores, he had seen evidence of a painted design on one of the cement floors of Mound E. As the mounds were being cut down by the municipal authorities, and the floor with the design destroyed by the passage of cart-wheels, it was decided to make a drawing of the object immediately. For the accompanying drawing Mr. G. F. Kaufmann is responsible. The design appeared to have been first executed in a reddish colour with a second coat of black paint over the former. The design had a total length of 270 cm. from east to west, and a width of 135 cm. in a north to south direction. The drawing is, of course, more perfectly executed than the original, but all possible care was taken to note or count the number of divisions in the "ladder-like" arrangement. The centre of the design consisted of an inner circle of 25 cm. to 36 cm. diameter divided into 24 segments. These segments were not quite equal, due to the roughness of the execution. The inside of this circle was joined by a ladder arrangement of six divisions in a north to south direction. On the outer circumference, connection was made on the east and west sides with a larger segmented circle of 49 cm. to 62 cm. diameter. This circle was divided rather unevenly into 34 setments. Connection was made by two lines between the larger circle and the rectangular part of the rest of the design. The drawing is self-explanatory, so that further description need not be entered into.

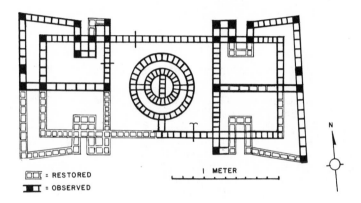

= RESTORED

= OBSERVED

I METER

N

Painted design on floor of a Huastec mound

An exposure of part of the immediately underlying cement floor showed that there was another painted design below the one described above. As it was quite obvious that the remainder of the mound would be destroyed when excavation was resumed by the workmen on the following Monday morning, it was decided to peel off the upper floor and expose the design below. This was done on June 21st, the drawing of the design being undertaken by Mr. Cecil Drake. It was similar in general outline to that on the floor above but more complete, as it had not been subject to the passage of cart-wheels, etc. It was slightly smaller than that in [the figure], being 250 cm. long from east to west, and 128 cm. in width. The position with reference to the points of the compass was approximately the same in both instances. In the second design the sides adjacent to the extreme corners were square with reference to one another, whereas on the upper floor the connecting lines formed a slight angle. The inside of the squares where the lines cross or intersect were painted in solid. This can be noted on the photographic reproduction of the north-west corner.

The writer is not able to state the purpose or use the pre-Columbian Huastecs had for these drawings. Until further research has been done and more evidence is forthcoming it must be largely a matter of conjecture.   At first glance the designs suggest something like the games now known as "Ludo" or "Parchesi. "

. . . .

• Pacific Islands

ON THE TOMBS ON THE ISLAND OF ROTUMAH
Wood, W. W.; *Anthropological Institute, Journal*, 6:5–6, 1876.

On reading Lieutenant Oliver's paper on "The Megalithic Structures of the Channel Islands, " I bethought me of some notes and sketches made years ago on the Island of Rotumah, in the South Pacific Ocean, where I met with some curious stone tombs, composed of masses so large that it was difficult to conceive the means by which the natives had been able to move and arrange them.   The Island of Rotumah is an outlier of the Fiji group, though at a considerable distance to the north.   The natives are of a different race and lighter colour than those of the Fiji's, and are distinguished (or were) for their amiable and inoffensive manners.   The island is a small one, and not very high, except towards one end, where there is a precipice overlooking the sea, with a large flat terrace at its base, overflowed at high tide.

. . . .

The megalithic monuments on the principal island were not far from the beach, near some very fine old trees.   The tombs consisted of a low platform of earth, enclosed by slabs of stone set verti-

Rotumah tomb, showing massive stone blocks (no dimensions given in article)

cally, and in the centre one or more huge stones of irregular shape
---mere masses of rock---some of which must weigh many tons.
The natives seemed shy of giving any information respecting these
curious structures, and from a European, who had settled on the
island, we could only learn that they were tombs. The remarkable
point was that these simple people should, without the aid of machinery, have been able to raise and arrange these great masses of rock.

. . . .

NOTES ON THE ANTIQUITIES OF TONGA

Thomason, Basil; *Royal Anthropological Institute, Journal*, 32:81-88,
1902.

The monuments in Tonga that have a claim to antiquity are the following:---(1) The Haamonga stones near Kolonga (East Tongatabu); (2) The
artificial hill near Holeva at the mouth of the Mua Lagoon and similar
mounds in various parts of the group; (3) The Langi, or tombs of the
sacred kings (Tui Tonga) at Mua.
    (1) The Haamonga stones have been so often described that I shall
only deal here with the question of their antiquity. The common tradition among the natives is that they were erected by the god Maui with
stones that he brought in a giant canoe from Uea (Wallis Island), which
is equivalent to saying that they know nothing at all about them, for on
the principle of omne ignotum pro magnifico, Maui is made to take the
credit for everything that they cannot explain. It is further alleged that
in the reef at Uea the holes from which these stones were quarried may
still be seen, and that the stone is of a kind not found in Tonga. This
is not the case; the stones are, in my opinion, merely weathered coral,
similar to that used in facing the Langi at Mua, but more roughly cut.
Similar, though smaller, blocks may be seen on the reef where they were
left lying ready for removal by the stone-dressing caste. In the Voyage
of the "Duff" (1799), p. 283, the then Tui Tonga, Futtafaihe (Fatafehi
Fuanu Nuiava) stated that the stones of the Langi were brought in a double
canoe from the island of Lefooga (Lifuka) in the Haapai group; possibly
some of the smaller stones were so brought, and the fame of the exploit
gave rise to the Maui myth.
    Such stone is soft enough to be cut with the chisel and the handsaw
when it is newly quarried, but, after a very few years of exposure to
the weather, the lime forms upon it an external crust of surprising hardness. I believe that the Haamonga stones were quarried from the reef
opposite their present situation, and set up by means of inclined planes
of earth. Their purpose will always remain a matter of conjecture. At
first sight they suggest a gateway to some sacred spot inland, but I have
examined the bush for some distance in their neighbourhood, and have
found no trace of ruins, or stones of any kind. Moreover, the memory
of sacred spots dies very hard in Tonga, and the natives do not believe
them to have been a gateway. I have lately received from Mateialona,

The Haamonga Stones, Tonga

the Governor of Haapai and cousin to the king, a letter in answer to one
of mine on this subject. He says: "Concerning the Haamonga of Maui,
they say forsooth that a Tui Tonga (the sacred line of chiefs), named
Tui-ta-tui, erected it, and that he was so named because it was a time
of assassination. And they say that he had it built for him to sit upon
during the Faikava (ceremony of brewing kava), when the people sat
round him in a circle, and that the king so dreaded assassination that
he had this lordly seat built for himself that he might sit out of the reach
of his people. And this, they say, is the origin of the present custom of
the Faikava, it being now forbidden for anyone to sit behind the king"
(the presiding chief sits at the apex of an oval). Mr. Shirley Baker told
me that he believed the Haamonga to have been erected as a <u>fakamanatu</u>
(memorial) to the son of some Tui Tonga, a view that finds support in
the fondness of Tongan chiefs for originality in the burial ceremonies of
their near relations---witness Mariner's account of the funeral of

Finau's daughter (vol. i, p. 373)---but on the other hand native traditions generally have a kernel of truth, and the legend of Tui-ta-tui and
its consequences finds an analogy in our own custom of guarding against
an assassin's dagger at the drinking of the loving-cup.

I have, unfortunately, mislaid my notes containing the measurements
of the Haamonga stones, but in 1884 the passengers of the SS. Wairarapa,
on a yachting cruise from New Zealand to the South Sea Islands, published an anonymous pamphlet entitled The Wairarapa Wilderness, from
which the following detailed account of the monument and its dimensions
is extracted:---

"The shape of the monument at first sight appears to be identical
with the form so well known at Stonehenge, namely, two upright stones
with a third one lying across the top of them, but a moment's observation shows a very marked difference. Instead of the upper one being
merely superimposed, in this case it is carefully inserted into the other
two. A groove about two feet wide has been cut in each upright stone,
and the upper stone, which has been carefully cut to the right size, has
been placed in it, so that the ends are about flush with the outside of the
perpendicular stones, while the top is about flush with the top of the
stones; but, owing to the easternmost stone being a little lower than the
other one, probably from breakage, it rises a little above it on that side.
The horizontal stone lies east and west, and it is noticeable that, either
by accident or design, there is a slight though perceptible inclination of
the faces of the perpendicular stones towards the north, i. e., the north
end of the opening between the stones is slightly narrower than the south
end. On the centre of the top of the horizontal stone a hollow has been
scooped out about the size of a cocoanut shell, and about 1-1/2 inches
deep, though whether this hollow has been part of the original design,
or has been made at a subsequent period, it is impossible to say. Owing
to the pressure of time and the absence of any correct tape or ruler, the
measurements taken must be considered as approximate; they are, however, roughly as follows:---Height of the perpendicular stones, 14 to
15 feet; depth of the horizontal stone, 4 feet 6 inches; distance between
the perpendicular stones, 10 feet; base of the perpendicular stones,
north-east side, 4 feet, north-west side, about 12 feet, or probably
less; breadth of the perpendicular stones at the top, 7 feet, probably
more. Thus it will be seen that the space contained between the three
stones is nearly a square, if not absolutely so. ... It seemed that there
were some indications of a trench on both the north and south sides, and
also that the trenches were part of a large circle, the stones being at
the northernmost end (the end nearest the sea), but these indications
are so faint that without further examination it would be impossible to
pronounce with any certainty upon this. The stones are situated about
80 yards from the seashore. "

Age. ---The fact that no detailed tradition of the origin of these stones
survives does not argue any great antiquity. Mr. Abraham Fornander,
it is true, professes to have traced traditional Polynesian history for
more than ten centuries, but my experience is that, beyond a doubtful
list of kings' names, tradition does not carry us back for more than
seven or eight generations, and that beyond this limit we are apt to step
into the region of mythology. The name of Tui-ta-tui does, however,
occur in Mr. Moulton's list of the Tui Tonga, as preceding Takalaua
(circa 1535) by eight generations. In historical times the generations
of the Tui Tonga averaged twenty-seven years, and on this computation

Tui-ta-tui was living in 1319. But in those troublous times the kings must have trod closer upon one another's heels, and Tui-ta-tui's reign may more plausibly be assigned to the latter half of the fourteenth century.

But though the Haamonga monument is thus assigned by native tradition to the fourteenth century, there are considerations which point to the later date. For the quarrying and mortising of stones weighing some 50 tons apiece the craft of stone-cutting must have been fully developed. In Mariner's time (1810) the Tofunga ta maka (stone-vault masons) were caste apart, but the despotic power of the chiefs was then declining, and they were not called upon to execute any notable public work. Their greatest achievement was the larger of the two Langi built in the reign of Telea, of which one contains his body, and the other is still tenantless. If this Telea is identical with Uluaki Matatelea, the successor to the king who entertained Tasman in 1643, the craft of stone-dressing may be said to have reached its culmination at the end of the seventeenth century. The Langis of the kings earlier than Telea are poor in comparison, and the stones are small, irregular, and roughly quarried. It is therefore difficult to conceive that so fine a work as the Haamonga can have been executed by craftsmen who could not build a decent tomb for their kings, unless the craft of quarrying had declined between the fourteenth and the seventeenth centuries, and had had a renaissance, which would be contrary to all our knowledge of native craftsmanship. Yet, when one is left to choose between a definite native tradition on the one hand and probability on the other for the assignment of a date, I would prefer the tradition. If the Tongans had invented the story as a mere expression for antiquity they would not have pitched upon Tui-ta-tui, about whom nothing else is recorded, in preference to Takalaua, Kau-ulu-fonua-fekai, or any of the kings who loom large in traditionary history. Whether the Haamonga was built for a throne or for a memorial, doubtless it is connected with the reign of Tui-ta-tui, who lived in the fourteenth century.

(2) The Artificial Hill near Holeva. ---This is, I think, the first time that attention has been called to what I believe to be the oldest monument in Tonga. Among the mangroves on the western side of the entrance to the Mua Lagoon and about half a mile south-east of the Roman Catholic Mission station at Maofanga, near Nukualofa, there is an artificial hill about 15 feet high. The mound is so heavily timbered that its real character can only be seen by visiting it, which few people do, as it lies at some distance from any road, and it can only be approached at low tide. I made a second and more careful examination of it in May, 1900. Leaving the beach road at the ford at Holeva Point (the place where Captain Cook pitched his instruments in 1777, naming it Observatory Point in his chart), we rode along the reef left bare by the tide until we came to a sort of wharf or causeway, which slopes down to high-water mark on the western shore of the lagoon. The causeway was built of coral lumps about the size of a man's head, about 6 feet wide on the top and from 40 to 60 feet long, sloping gently upward to the summit of the hill, and gradually widening to 12 feet. The hill itself is roughly quadrilateral, with rounded angles and almost perpendicular sides. It appears to be built entirely of rough lumps of coral, just as they are taken from the reef, but so carefully laid that, except in a few places, none had fallen out. The summit was quite flat and covered with black mould. It was so choked with undergrowth and creepers that it was impossible to measure it accurately, but it seemed to be about 60 feet from

north to south and 40 feet from east to west. The causeway joined it about the middle of the eastern side. In Captain Cook's time it was "overgrown with low trees and shrubs, " but the trees at present growing on it did not seem to be more than thirty or forty years old. In Cook's Third Voyage, vol. i, p. 289, it is described as follows:---"At this place is a work of art which shows that these people are capable of some design and perseverance when they mean to accomplish anything. This work begins on one side as a narrow causeway, which, becoming gradually broader, rises with a gentle ascent to the height of ten feet, where it is five paces broad, and the whole length twenty-four paces. Joined to this is a sort of circus whose diameter is thirty paces and not above a foot or two higher than the causeway that joins it, with some trees planted in the middle. On the opposite side another causeway descends, but this is not above forty paces long, and is partly in ruin. The whole is built with large coral stones with earth on the surface, which is quite overgrown with low trees and shrubs, and from its decaying in several places seems to be of no modern date. Whatever may have been its use formerly, it seems to be of none now, and all that we could learn of it from the natives was that it belonged to Poulaho, and is called Etchee. " On p. 357 of the same volume Cook describes another of these mounds in the island of Eua: "On the most elevated part of the whole island, we found a round platform, or mount of earth, supported by a wall of coral stones. . . . Our guides told us that this mount had been erected by order of their chief, and they sometimes met there to drink kava. They called it Etchee. " Again on p. 262 he describes similar mounds in the islands of Lifuka and Holeva in the Haapai group. At the foot of the former, he says, stood a stone which must have been hewn out of coral rock. It was 4 feet broad, 2-1/2 feet thick, and 14 feet high, "and we were told by the natives that not half of its length appeared above ground. They called it Tangata-arekee (Tangata eiki   Chief). . . . that it had been set up and the mount raised in memory of one of their kings. "

During my visit I questioned both Tungi and Fakafonua, the principal chiefs of this district and the repositories of much ancient lore, but neither was able to tell me anything about the hill on the Mua Lagoon. In the letter before referred to, however, Mateialona writes as follows: ---"Concerning the matter you have written about, namely, the origin of the series of mounds in Tongatabu and Haapai, which we in Tonga call the Jia. The Jia at Holeva, now used as a rifle butt, is attributed to a Tui Tonga of a very remote period, who ordered the people to erect this Jia and called it Suimafua'uta. The numerous Jia that are near Maofanga belonged to his daughter, and are ascribed to a feast that used to be celebrated by the chiefs of old time. " This is tantamount to a confession that the Tongans have no definite traditions about the Holeva mound, for if anyone could have got hold of a tradition it would have been Mateialona, who is very intelligent and takes some interest in antiquities. I have no doubt that the word Jia is identical with Cook's "Etchee." The J, which is now pronounced S, was used in Mariner's time as a hard Ch. Even in my time a few of the old men so pronounced it. Cook would have heard the word prefixed with the article "Koe Chia, " or " 'ae Chia, " and he would easily mistake the last syllable of the article for part of the word, and have written it down as Echia or "Etchee. " I am not sure of the etymology of the word, for the only Jia with which I am acquainted is an archaic word meaning "good, " used ironically for bad or indifferent.

It is probably connected with the Marquesan word for a public meeting-house, spelt "Ti" by Herman Melville ("Typee," p. 169).

. . . .

• Asia

PREHISTORIC JAPAN
Baelz, E.; *Smithsonian Institution Annual Report, 1907,* pp. 523–547.

A particular form of grave is represented by the imperial graves (Jap. "Misasagi") of the dolmen period. They would be more appropriately termed princely graves, since they do not occur only in central Japan, where the Emperor always lived, but also in all the districts where dolmens abound, and which must be considered as the seats of great feudal princes. These graves are often only a kind of unusually large dolmen mounds, yet they are prominent not only by their often enormous dimensions, but they have other peculiarities. In contrast to the position of the dolmens on hills, these graves lie principally on plains. They are double mounds of a characteristic form (as the accompanying figure by Gowland shows), consisting of a trapezoidal mound flat on top and often terraced, joined to a higher circular one likewise flat on top. Around the whole structure runs a large ditch or moat. The orientation of the long dimension is east and west. The entrance to the dolmen is in the south side about a third or half way up the circular mound. It contains one and often

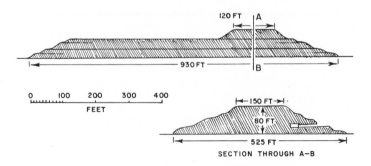

Section of a Japanese imperial grave

two stone or terra cotta sarcophagi. At other times the sarcophagi are buried in the mound without any real dolmen structure. The whole mound is surrounded at different levels by several rows of short, broad, hollow tubes of terra-cotta placed close together. The total number of these often runs up into the thousands. The terra cotta figures, called Tsutshinigyo (earth figures), are also found here, but only a few are preserved, since most of them soon crumble away in the open air.

An idea of the enormous labor which the erection of such grave mounds entailed may be obtained from the fact that one of these misasagi with its moat covers not less than 200 acres.

. . . .

The distribution of the dolmens is interesting and at the same time gives an idea of the political and social state of affairs at that time. A glance at the map shows that geographically Japan is divided into two almost equal parts, a western half (somewhat south, to be sure), which includes a part of the main island and the great islands Kiuschiu and Skikoku, and another half running almost north and south, which is made up of the larger part of the main island and of Jezo. The two parts are joined almost at right angles by a broad isthmus at 136-137° longitude east of Greenwich and 34-35° northern latitude. This isthmus forms an important ethnical and civilizational boundary. The bronze culture is absolutely and the iron culture nearly confined to the country west of the isthmus. Northward of it is the main region of neolithic culture; only here are found the well-finished stone weapons and neolithic human clay figures in any quantity. In this large northern territory we find, however, one well-circumscribed oasis of iron-age culture with dolmens---the fertile plain around Tokio with the surrounding mountainous country.

Besides this isolated group in the north, we can distinguish five other centers for the dolmens, two of which lie in the great southern island of Kiushiu. The smaller one is near the Pacific, in the province of Hiuga, where the grandfather of the first Emperor is supposed to have come down from heaven and whence he is said to have started on his victorious march. This took him first to the north of the Kiushiu. Here we find the second large dolmen region, including the island of Tsushima and the provinces lying opposite the southern point of Korea, a region where bronze weapons are especially frequent. This region was afterwards for a thousand years the seat of powerful vassals, who were often enough arrayed against the imperial court. From here, according to the Japanese annals, the first Emperor continued his journey across the bay of Shimonoseki to the main island and marched along the shores of the inland sea. On this road we encounter a third dolmen center in the province of Bizen. The conquest at last reached its goal in the central provinces, the Gokinai, which were from then the seat of the imperial rule for more than two thousand years. It is no wonder then that we find here the fourth and largest of the dolmen centers.

The fifth lies along the northwest coast of the principal island in and around the province of Idzumo, where, as mentioned above, the conquerors already found a civilized people. The sixth is that in and around the Tokyo plain.

Thus the legendary stories of ancient Japanese history are corroborated by the archeological finds. From these we learn that the invaders, a people in the iron-age culture, took possession of the fertile coast stretches in the southwest and spread out to the east and north along the ocean. In Yamato and Idzumo they encountered organized communities of a cultivated and probably related race; these they subdued only after a fierce struggle. The regions where we find the Dolmen centers were ruled by feudal princes who for a long time recognized the Emperor only as primus inter pares, since they were buried in a similar manner as the Emperor himself. Their power was gradually absorbed by the emperors in Yamato, and at last these were able to proclaim themselves "sole rulers by the grace of the gods."

The period of the imperial mounds as well as of the common dolmen mounds which are found in groups of 10 to 200 at the foot or on the slope of hills, probably began at least in the fourth century B. C., perhaps a good deal earlier. Its end is fixed about the year 700 A. D., since at that time an imperial edict was issued forbidding this form of burial. Cremation was then inaugurated under the influence of Buddhism.

It is noticeable in connection with the Japanese dolmens that (1) they are found in neither the stone nor the bronze age, but belong exclusively to the iron age; that (2) they are always of a megalithic nature, simple stone vaults or so-called cists not having been found so far in Japan, although they are numerous in Korea; and that (3) the country where they are found is entirely isolated from all regions with similar structures. It is necessary to go as far as the Caspian Sea or to the northern part of India to find anything like them. But their most similar counterparts existed in prehistoric Northern Europe. (pp. 538-547)

• Middle East

THE TUMULI OF BAHREIN
Cornwall, P. B.; *Asia and the Americas*, 43:230-234, 1943.

On Bahrein Island, in the Persian Gulf, there exist acre upon acre of round burial mounds. Usually referred to as "tumuli," these mounds exceed fifty thousand in number and cover a considerable portion of the northern half of the island. Some are only a few feet in height and diameter, but others resemble small pyramids, being as high as 30 feet, and having a diameter at the base of 76 feet or more. In general the mounds are so close together that only a few yards separate one from another, and at a little distance they present the appearance of a great, rolling sea of gravel heaps. Until very recently nothing quite like these tumuli fields was believed to exist anywhere else.

. . . .

The bulk of the island tumuli---those once labeled Phoenician---fall into two categories: first, a small cairnlike rock mound, usually not over four or five feet high, found principally on the heights near the central basin; second, a larger type constructed of dirt and limestone chips, which includes the so-called "pyramid mounds." On the average these gravel tumuli are two or three times the size of the rock mounds and, unlike them, are nearly always found closely grouped together on level or slightly slop-ing ground and at a distance from the central basin.

. . . .

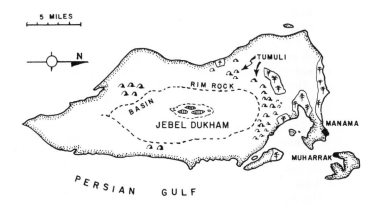

Distribution of Bahrein tumuli

The shape of a Bahrein tomb chamber is quite distinctive. Occasion-ally it is little more than an oblong cist---8 or 9 feet long by 3 feet wide and 3 feet high---with a simple doorway; but usually it is larger and has from one to four corner-recesses. As a rule, these recesses are small and empty, but in the really large tombs they are like anterooms and sometimes contain a skeleton. If there is only one recess, it is invariably in the northeast corner. No wholly satisfactory explanation for the re-cesses has yet been offered. It hardly seems likely that the Bahrein tombs were intended to reproduce the houses of the living, being simple or complex according to the rank or wealth of the individual. They are more apt to have some special religious significance.

. . . .

• Africa

BURIAL MONUMENTS OF NORTH AFRICA
Anonymous; *Scientific American*, 85:248, 1901.

In North Africa are found two great burial tumuli or mausoleums, which date even before the Roman occupation, and were, no doubt, built by the native kings of Mauretania and Numidia. The first of these, shown in the engraving, it situated near the coast of the Mediterranean, about thirty miles from Algiers, and was at that period near the ancient port of Caesarea (now Cherchell). It stands upon a high hill in the narrowest part of the Sahel range, and thus dominates the surrounding country. Its form is that of an enormous cylinder resting upon a square foundation and surmounted by a cone-shaped part which is built up of a series of steps reaching to the summit. At the base it measures 197 feet in diameter, and its present height is 102 feet, but it must have been over 120 feet high originally. For the construction, cut stone of large dimensions is used---disposed in symmetrical order and united by tenons of lead. The lower part is ornamented with sixty semi-circular pilasters, which appear to be applied against the wall, but really form part of it. The pilasters had Ionic capitals and supported a cornice of simple profile. At the four cardinal points were four ornamental panels or false doors, whose moldings imitated by their disposition a great cross inclosed in a frame. Before the eastern panel, and perhaps attached to the body, was an exterior structure or portico of rectangular shape, of which only the base remains. This monument remained an enigma for a long period. The Arabs called it Kbour-Roumia, or Tomb of the Christian, on account of the cross upon the northern panel, which was still preserved, and their imagination invented many legends in which were associated buried treasure, fairies and sorcerers. In the sixteenth century these legends were added to under the Spanish dominion, and it was assigned as the burial place of different important personages, but all without the slightest foundation. These legends excited the Pacha Salah-Rais (1552-1556) to try to find the hidden treasure, and he had the monument cannonaded; but, although he made a large breach in the western side, he was not able to lay bare the chamber containing the riches. Later on, Baba Mohammed ben Otsman, pacha of Algiers (1766-1791), demolished the revetment wall on the east side in the same way, but without any better result. What was more destructive to the monument than the cannonading was the removal of the lead tenons to make bullets, and thus a great number of the stones were overthrown.

The first regular excavations were made in 1865-66 by Berbrugger and McCarthy under Napoleon III. They cleared away a part of the outer wall, and made soundings to find an internal cavity, but it was only after four months that it was found. By a tunnel under the south panel they arrived in a vast gallery, admirably preserved, and thus discovered the internal arrangement of the structure. The entry is a low, rectangular opening below the ground and in the foundation masonry, in the rear of the rectangular structure previously mentioned. It was closed by three stones which were flush with the rest of the masonry. Beyond the entrance is a sliding door formed by a flat stone moving up and down in grooves, which could be held up by posts. After a short and low corridor, another such door leads into a vaulted chamber 16-1/2 feet long, 8 feet wide and 11 feet high. On the right-hand partition are sculptured in rather primitive fashion a lion and lioness facing each other above a second corridor. The latter is also closed by a stone door. At a short distance a stairway of seven steps leads up to the main gallery, which is on a level with the ground. This gallery is 6 feet wide and 7-1/2 high, and was lighted by lamps placed every 10 feet in niches, and traces of the smoke may still be seen. After making almost the entire circuit, the gallery turns abruptly and comes to the center, reaching a narrower corridor with a sliding door like the first. Beyond this is a small vaulted chamber 12-1/2 by 4-1/2 feet. A few beads of precious stone and pieces of jewelry in a vitrified material were found here. Another corridor with sliding door leads into the main chamber in the center of the monument measuring 10 by 12-1/2 feet. The three walls opposite the door have each a small niche. Unfortunately, nothing whatever was found in this vault. The gallery, chambers and corridors are paved with large flags and built of well-cut stone. The body of the monument is solid, and consists of rough stone and tufa blocks, irregularly placed and joined by a mortar of red or yellow earth. It was found that the monument had been entered once, or perhaps several times, for the purpose of pillage. The stone doors were broken, and whatever objects it contained were carried off long ago.

• Europe

THE BEE-HIVE TOMBS OF MEZEK
Filov, B.; *Antiquity*, 11:300–305, 1937.

Some important archaeological finds have been made in the course of recent excavations in Thrace, throwing a completely new light on its relations with Greece. Among the most important are the tholos-tombs or bee-hive tombs (Kuppelgraber) of Mezek.

Mezek is a village in southern Bulgaria, quite near the Greek frontier; it lies at the foot of the easternmost outlier of the Rhodope range, about 6 km. southwest of the railway station of Svilengrad, from which it can easily be reached in a car. Several tumuli can be seen near the village, chief among them being the hill called Mal-Tepe (the 'hill of the treasure'), 14 m. high and about 90 m. in diameter.

. . . .

It has been established that the hill was originally encircled with a
strongly built <u>krepis</u> of huge flagstones, of which only slight traces remain. The entrance to the burial-place (1.55 m. wide and 2.62 m. high)
was closed with great stone slabs; only the uppermost of these slabs is
missing, and it is demonstrable that this was removed or broken in
ancient times. A grown man could easily creep into the interior through
the aperture so formed. On either side of the entrance were unimportant
remains of late buildings; their function is not clear, but they show that
from the beginning the structure was not completely filled in, and that
its entrance was kept open for a long time, which suggests repeated use
of the burial-place.

The total length of the burial-place itself is 29.95 m.; it consists
mainly of a passage 21.50 m. long, 1.55 m. broad, and 2.60 m. high.
This passage is also constructed of huge flagstones (rhyolite and rhyolite-
tufa), joined horizontally with great iron rivets and vertically with strong
oak pins. The roof is made of corbelled flagstones, and in cross-section is of regular triangular formation. The passage leads directly to
two rectangular chambers, similarly roofed, the first measuring 1.50
m. by 1.26 m. by 3.20 m., the second 1.82 m. by 2.12 m. by 3.60 m.
The burial-chamber proper lies at the end of the passage; it is round,
with a bee-hive shaped dome, and in form and construction shows a remarkable resemblance to the Mycenaean bee-hive tombs (<u>e.g.</u> the tomb
of Atreus), in fact only differing in its smaller dimensions; it is only
3.30 m. in diameter and 4.30 m. high.

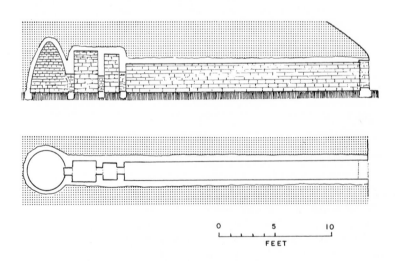

0   5   10

FEET

Beehive tomb, Mal Tepe

The entrance to this chamber (.72 m. broad and 1.50 m. high) was
closed by a folding bronze door, still standing in its original position;
a number of knob-shaped ornaments were originally fixed to it, giving

the appearance of large nails driven into the fabric, but these have now fallen off. The door-handle, which has likewise fallen off, has been preserved; it was shaped like a lion's head with a strong ring in the jaws.

At the rear of the burial-chamber, let into the floor, stands a coffin-rest, made from a single huge block of stone, measuring 2.40 m. by 1.12 m. by .76 m. To the right and left are two stone chests, originally closed with stone slabs. To the edge of the coffin-rest was fixed a single iron bar, still preserved in its entirety.

The coffin-rest stood empty, and the two chests had already been opened and contained no offerings. But on the floor of the domed chamber, and on the covers of the chests, which had been pushed on one side, were found several large bronze and clay vessels, while various other articles of gold, silver, bronze, and iron lay scattered in the other rooms. Plainly the tomb had not been rifled, but for some reason the original contents had already been removed or destroyed in antiquity.

NOTICE OF THE OPENING OF A TUMULUS IN THE PARISH OF STENNESS, ON THE MAINLAND OF ORKNEY

Petrie, George; *Archaeological Journal*, 18:353-358, 1861.

The Tumulus of Maes-how is situated about a mile to the northeast of the Ring of Stenness. Lieut. Thomas, in his Memoir on the Celtic Antiquities of Orkney, published in the Archaeologia, describes it as the most remarkable tumulus in Orkney, and "called M'eshoo or Meas-howe;" it is a very large mound of a conical form, 36 feet high and about 100 feet in diameter, and occupies the centre of a raised circular platform, which has a radius of about 65 feet. This is surrounded by a trench 40 feet in breadth.

Maes-how had evidently been previously opened. The recent excavations were commenced on the W. S. W. side. The covering stones (A and B, see ground plan and section) were reached, and lifted in the presence of Mr. Farrer and myself. We went down into the passage and proceeded to its inner end, which we found blocked up with stones and clay; but, as there were evidences of the existence of a chamber beyond the passage, and as it appeared easier of access from the top, excavations were then made from above (at D), and the walls of the building were soon found. They were carefully traced, and it then became evident that they formed a chamber about 10 feet square at the top, but widening towards the bottom. The chamber was completely filled with the stones which had originally formed the upper part of the walls and roof, and with the clay which had completed the top of the tumulus. Having been cleared out, it was found to be 15 feet square on the level of the floor, and about 13 feet in height to the top of the present walls.

The passage has been traced to the margin of the base of the tumulus, and runs inwards in the direction of E. N. E. It is 2 ft. 4 in. wide at its mouth (at E), and appears to have been the same in height, but the covering stones for about 15 feet were wanting. It then increases in dimensions to 3 feet 3 inches in width, and 4 feet 4 inches in height, and continued so for 26 feet, when it is again narrowed by two upright stone slabs (F F) to 2 ft. 5 in. These slabs are each 2 ft. 4 in. broad, and immediately beyond them (at G) the passage extends 2 feet 10 inches farther, and then opens into the central chamber, its width at the opening being 3 feet 4 inches. The dimensions of the passage, from the slabs to its opening into the chamber, are 3 feet 4 inches wide, and 4 feet 8 in. high, and the entire length 52 ft. About 34 ft. from the outer extremity of the passage, there is a triangular recess (I), in the wall, about 2 feet deep, and 3-1/2 feet in height and width in front, and, lying opposite to it was found a large block of stone of corresponding figure and dimensions. This block had probably been used to shut the passage, and had been pushed into the recess when admission into the chamber was desired. From the recess to the chamber the sides of the passage are formed by immense slabs of stone. One, on the north side, measures upwards of 19 feet long, and 4-1/2 inches thick (see K). The floor of the passage is also paved with flagstones, and when opened it was covered with lumps of stone, as for draining, to the depth of 18 inches.

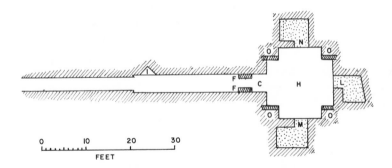

FEET

Chambered tomb at Maes How, Orkney

On emerging from the passage we enter the chamber. Immediately in front, opposite to the passage, is an opening (L, see ground plan) in the wall, about 3 feet above the floor. This is the entrance to a cell measuring 5 feet 8-1/2 inches, by 4-1/2 feet, and 3-1/2 feet in height. A large flagstone is laid as a raised floor between the entrance and the inner end of the chamber. The entrance is 2 feet wide, 2-1/2 feet high, and 22-1/2 inches long.

On the two opposite sides of the chamber, to the right and left, are similar openings nearly on a level with that just described. The opening on the right (M) is 2-1/2 ft. wide, 2 ft. 9-1/2 inches high, 1 foot 8 inches long, and 2 feet 8 inches above the floor of the chamber. The cell to which it gives admission measures 6 feet 10 inches by 4 feet 7 inches, and 3-1/2 feet in height, and it has a raised flag-stone floor 5-1/2 inches high, similar to that of the other chamber. The opening on the left (N) is 2-1/4 ft. wide, 2-1/2 ft. high, and 1-3/4 ft. long, and about 3 feet above the floor of the chamber. The cell which is entered through this opening, measures 5 feet 7 inches by 4 feet 8 inches, and 3 feet 4 inches in height. It has no raised floor like the other cells. The roofs, floors, and sides of the cells are each formed by a single slab; and blocks of stone corresponding in size and figure to the openings were found on the floor in front of them. These have been used no doubt to close the entrances of the cells.

The four walls of the chamber converge towards the top by the successive projection, or stepping over, of each course of stones beyond that immediately beneath it, commencing about 6 feet above the level of the floor, in a manner exactly similar to the construction of the so-called Picts-Houses of Quanterness and Wideford Hill, Kirkwall. By this means the chamber has been contracted from 15 feet square at the bottom to about 10 feet square at the present height of the walls, which are about 13 feet high, and when entire it was in all probability brought to a narrow aperture, a few feet square, at a height of 19 or 20 feet from the floor, and then completed by slabs or blocks of stone laid across the opening. Clay has been apparently been piled above and around the building, to the extent of several feet on the top, and many feet around.

A large buttress (O) stands in each angle of the chamber to strengthen the walls, and support them under the pressure of their own weight, and of the superincumbent clay. These internal buttresses vary somewhat in dimensions, and one of them is considerably lower than the others; but they appear to have been originally all nearly similar in height, and each has a large slab forming one of its sides.

With the exception of a quantity of bones and teeth of the horse, and a small fragment of a human skull, of unusual thickness, which were found in the debris in the chambers, no other relics were noticed. (pp. 354-356)

MIDWINTER SUNRISE AT NEW GRANGE
Patrick, J.; *Nature*, 249:517-519, 1974.

Newgrange is a passage grave in a Neolithic cemetery in County Meath, Ireland, about 30 miles NNW of Dublin (0 301 703). Two large samples of charcoal which were collected from caulking in between the roof slabs, yielded dates of 2475 ± 45 b.c. and 2465 ± 40 b.c. respectively. Depending upon which correction curve is used, this gives an age of 3100 ±100 BC for the building of the tomb. It consists of a huge, artificially constructed cairn of water-rolled stones, which is approximately 80 m in diameter. A passage, 19

m long, runs into the mound to give access to a large chamber about
3 m square and 6 m high. There are three recesses that open into
the chamber, so that the ground plan has a cruciform appearance
(Fig. 1). In each of these recesses is a large stone basin which was
used to hold the burnt remains of the interred occupants.

Carvings. The tomb has been open to visitors since 1699 and
an unknown amount of the original burial deposit may have been removed since then. In 1967 excavation of the tomb floor in front of
the basin stones revealed the burnt bone fragments of about five
people. These were accompanied by some grave goods characteristic of this type of tomb in Ireland, including stone pendants and
beads, stone 'marbles' and bone points. (Figures omitted.)

At the base of the mound is a continuous kerb of large slabs.
It is believed that dry-stone walling was built on top of the kerb to
a height of 3 m and that this wall was made of quartz for about 30 m
on each side of the entrance. The sun on the glistening white quartz
would have presented a spectacular sight from the surrounding
countryside. Most of this wall collapsed soon after completion of
the monument, and the kerb stones became completely buried and remained hidden until uncovered again at the start of this century. Outside the kerb, there are 12 large standing stones that may form part
of a circle, but their true relationship with the mound is not known
for certain. They may be older than the passage-grave.

One of the most outstanding features of Newgrange is the decoration on the stones. The Entrance Stone, set in front of the passage,
is regarded as one of the most impressive pieces of Megalithic art
in Europe (Fig. 2). The artist who executed this piece of work has
succeeded in using the shape of the stone to the utmost advantage in
creating its aesthetic appeal. Another small but remarkable design
is the three-spiral figure in the rear recess (Fig. 3). There are
many other decorations within the passage and chamber, and on the
kerbstones, virtually making Newgrange a Megalithic art gallery.

Astronomical alignment. Perhaps the most interesting feature
of Newgrange is the 'roof box'. Dry stone walling has been constructed on top of the passage orthostats to support the second roof-
slab at a higher level than the first, leaving a gap about 20-25 cm
high and 1 m wide. The gap is protected from the weather by a box
like structure of slabs supported on dry walls. This is open to the
front. For further protection against the weather, the rear edge of
the first roof slab and the front edge of the second roof slab have
water channels cut on them. The leading edge of the uppermost
roof slab of the roof box has an excellent relief carving of lozenges.

During the winter solstice in 1969 Professor M. O'Kelly observed
that 4 min after sunrise the Sun's rays shone through the roof box,
along the passage, and up to the rear recess of the burial chamber,
which became fully illuminated (Fig. 4). The spectacle lasted for
17 min before the sun moved out of alignment. Later, Mrs. O'Kelly
recalled a tradition that at a certain time of the year the sun lit up
the three-spiral figure in the end of the chamber.

In 1972 Professor O'Kelly asked me to make an accurate survey
of the roof box to see if this phenomenon would have occurred when
the burial chamber was first built. The passage is in the form of
two curves (Fig. 1), so that for a ray of light to travel directly from

the roof box to the back wall of the rear recess it must be in the azimuth range 133° 42'-138° 24'. The elevation of the distant horizon (0° 51') is the minimum elevation of which the Sun's direct rays can enter the slit. The floor of the chamber is about 15 cm lower than the roof box, so at the minimum elevation sunlight will extend across the floor and into the rear recess. Light rays will not enter the chamber when the elevation exceeds about 1° 40'. This range of azimuth and elevations, reliable to about 15' and 5' respectively means that the Sun's rays will shine directly into the chamber if its declination lies between -22° 58' and -25° 53'. It therefore seems that the sun has shone down the passage to the chamber ever since the date of its construction and will probably continue to do so forever regardless of secular changes in the obliquity of the ecliptic. It also means that the spectacle occurs for a number of days before and after the winter solstice.

Fortunately, the vagaries of time have had their effect on the passage and some of the stones are now leaning inwards, thus trimming down the width of the beam of light. At the time of construction the beam would have been about 40 cm wide whereas now it is only 17 cm. The two principal orthostats causing the obstruction are L18 and L20 (Fig. 1). The first 10 orthostats on either side of the passage have been straightened but there is no way of straightening the rest without dismantling the whole structure.

There are about 200 passage graves in Ireland with many more allied tombs in Scotland and Brittany, but to my knowledge none of them has a roof box like that at Newgrange. As this structure is unique, and as the whole monument is so grandiose, it seems likely that its orientation is deliberate.

The monument best known for its astronomical orientations is Stonehenge on the Salisbury Plain. After it had been built, it was remodelled several times, and the main astronomically oriented structures were erected in its third phase, which is dated at around 1800-2000 BC. This is about 1,000 years after the construction of Newgrange, and there is little connection between the two monuments or between the cultures which built them. The unambiguous definition of both direction and altitude at Newgrange is by far the most convincing evidence that some Megalithic structures were deliberately oriented on astronomical phenomena. This must lend greater credence to the theory that different cultures in the British Isles were investigating the basic solar cycles. It is quite possible that data passed between different cultures, so that Stonehenge eventually became an important repository of astronomical knowledge.

ANCIENT FORTS

All over Great Britain and much of Europe, hilltops are ringed with works that are apparently defensive in nature. In that part of the world, hilltop forts are considered anomalous only if of great size (Maiden Castle), peculiar design, or bizarre construction (the vitrified forts). In North America, where aborigines were not supposed to be so enterprising, we also have hilltop forts, but they are generally less impressive. Nevertheless, in their historical context, some American prehistoric forts must be considered truly remarkable in size and most surprising on a continent where man supposedly arrived late and is thought of in terms of wigwams and scalping parties.

Note that some of the walls presented in the next section may also be of military nature.

THE "OLD FORT" EARTHWORKS OF GREENUP COUNTY, KENTUCKY

Lewis, T. H.; *American Journal of Archaeology*, 3:375-382, 1887.

I.---Introduction. On the southern side of the Ohio River, in Greenup County, Kentucky, at a point about a mile and a half below Portsmouth, Ohio, and nearly opposite the old mouth of the Scioto River, there is a very interesting series of ancient earthworks, worthy of more attention than it has received of late years. The position was well chosen, for from the top of the highest walls or embankments a fine view could be had of the Scioto valley for several miles, and also for a few miles each way of the Ohio valley, were it not for the timber along the latter on the margin of the river. The main work, a large quadrangular enclosure, is locally known as the "Old Fort." This enclosure, together with its so-called covered ways or parallel walls, was described and mapped two-thirds of a century ago by Caleb Atwater of Circleville, Ohio. In 1846 these earthworks were re-surveyed by E. G. Squier and D. Morton, who discovered mounds and embankments not noted by their predecessor: a full account of them, with maps, will be found in the well-known work of Squier and Davis, The Ancient Monuments of the Mississippi Valley.

During the winter of 1885-6, I re-surveyed these imposing remains of antiquity. After a careful inspection of the ground beyond the ravine, at the end of the southwestern covered way, I became satisfied that there were earthworks, belonging to the series, not shown even in Squier's survey.. This fact has induced me to prepare the present paper, and to accompany it with a diagram or outline-map of this "Old Fort" and its entire accessories, thinking that they may interest students of North American antiquities.

II.---The Main Work, or Grand Square. The main work, central enclosure, or Grand Square as it deserves to be called, is situated on a terrace some forty feet above the river bottom, the distance to the river itself being about a quarter of a mile. In shape, it is a quadrangle with rounded corners, but instead of its sides agreeing with the cardinal points, as was first reported, it is rather the corners which look toward them. The inside area, though not level, is practically even---as even as ploughed land can be expected to be---and was probably shaped off to a reasonably perfect plane in the first place, for the convenience of the people using it: the inequalities of the ground having thus been removed the sky-line of the surrounding embankments is practically parallel with it. The top of each section of the wall, therefore, forms a straight line, excepting that portion of the N. W. wall which gradually rises from near the western gate to a point near the centre, and a slight depression in the S. W. wall near the south corner. While the N. W. and N. E. walls are, generally speaking, horizontal, the wall from the east corner and that from the west gate rise evenly to the south, where is the summit of the entire earthworks. The lowest part of the walls is at the western opening. The walls are not rounded at the top but there is a level space or walk of about eight feet in width, which can be readily traced along almost the entire length of the six embankments which constitute them.

These embankments, treated as four walls, are, in respect to their width at the base and vertical height, in mean dimensions, as follows: The N. E. wall is 60 to 65 feet wide, and 10 feet high. The S. E. wall has the same width and is 10 to 12 feet high, with the exception of a place near the southern corner, where it crosses the end of a spur of the slope of a higher plateau, which at that point overlooks the interior of the enclosure---most of that part of the slope which projected beyond the inside line of the wall was graded away and the material used in levelling the square. The S. W. wall ranges from 62 feet in width and 10 feet in height, at the south end, to 45 feet in width and 8 feet in height, at the west end. The N. W. wall is from 45 to 60 feet in width and from 8 to 10 feet in height.

There are six openings or entrances to this enclosure, the narrowest (the northern one) being 13 feet, and the widest (the N. E. one) 27-1/2 feet wide. The northern and southeastern entrances are not on a level with the natural surface, but are raised some two feet higher. Neither inside nor outside ditch entered into the plan of the builders here, for there are none, the walls being, generally speaking, equally elevated above the inside area and the outside natural surface, except at the narrow point described.

The larger dimensions of this Grand Square can now be given. From the centre of the S. E. to that of the N. W. opening a straight line, measured on the plan, gives a distance of 832 feet, and, between the other two openings, of 822 feet, making a mean diameter of 827 feet. The perimeter, or a continuous line traced entirely along the centre of the walls and across the openings, has a length of about 3,175 feet. The land contained within the inner lines of the embankments, but omitting any portion of the entry-ways, is about 13.20 acres in area.

Doubtless, when its architects first drew its lines on the ground, as they necessarily must have done, proper rectangles were formed, for it is even now, practically, an "exact square," as Mr. Squier called it. The following geometrical facts, deduced from plotted diagrams, will demonstrate this statement. The first diametrical line mentioned bears N. 47-1/4° W. (magnetic); the second one N. 42° E. ---the two lines intersecting within three-quarters of a degree of exact right angles. The latter line intersects the first precisely at its (own) middle point, but about three feet N. W. of the middle of the former, or N. E. and S. E.

dimension: were it, however, to run at right angles with it, it would cross about as far to the S. E., its termination striking within two feet of the right hand side of the N. E. opening, instead of half-way across it.

Considering the thousand years, approximately speaking, that have probably elapsed since these high embankments were raised, would it be rash to suggest that the builders of the same, of whatever tribe or race they were, had definite ideas of castramentation? Indeed, if we could see and test their original lines and should find them to be actually a degree or two out in angle, and ten or twelve feet in distance, for so large a square, we should have found blunders that could easily be paralleled in the work of more modern surveyors.

III. --- The North-Eastern Covered Way. The northeastern covered way extends a little over 2,000 feet from the wall of the enclosure, and its constituent embankments vary in width from 20 to 32 feet at the base, and in height from 1-1/2 to 3-1/2 feet---the narrowest parts being those on each side of the northern opening. Although, for convenience sake, occasionally called "parallel walls," here and elsewhere, like the southwestern ones, which are, for the most part, truly parallel, the walls of this covered way, at no place present any parallelism: the least distance between them, from top to top, is 176, and the greatest 320 feet. The walls intersect two ravines, both of which were undoubtedly in existence when they were built, for the embankments follow the slopes nearly to the bottom. The ends of the walls, at both crossings, show that they have been cut away by water coming from the adjoining high land.

The length of the N. W. wall, following along its central portion, is 2,135 feet, and that of the S. W. wall 2,320 feet. The northern opening or gateway is 15 feet wide, and the distance between the embankments at the southern end is 80 feet. The included area, as bounded by the lines forming the inside bases of the walls, continued across all the openings, as in the case of the Grand Square, is 8.80 acres.

IV. --- The South-Western Covered Way. The walls of the S. W. covered way run strictly parallel for nearly 1,100 feet, and are 191 feet apart (on centres) for that distance: the S. E. wall then makes a very slight angle to the left, or southward, but the other continues its course unchanged to the end. They are 35 feet wide at the base and from 2-1/2 to 3-1/2 feet in height. The length of the N. W. wall, both ends of which are finished, or rounded off, is 1,510 feet, and the farther end rests on the edge of the ravine, which is some 40 feet in depth and 500 feet wide, and has very steep sides. The end of the other wall has been destroyed by the falling away of the bank, leaving its present length exactly 1,190. The area, bounded by the lines forming the inside base of the walls and lines drawn between their extremities, is 4.90 acres.

V. --- Before describing the outlying earthworks, the extent and dimensions of the entire "fort" with its covered ways should be ascertained. From its extreme limits on the N. E. to the end of the finished embankment on the S. W. the distance is 4,500 feet in an air line, or .85 of a mile. The entire length of all the embankments, or walls, as built, omitting original openings or vacant spaces, is a few feet over 10,200 feet, or 1.93 miles. The land included within the square, and covered by the parallel walls, together equals 26.90 acres. A fair computation of the area covered by the bases of all these walls, and of the cubical

contents of the embankments raised on them---including the "traces"
and the spur crossed---according to the data furnished by this survey,
gives as follows:

For the grand square,	4 acres,	29,400 cubic yards.
" northeastern parallel walls,	3 "	6,700 " "
" southwestern " "	2 "	5,900 " "
Total,	9 acres,	42,000 cubic yards.

. . . .

PRE-COLUMBIAN STONE STRUCTURES IN SOUTHERN ILLINOIS
Coleman, Loren F.; *NEARA Newsletter,* 5:68, 1970.

At least nine pre-Columbian stone structures are known to exist in the
hills of southern Illinois. There may be others, the walls of which have
been razed down to ground level; in fact, the latest find was made when the
foundation courses were accidentally observed, three miles east of Cobden.

These walled structures, forming a rough alignment across the southern tip of Illinois between the Mississippi and Ohio rivers, have one striking feature in common---each is located on top of a high bluff where it projects outward. From the rear, they can be approached easily over gently
sloping ground; and it is across this approach that the walls are built. On
every other side, the structures border on sheer cliffs. This would suggest

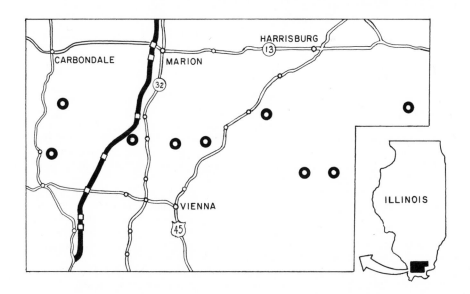

Locations of some enigmatic Illinois stone structures

that their primary purpose was as forts; however, only one (that near Stonefort in southern Saline County) has a water supply within it. Stone cairns and stone-lined pits are found beside the entrance gateways of all.

They are constructed of dry-stone masonry, using loose stones of moderate size, mainly from the beds of the brooks flowing along the cliff bottoms. Early records, and the recollections of very old people still living, indicate that the walls were originally six feet high and about as wide. They are now greatly diminished, due to farmers hauling away stones from them. Some, such as the one near Stonefort already referred to, were over 600 feet in length. The amount of labor necessary to build such walls, of stones that had to be carried up from the brook beds 200 feet below, is staggering.

The wall at the Stonefort structure forms half of an accurate ellipse with axes of 450 and 190 feet. It is not easy to see how it could have been so accurately laid out, if the area were as heavily forested at the time as it is now.

FORT MOUNTAIN
Shackleton, Robert, Jr., *American Antiquarian*, 15:295-304, 1893.

What Anthony Wayne is to the imagination of Ohio, De Soto is to that of Georgia. In Ohio, if a section of old corduroy road is discovered, it is likely to be at once ascribed to Wayne, even though he may never have been within a hundred miles of the spot. If an aboriginal fortification is found, that, too, must have been built by Mad Anthony. So important were his services to the state, by his march northward from the Ohio, and his overwhelming defeat of the Indians at the battle of Fallen Timbers, that the popular imagination has made his personality omnipresent.

So it is in Georgia with De Soto. No one knows where he marched; where he fought; where he met savage ambassadors. But he went somewhere through Georgia, and so there are fields and caves and valleys and mountains connected by legend or fancy with his name. Small wonder then that Fort Mountain, which bears upon its summit a curiously remarkable prehistoric stone fortification, should be deemed one of the places where he paused on his way to the Mississippi.

The earliest settlers found the fort there and asked the Indians to tell them by whom it was made. But the Indians could not. The traditions of their tribes said nothing of its origin. Their picturesque fancy had failed to frame a tale wild enough to fit the fort and its awe-inspiring location. They looked up at the rocky heights. They shook their heads. It was all a mystery. And perchance, as they gazed, some dark cloud flung its heavy folds about the jagged precipices, and the savages, gravely solemn, turned away, for their Manito would be angered should they question into what he so evidently intended to be hid.

From the top of the mountain there is a magnificent view. Other mountains stretch off into the distance, while below are tree-covered slopes and rocky precipices, and mile after mile of forests and fields and farms. The eye never wearies of the glorious sight, and as one glances over the magnificent expanse he tries to imagine what were the thoughts of the mysterious people who centuries since dwelt on this height.

For here their simple homes once stood. Here their household fires burned. Here wives welcomed returning husbands, and mothers watched tenderly over their little ones, and young people lived and loved, and children happily played. And here, to guard against the assaults of enemies, a stone wall was built across the broad top of the mountain.

The wall has been sadly shattered and broken. It has been flattened out. Many of its stones have been scattered. But it still marks plainly the original line, as made, centuries ago, by the Mound-builders who constructed it.

Fort Mountain is in Murray County, in northern Georgia, and the point from which it may best be reached is the town of Dalton. From the low hills overlooking that pleasantly situated town there is a wide spreading scene. To the westward are the steep heights of Rocky Face Ridge, which Johnston so successfully fortified and which Sherman tried in vain to pierce, while to the eastward the eye sweeps over fourteen miles of level country to the beautiful Cohutta Mountains, with Fort Mountain standing out from among them impressively distinct and grand.

. . . .

The northern end of the summit is separated from the rest of the mountain by the stone wall which constitutes the fort. The enclosed space

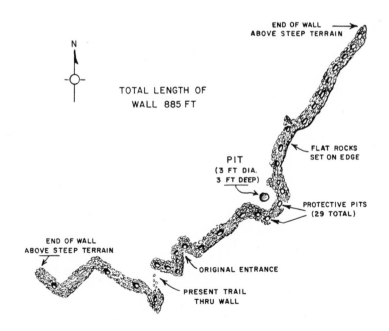

Plan of wall on Fort Mountain, Georgia

is some eight acres in extent, about one-half being almost level, and the remainder in easy slopes. The northern edge of this space needs no defensive wall, for there the cliffs descend in rocky inaccessibility. Rounding, too, on the eastern and western sides, the cliffs are wild and steep, and, although not so sheer and abrupt as at the northern end, are yet so abrupt as to make it impossible for an attacking party to scale them in the face of even the slightest opposition. Toward the south, however, there is no natural protection, and there it is that the wall is built, stretching from side to side of the ridge. And the construction of the wall is remarkable in the extreme, considering that it was undoubtedly the work of an aboriginal race. It is not straight. It is not curved. Instead, it is built in zigzag lines, and quite evidently with the intention of making it impossible for any assaulting force to advance without being taken in flank, unless they should charge right against the outer point of one of the angles.

The wall, while of zigzag shape, is yet not built with regularity. The angles vary greatly in degree and the zigzags are of different lengths. One salient angle, which projects a rounding outward, measures, on one side, fifty feet to the beginning of the curve of the point. On the other side it measures sixty-four feet. The diameter of the curve of the point is twenty-four feet. The height of the wall is now not more than from two and a half to three feet, but the stones lie scattered in a width of from fifteen to twenty feet, and the universal testimony of all who know anything of what it was in former days is that it was narrower and higher. One very old lady in particular remembers that her father, who, about the beginning of the century, climbed to the top of the mountain with one of the first Moravian missionaries that entered this section of the state, used to speak of the wall as having been, when he first saw it, quite carefully made and of a good height. But in the years that have passed since then the wall has been sadly shattered. Picnic parties have at times ascended the height; barbecues and camp meetings have been held there; and it seems to have been considered the duty and privilege of very many of those who made the ascent to indemnity themselves for the exertion by tearing down the wall. More than this, too, treasure-hunters have been at work. A fortified camp, occupied, as they believe, by De Soto, would, so it has seemed to them, be a place of deposit for much of mineral wealth, and so they have torn and dug, vainly seeking for what they can not find.

The wall is from a fifth to a sixth of a mile in total length. The stones were heaped up---not regularly and evenly piled, and in this respect the wall resembles that of Fort Hill, in southern Ohio. In the Fort Hill wall, however, there is a considerable admixture of earth, while the wall on Fort Mountain is of stone alone. There are but few small pieces in the wall. Most of the stones are from two to five inches thick, range from eight to eighteen inches in length, and are from six to twelve inches wide. In places advantage is taken of huge stones firmly set by nature into the mountain side, and at such spots the wall runs up to either side of the rock. There is but one entranceway in the wall, and that, so it is claimed by some, was made in recent years to allow of a passage into the fort by horse-back riders, there being a long and roundabout way to the summit by which, in some weather, it is possible for a good horseman to ride to the top. Others, however, believe that the entrance was left by the first builders, and this view seems to us correct, but the entranceway has been cleared in late years by some who found it blocked with scattered stone.

. . . .

ABORIGINAL WORKS AT THE MOUTH OF THE KLIKITAT RIVER, WASHINGTON TERRITORY

Whitcomb, T. M.; *Smithsonian Institution Annual Report, 1881,* p. 527

The works represented in the accompanying sketch consist of a stone wall 5 feet high, filled inside with earth, except the two squares within. These are 8 feet deep and 15 feet on each side, the whole work being about 200 feet on either side. There was formerly some kind of wooden structure on the stone wall, as the remains of cedar timbers occur at certain points on the top. The wooden work was evidently destroyed by fire, since all the cedar is charred.

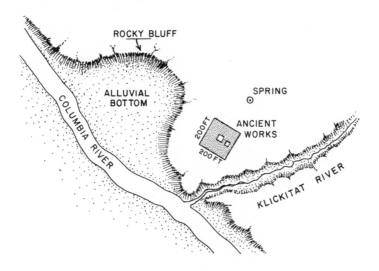

Map of works at Klikitat, Washington

None of the Indians in this country have any knowledge of the builders or of its use. There is a tradition among them that it was finished a long time ago. Large quantities of arrow-heads are found in and about the works. The place is eminently adapted for defense, being 100 feet above the river. The scarcity of aboriginal works of a permanent character on the Pacific coast makes this an object of peculiar interest to the archaeologist.

DEFENSIVE WORKS OF THE MOUND-BUILDERS
Peet, Stephen D.; *American Antiquarian*, 13:189-224, 1891.

IV. We now come to another class of strongholds, namely the "Stone Forts." These forts resemble the "Hill Forts" and may, by some, be regarded as identical.

....

Wherever they are located they are always characterized by the same feature. They are generally situated on eminences, where there are rocky precipices. (2.) In several cases the precipices are veneered with artificial walls which make a varrier against the wash of streams and furnish a foundation to the walls above. (2.) The gateways of the stone forts are frequently quite elaborate. The wall is generally four or five feet high and varies from twenty to thirty feet wide at the base. It is sometimes laid up in regular order, making a smooth even front with sharp angles, but generally is merely in the form of an irregular pile of stone, and resembles an earth wall, except that the material is different. The question has arisen whether the wall was surmounted by a stockade; on this point there is uncertainty. The stone walls generally conform to the nature of the ground. Stones were employed because they could be readily procured, although the hammer had nothing to do with the preparation of the materials, yet there is evidence of great labor and the place of location is selected with a military eye.

The stone forts may properly be considered as belonging to the village Mound-builders, and perhaps were designed as especial retreats for the villagers. It will be noticed, at least, that in Ohio this kind of fort is frequently situated in the midst of square enclosures, so giving evidence that they were built by the same people. In the Miami Valley there is a square enclosure on the terrace, and the fort is on the hill near by. So with the fort at Bourneville. This is situated in the midst of the valley of Paint Creek, and was surrounded by enclosures, which we have imagined to be villages of the sun-worshipers. The same is true of the fort on Massie's Creek, near the Big Miami River. The stone fort near Manchester, Tennessee, and that of Duck Creek, of the same state, may be regarded as specimens; yet these were located near the walled villages of the Stonegrave people and may have been built by that people. The same may be said of the stone fort of Southern Indiana. This last fort was located on the Ohio, somewhat remote from the region of the "sacred enclosure," so called, but there are on the White River many earth-works which resemble those on the Scioto, and so we place this stone fort among the works of the sun-worshipers.

....

1. One of the best specimens of the stone forts is at Bourneville. The description of this is given by Squier and Davis. It occupies the summit of a lofty, detached hill twelve miles west of Chillicothe. The hill is not far from forty feet in height. It is remarkable for the abruptness of its sides. It projects midway into the broad valley of Paint Creek, and is a conspicuous object from every point of view. The defenses consist of a wall of stone, which is carried around the hill a little below the brow, cutting off the spurs, but extending across the neck that connects the hill with the range beyond. The wall is a rude one, giving little evidence that the stones were placed upon one another so as to present

vertical faces, though at a few points the arrangement lends to the belief that the wall may have been regularly faced on the exterior. Upon the western side, or steepest face of the hill, the stones are placed so as to resemble a protection wall. They were probably so placed to prevent the creek from washing away the hill and undermining the fort. Upon the eastern face, where the declivity is least abrupt, the wall is heavy and resembles a stone heap of fifteen or twenty feet base and four feet high. Where it crosses the isthmus it is heaviest. The isthmus is seven hundred feet wide. Here the wall has three gateways.

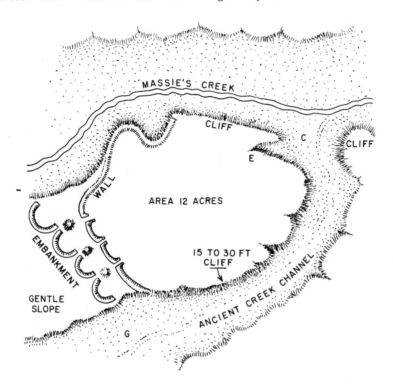

Stone fort on Massie's Creek, Ohio

The gateways are formed by curving inward the ends of the wall for forty or fifty feet, leaving narrow passages not exceeding eight feet in width. At other points where there are jutting ridges are similar gateways, though at one point a gateway seems to have been for some reason closed up. At the gateways the amount of stone is more than quadruple the quantity at other points, constituting broad, mound-shaped heaps.

These stone mounds exhibit the marks of intense heat, which has vitrified the surfaces of the stones and fused them together. Strong traces of fire are visible at other places on the wall, the point commanding the broadest extent of country. Here are two or three small stone

mounds that seem burned throughout. Nothing is more certain than that
powerful fires have been maintained for considerable periods at numerous points on the hill. There are several depressions or reservoirs,
one of which covers about two acres and furnishes a supply of water estimated as adequate to the wants of a thousand head of cattle. The area
enclosed within this fort is something over one hundred and forty acres,
and the line of wall measures upwards of two and a quarter miles. Most
of the wall and a large portion of the area was covered with a heavy primitive forest. Trees of the largest size grew on the line, twisting the
roots among the stones. The stones were of all sizes, and were abundant
enough to have formed walls eight feet thick. In the magnitude of the area
enclosed, this work exceeds any hill-work now known in the country,
although less in length than that of Fort Ancient. It evinces great labor
and bears the impress of a numerous people. The valley in which it is
situated was a favorite one with the race of Mound-builders, and the hill
overlooks a number of extensive groups of ancient works. (pp. 213-216)

• New Zealand

MAORI HILL-FORTS
Firth, Raymond; *Antiquity*, 1:66-78, 1927.

For comparative purposes it is interesting to note that the earthworks
of the Maori stronghold are strongly reminiscent of the British hill fortress of the Stone, Bronze and Iron Ages. On the average, perhaps, the
ramparts of these British forts, notably Eggardon and Maiden Castle, are
of greater size than those of the Maori, and owing to the less rugged
nature of the English countryside, they tend necessarily to be more elaborate. But to one who has spent many of his leisure summer days in
roaming among the ditches, terraces and ramparts of the pa maori, the
aspect of the British earthworks is by no means strange.
The function of these fortresses was apparently the same---to protect
their inhabitants from external danger and to serve as dwelling places in
normal life. In view of this fact their structural resemblance is noteworthy, raised as they were by the hands of people who are separated so
widely by geographical situation, by cultural achievement, and by the
span of the long-dead centuries. One needs to postulate no racial affinity
nor far-flung cultural contact between the builders of these earthworks;
the evidence warrants no such wild hypothesis of antipodal linkage. But
to the British archaeologist the description of a functionally cognate type
of earthwork fortification may prove of interest, especially as the type of

evanescent detail which has not been preserved for him in this country is still a matter of knowledge in New Zealand. The tools employed in fosse-digging, the structure of wooden stockades, the use of terraces, the relation of defence to water supply---on these and other points the description of Maori practice can perhaps initiate a fruitful comparison.

The pa or fortified village was by no means the characteristic form of settlement throughout New Zealand. As a culture trait of any importance it is to be found almost solely in the North Island, a very few examples occurring south of Cook Strait. Moreover, in its most developed form of hill-fort with earthworks, with which we are here concerned, it is very largely confined to the more northerly districts of this Island. Wellington, Hawkes Bay, Napier, do not display many examples, whereas in Taranaki, the Bay of Plenty, the Lower Waikato and the Auckland peninsula they seem to crown almost every prominent hill-top within sight.

· · · · · · · · · ·

It should be mentioned that these hill-forts vary greatly in age, some having been constructed only a few generations ago, while others have stood for several centuries.

· · · · · · · · · ·

Typical dimensions of a few of these earthworks may be given here to illustrate the range of achievement attained by these workmen of old with their primitive tools. A little fort examined by me some years ago at Tamahere in a bend of the Waikato river was defended by a single vallum and fosse, presenting in their eroded state a combined face of some 12 feet in height; a similar small defended position jutting out from the heights above Muriwai beach was fortified by a single wall some 9 feet high and 3 feet broad on the top. These are but small fighting posts, and represent comparatively insignificant examples of the Maori art of fortification. In the larger pa the ditch and rampart were often of great size. The accounts given of native forts by some of the earlier visitors to New Zealand are of especial interest in this connexion, since they saw these structures complete and often actually in use. Thus Cook mentions that the ditch and rampart of one pa at Mercury Bay presented a wall 22 feet high, while the inner vallum and fosse of another fort occupied by people at the same place gave a total height of 24 feet, to which must be super-added the stockade, noted by Banks as being 10 feet high. (pp. 67-70)

• Asia

EARLY DEFENSIVE WORKS IN CEYLON
Andrews, J. B.; *Man*, 9:181-182, 1909.

I wish to call attention to a fine cyclopean wall I visited in Ceylon recently, at the suggestion of Mr. J. Hill, of the Land Settlement Office, and formerly assistant to Mr. Bell, the Government archaeologist. It surrounds Mapagala Hill close to the famous rock fortress of Sigiri. It is similar to others found in various countries in England and on the French Riviera, such as are described and illustrated in the valuable publications of Dr. A. Guebhard, member of the Societe prehistorique of France. This wall was evidently constructed for defensive purposes; the enormous stones are piled unhewn on top of one another without the use of mortar. It dates probably from the Neolithic epoch, if not before. Similar fragments exist on Sigiri Hill itself, but most of the many walls thereon are quite different in style, the stones being much smaller, more regularly shaped, and put together with some order. These last are attributed to the parricide King Kasyapa, A. D. 500 circa. Doubtless other similar walls exist elsewhere in Ceylon and India, but, to my knowledge, they have not yet been noticed.

I also visited this winter the kadangas, long lines of huge earthworks situated in the mountains of Coorg, some hours' journey from the town of Mysore. I may confirm what Dr. Richter in his Manual of Coorg says of their resemblance to the so-called British earthworks and dykes, such as the Wansdyke, even in the occasional presence of supporting forts or camps. They are of unknown antiquity, thousands of years old according to the imaginative native traditions. The Coorg Chronicle narrates their being repaired three or four hundred years ago, in some small sections with stone, it is said. Some of the kadangas are of great length, traversing the province of Coorg from north to south. Their height is some 30 feet from the bottom of the fosse to the top of the vallum.

. . . .

• Middle East

TOWER OF BABEL
Anonymous; *American Journal of Science*, 1:37:352–353, 1839.

This is an immense pile of ruins,---at its base it measures 3082 feet (in circuit.)---width 150 feet; it presents two stages of hills; the first about 60 feet high, cloven into a deep ravine by the rain, and intersected by the furrows of ages. To the base of the second ascent is about 200 feet from the bottom of the entire pile, and from the base of this ruin to the top is 35 feet. On the western side, the entire mass rises at once from the plain in one stupendous though irregular pyramidal hill, broken in the slopes of its sweeping acclivities by time and violence. The south and north fronts are particularly abrupt towards the point of the brick ruin; on the north side there are large piles of ruins of fine and solid brick-work, projecting from among immense masses of rubbish at the base; the fine bricks were evidently part of the facing of this side.   The tower-like ruin of the extreme summit is a solid mass 28 feet broad, made of the most beautiful brick masonry, and presenting the apparent angle of some structure originally of a square shape, the remains of which stand on the east to the height of 35 feet, and to the south 22 feet.   It is rent from the top to nearly half way down; the remains of the masonry are furnace-burnt bricks: they are united by a calcareous cement about 1/4 of an inch in thickness, having in it a layer of straws, and so hard that it could not be separated.   The base of the structure was not altered, but the piles of fine bricks thrown down were vitrified with the various colors, and they gave the ringing sound belonging to the vitrifications of glass in the manufactories; the lines of cement are visible and distinct, and are vitrified.   The consuming power appears to have acted from above, and the scattered ruins fell from a higher point than the summit of the present standing fragment.

"The heat of the fire which produced such amazing effects, must have burned with the force of the strongest furnace; and from the general appearance of the cleft in the wall and these vitrified masses, I should be inclined, says the author, to attribute the catastrophe to lightning from heaven.   Ruins, by the explosion of any combustible matter, would have exhibited very different appearances."   The entire surface of the structure appears to have been faced with fine brick.

• Europe

VITRIFIED FORTS ON THE WEST COAST OF SCOTLAND
Hamilton, Edward; *Archaeological Journal*, 37:227–243, 1880.

On the west coast of Scotland between the headland, north of Loch Moidart and Arisaig, is a deep inlet of the sea.   This inlet, near its ter-mination, is divided by the promontory of Ardnish into two branches, called Loch na Nuagh and Loch Ailort.   At the entrance to Loch Ailort are two islands, one of which is called Eilean na Goar.

Loch na Nuagh trends to the east and terminates some four or five miles up, and washes the rocks on which runs the high road leading from Arisaig to Fort William.   At the point where Loch na Nuagh begins to narrow, where the opposite shore is about one-and-a-half to two miles distant, is a small promontory connected with the mainland by a narrow strip of sand and grass, which evidently at one time was submerged by the rising tide.   On the flat summit of this promontory are the ruins of a vitrified fort, the proper name for which is Arka-Unskel.

The rocks on which this fort are placed are metamorphic gneiss, with indications of trap, covered with grass and ferns, and rise on three sides almost perpendicular for about 110 feet from the sea level. The smooth surface on the top is divided by a slight depression into two portions. On the largest, with precipitous sides to the sea, the chief portion of the fort is situated, and occupies the whole of the flat surface. It is of somewhat oval form. The circumference is about 200 feet, and the vitrified walls can be traced in its entire length, but are most perceptible at A, B, C, and D. The width of the interior is fifty feet. At one part, A, the vitrified wall is seven feet high and about six feet in thickness. At C the wall

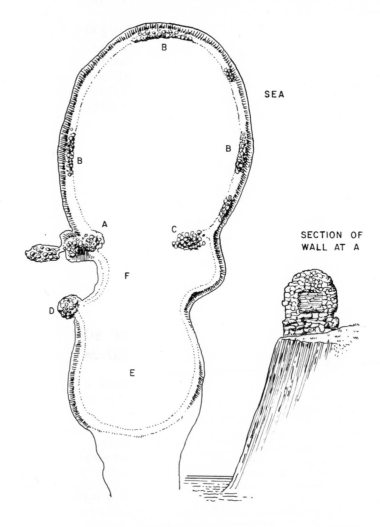

SEA

SECTION OF
WALL AT A

Plan of a Scottish vitrified fort

is three feet three inches high and five feet thick, and so continues through the whole of the walls, although they are not all so high. The wall at A appears to have been the termination on the east side of the first portion of the fort, as about twenty-five feet from this is another large mass of vitrified wall, D; the space between these two is without any signs of wall. It almost appears as if this might have been the entrance to the larger fort as well as the smaller, which is situated on the lesser portion of the rock, at E. This smaller fortress or portion of the larger is about 100 feet in circumference, 21 feet in width, and 24 feet in length, and appears to have been divided from the larger fort by a narrow strip, F; but although the line of ramparts may be traced there is no vitrified wall. On excavating at A, below the vitrified wall, we came upon a great mass of large and small boulders, all water-worn, and evidently brought up from the shore to form a foundation on which the vitrified wall rested. This foundation was three feet deep and five feet across, and rested upon the original gneiss rock.

We dug under the vitrified mass, and there found what was extremely interesting, as throwing some light on the manner in which the fire was applied for the purpose of vitrification. The internal part of the upper or vitrified wall for about a foot or a foot-and-a-half was untouched by the fire, except that some of the flat stones were slightly agglutinated together, and that the stones, all fellspatic, were placed in layers one upon another.

It was evident therefore that a rude foundation of boulder stones was first formed upon the original rock, and then a thick layer of loose, mostly, flat stones of fellspatic sand, and of a different kind from those found in the immediate neighborhood, were placed on this foundation, and then vitrified by heat applied externally. This foundation of loose stones is found also in the vitrified fort of Dun Mac Snuichan, on Loch Etive.

The other vitrified fort is much larger than that just described, is situated on the island at the entrance of Loch Ailort. This island, locally termed Eilean na Goar, is the most eastern and is bounded on all sides by precipitous gneiss rocks; it is the abode and nesting place of numerous sea birds. The flat surface on the top is 120 feet from the sea level, and the remains of the vitrified forts are situated on this, oblong in form, with a continuous rampart of vitrified wall five feet thick; attached at the S. W. end to a large upright rock of gneiss. The space enclosed by this wall is 420 feet in circumference and 70 feet in width. The rampart is continuous and about five feet in thickness. At the eastern end, A is a great mass of wall in situ, vitrified on both sides. In the centre of the enclosed space is a deep depression in which are masses of the vitrified wall strewed about, evidently detached from their original site.

Separated by a deep depression which is now a wet morass, and nearly parallel to the larger construction, is a smaller fort placed on another flat surface of the island. It is 100 feet in circumference and 25 feet across, entirely surrounded by the wall which in many parts remain in its original state.

One remarkable feature in these forts is their double form; none other previously described, as far as I am aware, having this peculiar character.

The examination of these two forts leads us to the consideration of the different opinions held by previous investigators as to weather

    1st. Were these structures built as a means of defence.

    2nd. Was the vitrification the result of design or accident.

3rd. How was the vitrification produced.

On looking at the plates which illustrate this paper and also at the plans of the great forts which illustrate some of these works I have quoted on the east coast, one can only come I think to one conclusion, ---that they were intended for places of defence. The regular design of these walls, their great extent and uniformity, the large area enclosed, all lead to prove that these early people had a design in their construction; and it is a curious circumstance that many of the most important of these works were re-occupied by the conquerors of the original designers, as places of defence. The remains of the wooden buildings in the vitrified fort of Dun Mac Uisen-achan, on Loch Etive, are the structures subsequently raised by the Irish conquerors of the builders of the original fort. In the ruins of the build-ing on Craig Phadric, some of the original vitrified walls have been built up in the structures of the second occupation. It is scarcely possible then to believe that these extensive walls, all vitrified, encompassing so large an area, could have been merely the site of beacon fires or that the vitri-fication was caused by such fires or by those for burnt sacrifices. An-other argument against the site being only used for beacon fires is that many of these forts are not placed on the highest points of land but gener-ally at the entrance of some strath or some inland loch.

2nd. Was the vitrification the result of design or accident? No doubt in the first instance the discovery that the stones were fusible was acci-dental, and was discovered probably as Mr. Williams suggests, by kin-dling great fires for burning their sacrifices; but I would also suggest another accidental mode by which this discovery might have been made. The aborigines of every country cooked or rather baked their food in ovens made in the ground. These ovens were lined with stones, and stones were placed over the object to be cooked, and then heat applied, oftentimes no doubt very intense. It may be that during this process of cooking the stones employed were of that fusible nature which we know exist in parts of Scotland, and that these were found agglutinated in their ovens, and vitrified. Very little acuteness on their part would lead them to apply this discovery to the building of their places of defence.

The investigation of these forts at Arisaig shew with what a regular design the builders worked. First the foundation of the water-worn boulders all brought up from the sea shore, then the stones known to be fusible, and generally brought from a distance, placed in regular layers on the top of the foundation of boulders to the prescribed height and thick-ness, and then the fire applied externally, both on the top and on every side; and thus we come to the question,

How was the vitrification produced? As we have seen, various theor-ies have been put forward, but I think we may conclude that in the two forts which I have described, the fire was applied externally and on all sides. This is proved by the internal part of the wall being unvitrified, solely because the heat did not extend so far, leaving the stones in their original condition, or only partly agglutinated, and only not fused because unable to be effected by the fire applied externally.

It is easy to suppose, in the then state of Scotland, that abundant fuel could be obtained from the great pine forests, which combined with sea-weed and earth would, with a proper amount of draught, cause heat in-tense enough to melt or vitrify the fusible material it came in contact with. (pp. 237-241)

A vitrified mass from the fort at Knockfarrel, Scotland (Janet & Colin Bord)

ON THE SUBSTANCES OBTAINED FROM SOME "FORTS VITRIFIES" IN FRANCE

Daubree, M.; *American Journal of Science*, 3:22:150–151, 1881.

M Daubree has made a critical mineralogical and chemical examination of materials obtained from several "Forts vitrifies" in different parts of France. This name is given to the walls or to the simple debris of walls, whose materials have been fused together by the action of fire.

The substance obtained from the neighborhood of Argentan was of a dark greenish brown color, opaque, and resembled certain slags. A section examined under the microscope revealed the presence of large numbers of crystals of an octahedral mineral, probably spinel, and also crystals of melilite, both formed by the process of fusion. An analysis showed a considerable amount of alumina and of soda, leading to the inference that the fusion had been accomplished by adding marine salt to the aluminous silicate in the clays and schists. Some partially fused granitic rocks from the forts of Chateau-vieux and of Puy de Gaudy (Creuse), also from the neighborhood of Saint Brieuc (Cotes-du-Nord), were especially examined. The specimens consisted of small fragments of the granite, some angular, others more or less rounded, and all forming a solid mass, with a glassy surface. They were in some cases similar in appearance to volcanic scoria.

When sections of the granite were examined in the microscope it was found that the orthoclase still acted upon polarized light, and the albite also was nearly unaltered, but besides them there were vitreous masses produced by the fusion. Of the minerals formed by the process, spinel was very common in regular octahedrons, sometimes transparent, sometimes opaque. There are also large numbers of microlites in geodes in the fused mica, which are probably to be referred to a triclinic feldspar. The small quantity of fluorine originally contained in the mica is regarded as having played an important part in the changes accompanying the fusion. These granites had been fused immediately by fire without the aid of soda, as in the first case named, and it is reasonably certain that the process of fusing together the small fragments was intentional although the means by which it was accomplished so thoroughly is less easy to understand.

MAIDEN CASTLE
Bord, Janet, and Bord, Colin; *Mysterious Britain,* London, 1972, pp. 92-93.

This aerial view of Maiden Castle gives an idea of the vast extent of this marvel of prehistoric engineering. It covers an area of 120 acres, with an average width of 1,500 feet and length of 3,000 feet. The inner circumference is about 1-1/2 miles round, and it has been estimated, as mentioned earlier, that it would require 250,000 men to defend it! It is hard therefore, to believe that this construction was originally intended to be a defensive position.

A great puzzle to archaeologists has always been the multiple and labyrinthine east and west entrances at each end of the enclosure, on the left and right sides of the photograph. Originally they may have been built as a way for processional entry by people of the Neolithic era. Later, when warriors of the Iron Age were using the site as a fortress they probably found them useful as a means of confusing the attacking force trying to gain entry. The fact that so many of these 'hillforts' have two entrances---one north of east and the other south of west---also suggest some form of Sun ceremonial.

ON A REMARKABLE FEATURE IN THE ENTRENCHEMENTS OF KNAP HILL CAMP, WILTSHIRE
Cunnington, M. E.; *Man* 9:49-52, 1909.

Recent excavations on the site of the small entrenchment known as

Aerial view of entrance to Maiden Castle "hill fort" in Dorset (J. D. H. Radford/Janet & Colin Bord)

Knap Hill Camp in Wiltshire revealed a feature which, if intentional, appears to be a method of defence hitherto unobserved in prehistoric fortifications in Britain.

Knap Hill is a bold conical-shaped hill, one of the series of capes or promontories standing out on the edge of the chalk plateau that borders, to the north, the Vale of Pewsey. On the south side, overlooking the valley, the hill is very steep and descends in one continuous slope from the summit to the level of the valley below, and on this side there is no evidence of defence, except that afforded by the natural steepness of the hill. But round the other side, where the hill slopes more gradually back to the level of the Downs that spread out behind it, is an entrenchment consisting of a single rampart and ditch, and this forms what is known as Knap Hill Camp.

The ditch has become silted up level, and there are six openings or gaps through the rampart. It was thought at first that, as often happens on ancient banks, some of these gaps were due to cattle tracks, or possibly had been made for agricultural purposes. There was, however, a certain regularity about them, and it was difficult to see why on such an isolated spot so many tracks should have been made.

The difficulty of accounting satisfactorily for these breaks in the rampart and for the ridges corresponding to them that were noticeable on the surface of the silted-in ditch suggested excavation at these points, and thus led to the discovery of the remarkable features to which it is desired to draw attention.

These excavations clearly showed that none of these gaps in the rampart are the result of wear or of any accidental circumstance, but that they are actually part of the original construction of the camp. The proof that the gaps are not the result of accident is that outside of, and corresponding to, each gap the ditch was never dug; that is to say, a solid gangway or causeway of unexcavated ground has been left in each case. Thus the entrenchment, consisting of the rampart and ditch, instead of being continuous, except for what might be deemed reasonable provision for ingress and egress, is broken up into short and irregular sections.

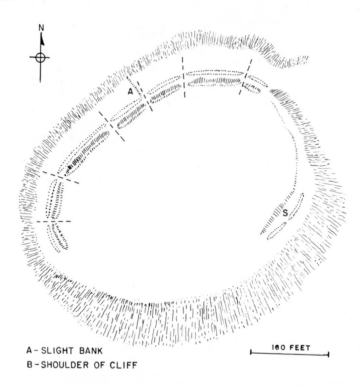

N

A – SLIGHT BANK
B – SHOULDER OF CLIFF

160 FEET

Plan of Knap Hill Camp. The many openings seem inconsistent with the fort interpretation.

The ditch of the main entrenchment is divided into seven sections. The unexcavated ground forming the causeway between each section is of a uniform width of 18 feet, although the length of the various sections of the ditch vary considerably. The first section, from the west, is 46 feet in length; the second, 92 feet, the third, 121 feet; the fourth, 98 feet; the fifth, 98 feet; the sixth, 122 feet; the seventh, 42 feet.

The main entrenchment ends on the eastern side of the hill at the seventh section of the ditch; this eastern side has been a good deal cut about by later settlers on the spot, and the rampart may originally have been carried further round the hill, but there never could have been a continuation of the ditch at this point.

But some little distance further round the hill, where the hill juts out and forms a shoulder, the ditch begins again, and there is a noticeable rampart. From end to end the shoulder is only some 130 feet in length, yet even here the ditch is not continuous, but is divided into two sections with a causeway of unexcavated ground between them of the usual width of 18 feet. The two sections of the ditch measure respectively 65 feet and 45 feet in length.

Given the need for an entrenchment at all, it seems at first sight inexplicable why these frequent openings should have been left, when apparently they so weaken the whole construction.

It has been suggested, by way of explanation, that the work of fortification was never finished, that the ditch was being dug and the rampart piled up by gangs of men working in sections, and that for some reason the work was abandoned before the various sections were completed, with the result now to be seen.

There is, however, considerable evidence in favour of these causeways being an intentional feature of the original design of the camp.

It is too improbable that on the isolated shoulder, as well as on the other side of the hill, the causeways should have been left accidentally as the result of an unfinished undertaking, and the position of the shoulder on the very steep side of the hill quite forbids the idea of an entrance there in any ordinary sense.

In every case the causeways are cut at a slight skew to the corresponding gap in the rampart, so that standing on or just outside the causeway, only an oblique view can be obtained into the camp. A line drawn through the gaps and out across the causeways indicates on the plan in which direction in each case the skew lies. The uniform width of the causeways alone almost affords sufficient proof of design.

The fact, also, that similar causeways have been noticed on several other sites, though not yet proved by excavation, strongly points to the conclusion that they were left for some definite purpose. It has been suggested that, as General Pitt-Rivers thought of the wide flanking ramparts at Winkelbury Camp, the causeways were intended in cases of emergency to admit a large number of cattle as rapidly as possible to the interior safety of the camp. But it would certainly be easier, and therefore quicker to drive a number of cattle through one or two wide openings than over half-a-dozen such narrow bridges as these.

It is then impracticable to regard these breaks in the entrenchment as due to an unfinished undertaking, or as entrances in any ordinary sense, and the only other feasible theory seems to be that they had some distinct purpose in the scheme of defence; that they were, indeed, a strenghtening and not a weakening factor in this seemingly not very strongly defended place.

The causeways may have been left as platforms from which to enfilade the ditch, the defenders being stationed upon them for this purpose. The distance from one causeway to another is not greater than would be within reach of hand thrown missiles. Any determined attempt to scale the stockade with which the rampart was presumably strengthened could probably be more effectually prevented from the gangways than if the defenders were themselves shut up behind the stockade, or forced to come out from some more distant entrance at risk of having their retreat

cut off. These causeways would be, in fact, sally ports admirably adapted for defence of the ditch. Even if the top of the rampart were not stock-
aded the same method of defence could have been adopted. A stockade or
paling carried across each causeway on a line with the outside edge of
the ditch would have served to shut out the enemy, and to protect the men
standing on the causeways. The gaps in the rampart need not have been
barricaded, but could have been left open to allow the defenders to pass
readily to and fro as they were needed at different points.

There is no sign of a beaten track leading to either of these causeways, but there is a much worn roadway leading to the eastern side of
the hill, and it is thought probable that the main entrance to the camp was
on this side to which the old road leads, but that the features of the actual
entrance have been obliterated by the later people who are known to have
lived on the spot.

Flint flakes and rude pottery have been found on the floor of the ditch,
and it is believed that the camp is of early date, that it belongs to the
bronze, or even to the late neolithic period.

The possible use which the gangways may have served is put forward
with all diffidence, and any suggestion on the subject would be welcomed.

Borough Hill hill fort, Leicester (Janet & Colin Bord)

WALLS, EMBANKMENTS, AND DITCHES

Robert Frost supposed that good fences made good neighbors.
Ancient man must have had a similar philosophy because he built long
walls and earthen banks on all continents. Some walls and ditches are
manifestly defensive in purpose. Hadrian's Wall in Britain is a classical example. Other walls are more mysterious and may have marked
boundaries long since overwhelmed by history. Herders built some
walls to keep their animals from straying too far. Some walls seem to
have no modern purpose whatever. Like most of the structural artifacts
included in this book, the walls that follow suggest extraordinary technology, the large-scale harnessing of manpower, or purposes as yet
undiscerned.

• North America

CERTAIN EARTHWORKS OF EASTERN MASSACHUSETTS
Willoughby, Charles C.; *American Anthropologist,* 13:566–576, 1911.

Besides the circular and square enclosures, there were evidently extensive areas of irregular form, sometimes subdivided into sections,
the direction of the stockade being determined by the contour and character of the land enclosed. The most extensive and best preserved
earthwork of this type known to the writer lies in the town of Millis,
about twenty miles south of Boston. It is situated on the shore of South
End Pond, an expansion of Boggestow Brook which flows into the Charles
River. The general character of the earthwork, and the contour of the
land enclosed is shown in figure 86. The hills which make up a greater
portion of the enclosed areas are covered with trees and the land has
never been cultivated. The greater part of the land bordering the hills
has been under cultivation for many years and it is quite certain that
portions of the embankments have been levelled and the corresponding
trenches filled. About 6,000 feet, or approximately 1-1/7 miles of embankments remain. The combined length of areas 1 and 2 is nearly
2,100 feet, and the amount of land in areas 1, 2, 3, 4, and 5 is approximately 31 acres. This land consists of glacial hills of irregular outline, with steep banks and deep gullies. Some of the depressions would
form a good protection from the winter winds. The embankment and
trench which undoubtedly enclosed the western end and the greater portion of the southern side of area 1 have been destroyed, probably by
cultivation. An extensive meadow borders the eastern edge of areas 3
and 4, and it is very probable that when the earthwork was built the

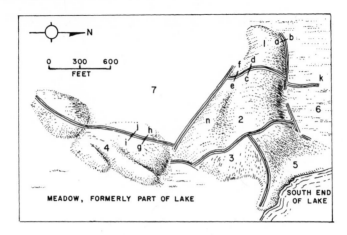

Embankments and trenches at South End Pond, Massachusetts

waters of the lake covered at least a portion of this meadow.   Area 5
is the only one now bordered by water.   The land at 6 is of medium
height and the embankment at k probably continued toward the water and
enclosed this section.   It is somewhat doubtful if the land at 7 was enclosed, although the turning of the southern extension of the embankment toward the west indicates that it may have been.   The land here is
fairly low and level and is under cultivation.

It will be noted that the trenches are on the inner side of the embankments only, with the exception of the northern side of area 1, where a
ditch may be traced on either side for nearly two hundred feet.   In the
neighborhood of these works, but beyond the limits of the sketch (fig. 86),
are a few indications of walls and ditches which may have formed parts
of this stronghold.

From the accompanying photographs and drawings of the embankments and trenches, a good idea may be had of the present appearance
of these remains.   It seems probable that the embankments supported
palisades, and that within the enclosures thus formed were many bark-
or mat-covered houses.   Apparently these works formed one of the most
extensive Indian strongholds thus far known in New England.

The existence of the earthworks at Millis has been known to local
archeologists for several years.   They were visited by Professor Putnam,
who made a sketch plan in 1887; a survey was made under the auspices of
the Peabody Museum, by A. D. Wyman in 1903; and a model which forms
the basis of figure 86 was prepared by the writer in 1909.

Sections of other embankments of a character similar to those described above have been brought to the writer's attention from time to
time, some of which are undoubtedly portions of Indian strongholds; but
generally not enough remains to give a comprehensive idea of the form
and extent of the enclosures.   Mr. Warren K. Moorehead, of the Phillips
Academy Museum of Andover, has recently called attention to several

earthworks in that town. Portions of these have been obliterated by cultivation, but enough remains to show some of them to have been extensive. (pp. 568–571)

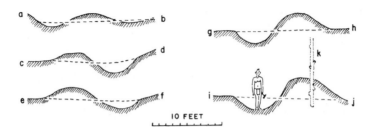

10 FEET

Cross sections of precolumbian earthworks in Massachusetts

COAST AND MARITIME STRUCTURES
Peet, Stephen D.; *American Antiquarian*, 22:157–180, 1900.

II. Another class of coast structures has been recently brought to light off the coast of Florida. We shall, therefore, take up the description of these as excellent specimens of the skill of the prehistoric people. They have been associated with the sand mounds and shell heaps of Florida, but they show a more advanced stage, and should probably be classed with the mounds and earthworks of the Gulf States, for it is the opinion of Dr. D. G. Brinton, Prof. F. W. Putnam and others that they were erected by the same people.

The object of these remarkable "shell keys" is unknown, but they appear to have been walls, which surrounded the seagirt habitation of an ancient and unknown people. The "reef raised sea walls of shell" surrounded central, half natural lagoons, or lake courts, with the "many-channeled enclosures," which, when surrounded by the dwellings of the people who erected them, must have made the island resemble a modern Venice. The houses were probably constructed altogether of wood, and perhaps covered with thatched roofs. The canals within the lagoon were dug out of low, swampy ground, and were lined with earth walls, which were covered with a tangled forest; making the ancient village resemble the villages on the coast of Benares or the Philippine Islands, more than the European Venice.

The islands lack the outside reefs which are found in the Caroline Islands, and there are no such artificial breakwaters, as are there; nor are there any such massive stone enclosures and shrines.

These were discovered and described by Mr. F. H. Cushing. The following is his account of his explorations and a description of their character and appearance:

I was not much delayed in securing two men and a little fishing sloop, such as it was, and in sailing forth one glorious evening late in May, with intent to explore as many as possible of the islands and capes of Charlotte Harbor, Pine Island Sound, Caloosa Bay, and the lower more open coast as far as Marco.

The astonishment I felt in penetrating into the interior of the very first encountered of these thicket-bound islets, may be better imagined than described, when, after wading ankle deep in the slimy and muddy shoals, and then alternately clambering and floundering for a long distance among the wide-reaching interlocked roots of the mangroves, I dimly beheld in the somber depths of this sunless jungle of the waters, a long, nearly straight, but enormous embankment of piled-up conch shells. Beyond it were to be seen (as in the illustration given) other banks less high, not always regular, but forming a range of distinct enclosures of various sizes and outlines; nearly all of them open a little at either end, or at opposite sides, as if for outlet and inlet.

Threading this zone of boggy bins, and leading in toward a more central point, were here and there open ways like channels. They were formed by parallel ridges of shells, increasing in height toward the interior, until at last they merged into a steep, somewhat extended bench, also of shells, and flat on the top like a platform. Here, of course, at the foot of the platform, the channel ended in a slightly broadened cove, like a landing place; but a graded depression or pathway ascended from it and crossed this bench or platform, leading to and in turn climbing over, or rather through another and higher platform, a slight distance beyond. In places, off to the side on either bank, were still more of these platforms, rising terrace-like, but very irregularly, from the enclosures below to the foundations of great level-topped mounds, which, like worn-out, elongated and truncated pyramids, loftily and imposingly crowned the whole; some of them to a height of nearly thirty feet above the encircling sea. The bare patches along the ascents to the mounds were, like the ridges below, built up wholly of shells, great conch shells chiefly, blackened by exposure for ages; and ringing like their potsherds when disturbed even by the light feet of the raccoons and little brown rabbits, that now and then scuddled across them from covert to covert, and that seemed to be, with the ever-present grosbeaks above, and with many lizards and some few rattlesnakes and other reptiles below, the principal dwellers in those lonely keys---if swarming insects may be left unnamed!

Wherever revealed, the surface below, like the bare spaces themselves, proved to be also of shells, smaller or much broken on the levels and gentler slopes, and mingled with scant black mold on the wider terraces, as though these had been formed with a view to cultivation, and supplied with soil from the rich muck beds below. Here, also, occurred occasional potsherds and many worn valves of gigantic clams and pieces of huge shells that appeared to have been used as hoes and picks or other digging tools, and this again suggested the idea that at least the wider terraces--- many of which proved to be not level but filled with basin-shaped depressions or bordered by retaining walls---had been used as garden plats, supplied with soil from the rich musk beds below. But the margins of these, whether raised or not, and the edges of even the lesser terraces, the sides of the graded ways leading up to or through them, and especially the slopes of the greater mounds, were all of unmixed shell, in which, as in the barren patches, enormous, nearly square-sized conch shells prevailed.

Such various features, seen one by one, impressed me more and more forcibly, as indicating general design---a structural origin of at least the enormous accumulations of shed I was so slowly and painfully traversing; if not, indeed, of the entire key or islet. Still, my mind was not, perhaps, wholly disabused of the prevalent opinion that these and like accumulations or capes of the neighboring mainland were primarily stupendous shell heaps, chiefly the undisturbed refuse remaining from ages of intermittent aboriginal occupation, until I had scaled the topmost of the plat-forms. Then I could see that the vast pile on which I stood, and of which the terraces I had climbed, were, in a sense, irregular stages, formed in reality a single, prodigious elbow-shaped founda-tion, crowned at its bend by a definite group of lofty, narrow, and elongated mounds, that stretched fan-like across its summit, like the thumb and four fingers of a mighty outspread hand. Beyond, moreover, were other great foundations, bearing aloft still other groups of mounds, their declivities thickly overgrown but their summits betokened by the bare branches of gumbo limbos, whence had come, no doubt, the lonesounding songs of the grosbeaks. They stood, these other foundations, like the sundered ramparts of some vast and ruined fortress, along one side and across the further end of a deep, open space or quadrangular court, more than an acre in extent, level and as closely covered with mangroves, and other tidal growths at the bottom, as were the entire swamps. It was apparent that this had actually been a central court of some kind, had probably been formed as an open lagoon by the gradual upbuilding on atoll-like reefs or shoals around deeper water, of those foundations or ramparts, as I have called them, from even below tide level to their present imposing height. (pp. 167-170)

. . . .

ANCIENT WORKS IN FLORIDA
Anonymous; *Scientific American*, 47:113, 1882.

The Travers Herald describes the finding of an ancient work in the digging a canal between Lakes Eustis and Dora, to open up the more southern lakes of the great lake region of Florida.

The first excavations revealed the existence of a clearly defined wall lying in a line tending toward the southwest, from where it was first struck. The wall was composed of a dark brown sandstone, very much crumbled in places, but more distinct, more clearly defined, and the stone more solid as the digging increased in depth. The wall was evidently the eastern side of an ancient home or fortification, as the slope of the outer wall was to the west. About eight feet from the slope of the eastern wall a mound of sand was struck, embedded in the muck formation above and around it. This sand mound was dug into only a few inches, as the depth of the water demanded but a slight increased depth of the channel at that point; but enough was discovered to warrant the belief that here on the northwestern shore of Lake Dora is submerged a city or town or fortification older by centuries than anything yet discovered in this portion of Florida. Small, curiously shaped blocks of sandstone, some of them showing traces of fire, pieces of pottery, and utensils made of a mottled flint were thrown out by the men while working waist deep in water. One spear head of mottled flint, five and a half inches long by one and a quarter inches wide, nicely finished, was taken from the top of the sand mound and about four feet below the water level of the lake.

AMONG THE ROCKY MOUNTAINS
Byers, Wm. N.; *American Antiquarian,* 1:16, 1878.

The native races have left but few lasting traces in this part of the territory. Such as I have observed I will answer under the numbers of your questions:
1. At certain "passes" over the main range of the mountains there are the remains of strategical works, about which the present Indians know nothing. At Boulder Pass, 55 miles west of Denver, an old trail or trace led where a wagon road is now built. It passes at 11,600 feet above sea level, and traverses, at that height, a plateau above timber line for between three and four miles. Its approaches are by spurs at right angles with the range, flanked by inaccessible canons. At the salient point in this pass there are long lines of breastworks---rough walls of stones such as cover the surface in the vicinity. They follow the natural 'vantage ground and at the many angles there are stronger defences of the same character, with enclosing walls and slight excavations within ---miniature forts or large rifle pits. These stone walls probably aggregate miles in length. Some have pronounced them military works; others think they were for killing game, and still others have maintained that they are moraines of the glacial period. Once in crossing with General Jno. M. Schofield, I asked his opinion and he replied: "It is very plain that they are military works."
Near what we now call Argentine Pass, about twenty miles further south on the same range, is a similar pass, by a transverse ridge, but of still greater length above timber line. Here is an old roadway which has evidently borne infinite travel of some kind. At intervals along it are circular works, apparently for protection or hiding places. Excavations of two or three feet, bordered by enclosing walls of stone, ten to twenty feet in diameter. But they are isolated and I never observed any trace of other walls.

THE MYSTERIOUS WALLS OF THE BERKELEY AND OAKLAND HILLS

Morrill, Sibley S.; *Pursuit,* 5:90–92, 1972.

For better than a century now, some ordinary looking stone walls in the Berkeley Hills overlooking San Francisco Bay have been a subject of speculation on three principal points: why were they built, by whom, and when.

They are found mainly in heavily wooded or chaparral-covered areas, but whether there or occasionally in the high grasslands, they appear to have served none of the usual purposes of walls---except in two or three places where it seems they may possibly form the remains of fortifications. They survive only in sections, ranging in length from 20 feet to 200 yards or so. Their height varies from 2 feet or less to 5 or a little more, the average probably being between 3 and 4 feet. Their breadth was great enough---4 feet in some instances---to make it a near certainty that the walls originally were much higher through the use of smaller stones along the top. Digging at their base, of which only a little has been done, reveals that the rock goes down as much as 10 inches below the surface.

While the sites of some of these walls, like those in the Vollmer or Bald Peak (1905 ft. elevation) and nearby Grizzly Peak (1750 ft. elevation) areas, suggest the possibility of a defense purpose, other sites, such as that of a wall which runs straight up the southeastern slope of Roundtop (1763 ft. elevation) through masses of underbrush and poison oak, offer no clue as to why they were constructed. Even if its present height of 3 feet was originally double that, Roundtop wall's length of nearly 100 yards would have made it of no use as a fortification. As to the possibility that it once extended much farther in either direction, there is nothing to suggest this at either end. And whoever constructed it certainly did not do it for fun; some of the rocks weigh easily over 200 pounds! Furthermore, it is unlikely that they did it for 'practice'. Those who built that and the other walls were persons of some skill and experience, for the walls are not just elongated piles of rock.

Seth Simpson, of Oakland, California, who has studied the walls as a hobby for several years, and his son Martin, a palaeontology student at Merritt College, say it is plain that some of the stones were chipped and fitted. In fact, a stone found in a wall near Vollmer Peak was actually bored through or holed, and because of the growth of a tree immediately in front of it, plus the length of time the stone must have been in situ, that operation was probably conducted generations ago, when or even before the wall was built. In any case, throughout the greater part of the length of these walls, it is generally evident that the rocks were placed in such a way as to give a locking effect.

Simpson's investigations indicate that the walls are found over an area extending for nearly 7 miles south into the Oakland hills, but he has been quite unable to relate them to any boundary markings. Water company survey maps show that none of the walls has any detectible relationship to boundary lines; except for one case in the Vollmer Peak area, boundary lines parallel no walls nearer than about 600 yards.

Nor is there anything in the construction of the walls to indicate that they are the remains of pens or corrals. They are, for the most part, straight. Some intersect at an angle, and there are instances of parallel walls separated by as much as 10 yards or so, but there are no indications whatever that they formed enclosures.

Simpson attempted to determine whether there were similar structures in other counties around the Bay, but discovered nothing except in the hills behind Milpitas, an extension of the Berkeley and Oakland Hills some 25 miles to the south. In a way, the walls there are still more baffling. They are in a gently rolling, comparatively treeless country, and except for the remains of one, they offer no suggestion of the usual purpose of a wall. In fact, from the nature of the terrain, which I have visited, it was not of a character to provide even the reason that New England farmers had for building their famous stone walls---primarily for "storage" of stones removed from fields to permit ploughing. When the New Englanders ran out of "wall space" they dumped excess rocks in the nearest gulley. The walls were virtually useless as fences, and grazing land was much more easily fenced by stumps or stakes and rails. In the Milpitas area, the stone walls just run their way for a few score or few hundred yards and then stop. Livestock have no difficulty in walking around them.

As to why and when those walls were built, ranchers in the area whom Simpson interviewed said they didn't know. They had always been there---and had been constructed by "the Mexicans, or Chinese, or some others", in every case long before the ranchers came into possession of the land. In brief, these ranchers know no more about the origin of their walls than the inhabitants of Berkeley and Oakland know about theirs.

That is the way it is today. But, since the walls in the Berkeley and Oakland hills have undergone a certain amount of attrition, even destruction, in recent years (a considerable part of one of them was removed in the construction of a botanical garden at Tilden Park), it is of interest to see what was thought of them fifty years ago or so.

On October 15, 1916, Harold French wrote in the Oakland _Tribune_ that, "since the Nineties, when my attention was first attracted by three ancient rock walls...I have asked many old timers what they knew about them. Two old tramping friends who have ranged these ridges since the Sixties have told me they were just as ancient in appearance then as in later years.

"One of them, the late Captain Albert S. Bierce, brother of Ambrose Bierce, dispelled the last lingering doubt in my mind when one day in 1904, he led me into a thicket of greasewood in a gulch draining the southern slope of Mt. Baldy, and in the jungle which has been growing there for ages he showed me a very distinct old wall completely hidden from view."

French reported that the walls to be found "at various points from the peak known as Round Top...to the northerly extension of Baldy Ridge" had a combined length that would "extend two miles in all". The largest walls French reported were those found "on the southerly slopes of Round Top, overlooking Redwood Canyon" where the walls "form a right angle, the longest line of which runs westerly down the slope for about 700 feet, the other points southward some 500 feet".

Noting that some of the "volcanic boulders" forming the walls weighed nearly a ton, French said that those forming the base of the walls "lie embedded in the soil for a foot or more", a matter which, when combined with the coating of lichens and the weathered surfaces of the rocks, "proves they have lain there a very long time".

As for the origin of the walls, French found nothing to indicate they were built by pioneers, Mexicans, or any other people who came after the arrival of the Spaniards in the 1770's. On the contrary, he notes that "there was a tradition among the Matalanes, tribesmen who made their homes among the Thousand Oaks [an area in the foothills of north Berkeley] and pounded their acorn mills on the rocks near Cerrito Creek...that the walls were fortifications built by 'the hill people' with whom they warred. The very name Matalanes sounds strangely similar to Atlanteans, to whom the Aztecs and their predecessors who lived about Mazatlan, down the Mexican Coast were reputed to be related."

Another source, an undated and unidentified, but very yellowed clipping found by the famous Oakland bookman, the late Harold C. Holmes, tells of walls found "half a mile east of Grizzly Peak" which form "two sides of a right angle, each side being about 100 yards in length and appear to terminate in the dense chaparral, although traces are found showing that they were at one time much more extensive...about 50 feet in length, although it may be seen that it was built to a length of about 280 yards...in the vicinity are the remains of other walls, at present of no considerable extent. The generally accepted belief is that the place was a city inhabited by some long-forgotten race...Certainly the people who built them understood stone cutting, as the boulders bear evidence of having been split and chipped in order to join compactly." Otherwise, the clipping gives much the same information as French gave.

A PREHISTORIC EARTHWORK IN THE HAIDA INDIAN AREA
Smith, Harlan I.; *American Anthropologist,* 29:109-111, 1927.

Near Rose Point, the most northeastern part of Graham Island of the Queen Charlotte Group, in the Haida Indian area of British Columbia, is an unusual prehistoric earthwork. Published accounts of earthworks in western North America are so rare that a note of this one may be useful. The information was collected during a brief visit made in 1919 for the Victoria Memorial Museum.

The exact location is about a mile and a half southward from the limit of trees on Rose Point. It is about a quarter of a mile east by north, on the trail from Mr. Bradley's ranch house to the east coast on a wooded flat among steep wooded moving dunes possibly thirty feet high. The site is probably a little northeast of the center of lot 1014. The earthworks consist of ridges of earth about twelve to eighteen inches high outlining long rectangles as illustrated in Fig. 1. Two low ridges in the northwest part of the earthworks, one of them at an angle to the other ridges, may be the remains of decaying timber. These are represented by dotted lines on the map. All of the complete rectangles are approximately one hundred feet long. Two complete rectangles and four parts are about fifty feet wide; one is about twenty-five feet wide, and another partial rectangle parallel to it at a distance of thirty-five feet, is thirty-five feet wide. All of the complete rectangles are longer easterly and westerly. It is surprising that lengths of these longitudinal ridges are equal, that they are an even hundred feet long, that the lengths of so many of the transverse ridges are equal, one rectangle being exactly

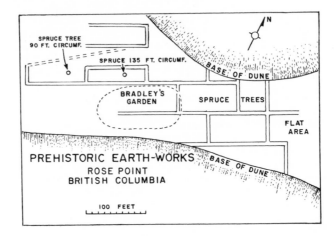

half as wide as the others, and that the width of an incomplete rectangle
is measurable in multiples of all of the other measurements.

Whether the dunes have covered part of the earthworks or whether
the ridges merely abut on the dunes was not ascertained. If the dunes
had been built out over part of the ridges it must have been long ago,
as there are large spruce trees on them at this place.   There are no
large trees on the ridges, but there are large spruce trees growing
within the earthworks as well as on the dunes, those northwest of the
earthworks being the larger. A spruce tree ninety inches in circumference stands about twenty-five feet westward from the top of the westernmost north and south ridge, and nearly twenty-five feet northward
from the top of the most western east and west ridge on a space that was
possibly enclosed, although we could not trace its western or northern
embankment. Another spruce tree one hundred thirty-five inches in
circumference stands within the most western complete rectangle.
This tree is, consequently, over forty-two inches in diameter and an
average spruce three feet in diameter on Graham Island is said by
foresters to be over one hundred seventy-five years old; it would seem,
then, that the earthworks were probably made before 1744, that is,
thirty years before the first European visit to the island. It is a possibility, however, that the tree was enclosed within the earthworks.

A spruce windfall to the northwest disclosed no village refuse, such
as shell-heap material, among its roots or in the hole formed on its
uprooting. The middle southern part of the earthworks is located in an
oval space about a hundred fifty feet long which the Bradleys have fenced
and cultivated as a garden. In this garden, stones burned and crackled
by fire were seen but no shells were found. Part of the skull of a whale
was seen imbedded in the earth near an embankment in the southeastern
part of these earthworks. On the whole, signs of habitation were so
scarce as to suggest that the period of occupation, if any, was short.

If these ridges are the remains of banking around houses, the houses
were not similar either in size or proportions to Haida houses. The
Haida houses were nearly square while those of Nootka and Salish tribes,
of the region much further to the south, were sometimes long and narrow.
Although these enclosures are parallel and in parallel rows, as were the
houses, there are no passageways between them except possibly in one

place. This place is the thirty-three foot space lying between the area walled on three sides as traced at the north and the enclosure to the south. Here there seemed to have been no ridges. Moreover, the rectangles are not arranged along the base of the dunes or with any symmetrical relation to them as would probably have been the case with houses built since these dunes were formed. The site is well sheltered by the dunes and in that respect, although rather low, is desirable for habitations on this point where both wind and driving sand are severe.

Mr. Carpenter, of Masset townsite, suggested that these walls were made up of sods removed in the making of gardens. At the Haida village of Masset I saw a wall about six feet long by two feet wide by two feet high consisting of sods taken up in the making of a garden. However, a wall of these earthworks, the one under cultivation within the enclosure fenced by the Bradleys, is of yellowish gray sandy soil rather than of black humus such as would result from the decay of sods.

Although many localities in the Haida area are referred to as forts, it is not known whether they include earthworks or not. The earthworks of the coast of southern British Columbia tend to be circular or semicircular except in places where they cut off promontories which could easily be fortified. The Rose Point earthworks do not appear to be fortifications and their true purpose has not yet been explained.

DEFENSIVE WORKS AT TIKAL

Puleston, Dennis E., and Callender, Donald W. J., Jr.; *Expedition*, 9:40–48, Spring 1967.

For the weeks, months, and even years one spends carrying out fairly routine work there is always the possibility of stumbling onto something important that is totally unexpected. The discovery of what appears to be a 9-1/2 km. long defensive earthworks 4.5 km. north of the Great Plaza of Tikal is an example of just such a chance. The earthworks lie directly between Tikal and the nearest large site, Uaxactun. These two sites are about five hours apart in terms of walking distance; the earthworks are one hour's walk north of Tikal. Frankly, a defensive barrier of this magnitude, or for that matter of any magnitude, was not one of the things we expected to find in the process of a project to explore and map the outlying areas of Tikal.

. . . .

The Tikal earthworks were discovered in the process of the systematic mapping of the remains of house platforms and other structures along the 1/2 km.-wide, 12-km.-long strip which extends north from Tikal's center. The trench is the most prominent feature of the earthworks, but when it was first discovered it appeared to be nothing more than a natural arroyo or ravine. As we followed it, however, it soon became evident that it was not a natural formation. First, it had a continuous raised embankment along the south side, and second, it passed up and down over hills, following a fairly straight line. At several points where we came to low ground it seemed to disappear, but by continuing on we were always able to pick it up again on the next piece of high ground. Otherwise, the earthworks were easy to follow. We soon found it easiest to walk along in the trench itself, though occasionally fallen trees of great size blocked our path, forcing us to crawl through a dense tangle of branches or make a detour. We followed the trench in this way for a total of three days. Compass bearings were taken every 40 to 50 meters and distances were paced off as accurately as possible, revealing finally that over their known length the earthworks extended for a total of 9-1/2 km. At both the east and west ends the earthworks disappeared into large swamps through which they may or may not have continued. We were particularly interested to note that the ends almost reached the two great logwood (Haematoxylum campechianum) swamps that lie to the east and west of Tikal.

With the realization that this new feature was not natural, but was something constructed with great effort by the Maya themselves, we were left with the question of why? What was the function of this great trench and embankment situated so far from the center of Tikal? At first we considered the possibility that it might have served as a canal in a water distribution system of some kind. However, this intriguing idea had to be rejected on the basis of two factors, both of which preclude the possibility that the trench could have held water: first, the extremely porous nature of limestone bedrock; and second, the way in which the trench goes up and down the sides of large hills without changing its depth.

On the other hand, its potential as a barrier to human movement was obvious for at least three reasons. (1) Though we did not know its depth before we began excavation, the four-meter width of the trench posed an obstacle few Maya could have crossed by jumping. To have tried to do so would have been additionally difficult for two reasons. First, over almost its entire length outsiders would have had to run uphill to approach the trench, and second, they would have had to jump upwards, as well as across the trench, to get onto the embankment which abutted the south lip. In looking at Fig. 2 it should be remembered that this embankment must have been considerably steeper and higher a thousand years ago than it is today. (2) The logwood swamps to the east and west would have made it difficult to get around the ends of the earthworks providing they were as unpleasant to struggle through in the days of the Maya as they are today. (3) Finally, that the trench was impassable is suggested by the fact that at four or five widely separated points along its length we found what appeared to be causeways across it. At each of these there was an equivalent gap in the embankment. If the earthworks were not a barrier to human passage these "gates" would have little reason to exist.

. . . .

A TRINCHERA NEAR QUITOVAQUITA, SONORA

Ives, Ronald L.; *American Anthropologist*, 38:257-259, 1936.

Stone walls on many of the hills of Papagueria have excited the interest of workers in that area for a number of years. The wall to be described below is of interest because it indicates a westward extension of the known range of the builders of these structures.

One mile southeast of Quitovaquita, a Papago town on the Arizona-Sonora border, the Sonoyta River enters a range of granitic hills, locally known as the Cerritos de Agua Dulce. At the point where the river enters the hills is a small isolated knoll separated from the main cerrito by an abandoned river channel about twenty feet above the present channel. On the east side of this knoll is a wall about 300 feet long, three feet high and two feet thick. Between this wall and the slope of the hill, material resembling sheetflood wash has accumulated or been placed. No other structures of any sort were found on or near this knoll.

The major portion of this wall has fallen, although it is firmly built. Earthquakes, which are, and have been for many years, common in this area, are probably responsible for the falling. Only a few hundred feet upstream, the bedrock in the river bed has been faulted so that the east (upstream) side is elevated four feet. This faulting occurred recently enough so that the broken edge of the uplifted portion is still sharp, but not within the last few years, as the scarp has been eroded away in the unconsolidated sediments close by.

This wall closely resembles the walls on the various "Cerros de Trincheras" described by McGee, Lumholtz, Sauer and Brand, and others, although it is west of the areas from which trincheras have previously been reported. Inquiries at Quitovaquita produced the information that this wall was built before the coming of "el Doctor Lumbo" (Lumholtz), and before that the "good padre" (possibly Kino). Further questions brought only "No comprendo" from the Papagos. At Sonoyta, Alberto Celaya, the Comisario, who assisted Lumholtz during his explorations in Papagueria, knew of the structure, but knew nothing of its origin. No description of this structure has been found in the literature of the area which goes back to 1698.

These walls have been described as fortifications by McGee and some of the early Spanish writers, but this wall, like many of the others known in Sonora, is poorly placed strategically. Three sides, the north, west and south, are open to attack. Sauer and Brand give evidence that some of the terraces described by them were inhabited, possibly by valley people who were driven from their homes. No evidence of habitation was found at the Quitovaquita trinchera. The structure was certainly not an irrigation dam, for it could not impound water, and there is no water to impound at this place except during the summer rains, and very little then. It was not a corral, for it is open at the ends, and could not confine any animal more active than a turtle. Lumholtz suggests that the trincheras were religious structures. Considering the location of some of these structures, and their apparent uselessness for any other purpose, this suggestion has its merits. Small pieces of red mericanite lava, found at the base of this wall, suggest a connection with Pinacate, twenty miles distant, where this lava is plentiful. Iitoi, one of the major Papago gods, is said to have made his home in a cave at Pinacate, and to have made his home in a cave at Pinacate, and to have burned away part of the peaks. No mericanite was found between the Quitovaquita trinchera and Pinacate, but in view of the lack of thorough exploration of the area, it cannot safely be said that there is no such lava nearer than Pinacate.

This wall is the most westerly of the trincheras in the Sonoyta valley and probably represents an outpost of the pre-Papago peoples who built them. Until a more thorough study of the outlying trincheras is made, and their relation to the structures further inland is determined, no age, other than pre-Papago, can be assigned to this structure.

• South America

THE "GREAT WALL OF PERU".....

Shippee, Robert; *Smithsonian Institution Annual Report, 1932,* pp. 461-473; and *Geographical Review,* 25:1-29, 1932. (Reprinted with permission from the American Geographical Society)

The appearance of "Peru from the Air," was followed by many requests for a continuation of the studies contained therein. In no field have the rewards of aerial survey been greater than in archeology, and the demand has been increasing for "more maps and more air photographs," as Crawford has phrased it. To meet this demand and the demands of geography were two of the chief objectives of the Shippee-Johnson Peruvian expedition of 1931. The expedition planned to record the most important ancient sites of Peru by oblique and vertical photographs and mosaic maps. We had little expectation of making really new discoveries in a country where exploration has already revealed so much. We were quite unprepared for the "Great Wall," as it has been popularly termed.

The Great Wall. While we were still operating from the base that we had established at Trujillo for the mapping of the well-known ruins of Chan-Chan, we made a flight with the photographic plane inland as far as the Maranon River and, on the return, circled southward around Mount Huascaran and then followed the valley of the Santa River to the coast. Our course was over the edge of the foothills bordering the narrow upper valley of the river on the north. Johnson, co-leader and photographer of the expedition, watching for photographic subjects, noticed what appeared to be a wall flowing up and down over the ridges beneath the plane, wondered for a moment as to the purpose of such a structure, decided that it was worth recording, and made a number of photographs of it. We hoped to be able to return later to make a more complete record of the wall but were not certain that we should have time to do so. The photographs, printed a few weeks later in our Lima laboratory, led to so much discussion, however, that just before our departure we arranged to make a special trip to relocate and examine the wall from both the air and the ground.

Johnson and I, with our Peruvian observer, Captain Ceballos, flew to Chimbote in the photographic ship and established a temporary base there. Chimbote lies on one of the largest bays of the Peruvian coast, a few miles south of the Santa Valley, of which it is now the principal port. The little town in the lee of three tall, barren sand hills can boast of two things only---a natural harbor that would make the most ideal naval, aviation, or submarine base imaginable and a level, hard landing field that is used by the Peruvian commercial air lines.

The natives of Chimbote assured us that they knew about the wall, that they had heard of it from their ancestors, and that it was pre-Incaic. They could tell nothing, however, of its purpose or its history and, indeed, gave little real evidence that they had ever even heard of it.

From Chimbote the flight to the mouth of the Santa River was a matter of a few minutes only. Turning inland from there we picked up the wall about 5 or 6 miles from the coast at the ruins of a small village. At that end the wall divides into two sections for a short distance. It may have once extended to the shore line; but, if it did, it has been

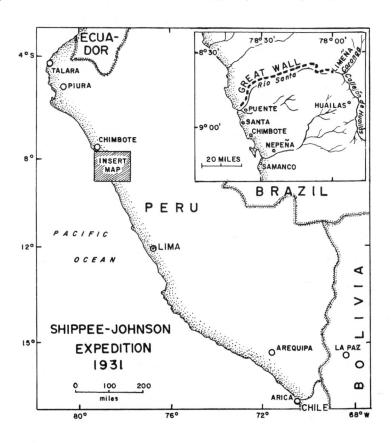

broken down, and the stones have either been removed for other building purposes or covered by the drifting sand.

From the ruined village, itself all but lost under the sand, the wall
leads away up the north side of the river, first across the level, sandy
plain of the river delta and then, as the valley narrows, over the edge
of the foothills bordering the valley. As the foothill ridges become
sharper and steeper, the wall rises and dips and in places is turned
slightly from its generally straight course. Its distance from the river
is in general about a mile and a half, although in one place at least it
dips down close to the edge of the river bed. In places it blends so
well with the background as to be almost indistinguishable.

It was impossible to make an accurate check on the distance we
followed the wall, for the air was so unusually rough that, as we approached the Andes, we had to circle and climb for more and more
altitude; but we followed it for at least 40 miles and possibly more.
Then we lost it. We had already passed over several short breaks,
but this time we failed to pick it up again. The light, which was poor
when we started---for the flight was made in August, a winter month,
when the coastal valleys are nearly always overcast and often filled
solid with fog---was getting rapidly worse; so we headed back for
Chimbote, taking only a few minutes out to get more close-ups of the
forts on both sides of the wall.

It so happened that none of our first photographs showed any of these
forts. But, on this second flight we noticed at irregular intervals on
both sides of the wall, but at short distances from it, a series of small
forts---some circular and some rectangular---most of which were
more or less inset in the top of small hills so as to be quite invisible
from the valley floor. Those on the south side, and they were the
larger, were located in the hills on the south side of the Santa River
opposite the wall. We believe that we located and photographed all of
these forts---a total of 14. The largest one appeared to be about 300
feet by 200 feet, with walls about 15 feet high and perhaps 5 feet thick,
and was of piled-stone construction. A few of the others were of the
same construction, but most of them appeared to be of adobe.

At Chimbote we at once began preparation for a trip to the wall
overland. From a rough sketch made while in the air we figured that
we could reach at least the western end of the wall by automobile.
There is a bridge over the Santa near its mouth, and, once on the other
side, it would be simply a question of how far the car could plow through
the sand. The next morning we loaded our equipment into an old Ford
and started off on a trip that was to take five hours of bumping over
crude roads, slithering down muddy cow paths, and pushing through
deep sand. Steering our course by a method of "dead reckoning"
especially devised for the occasion, we at last reached the sand-
covered ruins of the little village at the end of the wall. It was just by
chance that we did not miss them entirely. From the air we had been
able to make out the plan of the streets and the walls of the separate
houses. From the ground we saw nothing but a few sand-covered ridges.

Just beyond these ridges, which were crumbled adobe walls buried
beneath centuries of drifted sand, we saw the wall stretching away to
the horizon. We followed along it for several miles. Then the valley
began to narrow and the cross ridges to dip more sharply down to it.
The Ford could go no farther. We struggled on afoot for another mile,
lugging the cameras and stopping at intervals for still and motion pic-

tures showing construction details and the character of the terrain on which the wall stands.

The wall, as far as we followed it, now averages about 7 feet in height. It is built of broken rocks set together with adobe cement, and, where it has not been greatly disturbed, its outer surface is so well chinked with small rocks that it would be practically impossible to scale it without ladders. In occasional places, as seen from the air, the wall must still be 20 or 30 feet high where it crosses gullies. We found it impossible to make anything like accurate measurements. The rocks that have slipped from the top with the beating of the winds and the occasional rains spread away for a considerable distance on either side of the wall and aid the drifted sand in obscuring its base. We estimated that, in its original state, it was about 12 or 15 feet thick at the base and was built to taper upward to an average height of 12 or 15 feet.

Origin of the Wall. We were unable to come to any conclusion concerning the origin of the wall. As Dr. A. L. Kroeber remarks, that will require careful examination by an archeologist familiar with different types of construction and able to interpret potsherds or other fragments that may be found in association with the wall. If we had had time to carry our ground explorations farther and to investigate the forts, we might have found more definite indications as to its history; but we had already spent eight and a half months in Peru instead of the five months originally planned.

Further exploration to determine how far the wall extends into the Andes would be especially worth while. We estimate that when we finally lost sight of the wall we were in the neighborhood of Corongo. Wiener mentions strongly fortified hills in the Corongo region. We have, therefore, the possibility of a defensive wall joining the fortifications of the Corongo region with those at the mouth of the Santa River.

Clearly the wall with its double line of forts was erected as a defensive barrier. If it is true that the fortified hilltops at Paramonga, some 50 miles farther south, mark the southern limits of the domain of the Great Chimu, there are many guesses that can be made as to the origin and purpose of the wall. It may be an inter-tribal defense that antedates the consolidation of the Chimu kingdom. Or it may be a secondary line of defense erected by the Chimu against the Inca invader. If the latter is the case it may explain why, as tradition says, the Inca abandoned his invasions of the Chimu kingdom from the south along the coast and finally conquered it by advancing his armies through the Andes and laying direct siege to Chan-Chan, the Chimu capital.

The suggestion has been advanced by Dr. R. L. Olson, of the University of California, that the wall may represent one of a series of defense structures built by the Chimu as they extended their territory to the north and south. While engaged in field work in this part of Peru two years ago Doctor Olson noted a number of walls in the Chao Valley, about 20 miles north of the Santa Valley, mostly fragmentary and running for short distances only. He describes a larger wall cutting across the pampa between Trujillo and Chicama that was built presumably for the defense of Chan-Chan.

Prof. Marshall H. Saville suggests that the wall may have been erected by the Chimu or pre-Chimu occupants of the Santa Valley to prevent the neighboring tribes on the north, or possible invaders from the north, from gaining access to the river where, by damming or otherwise diverting the stream, they could cut off the water supply from the great aqueducts, still largely in fairly good repair, that irrigated the densely peopled Santa delta. In connection with this suggestion may be cited Montesinos's account that the Inca finally conquered the Great Chimu by cutting off his water supply. It may have been the supply to the Santa Valley that was cut off by the Inca, since Montesinos does not state which valley it was in which the Chimu finally capitulated, while Garcilasso de la Vega says that it was the Santa Valley, although he makes no mention of the cutting off of the water supply.

Dr. Julio C. Tello, director of the archeological museum of the University of San Marcos and a leading authority on the Inca and pre-Inca civilizations, states in reply to a letter addressed to him by the American Geographical Society that not only had he never heard of the wall until it was reported by the Shippee-Johnson expedition but that he has been unable to find anyone among the owners of the large haciendas in the Santa Valley who knows anything of it. Doctor Tello reports that he has discovered several walls similar to the Great Wall of the Santa Valley in valleys south of Lima, although none of them is more than a few kilometers in length. He also mentions the wall between Trujillo and Chicama described by Doctor Olson, but offers no suggestions as to the possible purpose of this or others of what he describes as the "mysterious walls of Peru."

It is still hard for us to believe that we have actually made a new discovery of such evident importance in a region whose ruins have been for more than 75 years the subject of frequent and careful explorations by a long list of noted archeologists, many of whom have made their reputations there. From the air, the wall and its forts are so striking a feature of the landscape that it is difficult to understand how they could have so long escaped notice from the ground. That this is the case seems less astonishing, however, when one considers that, even though the wall were noticed at its western end where it crosses the delta of the Santa River, it would appear only as one more wall in a region filled not only with the ruins of elaborate fortifications---fortified hills and defensive walls of various sorts---but also with the remains of cities, towns, and extensive irrigation works. Only when one looks down upon the wall from the air and thus is able to see long sections of it can one realize that it is a feature quite distinct from the short sections of wall characteristic of the Santa delta. This broad view presented to observer and camera is what makes the airplane so important an instrument in modern exploration. The aerial observer is afforded, and the aerial camera records frequently in a single exposure, a synthesis of details whose relationships might otherwise never be discovered.

. . . .

TRENCHES IN VENEZUELAN ARCHEOLOGY
Cruxent, J. M.; *Science*, 114:306, 1951.

During recent exploration in the Rio Negro region in the Territorio Federal Amazonas (Venezuela) the author was advised of the

existence, in a place known as "lugares viejos de los indios, " of man-
made trenches, about 300 ft. long, 6 ft. deep, and 6-9 ft. wide.
Sherds, some with anthropomorphic decorations, found in the immediate vicinity of these trenches are evidence of former human habitation. In this same zone and, probably, in the same locality or in
its immediate vicinity, lanceolate-shaped canoe paddles of hard wood
with anthropomorphic decorations on the handle have been found. A
wooden implement, decorated with a carved human face, has been
found in Cano Loro by Sr. Clemente Calderon of San Carlos de Rio
Negro and donated by him to Salesian Rev. Father Bombequio, who
in turn presented it to the convent of this order in Puerto Ayacucho.

Trenches of this type are reported to be present in many other
places, among which are the following: Caserio de Mayagua, Rio
Pasimoni, Caserio Solano, Cano Pasimoni, Capaco, Caserio Iguay-
nape, Cano Darigua, Caserio Urana, Cana Motuiti, Laguna de la Brega,
and Cano Bunte, all in Distrito San Carlos de Rio Negro. Wooden
paddles are said to have been recovered in all these places.

Recently the writer had an opportunity to study one of these trenches
in Santa Rosa de Amenodora. Considerably damaged by modern fill
from the surfacing of the adjoining village streets, it still retains its
ancient morphology and principal characteristics. Starting in the swampy
land near the bank of Rio Negro, it forms a shallow crescent in the general direction of the village square. Many of the natives remember it
when it was unencumbered by recent fill and when its entire length of 210
ft. was 9 ft. wide and 9 ft. deep.

According to popular belief, these trenches were filled with briars
or pointed sticks and loosely covered to serve as traps for an attacking
enemy. For lack of any evidence that would confirm or refute this
belief, the present author advances the hypothesis that these trenches
served as hiding places for the Indian dugouts at night or during war-
time. These dugouts would not be left in the river because, in the
eventuality of an enemy attack, the group that lost its canoes would find
itself in a precarious position indeed, in consequence of loss of mobil-
ity in forests that, flooded as they are during the greater part of the
year, offer very little facility for foot travel.

· · · · · · · · · ·

• Pacific Islands

CYCLOPEAN WALLS AND BASALTIC COLUMNS IN THE CAROLINES
Anonymous; *American Antiquarian,* 21:183-188, 1899.

A book published in Germany eighteen years ago, under the title
"Essay on South Sea Curiosities, " gave Professor Kubary's descrip-

tion of the wonderful prehistoric ruins discovered in the Caroline Islands, almost in the mid-Pacific. These ancient works are remarkable not only for the fact that the columnar shafts of basalt, many weighing several tons each, were transported from twenty to thirty miles to build up the defences, tombs and other structures, but also because the little islands themselves on which the walls were reared are mainly artificial in formation, having been built up out of the shallow waters of the lagoon by the heaping up of these shafts of basalt.

Professor Kubary's description of these ruins was the first written account of them. But he was able to visit only a part of them, and his studies on the ground were necessarily very incomplete. As the ruins are really among the world's prehistoric wonders, the recent studies of Mr. F. W. Christian at Ponape Island, near the eastern end of the Carolines, are particularly interesting and acceptable. The paper he read before the Royal Geographical Society, which is printed in the Geographical Journal for February, gives an excellent idea of these remains.

Ponape is the largest island of the Carolines. It is nearly surrounded by coral reef, with narrow openings here and there, and between the reef and the land, is a lagoon of very shallow water, most of it not over one to three feet in depth. The ruins are in this lagoon, off the east coast of the island and close to the south coast of the little island of Tomun.

Mr. Christian says:

The islets are mostly rectangular and are built up out of the shallow lagoons, and are enclosed in mangrove clumps. A network of shallow canals intersected the island labyrinth. The natives call them "waterways, " and the group of islets they call "waterways between the houses. " A massive breakwater runs along the edge of the deep sea, shutting in the woods and waters. Out to sea lie other islands, where there are scattered remains of another ancient sea wall. The most remarkable of all the ruins are on the Islet Tanack. The water front is filled with a solid line of massive stone-work about six feet wide and six feet above the shallow waterway. Above this is a striking example of immensely solid cyclopean masonry---a great wall, twenty feet high and ten feet thick, formed of basaltic columns laid alternately together and crosswise, and enclosing an oblong space, which can be entered only by one gateway in the middle of the west face. A series of rude steps leads up to the spacious court-yard, strewn with fragments of great pillars. Beyond this, and encircled by it, is a second terraced enclosure, tipped by a rude projecting frieze and cornice of stonework. The outer enclosure is 185 by 115 feet; the wall varies from twenty to forty feet in height; the inner court is parallelogram and measures seventy-five by eighty feet. Another rude flight of steps leads up to the great central vault or massive chamber, said to be the grave of an ancient monarch named Chan-te-Leur. This underground chamber faces the great gateway. It is about eight feet deep and roofed with enormous slabs of basalt. There are other vaults in the enclosure. Standing on the south-west angle, where the wall of the enclosure is about forty feet high, one looks down on the green abyss, with never a glimpse of canals, but the northwest angle, as we came out upon the canal, gives a happy impression of the style of architecture,

the two walls at the junction run high and bluff, like the bows of
a Japanese junk.

The names of some of the islands are significant. One means "The
Place of Loftiness"; another, "The Place of Cinder Heaps," from the
cooking fires of the workmen, who helped the demi-gods build the
walls; another means "The New Pavement."

These islands cover an area of about nine square miles. It will
be observed that most of them are rectilinear in form. It happens
that the break in the reef to the east is here unusually wide, and heavy
rollers would come in from the sea if it were not that a number of long
stone islands were built on the east, which serve as a seawall or breakwater. The massive walls of this breakwater are seen stretching southward for three miles, the masonry showing here and there through the
dense tangle of shrubs and mangroves that crown and encircle the islets.
The dense tropical vegetation that covers all the islands makes their
exploration difficult. A visitor who was not observant might visit the
spot and never know of the existence of the remarkable objects around
him. An immense amount of work had to be done to see the ruins at all,
and photographs could be taken only after a great deal of clearing away
of underbrush.

There are between fifty and sixty of these artificial islets. A network of shallow channels intersects the island labyrinth, the water in
which, for the most part, is deep enough merely to float a canoe. All
the islets and the walls, tombs and other structures on them were
built of basalt columns, commonly known as columnar basalt, of
which specimens may be found along our Palisades on the Hudson.
There is no basalt near the artificial islands, and the enormous quantity that was required by the ancient builders must have been carried
in great canoes or on rafts a distance of twenty to thirty miles along
the coast. Christian found the great quarries where these pillars and
blocks were obtained. The most distant of the two quarries is at
Thokach, thirty miles away, where the columnar basalt formation
is very strikingly marked. Here all the shafts and pillars required
were lying around ready shaped to the hands of the builders. They
had to be removed some distance to the sea from the dales at the foot
of a perpendicular scarp, whence they had fallen. Many of them weigh
at least three and a half tons. The problem of getting them to the sea
edge was probably the easiest part of the undertaking. It is likely
that large forces of workmen, equipped with levers, rolled them over
and over till they reached the water. Then, somehow or other, no one
knows how, they were placed on the rafts or in the canoes and transported to the spot where they were wanted. We can hardly realize the
prodigious amount of toil that was required to provide the material
with which to rear these fifty to sixty islets and the structures on them.
How were these columns, weighing tons, lifted to a height of twenty to
thirty feet to form the top of the walls reared on the islets?

Mr. Christian suggests that it was done by a large number of men
hauling or rolling them up over cocoa timbers covered with oil, and
thinks that the builders were an "intelligent minority" swaying an
"ignorant majority"; resembling, perhaps, the Inca kings who built
the cyclopean forts and the great temples and palaces of Peru, and
connected them with paved roadways and long suspension bridges, and
were able to make the industry of the people contribute to their wealth

and power.

The explorer was able to trace the course of the canoes or rafts which brought these great masses down to the building places. He found the bottom of the lagoon, from the quarries to the stone islands, strewn with blocks of basalt. The most reasonable explanation of their presence there, is that they fell from the canoes during the journey, or sometimes, being too heavy for the boats or rafts that carried them, sank with their craft.

The islands seem to have been reared beneath the water by dumping in the material with little regard to regularity, except that care was taken to provide a solid foundation and straight outlines. The interstices between the prisms of basalt were filled in with large blocks and then with rubble, the whole forming a compact mass. The island was reared above the water from five to ten feet, and on this foundation were erected great walls, the largest of which is on Nan-Tauach, where the wall rises to a height of thirty feet and is ten feet thick. All these walls were laid in the same manner. The prisms of basalt were placed close together, alternately lengthwise and crosswise. In old times the walls must have been considerably higher, but much of the masonry has now fallen into lamentable ruin. It is believed that these enclosed spaces were used for tombs, treasure chambers, and forts. The natives say that they were built by all the tribes of the island, united at the same time under a powerful line of kings, in the days when Ponape was much more populous than at present. In the course of time there was a great invasion of peoples from the south. According to this native legend the invaders must have come from some part of New Guinea, the New Hebrides, or some neighboring portion of the Melanesian area. The strangers came in fleets of canoes under the command of a fierce and terrible warrior. The savages poured in upon the peaceful inhabitants, and blotted out the ancient civilization after a great battle in which multitudes were slain on both sides. Part of these walls, behind which the natives fought, were thrown down, and their defenders were either slain in battle or offered in sacrifice to the war gods of their conquerors.

Mr. Christian was able to make a few excavations in the burial vaults within the spaces enclosed by the walls. His finds include many parts of shell fish-hooks, which were possibly broken and thrown into the graves at the time of the burial of some renowned chief, a considerable number of shell rings, a few of them elegantly carved, but most of them plain; a large number of shell beads; and the greatest prizes were ten or twelve ancient axes, three of them about a yard in length, rubbed down from the central shaft of the giant clam. Some of the smaller axes were of fine workmanship, white as polished marble, strong, and having keen cutting edges. Others had suffered great deterioration during their burial ages. He also extended his investigations to some other islands, for these ruins are not confined to Ponape, though seen in by far their largest development there.

In the island of Lele the ruins are of a different character, being built not of basaltic prisms, but of irregular blocks of stone, some of very large size. They are also on the land instead of the water.

On Strong Island are also the remains of cyclopean masonry. Here, also, was an enclosure formed of basalt blocks, and a network of canals intersecting a tract of low and which had been reclaimed from the sea.

Here the lofty walls exhibit an elaborate system of fortification, the product of native work, under the orders of a superior, and one who had a knowledge of engineering. The islanders use axes or adzes of excellent workmanship, laboriously ground and polished down from the great central piece of popol shell. In length they measure from six to nine inches, and two inches wide. These would be useful as hoes for agriculture, or as adzes for cutting wood, but would be of no use in hewing the hard basaltic blocks. There are, however, no signs of tool marks on the rocks. The columns were treated very much as logs of wood and were piled on top of one another in log-house fashion. In this they differ from the structures in Tonga, but they show considerable advance in skill beyond the piling of stones in a wall.

Admiral Bridge of the British Navy, who has seen some of these Caroline Island ruins and commented on Mr. Christian's paper, says it seems to him incredible that any people of the present race could have constructed these immense works. The defences all face seaward and not inland, which, to some extent, shows that they were built by residents and not by people attacking the island from the sea.

• Asia

ON NON-SEPULCHRAL RUDE STONE MONUMENTS
Walhouse, M. J.; *Anthropological Institute, Journal,* 7:21-43, 1877.

Closely akin to unsepulchral cairns must be the Mani, or long heaps of stones that excite the surprise of travellers in Thibet and Tartary. The late Mr. C. Horne, of the Bengal Civil Service, F. L. S., F. R. A. S., &c., who some years ago travelled over some of the highest Himalayan passes, wrote to me respecting them: "The Lama Tartars build long walls of loose stones, usually about 6 feet thick and 5 high; sometimes as at Nako, half a mile long. Every native passes them to his right; none seem to know why: hence there is a path worn on that side, and every one adds a stone; they must be the growth of centuries, every generation adding some yards. The heaps often have flags stuck on them and scraps of paper, with some sacred writing, as also horns of ibex, wild sheep, goats, &c., and round boulder-stones, inscribed with the Buddhist prayer in a circle, are often laid on the top. A great mystery attaches to them; none can explain their uses certainly; some say they are devotional, others that they were built on return from long journeys. The farthest object I saw in Tartary was a long double range of these walls." Mr. Wilson recently in his "Abode of Snow" mentions having passed hundreds of these Mani on his journey, sometimes in the most desolate situations, and remarks that the prodigious number of them in so thinly peopled a country indicates an extraordinary waste of human energy. Mr. Horne also mentioned that single heaps of stones abounded everywhere, "existing on every hill-top and pass; some evidently of great antiquity; in some places they are called Thor. * At the entrance of the province of Kurnawur there is a large field of them, all set up by grateful hill-men returning safe from the plains. Another cause of them is the setting of boundary marks by petty chiefs in old times. Presents too are sometimes given to wealthy people to erect stone heaps on apparently inaccessible peaks to commemorate their names. The highest I saw was on the Shatul peak (17,000 feet), near Kurnawur. The climber was paid 100 rupees by a rich merchant, but disappointed his employer, as the 'Thor' is called by his, and not the merchant's name. I never heard of people being buried under these heaps." The foregoing examples will suffice to show how cairns, both in ancient and modern times, may have had other than sepulchral purposes. The legend of Izdubar or Nimrod, between 2,000 and 3,000 B.C., in the Babylonian tablets, says of him, "He collected great stones; he piled up the great stones."

. . . .

On the Nilgiri hills, on the north declivity of the highest summit, on a spot of exceeding picturesque beauty, where several wooded slopes converge, there is a double circle, 35 feet in diameter, of stones of rather small size, none exceeding 3 feet above the ground, except two, which form an entrance on the south side. The stones are placed rather close together, and the inner and outer rings are a yard apart. No trace of an interment has been discovered in this circle, the only one of the kind known to me on those hills. The Irulas previously referred to have, however, two temples on the top of Rangaswami Peak, the highest eastern Nilgiri summit, where they twice a year worship Vishnu under the name of Rangaswami, with much ceremony. The temples are circles of rough stones, each enclosing an upright stone that represents the deity. One of the circles is of recent date. The Rev. Henry Baker, of the Travancore Mission, informed me that though tumuli and kistvaens abound on the Travancore Hills, in the extreme south of India, he had only seen one stone circle, much dilapidated, and that it contained no marks of interment. The natives called it a Rashi hill of Parasurama, from a tradition that when Parasurama (Rama of the Axe) created Kerala (the long strip of seaboard between the Western Ghauts and the Indian Ocean), rolling back the waters, he sowed the new land with rashies (the small spangle-like gold Hindu coins frequently found all over the country), and buried the surplus in this circle. The "Athenaeum" of 31st May, 1851, reported that Sir Robert Schomburgk had discovered in St. Domingo "a granite ring, 2,270 feet in circumference. In the middle of this circle lies an idol, nearly 6 feet in length, formed likewise out of granite. In all his travels in Guiana or the continent Sir Robert never met with such a monument." This too appears an instance of a devotional circle.

---

* The missionaries, Huc and Gabet, encountered similar large heaps on the great plateau in Chinese Tartary, there called Oboes, and stuck over with boughs on which strips of inscribed paper are hung. MM. Huc and Gabet say the Tartars worship the Spirit of the Mountain at them.

• Middle East

EARLY MAN IN NORTH ARABIA
Field, Henry; *Natural History*, 29:32-44, 1929.

Strange ruins which, from their form have been called "kites" by Group Captain Rees, are very numerous between Azrak and landing-ground "H." These "kites" are composed of walls with a round tower at intervals, and with long walls called "tails" which extend for miles across the country. There are many different kinds of "kites," but one of the simplest forms is shown in the following diagram.

Since these "tails" are sometimes eighteen miles in length, it does not seem plausible to suggest that they could have been fortresses of any kind, but rather traps for catching gazelle or some other animals. Group Captain Rees suggests that some of these "kites" whose "tail" opens upon a mud-flat some hundred yards away from the "head" were used as fortresses. To explain the dividing wall which sometimes runs

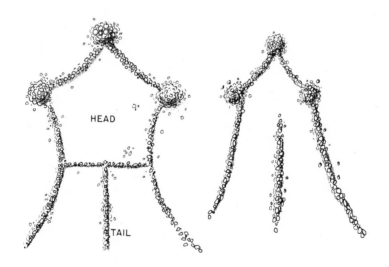

Typical forms of Arabian "kites"

down the center of the "tail" of the "kite" he suggests that domesticated animals were kept on one side of the wall and that rudimentary forms of agriculture were practiced on the other. Presuming that the mud-flat was at that time a small lake, it would have been possible to guard the wide area at the extreme end of the "tail" with one or two men, who could not fail to hear the approach of the enemy over water. At the first signal of alarm the animals would be driven into the "head" of the "kite," and the last wall hurriedly built up. In this position they would be safe from attack from any side. It is interesting to note that the walls connecting the towers are built on a curve with the highest part of the wall nearest to each of the towers. This would tend to make the attackers rush for the lowest part or center of the wall, and in their efforts to break through they could be attacked from the sides, as well as from the front. This is one of the principles of close fighting today. The machine guns are placed on the flanks, and every effort is made to make the enemy "bunch" at one place.

Flint implements are always found in these "kites," and these will have to be studied in detail. It is often very hard to follow or even to find these stone walls upon the ground, but air photographs help to overcome this difficulty. There are many types of "kites," ranging from the simple form described above to the most complex, which is only discernible from the air. (pp. 39-41)

SHEBIB'S WALL IN TRANSJORDAN
Kirkbride, Alec; *Antiquity,* 22:151-154, 1948.

Travelling by air over the Ma'an district, I noticed a stone wall running, for no obvious purpose, across country, from a point about twelve kilometres west of the twon of Ma'an and terminating near the edge of the scarp, known as Hagb Eshtar. The attached sketch map shows the alignment of this wall.

Enquiries from the local inhabitants showed that the wall was known as 'Khat Shebib' or, in English, Shebib's wall.

Shebib, its builder, was said to be the Amir Shebib el Tubba'i el Himyari, a prince of the Himyarite dynasty who conquered and ruled Transjordan before Islam, until he was killed by the Amir Hassan ibn Draid of the Beni Hilal at a battle which took place somewhere between Amman and Zerka.

To this Shebib also is ascribed a castle of medieval type, 'Qasr Shebib', at Zerka itself. The building consists of a square keep of three storeys with an outer bailey and, judging by its architecture, would seem to date from the 10th or 11th century of our era.

. . . .

Having collected all available information about Shebib, the next thing was to visit the wall itself. It proved to be a single layer of rough blocks of stone laid upon the surface of the ground, over a width of about two metres, with larger blocks standing upright in the centre of the strip at more or less regular distances of about five metres. Circular arrangements of similar rough stone appear to have existed at irregular intervals and, where the line crossed important tracks, there appeared to have been breaks or gates so as not to impede traffic.

While the line crossed a number of major valleys at right angles, its general alignment followed, as far as the topography of the country permitted, the crests of hills and ridges. In fact, it linked some of the most outstanding hilltops on which there were ancient ruins dating back to at least the second century A.D. judging by the sherds of Roman pottery found in their vicinity.

It is not, however, suggested that this fact is any more evidence of the age of the line than is the existence of innumerable palaeolithic flint implements lying on the surface of area through which it runs.

On the first visit, the line was found to extend further to the north than was first believed, and evidence was also seen, but not investigated, of a secondary wall. In view of the limitations of time it was decided to confine the inspection to that part of the line which lay to the south and to trace its extent to the north on another occasion. The line could, however, be seen reaching as far north as Jebel Jitha.

The line was followed on horseback from just north of the Ma'an-Wadi Musa road, to the Roman settlements at Moreigha, across the Ma'an-Aqaba road and to where it ended, with every appearance of an uncompleted project, two hundred metres short of the Roman settlement of Daouq, at a height of about 1600 metres above sea-level and some three kilometres east of the well of Abu Lisal on the Ma'an-Aqaba road.

Later in the year I had an opportunity of flying over the northern end of the wall and I was able to complete the map. Our earlier journey had followed the greater part of the alignment.

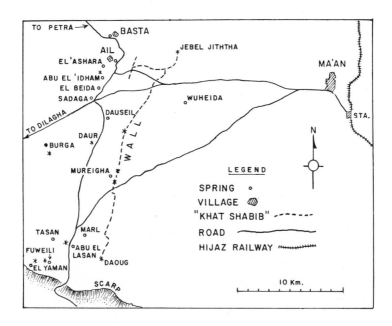

Map of long wall in Transjordan

The nature of its structure indicates that it could not be defensive; its general alignment, the presence in its centre of the upright stones and the fact that, at one point, it runs over a sheer cliff of some fifteen metres in height are conclusive evidence that it was a boundary line and not a causeway.

The line of upright stones forms indeed, a feature which is visible clearly for some distance, especially where the line runs along crests and hill tops.

It is noticeable that practically all the permanent water points lie to the west of the line, and so also does the cultivated land in the vicinity which is capable of raising rain-irrigated crops under existing climatic conditions. It is remarkable, in this connexion, that the 100 millimetre isohyetal of the average rainfall during the years 1937 to 1945 appears on the map in approximately the same position as that occupied by the wall.

There seems, therefore, some reason for accepting as true the local tradition that it formed the boundary between the land owned by cultivators and that at the disposal of their nomadic neighbors. While there is no evidence to confirm the date of its construction in the tenth century A. D. , there is none against that theory and the tradition crediting Shebib el Tubba'i with its construction is not, therefore, entirely valueless.

The most impressive thing about the line is the physical effort which must have gone to build so substantial a boundary mark. One is left with the feeling that the differences over ownership needed to goad the authorities to undertake such a work must have been serious indeed.

• Africa

EXCAVATIONS AT BIGO, UGANDA
Shinnie, P. L.; *Antiquity,* 33:54–57, 1959.

Legend has long associated Bigo with the people well known in the mythology of the area as the Bachwezi. Who the Bachwezi were and when they flourished are among the chief problem of Uganda's history, but the general concensus of opinion is that they were a cattle-owning, warrior aristocracy coming from the North (perhaps from south-west Abyssinia) and dominating the settled agriculturalists of Western Uganda. It may be that the present-day Bahima, nomadic and cattle-owning and of a markedly different physical aspect from the Bantu peoples amongst whom they live, are descendants of these Bachwezi.

The Bigo earthworks enclose an immense area and, with the limited

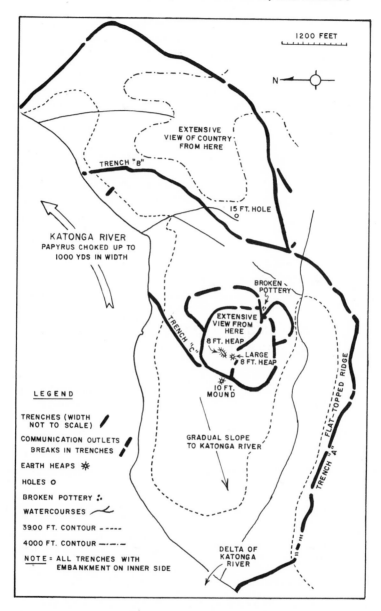

Plan view of ancient trenches at Bigo, Uganda

resources available, only a small preliminary investigation could be carried out.

Attention was concentrated on the centre of the enclosure where

earlier visitors had identified two mounds (the 'humps' of Wayland's plan). Clearance of the bush in this central area which took two weeks hard work by some twenty men, revealed that there were three mounds in the area enclosed by a ditch with a gap in it at the south side of Mound A. The stretches of ditch to the south of the mounds were almost completely silted up, and differ markedly from the other ditches of the site which, though heavily overgrown, still retain almost their original profiles.
. . . .

The most surprising discovery was that the silted ditch went down to a depth of twelve feet: cut into solid rock on which pick marks could be seen, it is most impressive testimony to the ability of its creators. The reason for the silting of this part of the ditch complex was soon clear. It had been used as a rubbish tip and the whole of the silt was full of pottery, animal bone and a few iron implements.
. . . .

RECENT DISCOVERIES IN EAST AFRICAN ARCHAEOLOGY
Gervase, Mathew; *Antiquity,* 27:215–216, 1953.

The Ntusi site lies approximately 7-1/2 miles within the Katonga line of fortification, the most elaborate system of earthworks reported in Africa. In each case these fortifications are concentric, and at Bigo the outer ring of bank and ditch is 2-3/4 miles in extent. Taken together, Kagogo, Bigo and Kasonko, all on the south bank of the Katonga River, command the river frontage for 5 miles on either side of Bigo ford. But Bigo at least is far more than a fortification. The ditches of the inner circuit are still 19 feet deep in some places, and a depth of 12 to 14 feet is usual. The normal width is from 6 to 8 feet. The earth bank that surmounts the inner side of the ditches nowhere rises higher than 4 or 5 feet. Much of the earth removed was used to make square earthen mounds within the bank, presumably as a foundation for grass houses. The elaborate system of elliptical bank within the circuit, and the occasional straight ditches, are best explained by the assumption that Bigo was primarily a royal village of the Zimbabwe type.

Two other sites of the same culture have been located, at Masaka a little to the north of Bigo, and on Mubende Hill. Eight more earthworks have been located in Mubende District, primarily through the enterprise of Mr. Lanning. It will be noted from the accompanying map that six of these earth-work systems seem to form a single line of fortification stretching south-westwards from Lake Albert to the Nabakasi River; the most northerly of these, Nsa bya Kateboha, was located by Mr. Lanning in Bunyoro shortly before Christmas, 1952.

Two shafts were found cut in the rock at Bigo four yards from each other and two hundred yards within the outer line of ditches. I consider that they are associated with a similar shaft not far off sunk into the quartz reef at Lusigate and with the group of shafts sunk through later-

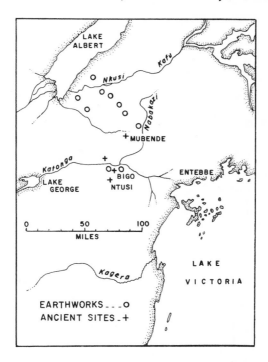

The Bachwezi site in Western Uganda

ite which I examined close to Masaka. If so, they represent some form of mine-working, since some of the Masaka shafts are linked by transverse galleries over 50 feet below surface, and some are so narrow that they could only have been used as vents.

It is the culture of an iron age people; five fragments of worked iron have been found, including an iron spear-haft from Ntusi. Stone implements were still in use; a chalcedony spear-head, a stone axe-head and some quartzite arrow-heads were among the surface finds at Bigo and Kagogo. The Backwezi (to give them their traditional name) were a pastoral people; cattle-bones, including skulls, have been found at Ntusi and within the outer earthworks at Bigo and in the area behind the Kinoni trenches. There is so far no evidence that they used cattle-flesh for food; when the Ntusi middens were opened all the bones found were small, and the ones so far identified are those of eland and of zebra. It is possible that they were attached to a fertility cult; an embossed clay cylinder from Ntusi and the round clay cylinder with lateral grooves found close by, are both probably phallic cult objects. They used beads, but their rarity suggests they were for ornament rather than for barter; a cylindrical glass bead from Bigo is in opaque Indian red over a clear green transparent core, 9.7 mm. in length, 7.6 mm. in greatest diameter. They used long pendants presumably also for ornament; a perforated pendant found at Bigo is a trapeze with rounded

ends, 77 mm. in length, 33 mm. at greatest width, made from sandstone with grey and black shadings and bearing traces of ochre decoration.

. . . .

• Europe

LYONESSE
Crawford, O. G. S.; *Antiquity,* 1:4–15, 1927.

Once upon a time (so tradition says) a region of extreme fertility
lay between the Scilly Islands and Cornwall. This land was called
Lyonesse; and where now roll the waters of the Atlantic there once
stood prosperous towns and no less than a hundred and forty churches.
The rocks called the Seven Stones, seven miles west of Land's End,
are said to mark the site of a large city. This country was overwhelmed
by the sea, and the sole survivor, one Trevilian, escaped destruction
only by mounting a swift horse and fleeing to the mainland.
Such, stripped to the bone, is the famous legend of Lyonesse. Had
it any real basis in fact, or is it merely an invention of the "dreamy
Celt"? There are good reasons for believing that the substance of the
legend is true, that within prehistoric times there did actually exist
land which is now covered by the sea, and that it has been gradually
overwhelmed. In one respect only does the modern critic disagree with
tradition. He believes that Lyonesse was the Scilly Islands themselves,
not a completely vanished region between them and Cornwall; and that
what is now an archipelago of islands was a single large island, surrounded perhaps by a few rocky islets.
The evidence, both archaeological and historical, is very strong.
It was my good fortune to be staying in St. Mary's last year, at the time
of the spring tides. One day I crossed in a boat to the uninhabited
island of Samson; and from the highest point I observed, stretching
across the uncovered sandflats between Samson and Tresco, a long
straight line of stones. I had not time to descend and make a closer
investigation; but when thinking the matter over on my return, I regretted it; for I could think of no natural explanation of the stones.
Further, it seemed probable that this was indeed one of those walls
described in 1753 by old Borlase. "The flats," he says, "which stretch
from one island to another, are plain evidences of a former union sub-
sisting between many now distinct islands. The flats between Trescaw,
Brehar and Samson are quite dry at a spring tide, and men easily pass
dry-shod from one island to another, over sand-banks (where, on the
shifting of the sands, walls and ruins are frequently discovered) on
which at full sea, there are 10 and 12 feet of water." The day follow-

ing next but one after my first visit to Samson was the day of lowest
spring tides (16 March 1926) and it seemed a chance not to be missed.
Accordingly I chartered the boat again, and accompanied by Mr.
Alexander Gibson with his camera, landed again on Samson. Our pro-
gramme was to photograph the line of stones first from the high ground
of Samson, then at closer quarters on the sands; and afterwards to
walk across to Tresco and thence to the island of Bryher. Such a
"submarine" walk is only possible at low spring tides.

We found, on walking out across the sands, that the line of stones
was undoubtedly the remains of a wall of human construction. It consisted of a number of boulders and stones of about the size and shape of
a milestone, some of them still standing upright. All round on either
side of the wall were scattered the smaller stones which once filled the
spaces between the larger uprights. Elsewhere the sands were almost
bare. The fact that some of these stones still remained standing proved
conclusively that the thing was artificial, but indeed its general appearance left no doubt whatever in our minds with regard to this.

It was one of those thrilling moments which occasionally occur
in the life of an archaeologist. Here before us was tangible proof
that the land had sunk since prehistoric times; for no one makes walls
like this below high water mark. While Mr. Gibson was taking photographs, I wandered about on the sands and picked up a few flint flakes.
Most of these were lying on the tide-scoured sand below the ordinary
low water mark. Their edges, originally sharp, have been smoothed
by the action of the sand and water, so that they have the appearance of
gravel-rolled flints. They are quite white and the surface is matte. A
few are illustrated here.

The wall was about 250 yards long, and ended at a bare, rocky
eminence called Black Ledge. On the further (north-eastern) side of
this rock, a line of stones was visible, half covered by the sea even at
this exceptionally low tide. I waded out to it in the hope of being able
to discover whether it was another of these walls; but the water was
over my knees and the tide was on the point of turning, so that I could
not satisfy myself on this point. * We duly reached Tresco---though
neither of us dry-shod!---but the tide was now rising and we were too
late by about ten minutes to continue on foot across to Bryher. My
reason for wishing to visit that island was that on the 25-inch map there
are marked some apparently very perfect examples of prehistoric stone
walls. We were not disappointed. We found them on the bleak hill
which forms the northern part of the island. They were precisely similar in character to the submerged wall we had just visited.

Such prehistoric walls occur on all the larger islands, and on some
of the smaller ones which are not now inhabited. A peculiar feature is
that at frequent intervals along them occur small round cairns of stones.
I observed these on St. Mary's, on Gugh, and on Samson, as well as on
Bryher, where the cairns are marked on the 25-inch map. They are
said to occur also on similar walls on the moors of Cromar, in Aber-
deenshire. The walls themselves are clearly field-walls. Even to-day
the field-walls of the Scilly Islands are made in exactly the same way.
I happened to see one being built. Large upright stones are set up some
few yards apart, and the space between is filled with smaller stones.
The materials are obtained, whenever possible, from the area to be
enclosed. The task of building these "stone hedges," as they are called,

is not so simple as it might appear to be; considerable skill is required, and no doubt the inherited experience of generations has been handed down by tradition from prehistoric times. (pp. 5-7)

---

* Since writing this, Mr. Alexander Gibson reports that he has been told of similar submerged walls between the west coast of Samson and White Island, and off the west shore of Tresco.

THE DORSET CURSUS
Atkinson, R. J. C.; *Antiquity,* 29:4-9, 1955.

Of all the early prehistoric monuments of Britain the Dorset Cursus is both the largest and at the same time one of the least known. Its claim to pre-eminence in terms of mere size is sufficiently established by the facts that it is six miles in length, contains an area of two hundred and twenty acres, and in its original state comprised a volume of earthwork amounting to some six-and-a-half million cubic feet. The significance of these figures may better be appreciated by a comparison with Avebury, which had originally an earthwork volume of about three-and-a-half million cubic feet, or with the Stonehenge Cursus, which is a little less than one-and-three-quarter miles in length, and encloses only seventy acres.

The Dorset Cursus follows an undulating and slightly sinuous course across the downs of Cranborne Chase, immediately SW. of the Dorset Wiltshire border. Its general direction is from SW. to NE., running roughly parallel to and half-a-mile SE. of the present main road (A. 354) from Blandford Forum to Salisbury. The central portion of the Cursus, a length of about three miles from the crest of Gussage Down to a point half-a-mile SW. of the village of Pentridge, has long been known and marked on the maps of the Ordnance Survey.

. . . .

Like similar monuments elsewhere, the Cursus consists of a long narrow enclosure, bounded on each side by parallel lines of bank and external ditch, with the short ends closed by transverse stretches of earthwork continuous with the sides.

. . . .

The association of the Cursus with no less than four long barrows, one of which (in the plantation) certainly, and another (on Gussage Down) probably antedates its construction, can hardly be fortuitous, and suggests not only that this remarkable structure should be referred to a late stage of the Windmill Hill culture, but also that its purpose must have been connected in some way with the cult of the dead, or at least with practices intended to ensure that the benign influence of the dead was transmitted, through the physical propinquity of their resting-places, to the living users of the Cursus. A similar association with a long barrow occurs at the Stonehenge cursus, and with analogous and apparently contemporary structures named 'long mortuary enclosures' in two cursuses in the upper Thames valley (Dorchester-on-Thames and North Stoke).

Although nearly a score of cursus monuments, certain and probable, are now known in Britain, no other proved example has been recorded of the addition of one cursus to another, end to end. Nor does any other cursus even approach in length either of the constituent portions of the Dorset Cursus, which represents a unique achievement in prehistoric construction. Though its over-all course is sinuous, long stretches are virtually straight, and can have been so laid out only after the clearing of a large area of thicket and other vegetation. This preliminary clearance must itself represent much labour, which should be added to that of building the earthwork itself in any assessment of the human effort involved.

The width of the earthwork, from centre to centre of the ditches, is fairly constant at about 300 feet. All the obvious local irregularities occur in the NW. ditch. From this it may be conjectured that the SE. side was the one to be ranged out and marked initially on the ground, the position of the other ditch being determined by offsets taken from the former at intervals, and evidently not always measured with equal accuracy.

. . . .

DURRINGTON WALLS
Crawford, O. G. S.; *Antiquity,* 3:49–59, 1929.

Probably not one in ten thousand of those who pass through the middle of Durrington Walls is aware of its existence. Though plainly visible when once pointed out, the earthen ramparts have been so greatly altered by ploughing as to be hardly recognizable, and the reconstruction of their original form is a very pretty exercise in field-archaeology.

The walls consists of a round enclosure, cut into two unequal parts by the road from Amesbury to Netheravon (Wilts), about a mile and a half north of Amesbury, on the west bank of the Avon. Woodhenge is only eighty yards to the south, close to and on the west side of the same road. The earthwork differs fundamentally from the ordinary defensive 'camp', for its encloses, not a hill-top but a coombe or hollow, and it has its ditch inside, not outside, the rampart. In this latter respect it resembles the circles at Avebury and Marden in Wilts, Knowlton in Dorset, Thornborough in Yorkshire, and Arbour Low in Derbyshire; though there are points of difference. In size, Durrington Walls compares closely with Avebury, whose great earthen circle is slightly smaller in diameter; from east to west the internal area of the Walls is 1300 feet across, and from north to south about 1160 feet. (The average diameter at Avebury is 1130 feet). Both too are within easy reach of a stream, the Avon being 100 yards from the eastern entrance of the Walls, and the Kennet 330 yards from the nearest point of the

great circle at Avebury. The enclosure at Marden actually touches the
banks of the Avon at a point higher up in its course.

. . . .

Originally, as I said above, Durrington Walls consisted of a circular
rampart and inside ditch whose larger diameter is from east to west.
The present condition of the remains however, as a result of ploughing,
varies in different sectors of the circumference, and each must be
separately analyzed. The whole may be divided into two portions, one
on each side of the modern road through it. The smaller, or eastern
portion, is that in which the best visible sector of rampart and ditch is
presented. Both are under plough; but the rampart is very plain, showing as a broad white chalky mound when looked at from the direction of
Amesbury and from Woodhenge itself. Here the real dimensions of
the bank and ditch can be appreciated; originally they must have been
colossal, to account for their present overall width of about 150 feet,
the ditch alone being 40 feet across (the present width of the rampart
and ditch at Avebury is exactly 150 feet). At the bottom of the coombe
enclosed is a gap, representing an original entrance, as Mr. Farrer
has pointed out. The break in the ditch is evident upon the ground; Mr.
Farrer has measured the entrance causeway between the two ends of
the ditch and finds it to be 30 feet wide. Air photographs do not show
this break in the ditch, probably on account of the greater depth of soil
at the bottom of the coombe; but they do show a break here in the rampart. Mr. Farrer was however mistaken in thinking that there was
'a gap of about 100 yards here'; the width of the gap was very much
less.

. . . .

THE DEWLISH TRENCH
Anonymous; *Nature,* 93:381, 1914.

The Dorset Field Club intends this month to reopen the Dewlish
Trench, about which there has been much discussion. This trench is
in chalk, and is filled with fine sand below, and above by loam with
bones of Elephas meridionalis. An open gash in soft chalk is so exceptional as to lead the Rev. Osmond Fisher to suggest lately that this
must be an artificial elephant-trap; other geologists take it to be natural,
though formed in some way not clearly understood. Should it prove to
be an elephant-trap, several interesting questions are raised. Elephas
meridionalis is not definitely known as Pleistocene; it occurs in Pliocene or pre-Glacial strata, and seems to have disappeared from Britain
at the incoming of the cold. The association of this elephant with man
would be a new point, though some supposed "eoliths" have been picked
up near the trench. The infilling of the trench is peculiar. The bones
belong to several individuals, and if they were trapped it seems to have
been for the meat alone, for the tusks remain. Below the elephant-
layer is fine dust-like desert sand, with highly polished flints. The

circular sent to us by the Earthworks Committee of the Dorset Field Club shows that the work will be properly done. Mr. Charles Prideaux will camp on the spot, which will be carefully enclosed. The trench will be opened from end to end, until the undisturbed chalk-bottom is reached. All fossils and flints will be carefully collected and examined. The Dorset Field Club proposes to visit the trench on June 30.

STONE CIRCLES, ALIGNMENTS, HENGES

Stonehenge comes to mind first, for it is the popular standard against which other henges are measured. But Stonehenge is only one type of ancient organized structure. There are fan-like alignments of stones, rectangles, medicine wheels, and many other geometries. No matter where he lived, ancient man had some compelling reason to organize stones into patterns. Astronomical applications are assumed almost automatically these days, but some simple stone circles more likely had ritualistic or artistic goals. The American tipi rings may have had only the mundane task of holding down tents.

The organized structures described here, though, seem to transcend such prosaic applications or, at the very least, demonstrate the diffusion of the henge-building urge. In all probability, ancient man was preoccupied with the sun, moon, planets, and stars and searched diligently for regularities in their motions. He probably did employ some of these organized structures to mark the limits of motion of the heavenly bodies, thus keeping track of the passage of time and possibly enabling the prediction of eclipses and other events. Whatever their true applications, ancient man invested considerable thought and labor in building these remarkable structures. It is our task to analyze them and read his thoughts.

STONE CIRCLES IN EUROPE AND AMERICA
Peet, Stephen D.; *American Antiquarian,* 23:371–377, 1901.

We turn now from these circles of the old world to those found in the new world, with the special object of tracing the analogies between them. We may say that there are in Peru certain stone circles, which very closely resemble those in Algeria, for they are arranged in terraces and furnish evidence of having been used in connection with sun worship. The near circle is ten feet in diameter, the further one has a grooved out-lying platform one hundred and fifty feet in diameter. The two show the prevalence of sun worship. Another locality in Bolivia presents a square two story burial tower (Chulpa) with hill fortress (Pucura) in the distance situated east of Lake Titicaca.(See p. 246.)

The most interesting locality where circles and circular enclosures are found is in the state of Ohio where was the center of the mound builders works. Here we find the burial mounds and altar mounds without circles, but there are many mounds and so-called temple mounds, which were surrounded by earth circles with a ditch upon the inside of the wall and a platform surrounding the mound, and a single entrance through the wall and across the ditch giving access to the burial place or altar. There are also earth circles, which were used only as village enclosures but in certain cases mounds have been seen occupying the very center of the village enclosure with a stone pavement surrounding them, showing that these were used either as a place of worship or burial too sacred for intrusion. The most notable and interesting of all the circles found in America are those near Portsmouth, Ohio. These are interesting because they so remarkably resemble the circles at Stonehenge and Avebury in Great Britain. They were explored when they were in good state of preservation by several parties. Squier and Davis gave a description of them as follows:

"The work consists of three divisions or groups, extending for eight miles along the Ohio River. Two of the groups are on the Kentucky side of the river, the remaining one, together with the larger portion of the connecting embankment is on the Ohio shore. The avenues or covered ways, extending from one work to the other, have induced many to assign them to a military origin and a design to protect communication between the different groups. The parallel embankments measure about four feet in height by twenty feet base. They are not far from one hundred and sixty feet apart. They run in three lines from the central group, one leading to the southeast, one to the southwest, and one to the northwest, each one of them pointing to important works on the opposite sides of the river. The total length of the parallels is eight miles, giving sixteen miles of embankment. The group upon the third terrace seems to be the grand center from which the parallel lines radiate. The two crescent or horseshoe-shaped walls constitute the first striking feature which presents itself. They are of about the same size and shape, and measure eighty feet in length by seventy in breadth. Enclosing them in part is a circular wall, about five feet high. A mound twenty-eight feet high, one hundred and ten feet base, truncated and surrounded by low circumvallation, stands near, from the summit of which a full view of the entire group may be had. The group on the Kentucky shore consists of four concentric circles, placed at irregular intervals in respect to each other, and cut at right angles by four broad avenues which bear very nearly to the cardinal points. A large mound is placed in the center; it is truncated and terraced and has a graded way leading to the summit. On the supposition that this work was in some way connected with the religious rites and ceremonies of the builders, this mound must have afforded a most conspicuous place for the observer. It is easy, while standing on its summit, to people it with a strange priesthood of ancient superstition. About a mile to the west of this work is a small, circular work of exquisite symmetry and proportion. It consists of an embankment of earth

five feet high, with an interior ditch twenty-five feet across by
six feet deep, enclosing an area ninety feet in diameter, in the
center of which rises a mound eight feet high by forty feet base.
A narrow gateway through the parapet and a causeway over the
ditch lead to the enclosed mound. A singular work occurs opposite the old mouth of the Scioto on the Kentucky side of the Ohio
River. The principle work is an exact rectangle, eight hundred
feet square. The walls are twelve feet high, by thirty-five or
forty feet base, except on the east where they arise above the
center of the area about fifty feet. The most singular feature
is the outwork which consists of parallel walls leading to the
northeast and southwest, each about two thousand one hundred
feet long. The parallel to the northeast starts from the center
of the main work and reaches to the end of the plateau or terrace.
To the left of the plateau is a singular redoubt or circular enclosure. The embankment of it is heavy, and the ditch, interior
to the wall, deep and wide, and the measure from the bottom of
the ditch to the top of the wall is twelve or fifteen feet. The enclosed oval area is only sixty feet wide by a hundred and ten feet
long. The object of the enclosure is difficult to divine.
Dr. Hempstead who was a resident at Portsmouth, and was familiar
with the works, has given the measurements a little more carefully, and
has suggested many things in reference to their orientation. He says:
"The chief peculiarity of the works is that the group in the
center is situated on an eminence three hundred and twenty-eight
feet above the water level and overlooks the valleys of the two
rivers, the Ohio and the Scioto. The circle here has four openings,
facing northeast and southeast, and northwest and southwest. Within the circle are two horseshoe formations, twelve feet high and
measuring one hundred and five feet at the open ends. The parallel embankments begin here and run for about four miles southeast to the river, and are continued on the opposite side till they
reach a large circular work which was probably a temple of the
sun. The outer circle of these works measures six hundred and
forty feet, the second one about four hundred feet, the third
about three hundred feet. In the center of the innermost circle
is a mound which rises forty-five feet above the surrounding surface. It has a spiral graded way leading to the top, which measures fifty feet east to west and seventy-five feet north to south.
This was probably the high altar, and ceremonies performed
on it could be readily witnessed from the surrounding mounds.
The "temple" consists of three embankments pierced by open
ways leading north, south, east and west. A center mound and
four ditches, the last to be passed only by the road leading from
the "citadel," the entire length of which was protected by parallel
walls. About a mile and a half west of the temple is a circular
embankment about six feet high, and an inner ditch twelve feet
deep. It has a center mound about seven feet high and the entrance to it is from the south. Beside it is an enclosure in the
form of an irregular hexagon. It measures one hundred and twenty
feet by seventy-five feet. The embankment is four feet high and
the ditch three feet deep. There are two entrances, facing northwest and southeast. All these have probably some connection

with the temple. "

Dr. Hempstead's view of the orientation was derived from the relative bearing of the so-called temple and the central group on the upper terrace where there was an altar and the horse shoes. He says:

"The temple when viewed from the group on the upper terrace on the north side of the river would mark the spot at which the sun arose and a square enclosure situated northwest would mark the sunset of the summer solstice. This last enclosure has also four entrances like those of the temple face north, south, east and west. This enclosure is on the west side of the Scioto River. There are also other parallel embankments, running from the central circle and horse shoe southwest terminating at the river but expanded so as to form a considerable enclosure, with small mounds constructed at the ends as if to fortify the entrances. Across the river and nearly facing the end of these parallels, is what has been known as the "Old Fort." A careful examination of this work will satisfy any one that it was never intended as a protection against enemies from without, but was calculated to keep any thing within, after it had once been decoyed or placed there. The whole work is commanded from the hills; the wall on the outside is only two or three feet high. An enemy having gained this eminence could annoy those within from all parts of the embankments. There are many strong reasons for believing that the enclosure was intended to entrap the large animals which roamed over the hills and ranged through the valleys at the time. The design of these circles and enclosures is difficult to determine but the general opinion is that they were erected for religious purposes, and considering the fact that sun worship was prevalent among the Mound-builders of this region, it is not unlikely that the enclosure on the southwest side was designed to keep captives taken in war, and that the whole group was designed for religious ceremonies, among which was the sacrifice of human victims, captives taken in war, as an offering to the sun.

Comparing these works at Portsmouth with those at Avebury in England, we find that the large circles which include the horse shoes correspond to the large circle near Silbury Hill, that is the large circle which contains two other circles. The concentric circle which contains the so-called temple mound corresponds to the circle at Kennet. The enclosure at the mouth of the Scioto corresponds to the work at Beckhampton, and the covered ways which connect these circles correspond with the alignments of standing stones which run from the large circle in the two directions, one toward Beckhampton, the other toward Kennet. The space between the parallel ways and the Ohio river corresponds with that at Avebury included between the large circle and the small stream, in the midst of which rises the artificial mound called Silbury Hill. These make important resemblances, though they do not prove an identity of form or design. They, however, suggest that there were important ceremonies which were connected with a form of sun worship which had many points of resemblance.

OHIO MOUNDS
Middleton, James D.; *Science*, 10:32, 1887.

Having recently made a survey on behalf of the Bureau of Ethnology, of some of the circles of the ancient works of Ohio, I wish to
call attention, by permission, to one or two facts brought to light.

This can best be done by an illustration, for which purpose the
'Observatory Circle' of the works of Newark, Licking County, is
selected (see 'Ancient Monuments,' by Squier and Davis, Plate xxv.
F.).

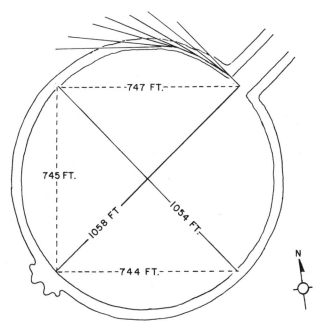

Dimensions of the Observatory Circle, Newark, Ohio

Running this by means of short chords of seventy-five feet in
length, taking the middle line of the top of the wall, I found the number to be 44, and twelve feet in addition, or the perimeter of the polygon 3,312 feet. The course of each chord was taken. While the variation from one to the other, if the figure were a true circle, should
be about 8° 9', it was found to vary from one to fifteen degrees. But,
somewhat to my surprise, it was found that these variations compen-
sated each other in short distances, so that in measuring the quarters
they almost wholly disappear, the angle of the first quarter being 44°
52', and its chord 747 feet; the angle of the second quarter 45°, and
its chord 745 feet; of the third quarter, 44° 52', and the chord 744
feet; the fourth quarter was not measured owing to obstructions. It

is therefore apparent that the figure as a whole is very near a true
circle.

But the most singular fact is presented by the diameters. These,
as taken by careful measurements from the quarter-stations, are
respectively 1,054 and 1,058 feet, the average of which is 1,056
feet, precisely sixty-four poles, or sixteen chains.

As there are several other circles of the size, this singular coincidence is, to say the least, interesting.

POSSIBLE MEGALITHIC ASTRONOMICAL ALIGNMENTS IN NEW ENGLAND
Morrill, Leon L., Jr.; *NEARA Newsletter*, 6:15, 1971.

The rising and setting points of the solstitial Sun---as well as other
astronomically significant dates throughout the year---may have been marked by man in stone circles and stone alignments located in New England.

The stone circles may consist of natural unshaped boulders or include
pointed monoliths. In at least one instance, there are two concentric rings
of stones; and sometimes stones are set up outside the stone circles. Or
stones may be set in or near the center of the stone circles.

These alignments---as indicators or pointers---may be combined with
a mountain peak, a large natural boulder on a ridge or a notch in an elevated
horizon. In some cases, the same alignments are used in both directions---
which would only be possible in hilly country. By clever choice of the position of the alignment, it could be made to define the desired declinations in
both directions. In some sites---such as Mystery Hill---the presumption is
that one looks from what in this case would be considered the center of the
circle, to a pointed standing stone and then beyond to the top of a hill.

. . . .

On Mt. Sunapee, New Hampshire, Robert Stone and I located in September 1967, a site which includes a dolmen, boulders-in-line, a ship carving
and a suspected earth-covered beehive. This site needs further investigation; the boulders-in-line certainly suggest an astronomical alignment.

On a suspected man-made mound in Hillsborough, N. H., is a twelve-
foot monolith which, when associated with a circle of boulders located nearby, indicates another alignment.

. . . .

The Raymond, N. H., site with its two circles of stones approximately
100 ft. apart has certain similarities with known megalithic astronomical
alignments in Britain. This site contains a circle of flat stones, 9 to 11
inches in diameter, surrounded by a semi-circle of stones 2 to 3 feet long.
There are five parallel tool marks on one stone in the circle of flat stones.
Within a smaller circle 100 feet away is an exact duplicate of this marked
stone; and its placement, with reference to the marks on it, is almost exactly the same. This would imply that these stones were designed to comple-
ment each other and were intentionally placed in these circles in a particular
position.

So far, fifteen stones within the Raymond site have been found to have drill holes which may have been bored in order to move these stones to the site, or they may have been done at a later date with the intention to eventually remove the stones elsewhere. It was also within this site that Jeff Morrill found a stone with markings similar to those on the Mechanicsburg Stones found in Pennsylvania by Dr. W. W. Strong.

Another probable alignment is located on Ragged Island in Lake Winnipesaukee near Tuftonboro, N. H. Here a monolith bearing a series of pit or cup marks lines up with two other nearby boulders on both the Winter and Summer solstitial sunsets. On Sandy Island, southwest of Ragged Island, is another monolith which---if the present trees were removed---could be seen from the first monolith and might line up with a further sighting point on the horizon.

The cup marks on the first monolith are of special interest, recalling the numerous cup-marked stones in the British Isles and Western Europe. The suggestion has been made that they were crude maps or diagrams of other sites or structures. Others feel that the cup marks have an astronomical meaning and may represent the constellations.

NEARA's assistant director of research, Mead Stapler, investigated the Kinnellon, N. J., dolmen which has two directional sightings. When sighting over the dolmen in a northerly direction, he noted two placed stones 39 feet beyond the dolmen, all three lining up with a V between two hills approximately three-quarters of a mile away. Another sighting, in a westerly direction, using a monolith 45 feet east of the dolmen, lines up with the peak of a hill approximately one-half mile distant.

The Groton, Conn., site, with a large double circle of boulders as the central sighting point, has at least five good alignments. The boulders in the double circle line up with several flat stones standing on edge, a beehive structure, and the right angle corners of several nearby stone walls.

Additional data from these and other sites may further prove that one of the purposes of their erection was to mark the rising and setting points of the solstitial Sun; and may establish that the builders also marked other settings and risings throughout the year, both stellar or lunar.

Note: In connection with the interpretations of the Ragged Island monolith pit marks mentioned above, we would like to add the following: According to the New York Times of January 20, 1971, a study of pit marks engraved on prehistoric bone and stone objects has revealed a system of notation used throughout most of Europe from 34,000 to 10,000 years ago. From his microscopic examination of these markings, Alexander Marshack of the Peabody Museum of Archeology and Ethnology, Harvard University, has concluded that almost all of the inscriptions are representations of the lunar calendar. It is possible, therefore, that the series of pit or cup marks appearing on the Ragged Island monolith may represent a similar notation. (Marjorie Kling)

THE TIPI RINGS OF THE HIGH PLAINS
Malouf, Carling; *American Antiquity*, 26:381-389, 1961.

Abstract. Stone circles known as tipi rings are a common feature of the Northern and Northwestern Plains of western North America. There are several types of stone circles: (1) a single course of stone in a simple circle; (2) more complex circles with several courses of stones; (3) circular walls made of piled-up stones; (4) corrals or forts of horizontal logs and stones; (5) stone circles of unusual size or with lines of rocks inside the circle. Studies of tipi-ring sites in Montana, Wyoming, and adjacent regions are summarized. The clusters of circles are usually found along main routes of travel and near water, fuel, and good hunting areas. Although many of these sites have been mapped, only a few of them have been excavated. Despite the paucity of cultural remains found in the excavations, the tipi-ring clusters are generally considered to be the archaeological remains of camps and villages of people who dwelt in conical, skin-covered lodges. The stones are believed to have been used to hold the skin lodge cover snug against the ground. Historical records, ethnographic observations, and the recollections of present-day Indian informants confirm these interpretations. Data from 136 recently studied tipi-ring sites along a 300-mile pipe-line from Greenriver, Wyoming, to Denver, Colorado, provide further archaeological demonstration of the domestic origin of the tipi rings. Only the very small or very large rings, or those with spokes or lines of rocks through them, such as the so-called medicine wheels, are considered to have served a ceremonial purpose.

THE COUNCIL CIRCLES OF CENTRAL KANSAS: WERE THEY SOLSTICE REGISTERS?

Wedel, Waldo R.; *American Antiquity,* 32:54–63, 1967.

Abstract. At five Little River focus village sites in Rice and Mc-Pherson counties, Kansas, so-called council circles are probably the most notable features present. Each consists of a low central mound surrounded by a ditch or a series of depressions (borrow pits) or both. No village site has more than a single circle. At the only one yet excavated (Tobias site), elongate house pits arranged around a patio within the ditched zone formed a structural complex which is apparently unique in Plains archaeology. The houses were built of poles and grass, earth-covered wholly or in part, and had evidently been destroyed by fire. The covering fill contained numerous large boulders and scattered human bones, some fire-blackened. From their plan and contents, it is suggested that these house complexes were special-purpose structures; from their demonstrated orientation, it is further suggested that one of their functions may have been to record solstitial sunrise (and sunset?) points on the horizon.

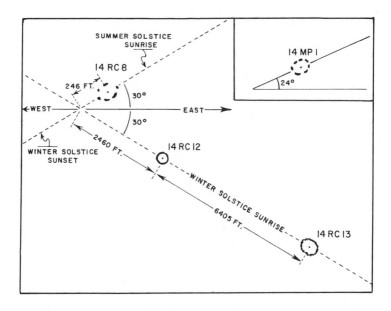

Alignment and orientation of circles, Rice County, Kansas

A WHEEL-SHAPED STONE MONUMENT IN WYOMING
Simms, S. C.; *American Anthropologist,* 5:107-110, 1903.

While on a visit, in the interest of the ethnological division of
the Field Columbian Museum, to the Crow (Ab-sah-ro-kee) Indians,
of Montana, during June, July, and August, of 1902, I was told of
the existence of what my informant termed a "medicine wheel" on
the summit of a mountain which he called "Medicine mountain," situated just across the Montana-Wyoming boundary line, in the Big
Horn range of mountains in the latter state.

Although I made many inquiries of the old men of the Crow tribe
regarding the "medicine wheel" and its significance, I found not one
who had ever visited it. A few of them had heard of it through their
fathers, but they could tell me nothing whatever of it excepting that
"it was made by people who had no iron." At different times I chanced
to meet with two Sioux Indians who were visiting the Crows, and they
also were asked about the wheel. After inspecting the diagram of it,
which I had hastily drawn in order to make clearer the questions asked
them through an able interpreter, each of the two Sioux drew a diametrical line through the wheel and, pointing to one half, said,
"Arapaho," and then pointing to the other half said, "Cheyenne."
Each one declared that he had not seen the wheel nor knew of its location, but had heard of it some time ago.

. . . .

The summit of the mountain is not extensive in area; it is irregu-

lar in shape, being broad at its western end and tapering with a jagged
outline to an abrupt point at the east. Within the narrow limits of
this eastern end we found the medicine wheel as it had been described.

This peculiar structure consists of a large number of limestone
slabs and bowlders of various sizes. Directly in the center, or at
what may be termed the hub, stands a circular structure about three
feet high, of the same kind of stone, radiating from which are twenty-
seven lines, or spokes, of stone leading to a well-formed perimeter.
Around the outer edge of this circular rim or "felly" of the wheel, at
irregular distances, are the remains of seven smaller stone structures, all of which come in contact with the perimeter except the most
southerly one which stands several feet away, although it is met by
an extension of one of the spokes beyond the rim of the wheel. Each
of these smaller stone structures is circular at the base with the exception of the easternmost, which is squarish and, unlike the others, has
a covering of stone slabs and an opening on the outer side through
which entrance may be gained by crawling.

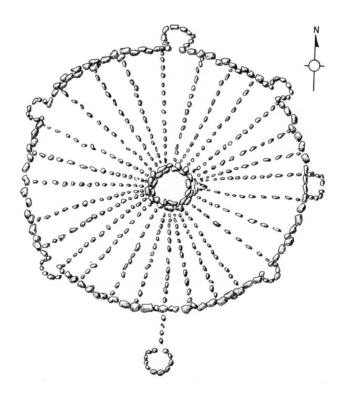

Wyoming wheel-shaped pattern of boulders (a "medicine wheel")

Upon the projecting slabs of the eastern side of the central structure rested a perfectly bleached buffalo skull which had been so placed
that it had the appearance of looking toward the rising sun. Resting
on the rocks near the skull were several other bones of the buffalo.

Within the central structure, which resembles a truncated cone,
there is a slight circular depression in the ground. This was carefully examined, as were the spaces within both the central and the
smaller structures, but the search yielded nothing. Measurements
showed the circumference of the wheel to approximate 245 feet.

. . . .

MEDICINE WHEELS AND PLAINS INDIAN ASTRONOMY

Eddy, John A.; *Native American Astronomy*, Anthony F. Aveni, ed.,
Austin, 1977, pp. 147–169.

An interesting rock alignment which may be a primitive wheel is
found in rugged mountains of northeastern Colorado, now within the
Rocky Mountain National Park (Husted 1963). It is apparently old, judging by the sunken rocks and their lichen cover. The alignment consists
of a small cairn on a hillock from which two lines, or spokes, of rocks
meander about 30 meters in roughly opposite directions, ending in
rough piles of stones. The alignment is unusual in that it lies on a
windy crest above Trail Ridge Road, at about 3,500-meters altitude.
Nearby is a reported Ute trail.

A brief investigation of the site with transit in 1973 revealed that a
line through the longer spoke to the central cairn as a foresight points
to the rising point of the summer solstice sun. The structure is crude
and alignment rough, and there is about a 1-in-20 chance that it could
be accidental. If it was intentional, however, it raises an interesting
question of motive. There are no tipi rings or other evidence of habitation in the area and, indeed, I cannot think that anyone would expect to
find them there. Trail Ridge was reported to be a major Indian route
across the Continental Divide, but I am surprised that anyone would
have stopped along its cold and windy reaches to mark the solstice sunrise. Perhaps more than anything else it says we shouldn't always
press for logical motives beyond joy, or personal satisfaction, or to
demonstrate that it could be done.

. . . .

By far the largest number of known medicine wheels are found in the
prairie provinces of Canada: at least thirty are known in Alberta and
ten in Saskatchewan. Many are not wheels but simply large cairns, some
without spokes, rings, or other associated features. The nearest to the
Big Horn or Fort Smith wheels is a month's walk to the north---a distance (600 or 700 km) almost as great as that which separates the Big
Horn site from the clearly distinct Pueblo culture to the south of it. Although some of the Indians of the short-grass plains surely roamed from
Wyoming to Canada, we should be cautious in assuming that the Big Horn

and Canadian medicine wheels had common builders, purpose, or eras of use. Nevertheless, an examination of the Canadian cairns and wheels for astronomical association seems obviously necessary in light of the claims made for the Wyoming and Montana sites.

. . . .

Our survey of the Alberta sites resulted in a number of general conclusions:

1. Most of the Canadian sites are wholly unlike the Big Horn Medicine Wheel in that they are dominated by the central cairn. Some of these cairns are huge and contain up to 100 tons of rocks (as compared with perhaps 1,000 lb. in the central cairn of the Big Horn wheel). Some of the sites consist of nothing but the cairn. These large central cairns often have a ring or rings about them, 5 to 30 meters in diameter and roughly circular.

2. The number of spokes varies, and we found examples with almost any number, including one and none. The only other wheel which like

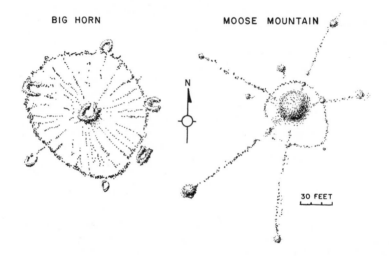

BIG HORN   MOOSE MOUNTAIN

N

30 FEET

Two North American medicine wheels. The Big Horn wheel is identical to the one of the preceding article, although the drawings differ somewhat.

the Big Horn site may have had 28 spokes is the Majorville Cairn in south-central Alberta, but it has been so badly rifled and rearranged that the number of original spokes is probably beyond recall. The central cairn contains an estimated 50 tons of rocks ranging in size from a few to several hundred pounds. Excavation by Forbis and Calder in 1971 found evidence of layered construction and possibly continuous use between about 4,500 and 500 years before the present (2500 B.C. to A.D. 1500).

3. Spokes point in almost all directions. They do not predominantly lie in the cardinal or the intercardinal directions, as is sometimes

claimed on cursory examination. There is a slight preference for south-west-directed spokes and other features which could be summer solstice sunrise oriented, were the central cairn a foresight, as at the Big Horn site. More than half of the wheels examined have spokes or other directional features which point within 2° of the summer solstice sunrise. There is also a tendency for spokes or other features to lie in those directions from center which would point to the rising places of the same three stars which were apparently marked at the Big Horn wheel: the brightest stars of the summer dawn, Aldebaran, Rigel, and Sirius. But many of the sites examined do not show these or other possible sky associations and do not seem to be strong candidates for astronomical use.

4. All the sites which we examined lie on hilltops or high mesas and all have clear horizons. They are almost always on the highest hill around, and in cases where we had difficulty in locating one we could usually find it by picking out the highest hill and looking there. (This does not mean, of course, that every high hill in Canada has a medicine wheel or cairn on it.)

5. Almost all the sites we examined had tipi rings in the general vicinity, indicating that they were near places of semipermanent encampment. This is unlike the Big Horn wheel, which is at an unlikely place for lengthy dwelling, although there, too, tipi rings, believed to be of an earlier era, are about 1 km away. Several of the medicine wheels had tipi rings within them, either as a central circle or on or near the spokes.

6. In Canada none of the known medicine wheels is in mountains or foothills or even within sight of the mountains. They are most often a feature of the bald and treeless prairie and would make good landmarks.

7. Medicine-wheel patterns seem diverse and seldom if ever repeated from site to site. Symmetry is unusual. Spokes seldom extend from the center in diametrically opposed directions. There seems to be no preference for an odd or even number of spokes, or for the number 4, as one might expect were they meant to point to cardinal or intercardinal directions.

8. The ages of the structures are almost completely unknown, for several reasons. They lie on hilltops where the deposition of soil by wind is not a simple function of time and where dating by stratigraphy is difficult. Few have been investigated professionally; systematic archaeology of the plains of Canada only began a few tens of years ago. Finally, all the cairns have been rifled to some extent. Only two sites which we examined in Canada are protected by anything but isolation, and neither of these is protected as well as the fenced but unguarded Big Horn wheel.

The most general conclusions one can draw from a survey of the medicine wheels of Canada is that they are quite definitely a "mixed bag" of things classified incorrectly under one rather miscellaneous heading. They were very probably built by different peoples over a long period of time and for possibly different or evolving purposes. A few (generally the most elaborate) seem of probable astronomical association; some are very likely burial mounds or commemorative structures like those described by Kehoe and by Dempsey; some may be landmarks; and some of the smallest may be simply decorations. The fact that an appreciable number of them show astronomical alignment on the directions of rise of a restricted set of summer-sky objects seems to me significant.

· · · · · · · · · ·

The Moose Mountain wheel is about twice as large and like most Canadian wheels has a massive central cairn, about 6 meters in diameter, built of an estimated 60 tons of piled-up rock. An egg-shaped ring of stones encompasses it. From the central cairn five long spokes extend, each ending in a small and partly sunken cairn, one or two meters across. One of the spokes extends farther than the others and ends in a slightly larger cairn; it stretches toward the southwest like the distinctive sunrise spoke of the Big Horn Medicine Wheel. Positions of the other Moose Mountain cairns seem to match the relative positions of other Big Horn cairns. In fact, if the spokes and rim of the Big Horn wheel were erased (and we think they are later additions) the Moose Mountain and Big Horn wheels would look much like twins, although hundreds of miles apart and in vastly different terrain. The cairn positions seem close enough to have been positioned from the same set of plans, although adjusted in size---scaled down for Wyoming, or up for Saskatchewan.

. . . .

STONE SQUARES IN ARIZONA
Brown, Herbert; *American Antiquarian,* 21:181, 1899.

In the March and April American Antiquarian, the article on "Prehistoric Stone Circles" has led me to write you of what may be called "Prehistoric Stone Squares." I enclose herewith a rough Sketch of my meaning. It is not meant to represent any particular place, but to convey an idea of these stone squares as they actually exist in southern Arizona. Occasionally I have found them on the desert, but, of course, always near a hill, for on the desert plain there is but little or no rock. On the mesas near the foot of the mountains, they are a common occurrence. In general appearance, they are perfect squares, and, practically, they are of all sizes, say from 10 to 300 feet. On some mesas there are perhaps, but one, and again, I believe, I have seen as many as a dozen within an area of ten acres. In some cases they are pretty well covered over by the wash from the hills above, and again they stand out bold and plain, as when first put in place. There are several fine specimens of these squares on the southern foot of the Santa Catalinas, about twenty miles east from Tucson. Some of the squares are made of rock quarried from granite by following the seams, and pieces five feet long and six to eight inches square, are not uncommon. These pieces are set firmly in the ground, a few inches apart, of equal elevation and straight sides. In some cases these squares are in the immediate neighborhood of old towns, but not always. These are not the Cliff-Dwellers, of which so much has been said, nor do they appear to have been the people who cultivated the great plains and built reservoirs and canals, but a people who cultivated narrow strips of land along water courses and fortified the hills above.

. . . .

STONE CIRCLES AND UPRIGHT STONES IN NEW MEXICO
Swan, A. M.; *American Antiquarian.* 21:206–207, 1899.

I have seen no mention, in any publication, of existing circles and lines of upright stones in New Mexico, and, therefore, conclude that their existence has escaped the eye of every scientist who has visited this country. There are two localities where very remarkable systems of upright stones may be seen, each of which appears to belong to a very early period.

One of these systems was discovered by Major George H. Pradt, while making a Government survey along the east line of the Socorro grant in Socorro county, New Mexico. Major Pradt has long been interested in archaeology of this country, and is a close observer. He describes the stone circles as located "on a low hill, an extension of the north end of the Oscura range." The inner circle was about thirty feet in diameter. The stones stood three or more feet above the ground, and from one to four feet apart. Some of them had fallen down. In the centre of this circle were three upright stones; and one that had fallen, forming a square. One broad stone had partly fallen, and without doubt had covered the four stones, forming a table or altar. Around this inner circle was an outer circle, many of the stones still standing. There were many petrified trees, some of great size, scattered around, lying on the same surface in which the upright stones were imbedded.

The second system of upright stones was discovered by Colonel Walter G. Marmon, while running the first correction line of the Navajo Reservation survey. This field is located about thirty miles northwest of Fort Defiance, and two miles east of the point where the correction line crosses Canon de Chelly, in the Navajo Reservation. Colonel Marmon describes this field as consisting of long lines of upright stones in parallel rows. The stones are about three feet high, and from five to ten feet apart. They stand in a dense pine forest, thus not easily attracting attention.

Near both of these systems of upright stones are extensive ruins that have not the characteristics of Pueblo remains---using the term, in a racial sense. These remains are, I think, worthy of investigation, especially as they bear so great resemblance to the stone circles of the old world.

MYSTERIOUS MOUNDS AT POVERTY POINT
Folsom, Franklin; *Science Digest,* 69:46–54, February 1971.

For as long as anyone can remember, unusual Indian artifacts have been turning up on an old plantation known as Poverty Point in northern Louisiana. Local citizens made collections of the "relics." A few professional archaeologists took an interest in Poverty Point stone tools, especially the tiny flint knives and curious little baked clay objects.

Some of this material came from the place where a road crossed a series of long, low earthen hummocks or ridges. The hummocks themselves seemed in no way remarkable---until an archaeologist happened to notice how they looked when viewed from above. Aerial photography revealed that the ridges formed a very definite geometric pattern. They could only be a series of well-planned terraces built by man in the form of six huge concentric octagons. The configuration measures three-quarters of a mile across, and its huge size conceals its real nature.

. . . .

The statistics of Poverty Point are staggering. To form the terraces, men and women and no doubt children carried earth in baskets and heaped it to a height of six feet or more. Each terrace measured about 80 feet wide at the base. The total linear measurement of the six concentric earthen ridges was 11 miles.

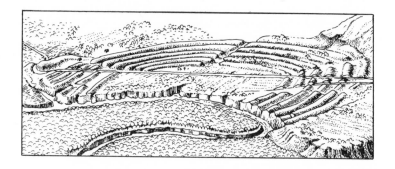

Immense concentric pentagonal ridges at Poverty Point, Louisiana

Nor was that the end of the earth-moving operation. On the west side of the terrace-complex these same people built a tremendous mound 640 feet by 700 feet at the base and 70 feet high. Although it is much eroded, there is some indication that they shaped the mound to resemble a colossal bird, and they connected it to one of the outer terraces by a huge sloping ramp. About a mile away stands another large mound and, close by, is a smaller cone-shaped one more than 20 feet high and almost 200 feet in diameter at the base.

In all, the builders of the mounds and terraces dug up and transported, perhaps 50 pounds at a time, at least 20,000,000 basketloads of soil. Why? Were the large mounds associated in some way with religious ceremonies? That was certainly true of mounds which the first Spanish invaders actually saw in use elsewhere in the South.

. . . .

Town-planning flourished in ancient Mexico, along with agriculture and the building of great pyramids. Often there was a strong link between farming, astronomy and certain Middle-American religious practices. Priests knew a good deal about the heavens and could forecast the right times for planting crops. With this in mind, James A. Ford has now studied the large Poverty Point mound and its ramp. They were, he found, oriented in a special way. If a man stood on top of the mound and sighted along the ramp, he would be in direct line with the rising sun at two times a year---about March 21 and September 21, the equinoxes. As in Mexico, dates were important to farmers who needed to know when to put seeds into the earth.

PREHISTORIC CITY HAD INDIAN "WOODHENGE"
Anonymous; *Science Newsletter,* 86:86, 1964.

Recent excavations at "Cahokia," the site of a thriving Indian civilization about 1000 A.D., have uncovered four huge circles of spaced wooden posts.

The discovery of these structures near "Monk's Mount," the largest prehistoric earthwork in North America, was reported by Warren L. Wittry, assistant director of the Cranbrook Institute of Science, Bloomfield Hills, Mich.

Comparing the post circles, called henges, to Stonehenge, Mr. Wittry emphasized the importance of a post found just five feet east of true center, in "Circle No. 2," discovered by Dr. Robert L. Hall of the Illinois State Museum.

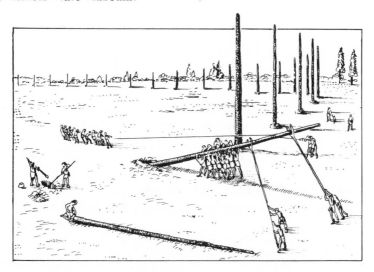

Sketch of how Indians might have erected the large posts at the Cahokia woodhenge site in Illinois

This woodhenge was 410 feet in diameter. "It was a very precise circle," Dr. Wittry reported, "and most certainly was laid out
with the use of a peg and rope compass."

An observer at the post in approximately 1000 A.D. would have
seen sunrise on mid-summer day, the summer solstice, directly
in line with one of the henge posts.

. . . .

Arrangement of Cahokia woodhenge posts, showing a possible roof.
(Adapted from *Scientific American* 223:30)

ASTRONOMY IN THE ANCIENT AMERICAS
Hicks, Robert D., III; *Sky and Telescope,* 51:372-377, 1976.

Warren L. Wittry has described an observing station at Cahokia, a
large Mississippian Period site (about A.D. 1000) located in modern St.
Louis, Missouri. Remains of holes dug to anchor large wooden posts
were found arranged in circles. The largest is Circle 2, which is 410
feet in diameter, and has been dubbed "an American Woodhenge" for its
superficial resemblance to European henge monuments.

This circle consisted of 48 posts, the arc between each of them being 7-1/2 degrees, while an additional post was about five feet east of the true center of the circle, apparently an intentional displacement. From this post, one would have been able to look due east in line with a post on the circle and witness sunrise at the equinoxes. Furthermore, from this same off-center post one could look past the fourth post north or south of due east to observe sunrise at the summer and winter solstices, respectively.

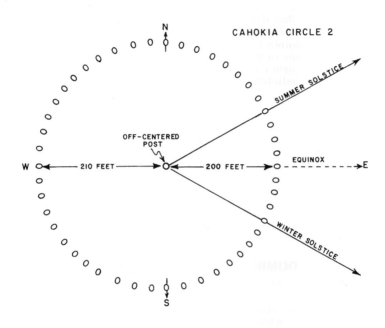

Alignments of Cahokia woodhenge Circle 2

Here the main problem is that the original heights of the posts are unknown, nor is it known whether observations were reckoned at the first gleam of sunrise, or when the solar disk was tangent to the horizon. Circle 2's 48 holes may have been concerned with solar eclipse prediction, in the manner attributed to the 56 chalk-filled holes of the Aubrey circle at Stonehenge. While Hawkins' interpretation of the latter has been strongly contested, possibly a similar system was implemented at Cahokia.

For example, if the postholes each represented a lunar month or lunation (month of the phases, averaging 29.53 days), 47 of them would equal 1387.9 days (3.8 years). This happens to be very nearly the length of 51 draconic months, which are measured by returns of the moon to the nodes of its orbit (where it crosses the ecliptic). For an eclipse to occur, the moon must be near a node and also close to either the new (solar eclipse) or full (lunar eclipse) phase. Hence, the lunation-draconic month relation produces a repetition of eclipses every 3.8 years.

While the ancients could thus predict eclipses, with up to half of the lunar ones visible at a single location, accumulated errors would upset such a system after about 16 cycles or only 60 years. An alternative scheme involves 581 lunations in 47 years, and is operable for up to 57 cycles, but its chance of detection by simple observations was less.

It seems to me that the likelihood of the 47-lunation cycle being used at Cahokia is considerable, for it was not too difficult to detect from the rising and setting points of the sun and moon, and eventually its users could work out cycles of longer duration and increased accuracy. In any event, absolute accuracy was not required; as long as eclipse danger periods could be predicted, when the likelihood of eclipses was great.

· · · · ·

• Mesoamerica

ANTIQUITIES OF DOMINICA AND SANTO DOMINGO
Palm, Erwin Walter; *Man,* 47:51-52, 1947.

In Man, 1946, 47, appears a note of the writer entitled 'Antiquities of Dominica (Haiti),' which is a somewhat hybrid combination of pieces of a correspondence on different civilizations.

(1) To begin with, Dominica, one of the lesser Antillan islands, situated in the British West Indies, has been confounded with the island of Santo Domingo (first known as Hispaniola, and often referred to under the indigenous name of Haiti).

(2) The writer's scope in addressing a British scholar was to find out whether the Haitian Negro tombhouses (Man, 1946, 47, fig. 3) could possibly be connected with West African types, and eventually be regarded as a distant echo of Roman sepulchral constructions in North Africa of the second and third centuries A. D. The easier alternative (as it seems to the writer) would be to derive the type from local timber-built constructions. The writer's correspondent kindly forwarded the inquiry to Man.

(3) The rest of the note consists of travel experiences and references (not intended for publication) to pre-Columbian remains. No continuity of artistic trends exists between them and the still practised Negro architecture, the Indians of the island having practically already died out before the middle of the sixteenth century. May I take this opportunity to straighten out several misunderstandings?

(4) The 'monumental stone,' which appears in fig. 1, is about the centre of the so-called Corral or Cercado de los Indios (Indian circus) at San Juan de la Maguana near the S. W. Haitian border of the Dominican Republic, the country which occupies the Eastern half of the island.

The vast stone circus, of a total circumference of about 2,270 feet, consists of two concentric rows of flat river-polished stones of 30-50 lb. each, which form a kind of continuous ring 20 feet wide. The spot was discovered and first described in 1851 by Sir Robert Schomburgk, British Consul in the then newly founded Dominican Republic, who made the measurements indicated. The 'centre stone,' 5 feet 7 inches high, actually somewhat out of focus in fig. 1, occupied its present situation already in 1851. The upper part of the slightly inverted stele is decorated by a circular-shaped face; its technique of engraving, often completed by other signs of anthropomorphization of the pillar, recurs in several (unfortunately unpublished) pieces in the island. A kind of road, the width of which in its present state varies between 30 and 58 feet, according to the writer's measurements, and which is paved by the same type of cobbles, leaves the periphery of the circle in a westerly direction, turning then sharply north and leading to a nearby rivulet. The 'circus' has long been associated with similar monuments on the American continent. As Schomburgk readily recognized, it can hardly be attributed to the Indians found on the island by Columbus. However, nothing definite can be stated until the whole complex is explored.

. . . .

ASTRONOMICAL OBSERVATORIES IN THE MAYA AREA
Ricketson, Oliver, Jr.; *Geographical Review,* 18:215-225, 1928.

The Uaxactun Observatory. These truly remarkable results seem the more significant when considered in connection with work done along the same lines at Uaxactun. Since the discovery of Uaxactun in 1916 it has been visited by several expeditions sent out by the Carnegie Institution of Washington. In 1923 the seventh Central American expedition, under the direction of the writer and Mr. Witherow Love of the Department of Terrestrial Magnetism, spent several months in the Peten District locating the exact geographic positions by latitude and longitude of twelve important ruins, of which Uaxactun was one. In 1924 the eighth expedition, directed by Mr. Frans Blom, made an accurate plane-table survey of the city. Although no excavation was possible at that time, Mr. Blom drew attention to the fact that the arrangement of buildings, mounds, and stelae in the easternmost plaza, called Group E on his map, suggested its probable function as a solar observatory.

The ground plan of this group, as it appeared before excavation, is shown in Figure 9. Making his observations from Stela 20 as he faced the east, Mr. Blom noted that the true east-west line passed through the estimated center of Mound E II, and that lines drawn to the apparent centers of Mounds E I and E III were 24° north and south of the true east-west line. The geographic position of Uaxactun having been determined the year before, it was possible to determine both the magnetic declination of the compass and the amplitudes of the sunrise points for

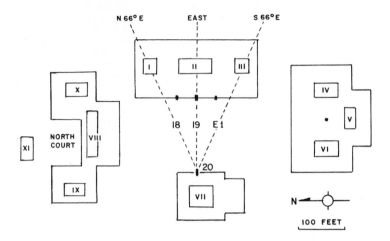

Structures of Group E, Uaxactun

that location. The latter were found to be 24.4° north of east and 24.9°
south of east (visible horizon) on June 22 and December 22 respectively
---i.e. the summer and the winter solstices. The true east-west line
gave, of course, the position of sunrise on both the vernal and autumnal equinoxes.

When excavation was begun in 1926, under the direction of the
writer, this group was selected for investigation. The results of two
seasons' work are summarized in Figure 10. [Not reproduced]
Mounds E I, E II, and E III were found to be temples, the floor levels
of which lay ten feet above the substructure platform which underlies
all three of them. This substructure platform is fifteen feet above the
plaza level. The true east-west line passes just within the north jamb
of the doorway of Temple E II and up the mid-line of the stone stairway which was found on the east slope of Mound E VII. The directions
for the amplitudes of the sun on June 22 and December 22 were found
to strike the front steps of Temples E I and E respectively if taken
from Stela 20. These directions are shown on Figure 10 as the lines
a n and a s. But, because of the fifteen-foot substructure platform
beneath Temples E I, E II, and E III, no observations of sunrise
points on the horizon could possibly be made from the plaza level,
and as a point of observation Stela 20 has to be abandoned. The directions taken from the top of the stairway on Mound E VII pass too far
outside the limits of Temples E I and E III. They are shown in Figure
10 as lines A N and A S. But from a point fifteen feet vertically above
plaza level on the mid-line of the stairway on Mound E VII the same
directions give the lines a' n' and a' s', which just touch the corners
of Temples E I and E III respectively. This point was arbitrarily
chosen because it is the lowest possible point from which a view could
be had of the horizon over the fifteen-foot substructure mound. (pp.
222-224)

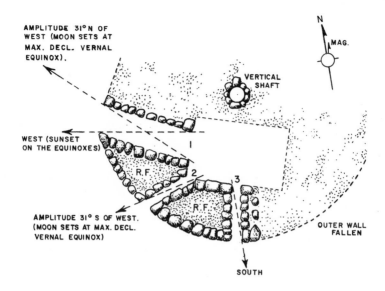

Diagram of Caracol windows, Chichen Itza. Dashed area supposedly represents the observing room. RF = rubble fill. (Adapted from an illustration in the preceding article.)

ASTRONOMY IN THE ANCIENT AMERICAS

Hicks, Robert D., III *Sky and Telescope,* 51:372-377, 1976.

Caracol Observatory, at the Mayan site of Chichen Itza, has been known for some time to display astronomical configurations. The limestone masonry of Caracol is set upon an elaborate platform substructure. The building itself is circular (a new design element of its period), being dedicated to the wind god Ehecatl. While the four lower room doorways are aligned with the cardinal points, the tower encloses an inner circular chamber, its four doorways being aligned midway between the first four. Most of a central stairway to the upper chamber has disintegrated, but three upper windows are intact, providing a total of six possible alignments.

Three of these are astronomical, one for the equinoxes and two for the moon. From repeated measurements of the alternate doorjamb sightings, Aveni believes the inside-left-to-outside-right alignment of Window 1 comes closer to the maximum northerly declination of Venus than to the maximum northerly declination of the moon. Likewise, Window 2 (inside left to outside right) may give a more precise determination for the southernmost declination of Venus when Caracol Observatory was built about A. D. 1000.

However, these positions of Venus are probably a secondary function of the windows, as the planet's extreme positions contribute little to aiding observations of its heliacal risings and greatest elongations. The latter phenomena are important in constructing Venus ephemerides, as in the famous tables of the Dresden Codex, a surviving Mayan document. Also, Venus positions are not related to eclipse prediction, assuming that this was the major function of the building.

Molloy believes the Carocol astronomers established a regional network of observatories, of which the Big House was one. Both have the same alignments with the sun and moon, and they include the same non-astronomical alignments. Both contain inner room chambers and have carefully-planned upper room chambers symmetrical with their substructures. Archaeologists have noted a diffusion of Meso-american cultural traits into the Casa Grande area.

Most notable is the cult of Quetzalcoatl, the Feathered Serpent, who was associated with the planets Mercury and Venus, and with eclipses. Another version of Quetzalcoatl was the already mentioned Ehecatl, the patron deity of the Caracol. If correct, Malloy's theory would establish a very important case for intercultural collaboration in pre-Columbian astronomical observation.

Caracol "observatory" at Chichen Itza (Robert D. Hicks, III)

RIDDLE OF COSTA RICA'S JUNGLE SPHERES
Harrison, James O.; *Science Digest,* 61:14-16, June 1967.

In a hot, tropical forest in Central America, some workmen for
a banana company were cutting their way through a thick tangle of
vines about 35 years ago.   They were searching in Costa Rica for new
land where they could plant bananas.   Coming to a small clearing,
they found a big round stone about six feet in diameter.   It was almost
perfectly round, and it was resting on a small platform paved with
river stones.

Fascinated, the men looked around in the underbrush and found
many more stones---some of them large, some small, but all of
them amazingly round and smooth.   The men wondered who had made
these stone spheres and where they were made.   The men had found
no places nearby where bedrock was exposed.   When they described
to others what they had found, they learned that few people had ever
seen these strange spheres and no one knew where they came from.

The land was found to be good for growing bananas, and the banana
company soon began clearing away the forest to make way for new
plantations.   As trees and underbrush were cleared away, more of the
stone spheres were found, as well as other small areas paved with
river stones.

But the spheres have remained a mystery.   Some people have
thought that the largest ones might mark the graves of Indian chiefs,
but digging showed there were no graves under them.

When scientists in other parts of the world learned about the stone
balls, they came to see them and try to find out more about them.
They found that most of the stone balls were made of granite, but a
few were made of limestone.   Some of the balls were only a few
inches in diameter and weighed only a few pounds; others were as
large as 8 feet in diameter and weighed more than 16 tons.   Some of
them were so remarkably round that it took very careful measurements
to show that they were not quite true spheres.

. . . .

The spheres were mostly found in groups of at least three and sometimes as many as 45.   Some were arranged in long straight rows,
others in circles, and others in triangles.   Some of the straight lines
point north and south.   Could it be that by looking along some of the
lines formed by the stones, people were able to keep track of the positions of the sun and other stars?

. . . .

• South America

THE PRIMEVAL MONUMENTS OF PERU COMPARED WITH THOSE IN OTHER PARTS OF THE WORLD
Squier, E. G.; *American Naturalist*, 4:1–17, 1870.

In connection with the group of chulpas at Sillustani, or rather on the same promontory on which these occur, are found a number of such Sun-circles, which seem strangely to have escaped the notice of travellers. The tradition of their original purpose is preserved in the Quichua name they still bear of Intihuatana, "where the sun is tied up."

Some of these circles are more elaborate than others, as shown in the engraving, from which it will be seen that while the one nearest the spectator is constructed of simple upright stones, set in the ground; the second one is surrounded by a platform of stones more or less hewn and fitted together. The first circle is about ninety feet in diameter; the second about one hundred and fifty feet, and has a single erect stone stand-ing in the relative position I have already indicated. A remarkable feature in the larger circle is a groove cut in the platform around it, deep enough to receive a ship's cable.

Intihuatanus or "sun circles" at Sillustani, Peru

I am well aware that many of the smaller so called Sun-circles of the old world are rather grave-circles, or places of sepulture; but that in no way bears on the point I am at present illustrating, namely: the close resemblance if not absolute identity of the primitive monuments of the great Andean plateau, elevated thirteen thousand feet above the sea, and fenced in with high mountains and frigid deserts, with those of the other continent. (pp. 10-11)

• Pacific Islands

STONE CIRCLES IN TONGAREVA
Anonymous; *Nature,* 130:742, 1932.

In an account of the ethnology of Tongareva, commonly known as Penrhyn Island (Bull. 92, Bernice P. Bishop Museum, Honolulu), by Te Rangi Hiroa (Dr. P. H. Buck), reference is made to two roughly circular arrangements of limestone pillars. Nothing is known of their uses and no name is applied to them by the islanders. It has been stated that stone circles of a Stonehenge type are present in Tongareva ---an erroneous interpretation of the word 'encircled' used by Lamont loosely in describing a marae which in reality was rectangular. The stones are not to be ascribed to an archaic civilisation; they are of the same type as those used in marae construction, and sun worship was unknown to the Tongarevans. The pillars, including the bilateral notched pillar of the Atutahi ellipse, are trimmed in the same way as the marae pillars. They must have been made by the ancestors of the present population. They are in fact extra-marae pillars set up near the marae for some subsidiary purpose which, it is suggested, were social gathering places on the way to or from the marae. Women and children were not allowed to enter the marae. The secular use of the circle may be borne out by the discovery of a partly worked shell fish-hook in one enclosure. The circle may have been used as the place in which was performed the dance and the wailing ceremony, an accessory performance outside the marae that required a clear space not far away. The circle probably arose from a desire to embellish the clear space where such dances were held. In function it would be subsidiary and complementary to the marae and not taboo.

• Australia

THE ORDERED ARRANGEMENT OF STONES PRESENT IN CERTAIN PARTS OF AUSTRALIA

Jones, Frederic Wood; *Royal Anthropological Institute, Journal,* 55: 123-128, 1925.

Permanent memorials of the culture of Australian aboriginals appear to be rare. When we have enumerated the rather limited number of painted and incised rocks, and considered the vast store of stone implements and ceremonial objects which are scattered all over Australia, we have exhausted most of the evidence of aboriginal enterprise which may be regarded as in any way permanent.

But in addition to these are other permanent works of the aboriginals, which, though designed at times on almost a grand scale, have received less attention than they deserve. Short of megalithic culture there are many manifestations of a stone cult which, though comparatively trivial in their display, are yet of the greatest interest.

The question of stone circles in Australia has been much debated in the past. In Philip Chauncy's Appendix to Brough Smith's Aborigines of Victoria (1878, p. 234) the following occurs:---"In one of Chambers' Tracts on the Monuments of Unrecorded Ages it is stated that 'Stone circles' are numerous in Victoria---that they are from ten to one hundred feet in diameter, and that sometimes there is an inner circle; also, that the aborigines have no traditions regarding them; that when asked about them they invariably deny knowledge of their origin. I can safely affirm that these statements are quite incorrect---there are no such circles, and never were. I am convinced that no structures of a monumental character were ever erected by any of the aborigines of Australia."

Mr. Chauncy was District Surveyor of Ballarat, and presumably had a wide knowledge of that part of Victoria. In thus dogmatically ruling out "stone circles" he evidently had in mind megalithic circles, for in the same article he himself calls attention to two very interesting cases in which stones have been quite definitely arranged in radiating, maze, or circular formations.

Concerning the first, he says:---"On a little basalt islet in Lake Wongan, about seven miles north-east from Streatham, I observed an ancient aboriginal work consisting of extensive rows of large stones, forming passages up and down, like a maze, at the foot of a little hill. A semicircular walk, 10 feet wide, has been made by clearing and smoothing the rough rocky surface up the hill and down again leading into the maze. This work was possibly executed for the purpose of carrying on some mystic rites, or probably only for the amusement of running between the rows of stones and up the hill and down again."

Of the second case he records:---"Mr. A. C. Allen, Inspector General of Surveys, has informed me that during a recent journey in the Tattiara country near the South Australian border, he noticed a number of stone walls 2 or 3 feet high, which had been constructed by natives, radiating from a little cave in the ground and forming irregular passages. I can only conjecture that these and other similar works have been used by the aborigines, in times past, for purposes of incantation."

The name Tattiara country is applied to the south-western district of Victoria, of which Bordertown may be taken as a centre. The stone formations which are described by Mr. Allen I have not seen, nor can I obtain any other account of them. I am therefore unable to state if they are in existence to-day.

Quite recently, however, I have had information about a very similar construction in another part of the country. At Durham Downs station, which is some 350 miles north-east of Farina and 400 from north of Broken Hill, is a very remarkable arrangement of stones laid down as pathways. The existence of some place which was held in special superstitious regard by the station blacks has been for long known to the manager, Mr. McCullagh, but it is only within the present year that the actual spot has been localized, and its finding was the outcome of pure accident. The place is within ten miles or so of the station homestead. In nearly all the details this Durham Downs structure appears very similar to the stone work described by Mr. Allen. Owing to the kindness of Mrs. McCullagh I have been permitted to see photographs of the site, and to have a first-hand description of the stonework.

As in the Tattiara example the low stone walls radiate from a cave, and here the mouth of the cave (which has partly fallen in, and has not been entered by the station owners) is described as being greasy or shiny, as though something had rubbed against its sides in coming and going. Judging by the photographs, the stones that mark the edges of the paths are about knee high, though here and there a considerably higher one is conspicuous. The paths themselves appear to be arranged in a most intricate maze-like fashion, though there are evidently some which proceed more or less directly in a radiating manner from the mouth of the cave. The present station blacks, who number about thirty, are said to have a tradition that these paths were used by people who lived in the district before the time of their old people. These folk, they say, had blue eyes, and they lived in the cave by day, emerging in the evening to dance among the stones. The present blacks evidently hold the spot either in some dread or in some special esteem, and would not make its whereabouts known to the white people. I have had neither time nor opportunity to make the journey to Durham Downs to inspect this very interesting place; but it is much to be hoped that it will be visited and recorded by some Australian ethnologist, and that it will be preserved intact as a permanent monument.

A rather different form of what is evidently the same basal type of stone structure is described by A. W. Howitt (Brough Smith, App. D, Notes on the Aboriginals of Cooper's Creek). According to Howitt this type of stonework was common, for he says "in many places where the ground was bare---as on extensive clay flats---I have seen circles and circular figures formed with stones of various sizes, generally as large as a 2-lb. loaf. They are laid on the ground, and were explained by the blacks to me as being play. I think they require more explanation." No individual claypan is instanced by Howitt, and it is difficult to be certain as to the exact district of the Cooper's Creek area he is describing. In May, 1920, I did the journey from Hergott Springs (Marree) to Cooper's

Creek, but did not notice any artificially ordered arrangement of stones anywhere along that portion of the great Queensland cattle route known as the Birdsville track. In 1921, and again in 1922, I visited the gigantic claypans to the south and west of Lake Eyre, known as Bamboo Swamp and the Devil's Playground. Bamboo Swamp is too much covered with harsh cane grass to permit an examination of its floor; but the Devil's Playground is strewn with stones ranging up to large masses as big as an ordinary suit-case. The native account has it that these stones were tossed about by a former race in some sort of play; but if they were at any time arranged in definite order they must have been disturbed since, for to-day they appear to be merely scattered at haphazard. It must be remembered that claypans fill during rains, and large pans, such as these, hold a considerable sheet of water that remains for many months even in the climate of the centre. Again the trampling of cattle as they come to the claypans to water might easily disturb the loosely piled stones.

Quite recently (May, 1923) I have had the good fortune to visit another claypan, the native name of which is Gungra. This pan lies about 10 miles north-west of McDouall's Peak on the track to Lake Phillipson, about 540 miles in a straight line north-west of Adelaide (Railway Map, 1921). This claypan is not marked or named on any map or Pastoral Plan that I have had access to. Gungra is not a large claypan, for it measures some 800 yards long and some 600 yards wide; it is very shallow, and, save for one hole in which a mulga bush grows, it probably does not retain water long, even on those rare occasions when it is filled. The astonishing thing about this claypan is that of the millions of stones which strew its even surface the vast majority have obviously been placed in their present position by human hands. The complexity of the arrangement is so great that no concrete notion can be had of the general plan; but the main lines of arranged stones, and the cairns are

Line of stones, Gungra Claypan, Australia. Four rock cairns (not shown) are at the far end.

obvious at a glance. The main complexity of the design is towards the south-east side of the pan, and from this centre long lines of stones, in straight or waved lines, radiate right across the claypan and are lost in the sandhills beyond. Some lines of stones are several hundred yards in length, and the stones themselves are so carefully selected and placed in position as to make almost even and nearly perfectly straight tracks, like rows of bricks placed along the border of a path. I could detect no general geographic orientation in the pattern. One rather obvious line runs nearly due east and west, but so many others run at varying angles to it that this is probably only a coincidence. One line, however, which is lost on the sand on the north-west side of the claypan appears to point to another claypan about a mile further on. Some of the lines are evenly waved, being composed of a series of crescents, and at one time the junction of the crescents was marked with little heaps of stones which have now fallen down. As the central portion of the pattern is approached the arrangement of the lines becomes bewildering; some are looped, running from the centre and then back again; some appear to unite the various rays as do the strands in a spider's web; and some run out to a point and then sharply return. The central portion of the maze-like area has been marked by a series of cairns about 4 feet high and solidly compacted---very much like the cairns erected by the surveyors on prominent spots. Of these cairns only four are now standing, but the sites of many more can be detected by the mass of disordered stones caused by their collapse. The main features of the claypan and the cairns, and linear arrangement of the stones are shown in the two illustrations, but nothing short of a prolonged survey or an aerial photograph could give any connected idea of the plan of the whole curious structure.

. . . .

NATIVE MONUMENT IN CENTRAL AUSTRALIA

Butement, W. A. S., and Pither, A. G.; *Antiquity,* 30:116, 1956.

During a recent visit of an official party to a remote part of Central Australia in connection with defence requirements, a very interesting native relic in stone was discovered.

It was located approximately 250 miles inland from the Great Australian Bight and about 200 miles east of the West Australian border. At the actual site there were two large claypans, which probably became shallow lakes in wet periods. These were bounded on the south-west by a low range of hills. The hills presented a rather striking appearance from a distance giving the impression of terraced surfaces. Close inspection showed that this effect was due to differential weathering of the strata. Hard bands of slate three to four inches thick had proved much more resistant to attack than the adjoining clays and gravels, and consequently stood proud of the surface, giving the effect of terraces.

The site of the monument is about 100 yards from one of the lakes and lies along a small dry creek bed leading into the lake. It consists essentially of a series of stone piles, all of which show a characteristic style of construction. These piles are grouped in two areas. In one area they are placed in a straight line and spaced at intervals of approximately 12 feet. Some twelve piles are discernible on the ground. The line runs on a bearing of about 9° true. The second area lies on the opposite side of the creek and is roughly 50 yards square. There is a large number of piles which, in general, are considerably bigger than those in the first area. However, as far as can be ascertained, these are not arranged according to any particular pattern. The characteristic form of construction of the piles can be seen on Plate X, A. [Plates not reproduced.] Basically they consist of a central slab approximately 3 feet to 4 feet high, 2 inches to 3 inches thick and 6 inches to 12 inches wide. This has been placed vertically on the ground and held in position by a collection of stones piled around its base.

Stone monument in Central Australia

Associated with the second area there is an individual feature of considerable interest. This is a natural platform formed by an outcrop of the slate in the highest horizon exposed. This gives the impression of having been used as a rostrum or conducting platform and in fact the party nick-named it the 'High Priests' Platform'. Some weight is given to its possible use for such a purpose by the presence of slate slabs, one on each side, now being flat, but which had evidently stood erect at some time past. A general impression of the platform is given by Plate IX, B.

The piles of stone in the second area have the appearance of having been added to progressively. Plate X, B shows one of the largest piles, while those seen on Plate X, A may represent earlier stages of development.

Possibly an estimate of the age of the relic might be made from geological considerations. It seems clear that the whole of the stone was drawn from the slate out-crops in the creek bed. In view of the comparatively large amount of stone involved, it can be assumed that there was considerable activity in the area and the stone as produced was sound. However, the present outcrops have weathered to such an extent that many of the stones there can now be dislodged at the touch of a finger. It would therefore appear that an estimate of the time required for this weathering might throw some light on the age of the relic. A feature which may have considerable significance is that various piles have the appearance of having had fires built around them.

• Asia

THE STONE CIRCLES OF OYU

Kidder, J. Edward; *Archaeology,* 11:232-238, 1958.

Oyu is a small hot-spring town, undistinguished in every way, from which one may take the road to Hanawa up a steep hill and across a cultivated plain for a distance of approximately three miles. Here one finds two sets of stone circles, one on either side of the road, about eighty yards apart. These have received the names of the microscopic communities nearby, Manza for the northern one, Nonakado for the one to the south. The stones were brought from the bed of the Oyu River, which at its nearest point is only a few hundred yards away.

The Nonakado and Manza circles are roughly the same size, though the irregularity of the remains makes measurements only approximate. The outer circle of the former measures about 135 feet in diameter, the inner circle thirty-five; Manza is a little larger, the diameter of the outer circle being some 150 feet, of the smaller nearly forty-seven. Even though man and nature have combined to destroy many of the formations, in numerous cases the groups of stones within the outlines of the circles are still intact in patterns more or less oblong or circular, in some instances with one or more standing stones. At times the horizontally laid stones outline a pit below, or the uprights disposed at four or more points are connected by horizontals, as if marking graves. Presumably the hundreds of loose stones in haphazard positions may also have formed part of recognizable patterns. The

Oyu double circles have a feature that is without doubt of considerable significance inasmuch as its relative position is the same in both sets of circles: a sun-dial construction stands apart from the rings, at Nonakado quite isolated, at Manza more nearly within the outlines of the outer ring. Each is located in the northwestern sector of the circle, Nonakado at 302°, Manza at 296°. A difference of six degrees does not alter the apparent calendrical significance of the arrangement. (p. 233)

Locations of stone circles reported in North Honshu

THE STONE ALIGNMENTS OF SOUTHERN HYDERABAD
Allchin, F. R.; *Man,* 56:133-136, 1956.

The first notice of the Indian 'megalithic' monuments which are discussed in this paper was in Colonel Meadows Taylor's account of the ancient remains in Surapur (1852). Taylor recorded four places at which lines or diagonal lines of stones were to be seen. Eighty years were to elapse before the Hyderabad Geological Survey, under the leadership of Captain Leonard Munn, published reports of many further alignments in its Journal (1934-41). A number of sites were also reported in the

<u>Annual Report</u> of the Hyderabad Archaeological Department. From all
these sources 24 are known. During my fieldwork in Hyderabad in 1952
a further 19 sites were discovered, of which this is the first report.
The resulting distribution map shows that so far alignments have only
been found to the north of the Krishna and Tungabhadra rivers in the
Raichur, Gulbarga, Nalgonda, Mahbubnagar and Atraf-i-Balda districts
of Hyderabad state. It is certain that many more sites await discovery
in this area and it would be interesting to make further exploration in
the adjoining districts to the south and east. Indeed until a search has
been made there it is impossible to determine whether the absence of
sites south of the rivers is a fact or merely the result of limited research.
The alignments consist of parallel lines of standing stones set out
with mathematical precision. The lines are approximately oriented on
the cardinal points in all recorded cases. The stones are spaced at carefully regulated intervals which may differ on the north-south and east-
west axes. The intervals so far recorded vary between 15 and 40 feet.
In one case an alignment is reported to have stones still standing of 14
to 16 feet in height; in another a single fallen stone has been noticed of
25 feet: but the most common heights for the stones are from three to
six feet. The cross section of the longer stones is sub-rectangular,
polygonal or near circular, whilst the shorter ones are often barely worked boulders of conical form and irregular section. The diameter varies
between two and four feet. The shorter stones are often mere boulders
with little or no dressing; the longer ones are blocks which must have
been quarried by means of fire-setting. The marks of chisels or drills,
which are so often to be seen on mediaeval or modern stonework, have
never so far been reported. The rock chosen was usually local granite
or gneiss or more rarely dolerite. In a few cases from Gulbarga district the local sandstone was used, as it was for stone-cist graves in
the same area. In a very few instances the stones were carried to the
site from a short distance, probably not more than a couple of miles
(e.g. Nos. 8 and 12 of the Gazetteer). Although no accurate survey has
yet been made of any site, it is possible to discern two varieties of
arrangements, which we may term 'square' and 'diagonal.' In the first
the stones are set in lines which form rectangles. The smaller alignments are mainly of this sort and thus we find two with three rows of
three stones, three with four rows of four, three with five rows of five,
two with six rows of six and one with seven rows of seven stones. Some
have other ratios as three rows of four, or four rows of five. In the
second variety the stones of the even-numbered rows are offset half an
interval, or rather are set in the centres of the squares formed by those
of the odd numbered rows. The effect is thus to stress the diagonal lines.
The old examples which are known to belong to this variety are those
with larger numbers of stones and it is probable that careful survey
would reveal that these also had regular numbers of stones in the rows
and that the even-numbered rows contained one less than the odd.
It has already been noticed that the rows are oriented roughly on
the cardinal points. As far as can be determined this applies also to
the diagonal alignments, although I have been unable to verify it. Of the
ten examples which I was able to measure, no less than six lie between
15° and 20° east of north. I noticed a similar variation in the orientation of some of the stone-cist graves of Raichur, and Dr. Hunt recorded
comparable figures for the graves east of Hyderabad. The meaning of

this variation is not clear but it would seem to relate to the method adopted to establish the cardinal point. It may well be that the sunrise was employed as it is still in some Buddhist countries to orient religious structures, but the problem merits further study.

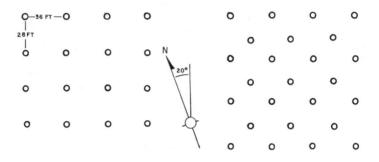

Square and diagonal types of stone alignments in India

In considering the age and original purpose of the alignments it may be useful to notice their relationship to other sites. More than half the recorded examples are in the immediate vicinity of, or even adjoining, stone-cist or circle graves. The circle graves either may or may not have a cist buried in a pit. Several of the alignments lie on the outskirts of major settlement sites. Several are on the banks of streams. No less than eight sites have been recorded along about 50 miles of the modern road from Raichur to Mahbubnagar. The meaning of these observations is not clear as systematic search has mainly been limited to the vicinity of the roads, but it seems clear that the graves, alignments and settlements all stand in regular relationship and that the graves and alignments would appear to be generally contemporary. A clear picture of the relationship can be had at Piklihal, Maski or Jamshed and is briefly indicated in the Gazetteer of sites below. The hypothesis of the general contemporaneity of circle graves and alignments is reinforced by the excavation of a ten-foot square around one of the stones in Piklihal I. Immediately below the modern turf and humus the disintegrated granite subsoil was encountered. The stone itself had been erected in a pit of about 18 inches in depth. On the surface of the subsoil were several shallow depressions less than six inches deep and in one of these depressions was found a sherd of red-and-black ware of a type well known from the grave sites of the entire Peninsula. The hollows were perhaps connected with the mechanics of erecting the stone. The excavation revealed no further evidence, but seems to support the hypothesis that the alignments may be dated to roughly the same period as the graves. This would perhaps indicate that they may date from the last centuries B.C. or first centuries A.D., but when further evidence is available these limits may well be extended in either direction.

We have seen that the Hyberabad alignments are rows, or diagonal rows, of rough-hewn stones or boulders set out with mathematical precision and oriented to the cardinal points. With such features as criteria it is not easy to find comparable monuments in India. The nearest comparison to the plan is to be found in the nava graha (nine planets), carved in stone in human form, standing in three rows of three, and to be found in many South Indian temples. None of these, however, has any great antiquity. There is a solitary reference to a line of four standing stones in Cochin, but apparently it is a single line only. The Dimapur alignment, together with the other examples recorded by Hutton in Assam, is also clearly different. There are two types of stone, male and female, either of phallic form or forked. Stones of both types are carved in a manner which suggests the mediaeval temple stone mason. The characteristic plans of the Hyderabad specimens are not comparable with these twin lines of carved stones, and it is difficult to assign any comparable date to the Assam monuments. Moreover, as Hutton has convincingly shown, there is a close connexion between them and the neighbouring Naga stone and wood memorial pillars, to which bulls were tethered for sacrifice.

What was the purpose for which these lines of great stones, often weighing several tons, were set up? Within my knowledge Sanskrit literature supplies no answer, nor does ancient Tamil. There are many references to stone memorial posts, warrior stones, and stones to which offerings are made, but never to alignments of such stones. Modern traditions in Hyderabad are not particularly helpful. The villagers refer to the stones in Telegu as nilu ralu or enugu ralu, standing stones or elephant stones, and one case the story is told of villagers and their cattle petrified by curse. Taylor mentions the tradition that they mark the sites of kings' camping places and that horses and elephants were tethered to the stones. Dr. Mahadevan records an interesting custom associated with the monument at Hegratgi. It is known as mantraki (Sanskrit: mantra, a charm, hence perhaps charm field or magician) and in times of epidemic the herds are driven around the stones to ward off disease. This recalls the 'cattle stones' of the Mysore country to which offerings are made in similar circumstances. Among the Koyis of Godavari district it is reported that great stones are set up for commemorative purposes and that the tail of a cow or bullock which has been sacrificed is tied to the top. These customs seem to suggest commemorative and perhaps magical and prophylactic functions for the stones, and call to mind Hutton's conclusions. They also raise an interesting question of relationship of stone alignments and stone yupas (sacrificial pillars) for in at least one case such pillars were set up in a group of four. The repeated proximity of graves and alignments might support the theory. There is, however, a second broad possibility which also deserves attention. The sites occur on the outskirts of settlements and on the lines of roads. Is it possible that they represent caravan halting places (or dharma-sala) or that they were the sites of periodical markets or fairs? It is even possible that they combined these functions with those of commemoration and prophylaxis, but these are fields of speculation which at present are unpromising. The need is for further survey, particularly air survey, of the region, and for the accurate recording of sites. It is then for careful and complete excavation of a selected example. After this it may be possible to supply further information on the function of these unique and interesting monuments.

• Africa

NOTE ON STONE CIRCLES IN GAMBIA
Todd, J. L.; *Man,* 3:164–166, 1903.

We know altogether of four localities in which perfect stone circles occur in the Gambia. In isolated instances in the bush, on both sides of the river, we have seen single stones similar in every way to those composing the circles. In two instances careful search revealed no stones accompanying these monoliths---on the surface, at least.

The first circle which we saw was at Kununko, a small village on the south bank of the Gambia, almost opposite to the town of Sukuta. This circle is about four miles from the river. It is situated on the eastern slope of a small hill, about half way towards the top. The stones composing this circle are about half the size of those forming the circle near Manna. It contains, I think, 13 stones (notes have been mislaid, and the photograph was not a success). At the western side two stones were further apart than elsewhere, so as to form some

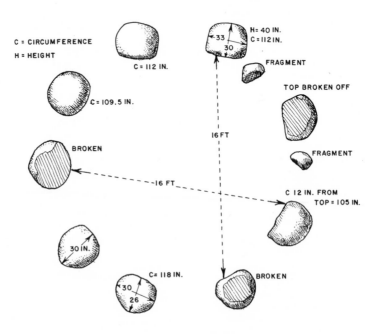

Plan view of a Gambia inner stone circle

sort of an "entrance." The width of this circle was about 12 feet 6 inches (paced).

At Niamimaru there are, so I have been told, four or five stone circles composed of stones much larger than even those at Manna. It was one of these which Mr. Ozane investigated. The circle at Manna is situated on the northern bank, about a mile from the river, and is on rising ground.

At Maka---called by the French Makacolibantan---the chief town of the Cercle de Niani-Ouli, there are two quite complete circles placed side by side, and, approximately to the east, there are some evidences of there being a much larger outer segment of a circle, indicated by taller columns, as at Manna, which springs from the small central circles, and so forms, as it were, a court or approach, in the manner indicated by the accompanying little plan. The stones composing these circles are about as large as those at Kununko, which are about 2 feet 6 inches to 3 feet in height, and about 9 inches in diameter.

The stone of which all these circles are made is the ordinary red volcanic "ironstone," which is so common in Senegambia. At none of the places where we saw circles would it have been necessary for the builders of the circles to go more than a few hundred yards for their material.

That the stones of the inner circles are worked into an approxi-mately D-shaped form is certain.

The natives have absolutely no idea by whom or for what purpose these blocks of stone were arranged in this way. When questioned they say simply that the olden people did it. They do not look upon the circles with any particular awe, although they are sometimes used by the Mohammedan blacks as praying places. In spite of this they have not in many places any compunction in planting their crops near and around them.

• Europe

MEGALITHIC RINGS: THEIR DESIGN CONSTRUCTION

Cowan, Thaddeus M.; *Science,* 168:321-325, 1970. (Copyright 1970 by the American Association for the Advancement of Science)

Sometime between 3500 and 1000 B.C. several thousand megalithic structures were erected in western Europe. Some of those in the British Isles, such as Stonehenge, are thought to have served as as-tronomical observatories, while others, like the mound at New Grange,

Ireland, seem to be burial places. Those that are ring-shaped fall into four categories of design: circles, flattened circles, ellipses, and eggs. Thom in an investigation of the geometry of these designs has made a substantial contribution to the solution of these enigmatic shapes; he has given us a tractable geometrical analysis which is esthetic in its simplicity. Essentially, he has considered each ring perimeter as a set of arcs drawn from various centers within the design. Thom's geometrical analysis is given in Fig. 1; only the geometry of the ellipse and that of the type II egg are not his.

In this article I extend Thom's proposal and suggest the manner in which the designs were scribed. I confine my remarks to the simpler rings and do not discuss the compound rings, exemplified by the Avebury monument in Wiltshire, although there are features which suggest that even these fit the pattern of construction described here.

Thom's geometry suggests that ropes attached to anchor stakes placed at the arc centers were used to scribe the designs. Surprisingly, Thom has questioned the use of the rope and stake as a scribing tool. He claims that the rings are too accurate to have been scribed by such a procedure. Presumably, he is referring to the propensity rope has for stretching. He suggests that the megalithic designers used two rods of standard length (a "megalithic yard") and measured the distances by carefully laying out the rods end to end much as one would use a yardstick. There are two sources of cumulative error in such a procedure. One is associated with the picking up and placing of the rods; the other is the problem of trying to keep the rods properly aligned. On the other hand, a little experience with a rope would quickly tell how much tautness is needed to keep the stretch to a minimum.

The assumption here is that two anchor stakes and two other stakes, "pivot stakes," were used in the construction of each simple ring, with the possible exception of the circle. Furthermore, it is assumed that the anchor stakes and the pivot stakes were always aligned at right angles. On the surface, this relationship is of minor interest, but further consideration shows that, in constructing the various rings, the needed placing and movement of the anchor and pivot stakes may follow an evolutionary pattern.

Thom convincingly argues that the people who built these structures were obsessed with a concern for perfection---so much so that all their measures were laid out in integral units. The circular megalithic ring, with its perfect radial symmetry, must have especially appealed to them, particularly since its construction represents the utmost in simplicity. To a geometer, probably few things are more intuitively satisfying and esthetically appealing than an absolutely perfect circle drawn by rotating a radius around a point. Undoubtedly discovery of the irrational ratio between the diameter and the circumference was frustrating to the megalithic geometers. Quite possibly this discovery instigated the search for rings whose perimeters were such as to make this ratio integral. Perhaps it was at this point that the flattened circle was developed.

The Flattened Circles. Figure 1 shows the various simple rings, their geometry, and the proposed methods of construction. For the flattened circle of type A, Thom suggests four centers (a_1, a_2, p_1, and p_2) from which four arcs are drawn. Suppose an anchor stake was placed at point a_1 and two pivot stakes were driven at points p_1

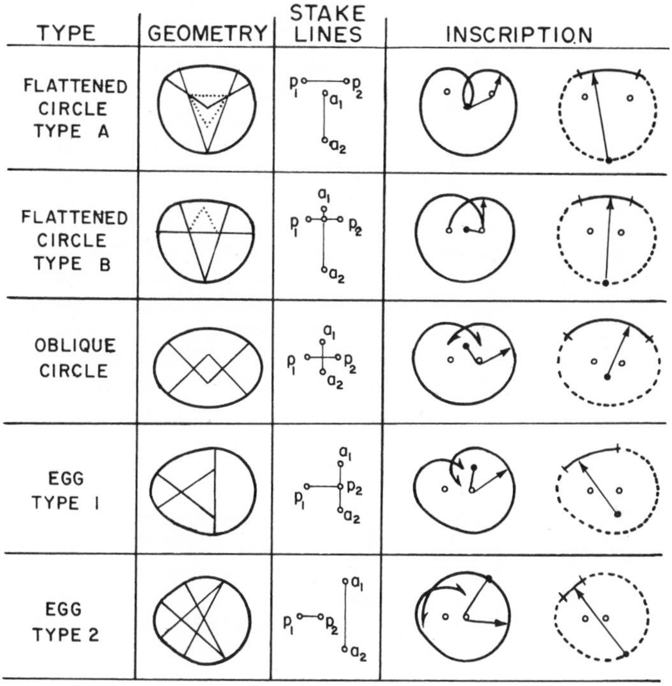

TYPE	GEOMETRY	STAKE LINES	INSCRIPTION
FLATTENED CIRCLE TYPE A			
FLATTENED CIRCLE TYPE B			
OBLIQUE CIRCLE			
EGG TYPE 1			
EGG TYPE 2			

The geometry, stake lines, and scribing methods for five classes of megalithic rings

and p_2. With a rope of appropriate length tied to stake a_1 the designer could, in one sweep, inscribe all of the type A ring, except for the top arc, by moving the rope so that it swung around the pivot stakes when it came against them. The resulting figure is very nearly a perfect cardioid. The design could be completed by re-anchoring the rope at a_2 and marking the top arc.

Since the top arc smooths over the indention in the cardioid, one might guess that the builders dismissed this shape because it served as merely an auxiliary figure. There is evidence from other megalithic structures, however, that this was not the case, and indeed the cardioid may have been regarded as quite exceptional. The structures in which cardioid shapes seem to be important are the numerous passage tombs found throughout Britain and Ireland. Examples include the chambered tombs of the Severn Cotswold culture. One of these, the tomb at Parc le Breos Cwn at Glamorgan, is obviously cardioidal, albeit misshapen.

Figure 3 is an outline of the exquisitely chambered passage tomb at New Grange, Ireland. This is considered to be one of the finest of the passage tombs; its date of construction has been placed at about the third millennium B.C. The end of the tomb is in line with the pivot points, and the entire chamber (exclusive of the passage-

way) just fits between the arcs below the cusp of the cardioid used
to construct the design. These fits require the assumptions that the
passage marks the vertical diameter and that the center of the finishing arc is located within the ring rather than on the perimeter.

How were the positions of the anchor and pivot stakes found? In
all type A rings, points a_2, p_1, and p_2 lie on radii that divide the
circle with center a_1 into three equal sectors. Thus the ring is a
two-thirds-perfect circle with a flattened arc over the remaining
third. Someone has remarked that perhaps all of these misshapen
rings were attempts to make ring structures such that the ratio of
circumference to diameter would be 3. That the radial lines divide
the ring into thirds suggests that an equilateral triangle was constructed with p_1 and p_2 occupying two vertices and with the third
vertex located at a point below a_1, the center of the triangle. The
intersection of lines drawn from any two vertices to the midpoint of
their bases would locate a_1. The construction of this triangle and
its center would not be difficult, and it may be said with some confidence that the type A design construction was based on an equilateral
triangle.

Neither the lower vertex of the triangle nor the cardioid cusp
point in the type A ring are conspicuously evident in the final construction. Nor did they necessarily serve as pivot points during the
construction as did the other triangle vertices. Their importance
might have been enhanced if one served to mark the other. If the
lower type A triangle vertex was located at the cusp point and the

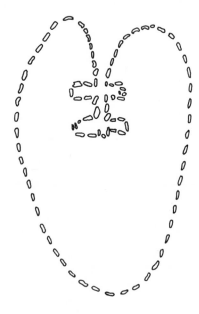

Outline of tomb at Parc le Breus Cwn

other two vertices, which remained pivot points, were placed in line with a_1, then a type B circle could be drawn in much the same manner as a type A circle. In a type B circle the length of rope needed for scribing the circumference was determined by measuring the distance from the anchor stake to the top vertex of the equilateral triangle by way of the outside of one of the pivot stakes. This procedure would give a correct measure of the needed length of rope only if the pivot stakes were placed, as most of them were, one-third of the radial distance from the center. Only one of Thom's type B sites did not conform to this plan. Thus, as in the case of the type A design, one may say with some assurance that the equilateral triangle played a role in the construction of the type B rings.

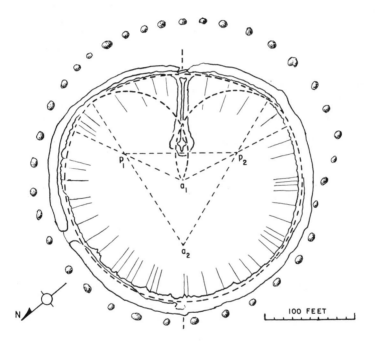

Plan of New Grange passage tomb with superimposed geometric analysis

The Ellipses or Oblate Circles. Thom and others describe a number of rings as "elliptical." These are nearly circular, but one axis seems to be slightly shorter than the other. However, if the anchor and pivot stakes were used, aligned at right angles for all designs, then the rings cannot be true ellipses; rather, they must be regarded as oblate circles.

Where were the stakes placed in constructing these sites? Note that the flattened circles are symmetrical about their lesser diameter, whereas the egg-shaped rings, dealt with below, are symmetrical about their greater diameter. The oblate circles, while not radially symmetrical, have a bilateral symmetry with respect to both their major and minor axes. This suggests two things: first, the anchor and pivot lines reflect this double symmetry, and second, the oblate circle represents an evolutionary midpoint between the flattened circles and the eggs. If the anchor and pivot lines were made to intersect perpendicularly at their midpoints, then a rope tied to a_1, and then to a_2 could scribe the design in the same way that the flattened circle designs were constructed. Experimentation with a compass quickly demonstrates that an oblate circle can be constructed from these points---one which, to the eye, is indistinguishable from an ellipse.

A pattern to the shift of anchor and pivot lines begins to emerge. The anchor line seems to be drifting upward from its position in the type A flattened circle to its position in the type B ring, and finally in the oblate circle the two lines bisect each other. From here on, the only movement the anchor line can make to produce a new figure and yet remain at right angles to the pivot line is a lateral shift. This is precisely the step taken in the production of the egg designs.

The Egg-shaped Rings. The construction of a type I egg seems to have involved a shift in the anchor line just to the end of the pivot line. Before the design was scribed, a rope would be attached to a_1, then placed on the inside of p_2 at the right angle of the triangle formed by a_1, p_1, and p_2, and allowed to loop back to a_1. From this position all but one of the side arcs could be drawn in one sweep as before. The remaining arc could be drawn by re-anchoring the rope to a stake placed at a_2.

This shift of the anchor line carried with it a number of consequences. The most obvious one is the change in the orientation (symmetry) of the ring from its anchor line to its pivot line. Also, the pattern of the lines seems to mirror that of the type B flattened circle; in both, one line is at the end of the other. Despite these changes, the stake lines remain at right angles, and the arcs of the perimeter remain in the same positions relative to themselves and their centers (or, equivalently, the lie of the scribing rope relative to the four points is the same). This points to a certain topological equivalence between the simple rings discussed so far. Thom suggests that the megalithic geometers knew rudimentary trigonometry. Perhaps they were nibbling at the edges of topology as well. They must have been impressed by the peculiar changes in the perimeters of these rings made by the straightforward manipulation of the stake lines---a quasi-topological observation at the very least.

A common feature of the type I egg is the appearance of perfect Pythagorean triangles formed by the stake points. Thom has discovered a number of these, particularly of the 3, 4, 5 variety. The perfect right triangle is conspicuously missing in the flattened circles. How did the Pythagorean triangle come into being here? In all likelihood it did not, like Athena, spring fully matured from the brow of its creator. Probably there was a good deal of experimenting, perhaps starting with the equilateral triangles. If the builders were an inquisitive lot, as no doubt they were, they must have contemplated the distance between, say, the point at the cardioid cusp of the type B ring and the anchor point directly below. The side and altitude of an equilateral triangle and half of the base are in the ratio $1 : 3\text{-}1/2 : 2$, which is close to 4 : 7 : 8 in quarter units. This is nearly Pythagorean $(4^2 + 7^2 = 65 \approx 64)$ but not so close that the difference would escape detection. If, as Thom suggests, these people were obsessed with integral measurement, the discovery of the nonintegral altitude of the equilateral triangle may have motivated them to seek a right triangle with integral sides.

The geometry suggested by Thom for the type II egg is considerably different from that given here. Our scribing method could not be reconciled with Thom's geometry, and this necessitated a search for another solution. Once the pattern of stake-line variation was established, the solution was quickly found. If the orientation of the stake lines of the type B circle had its counterpart in the type I egg, the stake lines of the type A circle should have its counterpart in the type II egg. That is, the anchor line of the type II egg should lie outside the pivot line, just as the pivot line lies outside the anchor line in the type A circle. This was indeed found to be the case.

There remained the problem of how far away from the pivot point the anchor line was placed. Since the distance between a_1 and the pivot line in the type A circle was determined by an equilateral triangle, it was thought that the same thing might be true for the type II egg. Unfortunately, any number of equilateral triangles can be constructed around the pivot stake p_2. As Fig. 1 suggests, the anchor stake might have been positioned at the intersection of the circumference of the larger circle and two of its trisecting radii. The principal differences in the perimeters of the type II egg produced by Thom's geometry and by the geometry suggested here is that Thom assumed that the top and bottom sides were straight, whereas here they are very shallow arcs. The use of shallow arcs rather than straight lines has precedent. Thom suggested such arcs in considering Woodhenge, and so did Borst in his analysis of the crypt of William the Englishman.

The designs of the four type II eggs listed by Thom were reconstructed on the basis of the geometry suggested here. Thom's measurements of the distance between the centers of the large and small nearsemicircular ends and the radius of the large end arc were kept. With the geometry proposed here, the designs of two rings (Leacet Hill and The Hurlers in England and Wales, respectively) were virtually identical to the designs proposed by Thom. On the other hand, the designs of the Borrowston Rig and Maen Mawr monuments in Scotland and Wales could be constructed on the basis of Thom's measurements only if the locations of a_1 and a_2 were free to shift on the circumference of the larger arc. There are rationales for these diversities, however.

The passage tomb at New Grange had an outside megalithic ring which was possibly a type II egg. A good construction of it can be produced if an equilateral triangle is used. There are three places where the construction seems to miss its mark---the north, southeast, and southwest locations. This makes it uncertain that the type II egg was its model. However, this construction fits as well as, or better than, any of the others, including Thom's type II geometry.

If the passage tomb at New Grange is a type II ring, then an interesting question arises regarding the apparent evolution of the designs, for here the earliest (a type A flattened circle) and the latest are present in the same site. There are a number of ways in which this could have come about. The outside egg could have been constructed

well after the inner flattened circle. It is difficult, however, to think
why such a ring would be added to a site already occupied by a tumulus.
If it should be found that the tumulus was built within an existing ring
(whose presence perhaps indicated hallowed ground), this would be far
more understandable. If the type A inner ring was developed (hence
built) after the type II egg, implying a structural evolution in the reverse order of the one proposed here, then we must conclude that the
Pythagorean triangle was discovered and then suddenly abandoned---
a possibility which seems untenable. Such a conclusion also runs contrary to the earlier proposition that the Pythagorean triangle evolved
from the type-B-ring equilateral triangle.

**Arbor Low, Derbyshire, with its recumbent stones and surrounding
ditch (Janet & Colin Bord)**

Of course, the tumulus and the outer ring could have been constructed at the same time. In this case all ring types would have been
known and used concomitantly. This could have happened if the different types evolved fairly rapidly, or if each ring design served a unique
function. The specific function each design served remains a mystery.
Despite the difficulty in eliciting a rationale, there are reasons for
believing that the outer ring was constructed after the tumulus. Although the center triangles of the ring and the tumulus are oriented in

approximately the same manner, they do not coincide or share a common center. If the ring and the tumulus were built simultaneously, they undoubtedly would have the same center. If the ring had been built first, then its center could have been found fairly easily, and the design of the tumulus built around that center. Suppose the tumulus was constructed first, however. During the later construction of the ring it would have been necessary to ascertain the center of the tumulus from the top of the mound, if a common center was desired. This would have been difficult at best.

Final Comments. I have attempted to show how some of the simple megalithic rings were drawn, and this attempt, I believe, not only affects existing analyses of these sites but leads to new conjectures concerning the mathematical talents of the designers. Were the hypothesized scribings really used? Or are they another of a number of explanations that merely fit the field data? There are two indications that the evidence for the scribing method is more than circumstantial. The first is the existence of sites in which the cardioid appears to have been used. The second is the fact that the change in the pattern of the stakes from one ring to another is too orderly to be circumstantial.

Perhaps the best witness to the talents of these megalithic builders is the scribing method itself, for here is a procedure for geometric construction that is unique. There are only three known nonalgebraic or nongraphic geometric constructions: the Poncelet–Steiner circle method, the fixed compass or Mascheroni method, and the common method involving use of the flexible compass. No existing technique approaches that of the megalithic geometers, except for the well-known method of scribing an ellipse. The Poncelet–Steiner circle is the most restricted of the known constructions; it requires only a straightedge and a fixed circle. The Mascheroni method allows the use of any number of circles or arcs with a fixed radius, and the flexible compass further allows the use of arcs of varying radii. If all restrictions on radius length were removed so that the radius could be of any length at any time during the construction, then virtually any two-dimensional figure could be drawn. The proposed megalithic scribing method allows the length of the radius to change discretely and in one direction (toward shorter lengths) in the middle of a sweep. For this reason this technique might possibly constitute the next step in a hierarchy of construction methods. While this scribing method may not contribute profoundly to mathematical theory, it may at least have consequences of interest to recreational mathematics.

The megalithic geometers knew rudimentary trigonometry and may have had a grasp of simple topology. They had a standard length which, for all we know, may have been the precursor of the yard, and they had a unique method of geometric construction.

Is there something more? Perhaps much remains hidden in these remarkable sites.

THE CAITHNESS FAN-SHAPED ARRAYS

Brown, Peter Lancaster; *Megaliths, Myths and Men*, New York, 1976, pp. 203–204.

One of the most remarkable aspects of Thom's Megalithic studies at Scottish sites was his interpretation of the curious fan-shaped stone arrays in Caithness. In several of these arrays the slabs are positioned with their long axes laid parallel to the direction of the row. These stone rows had been surveyed in 1871, but their curious layout, with the indi-

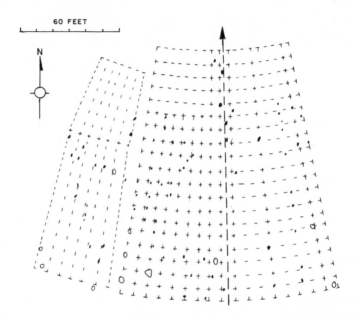

The sector arrays at Mid-Clyth, Caithness, Scotland, which may represent a primitive stone computer for analyzing lunar motion

vidual stones seldom more than 45 cm (18 inches) high, had long provided an even bigger puzzle as to their true purpose than had Megalithic circles. However, according to Thom these rows perhaps represent primitive stone computers used by the astronomer-priests to solve complex problems involving extrapolation which arises as a consequence that the Moon's maximum declination may be reached when it is not at its rising or setting point. Owing to the 27·21-day factor, lunar declination undergoes a relatively fast monthly change (passing through declinations $\pm23°51'09''$). The result is that the Moon may reach a maximum declination and then start to decrease again between two observations which normally would be separated by at least an interval of a full day. Without recourse to some extrapolation method this could lead to an error up to 10' of arc in an azimuthal fix when the astronomer-priests were attempting to fix an extreme lunar position by two (before–and–after) observations. Thom's interpretation of these fan–arrays perhaps represents the greatest degree of sophistication yet claimed for Megalithic man, and for good reason they have been referred to as 'Megalithic graph paper'.

STONE ROWS IN SCOTLAND

Burl, Aubrey; *The Stone Circles of the British Isles,* New Haven 1976, pp. 157–159.

The stone rows of Caithness and Sutherland, which occupy roughly the same areas as the preceding Orkney-Cromarty tombs, particularly around Lybster on the coast, differ from those of Dartmoor in one respect. Whereas the latter are always parallel those in northern Scotland may be either parallel or splayed. Yet they have common traits with those in Devon. They

One of the Caithness stone rows (Janet & Colin Bord)

are on hillsides, often connected to an unencircled cairn or cist, and are built of unobtrusive stones unlikely to have been chosen as sighting devices. The settings contain as many as twenty-three rows at Mid Clyth but these, like their southern counterparts, are composed of several groups. The orientations vary. With their short lengths, averaging about 36.6 m and their ankle-high stones they appear to be parochial variations as peculiar to the region as the megalithic horseshoe-shaped settings like Achavanich and Broubster, fifteen miles apart in central Caithness which, too, possess the local trait of having stones at right-angles to the perimeter.

. . . .

Returning to the Caithness rows of tiny stones, these may be arrangements designed to lead the eye up the slope to a surmounting cairn just as the Dartmoor rows perhaps provided a line to walk along to the burial place. There are, however, more involved astronomical interpretations. At Mid Clyth, 'the hill of many stanes', the fanned rows have a central north-south axis. Thom thought the rows might be aligned on the risings and settings of Capella (α Aurigae) between the years 1900 and 1760 BC. Certainly such observations, by bisecting the angle between them, could have established a north-south line much as the pyramid-builders of Egypt may have done, the more so as the need for a level horizon to ensure an accurate bisection is fulfilled at Mid Clyth. Little stones could then have been set in rows not for observation but to record the lines.

. . . .

Groups of stone rows, usually single and short but megalithic, are known in many other regions of the British Isles: Northumbria; Ulster; south-west Wales; Dartmoor; Cork and Kerry; as well as the awesome rows of Brittany, some of which are splayed. There are also isolated sites like the Old Castle Hill Stones on Moorsholm Moor, Yorkshire. Fan-shaped examples are uncommon outside northern Scotland but there are, of course, radiating avenues like that at Callanish and the four rows running to the Circles A and B at Beaghmore, Tyrone. One must conclude that each region developed local variants having only the most general resemblance to others.

BRONZE AGE STONE MONUMENTS OF DARTMOOR
Brailsford, J. W.; *Antiquity*, 12:444-463, 1938.

The lofty expanse of heather, bog and bare granite which forms the region under discussion in this paper, contains a numerous and in many ways unique group of prehistoric antiquities. Although Devonshire archaeologists have for many years been doing good work in this district, it has never, to the best of my knowledge, been comprehensively dealt with in the light of modern methods and experience. Consequently, the prehistory of Dartmoor still presents something of a mystery. After describing the material at our disposal, I shall here make a few tentative suggestions which seem to resolve some of the

difficulties encountered in the interpretation of the archaeological
evidence, and which may throw some light on the prehistory of the
rest of southwest England.

The types of stone structure on Dartmoor which seem to belong
to the Bronze Age are as follows:---

(A) Alignments or Stone Rows	(D) Cairns
(B) Stone Circles	(E) Menhirs
(C) Cists	(F) Hut-circles and pounds

The last group are not strictly speaking monuments, but they unquestionably belong to the same complex as the sepulchral structures,
and since they have yielded evidence for dating, their omission could
hardly be justified. Other prehistoric structures, hardly referable
to the Bronze Age, but which have some connexion with the matter in
hand, are 'Dolmens' and 'Camps'.

A, Alignments. Monuments of this type are very rare in Britain
outside Dartmoor, where, however, about sixty known examples occur.
They consist of single, double, or multiple rows of stones, usually,
and probably originally always, in association with a burial. The
cairn which usually marks the starting point of the alignment is most
often more or less on the summit of a ridge, from which the row or
rows run downhill. The stones nearest the beginning are usually larger
than the average, and the first is sometimes a fine menhir as at

Stone row, Merrivale, Dartmoor (Janet & Colin Bord)

Drizzlecombe, Langstone Moor and other sites. The end of the alignment is almost invariably marked by a transverse 'blocking stone'.
The intermediate stones have their long axes along the line of the row;
sometimes the first as well as the last stone is placed transversely,
as at Assycombe, Cosdon, Trowlesworthy Warren 2, and some other
sites. One of the Drizzlecombe blocking stones is the highest menhir on the Moor, being 17 ft. 9 ins. long overall. The stones which
form the body of the row may be only a few inches high, and are rarely
over two or three feet, though many of those on Stall Moor are 6 ft.
to 8 ft. 6 ins. high. Here the stones are spaced at intervals of 3-15
yards, but usually they are only about 5 ft. apart. There is great
variety in the total length of these alignments. That connected with
the large kist on Lakehead Hill is only 40 ft. long, but is probably incomplete. The most usual length is about 150 yards. Of those I have
surveyed, nine are between 130 and 165 yards, 4 are between 400 and
413 yards, and the others, excepting the second row, also incomplete,
on Lakehead Hill, are 266 yards, 62 yards (Harter Tor), 85 yards
(Trowlesworthy Warren), and 83 yards (Drizzlecombe). The small
row at Merivale, which appears to be complete, is only 46 yards long.

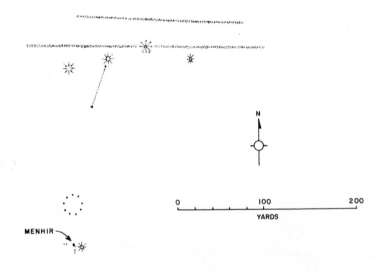

MENHIR

N

0   100   200
YARDS

Plan of stone rows at Merrivale, Dartmoor

There is a row, consisting of small, but closely set, stones, which
starts with a circle on Staldon Moor, and ends with a small cairn on
Green Hill, some 2-1/4 miles distant. Another on Butterdon Hill is
over a mile long.
　　The stone rows tend to run approximately east and west, as at
Drizzlecombe, Merivale, Assycombe, Harter Tor, Trowlesworthy
Warren 2, Down Tor, Cosdon Beacon, Lakehead Hill, etc. In other

cases the direction seems to be governed by the form of the ground.
The Erme Valley group, including the Stall Moor and Staldon Moor---
Green Hill examples, all run north and south, parallel to the river,
but following the undulations of the Moor on either side. Those at
Challacombe (N-S), Hurston Ridge (SW-NE), Ringmoor Down and
Trowlesworthy Warren I (NNE-SSW), also follow the slope of the
ground.

It is impossible to do more than conjecture the purpose of the stone
rows, though many theories have been put forward. It has been suggested that they were processional ways, but it is difficult to apply
this interpretation to the many examples of single alignments. They
may simply represent a connecting link between the circle and outlier
which is such a common type in Scotland, or a trace of the passage
found in the chambered tomb from which the Dartmoor type of monument is probably derived. Fergusson considered that the Merivale
rows were a memorial of some great battle, and represented two
armies drawn up face to face, but this theory has found little favour,
even as regards this specific instance. Worth believed that the
alignments marked the resting-place of some great chief, and that the
number of stones represented the size of his retinue. The practice
of setting up rows of stones is followed today on the island of Atchin,
where they are used as symbols for ancestors in religious rites. On
the same island a menhir, which replaces an original carved wooden
image, is set up to represent the general ancestral spirit.

Alignments of carved stones are also found in Assam, where they
are connected with a fertility cult and serve as vehicles for the souls
of the dead. (pp. 444-447)

ALIGNMENTS AT ASHDOWN

Fergusson, James; *Rude Stone Monuments in All Countries,*
London, 1872, pp. 121-124.

In the neighbourhood of Uffington, in Berkshire, there are three monuments, two at least of which still merit a local habitation and a name in
our history. One of these is the celebrated white horse, which gives its
name to the vale, and the scouring of which is still used by the inhabitants
of the neighbourhood on the occasion of a triennial festival and games,
which have been so graphically described by Mr. Thomas Hughes.

The second is a cromlech, known as Wayland Smith's Cave, and im-
mortalized by the use made of it by Sir Walter Scott in the novel of
'Kenilworth.' The third is as remarkable as either, but still wants its
poet. The annexed woodcut will give a fair idea of its nature and extent.
It does not pretend to be minutely accurate, and this in the present instance is fortunately of no great consequence. All the stones are overthrown: some lie flat on the ground, some on their edges, and it is only
the smallest that can be said to be standing. The consequence is, that
we cannot feel sure that we know exactly where any of them stood, nor

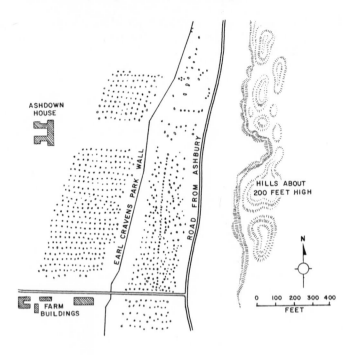

Stone alignments at Ashdown

whether they were arranged in lines, like those at Carnac; nor if so, in how many rows, or whether they always had the confused appearance they now present. They are spread over an area of about 1600 feet north and south, and of half that distance east and west. The gap in the centre was made purposely to clear the view in front of the house when it was built, and many of the stones it is feared were employed in the erection. They are the same Sarsens as are used at Avebury and Stonehenge, and the largest are about 10 feet long from 6 to 9 wide, and from 3 to 4 feet high (in their present recumbent position); but there are few so large as this, the majority being from 2 to 4 feet in length and breadth, and from 1 to 3 high. (pp. 121–123)

AN ATTEMPT TO ASCERTAIN THE DATE OF THE ORIGINAL CONSTRUCTION OF STONEHENGE FROM ITS ORIENTATION

Lockyer, Norman, and Penrose, F. C.; *Nature,* 65:55–57, 1901.

This investigation was undertaken in the spring of the present year, as a sequel to analogous work in Egypt and Greece, with a view to determine whether the orientation theory could throw any light upon the date of the foundation of Stonehenge, concerning which authorities vary in their estimate by some thousands of years. We beg to lay before the Royal Society the results derived from a careful study of its orientation for the purpose of arriving at the probable date of its foundation astronomically. This is not, indeed, the first attempt to obtain the date of Stonehenge by means of astronomical considerations. In Mr. Godfrey Higgins' work the author refers to a method of attack connected with precession. This furnished him with the date 4000 B. C.

More recently, Dr. W. M. Flinders Petrie, whose accurate plan is a valuable contribution to the study of Stonehenge, was led by his measures of the orientation to a date very greatly in the opposite direction, but, owing to an error in his application of the change of obliquity, clearly a mistaken one.

As the whole of the argument which follows rests upon the assumption of Stonehenge having been a solar temple, a short discussion of the grounds of this view may not be out of place; and, again, as the approximate date which we have arrived at is an early one, a few words may be added indicating the presence in Britain at that time of a race of men capable of designing and executing such work.

As to the first point, Diodorus Siculus (ii. 47) has preserved a statement of Hecataeus in which Stonehenge alone can by any probability be referred to.

"We think that no one will consider it foreign to our subject to say a word respecting the Hyperboreans.

"Amongst the writers who have occupied themselves with the mythology of the ancients, Hecataeus and some others tell us that opposite the land of the Celts there exists in the Ocean an island not smaller than Sicily, and which, situated under the constellation of The Bear, is inhabited by the Hyperboreans; so called because they live beyond the point from which the North wind blows....If one may believe the same mythology, Latona was born in this island, and for that reason the inhabitants honour Apollo more than any other deity. A sacred enclosure is dedicated to him in the island, as well as a magnificent circular temple adorned with many rich offerings.... The Hyperboreans are in general very friendly to the Greeks."

The Hecataeus above referred to was probably Hecataeus of Abdera, in Thrace, fourth century B. C.; a friend of Alexander the Great. This Hecataeus is said to have written a history of the Hyperboreans: that it was Hecataeus of Miletus, an historian of the sixth century B. C., is less likely.

As to the second point, although we cannot go so far back in evidence of the power and civilisation of the Britons, there is an argument of some value to be drawn from the fine character of the coinage issued by British kings early in the second century B. C., and from the statement of Julius Caesar (de bello Gallico, vi., 13) that in the schools of the Druids the subjects taught included the movements of the stars, the size of the earth and the nature of things.

....

Studies of such a character seem quite consistent with, and to demand, a long antecedent period of civilisation.

The chief evidence lies in the fact that an "avenue," as it is
called, formed by two ancient earthen banks, extends for a considerable distance from the structure, in the general direction of the sunrise at the summer solstice, precisely in the same way as in Egypt
a long avenue of sphinxes indicates the principal outlook of a temple.

These earthen banks defining the avenue do not exist alone. As
will be seen from the plan which accompanies this paper, there is a
general common line of direction for the avenue and the principal axis
of the structure, and the general design of the building, together with
the position and shape of the Naos, indicate a close connection of the
whole temple structure with the direction of the avenue. There may
have been other pylon and screen equivalents as in ancient temples,
which have disappeared, the object being to confine the illumination
to a small part of the Naos. There can be little doubt, also, that the
temple was originally roofed in, and that the sun's first ray, suddenly
admitted into the darkness, formed a fundamental part of the cultus.

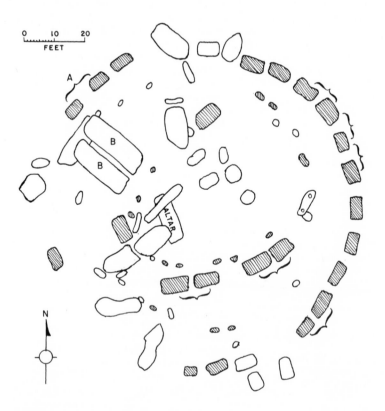

Plan of Stonehenge shortly after the turn of the Century. A = fell
in 1900; B = fell in 1797.

While the actual observation of sunrise was doubtless made within the building itself, we seem justified in taking the orientation of the axis to be the same as that of the avenue, and since in the present state of the south-west trilithon the direction of the avenue can proba- bly be determined with greater accuracy than that of the temple axis itself, the estimate of date in this paper is based upon the orientation of the avenue. Further evidence will be given, however, to show that the direction of the axis of the temple, so far as it can now be deter- mined, is sufficiently accordant with the direction of the avenue.

The orientation of this avenue may be examined upon the same principles that have been found successful in the case of Greek and Egyptian temples---that is, on the assumption that Stonehenge was a solar temple, and that the greatest function took place at sunrise on the longest day of the year. This not only had a religious motive; it had also the economic value of marking officially and distinctly that time of the year and the beginning of an annual period.

It is, indeed, probable that the structure may have had other capabilities, such as being connected with the equinoxes or the winter solstice; but it is with its uses at the summer solstice alone that this paper deals.

There is this difference in treatment between the observations re- quired for Stonehenge and those which are available for Greek or Egyptian solar temples---viz. that in the case of the latter the effect of the precession of the equinoxes upon the stars, which as warning clock stars were almost invariably connected with those temples, offers the best measure of the dates of foundation; but here, owing to the brightness of twilight at the summer solstice, such a star could not have been employed, so that we can rely only on the secular changes of the obliquity as affecting the azimuth of the point of sunrise. This requires the measurements to be taken with very great precision, towards which care has not been wanting in regard to those which we submit to the Society.

The main architecture of Stonehenge consisted of an external circle of about 100 feet in diameter composed of thirty large upright stones, named sarsens, connected by continuous lintels, and an inner struc- ture of ten still larger stones, arranged in the shape of a horseshoe, formed by five isolated trilithons. About one-half of these uprights have fallen and a still greater number of the lintels which they origin- ally carried. There are also other lines of smaller upright stones respecting which the only point requiring notice in this paper is that none of them would have interrupted the line of the axis of the avenue. This circular temple was also surrounded by an earthen bank, also circular, of about 300 feet in diameter, interrupted towards the north- east by receiving into itself the banks, forming the avenue before men- tioned, which is about 50 feet across. Within this avenue and looking north-east from the centre of the temple, at about 250 feet distance and considerably to the right hand of the axis, stands an isolated stone, which from a mediaeval legend has been named the Friar's Heel.

The axis passes very nearly centrally through an intercolumna- tion (so to call it) between two uprights of the external circle and be- tween the uprights of the westernmost trilithon as it originally stood. Of this trilithon the southernmost upright with the lintel stone fell in

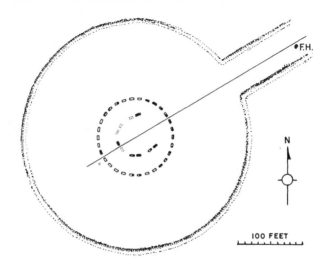

N

100 FEET

Stonehenge and surrounding earthwork

the year 1620, but the companion survived as the leaning stone which
formed a conspicuous and picturesque object for many years, but happily now restored to its original more dignified and safer condition of
verticality. The inclination of this stone, however, having taken
place in the direction of the axis of the avenue, and as the distance
between it and its original companion is known both by the analogy of
the two perfect trilithons and by the measure of the mortice holes on
the lintel they formerly supported, we obtain by bisection the measure
(viz. 11 inches) from its edge of a point in the continuation of the central axis of the avenue and temple, and which has now to be determined very accurately. The banks which form the avenue have suffered much degradation. It appears from Sir Richard Colt Hoare's
account that at the beginning of the last century they were distinguishable for a much greater distance than at present, but they are still
discernible, especially on the northern side, for more than 1300 feet
from the centre of the temple, and particularly the line of the bottom
of the ditch from which the earth was taken to form the bank, and which
runs parallel to it. Measurements taken from this line assisted materially those taken from the crown of the bank itself. With this help and
by using the southern bank and ditch whenever it admitted of recognition, a fair estimate of the central line could be arrived at. To verify
this, two pegs were placed at points 140 feet apart along the line near
the commencement of the avenue, and four others at distances averaging 100 feet apart nearer the further recognisable extremity, and their
directions were measured with the theodolite, independently by two
observers, the reference point being Salisbury Spire, of which the
exact bearing from the centre of the temple had been kindly supplied
by Colonel Johnston, R. E., the Director-General of the Ordnance
Survey. The same was also measured locally by observations of the

sun and of Polaris, the mean of which differed by less than 20" from the Ordnance value. The resulting observations gave for the axis of the avenue nearest the commencement an azimuth of 49° 38' 48", and for that of the more distant part 49° 32' 54". The mean of these two lines drawn from the central interval of the great trilithon, already referred to, passes between two of the sarsens of the exterior circle, which have an opening of about 4 feet, within a few inches of their middle point, the deviation being northwards. This may be considered to prove the close coincidence of the original axis of the temple with the direction of the avenue.

This value of the azimuth, the mean of which is 49° 35' 51", is confirmed by the information also supplied from the Ordnance Office that the bearing of the principal bench mark on the ancient fortified hill, about eight miles distant, a well-known British encampment named Silbury or Sidbury, from the centre of the temple is 49° 34' 18", and that the same line continued through Stonehenge to the south-west strikes another ancient fortification, namely Grovely Castle, about six miles distant and at practically the same azimuth, viz. 49° 35' 51". For the above reasons 49° 34' 18" has been adopted for the azimuth of the avenue.

The present solstitial sunrise was also watched for on five successive mornings, viz. June 21 to 25, and was successfully observed on the latter occasion. As soon as the sun's limb was sufficiently above the horizon for its bisection to be well measured, it was found to be 8' 40" northwards of the peak of the Friar's Heel, which was used as the reference point, the altitude of the horizon being 35' 48". The azimuth of this peak from the point of observation had been previously ascertained to be 50° 39' 5", giving for that of the sun when measured, 50° 30' 25", and by calculation that of the sun with the limb 2' above the horizon should be 50° 30' 54". This observation was therefore completely in accordance with the results which had been obtained otherwise.

The time which would elapse between geometrical sunrise, that is, with the upper limb tangential with the horizon, and that which is here supposed, would occupy about seventeen seconds, and the difference of azimuth would be 3' 15".

The remaining point is to find out what value should be given to the sun's declination when it appeared showing itself 2' above the horizon, the azimuth being 49° 34' 18".

The data thus obtained for the derivation of the required epoch are these:---

(1) The elevation of the local horizon at the sunrise point seen by a man standing between the uprights of the great trilithon (a distance of about 8000 feet) is about 35' 30", and 2' additional for sun's upper limb makes 37' 30".

(2) −Refraction + parallax, 27' 20".

(3) Sun's semidiameter, allowance being made for greater eccentricity than at present, 15' 45".

(4) Sun's azimuth, 49° 34' 18", and N. latitude, 51° 10' 42".

From the above data the sun's declination works out 23° 54' 30" N., and by Stockwell's tables of the obliquity, which are based upon modern determinations of the elements of the solar system, the date becomes 1680 B.C.

It is to be understood that on account of the slight uncertainty as to the original line of observation and the very slow rate of change in the obliquity of the ecliptic, the date thus derived may possibly be in error by ± 200 years.

In this investigation the so-called Friar's Heel has been used only as a convenient point for reference and verification in measurement, and no theory has been formed as to its purpose. It is placed at some distance, as before-mentioned, to the south of the axis of the avenue, so that at the date arrived at for the erection of the temple the sun must have completely risen before it was vertically over the summit of the stone. It may be remarked further that more than 500 years must yet elapse before such a coincidence can take place at the beginning of sunrise.

. . . .

STONEHENGE: A NEOLITHIC COMPUTER
Hawkins, Gerald S.; *Nature,* 202:1258-1261, 1964.

Diodorus in his History of the Ancient World,[1] written about 50 B.C. said of prehistoric Britain: "The Moon as viewed from this island appears to be but a little distance from the Earth and to have on it prominences like those of the Earth, which are visible to the eye. The account is also given that the god [Moon?] visits the island every 19 years, the period in which the return of the stars to the same place in the heavens is accomplished.... There is also on the island both a magnificent sacred precinct of Apollo [Sun] and a notable temple... and the supervisors are called Boreadae, and succession to these positions is always kept in their family".

I am indebted to the British archaeologist R. S. Newall for directing my attention to this classic work. The statement of Diodorus is secondhand and has sometimes been dismissed as a myth, but there is a possibility that it refers to Stonehenge.

The Moon rises farthest to the north when it appears over stone $\underline{D}$ as seen from the centre of Stonehenge[2], similar to the rising of the midsummer Sun over the heel stone. In a period of 18.61 years the extreme moonrise will shift from $\underline{D}$ to the heel stone to $\underline{F}$ and then return to $\underline{D}$. The extreme moonrise thus swings from side to side in the avenue because of the regression of the nodes. When we consider a particular moonrise, such as the nearest full moon to the winter solstice, which we will call 'midwinter moonrise', then the cycle takes either 19 or 18 years.

The position of the Moon has been computed using first-order terms[3] from 2001 to 1000 B.C. and the azimuth of moonrise has been determined for each winter solstice during this period. A sample of the results from 1600 to 1400 B.C. is shown in Fig. 1. Mrs. S. Rosenthal assisted with the programming of the I.B.M. 7094, and I thank the Smithsonian Astrophysical Observatory for the donation of 40 sec of machine time for this problem.

With midwinter moonrise the cycle is primarily one of 19 years with 38 per cent irregularity. For example, the Moon rises over F̅ in 1671, 1652, 1634, 1615, and 1596 B.C. The intervals are 19, 1̅8̅, 19 and 19 years respectively. Actually, from 2001 to 1000 B.C. the winter Moon is over F 52 times, and there are 32 intervals of 19 years and 20 of 18 as shown in Table 1. Similarly the cycle is primarily one of 19 years for moonrise over D̲ at the winter solstice (Table 1).

The winter Moon rises over the heel stone with twice this frequency. For example, in 1694, 1685, 1676 and 1666 B.C. the intervals are 9, 9 and 10 years. Over the period 2001 to 1000 B.C. the '10' irregularity occurs with a frequency of 33 per cent. However, if we consider second intervals, 1694 to 1676 and 1685 to 1666 B.C., then the cycle is again 19 years with 18 occurring as an irregularity as shown in Table 1.

Table 1. Interval in Years Between Winter Moonrise Over Stones D, F and the Heel Stone

Interval (years)	Frequency of interval (stone F)	Frequency of interval (stone D)	Frequency of interval (heel stone)
8	0	0	2
9	0	0	70 (65%)
10	0	0	35
18	20	20	40
19	32 (62%)	33 (62%)	66 (62%)
37	39 (77%)	40 (77%)	80 (77%)
38	12	12	24
54	0	0	1
55	8	8	15
56	42 (84%)	43 (85%)	86 (84%)

This cycle would also govern the return of the Moon to the other important alignments such as 94–91, and the trilithon positions. Even the moonrise along 92–93 at the time of the summer solstice would be governed by this 19, 19, 18 cycle. The Sun would return to the trilithon and heel stone at the winter and summer solstice each year. Thus the 19-year cycle was the main periodicity and seems to account for celestial objects returning to their positions as Diodorus implies. A rigid 19-year cycle gradually becomes inaccurate, however, and the winter moon deviates from the heel stone (Fig. 1) unless a correction is made every 56 years.

Eclipses of the Sun and Moon also follow this cycle. An eclipse of the Sun or Moon always occurs when the winter Moon rises over the heel stone; actual winter eclipses[4] from 1600 to 1400 B.C. have been indicated in Fig. 1. It should be noted that not more than half of these eclipses were visible from Stonehenge, and so moonrise over the heel stone primarily signals a danger period when eclipses are possible.[2]

Now I cannot prove beyond all doubt that Stonehenge was used as an astronomical observatory. A time machine would be needed to prove that. Although the stones line up with dozens of important Sun

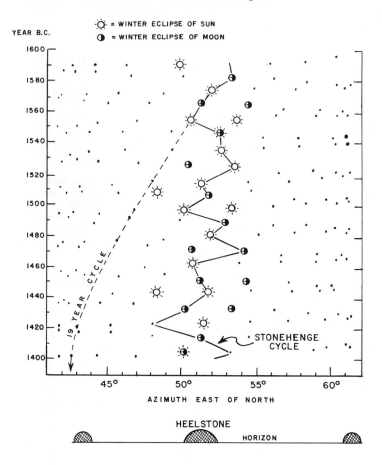

YEAR B.C.

☀ = WINTER ECLIPSE OF SUN

◑ = WINTER ECLIPSE OF MOON

Azimuth of winter moonrise, 1600-1400 B.C.

and Moon positions the builders of Stonehenge might somehow have remained in ignorance of this fact. The statement of Diodorus might be a meaningless myth. But perhaps I can reduce the doubt to a shred by showing how other features of Stonehenge are explained by the astronomical theory.

If we take second intervals between the years when the Moon is over the marker stones there is no clear periodicity; in Table 1 the Moon is over D̲ and F̲ every 37 or 38 years. However, a surprising condition exists for the next interval in extreme azimuths---it is almost always 56 years! Similarly, winter moonrise over the heel stone and eclipses also occur exactly 56 years apart on 84 per cent of all occasions (Table 1). This means that the winter Moon will return to its position over a certain stone every 56 years, and there are many such cycles which will become due in the span of a human lifetime. For example, during 20 years of observation the Moon would take up the ten positions which I have noted[2] in both the sarsen circle and station stones. Each of these occurrences would have been a part of a sustained 56-year cycle and therefore could have been predicted by a person with knowledge of the cycle-knowledge "kept in their family" as Diodorus says.

The number 56 is of great significance for Stonehenge because it is the number of Aubrey holes set around the outer circle. Viewed from the centre these holes are placed at equal spacings of aximuth around the horizon and therefore, they cannot mark the Sun, Moon or any celestial object. This is confirmed by the archaeologies' evidence; the holes have held tires and cremations of bodies, but have never held stones. Now, if the Stonehenge people desired to divide up the circle why did they not make 64 holes simply by bisecting segments of the circle---32, 16, 8, 4 and 2? I believe that the Aubrey holes provided a system for counting the years, one hole for each year, to aid in predicting the movement of the Moon. Perhaps cremations were performed in a particular Aubrey hole during the course of the year, or perhaps the hole was marked by a movable stone.

Stonehenge can be used as a digital computing machine. One mode of operating this Stone Age monument as a computer is as follows:

Take three white stones, $\underline{a}$, b, c, and set them at Aubrey holes number 56, 38 and 19 as shown in Fig. 2.

Take three black stones, $\underline{x}$, $\underline{y}$, $\underline{z}$, and set them at holes 47, 28 and 10.

Shift each stone one place around the circle every year, say at the winter or the summer solstice.

This simple operation will predict accurately every important lunar event for hundreds of years. For example, to the question: "When does the full Moon rise over the heel stone at the winter solstice?", the answer is: "When any stone is at hole 56". (Hole 56 is a logical marker because it lines up with the heel stone as viewed from the centre.) In Table 2, I have given the critical years as predicted by the Stonehenge computer for the period 1610 to 1450 B. C. with the stones set so that '$\underline{a}$' was at hole 56 in 1610. This period was chosen because 1600 B. C. is the earliest year for which eclipses have been computed[4]. Table 2 shows the remarkable accuracy of the Stonehenge computer. The correct year was predicted on 14 occasions out of 18 and the maximum error was only one digit. It also gave the years when the nearest full Moon to mid-summer set through the great trilithon (55-56). Incidentally, a stone was at hole 28 at this time, lining up with the great trilithon.

The stones at hole 56 predict the year when an eclipse of the Sun or Moon will occur within 15 days of midwinter---the month of the winter Moon. It will also predict eclipses for the summer Moon. In 1500 B. C. the winter solstice occurred on January 6, Julian calendar, and so the 30 days between December 22, 1501, and January 21, 1500, were the period of the winter Moon. Similarly, the summer Moon and other seasons in 1500 B. C. occurred 15 days late by our present Gregorian calendar. Table 2 gives actual eclipse data showing how Stonehenge scored 100 per cent success in predicting winter and/or summer eclipses. When more than one eclipse occurred, only one is

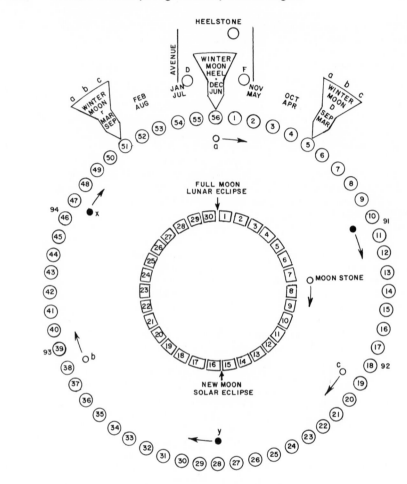

Stonehenge computer plan

listed in Table 2.

To summarize the mode of operation for the reader six movable stones give intervals of 9, 9, 10, 9, 9, 10.... years after 1610 B.C. The a, b, c stones give intervals of 18, 19, 19.... years. The Stonehenge cycle keeps in step with the Moon because it gives an average period of 18.67 years and the regression of the nodes of the Moon's orbit is close, 18.61 years. It keeps in step with eclipses because the metonic cycle of 19 years and the saros of 18 years are both eclipse cycles. The metonic cycle has not been previously recognized as an eclipse cycle, probably because it runs for only 57 years or so. It is, however, a remarkable cycle because eclipses repeat on the same calendar date. The lunar eclipse of December 19, 1964, for example, follows the lunar eclipse of December 19, 1945.

Table 2. Winter Moonrise over the Heel Stone and Eclipses
at the Summer and Winter Solstices

Stonehenge cycle Year B. C.	Moon over heel B. C.	Lunar eclipses	Solar eclipses
1610	1610	No data available	
1601	1601	No data available	
1592	1591	Jul. 14, '92	Dec. 24, '92
1582	1583	Dec. 30, '83	--
1573	1573	--	Jan. 4, '73
1564	1564	Jan. 10, '64	--
1554	1554	--	Jan. 4. '54
1545	1545	Jan. 10, '45	--
1536	1536	--	Jan. 14, '36
1526	1527	Jul. 16, '27	Jan. 5, '27
1517	1517	Dec. 31, '18	--
1508	1508	--	Jan. 5. '08
1498	1498	Dec. 31, '99	--
1489	1489	--	Jan. 6, '89
1480	1480	Jan. 10, '80	Jun. 21, '80
1470	1471	Dec. 22, '71	Jul. 12, '71
1461	1461	--	Jun. 21, '61
1452	1452	Jan. 1, '52	Jul. 12, '52

When does the winter Moon rise over stone F, and set along 93-91?;
when does the summer Moon rise over 91 as seen from 93?; when does
the equinox[5] Moon rise and set along 94-C, and when do eclipses occur
at the equinoxes? Answer: When a white stone is at hole 51. A comparison of the Stonehenge prediction and the actual dates is given in
Table 3. Again the accuracy is very satisfactory.

Table 3. Winter Moonrise over Stone F, and Eclipses of the
Harvest and Spring Moon

Stonehenge cycle Year B. C.	Moon over F B. C.	Lunar eclipses	Solar eclipses
1597	1596	Apr. 13, Oct. 6, '97	Mar. 18, '96
1578	1578	Apr. 13, Oct. 7, '78	--
1559	1559	--	Mar. 29, Sep. 22, '59
1541	1540	--	Apr. 9, Oct. 2, '41
1522	1522	--	Apr. 9, Oct. 3, '22
1503	1503	Mar. 25, '03	Apr. 9, Oct. 3, '03
1485	1485	Apr. 4, Sep. 28, '85	Apr. 19, Oct. 13, '85
1466	1466	Apr. 5, Sep. 29, '66	--
1447	1447	--	Mar. 20, '47

When does the winter Moon rise over stone D, and set along 94-91?;
when does the summer Moon rise over mound 92 as seen from 93?; when
does the equinox Moon rise and set along 94-C, and when do eclipses
occur at the equinoxes? The answer to all these questions is: When
a white stone is at hole 5. A sample run (Table 4) shows the accuracy
of the stone machine.

Needless to say, Tables 2, 3 and 4 also predict the appearances
of the moonrise and moonset in the trilithon and archways of the sarsen

Table 4.   Winter Moonrise over Stone D, and Eclipses of Harvest
and Spring Moon

Stonehenge cycle Year B. C.	Moon over D B. C.	Lunar eclipses	Solar eclipses
1605	1606	No data available	
1587	1587	Apr. 13, Oct. 7, '87	Apr. 7, Oct. 1, '87
1568	1568	Mar. 23, '68	Apr. 7, '68
1549	1550	Mar. 23, '49	--
1531	1531	Apr. 3, Sept. 28, '31	--
1512	1512	--	Mar. 20, Oct. 12, '12
1493	1494	--	Mar. 19, Sep. 24, '94
1475	1475	--	Mar. 30, Sep. 24, '75
1456	1457	--	Mar. 30, Sep. 23, '56

circle, because this later construction repeats the 10 lunar-solar alignments of the station stones.

In what years will eclipses occur between the solstice and equinox?
In terms of our calendar, take the months of April and October as an
example. When any stone is at holes 3 or 4, eclipses occur during
these months. The sector between 51 and 5 has been marked appropriately in the diagram so that it predicts the eclipse seasons according to our present-day calendar.

One remaining requirement was to be able to determine which full
Moon was nearest to the solstice or equinox. The average time between one full Moon and the next is 29. 53 days and the Stonehengers
would need to count that interval. A movable stone in the 30 archways
of the sarsen circle would be sufficient. If it were moved by one position each day, full Moon could be expected when the stone was at a
particular archway, such as 30-1. The stone would require resetting
by ±1 position every two or three months to stay in time with the somewhat irregular Moon. As the solstice or equinox approached (shown by
solar observations), the Stonehenger could decide which full Moon was
going to be the critical one. The sarsen circle could also have been a
vernier for predicting the exact day of an eclipse. A lunar eclipse
occurs when the Moon stone is in archway 30-1; a solar eclipse when
the Moon stone is in 15-16.

A complete analysis shows that the stone computer is accurate for
about three centuries, and then the Moon phenomena will begin to
occur one year early. This would be noticed by the Stonehengers and
could have been corrected simply by advancing the six stones by one
space. The process is known to-day as resetting or recycling, and is
used by all modern computers and logic circuits. A simple rule to
add to the operating instructions would be to advance all six stones by
one hole when the Moon phenomena are a year earlier than the prediction of a particular stone, say stone a. This is not a critical adjustment. If the error was not noticed with stone a, because of clouds for
example, the error could still be corrected with the following stones,
x, b, y, etc. The adjustment becomes due once every 300 years or so,
in 2001, 1778, and 1443 B. C. , for example.

Precession does not affect the accuracy, and the change of obliquity of the ecliptic and Moon's orbit also have very little effect. In 1964, for example, stone <u>a</u> is at 56. The full Moon rises over the heel stone on December 19, will be eclipsed at 2.35 a.m., and will set along 94-<u>G</u>. The next winter eclipse is also visible at Stonehenge, and is marked by stone <u>x</u>, 9 years later on December 10, 1973. The Stonehenge computer will function until well beyond A.D. 2100, when it will require resetting by one hole. It will then function for at least another 300 years before further resetting is required.

[1]<u>Diodorus of Sicily</u>, Book II, 47 (Harvard Univ. Press, Cambr., 1935).
[2]Hawkins, G. S., <u>Nature</u> 200, 306 (1963).
[3]<u>Explanatory Supplement to the Astronomical Ephemeris</u> (H.M.S.O., London, 1961).
[4]Van den Bergh, G., <u>Eclipses -1600 to -1207</u> (Tjeenk, Willink and Zoon, Holland, 1954).
[5]Newham, C. A., <u>The Enigma of Stonehenge</u> (private publication, 1964).

DECODER MISLED?

Atkinson, R. J. C.; *Nature,* 210:1302, 1966.

This book [<u>Stonehenge Decoded</u>] is an expansion of two articles in <u>Nature</u> (200, 306; 1963, and 202, 1258; 1964). It is tendentious, arrogant, slipshod and unconvincing, and does little to advance our understanding of Stonehenge.

The first five chapters, on the legendary and archaeological background, have been uncritically compiled, and contain a number of bizarre interpretations and errors. The rest of the book is an unsuccessful attempt to substantiate the author's claim that "Stonehenge was an observatory; the impartial mathematics of probability and the celestial sphere are on my side". Of his two main contentions, the first concerns alignments between pairs of stones and other features, calculated with a computer from small-scale plans ill-adapted for this purpose. Their directions were compared with the azimuths of the rising and setting Sun and Moon, at the solstices and equinoxes, calculated for 1500 B.C. Any alignment falling within $\pm 2^{\circ}$ of one of these eighteen azimuths is accepted, arbitrarily, as "significant". The limit of error adopted is unrealistically large, since experiment shows that such alignments can be laid out with a pair of sighting-sticks to a repeatable accuracy of ± 5 min. Moreover, the assumption that the builders aimed at the full orb of the Sun and Moon, tangent to the horizon, instead of at the first or last flash, is not confirmed by an analysis of the author's (unpublished) tables of vertical errors.

In claiming to have found thirty-two "significant" alignments, Hawkins has in five cases exceeded his own limits of "significance". Furthermore, he has failed to show that his results are due to anything but chance. Even with the most favourable choice of data, no more than six of his alignments can be shown to be significant in the statistical sense. Before these can be accepted, they need to be measured on the site, and not from plans.

Hawkins's second contention is that the fifty-six Aubrey Holes were used as a "computer" (that is, as tally-marks) for predicting movements of the Moon and eclipses, for which he claims to have established a hitherto unrecognized 56-year cycle with 15 per cent irregularity; and that the rising of the full moon nearest the winter solstice over the Heel Stone always successfully predicted an eclipse. This, if substantiated, will provide the best explanation so far of this stone, though it should be noted that no more than half these eclipses were visible from Stonehenge. As for the suggested use of the Aubrey Holes, it may be remarked that a ring of pits, filled up as soon as they had been dug, is not a very practicable form of permanent tally. Moreover, it is questionable whether a barbarous and illiterate community (for this is Stonehenge I, not Stonehenge III), which has left us no other evidence of numeracy, could successfully have recorded the data needed to establish a cycle which exceeded the contemporary life-span, and could not even have been recognized as a cycle until several generations had elapsed.

The fundamental objection to this and to other equally unconvincing suggestions in this book arises from the false logic of Prof. Hawkins's working hypothesis, declared in the preface. "If I can see any alignment, general relationship or use for the various parts of Stonehenge, " he says, "then these facts were also known to the builders." As he so truly adds in the next sentence, "Such a hypothesis has carried me along over many incredible steps".

STONEHENGE---AN ECLIPSE PREDICTOR
Hoyle, Fred; *Nature,* 211:454-456, 1966.

The suggestion that Stonehenge may have been constructed with a serious astronomical purpose has recently received support from Hawkins, who has shown that many alignments of astronomical significance exist between different positions in the structure. Some workers have questioned whether, in an arrangement possessing so many positions, these alignments can be taken to be statistically significant. I have recently reworked all the alignments found by Hawkins. My opinion is that the arrangement is not random. As Hawkins points out, some positions are especially relevant in relation to the geometrical regularities of Stonehenge, and it is these particular positions which show the main alignments. Furthermore, I find these alignments are just the ones that could have served far-reaching astronomical purposes, as I shall show in this article. Thirdly, on more detailed investigation, the apparently small errors, of the order of $\pm 1°$, in the alignments turn out not to be errors at all.

In a second article Hawkins goes on to investigate earlier proposals that Stonehenge may have operated as an eclipse predictor. The period of regression of the lunar nodes, 18.61 years, is of especial importance in the analysis of eclipses. Hawkins notes that a marker stone moved around the circle of fifty-six Aubrey holes at a rate of three holes per year completes a revolution of the circle in 18.67 years. This is close enough to 18.61 years to suggest a connexion between the period of regression of the nodes and the number of Aubrey holes. In this also I agree with Hawkins. I differ from him, however, in the manner in which he supposes the eclipse predictor to have worked. Explicitly, the following objections to his suggestions seem relevant:

(1) The assumption that the Aubrey holes served merely to count cycles of 56 years seems to me to be weak. There is no need to set out fifty-six holes at regular intervals on the circumference of a circle of such a great radius in order to count cycles of fifty-six.

(2) It is difficult to see how it would have been possible to calibrate the counting system proposed by Hawkins. He himself used tables of known eclipses in order to find it. The builders of Stonehenge were not equipped with such <u>post hoc</u> tables.

(3) The predictor gives only a small fraction of all eclipses. It is difficult to see what merit would have accrued to the builders from successful predictions at intervals as far apart as 10 years. What of all the eclipses the system failed to predict?

My suggestion is that the Aubrey circle represents the ecliptic. The situation shown in Fig. 1 corresponds to a moment when the Moon is full. The first point of Aries γ has been arbitrarily placed at hole 14. $\underline{S}$ is the position of the Sun, the angle $\odot$ is the solar longitude, $\underline{M}$ is the projection of the Moon on to the ecliptic, $\underline{N}$ is the ascending node of the lunar orbit, $\underline{N}'$ the descending node, and the centre $\underline{C}$ is the position of the observer. As time passes, the points $\underline{S}$, $\underline{M}$, $\underline{N}$ and $\underline{N}'$ move in the senses shown in Fig. 1. $\underline{S}$ makes one circuit a year. $\underline{M}$ moves more quickly, with one circuit in a lunar month. One rotation of the line of lunar nodes $\underline{NN}'$ is accomplished in 18.61 years. In Fig. 1, $\underline{S}$ and $\underline{M}$ are at the opposite ends of a diameter because the diagram represents the state of affairs at full Moon.

If the Moon is at $\underline{N}$, there is a solar eclipse if the Sun is within roughly $\pm 15^{\circ}$ of $\underline{N}$, and a lunar eclipse if the Sun is within $\pm 10^{\circ}$ of $\underline{N}'$. Similarly, if the Moon is at $\underline{N}'$, there will be a solar eclipse if the Sun is within $\pm 15^{\circ}$ of coincidence with the Moon, and a lunar eclipse if not within roughly $\pm 10^{\circ}$ of the opposite end of the line of lunar nodes. Evidently if we represent $\underline{S}$, $\underline{M}$, $\underline{N}$ and $\underline{N}'$ by markers, and if we know how to move the markers so as to represent the actual motions of the Sun and Moon with adequate accuracy, we can predict almost every eclipse, although roughly half of them will not be visible from the position of the observer. This is a great improvement on the widely scattered eclipses predictable by Hawkins's system. Eclipses can occur as many as seven times in a single year, although this would be an exceptional year.

The prescriptions for moving the markers are as follows: (1) Move $\underline{S}$ anticlockwise two holes every 13 days. (2) Move $\underline{M}$ anticlockwise two holes each day. (3) Move $\underline{N}$ and $\underline{N}'$ clockwise three holes each year.

We can reasonably assume that the builders of Stonehenge knew

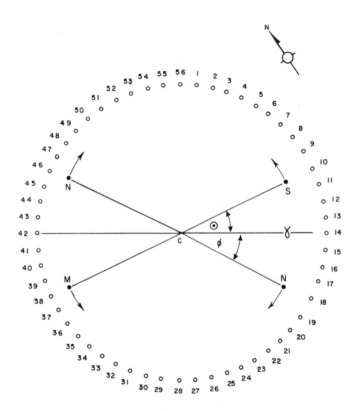

Hoyle's concept of the Stonehenge "computer"

the approximate number of days in the year, the number of days in the month, and the period of regression of the nodes. The latter follows by observing the azimuth at which the Moon rises above the horizon. If in each lunar month we measure the least value of the azimuth (taken east of north), we find that the "least monthly values" change slowly, because the angle $\odot$NCγ changes. The behaviour of the "least monthly values" is shown in Fig. 2 for the range $-60° <<$ $\phi << 60°$. The azimuthal values in Fig. 2 were worked out without including a refraction or a parallax correction. These small effects are irrelevant to the present discussion.) The least monthly values oscillate with the period of ϕ, 18.61 years. By observing the azimuthal cycle, the period of ϕ can be determined with high accuracy by observing many cycles. At Stonehenge sighting alignments exist that would have suited such observations. With the periods of $\underline{S}$, $\underline{M}$ and $\underline{N}$ known with reasonable accuracy the prescriptions follow immediately as approximate working rules.

Suppose an initially correct configuration for $\underline{M}$, $\underline{N}$ and $\underline{S}$ is known. The prescriptions enable us to predict ahead what the positions of $\underline{M}$, $\underline{N}$ and $\underline{S}$ are going to be, and thus to foresee coming events---but only for a while, because inaccuracies in our prescriptions will cause the markers to differ more and more from the true positions of the real Moon, Sun, and ascending node. The lunar marker will be the first to deviate seriously---the prescription gives an orbital period of 28 days instead of 27.32 days. But we can make a correcting adjustment to the $\underline{M}$ marker twice every month, simply by aligning $\underline{M}$ opposite $\underline{S}$ at the time of full Moon, and by placing it coincident with $\underline{S}$ at new Moon. The prescription for $\underline{S}$ gives an orbital period of 364 days, which is near enough to the actual period because it is possible to correct the position of $\underline{S}$ four times every year, by suitable observations made with the midsummer, midwinter, and equinoctial sighting lines that are set up with such remarkable accuracy at Stonehenge.

Stonehenge is also constructed to determine the moment when $\Phi = 0$, that is, when $\underline{N}$ should be set at Υ. The fine $\underline{C}$ to $\underline{A}1$ of Fig. 1 is the azimuthal direction for the minimum point of $\overline{\text{Fig. 2}}$. By placing $\underline{N}$ at Υ when the Moon rises farthest to the north, the $\underline{N}$ marker can be calibrated once every 18.61 years. The prescription implies only a small error over one revolution of $\underline{N}$. If $\underline{N}$ started correctly, it would be out of its true position by only 1° or so at the end of the first cycle. The tolerance for eclipse prediction is about 5°, so that if we were to adjust $\underline{N}$ every cycle, the predictor would continue to work indefinitely without appreciable inaccuracy. The same method also serves to place $\underline{N}$ at the beginning.

But now we encounter an apparent difficulty. The minimum of Fig. 2 is very shallow and cannot really be determined in the way I have just described. Angular errors cannot have been less than $\pm 0.25^{\circ}$, and even this error, occurring at the minimum of Fig. 2, is sufficient to produce an error of as much as $\pm 15^{\circ}$ in Φ.

The correct procedure is to determine the moment of the minimum by averaging the two sides of the symmetrical curve, by taking a mean between points 2, for example. The inaccuracy is then reduced to not more than a degree or two---well within the permitted tolerance.

What is needed is to set up sighting directions a little to the east of the most northerly direction. The plan of Stonehenge shows a line of post holes, $\underline{A}1$, 2, 3 and 4, placed regularly and with apparent purpose in exactly the appropriate places.

The same point applies to solstical measurements of the Sun. In summer the sighting line should be slightly increased in azimuth, in winter it should be slightly decreased.

Hawkins gives two tables in which he includes columns headed "Error Alt.". These altitude errors were calculated on the assumption that the builders of Stonehenge intended to sight exactly the azimuthal extremes. The test of the present ideas is whether the calculated "errors" have the appropriate sign---on the argument given here "errors" should be present and they should have the same sign as the declination. In ten out of twelve values which Hawkins gives in his Table 1 this is so. The direction from $\underline{C}$ to the Heelstone is one of the two outstanding cases. Here the "error" is zero, suggesting that this special direction was kept exactly at the direction of midsummer sunrise, perhaps for aesthetic or ritualistic reasons. The other discrepant case is 91 → 94. Here my own calculation gives only a very small discrepancy, suggesting that this direction was also kept at the appropriate azimuthal extreme.

Negative values of the altitude error correspond to cases where it would be necessary to observe below the horizontal plane, if the objects in question were sighted at their extreme azimuths. This is impossible at Stonehenge because the land slopes gently upward in all directions. Such sighting lines could not have been used at the extremes, a circumstance which also supports this point of view.

It is of interest to look for other ways of calibrating the N̲ marker. A method, which at first sight looks promising, can be found using a special situation in which full Moon happens to occur exactly at an equinox. There is evidence that this method was tried at Stonehenge, but the necessary sighting lines are clearly peripheral to the main structure. Further investigation shows the method to be unworkable, however, because unavoidable errors in judging the exact moment of full Moon produce large errors in the positioning of N̲. The method is essentially unworkable because the inclination of the lunar orbit is small. Even so, the method may well have caused a furore in its day, as the emphasis it gives to a full Moon at the equinox could have been responsible for the dating of Easter.

An eclipse calibrator can be worked accurately almost by complete numerology, if the observer is aware of a curious near-commensurability. Because S̲ and N̲ move in opposite directions the Sun moves through N̲ more frequently than once a year, in 346.6 days. Nineteen such revolutions is equal to 6,585.8 days, whereas 223 lunations is equal to 6,585.3 days. Thus after 223 lunations the N̲ marker must bear almost exactly the same relation to S̲ that it did before. If the correct relation of N̲ to S̲ is known at any one moment N̲ can be reset every 223 lunations; that is, every 18 years 11 days. The near-commensurability is so good that this system would give satisfactory predictions for more than 500 years. It requires, of course, S̲ to be set in the same way as before. The advantage is that in the case of N̲ it obviates any need for the observational work described above. But without observations the correct initial situation cannot be determined unless the problem is inverted. By using observed eclipses the calibrator could be set up by trial and error. This is probably the method of the Saros used in the Near East. There is no evidence that it was used at Stonehenge. The whole structure of Stonehenge seems to have been dedicated to meticulous observation. The method of Stonehenge would have worked equally well even if the Saros had not existed.

Several interesting cultural points present themselves. Suppose this system was invented by a society with cultural beliefs associated with the Sun and Moon. If the Sun and Moon are given godlike qualities, what shall we say of N̲? Observation shows that whenever M̲ and S̲ are closely associated with N̲, eclipses occur. Our gods are temporarily eliminated. Evidently, then, N̲ must be a still more powerful god. But N̲ is unseen. Could this be the origin of the concept of an invisible, all-powerful god, the God of Isaiah? Could it have been the discovery of the significance of N̲ that destroyed sun-worship as a religion?

Could M, N and S be the origin of the doctrine of the Trinity, the "three-in-one, the one-in-three"? It would indeed be ironic if it turned out that the roots of much of our present-day culture were determined by the lunar node.

ASTRONOMICALLY ORIENTED MARKINGS ON STONEHENGE

Brinckerhoff, Richard F.; *Nature,* 263:465–468, 1976.

Abstract. In view of the years of careful study that have been devoted to Stonehenge it may seem unlikely that any more information could be extracted from the monument, or at least from that part of it above ground. During the past two years, however, further markings have come to light that are, at least, interesting, and possibly important. These markings are a series of at least 11 pits on the upper surfaces of the three contiguous lintels (130, 101 and 102) that span the well-known line of sight from the centre of the sarsen circle north-eastward towards the heel stone. For an observer diametrically across the circle, 9 of these pits identify directions of the rising moon at significant points in its 18.6-yr cycle.

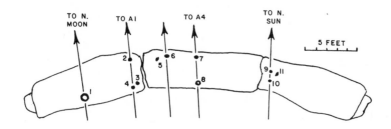

Pits on tops of Stonehenge monoliths and alignments through them. Directions are approximate.

CALLANISH, A SCOTTISH STONEHENGE

Hawkins, Gerald S.; *Science,* 147:127–130, 1965.

Conclusion. On the basis of the stone record it appears that the Callanish people were as precise as the Stonehengers in setting up their megalithic structure, but not as scientifically advanced. Callanish is, however, a structure that could have been used much as Stonehenge was. It would be interesting to obtain a date, by the

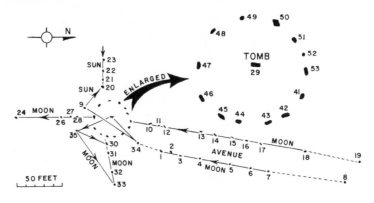

Plan of Callanish, Island of Lewis, Outer Hebrides

radiocarbon method, for the peat in the area of Callanish, to determine how much older, or more recent, than Stonehenge this structure is. Perhaps the knowledge gained at Callanish was later used in the design of Stonehenge.

These structures are both at critical latitudes. Callanish is at the latitude where the moon skims the southern horizon. Stonehenge is at the latitude where at their extreme positions along the horizon the sun and the moon rise at a right angle on the horizon. From the standpoint of astronomical measurement Stonehenge could not have been built further north than Oxford or further south than Bournemouth. Within this narrow belt of latitudes the four station stones make a rectangle. Outside this zone the rectangle would be noticeably distorted. Perhaps these latitudes were deliberately chosen, and perhaps these people were aware that the angles of the quadrangle formed by the station stones would change as one moved north or south. If Stonehenge and Callanish are related, then the builders may have been aware of some of the fundamental facts which served later as the basis of accurate navigation and led to a knowledge of the curvature of the earth. But if they possessed knowledge of such importance it must have been passed along by word of mouth; no record of it is found in the stones.

A STATISTICAL EXAMINATION OF THE MEGALITHIC SITES IN BRITAIN

Thom, A.; *Royal Statistical Society, Journal,* 118:275-295, 1955.

Introduction. In the past twenty years I have visited some 250 megalithic sites in England and Scotland, and made accurate surveys where there appeared to be anything worthy of survey. The surveys were carefully made plans showing the position of every stone except those obviously loose. Particular attention was paid to the orientation of the plans, the azimuths being determined in nearly every case astronomically by theodolite observations of the sun. This mass of material provides data for a geometrical and statisical study of the sites. The sites examined consist mainly of circles of standing stones, of rows of standing stones, here called alignments, or of a combination of the two. Many of the circles have one or more outliers, i. e. single upright stones outside the ring.

Of the published plans of stone circles, some are lacking in accuracy, and only one or two contain determinations of azimuth and horizon altitudes. Thus, in a study of the possible astronomical significance of stone alignments, etc., they are quite useless. There is also the danger that if published surveys are used the data may be biased and unsuitable for statistical examination. Accordingly in the present paper the material is restricted to sites I have been able to visit, and strict attention has been paid to laying down and adhering to terms of reference in selection. In the analysis presented here, nothing has been excluded which has a bearing on the subject, except one or two sites which I am assured are fakes.

. . . .

Conclusion. The study of a single megalithic site can only provide a limited amount of information, more especially as it is unlikely that there is such a thing to-day as a completely undisturbed example. We must examine many, and this immediately makes it necessary to introduce statistical methods of analysis. There are a number of problems to be solved and some of these are presented in such a form that they seem to call for special treatment and methods.

From an examination of three of these problems it appears that many of the circles follow certain geometrical designs; that a universal unit of length was used in setting these out on the ground and that many of the constructions carry indications of astronomical uses beyond those associated with the sun. Existing statistical theory allows us to be reasonably certain about the last two statements, but there seems to exist no method of attaching a value to the probability that the geometrical designs suggested were intended.

ANCIENT STONEWORKS FOUND IN LOCH NESS

Anonymous; *Science News,* 110:103, 1976.

Scientists searching for the Loch Ness monster have stumbled upon several large, prehistoric manmade stoneworks submerged in the Loch. The structures include a stone wall, several ancient mounds (locally called cairns) and possibly an ancient fortified island (called a crannog). Though such cairns and crannogs are common in the area, the discovery of such structures some 30 feet below the Loch's surface indicates the water level has risen sharply over the centuries. Also, since most cairns have long since been pillaged of whatever remains they might have contained, the discovery of several apparently intact structures may allow archaeologists to learn more about the area's ancient inhabitants.

The cairns are made of piled stones, varying in size from nearly one foot diameter down to pebbles. Such structures were presumably built as burial and religious mounds three or four thousand years ago. The mounds are generally laid out in series of concentric circles, as much as 100 feet in diameter, but one complex series stretches 250 feet.

. . . .

THE ASTRONOMICAL SIGNIFICANCE OF THE CRUCUNO STONE RECTANGLE

Thom, Alexander, et al; *Current Anthropology,* 14:450–454, 1973.

While we were engaged on extensive surveys in the Carnac area in Brittany in July 1970, three of us (A. S. Thom, R. L. Merritt, and A. L. Merritt) decided to take a look at an unusual geometric configuration of megaliths---the rectangular Cromlech de Crucuno, referred to by Niel as amongst the most remarkable megalithic monuments in

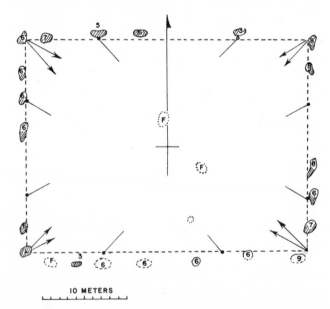

10 METERS

The Crucuno rectangle. Dotted lines indicate stones with uncertain outlines due to covering vegetation. Numbers indicate stone heights in feet. F = fallen stone. Arrows and dots indicate directions of the rising and setting points of lunar extremes.

the world. As a result we produced a large-scale survey which is
shown on a reduced scale in figure 1. Astronomical observations were
made for azimuth so that the plan could be accurately orientated. The
dotted rectangle was superimposed on the plan with its short sides exactly on the meridian. The rectangle as drawn is 30 x 40 megalithic
yards and so has a diagonal of 50.

It is probably not coincidence that the two 3-4-5 Pythagorean
triangles formed by the diagonal have sides which are multiples of
10 megalithic yards. Thom has shown that megalithic man, when constructing stone circles and rings in Britain, often dealt in multiples
of 2-1/2, 5, and 10 megalithic yards, and employed perfect Pythagorean triangles in the geometry of the construction of numerous stone
rings. Thom and Thom have shown that the main Carnac alignments
were set out with a unit of 2-1/2 megalithic yards, and this is also
found in the perimeters of practically all megalithic rings in Britain.
The Crucuno rectangle thus falls into line metrologically with other
megalithic remains in both Britain and Brittany.

. . . .

It should be understood that Crucuno, unless it had foresights
some distance away, could never have been more than a symbolic observatory like Castle Rigg in the north of England near Keswick,
Cumberland. In the absence of such foresights the rectangle would
have been useless as a scientific observatory, although precise lunar
observations such as are required for eclipse predictions were made
elsewhere in the neighborhood. It could have been used, however, to
give the calendar dates corresponding to the equinoxes. A second
visit, in 1972, showed that the necessary foresights may indeed have
existed.

. . . .

THE CARNAC ALIGNMENTS

Thom, A., and Thom, A. S.; *Journal for the History of Astronomy,*
3:11–26, 1972.

Conclusion. The original geometrical layout of the Menec alignments and cromlechs has been established. A remarkable feature is
the great accuracy of measurement with which the rows were set out.
It cannot be too strongly emphasized that the precision was far greater
than could have been achieved by using ropes. The only alternative
available to the erectors was to use two measuring rods (of oak or
whale bone?). These were probably 6.802 ft. long, shaped on the ends
to reduce the error produced by malalignment. Each rod would be
rigidly supported to be level but we can only surmise how the engineers
dealt with the inevitable 'steps' when the ground was not level.

It may be noted that the value for the Megalithic yard found in
Britain is 2.720 ± 0.003 ft. and that found above is 2.721 ±0.001 ft.
Such accuracy is today attained only by trained surveyors using good
modern equipment. How then did Megalithic Man not only achieve it

Some of the stone alignments at Carnac (French Government Tourist Office)

in one district but carry the unit to other districts separated by greater distances? How was the unit taken, for example, northwards to the Orkney Islands? Certainly not by making copies of copies of copies. There must have been some apparatus for standardizing the rods which almost certainly were issued from a controlling, or at least advising, centre.

The organization and administration necessary to build the Breton alignments and erect Er Grah obviously spread over a wide area, but the evidence of the measurements shows that a very much wider area was in close contact with the central control. The geometry of the two egg-shaped cromlechs at Le Menec is identical with that found in

British sites. The apices of triangles with integral sides forming the
centres for arcs with integral radii are features in common, and on
both sides of the Channel the perimeters are multiples of the rod.

The extensive nature of the sites in Brittany may suggest that this
was the main centre, but we must not lose sight of the fact that so far
none of the Breton sites examined has a geometry comparable with that
found at Avebury in ambition and complication of design, or in difficulty
of layout.

It has been shown elsewhere that the divergent stone rows in Caithness could have been used as ancillary equipment for lunar observations, and in our former paper we have seen that the Petit Menec and
St. Pierre sites were probably used in the same way. We do not know
how the main Carnac alignments were used but we do know that careful
and continued use of observatories like those in Argyllshire and Caithness would have presented problems which must have intrigued and
probably worried the observers. Did they solve these in Carnac?

THE ASTRONOMICAL SIGNIFICANCE OF THE LARGE CARNAC MENHIRS

Thom, A., and Thom, A. S.; *Journal for the History of Astronomy,*
2:147–160, 1971.

Er Grah, or The Stone of the Fairies. This stone, sometimes known
as Le Grand Menhir Brise, is now broken in four pieces which when
measured show that the total length must have been at least 67 ft. From
its cubic content it is estimated to weigh over 340 tons. Hulle thinks
it came from the Cote Sauvage on the west coast of the Quiberon Peninsula. His suggestion that it was brought round by sea takes no account
of the fact that the sea level relative to this coast was definitely lower
in Megalithic times; neither does he take account of the fact that a raft
of solid timber about 100 x 50 x 4 ft. would be necessary---with the
menhir submerged. It is not clear how such a raft could be controlled
or indeed moved in the tidal waters round the Peninsula. Assuming that
the stone came by land, a prepared track (? of timber) must have been
made for the large rollers necessary and a pull of perhaps 50 tons
applied (how?) on the level, unless indeed the rollers were rotated by
levers. It took perhaps decades of work and yet there it lies, a mute
reminder of the skill, energy and determination of the engineers who
erected it more than three thousand years ago. Its commanding position on a peninsula in the Bay of Quiberon is shown in Figure 2.

In Britain we find that the tallest stones are usually lunar backsights, but there seems no need to use a stone of this size as a back-
sight. If, on the other hand, it was a foresight, the reason for its
position and height becomes clear, especially if it was intended as a
universal foresight to be used from several directions. There are
eight main values to consider, corresponding to the rising and setting
of the Moon at the standstills when the declination was $\pm(e \pm i)$. A
preliminary examination has been made of all eight lines (Figure 2).

. . . .

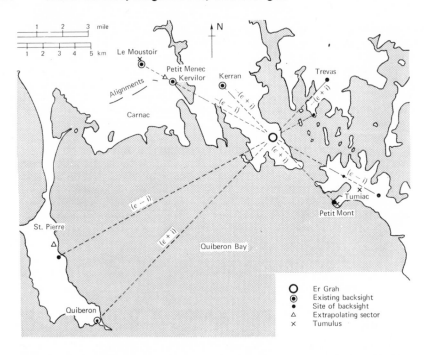

Er Grah, a large standing stone, conceived as a universal lunar foresight. Note the location of the Carnac alignments.

It has now been shown that there is at least one site on each of the eight lines which has the necessary room for side movement. The results obtained at those sites where there are menhirs or stones are summarized in Table 3.

We must now try to think of how a position was found for Er Grah which would have satisfied the requirements. Increasingly careful observations of the Moon had probably been made for hundreds of years. These would have revealed unexplained anomalies due to variations in parallax and refraction, and so it may have been considered necessary to observe at the major and minor standstills at both rising and setting. At each standstill there were 10 or 12 lunations when the monthly declination maximum and minimum could be used. At each maximum or minimum, parties would be out at all possible places trying to see the Moon rise or set behind high trial poles. At night these poles would have needed torches at the tops because any other marks would not be visible until actually silhouetted on the Moon's disc. Meantime some earlier existing observatory must have been in use so that erectors could be kept informed about the kind of maximum which was being observed; they would need to know the state of the perturbation.

Then there would ensue the nine years of waiting till the next standstill when the other four sites were being sought. The magnitude of the task was enhanced by the decision to make the same fore-

Table 3. Sites with menhirs or stones which may be backsights, to be used with Er Grah as a foresight, for lunar observations.

Site	Lat.	Az.	Alt.	Decl.	'Expected' decl.	
Kerran, small menhir	47°35'.9	136°13'	3'	-28°46'	-(e + i - s)	-28°47'
Kerran, dolmen	47°35'.9	136°29'	3'	-28°54'	-(e + i - s+ △)	-28°56'
Le Moustoir, menhir on dolmen	47°36'.7	118°31'±	-3'	-18°33'±	-(e - i - s)	-18°30'
Le Moustoir, menhir near dolmen	47°36'.7	118°09'±	-2'	-18°18'±	-(e - i - s - △)	-18°21'
Kervilor, stone C	47°35'.2	119°08'	-1'	-18°53'	-(e - i + s - △)	-18°52'
Kervilor, stone D	47°35'.2	118°27'	0	-18°27'	-(e - i - s)	-18°30'
Quiberon, Goulvarh	47°28'.4	46°02'	2'	+28°20'	+(e + i - s - △)	+28°38'
Stone near Goulvarh	47°28'.4	45°22'	3'	+28°43'	+(e + i - s)	+28°47'

Note: The 'expected' declinations assume e = 23°53'.8 (1700 B.C.), i = 5°08'.7, s = mean semidiameter = 15'.5, △ = 8'.7.

sight serve both standstills.   We can understand why this was considered necessary when we think of the decades of work involved in
cutting, shaping, transporting and erecting <u>one</u> suitable foresight.
It is evident that whereas some of the sites, such as Quiberon, used
the top of the foresight Er Grah, others, such as Kerran, used the
lower portion.   This probably militated against the use of a mound
with a smaller menhir on the top.   Much has rightly been written
about the labour of putting Er Grah in position, but a full consideration
of the labour of finding the site shows that this may have been a comparable task.

We now know that for a stone 60 ft high the siting is perfect.   We
do not know that all the backsights were completed.   But the fact that
we have not yet found any trace of a sector to the east does not prove
that the eastern sites were not used because the stones may have been
removed.   Perhaps the extrapolation was done by the simpler triangle
method or perhaps it was done at a central site like Petit Menec.

No one who sees Er Grah can fail to be impressed, or to ask the
reason for its being there.   Many explanations have been advanced but
they all fail to account for the sheer size of the stone or indeed for its
position.   The explanation we have given covers both size and position.
In use, both the height of the top and the vertical length were needed---
the top for backsights where the hills appeared behind the stone and
the bottom for the nearer backsights when the horizon was lower.   The
reasons for the choice of the position have already been given.

It is for the reader to decide whether or not we have collected
enough evidence to permit acceptance of our explanation.

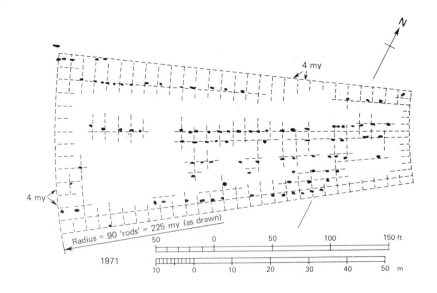

Part of the sector alignments at Petit Menec

THE OTHER PYRAMIDS

One anomaly of this book of anomalies is the de-emphasis of the Great Pyramid and other Egyptian pyramids. Not that these edifices are not marvels of ancient engineering, but rather that other pyramids are not less remarkable for their times and places. Indeed, pyramids are everywhere. In North America they are huge truncated earthen mounds. In Mesoamerica they are of masonry, with long flights of stairs leading up to diminutive enclosures. Pyramids on the Pacific isles are not so much impressive in size as they are startling in their appearances thousands of miles from continental influences. In England, Sillbury Hill is an immense pile of earth truncated at the top somewhat like America's Cahokia Mound. Was the urge to build pyramids carried around the world by a single culture? Why are all truncated? (Note that the Great Pyramid lacks a capstone and is thus truncated.)

Whatever the answers, pyramid building consumed a great deal of manpower and materials. Like the menhirs, dolmens, and stone circles, the pyramids seem to represent a global motif---something with ritual and occult significance. The crucial question may not be how the pyramids were built but why?

• North America

THE GREAT CAHOKIA MOUND
Peet, Stephen D.; *American Antiquarian,* 13:3-31, 1891.

One of the most interesting localities for the study of the prehistoric monuments of this country is the one which is found on the banks of Cahokia Creek, some twelve miles from the City of St. Louis. Here the largest pyramid mound in the United States is to be seen, and with it many other mound structures, which are as curious and interesting as the great mound itself. It should be said that this is the northernmost point at which any genuine pyramid mounds of the southern type have been recognized, but it is a locality in which all the peculiarities of that class of earth-works are exhibited. There is certainly a great contrast between these works and those situated in the northern districts; but the fact that this large group has been introduced into the midst of the northern class, and in close proximity to many specimens of that class, makes the contrast all the more striking and instructive.

The conditions of life in the different parts of the Mississippi Valley seemed to have varied according to the climate, soil and

scenery, but they are so concentrated into a narrow compass that one
may, by the aid of steam and the railroad train, pass in one day from
the midst of the wild savage hunters of the north into the very midst
of the works of the semi-civilized agricultural people of the south,
and may find the whole panorama of the prehistoric races unrolled and
the whole condition of society in prehistoric times rapidly brought before the eyes. Cahokia mound is at first disappointing, for it is not
as imposing as some have represented it to be, and yet the consciousness that a great population once swarmed here and filled the valley
with a teeming life made the spot a very interesting one. There was
also a double presence which was forced upon the mind---the presence
of those who since the beginning of historic times have visited the region and gazed upon this very monument and written descriptions of
it, one after the other, until a volume of literature has accumulated;
and the presence of those who in prehistoric times filled the valley
with their works, but were unable to make any record of themselves
except such as is contained in these silent witnesses. There is,
perhaps, no spot in the Mississippi Valley which has been oftener
visited by distinguished persons and no monument which has oftener
gone into history. Descriptions of it began as early as the time of
Marquette and the French missionaries; they appear again in the time
of Gen. Rogers Clark and the conquest of the country from the Indians;
they come out again in the time of the early explorers and travelers,
Brackenridge, Latrobe and others, and continue to the present day, ---
missionaries, early travelers, military generals, historians and
modern archaeologists vying with one another in describing the scene.
We shall offer no minute description of our own, but shall quote from
different travelers who have visited the spot and who have seen the
earthworks before they were so sadly despoiled by the aggressions of
modern days. Probably not one fifth of the mounds and earthworks
which formerly covered this broad valley, and which also surmounted
the bluffs adjoining, can now be seen. The growth of the great City
of St. Louis has destroyed the last vestige of the large group which
could once be seen there, and all of the pyramids, cones, "falling
gardens," terraces and platforms, which once attracted attention,
have disappeared. Twenty-seven large mounds once stood on the bluff,
making it memorable as the location of a large village, which was
similar in many respects to the one where the great mound now stands,
but they have been destroyed and can not now be studied.

We shall go back for our descriptions to the author who has given
the earliest and fullest account---J. M. Brackenridge. He says:
"There is no spot in the western country capable of being more highly
cultivated or of giving support to a numerous population than this
valley. If any vestige of ancient population could be found this would
be the place to search for it; accordingly this tract, as also the tract
on the western side (Mound City, now St. Louis), exhibits proof of
an immense population. The great number of mounds and the astonishing quantity of human bones dug up everywhere or found on the surface
of the ground, with a thousand other appearances, announce that this
valley was at one time filled with inhabitants and villages. The whole
face of the bluff or hill which bounds it on the east appears to have
been a continued burying ground. But the most remarkable appearances are the two groups of mounds or pyramids---the one about ten

miles above Cahokia (a village nearly extinct), the other nearly the
same distance below it---which in all exceed in number one hundred
and fifty mounds of various sizes. (See map.) The western side
(St. Louis) also contains a considerable number. A more minute
description of those above Cahokia, which I visited in 1811, will give
a tolerable idea of them all. I crossed the Mississippi at St. Louis.
After passing through the wood which borders the river, about half a
mile in width, I entered on an extensive plain and found myself in the
midst of a group of mounds, at a distance resembling enormous hay-
stacks scattered through a meadow. One of the largest, which I
ascended, was about two hundred paces in circumference at the
bottom. The form was nearly square, though it had evidently undergone some alterations by the washings of the rains. The top was level,
with an area sufficient to contain several hundred men. The prospect
from the mound was very beautiful. Looking toward the bluffs, which
are dimly seen at a distance of six or eight miles, the bottoms at this
place being very wide, I had a level plain before me, bounded by islets
of wood and a few solitary trees; to the right (the south) the prairie is
bounded by the horizon; to the left the course of the Cahokia River may
be distinguished by the margin of wood upon its banks. Around me I
counted forty-five mounds or pyramids, beside a great number of
small artificial elevations. These mounds form something more than
a semi-circle a mile in extent, to the open space on the river. Pur-
suing my walk along the bank of the Cahokia I passed eight others in
a distance of three miles before I arrived at the largest assemblage.
When I reached the foot of the principal mound, I was struck with a
degree of astonishment not unlike that which is experienced in contem-
plating the Egyptian pyramids. What a stupendous pile of earth! To
heap up such a mass must have required years and the labor of thousands. Were it not for the regularity and design manifest, the circumstance of its being alluvial ground, and the other mounds scattered
around it, we would scarcely believe it to be the work of human hands. "
Brackenridge also says: "The shape is a parallelogram, standing
north and south. On the south side there is a broad apron or step, and
from this another projection into the plain which was probably intended
as an ascent to the mound. The step or terrace has been used for a
kitchen garden by some monks of LaTrappe settled near this, and the
top of the structure is sown in wheat. Nearly west was another of
smaller size, and forty others were scattered about on the plain.
Two were seen on the bluff at a distance of three miles. I every where
observed a great number of smaller elevations at regular distances
from each other, and which appeared to observe some order. I concluded that a populous city had once existed here, similar to those of
Mexico described by the first conqueror. The mounds were sites of
temples or monuments of great size. "

We have given the quotation for the sake of showing the impressions
which were formed by the works when they were first visited and when
the country was in its native wildness, with no work of modern civilization to mar the scene. It will be learned from the description that
there were at the time several large groups of mounds---one situated
on the bluffs where St. Louis now stands; another on the bank of the
Mississippi River, not far from the present site of East St. Louis; a
third on the bottom lands, about ten miles below the old village of

Cahokia; the fourth about ten miles above the old village, which is
the group in which we are especially interested. We speak of this because there has been a general impression that the celebrated "Cahokia"
mound, or more properly "Monk's" mound, is a solitary pyramid, and
that it has no connection with any of the works in the vicinity. Mr.
Brackenridge unconsciously corrects this impression, for according
to his description the works of the entire region were all of them of the
same class, the majority of them having been truncated pyramids. It
should be said that there are lookout mounds at various points on the
bluffs, which command extensive views across the country into the
interior, and which must also have served as beacons or signal stations
for the villages which were scattered throughout the bottom lands. Two
of these are mentioned by Mr. Brackenridge as in plain sight from
Monk's mound. One of these is now called "Sugar Loaf." It forms a
prominent mark in the landscape, as its towering height can be seen at
a great distance. So favorable was the mound as an observatory that
the Coast Survey took advantage of it and made it a station for triangu-
lating. Our conclusion is that the whole system of works on the great
American bottoms was connected together, and that here at the mouth
of the Missouri, a colony resembling the race of southern mound-
builders had long made their home, but were driven off at some time
preceding the date of history by the hunter tribes, who came down upon
them from the north.

The terraced structure of Cahokia or Monk's Mound in Illinois

We here make a record of an observation which amounts to a new
discovery. It was noticed by the writer as he ascended the great mound
that it was in the midst of a large group of similar mounds; that the
mounds surrounding it were arranged in pairs---a conical mound and
a pyramid constituting a pair---and that each one of these separate
pairs was placed on lines which are parallel to the sides of the great
pyramid, and that they were all orientated, the sides always facing the
points of the compass. It was noticed also that in some cases the ground
was raised between the truncated pyramid and the conical mound, giving
the idea that there may have been here a chunky yard or play-ground,
the same as there was between the public squares and the rotundas,

which have been described by Adair and Bartram as common in the villages of the southern Indians. In one case, about half a mile to the east of the great pyramid, there was a high platform or pyramidal mound, and immediately adjoining it on the north was a large platform, but at a lower level and on the northeast corner of this platform, was a large conical mound, the three parts being in close proximity, the arrangement of the three reminding one of the relative location of some of the so-called sacred enclosures of Ohio, where a large circle intervenes between a small circle and a large square enclosure, the three being joined together by protecting walls. This discovery of the peculiar grouping of the surrounding mounds was made while looking down upon the scene. A very beautiful pair of earth-works stands immediately south of the great pyramid, each one presenting its sides covered with varied foliage, the golden autumnal tints being set-off against the silvery radiance of the little artificial lake which lay in the background. The size of the pyramids adjoining the great pyramid can be learned from the circumstance that nearly all of the large farm-houses in the region are built upon the summits, the pyramids being large enough to accommodate the houses, with their out-houses, barns, lawns and other conveniences of residence. One of these, the one at the west had been graded down about eight feet, but others were left at their natural height. The houses are arranged along the sides of the common highway, which here constitutes the line between two counties, the distance from one end of the group to the other being about three miles from east to west, and two miles from north to south. The arrangement of the group is peculiar. There are pyramids and conical mounds close by the side of the great pyramid; beyond these are similar works, making several pairs east and west and several pairs north and south of the great pyramid, all of them arranged with their sides facing the sides of the

Cahokia Mound as it appears today. (Illinois State Museum)

central pyramid, and all of them overlooked by its towering height.
There are also many artificial ponds, whose waters glisten beneath
the dark shadows of the many earth-works, making a varied scene.

2. As to the size and shape of the great mound, we shall give the
descriptions of others, for the reason that many of them have had
better opportunities for observing and measuring them than we have.
It may be said, however, that the descriptions which have been written
so vary in their details that we are uncertain which account to believe.

Squier and Davis speak of the mound, but seem to have given the
wrong dimensions. They say: "It covers not far from eight acres; its
summit has an area of about five acres; its solid contents may be roughly
estimated at 20,000,000 cubic feet. It is nearly ninety feet high, is
built in terraces, and is reached by a graded way which passes up at the
south end."

Mr. William McAdams says: "We have surveyed the group, and
found that the great pyramid is surrounded by seventy-two others of
considerable size within a distance of two miles. The largest axis of
the pyramid is 998 feet, the shortest is 721 feet, and it covers sixteen
acres, two rods and three perches of ground. He says: "After many
days of exploration and study, we believe the evidence to prove this to
be a group of the greatest mounds on this continent and perhaps in the
world, and possibly this was the Mecca or great central shrine of the
mound-builders' empire. Upon the flat summit of the pyramid, one
hundred feet above the plain, were their sanctuaries glittering with
barbaric splendor, and where could be seen from afar the smoke and
flames of the eternal fire, their emblem of the sun."

Prof. Putnam says: "Situated in the midst of a group of about sixty
mounds of more than ordinary size, several in the vicinity being from
thirty to sixty feet in height, and of various forms, Cahokia mound,
rising by four platforms or terraces to a height of about one hundred
feet, and covering an area of about twelve acres, holds a relation to
the other tumuli of the Mississippi Valley similar to that of the great
pyramid of Egypt to the other monuments of the valley of the Nile."
Dr. J. J. R. Patrick, residing in the vicinity, has made a survey of
the group and prepared two accurate models of the mound itself---one
of them representing the mound as it now exists.

Featherstonaugh visited the mounds in 1844, and says that the
settlement of the monks was on a smaller mound to the west, but at the
time of his visit the building in which they had lived had been leveled
with the ground. He also states that a Mr. Hill was living in a house
he had erected on the top of the great mound; that upon digging for the
foundation, "he found large human bones, with Indian pottery, stone
axes and tomahawks." We judge from Brackenridge's account that
there was no roadway to the summit in his time, but that the one which
now appears must have been made by Mr. Hill, the owner, and that the
well which is now in ruins was dug by him.

In reference to the present condition of the mound, we have to say
that an air of waste and ruin surrounds it; deep gullies are worn into
its sides, and it seems to be wrinkled and ridged with the marks of its
great age. See Plate I. Though surrounded by many other structures,
on which there are signs of modern life, this seems to be deserted.
The very house which was found upon its summit has been leveled to
the ground, and the home of the present owner, situated a little to the

rear of it, seems to hide itself in the shadows of the great monster.
It stands like a solemn monarch, lonely in its grandeur, but imposing
in its presence. Though the smoke of the great city may be seen in
the distance, and many trains go rumbling across the valley and through
the great bridge which spans the river, yet this monster mound stands
as a mute witness of a people which has passed away. It is a silent
statue, a sphinx, which still keeps within its depths the mystery which
no one has as yet fathomed. It perpetuates the riddle of the sphinx.
(pp. 3-9)

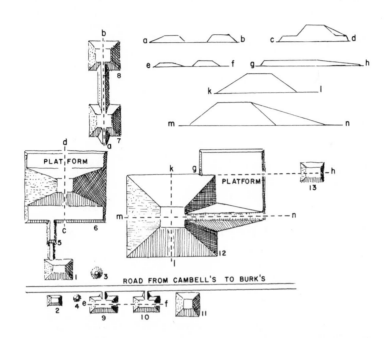

Complex of mounds at Seltzertown, Mississippi, taken from a later
section of the above article

TRACES OF AN UNKNOWN EVERGLADES TRIBE
Anonymous; *Science,* 73:sup 14, May 22, 1931.

First traces of the unknown prehistoric Indians who lived in the
Everglades have been discovered by Mr. Matthew W. Stirling, chief
of the Bureau of American Ethnology. Mr. Stirling has returned
from several months of archeological exploration in Florida.

On the very edge of the Everglades, near Lake Okechobee, Mr.
Stirling encountered a great plan of earthworks, elaborately laid out
in embankments and mounds, and covering an area a mile square.
So large and conspicuous are these earthworks, Mr. Stirling said,
that it is surprising that no previous explorer has ever reported

their existence or their significance. The nearest approach to anything like them are the famous Fort Ancient earthworks in Ohio, which
were also made by prehistoric mound-building Indian tribes.

The most prominent feature of the Everglades site is a flat-topped
rectangle of earth built 30 feet high and 250 feet long. This was
apparently the focusing point of attention for whatever ceremonies
were held at the site. Earthen embankments enclose a court in front
of this high place. Back of it a semi-circular bank of earth was
raised.

This is only a small portion of the earthworks. A curious formation consisting of a large semi-circular bank extends in front of
the high place and its court. And out from the semi-circle start a
number of parallel lines of banks with circular mounds at the ends.
Within the great semi-circle is a platform of earth six feet high and
a quarter of a mile long.

"The whole plan is laid out with remarkable precision," Mr.
Stirling reported. "The parallel lines are straight as a string, and
the semi-circles are so perfect that we can imagine some Indian
walking around a fixed point with a string held taut, to mark the
outline."
. . . .

THE LOST PYRAMIDS OF ROCK LAKE
Whitcomb, Ben; *Skin Diver*, 24–25, January 1970.

So, there were these seven divers 40 feet beneath the surface of
Rock Lake in Wisconsin on July 30, 1967. Above a dying afternoon sun
arrowed the last of its heat at kids hollering across bathing beaches
and hiding from their folks because they knew it was time to go home.
A few fishermen slumped on the blue surface, lines slack, drowsing
out the end of a fine July day.

But, 40 feet below it was already dark and cold enough to require
wet suits. The seven men moved through a thin fog of sediment that
hangs suspended in the lake throughout much of the year. On clear,
cold days the fog vanishes, and then you can look down deep into the
lake to its bed.

The seven were running out of light as the thin daylight filtering
to 40 feet began to wane, and they lacked more than light. A diver on
the right flank pulled his forefinger across his throat in the well-known
signal which meant his air supply was gone. He moved up from the line
of divers, exhausting a trail of balloon-sized bubbles as he huffed air
under pressure from his lungs.

The formation shrank. Man after man pulled his head back, aiming
upward for the surface, until only one man was left in the grey quiet,
flippers stirring ghost veils of suspended mud where they touched
bottom. He pulled his left arm back behind him and yanked at the ring-
handle of his five minute reserve air supply. A bleak darkness shaped
in the water ahead. His palm shot forward, made contact, and his

fingers crawled across a slanting rise of stone wall.

The diver struggling to eke out his air supply in the cold gloom of Rock Lake was John Kennedy of Lombard, Illinois. A government plant inspector at O'Hare International Airport, Chicago, John is a trained botanist who also is a cracking good scuba diver and a certified instructor. His lungs now tight with excitement, John angled across the long wall and followed its shape with his hands while his flippers drove him forward. He moved across a low platform rising five feet above the lake bottom. The stone sides slanted inward as they rose. He estimated the formation to be about 20 feet across and probably 40 feet from its shoreward end to the point where the slanting rock wall plunged down into the lake bottom mud.

John Kennedy had just relocated the Lost Pyramids of Rock Lake--- if that's what they really are. With his discovery, a half-century-old legend leaped back to life. He came up hugging three grapefruit-sized lumps of rock he'd pried from the low wall below. They were a necessary proof that there was something down there, and excellent proof it was, because that area of the lake is a mud bottom. There is an exposed rock-bottom in the east half of the lake, but not in the west half where John and his crewmates had been.

John's grapefruit-sized rocks continued to be valuable proof in the months that followed. Other divers went down but were unable to relocate John's rock platform. Diving buddies kidded him about "shallow water narcosis" until even John's ready grin looked a little tired as repeated efforts to relocate his lost bearings from the lake surface and from the air failed to turn up Rock Lake's lost pyramids.

The atmosphere turned even stickier when Lon Mericle's crack archaeological dive team from the Milwaukee Museum announced that it had spent four days diving in the lake after interviewing the numerous Lake Mills natives as to the likeliest spot for the pyramids to be found. They had come up with a clear zero.

Diver Mericle told a Chicago diving symposium on March 30; 1968, "We've spent a lot of time and we have interviewed a lot of local residents. I can only say that there is no trace of a pyramid in the area searched by our group. We laid our grids with divers in a line swinging about a central point. In many weeks of work, I'm sorry to say, we failed to find anything in the lake in the spots in which we worked."

No one just writes off the Milwaukee Public Museum as one more opinion. The Museum is famous for its underwater archaeological work---probably as famous in the midwest as is the University of Pennsylvania in the east. Milwaukee divers representing the Museum have uncovered a wealth of lost artifacts in the inland waters of Mexico.

At that point, John Kennedy might as well have given up and the pyramid tale would have gone back to sleep. Instead, he went airborne again. This time he came back with a series of color shots that picked out something dark and square on the pale mud of the lake floor.

But the real discovery came when Chicago diver M. R. (Mike) Kutska led his Narcosis Knights in a major assault on the lake. It was a cold Sunday when Mike's ten divers assembled in three teams to work across a promising area that had been pre-surveyed in reports that the Knights had carefully fitted together.

Kitska and two other men of his team dropped from their boat and began a sweep, positioning themselves along a 30-foot line. John made his mistake the previous July by not rechecking his bearings after he had made contact with his pyramid. Now, the Knights carefully held a line of reference, using a bearing due west of Bartell's Boat Rentals, a boat livery on the lake.

The three teams were having no luck when a pair of local fishermen suggested that they were probably 150 yards off the true site. These obliging and unsung pathfinders (Mike's eager crew failed to get their names) put Mike's teams over the formation using a fish fathometer as bottom sounder.

The Knights moved onto the new site and were down on the bottom within minutes. Like John Kennedy, the Kutska group found mud bottom. This in itself was encouraging, for the Milwaukee Museum team had reported that their unsuccessful search had been over a rocky bottom.

Mike's three divers came down almost directly atop a formation of heaped boulders that he guessed very roughly as 10-15 feet in height. Visibility was remarkably good in the lake that day (15 feet) and it was still early afternoon, only 2 p. m. The dying light that had hampered the Kennedy team search was not to be a problem now.

Mike carefully pointed out that he could only get a rough impression of the heaped rubble. It appeared to be 50-70 feet long and half that wide. The edges of the boulder formation ran in a straight line and ended in squared corners.

Minutes after Mike's team located the first mound, a second Knight's team located another which was more square-shaped than the first rock mound. Both mounds lay in 37 feet of water. Two other finds which were important were broken clam shells found deposited in one wall of the first sunken structure, along with a broken length of bone. History reveals that there was a Pre-Columbian Indian city near the lake called Atzalan. The inhabitants of Atzalan used shells and had a habit of eating their enemies and cracking open the long bones for the marrow. They also built low earth step-pyramids, leaving one at Atzalan.

Atzalan got its name from Nathaniel Hyer, who discovered a mounded formation east of Lake Mills in 1836. He named it after the legendary Aztec homeland which was abandoned when the Aztecs drifted south to Mexico City. Early scholars believed the Hyer mound pyramid at Atzalan dated to about 1300 or 1400 A. D. However, recent carbon datings at St. Louis pushed the age of the pyramids back to before 1000 A. D., 300 years earlier than previous estimates.

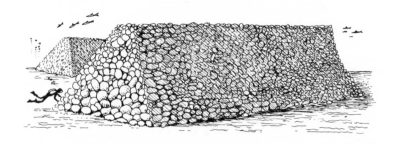

Artist's concept of the Rock Lake pyramids

The men who built Atzalan were outlanders. They came from the south and built a fort and an earth pyramid. They were uncomfortable neighbors, thought to be cannibals who fed on their victims. They may have died when their fortified city was besieged and burned, because the log walls were reduced to charred carbon at some point in its history.

It's now known that Atzalan was misnamed, that the dead city had no connection with Mexico's Aztecs. But it did have connections with earth pyramid builders to the south. The stones in the formations in Rock Lake is another question mark. The Mississippian mound builders worked with earth, not stone. Only Central America's pyramids are stone.

The whole Rock Lake problem simply lies in the question, "Why pyramids?" In the history of the world, nobody, nowhere, has made a practice of putting pyramids on lake bottoms. And it's not likely they could have built it before there was a Rock Lake, because the lake is a glacial lake, created by the Wisconsin glacier, making it 10,000 or more years old, according to geologists. Even though some divers have found tree stumps at the bottom of nearby Lake Michigan that are 6,500 years old, nobody was building pyramids even then---not anyone that archaeologists know of.

The pyramids are illogical. They shouldn't be there. They would be too old, and in a place where no person could have built them, so logically they can't exist. However, history is seldom logical, and logic or not, the pyramids of Rock Lake keep popping out of oblivion often enough to trouble the most logical students of American prehistory.

The records of pyramid sightings in Rock Lake began when brothers Claude and Lee Wilson returned from duck hunting on the lake in the early 1900's, before World War I. They told of seeing the top of a "pyramid" in the lake. A drought had baked the lake that year, and the water was six feet lower than normal. The Wilsons said they were able to touch this pyramid apex. They poked an oar over the side of their boat and about six feet down in the water they could push with the oar against the hard stonework of the pyramid. They described the stones as "teacup sized."

There is no record of an immediate rush of observers to the lake, but their story did begin the pyramid legend. Claude, later mayor of Lake Mills, never lost faith in the pyramid.

On April 11, 1936, Dr. Fayette Morgan, a Lake Mills dentist who was badly bitten by the flying bug, spotted the pyramids from his open cockpit biplane. It was one of those peculiarly clear days when the sky remains overcast but the lake water seems to grow as transparent as air. Morgan saw three formations he only called "bumps" on the lake floor.

He talked about it though, as did Mayor Wilson. Max Gene Nohl, holder of the world's diving depth record in 1937, heard about it in Milwaukee, Wisconsin. Nohl was interested because a little earlier that year, he had located one of the Rock Lake pyramids by dragging. His descriptions tallied with those of Claude Wilson. Nohl described a high-peaked narrow-topped pyramid:

"The pyramid is shaped in the form of a truncated cone. Approximate dimensions: diameter upper base, 3 feet; diameter at bottom, 18 feet; altitude, 29 feet. The construction is apparently of smooth stones set in a mortar. It is covered with a greenish, thin scum that rubs away easily and is bare in parts. "

John Kennedy had found a low platform with sloping sides of loose quartzite rock. The three boulders John salvaged are of water-rounded quartzite, typical of rock deposited in a stream bed. They don't resemble the "teacup-sized stones" of Nohl or the Wilsons. But Nohl and Kennedy do agree that the formation, or formations, lie on a mud bottom.

The ice-cream cone Max Gene Nohl and Claude Wilson described is like no Indian pyramid. Moundbuilder pyramids of the Mississippian group were squat, broad, low, with a flat top. The top was a ceremonial platform on which a thatch temple was probably built since all of the pyramid builders right up through the Maya and the Aztecs of Mexico used their pyramids for worship.

By early 1968, over six men had seen formations of some kind on the bed of Rock Lake. There is no longer any doubt that something is down there waiting to be found. However, even though the Wilsons, Dr. Morgan, Nohl, Kennedy and Kutska have reported the pyramids, many professional geologists and archaeologists say that the formations are nothing. It looks as if the diving fraternity will have to supply the additional needed evidence.

The odds of finding the strange "ice cream cone" pyramids made of cemented, teacup-sized stones described by Max Gene Nohl and the Wilson brothers seem low. But the odds that the typical low, four-sided pyramid mounds are down there seem to be rising. If they are there, why and how they got there will be even more puzzling than their existence.

Divers don't need to go to Central America for an adventure in archaeological mystery. Right in the Mississippi basin is the beginning of a trail of mysteries as ole as recorded time. And it's only 40 feet down.

THE GREAT MOUND ON THE ETAWAH RIVER, NEAR CAR—TERSVILLE, GEORGIA

Whittlesey, Charles; *American Naturalist,* 5:542-544, 1871.

This mound is situated on the river bottom, on the north bank, about three miles below where the railroad from Chattanooga to Atlanta crosses the Etawah river. Its base is an irregular figure, five hundred and eighty-five poles in circumference, covering about three acres. The bottom on which it stands is elevated eighteen to twenty-three feet above low water, and is seldom invaded by high water in any part. The mound is truncated, nearly flat on the top, which embraces about an acre of ground. This area is elevated fifty feet above the base, and seventy-three feet above low water. There is no high land within a quarter of a mile on either side of the river. Its slopes are very perfect and steep. Bushes, grass, vines, shrubs and trees grow luxuriantly on its sides and the level space on the top is annually planted in corn or cotton. There is a broad ramp or road fifty feet wide, commencing at the southeast corner which winds around the southerly face bending to the right, and reaches the summit on the west side. It has an easy grade for footmen and horses, but is too steep for vehicles. The mass of this mound I estimate at about one hundred and twenty thousand cubic yards, or about four-fifths of the contents of the British earth pyramid raised on the field of Waterloo. Rising over the alluvial valley where it is isolated it has an impressive aspect, like that of the pyramids of Egypt on a sandy desert. This valley, however, is everywhere rich and beautiful.

Like some of the larger pyramids it has two smaller ones which appear to be tenders. One is a square, truncated pyramid which stands one hundred feet east of the foot of the ramp and is twenty-two feet high, its flat top being about eighty feet on a side; its slopes, steep and perfect like the great mound. To this one there is no ramp or place of ascent.

The other is about one hundred feet due south of the southwest corner of the great mound, and is of about the same dimensions but has on its east side a ramp or graded way by which to ascend to the flat space on the top. Its sides and that of the other tender are from five to ten degrees west of the magnetic meridian.

All of this group are composed of the rich black alluvial earth of the adjacent bottom, with occasional lumps of red clay which constitutes the base of the river terraces that border the valley. About two hundred yards from the mounds on the north there are the remains of a ditch which has been mostly obliterated by cultivation and which encircles the group in a circular form a distance of about one-fourth of a mile, coming to the river below but not above. Within and without the trace of this ditch which the owner says had an interior embankment, there are low mounds partly plowed down. Near its upper or the easterly end, there are two large, oblong pits from which a part of the earth of the mounds may have been taken.

There are other small mounds in the valley below on both sides of the river. The valley is bordered by limestone bluffs about two miles apart which rise two hundred to two hundred and fifty feet above the river. On a rocky summit about two miles west of the great mound is what is called the "Stone Fort." It consists of a wall or heap of loose blocks of limestone surrounding the summit in an oval form, the largest diameter of the enclosure being two hundred and twenty poles. There are numerous openings in it at irregular intervals, some of them fifty feet broad. The space around the crown of the hill is clear of loose stones and this explains the existence of the wall, which has the appearance of a stone fence fallen down.

It does not have the appearance of a fort or stronghold, but of a high place dedicated to imposing ceremonies to which the people came up in all directions through the openings or passes in the line of stones. Probably, it was then as now covered with oaks. The crown of the hill is about fifty feet above the encircling wall, and presents from its summit a view of the valley and the country opposite that is hardly equalled for scenic beauty.

It is probably the work of the red man of our times and has no connection with the great mound or its builders.

....

• Mesoamerica

"CUICUILO---"
Willis, Ron; *INFO Journal*, 3:1-7, 1973.

In perusing archeological textbooks on ancient Mexico, you may come across a reference to a site called Cuicuilco, once south of the suburbs of Mexico City, now in danger of getting swallowed up in the city's urban sprawl. Cuicuilco is a four-step pyramid, round in form, now restored and slickified for the tourists to come and gape at. The books ascribe its construction at the earliest to perhaps 300 B. C. , a fairly respectable age, but they don't mention the fact that it is quite possible that Cuicuilco is one of the earliest "pyramids" in the world, perhaps antedating the great Egyptian pyramids by thousands of years.

Cuicuilco was hardly more than a shapeless mound with some scraggly trees growing on it back in 1922 when Byron Cummings received permission from the Mexican Government to begin excavation at the site. (1) The most significant thing he noticed about Cuicuilco before beginning to dig was that the great lava flow known as the Pedregal had partially engulfed and surrounded the structure. Cummings was particularly interested in the site when he learned that George E. Hyde, a geologist, had estimated the date of the Pedregal lava as being 7,000 years old. This would have meant that the structure had been in existence 2,000 years before the great pyramid-building epoch of the Egyptians.

A few days after his workers began to excavate, an unidentified light was seen over the top of Cuicuilco, which then passed slowly across the rocky surface of the Pedregal to the hill of Zacatepec. Cummings did not speculate on this mysterious light other than to say that it only reinforced his Mexican laborers in their idea that Aztec treasure must lie in the mound.

Slowly trenches were cut down through the Pedregal lava towards the base of the pyramid. Trenches were also cut on the top and sides of the structure since it was covered in places on top with dozens of feet of volcanic ash and detritus. To begin with, Cummings was not entirely sure that any structure of significant size actually lay beneath this mound, even though there were probably surface artifacts present. But in the Valley of Mexico, one can hardly take a step without treading on a relic of ancient man.

As the trenches deepened, several layers of archeological occupation were found interspersed with layers of volcanic ash. Gradually the shape of the pyramid was uncovered. It was a truncated cone, with four steps, 387 feet in diameter and stood 60 feet in height. The top step formed a circular platform 290 feet in diameter. The name Cuicuilco is an Indian name which signifies dancing, alluding perhaps to ancient religious rituals. It is curious that if the name really derives from its ancient usage, it has survived thousands of years when the structure was unused and covered with ashes and lava. It is also rather humorous that the name in Cumming's day was San Cuicuilco, or Saint Cuicuilco, a remnant of the Church's attempt to incorporate all profane religious places under their own wing. Did the Indians still recognize the spot as sacred?

Figure 1 gives a sketch of what Cummings found as he dug down through the approximately 25 feet of lava, ashes and other materials that partly surrounded and covered the sides of the structure. Below the Pedregal lava was found an archeological stratum today classified as Early Classical, 200 to 400 A. D. Below this was a layer of volcanic ashes. Below that were the remains of an intermediate culture. Below that was another thick layer of volcanic ash. Below that were the artifacts of a very primitive culture. Below that was a solid pavement which surrounded the pyramid which must be as old as the last construction period of the structure.

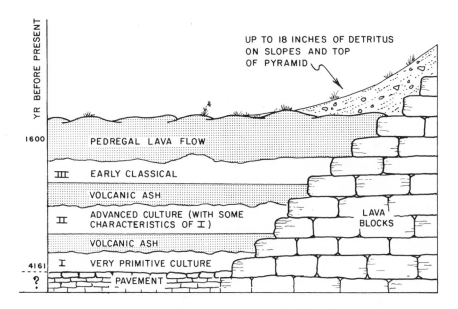

Layers of lava and ash engulfing the Cuicuilco pyramid near Mexico City

The pyramid itself was constructed of unformed chunks of lava, not of the Pedregal, which was much later of course, but of other lava which is found in the neighborhood. It was carefully laid with no filler, the sides of the pyramid forming a 45 degree angle. At the top the thickness of this lava facing was 70 feet; it is obviously much thicker at the base. The interior was filled with earth. Later work by Cummings showed that the structure had been enlarged at least two times, each time a new facing being put on it from the pavement up.

· · · · · · · · · ·

Cummings found 18 feet of sediment and ashes between the bottom of the Pedregal layer and the pavement surrounding the temple pyramid. He tried to estimate as well as he could how long it would have taken to accrete all these layers, and came up with the remarkable figure of 6, 500 years. This added to the 2, 000 year age of the Pedregal, means the pyramid would

Table 1

CUICUILCO RADIOCARBON DATES

Sample Numbers	Depth (Approx.)	Age	Error Margin (in years)
UCLA-228, Cuicuilco A-2	Associated with the Pedrigal Lava	414 A. D.	65
UCLA-206, Cuicuilco B-1	4 ft. 6 in.	160 A. D.	75
UCLA-205, Cuicuilco B-2	7 ft. 6 in.	15 A. D.	80
UCLA-602, Cuicuilco B-17	7 ft. 6 in.	240 B. C.	80
UCLA-208, Cuicuilco B-4	7 ft. 8 in.	150 B. C.	150
UCLA-603, Cuicuilco B-18	7 ft. 11 in.	280 B. C.	80
UCLA-207, Cuicuilco B-3	8 ft. 1 in.	650 B. C.	70
UCLA-209, Cuicuilco B-5	8 ft. 8 in.	350 B. C.	70
UCLA-594, Cuicuilco B-9	14 ft. 3 in.	610 B. C.	80
UCLA-210, Cuicuilco B-6	15 ft. 0 in.	2030 B. C.	60
UCLA-595, Cuicuilco B-10	15 ft. 0 in.	540 B. C.	100
UCLA-596, Cuicuilco B-11	15 ft. 4 in.	610 B. C.	100
UCLA-597, Cuicuilco B-12	16 ft. 8 in.	1870 B. C.	100
UCLA-598, Cuicuilco B-13	16 ft. 8 in.	1870 B. C.	100
UCLA-211, Cuicuilco B-7	17 ft. 6 in.	4765 B. C.	90
UCLA-212, Cuicuilco B-8	19 ft. 0 in.	2100 B. C.	75
UCLA-600, Cuicuilco B-15	20 ft. 8 in.	1980 B. C.	100
UCLA-599, Cuicuilco B-14	21 ft. 6 in.	1900 B. C.	200
UCLA-601, Cuicuilco B-16	21 ft. 6 in.	2161 B. C.	120

have existed 8, 500 years ago, or more. Though attracting a bit of notice at the time, archeologists fell over themselves ignoring a structure that would have required a fairly complex civilization in the Valley of Mexico several thousands of years before Sumeria or archaic Egypt flourished.

But there's more. Table 1 shows the result of recent C-14 datings on organic materials found not in the site, since this had been cleared by Cummings, but under the Pedregal lava in the same sequence nearby.

There are anomalous dates in the series which do not fit. This is common in the C-14 process. Like any good archeologist, I will ignore the dates that do not fit. But in general, the farther down one gets, the older the material is dated. The material at the level of the pyramid pavement is dated 4161 before the present. This indicates that a reasonable minimum age for the pyramid is not 2, 000 years ago, but over 4, 000. And it is probably much older.

. . . .

Around the pavement area to the south are two lines of upstanding stones which Cummings called "cromlechs." He speculated from this and other structures about the pyramid that, being very close to the great lake system of the Valley of Mexico, probably in ancient days nearly on the border of Lake Xochimilco, it indicated that there may have been danger of inundation at times, and that these were part of a dike system. Indeed, Cummings found fine, water-deposited silt between the facing stones, so that the pyramid at one time must have been immersed up to six feet deep in water.

Again we have positive indications that the ubiquitous "flood" story had some basis in fact.

There have since been found four smaller mound structures in the vicinity of Cuicuilco which are considered connected with the larger one. It is suggested that the whole site formed a rather large temple complex and possibly a city existed there. The difficulty in finding just what lies under the Pedregal, most of which is unmoved, is that it is difficult and expensive to dig and even blast through the lava flow and this is only done where there is some indication something will be found. We simply do not know what lies below these broad stretches of lava.

(1) Cummings, Byron; "Ruins of Cuicuilco May Revolutionize Our History of Ancient America, " National Geographic Magazine, 44:202-220, 1923.

THE LA VENTA FLUTED PYRAMID
Heizer, Robert F., and Drucker, Philip; *Antiquity*, 42:52-56, 1968.

In July 1967, the present writers saw the Great Pyramid of the Olmec archaeological site of La Venta in the state of Tabasco for the first time. This statement would be unremarkable were it not for the fact that we had looked at this impressive man-made hill of clay on many previous occasions; one of us during the excavation season of 1942, and both of us during that of 1955, and as well during several subsequent brief visits to the site, including one as recently as January 1967. The significant difference was that in July 1967, the Pyramid had been cleared of most of its heavy vegetative growth so that the actual surface and outline of the structure could be observed.
. . . .

First of all, geometrically the structure is not a 'pyramid' at all. The most precise definition of its form is that of a fluted (or grooved) conoidal frustum. However, to avoid use of this lengthy and unfamiliar designation, we continue to refer to it as the 'Pyramid'. On each of three exposures---they cannot properly be termed 'sides'---north, west, and east, occur three depressions which produce or set off four ridges or lobes, the outermost of each set forming a point of marked change of direction. If the basic plan were viewed as rectangular, though we do not believe that it should be, these outer lobes could be considered the corners.
. . . .

The northern exposure comes nearest to presenting a flat face. Its three depressions are shallower and the two central lobes smaller and less divergent in declination than those of the east and west exposures. The southern exposure is the only markedly irregular one, consisting as it does of two depressions marking off a comparatively large lobe which is 90 ft. wide at the base, and a straight, featureless border extending about 80 ft. out to the southeastern-most ridge.   The effect produced is one of incompletion---this is an impression, of course, and not a demonstrated fact.

The peculiar grooved or fluted form of the Pyramid cannot be explained satisfactorily until excavation is done.

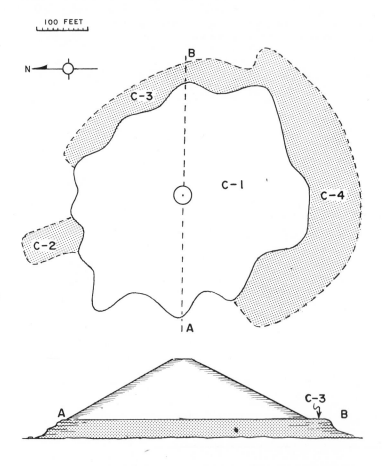

La Venta fluted pyramid, showing platforms C2-C3-C4

AN INTERPRETATION OF THE CAVE UNDERNEATH THE PYRAMID OF THE SUN IN TEOTIHUACAN, MEXICO

Heyden, Doris; *American Antiquity,* 40:131–147, 1975.

Discovery and Description of the Cave.   Toward the end of 1971 a depression at the foot of the main stairway of the Pyramid of the Sun in

Teotihuacan was examined by Ernesto Taboada, then in charge of the archaeological zone, who found the entrance to a seven-meter deep pit that had been filled in with rocks and rubble many centuries ago. When cleared, it revealed an ancient, semi-destroyed stairway cut out of bedrock, leading down the pit. This man-made stairway led to a natural cave-tunnel penetrating the bedrock underneath the pyramid and ending in a series of chambers in the form of a cloverleaf. Like the main facade of the pyramid, the mouth of this tunnel faces west. Archaeologist Jorge Acosta of the Institute Nacional de Antropologia was in charge and consolidating the find.

Federico Mooser, a geologist of the Mexican National University's Institute of Geology and consultant to the Institute of Anthropology, examined the cave. In his opinion it is a natural formation, the result of a lava flow that occurred more than a million years ago. As it flowed into the Teotihuacan Valley, bubbles were formed, and when new lava flowed over them, the bubbles remained as subterranean caves and often served as outlets for springs. The tunnel and four end chambers were formed this way, although the latter show man-made modifications. In addition, two other chambers branch off on either side of the tunnel about midway. Ancient Teotihuacan man also plastered the walls with mud and roofed parts of it with basalt slabs. Some of these slabs are in situ on part of the ceiling.

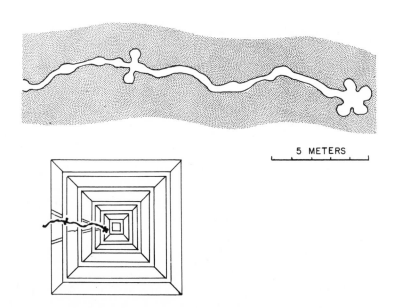

5 METERS

Curious tunnel under the Pyramid of the Sun, Mexico

The existence of this cave must have been known when the Pyramid of the Sun was built, inasmuch as the entrance to the 103 meter long tunnel coincides with the middle of the pyramid's original central stairway (discovered recently by Acosta during Son et Lumiere installations) and the tunnel itself ends in a series of chambers almost directly under the center of the pyramid.

Although no remains of mural painting or decoration are visible, the cave-tunnel once was partitioned by a series of walls that crossed from one side to the other. These walls indicate that parts of the grotto were closed off at different times. Originally 25 to 30 chambers were formed this way. Walls in situ when the archaeologists penetrated the cave contained openings in the upper half that from all indications were made long ago by vandals. The cloverleaf, or four-petal flower, at the far end of the tunnel is formed of four chambers. If different sections were sealed off one by one, this natural cloverleaf would have been the first to be closed. This suggests an early cult to caves in which these end chambers would have constituted the sancta sanctorum.

In these chambers numerous vessels of crude manufacture were found, together with two thin basalt discs beautifully engraved with anthropomorphic figures, one dressed in a jaguar costume, another as a bird. These discs have Gulf Coast stylistic influence and show evidence of having been inlaid with other material, which is missing. Both the clay vessels and discs were broken intentionally when placed in the chambers. The discs appear to have been mirror backs. (Excerpt)

• South America

THE ARCHITECTURE OF THE CIVILIZED RACES OF AMERICA
Peet, Stephen D.; *American Antiquarian,* 11:205–235, 1889.

The specimen which we first select in America for comparison is that of Cholula. This is one of the largest and perhaps one of the most ancient of the American pyramids. What is more, there is a tradition of the deluge connected with it. The method of constructing this pyramid was by terraces, the terraces being made on the sides of a natural hill, but the summit crowned by an artificial pyramid and temple. We here call attention to the resemblance between the American and the Chaldean pyramids. One peculiarity of the American pyramid was that it was partly natural and partly artificial. This was also the case with the Oriental pyramids. Reber says "that the terraced pyramids of Koyundjic was a terraced structure of three or four steps,

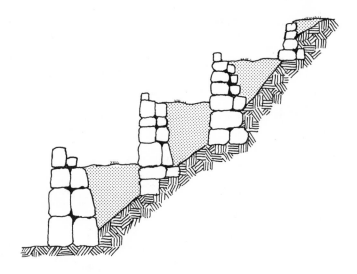

Terraces forming part of the "fortress" at Cuzco

situated upon a natural elevation. " The lower terrace is decorated
with pilasters in low relief. This is one of the earliest of the Oriental temples.

We refer to another specimen of an American pyramid to illustrate
this point. It is a pyramid found in Peru---a pyramid built in terraces,
the terraces on the side of a natural elevation. We do not claim this
to have been a temple, for it was a fortress---the fortress of Huatica.
Yet terraces on the side of the hill show how the pyramids in America
are constructed. There is another heap of ruins in Peru, a cut of
which we do not present. This was the temple of Pachacamac, twenty
miles south of Lima. It was constructed of terraces and was devoted
to the worship of a fish-god, and is said to have been resorted to by
pilgrims from all parts of the coast. Some maintain that the Incas
erected on the summit of this hill, a temple of the sun. There are
rooms in this temple which are filled with enormous quantities of
earth, though how it came to be there is unknown. The ruins are
largely artificial, but it is supposed that the central core of them is
natural, but that the terraced pyramids sustained or supported an
ancient temple of magnificent proportions.

Other specimens of American pyramids are found in widely separated localities and embrace structures which were devoted to very
different uses, but they show the American peculiarities. The pyramids were used here for fortresses as well as for temples. In fact
pyramids sustained palaces as well as temples and both were regarded
as fortresses. In Peru the differentiation may have been more marked,
for there are pyramids which were used for fortresses, others for
burial towers, and still others for temples, while in Central America
they were all combined in one.

Another point in connection with the pyramid in America is that

in finish and elaborateness it was unexcelled by any of the pyramids
of the Old World.   The Egyptian pyramids were very plain structures.
They were never covered with carving and never showed art or architecture at a high stage.   The terraced pyramids of Assyria were
much more advanced than these, but the pyramids themselves, if we
leave off the palaces which were built upon them, were not at all equal
to those in America.

We give two specimens of perfect pyramids which have been found
in America, namely, the pyramids of Copan and those at Teotihuacan;

Ruins of a stepped pyramid, Chicana Valley, Peru

these we think compare with any of the Egyptian pyramids in symmetry and beauty, though they are not as large.   If, however, we were
to restore the palaces which formerly stood near these pyramids and
could show the broad path of the dead, so-called, lined with the elaborate structures which have now disappeared, we should conclude that
the American civilization was fully equal to the Egyptian at the time
that the pyramids were built.   These pyramids are, however, not the
best.   There are pyramids at Tusapan and Papantla, which have their
exteriors built up with seven terraces, each terrace having an elaborate
cornice, with panels below the cornice.   Tall buttresses also project
from the terraces, forming a massive and elaborate finish to the whole
structure.   There is at Chichen Itza also a pyramid which has a stairway running up its entire side, which in massiveness and breadth and
elaborateness of detail is not exceled by any of the stairways of the
Assyrian palaces.   Charnay has spoken of this pyramid and has given
a new and interesting description of it.   The same is true of the pyramid of Uxmal, at Tikal, Kabah, Izamal and several other places.   The
south side of the pyramid at Izamal is built up of stone, laid without
mortar and rounded off at the corners.   On its side near the basement
stands a gigantic face, which was reproduced by Stephens, 7 feet 8
inches high, the features rudely formed by small rough stones fixed
in the side of the mound by mortar, and afterwards perfected by stucco.

The pyramid at Ake has also a face, and has also in its side a colossal head 13 feet high, formed by rough stones coated over with mortar, and one of the finest bas-reliefs, its principal subject being a crouching tiger with a human head, reminding us of the order of knighthood in which the tiger had the pre-eminence. It would appear from this that the pyramid in America combined the massiveness and solidity of the Egyptian, the terraced form of the Chaldean, the walled and palace-crowned quality of the Assyrian, and at the same time embodied the carved specimens which resemble the sphinxes of Egypt, and sustained on their summits temples and palaces which remind us of the Medean and Persian. There is certainly nothing in all this to show that the American architecture was of an inferior or low grade, but there is everything to show that it was equal to that of the civilized races of the ancient monarchies even in their most advanced stage. (pp. 212-215)

• Pacific Islands

SUN-CULT AND MEGALITHS IN OCEANIA
Rivers, W. H. R.; *American Anthropologist,* 17:431-445, 1915.

The conclusion so far reached is that the secret rituals of Oceania which have the sun as their object belong to an immigrant culture which has come from a widely distant part of the world. I have now to consider whether it is possible that this same people may also have been the architects of the stone buildings and images which form so great a mystery of the islands of the Pacific.

Here again I will begin with eastern Polynesia. The Areoi societies held their celebrations in an enclosure called marae or marai at one end of which was situated a pyramidal structure with steps leading to a platform on which were placed the images of the gods during the religious celebrations of the people. The marae was used for religious ceremonial unconnected with the Areoi societies, but there seems to be no doubt that the Areois were of especial importance in connection with it. In the pyramid of the marae we have one of the best examples of the megalithic architecture of Polynesia. One such pyramid in the western part of the island of Tahiti was 267 feet in length and 87 feet in breath at the base. All were built of large stones without cement, but so carefully shaped that they fitted together closely and formed durable structures.

In the Marquesas, another home of the Areois, there were platforms similarly constructed a hundred yards in length, and many of them shaped and closely fitting blocks of which these structures were composed were as much as eight feet in length. On these platforms were pyramidal "altars" and they were surrounded by enormous upright stones. This association of the distribution of the Areois with the presence of megalithic structures suggests that the immigrants to whom I have ascribed the cult of the sun may also have been the people who introduced the art of building the stone structures which have so greatly excited the wonder of visitors to Polynesia.

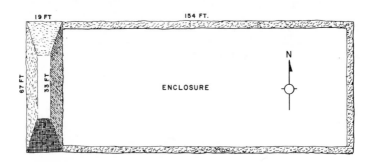

Marae Horoa, Moorea. Note the prominent pyramid

The part of the Pacific ocean where these stone structures have reached their acme in size and complexity is the Caroline islands. If there be anything in my hypothesis, we should expect here also to find manifestations of the religious ideas of those who founded the Areoi societies, and they are not lacking. In the Marianne or Ladrone islands there were associations of persons which seem to furnish an intermediate condition between the Areois of Tahiti and the occupants of the clubhouse of Melanesia. We know very little about these associations, but their relation to the Areois of the east is shown clearly by the name they bore, Urritois or Ulitaos, which is merely another form of the Tahitian word, Areoi, the latter word having suffered the elision of a consonant so frequent in Polynesia. Similar associations flourished in the Carolines, and though we know still less of them than of the Urritois of the Ladrones, we can be confident that they had a similar character. Societies very closely related to the Areois thus existed in this region in conjunction with stone structures similar to those of eastern Polynesia.

There is a remarkable point of similarity between the traditions concerning the origins of these stone structures and of the Areoi societies of Tahiti. The ruins of Nan-matal on the east coast of Ponape in the Carolines are reputed to have been built by two brothers, Olo-chipa and Olochopa. In the tradition of the foundation of the Areois of Tahiti, a very prominent part was taken by two brothers Orotetefa and Urutetefa. The interchanges between r and l, t and ch and p and f are so frequent in Oceania as to suggest that these two pairs of names are variants of one original, so that we should have in the traditions of these two groups of islands nearly four thousand miles apart a most striking similarity of the names of pairs of brothers to whom prominent features of the culture are ascribed. In one case the brothers founded societies whose aim it was to celebrate the annual changes of the sun, while rude stone buildings were the handiwork of the others.

A recent account by Hambruch shows that the resemblance between the Ponape and Tahiti names is not quite as close as would appear from previous records. Hambruch calls the two founders of the stone buildings, Sipe and Saupa but to put against this, he states that the place, Matolenim, where the structures were built, was formerly called sau nalan which means "the sun."

Though the resemblance in the names of the two culture heroes of Ponape and Tahiti is not as close as once seemed to be the case, it cannot be neglected. It may be that the two words have some meaning which would reduce the importance of the similarity, but taken in conjunction with the close resemblance of the names of the societies in the two places, it affords striking corroborative evidence supporting the conclusion suggested by the distribution of societies and monuments that both are the work of one people.

If the stone monuments and secret societies of Polynesia have had a common source, we should expect to find an association between the two elements of culture in Melanesia, and so it is. We know of stone structures in several parts of Melanesia, viz., the northern New Hebrides, Santa Maria in the Banks islands, Loh in the Torres islands, Ysabel in the Solomons, and Fiji. The Banks and Torres islands and the northern New Hebrides are strongholds of the secret cults, and though the only island in the Solomons in which we know of the existence of secret societies is Florida, there is a definite tradition that this society came to Florida from Ysabel. The distribution of stone structures in Melanesia is just as it should be if the ghost societies and the stone buildings were the work of one and the same people.

The evidence for the connection of stone structures with secret societies is even more definite in Fiji. The Nanga societies of Viti Levu take this name from their meeting places, oblong enclosures, consisting of two or more compartments, surrounded by stone walls. The resemblance of these enclosures to the marae of Polynesia has struck more than one observer and the similarity extends to detail. At one end of each main compartment of the nanga there were truncated pyramids which served as platforms, evidently representatives of the pyramids of the marae of Tahiti measured by Captain Cook. Further, both marae and nanga were oriented with their long axes east and west, though the two differ in that the pyramids were at the western end of the marae and at the eastern end of the nanga.

There is thus a remarkable correspondence between the distribution of stone structures and secret societies in Oceania which points strongly, if not yet decisively, to the introducers of the secret cult of the sun having been the architects of the stone buildings which form one of the chief mysteries of the islands of the Pacific.

It is even possible that we may have here the clue to the greatest mystery of all, the great stone statues of Easter island. There is reason to suppose that these statues are not so unique as is often supposed. According to Moerenhout, similar statues, though not so large, exist in the islands of Pitcairn and Laivaivai; he believes that such colossal figures once existed in many other islands, but have been destroyed or have fallen into ruins. In the Marquesas and Society islands, also, stone figures in human form have been found which are sufficiently like those of the smaller and more eastward islands to suggest a common origin. Moerenhout believes that such stone figures and statues had a common meaning and were all representatives of beings called tii whose function it was to mark the limits of the sea and land, to maintain harmony between the two elements and prevent their encroachment upon one another. I venture, though very diffidently, to extend the comparison. At one end of a clubhouse of Santa Maria in the Banks islands there are ancient stone figures which, in one respect at least, resemble the colossal statues of Easter island. In each instance the head is covered. This head-covering is very frequent in one variety of the representations of the human figure found throughout Melanesia, and is almost certainly connected with the importance of head-coverings in the ritual of the secret societies. It is therefore of interest that a head-covering should be a prominent feature of the statues of Easter island. Such a point of resemblance standing alone would have little significance, but taken in conjunction with the other correspondences and similarities pointed out in this paper, we must not ignore the possibility that we may have here only another expression of the art of the people I suppose to have introduced the cult of the sun into Oceania.

I cannot consider here how far it is possible to connect the stone work and sun-cult of Oceania with the megalithic monuments and sun-cults of other parts of the world. Megalithic monuments elsewhere are associated with a cult of the sun and the occurrence of this association in the islands of the Pacific ocean must serve to strengthen the position of those who hold that the art of building megalithic monuments has spread from one source. I must be content here to mention certain megalithic monuments of Polynesia which raise a difficulty.

The island of the Pacific which holds examples of megalithic structures most closely resembling those of other parts of the world is Tongatabu, where there are trilithic monuments so like those of Europe that the idea of a common source must rise to the mind of even the most strenuous advocate of independent origin. It is not possible at present to bring these monuments into relation with those of other parts of Oceania by connecting them with a cult of the sun, but Hambruch tells us that tradition points to the builders of the stonework of Ponape having come from Tonga. It may be that Tongatabu forms the intermediate link between the stonework of the Carolines and the megalithic monuments of other parts of the world.

I have dealt elsewhere with the relation between these Tongan monuments and the pyramids of other parts of Oceania, and have suggested that these two ancient forms of monument may be expressions of the ideas of two different streams of the megalithic culture. I cannot deal with this matter here; to do so would take me far beyond the relation of sun-cult and megaliths which is the subject of this article. (pp. 440-445)

• Europe

SILBURY HILL
Atkinson, R. J. C.; *Antiquity,* 41:259-262, 1967.

Silbury is the largest ancient man-made mound in Europe. It stands beside the Bath Road (A4) in north Wiltshire, about six miles west of Marlborough. It forms a regular truncated cone, with a flat top 100 ft. (30.5 m.) in diameter and 130 ft. (40 m.) high above

Silbury Hill, Wiltshire (Janet & Colin Bord)

the surrounding meadows. The base covers about 5.25 acres (2.1 hectares). A little below the top the profile is broken by a marked step or terrace; and there are traces of what may have been similar terraces lower down, on the north and east sides. It may be that the mound was built originally in the form of a stepped cone.

The material was obtained from an enormous encircling ditch, now largely silted up. On the east and north it is about 120 ft. (37 m.) wide, while to the west an extension reaches to 490 ft. (150 m.) from the base of the mound. To the south, where the ground rises, it is narrower and doubtless shallower, and is separated from the main ditch by two causeways of solid chalk. Most of it appears to be at least 16 ft. (5 m.) deep, with a drop to 21 ft. (6.4 m.) near the base of the mound.

The apparent volume of the mound today is about 12.5 million cu. ft. (350,000 cu. m.); but the volume actually piled up artificially is smaller, because the site stands on a sloping spur of chalk, the sides of which were scarped to continue the slope of the mound downwards. The present piled volume is about 8.7 million cu. ft. (250,000 cu. m.); but to this must be added a large part of the silt in the ditch, consisting of chalk rainwash derived mainly from the sides of the mound. The present volume of silt exceeds 5.5 million cu. ft. (155,000 cu. m.). We may therefore suppose that the original piled volume was, like the apparent volume today, about 12.5 million cu. ft. or 350,000 cu. m.

Excavations have been made in the mound or ditch on five previous occasions. In 1776 a shaft 8 ft. square was sunk from the centre of the top to the old ground surface, but apparently found nothing apart from a fragment of oak. In 1849 the Archaeological Institute, as an adjunct to its Salisbury meeting, sponsored the driving of a tunnel along the base of the mound to the centre. This revealed at the centre a primary barrow of chalk, clay-with-flints and turf, which was at least 80 ft. in diameter and 8.5 ft. high, and may be larger if the sec-

A terraced earthen pyramid, Merlin's Mount, Marlborough, Wiltshire (Janet & Colin Bord)

tion then recorded proves to lie on a chord and not a diameter [3]. Short lateral galleries showed that a part of the interior of this barrow was surrounded, and perhaps capped, by a convex layer of sarsen boulders. Apart from animal bones, nothing was found except some fragments of string, apparently made of grass. This and other indications suggest that organic material is exceptionally well preserved beneath the mound.

·········

As this article was being written, the BBC received from Isotopes Inc. of New Jersey a radiocarbon date (I-2795), for a mixture of antler fragments from the 1867 and 1922 excavations, of 800 BC ± 100. This is unexpectedly late, and we must await confirmation, or contradiction, from further material to be obtained from the forthcoming excavations, before we apply it unequivocally to the building of the mound. The Late Bronze Age, as at present understood, provides no suitable context for a major work of civil engineering of this kind.

·········

UNUSUAL ANCIENT BUILDINGS

If the pyramids of the preceding section had obscure purposes, so did many of the lesser buildings described in this section; viz., Scotland's brochs and Minorca's talayots. Another mysterious class of buildings consists of the rough-laid masonry structures in North America. Are all of these structures merely colonial root cellars, or were they built 2,000 years ago by wandering Europeans? Most impressive of all, however, are the great deserted cities, the ruins of which stand on lonely plains in Asia Minor, high in the thin air of the Andes, and on storm-swept Arctic shores. Here are signs of great civilizations that once prospered and raised magnificent walls, buildings, and monuments. Perhaps we have acclaimed the Greeks and Romans too loudly. Used to a sunny Mediterranean clime, could the engineers of classical antiquity have built Tiahuanaco at 12,000 feet?

• North America

WHO BUILT THE NEW ENGLAND CLOCHANS?
Perry, Phillip M.; *Popular Archaeology*, 2:4-9, no. 4, 1973.

Hidden deep in the woods of a New England village is a man-made hut, formed from local granite stones in the side of a hill. It's not a large cave, but it is an unusual sight in the otherwise untouched forest.

Noticing the dark hole in the side of the hill, you walk closer and inspect the cave. With some surprise, you see the blocks of stone have been fitted together without the use of mortar. You move closer and gaze into the cave with the small opening. Five feet down you see the stone blocks curve upward toward the ceiling, which is really the point where the curved walls of the beehive-like structure come together. At the very entrance to the stone house, a large rock rests on top of the opening.

Who built this eerie hut in a hill? you ask. How long has it been here? How many others like it can a person see in New England? What was it used for?

Alas, the answers to these questions cannot be given as readily as they can be demanded. These beehive, underground huts in New England hillsides have been the object of heated study, conjecture and counter-conjecture for decades. They can be seen in Massachusetts, Vermont, New Hampshire and Connecticut. But no one can give satisfactory explanations for their existence.

. . . .

There are really two types of these stone huts in New England. One is the underground variety, with the stone lintel at the opening and the heavy capstone at the top of the cave. A second variety is built above ground, always on the top of a hill. These are made of huge slabs of rock weighing several tons each, which are not indigenous to the area. Found within a range of 150 miles north and south in the New England states, the largest such cave is in Upton, Massachusetts. The cave itself is 10'5" high, and it has a tunnel 14' long and 6' high.

. . . .

A REPORT ON THE PEARSON STONE CHAMBER, UPTON, MASS
Whittall, James P.; *Early Sites Research Society, Bulletin*, 1:12-22, 1973.

On April 26, 1893, under the non-de-plume "Pratt Pond, Jr.", Daniel Fiske wrote the following story for the Milford Journal.

A Deserted Haunt of Unknown Origin

"Our main object in penning this legend is to rescue from oblivion a relic of the unknown past within our own environments, forgotten by a few of our oldest citizens and unknown to all others around which may linger an atmosphere of mystery or of romance.

We venture to assert that on account of its secluded location there are not fifty living citizens who have ever been within this mouldering enclosure and many hundreds who born in Upton for a period of four-score years, were ignorant of its existence.

In our younger days in company with other small boys, when playing "Injun", we should occasionally enter its portals and ruminate on its unknown origin, the object of its construction, and its occupants as our untutored intellects would admit. It was one of the fine days of last October that we in company with an old schoolmate visited this haunt for the first time within the past forty years and after considerable perambulation among rocks and brush, one succeeded in finding the entrance to the walled cavern, and we compelled to here acknowledge our lack of courage, for we insisted on our companion entering first for fear we might be a victim of some venomous reptile. If our pen has already created a desire in the mind of the

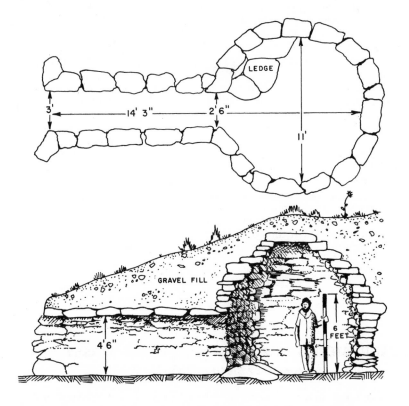

The dry masonry underground chamber at Upton, Massachusetts

reader to visit this relic we advise no one to make this attempt without a guide and with a lighted lantern. The best time to visit it is in October or November when the foliage of the trees and brush has fallen. It has been completely obscured by the snow the past winter. Its location is near the old Hopkinton road which is well known to have existed nearly 200 years. From our youth we have occasionally sought information of our oldest citizens whose ancestors lived on this road from 150 to 200 years ago and they were as ignorant of its origin as we of today. In outward features it resembles the mounds of western states and may have been constructed by the same race existing before the red men.

Though the entrance is partially obstructed by crumbling rocks, enough remains to indicate that it was originally in the form of a common door. From the entrance is a narrow rolled passage of some twelve feet in length leading to the cavern or chambers some fifteen feet in dimensions. The walls are built of small stones easily handled, but the canopy is of stones mammoth in size, which in our imagination could only be placed in position by sliding down from the declivity above.

The floor is of the same material. The mind of the visitor on entering this mysterious place, is immediately led to muse or ponder on its origin, its builders and purpose of erection. Speculation only may lead to a conclusion that may be some consolation for lack of historical proof.

It is well known that the eastern portions of Massachusetts and Rhode Island were visited by Norwegians at the beginning of the eleventh century and it is thought the stone tower at Newport was erected by them and the hieroglyphic marks on the Dighton rock are their work. They may have visited distant inland portions leaving their imprint in lasting monuments. It has been thought by some that this relic was erected as a place of refuge from the attack of some warlike nation previous to the Indian race. Since its abandonment by man, no doubt it has been a refuge for bears, wolves and other wild animals, as well as of the bat, lizard, venomous reptiles or worms of the slimy brood. Near by the entrance is a portion of a curiously wrought stone, partially imbedded in the earth. Some of the lines represent portions of a circle, others resemble those of the Dighton rock. It is possible this stone may have been a part of the original gate or door.

If one well versed in anthropography or in archaeology could have a chance to inspect and give a thorough study to this curious stone, it is possible some insight might be gained that would lead to an interesting local history of the past. Till then doubtless the origin of the subject of this legend will remain as oblivious as to those of former generations. "

THE SANDYSTON STONE CHAMBER IN NEW JERSEY
Lenik, Edward J.; *NEARA Newsletter,* 7:56-57, 1972.

This underground chamber was formed by a natural crevice in the bedrock. The roof was made by capping the crevice with thirteen large flat stones. Earth and brush now cover the roof.

In 1966, my acquaintance Mr. Milton Monks reported that the back of the chamber opened up into a "large room". He had visited the site "15 years ago". However, our examination showed that the rear of the chamber terminates in bedrock with no "large room" present.

About 30 feet to the north of this underground chamber is a small rock-shelter and a possible second underground chamber. The roof of this second chamber has collapsed. Perhaps this possible second underground chamber might contain a "large room" as reported by Mr. Monks.

The famous Indian site known as the Bevans Rockshelter, is approximately 100 yards south of the underground chamber. This rockshelter is at the bottom of the bedrock ledge and borders a present day swamp. The Bevans rockshelter was excavated approximately thirty years ago by Dr. Dorothy Cross of the New Jersey State Museum.

The area to the north of the underground chamber was farmed in previous years. A stone barn foundation lies just to the east of the chamber and a second stone foundation is about fifty feet to the southwest.

A large area in front of the entrance to the chamber has been filled with domestic trash. This trash is approximately two to three feet deep and consists of coal, coal ashes, glass and pottery fragments. An examination of the surface material indicates a 19th century date for the dump.

According to Mr. Milton Monks, the interior of the underground chamber has been dug several times by Indian relic collectors. Further exploration should be done on the roof of the chamber, hopefully to get some charcoal for a carbon date. The area in front of the chamber should also be excavated in order to accurately date the period of trash dumping, and farm occupation nearby.

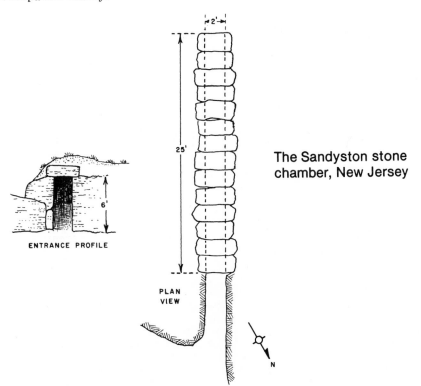

ENTRANCE PROFILE

PLAN VIEW

The Sandyston stone chamber, New Jersey

ARCHITECTURE IN THE STONE AGE

Peet, Stephen D.; *American Antiquarian,* 22:367-382, 1900.

There are stone-heaps, or rock-circles, in North Carolina which are very well built, but which retain the shape of a primitive hut. Dr. Thomas says:

"They are placed upon the solid rock foundation, the earth having been removed, and a level space left, from ten to thirty feet in diameter. Centrally in this was placed a layer of flat stones, with the best edge inward, around a circle about three feet in diameter. Upon the outer edge of these, others were placed with their outer edge resting upon the prepared foundation, running entirely around the circles, the stones of one layer breaking joints with those below. Outside of the inner row, with the edges resting

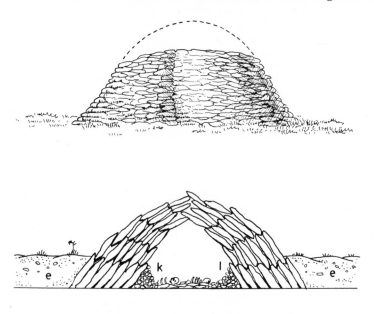

Stone burial vaults in North Carolina

on it, other circles were added, until a diameter ranging from twenty to fifty feet, and even more, was attained. The height of these piles was found to vary from four to eight feet, sometimes ten feet; but in all cases the circular space, or opening in the centre, continued to the top. These stone heaps were built at a point overlooking the Kanawha River, from which the valley could be distinctly seen for several miles. A somewhat different type of these heaps have a triangular cavity, and were undoubtedly burial places, and were not built up with as much care."

Dr. Thomas also speaks of conical stone chambers as situated in North Carolina. They were located on the farm of Rev. T. F. Nelson, in Caldwell County, and were covered over with a mound, but were placed in a

circular pit about thirty-eight feet in diameter, which had been excavated
to the depth of three feet. The stones were built up around the bodies,
which were found still standing, and they showed more or less evidence
of fire, as did the skeletons. (pp. 376-377)

FIRE-SWEPT CITY OF ANCIENT MAN IN TENNESSEE
Anonymous; *Science,* 58:sup 8, July 20, 1923.

Charred and blackened remains of a beautiful prehistoric Indian
city, destroyed by fire long before the advent of the white man, but
formerly covering an area of 500 acres and defended by a palisaded
wall and breastworks more than a mile in length, have been discovered in two bends of the Harpeth River near Kingston Springs, Tennessee,
by W. E. Myer, special archeologist of the Smithsonian Institution.

Mr. Myer, who has just returned to Washington after two and a
half months' excavation at this ancient site, declared that no other old
Indian town in the United States was laid out with such artistic skill as
is evidenced in the structural plan of the great mounds of this large
fortified place.

On one bed of the river is a great hill which was artificially shaped
by the ancient builders from bottom to top. Three wide terraces were
built at various levels along this hill, and its original summit was cut
away until a level plaza, about 1,000 feet in length and 500 in breadth,
had been formed. On this level plaza they had erected a large mound.
Around the edge of the plaza and the terraces other mounds had been
formed. The sun-baked clay used in the construction of ancient earth
lodges was found surrounding the open plaza and along the terraces.

In addition to this great central mound on the bold terraced hill,
which formed the most striking feature of the city, there were within
the walls five other eminences which had also been leveled into plazas.
These yielded many traces of the ancient earth lodges and other evidences of the former inhabitants. The remains of about thirty mounds
of various sizes have been found. On the edge of the terraces were the
earth lodges of the common people. The sacred temples and council
houses and the earth lodges of the chiefs and sub-chiefs had probably
been placed on the summits of ten of the largest mounds.

The upstream portion of the ancient city was defended on the water
side by perpendicular cliffs of the Harpeth River. On the land side
many traces still remain of the ancient breastworks, which extended
for about a mile and a half and originally had wooden palisades about
10 feet in length firmly embedded in their tops. These palisades
formed a wooden wall which had been plastered on the outside in order
to make scaling difficult by an enemy. Along this wall at intervals of
about 150 yards were found earth bastions which had formerly supported semi-circular wooden towers. The enemy advancing to attack was
therefore subjected to fire from the defenders along the main wall
and also an enfilading fire from the warriors in the towers on these

bastions.   Faint traces of the wooden towers and of the wooden palisades were found.   The great length of the wall to be defended indicates that the city must have contained several thousand inhabitants.

All the buildings whose traces were uncovered appeared to have
been burned.   Under an overturned wall the charred remains of the
woven-reed tapestry which had formerly hung on the walls of the building were discovered, and Mr. Myer and his assistants secured plaster
casts of this ancient work of art for the Smithsonian Institution.   No
object of white man's manufacture was found on the site.   Everything
denoted great age.

Beyond all question this town had been lived in and destroyed long
before the coming of the whites into the region, while the Indians who
claimed this section of Tennessee stated to the first whites that their
Indian forefathers had found these remains lying silent and deserted
when they arrived.
· · · · · · · · · ·

PHOTOARCHAEOLOGY

Strandberg, Carl H.; *Photogrammetric Engineering,* 33:1152-1157,
1967.

About 130 years before Columbus landed in the New World, the inhabitants of the village site shown in Figure 1 constructed bastioned fortifications, surrounded by dry moats.   This site is located in Lyman County,
South Dakota, about 22 miles south of Pierre, the state capital.   During
this same period in history, my ancestors from southern Sweden constructed similar fortifications in Finland, Western Russia, and other

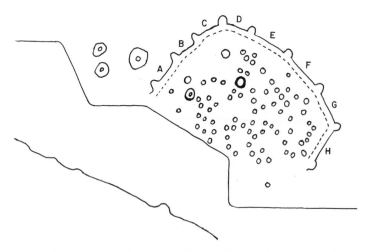

Sketch of soil marks caught by aerial photography, Lyman County,
South Dakota. The markings apparently indicate elaborate pre-
columbian fortifications.

areas then under Swedish control. I bring this point out because this similarity, and other evidence, tend to prove that early Norse explorers visited the New World between the year 1000 AD and at least as late as 1362 AD. This thesis is controversial; particularly to Italians as evidenced by their reaction to the Vinland Map. I reopen this controversy, however, because many bits of evidence, for which archaeologists have no satisfactory explanation, indicate the possibility of late Viking age Scandinavian penetration into the middle of North America.

THREE DRY-LAID MASONRY STRUCTURES IN THE NORTHERN ROCKY MOUNTAINS
Kehoe, Thomas F.; *American Antiquity,* 23:430-432, 1958.

The features consisted of 3 small hemispherical structures of dry-laid masonry. Structure 1 was built of tabular sandstone slabs laid horizontally in even courses to form a dome. The profile of the broken wall suggests that the slabs were more carefully aligned for the interior surface, and that earth may have been mounded up on the outside. The slabs were of varied sizes, and in places smaller stones appear to have been used for chinking. The entire structure exhibited the same careful construction; it is possible that the slabs were roughly trimmed for greater uniformity before being laid. The floor was lined with sandstone slabs 1 inch in thickness and 1 foot in length, producing a regular flagged surface. Apparently no mortar of any type had been employed in the construction. The dimensions were: diameter, 4.7 feet at the base (north-south); height, 1.7 feet at the center. Although one side of the wall had been destroyed, the east-west diameter was 3.6 feet to the break, and no doubt had once extended at least an additional foot. The top of this structure was 6 inches below the ground surface, and a large tree, 1.5 feet in diameter, was growing over it, one of the roots causing the dome to sag. The western side of the structure may have been exposed, since it lies on a hill slope. An entry may have been placed in this side, but the activities of the road crew had demolished it. Subsequent to the visit the entire structure was buried under rock debris from the road.

Structure 2 lay about 50 yards east of Structure 1 on the same terrace. This structure had collapsed prior to current road construction, though perhaps from earlier road building---if not from natural causes or a defect in construction. At present the feature appears as a mound of dirt and slab rock debris, 10 feet east-west by 8 feet north-south. A depression in the center of the mound about 3 feet across consists principally of the slab rock debris, presumably the remains of the collapsed structure. A large slab located on the lip of the depression suggests that an entry may have been present in the top, closed by this slab. In effect this structure appears to have been similar to the first.

Structure 3 is located on a higher terrace, in an area of dense brush,

overlooking Crystal Creek and about 1/4 miles west of the first 2 structures. It is in an excellent state of preservation and under no immediat e
threat of destruction. It is a semisubterranean, roughly hemispherical
vault, of dry-laid masonry but significantly different from Structure 1 in
construction: the walls of this structure were built of large unshaped
blocks of stone, varying in size, heterogeneously laid in uneven horizontal courses, leaving an irregular interior face and a corbelled effect.
There was a little chinking with rocks, but no evidence of mortar.
Fallen wall material lay on the interior floor. The maximum interior
width at the base was 4.4 feet and the maximum height 2.2 feet. An
opening faced approximately northeast. The structure, on flat ground
rather than on a hill slope, was capped by a large, thick slab.

· · · · ·

MYSTERY PEOPLE OF THE ARCTIC

Rainey, Froelich G.; *Natural History*, 46:148-155 +, 1941.

We have now found an "Arctic metropolis," many times larger
than anything previously thought possible in this part of the world
and inhabited by people whose material culture differed markedly
from that of the Eskimos as we know them.

· · · · · · · · · ·

One morning in June, 1940, when Magnus Marks and I returned
to begin the second season of digging at Ipiutak, we became aware
of the astonishing extent of the ruins---and through a peculiar circumstance. At that time of the year the grass and moss on the bar were
just beginning to turn green. Owing possibly to the fertility action
of the refuse beneath, the growth over the house ruins was slightly
taller than on the surrounding plain, and consequently it retained the
yellow cast of dead grass for a few days longer than that on most of
the bar. Thus we could see long avenues of yellow squares, marking
the house sites, extending east and west along the north shore.
Within the next few days we hurriedly charted the location of the yellow
squares and found that there were five "avenues" lined with houses,
as well as short cross-blocks of houses arranged at right angles to
the thoroughfares. There were over 600 houses on the completed
chart. Later numerous test pits disclosed that there are probably
200 additional houses buried beneath so much sand from the beach
that they cannot be discerned on the surface. The town was nearly
one mile long and a little less than a quarter of a mile wide.
The arrangement of the houses, the similarity of the implements
found in all 23 houses excavated, the fact that none were superimposed
over older structures, and the absence of any large refuse deposits
covering any of the village, lead us to believe that the majority of the
houses were actually occupied at the same time. With an average of
five persons to a house, the village would have a population of 4000,
a seemingly incredible number of inhabitants for a hunting village on
the Arctic coast.

· · · · · · · · · ·

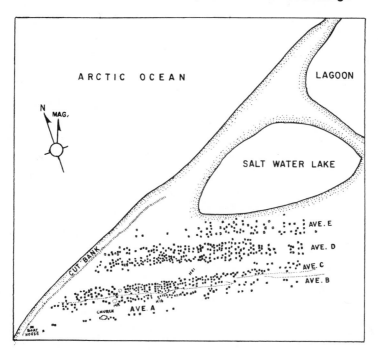

Plan of the buried Arctic city of Ipiutak. Approximately one mile long.

One of the most striking features of the Ipiutak material is the elaborate and sophisticated carving and the beautiful workmanship, which would not be expected in a primitive, proto-Eskimo culture ancestral to the modern. This suggests that the people of this Arctic metropolis brought their arts from some center of cultural advance and that they were immigrants from some southern region where their forebears had a well-developed Neolithic or New Stone Age culture adapted to the hunting of both land and sea mammals. Higher centers of primitive culture lie closer to the Arctic coast in eastern Asia than they do in America. Therefore it is toward Asia that we turn in our search for the origin of the Ipiutak people. A peculiar motif in their carved objects, which has not been uncovered anywhere else in America, is a spiral made of two elements carved in the round. Such a motif does occur, in relief, on carvings of the historic Ainu people of Japan and among the Amur River tribes of northeastern Asia. Furthermore, the exceptionally fine flint tools of Ipiutak appear to be more closely related to Neolithic flint work in northeastern Asia than to the coarser work of northern North America.

. . . .

PREHISTORIC TOWERS AND CASTLES OF THE SOUTHWEST
Fewkes, J. Walter; *Art and Archaeology,* 7:353–366, 1918.

One aim of the student of the antiquities of the Southwest is to answer satisfactorily three questions: Who were the Cliff Dwellers? When and how long did they flourish? and, What became of them? In other words the archaeological student of a particular area is called upon to determine the condition and relationship of man's culture when he first entered that area, at what time he developed its pecular character, when it reached its zenith, and when, declining, it ceased in what form or geographical locality supposed survivals of this phase of growth still exist, and what condition of human culture preceded it in other areas most closely allied to its pristine condition, are problems connected with other culture subareas. At present these questions cannot be answered, decisive data being wanting; but we can collect facts bearing on them and scientifically study the new material which may ultimately afford a solution of the problems involved.

The character of the prehistoric human population of the area considered in the following pages is a problem in the domain of the archaeological methods of research. The population of this region left no recorded history; we do not know even the language of the people, but simply that they were unfamiliar with letters and destitute of hieroglyphic methods of transmitting their thoughts. There are but two methods of rehabilitating the past of this long-forgotten race: The objective material from which we can gather information of their culture are architectural and ceramic remains, and minor objects associated with them. The architectural material is of the finest character; for the buildings of this prehistoric people were not surpassed by the products of any aboriginal tribe north of Mexico. The pottery belongs to the most ancient, often extinct types, antedating the more highly differentiated products of more modern epochs. The testimony of both architecture and ceramics indicates a people in an autochthonous condition, unmodified by acculturation of alien tribes. The object of this article is to discuss the structure of one type of prehistoric building confined to a limited area and to compare the various modifications of this type. The material upon which it is based was obtained in 1917 in field work for the Bureau of American Ethnology.

The situation of towers in caves, on mesa tops, on bowlders, or at the bottoms of canyons is not regarded as important in a study of their morphology. The main thing is their structural characters, their external forms and annexed rooms. For convenience in study they are considered under five more or less artificial divisions.

1. Simple towers of round, semicircular or rectangular ground plan without annexed rooms.

Although towers are widely distributed in the Southwest there is no better locality in which to study their differences in form than in the Hovenweep district, Utah. Here the walls of the several types show exceptional preservation and excellent masonry. None of these, however, still have roofs or floors in place, although elsewhere the ends of roof beams project from the sides of piles of rock, evidently remains of towers. Rows of small openings in the standing walls show the position of former floors or roofs, and indicate that these buildings were often two or three stories high.

The stones of which towers are built exhibit both the excellence and the defects of aboriginal masonry. They are almost without exception artificially dressed, and their exposed surfaces are covered with pits, the markings of rude stone hammers. They were laid in horizontal courses, sometimes emplecton, often not tied or bonded, the masonry showing other defects of the aboriginal mason. The size of these stones varies at different heights; in some instances the lower courses were constructed of stones some of which might be classed as megaliths. The foundations were sometimes made of small flat slabs of rock, above which were laid courses of larger stones capped by smaller ones. Superficial incised figures no doubt formerly existed on their surfaces, but these, if present, have now become illegible. The masonry is not equally good in all sections of the walls.

The stones were laid in adobe mortar, some of which is now washed out, and the intervals between courses were chinked with spalls, many of which still remain in place, but the majority have fallen out, judging from their presence at the foot of the walls. The rooms within show signs of former plastering which has almost completely disappeared from the surface of the outer walls. Here and there the walls are pierced by small openings, irregularly arranged, probably formed by the omission of stones. These openings are easily distinguished from the holes for ends of floor beams, being as a rule round and lined with adobe plaster. Their directions are at all angles to the face of the walls. Larger openings, as rectangular doorways and windows, also occur. These have well-made stone lintels and thresholds, the latter sometimes slightly raised above the foundation, as in cliff-dwellers' doorways. These openings in a few instances have been filled in by masonry which rarely shows as good work as the original wall. The uprights and tops of many openings have been enlarged by mutilation of vandals or by natural destruction since the towers were deserted. T-shaped doorways, or those in which the lower part is narrower than the upper, occur in the walls of upper stories in several towers. The foundations were constructed on a solid base, whose surface was not leveled by cutting down the rock; in order to bring the foundation for the first course to a proper level flat stone slabs were introduced with no regularity. The angles of square and semicircular towers are plumb, their surfaces perpendicular, slanting slightly inward from base to top, and often showing a slight bulge or curve which adds to their picturesqueness. Whether this marked entasis was intentional with the builders was not determined. A settling of the walls, especially when the foundation walls were constructed on fallen bowlders, has occasionally thrown walls once vertical several degrees out of plumb.

Both square and rectangular towers sometimes have their angles rounded, affording an easy gradation from angular into oval, rounded, and semicircular forms. Many of the angular-walled or rectangular towers have two or more rooms annexed in such a way as to suggest a later addition (fig. 1). In the case of multi-roomed, oval and D-shaped towers there is no evidence of secondary outside additions, as the external lines of the outer wall are regular. The semicircular tower in the west wing of Hovenweep Castle shows evidences that the square room now found on its south side was constructed after the tower was built.

Two large buildings on the south rim of Square Tower Canyon, popularly called the Twin Towers, are good examples of towers with multiple rooms. The ground plan of the smaller one is horseshoe-shaped, with an entrance on the east or straight side; the larger has a like form, but

Square type of tower, Hovenweep National Monument, Utah

the doorway is on the south. Both stand on a rock separated a few feet from the edge of the cliff. Their interiors are divided into a number of rooms by a median wall with cross partitions. Somewhat similar multi-chambered towers more regularly semicircular in form occur in Yellow Jacket Canyon, the typical one here figured standing on a terrace of the canyon side, near the Littrell Ranch. The falling of the straight wall on its south side has revealed the partitions of rooms in its interior showing an arrangement not very unlike that of the larger of the Twin Towers of the Square Tower Canyon group. It is evident that these multi-chambered towers are morphologically unlike pueblos and cannot be classed as such, if we limit the term to buildings having a circular subterranean room with mural banquettes and pilasters, enclosed by rectangular rooms. Moreover, they have lateral entrances which are also foreign to the pure kiva type. While evidences of habitation are not wholly absent, their forms depart so radically from that of permanent dwellings that we may well doubt whether they were primarily constructed for domiciles.

Nearly opposite the mouth of Dawson Canyon, a tributary of the Yellow Jacket, there is a simple semicircular tower, accompanied by a circular depression on a terrace halfway down the side of the cliff. Scanty evidences of rectangular rooms occur in the neighborhood, but a pueblo of considerable size formerly stood on the edge of the canyon far above it. When towers are not united to pueblos the pueblo to which they belong is generally found not far away, showing that while they are not habitations they stand in intimate relationship to pueblos, whose inhabitants we have every reason to believe erected them. [In the interest of brevity, only the first of the five classes of towers is described.]

• Mesoamerica

A NEW TYPE OF ARCHAIC RUINS IN CHIAPAS, MEXICO
Russell, S. Robert; *American Antiquity,* 20:62-64, 1954.

This report outlines the discovery, in 1953, of ruins in the state of Chiapas, Mexico. In ground plan, architecture and construction these ruins, so far as I can determine, show no obvious relationship to old empire Maya ruins some 100 miles to the east. Neither do they exhibit easily identified similarities with the Valley of Mexico sites.

The ruin most thoroughly studied consists of a 200 by 680 foot integrated rock complex of very squat structures inclosed by a low wall or rampart. No structures exceed 15 feet in height. The commanding elevation of the complex was obtained by building in on top of a great, field-rock mound, which in turn was built on an elongated natural hill. At the base the mound is approximately 700 feet long, with a varying width between 300 and 400 feet. In one place, on the south side where the hill was indented, the mound is approximately 70 feet high. Its average height is probably about 25 feet.

The builders utilized multiton, weather-formed boulders lavishly in foundations and supporting walls. Some of them have been rough-squared. Structures and the rampart are built of, or faced with, rough-squared limestone slabs. A size of between 3 and 4 feet square by 8 to 10 inches thick appears to have been almost standardized.

. . . .

This complex is built upon a large foundation-mound of piled field rock and is oriented almost east-west. The north side of this mound slants up to a massive vertical wall upon which the complex stands. This wall is built of large, weather-made boulders some of which are multiton. A few appear to have been roughly-squared. Because the complex floor rises in a series of four levels, the height of this supporting wall increases from 15 to approximately 50 feet. It is 650 feet long.

. . . .

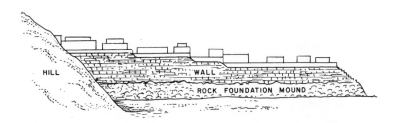

HILL   WALL   ROCK FOUNDATION MOUND

Complex #2, Chiapas, Mexico, showing the great north wall

PREHISTORIC RUINS OF HONDURAS AND YUCATAN
Maudslay, Alfred P.; *Nature,* 57:568-571, 1898,

In a country where water is so scarce, it is only reasonable to suppose that the inhabitants would have devised some means of storing the
precious fluid; and in the existence of numerous "chaltunes" we have almost certain evidence of the means of storage most commonly employed.
These chaltunes are "single chambers of a vault-like appearance, built
from ten to fifteen feet beneath the surface of the ground, and communi-
cating with the outer world by means of a narrow well-like opening placed
near the apex of the vaulted roof." They are somewhat irregular in shape,
but the prevailing form is shown in the following section.

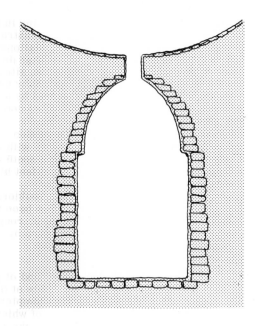

Section of a chaltune

Mr. Thompson paid particular attention to the chaltunes amongst the
ruins of Labna, a neighbourhood where---if the opinion that they were
used for the storage of water be correct---it is likely that they would be
found in considerable numbers, as the nearest permanent water supply
is found at the Cave of Loltun, twelve miles distant. Mr. Thompson is
of opinion that many of the rougher class of chaltunes were formed in the
cavities or pockets from which the white earth, called by the natives
"zahcab," had been taken. "This earth is of a peculiar character, and
served the ancient builders, as it does those of the present day, as a
building material to mix with lime in place of siliceous sand, which is

practically unknown in Yucatan. " The other chaltunes are well-built
chambers, having their walls, roof, and floor of dressed stones, and
finished with a coating of fine, hard stucco. In the ruins of Labna, each
edifice and each terrace was found to be provided with one or more of these
subterranean chambers, the largest of which, however, would not hold
more than 10,000 gallons.

Many of the chaltunes had become hopelessly ruined, and many were
filled up with earth and rubbish; but some of them had been purposely sealed up by the ancient inhabitants, and these presented a new and interesting
field for investigation. Human bones and various objects of human workmanship were found among the deposits at the bottom of the chambers; and
Mr. Thompson is led to the conclusion that many of these singular structures, after having been first used as reservoirs, were finally used as
depositories for human remains, probably secondary burials, in connection with some special rite, after which the entrance of the chaltune was
closed and cemented.

ATLANTIS UNDISCOVERED---BIMINI, BAHAMAS
Harrison, W.; *Nature*, 230:287-289, 1971.

In 1969, J. M. Valentine described what he called an "archaeological
enigma" consisting of "pavement-like stones---15 feet off North Bimini".
Since then, newspaper reports, at least one magazine article and two
books have suggested, first, that there is a seawall or roadbed submerged at about 7 m off the north-west coast of North Bimini and,

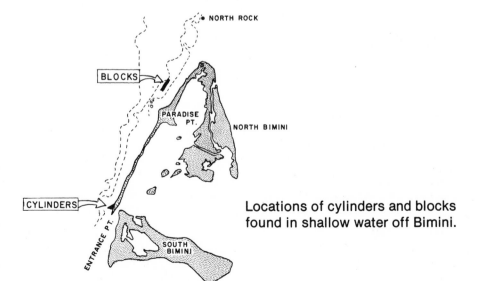

Locations of cylinders and blocks
found in shallow water off Bimini.

second, that sections of pillars which seem "to have been carved from natural stone" lie at shallow depths off Entrance Point. Last October an advertisement for one of the books, <u>Atlantis</u>, by R. Ferro and M. Grumley, appeared in the <u>New York Times</u>, confidently reporting that although ultimately it may turn out that Atlantis is no more than a legendary pot of gold . . . Ferro and Grumley discovered unmistakable traces of an ancient civilization---exactly where and when Edgar Cayce prophesied the re-emergence of Atlantis.

These occurrences have now been carefully investigated, using SCUBA gear, underwater cameras and hand tools. Most of the underwater work was done by Dr. R. J. Byrne and Mr. M. P. Lynch, who also helped in the interpretation of the data. We were guided to the sites by Mr. Pino G. Turolla, said to have been the original discoverer.

The most obvious "pavement-like stones" or blocks form single or double lines roughly parallel to the present shoreline. The blocks here are between 60 and 90 cm thick, somewhat pillow-shaped in cross section, their originally right-angled corners having been trimmed back, chiefly by boring molluscs and sea urchins. All of the blocks are of coarse-grained limestone lying on a stratum of denser limestone of finer grain. Shifting sands cover this underlying formation in most places, giving the impression that the blocks have been placed there. Erosion at the interface of the two rock types has caused many of the largest blocks to fracture, either under their own weight or when storm swells have caused heaving and fracturing.

Although casual inspection of structures such as the fractured rock of Fig. 2B might suggest small slabs that have been cut and fitted, closer examination of the opposing faces of the lifted and the unmoved pieces indicates an exact correspondence of bedding planes and surface morphology, so that all pieces are from the same original block. Similarly, the margins of adjacent large blocks correspond to one another, indicating that all blocks have developed by fracturing of an originally coherent formation. At no place are blocks found to rest on a similar set beneath. Samples of several blocks indicate that all are composed of shell-hash cemented by a blocky calcite, a type that originates only in the fresh water vadose or phreatic zones. The rock was thus almost certainly lithified during the lower relative sea level of the Pleistocene.

The geological setting of the blocks is important. The three small islands off Paradise Point are composed of a cemented wind-blown sand (eolianite) above a cemented shell-hash, with an interface roughly 1 m below low water. The beds of cemented shell-hash gravels and marine sands extend to at least 2 m below MLW, wo that the sequence of blocks of coquina limestone overlying marine sand limestones to the north-east of the islands is not surprising.

The blocks are believed to have originated as follows. A shell-hash gravel was deposited in shallow water as relative sea level fell during the most recent emergence of the Bahama Banks, and later brought into the fresh water environment. The materials were cemented and joints formed in the material, as is usually the case with limestones. After two sets of practically right angle joints had developed, submergence of the area brought the jointed coquina limestone first into the breaking zone of waves and then the offshore zones. Wave action probably caused much of the initial separation into blocks, but when the formation was farther offshore the destructive activity of marine life would have become dominant.

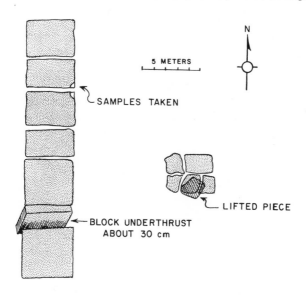

The overall result is a field of blocks that at first sight appear to have been fitted together, and this has led to statements such as, (some) "human agency must have been involved". The blocky remains of the limestone outcrop are, however, no more enigmatic than other subaerial or subaqueous outcrops of jointed limestone found in various stages of fracture and decay in the north-western Bahamas.

The cylinders, previously called "pillars", raise different considerations. They were found in grooves in the limestone country rock running roughly perpendicular to the present shoreline. Such grooves are common at Bimini and other Bahamian islands. Two of the cylinders are composed of marble and have flute-like marks parallel to the long axis. The wavelength of the crests is about 15 cm and their height about 1.5 cm. The remaining cylinders consist of what is most probably an early natural cement. All of the cylinders are encrusted with a layer of whitish $CaCO_3$, a few mm thick. Although several of them have been attacked by boring molluscs and sea urchins, destruction has been hindered by periods of burial by sand.

Table 1 Eight Measurements of the Circumference of
a 68.5 cm Long Cylinder, by 10 cm intervals

Incremental distance (cm)	Circumference (cm)
0.0	135 (end)
10.0	152
10.0	160
10.0	165
10.0	163
10.0	157
10.0	147
8.5	142 (end)

Thin section examination of one of the marble samples indicates that it consists of calcite (90%) and quartz (8%) together with muscovite, pyrite and sphene.   It is the melamorphosed equivalent of a calcite-rich lime-stone containing a small amount of clay.   The marble is not native to the Bahamas, so that it would have had to be transported at least a few hundred miles to Bimini.   Georgia is probably not the source and there is only a small chance that it could have come from Vermont (unpublished communication from J. B. Lyons).   A possible clue to its origin is the pyrite content.

The cement cylinders are also composed of material which is not indigenous to the Bahamas (unpublished communication from R. Perkins).   On balance, the material seems to be a hydrated natural cement.

Mr. P. Klieger of the Portland Cement Association, Skokie, Illinois, has supported this opinion on the basis of X-ray and petrographic analy-sis, as has Dr. R. C. Mielenz (Master Builders, Cleveland, Ohio) on the basis of petrographic analysis.   Dr. R. Nurse of the Building Re-search Station (England) has examined a thin section and concludes that it is a high temperature product and not an oxychloride cement and that "it resembles the 'grappier' made from the overburnt product of lime kilns".

Mrs. Bryant Mather, US Army Corps of Engineers (unpublished com-munication), says that the material consists of "calcite, brucite, a com-plex calcium aluminum hydrate, quartz, hydrogarnet, a little ettringite and some sort of calcium aluminoferrite", suggesting that the material is a hydrated natural cement manufactured after about 1800.   The material also contains widely separated particles of partially carbonized coal, supporting the belief that it is a simple natural cement from lime kilns in the United States, England, France or Belgium.   Long-term action of seawater on the set material would account for sulphate, chloride, and perhaps part of the magnesium, but an important proportion of the mag-nesium is an original constituent of the cement.

The most striking aspect of the cylinders is the constancy in size and shape of the whole ones.   They are all barrel-shaped, about 70 cm long and 50 cm in diameter (Table 1).   It seems most likely that the objects were formed by cement hardening in barrels or casks.   The wooden con-tainers would have by now been broken up and lost.   The most likely ex-planation of the marble and cement cylinders is therefore that they are construction materials that were being transported by ship when, either by shipwreck or design, they came to rest on the seafloor off Entrance Point.

• South America

THE PRIMEVAL MONUMENTS OF PERU COMPARED WITH THOSE IN OTHER PARTS OF THE WORLD
Squier, E. G.; *American Naturalist*, 4:1-17, 1870.

The arid plain to the south of the town of Acora, near the shores of Lake Titicaca, and twelve miles distant from the ancient town of Chucuito, is covered with remains of this kind, of which Fig. 1 is an example; and on the western border of the plain, at the base of the mountains which bound it in that direction, are some of the better class of chulpas, round and square, built of worked stones, to which I shall have occasion to allude in another place.

A modification of the second class of chulpas, which I have described, or rather an improvement on them, is to be found among the ruins, so called, of Quellenata to the northeast of Lake Titicaca, in Bolivia, and at many other places in the ancient Collao. Here the inner chamber or vault is formed, as in the case of those already noticed, by a circle of upright stones, across the tops of which flat stones are laid, forming a chamber, which often has its floor below the general level of the earth. Around this chamber a wall is built, which is carried up to varying heights of from ten to thirty feet. The exterior stones are usually broken to conform to the outer curve of the tower, and the whole is more or less cemented together with a very tenacious clay. Nearly all are built with flaring or diverging walls; that is to say, they are narrower at their bases than at their tops. Sometimes this divergence is on a curved instead of a right line, and gives to the monument a graceful shape. In Quellenata I found only one skeleton in each of the chulpas I examined; and none of the chulpas had open entrances. Similar structures in shape and construction occur in great numbers among what are called the ruins of Ullulloma, three leagues from the town of Sta. Rosa in the valley of the river Pucura. But here the chulpas have openings into which a man may creep, and all of them contained originally two or more skeletons.

Returning now to Acora. As I have intimated, within sight of the rude burial monuments already noticed as existing there,---and which so closely resemble the cromlechs of Europe,---are other sepulchral monuments, showing a great advance on those of Quellenata and Ullulloma. They are both round and square, standing on platforms of stones regularly and artificially shaped, and are themselves built of squared blocks of limestone. In common with the primitive and typical forms of the same class of monuments already described, these also have an inner chamber, vaulted by overlapping stones, after the fashion of the earlier approximations towards the arch. They differ, however, in having each four niches in the chamber or vault, placed at right angles in respect to each other. The sides of these niches converge a little towards their tops, as do most of the Inca niches, windows and doorways. In these niches were fastened the bodies of the dead, in squatting or crouching postures.

Figure 4 is a view of a double-storied, square chulpa, with a pucura or hill fort in the distance, occurring near the Bolivian town of Escoma, on the eastern shore of Lake Titicaca. I introduce these cuts to show some of the variations in this class of monuments. Escoma is on the same side of Lake Titicaca with Quellenata, bur sixty miles to the southward; and it is a curious fact, that while at the latter place all the chulpas are round, at the former they are all square.

Pucura or hill fortress of Quellenata with chulpas

The sides of all the square chulpas appear to be perfectly vertical, and near their summits we find a projecting band or cornice. Their tops seem to have been flat. On the other hand the round chulpas here swell out regularly up to the ornamental band or cornice, and terminate in a dome.

These features, however, are still better marked in the ruins of Sillustani, where the chulpas, in respect of size, elaboration of design and workmanship, take their highest form. Here we find them built of great blocks of trachyte and other hard stones, fitted together with unsurpassable accuracy, the structure nevertheless preserving some of the characteristic features of the first and rudest form of the chulpa. The lower course of stones is almost invariably composed of great blocks of which the unhewn portions are set in the ground, and these support a series of layers, not always regular in respect of thickness, nor uniform in respect of size, but which have their sides cut on exact radii of the circle, and their faces cut with an accurate bevel upward to correspond with the swell of the tower. The stones forming the dome are not only cut on accurate radii, but the curve of the dome is preserved in each, and they are furthermore so cut that their push or plunge is inward towards the centre of the structure, thereby tending to give it compactness and consequent strength. There are many other interesting architectural features connected with these remains of Sillustani, the enumeration of which is not necessary in order to illustrate the particular question before us.

Some of the chulpas of Sillustani have double vaults or chambers, one above the other, and others have a double row of niches, in a single chamber, with a cist, carefully walled up, sunk in the earth below. There are a few built of rough stones plastered and stuccoed over, and painted, with inner chambers also stuccoed.

Cross section of a chulpa

Now, in all these varieties of the burial monument called the chulpa, from the rude pile of rough stones at Acora, so much resembling the European cromlech, through every variety of form and phase of skill to the fine towers of Sillustani we discover common features, a common design, and many evidences that all were equally the work of the same people. If so, do the ruder monuments mark an earlier and possibly very remote period in the history of that people? And do the various stages of development which we observe in this class of monuments, correspond with like stages in the development of their builders? Or did they build the rough tomb for the poor and insignificant, and the grander and more elaborate monument for the rich and the powerful, as we do today? (pp. 3-9)

THE TRUE ARCH IN PRE-COLUMBIAN AMERICA?
Befu, Harumi, and Ekholm, Gordon F.; *Current Anthropology*, 5:328-329, 1964.

While Chichen Itza does not provide the example to prove incorrect the

often stated "rule"---that the true arch was unknown in the New World---
there is fairly good evidence that the principle was understood and applied
at least once by the Maya.   This occurance is in Structure XII, Room 2,
at the site of La Muneca in southeastern Campeche, that was discovered
by a Carnegie Institution survey of the region in 1933 (Ruppert & Denison
1943:8, 25-26, Fig. 22, 23, plates 3, 4A).   The vault was incomplete, unfortunately, but the evidence leaves little doubt that a true arch is indicated.   Section and elevation drawings taken from Fig. 22 and 23 of the
report are reproduced here.

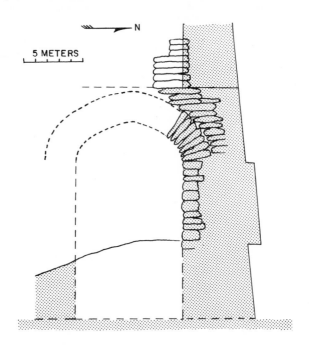

True arch in precolumbian America?

THE ANCIENT RUINS OF TIAHUANACU

Anonymous; _Pan American Union, Bulletin,_ 37:513-532, 1913.

A city so old that even the legendary lore of the Incas, who traced back
an unbroken line of kings to the eleventh century, is dumb concerning the
people who built it; a city which 1,000 years ago had been so long dead that
even song, story, and tradition had forgotten every vestige of its history.
Such is the old city of Tiahuanacu, whose ruins are crumbling surely, but
very slowly, into dust not far from the southern shore of Lake Titicaca.
When the first of the invading Spaniards saw the ruins and splendid
masonry of the time-scarred walls they asked the native Indians who had
built these monuments of a long-forsaken city and some answered: "They

existed before the sun shone in the heavens, " others said they had been raised by a mythical race of giants; still others that they were the remains of an impious people, whom an angry deity had converted into stone because they had refused hospitality to his messenger or viceregent.

The first authentic account handed down to us anent these particular ruins is that of the observant Spaniard, Cieza de Leon, who investigated them during his stay in the country about 1540, while they were still in a better state of preservation and had not yet become the prey of vandals and other thoughtless folk who, for over three and a half centuries have utilized the beautifully carved stones of these ancient temples, palaces, doorways, and walls as legitimate rock quarries from which to gather building material for everything from hovels to public buildings, from pavements for patios to church walls. Garcilasso de la Vega is another of the old Spanish chroniclers who notes these ruins and adds to our little store of knowledge of pre-Incaic civilization.

Among the archaeologists of more recent times who have been fascinated by the problem of Tiahuanacu may be mentioned E. George Squier, who, in his "Peru---Incidents of Travel and Exploration in the Land of the Incas, " goes into most gratifying details and gives us many original illustrations of the ruins. E. W. Middendorf, a German scholar and student of archaeology, who lived in Peru for some 25 years, gives a splendid account of them in the third volume of his "Peru-Beobachtungen und Studien uber das Land und seine Bewohner, " illustrated with original photographs and drawings. Sir Clements Markham also gives a brief description of some of the most interesting features in "The Incas of Peru, " while the latest publication, and the most elaborately illustrated, dealing with the problem, is that of Arthur Posnansky, in his "Guia General illustrada para la investigacion de los Monumentos prehistoricos de Tiahuanacu e Islas del Sol y la Luna, " published in La Paz in 1912.

The little present-day village of Tiahuanacu is located on the railroad which connects La Paz, the modern capital of Bolivia, with the port of Guaqui on Lake Titicaca, and may be reached in about two hours from the former place. The ruins of ancient Tiahuanacu, covering an area of about a square mile, are not over a half mile from the village.

A traveler stopping in the little town, and ignorant of the close proximity of the ruins, would be astounded to observe the number of beautifully cut stones built into parts of adobe huts of the most primitive character, and sometimes forming portions of a squalid patio. A doorway to a dilapidated, thatch-roofed hut, may have a lintel or jamb formed by an artistically carved stone. In the walls of the little Catholic Church and in those inclosing its yard, and even in the paving, may be seen these smooth stones. The pedestal on which is mounted the stone cross in front of the church is made up of them, while on either side of the gateway to the inclosure stands a carved stone idol whose lines, marred by the ravages of time, still show the artistic skill of the ancient sculptors who wrought them.

Thus the ruins of the ancient city have furnished much of the material to build the village of to-day, and while the strict utilitarian may find no fault with this work of destroying the artistic monuments of a hoary antiquity to cater to present needs, to the student of archaeology it seems almost like desecration. The writer has been informed that the Bolivian Government has recently enacted a law forbidding the carrying off or injuring of the portions of the ruins still left intact by vandal hands.

A description of all of the antiquities found in these interesting ruins can not be attempted in a short magazine article, so only the most striking features may be dealt with.

As stated, the ruins lie about a half mile southward from the village and are separated from it by a shallow valley and a small brook, on a broad and level plain. Probably the first objects that would attract the attention of the visitor are the rows of erect stones, some of them but roughly shaped, while others are accurately squared and cut and fitted into walls of fine workmanship. Closer inspection reveals long sections of foundations, with piers and lower portions of stairways; great blocks of stone with moldings, cornices, and niches cut with geometric precision; great monolithic doorways, ornamented with symbolical figures cut in high relief; and hundreds of smaller, rectangular and symetrically shaped stones lying promiscously about the plain.

The central and most conspicuous feature of the ruins is a great rectangular mound of earth, originally terraced, each terrace being supported by a massive wall of cut stones, the whole evidently having once been surmounted by stone structures, parts of the foundations of which are still to be seen. This section of the ruins is called the "fortress" by some archaeologists, while Posnansky gives it the name of the "Cerro Akapana." Its sides, like those of all the other ruins found here, coincide very nearly with the points of the compass.

Immediately to the left of this great mound is another area slightly elevated above the level of the plain and further defined by long lines of stones. Somewhat in advance of the eastern front of this area, generally called the "temple," stands a row of massive pilasters, and in front of these in turn are the deeply embedded piers of a still smaller building of squared stones, with traces of an exterior corridor, which is called the "palace" by Squier.

The area called the "temple" forms a rectangle 388 by 445 feet, defined by the stones alluded to above. These are mostly of red sandstone and are between 8 and 10 feet in height, 2 to 4 feet broad, and 20 to 30 inches thick. Some are still erect, some have fallen, and others have doubtless been carried away, but enough remain to show that they formed part of a rough wall built in between them. They had been placed about 15 feet apart and inclined slightly inward. These walls, evidently, once supported a terreplein of earth about 8 feet above the general level of the plain. On the eastern side of this terreplein is a lower terrace 18 feet broad, along the edge of which were raised 10 great stone pilasters, 15-1/2 feet apart, all of which except one, which has fallen, stand in perfect alignment to-day. They are of different sizes and height. The tallest is nearly 14 feet high, 4 feet 2 inches wide, and 2 feet 5 inches thick; the shortest, 9 feet high, 2 feet 9 inches wide, and 2 feet 5 inches thick. They are accurately cut and smooth in front, while the backs are rough and only partly worked. The tops of the taller ones have shoulders cut in them as if to receive architraves, indicating that at one time all were perhaps of equal height and formed part of the masonry of a building or corridor of some kind. Another feature of this colonnade is that the sides or edges of each of these stones are cut away to within 6 inches of its face, so as to leave a projection of about an inch and a half, in order to retain in place the slabs of stone fitted in between them and prevent their falling outward.

A little over 50 feet from this colonnade are the traces of a rectangular structure alluded to as the "palace," composed of blocks of trachyte finely cut 8 to 10 feet long by 5 feet broad, with remains of what appears to have been a corridor some 30 feet wide extending around it. The piers which supported the "palace" still remained some years ago, sunk deep in the ground, and resting on an even pavement of cut stones. In speaking of these foundations Squier, who examined them in 1864, writes:

Remove the superstructures of the best-built edifices of our cities, and few, if any, would expose foundations laid with equal care, and none of them stones cut with such accuracy or so admirably fitted together. And I may say, once for all, carefully weighing my words, that in no part of the world have I seen stones cut with such mathematical precision and admirable skill as in Peru, and in no part of Peru are there any to surpass those which are scattered over the plain of Tiahuanacu.

On the great mound which Squier calls the "fortress" are found sections of foundations and some portions of the outer or lower wall which are nearly intact. An examination of these shows that the large upright stones planted in the ground formed portions of the walls, and that the intermediate stones forming the wall are each cut with alternate grooves and projections, like mortise and tenon, so as to fit immovably into each other horizontally. Vertically they were held in position by round holes drilled into the bottom and top of each stone at exact corresponding distances, in which, there is reason to believe, were placed pins of bronze. This shows the intelligent devices of a people unacquainted with the use of cement to give strength and permanence to their structures.

Tradition has it that once there were large subterranean vaults in this area, filled with the treasures of this lost race, and that a subterranean passage led from here to Cuzco, but Squier found no such vaults or passage.

To the southeast of the "fortress," and about 250 yards from it, is a long line of wall in ruins. Beyond this are the remains of buildings of whose plans but an inadequate idea can now be formed. One of these was still in a fairly good state of preservation when D'Orbigny visited the ruins in 1833. This was called the "hall of justice" and D'Orbigny's description is as follows:

It is a kind of platform of well-cut blocks of stone, held together by copper clamps, of which only the traces remain. It presents a level surface elevated 6 feet above the ground, 131 feet long and 23 broad, formed of enormous stones, eight making the length and two the breadth. Some of these stones are 25-1/2 feet long by 14 feet broad, and 6-1/2 feet thick. These are probably the ones measured by Cieza de Leon, who describes them as 30 feet long, 15 in width, and 6 in thickness. Some are rectangular in shape; others of irregular form. On the eastern side of the platform and cut in the stones of which they form a part, are three groups of alcoves or seats. One group occupies the central part of the monument, covering an extent of 53 feet, and is divided into 7 compartments. A group of 3 compartments occupies each extremity of the monument. Between the central and side groups were reared monolithic doorways, similar in some respects to the large one, only more simple, the one to the west alone having a sculptured frieze similar to that of the great gateway. In front of this structure, to the west, and about 20 feet distant, is a wall remarkable for the fine cutting of its stones, which are of a blackish basalt and very hard. The stones are of equal dimensions, having a groove running around them, and each has a niche cut in it with absolute precision. Everything goes to show that the variety of the forms of the niches was one of the great ornaments of the walls, for on all sides we find stones variously cut, and evidently intended to fit together so as to form architectural ornaments.

The most remarkable monument in Tiahuanacu, the "piece de resistance" from an archaeological point of view, is the great monolithic gateway which stands in the northwest corner of the area called the "temple." D'Orbigny says that when he visited the place (1833) it had fallen down. Every traveler that has visited it since then has found it standing erect. Who raised it, or for what purpose, is unknown. Entirely disconnected from any building or wall and facing inward toward the court the presumption is that it has been moved from its original position. In all likelihood it once formed the entrance to one of the massive structures, perhaps the temple itself. Squier's description of this relic of American antiquity is so comprehensive and so clear in its details that most of the following is taken from his work.

The top of the monolith has been broken, some say by lightning and others by an earthquake, so that the two parts lap by each other, causing the sides of the doorway to incline slightly toward each other. Imagine a block of stone, somewhat broken and defaced on its edges, but originally cut with precision, 13 feet 5 inches long, 7 feet 2 inches high above ground, and 18 inches thick. Through its center is cut a doorway, 4 feet 6 inches high and 2 feet 9 inches wide. Above this doorway, on its southeast front, are four lines of sculpture in low relief, like the Egyptian plain sculptures, and a central figure, immediately over the doorway, sculptured in high relief. On the reverse we find the doorway surrounded by friezes or cornices, and above it on each side two small niches, below which, also on either side, is a single larger niche. The stone itself is a dark and very hard trachyte. It is faced with a precision that no skill can excel; its lines are perfectly drawn, and its right angles turned with an accuracy that the most careful geometer could not surpass. Barring some injuries and defacements and some slight damages by weather, I do not believe there exists a better piece of stonecutting, the material considered, on this or the other continent. The front, especially the part covered by sculpture, has a fine finish, as near a true polish as trachyte can be made to bear.

The lower line of sculpture is 7-1/2 inches broad, and is unbroken. The three above it are 8 inches high, cut up in cartouches, or squares, of equal width, but interrupted in the center, immediately over the doorway by the figure in high relief mentioned above. This figure, with its ornaments, covers a space of 32 by 21-1/2 inches. There are consequently three ranges of squares on each side of this figure, eight in each range, or 48 in all. The figures represented in these squares have human bodies, feet, and hands; each holds a scepter; they are winged; but the upper and lower series have human heads wearing crowns, represented in profile, while the heads of the 16 figures in the line between them have the heads of condors.

The central and principal figure is angularly but boldly cut in a style palpably conventional. The head is surrounded by a series of what may be called rays, each terminating in a circle, the head of the condor or that of a tiger, all conventionally but forcibly treated. In each hand he grasps a stave or scepter of equal length with his body, the lower end of the right-hand scepter terminating in the head of the condor, and the upper in that of the tiger, while the lower end of the left-hand scepter terminates like the other, and the upper is bifurcate and has two heads of the condor. An ornamental girdle surrounds the waist of this principal figure, from which depends a double fringe. It stands upon a kind of base or series of figures approaching nearest in character to the architectural ornament called grecgues, each extremity of which, however, terminates in the crowned head of a tiger or condor.

The winged human-headed and condor-headed figures in the three lines of squares are represented kneeling on one knee, with their faces turned to the great central figure, as if in adoration, and each one holds before him a staff or scepter. The scepters of the figures in the two upper rows are bifurcate, and correspond exactly with the scepter in the left hand of the central figure, while the scepters of the lower tier correspond with that represented in his right hand. The relief of all these figures is scarcely more than two-tenths of an inch; the minor features are indicated by very delicate lines slightly incised, which form subordinate figures, representing the heads of condors, tigers, and serpents.

The fourth or lower row of sculpture consists of repetitions on a smaller scale and in low relief of the head of the central figure, surrounded by corresponding rays, terminating in like manner with the heads of animals. The three outer columns of winged figures, and the corresponding parts of the lower line of sculpture, are only blocked out, and have none of the elaborate, incised ornamentation discoverable in the central parts of the monument. A very distinct line separates these unfinished sculptures from those portions that are finished, which is most marked in the lower tier. On each side of this line, standing on the rayed heads to which I have alluded, placed back to back, and looking in opposite directions, are two small but interesting figures of men, crowned with something like a plumed cap, and holding to their mouths what appears to be trumpets. • Although only 3 inches high, these little figures are ornamented in the same manner as the larger ones, with the heads of tigers, condors, etc.

Besides this elaborately sculptured gateway and another of similar character, but not quite so profusely ornamented, which has been moved from its original location and now forms the entrance to a cemetery of the modern village, there are several stone idols which have been unearthed since the time of Squier's visit. Among these are three which were found partially embedded in the earth near the railroad. The Geographical Society of La Paz has had them unearthed and raised to an erect position. On one of these the sculptured designs are still comparatively well preserved and are plainly shown in the accompanying photograph of the detail. Another large monolithic idol was accidently unearthed in plowing near the foot of the "fortress" for agricultural purposes. It is over 8 feet in height and the encircling belt about the waist of the figure is finely carved.

As stated, the entire ruins cover something over a square mile of the plain. These are the ruins of temples, palaces, and great structures of what once must have been a large, densely populated city. Not a vestige remains of the dwellings and less pretentious houses in which this population must have lived. These were naturally of a more temporary character and the relentless agents of destruction, working through countless centuries, have obliterated all traces.

The question which confronts the archaeologist is---how could a population sufficiently numerous to accomplish the building of such a city have maintained itself in this region? The city was located 13,000 feet above the level of the sea on a vast plateau, where the cold is constantly so great that corn and other grain will not ripen. During present times crops of potatoes and oca and some other edible roots are grown, but at best the region is such that it is only capable of sustaining a scanty mountain population. Concerning this phase of the Tiahuanacu mystery Sir Clements Markham writes:

The city covered a large area, built by highly-skilled masons, and with the use of enormous stones. One stone is 36 feet long by 7, weighing 170 tons, another 26 feet by 16 by 6. Apart from the monoliths of ancient Egypt, there is nothing to equal this in any other part of the world. The movement and placing of such monoliths point to a dense population, to an organized government, and consequently to a large area under cultivation, with arrangements for the conveyance of supplies from various directions. There must have been an organization combining skill and intelligence with power and administrative ability.

Inca stonework in Peru showing close-fitting odd-shaped blocks

• Pacific Islands

PREHISTORIC STRUCTURES ON PONAPE
Anonymous; *Science,* 5:284, 1885.

Capt. L. U. Herendeen of San Francisco communicates the following notes on prehistoric structures in Micronesia. American missionaries recently settled at Ponape, may, it is hoped, furnish additional details hereafter.

A few years ago I visited Ponape Island in the Pacific, in east longitude 158⁰ 22', and north latitude 6⁰ 50'. The island is surrounded by a reef, with a broad ship-channel between it and the island. At places in the reef there were natural breaks, that served as entrances to the harbors. In these ship-channels there were a number of islands, many of which were surrounded by a wall of stone five or six feet high; and on these islands there stood a great many low houses, built of the same kind of stone as the walls about them. These structures seem to have been used as temples and forts. The singular feature of these islands is that the walls are a foot or more below the water. When they were built, they were evidently above the water, and connected with the mainland; but they have gradually sunk until the sea has risen a foot or more around them. The natives on the island do not know when these works were built: it is so far back in the past, that they have even no tradition of the structures. Yet the works show signs of great skill, and certainly prove that whoever built them knew thoroughly how to transport and lift heavy blocks of stone. Up in the mountains of the island there is a quarry of the same kind of stone that was used in building the wall about the islands; and in that quarry to-day there are great blocks of stone that have been hewn out, ready for transportation. The natives have no tradition touching the quarry, ---who hewed the stone, when it was done, or why the work ceased. They are in greater ignorance of the great phenomena that are going on about them than the white man who touches on their island for a few hours for water. There is no doubt in my mind that the island was once inhabited by an intelligent race of people, who built the temples and forts of heavy masonry on the high bluffs of the shore of the island, and that, as the land gradually subsided, these bluffs became islands. They stand to-day with a solid wall of stone around them, partly submerged in water.

NAN MATOL: ANCIENT VENICE OF MICRONESIA
Brandt, John H.; *Archaeology,* 15:99–107, 1962.

The fantastic early stories of the ruins called Nan Matol were expanded by equally fantastic true findings. The ruins contained over ninety man-made islands, covering some eleven square miles, built by cribbing huge basaltic splinters in "log cabin style." The interiors of the retainer walls were filled with coral boulders and earth. Thatched buildings were presumably built upon these walls. Canals interlaced the islands. None

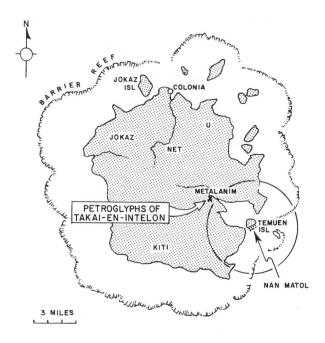

Map of Ponape Island, pinpointing the extensive ruins at Nan Matol

of the structures, with the exception of Pei-En-Kitel, a burial island, were built on solid land; all were laboriously constructed by dragging materials long distances to complete this monumental work.

. . . .

The oft-repeated question of the true age of Nan Matol must still go largely unanswered. That the ruins are of great antiquity seems unlikely, although Carbon 14 tests in the Mariana Islands have indicated the presence of man in Micronesia possibly as early as 1500 B.C. Comprehensive archaeological investigation would shed light on the prehistory of Nan Matol, but none has yet been undertaken.

. . . .

Shortly after penetrating the ruins one finds oneself at the west wall of the main burial chamber. The huge outer walls of Nan Towas loom thirty feet above the main gateway from the canal. Outer walls, fifteen feet thick, are made of criss-cross basalt blocks. These huge polygonal

Part of the "temple" at Nan Matol built of prismatic basalt "logs" (Bishop Museum)

"logs" of natural prismatic formation were quarried principally in the districts of Lot, Metalanim and U. Presumably the miners heated the cliff face with huge fires and then drenched the surface with cold water. The resultant expansion and contraction broke off the splinters desired for construction. Many were undoubtedly lost in transport since in places the reef is strewn with basalt "logs," indicating the site of swamped rafts en route to Nan Matol with loads of building stone.

The huge walls form a rectangle oriented north-south and east-west. It is the only building apparently so laid out in the area. The north wall of Nan Towas remained unfinished. Passing through the main gate, one encounters the inner wall, surrounded by courtyards and terraces, now largely overgrown with vegetation. A small gateway in the west wall leads to the main vault where lie buried the Satalurs, or kings, of Nan Matol. In the north, south and east courtyards are three more burial vaults lined with basalt logs. The inner wall, on the south, has a small passageway through which one can enter by stooping. The outer dimensions of Nan Towas are roughly 185 x 115 feet, with walls of varying heights. The oblique inward pitch of several walls shows that they were probably erected by sliding the ponderous basalt splinters up a ramp of logs. The main grave, in the center, is covered with huge parallel stone logs. Although Nan Towas is rectangular, as are most of the ruined building sites, some structures are irregular, such as Us-En-Nam, which has ten sides, and Pei-To, which has three.

. . . .

• Middle East

AN UNNOTICED ANCIENT METROPOLIS OF ASIA MINOR
von der Osten, H. H.; *Geographical Review,* 18:83–92, 1928.

The "unnoticed metropolis" of this paper is a remarkable site, the existence of which has long been known but which has apparently never been described. Yet it is the site of the largest pre-Greek city of Asia Minor, a city that in its day must have been one of the chief cultural and political centres of the great Hittite Empire that flourished in the second millennium before the Christian era. In the last few years the decipherment of Hittite cuneiform records has greatly stimulated our interest in that Empire and its mysterious and little-known people. Its survivals, however, cover a vast territory, scattered as they are from one end of Asia Minor to the other, and little has heretofore been done to recover and study them.

. . . .

As to the silent ancient city immediately before us, it is nothing short of imposing. The surrounding walls, which when viewed from the kaleh at the easternmost angle of the city appear like long walls of piled-up rocks, enclose an area approximately three times the size of Boghaz Koi, the ancient Hittite capital. The great expanse of ruins, once a city teeming with the life and resounding with the voices of a powerful people who dominated most of Asia Minor, now lies mute and barren. A few scrub trees, stunted by the harsh winter winds which sweep over this now deforested region, timidly sprout from amongst the jumble of rocks at the base of the kaleh immediately below us. Otherwise the great enclosure is a picture of desolation. Northwest from the steep kaleh the ribbon of tumbled wall stretches away in gentle undulations until it reaches what was the northernmost limit of the city, where it turns back sharply upon itself southwestwards, and from the kaleh can be seen, almost a mile away, continuing southward until it reaches the abrupt, steep slope of Kiramitlik which for a short distance serves to break its continuity (stations 35 to 38). East of Kiramitlik, the city's southern limit, the wall is resumed, winding sharply northward again toward the kaleh, to complete an enclosure nearly a mile in width and over a mile and a half in length (1520 meters by 2564 meters).

The enclosure walls follow the natural elevations rising from the plateau; and within them well-marked contours of ancient structures are visible, although here and there at higher points the bed rock comes to the surface. On the kaleh itself room divisions are well defined by rectangular lines, once building walls but now simply piles of stones. In some places can still be seen remnants of the actual walls, with stones still in situ, the thickness of the wall at such points measuring about 1.85 meters.

. . . .

The survey of the wall was achieved by "shooting" 133 stadia lines. At each station thus secured the width and height of the fallen wall was measured, as well as the dimensions of any other adjacent construction. The height of the now fallen wall averaged 2.50 meters, sometimes attaining 3.50 meters, while in its present tumbled and dispersed condition the width of the debris varied between 10 and 16 meters, the sections near stations 90 and 105 bearing evidence of having been especially massive. Near the slope to the east (stations 118 to 122) only very scanty remains of the wall are to be found. In

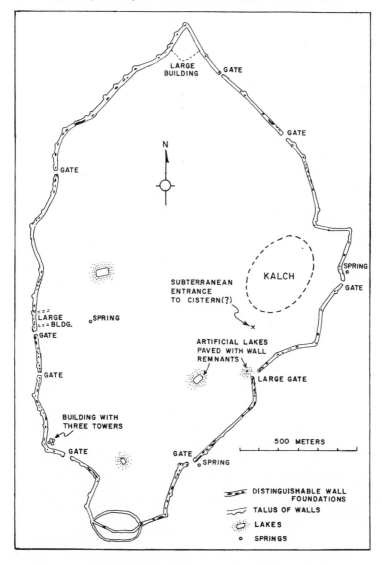

Plan of the deserted ancient city of Kevkenes Dagh

addition to the stadia lines a few triangulation lines also were "shot," in order to locate some artificial lakes and a subterranean spring at the foot of the kaleh. Of interest was the fact that on the Kiramitlik side of the wall was for some distance discontinued (stations 35 to 38). At the same time we prepared also a small map showing the general situation of the city and its relation to surrounding tumuli and huyuks.

Closer investigation of the outer wall, as partially preserved in some places, revealed that it was built upon a massive stone foundation some 5 or 6 meters thick at its top. To determine the original thickness at the base of the foundation would have required the removal of much fallen masonry, often consisting of very large stones. The angle of the outer slope of the foundations averaged about 60 degrees. Upon this foundation was built the city wall, which varied in thickness from 4 to 4.5 meters.

Protective towers had been built at irregular intervals, usually at points of obvious strategical or tactical advantage or near gates (stations 59 and 89). I found only one tower whose walls were in the least preserved (station 52); all the others could be recognized only as great heaps of stones which had fallen outward from a structure of indeterminate height, the stones in some instances having tumbled to a distance of 17 meters from the actual tower wall. Apparently the towers were round or, at least, had rounded corners.

. . . .

As to the origin and history of this city, or regarding its possible name and identity, I would not venture to hazard any premature statement at this time. I would only call attention to the fact that the character of its walls, the rounded corners in much of the construction, and the slope of the foundation walls, are reminiscent of the ruins at Akalan, near Samsun; while the general emplacement of the site reminds one of Boghaz Koi. In other respects, however, this city on the Kevkenes Dagh is not only very different from Boghaz Koi but encloses an area three times the size of the latter.

THE GERMAN EXCAVATIONS AT BAALBEK
Paton, Lewis Bayles; *Art and Archaeology,* 1:121-129, 1914.

One of the chief results of excavation has been the disclosure of the original ground-plan of the temple-complex. The buildings stood upon a raided platform that was enclosed with a massive retaining wall. Instead of filling in this area with earth, arched vaults were constructed that were used as shops and storehouses. The sacred enclosure was reached by a grand staircase at the eastern end, at the head of which stood the Propylaea, consisting of a portico flanked by two towers. Within this was an hexagonal Forecourt from which three doors led into the Great Court of the Altar (fig. 1). In the center of this court over the altar one sees the ground-plan of the later Basilica of Theodosius. On the west side of this court a flight of steps and a single portal led up to the Temple

Court. Here, in line with the axis of the sanctuary, stood the Great
Temple, traditionally called "the Temple of the Sun," but now known to
have been dedicated to Jupiter and all the gods of Heliopolis. South of
this lay a smaller temple, traditionally called "the Temple of Baal," but
now known to have been dedicated to Bacchus.

The lowest course of the outer retaining wall consisted of moderate-
sized stones. Above these came three courses of stones, each about
thirteen feet in length. The middle courses remain only on the western
side, and there consist of three of the largest stones ever used by builders. One is sixty-four feet long, another sixty-three and one-half and the
third sixty-two and one-half. All are about thirteen feet high and ten feet
thick. The inner surface of one of these stones has been exposed by the
excavations on the west side of the Temple Court. From these remarkable stones the temple probably received its ancient designation of Trilithon. A similar stone seventy by fourteen by thirteen feet and weighing
at least one thousand tons remains in the quarry from which the other
stones were obtained. How these gigantic blocks were transported and
raised to a height of twenty-six feet in order to rest upon the lower courses,
is an unsolved problem. The method of quarrying by which they were cut
out like columns from the native rock and then split off may still be
studied in situ.

. . . .

Baalbek Temple, Lebanon, showing the immense foundation stones

• Africa

ARCHAEOLOGICAL EXPLORATION IN AFRICA
Anonymous; *Nature,* 136:213, 1935.

Further particulars are now to hand of an archaeological discovery in Tanganyika reported early in July. According to a dispatch
from Nairobi in The Times of August 1, Commander Nino del Grande,
leader of an expedition collecting snake poison for the preparation of
a snake-bite serum, camped for five days on the site of the ancient
city discovered near Nguruka. He reports that the city is four and a
half miles long by one and a half miles broad and is constructed
terrace-wise on the wall of the Great Rift escarpment. Remains of
houses, estimated to number four thousand, were found. Each had
three or four rooms and stone walls four feet in thickness. Large
stone tombs, one containing a skeleton, were found in the valley below. It is given as the opinion of Commander del Grande that no very
high antiquity is to be assigned to these remains. It is thought that
they may be about five hundred years old and the work of an advanced
tribe, possibly the ancestors of the Wambulu now living some fifty
miles away. The site is being examined by Dr. L. S. B. Leakey,
whose verdict on the relation of these remains to other vestiges of
stone structures found in various parts of East Africa should be of
signal importance for the cultural history of the southern half of the
continent.

RECENTLY DISCOVERED RUINS IN RHODESIA
Geare, Randolph I.; *Scientific American,* 94:231-232, 1906.

Spreading over an area between 18 deg. and 22 deg. south latitude and
about 27 deg. to 33 deg. east longitude some puzzling ruins have lately
been discovered, concerning which very little has so far been published.
More than one hundred and twenty separate localities show evidences of the
same character of remains, while minor ruins of forts and what were
probably guardhouses are scattered for a considerable distance beyond the
limits above indicated. Most of the ruins are in or near a region liberally
supplied with granite, whose huge bowlders form parts of the walls, which
it would seem were erected for defensive purposes. Most of the blocks of
granite measure from seven to eleven inches in length, and from 2-1/2 to
5 inches thick, roughly worked into a rectangular shape, while larger ones
were often used in building the lower courses. The blocks were carefully

laid in the walls, many faced on both sides, the interior being filled up with loose rubble. No cement or mortar was used, but the excellent and solid character of the masonry is proved by the fact that some of the walls, 30 feet high and 16 feet thick at the base, stand as firmly to-day as when they were built---probably as far back as 1,000 to 2,000 years before the Christian era.

The extent of some of the ruins, such as Zimbabwe, Mundie, M'Popoti, Chum, Dhlo-Dhlo, and Khami, would indicate that they were important centers, the first being by far the greatest. The so-called "temple" at Zimbabwe (houses of stone) is perhaps the best example of the architecture employed. It is an elliptical figure of three hundred feet by two hundred and thirty feet. Several ingenious theories have been propounded as to the significance of the curves, of orientation, of the special object of the ornamental work in its walls, and as regards the standard of measurement used, but it is a question how far they can be relied upon. Thus, one explorer states that his measurements of the celebrated cone in the temple differ materially from others that have been made, and on which latter was founded the theory that the unit of measurement was the cubit of 1.717 feet.

It is regarded as strange that none of the buildings is square or rectangular in form. The older ruins are characterized by round ends to the walls and entrances, elaborately ornamented, while those of apparently recent date have square corners and straight walls. Several of the entrances were found to be covered in. At Zimbabwe passages or openings through the walls can be seen, the roof or top being supported by beams or slabs of stone. In the entrances of some of the ruins stout hardwood posts still remain, lying partly in recesses which were left in the wall at the time of their construction, the blocks being laid carefully against the timbers. The theory has been advanced that the entrances to these ruins face the rising or the setting sun, which might indicate some form of sun-worship, but others affirm that these openings point to all parts of the compass, and were evidently placed where best suited to the special locality.

In the older type of ruins the walls generally run in one face from the foundations to the top, while in later ruins the walls are built in two, three, or even four tiers, stepped back, and forming terraces two to ten feet in width, and originally covered with a concrete or cement pavement made of crushed burnt granite.

The most characteristic feature of the buildings is the way in which they were ornamented. Spaces were left in the courses by introducing sloping tiles or thin slabs of stone of different colors, or by laying some courses of a different colored rock. Explorers report that they have discovered several distinct types of ornamental work, which they have named and classified as (1) dentelle, (2) chevron, (3) herring-bone, or double line of sloping blocks, (4) sloping block, (5) check or chess-board pattern, and (6) courses of different colored rocks. The first of these styles of ornamentation---the least common of them all---is formed by placing blocks with an angle facing outward, as is often seen in modern brickwork. The second is a kind of inverted V (the apex uppermost). In the third the V lies sidewise, one following another. In some instances the slabs or tiles of each "herring-bone" are of granite or ironstone, or occasionally a section of granite tiles is followed by one of ironstone. In others the herring-bone figure extends for a long distance, while in others each pattern is separated by one or more full-sized blocks of granite. The "sloping block" is similarly varied. In the check or chess-board style the pattern is formed by leaving out alternative blocks, the dark cavity which remains forming a marked contrast with the gray face of the wall.

At Zimbabwe is seen a special style of ornamental work, consisting of large beams or posts of granite and soapstone fixed into the top of the walls, generally in an inclined position. The objects found in these ruins embrace a large variety, including iron and brass cannon, silver utensils, crockery, beads, glass, etc. These would indicate the presence of the Portuguese at some time. Articles of iron and copper are supposed to represent comparatively recent Kaffir occupation; while worked gold in plates, bangles, beads, tacks, ferrules, etc., are considered to be typical of the ancient builders who, in search of the precious metal, penetrated into what was to them the uttermost part of the world. Such articles as the beads, gold work, roughly carved stone emblems, etc., are claimed by some to establish the antiquity of the ruins beyond doubt on account of the similarity between them and other like objects found in Egypt and Arabia, although it is of course possible that these articles may have been brought from Northern Africa by Arab traders or by migrating tribes in comparatively recent times. This is a problem which further investigation alone can solve.

Mr. Randall McIver, who largely through the assistance of the Rhodes trustees has made extensive explorations in this region, divides these ruin-sites into two groups, the first including the Rhodes estate, the Niekerk ruins, and Umtali; the second embracing Dhlo Dhlo, Nanateli, Khami, and the celebrated Zimbabwe. Dhlo Dhlo is easily accessible from Bulawayo, being only sixteen miles from the railway station of Insiza. Round the citadel there runs a girdle-walk, built of rough, unworked stones, carelessly piled on one another. Viewed as a whole, with the citadel on high ground in the middle, and this rough wall surrounding it, Dhlo Dhlo strongly resembles the eastern fort at Inyanga, whose antiquities have been described as "hill forts," "slave pits," and "water furrows." Some explorers believe that these pit dwellings not unfrequently contained a subterranean passage, but others affirm that they were built up, and not excavated. The builders commenced by raising a massive platform, whose exterior platform was composed of large, unhewn rocks, carefully selected and fitted, while the inside was filled with earth and rubble. On continuing the work down hill, the builders did not content themselves with maintaining the same height of platform all the way, but added extra courses in proportion to the increase of the gradient, so as always to maintain a horizontal surface over the top. On the upper side of the incline the artificial structure might only be a meter high, but on the lower side it was often two or three meters high. So it was possible, by leaving a space within the platform itself on the lower side, to make a pit without excavating at all, and this the ancient builders appear to have continually done. Thus the floor of the circular or elliptical pit is always found on the actual level of the ground outside, though its sides may be as much as eight feet in height.

The cement walls of Dhlo Dhlo are still partially intact, and the circular ones were foundations and floors of huts, but where the circumference of one circle abutted on another, a horseshoe or wedge shaped piece was often inserted to fill the space which otherwise would have been left vacant. Excavations showed these hut-foundations to have been constructed as follows: On the bed-rock was first put a layer of large, rough stones mixed with earth, and a flooring of cement some 40 centimeters thick was laid upon this. Then the cement walls of the round hut were erected upon this floor, and divisional walls of the same material were inserted to divide it into compartments. The walls of the huts bear the clear impress of wooden stakes, against which the cement had been plastered, and stakes were also used to hold together and strengthen the cement of the platform while it was drying. In all these platforms wooden stakes are found within the cement of the floor, generally running clear down to the foundation. There is therefore nothing surprising in the presence of wooden posts standing up above the ground to support the sides of the stone walls at the main entrance.

Some idea of the vast extent of these ruins may be had from the fact that the Niekerk ruins alone cover an area of not less than fifty square miles, and it is said that within their limits it is hardly possible to walk ten yards without stumbling over walls or buildings of rough, undressed stone. The general principle of these ruins is described as embracing nine or ten hills, each of which constitutes a separate unit, complete with its own buildings and divided at the bottom from its neighbor by a boundary wall. Such a boundary is the first in a series of concentric lines which rise one behind the other, at first low and wide apart, then higher and closer together, until the crown of the hill is reached. On one of the lower hills there were counted fifty distinct concentric lines from the valley to the top.

For what purpose could these walls have been built? Mr. McIver disposes of the idea that they were built for purposes of cultivation or irrigation, and concludes that they were intrenchment lines, which leads to the supposition that the inhabitants were subject to sudden attacks from hostile tribes.

In many of these fortified places objects of different kinds were found, including articles of copper, bronze, and iron; also stone implements, quartz and crystal arrow-heads. In one excavation Mr. McIver found the remains of ceremonial feasts, consisting chiefly of bones of antelope. They had been partially burned, and the great logs of the fire were discovered in several cases. There they had been placed, with the ashes from the fire and various small articles and implements, in large earthenware jars, which were found buried in groups of varying number, or sometimes in layers, one on the top of the other.

· · · · · · · · · ·

THE RIDDLE OF ZIMBABWE
Holz, Peter; *Natural History*, 65:268-273, May 1956.

Many remarkable and ancient ruins have been discovered in the British territory of Southern Rhodesia, but none are more massively built, more extensive, or better preserved than those at Zimbabwe. The origin of these relics of a vanished culture is hidden in the mists of time. Three-quarters of a century of speculation and investigation have failed to show conclusively who built these astonishing walls, which cast their spell over a valley fifteen miles from the end of the railroad in southeastern Southern Rhodesia.

The Zimbabwe Ruins were vaguely known to early Arabian and Portuguese explorers, but so meager was the information that when the hunter Adam Renders reached them as late as 1868, he was considered to have discovered them.

The word "Zimbabwe" is really of Bantu origin and means "houses of stone," a name applicable to any of the 500 other smaller ruins scattered over the length and breadth of Southern Rhodesia. By custom, however, the name is today associated chiefly with the largest site.

. . . .

Some have claimed that the Zimbabwe Ruins are culturally linked with India, while others hold them to be of purely local origin. The ruins have at times been dated as far as 3000 years back and identified with the ancient Ophir from which King Solomon obtained his gold; and a host of authors have ascribed them to the Sabaeans or the Phoenicians. But trained archeologists were inclined to date Zimbabwe as late as A.D. 1550. How close they came has recently been shown by the Carbon 14 method of determining age by examining organic materials. Two pieces of timber, taken from an inner wall, were subjected to this test independently in Chicago and London. Their age was thus stated without doubt to be A.D. 1361 (plus or minus 120 years) and A.D. 1252 (plus or minus 92 years).

. . . .

ON THE RUINS OF DHLO-DHLO, IN RHODESIA

White, Franklin; *Royal Anthropological Institute, Journal,* 31:21-29, 1901.

In the central portion of Rhodesia there are numerous stone constructions, now more or less in ruins, scattered over a considerable area. So little is accurately known about them that it is not possible to say definitely with what object they were built. The native races of the present day attribute to them mysterious origin of the class which usually appeals to the ignorant imagination.

The occupants most certainly not only possessed but also smelted and worked gold.

The ruins are generally found on or near granite knolls or bosses, not as a rule actually in the gold-bearing districts, although auriferous veins are often found at no great distance away. The builders seem to have selected in preference an agricultural country with positions easily defended. The granite areas, with their numerous streams, bare knolls, and scattered boulders, would best comply with these requirements.

In his Ruined Cities of Mashonaland Mr. Theodore Bent records the results of his exploration of the Zimbabwe ruin, the most extensive yet discovered, and it is to be regretted that such systematic research has not been continued. Now, additional knowledge can only be gained from occasional visits of travellers to ruins lying near their routes or from work carried on chiefly in search for gold and ornaments. The latter is fortunately conducted in such a way as to do the least damage compatible with the treasure-hunting, but it naturally is not done with the object of collecting information or of investigating points of interest.

General Description. The Dhlo-Dhlo or Mambo ruins, the subject of this paper, are located some 50 miles north-east of Bulawayo, or say 19-3/4 degrees south and 29-1/4 degrees east.

The level above sea is about 4,500 feet.

They occupy a commanding position on a granite plateau between two streams forming part of the head waters of the Inciza River, a tributary of the Limpopo.

The name "Mambo" is derived from the designation of the tribe of Kaffirs who occupied this country before the Matabeles conquered it.

I was able to make a fairly accurate plan of the most important part of these ruins and to take some photographs which show the construction of the walls and the different styles of ornamentation used by the builders.

Some prominent bosses of bare granite were made use of as base for the walls, and the builders were fully aware of the tendency of granite to peel off in slabs under atmospheric influences, perhaps assisted by fire. They thus obtained a large supply of material well suited for their purpose and close at hand. From the hills a few miles away they brought slabs of banded ironstones, which were ingeniously used to form a contrast with the grey of the granite.

A reference to the plan will show that the main building is of a rough egg-shaped form 350 feet long and 200 feet wide, the longer axis running north-west and south-east. There are two outer enclosures attached to the main building, one being on the north-eastern and the other on the south-western side.

The northern and south-western sides of the ruin show the finest as well as the highest walls. The main entrance was undoubtedly on the north side. There are several isolated buildings surrounding the main ruin, of inferior construction.

Style of Construction. The buildings are made of blocks or small slabs of granite varying generally from 7 to 11 inches in length and 2-1/2 to 5 inches in thickness. The lower courses are generally made of larger blocks. Smaller pieces are used for the ornamental work.

There are no real foundations to the walls; they just begin on any ground firm enough to carry them. As they are seldom more than 8 feet high in any one face the weight is not great. Where additional height was required the walls were raised in tiers, the upper one being stepped back, leaving a ledge varying from 1 to 12 feet in width, widening and narrowing without any apparent reason. No mortar or clay was used in the wall proper, but the top was covered with a layer of clay and ground-up granite.

Although curves and rounded endings-off to the walls were apparently preferred, still angular corners and straight lines could be made when considered advisable.

The batter of the walls varies, but is generally slight. At one point the top actually overhangs the base.

Some walls were made with two faces, the intervening space being filled up with rubble.

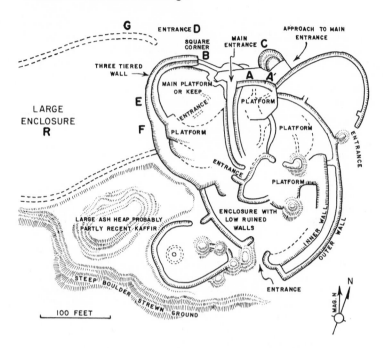

Plan of the Dhlo-dhlo ruins in Rhodesia

The courses preserve their thickness fairly well. In some cases a course widens, and in others disappears.

Boulders of granite lying on the surface were made use of as part of the wall whenever possible.

The most striking feature of the walls is the attempt made to introduce some style of ornamentation. In these ruins the following variations can be seen:---

    1st.   Lines of a different coloured rock.

    2nd.   The chess board, or chequered pattern.

         This varies from the ordinary gap and stone in one to eight courses, and groups of three spaces with thin blocks in two courses, separated by two thicker blocks.

    3rd.   The zigzag pattern.

    4th.   The sloping block varied by alternating granite with red banded ironstone slabs.

    5th.   The chevron or fish-bone pattern varied by alternating red and grey blocks, either in patches or singly and in patches separated by thick granite blocks.

         It will be noticed that the sloping blocks incline respectively to the west and to the east, or in different ways on each side of the main entrance.

As far as I have been able to observe the ornamented patches commence and finish off in an arbitrary or capricious manner and are not confined to any one part of the walls.

Description of Ruins. To the south and south-west of the main ruin
there are numerous and extensive enclosures, the walls of which seldom
exceeded 6 feet in height and were of somewhat inferior construction.
As the grass was high no careful examination could be made. They were
probably cattle pens or locations for slaves.

The large enclosure (R) on the western side of the ruin is surrounded
by a wall considerably destroyed, but in parts still showing a height of 7
feet. It was well built and was ornamented with a band of red stone and
also a course of sloping blocks.

About 100 feet to the north of the main entrance is a roughly built enclosure (M) 75 feet by 90 feet with one entrance on the east side.

To the north-east of the main entrance and about 155 feet away is a
circular platform (N) considerably destroyed, but apparently 4-1/2 feet
high and 30 feet in diameter. Behind this there is another enclosure (O)
some 80 feet by 60 feet, with two entrances, one on the north-east and
one on the south-west.

On the south-west side of the main ruin there is a well-built enclosure or platform (P) 95 feet wide by 100 feet long. It is built up on a
rather steep slope strewed with granite boulders, some of which have
been utilised as part of the walls. Only one entrance can now be seen,
outside the main wall. There may have been a communication with the
main ruin, but the wall at this point has been pretty thoroughly broken
down, and no signs of a doorway can be seen.

About 100 feet from P is the large area (R) 300 feet long by 190 feet
wide. It had clearly a main entrance at D, and others may have existed
in the parts of wall now broken down. The ground here is flat and good,
and this enclosure was probably a garden or cattle pen.

Between P and R there is a mound of ashes, broken bones, potsherds,
etc. It is evidently the refuse heap of the later Kaffir occupants of the
ruins and is now higher than the top of the wall of platform P. It probably lies over a small ridge or granite boss.

Some 300 feet north-west from the main entrance is another stone
construction (H) perched in a commanding position on the precipitous
northern face of a granite boss which slopes gradually southwards. The
wall is well made, but it apparently did not form a complete enclosure.
There is a rather elaborate entrance at H, and some very regular ornamental work.

On the east side of the main ruin there is a large enclosure 120 feet
along the wall and 95 feet in depth. It had apparently one gateway on the
southeast side. There are indications of interior divisions of walls, but
the whole is too much destroyed and grown over by bushes to be properly examined without considerable labour.

Description of the Outer Walls. The main approach was evidently on
the north side, where there is an arrangement of roughly built slopes
and platforms leading up to what is certainly the main entrance (C). A
long narrow passage running to the centre of the ruin attracted our attention, and a little work spent in clearing away the fallen stones and rubbish showed the remains of two stout posts of hard red wood 5-1/2 feet
apart on the west side. The tops of the posts are burnt. They lie partly
in recesses carefully built in the wall. On the east side can be seen
similar recesses. The opening is 11 feet in width, and goes back 15
feet, where there are signs of another pair of posts, and the passage
commences 7 feet in width.

The wall to the east of the entrance is still 8 feet high and is apparently nearly its original height. About 25 feet from the main entrance a chessboard pattern of seven courses commences in a somewhat irregular manner. Over this and separated from the top by three courses runs a line of dark ironstone, and three courses above this there is another row of dark stones changing suddenly into a course of chevron pattern formed of white and dark stones in patches, the points being to the east. Three courses above the chevron and commencing over the western end is a row of sloping blocks dipping to the west. Four courses above this and more or less over it is a three-course line of chess-board pattern also commencing at the end of a line of dark stones. Two of these bands of dark stones run nearly to the main entrance, but this portion of the wall is built in a somewhat slovenly manner, although it cannot be said that there is distinct evidence that it has been pulled down and rebuilt. The ornamentation cannot be traced eastwards, as the wall is partially destroyed and partly hidden by the fallen stones.

On the western side the walls attain greater height, being in three tiers, the top being some 16 feet above the base. At about 16 feet from the side of the entrance the walls turn outwards for say 5 feet and then run west for 30 feet to a carefully constructed corner. The first corner is partially filled up by a diagonal wall roughly built.

This section of the wall is ornamented as follows:---At the base of the lower tier there is a row of chevrons spaced off by thicker blocks. The chevrons are formed of alternate dark and white blocks and point to the west. Eight courses above this is a row of sloping blocks (white and dark) dipping to the east. Three courses over this runs a three-course line of chequers.

The upper tiers were no doubt ornamented, but the faces are much damaged now.

To the west of the second corner we see the first piece of the zigzag pattern commencing near the top and about 3 feet from the corner. It can be traced westwards as far as the wall is intact, but does not appear to have continued right round to the western face. Three courses below the zigzag is a line of sloping blocks dipping east, and three courses below this is a two-course chequer pattern. There is, therefore, no continuity of pattern to be seen in the lower tier. The chevron pattern is also missing to the west of the corner.

The two upper tiers were ornamented, the upper one with a zigzag pattern apparently corresponding to that on the western face. There are patches of zigzag pattern in the middle tier, but the walls are too much destroyed for me to be able to trace if the patches on the upper and lower walls correspond at all.

The western face is very fine, the tiers being 7 feet, 5 feet and 4-1/2 feet high, standing back each from 12 to 5 feet at the widest part, thus leaving broad platforms or ledges, which, however, narrow considerably at the turn (D).

The upper tier finishes off at a corner, where there were probably steps leading to the top platform. The ornamented courses finish about 3 feet from this corner.

The patches of ornamentation follow more or less regularly along the north and west wall of the building, and are most abundant where the walls are most bold.

The high western wall gradually alters beyond the corner. The upper tier apparently turned eastwards, enclosing the upper platform, about 80 feet in diameter.

The second tier continues southwards for about 50 feet, then turning eastwards to form the second platform.

The bottom tier runs on for about 120 feet, then a part turns east at right angles and forms another platform and part of the inner line of defence. An extension of it ran some 100 feet to the south-west, finishing off at a huge granite boulder which forms one side of the southern entrance.

At the western side of this entrance a well built wall commences. It is 6 to 8 feet high and about 5 feet wide at the top. It runs without a break round the south and eastern side until it butts up against the continuation of the north-eastern wall. Inside the wall is a passage or ditch 8 to 15 feet in width, blocked at both ends. Apparently the idea was to catch the enemy between the outer and the inner walls.

Central Passage. This commences at the northern or main entrance and runs about due south (magnetic) for 100 feet with a width of 5 feet to 7 feet. It then turns off a short distance to the south-east. The two walls finish with well made square ends.

The walls of the passage are now about 6 feet high, but there is some rubbish on the bottom.

A large heap of stones blocks the main entrance. It is possible that it was originally covered over with wooden beams carrying a stone parapet.

The recesses in the wall in which the posts are partially imbedded may correspond to what Mr. Bent saw at Zimbabwe and considered as grooves for a portcullis.

Platforms. The top of the main platform was evidently covered over with cement or fine concrete made of clay and ground-up granite. Treasure seekers have dug a hole near the centre, exposing chiefly loose stones. On the top of the platform are several raised ledges or benches of concrete.

On the platform east of the main entrance there are indications of a large circular dwelling which evidently had hard wood posts built in a cement wall. The same thing can be seen on the platform to the south.

In the enclosure P are the remains of a circular clay wall 10 feet in diameter, with a small hole about 2 feet in diameter in the centre.

On the top of the granite boss at H are remains of three circular clay walls or floors.

It is impossible to say whether these clay or cement structures belong to the same age as the stone walls. Some are of much better construction than others, the better being probably older Kaffir work. The stone wall builders may have used circular dwellings, and the idea would be copied by the natives of the country, although in an inferior class of work.

In the Khami ruins, near Bulawayo, are remains of a superior class of circular dwellings which I am told are similar in character to huts in use at the present day by Kaffirs living near Lake Ngami; on the granite hills near Khami can be seen remains of very inferior circular mud huts built by natives of the present day.

There is a notable absence in the Dhlo-Dhlo ruins (as in all others) of the remains of dwellings and of places of burial corresponding to the number of persons who must have been employed in their erection and occupation.

MEGALITHIC MONUMENTS IN NORTH AFRICA

Fergusson, James; *Rude Stone Monuments in All Countries,* London, 1872, pp. 395–405.

It would be difficult to find a more curious illustration of the fable of "Eyes and no Eyes" than in the history of the discovery of dolmens in northern Africa. Though hundreds of travellers had passed through the country since the time of Bruce and Shaw, and though the French had possessed Algiers since 1830, an author writing on the subject ten years ago would have been fully justified in making the assertion that there were no dolmens there. Yet now we know that they exist literally in thousands. Perhaps it would not be an exaggeration to say that ten thousand are known, and their existence recorded.

     · · · · · · · · · ·

It need hardly be added that no detailed map exists showing the distribution of the dolmens in Algeria, and as many of the names by which they are known to French archaeologists are those of villages not marked on any maps obtainable in this country, it is very difficult to trace their precise position, and almost always impossible to draw with certainty any inferences from their distribution. In so far as we at present know, the principal dolmen region is situated along and on either side of a line drawn from Bona on the coast to Batna, sixty miles south of Constantine. But around Setif, and in localities nearly due south from Boujie, they are said to be in enormous numbers. The Commandant Payen reports the number of menhirs there as not less than ten thousand, averaging from 4 to 5 feet in height. One colossal monolith he describes as 26 feet in diameter at its base and 52 feet high. This, however, is surpassed by a dolmen situated near Tiaret, described by the Commandant Bernard. According to his account the cap-stone is 65 feet long by 26 feet broad, and 9 feet 6 inches thick; and this enormous mass is placed on other rocks which rise between 30 and 40 feet above the surface. If this is true, it is the most enormous dolmen known, and it is strange that it should have escaped observation so long. Even the most apathetic traveller might have been astonished at such a wonder. Whether less gigantic specimens of the class exist in that neighbourhood, we are not told, but they do in detached patches everywhere eastward throughout the province. Those described by Mr. Rhind are only twelve miles from Algiers, and others are said to exist in great numbers in the regency of Tripoli. So far as is at present known, they are not found in Morocco, but are found everywhere between Mount Atlas and the Syrtes, and apparently not near the sites of any great cities, or known centres of population, but in valleys and remote corners, as if belonging to a nomadic or agricultural population.

When we speak of the ten thousand or, it may be, twenty thousand stone sepulchral monuments that are now known to exist in northern Africa, it must not be understood that they are all dolmens or circles of the class of which we have hitherto been speaking. Two other classes certainly exist, in some places, apparently, in considerable numbers, though it is difficult to make out in what proportion, and how far their forms are local. One of these classes, called Bazina by the Arabs, is thus described by Mr. Flower:---"Their general character is that of three concentric enclosures of stones of greater or less dimensions, so arranged as to form a series of steps. Sometimes, indeed, there are

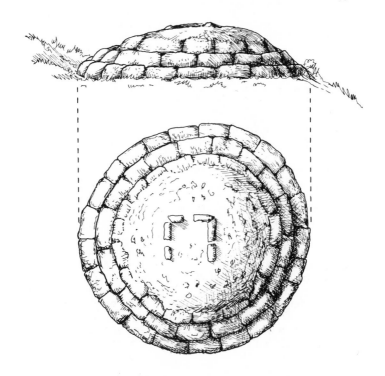

Bazina, a type of megalithic monument found in North Africa

only two outer circles, and occasionally only one. The diameter of the
larger axis of that here represented is about 30 feet. In the centre are
usually found three long and slender upright stones, forming three sides
of a long rectangle, and the interior is paved with pebbles and broken
stones.

"The Chouchas are found in the neighbourhood of the Bazinas, and
are closely allied to them. They consist of courses of stones regularly
built up like a wall, and not in steps like the Bazinas. Their diameter
varies from 7 to as much as 40 feet; but the height of the highest above
the soil does not exceed 5 to 10 feet. They are usually capped and
covered by a large flag-stone, about 4 inches thick, under which is a
regular trough or pit formed of stones from a foot and a half to 3 feet in
thickness. The interior of these little towers is paved like the Bazinas;
and indeed M. Payen considers that they are the equivalents in the mountains of the Bazinas in the plains."

In many instances the chouchas and bazinas are found combined in
one monument, and sometimes a regular dolmen is mounted on steps
similar to those of a bazina, representing one existing halfway between
Constantine and Bona. But, in fact, there is no conceivable combination
which does not seem to be found in these African cemeteries; and did we
know them all, they might throw considerable light on some questions
that are now very perplexing.

The chouchas are found sometimes isolated, and occasionally 10 to 12 feet apart from one another in groups. In certain localities the summits and ridges of the hills are covered with them, while on the edges of steep cliffs they form fringes overhanging the ravines.

In both these classes of monuments the bodies are almost always found in a doubled-up posture, the knees being brought up to the chin, and the arms crossed over the breast, like those in the Axevalla tomb described above.

The most remarkable peculiarity of the tumuli and circles in Algeria is the mode in which they are connected together by double lines of stones---as Mr. Flowers expresses it, like beads on a string. What the object of this was has not been explained, nor will it be easy to guess, till we have more, and more detailed, drawings than we now possess. Mr. Feraud's plate xxviii. shows such a line zigzagging across the plain between two heights, like a line of field fortifications, and with dolmens and tumuli sometimes behind or in front of the lines, and at others strung upon it. At first sight it looks like the representation of a battle-field, but, again, what are we to make of such a group as that [pictured]. It is the most extensive plan of any one of these groups which has yet been published, but it must be received with caution. There is no scale attached to it. The triple circles with dolmens I take to be tumuli, like those of the Aveyron, but the whole must be regarded as a diagram, not as a plan, and as such very unsafe to reason upon. Still, as it certainly is not invented, it shows the curious manner in which these monuments are joined together, as well as the various forms which they take. (pp. 395-400)

A choucha from North Africa

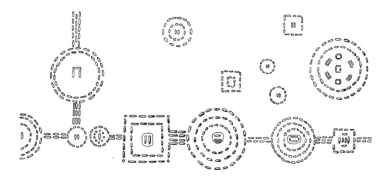

A group of megalithic structures in Algeria

• Europe

MALTA'S MEGALITHIC CITIES

Fergusson, James; *Rude Stone Monuments in All Countries,* London, 1872, pp. 415–419.

The best known monuments of the Maltese groups are situated near the centre of the Isle of Gozo, in the commune of Barbato. When Houel wrote in 1787, only the outside wall with the apse of one of the inner chambers and the entrance of another were known. He mistook the right-hand apse of the second pair of chambers for part of a circle, and so represented it with a dolmen in the centre, led to this apparently by the existence of a real circle which then was found at a distance of 350 yards from the main group. This circle was 140 feet in diameter, composed of stones ranged close together and alternately broad and tall, as shown in the next woodcut, which represents the rear of the principal monument. The entrance was marked by two very tall stones, apparently 20 feet high. The interior was apparently rugged, but there is nothing in the plates to show from what cause. When Houel made his plan, it had all the appearance of being what was styled a regular "Druidical circle," and might have been used as such to support any Druidical theory. It is now however evident that it really was only the commencement of the envelope of a pair of chambers, such as we find in all the monuments of this class on these islands. If the plan is correct, it was the most regular of any, which, besides its having every appearance of never having been completed, would lead us to suppose that it was the last of the series. This monument has now entirely disappeared, as has also another of even more megalithic appearance which stood within a few yards of the principal group, but of which unfortunately we have neither

The Giant's Tower at Gozo, Maltese Islands

plan nor details. It is shown with tolerable distinctness in a view in Mr. Frere's possession, and in the plates which are engraved from drawings by a native artist, which Admiral Smyth brought home in 1827, and which are engraved in volume xxii. of the 'Archaeologia.' Unfortunately the text that accompanies these plates is of the most unsatisfactory character. This he partially explains by saying that he had left his measurements with Colonel Otto Beyer, who had just caused the principal pair of chambers to be excavated. (pp. 415-416)

THE PREHISTORIC REMAINS OF THE MALTESE ISLANDS
Zammit, T.; *Antiquity,* 4:55-79, 1930.

The Complete Megalithic Buildings. Besides noticing the minor neolithic remains of these islands it is well to give a cursory glance at the megalithic buildings methodically arranged for a definite purpose such as dwellings or sanctuaries. It is astonishing how numerous these buildings must have been in the Maltese islands. Some of them in the course of ages have partly or completely disappeared; but those that still remain are sure evidence of the activity of a race already formed into a large, organic and peaceful society.

The number of buildings is more bewildering than their magnificence. If the islands had only one or two complete megalithic structures one would feel that the neolithic population had raised a monument to the Power they believed in, or in honour of a hero or for the hero's use, but when these complete dwellings, towers or temples, whatever they may be thought to be, are met with all over the island the explanation of their presence is certainly perplexing.

In this work of compilation, however, it is useless to go deeply into this interesting question, and the author feels that he must confine himself to a simple list of these extraordinary monuments.

Standing on the shores of the Grand Harbour the importance of this splendid haven is shown by the number of megalithic monuments surrounding it. We can only mention what remains on the southern shores, for those that were probably raised on the northern side were completely demolished when Valletta was built on the Mount Sceberras in 1568. The southern heights of the harbour are known as Il Kortin, a name which later was changed to Cordin or Corradino. [Limited space permits us to include only one group of these magnificent Maltese ruins.] (pp. 63-64)

A Maltese megalithic building

The Tarxien Groups. Not far from the Corradino ruins, another group of megalithic buildings can now be seen to the southeast before reaching Tarxien (Tarshien).

The monument was completely buried under field soil until 1914, and nothing on the surface pointed to its existence. The farmer who rented the fields near Tal-Erwich cemetery volunteered the information that a certain depth below the surface his tools struck blocks of stone; this led the Curator of the museum to investigate the site, which was completely excavated in about six years.

This magnificent megalithic monument consists of three groups of buildings which the excavator believes to be temples, of three different periods, but all of them in the Stone Age, or at least before the diffusion of the Bronze Age culture. The temples are freely connected with each other, and at present they have a common approach from a large semi-circular forecourt.

The first temple, supposed to have been the earliest of the three to the northeast, had a regular entrance flanked by upright blocks of stone across which a high step was laid. This led to a central corridor in a

NW-SE direction along which two sets of semicircular apses are disposed. No decorations whatever are to be seen in this building but the northeast apse was connected with a room which was probably used as an oracular chamber.

The second temple was originally reached from the south, where the third temple was later on constructed and which, probably, occupies the site of its forecourt. A passage, over 20 ft. long, leads to an elliptical space about 50 ft. long at right angles to it, ending in an oval apse at each end with a circular fireplace built in the middle in front of the passage. The southern wall of this elliptical enclosure is pierced by two gateways, one to the right and one to the left of the corridor, leading into two comparatively small rooms. On the walls of the room on the east side the figures of two bulls and a sow are cut in relief.

Beyond this elliptical space a high threshold is laid in front of a ten foot corridor flanked by two semicircular apses, in which two stone screens decorated with spirals in relief are still standing (plate III). Beyond this, another high threshold is found before one reaches a pair of circular apses of smaller dimensions. This second temple is built with great care and some of its stones are decorated with spirals in relief.

The third temple, reached from the forecourt to the south, has a huge convex slab for a threshold, beyond which is a short passage paved with a single block of stone. The passage leads to a square space flanked by an apsidal room on each side, in front of which are beautifully decorated blocks. The remains of a colossal stone idol stands on the side of the right apse. In the left apse are the remains of an elaborate chapel in which carved blocks and two friezes representing sacrificial animals are still to be seen. (Plate VI)

The main corridor extends further north to a semicircular shrine on a high platform, of which the front is decorated with a delightful pattern of spirals. An apse to the left of this platform is connected with an archaic shrine, and, to the right, the eastern apse, symmetrical to the one to the west, was modified to afford an entrance to the second temple.

During the excavation of this site it was found that the floor of these temples was covered with about 3 ft. of silt, a sandy dust that had spread over the site in the long length of time during which the monument was a heap of ruins. After this accumulation of soil a Bronze Age people made their appearance in Malta; they disposed of their dead by incineration, and utilized the open space under which the Stone Age remains were buried for the deposition of their cinerary urns. (pp. 67-69)

STONE MONUMENTS OF MINORCA
Anonymous; *Nature,* 119:61, 1927.

It has generally been held that the talayots of Minorca, great mounds of huge, rough uncemented stones 26 ft.-30 ft. high, were comparable with the better known nurhags of Sardinia. This comparison was based

Talayot at Trepuco, Minorca, off Spain

on the view that the talayot in some, if not all, cases was built hollow with an entrance, resembling in this respect a chambered cairn. Mr. Chamberlin examined 186 talayots, some previously unknown. Of these, 107 were in a sufficiently good state of preservation to permit him to say that 32 only, or one out of three, had ever had an entrance of any sort, while three alone had an interior chamber, and only one more than one apartment. It is clear, therefore, that the talayot is not comparable to the nurhag and, indeed, is a monument without a parallel. Associated with the talayot, and usually within a hundred feet of it, is a class of monument known locally as a taula---a two-stoned monument 5 ft.-12 ft. high in the shape of a Greek T, the flat top stone being fully 12 ft. long. Ten of these are now known. Each is surrounded by a horse-shoe-shaped wall pierced by a doorway surmounted by a single-stone lintel. The two classes of monument clearly stand in relation one to another, though there does not appear to be any evidence of orientation. Sir Wallis Budge has expressed the opinion that the talayots are pyramids of a funereal nature, and the taulas altars for sacrifice or other funereal ceremonies. A third class of monument, called naus from its resemblance to a ship, of which sixteen are known, has an elliptical chamber 15 ft. long by 7 ft. high, and appears to have served as a tomb for dwellers in the numerous caves in the neighbourhood.

SCOTTISH BROCHS
Anonymous; *Nature*, 120:563, 1927.

In Antiquity for September, Mr. Alexander O. Curle discusses the origin and structure of the broch---the characteristic defensive structure of the north and west of Scotland, consisting of a circular tower surrounding an open court, built of dry masonry without mortar or other binding material, and of which the height originally in some cases must have been as much as 60 feet. The walls at the base are usually 15 feet thick and contain series of superimposed galleries. A puzzling feature, a ledge projecting about 12 inches from the interior of the wall, is now explained in the light of excavations at Dun Troddan, as the resting place for beams extending to posts circling the interior and forming the roof of a closed colannade around a central hearth open to the sky. The brochs have no relation to the Nurhagi of Sardinia, which differ from them essentially in structure and purpose. Their closest analogies are to be found in the galleried duns or promontory forts and the so-called 'semi-brochs' of the west of Scotland. The distribution of the broch points to its origin in the north and west of Scotland, those found outside this area being due to an extension of tribal influence from the north. In date they are to be regarded as not earlier than the Iron Age, while the occurrence of Samian ware, Roman coins, and other objects, indicates that they were occupied at the time of the Roman invasion and in the second century A.D., though probably they date back some hundreds of years before that time. They probably were occupied for some time later, but from the absence of wheel-made pottery and Viking relics, it cannot be asserted that they survived to the eighth century.

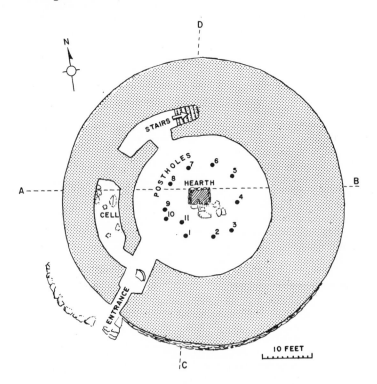

Horizontal section of the Broch of Dun Troddan, indicating the galleries and circular openings

LARGE-SCALE PATTERNS OF STRUCTURES

At dimensions of tens to a few thousand feet, ancient structures display many different geometries---circles, pyramids, etc.---suggesting that ancient man was fascinated by such regularities long before Euclid. The "macroforms" described in Chapter 3 prove that "primitive" peoples could extrapolate geometric creativity to distances of several miles, so large that their patterns could be appreciated only from the air. Some artistic or geometric urge also impelled them to build regularities into the ways they located their structures. To illustrate, the Mayans seemed to like their cities arranged on a hexagonal grid. In Britain, the tendency was to align megalithic structures along straight lines (the controversial "leys"). Other such "large-scale" systematics may exist, for we are just beginning to look for this unusual macroscopic type of order that ancient man used to guide his planning.

• Mesoamerica

TERRITORIAL ORGANIZATION OF THE LOWLAND CLASSIC MAYA

Marcus, Joyce; *Science,* 180:911-916, 1973.

Summary and Conclusions. Thus far I have discussed ancient Maya sociopolitical structure from the upper levels of the hierarchy downward. Let me now summarize their territorial organization from the bottom upward, starting at the hamlet level (Fig. 8).

The smallest unit of settlement---one usually overlooked by archeological surveys in the lowland rain forest---was probably a cluster of thatched huts occupied by a group of related families; large clusters may have been divided into four quadrants along the lines suggested by Coe. Because of the long fallow period (6 to 8 years) characteristic of slash-and-burn agriculture in the Peten, these small hamlets are presumed to have changed location over the years, although they probably shifted in a somewhat circular fashion around a tertiary ceremonial-civic center for whose maintenance they were partly responsible. These tertiary centers were spaced at fairly regular intervals around secondary ceremonial-civic centers with pyramids, carved monuments, and palace-like residences.

In turn, the secondary centers occurred at such regular intervals as to form hexagonal patterns around primary centers, which were still larger, with acropolises, multiple ceremonial plazas, and greater numbers of monuments. In some cases, the distance between secondary centers was roughly twice the distance between secondary and tertiary centers, creating a lattice of nested hexagonal cells. This pattern, which conforms to a Western theoretical construct, was presumably caused by factors of service function, travel, and transport. The pattern was not recognized by the Maya at all. They simply recognized that a whole series of smaller centers were dependent on a primary center and therefore mentioned its emblem glyph. Linking the centers of the various hexagons were marriage alliances between members of royal dynasties, who had no kinship ties with the farmers in the hamlets.

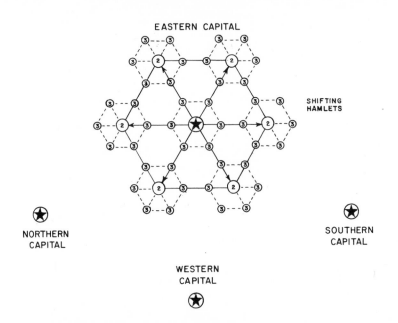

Idealized diagram of the territorial organization of lowland Classic Maya, from regional capital to outlying hamlet. Stars indicate regional capitals; 2s, secondary centers, etc.

Out of the large number of primary centers available to them, the Maya selected four as regional capitals. True to their cosmology, the Maya regarded these capitals as associated with the four quadrants of their realm, regardless of their actual location. Each was the home city for a very important dynasty whose junior members probably ruled secondary centers. Since the hexagonal lattices were probably adjusted to variations in population density, each of the four quadrants of the Maya realm probably controlled a comparable number of persons. So strong was the cognized model that, despite the rise and fall of individual centers, there seem always to have been four capitals, each associated with a direction and, presumably, with a color.

There is still a great deal to learn about the social, political, and territorial organization of the lowland Maya, and parts of the picture presented here need far more data for their confirmation. What seems likely is that the Maya had an overall quadripartite organization (rather than a core and buffer zone) and that within each quadrant there was at least a five-tiered administrative hierarchy of capital, secondary center, tertiary center, village, and hamlet. Perhaps most significant, there was no real conflict between the lattice-like network predicted by locational analysis and the cosmological four-part structure predicted by epigraphy and ethnology. (p. 915)

• Europe

NOTES ON ANCIENT BRITISH STONE MONUMENTS. I
Lockyer, Norman; *Nature,* 77:56-59, 1907.

The Inter-relation of Monuments. In my "Notes on Stonehenge" Nature, vol. lxxi., p. 391) I referred to some remarkable relations between Stonehenge and the surrounding localities which had been communicated to me by Colonel Johnston, the late director-general of the Ordnance Survey. These are rendered manifest by the accompanying diagrams which I reproduce.

Fig. 1 shows that Stonehenge is (1) on the same straight line which contains Sidbury, Grovely Castle and Castle Ditches; (2) at the apex of an equilateral triangle of exactly six miles in the side; (3) that Salisbury, i. e. Solisbury Cathedral, from its name an old solar temple, was on the same straight line which contained Stonehenge and Old Sarum.

Fig. 2 shows that the oldest cross-roads on Salisbury Plain exactly occupy the centre of the triangle referred to.

Such relations as the above, but on a smaller scale, are often to be noticed, in some cases between monuments, in others between monuments and decided natural features on the sky line as seen from them.

I give some examples from Cornwall.

At Trevethy is one of the most famous cromlechs in that county, and it has not been restored, so that we need not hesitate to measure it to try to determine its meaning. Close by, at St. Cleer, is a renowned holy well, and a little further away King Doniert's stone.

The accompanying photographic reduction of the Ordnance map shows the strict relation of these monuments. The entrance of the cromlech is directed towards the November sunrise, az. S. 63⁰ E. ; looking in the opposite direction it commands the May sunset. I shall refer to this later. As seen from the holy well the cromlech marks the azimuth of the May sunrise. The monolith, King Doniert's stone, is true west from the cromlech, and so marks the equinoctial sunsets.

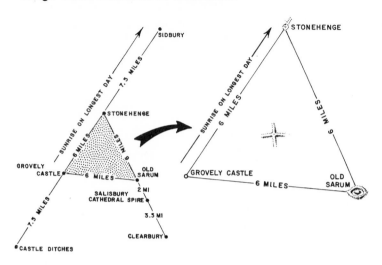

Pattern of some ancient British sites

In the Bodmin district are two famous circles, the Stripple stones and Trippet stones, some half-mile apart.

The following table shows the relation of the latter to the former, and also to the surrounding hill-tops, as I believe was first noticed by Mr. A. L. Lewis. We indeed learn why the circle was erected on the precise spot it occupies.

Trippet Stones, Blisland, lat. 50° 33' N.

	Az.		Hill	Dec.	Star	Date
To Stripple Stones.	N. $81^{\circ}30'$E		2°	N. 6° 42'	Pleiades	1720 BC
" Rough Tor	N. 15°	E	1-$1/2^{\circ}$	N. 39° 1'	Arcturus	1700 BC
" Brown Willy	N. 31°	E	1-$1/2^{\circ}$	N. 34° 5'	Capella	1420 BC
" Hawks Tor	N. 63°	E	2-$1/2^{\circ}$	N. 18° 34'	May Sun	May 14
" Barrow	N. 63°	E	1-$1/2^{\circ}$	S. 19° 31'	Nov. Sun	Nov. 21
			assumed			

My wife and I visited the Trippet stones in April, 1907, in the company of Mr. Horton Bolitho and Mr. Collings. A hail-storm made observations difficult, and this may explain the departure of the May and November days from the normal. The coincidence of the dates of the possible observations of Arcturus and Capella suggests that we have then the true date of the erecting of the circle, Brown Willy being subsequently used with Capella when the old alignment of Arcturus on Rough Tor became useless in consequence of the precessional movement.

I shall have more to say on the inter-relation of monuments and double and multiple circles on a future occasion.

Ancient Connection between Stonehenge and Grovely. Figs. 1 and 2 suffice to show the old association between Stonehenge and Grovely.

Canon Wordsworth, in a paper on "Grovely Customs," communicated to the annual meeting of the Wiltshire Archaeological Society held in July, 1906, at Wilton, has brought together some additional particulars touching this association.

Some of the new information refers to the gathering of wood in the valleys near Stonehenge; this, I think, may be accepted as strengthening the evidence that the plain at Stonehenge was not wooded, contrary to the opinions of many that the monument was built in a sacred grove of oaks. My argument against this view was that if the monuments had any astronomical use at Stonehenge, Dartmoor, or elsewhere, they would not have been erected among trees, which would have spoiled the observations which were always made on the horizon.

. . . .

STONEHENGE: ITS RELATIVE POSITION WITH REGARD TO OTHER ANCIENT WORKS
Spencer, Joseph Houghton; *Antiquary,* 1:144-145, 1905.

The axis of the temple, which is practically in the same line as that of the avenue, points north-eastward to the horizon in one direction, where the sun rises at the summer solstice, and, consequently, in the opposite, or south-western, direction to where it sets at the winter solstice; and it can be seen by reference to Ordnance Maps that the line thus obtained connects the British encampment named Sidbury, 735 feet above the sea, about eight miles distant from the temple to the north-east, with Grovelly Castle, another ancient work, 500 feet high, and about six miles distant, to the south-west of the temple.

The fact that Stonehenge is thus connected with two other ancient works is referred to in "An Attempt to Ascertain the Date of the Original Construction of Stonehenge from its Orientation," published in Nature, November 21, 1901, when the conclusion arrived at was 1680 B. C., with a possible error of ±200 years.

A straight and clearly-defined line, some fourteen miles long, which may be regarded as the prolonged axis of the temple, is thus derived from the positions of the sun at the summer and winter solstices, and joins two ancient fortifications with the temple.

It is not proposed to continue this line in a north-eastern direction at present, but to extend it, on the Ordnance Map (scale 1 inch to a mile), to the south-west, when it will be seen to cross a Roman road about one and a quarter miles from Grovelly Castle, and to pass, about the same distance further to the south-west, close to the Ordnance Trigonometrical Station, marked 449 feet above the sea.

The line, if continued further, would cut Teffont Manor and Castle Ditches, the latter an ancient work 630 feet high, and pass through the old castle in Wardour Park. Between this point and where it crosses the river Don it would be within three miles of Winkelbury Camp, and about three and a half miles after crossing the river, and at a distance of one and a half miles from Shaftesbury, pass through West Melbury, near Melbury Hill, which has an altitude of 863 feet.

Thence, passing between West Orchard and Manston, it runs by the castle near Sturminster Newton, through Fifehead Neville, and Kingston, to Buckland Newton, between Knoll, 651 feet high on one side, and Ridge Hill, 700 feet high, on the other.

Being still continued, it passes between Cerne Abbas and Up Cerne, through a camp in Cerne Park, where are some ancient ditches, having an altitude of 700 feet, to the Court House at Sydling St. Nicholas, and to a point beyond, 581 feet high, near Maiden Newton.

Thence, by Hill Barn, 608 feet high, it passes between a cromlech and a British village, crossing the road at 707 feet above the sea near a tumulus, and, if continued to Higher Coombe, near Chilcombe Hill, it there crosses the line from Weymouth Bay to Porlock Bay, which passes through Castle Neroche, and is derived from the setting sun at the summer solstice, and the rising sun at the winter solstice and upon which line the "Monks' Walk," Corfe, is situated, as described in the Proceedings of the Somersetshire Archaeological Society last year.

Within an area of about half a square mile adjoining the point of junction of these two lines lie the camp on Chilcombe Hill and the site of a British village, earthworks, and tumuli on Askerswell Down. And if the line from Stonehenge be continued to the English Channel, it terminates at a point on the coast between Burton Bradstock and Swyre, marked Cliff End.

A third line is also connected with Higher Combe.

There is in Melbury Park near Evershot, which must be distinguished from Melbury near Shaftesbury, a group of eight roadways or drives, radiating from a central point 460 feet high, in an open space in Great High Wood, named "The Circle," arranged upon the same principle and connected with the sun as are the crosses of the "Monks' Walk" upon the Weymouth Bay to Porlock Bay line, before referred to.

For a fuller description of this figure see the Antiquary, No. 117, vol. xx., p. 99, article, "Ancient Trackways in England." It is wished to direct attention to the fact that a line drawn from the centre of "The Circle" in Melbury Park through the middle of the road or drive running south by west, nearly, if continued to the English Channel, touches it near "The Knoll," 500 feet high, above Puncknowle, and on its way passes by Rampisham and through the camp on Eggardon Hill and the site of a British village, before it cuts the point of junction of the other two lines at Higher Coombe.

Thus there are three lines---one radiating from the centre of Stonehenge, about forty-eight miles from Higher Coombe; another from the centre of the "Monks' Walk," about twenty-five and a half miles from Higher Coombe, on the Weymouth Bay to Porlock Bay line, which passes through Castle Neroche; and the third from the centre of "The Circle" in Melbury Park, about nine and a half miles distant---all meeting at Higher Coombe, which adjoins an elevated point in the immediate neighbourhood of the camp on Chilcombe Hill, the site of a British village, earthworks, and tumuli, thus marking it as a position of some importance.

The inference may be drawn from the foregoing facts that these three lines connected with Stonehenge and other primitive works, also with the sun at the summer and winter solstices, meeting at Higher Coombe, where there are also remains of ancient works, is not a mere coincidence, but a factor in a well-considered and skilfully-designed system.

Consequently, it is suggested that Stonehenge is not simply an isolated monument of ancient art, but an integral part of a comprehensive and far-reaching whole; therefore, in determining the date of Stonehenge, the period of the formation of those earthworks so evidently connected with it would also be decided.

THE ORIGINS OF THE LEYS

Brown, Peter Lancaster; *Megaliths, Myths and Men,* New York, 1976, pp. 222-223.

The cult of the leys via Watkins' theories had its genesis one hot summer's day in the early 1920s. On that afternoon, Watkins recalled, he was riding across the Bredwardine hills some 19km (12 miles) west of Hereford and stopped on a crest for a moment in order to take in the sweep of the panorama before him. It was then he noticed something which he believed no one in Britain had seen for thousands of years: it was as if the more recent surface of the great landscape had been stripped away, revealing an unambiguous web of lines linking the ancient sites of antiquity that stretched out before him. Each fell into place in the whole scheme of things; ole stones, holy wells, moats, mounds, crossroads, and pagan sites obscured by Christian churches stood in exact alignments that ran on for as far as the eye could trace. In a single all-powerful visionary moment, Watkins, as a self-appointed cult leader, was witness to what one of his later disciples described as 'the magic world of prehistoric Britain', but which Watkins less histrionically described as 'a glimpse of a world almost forgotten when the Roman legions marched across it'. He related that 'like Him Hawkins in Treasure Island, I held in my hand the key plan of a long-lost fact...'

However, it seems likely too that Watkins was affected by the same muse as that which caught Wordsworth when he composed his great nature poem 'Prelude' (1805 version):

> I had a reverie and saw the past...
> To have before me on that dreary Plain
> Lines, circles, mounts, a mystery of shapes
> Such as in many quarters yet survive,
> With intricate profusion figuring o'er
> The untilled ground, the work, as some divine
> Of infant science, initiative forms
> By which the Druids covertly expressed
> Their knowledge of the heavens, and imaged forth...

I saw the bearded Teachers, with white wands
Uplifted, pointing to the starry sky
Alternatively, and Plain below...

Watkins maintained that the so-called old straight tracks which
crossed the landscape of prehistoric Britain over mountains, dales, and
lowland woods and decided the site of almost every kind of human communal activity.

PREHISTORIC ROADS

Modern roads are built to facilitate travel and the movement of goods;
and we may assume that ancient man built them for the same reasons.
Unfortunately, some prehistoric road terminals have not been found,
making the purposes of the roads questionable. In some ancient highway
systems, the actual purposes can only be guessed at. For example, the
enigmatic Maltese "cart ruts" have no obvious utilitarian purpose, nor
do we have a good idea what vehicles used them. The Mayan causeways
run straight as a die for miles and are magnificent engineering accomplishments. Since wheeled vehicles were rarely if ever employed for
practical transportation by the Mayans, we must assume these roads
were mainly for foot traffic and the hailing of construction materials and
farm produce. The discovery of well-preserved wooden trackways over
3,000 years old in Europe demonstrates the existence of a surprising
commerce for that period and locale.

• Mesoamerica

THE ANCIENT MAYA CAUSEWAYS OF YUCATAN
Saville, Marshall H.; *Antiquity,* 9:67-73, 1935.

On the expiration of my work at Labna, April 1891, my friend Don
Antonio Fajardo, in Ticul, urged me to undertake a trip to Chemax
in order to investigate a great ruined city which he stated was near a

large hacienda owned by him, some distance to the east of Chemax.
In September of the same year Teobert Maler saw this ancient causeway running to Coba; he reached the ruins and made several photographs, but he kept his knowledge to himself, issuing no description
of his visit. As Maler lived in Ticul and was on very friendly terms
with Don Antonio, it is probable that he learned of the ruins from his
neighbour. Hence we see that knowledge of the causeway and Coba
was not confined solely to the Indians. However, only in recent years
has it been safe to go into this region, as the Indians of Chan Santa
Cruz were in control of the country, and no extensive explorations
could have been carried out.

It remained for Dr. Thomas Gann to be the first to visit the site,
under the auspices of the Carnegie Institution of Washington, in the
winter of 1926. In the report on four expeditions to Coba during that
year by different investigators no mention is made of the causeway,
but, in his book published during the autumn, Dr. Gann speaks of it.
He says that the road is 32 feet wide and varies from 2 to 8 feet in
height. He first encountered it about 6-1/2 leagues beyond Chemax
and followed it about 4 leagues towards Coba. He writes; 'the road
represents an enormous expenditure of time and labour, involving
the quarrying, transport, facing, and building in, of nearly a million
tons of stone, and is unique throughout the whole of the Maya area,
for though cement covered roads exist in and around many of the ruined
cities, no such elevated causeway has been found elsewhere'. Again
he writes: 'on each side of the road were great quarries from which
the stone used in its construction had been taken. Holes were apparently sunk round the great blocks, in which they built fires, and then
pouring water into the red-hot holes, cause the rocks to split, so that
slabs of it could be easily dug out. The sides were built of great blocks
of cut stone weighing hundreds of pounds; the central part was filled
in with unhewn blocks of limestone, and the top covered with rubble,
which, as is indicated by the traces of it which remain here and there,
was once cemented over....It was convex, being higher in the centre

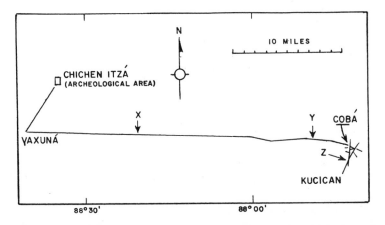

Map of the Yaxuna-Coba causeway, greatest of the ancient Mayan
roads; 62½ miles long, 30-34 feet wide, built of stone and surfaced
with cement.

than at either side, and ran so far as we followed it, straight as an arrow, and almost flat as a rule'.

A member of the third Carnegie Expedition to Coba in 1926, was J. Eric Thompson, who has recently published a much fuller account of the causeway. From Thompson's account, published in Spanish, I quote as follows: 'noteworthy are the great number of roads which appear to radiate from the metropolis of Coba, undoubtedly one of the most important of Maya cities, being only surpassed by Tikal in the extension and number of temples and mounds which it contains. Of these roads, we counted eight, and Indians of confidence who have travelled in the mountains told us of two or three more. They are of variable height, but the great road seen by Dr. Gann, which was discovered by the Austrian archaeologist Teobert Maler, has a width of approximately ten metres. Another road which united the city of Coba with the sacred ward of Macanxoc has, however, a width of twenty metres more or less, but this is exceptional.

The great road called by Dr. Gann the Camino Real de Occidente, does not, so far as we could determine, connect Coba with the ruins of Chichen Itza, but it seems to end at Yaxhuana, a ruin whose architecture very much resembles that of Coba. It is situated about ten miles south of Chichen Itza. The distance between these two cities is some sixty miles. On account of lack of time and scarcity of water, we were not able to go over the road more than a distance of ten or eleven miles, the road running in a straight line without any curves or deviation due east in the direction of Coba. In the last half-mile which we traversed when we were already entering the wards of Coba the road is divided into two sections: one goes towards the ward of the north called Nohoch Mul, and the other in an extended curve ended at the foot of the highest hill in the city proper of Coba, situated on the isthmus between the two lagoons of Coba and Macanxoc. In nearly all the entire road which we traversed it reached an elevation of a metre more or less, but when we came to depressions it maintained its proper level, undoubtedly to contend with the peril of inundation during the rainy season. So that in various places where there are depressions the road reaches a height of three to four metres.

The bed of the road consists of the typical mixture of stones such as are found in ruins of the ancient Mayas; that is to say, great unworked stones. Above this is a layer of smaller stones held together with a mixture of lime and saccab, and over this is a typical pavement of plaster made of lime and saccab which appears to be almost a cement. Of course the floor has been almost completely destroyed. The sides of the road were made of walls of stones roughly squared, and of sufficiently regular size. It seems certain that these walls were formerly covered with plaster in ancient times, but today there remain no signs of it. These roads are much damaged by the great trees whose roots have thrust into the cement, tearing up the stones, and as the trees have fallen they brought up great masses of mixed stones cemented together. Without doubt, however, with only a little repairing these roads would serve well for automobiles.

There is another road which unites Coba with Kucican, a ruin which we found some ten miles to the south, and for a number of miles has an elevation of six to seven metres. Near Kucican there are various passages made under the road, constructed with the typical Maya roof of the ancients. These tunnels would permit travellers to go from one side of the road to the other without having to climb over them. A short distance from Coba this same road joins another which seems to come out from the sacred ward of Macanxoc. The roads connect at an angle of 35 to 40 degrees, and in the angle forming this junction is a small ruined building. (pp. 69-72)

THE SACBE SYSTEM

Roys, Lawrence, and Shook, Edwin M.; *Preliminary Report on the Ruins of Ake, Yucatan,* bound in *American Antiquity,* vol. 31, 1965, pp. 43-45.

In summary, Sacbe I begins at the east edge of Str. 8, near the middle of Ake, and runs 7 km. in a straight line slightly north of east to Xemna. There it makes the only change in direction observed and continues to Izamal in an almost dead east direction north, 87-1/2° east, magnetic. The sacbe has practically the same width, 13.2 m., and identical construction at every point checked. Its surface appears level throughout, the actual height varying with the irregularities of the limestone plain. The minimum height noted is 30 cm., and the maximum about 1.5 m.

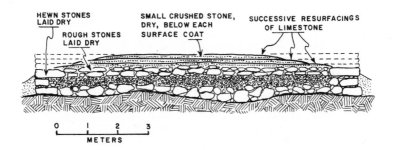

Section of Scaba raised road from Ake to Izamal

The edges are faced with large blocks, roughly hewn or broken to shape, and occasionally exceeding 2 m. in length. One has a vertical depth of fully 1 m. The fill between consists of uncut rubble from bed-rock up to a predetermined height, then a stratum of well broken-up rock, then another layer of uncut large stones more carefully laid than the bottom fill, and finally a topping of finer crushed rock apparently temped. The cross section shows enough camber to insure rapid drainage. Two resurfacings of a major nature increased the height of the road about 16 cm. each time. These must have been enormous undertakings considering the width of the road and its probable length of 32 km.

The Indian laborers at Ake know of the <u>sacbe</u> going to the east. They recounted to Segovia a delightful modern folk tale of its origin. In ancient times, two cousins were kings at Ake and Izamal, and the causeway connecting these cities was built in order to speed the delivery of the super-excellent tortillas from the kitchen of the King of Ake to his royal cousin at Izamal.

However, there is no present knowledge of such a road leading westward. In the limited time available, Shook sought it where a west-bound continuation would logically fall, but without success. Segovia repeated and widened the search and located Sacbe 7, but that terminated as shown on the map. In March, 1953, he spent the good part of a day criss-crossing the area west of our map, away from roads and paths, but again was unrewarded. (pp. 44-45)

• New Zealand

ANCIENT ROADS AND STONE SEATS IN NEW ZEALAND
Anonymous; *American Antiquarian*, 26:196, 1904.

The Journal of the Polynesian Society for December, 1903, contains a description of an ancient road called the "Great Road of Toi." It follows, generally, the foot of the hills, cutting across the mouths of the valleys, leaving the level flat to the seaward. It is about 22 or 23 miles in length, and is paved with flat volcanic or coral stones. Its width is about 15 or 20 feet. In several places, at the sites of old villages, are to be seen stone seats, where local gossips used to sit and learn the news of the passers by. The principal temple or marae, where the ruling chief often dwelt and where the sacrifice to the gods were made and the annual Feast of the Presentation of the First Fruits was held, was located at Araltetunga. This was probably at one time enclosed with a wall. At Arerangi, where the high chief usually lived, is a platform, about two feet above the level of the road, the face of which is lined with stone seats having backs to them. When the minor chiefs used to visit the high chief (Ariki) they occupied those seats, and they lodged in a seven-roomed house on the opposite side of the road, which was called a house of amusement. At Araitetinga there was a seat on which the chief pontiff sat when offerings were made. On his right, was seated a priest, and further away, was a seat which was called <u>puera</u>, meaning to open or disclose, because it

was through this priest that the decision was announced. Another
seat was called <u>Maringi-toto</u>, or blood-spilling, because on this
stone was laid the heads of the human victims which were brought here
to be sacrificed to the gods. These seats remind us of those which
were common in Peru and Mexico, though it is not known that there
is any connection between them.

• Africa

ANCIENT CIVILISATION IN THE RIFT VALLEY
Anonymous; *Nature,* 130:969, 1932.

Capt. G. E. H. Wilson discusses in <u>Man</u> for November the evidence for the existence of a forgotten civilisation in the Rift Valley,
East Africa. The existence of ancient works, terracing, grading
roads (the so-called elephant tracks) and irrigation works---canals
and drainage---is now established not only in Tanganyika, but also
in Abyssinia, Uganda, Kenya and Northern Rhodesia. The terraces,
averaging in width at the top about one foot, but probably originally
about three feet, follow the contours of the hills. The depth between
terraces is about three feet. The roads, clearly not elephant tracks,
point to a high state of civilisation. They are difficult to locate,
though in places they are part of roads in use to-day. The points at
present located suggest a system of communication running north
and south on the eastern side of the Great Lakes, pointing to outlets
by way of the Nile in the north and by Rhapta in the south, with possibly an intermediate route via Mombasa, the origin of which may prove
very much more ancient than is thought. There are traces of an extensive system of irrigation at Uhehe, and in low-lying districts, such
as the Mgeta River near Kisaki, there are river diversions which may
be artificial. As to the authors of this civilisation, there are legends
of an alien race dominating local peoples in both north and south Tanganyika. At present there is a great diversity of language and culture
where these ancient works are found; but at some time the people may
have been more homogeneous. If there has been an alien immigration,
it is possible that it may have taken place so early as 1500 B. C. , and
that by the time of Solomon (970 B. C.) a flourishing trade already
existed and the Sheban port of Rhapta had been established. It is
suggested that this ancient civilisation may have originated in the north,
spread through the Rift Valley over the highlands of the Great Lakes,
and have reached Zimbabwe.

THE AZANIAN CIVILISATION OF KENYA
Huntingford, G. W. B.; *Antiquity,* 7:153–165, 1932.

IV.   Under the term Linear Earthworks are included (A) artificial
works which are beyond doubt roads; (B) works which appear to be
ditches rather than roads.   Undoubted roads, which in some places
are graded, and in others pass through hillsides in cuttings not unlike railway cuttings, and cross swampy ground over carefully made
embankments, occur in Kenya and Tanganyika.   Such a road, with
cuttings and embankments, crosses the east side of the Uasin Gishu
plateau.   Sometimes a ditch may be really a sunk road, as in the case

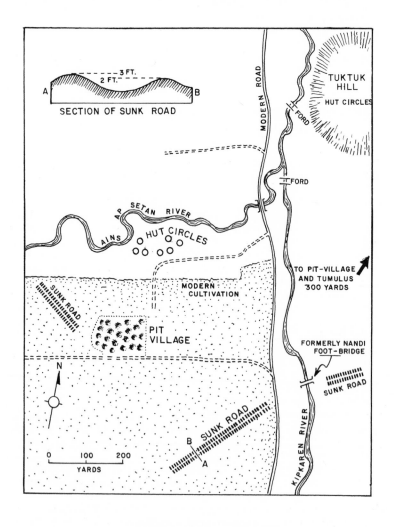

Sunken roads in Kenya

of a series which encloses on two sides the farm where I live. Here in 1922, before the land was ploughed, two lengths of ditch were visible for a distance of over 600 yards, running between low banks from one river to another, and re-appearing across the river, which must have been crossed by a wooden bridge, as it is not fordable there. On Tilolwa Ridge in Nandi occurs a ditch which is plainly not a road, and equally plainly not of natural origin; a length of some 250 yards (no more is recorded) has a higher bank on the upper side than on the lower. (pp. 158-159)

EXPLORATIONS IN THE NORTHERN FAYUM
Caton-Thompson, G.; *Antiquity*, 1:326-340, 1927.

The bones of strange ancestral mammals strengthen the overwhelming impression of a return to an extinct, uncanny, strangely beautiful, pre-human world. The region shows, compared with the low desert, few traces of human visitation. The little-used camel track to the Baharia Oasis passes through it for some distance: ancient flintmine workings on a hill top: remains of a stone circle of roughly-piled up blocks of basalt: an inscription on a rock, ||| ⁝ᵢᵢ V = ₒ ||||: the 25-year-old traces of the Beadnell-Andrews camp: these, and above all in arresting interest, a long straight four-mile thread of ancient road running north.

This road was first noted by Beadnell in his official survey memoir, but he gives no photographs or details as to structure or probable age, beyond its label on the map "ancient quarry road." Since then no further details have, to my knowledge, been added. The road, at its lower extremity, availing itself of gaps in the scarp immediately west of the little dynastic temple of Qasr el Sagha, is not, in fact, recognizable as man's handiwork until it emerges on the level of the middle scarp, whose main features we have already indicated. Here, with the unbroken width of the scarp plain to cross in its progress northwards to the hills---its ultimate destination---it straightens out into a line of paved track, about 7-8 feet broad, carefully laid with slabs of whatever rock was handiest to collect at that point of its course. Much of this is rather friable sandstone, which has weathered badly, and forms a surface, compared to which the stony desert on either side is smooth going. The slabs, however, though wide interstices separate them, still lie fairly flat.

At another point the sandstone paving is succeeded by a stretch of unusual---perhaps unique---road metal, the logs of fossil wood already referred to laid side by side, sleeper fashion across the road. The trunks naturally vary in size, but the average diameter is about 1 foot. Two big dumps of basalt blocks by the wayside give a clue as to the road's ultimate destination; but no pottery has yet been found to give a clue as to its makers. Nearing the final hills, the road becomes more broken---in places even difficult to trace---owing to destructive drainage from the hill slopes; but we picked it up again under the frowning peaks of Widan el Faras, at a point where it is raised and cambered above the surrounding level, in order, presumably, to avoid the racing spates in time of storm. Following on another 1/4 mile we suddenly come to the abrupt termination of our quest, sharply brought up against a steep hill-side, down which has shot a dark mass of basalt blocks from their sill-bed upon the summit: a nature-worked quarry. Not far away a large, sunk, sand-filled hollow, fringed with corrugated Roman pottery litter, gives a first clue as to the probable quarrymen. The presumptive evidence seems strong, supported as we were afterwards to find it, by lumps of basalt, and Roman sherds at a low level, far away, near the present lake. On the other hand, none of the Graeco-Roman towns and temples to the Fayum show any trace of basalt in structure or decoration. Dime, an important and extensive ruin calling for excavation, lying 4 miles nearly due south of the road's termination near Qasr el Sagha, shows, superficially at least, not a trace of this material; nor does the other nearest Ptolemaic town of Kom Ashim, though this has been extensively excavated, and lumps of basalt may actually be found on the low desert in its direction. Road metal for export? We know of none.

The only possible alternative to the road's Roman origin would seem to lie in connexion with the dynastic temple of Qasr el Sagha: its termination, a great elongated dump of colossal, weathered basalt blocks, is within a stone's throw of the building. The temple is built of giant blocks of sandy limestone, and is stripped of all adornment; its very date is uncertain. But such passing attention as we---not Egyptologists and engaged on other work---were able to give it, indicates that it is not later than the Middle Kingdom: I would myself suggest that it was originally built in Old Kingdom times, and continued in use till the Middle Kingdom, my reasons being based on the presence in its immediate vicinity, concentrated in regular "workshops" of limestone and alabaster debris, of great quantities of crescentic, hollow flint grinders, which are known to date from protodynastic to Old Kingdom times; and fragments of contemporary, spouted vases. That the place, however, was also occupied in the XI–XII dynasties is certain. Not only are shaft-graves of that age within a stone's throw ---we collected a scarab, and elements of a wooden funerary boat from old spoil heaps and ravaged fillings---but we discovered during the first season a small cemetery of 41 graves of this age at the base of the lowest scarp.

Now, in addition, a fragment of inscribed, polished basalt from the temple area seals the evidence for the later date. But this basalt is a fine-textured stone, unlike our coarse-grained local material, and seems unlikely, curiously enough, to have the same source. The probabilities of our road origin, therefore, seem to lie with the Romans; but the subject is well worth following up in further study and greater leisure. (pp. 338–340)

EGYPTIAN SHIP RAILWAY
Anonymous; *Science,* 18:47, 1891.

It is more than probable, says <u>Iron</u>, that the Egyptians were in
the habit of transporting vessels overland across the Isthmus of Suez,
and tradition records that twenty-three centuries ago a true ship-
railway, with polished granite blocks as rails, existed and was
worked across the Isthmus of Corinth, where the construction of a
ship-canal has been projected.

• Europe

THE CART-RUTS OF MALTA
Murray, M. A.; *Man,* 28:20-22, 1928.

The ancient wheel-tracks which are found in many parts of Malta
have long been of interest to archaeologists. As they are being rapidly
destroyed---owing to road-making, increase in the area of cultivation, and other causes---it seems worth while to record at least a
few of them. Professor Zammit and Commodore Clark Hall hope to
make a complete map, from air-photographs, of all the known tracks
on the island. This paper must, therefore, be considered only as a
preliminary introduction to the study of the subject.

The first point to be considered is whether the ruts are natural or
artificial. It is, of course, well known that parallel fissures often
occur in limestone, and, if these ruts were only straight lines of varying gauges, there might be considerable doubt as to their origin. But
they often curve, and when they do so the distance between the two
parallel lines remains the same; in other words, a pair of tracks
are always equidistant throughout their length, whether straight or
curving. The gauge is also fairly constant, being rather wider than
a modern Maltese cart.

The depth of the ruts is not very great: one of the deepest is seen
in fig. 2 [photos not reproduced]. The photograph shows the section
of the cutting for the footpath and steps which join two of the zigzags
on the Military Road near Nashar (Naxxar). The rut is about a foot
deep.

The archaeological evidence for the human origin of the tracks is
fairly strong. In ancient Greece such ruts were cut in the rocky slopes
of hills for the passage of wheeled traffic, which could not otherwise
surmount the uneven surface. (The kind of surface to be traversed is

seen in almost all the photographs). Caillemer, in his description
of ancient Greek roads, speaks of these tracks as "Ornieres artifi-
cielles, profondes de quelques centimetres." He states that the
Greeks "creusaient pour les roues des rainures qu'ils nivelaient avec
grand soin. Entre les deux rainures, lorsque le sol etait trop raboteux
ou trop inegal, on repandait du sable ou du gravier." The ruts were
probably cut quite shallow and were deepened by wear. "Pour remedier
a l'inconvenient des rencontres de chars, il suffisait d'etablir deux
voies paralleles, ou meme, en se contentant d'une voie unique, de
disposer de place en place des courbes d'evitement." The parallel
pairs of ruts are a common phenomenon in Malta, but the curves for
passing do not occur in any of those which I have seen. Caillemer
gives instances of such artificial cart-tracks in Italy and in the south
of France.

There seems to have been a network of these roads over the whole
island. The best examples now remaining are on the rocky slope near
the Nashar (Naxxar) Gap, close to San Paul tat Targia, down which the
new Military Road has been constructed. Another group is at Ta
Frattita on the west side of the Bin Gemma hills. Short lengths of
such roads are often found in connection with megalithic monuments,
apparently leading directly to the monument, as at Santa Sfia and
Santa Maria tal Bakkari (see my "Excavations in Malta," Part II,
Pl. XXXIII). In each of these cases the remainder of the road has been
obliterated by modern alterations, such as the making of fields, construction of metalled roads, building of houses, and so on.

The age of these ancient roads seems to be indicated not only by
their connection with the megaliths, but by the fact that they were
made when the configuration of the island was different from its
present condition. At St. George's Bay near Birzebuggia a cart-
track crosses a little spit of land which juts out into the Bay. Before
the houses and Marina were built, this track could be traced on each
side of the Bay. It is evident that at one time the sea had not advanced
so far as it has now and that there was a road across the valley. (For
photograph see "Excavations in Malta," Part II, Pl. XXXIII). Tracks
are also found leading to the edge of the cliffs, where they end abruptly
owing to a fall of rock into the sea. On the south side the island is
continually losing by the breaking down of the rocks and cliffs. (The
temple of Shrobb-in-Ghagin is rapidly disappearing in this way; only
a small part of it still remains).

In considering the series of photographs given here, Figs. 1-4 are
perhaps the most convincing; Figs. 1, 6, and 7 show the broken type
of surface, with small fissures at every angle, in contrast with the
straight or evenly curved lines of the tracks; these photographs also
show the rugged uneven surface between the ruts where the traction
animal must have walked, the hollows, according to Caillemer, having
been filled up with stones and sand. Such a surface would have given
the animal a good foothold; at the present day on rock-cut country
roads, where cart tracks are formed nearly as deep as the ancient
ones, the middle of the road is deeply scored across horizontally to
prevent the animal from slipping. The modern cartwheel is unusually
large, and this was probably the case anciently; the body of the cart
would then be lifted well over the high part in the centre of the road.

A map of the tracks will give the centres of population in early,

possibly neolithic, times; and will throw light on many of the archaeological problems connected with Malta.

There remains a tradition in the island that the tracks were made
for "a boat which went on wheels, " a kind of via sacra. The tradition
is, perhaps the origin of Father Magri's theory that the motive power
for the ancient vehicles was sails. But, as Caillemer has noted in
the Greek examples, there would be no difficulty for an animal to draw
a cart along these artificial ruts when the surface on which the animal
walked was made more or less even.

Like almost every country, Malta has retained little memory of
her ancient past, and on this particular point there is but the one tradition already mentioned. A great change came over the island in
Roman times. The Romans were distinguished from all other nations
by their ability in road-making, and the primitive roads of Malta were
probably superseded then. It is perhaps significant that Maltese folk-
memory and tradition date from St. Paul's shipwreck during the
height of the Roman domination.

THE ANCIENT CART-TRACKS OF MALTA
Gracie, H. S.; *Antiquity,* 28:91-98, 1954.

The barren hill-tops of Malta are scored in many places by
ancient ruts cut deeply into the rock. They can be seen also on the
slopes and on the lower plains, but less frequently because these
areas are normally under agricultural soil. They always occur in
pairs from 52 to 58 inches apart and were quite clearly used by
vehicles. They have been discussed in print for 300 years but no
agreement has been reached on how, when or why they were made or
what vehicles used them. In fact, there are as many theories as
there are authors. Of these writers only Captain E. G. Fenton and
Professor Sir T. Zammit appear to have done any serious field work,
and none has published a map. The present writer, therefore, decided to attempt the laborious task of plotting them, making such
other observations and measurements as he could. Zammit, in the
paper cited, reproduced some excellent photographs from both the
ground and the air, to which the reader is referred.

. . . .

The depths of the ruts range from a mere smoothing of the surface to more than 2 feet. The greatest depth noted was 27 inches and
there were several measurements between 22 and 24 inches. These
are the mean depths of a pair of ruts taken from the highest point of
the intervening rock. A wheel to negotiate such ruts would need to
be 5 feet in diameter, allowing only 6 inches for the hub.

There are a number of instances of sharp turns in the tracks,
including one shown in the lower middle part of Fig. 1. In four such
turns the radii were 38, 38, 24 and 14 feet. In no case was there
any widening or flattening of the bottoms of the ruts such as would

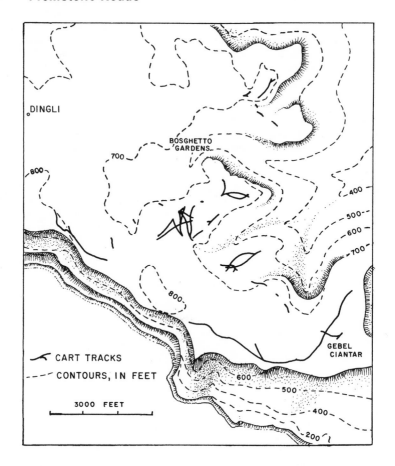

Prehistoric Maltese "cart tracks"

necessarily have been formed by a sledge runner. Sledges, therefore, could not have been used. Fenton excluded sledges on account
of the undulatory nature of the bottoms of the ruts.

Frequently a track will bifurcate, the two parts coming together
again after a short distance. Sometimes the two will separate widely
enough to enable two vehicles to pass, but more often the separation
is only a few inches and may even show only as a widening of the ruts.
These last are said to be duplicated. Triplicated tracks occur and,
on the same track just beyond (C), an example of quadruplication can
be seen. Zammit concluded that the wider of these bifurcations were
deliberately made shunts and shows an air photograph of Tal Minsia
as an example. In this particular case, and there are other instances,
the two parts meet at different levels and could not have been contemporary. Plate I, D shows the southern junction and a drop of 6 inches
from one rut to the other. Duplications are very frequent and were

observed in 25 of the 32 suitably preserved sites examined. The large numbers of groups of parallel tracks were not there for several carts to use the route at the same time. Whenever such a group can be traced for any distance it will be found to coalesce into one track in each direction. In particular the tracks shown in Zammit's plate III--- twenty-three can be counted on the ground---all coalesce into three before they are lost under present cultivation. It is interesting to compare this plate with the frontispiece of O. G. S. Crawford's Archaeology in the Field. The two photographs show what one would expect in the formation of natural tracks---a multiplication of routes fanning out from a fixed point at the bottom of a rise and coming together again further on. In the one case parallel ruts are formed in limestone and in the other sunken roads appear in the comparatively soft chalk.

. . . .

The date of this road system is more difficult to arrive at. Tracks pass over Punic graves at at least four places. At Imtarfa, the lip of the rut is a sharp right angle, indicating that the rut is older than the grave, which has cut through and truncated the rut. Professor Zammit claimed that the grave goods dated from 600 B. C., but Dr. Baldacchino, Director of the Valletta Museum, considers that they may be up to a few hundred years later than this. We have seen above that the tracks are older than the bulk of the terracing but the date of this work is not known. Zammit found traces of its going on in Roman times at Tarxien. Finally the land at St. George's Bay has sunk at least three feet since the tracks were made. Unfortunately one cannot say how long this might have taken. Local movements in this area can be quite rapid, but one would expect such a subsidence to have been noticed had it taken place in historical times. It seems reasonable to put the date before the advent of the Romans in 217 B. C.

. . . .

To sum up, it appears that a simple system of natural tracks joining settlements with each other and with springs and the sea was formed about the beginning of the first millennium B.C. but possibly earlier. The land was soil-covered and only one track of a group was visible at any one time. The tracks were worn down by friction and not deliberately cut. The vehicle in use was some form of slide-car, which became larger and more strongly made as time went on.

RADIOCARBON DATING OF PREHISTORIC WOODEN TRACK-WAYS

Godwin, H., Willis, E. H.; *Nature,* 184:490-491, 1959.

The purpose of building corduroy tracks is to avoid detours, and prehistoric examples of these wooden structures have been preserved by continuous water-logging. It is not surprising, therefore, that increased wetness of climate should have caused many former routes to be flooded, and have induced first the construction and then the preservation of wooden trackways. Thus there is an expectation that, were it possible to determine the age of a number of trackways, their ages would be grouped at distinct periods of climatic deterioration.

Corduroy tracks, however, have not been studied typologically, and apart from axe-marks on the timber and the chance of associated archaeological finds, they have been very difficult to date, until the advent of pollen-analysis, and, more recently, of radiocarbon dating.

Both techniques have been applied to the problem of dating several of the wooden trackways revealed in recent years by peat-cutting in the derelict raised bogs of the Somerset Levels. Some of these have been described already, and descriptions of others are being prepared for publication (Phil. Trans. Roy. Soc. Edinburgh). They run between the Mendip and the Polden Hills and the low islands that project through the intervening flat lowlands of the Glastonbury Levels.

The six Somerset trackways so far dated, and also certain associated wooden platforms, all occur at a comparable stratigraphic horizon in the bogs. This is at the surface of a very dark, highly humified Sphagnum-Calluna-Eriophorum peat, and its junction with a Cladium-Hypnum peat. The lower peat is indicative of the growth of heather-clad bogs receiving water only as rain or snow, in a condition of arrest or slow growth: their gentle convex surfaces could easily have been traversed on foot and offered little obstacle to passage across the levels. The over-lying Cladium-Hypnum peat by contrast points unmistakably to flooding by calcareous water from the big catchment area of the Mendips and Polden Hills. Such flooding imposed very circuitous routes between one hill ridge and another and the evidence suggests that the wooden trackways were built in consequence of the flooding and that their preservation was ensured by its continuance.

Several of the trackways were also shown to be close to the same pollen-analytic zone-boundary, and upon this evidence it was suggested that the tracks were probably built about the transition between the Bronze Age and the Iron Age. This supposition was strengthened by the occasional discovery upon the timber of the markings of the small thick axes of Late Bronze Age type, and by the recovery of two bronze spearheads at comparable stratigraphic levels, one of the Late Bronze Age and the other of late Middle Bronze Age.

Radiocarbon dates have now been obtained for the wood of the trackways and also of the peat in which they are embedded. The assays were made with carbon dioxide at 2 atmospheres pressure in a copper proportional counter of about 2-litres volume.

Table 1. Dating of Wood from Trackways

		Years B. P.
Q52	Meare Heath track (Bulleid's)	2840 ± 110 2850 ± 110
Q39	Shapwick Heath track (Foster's)	2470 ± 110
Q308	Westhay track (Sandford's)	2800 ± 110
Q306	Blakeway Farm track	2600 ± 110
Q7	Vipers track (Dewar's A)	2520 ± 110

Q312	Vipers track (Dewar's A)	2630 ± 110
Q313	Nidons track (Dewar's B)	2585 ± 120
Q311	Vipers platform	2410 ± 100
		2640 ± 110

It will be seen that these all lie between 450 and 900 B.C., which is certainly Late Bronze Age in this part of Britain. The datings are supported by those of the associated peat.

Table 2. Dating of Peat Associated with Trackways

		Years B.P.
Q53	Meare Heath track---subjacent peat	3230 ± 110
Q44	Shapwick Heath track---subjacent peat	3310 ± 110
Q309	Blakeway Farm track---subjacent peat	2790 ± 110
Q316	Nidons track---peat at track level	2590 ± 120
Q318	Nidons track---subjacent peat	2642 ± 120
Q319	Nidons track---subjacent peat	2482 ± 120
Q317	Nidons track---superjacent peat	2628 ± 120

Whereas the results from Nidons track suggest close contemporaneity between the track itself and adjacent peat, at the other sites the greater age of the underlying peat supports the field evidence that some erosion or wastage of the peat surface had occurred before the trackways were constructed.

As long ago as 1906 a monoxylous boat had been recovered from the bog deposits near Shapwick Station, but under conditions that did not allow any dating or reference to a stratigraphic horizon. It was apparent that it could not have been embedded while the bogs were covered by heather and cotton-grass and it seemed likely that it related to a substantial flooding period. The curator of Taunton Castle Museum, where the boat is now preserved kindly provided enough wood for the following radiocarbon assay:

| Q357 | Shapwick boat | 2305 ± 120 years B.P. |

It will be seen that this assay places the boat within the Early Iron Age, so that it is younger than the wooden trackways and indeed corresponds in age with the Cladium-Hypnum peat of the major flooding episode of this time.

There is a good deal of evidence in various parts of north-western Europe that about 600 B.C. there was in progress a change of climate towards increasing rainfall and lower temperatures. It has been made the boundary between the Sub-boreal and Sub-atlantic climatic periods; it is an important pollen zone boundary and is often marked by 'recurrent surfaces' in peat bogs. In view of the likelihood that this climatic change was also widespread in Britain, it is interesting to append the radiocarbon date from three further wooden trackways that we determined.

It was already known from associated prehistoric finds that the Brigg trackway clearly belonged to the Late Bronze Age to Early Iron Age transition. Pollen-analytic evidence and a single sherd from the Fordy trackway had already suggested a similar age for that

Table 3.   Trackways Outside Somerset

		Years B. P.
Q310	Fordy---Little Thetford, Cambs.	2560 ± 110
Q77	Brigg, Lincs.	2552 ± 120
Q68	Kate's Pad, Pilling, Lancs.	2760 ± 120

structure. It is now strikingly evident that indeed all the trackways belong to the one archaeological period.

Of course, prehistoric trackways were built at other periods than this, and the Groningen laboratory has dated an Irish example as follows:

GRO272   Corlona, Co. Leitrim   3395 ± 170 years B. P.

None the less, the consistency of the English results is striking and strongly underlines the importance of carefully recording and dating these unregarded prehistoric monuments.

CANALS, DAMS,
AND OTHER WATERWORKS

Almost all waterworks of prehistorical origin were designed to control water for agricultural purposes. Such usage is not anomalous because we know that some ancient population centers were surprisingly large---even where desert and jungle now reign. It is the magnitude and engineering sophistication that are startling, particularly in the "backward" Americas. Truly immense quantities of earth were moved in constructing Michigan's garden beds, Arizona's canals, and Mesoamerica's hydraulic systems. The civil engineering and agricultural finesse are amazing. More puzzling as to application are Florida's canals, which seem to be oriented toward shipping instead of agriculture. Just what sort of ancient commerce required the excavation of miles of canals is beyond conjecture at the present time. The ancient waterworks in the Middle East are agricultural in purpose and suggest that ancient man made better use of Nature's limited water supplies in that region than we do today. Finally, Britain's dew ponds have always stimulated controversy. Who designed these clever traps for atmospheric moisture?

ANCIENT CANALS ON THE SOUTH-WEST COAST OF FLORIDA
Douglass, Andrew E.; *American Antiquarian, 7:277–285, 1885.*

While exploring the South-west coast of Florida, I was much interested in two ancient canals which I examined, and whose object seemed quite inexplicable. The first occurs about three miles north of Gordon's Pass, an inlet thirty-three miles south of Punta Rasa, and twenty miles north of Cape Roman.

....

I entered Gordon's Pass, and for some days was occupied in examining the evidences of Indian occupation in the shell and earth mounds to be found there, and while awaiting a fair wind for Punta Rasa, devoted a day to the examination of the Canal. With two of my men I walked northward along the beach, which was a perfectly straight line to the next Pass. For the first half mile this beach was skirted by a beautiful grove of cabbage palmetto, under whose shade was the ranch of Mr. Madison Weeks, an intelligent settler, who was cultivating the surface of an extensive shell mound, just north of the Inlet, and who courteously gave me much information about the country. The Palm Grove was on a plateau about eight feet above the sea level, but beyond the grove the land sank into a low marsh not more than half that elevation. The storms of many years had created a levee of sand, which defended this morass from the sea, and was at least one hundred feet in breadth. It was apparent, however, that erosion of the coast had here occurred to a great extent, for stumps of dead palms could be seen a hundred yards or so to sea, and suggested the probability of a great change in the contour of the land during not remote years. One of our party followed the line of embankment or sand-dune while the other two kept along the beach. At a distance of three and a-half miles from the Inlet the former announced the Canal, and we soon joined him and saw the object of our search before us. Where we stood it was buried in the sand embankment, but from that it was plainly visible straight as an arrow, crossing the low intervening morass and penetrating the sandy pine ridge, half a mile, or nearly so, away. The bottom was moist and full of tall grass; the sides and summit of the embankment covered with a dense chapparal of oak scrub and scrub palmetto. Its direction from our standpoint was about one point South of East. We could see in the distance, pines growing upon the inner and outer sides of its banks. With infinite labor we worked our way through the dense scrub for a hundred yards or so, and took our measurements. The width from the summit ridge upon each bank was 55 feet, and the depth from that summit level to centre of the excavation 12 feet. At the bottom the width was 12 feet, the banks being almost perpendicular for some 5 feet, and then receding on an easier angle at the summit. This summit was about eight feet above the level of the meadow, through which for nearly half a mile it was excavated, till it reached the higher level of the sandy pine land beyond. Owing to considerable indisposition on my part, this was the end of our exploration for that day, but on the day following we rowed up the Interior Lagoon with a view of examining its eastern terminus. Mr. Weeks, the resident settler, kindly accompanied us and gave us all the information he possessed as to its structure and peculiarities. He had often hunted through the pines, and had crossed it at various points not at present accessible to us. A long pull of about four miles from the Inlet along the Lagoon brought us to a little bay on the west shore where we landed, and penetrating the thickets reached a swamp of saw grass and water, where we found the Eastern terminus of the canal, though much reduced in dimensions, as probably it was here more exposed to the wash of the Lagoon in the rainy season. The banks were covered with a growth of cabbage palms, and as it progressed toward the pine barren, it increased in size and height. We found that at this end the trench curved to the South as it approached the Lagoon, and about two hundred yards from the shore it was intersected by a cross ditch or trench, as if to allow it to receive the waters from the level on either side. If this cross opening has not been a modern adjunct, designed to allow the swamps to discharge into the Lagoon, as we found was now the case, it would seem to indicate that the whole of these interior waters were expected to find an outlet to the sea by means of this very considerable drain or canal. Mr. Weeks gave us the following information about the canal in its passage through the pine land. The whole canal is about one mile and a half in length, reaching from the Lagoon to the Sea.

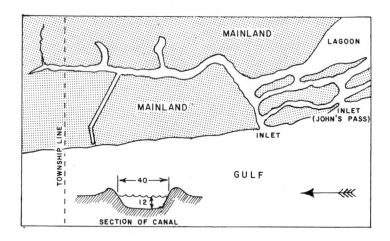

Ancient canal on the Florida Gulf Coast

With the exception of the curve at the Eastern terminus it is perfectly straight. In passing through the pine woods it intersects sand ridges, in which it is excavated to a depth of forty feet. The bottom is everywhere of the same width I have described, but at points where he has crossed it in hunting, he finds a trench about four feet in breadth, and at present, two feet deep running along the center, leaving a breadth of about four feet on each side. Mr. Weeks was of the impression that this supplementary trench was designed to accommodate the keel of a boat as it ran along the conduit. Leaving the Canal, we crossed the Lagoon and found and ascended a creek with rocky banks and bottom for some two miles, into the pine woods of the mainland. Mr. Weeks was of the opinion that it formerly connected with the Canal, and the latter was constructed to carry it to the sea, but I see no indication of that being even remotely possible, though it is as good a guess as any other that can be made in the apparent absence of any more plausible theory. The trench in the middle of the main canal appears to me to indicate that the canal has been made by civilized men, and within a comparatively recent period. It is a work of enormous labor indeed, but in trenching through the sands of these regions, it is quite usual to make an interior ditch, that the tables left on each side may intercept the drifting sands brought down the sides by heavy weather, rains or wind. But the question is, what was the purpose of such an expense of labor, and who in this sparsely settled country could have undertaken it. As regards drainage, the Lagoon already empties into the Inlet, and through that into the sea. If for the admittance of vessels, the Inlet of Gordon's Pass gives far greater accommodation. And who would not be aware that an opening of the kind at right angles to the shore, without some very massive artificial breakwater and continually dredged channels, would be choked up by the sand on the first storm, and show the same obstruction at its mouth as we have just seen. My own idea is that by whomsoever constructed, it was designed to relieve the lowlands to the eastward of great accumulations of fresh water in the rainy season, at some remote period when there was no Gordon's Pass, and when the exterior conformation of the coast was far different from what it is at present. Inlets in the Florida coast, particularly on the Atlantic side, open and close unexpectedly. In St. Johns County a couple of miles south of Mantanzas Inlet, an inlet, known as Hughes', closed up in heavy gales an hundred years since, and that region was rendered very unhealthy by the stagnant fresh water. A few Spanish soldiers with shovels, opened a channel through the marsh back of the Sand Dunes, and in a short time the waters had worn a course into the Matanzas river, which has so remained ever since. Heavy storms on the Gulf Coast may have choked up several Inlets on the west coast, and filled up channels among the Mangrove Islands, or on the other hand, the mainland which now confronts Gordon's Pass only a mile or so to the eastward, may have reached the sea in bygone ages, and enclosed a fresh water lake where is now the Northern Lagoon. Who were the constructors, is a question, even more difficult to settle. There is no record of such a work in any local tradition, or in any history that we now possess. Indeed, there is nothing more obscure than the history whether ancient or modern, of the Southwest Coast of Florida.

. . . .

The other canal I visited, is quite as inexplicable, and even more surprising for its extent and dimensions than this. It has been occasionally noticed in accounts of hunters and sportsmen, who have not infrequently encountered it in a more accessible and better known region. The sheet of water on the coast north of Caloosahatchee river known as Charlotte Harbor, Charlotte Sound and Carlos Bay, has on its eastern border a long island known as Pine Island. It is about 18 miles long, and from three to five miles broad, extending in a direction nearly north and south. On its east side it is separated from the mainland by a shoal channel, obstructed by oyster and sand bars, from half a mile to a mile in width. On the west, Charlotte Sound intervenes between it and the outside or coast-line of keys with a width of from three to five miles. Just on the verge of Pine Island, a maze of mangrove keys or islets stretch along the entire distance, and some of these have been occupied by the Muspa Indians as late as fifty years since. Pine Island itself is clothed in pines, and is a sandy level fringed along the water by mangrove thickets. Some of the adjacent islets are occupied here and there, by a solitary settler, who finds cultivatable ground on the shell mounds left by the Indian inhabitants of prehistoric or more recent days. One of the largest of these shell mounds which I have ever seen, is found on the west coast of Pine Island, some four miles from its northern end. The heaps cover a space of several acres, and rise in steep ridges to the height of, in some instances, twenty-five feet. Their flanks run off frequently on very slight inclinations, and have been dwelt on by Indian residents long subsequent to the era of original construction, until the debris accumulated over the shells has resolved itself into a very fertile mould, tempting to the settler of the present day. This shell heap had been so utilized, that around the steep ridges, rows of lime and lemon trees, with pomegranates and fig trees, spread out on the long levels. But all was now deserted and on landing I found it a maze of wild luxuriance; briars and the American Aloe, and cacti innumerable, filled up every vacant space, and these with the "Spanish bayonet," render it a danger as well as labor to explore.

I had but little time to spare, owing to the delays forced upon us by a long period of unusually inclement weather, and could only make a hasty inspection. We had expected to find two settlers at the ranch, but it was vacant, and our work had to be done without the aid of a guide. We made for the mangrove swamps to the south, and the tide fortunately being out, we worked through the damp thickets till we emerged into the tangle of scrub palmetto which covered the surface of the sandy upland of the Island. Catching a glimpse of a sand mound glistening with whitened crest, among the pines a quarter of a mile away to the eastward, we plunged in through the chapparal and made for that object. On our way we rose upon a slight ridge and then descending into a hollow level for some thirty feet, again surmounted a ridge and then realized that this was the Canal. It was thus we found it, much to our surprise. A thin growth of tall pines covered it and the surrounding sand level, an occasional palmetto rose here and there along the bottom, all else was a thicket of scrub palmetto. The position of this end of the canal was of some interest, as enabling us to estimate how far it was coeval with the sand or shell mounds at its western terminus. So far as it can be described without the aid of a diagram, the arrangement of these objects was as follows: On the western verge of the Island in a mangrove swamp, rose the various masses of shells constituting the Shell mound spreading over an area of eight or ten acres; due east of these ridges at a distance of some 300 feet, but upon the sand level of the Island, rose a sand mound 35 feet in height and 200 feet in base diameter, (one of the largest of these constructions which had come under my observation anywhere in Florida.) Looking eastward from its summit, we could discern about 460 yards distant, the sand mound, as I afterward ascertained, 20 feet in perpendicular height, with a depression of 8 feet between the two summits, and the longest diameter of its base 300 feet. While these two mounds lay on a line due east and west, the canal passed between them angularly, coming from the south-east. The dimensions of the latter were at this point 30 feet in width from the bottom of the opposite banks, and seven to eight feet in height to the summit of the banks, which was also at an elevation of some three or four feet above the level of the adjacent sand of the Island surface.

Far as the eye could reach, we could trace this canal in a direct line through the sparse pine woods; its course being especially marked by the tall fronds of the cabbage palms, which the moisture of the depression tempted to grow within the banks, and were confined to that level. After passing between the two sand mounds in an angular direction, the western terminus of this interesting construction, faded away in the general level of the surface to the north of the larger mound, and this level, within a few rods, sank into a creek which continued straight through the mangroves into Charlotte Sound, emptying two hundred yards north of the ranch where I had landed. These were all the local characteristics of this Canal that I was able personally to inspect. I was assured by an old settler that it crosses the entire Island in a direct line on the course which I observed. At this point, the direct width of Pine Island is three and a half miles. The Canal however, crossing at the angle indicated, must exceed five miles in length. It was a source of great regret that indisposition on one hand and delays incident to an unusually rough and inclement winter on the other hand should have prevented my making a more thorough survey of this interesting and inexplicable work.

. . . .

ANCIENT GARDEN BEDS OF MICHIGAN
Hubbard, Bela; *American Antiquarian,* 1:1-9, 1878.

The so-called "Garden Beds" were found in the valleys of the St. Joseph and Grand Rivers, where they occupied the most fertile of the prairie land and burr-oak plains, principally in the counties of St. Joseph,

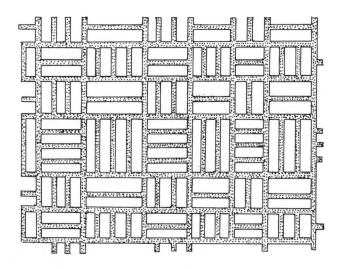

Ancient garden bed, Kalamazoo, Michigan

Cass and Kalamazoo.

They consist of raised patches of ground, separated by sunken paths, and were generally arranged in plats or blocks of parallel beds. These varied in dimensions, being from five to sixteen feet in width, in length from twelve to more than one hundred feet, and in height six to eighteen inches.

The tough sod of the prairie had preserved very sharply all the outlines. According to the universal testimony, these beds were laid out and fashioned with a skill, order and symmetry which distinguished them from the ordinary operations of agriculture, and were combined with some peculiar features that belong to no recognized system of horticultural art.

In the midst of diversity, sufficient uniformity is discoverable to enable me to group the beds and gardens, as in the following classifications:

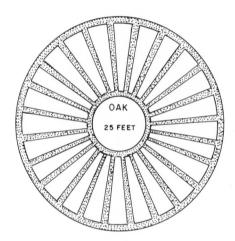

Prehistoric garden plats,
Kalamazoo, Michigan

1. Wide convex beds, in parallel rows, without paths, composing independent plats. (Width of beds 12 feet, paths none, length 74 to 115 feet.)
2. Wide convex beds, in parallel rows, separated by paths of same width, in independent plats. (Width of bed 12 to 16 feet; paths same; length, 74 to 132 feet.)
3. Wide and parallel beds, separated by narrow paths, arranged in a series of plats longitudinal to each other. (Width of beds 14 feet; paths, 2 feet; length, 100 feet.)
4. Long and narrow beds, separated by narrower paths and arranged in a series of longitudinal plats, each plat divided from the next by semi-circular heads. (Width of beds 5 feet; paths, 1-1/2 feet; length, 100 feet; height, 18 inches.)
5. Parallel beds, arranged in plats similar to class 4, but divided by circular heads. (Width of beds, 6 feet; paths, 4 feet; length, 12 to 40 feet; height, 18 inches.)
6. Parallel beds, of varying widths and lengths, separated by narrow paths, and arranged in plats of two or more at right angles N. and S., E. and W., to the plats adjacent. (Width of beds, 5 to 14 feet; paths, 1 to 2 feet; length, 12 to 30 feet; height, 8 inches.)

7. Parallel beds, of uniform width and length, with narrow paths, arranged in plats or blocks, and single beds, at varying angles. (Width of beds, 6 ft; paths, 2 feet; length, about 30 feet; height, 10 to 12 inches.)
8. Wheel-shaped plats, consisting of a circular bed, with beds of uniform shape and size radiating therefrom, all separated by narrow paths. (Width of beds, 6 to 20 feet; paths, 1 foot length, 14 to 20 feet.)

....

A STONE DAM IN IOWA
Jordan, Cora M.; *American Antiquarian,* 14:226-227, 1892.

In regard to the stone crossing it is so constructed as to dam the creek or river, it has been, part of it, taken away, but enough remains to make what the people here designate "The Ripple." The evidence that it is not natural is that the stones are laid in evenly and the river has but very little rock in it, the nearest above veing one-half mile.

Some of the citizens of our village are very old settlers; have been here when there were only three families within the limits of what is now Ringgold County. I have taken pains to inquire and they inform me that no mill was ever situated at this point, and that the dam or ford is not the work of white men.

THE HOHOKAM CANALS AT PUEBLO GRANDE, ARIZONA
Woodbury, Richard B.; *American Antiquity,* 26:267-270, 1960. (Reproduced by permission of the Society for American Archaeology from *American Antiquity,* 26(2), 1960)

Interest in the surviving, visible remains of ancient irrigation canals in southern Arizona and northern Sonora has been long and intense, going back at least to Manje's careful notes on the canal at Casa Grande ruin in 1697, and including such observant travelers as Rusling (1877) and the records of several local residents, particularly Patrick (1903) and Turney (1929). Nevertheless, the body of information available has consisted largely of unsystematic comments on the surface appearance of these canal remnants, and the investigation of Hohokam irrigation by archaeological techniques has proceeded very slowly. The work that Cushing directed at Los Muertos was reported by Hodge (1893) and supplemented by Haury's monograph (1945) which also summarized the available information on the subject. The only thorough excavation of a Hohokam canal that has been reported is the cross sectioning at Snaketown in 1935 which provided clear association between the stages of construction and use of the canal and the ceramic sequence being worked out at the site. On this basis it was possible to assign the beginning of the Snaketown canal to about A. D. 800 and suggest that it was in use for about 500 years. Careful mapping of the entire surviving Hohokam canal system, making use of aerial photographs, was begun by the Smithsonian Institution in 1930 but never completed due to the pressure of other activities and the lack of funds.

....

Excavation of a cross section of these canals was greatly aided by the generous loan of a Gradall, with its two operators, by the Salt River Valley Water Users Association. The 60-m. trench with sloping sides which the Gradall dug to a depth of two to three meters was further deepened by hand where it crossed the filled channels of the two canals, and one wall was cleaned to permit observation of the straitigraphy.

One of the most impressive revelations of this trench was the size of the original canals, about 10 and 6 m. wide at the former ground level, and about 26 and 18 m. wide from crest to crest of the banks. Also, the fact that subsequent filling of the channels had raised the level between the banks to slightly higher than the original ground level is of interest, since it vitiates inferences that have been made in the past concerning the relationship of river channel elevation and canal elevation. Such inferences have been based only on observations of present surface indication, which this cross section shows to be inadequate for estimating original depth (or profile).

The North and South canals proved to be quite different in profile, the North Canal being flat-bottomed with the sides sloping at about 35°, the South Canal V-shaped in profile with the lower part of the sides sloping at 50° to 60°. Nevertheless, they contained rather similar fills, ranging from coarse sand through fine sand to silt, much of it laminated and indicating successive phases of deposition, with either periodic intentional cleaning or natural removal of the deposits. Both canals were dug through an otherwise undisturbed layer of finegrained, river-laid sand ranging in thickness from 1.5 to 2.0 m., and both were dug into underlying coarse gravel, a most unpromising material for holding the water that the canals were constructed to carry. There is, of course, a possibility that the water table was high enough in ancient times for the canal bottom to have

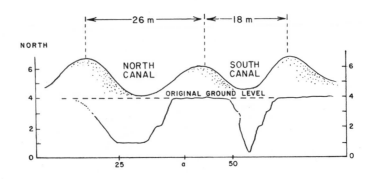

Cross sections of Hohokam canals, Arizona

penetrated it, and thus considerably reduced the loss of water in transit.
However, in the North Canal, the remains of a substantial clay lining were
found resting on the lowest of the sandy fills in the channel. The lining
consists of a compact, homogeneous layer of chocolate brown clay, from
5 to 9 cm. thick, with a cracked and uneven upper surface as though exposed to the sun. Careful examination revealed no lamination or horizontal structure within the clay, such as would indicate that it was naturally
deposited in standing water. Furthermore, although the layer of clay was
not traceable across the bottom of the canal, where it had probably eroded
away, it was well preserved for a considerable distance up the sides; if
this were the remnant of a water-laid layer it would have originally been
over a meter thick, a wholly unreasonable deposit in such circumstances.
Instead, the evidence points clearly to its having been laid by hand, with
clay brought from a source not yet identified but possibly within a few
miles. The total extent of this clay layer can only be guessed, but its
presence was verified in test pits 40 and 145 m. to the west. With an observable width of at least 8 m., and assuming a minimum thickness of
5 cm., such a lining would have needed at least four-tenths of a cubic
meter of clay for every linear meter of canal. Only a very critical need
could have justified bringing in such a quantity of material. The need was
undoubtedly for a canal bottom that would lose less of its water in transit,
as the channel is here dug into coarse material into which water would
percolate easily. Many modern irrigation canals are, of course, lined
with concrete for the same purpose, the cost being more than offset by
the saving in water. No other Hohokam canal has been found with an
identifiable lining, although some early and unsubstantiated reports mention the use of adobe or clay for this purpose. It is doubtful if this was
ever a common practice but in this instance there seems little doubt that
at least part of a large canal was carefully lined to render it practically
watertight, even though the cost in labor must have been enormous. It
should be noted that the canal saw use for at least a short time prior to
the addition of the lining, as shown by the deposit underlying it (number
1 in the cross section).

. . . .

Dating the construction and use of the canals has proved difficult.
Their proximity to Pueblo Grande would suggest use during its occupation, which probably extended from the 12th century to the end of the 14th,
with a large part of its construction during the Soho phase, approximately
1150 or 1200 to 1300. However, examination of the few sherds found in
and under the canal banks and in the canal fills shows no evidence of construction before the Soho phase or of use after it. The small number of
sherds makes such a conclusion somewhat less than final, and the possibility cannot be eliminated of a much earlier canal having been completely cleaned out or totally re-excavated and enlarged, thus removing evidence of its original date.

The total extent of these canals was recorded by both Patrick (1903)
and Turney (1929), Turney probably depending heavily on Patrick's much
earlier first-hand observations. The North Canal is shown as extending
for about 9 miles, the South Canal about seven. Both are shown heading
about a half mile east of the Park of Four Waters. There is an apparently reliable local recollection, however, that before the end of the last
century one of these canals could be traced another two miles eastward,
to a point opposite Tempe Butte. It may never be possible to establish
the original length of these canals precisely, but the general order of

magnitude suggested here is undoubtedly correct. Both canals are comparable in length to some of the modern canals in use today. It might be
expected that canals of such size, involving substantial and probably pro-
tracted labor in their construction, would have been used for more than
the century or so suggested by the ceramic evidence. On the other hand,
many causes may have been responsible for their abandonment after a
relatively brief span of service---excessive silting, waterlogging of the
fields they served, or changes in the river.

. . . .

A GIGANTIC EARTHWORK IN NEW MEXICO

Gaillard, D. D.; *American Anthropologist,* 9:311-313, 1896.

During the progress of the survey of the international boundary line,
United States and Mexico, in July, 1892, there was encountered in Animas
valley, Grant county, New Mexico, about 11 miles east of the point where
the boundary line between New Mexico and Arizona intersects the international boundary line, a peculiar topographic feature, which appeared to be
artificial, and if so was probably a prehistoric dam.

. . . .

Description of the Dam. Measured along the axis of its crest, the dam
is 5.5 miles in length, while its crest is from 22 to 24 feet higher than the
foot of its eastern slope. At the point where the change of direction in the
dam occurs is a breach through which passes the drainage of a watershed
of about 25 to 30 square miles. Were this breach repaired and the adjacent
portions of the dam brought up to the prevailing height, it would be capable
of forming a reservoir with an average length of five miles and a width of
one-quarter of a mile. The maximum depth would be about 20 feet and the
mean depth about 10 feet. The area would be one and one-quarter square
miles only. Practically all of this water could be drawn out at the point
where the breach occurs and used to irrigate the portions of the valley to
the eastward.

The dam is composed, as judged by surface indications only, of the
stiff sedimentary material of the surrounding valley. Its slopes and crest
are regular and covered during the rainy season with a luxuriant growth
of grass, but are entirely bare of trees or bushes. It has the appearance
of great age, and there is now no evidence either of irrigating ditches or
of excavations from which material has been obtained. As shown in the
distorted sections, the foot of the western slope is from zero to 4.96
meters (average 2.92 meters) higher than that of the eastern slope,
apparently due to deposits which in the course of time have been collected
by the dam and have covered the lower portions of the original western
slope. If such is the case, deposits might also account for the absence
of evidences of irrigating ditches and exc avations and for the present
small width of the body of water which would be impounded were the breach
in the dam repaired and the reservoir filled.

At Y a small pool of water remains for several days after rains and is eagerly sought by hundreds of cattle, which have trampled down the slopes in the vicinity, so that the latter are somewhat irregular.

The materials of the dam, the direction of its axis, the regularity of its slopes, the uniformity in elevation of its crest (for 3.5 miles north of K there is an extreme variation of but 0.76 meters in elevation), the fact that it joins high ground at both ends, and its location at a point where it seems very unlikely that it could have been caused by natural agencies, all seemed to indicate that this remarkable earthwork was of artificial construction, and such was the impression of almost every official of our party; but, on the other hand, so gigantic is the work---requiring, if the western slope once continued as indicated by the dotted line in the distorted cross-sections, the handling of from 8,000,000 to 10,000,000 cubic yards of material---that it seems almost impossible that it could have been the work of human hands. Again, if constructed for a dam, one is at once struck by its extremely flat slopes and by the immense linear development of dam constructed to impound such a comparatively small volume of water.

One of our rodmen stated that from the summit of a small hill he thought he observed a continuation of this dam, or possibly another dam, several miles to the northwest and north of the one I have described. I myself thought I could faintly distinguish some such feature about eight miles north of monument 67.

ROCK PILES AND ANCIENT DAMS IN THE KLAMATH VALLEY
Clarke, Wm. J.; *American Antiquarian,* 7:40-41, 1885.

In traveling through the Klamath Lake country one continually sees rocks piles up one upon the other in the most grotesque and singularly simple manner. They assume all kinds of shapes, and it is almost impossible to dislodge them, they are so stationary. The common form is where several flat and at the same time rounded rocks, the size of a hat or larger, are placed on each other to the number of four or five. We should say that the piling process is generally upon large boulders. There is quite a pretty story or legend connected with this rock-piling. Mr. O. C. Applegate says that some of the Indians claim that it is done by the children; that it is an emblem of bravery; that the children do it after dark, and that the one who goes the farthest from the lodge and erects a pile of rocks is considered the most brave. Others say it is done as a religious rite; and still others hold that it is done to mark a camp and show that it has been occupied. One thing that gives us reason to believe it is a religious rite is, that under no circumstance will any other camp or tribe disturb them. We found evidence of a race of people, of whom the present Indians at Klamath know nothing, who inhabited the Klamath Lake country many years ago. All that remains are the ruins of dams, one of which is located on Link river, within a stone's throw of Linkville, and a number of others, notably, one on Lost River. The Indians claim no knowledge of the formation of these dams, and their symmetry of architecture show that they are not freaks of nature. We can not describe as well as we could wish the shape of the dam at Linkville. It is a semi-circle, pointing down stream, with a narrow channel extending some distance down stream.

The water barely covers the wall, but its outline is plainly visible. The only surmise we can make is that channels were used to put willow or reed nets in, and that the dam was built for fishing purposes. There is another very peculiar feature about Link river, and that is that it is occasionally blown dry. This must seem astounding to our readers, but such is the fact. It is caused by a steady wind blowing from the south and up the river---this through a seemingly canyon---and the waters of Big Klamath Lake roll up towards the north, and the water is literally all blown down toward the northern end of the lake, and there being but a shallow outlet into Link river, and the water being blown up the lake, leaves no water, and so the river runs dry. The shallow outlet of Big Klamath Lake has been caused by the aforesaid Indians, who wish to confine the waters of the lake for the sake of the tule lands. There is a movement on foot to remove these obstructions at the mouth of Link river. Such being done would decrease the depth of the lake a foot or so, and make thousands of acres of land arable that are now nothing but tule.

THE "ANCIENT STONE FISH TRAPS" OF THE COACHELLA VALLEY, SOUTHERN CALIFORNIA

Treganza, Adan E.; *American Antiquity*, 10:285-294, 1945.

A group of small stone enclosures, supposed by some to be of natural origin and by others to be the works of man, lies on a rocky travertine-encrusted talus slope at the base of the Santa Rosa Mountains on the west side of the Coachella Valley in Riverside County, California. These phenomena are known locally as the "Ancient Fish Traps." They occupy a series of rocky terraces some 90 feet below the maximum high-water shore line of Ancient Lake Cahuilla (called by some Blake Sea), whose basin is now partly occupied by the Salton Sea. The "traps" consist of 85 to 100 bowl-like depressions composed of a travertine-encrusted granite talus debris. They are arranged in three rows, each of which follows the exact contour of one of the old recessional terraces of the lake.

• Mesoamerica

MAYA LOWLAND HYDRAULIC SYSTEMS
Matheny, Ray T.; *Science,* 193:639–646, 1976.

Hydraulic Construction at Edzna. Edzna lies in a central Campeche valley where surface water is found only in an occasional aguada. Groundwater is 20 m below the surface in limestone formations. Apparently the Maya could dig wells through 20 m of soil and rock, but they chose not to do it at Edzna. Only 12 chultuns of the Lake Classic period have been found at the site, suggesting that this method of obtaining water was too difficult to exploit. Soil in the Edzna Valley consists of stratified clay and has a high impermeability to water once it becomes soaked during the rainy season.

The first settlers at Edzna were Pioneers of the Middle Preclassic period. Although evidence for the Middle Preclassic period is moderate, it seems to parallel similar manifestations found at nearby Dzibilnocac, Santa Rosa Xtampak, and Becan. We assume that Pioneers settled at Edzna because naturally occurring aguadas could be developed into dependable water sources and, secondarily, because the valley soil was unusually deep for central Campeche.

During the Lake Preclassic period a huge hydraulic system, consisting of more than 20 km of canals and an extensive array of reservoirs, was constructed at Edzna. Excavations and analysis of artifacts suggest that this system was operational by the time of Christ. The main canal ends (begins?) at a savanna 12 km south of Edzna. This canal is large--- 50 m wide for at least 6 km of its length. It may be equally as wide at the 12-km point, which has not been measured. Test trenches show that the canal was originally excavated to about 1.5 m below ground surface. The north end of the canal joins a huge moat system that surrounds an earthen fortress. The moat in turn joins to a canal that runs north to within 250 m of the ceremonial center of the site. Other smaller canals join the main canal and moat system.

From the southwest corner of the moat the main canal is oriented nearly north-south for its first 4 km, aligning exactly on the main temple structure known as Cinco Pisos. The alignment is deliberate for this entire distance but then becomes less exacting as a crooked section of the canal leads to the savanna. The canal alignment was part of an overall plan for the ancient city.

There are seven large canals (averaging 40 m wide and from 0.6 to 1.5 km long) and two smaller ones in the northwest and northeast sectors of the site. These canals, identified first as radiating lines on aerial photographs, are only nine of a larger number of lines that converge on the city center like the spokes of a wheel. Some of the lines may prove to be ancient roads or trails, but these nine are definitely canals.

Excavations in some of the converging canals show they were dug to a depth of 3 m. Earth from the original digging was used in constructing

house platforms on or near the canal banks.   Excavations in these platforms suggest that a Late Preclassic farming population lived along the
canals adjacent to the city center.   (pp. 640-641)

• South America

ANCIENT RIDGED FIELDS IN THE REGION OF LAKE TITICACA
Smith, C. T., et al; *Geographical Journal,* 134:353-367, 1968.

Minor landscape features which are apparently the result of pre-
Columbian cultivation on poorly drained terrain have recently been described in various parts of lowland South America.   The most spectacular vestiges of these ancient ridged fields are in the seasonally inundated
tropical savannas of the San Jorge floodplain of northern Colombia and
the Llanos de Mojos of north-eastern Bolivia.   Similar fields have been
traced in the Orinoco Llanos, in Surinam and near Guayaquil in Ecuador.
They consist of parallel or irregular groupings of raised ridges of variable height, width and length: from a few inches to several feet in height,
from about 10 to 70 feet in width, and up to several thousand feet in
length.   They are indicative of a careful and laborious reclamation of
marshland for intensive tropical agriculture in areas which are considered marginal for agriculture goday, or in which crop cultivation has
been entirely abandoned.
The reclamation of marshland for agriculture was also practised in
the higher cultures of the New World in the highlands of Mexico and the
Andes.   The chinampa or 'floating garden' agriculture of the Valley of
Mexico is well known, and the form and patterns of dry, abandoned
chinampas are remarkably similar in appearance to some of the ridged
fields of South America.   A few elevated crop platforms have also been
observed in poorly drained parts of the Sabana de Bogota in Colombia.
But the largest area of ancient ridged fields so far discovered in the
Americas is in the region of Lake Titicaca in Peru and Bolivia on level
ground at 3800 and 3890 m (12,500 to 12,800 ft) above sea level.   These
previously undescribed features, now used mainly for pasture, are almost certainly of pre-Inca origin, and their existence helps to confirm
other indications of a dense pre-Columbian Indian population in the area.
(p. 353)

• Asia

GIGANTIC WATER-WORKS IN CEYLON
Anonymous; *Scientific American,* 6:360, 1851.

We have held the opinion that the Croton Works were the most gigantic in the world, and we have heard the assumption made that no works of such magnitude ever existed in the days of old. So far as the latter assertion is concerned, it is not correct. Mr. Tennant, in his recent travels in the Island of Ceylon, describes some ancient Water Tanks, besides which our Croton Works are as some small creek compared to the Hudson river. One tank, named Pathariecolorn, is seven miles long, three hundred feet broad and 60 feet high. The tank was faced throughout its entire length with layers of square stones. This huge tank is but one of a great many scattered over the country, and had been erected for irrigation. It is partly in ruins, as the waters flow freely out of a huge breach two hundred feet wide, which appears to have been made centuries ago. The race which constructed these tanks has passed away, and the country where, at one time, there existed a highly civilized and skillful engineering people, is now the abode of wild Veddahs, a race whose homes are in tents and who wander about from place to place. An engineer has calculated that it would cost more than \$4,000,000 to construct the front embankment to this huge water reservoir. What must have been the causes which exterminated the people who erected these works (and they must have been numerous) and left them to fall into ruins, tenanted only by the buffalo and the unclad savage? The savage is surely not the natural but the unnatural state of man---the savage is man shipwrecked in social position.

• Middle East

THE ROCK-HEWN WELLS IN FIKA EMIRATE
Reynolds, F. G. B.; *Man,* 30:221-224, 1930.

The small independent Emirate of Fika, in which the wells herein described are found, lies between latitude 11 and 12° N. and longitude 10° 50' and 11° 30' E. The Emirate has maintained its independence, in spite of neighbours much more powerful than itself, owing to its geographical features which have made hard the way of the would-be invader.

. . . .

The wells described herein, all of which are cut in solid rock, may be divided into three distinct categories:
    (i)   Large systems of cisterns.
    (ii) Small groups of single-shaft water-holes, found esclusively in the hill area, and of no great depth.
    (iii) Single isolated wells, which are wells proper in that they tap a water supply and can be used all the year round.

Categories (i) and (ii) merely serve to store such water as they collect during the rains, and run dry before the ensuing rains.

All three categories have this much in common, that the present inhabitants have no tradition as to how or when they were made, nor have they tools with which they could make them. They are alternatively ascribed to Allah, the Prophets, or a legendary race of giants named the Sau (or So). This mythical race, variably round as Shaushau, Susu and Seu, is merely a generic term for aboriginal tribes, and we may surmise that the actual diggers of the wells were a people known as the Bum or M'bum of whom the present Boliwa of Fika are descendants.

These same Bum are referred to in an extant Arabic document as being the diggers of the wells at Kutushi (or Koutous) to which reference is made hereinafter.

The most interesting of these wells are the huge systems of what are presumably cisterns. (It has been suggested that they are not cisterns at all, but corn-stores. Be this as it may, they are used as cisterns now). These cisterns are of two different types, although the main idea is the same. Those at Mele and at Gana Agado represent the different types.

The Mele cisterns, of which there are some 200, consist of a single shaft varying from 6-10 feet deep and 3-5 feet in diameter. The shaft opens into a large compartment which is divided by low walls into smaller compartments. These compartments which extend in different directions and at different depths contain the water-holes which number from two to three holes per compartment with a depth of 6-10 feet each. Thus such a cistern comprises a work of no little magnitude even for modern tools.

Assuming that these excavations were intended as cisterns, it is presumed that this rather complicated plan was devised to shield the water from the rays of the sun. Alternatively, it may be that the shape was adopted to lessen labour in places where a hard cap of rock existed on the surface with a stratum of softer rock beneath it. Some of the cisterns are connected by underground passages. At Gana Agado some 300 similar cisterns are found, cut in a slightly different plan. Here we find the single shaft as at Mele, 7-12 feet deep, but opening into one central chamber which runs horizontally from the shaft in one direction only. This chamber may contain from 2-19 water-holes at different elevations, with an average depth of 12 feet each.

Similar cisterns to those of Mele have been located at Bainu (30 cisterns), and one mile east of Zai (55 cisterns). Systems similar to that of Gana Agado are Shula (40 cisterns) and Akoli.

. . . .

In looking for further reasons for the existence of these workings, other than as cisterns or as corn stores, the possibility of their being either hiding places or ancient mine workings cannot be overlooked. The fact that some of them are joined up by subterranean passages makes either suggestion conceivable, and it is also possible that they were originally more inter-connected than at present appears, the passages having become blocked up.

It should be noted that the terms "wells" and "cisterns" are used in describing these curious workings simply for want of a better word, and the writer would welcome suggestions as to their original use. The present-day inhabitants use them for water storage, and have no traditions of any other use of the workings.

• Africa

RHODESIAN CULTIVATION TERRACES
C., O. G. S.; *Antiquity*, 29:96–99, 1950.

The photographs which we publish here [not reproduced] show portions of a vast system of terrace cultivation, and the homesteads of the cultivators, near Inyanga in Southern Rhodesia. By the time that the following remarks appear in print it is probable that excavations will have begun, so that a full account of the remains would be premature. Our object in publishing this note is two-fold: (1) to give readers some general information about a matter of topical interest which may be mentioned in the press; (2) to enlist support for the Inyanga Research Fund, which has been founded under the patronage of the Governor of Southern Rhodesia, who recommends it as 'deserving the strongest support'. We do so too, and would urge those of our readers who wish to help to send their contributions to the secretary of the Fund (Mr. Neville Jones), P. O. Box 240, Bulawayo, Southern Rhodesia.

It will be obvious at a glance that the remains consist of thousands of terraces deliberately constructed on the steep slopes of the hills, of roughly circular and oval stone enclosures, and of paths leading between walls to those enclosures. The terraces are not lynchets---which are formed by the natural accumulation of soil on the lower sides of fields--- but strips of ground on whose lower side a wall has been built to reduce the steepness of the slope and to hold the soil. Only by such measures could the cultivation of such steep slopes be possible. The construction of these terraces must represent an enormous amount of labour, and it is legitimate, even without the evidence of excavation (which alone can be decisive) to conclude that the whole complex must be measured in centuries. But it would be rash to suppose that it must have covered many centuries and still more so that it is very ancient. In fact in a climate of heavy rainfall which is continually eroding the surface any great antiquity is ruled out.

....

We would warn our readers that the forthcoming excavations will probably be the signal for an outburst in the press of the usual mystery-mongering and the re-hash of stale speculations about King Solomon's mines and similar fantastic rubbish. Excavation has twice over disproved the great antiquity of the Zimbabwe culture, and has shown good reasons for regarding it as ancestral to the recent African culture of the region. The date of the beginning of the Zimbabwe culture has not yet been determined; but it was certainly flourishing at the beginning of the 16th century and may be a few centuries older---it is unlikely to be more.

....

WELLS, CAIRNS, AND RAINPOOLS IN KENYA COLONY
Watson, C. B. G.; *Man*, 27:50-53, 1927.

In the easterly parts of the country known as the "Northern Frontier Province" of Kenya one finds wells bored through from 16 to 40 feet of limestone rock, and others taking the form of pits with underground passages leading to the water dug through clay. In certain parts barrows or cairns occur in large numbers. If there is a hill in the desert there is sure to be an excavation at its foot which, in the rare event of rain, soon becomes a lake of sometimes half a mile in diameter.

Among the officials there are two schools of thought. The first attributes the cairns and the wells to volcanic origin and the rainpools to natural hollowing out of the ground by tropical deluges. The opposition believe in an ancient civilisation of a people who have left behind them no trace save their feats as water engineers and cairns that yield no bones, implements or records of any kind. This tribe has been called "The Medenli."

A rough description of the country will not be out of place. Vast areas of desert, open in places, but for the most part covered with dense bush standing 8 to 10 feet, with occasional trees. The ground is either soft sand, white rock or, in the open spaces, "black cotton" soil. Much of the bush is dead and firewood is always to hand. The rest is barren, save for three months after a good rainy season. It is everywhere obvious that the country was once fertile. In certain parts dry river beds of perhaps 30 yards breadth are common.

The present inhabitants---Boran to the west and south, Ogaden Somalis to the east---are bone-idle and only work sufficient wells for their needs, not attempting to repair them or to dig out those that go dry.

Figures will show that the Medenli must have been:

(a) immensely numerous and wealthy;
(b) clever water diviners;
(c) cunning engineers;

and that their country was fertile, though now a barren desert.

Wells. At El Wak (the wells of the Wak tree) are some 50 wells spread over an area of about 20 square miles. Only a dozen are now used by a mixed Galla-Somali tribe called Gurre. They consist of (a) a deep pit averaging 60 feet deep and 15 broad at the top, (b) underground passages varying in number and length. Wanderers have been known to have been lost forever in these passages.
. . . .

We travel southwards to Katulu, Wajir and Arbo. Eastwards for two days from Wajir to Wajir Bor and north-west from Wajir for five days to Buna. All these places have wells of identical structure, totally different to the rough and ready ones at El Wak.

At Katulu there are some 50 wells, all now run dry. They occupy an area of about 2 square miles. They have been sunk through 12 or 16 feet of limestone rock by this means, it is said. A fire is lit and on burning itself out the crumbled rock is scraped away. The process is repeated until water is reached. This theory is backed by the peculiarly shaped walls of the wells, which are practically perfect circles.

At Wajir one can give figures which give an idea of the size of the Nedenli tribe and its stock.

In an area of about 2 square miles there are known to be more than 400 wells of this type, all of which could be used if required to-day. Now in the Government boma a few whites and about 300 natives get all the water they require from two wells. Water can be pulled up by tribesmen for a day continuously before a few hours' rest is needed for the water to filter through the sandy subsoil to restore the level. Who then could these people have been who required this immense water supply obtained by such laborious feats of engineering?

At Arbo the wells number about sixty. At Buna we see wells made on the same lines but about 40 feet in depth. To my mind they explode the "volcanic" theory. At Wajir water is not far down and a goatskin bucket can easily be lowered. Therefore the wells are narrow. At Buna, where the water is deep down, they are about 4 feet across and are worked by a dozen men and women, who descend and, standing on ledges, throw giraffe-hide buckets from hand to hand. Nature could never have worked such a convenient fluke.
. . . .

JOSEPH'S CANAL IN EGYPT
Anonymous; *Scientific American*, 177:138, 1897.

How many of the engineering works of the nineteenth century will there be in existence in the year 6000? Very few, we fear, and still less those that will continue in that far-off age to serve a useful purpose. Yet there is at least one great undertaking conceived and executed by an engineer which during the space of 4,000 years has never ceased its office, on which the life of a fertile province absolutely depends to-day. We refer, says Engineering, to the Bahr Joussuf---the canal of Joseph---built, according to tradition, by the son of Jacob, and which constitutes not the least of the many blessings he conferred on Egypt during the years of his prosperous rule.

This canal took its rise from the Nile at Asiut, and ran almost parallel with it for nearly 250 miles, creeping along under the western cliffs of the Nile Valley, with many a bend and winding, until at length it gained an eminence, as compared with the river bed, which enabled it to turn westward through a narrow pass and enter a district which was otherwise shut off from the fertilizing floods on which all vegetation in Egypt depends. The northern end stood seventeen feet above low Nile, while at the southern end it was at an equal elevation with the river. Through this cut ran a perennial stream, which watered a province named the Fayoum, endowing it with fertility and supporting a large population. In the time of the annual flood a great part of the canal was under water, and then the river's current would rush in a more direct course into the pass, carrying with it the rich silt which takes the place of manure and keeps the soil in a constant state of productiveness. All this, with the exception of the tradition that Joseph built it, can be verified to-day, and it is not mere supposition or rumor.

Until eight years ago it was firmly believed that the design has always been limited to an irrigation scheme, larger, no doubt, than that now in operation, as shown by the traces of abandoned canals, and by the slow aggregation of waste water which had accumulated in the Birket el Querum, but still essentially the same in character. Many accounts have been written by Greek and Roman historians, such as Herodotus, Strabo, Mutianus, and Pliny, and repeated in monkish legends, or portrayed in the maps of the middle ages, which agreed with the folk lore of the district. These tales explained that the canal dug by the ancient Israelites served to carry the surplus waters of the Nile into an extensive lake lying south of Fayoum, and so large that it not only modified the climate, tempering the arid winds of the desert and converting them into the balmy airs which nourished the vines and the olives into a fullness and fragrance unknown in any part of the country, but also added to the food supply of the land such immense quantities of fish that the royal prerogative of the right of piscary at the great weir was valued at L250,000 annually. This lake was said to be 450 miles round and to be navigated by a fleet of vessels, and the whole circumference was the scene of industry and prosperity.

EXCAVATIONS AT ABYDOS

Naville, Edouard; *Smithsonian Institution Annual Report, 1914,* pp. 579-585.

There is no longer any doubt, then, that we have discovered what Strabo calls the well or the fountain of Abydos. He spoke of it as being near the temple, at a great depth, and remarkable for some corridors whose ceilings were formed of enormous monolithic blocks. That is exactly what we have found.

These cells were 17 in number, 6 on each of the long sides. There was one in the middle of the wall at the back; in passing through it one came in the rear to the large hall which was the tomb of Osiris. A careful study of the sculptures confirmed the opinion that this was a funeral hall where the remains of the god were expected to be found. But this hall did not form a part of the original edifice. It must have been constructed under ground when Seti I built the temple of the god. The tomb of Osiris was very near the great reservoir. Nothing revealed its presence; the entrance to it was exactly like that to all the other cells, the back of it being walled up after they had dug through it.

The discovery of this subterranean reservoir, constructed of huge building stones, presents many questions, some of which let us hope may be solved by the completion of these excavations. At present we are checked. We could not get to the bottom of the basin, as it is obstructed by a numer of large blocks thrown there at the time the edifice was destroyed. There are some millstones weighing several tons and other fragments just as heavy. We must get to the bottom in order to find out where the wall of magnificent masonry inclosing the water may lead, whether it ends at a flagstone pavement, and also whence comes the abundant supply of water that we see in our excavations. Hydraulic engineers are now studying the sheet of water which extends under Egypt, under the desert as well as under cultivated land. Is it that water that we find in the reservoir? Or has it a conduit which emanates from no one knows where? The word that Strabo uses might apply to a spring.

We have as yet no certain indications of the date of the construction; but the style, the size of the materials, the complete absence of all ornamentation, all indicate very great antiquity. Up to the present time what is called the temple of the Sphinx at Gizeh has always been considered one of the most ancient edifices of Egypt. It is contemporaneous with the pyramid of Chefren. The reservoir of Abydos being of a similar composition, but of much larger materials, is of a still more archaic character, and I would not be surprised if this were the most ancient architectural structure in Egypt. The pyramids are perhaps of the same age, but a pyramid is simply a mass of stone and is not a complicated design like the reservoir.

If we have here the most ancient Egyptian structure that has been preserved to us, it is curious that it should be neither a temple nor a tomb, but a reservoir, a great hydraulic work. This shows that the ancients well understood the flow of subterranean waters, the laws which control their rise and fall. It is very probable that this reservoir played some role in the worship of Osiris. The cells are perhaps those which appear in the Book of the Dead; it is possible also that the water was believed to have a curative property and that it was of service to invalids who came there to seek a cure. Did the barque of Osiris sometimes float on this reservoir, towed by the priests who followed the footpath?---for the solar barque such as one sees in the tombs of kings was always pulled along by a tow line, stopping at some of the doors or chambers. Such are the questions which arise and to which we can not yet reply.

The few travelers who have already seen the reservoir of Abydos have been struck with the grandeur and dignity of the edifice, in spite of the ruined condition in which it was found. Who would have thought a few months ago that at 10 meters underground there would appear a structure such as this, surpassing in grandeur the most colossal Cyclopean edifices? What a strange country this Egypt is! We were beginning to believe that we had found all the great structures and that nothing more remained to be discovered. Who can say that this region does not conceal beneath the ground some majestic work of the most ancient Egyptians that may bring surprises as astonishing as those of Abydos? (pp. 584-585)

• Europe

PREHISTORIC ENGINEERING AT COPAIS
Champlin, John Denison; *Popular Science Monthly,* 48:209-219, 1895.

To guard against the recurrence of a similar catastrophe [flooding around Lake Copais, Greece], the ancient engineers planned several cuttings and tunnels through the hills, which, if they had been carried to completion, would have rounded out the original design and accomplished what the Greek Government is to-day trying to effect---the thorough reclamation of the basin and its protection from any contingency of flood. On the southeast shore of the lake are vestiges of an immense cutting, thirty metres deep, through the Hill of Carditza toward Lake Hylicus, and beyond that traces of works to connect Hylicus with Paralimni, and the latter with the sea. Across the Hill of Carditza, too, are a series of excavated shafts marking the line of a tunnel through the hill constructed with an object similar to that of the cutting---to convey the waters to the sea through the smaller lakes; but the shafts are now filled up and there are no indications that the work was ever completed.

This route is the one adopted by the modern engineers, who, by a tunnel through the Hill of Carditza, not far from the line of the ancient tunnel, seek to carry the waters into Lake Hylicus, thence into Paralimni, and finally through another tunnel into the sea. There is also a plan to deflect a portion of the waters for use in irrigating the plain of Thebes.

A still more ambitious undertaking of the ancient engineers was an attempt to penetrate the Hill of Kephalari in the northeast end of the lake by a tunnel more than a mile and a quarter long. This hill, a depression on the flank of Mount Ptoum, has a maximum height of one hundred and forty-seven metres above the sea and fifty-two metres above the bottom of Lake Copais. Across this depression, from near the openings of the

Katabothra of Bynia in the Bay of Kephalari, runs a line of ancient wells or shafts in a general direction from southwest to northeast, not in a straight line, but following the contour of the hill, ending on the east side not far from where the katabothra opens into the Valley of Larymna. There are sixteen of these wells, cut through the hard, gray limestone of which the mountain is composed, and carefully squared, with an average horizontal section of three to four metres. The first shaft, on the west side, two hundred and twenty-five metres from the opening. The wells are at an average distance from each other of about one hundred and sixty metres, and the whole distance from opening to opening is about twenty-four hundred metres.

These shafts are not mentioned by any ancient writer, but have been frequently described by modern travelers, notably by Forchhammer, who has given the most complete description of them. The general conclusion in regard to their object was that they were designed to facilitate the clearing of the katabothra when, from caving or other causes, it had become clogged; but in 1846, M. Sauvage, who examined the shafts critically and cleared several of them, came to the conclusion that they were part of a tunnel scheme, and were sunk with the purpose of giving many points of attack to the workmen engaged in excavating the tunnel instead of a single one at each end. To the ancients, ignorant of the use of explosives, this was of great importance, for the cutting with hammer and chisel was arduous and slow. Even with these numerous shafts, which must themselves have been a difficult undertaking, the excavation of so long a tunnel would have cost the labor of many years. In 1882 several more were

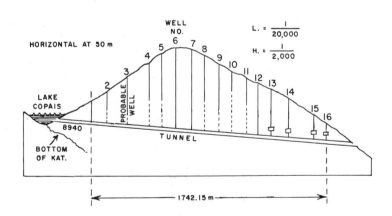

Ancient shafts and tunnel at Lake Copais, Greece

cleared and thoroughly examined---the first and the second on the west slope toward the lake and the thirteenth, fourteenth, fifteenth, and sixteenth on the east slope of the hill. The first and the sixteenth wells are each eighteen metres deep, while the sixth, at the summit of the hill, is sixty-six metres deep.

Sauvage concluded that the tunnel had been left unfinished, which later examinations have fully proved. The fact that the first and second wells contain water indicates that it had been completed on the lake side for at least five hundred metres. The exploration in 1882 of the thirteenth well, whose orifice is at an elevation of 107.68 metres, discovered, at a depth of 28.35 metres, a horizontal gallery, 1.60 metre wide and 1.65 metre in the axis, cut in each direction about six metres. At 2.15 metres below this was found a second gallery of the same section, cut in the same direction, and the shaft was excavated 2.70 metres farther down, probably for use as a drainage well, ending in a level bottom, its total depth being 36.50 metres. The fourteenth, fifteenth, and sixteenth wells, at decreasing altitudes, show a similar interior disposition, save that in the fourteenth the gallery has been but slightly advanced and there is no drainage well. In the fifteenth shaft, which has a total depth of 78.93 metres, the upper gallery is cut to a depth of five metres on the west and two metres on the east, and the lower one 10.30 metres on the west and 10.70 on the east, while the well is 4.70 metres deep. In the sixteenth well the upper gallery is cut only two metres on the west and none on the east, the lower one seven metres on the west and 7.30 on the east, with a well of 4.20 metres in depth. In the last shaft the two galleries are three metres apart, and in the fifteenth only 2.15 metres, thus showing a tendency to diverge. This would seem to prove that there was no intention of ultimately uniting the two galleries by cutting away the rock between. It is more probable that the upper galleries were begun first, and that some consideration induced the engineers to change the grade and give a greater fall to the tunnel. The mean section of the lower gallery is about two metres, the fall from Copais to its mouth is 0.011 metre to the lineal metre, and its total length completed would have been about twenty-four hundred metres. The cutting of so long a tunnel through so hard a rock with the primitive means at the disposal of the ancients shows not only an audacity of plan and a persistent obstinacy in execution, but also a skill in the art of the engineer and the miner that would be no discredit even to the present age.

Who were the authors of these great works concerning which history is silent and which are themselves their only witnesses? Perhaps this question will never be satisfactorily answered. Leake and others attribute all the wells of Kephalari as well as the canals, to the Minyans, while some believe that Crates of Chalcis was responsible for the parts exhibiting the most engineering skill, and others ascribe them to some of the earlier Roman emperors. Curtius, in his Die Deichbauten der Minyer, a paper read before the Berlin Academy in 1892, carefully distinguishes two distinct works and methods of work: (1) the utilization of the natural exutories toward which the waters were led by means of dykes and canals, and (2) the formation of an artificial emissary to draw off either all the water or the excess of water from the lake. The first, grand and simple in design, he attributes to the primitive or Homeric age; the last, marked by careful calculation and executed with the skill of the practiced engineer, he ascribes to the age of Alexander, and presumably to Crates, the only name mentioned in connection with it. Unless the future shall bring to light some inscribed stone or other monument which shall give us definite information concerning the promoter who planned or the engineer who executed these vast works, we shall have to accept the judgment of Curtius and give the credit of them to Crates, the miner of Chalcis. (pp. 216-219)

AN ANCIENT TUNNEL
Anonymous; *Knowledge,* 6:370, 1884.

The Governor of Samos, Abyssides Pasha, has at last succeeded, after years of work, in uncovering the entrances to a tunnel of which Herodotus speaks with admiration as the work of Eupalines and Megaira, and which, according to the same authority, was built during the tenth century B. C. The tunnel, about 5,000 feet long, was intended to secure a supply of fresh water to the old seaport town of Samos, and consists of three parts. They are the tunnel proper, 5-1/2 feet high and 6 feet wide; a canal about 5 feet deep and nearly 3 feet wide, which runs in the middle or on the side of the base of the tunnel; and the aqueduct running in this canal. The aqueduct consists of earthen pipes, each 2-1/2 feet long, 32 to 33 inches in circumference, the sides averaging about 1-1/2 inch in thickness. Every other joint has a hole, for what purpose has not yet been fully explained. Mr. Stamatiades, a Greek archaeologist, believes that they were intended to facilitate the cleaning of the pipes, and to make the flow of water easier. The canal is arched over, but twenty-eight manholes were provided to admit the workmen who were charged with cleaning and repairing the aqueduct. The tunnel is not quite straight, forming an elbow about 1,300 ft. from one of the entrances. This elbow, according to Mr. Stamatiades, was caused by a mistake in the calculations of the engineers, who had none of the instruments used in tunnel-building nowadays. The tunnel starts near a small water-course, which may have been quite a stream in olden times, pierces the mountain Kastri, which was formerly crowned by the fort Samos, and ends a few hundred yards from the old town of Samos, about 10 ft. below the surface. From the mountain slope to the city, this subterranean aqueduct is profected by a massive stone structure, ending within the walls of the present convent of St. John. The preservation of this work---which is truly wonderful, considering the imperfect mechanical resources at the disposal of the builders---for nearly three thousand years is probably due to the care taken by Eupalinos, who, in all cases where the rock did not seem of sufficient firmness, lined the tunnel with several layers of brick, running on the top into a peaked arch.

DEW-PONDS
Martin, Edward A.; *Antiquity,* 4:347-351, 1930.

A great antiquity has been claimed for dew-ponds, or rather for those ponds which have passed as such. They are found on the higher parts of the chalk downs of Southern England, and sometimes indeed on their very summits. They first came to be noticed by reason of the fact that in dry weather, when by all reasoning from their exposed position they ought quickly to dry up, they are the very ponds that still carry water, whereas other ponds on the lands below, which are fed by runnels and other drainage, are the earliest to suffer from drought. This is a very real distinction, for the old dew-ponds, to call them by their better-known name, have no drainage beyond the collecting area of their own banks. That observant student of natural history, Gilbert White, was almost the earliest writer to call attention (in the middle of the eighteenth century) to the ponds on the common above Selborne, which, although used for the watering of innumerable cattle and sheep, had never been known in his time to fail. His attempted explanation need not trouble us here, but it is noteworthy that he did not call them by the name of dew-ponds, and this name did not appear until well on into the nineteenth century. Pseudo-scientific people gave this name to something which they could not explain and so the mysterious dew-pond was christened. They still give it the same name, although those living in their immediate neighbourhood still know them as mist-ponds or fog-ponds. The worst of it is that the mystery of the dew-ponds is constantly cropping up in print, and it really seems as if the general public does not want to know the truth of the matter. Mystery always appeals to them and I fear that editors do not always desire to deprive their readers of its fascination.

Many of these ponds are found inside or in close association with earthworks. But the majority are not so found. Early archaeologists were much concerned, as well they might be, to discover the source from which the inhabitants of earth-walled encampments drew their water. A certain quantity was needed, although we need not imagine that these early men in Britain washed themselves so frequently as modern men do. For drinking purposes and perhaps for cooking, rain-storage within the camp sufficed as a general rule. When this failed, it was necessary to have a reserve and so they fell back on their ponds.

An attempt has been made to show that neolithic man was the first to make and use these ponds, and he may have done so, but that is a very different thing from saying that he made the identical ponds that now exist. With the possession of cattle he would find that any spot much frequented by them would become so puddled that the spot would hold water. If driven at night through a narrow entrance to a camp, that entrance would soon become a quagmire, and so the puddled bottom of a pond would be revealed to him. This might have induced him to dig ponds elsewhere where they would be less of a nuisance, and so sometimes one is found within the enclosure. There is a pond some two hundred feet below the north side of Cissbury camp, but it is not worthy of the name of a dew-pond, as it is sheltered from the incoming southerly moisture-laden winds, and it is not to be imagined that the occupants of the camp would come down all that distance to carry up to the top the desired water, especially whilst they had the whole area of a large enclosed camp in which to make all the ponds they needed.

....

Without attaching much credence to the remarkable stories of new ponds becoming filled in a single night, the fact remains that there is some recruiting agent which keeps them fairly well supplied in times of drought, when those at a lower level have ceased to hold water. First of all, of course rainfall is responsible for most of the water. Unfortunately the rainfall is least in the months when it is most needed, and when evaporation is greatest. My experiments made some years ago naturally began with a view to ascertain if dew had anything to do with their filling.

I mean real dew, and not other forms of condensation from the atmosphere. A thorn-bush overhanging a pond will condense moisture which will drip into a pond. But this is not dew. Low-lying clouds and fogs, which are no doubt the real recruiting agents, cannot be classed as dew. Dew is produced on good radiators of heat, when those radiators have been reduced in temperature to below a certain point called dew-point. This is familiarly produced on grass in the evening after a hot day, through the rapid chilling of the layer of air in contact with the earth, and the condensation of the moisture which is rising from the soil. Grass, straw, and the like are good radiators of heat, and quickly receive dew. I need not enter into the question that sometimes arises, as to whether dew falls or rises. It is simply deposited. The moisture in the air may rise or it may fall, and so sometimes the dew is on the under surfaces and at other times on the upper surfaces of good radiators. The point to consider is whether it can ever be deposited on the surface of water already in a pond, or on the smooth surface of the chalky banks of the best-kept ponds. Sometimes the grassy surface of the bank has seemed to be quite moist with dew, but it would require a great amount of dew to be formed before it began to run down into the pond. Much of the moisture thus found on a bank sinks at once through the material of the bank. Any vegetation growing in a pond might add a small quota to the water in the pond, as long as the roots of such vegetation do not perforate the bottom. But the best-kept ponds are perfectly clear of vegetation, and we are driven to ask if the water-surface itself receives dew. This is not an easy problem to tackle. But repeated experiments showed that although the grass around was wringing wet with dew after night-fall, only on very rare occasions did the water-surface temperature go below dew-point. Taking July, August, and September as the months of greatest dew and least rainfall, and dewy nights as on the average one in three, there would be a possible thirty nights of dew. On each night there might be a possible six hours of dewfall, or 180 hours altogether. During the course of my investigations there was a possible five hours in those months when the surface water went down below dew-point.

Although fogs and mists are to my mind the critical factors in keeping ponds alive, these would be of little avail were it not for the rainfall. The rain-gauges that I kept on the top of the downs showed that rain was there precipitated some thirty per cent. more than in the Weald below. But apart from this increased rainfall, the great collecting area of a pond has often been overlooked. There is a level higher than which a pond never seems to rise. Above this there are the collecting areas of the banks, and in cases I have met with, the area of the surface of the water has to be trebled or quadrupled in order to arrive at the area of the banks. Nearly all the water from heavy rains runs at once down into the pond. When there are only moderate rains a good deal of the water goes through cracks, or goes to saturate the surface of the dry puddle, after which it begins to go down into the pond. Downland mists and low-lying clouds settle in hollows on the downs, and are the last to disappear thence. Although difficult of proof, I have no doubt that it is to these that we are indebted for the maintenance of ponds in the drier months.

One thing is certain. It is obvious that a pond can never receive any dew worth mentioning, and therefore there is no such thing in nature as a real dew-pond.

ANCIENT MINES AND QUARRIES

Ancient man quarried his flint, quartzite, and similar minerals wherever he could. He manufactured tools and tool blanks and traded them over wide areas, as evidenced by the discoveries of "workshops" and impressive hoards of implements. In fact, flint was in such good supply that it was used for ritual and other nonutilitarian applications. (See Chapter 2.) Metal mining, especially in the New World, was practiced by prehistoric man at surprisingly early dates and with great ambition. The famed aboriginal copper mines of the Lake Superior region must have yielded many times the amount of copper found in American Indian mounds. Where did it all go and who were the miners? Even more startling are hints of early iron mining in North America. In Africa, too, iron mining seems incredibly ancient. Then there are those excavations that do not seem to be mines at all but whose real purpose escapes us; such as the English dene holes.

• North America

THE GOSHEN STONE MYSTERY

Rothovius, Andrew E.; *NEARA Newsletter,* 7:52, 1972. Summarized from: Leland H. Godfrey, *Yankee,* November 1971.

Built into the side of a hill on the west side of the cemetery in Goshen, Mass., and constructed entirely of unmortared, closely-fitting fieldstones, is an extraordinary underground structure. The few extant references to it usually term it "Counterfeiters Den", in allusion to a tradition that a band of counterfeiters was apprehended a few miles to the southwest. There is however absolutely no evidence to link the structure with this story, or with the pre-Civil War "Underground Railroad", since it has no connecting passage to any houses; the nearest one being the John Williams farm, about 1000 feet to the northwest. (The elevation of the site above sea level is 1500 feet.)

In the Hampshire County History, it is suggested that the structure was a hideout from Indian raids; but the area was not subject to them, nor is the structure suitable for the purpose. The History also speaks of it as a "dry well", which superficially it is; but an on-the-spot inspection will quickly dispel that impression. The main shaft, sunk into a clay hardpan soil so dense it can be worked only with a pick, is 15 feet deep and 3-1/2 feet in diameter. At the bottom, two tunnels lead out in opposite directions; the upper one, with its opening 3-1/2 feet above the shaft floor, is 2 x 2-1/2 feet in size, barely large enough to admit a crawling adult. It runs eastward some 90 feet toward the cemetery, but stops short of it. According to Mr. Godfrey, when he was about 16 he was informed by an old man of 90, resident of Goshen all his life, that the tunnel originally opened into an underground chamber 10 feet square. Now, however, the further end has fallen in and it is impossible to get into this chamber.

The lower tunnel, running about 70 feet toward the Williams farm, appears to have been intended as a drain to prevent water from building up in the main shaft. Both tunnels, stone-lined on the sides, are roofed with flag-stones of two to ten-inch thickness, that could have been quarried out of a protruding ledge about 200 feet to the south.

Local tradition affirms that the structure was discovered nearly two centuries ago by two boys who chased a rabbit into its burrow and while trying to dig it out, uncovered the flagstone cover of the main shaft, which had become completely sodded over, with bushes growing above it. This discovery took place long before the cemetery was located in the vicinity.

There would appear to be no possibility of Colonial origin or purpose for this enigmatic structure, built of many tons of stones with an enormous expenditure of labor. Finding its true nature and date is one of the most important tasks confronting NEARA.

ANCIENT IRON-SMELTING FURNACES IN OHIO

Keeler, Clyde E., and Kelley, Bennett E.; *NEARA Newsletter,* 6:28-32, 1971.

Arlington Mallery, in his <u>Lost America</u>, described his opening of many prehistoric sites, most of them in mounds, giving evidence of the making of moulded brick and the smelting of bog iron. He had analyses made by employees of the Battelle Institute and the Bureau of Standards. His greatest mistakes were that (1) he failed to publish the analyses, (2) did not preserve his specimens in one place where later investigators could examine them, (3) stoutly maintained without sufficient evidence that the Vikings smelted the iron, and (4) saved no charcoal or bone specimens that could have been carbon dated. Mallery died in 1968.

The present authors became convinced in the early 1960's that, in spite of Mallery's mistakes, his demonstration of the existence in Southern Ohio of many prehistoric bog iron furnaces is correct, and we have sought thereafter to collect information on furnaces dug by Mallery, as well as new sites.

Table 1 will give a quick summary of materials found at such sites.

It will be noted that glazed stones, iron slag, baked clay, bog iron ore, charcoal, cast iron, bricks, iron tools and even intact furnaces are likely to be present, a number of the furnaces being inclosed in mounds.

. . . .

Prehistoric refractory brick were found by Mallery in the Deer Creek Furnace, the two Haskins Furnaces, the Arledge Furnace mound, and the Walled Village on Paint Creek six miles west of Chillicothe. Kelley found brick at the two Waters furnace sites.

John Haywood (1823) reported: "On the inside of the wall (around the

Table 1

Investigator	Mound or Furnace Site	Glazed Stones	Slag	Baked Clay	Iron Ore	Charcoal	Iron	Bricks	Iron Shovels	Iron Axe	Intact Iron Furnace
Atwater	Circleville	X	X			X	oxide of iron knife iron plate	X			
Atwater	Newark?	X		X		?		X			
Haywood	Spruce Hill	X	X	X	X	X					
Neff	Several	X	X	X	X						X
Putnam	Turner	?	X			X	iron bar					2 connected furnaces
Mallery	Arledge	X	X	X		X	63 Lb. iron bar	X				2 furnaces
Mallery	Allyn	X	X	X		X						X
Mallery	Haskins	X	X	X		X	32 Lb. Bar 55-3/4 Bar	X X				4 furnaces
Mallery	Spruce Hill	X	X	X		X						5 Sites 1 furnace
Mallery	Deer Creek	X	X	X		X		X				
Kelley	Waters	X	X	X		X	Iron plate ? lbs.	X				X
Kelley	Caldwell	X	?	X		X						
Kelley	Waters 2	X	X		X		X					
Kelley	Haskins 2	X	X		X		X					X

summit of Spruce Hill) at line D. there appears to have been a row of furnaces or smith's shops, where the cinders now lie many feet in depth.

"I am unable to say with certainty, what manufactures were carried on here, nor can I say whether brick or iron tools were made here, or both. It was clay that was exposed to the action of fire; the remains are four to five feet in depth, even now in some places. Iron ore, in this country, is sometimes found in such clay; brick and potter's ware are manufactured out of it, in some other instances".

"There can be no doubt that the ancient people selected prominent and elevated positions upon which to build large fires, which were kept burning for long periods, or renewed at frequent intervals. For what purpose they were built, whether to communicate intelligence or to celebrate some religious rite, it is not undertaken to say. The traces of these fires are only observed upon the brows of the hills; they appear to have been built generally upon heaps of stones, which are broken up and sometimes partially vitrified over a large area and several feet thick. They are vulgarly supposed to be the remains of "furnaces". Squier and Davis (1847).

"Some are singularly constructed of stone and earth, and when opened, present a three-fold arch of clay and stone, and in the center, on the natural ground, an altar or pile of iron ore-no ashes, but little traces of fire, and yet the sand stone in places shows evidence of being in the fire---. Why did they cast up a mound 5 or 8 ft. high, and 10 to 30 ft. in diameter? Peter Neff (1880).

Although Neff described the "furnaces" so accurately, he accepted the interpretation of the professionals of his day and called them "signal fires". Why were the intact furnace-like structures in the middle of low mounds? Possibly to keep in the heat and provide a ramp for workers bringing bog iron ore and fuel. Also so that there would be access to the furnaces from the top to observe and aid the smelting process.

Observation signal fires would never have been built five feet deep down in a furnace-like structure buried in a mound.

"But the position of the so-called 'Signal Mounds' or 'Mounds of Observation' is opposed to their implied use rather than confirmatory of it. When a point already overlooks the surrounding country for many miles, no possible advantage could be gained by raising a signal fire a few feet higher, or elevating a sentry to a slight extent when his horizon was already far beyond the limit at which he could discern any moving object. Head lands and high peaks have always been favorite burial spots with Indians, even till the present generation; and human remains are of such common occurrence in mounds thus situated as to warrant the assertion that all were intended as tumuli". (Gerard Fowke, 1902.) This general conclusion is entirely too inclusive for the facts.

Fowke goes to great pains to show that "bricks" reported by Atwater and others as being found in mounds are not moulded and fired bricks at all, but simply portions of mud walls plastered onto frames of withes woven horizontally on upright sticks set in the ground. He thinks that a ravaging accidental fire baked the clay wall which then fragmented at right angles into blocks that resembled bricks. Evidently, Fowke had never examined the true hard baked bricks taken from any of the furnace-bearing mounds of southern Ohio or he would not have given such an explanation.

True bricks were encountered by Mallery in several Ohio furnaces including the Deer Creek furnace in which worked iron was found. True bricks were recovered recently by B. E. Kelley from Waters furnace No. 1 at

Washington Court House in which a circular cast iron mass was found together with slag and glazed stones. This mass reminds one of Atwater's plate of iron "which had become an oxyde". True bricks were also found in Waters furnace No. 2. Mr. Kelley has some of these bricks, and C. K. has several specimens.

Whoever constructed the furnaces must be credited with the ability to make moulded hard-fire brick. . . . .

"The Allyn mound is what intrigues me the most. I helped some there. That dome-shaped burned clay structure - call it a furnace or what you like to - was without a doubt in my mind prehistoric. The ashes and charcoal which apparently had been raked away from it extended some distance out from it on the south side, and lay under the three skeletons which were laid directly one on the other, with no earth fill between them. A short distance from the "furnace" N. W. in some charcoal and ashes but not in the main deposit on the south side, was found a small chunk which to me looked like a clinker from a coal heating stove. This was broken up to see its consistency, and it would jump to a small magnet". The "furnace" had a round opening 7 or 8 inches in diameter through the center of the top". Donald McBeth, 1962. See Fig. 1 taken from Mallery (1951).

It so happens that of 14 furnaces opened by Mallery, only one contained skeletons, refuting Shetrone's belief that they were all burial tumuli. The furnaces are not confined to hilltops as declared by Squier and Davis and others who thought them to be signal fires, but may be found at any level

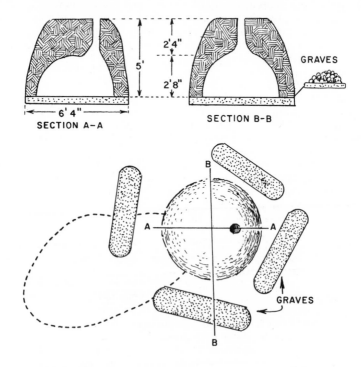

Plan view and sections of the Allyn Mound Furnace, Ohio

including the banks of streams. And so we return to the position of Atwater who described the structures under consideration as "shops or furnaces" for the baking of brick or the smelting of iron. One might also suggest that some of them might have been built for the production of lime.

Were the furnaces built before the time of the Moundbuilders, contemporaneously with them or after their disappearance? The answer to these questions would distinguish between the possibility of several peoples who are now suspect.

The only way to distinguish between the times of Phoenicians, Romans or Vikings at present is by carbon-dating and by magnetic dating. Charcoal and bones may be carbon dated readily. Undisturbed parts of the furnace wall and floor, after placing on them a magnetic north-south line, may be used for magnetic dating. . . . .

References
Adams, H. H. Personal Communication. 1962.
Atwater, Caleb. A description of the antiquities of Ohio. Archaeologia
    Americana 1820.
Fowke, Gerald. Archaeological History of Ohio. Columbus. Fred J. Heer.
    1902.
Haywood, John. Natural and Aboriginal History of Tennessee. Nashville.
    George Wilson. 1823.
Mallery, Arlington. Lost America. Columbus. Overlook Co. 1951.
McBeth, Donald. Personal Communication. 1962.
Neff, Peter. American Antiquarian. 1880.
Shetrone, Henry C. The Moundbuilders. New York, Appleton. 1930.
Squier, Ephriam G. and E. H. Davis. Ancient Monuments of the Mississippi
    Valley. Smithsonian Contributions to Knowledge. Vol. 1. 1847.

Excavation of Haskins #2 Furnace, Ohio (Clyde E. Keeler)

Ax and iron bar from Haskins #1 Furnace (Clyde E. Keeler)

ANCIENT MINING IN NORTH AMERICA
Newberry, J. S.; *American Antiquarian,* 11:164–167, 1889.

The ancient copper mines on Lake Superior have been fully described by many writers. I have been much in that country and can testify to the accuracy of the descriptions of the ancient copper mines given by Whittlesey, Foster and others, as well as the review of the subject now presented by Mr. Appy. I will only add that so far as my observation has extended all the ancient workings on Lake Superior were abandoned many hundred years ago, for the heaps of debris that surround the pits made by the ancient miners were covered with forest trees which had obtained their maximum size, and I have never heard of any of the old mines which did not show evidence of abandonment at least four hundred years ago.

The old mica mines of North Carolina and the quarries of serpentine in the Alleghanies, worked by the ancient inhabitants to procure materials for their pots, pipes, etc., show the same rude processes and I may add the same antiquity as the copper mines of Lake Superior, for they, too, were overgrown by what seemed the primeval forest when first visited by the whites.

To all the evidences of ancient mining industry in our country cited by Mr. Appy, I will add that some population of the Mississippi valley in ancient times worked our oil fields in many places, and at least in one case opened and extensively worked a vein of lead. This lead vein is situated on the Morgan farm, about six miles northeast of Lexington, Kentucky. Part of the area traversed by it has been long cultivated and the evidences of excavation have been thereby to some extent obliterated, but a part of the course of the vein runs through a tract of woodland which has never been touched by the axe. Here the ancient working is in the form of an open cut, six to ten feet wide, of unknown depth, and now nearly filled with rubbish. On either side of this trench the material thrown out forms ridges several feet in height, and these are everywhere overgrown by trees, many of which are as large as any found in the forests of that section. We learn from this that the work was abandoned at least five hundred years ago. Galena has been found in a great number of the ancient works in Ohio, both in mounds and fortifications. It has never been smelted, however, and seems to have been valued merely for its brilliancy, though it may have been calcined and used for the production of a pigment.

In regard to the working of our oil fields in former times, I would say that I have found conclusive evidence that wells were sunk and oil collected on Oil Creek, near Titusville, Pennsylvania, in Mecca, Ohio, and at Enneskillen, Canada. In 1860 the first fountain well was opened by Brewer and Watson, just below Titusville. I then resided in Cleveland, Ohio, and went to Titusville to examine the interesting geological phenomena presented by the newly-opened oil wells. In passing down the valley of Oil Creek I noticed that the surface of the ground was pitted in a peculiar way; it was in places completely occupied by shallow depressions, ten to fifteen feet across and from one to three feet in depth. At first I thought they must have been produced by a wind-fall, in which the trees were all up-rooted, but I was familiar with the character of the depression made by the overturning of a large forest tree, and knew that the pit thus formed was oval, with a ridge on one side and none on the other. These pits were, however, quite symmetrical and were a puzzle to me. While I was talking with Mr. Brewer or Mr. Watson about them and asking questions to which I got no satisfactory answers, a man standing near told me if I would go with him to his well one hundred yards away the mystery would be solved. I did so, and found that he had begun the excavation of a well in one of these pits, and had sunk through the superficial material some twenty-five feet to the rock where he was to begin drilling. In sinking his pit he followed down an old well, cribbed up with timber, and in it stood a primitive ladder, such as was so often found in the old copper mines of Lake Superior; a tree of moderate size, with many branches, had been felled and the limbs cut off a few inches from the trunk, thus forming a series of steps by which one could ascend or descend. The cribbing of the ancient well was rudely done with sticks six to eight inches in diameter, either split from a larger trunk or lengths cut from a smaller one. The sticks had been cut by a very dull instrument, undoubtedly a stone hatchet.

The method of gathering the oil practiced by the ancient inhabitants was evidently that followed in the Caspian region up to the time when the American method of drilling and pumping was introduced, viz.: a pit was sunk in the earth, and the oil skimmed from the water.

What use was made of the oil we can only conjecture, possibly it was employed only medicinally, as the oil from the spring at Cuba, New York, was used by the Indians in that region; possibly for burning, as petroleum has been used from time immemorial in Persia, India and China. The large number of pits sunk in the valley of Oil Creek indicate, however, that the quantity taken out was large and that the oil served some important purpose among the ancient people. The pits

described above were located in a dense hemlock forest in which many
of the trees were three feet and more in diameter.

At Enneskillen, Canada, the oil was collected much as an Oil Creek,
that is by sinking wells in the superficial clay. At the time of my visit
to Enneskillen a pit six by twelve feet had recently been sunk to a depth
of about fifty feet, and one corner of this pit was cut in an ancient one
that had been filled up with rubbish, leaves, twigs, etc.; at the depth of
thirty-seven feet from the surface a pair of deer's antlers had been taken
out from this pit, showing conclusively that it had once been opened to
that depth. Over this old well, as well as upon depressions which marked the sites of others, full-sized trees were growing, proving that the
pits had been abandoned and filled many hundred years before.

At Mecca and Grafton, Ohio, I found a few depressions in the surface that seemed to me quite like those on Oil Creek, and I have no
doubt they were ancient oil wells, but the quantity of oil which came to
the surface in these localities was small and therefore the wells were
few.

Who the people were who worked these oil wells I will not pretend to
say; doubtless they were some members of the great American family
of nations, but I can not at all agree with those who would regard them
the same as our modern nomadic Indian. I have been much among our
Indians, having visited about forty tribes, and I have been from boy-
hood studying the works of the so-called Mound-builders, and I find
indications of strongly marked differences between them. The Mound-
builders were doubtless not one, but many tribes, and they were but
little way advanced on the road to civilization; still they differed from
the present Indian in this, that they were far more sedentary, agricultural and industrious.

The modern Indians of New York, Ohio, Kentucky, Indiana, etc.,
had their fields of corn and pumpkins when the white man appeared,
but they were essentially the children of the forest, and the clearings
they made and cultivated were utterly insignificant as compared with
the great breadth of forest growth. The modern Indians never built any
such works as those of Marietta, Newark and Circleville and were not
found working the copper mines, the oil wells or lead veins when they
were first observed by the white man. On the other hand we may say
that the characteristic works of the Mound-builders had been abandoned
a thousand years or more before the white man set foot in the Mississippi
valley. This we know because their walls and mounds, copper mines
and oil wells are not only covered with a generation of trees which had
attained their maximum size, but the roots of these trees had overgrown
the trunks of a preceding generation, which grew and died before them.
How many such generations of forest trees have succeeded each other
since the fields and towns and fortifications were deserted, we have no
means of knowing, but we have positive evidence of two.

From the facts which have come under my observation I am convinced that the modern Indians of the states I have mentioned are not the
descendants of those who have left these records behind them, but that
they are invaders and usurpers who, like the barbarian hordes that
overran and nearly effaced the civilization of the shores of the Mediterranean, came from the north and dispossessed a more sedentary,
peaceful and industrious people or peoples that had long occupied the
best portion of the Mississippi Valley. That the Mandans, Natches,

and perhaps other tribes may be the descendants of the Mound-builders, I can very well believe, but that the Iroquois and Algonquins are their modern representatives will, I think, not be credited by any one who has studied the ancient works and has by personal observation made himself familiar with the Indian of to-day.

PREHISTORIC MINES OF LAKE SUPERIOR

Lathrop, J. H.; *American Antiquarian,* 23:248-258, 1901.

The traces which the ancient miners have left of their work in the Lake Superior copper country indicate that they were a most industrious and intelligent race, and that their manual labors must have extended through centuries of time, as they cover an area in Michigan, known as the trap-range, having a length of nearly one hundred miles through Keweenaw, Houghton, and Ontonagon counties, and with a width varying from two to seven miles. Their works were also very extensive on the island in Lake Superior, some forty miles from the Michigan shore, known as Isle Royale. This island is about forty miles in length, by an average of five miles in width. Their works here will be spoken of more in detail later.

From examination of their ancient pits we can get a fair idea of their methods of mining, which are crude and primitive to our eyes, but which show wonderful perseverance on their part. The process was to heat the rock containing the embedded copper by building fires along the outcrop of the vein, and then, removing the coals, to dash water on the heated rock, thus cracking it, and afterwards taking out the broken pieces of rock; then, by breaking away the remaining rock with stone hammers, they released the copper. This method is shown plainly, in all the ancient workings, by the presence of quantities of charcoal and of stone hammers. In some places remains of birch-bark baskets have been found. These were used to carry water to the fires, or the pieces of copper to the boats. It is assumed that the ancient miners had no knowledge of raising water otherwise than by hand, for the pits have only been sunk to a depth where water could be baled out with comparative ease by sets of men.

All along the trap-range the vestiges of ancient miningworks are very numerous. As far back as 1771, a large mass of native copper weighing about four tons was found near the bank of the Ontonagon River. It is supposed that this mass was moved from its native resting-place to the place near the river where found. In 1845 it was floated on a raft down the river by James K. Paull, who thus became the first shipper of modern times of a large amount of copper from the Lake Superior District. Unfortunately for Mr. Paull, this mass of copper was appropriated by an agent of the United States Government, by him shipped to Detroit, and later to Washington, where it now reposes in the Smithsonian Institute.

The earliest record in detail of the work of the ancient miners was the discovery in 1846 by the prospector, Albert Hughes, on the Minnesota mine location in Ontonagon county, and thus described by Samuel O. Knapp, then agent of the Minnesota mine:

> When he had penetrated to a depth of eighteen feet, he came to a mass of a native copper, ten feet long, three feet wide, nearly two feet thick, and weighing over six tons. On digging around the mass it was found to rest on billets of oak, supported on sleepers of the same material. The wood, from its long exposure to moisture, was dark-colored and had lost its consistency. It opposed no more resistance to a knife-blade than so much peat. The earth was so firmly packed as to support the mass of copper. The ancient miners had evidently raised it about five feet, and then abandoned the work as too laborious. The number of ancient hammers he took from this and other excavations exceeded ten cartloads. They were made of greenstone or porphyry bowlders.

From further explorations in this pit, it appeared that the original work was about thirty feet in depth. On the debris outside the mouth of the pit were trees showing three hundred and ninety-five rings of annual growth.

In 1857, while exploring on the lands of the North Cliff Company at Keweenaw Point, west of Eagle River, Edwin J. Hulbert and Amos H. Scott discovered evidence of the work of ancient miners which was described by Mr. Hulbert as follows:

> The opening was a perfectly-formed underhand slope. The vein was rather in the form of a large cross course. The ancient miners had excavated between the walls of this vein, a width varying from two to three and one-half feet, almost the entire matrix for a distance of some thirty feet in length, and in some places six feet in depth. They carried away with them the entire product of their copper, the excavation containing only decomposed leaves.

A large mass of float-copper was found in the woods on the land of the Mesnard Mining Company, located to the northeast of the Franklin mine. This mass had been worked at by the ancient miners, as much charcoal was found around it, and the top and sides had been beaten smooth by stone hammers, the marks of which were plainly visible. All projections, and every particle of copper which could be beaten off, had been carried away. The ancient miners must have felt much regret at having to abandon such a treasure. This mass weighed about eighteen tons, and was cut up under direction of Mr. Jacob Houghton, agent of the Mesnard Company.

The most extensive series of continuous workings as yet discovered were those found on Isle Royale, on what is known as the Minong Belt. Here, for a distance of about one and three-quarter miles in length and for an average width of nearly four hundred feet, successive pits indicate the mining out of the belt of solid rock to a depth of from twelve to thirty feet. Between the rows of pits are ridges of rock and soil, taken from successive pits, and indicating that they were left as dams to prevent the passage of water from one pit to another while the latter was being wrought. In another place a drain sixty feet long had been dug and covered with timbers, felled and laid across. In one place the vein had been followed on an incline to a depth of more than thirty feet, and some thirty inches in width, with large bowlders rolled in and wedged to keep the rock above from falling in on the miners, thus taking the place of timbering, as in our modern mines.

These discoveries on the Minong Belt, first noted in 1867, and more extensively explored in 1871 and 1872, led to the formation of the Minong Mining Company in 1874; and in the work of clearing out the old pits much barrel-work and stamp copper was found, also a mass weighing nearly three tons, which had been detached from its bed by the ancient miners, as it showed the marks of stone hammers, but was evidently too heavy to be carried away. From the extent of these workings on Isle Royale, it would indicate that a large number of men must have been employed for a long series of years, and as Lake Superior is a treacherous sheet of water, the crossing of the intervening forty miles between Isle Royale and Michigan must have been risky work for small boats or canoes.

Nothing has ever been found on either Isle Royale or in the Lake Superior region, to indicate that the ancient miners were permanent dwellers in the copper country. The climate is severe, and the best of protection has to be given to the people at the mines. When one considers the length of time which had to be taken in making the long journey from even Southern Michigan to the copper region, unless the seasons were different in those ancient days than at the present, it is safe to infer that the actual mining in the Lake Superior Country, and particularly on Isle Royale, could not have exceeded three months in the year. These ancient miners were doubtless well posted as to the advantages of the organization of labor, particularly in these extensive works at Isle Royale. There were probably parties who were expert in the extraction of copper from the rock, others whose time was occupied in bailing water from the pits, or carrying it to the heated rocks, and still others who were engaged in the manufacture of stone hammers, sledges, and other implements from the water-worn bowlders from the beach. Other parties, also, were busy in procuring food from the lake, and from the woods surrounding the workings.

A peculiarity of the immense numbers of stone hammers which were found in and about the Isle Royale workings, and which has often been commented upon, was the absence of a groove around the stone. This groove was for the purpose of bending a piece of flexible wood around it and then holding it firmly in place by thongs of deerskin, thus providing a handle which could be reinforced by stiffer pieces of wood. The stone hammers found on the mainland of Michigan almost invariably have the grooves. In some explorations made during the summer of 1899 on the Ontonagon Range, one of these hammers was found with a part of the handle still intact, held in place by the thongs of skin. It may be that the miners at Isle Royale found the stones on the beaches so well shaped by nature and the attrition of the waves that they made excellent hammers just as they were picked up, so that no time was taken to fit them with handles. On the mainland, near the Ontonagon River, there was found quite an area of ground strewn with stone chips and broken and discarded pieces of porphyry, showing that at some time in the distant past it had been a sort of workshop for the purpose of preparing the stone hammers and other implements for transportation inland.

. . . .

ANCIENT MINING IN AMERICA
Appy, E. P.; *American Antiquarian,* 11:92-99, 1889.

We now come to other mines besides those of Lake Superior. We not only find traces of ancient mining operations in the copper-bearing district of Lake Superior, but in California, Lower California, Arkansas, New Mexico, Missouri, Illinois, Indiana, Georgia, New Jersey, and Ohio. In California a shaft was discovered in 1849 that was two hundred and ten feet deep, at the bottom of which were found the bones of a human skeleton. An altar was also discovered in the shaft, which would point more closely to the Indian period than to the early Spanish adventurers. This mine had been so thoroughly worked that the discoverers deemed it unprofitable to work it farther. The mines of Seven Cities of Cibola, New Mexico, have lately been found, from which large quantities of gold are now being taken. The former operations in these mines are described as crude and primitive. In the Wabash Valley, Indiana, several rude attempts at mining have been discovered. Those in Arkansas, Missouri and Illinois consist of wells, dug to obtain a more plentiful supply of salt. The largest of these was discovered near the Saline River, in Illinois. It is known as "Nigger Well," or salt works, as it was worked by slave labor, while Illinois was a territory. It is a curbed well, eight feet square and forty feet deep. These works with their surroundings have been very thoroughly examined by Mr. Sellers, who is of the opinion that they do not show the signs of high civilization that Mr. Foster and others would have us believe. In ancient times salt was obtained in the following way: The salt water obtained from the well was carried up the hill just back of it, where the water was evaporated in large earthen kettles by means of the sun's rays and heated stones plunged into it. Mr. Sellers, in closing his description of these works says: "You may say I am indulging my imagination. Well, be it so. If I am, my imagination keeps within the bounds of possibility; while yours (meaning Mr. Foster's remarks) would endow these primitive people, whose only implements or tools seem to have belonged to the rude age of stone, with a skill in handling them far beyond what we, in this enlightened age, possess, with all our appliances; and you do this to give a color of truth to an entirely imaginary process, not sustained by a single fact."

There are those who even go so far as to make the assertion that the flint mines found all over the country were worked by the Mound-builders, and not by the Indians. They are compelled to make this assertion for, if the Indians were capable of mining flint, they would also be capable of mining copper. No reasonable mind can doubt that the flint mines or pits found at Flint Ridge, Licking county, and those in Perry county, Ohio, were worked by the red men. They used enormous quantities of flint, as the innumerable fragments scattered over the surface of the ground in almost every portion of the state attests.

Nearly all the men who have examined these ancient mining pits of different kinds say that most of them show that they have been abandoned quite recently. Their conclusions are well sustained by the presence of wood and other perishable materials in many of the pits. A few of the pits in the Lake Superior region show that they have been abandoned for several centuries, which proves conclusively that they were not all worked at the same time. In forming our opinions in regard to any of these ancient works, we must bear in mind the enormous changes that have taken place in the last two centuries; and we should strive to bring out the facts and not the mysteries. In science, mystery counts as naught. (pp. 98-99)

TRACES OF ABORIGINAL OPERATIONS IN AN IRON MINE NEAR LESLIE, MO.

Holmes, W. H.; *Smithsonian Institution Annual Report, 1903*, pp. 723-726.

Early in April, 1903, a communication was received by the Bureau of American Ethnology from Dr. S. W. Cox, of Cuba, Mo., stating that evidences of ancient mining operations had been discovered in an iron mine operated by him near Leslie, Franklin County. This report was confirmed by Mr. D. I. Bushnell and other St. Louis archeologists, and the present writer, who is especially interested in the quarrying and mining industries of the aborigines, repaired at once to Leslie to make a study of the interesting phenomena.

It was found that the miners had encountered a body of iron ore, of unknown depth and horizontal extent, lying immediately beneath the surface of the soil on a gentle slope reaching down to the banks of Big Creek, a branch of Bourbois River, and that they had removed the ore from a space about 100 feet wide, 150 feet long, and to a depth at the deepest part of between 15 and 20 feet. In beginning the work traces of ancient excavations were observed penetrating the soil which covered the surface of the ore body to a depth of from 1 to 5 feet, and as the work progressed it was found that the ore had been fairly honeycombed by the ancient people, the passageways extending even below the present floor of the mine, as at the right of the figure in the plate. There were many partially filled galleries, generally narrow and sinuous, but now and then larger openings appeared, two of these being of sufficient dimensions to accommodate standing workmen.

In the debris of the old excavations many rude stone implements were encountered, and upward of 1,000 of these had been gathered by the miners into a heap on the margin of the mine. These sledges are exceedingly rude, consisting of hard masses of stone or hematite weighing from 1 to 5 pounds, and roughly grooved or notched for the attachment of withe handles, no traces of the latter remaining, however. The great number of these implements made it certain that extensive operations had been carried on by the ancients, but the exact nature of the work was not readily determinable. The first impression was that the compact masses of hematite were sought for the purpose of manufacturing implements such as were employed by the mound-building tribes in many parts of the Mississippi Valley, but examination revealed few traces of the shaping of the material, save that it had been used in making the rude sledge heads or hammers found in the mine. In break-

Rude mining implements from Missouri mine

ing up the ore the white miners encountered small, irregular seams and masses of flint, but these were too limited in extent and too brittle in texture to have been utilized successfully in the manufacture of implements. Some workable flint was observed in the vicinity of the ore body, and flakes and rejectage of blade making, as well as a number of well-finished spearheads, arrow points, and leaf-shaped blades were intermingled in the filling of some of the superficial pits, but this flint shaping appears to have been an incident only of the work on the site. The evidences of this shaping work are not sufficient to warrant the conclusion that the extensive tunneling was carried on for the purpose of obtaining material for that purpose. Besides, this flint is found in large bodies in many sections of the general region and could readily have been obtained in quantity by the Indians.

It was observed, in approaching the mine, that the exposed surfaces of the ore and the ground about were everywhere a brilliant red. The workmen were red from head to foot, and anyone venturing to handle the ore soon found his hands smeared with red oxide, repeated washing being required to remove it. The prevalence of the red color suggested at once the idea that the site had been an aboriginal paint mine and that the red and yellow oxides were mined and carried away to be used as paint---an article of utmost importance in the aboriginal economy.

As the charges of dynamite used by the miners broke down the walls of the mine it was observed that the deposits were of irregular hardness, that certain portions of the ore were very compact and flinty, containing much quartz, and of dark-bluish or purplish hue, while the larger part was so highly oxidized as to be easily broken up. Extending through the ore body in all directions were pockets and seams of soft red and yellow oxides, and in places there were irregular openings and partially filled cavities. Two of these openings are shown in plate III, a view of the face of the mine taken by Mr. Clark McAdams, of St. Louis. The miners would drill with great difficulty through the hardest of ore, to have the drill drop suddenly into a cavity of unknown depth. This occurred at the spot shown in plate IV. It was difficult to discover

just which of these openings and cavities were artificial, or whether or
not they had been penetrated by the ancient workers, as changes are
constantly taking place in such ore bodies. Percolating waters fill up
or clear out the passageways. Generally, however, as the walls were
broken down by our miners the openings were found to connect with
the superficial pittings, as indicated in plate V. (Plates omitted.)

It appears certain that the larger tunnels or galleries in which the
sledges were found had been opened up or enlarged by the ancient miners
and that, in the search for other bodies of the desired product, they had
followed weak lines and partially filled passageways, removing the projecting masses of hard ore, where these interfered with the work, by
means of the sledges. It is apparent that the sledges could have had no
other function than that of crushing and breaking up the solid masses
of ore to be used in the manufacture of implements or in opening new
passageways through the ore body. Although these sledges were made
in the main of compact bits of the ore and of the flinty masses associated
with it, they correspond very closely in general characteristics with the
bowlder sledges used in such great numbers in the copper mines of Lake
Superior. Nearly all appear to have been hafted for use, and the majority show the rude grooving or notching necessary for the attachment of
the withe haft. It would seem that in the narrow passages of the mine
the use of hafted implements would be inconvenient if not entirely impracticable, and we are left to marvel at the feat accomplished by the
ancient workmen of penetrating a compact ore body in dark, sinuous
passages hardly roomy enough to admit the body of a man, with the aid
of rude bits of stone held in the hand. The character of these openings
is indicated clearly in plate III, which shows the face of the mine as
freshly exposed by the mining operations; and plate V indicates somewhat
imperfectly the manner in which the tunnels or borings penetrate the ore
body connecting with the superficial pits and extending to unknown depths
beneath the present floor of the mine. Three of these borings are seen
in the wall of the mine shown in plate VII. One is exposed at the right of
the right-hand figure, and a second occurs beyond this, extending from
the stump on the margin of the mine down to and beneath the feet of the
man whose back is turned toward the observer, and a third passes down
from the second stump, being the same opening as that shown at d d in
plate V.

Numerous examples of the implements found and specimens of the
ore in its various phases, together with a large mass of the compact ore,
one surface of which shows the markings of the mining tools of the aborigines, were presented to the U. S. National Museum by the proprietor
of the mine, Dr. S. W. Cox.

I have now examined mines and quarries of the aborigines in twelve
distinct materials, and each new example has added to my former high
estimate of the enterprise and perseverance of the native peoples when
engaged in the pursuit of their normal industries.

ABORIGINAL NOVACULITE QUARRIES IN GARLAND COUNTY, ARKANSAS

Holmes, William H.; *American Anthropologist,* 4:313–316, 1891.

In the State of Arkansas, and extending from near Little Rock to the western limits of the State, is a broad belt of highland made up in great part of a peculiar species of rock known as novaculite. This rock closely resembles chert and flint in character and appearance, but is more attractive to the eye, and on account of its purity and massiveness is more conveniently worked. It occurs in strata, often 50 to 100 feet in thickness, interbedded with silurian slates, sandstones, and quartzites, and outcrops nearly continuously for many miles at a time. Certain varieties of the rock are now extensively quarried for whetstones, as is shown in the report to the 11th Census by Mr. L. S. Griswold, of the Arkansas Geologic Survey. The more flinty or glassy varieties were quarried extensively by the aborigines in past centuries, and employed by them in the manufacture of flaked tools and projectile points and, to a limited extent, of polished tools. The appearance of the rock is most attractive, passing as it does from translucent and milky forms resembling agate into all shades of delicate reds, yellow, grays and blacks. Forming a large share of the exposed rock of the region, erosive agencies have broken it up extensively and have distributed the worn or partially worn fragments over the slopes and along the stream courses. Everywhere the aborigines found and worked these transported masses, and hundreds of square miles are strewn with flakes, fragments, failures and rejected pieces, and the country around, from the mountains to the gulf, is dotted with the finished forms that have been used and lost.

The natives did not stop, however, with the utilization of detached and transported masses. Not finding upon the surface material in suitable quantities, they essayed to quarry it from the hills, and the recently discovered evidences of this work are of unusual interest. The quarries surpass in extent any similar achievements of the aborigines in this country, if not in America.

The quarries are numerous and widespread, but the whole class may be illustrated by a single example, which, though not the most extensive, is unsurpassed in its interest. The example referred to is a group of quarry pits located on the crest of a high forest-covered ridge about three miles east of Hot Springs, Arkansas. The evidences of ancient quarrying consist of a number of pits and excavations dug in and about the crest of the ridge. This ridge is a solid formation of the novaculite weathering out in irregular grayish flinty-looking masses which protrude from the crest or project on the slopes, forming short broken cliffs from ten to twenty feet in height. When we come to realize the true character of these rocks, their slight outcrops, their massiveness and flinty texture, we marvel at the courage of the workman, who with rude stone tools and wooden pikes essayed the work of quarrying; but the beginnings were probably small and the progress of the work so gradual that the workmen did not realize the difficulties that seem so apparent to us.

The largest excavation as seen to-day is on the crest of the narrow ridge near the highest point. It is almost circular and about 150 feet in diameter. The rim of the conical depression is irregular, being

higher at the center of the crest of the ridge and lower at the sides.
The greatest depth is about 25 feet. On the east side the rim is broken
down as a result of the digging of a large pit on that side of the crest.
The process of excavating this great conical pit has been, no doubt,
about as follows: An outcrop of particularly desirable rock was discovered upon the surface. Gradually it was worked down and followed beneath
the surface. The process of uncovering the ledge and breaking up the
rock was most tedious; the latter was accomplished by means of hammers,
aided by the use of fire. As fragments of suitable size and quality were
obtained they were thrown or carried to the margin of the pit, and broken
up and trimmed into approximate shape for the desired tools, and the
refuse gradually formed heaps and ridges about the excavation. At the
present time the enormous accumulations of this refuse have descended
upon the interior of the mine, partially filling it, and upon the exterior
form slides of broken bits of the richly colored rock, reaching far down
the slopes of the ridge. This encircling wall of refuse is composed
greatly of partially shaped fragments, all indicating the intention to produce leaf-shaped blanks or blades, suitable for final specialization into
spear or arrow points, or knives, scrapers, or like tools. Hundreds of
tons of these failures could be collected, and freely intermingled with
them are the rude hammers of quartzite made by slightly reshaping
bowlders of tough quartzite from the valleys below. This particular pit
was entered by the whites in recent years and a shaft was sunk in the
center for the purpose of determining whether or not the rocks contained
gold or other precious metal, for it was popularly believed that these
pits were old Spanish diggings where the early adventurers obtained the
fabled gold. It would seem that a very slight experience with the barren
flinty novaculite must have discouraged the unlucky prospectors, for
little was accomplished. Some of the shaft timbers are still in place
in this pit, and the careless observer might readily be led to believe
that the excavations were wholly due to modern enterprise. That the
recent work has not seriously changed the contour of the ancient quarries
is evident from the fact that the entire mass of ejected material, interior, is composed of the partially shaped fragments derived from ancient
flaking.

Connecting partially with the main pit and on the south side is another
pit, larger in area, but less regular and not so deep. The symmetry of
the basin is interfered with by a series of masses of gnarled rock not
removed by the quarrymen. Other smaller excavations occur on the
crest north and south of these, and a good deal of work has been done
at the sides, especially at a point directly beneath the main pit on the
east. Photographs were taken, but fail to give a clear notion of the
phenomena of the ancient quarries.

Evidence of the use of fire in quarrying is found in some of these
lateral diggings, where there has been undermining. Here certain faces
of the novaculite, protected from the weather by overhanging ledges,
still retain the blackened patches left by the fires. The freshly quarried
rock was carried out of the pits to be worked. High ridges of refuse,
marking the favorite positions of the flakers, encircle the pits, but much
work was done on all the level spots about the crest of the ridge. The
refuse is identical with that of similar sites in other parts of the country.
It is like that of the quarries of the District of Columbia, insomuch as it
contains no fragments or pieces indicating that more than the merest

roughing out was done on the spot.   Like the District of Columbia sites, this was in a wild region and some distance from habitable spots.

. . . .

A NOTE ON SOME LARGE PITS IN CERTAIN SITES NEAR DALLAS, TEXAS

Stephenson, Robert L.; *American Antiquity,* 15:53–55, 1949.

It was noticed some years ago that each of the large village sites along the East Fork of the Trinity possessed one feature in common. Each contained a single, large, circular pit near its center.   These pits now are somewhat difficult to see as a cultivation and river overflows have tended to level them off considerably.   Nevertheless, they are still discernible.   The writer visited eight of these sites and was told of three others.   None of the small campsites appear to have contained these large pits.   The pits are all very much alike in size, shape, and location within the site, and as the feature was quite unusual it was decided that one should be test-trenched for further information.   Members of the Dallas Archaeological Society assisted the writer in this trenching, and the pit at Hogge Bridge site (41-18C9-1) in Collin County, within the Lavon Reservoir, was selected as being most typical.

This site is located on the north side of the East Fork of the Trinity River and covers approximately 3 to 4 acres from the river north to the edge of the uplands (shown as fields in the sketch map), and from an overflow slough on the west a distance of roughly 400 feet to the east. It is entirely within the present floodplain of the East Fork and is subject to annual overflow from that stream.   The pit is located near the center of the site and is a very symmetrical circle in shape with a concave, excavated interior, the soil from which was used to build up the rim.   The entire area in which the pit is located, including the pit itself, has been cultivated, sporadically, for some 50 years and this cultivation, coupled with annual flooding, has removed a considerable quantity of the surface soil.

At present the pit is 90 feet in diameter, measured from the crests of the rim, and the surface of the center of the pit is now 1 foot below the general level of the surrounding ground.   The crest of the east rim is 4.5 feet above the interior surface and the north, west, and south rims have eroded gradually down to 2–3 feet above the interior surface. The impact of flood waters first hits the west rim of the pit causing more erosion here than on the east rim.   An east-west test trench was excavated through the center of the pit and showed that 26 inches of fill had been washed into the pit in the process of erosion of the rim.   Assuming an erosional loss of 2 feet of elevation at the crest of the east rim, a total depth of 8.5 feet can be postulated for the pit while it was in use (see profile).   The test trench further showed that the original interior surface was concave with gradually sloping sides, and on this surface were found numerous concentrations of mussel shells, broken bones, and flint and chert chips.   There were also three nondescript scrapers, a clay-tempered, brushed potsherd, and several small fragments of burned clay. Similar material plus shell-tempered potsherds and fragments of broken glass bottles were found scattered sporadically through the depositional fill, as well as on the surface of other sections of the site. No post holes, fire hearths, or other evidences of a superstructure were found.

The landowner stated that the pit was 10 or 12 feet deep when the land was first put into cultivation, and that no overflow water ever entered it at that time, the rim being of a uniform elevation. Nearly all of the interior fill, as well as the rim erosion, has occurred in the past 50 years. Landowners at other sites where these pits occur made similar statements regarding the size and descriptions of the pits in pre-cultivation times.

The purpose of these pits is still unknown.

. . . .

THE ALIBATES FLINT QUARRY, TEXAS
Shaeffer, James B.; *American Antiquity,* 24:189-191, 1958.

The quarries are located about 35 miles north of Amarillo on the Bivins Ranch in Potter County, Texas. The outcrop of horizontal flint beds which form the quarry source is about a mile south of the Canadian River in the "brakes" or canyon country parallel to Alibates Creek, a tributary of the South Canadian. This remarkable concentration of exposed flint, approximately 3/4 mile in length, was first discovered by Studer nearly 35 years ago while surveying for sites of the Panhandle Puebloid.

. . . .

The flint formation appears on the surface mainly along the back and eastern slopes of a spur or ridge which runs in a southerly direction between 2 canyons. Most of the exposure is along the eastern side of the ridge which slopes steeply but not vertically to a narrow alluvial valley some 100 feet below. The quarry averages 50 to 300 feet in width. Flint outcrops are especially prominent on the noses of the hills which jut into this narrow valley and which, allowing for irregular projections, form a slight arc. From the top of the ridge the South Canadian River is clearly visible. The exposure, while fairly extensive, is local in character. There is another outcrop to the north and east on Antelope Creek. There are, also according to Studer, flint outcrops which extend for 1 or 2 miles directly across the Canadian on the northern bank, but back in some instances as far as 3 miles. This material is inferior to that of the Alibates quarry and there is much less evidence of working. The only other known major prehistoric quarry source in the Texas Panhandle is at Quitique, some 70 miles southeast of Amarillo in Briscoe County. The flint is again of an inferior sort and the exposure is limited. Quarrying on a small scale is also reported from a number of other scattered sites in the Panhandle but they are of limited extent and of material which is inferior in quality to that of the Alibates quarry.

Quarry evidence at the Alibates site is of 2 kinds. First, there is an enormous concentration of flint chips, flakes, and cores mixed together with occasional large hammerstones, scrapers, knives, and points which litter the ground. In places this deposit is several feet thick. The debris is sporadic in distribution. It occurs mostly on the sides of some of the hills and in more favored locations although chips can be found almost anywhere. Second, the sides of many of the hills are pitted with depressions 5 to 20 feet across which are now almost filled with top soil. The depressions which are 1 to 2 feet deep represent the prehistoric quarry sites. In fact some of these hillsides look from a distance as if they had been peppered with artillery concentrations. Around the peripheries of these workings there is scattered flint debris which in some cases actually surrounds the depressions with low mounds. One of the larger workings which has possibly been enlarged through the curiosity of white prospectors is several feet deep and ringed by a mound 2 to 4 feet high. Altogether the amount of flint debris is considerable and together with the amount removed from the quarry must represent tons of material. The flint beds themselves appear to be almost horizontal but it is difficult to judge the exact thickness of the formation. Its greatest present exposure is about 4 or 5 feet. Some large boulders, which have been pried out or have weathered loose, are 3 to 4 feet in thickness.

. . . .

PREHISTORIC QUARTZITE QUARRIES IN CENTRAL EASTERN WYOMING
Knight, Wilbur C.; *Science,* 7:308–311, 1898.

In July, 1894, while our scientific expedition was passing through eastern central Wyoming, we came upon some prehistoric quarries, which, owing to their number and extent, are of more than usual scientific interest. They are located some forty or fifty miles north and east of Badger, a station on the Cheyenne and Northern Railroad, one hundred and twenty-five miles north of Cheyenne. There are no roads or trails leading to this discovery, but the old overland trail, following the north side of the North Platte River, passes some four or five miles west of the largest quarries. The drainage from the quarries is to the northward, into Muddy Creek, which flows westward to the Platte River. In the vicinity of the quarries the stream is dry, and water is found running only in the spring and during heavy rains. The country about is very arid, and there is but a scanty supply of both water and vegetation.

Passing through this region from the northeast to the southwest is a very prominent bluff, with precipitous slopes facing the north. The bluff is five or six miles in length, and scattered along nearly its entire distance are the quarries of various sizes and shapes. The bluff has been caused by a fault which brought the Dakota sandstone to the surface. This sandstone has been metamorphosed into a great variety of quartzites. In color they shade from white to nearly black, and from a light pink to a dark red. They are very fine grained and work so easily by chipping that a novice can make a very good-looking implement in a few minutes.

In the preliminary examination, which was necessarily very limited, nineteen openings were visited. The nature of the openings varied so much that it has been thought best to classify them as follows: 1. Superficial; work of great surface extent where exposed blocks of quartzite have been dug up. 2. Shallow quarries; which are quite extensive, but have not been worked to a depth of more than two or three feet. 3. Deep quarries; worked to a depth, varying from fifteen to twenty feet or more. 4. Tunnels; but one of this class was seen. 5. Shafts; resembling the modern mining shaft, but not appearing to be very deep. All of the work has been done in a very systematic manner, and does not resemble the ordinary quarries so common in Wyoming, and from which the Indians secured most of the material to manufacture implements. In place of delving here and there, these quarrymen opened a quarry along the outcropping quartzite and worked it into the bluff, or dug a hole deep enough to reach the valued stone. In all the openings they had evidently maintained a clean face to work on. The refuse rock was carried back as by modern quarrymen. In fact, one could easily imagine that these quarries were old modern ones.

The largest quarries are located near the center of the bluff and near a very small spring. A description of the largest of this group will give a general idea of the excavations. It covers several acres of ground which slopes gently to the north and east. The workmen had commenced the excavation on a point, but when operations were suspended the quarry face was several hundred feet wide. The ground that has been worked over is covered with irregular mounds of refuse, which in the majority of cases is grass grown. In exposed places, where the wind

Map of some Wyoming quartzite quarries

has had free access, the refuse heaps are as the quarrymen left them.
No fragments of rocks were seen that would make a heavy load for one
man to carry. Near the old quarry face, which in most places was
entirely obliterated, and where the fragments of rock have not been
covered with the drifting sand, there were numerous circular depressions. These had been made with rock fragments, and were from two
to three feet in diameter and from twelve to sixteen inches in depth.
Within these depressions were numerous roughly formed implements.
These pits were beyond question collecting places for the quarrymen,
and the pieces left behind were rejected on account of some defect.
Near the old quarry face some enthusiastic prospector has in recent
years sunk a shaft, probably in search of gold. This shaft, although
partly caved, was nearly twenty feet deep. On one side rock in place
could be seen, but the shaft had been sunk in the debris.

The implements found about the quarries were unusually large and
rudely made. No finely finished implements of any kind were found.
The hammers and mauls were all made from boulders of quartz and
granite that had been brought from the neighboring mountains, some
twenty miles away. With the exception of the mauls and hammers,
all of the implements found were made of quartzite. Spear points,
scrapers, axes and anvils were all of the implements found that have
been classified. The axes are exceptionally rude, and according to
Dr. Wilson, of the Smithsonian, are the first reported from the Rocky
Mountains. Some three hundred implements were collected. For some
distance about the quarries the ground was strewn with chips and fragments of quartzite, but in no instance were any heaps of chips and refuse,
as are usually seen where the implement maker has labored.

There were no signs of any habitation except the tepee rings, which
were scattered all around the quarries, in valley and on hill alike. No
burial places were found. On the northeast slope, leading from the
largest quarry, the workman left a very peculiar figure. It faces the
east, and has been made by arranging fragments of rock along the
ground. There were circular piles of stone at either end of the figure.

**Boulder mosaic near Wyoming
quartzite quarry. a = stone pile**

The most striking points associated with these quarries are as follows: The vast amount of work done, the absence of chip heaps, the rude nature of the implements and their great size. All estimation of the tonnage of rock moved must be left for some future investigation. Suffice it to say that it will be estimated by the hundreds of thousands, if not by millions, of tons. The absence of chip heaps leads one to suppose that the quarrymen carried the quartzite away to manufacture. Which, if true, would signify that these quarries were neutral ground where the aborigines from all quarters worked for the implement stone, and that they took it to their respective haunts to work up. The unusual positions of many of the tepee rings also strengthens this supposition. Quartzite implements made from quartzite resembling that quarried from this region are very common on the plains and in the mountains. The rudeness of the implements can not be explained satisfactorily at this time. It might have been due to the age in which they were made, or it may be possible that only rejected implements have been found. The size is, no doubt, due to the nature of the stone. It would make a large implement, but possibly not a small one.

The quarrymen must have been the aborigines, but unlike the Indians of modern times, they must have been laborers, and have worked for centuries to have accomplished so much, with the very crude tools that they used. Who they were will never be known. The trails over which they traveled are entirely obliterated, and most of the quarries are covered with drifting sand and overgrown with the scanty vegetation of an arid region.

Central eastern Wyoming is a very noted place for prehistoric quarries, but as a rule they are small and very shallow and are in no way comparable to the recent discovery. Usually the Indians have worked for jasper and agate and have dug irregular openings that do not represent systematic development. Quartzite quarries are extremely rare and these are by far the largest that have been reported from Wyoming.

STUDY OF THE SPANISH DIGGINGS, ABORIGINAL FLINT QUARRIES OF SOUTHEASTERN WYOMING

Saul, John M.; *National Geographic Society Research Reports, 1964 Projects,* Washington, 1969, pp. 183-189.

Conclusions and Inferences.

(1) Spanish Diggings materials have been used by peoples of the Clovis culture onward.

(2) The Spanish Diggings were almost certainly quarried from the time of the McKean Complex, about 2000 B.C., and may have been quarried much earlier. (This date may be compared with the carbon-14 date of 1025 B.C. for a bone-quarry tool.)

(3) A marked change in the size of projectile points manufactured took place in the area during the Woodland Period or shortly before. Perhaps this change resulted from the introduction of the bow and arrow.

(4) All peoples of the region used Spanish Diggings chert in preference to Spanish Diggings quartzite for projectile point manufacture, but because the quartzite quarries are large and the workshops associated with them are also large it is probable that Spanish Diggings quartzite was a favored material for the manufacture of some non-projectile point artifacts.

(5) The "Morrison Agate" was a material imported into the area with regularity and in quantity since earliest times. It was imported in the form of finished products, projectile points and other artifacts. Of the materials grouped under "other," virtually all are from known or readily known sources. (1)

Aerial view of the "Spanish Diggings," a Wyoming flint quarry (John M. Saul)

ABORIGINAL TURQUOISE MINING IN ARIZONA AND NEW MEXICO

Blake, William P.; *American Antiquarian,* 21:279–284, 1899.

Recent explorations for turquoise at Turquoise Mountain in Mohave County, Arizona, twenty miles from Kingman, show that mining operations were carried on there during the Stone Age. It is evident that the object of this mining was to secure a supply of chalchihuitl, or chalchuite, more generally known as turquoise. The outcropping rocks at this locality are seamed and veined with this gem so highly prized and generally used by the Aztecs and aboriginal tribes of this region and Mexico.

The ancient mining is made evident not alone by the ancient excavations in the form of trenches, cuts, and pits, now filled in with rubbish and overgrown with mezquite trees but by an abundance of stone implements.

There are benches or terraces cut in the side of the mountain, where, apparently, the ancient miners lived, or camped, and probably sorted out the best pieces of chalchuite. In making an excavation upon one of these terraces, a pit or shaft was found by Mr. A. B. Frenzel, of New York, who has recently published a notice of the discovery in the columns of the Engineering and Mining Journal of New York, to which I am indebted for the accompanying illustrations from photographs taken by Mr. Frenzel. These pictures show the mouth of the chief pit, or shaft, and a number of the stone hammers, or mauls, picked up nearby. The shaft was filled up with earth without stones, and apparently with the object of concealing it. It is well cut into the hard rock, and appears to have been made not only by pounding away the rock but, also, by the use of fire. There is also a cut, some twenty-five feet in length, extending into the side of the hill.

In cleaning out the openings a variety of implements were found, but mostly mauls, or stone hammers, of various sizes, from four or five inches to nine or ten inches in length, and weighing from four pounds to over fifteen pounds each. The great size and weight of some of these implements indicate great strength of the men who used the hammers. The photograph shows the general form of the hammers. In some of them the groove around the boulder (for boulders they probably originally were), made to receive the raw-hide band, or with handle, is about half the distance from end to end, or midway of the stone, but in others, it is cut nearer to one end than to the other, conforming in this respect to the general form of the stone axes of the Salt River Valley.

All the implements bear evidences of hard usage. But few of them are in a perfect state. Great flakes of the stone have been split off the sides, from the points or ends backwards toward the groove, and some are broken across. These implements closely resemble those found in the prehistoric pits and cuts upon the croppings of some of the copper bearing veins on the borders of Lake Superior.

Another locality of chalchuite in Arizona, which shows aboriginal workings, is in Cochise County, twenty miles east of Tombstone, on the eastern slope of the Dragoon Mountains, in the district known as Turquoise. Here there are large excavations and dumps giving conclusive evidence of extensive working.

Chalchuite was also obtained across the Arizona line in New Mexico, not far from Silver City, in the Burro Mountains; but none of these localities compare, for extent, with the great excavations at Las Cerrillos, not far from Santa Fe, in New Mexico, which appears to have been one of the chief sources of the gem in Aztec times. Its extent and the over growth of trees indicate great antiquity for the chief excavations. There is, however, a tradition that in the year 1680, a large part of the mountain, which had been honey-combed by the long continued excavations of the aboriginal miners, caved in, burying many of the miners, and precipitating the uprising of the Indians and the explorations of the Spaniards. Modern explorations of this locality, by shafts and tunnels, have revealed caves, or subterranean chambers, made by the ancients. (pp. 279-280)

ANCIENT SALT MINES OF THE INDIANS

Harrington, M. R.; *Scientific American,* 135:116-117, 1926.

That mines were operating in Nevada many centuries before the days of Aurora and Pioche---of Virginia City, Tonopah and Goldfield, is one of the interesting discoveries made by archeologists now delving in the ruins of Pueblo Grande de Nevada, popularly known as the "Lost City," in the southern part of that state. "Many centuries" is putting it mildly, for the finds show that mining was in progress about the beginning of the Christian Era, some twenty centuries ago, and there are indications which point to work at an even earlier period.

A Mystery to be Solved. It was a salt mine, or rather, a series of salt mines, that has just been explored by the expedition sent out by the Museum of the American Indian, Heye Foundation, of New York City, working in cooperation with the State of Nevada. The principal mine is situated in a peak of solid rock-salt owned by the Virgin River Salt Company, about four miles south of St. Thomas, Clark County, Nevada, and some six miles from the expedition headquarters at the Lost City.

The entrance to the principal cavern proved to be through a low, tortuous underground passage, a natural drainage channel which may be followed completely through the mountain. But we left it about a hundred yards from daylight, clambering up out of it into a series of valuted chambers, hot, dark and silent, and smelling strongly of bats.

Turning our lights upon the walls, we were astonished to find them covered with markings, apparently made by the hand of man---curious circles and ovals, a foot or so across, outlined by grooves cut into the salt. Some were separate, some overlapping, and some strung together like links in a chain, and all were especially numerous wherever the salt outcrops seemed purest. What could they be? Were they ceremonial symbols of some sort? Certainly they were utterly unlike any of the several types of ancient rock-writings or petroglyphs we knew to be characteristic of the district.

We looked about us for evidence bearing on the problem and observed that the floor of the chamber where we stood was covered with a dry, dusty deposit. Surely, if human hands had carved the circles, a great many hours must have been spent in the work, and the carvers must have left some traces of their visit in the loose deposit underfoot--- traces that an archeologist might interpret, and from which he might hope to learn the identity of the carvers, even, perhaps, the purpose of the carvings. So we applied for, and obtained, permission to investigate the caverns.

The Mystery is Solved. The systematic digging had not proceeded far, when it dawned upon us that the place was nothing more nor less than an ancient salt mine, and that the deposit was merely a mass of salt mine refuse, consisting mainly of discarded salt, ranging from large chunks down to dust, and profusely perfumed with bat droppings and somewhat mixed with other things.

We were led to this conclusion first of all by the finding of hundreds of stone picks and hammers scattered throughout the mass which surely were not there by accident. The picks were waterworn boulders six or eight inches long, with one end chipped to a point. They had evidently been held in the hand. Some of the hammers had been held in the hand also, but most of them were provided with notches or with rude grooves for the attachment of wooden handles; while a few, to our astonishment and delight, still retained their wooden handles in perfect condition, due to the dryness of the cave plus the preservative action of the salt.

We finally learned the significance of the mysterious circles which had puzzled us at first, when we reached the original bottom of the cavern, a ledge of solid rock-salt, and carefully laid it bare. It was covered with just such circles and ovals as those we had seen on the walls, but with every little mark and detail beautifully preserved by the dust and refuse that had covered them.

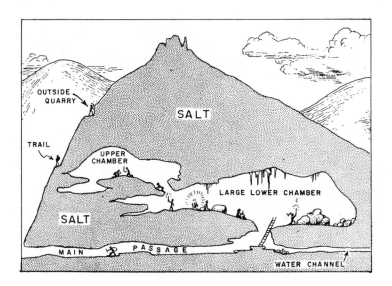

Ancient salt mine south of St. Thomas, Nevada

When we examined these carefully, we found that the circles had been carved into the salt with the stone picks, grooved around and around, deeper and deeper, until a raised circular block of salt was left in the center. Then this block had been broken out with the stone hammer to be taken home by the miner. We were able to prove this by fragments of just such salt blocks, found in the mine refuse, which showed parts of the encircling groove with the marks of the stone pick still plainly visible.

After the excavation was finished, and we had laid out and classified all the specimens we had found in the cave, we discovered that nearly everything we had found had to do with salt mining, directly or indirectly.

. . . .

• Mesoamerica

PUZZLE OF MINES
Anonymous; *Rocks and Minerals,* 892, December 1968.

Puzzle of Mines. Then there's the puzzle of the mines, a series
of large excavations in western Zacatecas. They had first been studied
in 1910 by a passing archeologist who interpreted them as caverns,
used by the Indians as hiding places when they were under attack.

Kelley and other field workers combed the region from 1961 thru
1963, discovered more mines and correctly identified their function.

"The whole area is as large as the S. I. U. compus. It's as if someone were to discover Southern Illinois.

Stripmines had been in existence before metal tools were used.
What were they for? What were they getting out of the mines?" Kelley
asks.

Possible Gem Hunt. Speculation is that some empire in southern
Mexico sent technicians and soldiers into Zacatecas and put the local
Indians to work, perhaps to excavate low grade gem stones. Or maybe
they were looking for emeralds.

The strange mines were worked between 300 and 900 A.D., it is
suspected. An S. I. U. graduate anthropology student, Phil Weigand,
now curator of North American archeology at the museum, explored
some of the dangerous, unbraced tunnelings. He found axe handles,
sorting piles, and burned torch splints. Radiocarbon tests dated the
torches at 390 and 600 A.D.

While most of the S. I. U. work in Mexico was marked by arduous,
routine digs, some of the discoveries, according to Kelley were dramatic moments. One of them was the unearthing of a 20-inch-high stone
statue of a god in an intact altar at Motehuma. It was a big find because
the Indians usually destroyed their religious centers when leaving a
community.

· · · · ·

RECENT DISCOVERIES IN MEXICO AND GUATEMALA
Anonymous; *Nature,* 131:101, 1933.

Excavations on Monte Alban in the State of Oaxaca, Mexico, the
site on which the rich grave treasure of gold and other ornaments was
found in January of last year, were resumed at the end of October by
Senor Alfonso Caso on an extended scale immediately the decision of
the Supreme Court on the question of State jurisdiction over antiquities

had been made known.   . . . .

It remains only to describe what is up to the present the most remarkable feature of the site, of which the purpose is at present obscure.
This is a series of stone-lined tunnels too small to serve as emergency
passages, as was at first suggested, and not apparently intended for
drainage. The first was discovered at the close of last season's work,
but its exploration left until this year. When it was entered on the re-
sumption of work, it was found to be so small---20 in. high by 25 in.
wide----that the explorers had to proceed stretched at full length on
their backs and work their way along by elbows and toes. At a distance
of 195 ft. in the tunnel a skeleton was found, accompanied by an incense
burner, funerary urns and ornaments of jade, stone and turquoise as
well as a few pearls. Some yards further the tunnel was found to be
blocked and had to be entered again by a shaft sunk from the surface
25 ft. above for the purpose. A second skeleton was found 320 ft.
from the entrance, just before the tunnel terminated at the side of
the north terrace. It was found that a number of even smaller tunnels,
not more than a foot high, led into the larger tunnel. Of these one had
tiny steps leading down to it.

Two further tunnels of similar character to the first were found,
but packed with earth or clay. Finally, a complex of miniature tunnels
was found to the east of the famous treasure tomb. All are stone-
lined and some are less than a foot high. Some, but not all, have the
inverted V roof. The application of a smoke test revealed a number of
unexpected exits.

• Africa

AMAZING ANTIQUITY OF MINING IN SOUTHERN AFRICA
Dart, R. A., and Beaumont, P.; *Nature,* 216:407–408, 1967.

The only ancient manganese mine yet recorded is in southern Africa,
at Chowa near Broken Hill, Zambia. Its rubble infilling contained crudely flaked mining tools chiefly of manganese, used as choppers, wedges
and chisels, together with hammerstones, perforated stones, upper
and lower grindstones and a single polished stone axe, but no metal objects or potsherds. The Kafulamadzi Hills 3 miles away revealed Later
Stone Age assemblages in quartz, together with manganese tools identical to those found in the working. On this basis, Dart postulated in
1934 the existence of stone age mining in southern Africa.

In 1964 Boshier conducted trial trenching in workings at the Ngwenya
Iron Mine in western Swaziland. Sites there yielded flaked stone mining
tools similar to those from Chowa found in 1934.

So far forty excavations have been completed, seventy collections made and 300,000 artefacts recovered. It has unexpectedly emerged at Ngwenya, particularly from the site called Lion Cavern, that the mining is of great antiquity.

Lion Cavern is at the southern end of a steep scarp face of the haematite hill, Lion Peak, where ancient miners cut into the face of a cliff, more than 500 ft. high, a shelter-shaped working about 25 ft. wide, 30 ft. deep and 20 ft. high. The floor of the shelter was covered by haematite soil and rubble. The first excavation, just inside the cavern's drip-line, bordered on the inner aspect of a large 5 ton haematite boulder fallen from above and almost blocking the entrance to the cavern.

The deposit, 9 ft. deep in this area, had the following characteristics: (a) 0-7 ft. contained stone-mining tools with a few sherds, which were restricted to the upper 4 ft.; (b) 7 ft. of worked bedrock 9 ft. down contained an atypical assemblage of stone artefacts chiefly quartzite and quartz. Irregular flakes predominated, and there were a few chisels. The industry was ascribed provisionally to the Later Stone Age.

Dr. Minze Stuiver gave as the date for the basal level Y-1713, 9640 ± 80 B.P./7690 ± 80 B.C. We therefore decided to remove the obstructing haematite boulder by undercutting it on its talus-slope side and excavated the underlying deposit. Here the deposit had a maximum depth of more than 11 ft., with details as follows: (a) 0-6 ft. contained a few mining tools; (b) 6-8 ft. contained undoubted Middle Stone Age artefacts and possible Later Stone Age tools; (c) 8 ft. of worked bedrock deeper than 11 ft. yielded 23,000 artefacts belonging unquestionably to a middle stage of the Middle Stone Age. Occasional stone mining tools were also found. Well defined ash levels showed that the assemblage was in situ.

Quartz, white quartzites, grey and white dappled quartzite, black indurated shales and greenish cherts were the principal materials used by the miners. These rock types occur mostly on a ridge overlooked by, and about 0.25 miles from, the cavern. The exposures there are patently flaked. Dappled grey and white quartzite exposures occur about a mile and more northwest of the site.

Samples of charcoal nodules from the middle to lower levels of the Middle Stone Age level were sent to the Yale and Groningen Laboratories, and the following dates were given:

Y - 1827,   22,280 ± 400 B.P./20,330 ± 400 B.C.
GRN - 5020, 28,130 ± 260 B.P./26,180 ± 260 B.C.

The dates harmonize with the archaeological evidence and suggest that there was mining here for a very long time, terminated perhaps by the fall of the haematite block.

....

These datings demonstrate that haematite has been mined at Ngwenya, on and off, for at least 28,000 yr. They afford the first dated presumptive evidence that all foreign ores and pigments found in prehistoric deposits all over the world were the result of deliberate mining. Dates of cavern strata containing haematite in Rhodesia and South Africa have ages ranging from 37,000 to 42,000 B.P. Incidentally, the claim made almost 35 yr. ago, that "manganese was being deliberately mined in Zambia by a foreign people familiar with its potentialities in Late Stone Age times", and Boshier's expectation that "In this field (of ancient mining) Bomvu Ridge (Ngwenya) is of supreme significance; its thorough investigation might well furnish us with knowledge of the genesis of South African mining", have been fully justified.

. . . .

STONE FORT AND PITS ON THE INYANGA ESTATE, RHODESIA

Hall, R. N.; *Anthropological Institute, Journal,* 35:92-102, 1905.

The Inyanga Range lies in south-eastern Zambesia, and is a wild mountainous country rising to 10,000 feet above sea-level. The district is 250 miles north of Great Zimbabwe, and 300 north-east of the Matoppo Hills. The Inyanga Mountains cover an area extending about 100 miles from north to south and 60 miles from east to west, and lie inland 200 miles west of the shore of the Indian Ocean. An area of this range, some 60 miles by 40 miles, is covered with the traces of some long-forgotten people.

The hills are of both granite and blue slate. Their form is that of long lines of very high perpendicular cliffs, each line of cliffs extending for miles. The hills on the granite formation are rugged and most fantastic in shape. Those on the slate formation have graceful curves and are gently rounded. Between the lines of cliffs are rolling downs of great extent. On the summits of the hills are stone forts, possibly a hundred of these structures, while up the sides of the hills, from base to summit, are stone terraces. Round their lower flanks run old aqueducts, each one two or three miles in length. On the downs in the valleys and on the lower flanks of hills are very many hundreds of stone-lined pits, and, also in the valleys, at every 50 yards, are the most obvious evidences of old occupations, while almost every stone appears to have passed through human hands.

The great extent of country covered with these remains is simply marvellous. They have no similitude whatever to the remains of ancient buildings found in any other part of Rhodesia. In every feature they are altogether dissimilar.

. . . .

Stone-Lined Pits on the Inyanga Estate, Mashonaland. These structures, which are so numerous throughout the whole of the Inyanga Range, are proportionately numerous on Mr. Rhodes' estate. For instance, within the small radius of two miles only from the farmstead, there can be no less than one hundred of these pits and passages, if not very considerably more. This is thought to be a modest estimate, yet it serves to demonstrate the vast number of such pits which are to be found distributed, in similar, if not in greater, proportion, throughout an area of hill country some 60 miles in length by 40 miles in width.

Generally the pits are found in clusters of twos and threes, or singly at 100 yards distance, but sometimes at a distance of 50 yards apart. Their position can be ascertained from a distance, for wherever a clump of large trees is to be seen breaking the view on the downs and lower hillsides, there is almost certain to be found one of these pits, and the trees on being approached will invariably prove to be figs of great girth growing on the floors or from the wall-masonry of the pit. The wood of this kind of fig is soft, the trees though tall and gnarled are not of very great age, and are probably the descendants of similar trees which once grew even more plentifully over this district than they do to-day. The presence of these trees in and near the pits is most striking.

The majority of the pits are either dilapidated or almost completely filled with silted soil from higher ground, and only one in twenty is in such a state of preservation as to admit of even partial examination. A pit in an almost perfect condition, undamaged and unfilled, is only met with in this district at rare intervals.

The pits are mostly found on the gentle slopes of low hills, also along the upper ridges of rolling downs where the soil is of a bright red gravelly nature. This is shown in the numerous narrow and deep gorges which run from kloof-like positions on the sides of the hills to the streams at the base. These deep cuttings appear to have been scoured out in some past age by waterspouts, for the great majority start from the top at spots which are waterless. The precipitous sides of these gorges bear rich red soil at least 20 feet deep, with thin horizontal strata of clay stone, very much resembling soapstone, which the natives use as material for carving, while at the bottom of these gorges water has exposed large rounded boulders of blue slate.

The original builders have sunk their pits some 9 feet to 12 feet in depth, with diameters varying from 16 feet to 30 feet. The soil from each pit has been thrown up on the hillside, making a semicircular rampart of some 20 feet to 30 feet in width, which increased the depth of the pit on the outer side, making the height of that side of the pit correspond with that of the higher ground on the hillside of the excavation. Where pits have been sunk on practically level ground the excavated soil has been piled all round, forming a rampart of equal width, thus bringing the top edge of the coping stones of the pit to a level slightly above that of the surrounding veldt.

Inside the pit, and forming a lining, a circular wall was built up to the height of the earth rampart, where a coping of much larger stones, well fitted together, was made. This firmly binds the summit of the wall all round the pit. The wall is a facing of single stones only, and some of the long stones, which are built in lengthways from front to back, run from the face of the wall right into the soil behind. The appearance of these walls, which in many instances and for several reasons have partially collapsed into the pit, shows that, at several stages in the building of the wall, soil was dragged down and rammed into the space behind the wall, for unless this had been done these long and heavy stones, without some support, would have levered out the face of the wall. The effect of this occasional arrangement of larger stones would naturally be to bind the wall and render the perpendicular lining and single blocks of irregular size and shape less liable to collapse inwards. The builders of these walls made no attempt to build in courses, as stones of all sizes and shapes were employed, causing large gaps and chinks which were filled in with smaller fragments. In no single instance has there been found the slightest evidence of any building stone having been worked.

When the pit was excavated a cutting was made in the soil some 30 feet long, usually on the higher side of the pit, from its interior at the base to within 4 feet of the ground at its outer and upper extremity. The length of the passage from end to end in a direct line is usually about 26 feet, the length of 30 feet being reduced by a curve invariably present in these passages. Standing in the pit and looking along the passage the curve is found to correspond, in most instances, to the left hand upper quarter section of a circle. The close similarity between the length of the curve and its direction, and the relative position of the passage to the pit, are most remarkable. Possibly this was intentional, in order to place the outer entrance to the passage to the lee-side, where it was protected from the prevailing cold winds and rains, in the same way that to-day the position of hut doors is fixed with the purpose of avoiding exposure to the prevailing winds and rains.

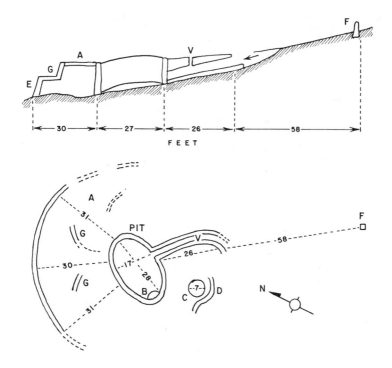

Representative plan and section of rock-lined pit, Rhodesia

After the construction of this passage it was paved throughout with slabs of stones, on which and on either side parallel walls of single stones were built to an average height of 3 feet above the paving, with a space of 2 feet 2 inches to 2 feet 8 inches between them. The passage was then covered over with large stone beams placed close together throughout its whole length, except at a point about 10 feet from the pit, where, in almost every instance of such pits in this locality, there is an aperture or ventilating shaft some 14 inches wide in the roof of the gallery or passage.

The similarly relative position of these apertures in the passage roofs in so very many pits is also extremely striking. The floor of the passage where it enters the pit is from 6 inches to 12 inches above the stone pavement of the pit. The fall in the passage floor averages 8 inches to 12 inches in 10 feet.

No steps have so far been found inside these passages, but in the circular space enclosing the upper entrance, which is very frequently formed by the continuation of the outer wall, there are often two or three shallow steps leading down from the floor of the circular space to the floor of the passage. The object of this circular space appears to have been to prevent rain water from the higher ground running in to the passage, and thence into the pit. This circular chamber is deeper by 2 feet or 3 feet than any other of the circular enclosures of stone built on the upper edges of the pit, which evidently form part of the original structure, and it seems to have served as a vestibule to the passage and pit.

After the completion of the passage roof, one or two layers of large stones were piled so as to cover the cross beams, and these extended for some distance on either side, thus completely burying the passage. On this paved floor was another circular enclosure of stone, some 20 feet in diameter (external measurements), and in the floor of this enclosure is almost sure to be found the ventilating hole into the passage below. This enclosure, containing the ventilating shaft, occupied the space between the vestibule and the pit, reaching to within 3 or 4 feet of the edge of the latter.

The rampart of soil from the pit was supported on the outer and down side by a semicircular retaining wall, providing a flat surface round the pit. The retaining walls vary from 3 feet to 6 feet in height, according to the slope of the side of the hill. Frequently there are two retaining walls, one above and at the back of the other. The surface of the rampart was in almost every instance paved, and on it one of two different classes of structures was raised: (1) Ordinary stone huts, as made by natives in Mashonaland, with diameters varying from 10 to 18 feet, and walls still standing 2 feet high. One half of each floor is paved, the other half is a raised floor of daga (clay) with a raised rim of daga. The huts are thus divided into two parts, one for the family and the other for the goats. Only very common native articles, of to-day's make and use, have so far been found in those huts. (2) Stone foundations of granaries similar to those made by natives of to-day. These are formed by erecting stones in a vertical position to carry a floor of other flat-stones, which are placed from point to point of the vertical stones, thus making a raised floor with an open space underneath. On this floor was laid a daga floor of about 6 feet in diameter (exterior measurement), and a daga and thick granary was built up, exactly similar to those seen in many hundreds of villages to-day, with the sticks in some instances still standing upright in the daga.

The number of circular enclosures built on the ramparts of these pits varies considerably. At some pits only two are found, and these are the enclosures containing the ventilator and the upper entrance to the passage. At other pits as many as six or eight circular enclosures are definitely traceable, but in the majority of instances four or five enclosures only have existed.

With regard to the age of these circular enclosures (excepting the enclosures with the ventilator and passage entrance respectively, which appear to form part of the original structure), some are most obviously of later construction than the pit; others bear a striking similarity in workmanship to that displayed in the construction of both pit and passage, while it must not be forgotten that it is a common practice among the natives on moving the site of their kraals to build their huts round such pits as may be still in a fair state of preservation, and use the pit for their goat and sheep kraal. Instances of this practice can be seen in this locality.

In several pits a drain will be found running through the rampart out on to the veld below. This drain faces the entrance to the pit, and is at the lowest point of its paved floor. On the outside of the rampart, where the drain emerges, a deep depression in the earth some yards long runs outward to the lower ground. It is believed that such a drain will be found in every pit.

The floors of the pits are paved with close fitting stones sloping from the entrance of the passage towards the drain on the opposite side, the fall averaging 6 inches in 10 feet. The paving stones are laid on the surface left by the excavators of the pit, and experience has shown that there is nothing to be found on removing any of the paving stones and digging beneath them.

A curious feature connected with these pits is the erection near some of them of a plain stone beam or monolith, which averages 2 feet 6 inches to 3 feet 6 inches above the ground, into which it is fixed with stones. On higher ground, at a few yards distance, there is generally a retaining wall, sometimes 50 yards in length. These upright stones which occupy isolated positions stand at 50 feet to 60 feet distance on the higher side of the pit. In two instances the distances from the pit and positions of these monoliths are respectively as follows: 51 feet 8 inches south south-east of pit, and 58 feet south south-east of the pit.

In these structures the walls of both pits and passages are perpendicular, and portcullis grooves in the entrances are altogether absent.

. . . .

Old Aqueducts. One of the most extraordinary features of the Inyanga Range is the vast number of old aqueducts, some two miles or more in length, running from artificial dams on the mountain streams, and crossing from hill to hill in a most remarkable manner.

Whoever constructed these aqueducts must have been a people thoroughly conversant with engineering, for their levels are beautifully and exactly carried out in spite of all natural obstacles, and not an inch of fall is wasted throughout the length of their courses. These are a marvel to all modern engineers who inspect them. Evidently they were used for purposes of irrigation. The hardest material pierced in their construction appears to have been shale or clay stone.

They are all about 16 to 24 inches wide, and are about 2 feet in depth. They have no paving or built sides.

Hill Terraces. Perhaps the feature which most strikes the visitor to this district is the hill terraces. These are found in hundreds throughout Inyanga.

These terraces cover the hills from base to summit, but mainly on their northern side. As many as forty terraces, one above and behind the other, are to be found on any one hill. Most of these have earth behind them, but from the inner sides of some the soil has in the course of time been washed away. They have retaining walls, and most probably were used for horticultural purposes. Hill terraces also occupy a small area as far south as Swaziland, while similar hill terraces are found in South Arabia.

Many of the trees found in this area, wild vines, figs and lemons, are not indigenous to South-East Africa.

• Europe

PREHISTORIC FLINT MINING
W., A. S.; *Nature,* 96:316–317, 1915.

The numerous pits in the chalk at Weeting, Norfolk, commonly known as Grime's Graves, have long attracted attention, but the only exhaustive study of them made until last year was that of Canon William Greenwell, who proved in 1870 that they represent prehistoric flint mines. In the account of his results Canon Greenwell remarks that there "can be no doubt that the whole space occupied by the pits is a complete network of galleries," and he shows that the flint obtained from the mines was worked into implements on the spot. How extensive was this industry may be realised from the fact that the pits are from three to four hundred in number, and occupy an area of not less than twenty acres. They vary from about nineteen to more than eighty feet in diameter, and all are filled to within a few feet of the surface with material which seems for the most part to have been thrown in by the miners themselves.

From the whole of the evidence Canon Greenwell concluded that the flint-working was of Neolithic date, and subsequent researches at Cissbury and other localities where flint was mined seemed to confirm this conclusion. When, however, discoveries in the French and Spanish caverns revealed a regular succession of fashions in the making of stone implements, a study of the worked flints from Grime's Graves and Cissbury suggested that many of these were of the late Palaeolithic Society of East Anglia, therefore, with characteristic energy, decided to examine the question further, and in the spring of 1914 it undertook a most painstaking excavation and examination of two typical pits in the group of Grime's Graves. The work was done under the immediate direction of Mr. A. E. Peake, whose exhaustive report, accompanied by the valuable notes of several specialists, has now been published by the Society.

The mining seems to have been done chiefly with picks made of red deer antlers, of which no fewer than 244 were discovered in the two

shafts and the galleries connected with them. Three of these picks, as
they were left by the miners, are shown in the accompanying photograph (Fig. 1). Some were found to be so well preserved that even
finger-prints could be distinctly observed on the adherent mud. The
blocks of flint were brought to the surface and chipped into implements
on the spot, as indicated by the numerous spoil heaps or "floors," of
which fourteen were examined. (Figures omitted.)

Both in the spoil heaps and in the earth filling the shafts numerous
flint implements were collected, and the chief forms are described,
with fine illustrations, by Mr. Reginald A. Smith. None are polished,
but some of them (Fig. 2) are of the typically Neolithic pattern, while
others (Fig. 3) are more suggestive of the Palaeolithic period. One is
noted as being "a not uncommon type in the period of La Madeleine";
one resembles "the tapering portion of a Chelles ficron"; another has
a "facetted butt in the Northfleet style"; others "cannot be matched anywhere but in Le Moustier deposits"; while at least two can only be compared with implements from St. Acheul. A typical Celt-like Neolithic
implement "might well be regarded as an intruder" if the position of
its discovery had not been known, and if a second exactly similar specimen had not been met with.
        . . . .

THE ESSEX DENEHOLES
Anonymous; *Science,* 5:113–114, 1885.

The word 'denehole' means 'denhole,' and is pronounced 'danehole.'
Those of Kent and South Essex may be described as consisting of narrow
vertical shafts leading to artificial chambers excavated in the chalk,
their depth varying with the distance of the chalk beneath the surface.
They are found singly, in groups of twos and threes, or in larger collections of perhaps fifty or sixty pits.

Our illustrations show two types of the varieties of form exhibited
by deneholes. The beehive shape is especially common in the shallower
pits, which are wholly, or almost wholly, in chalk. A drawing of a pair
of such pits discovered in a chalk cliff at Crayford brickfields is given.
Their depth was thirty-seven feet, and the greatest width eighteen feet.
The walls showed no signs of metal picks, and the chalk blocks must
have been prized out, but they were well and symmetrically worked.
In one was a layer of very hard clay, washed into a cone at the bottom,
and containing flint flakes, scrapers, and a 'core:' above that a layer
of Roman pots and pans (a Samian dish, etc.) rested, followed by
some very fragmentary and coarse potsherds and confused rubbish,
apparently intended to fill the hole up to the surface of the ground. The
sister-cave did not show an equal stratification of debris, and appeared
to have fallen in at an early period.

Of the deeper deneholes existing in Hangman's Wood, one is eighty
feet deep. In three examples at Hangman's Wood (not figured) there
were six chambers, while in two at Bexley only three chambers radi-

ated from the shaft. A final stage in denehole evolution seems to have
been the removal of the greater portion of the partitions separating the
chambers, pillars of chalk only being left to support the roof. The
usual height of denehole chambers may be said to be from ten to twenty
feet. A leading characteristic of deneholes is the separation of each
pit from its neighbor, though they are often so close together that much
care must have been exercised to prevent intercommunication. Another
is the fact, that, while they are here and there abundant in bare chalk,
they are often especially numerous where the top of the chalk is fifty
to sixty feet below. Thus at Hangman's Wood, for example, the top of
the chalk is fifty-six or fifty-seven feet below the surface, while there
is plenty of bare chalk within a mile.

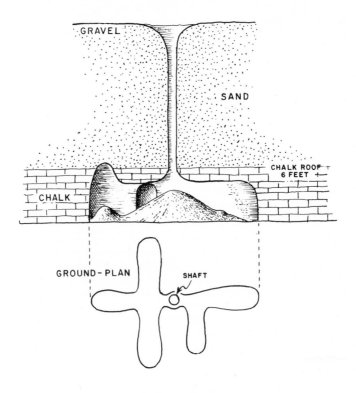

An English dene hole

Though there are more than fifty separate deneholes in Hangman's
Wood, each shaft being at an average distance of about twenty-five yards
from its nearest neighbor, only five shafts are now open, the rest having fallen in at various times. In most instances, however, there is
nothing to suggest that the chambers below have been materially, if at
all, injured, the funnel-shaped hollow at the surface being but little
greater than those around the mouths of shafts still open. This closing

of the great majority of the shafts is not by any means simply disadvantageous to denehole explorers, though it certainly increases the cost of exploration; for it is obvious that closed pits necessarily afford more satisfactory evidence than such as have been visited from time to time, either from curiosity or to recover a lost sheep or hound.

Preliminary examinations of six of the deneholes in Hangman's Wood were made during the summers of 1882 and 1883. A more thorough investigation is now in progress.

THE WILSFORD SHAFT
Ashbee, Paul; *Antiquity,* 37:116-120, 1963.

Excavation of the pond barrow at Normanton Gorse, Wilsford, disclosed the weathered top of a circular and vertical shaft which proved to be nearly 100 ft. in depth. Its fill, the result of natural silting processes, contained pottery in the upper part and, at the waterlogged bottom, broken wooden vessels and other objects, besides a mass of rotted wood, seeds, leaves and other organic remains. The dished and funnelled top of the shaft as well as the uneven sides were, for more than a third of their depth, the product of natural weathering. Below here distinctive antler-pick marks and the clear traces of a broad-bladed metal axe showed that the shaft had been dug in short sections, checked by template and plumbline. No positive trace of how the prehistoric engineers moved up and down their sophisticated shaft remained.

. . . .

The shaft was just under 100 ft. in depth from the estimated ancient surface and was almost 6 ft. in diameter. Some 2826 cu. ft. of chalk had been hewn out by the prehistoric engineers, which means that when broken up some 4945 cu. ft. of chalk rubble had to be brought to the surface. This would presumably have formed the surrounding bank of the pond barrow. There were no traces at any point in the shaft of beams or foot-holds. Thus access and egress as well as spoil removal can only have been via some form of winching or hauling gear. All traces of posts or beams at surface level would have been removed by the weathering back of the shaft lip.

Once emptied of its silting, it could be seen that the shaft had been dug in short vertical lengths. The beginning and perhaps the limit of each must have been checked by plumbing and template to preserve the perpendicularity and circularity of the shaft as its diggers descended. Each stage strayed slightly from the perpendicular but deep vertical antler pick marks showed correction for a fresh stage. These deep marks and their progressive ridging suggest punch use as in the flint mines. The sides at each stage, where such a record survived, had been dressed with a broad-bladed axe or palstave. Seams of flint had been dug through and projecting nodules had been broken off neatly by percussion and even slightly dressed. In the lower part of the shaft the tool marks were clear and constant, in the upper part they were presum-

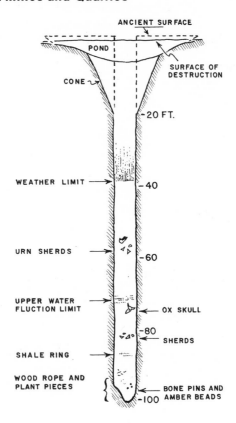

ANCIENT SURFACE

POND

CONE

SURFACE OF
DESTRUCTION

-20 FT.

WEATHER LIMIT ——→

-40

URN SHERDS ——→

-60

UPPER WATER
FLUCTION LIMIT ——→

——← OX SKULL

-80

——← SHERDS

SHALE RING ——→

WOOD ROPE AND
PLANT PIECES

——← BONE PINS AND
-100 AMBER BEADS

Section of the Wilsford Shaft, England

ably destroyed by weathering before they were covered by the progressive silting process.

The narrow bottom section, honeycombed and scored with pick marks,
pointed to unfinished work. Indeed, a roughly hewn pit later trimmed to
the requisite diameter would seem to be the digging procedure. A
reason for abandonment of the shaft was suggested by the fact that this
bottom section had impinged directly upon a water-bearing fault in the
chalk. A patina of iron oxide all over the bottom 25 ft. of the shaft
indicated seasonal fluctuation of the water level. This was also reflect-
ed by the character of the fill.

In the absence of a specific deposit such as a burial, one is posed
with the problem of the shaft's function. A deep circular shaft into the
chalk might seem to be a well. Indeed, Roman wells of modest diameter
dug into the chalk are well known and as far as can be seen the pattern
of north-western European well-sinking was brought about by Roman
innovation of influence. Mitigating against the shaft being a functional
well is scale and sophisticated finish as well as the not inconsiderable
effort needed for its execution. The use of a broad-bladed axe in the

shaft cannot but recall the circumstance of an alleged 'archaizing ritual axe' recorded in connexion with the later Bronze Age sanctuary at Bargeroosterfeld in Holland. Water might have been obtained much more readily in the region. In addition it seems that a deep shaft in the chalk can be no automatic guarantee of water as many unproductive wells show. The possibility that other pond barrows in the region, some of considerable relative size are the tops of silted-up shafts must be seriously considered. This would account well for the circular dish-like depression surrounded by a bank which is their form. Careful measurement of bank volumes and comparison with pond capacity would perhaps give some indication which geophysical methods might test. Barrows considered pond have been excavated during the past decade in Dorset and at Snail Down. In the circumstances they could be seen as monuments embodying different principles.

Deep graves have been met with under Bronze Age barrows while more modest pits recur regularly beneath barrows long and round as well as with henge monuments. Indeed, the only shafts directly comparable with the present example were within Maumbury Rings, at Dorchester. Excavations, never fully published, revealed that within the bank the 'ditch' had been a series of conical pits, recorded as up to 35 ft. in depth. Weathering could well have produced the conical form and the intersection of the pits had the monument, in its original form, been a series of cylindrical pits with a bank about them.

Pits loomed large in early European lore. Philostratus says how the cthonic gods welcomed ceremonies done in the hollow earth. Pausanias in his guide-book describes how at Titane, a town in Sicyonia, a priest performed secret rites in four pits to soothe the winds. It was the custom in Italian cities to dig a pit known as a mundus, which was closed with a stone and symbolized the abode of the rulers of the nether world. May not the Wilsford shaft-diggers have thought that they had breached the Styx when water made further descent impossible?

THE SALTING MOUNDS OF ESSEX
Stopes, H; *Anthropological Journal,* 36:369-372, 1879.

There has been, as yet, no scientific notice taken of the numerous ancient mounds of burnt earth in the marshes on the Essex and Suffolk coast. They just fringe the full-tide line of the rivers and estuaries, being only occasionally covered by exceptionally high tides. They consist of a reddish clay mixed freely with broken pottery of the rudest type, and wood ashes and charcoal. It is very strange that they should have for so long a time failed to excite the attention of antiquaries or archaeologists, for it is just possible they may be able to fit the key to some of the ciphers of our half-revealed past history.

These mounds exist only in this one peculiar position. I have examined many, and I never saw one more than five feet above high-water mark, and never reaching to low-tide mark. They seem all very uniform in character and composition. Those I have seen are from 2 feet to 4-1/2 feet deep, and have the same appearances at the surface as when worked down to the base. I have not yet examined them sufficiently to tell the full number and extent of them; but among those I have dug into, the largest was, as nearly as I could judge, about 30 acres. It consists almost entirely of this red burnt clay, and contains an enormous number of fragments of pottery, bricks and vessels, although not one of them seems to be entire. An old man in the neighbourhood has been for years in the habit of carting away the soil from this mound, or "Red Hill," as he called it. He told me he had moved away many hundreds of loads, but he had never found a single piece of whole pottery, nor a coin. I showed him the largest piece I had picked up, and he said it was much larger than most pieces, although he remembered having seen a few pieces nearly as large again. Mixed with the earth, though irregularly, are large quantities of charcoal and wood ashes, but I could find no trace of coal. Clinkers seemed common, and they showed that great heat must have been thrown out by the fires that have burnt them.

. . . .

Altogether, these mounds covered about thirty acres, and, with the others I visited, making upwards of forty acres, as nearly as I could judge; and this extent has been considerably reduced during the lifetime of the one old man I talked to, as the soil is valuable to apply to clay, and also to dress the land after an exceptionally high tide. I have no idea of the total number of these mounds, but their number may be imagined when, after the destruction of centuries, eighteen still remain between Strood and Virley, a distance of only six miles. I am told they exist on the Norfolk coast, along the wide rivers of Suffolk, and also in Kent. Still, I believe we have them in the greatest number and the largest size in Essex. They are quite peculiar to our own coasts, and are entirely distinct from the kitchen middens of Denmark and Scotland.

They present an interesting field of investigation, and I cannot pretend to account for them, but may give a few facts further, and possible suggestions therefrom.

These mounds invariably reach right down to the London clay, showing either that the clay, at the time they were deposited, was not covered by mud, or that the men who made them always first cleared down to the clay. When we remember the acreage they cover, this would be no small task.

I have tried for some years to collect the traditions and popular opinions about them, and they are various. Some say they were Roman brick-yards; others that they were Saxon potteries, under Alfred the Great. Some believe that they were the base of the camp-fires of Boadicca or of Alfred at the Danish invasion; while others fancy the Danes brought their dead to be buried there, and that the broken pottery was the shivered vessels of the dead. All these fancies are equally absurd; but what are they?

. . . .

Chapter 2
FLINTS, TOOLS, AND OTHER SMALL ARTIFACTS

INTRODUCTION

The marvelous buildings, canals, stone circles, walls, and other structures of Chapter 1 testify amply to the engineering capabilities of ancient man. But a pocket computer betrays a higher technology than a superhighway. Thus, we have the present chapter on "small artifacts." Entries have been selected in part because they seem to be out-of-time or out-of-place and consequently do not fit current archeological conceptions. Manufactured articles suggesting even an elementary knowledge of metallurgy, electricity, and other elements of sophisticated technology are particularly significant. Still another criterion emerges here: <u>mystery</u>. Some small artifacts are totally perplexing and without reasonable application. These seem to lead to artistic, mystical, and religious interpretations, indicating that we do not really understand how ancient man conceived the cosmos or viewed beauty or faced death. All we can do is keep collecting and organizing in hopes of seeing some overall pattern.

SMALL STONE ARTIFACTS

Raw stone was the primary working material of the ancient artisans. At least it seems that way because stone was the material that survived the elements down the long centuries. How can stone artifacts be sufficiently anomalous to be included here?

1. They can be located in geological deposits of such antiquity that they cast doubt upon prevailing timetables of human evolution and dispersal. This is particularly significant in North America where man is supposedly a very recent addition to the fauna.
2. They can be strictly nonutilitarian or of problematical use, as in the case of the so-called "eccentric flints."
3. They can be so small that they would seem to be of little practical use to men of normal stature; i.e., the "pigmy flints."

4. They can be found in immense quantities or arranged in
    patterns that apparently had mystical or ceremonial mean-
    ings.

Each class of anomaly focusses on some character of ancient man that
seems out of keeping with modern archeological and anthropological
theories. At the very least, these curious stone artifacts suggest extra
dimensions of prehistoric man that should be explored.

• Antiquity of American Man

ON THE OCCURRENCE OF STONE MORTARS IN THE AN—CIENT (PLIOCENE?) RIVER GRAVELS OF BUTTE COUNTY, CALIFORNIA

Skertchly, Sidney B. J.; *Anthropological Institute, Journal,* 17:332-
337, 1888.

During a visit to the Spring Valley Gold Mine at Cherokee, Butte Co.,
California, my friend Mr. Louis Glass, the Superintendent of the mines,
directed my attention to the discovery of stone mortars in the undisturbed gravel of the old river system of California. As this bears upon the
question of the antiquity of man in North America the following notes
may be interesting. I may add that being away from books references
are unobtainable, but I believe Mr. Bowman has examined some of the
finds and is satisfied that the mortars occur in situ. I am bringing one
home with me.
    1. Geological Position. The Spring Valley Mines are situated on
the Foot Hills of the Sierra Nevada, in one of the valleys of the Sacramento River system, which are here excavated to a depth of over 2,000
feet.
    The following is a section in the deepest part of the channel:

Spring Valley Gold Mine.

1.	Basalt cap	25 to 100 feet.
2.	White quartz sands with lenticular masses of pipe-clay	450 feet.
3.	Blue gravel, full of decomposed meta-morphic or eruptive rock boulders	2 to 15 feet.
4.	Blue gravel with large undecomposed boulders, much cemented	50 feet.
5.	Bed rock, metamorphosed cretaceous slates.	--

The mortars, of which about 300 have been found since the year 1849,
occur in the white sand or gravel No. 2, and one, examined by Mr. Bow-

man, is said to have occurred in No. 3.

The beds 2 to 4 constitute part of one of the old rivers which drained the country prior to the establishment of the present river system. This particular "Cherokee River" cuts across the valley of the Feather River, as shown in the section, and has been proved beneath the Sacramento River at the place marked "well."

The gravel is for the most part well water-worn, even the large boulders, some of which weigh eight tons, being rounded, with the exception of those in bed 4, which are only sub-angular.

I could detect no trace of ice action, and the whole deposit bears evidence of its fluviatile origin. The pebbles and boulders are "shingled," or lie pointing down stream.

At the top of bed No. 3 impressions of leaves are sometimes obtained in a sandy loam very full of black vegetable matter. These have been examined by Prof. L. F. Ward and very doubtfully referred to Cinnamomum or Paliurus, but he remarks, "The specimen may possibly represent a Populus unlike any modern form."

The blue (and more highly auriferous) gravels are sharply distinguished from the overlying white beds, there being often a "pan" of cemented gravel between the two, the cement being red iron oxide. The general opinion is that these blue gravels are of distinct age, and much older than the white. This seems borne out by the characters of the two deposits. The blue gravels contain many very large boulders of metamorphic and eruptive rocks with much black sand (ilmenite), while the white gravels are entirely free from boulders and contain but little black sand.

2. Age of the Gravels. Prof. Whitney considers the white gravels to be of Upper Pliocene age, and that with the blue gravels these auriferous deposits may represent the whole of the Tertiary. Dr. C. A. White, quoted by Mr. Diller, suspects the whole to be of Upper Pliocene age; and Mr. Diller remarks that "all that can be definitely stated at present concerning the strata containing the leaf impressions is that they are more recent than strata known to belong to the Chico group, and that their flora, as far as Prof. Ward can judge from the few imperfect specimens at hand, has a pre-Pliocene aspect."

These conclusions are based upon the determination of the age of the lava flow which overlies the gravels, and from the age of the faults in the neighbouring Sierras. The lava flows are derived from the vicinity of Lassen's Peak (60 miles north of Cherokee) and are certainly not older than the close of the Pliocene; and as these lavas are faulted the dislocations are probably post-Tertiary. Part of the upheaval of this portion of the Sierras is thus of very recent geological date, and it is quite possible that the ancient river beds may have partaken somewhat in these movements, for I find from observations on the transporting power of the sluices at Cherokee that the present grade of the old channel (about 6 per cent.) could be much reduced and still afford sufficient transporting power to move the larger boulders in the blue gravels.

Whatever be the absolute age of these gravels from a geological standpoint, their immense antiquity historically is beyond question. The present great river system of the Sacramento, Joaquin, and other rivers has been established; canons 2,000 feet deep have been carved through lava, gravels, and into the bed rock; and the gravels, once the bed of a large river, now cap hills 6,000 feet high. There is ample ground for the belief that these gravels are of Pliocene age, but the presence of objects of human fabrication invests the gravels with a higher interest to the anthropologist than even to the geologist, and may suggest new views.

3. Occurrence of the Mortars. The working face of the mine is an artificial cliff of from 400 to 600 feet in height, the whole of which is fetched down by the water jets of hydraulic giants. The material is washed into the sluices and the mortars are found with the rest of the mass. They are thus not quarried out by hand, but fairly washed out from the gravel. They cannot have come from the surface, for none are ever found there, and many of them have been seen by Mr. Glass with the original gravel adhering to them. They are readily noticeable as being the only large stones in the white gravel. I may add that the top soil overlying the lava cap is very thin and certainly does not contain these mortars.

Occasionally mortars are found on the surface in the neighbouring gulches, but only where the gulch has intersected the gravels, and these mortars are clearly derived from the old white gravels.

4. Description of the Mortar. The mortar I obtained is composed of some eruptive or metamorphic rock, which has become so decomposed as not to be easily determinable. Its outside measurements are 9-1/2 inches by 7-1/4 inches by 6-1/4 inches, but some specimens are rather larger, others somewhat smaller. The hollow measures 6 inches by 5 inches and is about 5 inches deep. It still retains traces of having been used for grinding. The external shape is irregularly oval and shows distinct traces of chipping. The rock has disintegrated to a light brown colour like many acid rocks, and this and the very rolled character of the utensil gives the appearance of great antiquity.

5. The Digger Indians. This country was inhabited by the Digger Indians until about the year 1865. My friend, Mr. Glass, was well acquainted with them, and assures me that they did not use such mortars: they hollowed out rocks in situ, and therein pounded the acorns on which they so largely subsisted. They were acquainted with these mortars, but knew nothing about the makers of them, and held them in such superstitious dread that on no account could they be induced to touch one. This dread of the relics of past ages seems to be everywhere common and is of itself proof of antiquity.

6. Age of the Gravels. If these mortars had not been found in the gravels American geologists would never have doubted their Tertiary age, but when relics of man are demonstrated to exist therein, even in the older blue gravels, one may well hesitate to ascribe to them so great an antiquity.

Even before visiting California I had suspected these old river gravels might be contemporaneous with the glacial epoch, and I still think this possible. This area was not glaciated and these old gravels, hundreds of feet in thickness, may very well represent that great interval of time occupied in other regions by the glacial periods.

This would bring the mortars to approximately the same age as the palaeolithic implements discovered by me in East Anglia. It must be admitted that this is only a surmise, but if it be rejected there remains no alternative but to ascribe these relics to Tertiary times.

7. Conclusions.

1. These mortars are undoubtedly artificial.
2. They come from the old valley gravels.

3. These gravels are universally believed to be at least as old as Pliocene times.

4. I would suggest they may be of glacial age.

5. The immense antiquity of the gravels is shown---
    (a.) By the present river system being of subsequent date, sometimes cutting through them and the superincumbent lava-cap to a depth of 2,000 feet.
    (b.) By the great denudation that has taken place since they were deposited, for they sometimes lie on the summits of mountains 6,000 feet high.
    (c.) By the fact that the Sierra Nevada has been partly elevated since their formation.

THE EARLIEST AMERICANS
Haynes, C. Vance, Jr.; *Science,* 166:709-715, 1969.

Recently, at the Calico Hills site, near Yermo, California, very crude flints, reported to be artifacts, have been found in alluvial-fan gravels of Pleistocene age. Because this site exemplifies most of the problems encountered with possible archeological sites thought to be of early Paleo-Indian age, I consider it here in some detail. The ancient alluvial-fan gravels, containing up to 10 percent of chert derived from bedrock which crops out in the Calico Hills 3 miles (3.8 kilometers) to the west, have been intensely weathered to a depth of over 6 meters. This ancient soil has superimposed upon it a calcareous red B-horizon and a vessicular A-horizon in the upper half meter, which indicates a second episode of weathering. The strength of soil-profile development shown by the upper red soil is as great as, or greater than, that of mid-Wisconsinan soils elsewhere in the southwestern United States, and many geologists, including myself, believe that the deposit is no younger than Altonian. The additional factor of 6 meters of rotten gravel below the red soil is convincing evidence that the deposit is of pre-Wisconsinan age (more than 70,000 years old), because such a depth of weathering is not known in Wisconsinan deposits. Some geologic age estimates of between 30,000 and 120,000 years have been made, but an age of 500,000 cannot be precluded.

The origin of what have been called artifacts within the deposits is even less certain, but some authorities, including those conducting the excavations, appear to be absolutely convinced that some of the fragments of chert show flaking that could only have been done by man. Others contend that even the best specimens could have been chipped and flaked naturally, especially in view of the fact that each "artifact" has been selected from literally hundreds or thousands of individual pieces of chert, excavated from gravels which, when fresh, experienced intergranular percussion and pressure at various times during their transportation from outcrops in the Calico Hills. Natural flaking would have been further aided by the igneous-rock cobbles which make up a significant percentage of the rocks and which, when fresh, would have served as natural hammerstones. (pp. 712-713)

ARTIFACTS OR GEOFACTS?
Brewer, Frederic; *Science,* 181:1202, 1973.

Charles Dawson, presumed architect of one of the greatest scientific hoaxes---Piltdown man---devised in the early part of this century a simple experiment that now could be used to support one facet of the argument Vance Haynes advances (27 July, p. 305) about the origin of the chipped flints at the Calico site.

A lawyer, Dawson belonged to a local society of science hobbyists and antiquarians in Lewes, East Sussex, England. He was annoyingly insistent that the stone artifacts proudly displayed by fellow members could have been the result of geologic processes. One day, Dawson arrived at a meeting of the society, a sackful of flint in hand. He placed the sack on the floor and then proceeded to jump up and down on the rocks, crunching them to fragments. In a little while, he removed the stones and, with a triumphant smile on his face, showed them to his incredulous colleagues. Many of the newly splintered rocks exactly resembled the so-called hand tools.

Thereafter, Dawson was snubbed by the society. A few years later, in 1912, he made an amazing discovery that propelled him to fame---the skull and jaw fragments of the Piltdown man.

It is curious, and refreshing, to note that K. P. Oakley---mentioned in Haynes's article as having examined the Calico specimens---defrocked the spurious Eoanthropus dawsoni, using a fluorine dating technique, in 1949.

A STONE IMPLEMENT FROM A WELL IN ILLINOIS
McAdams, William; *American Association for the Advancement of Science, Proceedings,* 29:720-721, 1880.

Last year an old gentleman from Green County, Ill., came to my house and told a curious story of the finding of a stone axe in the base of the drift while digging a well. It seems that, during the dry weather in the fall, Mr. Abraham Young undertook to dig a well on his farm, and near his residence.

At the depth of seventy-two feet the rock in place was reached, and in cleaning off this, preparatory to blasting, the axe in question was found. Thinking from the character of the parties, who are well-to-do farmers, and known to me, that possibly there might be some truth in the matter, I visited the locality, obtained the relic, and the following information in relation to its discovery: Four wells have been dug at different times in fruitless search for water. The depth of these wells is given as from thirty to seventy-two feet. The one in which the axe is claimed to have been found is seventy-two feet in depth. I examined the earth thrown out from the well, and could easily see that it was almost entirely loess. Just before the bottom of the well, or rock, was reached, the loess assumed more of a clayey character, and contained angular fragments of chert, not apparently water-worn. Lying on the surface of the rock, covered with clay and fragments of chert, the axe is claimed to have been found.

The finders of the relic seemed not to have much interest in the matter, and would receive no compensation for it, and when I wrote out a statement of the time and manner of the discovery they signed it without hesitation, and apparently in good faith. Afterwards they went of their own accord before a justice, and made the following affidavit:---

Green County, Ill., Feb. 1, 1880

Be it known by these presents that J. R. Cade, A. B. Young, David Mateson, and Rowel Hunnicutt, all of Walkerville Township, County of Green, State of Illinois, appeared before me, John Painter, a Justice of the Peace in Green County, Ill., and, after being duly sworn, said parties state that on or about the 20th of May, 1879, while engaged in digging a well on the farm of A. B. Young, in Green County, Ill., at the depth of seventy-two feet, J. R. Cade found, while digging, an ancient stone axe, which was raised from said well by A. B. Young and David Mateson, and preserved for curiosity.

Rowel Hunnicutt states that he was present a short time after said discovery, and measured the depth of the well and found it to be about seventy-two feet to where the axe was found, and that he took said axe in his possession and placed the same in possession of one William Mc Adams, of Jersey County, Ill.

Signed, J. R. Cade,
A. B. Young,
David Mateson,
Rowel Hunnicutt.

Subscribed and sworn to before me this 1st day of February, 1880.
John Painter, J. P.

I examined the well closely, to see if by any possible means the axe could have fallen in from the top while they were at work, but, from the very top down, the excavation was as smooth and almost as hard as a cemented cistern; and the discoverer of the relic says he found it covered with the hard, undisturbed clay on the rock.

I am inclined to believe they found the axe as stated.

I asked the men how they supposed the axe came to be in that position, and one of them replied that he could think of only one possible way by which its presence could be accounted for where they found it: "Some half-mile north of the well was a sink hole; possibly the axe might have been washed into this, and conveyed by some channel or watercourse to where it was found. "

MAN AND THE GLACIAL PERIOD
Wright, G. Frederick; *Science*, 20:275-277, 1892.

I acknowledge with pleasure the courtesy with which Dr. Brinton, in his review of "Man and the Glacial Period," has dealt with the question of the genuineness of the reported discoveries of implements in the glacial gravels of the United States. This, of course, was the first question to be settled, Were implements of human manufacture really found in undisturbed strata of gravel which was deposited during the glacial period? If this question is settled in the affirmative, then all glacial geology has direct bearing upon the question of archaeology. If it is decided in the negative, glacial geology remains the same, but it ceases to have interest in connection with archaeology. I am glad to have the issue so clearly made by Dr. Brinton, and thereby to have occasion to present more specifically my reasons for belief in the genuineness of these discoveries.

The evidence naturally begins with that at Trenton, N.J., where Dr. C. C. Abbott has been so long at work. Dr. Abbott, it is true, is not a professional geologist, but his familiarity with the gravel at Trenton where he resides, the exceptional opportunities afforded to him for investigation, and the frequent visits of geologists have made him an expert whose opinion is of the highest value upon the question of the undisturbed character of the gravel deposit. The gravel banks which he has examined so long and so carefully have been exposed in two ways: 1st, by the undermining of floods on the river-side, but principally by the excavations which have been made by the railroad and by private parties in search of gravel. For years the railroads have been at work digging away the side of the banks until they had removed a great many acres of the gravel to a depth of twenty or twenty-five feet. Anyone can see that in such conditions there has been no chance for "creep" or landslides to have disturbed the stratification; for the whole area was full of gravel, and there was no chance of disturbance by natural causes. Now Dr. Abbott's testimony is that up to the year 1888 sixty of the four hundred palaeolithic implements which he had found at Trenton had been found at recorded depths in the gravel. Coming down to specifications, he describes in his reports the discovery of one (see "Primitive Industry," 492) found while watching the progress of an extensive excavation in Centre Street, which was nearly seven feet below the surface, surrounded by a mass of large cobble stones and boulders, one of the latter overlying it. Another was found at the bluff at Trenton, in a narrow gorge where the material forming the sides of the chasm had not been displaced, under a large boulder nine feet below the surface (ib. 496). Another was found in a perpendicular exposure of the bluff immediately after the detachment of a large mass of material, and in a surface that had but the day before been exposed, and had not yet begun to crumble. The specimen was twenty-one feet from the surface of the ground.

In all these and numerous other cases Dr. Abbott's attention was specially directed to the question of the undisturbed character of the gravel, having been cautioned upon this point in the early part of his investigations.

Nor is he the only one who has found implements which were clearly in those undisturbed gravel deposits. Professor Shaler (Report of the Peabody Museum at Cambridge, Vol. II., p. 45) found two of the implements twelve feet below the top of the bank, where he says that it was difficult for him to believe that they could have travelled down from the superficial soil, and he expresses it as his opinion, after having gone over the ground with Dr. Abbott, that the implements which Dr. Abbott had found occurred under conditions that make it "quite unquestionable that they were deposited at a depth of many feet below the soil, and are really mingled with the drift matter that forms the section before described." This is the description which I have quoted in my volume (p. 242). Professor Putnam, also, personally found implements in position which he decided to be certainly undisturbed gravel (see 14th Annual Report of Peabody Museum, p. 23, and Proc. Boston Society of Natural History for Jan. 19, 1880).

The question of the occurrence of these implements in undisturbed gravel was so thoroughly discussed by the scientific men in Boston who visited the region about 1880 that I had supposed there was no longer any reasonable doubt concerning the facts, and I feel sure that anyone who goes through the records of the Peabody Museum and the Boston Society of Natural History about that time will be convinced. At the same time I would say that I have been unable myself to find any implements in place, though I have frequently examined the bank. But I have not felt at liberty on that account to doubt the abundant testimony of others who have. If we are limited to believing only what we ourselves have seen, our knowledge will be unduly circumscribed; and though I might be more certain of the facts if I had seen them myself, I do not see how I could increase the confidence, in the facts, of other people who could disregard the testimony already in hand.

Passing now from the discoveries at Trenton, N. J., to those in gravels of corresponding age in Ohio, we do not come to the subject with the same amount of incredulity with which we first encountered the evidence at Trenton. Dr. Metz has been for years co-operating with Professor Putnam in various investigations, and the discovery of a flint implement by him in excavating for a cistern in his own yard was such that no reasonable question can be raised as to its having been undisturbed since the deposit was made, and there can be no reasonable question that the deposit was made during the continuance of glacial conditions in the State. I have described the conditions in a report to the Archaeological Society of Ohio for December, 1887.

The discovery of a palaeolithic implement at New Comerstown, Ohio, by Mr. W. C. Mills, is an equally well-attested case. Mr. Mills, like Dr. Abbott, resided in close proximity to an extensive glacial terrace to which the railroad was resorting for ballast. Many acres of the gravel have been removed. During the progress of these excavations Mr. Mills repeatedly visited the pit, and after a fresh excavation discovered this implement in a perpendicular face of the bank fifteen feet below the surface. The facts were recorded in his diary and the implement placed in the general collection of Indian relics which he was making. Mr. Mills was at that time engaged in business in the place, but he had been a pupil of Professor Orton in geology, and was well qualified to judge of the undisturbed character of the gravel in which this implement was found. As anyone can see by consulting the photographic illustrations on pp. 252 and 253 of my volume, the implement itself is an exact duplicate, so far as form is concerned, of one which I have in my own collection, from Amiens, France, and which came to me, through Professor Asa Gray, directly from the collection of Dr. Evans in London.

The New Comerstown implement was submitted to Professor Haynes of Boston and to others at a meeting of the Boston Society of Natural History, and by them pronounced to have all the essential characteristics of palaeolithic age. The full report upon this is found in Tract No. 75 of the Western Reserve Historical Society, Cleveland.

As to Miss Babbitt's discoveries at Little Falls, Minn., I have nothing further to say than that up to the present year no serious question had been raised concerning the glacial age of the gravel in which her implements were found. But as questions have now been raised in view of recent examinations, I will not attempt to discuss the matter until the facts are more fully published. But the removal of this case from the category would not disturb confidence in the evidence connecting man with the glacial period in New Jersey and Ohio.

The statement of Dr. Brinton that a well-known government geologist had recognized the Nampa image "as a clay toy manufactured by the neighboring Pocatello Indians" is news to me, and it is due to the public that this official's knowledge of the subject should be more specifically detailed. The facts as I have brought them out by prolonged and minute inquiry do not warrant any such flippant treatment of the evidence. Professor Putnam, to whose inspection the image was subjected when it first came into my hands, at once pronounced it an antiquity of some sort, unlike anything which he knew to be in existence among the aboriginal tribes. I need not say that Professor Putnam's opinion upon a question of that sort is of the very highest value. There were upon the image patches of the anhydrous oxide of iron, which to him and other experts were indubitable evidence that it had lain for a long time in the earth. Subsequently I ascertained, while on the ground at Nampa, that the shade of color in this iron oxide upon it corresponded exactly to that which had formed upon the clay concretions which came up in large quantities from the same stratum in which the image was alleged to have been found. I have also, I think, made it evident that the burying of human relics even to the great depth of 320 feet in the Snake River Valley may not be much more surprising than the burial of the remains of man in Pompeii and Herculaneum, and that the date of this burial may not have been very many thousand years ago. The direct evidence to the fact that this little image, an inch and a half long, came up from the depth reported is about as convincing as we can have for any fact which depends for credence upon human testimony. There has been nothing with regard to the appearance of the parties suggesting fraud. Mr. Cumming, the superintendent of that division of the Union Pacific Railroad, whose attention to the facts was called the day after the discovery, is a Harvard College graduate, of extended legal education and wide practical experience, who knew all the parties and was familiar with the circumstances, and investigated them upon the ground. Charles Francis Adams emphatically affirms that Mr. Cumming's evidence in this matter is entitled to as much consideration as the evidence of any scientific man would be. Anyone who wishes to get my detailed report of the evidence will find it in the Proceedings of the Boston Society of Natural History for Jan. 1, 1890, and Feb. 18, 1891.

The discoveries of human implements under Table Mountain in California are in close analogy with this discovery at Nampa, in the Snake River Valley, and the same remarks have been made respecting them that Dr. Brinton reports concerning the Nampa image, namely, that they are modern implements at present in use among the local tribes of

Indians. But no such offhand opinion as this can break the force of the evidence which has accumulated in support of their having been found in deposits which have been undisturbed since the great lava outflows which constitute what is called the Sonora Table Mountain. The evidence concerning the Calaveras skull has been exhaustively discussed by Professor Whitney of Harvard College, who pronounces the facts to be beyond all reasonable doubt. At the meeting of the Geological Society in Washington in January, 1891, three independent discoveries of human implements in conditions similar to those assigned to the Calaveras skull were presented. I had myself obtained information at Sonora of the discovery of a stone-mortar in the tunnel of the Empire mine of which the evidence was satisfactory beyond reasonable doubt. The discovery was made by the assistant surveyor of the county in the tunnel of a mine under Table Mountain, which was owned by his father and where work is still prosecuted. The mortar had been given away to another person, but it has since come into my hands and is preserved in the Museum of the Western Reserve Historical Society of Cleveland.

At the same meeting Mr. George H. Becker of the U.S. Geol. Survey presented a similar mortar found under Table Mountain some years before by Mr. Neale, a mining engineer. Mr. Neale signed an affidavit detailing the particulars, and his remembrance of the situation was so minute that there could be no question of the undisturbed character of the deposits. Mr. Becker well remarks that Mr. Neale's judgment as mining-engineer concerning the undisturbed character of the deposit is the highest evidence that can possibly be obtained, for that is a point to which the miner's attention is constantly directed, on account of the danger attending the opening of any old excavation.

The third new evidence offered was that of Mr. Clarence King, who had just presented to the Smithsonian Institution a fragment of a pestle which he had taken with his own hands, in the vicinity of the two previous places mentioned, from the undisturbed gravel beds underlying Table Mountain. I need not say that Mr. Becker and Mr. King are two geologists of the very highest standing in the country, and that they both have unusual familiarity with the phenomena of that region, and they both, together with Professor Marsh, Professor Putnam, and W. H. Dall, express their unqualified belief in reference to the Calaveras skull that it was found in place in the gravel beneath this same stream of lava.

But I have already made my communication too long. I trust, however, upon your forbearance in publishing it, since the facts are too numerous to be compressed into less space of description, and a volume would be required to give all the evidence in detail. In my book upon "Man and the Glacial Period" I was called upon to discuss a very broad subject in a very small volume, and so could not enter into details. I endeavored, however, to limit myself to facts of which there was abundant proof, if they should ever be called in question. And I would repeat that I am glad of the revival of interest in the subject which will be created by the expression of such doubts as still remain in Dr. Brinton's mind. I have no question but full discussion will dispel the uncertainty that may exist.

ARTIFACT FROM DEPOSITS OF MID-WISCONSIN AGE IN ILLINOIS

Munson, Patrick J., and Frye, John C.; *Science,* 150:1722-1723, 1965.

An artifact of almost undeniable human manufacture has been discovered in west-central Illinois (SW1/4NW1/4SE1/4 sec. 19, T5N, R3E, Fulton County), well-imbedded in the nearly vertical face of a fresh road cut. If the artifact is the same age as the stratum where it was found, 35,000 to 40,000 years, it is extremely important in determination of the age of man in the New World.

Because this is an isolated artifact and because the road cut was made by heavy machinery, there is, of course, the unlikely possibility that the specimen was dragged from another area or fell from the surface above and was pushed into the face of the cut by the machinery. A thin scattering of archeological materials attributable to Archaic occupation (10,000 to 3,500 years ago) on the surface adds some credibility to this possibility. Due to the sheerness and fresh condition of the cut at the time of discovery, however, it would appear to be impossible that the artifact fell from the surface and lodged after completion of the cut. Another equally implausible possibility is that the specimen was intruded by natural means (for example, burrowing animals, uprooting of trees) from the bottom of the Peoria loess 1.1 meters above, which dates after 20,000 years ago.

The artifact, one end of which is broken by an old fracture, is plano-convex, well-trimmed, and percussion flaked; and the material is a rather poor-grade gray chert which occurs as pebbles in the local glacial tills.

The Pleistocene stratigraphy in the road cut was studied, the deposits were sampled, and the fractions of the samples of diameter less than 2 microns were analyzed by x-ray diffraction. The stratigraphy at the locality and significant data from the x-ray analyses are shown graphically in Fig. 2. The stratigraphic units are characteristic of the Illinois Valley region and have been described in detail through this part of Illinois. The Peoria loess consists of yellow-tan massive silt with a relatively deep surface soil at the top. It has been leached of carbonate minerals except in the lowermost 50 centimeters, which contain a minor amount of dolomite (determined by acid in the field and checked by x-ray diffraction). In the lowermost 30 centimeters is a crenulate zone of charcoal flecks; the peaty zone that is typical of the Farmdale is not present in this locality. The Roxana silt consists of loess in the upper two-thirds (zones II to IV) and sandy silt grading downward into sandy, pebbly silt at the base (zone I). The Roxana has been entirely leached of its carbonate minerals and contains a soil at the top and one or more soils in the basal part. Below the Roxana silt is a strongly developed Sangamon soil at the top of Illinoian till; this soil grades downward into typical, calcareous, Illinoian till in the lower part of the cut.

The age of the stratigraphic units has been determined by numerous radiocarbon dates, both on snail shells and on wood, in western and central Illinois. Several ages from the lower part of the Peoria loess have ranged from 17,000 to 20,000 years ago. A large number of dates from the Farmdale peats and silts fall in a range between 22,000 and 27,000 years ago. Although Farmdale peat does not occur in this section, its

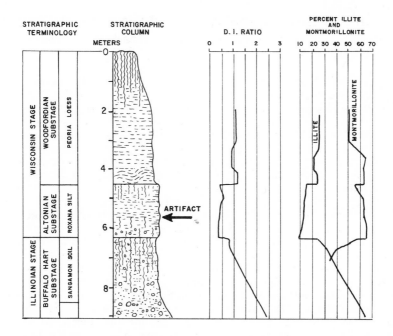

Site stratigraphic succession. The diffraction-intensity ratio (D.I. ratio) and percentages of illite and montmorillonite in the fraction of particles less than 2 microns in diameter are shown graphically.

stratigraphic position is between the Peoria loess and Roxana silt. For the Roxana silt, two ages from the upper part of zone II and the lower part of zone III in southwestern Illinois, determined from snail shells, were 35,000± 1,000 and 37,000 ±1,500 years (samples W-729 and W-869), and ages for peat in a comparable stratigraphic position in northern Illinois have been determined at 35,000± 2,500 and 38,000± 3,000 years (samples W-1450 and I-847). Because the stratigraphic position in which the artifact occurred was just above zone I in the Roxana loess and below the bulk of zones II to IV, its inferred age is in the range of 35,000 to 40,000 years.

THE FIRE AREAS ON SANTA ROSA ISLAND, CALIFORNIA

Orr, Phil C., and Berger, Rainer; *National Academy of Science, Proceedings,* 56:1409–1416 and 56:1678–1682, 1966.

In about 3 km of sea cliffs, up to 30 m high, and badlands on the NW coast of Santa Rosa Island, California (34°N Latitude; 120°11'W Longitude), there are found approximately 100 red fire areas. The base of the cliffs is composed of resistant Rincon shales of Miocene age capped by unconsolidated Pleistocene alluvium deposited as fangiomerates emanating from the canyons of the island. As described previously, the Miocene shales are topped by the Santa Rosa Island formation composed of the oldest Garanon member, the intermediate Fox, and the most recent Tecolote member.

The Fire Areas.---A major characteristic of the fire areas is their brilliant to dull brick-red appearance, easily recognized in the buff clays of the Tecolote in which almost all the fire areas occur. None are observed very far upstream in the canyons beyond ca. 800 m. The stratigraphic correlation of the fire areas in the sea cliff is made relatively easy by the undisturbed horizontal layers of the Tecolote, as determined by on-foot and helicopter measurements. Only a few fire areas have been recognized in the other location on Santa Rosa, near China Camp on the south coast. On Santa Cruz Island, a few fire areas can be seen near Christies Ranch. One site on the mainland has been found on the Hollister Ranch, 65 km west of Santa Barbara, and others, by Hubbs, in the vicinity of La Jolla.

There is a certain uniformity in the structure of the fire areas irrespective of their stratigraphic position in the height of the sea cliff. One type is a U-shaped pit about 60 cm in diameter and depth, of which the lower 20-30 cm are reddened clay. The other is found in the shape of a saucer generally 3.50-5 m in diameter with similar reddening. The most intensive red coloration is in the center, with the brightness gradually changing to a dull rich brown at the rim. The shape of the pits in the vertical has been ascertained in numerous cases in the face of the cliff. Occasionally, fire areas appear as elliptical or circular features on the horizontal top surface of the cliff after the overburden has been eroded away. Infrequently a thin horizontal band can be seen in the face of the cliff. This is thought to be due to erosion of fire areas by rain, which washed away and spread the brick-red clay, as will be discussed later.

Within the fire areas, bands of dark soil containing charcoal are often found. One of the very first fire areas discovered, found in 1946 in the face of the sea cliff at an elevation of some 25 m, appeared to have a ring of stones associated with it as is often found with man-made hearths. However, due to the lack of suitable equipment, this site could not be inspected before the cliff caved in. No other fire area of this type has been found since, although sandstones burnt red in the fires were observed occasionally. The extent of the number of fire areas lost to the sea cannot be estimated today.

During many years of investigation of the Santa Rosa fire areas, 24 were found to contain bird bones, 14 dwarf mammoth bones, and 5 bird and mammoth bones together. On the basis of 100 counted fires, this indicates that more than one third contain bones; but the real percentage may be considerably higher. The size of the bones found varies from large dwarf mammoth bones to small fragments of centimeter size from birds. (pp. 1409-1410)

A number of fire areas on Santa Rosa Island, California, have been dated by the radiocarbon method. In all probability these very early fire areas, reaching in age beyond the scale of radiocarbon dating, are the result of the activities of early man in America. Therefore the question of man's arrival in America should be examined in the light of newer considerations. The status of Pacific Coast field archeology up to 1965 has been summarized and reviewed by Meighan. Haynes discussed the entry of man into North America from Asia 12,000 years ago when the Cordilleran and Laurentide ice sheets separated to permit passage onto the continent from Asia. Recently, Muller-Beck concluded that the paleohunters of Eurasia probably crossed the Bering land bridge about 28,000-26,000 years ago into North America, but were isolated from the Old World by the glaciation of the following maximum until the ice melted again and permitted renewed access into this continent 12,000 years ago. Chard favors two basic movements into the New World, one near 40,000 years ago and a subsequent one in the Middle Paleolithic. Other arguments favor man's presence in America as early as the Third Interglacial (now dated by Pa^{231}/Th^{230} near 100,000 years ago as discussed by Curray) based on genetic studies by Birdsell and perhaps linguistic considerations.

Since one of the Santa Rosa fire areas, UCLA-749 at ~ 37,000 years, is of infinite radiocarbon age, very early land connections and migrations are likely. On stratigraphic grounds, UCLA-749 appears to be considerably older than 37,000 years on the order of some tens of thousands of years rather than a few millenia. The height of the sea cliff for L-290R is very closely that of UCLA-749, but the latter is at a depth of 24.5 m rather than 11.5 m for the ca. 30,000-year level. The question arises, therefore, when land bridges existed in the region of today's Bering Strait. (p. 1678)

SHEGUIANDAH AS VIEWED IN 1974
Lee, Thomas E.; *NEARA Newsletter,* 9:34-37, 1974.

How, then, does Sheguiandah fit into today's evidence? Let us see. To make the situation clear, a brief description of the site is needed. It occurs at the east end of Manitoulin Island, in northern Lake Huron, a lightly glaciated area, and occupies some 26 acres of a quartzite hill. While part of the hilltop is forested, the upper portions are almost free of trees, and it is seen that enormous quarrying operations there have removed entire ridges of the white rock and left the area littered with discarded rubble. This ends downslope, however, at a Great Lakes Nipissing notch on the hillside, which thus gives us a minimum date of 4,000 years for the latest major occupation of the hill. There are many hillside dumps, and we now know that deep quarry pits are concealed beneath them. There is an area, too---sheltered from all winds---that we can consider as the principal place of habitation. Further, by a rare stroke of good fortune, four small swamps are trapped in pockets in the rock near the top of the hill. The site is an unbelievably well equipped and supplied outdoor laboratory.

Trenching into the swamps to a depth of nine feet revealed a deposit of peat just over five feet thick, containing artifacts, among other evidences. The bottom one-inch layer of peat, in 1955, produced a radiocarbon date of 9130 ± 250 years. At first hailed enthusiastically by the USGS, because it seemed, as they fondly hoped, to prove Antevs wrong about the date of the Cochrane glacial advance, this date was then suppressed by them for two years! And small wonder. The position or altitude of the sample, when they stopped to think about it, showed that glacial Lake Algonquin had already fallen 300 feet before the peat began to form, even if they ignored the facts that vegetation would not catch on immediately on the quartzite, and that the first inch of dense greasy material could not have been formed instantane- ously. How long did it really take? A thousand years? Two thousand? More? Yet there were several well known radiocarbon dates that placed the peak of Algonquin waters at only 3,600 years. And there were numerous fanatics in both professions prepared to die for the principle that radiocarbon was consistent and therefore, in some mysterious manner accurate! Con- sistent? What to do now with a 6,000-years discrepancy? Obviously, bury it! What else?

Beneath the peat were glacially-deposited gravels---and in them, man- made flakes and cores. But all of these things we did not know until the third year of excavations, when the swamps were first examined.

The habitation area was a far more complex problem. First, there was some Point Peninsula evidence---never more than three or four specimens in the four years of excavation---but quite enough to set the armchair ex- perts to crying loudly, "Point Peninsula workshop!" Their absurd clamor came close to cutting off financial support and ending the work, for there were always lots of foolish people to listen to them.

Then came prolific material that was closely related to George Lake I, probably dating around 4,000 to 6,000 years old. It was then said in the Canadian press by Michigan opponents, who were green with envy, that the site was neither old nor important.

A more interesting cultural layer was then revealed, only about one inch thick, made up of yellowish wind-deposited Algonquin sediments. It contain- ed projectile points ranging from Laurentian types through most of the Plano types of the West. There were even two fluted points, one with ears. At this stage a visiting anthropologist said, "If there are such things as early projectile points in Ontario, you have them!" He was right, of course. But he then urged me to go after the projectile points and to forget about the tools of man in the gravels beneath them! It is these scorned gravels---and still deeper deposits---that form the basis for this paper.

In our early digging, in 1952, we were going only a short distance into underlying gravels, in order to be sure that sterile soil had been reached. It looked sterile---but an occasional artifact and a number of flakes turned up. I was genuinely puzzled, since my reading, training, and experience had not prepared me for this. I saw at once that the gravels and scattered bould- ers had not been put there by man. But by what natural agency? The arrival of a geologist, Dr. John Sanford of Wayne University, had me in a fever of excitement. His considered judgment and pronouncement, after careful study, staggered me. "This is unsorted glacial till," he said, "and it is in primary position. The contained artifacts are older than the till, hence older than the last glacial advance over this site." I had no alternative explanation. Yet I had been taught, in the great and infallible universities, that glaciers destroy all trace of man in their advance!

The trenches were dug through the gravels, and artifacts were found throughout, though in sharply declining numbers downward. In the next three years, with increasing familiarity, I became aware that there were two bodies of till, containing two greatly different quantities and kinds of artifacts. One till must have slid over the frozen mass of the other, perhaps planing away the top of it.

In the second year over 60 geologists saw these open trenches on one occasion, and numerous others came singly or in small groups, year after year. None objected to the designation, with a single exception in 1955 (I proved him wrong), and some vigorously supported the identification as till. The question of mud-flow was considered and rejected on grounds that there was no higher area large enough to produce the mud, and that sharp ridges of quartzite lay across the slopes above the area of the habitation site, blocking any proposed movement downward. The famed Dr. Ernst Antevs, whose specialties included studies of mud-flow, laughed to scorn the mere suggestion. "How can you have mud-flow," he said, "if you don't have mud? And how can you make mud out of these sands, gravels and boulders that will not hold water in your trenches, even in the heaviest rains?" In absolute agreement were Dr. Bruce Liberty and Dr. Jaan Terasmae, both of the Geological Survey of Canada, who studied the trenches intensively---Liberty over a long period and daily or even twice daily.

Beneath the tills were sorted materials that I would describe as sands and fine gravels. They contained one definite bifacial artifact and numerous man-made flakes. Pleistocene experts of the G. S. C. identified the deposits as "meltwater-laid"---put down by water right at the edge of the ice.

But there was more. The meltwater deposits rested upon a boulder paving of unknown age---boulders resting side-by-side, up to 35 inches in diameter. Geologists could only describe them as "a major geologic event" that might go back to a still earlier glaciation.

The boulders were removed, exposing water-laid clays. The upper portion of the clays produced one definite bifacial artifact, several rolled and battered objects that I regarded as former bifaces, and a number of man-made flakes. Who can guess what extreme age should be assigned to them?

Privately, the geologists most closely concerned expressed the opinion that the artifacts were interglacial, perhaps 150,000 years old. But the wise and experienced Antevs, who knew all too well the mental limitations of the archaeological profession, said "If you tell them this, not one will believe it. Try 30,000 minimum---a few of them may believe it."

SOME PALEOLITHIC TOOLS FROM NORTHEAST NORTH AMERICA

Raemsch, B. E., and Vernon, W. W.; *Current Anthropology,* 18:97-99, 1977.

Research on an early-man site in the Catskill Mountains of New York has, over the past six years, demonstrated the presence of core and flake tools associated with glacial deposits of different ages. Through analysis of paleosols, an estimated age of 70,000 years B. P. has been considered reasonably accurate for the oldest of the artifacts. This figure was arrived at on recognizing, in the oldest soil excavated, a marked weathering profile as determined by field and chemical analysis. The defined paleosol is overlain by a till sheet believed at the time it was discovered to be of early Wisconsin (Wurm) age. Geologic studies (pebble counts, pebble orientation studies, and correlation with already dated tills) done most recently on this till sheet confirm that it is early Wisconsin (termed Olean in New York State), thus dating the oldest arti- facts as being of pre-Wisconsin age.

The oldest of the artifacts closely resemble flake tools commonly referred to in Europe and Africa as Upper Acheulean, and they include

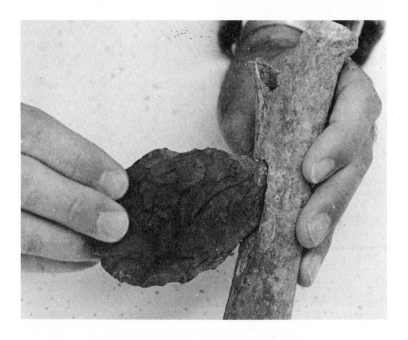

Handax in bovoid leg bone as it was found in New York State. Esti- mated age about 70,000 years. (B. E. Raemsch)

cordiform points, type side- and end-scrapers resembling those of Mousterian assemblages, and core knives and other core tools having specialized functions judged by the presence of complex structural features. Since the site (referred to as Timlin after its discoverer) incorporates a 60-ft. (18-m) terrace, the surface of which (considered to be Binghamton, or late Wisconsin, till) appears to have been in more recent times an area of occupation, we have been able to trace temporal sequences of stone tool cultures up to the Archaic stage. The latter is a biface stone tool culture, whereas all other cultures examined on the site are of flake and core types.

· · · · · · · · · ·

• Pigmy and Eccentric Flints

PIGMY FLINTS
Gatty, Reginald A.; *Science Gossip,* 2:36, 1896.

I will not venture to enter on the question of how long ago it was that the primitive inhabitant of Britain used flint, because he was ignorant of the existence of bronze or iron. This must be left for future determination. At present we are much in the dark, and what is wanted is some better classification of flint implements. I have styled this paper pigmy flints because I propose leaving the beaten track of ordinary flint weapons, and entering upon what is almost a novel phase. For some years past I have carefully preserved all specimens of flint implements I came across, both small and great. It was easy work to put out in drawers the arrowheads, some barbed, some leaf-shaped, some broad-tipped; and in another drawer to range the knives and scrapers in their order. When it came to minute specimens; to flint implements carefully and perfectly made, no bigger than half-an-inch, and many much less, I am bound to say I was completely puzzled. The first question which arose was: Are these genuine? Is there not some mistake? They might be accidental chippings, struck off at random when the ancient flint worker was framing his tools. A closer inspection with a magnifying glass proved that this was impossible. Whoever the people were who made these implements, they spent an enormous amount of skill and patience in their construction. They designed them with a purpose, and the flints must in some way have supplied a requisite want. I will take one specimen, which I will call a crescent-shaped knife, for examination. To show the size of this perfect tool it exactly covers in length the word "examination" as printed on this page, and its breadth is a trifle broader than the printing. I am led to give it the name of crescent because it has that form, and also in a pamphlet written by Dr. H. Colley March, of Rochdale, entitled, "The early neolithic floor of East Lancashire," I find reference to similar implements discovered in India. He says: "In the Colonial Exhibition, at South Kensington, there were shown, last year, as the work of Bushmen, Hottentots, and Kaffirs, some diminutive tools of flint, labelled 'drills.' Similar flint implements have been met with in Egypt; in the Exeter Museum are some slender points of worked flint that were discovered beneath a submerged forest near Westward Ho! and small worked crescents of flint and agate have been found in caves of the Vindhya Hills of India. But all these are far surpassed, as regards minuteness and delicacy of workmanship, by the implements of the East Lancashire floor. Indeed, in some of them, the secondary flaking is so fine that it cannot well be seen without a magnifying glass. Roughly speaking these minute implements are divisible into two classes, and are probably borers or gravers."

The peculiarity of these discoveries of Dr. Colley March is, that they were made at a depth of six feet under peat, and at an altitude of thirteen hundred feet above sea level. The weapons found by myself were all taken from the ploughed fields, none of which exceeded two hundred feet above sea level. I must except a few which I found on the moors quite one thousand feet above the sea. It is very difficult to classify the pigmy flints, or to assign them a definite use. Many are like tiny knife blades, and I have also many borers. They differ considerably in shape: some are oval, some squared at the edges, but all show working of such a delicate character, that it requires a magnifying glass to detect the flakings on the edges. I tried to count the flakings on the crescent-shaped knife above alluded to, and I found there must have been above a hundred along the edges. The quantity of pigmy flints obtained is surprising, and I have a collection of some hundreds. You may be tempted to throw aside small fragments when you pick them up in the fields, but this is never wise to do, until you have washed your flint, and then subjected it to careful examination under a strong magnifying glass. When you have got what I may term a "worked" flint, it is quite unmistakable. No process of nature can ever imitate the delicate flakings by which the edge, say of a flint knife, has been brought to perfection. The work is no doubt due to pressure. A hard body is pressed against the side which it is intended to sharpen, and fragments fly off leaving a scar behind in the form of a slight indentation. This is readily observed on a flint some inches in length, but shen you get down to very minute sizes, to little well-formed flints less than a quarter of an inch, you need a magnifying glass to discover the workmanship. What hands, what eyes, these pre-historic flint-flakers must have had to frame such delicate tools! I often look in amazement at a drawer of these pigmy flints. Perhaps sixty or seventy knives and borers will make one row, and when seen together, row after row, you realise that these flints were fabricated with a design and purpose, and whoever the people were who made them, dwarfs or fairies, they certainly were handicraftsmen of no mean order. It is very difficult to give any idea of the various forms which these flints take. I think the pervading notion seems to have been to use them fixed in some sort of handle. In fact, without such aid, they could do nothing with the fingers. It would be possible, I think, to arrive at some solution of this difficulty if we could place the pigmy flints before a tribe of savages, such as the Bushmen of Africa. Perhaps in time to come, when more is known on this subject, such may be done.

Collections are wanted from all parts of the world. By comparing notes, by steadily accumulating evidences, much might be brought to light. The migration of man from one part of the world to another could be traced, and the pre-historic story of our race might have considerable light thrown upon it. I have alluded to the pamphlet, by Dr. Colley March, on the early neolithic floor of East Lancashire, in which he states that small crescent-shaped knives have been found in the Vindha caves of India, similar to those of Lancashire, and similar again to those which I have found on the ploughed fields. There is an immense distance to be covered between India and England, but vast as the space may be, to what lengths of time must we go to date the formation of the peat 1,300 feet above sea-level, under which such knives have been found? And these are pigmy flints we are dealing with, not the big palaeolithic weapons of the drift. In these substantial implements there is something tangible and reasonable. We can imagine a savage breaking a hole in the ice to let down his fishing line, or raising it aloft to hit his enemy on the head. But a crescent knife has no such ostensible use. It faintly resembles the crescent of a new moon, and may have been copied from that luminary. It is worked, or rather flaked all round, giving a cutting edge every way, and its horns are very sharp. That his should be found in India and England, and, more than all, below a peat stratum, is certainly a most remarkable fact.

PYGMY IMPLEMENTS FROM AUSTRALIA
Johnson, J. P.; *Man*, 14:147, 1914.

I can sympathise with Mr. Lewis Abbott in his surprise (expressed in his paper on "Pygmy Implements from Cape Colony" in the September number) at learning that pygmy implements similar to those of South Africa occur in Australia. I experienced a similar surprise on recently seeing examples from Western Australia in the Perth Museum, and others from Eastern Australia in the Sydney Museum.

It does not seem to be realised by writers on this subject that the South African pygmies, with the exception of the crescent type, are merely diminutive forms and varieties of what the French archaeologists term the Audi, Chatelperron, and Gravette pointes or couteaux. These are characteristic of the Aurignaco-Magdalenien assemblages of Northwestern Europe where the crescent is absent, and are prominent in the Capsian assemblage of Sicily where the crescent is present.

I am now able to announce that this is also the case with the Australian pygmies. They are all varieties of the Audi, Chatelperron, and Gravette pointes, the crescent being absent. The accompanying drawing

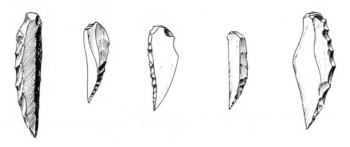

of specimens collected by Mr. Whitelegge, of Sydney, and now in my possession, will demonstrate this. These, it should be noted, are of more than average size. In Australia, however, they do not appear to be associated with "scrapers" as in Europe and South Africa.

SMALL FLINT IMPLEMENTS FROM BUNGAY
Dutt, W. A.; *Nature*, 77:102-103, 1907.

The small flint implements figured in the accompanying drawing were found in a sandy hollow about 2 feet deep at Bungay, in Suffolk. The sand in this hole was littered with minute flakes; in a few minutes I picked up between fifty and sixty, of which the figured ones are typical examples. I hesitate to describe the implements as "pigmy flints," because their fine secondary chipping is not confined to the thicker edge or "back" of the flakes, but, judging from photographs I have seen, they closely resemble some pigmies found recently near Brighton by Mr. H. S. Toms. So far as the untrimmed flakes are concerned, it is impossible to distinguish them from typical pigmy flakes, while the trimming of implements 3 and 5 is identical with that of the pigmies.

In consequence of nearly all the English pigmies having been found on the surface of the ground, it has been impossible to say with any confidence whether they belong to the Neolithic, Bronze, or Early Iron period. In view of this, it is interesting to know that the small flakes and implements from Bungay were found in association with a polished axe of grey flint, a black flint lance-head of very delicate workmanship, one of the rare and finely chipped triangular "knives," and some small convex scrapers showing very delicate secondary chipping. These implements were found in the same sandy hole when the small implements were discovered, and from an examination of the sides of the hollow it was evident that they all came from what might be called a "Neolithic floor" about 18 inches from the surface of the ground. Nowhere on the surface of the surrounding ground could I find a single flake or implement, and if the ground had not been disturbed in order that a small quantity of sand might be carted away, not one of the implements would have been brought to light. As it happened, they were all found within an area of about six square yards. Some small bones found on the same site have been identified as those of a girl or a small woman.

The makers of the small flint implements evidently had their home or their "workshop" on a sandy knoll only a few feet above the level of the marshes of the Waveney Valley. On this knoll and a neighbouring one there are some saucer-shaped depressions in the ground very suggestive of hut-circles.

DEPOSITS OF FLINT IMPLEMENTS
Snyder, J. F.; *Smithsonian Institution Annual Report, 1876,* 433–441.

In the "Ancient Monuments of the Mississippi Valley" is mentioned a strange class of deposits of stone implements and other objects, differing in the motive of interment from the simple caches which I have described. The interest of that valuable work culminates in the chapter devoted to "sacrificial mounds," the arrangement and contents of which exhibit the plane of religious thought attained by the moundbuilders. The "altars" of burnt clay; the votive offerings, through fire, of their choicest works in stone, copper, mica, and shell, doubtless together with many articles of less durable materials which were consumed by the intense heat; the cremation of human bodies; the heaping of earth upon the glowing mass; and the introduction of strata of sand in the enveloping tumulus, with the outward covering of coarse gravel, together constitute a record wonderful and unparalleled. Certainly the most plausible solution of this interesting problem rests in the view ascribing the origin of this class of monuments to ideas of propitiation or devotional fanaticism. In either case we feel tolerably certain of the fact that the inclosures of the so-called sacrificial mounds were intended by their constructors to be final. We have here no stores of hidden goods to be withdrawn at pleasure, for use or traffic, but a deposit of objects made in accordance with some superstitious rite or religious notion, and designed to remain there undisturbed to the end of time.

Associated with the sacred mounds which covered the burnt offerings, and in the same inclosure, Squier and Davis, (page 158, l. c.) describe one which contained no burnt altar, but in the place of it a great number of curiously wrought disks of black flint, which appeared to have been buried without the accompaniment of fire, but with the same precision, and covered by the same strata of sand and outward layer of gravel as were the clay altars of the other mounds with their treasures of polished implements, utensils, and ornaments. The account given by Mr. Squier of this deposit, on page 158, "Ancient Monuments," &c., is as follows: "Another singular mound, of somewhat anomalous character, of which a section is herewith given, occurred in the same inclosure with the above. It is remarkable as being very broad and flat, measuring at least 80 feet in diameter by 6 or 7 in height. It has two sand strata, but instead of an altar there are two layers of disks chipped out of hornstone, some nearly round, others in the form of spear-heads.

They are of various sizes, but are for the most part about 6 inches long by 4 wide, and three quarters of an inch or an inch in thickness. They are placed side by side, a little inclining, and one layer resting immediately on the other. Out of an excavation 6 feet long by 4 wide not far from six hundred were thrown. The deposit extends beyond the limits of the excavation on every side. Supposing it to be 12 feet square, (and it may be 20 or 30,) we have not far from four thousand of these disks deposited here. If they were thus placed as an offering, we can form some estimate, in view of the fact that they must have been brought from a great distance and fashioned with great toil, of the devotional fervor which induced the sacrifice, or the magnitude of the calamity which that sacrifice was perhaps intended to avert. The fact that this description of stone chips most easily when newly quarried, has induced the suggestion that the disks were deposited here for the purpose of protecting them from the hardening influences of the atmosphere, and were intended to be withdrawn and manufactured as occasion warranted or necessity required. It is incredible, however, that so much care should be taken to fashion the mound and introduce the mysterious strata, if it was designed to be disturbed at any subsequent period. There is little doubt that the deposit was final, and was made in compliance with some religious requirement. An excavation below these layers discovered traces of fire, but too slight to be worthy of more than a passing notice, " It may be here noted that the disks in this deposit had never been used.

In the year 1860 a similar deposit of hornstone disks was discovered in this vicinity, in the town of Frederickville, in Schuyler County, on the west side of the Illinois River. This locality was a favorite abiding-place of the Indians, and the center of a dense population. Relics of their works are still found in abundance throughout this region. A small ravine near the foot of a bluff, one day, after a heavy rain, caved in on one side, and the displacement of a large quantity of earth in consequence exposed to view a few strange-looking flints. They had been buried about 5 feet below the surface of the hillside, laid together on edge, side by side in long rows, forming a single layer of unknown extent. The discovery of such novel objects attracted some of the villagers to the place, who dug out about thirty-five hundred of the unique implements, and, their curiosity satisfied, abandoned the work without reaching the limits of the deposit. From diligent inquiries of persons who were present at the time, I learned that the flints had apparently been placed in an excavation made for the purpose 'at a point of the bluff above the highest water-level, and about two hundred yards from the river-bank. No traces of fire above or below were seen, and no peculiar arrangement of the superincumbent earth was noticed, nor was any mound or other mark of any kind discernible over or about the place to designate their hiding-place. It was several years after this occurrence when, in 1871, I first heard of it. Several visits to the place were rewarded with but a few badly mutilated specimens of the disks which I obtained from the citizens; the rest of the large number had disappeared. At length I found in the possession of Mrs. Charles Farwell (whose husband owns the premises where the deposit was found) ten of the flints, two of which she kindly gave me. The stone of which these disks are made is a dark, glossy hornstone, undistinguishable from the disks of the sacrificial mound in Ohio, and, like that deposit, these Frederickville flints had been buried without having been used.

. . . .

"ECCENTRIC" FLINTS OF OKLAHOMA

Clements, Forrest E., and Reed, Alfred; *American Antiquity,* 5:27–30, 1939.

During the past two years the attention of archaeologists and collectors has been directed toward peculiar types of chipped stone objects purportedly found in Delaware County, Oklahoma. Professional opinion is divided as to the authenticity of these specimens and various stories about them are in circulation. Although the specimens exhibit a large variety of shapes, the general pattern and type of workmanship recalls the so-called "eccentric flints" of British Honduras and Guatemala. For these reasons, it is felt that the facts so far as they are known should be presented.

Typical eccentric flints

Mr. Alfred Reed, co-author of this paper, is especially fitted to speak with authority on the subject for the supposed location of the finds is within a short distance of his home; he has personally interviewed the discoverer and acquired from him about 900 of the specimens. Dr. Clements has also talked with the man who claims to have found the eccentrics (a mixed-blood Indian, Mack Tussinger, who has lived in the locality all his life), and has examined closely about 200 of them.

Tussinger says that in 1926 he came across a low circular mound about four feet high and twenty-five feet in diameter in the second bench on the north side of the Elk River approximately six miles up from its junction with Grand River. This is in the northern part of Delaware County, situated in the northeast corner of the state. He dug a small shaft in the center of the mound and at a depth of four feet struck a cache containing 3,500 of these eccentric flints. They were between the skulls of several burials which were laid with the heads together, the bodies extending out from the center of the mound like spokes from the hub of a wheel. He does not remember how many skulls he found but thinks there were probably half a dozen. He gathered up the flints which were all heaped together in a pile and carried them home where he buried them in several small caches. During the interval from 1926 to 1931, he sold pieces to Dr. Barnard purchased approximately 800 eccentrics, selecting these pieces from groups exhibited to him by Tussinger from time to time. Apparently Tussinger made no effort to sell to anyone else during this period but in 1930–31 he became almost destitute and decided to seek a wider market, as he had more pieces than Dr. Barnard wished to buy. At this time he approached Mr. Reed who though by no means convinced of the authenticity of the specimens believed that they offered a problem worthy of serious consideration. He purchased nearly all of his 900-odd eccentrics direct from Tussinger. Mr. Reed paid from $1.00 to $3.00 for about 600 of his points with an average of $2.25 each including two dozen for which he paid from $8.00 to $10.00 apiece. His remaining 300 points ran from twenty-five to seventy-five cents and the average paid for the 900 eccentrics in the collection was about a dollar and a half each.

From 1931 to 1937, Tussinger gradually disposed of his alleged find to various collectors. Sometime during this period he entered into informal partnership with a man named Robertson who runs a gasoline station on U.S. Highway 66 just across the Oklahoma line in Kansas and not far from Miami, Oklahoma. During the last two or three years Robertson has done most of the peddling and the price has increased until the eccentrics now sell for several dollars each and there is one rumored to have sold for fifty dollars. At the present time Tussinger claims to have no more of the points in his possession and Robertson is supposed to have disposed of all but about 200. As stated above, Mr. Alfred Reed has around 900 in his collection. Dr. Barnard is reported to have about 800 and Mr. Clark Field of Tulsa, Oklahoma, has about 200. This accounts for around 2,100 of the supposed original 3,500 specimens. The remainder seem to have been sold in small lots to tourists along the highway and are no doubt widely scattered.

. . . .

FLINT DISKS

Anonymous; *American Antiquarian,* 13:304, 1891.

Seven thousand two hundred and thirty disks and leaf-shaped implements were recently taken from a mound near Clarke's Fort. Mr. W. K. Moorehead, with a corps of explorers, has been at work on the mounds near this celebrated earth-work, where Squier and Davis formerly found so many interesting relics. The deposit was in an elliptical mound, "No. 22." It is suggested that the shape of the mound was the same as that of the disks and that there was a symbolism in the whole deposit. The only discrepancy in this theory is that the apex of the heaps of disks did not correspond with that of the mound, the ovoid mound having its axis north and south, but that of the heap trended to the west. The Chillicothe Leader has an account of the find. The disks, when taken out, are said to constitute a pile twelve feet long, three feet high and four feet broad, and are reckoned as about half a car-load.

GIANT FLINTS
Anonymous; *American Antiquarian,* 2:48, 1879.

One of the greatest archaeological puzzles in our country is the large flaked flints, usually called leaf-shaped implements. They are from 4 to 9 inches in length, 3 to 5 wide, and about half an inch thick, round at the base, and very obtusely pointed at the opposite extremity, the apex being slightly to one side. They show no signs of use whatever, and are found in masses from a few to many hundreds. Mr. Thomas Thodes, of Akron, Ohio, has lately discovered a cache of these objects about three miles west of that town, under an old tamarack stump, about two feet below the surface, in peat or muck. There were 197 in the nest. The largest is 8-1/2 inches long by 3-1/2 wide; the smallest is about 2-1/2 inches long.

• Sundry Curious Artifacts

STONE YOKES FROM MEXICO AND CENTRAL AMERICA
Lothrop, S. K.; *Man,* 23:97-98, 1923.

Archaeological studies in Mexico and Central America have placed on record certain classes of objects of unusual and definite shape and of wide distribution, the function of which is unknown. Stone yokes form one of the most important and mysterious of such groups.

The stone yoke is shaped like a letter U, and is about two feet in height (Fig. 1). The bevelled outer surface is often carved with elaborate designs, which have been analysed by Strebel, Parry, Holmes, Fewkes, and others. The distribution extends from Salvador across Guatemala, Chiapas, and Oaxaca to the central Mexican plateau, and thence eastward to the Gulf of Mexico. The centre of manufacture was the Totonac region, including the states of Vera Cruz, Puebla, and Tlascala, to which the stone yoke is connected not only by the number of specimens found, but also by the character of the decorative motives. Fragmentary specimens have been found at Copan, Palenque, and other Old Empire Maya cities, from which fact it is evident that the stone yoke was evolved before the abandonment of these cities at the close of the sixth century. A. D. On the east coast of Mexico, in the Totonac region, stone yokes have been found in graves, placed around the bodies of the dead. Such are the general facts now known.

An aura of mystery has surrounded the stone yoke because it has been impossible to identify this object either in the native manuscripts or in the many available examples of sculpture in stone and clay.   In consequence, there has been much speculation as to its function.   The question of how it was used is answered by the figurine shown in Plate H, which was recently purchased by the writer in the city of Guatemala. The exact finding place of this specimen is unknown, but it is said to have come from the Department of Quiche.   This is quite in keeping with the nature of the clay, thin and well fired, and of the peculiar creamy grey colour which characterises some of the pottery of the region named.

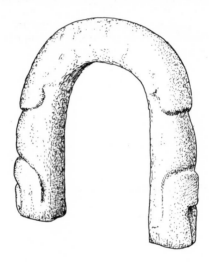

Stone yoke from Motzorongo, Vera Cruz, Mexico

The figure is clad in a breech clout and a heavy sheet-like garment which reaches from the breast to the thighs.   Spiral bandages cover the arms and legs.   This peculiar dress gives ground for the belief that the figure represents a warrior clad in the cotton armour described in all early accounts of the natives, but of which no actual examples remain. The stone yoke is placed around the waist with the open end at the right side of the body.   It exhibits not only the typical outline but the typical cross-section, which resembles a truncated triangle.   Some small object, now broken off and lost, was attached to the yoke at the base of the arched portion.

With the knowledge in mind that the stone yoke was worn around the waist, an examination of Middle American sculpture is singularly barren of representations of this object which can be identified.   It is true that many figures seen on Maya stelae and lintels wear about the waist a heavy projecting belt with numerous heads attached to it.   These suggest the yoke, but not with great exactness.   On several of the sculptured slabs from Santa Lucia Conzumalhualpa, however, stone yokes are certainly represented.   This site lies on the Pacific slope of the Cordil-

leras in Guatemala, not far from the town of Escuintla. The sculptured
slabs to which we refer, some of which are as much as twelve feet high,
characteristically represent a deity to whom an offering of a human head
or heart is made by a man wearing a yoke. An example is shown in Fig.
2. The yokes, it will be observed, exhibit the characteristic bevelled
outer surface and are placed with the broad side up, as is also the case
in Plate H. (Plates omitted.)

From the evidence which has been adduced it is manifest that the
stone yoke was worn around the waist. From the nature of the object
itself it is clear that it served no utilitarian purpose, and the problem
has only been half solved until the purpose and symbolism have been
explained. To this phase, however, we have no contribution to make.
The personal belief of the writer is that the yoke may represent the
underworld, because the outline resembles the Mexican symbol for that
region and also because the yoke is associated with death and sacrifice
in the Santa Lucia sculptures. This, however, is only speculation, and
proof must await the presentation of new facts.

PROBABLE USE OF MEXICAN STONE YOKES
Ekholm, Gordon F.; *American Anthropologist,* 48:593–606, 1946.

The stone yokes of Mexico have always presented a difficult problem.
Their curious though definite shape suggests a specific function and always stimulates the question of how they might have been used. This
paper attempts to answer this question, disregarding for the moment the
other problems involved in the study of stone yokes, such as the symbolism of their carved designs or their distribution and chronological position in Middle American prehistory.

The usual form of the stone yoke is that of the letter U. There are
also a few yokes which are generally oval in shape except for a straight
bar across one end. Those of the first type will be referred to as open
yokes, the second as closed yokes. Cut from diorite, basalt, or other
fine and hard stones, they are often elaborately and beautifully carved,
and are highly prized items in collections of Middle American art objects.
They have been found from as far north as the Mexican State of San Luis
Potosi to as far south as El Salvador and Honduras, but since they are
most common on the Mexican Gulf coast in central and southern Vera
Cruz, they have been loosely though not necessarily correctly identified
with the Totonac. Very few of the perhaps several hundred stone yokes
known in collections have been found in regularly conducted excavations,
so we can gain little assistance in explaining their use from whatever
position or associations they may have had in the ground.

There have been several suggestions for the probable use of stone
yokes, other than the one to be discussed here, but none of them is very
convincing. Since these ideas are generally well known, they will be
mentioned but not discussed in detail. The most commonly suggested
use, which is however without any real foundation, is that they were used

in human sacrifice to put about the neck of the victim to render him im-
mobile and unconscious. Another theory, now widely current, is that
stone yokes were mortuary offerings, "mortuary crowns," made especially to be buried with important persons. This idea is based largely
on the excavation of one grave reported by Genin where an open yoke was
found placed around the skull of the skeleton. Such a find is of course,
interesting, but in my opinion it does not necessarily have any bearing
on the primary use intended for the object. Many things are found in
graves which were not originally intended for burial.

A seemingly much more logical explanation of the use of Middle
American stone yokes, the one to be discussed here, is that they were
worn around the waist in the form of a belt, probably for some ceremonial purpose in connection with the ball game. The idea that stone
yokes were worn about the waist is not original with me; it was first
proposed by Lothrop on the basis of two very straightforward pieces of
evidence which I shall present again and to which I shall make additions.

· · · · · · · · · ·

The best available evidence that stone yokes were worn around the
waist, and to my mind this is incontrovertible, is the remarkable effigy
vessel in the Museum of the American Indian, Heye Foundation, which
was well illustrated by Lothrop. Tracings from his photographs are
shown in Plate 3, a. b. The vessel, fifteen inches in length, portrays
a man reclining on his left elbow, the orifice of the vessel being at the
waist on the right side. Of primary interest to us here is the heavy belt

Stone yokes shown on Mexican figurines

around the waist that has precisely the form of an undecorated open stone
yoke. The ends of the yoke are cut off squarely, and it is quasi-triangu-
lar in cross section, thick at the top and thin at the bottom, a form characteristic of most stone yokes. Underneath the yoke, the individual wears
a sheath-like garment extending from the middle of the chest to as far
down as the knees in back and to the middle of the loin cloth in front. It
will also be noted that what appears to be the end of a sash of some kind
hangs partly over the yoke at the left front side of the figure. The left
arm, from the palm of the hand to a point near the shoulder, is spirally
wrapped with some heavy material, and there are pads or protecting devices on both knees. The feet are shod with what resemble shoes, but
the legs are not wrapped as stated by Lothrop.

· · · · · · · · · ·

PORTO RICAN COLLARS AND ELBOW STONES

Lothrop, R. W., and Lothrop, S. K.; *Man,* 27:185-186, 1927.

Archaeological investigation in Porto Rico has brought to light various objects of stone which, although exhaustively described by various writers, have never been satisfactorily explained. Among these the most perplexing are the so-called collars and elbow stones. The collars, in size and shape not unlike a horse collar, are classified as massive or slender. These types we illustrate in Plate K, b and c. Various skeuomorphic markings on the surface of these stone collars have led Mason and subsequent writers to the belief that their curious shape had its origin in wood. Joyce has established that the prototype of the slender class of collars was a √-shaped wooden section, cut from the trunk and abutting branch of a tree, bent to form a pear-shaped loop, and lashed to retain this shape. The massive collars seem originally to have been made from a single stout staff, curved until the ends met, and bound in that position.

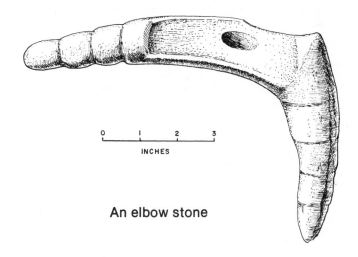

An elbow stone

Elbow stones apparently form part of composite collars made of both wood and stone. The normal type (Fig. 1, b) corresponds in a general way to the shoulder of the slender type of collar, although the decorative details are not always displayed in identical fashion on the collar and elbow stone. Both ends of the elbow stone are often cut by a longitudinal trough encircled by small transverse grooves. The trough, we judge, received the butt of the wooden arch which completed the collar, while the small grooves prevented the lashings from slipping. A hole drilled through the bottom of the trough---in the right hand side of Fig. 1, b---probably socketed a peg to make the juncture more secure.

In Plate K, a, a[1], we illustrate a unique elbow stone. On one arm is carved a boss suggesting the projections seen on the collars in the same plate. At the other end there is an opening, which may well have served for the insertion of a peg.

We have presented the specimens depicted not with the purpose of adding to the already multitudinous theories concerning their use, but to make them available to students. It seems probable that the questions raised by the mysterious products of Porto Rican archaeology will eventually reach solution through interpretation of such aberrant and highly specialised examples rather than through further scrutiny of normal types.

CEDAR COLLARS OF THE NORTH PACIFIC COAST INDIANS
Mason, O. T.; *Science,* 11:831, 1900.

Can any one tell me whether the cedar collars of the North Pacific Coast Indians are made rights and lefts. In Dr. Boas's paper in Report of U. S. National Museum for 1895, on the Kwakiutl Indians there are many examples of the cedar bark collars figured, but it does not appear from the drawings whether they are worn indifferently on the right or left shoulder, that is, whether the ornament is worn on a particular side. The reason for asking is this: The Porto Rican stone collars are rights and lefts. In the National Museum collection of thirty, every one of them is carefully carved to imitate the splice joint shown perfectly in Dr. Boas's examples of cedar bark. In the drama of the expulsion of the Cannibal, acted with so much spirit by these Indians in Chicago, two men led the Cannibal to the fire, each wearing a cedar bark collar. It requires little imagination to transfer this scene to Porto Rico, where stone collars in likeness of those of bark would surround the necks of the captors, one on the right hand, the other one the left, wearing each the decoration outside. I discovered twenty-five years ago that the Porto Rican collars were rights and lefts, also that the overlapping ornament at the side of each stood for the sizing or wrapping of a hoop, but then did not know that Dr. Boas's Kwakuitl Indians were wearing homologous decorations.

A PORCELAIN BATON
Greenman, E. F.; *American Antiquity,* 2:204-205, 1937.

Three years ago I published an account of two objects of porcelain acquired by the Ohio State Museum, in a periodical of that institution known as Museum Echoes (for June and October, 1933). Inasmuch as their origin has not yet been cleared up, I should like to see them again put on display in American Antiquity.

. . . .

It is eleven and three-quarters inches long; the cross section is oval, with diameters of one and one-quarter and one and one-half inches. It is hollow, the hole being also oval in cross section with diameters of about three-eights and five-eights inches. Professor Watts, of the Department of Ceramics of Ohio State University, describes this specimen as follows:

"It is a nearly vitreous earthenware body covered with a light blue cobalt glaze, probably matured with the body at about 1300 degrees centigrade. Made in two parts and pressed together with a clay slip joint."

The surface of the specimen is ridged, or fluted, in relief of about three-sixteenths of an inch. The other specimen is similar in all respects to this one.

Both pieces were found near the village of Garrettsville, Portage County, in northern Ohio. The one illustrated was first described by M. C. Read in Archaeology of Ohio (Western Reserve Historical Society, Tracts 73-84, Vol. III. p. 118). According to Read, it was plowed up in a field "...at a place where several 'Indian relics' had previously been found."

In certain early French records concerning the region of the Great Lakes, there are references to the use of objects apparently similar to these, by the whites and the Indians, in the seventeenth and eighteenth centuries. These objects were called "porcelain sticks," and were used as presents, or as credentials of speakers at important councils.

In two volumes of the Jesuit Relations (Vol. 11, p. 257; and Vol. 40, p. 205), the French word which has been translated into English as "stick," is baston, or the modern baton. But both of these references indicate that the objects described were small enough to be enclosed in the hand or worn in the ear.

The following appears in the record of a council of Cadillac with the Ottawa Indians at Detroit in 1707 (See Michigan Pioneer and Historical Collections, Vol. 33, p. 349): "Monsieur de la Mothe, with three sticks of porcelain, speaks to the Outtavois; this porcelain represents the black robe (a Jesuit), as if it were present at the council...."That the term "porcelain" did not necessarily refer to "shell" in the French of New France is indicated by the use of both terms in an inventory of Cadillac's property at Detroit in 1711, in which there is an item of "1 white shell with two divisions of blue porcelain" (Michigan Pioneer and Historical Collections, Vol. 33, p. 524. The original is not given). Note here that the porcelain is described as blue, which is the color of the two specimens under discussion.

All efforts to find some explanation for these two objects other than that suggested in the above quotations has failed. Two visits to the village of Garretsville failed to discover anyone who knew exactly where they were found, and there is no record of any local pioneer pottery manufactures where such things might have been made. The writer saw a fragment of another specimen in the Paine collection at Springfield, Illinois, a couple of years ago. It was identical with those herein described except for the short diameter of the cross section: about one-quarter of an inch less. It was marked "Ohio," and there is no mention of it in the Paine catalogue. C. B. Moore (Certain Aboriginal Remains of the Northwest Florida Coast, p. 241) describes an object somewhat similar to these from Ohio, taken from a mound in Florida. It was eleven inches long and two and one-half inches in diameter, with a rounded enlargement at both ends. The material was impure kaolin. It was not fluted or grooved, but showed "...traces of decoration in low relief."

....

ANFORETAS RECOVERED IN MAINE

Whittall, James P., II; *Early Sites Research Society, Bulletin,* 5:1-5, 1977.

In July 1971 Norman Bakeman of Castine, Maine was scuba diving in search of old bottles or anything else of value which might have been thrown overboard from a ship. In the Bay of Castine at a depth of about 12 meters he recovered two curious ceramic storage jars. They rested on the mud bottom about 15 meters apart, one partially buried, the other on the surface. After the recovery of the two jars he left the area. Mr. Bakeman puzzled over both the origin and use of the two jars as he had never seen anything like them before. Persons he showed the jars to couldn't shed any light on their origin. Many suggestions were forthcoming from whale oil lamps to small powder kegs. For awhile they were on display at the University of Maine; later, they were packed away and forgotten.

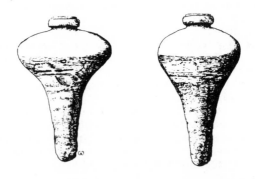

Anforetas recovered off Maine coast

In November 1976 Dr. Barry Fell, President of the Epigraphic Society, gave a lecture at the University of Maine on material covered in his new book America B.C. During the course of the lecture Dr. Fell mentioned the Hinge-Ogam inscription on Monhegan island "Long-ships from Phoenicia; Cargo-lots landing-quay." (1) and he also made reference to the passage quoted above from America B.C. After the talk he was approached by a local archaeologist who told him about "two unusual amphoras" he had seen. Dr. Fell was interested in finding out more on the subject and he requested Dr. Sentiel Rommel, a faculty member at the university and Epigraphic Society member, to track down the present location and owner of the jars. Dr. Rommel was successful in his search. The information he presented to Dr. Fell was relayed on to me. I then contacted Mr. Bakeman, who still had the jars. Then Malcolm Pearson, research photographer for Early Sites, and I went to Maine to make a photographic record of the two jars.

Upon seeing the two jars I recognized them as being identical to an Anforeta recovered in the Iberian Penninsula at Lagos, Portugal. Another similar Anforeta was recovered in Evora, Portugal. Both these jars were classified as Roman Period by Portuguese archaeologists in the 1890's. The probable use of these was storage for wine, oil, or honey.

Maine Anforeta No. 1 measures .314 meters in height and .202 meters at the widest bulge. Anforeta No. 2 measures .33 meters by .18 meters. Anforeta No. 1 has a small hole punched out of one side. Both the Anforetas, though they vary in shape, hold exactly the same amount, 1200 milliliters, equivalent to two Roman sextarius. The clay paste and grit of the Maine artifacts is similar to material in sherds I have recovered in the Iberia Penninsula which date to the Roman Period. Whether these particular jars were made in the Iberian Penninsula or not we do not as yet know. Extensive research has failed at this time to have turned up any more examples of this design. A storage jar somewhat similar to these Anforetas was recovered off the fishing village of Marzamemi in Sicily. The wreck was considered to be an early Byzantine ship and the jar is considered part of the ship's gear and is called a "wine thief." It is quite possible that the Anforeta found in Lagos, Portugal was an import as that seaport has been a major port of call on the Algarve coast since the time of the Phoenicians.

There are no markings on the Maine Anforetas. However, Anforeta No. 1 has a wear mark just under the main body of the vessel which I feel was made by a metal ring in which the vessel was stored on a ship. The wear was caused by the motion of the ship at sea. Associated with the worn area is some rust staining. The other Anforeta hasn't any such wear.

A REPORT ON PERFORATED SHERDS FROM CENTRAL NEVADA.....

Magee, Molly; *American Antiquity*, 32:226-227, 1967.

Unlike the perforated sherds from riverine culture sites on the Upper Mississippi in northwestern Indiana, reported by Charles H. Faulkner (1965) in the July issue of American Antiquity, perforations do not occur in the vessel base of any of the central Nevada sherds which have been found to date. The holes are scattered below the rim and throughout the body. The perforations are drilled from the exterior of the vessel after firing. The holes are tapered. Exterior measurement is 8 mm. in diameter, and interior measurement is 5 mm. in diameter. The holes are fairly uniform in size.

None of the perforated sherds recovered from central Nevada shows evidence of having come from a vessel which had been used for cooking. These sherds are not fire blackened. They contain no charred food remains.

While the use of perforated earthenware vessels as colanders may be feasible in the riverine cultures to which Faulkner refers, such use seems singularly farfetched at the specific central Nevada sites where such sherds have been found. Moreover, even if perforated sherds were to be discovered near flowing springs and perennial creeks at some later date, a culture such as the Plateau Shoshone, with a basket weaving tradition going back for centuries, would certainly be straining its food the hard way if it used drilled earthenware pots instead of loosely-woven willowware baskets for the purpose.

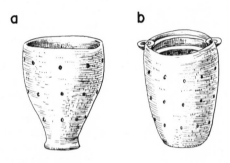

Perforated vessels from Nevada

Upon consideration of the known diet of historic and prehistoric Plateau-Shoshone for determining possible uses of perforated earthenware vessels, the Shoshones' predilection for eating small rodents springs to mind.

Among the handful of animals known to have been domesticated by neolithic societies in the North and South Americas was a small rodent, the guinea pig. I do not suggest anything so exotic as the importation of domesticated guinea pigs into central Nevada, although they did spread from the Inca Empire to many parts of the world after the Spanish Conquest. Nevertheless, the snaring of indigenous rodents, such as chipmunks and packrats, both of which abound in the jumper-pinyon belt of central Nevada, was known historically among local Shoshones, either for pets or food, or possibly for a combination of the two (personal communications too numerous to cite).

The capture of such small rodents immediately poses the question: how were they domiciled in captivity?

Cages constructed of wood solid enough to resist the sharp teeth of these resourceful little animals would have been too cumbersome to carry around between the transitory summer camps of the high canyons.

No willow basket would have held a chipmunk or packrat overnight. But another receptacle, hallowed by tradition, suggests itself: the perforated earthenware pot called a <u>dolia</u> and used by the Romans to house domesticated dormice.

John Howland Rowe's challenging study in the January issue of <u>American Antiquity</u>, "Diffusionism and Archaeology" states the case for comparative studies as opposed to claims of diffusive distribution better than I could. But along similar lines, I would propose that the dormouse confronted the Romans with the same sort of problem with which the chipmunk and packrat confronted the Plateau Shoshone, and that they both proceded independently to solve it. I would welcome any information on how the Incas housed their guinea pigs, which might throw additional light on the domiciling of small rodents.

The Roman <u>dolia</u> and the Shoshonean perforated vessel present striking similarities. These similarities encourage speculation that the perforated vessel described by Faulkner as a colander may have been used to house either a small animal or fish, even if the holes were drilled only in the bottom and not on the sides of the vessel.

ON THE DISCOIDAL STONES OF THE INDIAN MOUNDS
Squier, E. G.; *American Journal of Science,* 2:2:216–218, 1846.

In the paper contributed, by Dr. Morton, to the last number of the American Journal of Science, reference is made to certain "discoidal stones," some of which are figured. Exact counterparts of these stones, are in the possession of Dr. Hildreth of Marietta; in fact, they occur in considerable numbers, all over Ohio, and may be found in the cabinets of almost every collector of aboriginal remains. After extensive exploration, I have reason to think it extremely doubtful whether discs of this description were ever found in the mounds, except in cases when they were deposited by the modern (existing) race of Indians. The stones met with in a mound near Chillicothe, to which Dr. Morton alludes, are very unlike those figured in his paper, as they are of horn-stone, rudely blocked out, while the others mentioned, are of great symmetry and manifestly the result of much labor.

Nor is there, apparently, much mystery as to the use made of these stones. I am assured, by Rev. Mr. Finley, "the Syandot Chief," (distinguished for his zealous efforts in christianizing the Indian tribes of Ohio,) that among the tribes with which he was acquainted, stones of this description were much used in a popular game, somewhat resembling our game of "ten pins." A smooth and well packed area of earth was selected, at one extremity of which a small wooden pin was stuck, while the player stationed himself at the other. The point of the game consisted in striking the pin oftenest in a given number of trials. The form of the stones suggests the manner in which they were held and thrown, or, rather, rolled. The concave sides received the thumb and second finger, the forefinger clasping the periphery.

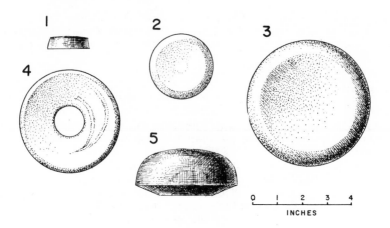

Discoidal stones

Adair, in his account of the Indians along the gulf, gives a minute, and graphic account of a game, somewhat analogous to that described by Mr. Finley, in which stones of this description were used. He says: ---"The warriors have another favorite game, called Chungke; which, with propriety of language, may be called "Running hard labor." They have near their state house, a square piece of ground well cleared, and fine sand is carefully strewn over it, when requisite, to promote a swifter motion to what they throw along the surface. Only one or two on a side, play at this ancient game. They have a stone about two fingers broad at the edge and two spans round; each party has a pole about eight feet long, smooth and tapering at each end, the points flat. They set off abreast of each other, at six yards from the edge of the play ground; then one of them hurls the stone on its edge, in as direct a line as he can, a considerable distance towards the middle of the other end of the square: when they have run a few yards, each darts his pole, anointed with bear's grease, with a proper force, as near as he can guess, in proportion to the motion of the stone, that the end may lie close to the same---when this is the case, the person counts two of the game, and in proportion to the nearness of the poles to the mark, one is counted, unless, by measurement, both are found to be an equal distance from the stone. In this manner the players will keep moving most of the day, at half speed, under the violent heat of the sun, staking their silver ornaments, their nose, finger and ear-rings, their breast, arm and wrist plates, and all their wearing apparel, except that which barely covers their middle. All the American Indians are much addicted to this game, which appears to be a task of stupid drudgery; it seems, however, to be of early origin, when their forefathers used diversions as simple as their manners. The hurling stones, they use at present, were, from time immemorial, rubbed smooth on the rocks, and with prodigious labor; they are kept with the strictest religious care, from one generation to another, and are exempt from being buried with the dead. They belong to the town where they are used and are carefully preserved. "---<u>Adair</u>, p. 402.

Dr. Morton is, I think, mistaken in supposing the occurrence of these stones to be circumscribed. They certainly occur throughout the west, as do also, the spheroidal stones mentioned, which, it is quite evident, were used for similar purposes.

It will be seen, from the above, that Dr. Blanding was right in his suggestion, that these stones were used in the games of the aborigines.

Chunky stones from Tennessee

A PRELIMINARY REPORT ON THE SO-CALLED "BANNER-STONES"

Baer, John Leonard; *American Anthropologist,* 23:445–459, 1921.

For the past half century American archaeologists have been amazed at the beauty and puzzled over the use of certain problematical forms left by primitive men about their camp sites and buried with their dead in eastern North America. From Ontario to Florida, from Maine to the Mississippi Valley, have been found hundreds of beautifully wrought and highly polished pierced objects of stone somewhat resembling the drilled stone axes of the Old World. Here, however, these artifacts are usually of too soft a material and of too delicate workmanship to be weapons, tools, or implements of practical use. The carefully selected material, the elegant and symmetrical shape, and the high polish of these relics have led many to believe that their use was of a ceremonial nature.

Many fanciful names such as bannerstones, ceremonial axes, maces, butterfly stones, thunder-bird emblems, totems, whale-tail emblems, totems, whale-tail emblems, baton or sceptre heads, equipoise stones, and mesh gauges, have been applied to these mysterious relics. The name bannerstone, applied by Dr. C. C. Abbott, is the one most generally accepted because of its priority and because of the fact that most of the stones seem to have been shaped and drilled for mounting upon handles so as to be carried during ceremonies as standards or banners.

In support of this name, is the discovery of a cache of three bannerstones all mounted upon engraved stone handles about a foot in length. They were plowed up in a field near Knap of Reeds, Granville Co., N. C., in the year 1908. One of them (fig. 74, a) has been on exhibition in the North Carolina historical collection at Raleigh, N. C., for a number of years and was discovered by Mr. W. E. Myer who kindly brought the knowledge to the writer's attention. He described this interesting find as follows:

There is one banner stone mounted on a stone staff... in the above collection. The material of both the banner stone and staff is a micaceous shale. The material is coarser in the banner stone than in staff. Staff about 7/8 inch in diameter at largest point, a to b about 4-1/2 inches, e to d about 12 inches. The record attached to this banner stone is: "Three banner stones, all handles complete, plowed up in one spot, in a field on the farm of Mrs. Mary P. Waller, near Knap of Reeds, Granville Co., N. C. Not far away in [is?] Indian burial mound. Lent by Mrs. Waller." The staff fits the hole in banner stone exactly. It extends to x in the hole. In fact, the staff and hole appear to have been made to fit perfectly by means of turning the staff in the hole and thus grinding to a more perfect fit. This grinding has some slightly modern appearance, as if people handling it had turned it somewhat in the hole. But the modern grinding is not sufficient to hide evidences of the old aboriginal grinding.

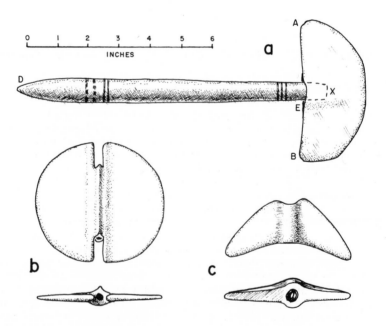

Bannerstones from: (a) North Carolina; (b) Pennsylvania; and (c) Florida. Drawn half size

The above record has been substantiated in letters from Mrs. Mary P. Waller and Col. Fred A. Olds. Mrs. Waller states: "These banners were plowed up together. The handles were in two, but one handle was broken and apart from the head. One of the perfect stones and the broken one have been lost." Col. Olds adds to the above information, "the handle is well made and slightly ornamented with rings." The writer is indebted to him for a photograph of the specimen from which the illustration was drawn. This find strikes the writer as one of the most important bearing upon the use of the bannerstone.

While the material used for making bannerstones was usually slate, ribbon or colored slate preferred, many other materials were used such as shell, steatite, shale, serpentine, diabase, granite, quartzite, jasper, crystallized quartz, rose quartz, or any other stone which was capable of taking on a high polish and reflecting brilliant or pleasing colors. Mr. Clarence B. Moore has in his remarkable collection at the Academy of Natural Sciences, Philadelphia, a beautiful bipennate specimen made of shell (Strombus gigas) which was found in Volusia Co., Florida. In the same collection is a butterfly-shaped piece made of crystallized quartz, found near Red River. One wing has been broken off near the perforation and the fractured surface carefully polished, showing the esteem with which even broken bannerstones were regarded. A similar unfinished specimen of crystallized quartz from Louisiana is in the collection of the U. S. National Museum. One wing of it was broken in the making and the hole therefore, was never drilled.

The aboriginal artisan showed great skill in selecting the stone best suited for his particular purpose. As stated above, a large percentage of bannerstones was made of slate, green or banded being preferred to the common gray variety. In choosing ribbon slate, the bannerstone maker showed excellent taste in securing, when possible, blocks in which the bands ran parallel with the cleavage. When these blocks were pecked into shape and polished, the ribbons crossing the gracefully curved wings at different angles made beautifully matched patterns. In addition to its pleasing effect, the east with which it could be worked was undoubtedly a factor in the choice of slate. While water-worn pebbles were made use of when available, slate, serpentine, and diabase were to the writer's knowledge quarried particularly for the manufacture of bannerstones. Blocks of slate were split into the required shape for transportation to the camp site where they were fashioned with flint hammer stones, scrapers, drills, and polishing stones into beautiful works of art.

. . . .

The mystery surrounding the origin, significance, and use of these so-called bannerstones makes their study all the more interesting. No record has appeared of early explorers having seen such objects among the Indians of post-Columbian times. No reference to prehistoric artifacts which can be identified as bannerstones has been discovered in Indian cosmology, mythology, or folklore. Thus a number of theories have arisen as to the possible use of these problematical forms. While a few still claim that they were specialized implements, most archaeologists agree that they must have been for ceremonial purposes. Many of the forms, and especially those made of fragile material such as steatite, slate, shell, etc., would not have served for any rough or even mechanical use. Neither would mere implements have been so symmetrically wrought or so highly polished. The specimen with a stone handle described at the beginning of this article shows no evidences of having been used as a weapon. Nor have the wings of this or any other banner-stone within the writer's knowledge been reduced to cutting edges. The polished handle with incised rings surely places this specimen in the ceremonial class. The fact that a bannerstone as crude as this one should have been used for ceremonial purposes should bespeak a high and important place in religious festivals for the more beautiful and more delicately wrought specimens. Space does not permit entering into the numerous theories as to the origin and significance of the bannerstone. Until more material is available, more argument would be mere speculation, but whatever the various types of bannerstones may have symbolized, it is quite evident that they were to be mounted upon handles for ceremonial use.

THE COGGED STONES OF SOUTHERN CALIFORNIA
Eberhart, Hal; *American Antiquity,* 26:361-370, 1961.

Abstract. Cogged stones are one of the few classes of artifacts which are limited in occurrence to the "middle" period in southern California's prehistory. They are stone discs, 6-1/2 inches or less in diameter, characterized by grooves or indentations in the edge. On the basis of the nature of the latter and of the presence or absence of perforation they are described in four types. Some of the variations may have historical significance, but this cannot be proven with the data at hand. Few specimens have been excavated under controlled conditions. The distribution is virtually limited to the coastal drainage south of Ventura County and appears to center along the Santa Ana River Valley. According to the interpretation of coastal chronology employed, cogged stones were made during the period 6000-3500 B.C. Their use is unknown, but the absence of any pattern of wear and the conjunctions of certain of the specimens suggest that they served some ritual function.

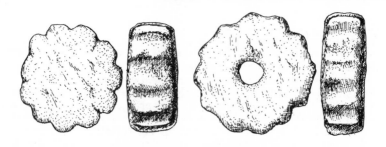

California cogged stones

PREHISTORIC ROCK BASINS IN THE SIERRA NEVADA OF CALIFORNIA

Stewart, George W.; *American Anthropologist,* 31:419–430, 1929.

Among the many unsolved riddles that have been handed down by the early inhabitants of this continent to the present occupants is one which, so far as known, is confined to a single county of California, in fact, to a small section of the Sierra Nevada in and adjacent to Sequoia National Park.

In that region there occur numerous smoothly rounded basins artfully hollowed out of the solid granite, the work of a prehistoric race of men of whom the present Indians know nothing. These cavities measure as a rule from four to five feet in diameter and from one to two feet in depth, and are shaped like huge wash bowls with smoothly curving sides and bottoms. To local residents they have been known for many years. But no critical examination of them has been made hitherto. At first they were thought to have been worn by the action of running water, and reports of the occurrence of such basins in locations where streams cannot have existed were given but scant credence.

The basins in question are found in groups at altitudes ranging from 4,000 to 9,000 feet above sea level, and scattered over an area about 35 miles long from northwest to southeast in that part of the Sierra Nevada in Tulare county which is drained by the Kaweah and Tule rivers (see accompanying map). (Map omitted.)

In the summer of 1925, while camping at Redwood meadow with a party under the leadership of Mr. Stephen T. Mather, Director of the National Park Service, the author was invited by Mr. Mather to inspect some of these mysterious basins which are excavated in the tops of small knobs of granite scattered among the sequoias, pines, and firs adjoining the meadow. The knobs consist of essentially unfractured, massive granite and measure from five to fifteen feet in height and from twenty to thirty feet in major diameter. The basins are almost perfectly circular in outline, and smoothly concave. In a general way they resemble the well known mortar holes in which the Indians grind acorns and seeds, but they are many times larger and more smoothly finished.

The granite knobs, being free from joints, are exfoliating in the manner characteristic of massive granite throughout the Sierra Nevada, and consequently have each of them two or three concentric scales or shells that envelope the main mass, curving around it like the layers of an onion. These shells are from a fraction of an inch to three or four inches in thickness, and the basins are sunk through them into the massive granite beneath. The smooth curvature of the basins is, however, scarcely marred by the partings.

All the basins were found deeply filled with a litter of twigs, leaves, and fragments of bark from the neighboring trees. Excavation of several of the basins revealed underneath this litter some bits of charcoal and ashes, some humic earth, comminuted granite and, at the bottom, a deposit of fine-grained, cream-colored material five or six inches deep, which according to analyses made by Dr. C. S. Ross, mineralogist of the U.S. Geological Survey, consists of volcanic ash (rhyolite). Throughout the litter, except at the bottom, were occasional fragments of granite derived from the sides of the basins.

In one basin was found an angular block of granite about twenty inches long and twelve to fifteen inches thick, that showed no evidence of abrasion. In several other basins were small blocks of granite six to eight inches long and four or five inches thick that exhibited slight evidence of wear; and on one of the larger knobs, near a group of basins, were two ordinary mortar holes and beside them several small stones which appeared to have been used for pestles. A growing fir tree seventeen years old was taken from one of the basins.

It was apparent from the outset that the basins are of artificial, not natural, origin, and this fact was verified by Mr. F. E. Matthes of the Geological Survey, who assisted in the excavating of the basins. According to him there are in the Sierra Nevada two types of natural rock basins with which those here discussed might possibly be confounded, namely, the familiar pot-holes that are worn in stream beds by rotating cobbles, and the less well known but common weather pits that are produced in bare surfaces of granite by localized disintegration and the solvent action of standing water. However, the basins in question are readily distinguished from both pot-holes and weather pits by the wonderful regularity and perfection of their shapes. Pot-holes, being literally bored by rotating cobbles, tend to assume cylindrical forms and sometimes are broader at the base than at the top, but seldom shaped like wash bowls; and weather pits expand as a rule laterally more rapidly than downward, and therefore tend to acquire somewhat irregular outlines and flat bottoms.

Measurements were made of two of the larger masses of granite and of the basins sunk therein, and diagrams were prepared by Mr. Matthes showing the dimensions. Figure 1 represents the ground plan of one of these rock masses and the relative positions of the basins excavated in its surface, and figure 2 is a cross-section of another granite mass, showing several shells detached, or becoming detached, by the process of exfoliation, and a basin sunk through them into the solid rock underneath.

In the Giant Forest, near the rangers' headquarters in the Sequoia National Park, is a group of twenty basins, from three and a half to six

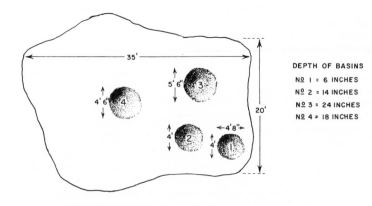

DEPTH OF BASINS

NO 1 = 6 INCHES
NO 2 = 14 INCHES
NO 3 = 24 INCHES
NO 4 = 18 INCHES

Ground plan of some California rock basins

feet in diameter but not so deep as those at Redwood meadow. They
occupy a space about sixty feet square on a long sloping surface of bare
granite.
. . . .

At the lower end of Crescent meadow in the Giant Forest, and also
on the South fork of the Kaweah river at an altitude of about 4,000 feet,
are basins which have not been measured.

A small group of basins with ordinary mortar holes associated with
them occur, further, on a rock platform near Dorst creek, five miles
northwest of the Giant Forest, and a similar group occurs on a ridge between Eshom and Pierce valleys, ten miles northwest of the Giant Forest. On a high granite rock near Oriole lake are five basins reported
to be five feet deep and only two and a half feet in diameter. In a mass
of granite near Atwells mill are two basins, of which one, measured by
Rodney S. Ellsworth, is over six feet across at the top and four feet
deep, circular in outline, tolerably perfect in form, with smoothly
curving sides. The other basin is smaller and less perfectly shaped.

Near Salt creek, a mile from the west boundary of Sequoia National
Park, are three large basins and several smaller ones, and on the high
ridge between the South fork and the Mineral King fork of the Kaweah,
a mile east from the above small group, are said to be seven "stupendous mortars" five to seven feet deep and averaging three feet in diameter. Two basins on a granite surface near-by, and one situated half a
mile to the east, are said to be larger than any herein described. These
basins appear to have the shape of a deep vase rather than that of a bowl.

The late Orlando Barton mentioned the existence of a group of eleven
basins situated about three miles southeast from the last described, at
an altitude of 9,000 feet, on the top of a bold landmark known as Homer's
Nose. One "large mortar" at this place he reported to be in an unfinished state, the rock having been removed from it to a depth of only about
one and a half inches. The periphery of the excavation, as far as completed, he described as the segment of a circle three feet in diameter.
The bottom of the hole he stated to be quite rough, as if the work had
been done with a chisel, but the sides just below the rim were smooth.

Groups of basins occur also at several places in the watershed of
Tule river, namely on the divide west of the Middle fork, on a high block
of granite, at an elevation of 5,800 feet; on Black mountain, south of
Camp Nelson, at an elevation of 6,500 feet; in Balch Park; and a short
distance to the south thereof. These groups are similar to those already
described, but their contents have not been examined.

Thus far nothing definite is known of the use that the Indians made
of these basins. It has been suggested by different persons that they
may have been used for grinding gold-bearing quartz, for tanning hides,
for sweat-houses, for roasting seeds or meat, for baking pottery, and
for storing supplies.

Debris from the bottom of some of the basins has been "panned out"
without showing any color of gold, and as most of the basins are situated
at great distances from quartz veins, none of which bear evidence of
having been anciently worked, and as no fragments of quartz have been
found in or near any of the basins examined, there appears to be no
support for the supposition that the basins were used for the extraction
of gold.

Indians made buckskin, and cured pelts without removing the fur, but it is not known that they made leather by immersing hides in vats with tannin; nor are the interiors of the bowls stained, as would be the case if tannin had been used, particularly the red sap of the sequoia, which carries a high tannin content. Therefore, the theory that the basins were used for tanning vats does not appear well founded.

If utilized for baking bread or roasting seeds, nuts, or meat, the basins were large enough and sufficient in number to serve a great multitude; but no bones or charred pieces of bones have been found in or about them.

That they were made expressly for sweat-houses seems quite improbable, for a serviceable sweat-house can be constructed with much less labor, and few if any of the basins are located near streams or bodies of water suitable for bathing. Had they been used for sweat-houses, or for the baking of pottery, small scales of granite would have become detached from the sides and bottoms, leaving them rough and discolored, whereas the interiors are remarkably smooth.

If used for storing acorns, seeds, flour, or other articles of food, the dampness would have impaired the quality of the contents or would have utterly ruined them; and satisfactory receptacles for storage could have been constructed with less trouble.

When the basins were first examined it was supposed that their excavation was begun by building fires on the granite and by throwing water on the heated surface, so as to cause it to fracture and scale off. If so, they must have been completed by other means, for the sides and bottoms of those finished are very smooth. They might have been made by pounding or rubbing with blocks of rock. Perhaps the stones shown in plate 28, which exhibit wear, were used for this purpose. The rough interiors of the unfinished basins observed by the writer in the Giant Forest and by Mr. Barton on the promontory known as Homer's Nose, however, lead to the belief that excavation was effected in part by some method similar to chiseling, but no implements have been found which could have been so used.

The basins in the southern groups, it would appear from the reports, are much deeper than those which have been measured further north. The question, therefore, suggests itself: Do the increased size and depth of the southern basins indicate that the people who made them came from the southeast or east, and that they had occupied the southern portion of the area described for a longer period than the northern?

All the basins are situated at considerable altitudes, the majority of them in the zone in which the forests of Sequoia Gigantea occur. Is it merely a coincidence that these basins occur only in the Sierra Nevada where the sequoias flourish in greatest numbers? Was the purpose for which they were made connected, possibly, in any way with the proximity of the sequoias?

The deposits of volcanic ash found at the bottom of the basins at Redwood meadow and in some of those in the Giant Forest were notably undisturbed, and unmixed, or only slightly mixed, with other materials.

There was, moreover, no other loose material under the layer of ash. Evidently, then, the basins were empty and clean when the volcanic shower fell, and this would show that they had been used only a short time before the eruption took place. Furthermore, the fact that this material has not been removed is proof that the people have never returned to the mountains, though they must have lived there for a long period. It may be reasonably presumed, however, that a heavy fall of suffocating volcanic dust would have driven the inhabitants of the region in haste from their homes.

From which volcanoes the ash may be derived is as yet uncertain. The volcanic cones nearest to Redwood meadow are those situated in the basin of Golden Trout creek, east of the Kern River canyon. They lie about 22 miles to the southeast. These cones have in the past discharged large flows of lava, but volcanoes of this type are explosive at times, and it is not improbable, therefore, that they have emitted great volumes of ash, the finer particles of which were carried to great distances by the wind. As the winds in this part of the Sierra Nevada blow frequently from the south or southeast, the ash from these volcanoes would naturally have been carried in the direction of Redwood meadow and other portions of Sequoia National Park.

As yet no information is at hand that permits us to answer the questions which naturally arise: Who were the remarkable people that excavated the basins? For what purpose did they make them? At what date did the volcanic eruption take place which put these people to flight? Whither did they go? Who are their descendants?

SOME RELICS OF THE INDIANS OF VERMONT
Perkins, George H.; *American Naturalist,* 5:11-17, 1871.

Fig. 6 seems to be a badge of office, amulet, or something of the sort. It is made of a very pretty breccia composed of light and dark

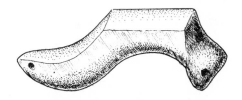

material. It is finely wrought and very smooth, though not polished. The upper side is worked to a sharp edge, from which the sides round outwards towards the rectangular base, which latter has a hole at each end running obliquely through the ends. The length of the relic is 4.5 inches and the height nearly 2 inches. This was found about a mile north of Burlington, Vt. All these articles, except Fig. 2, are in the Museum of the University of Vermont. Besides such remains other traces of the Indian tribes are seen in the hieroglyphics. At Bellows Falls two rocks were found many years ago on which were rudely traced heads, a large group on one and a single head on the other. Some of these had rays coming from the top. Near Brattleborough, by the side of the river, a large rock was found which was covered with tracings of animals, as snakes, birds, etc., in all, ten figures, some not recognizable as representing any animal.

Such are some of the works which tell us of the former occupants of Vermont. (pp. 16-17)

POTENTIAL INTERPRETATIONS OF "STONE GORGET" FUNCTION
Curren, Cailup B,. Jr.; *Antiquity,* 42:97–101, 1977.

Certain artifacts, which are relatively flat, variously shaped, ground, and polished slate, limestone, greenstone, lematite, or steatite, many times with one or two holes drilled through their breadth, have had a variety of labels attached to them: "stone gorgets," "bannerstones," "atlatl weights," and "forearm bowguards." Some were found in burial associations which seemed to indicate each of these labels at one time or another. However, archaeologists in general are still puzzled today by these objects of prehistoric Indian design. Morphological considerations, however, may indicate that these objects were ceramic tools.

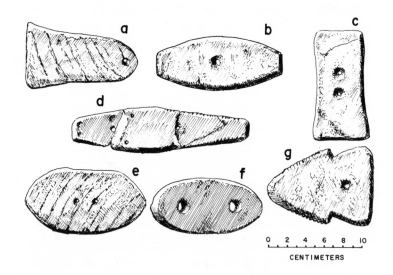

Stone gorgets from eastern U.S.: (a, e) Adena gorgets; (b, c, f) Woodland period gorgets; and (d, e) Tennessee gorgets from Woodland period.

THE STONE IMAGES AND VATS OF CENTRAL CELEBES
Raven, H. C.; *Natural History*, 26:272-282, 1926.

The first stone vats I found in Besoa were near the image "Tadoe Lakoe" where there were four or five together. The most interesting one was cracked and had more or less recently been turned on its side. It was of average size, about five feet in diameter by six in height, but its peculiar feature was a concave shelf about eight or ten inches wide inside the vat a few inches from the upper rim, as shown in the accompanying photograph and diagram. Except for this shelf the inside of the vat was perfectly smooth and well worked, the outside somewhat weathered and less smooth on that account. The bottom of the vat outside was flat, with the edge bevelled off hexagonally. The vats in nearly every case were encircled by consecutive raised rings, and it is possible that in the few cases where these were lacking they had been weathered off, as all were in low relief.

Across the plain nearly five miles from Boeleli were nineteen more stone vats of various sizes, the largest one standing about seven feet above the ground and measuring more than that in diameter. I dug under the lower edge of this and made certain that it too was bevelled hexagonally below. On this vat, the only one having any ornamentation other than the raised rings, was a series of faces resembling those of the statues and executed in relief around the upper third of the vat. Each of the faces was separated from its neighbor by a shallow vertical groove and the series bounded below by another groove encircling the whole vat, clearly seen in the photograph. All the vats that still remained upright were filled with mud and water in which there was a dense growth of sedge. I emptied some of these but found only mud and soft earth except in one in which there were in addition wood ashes and fragments of a clay pot. The simplest cover, made for one of the small vats, was smooth and flat below, evenly convex above but somewhat wheathered, with a thin edge all around. Near-by was a squat, barrel-like vat much less in diameter at the top than through the middle, which if fitted with this convex cover would have appeared nearly spherical or at least domelike in side view. The three remaining covers were of about the same size, huge stone discs more than six feet in diameter and seven or eight inches in thickness, bevelled so that the diameter above was slightly more than that below. The simplest of these was decorated in the center with a nicely hewn knob more than a foot in diameter and six inches high. Another cover was carved with images of three large monkeys and one small monkey hewn in a row across the middle. The most elaborate cover was also decorated with images of these black monkeys peculiar to Celebes. The figures were well modeled, arranged symmetrically around the periphery, and in the center was a raised circular boss, flattened on top.

In the nine years since I left Celebes I have occasionally inquired among my friends and colleagues regarding these stone objects. All supposed them to be well known but none could tell by whom they were made, when, or for what purpose. Recently I have searched through much of the literature on the archaeology of the Oriental-Indo-Malay-Pacific region in an effort to find out, if possible, to what culture they belong. I am now able to compare them with somewhat similar stone objects in various other localities.

The literature reveals the fact that some of the stone objects shown here were briefly described in 1908 by Mr. J. Th. E. Kiliaan, an official of the Netherlands East Indian Government.   Later the same year another brief notice was published by the Reverend Dr. Albert C. Kruyt, who better understood the inhabitants of the country and on that account was able to learn more from them and to correct certain statements made by the original discoverer of the stones as well as to add new facts. Doctor Kruyt also reports three fallen images from Besoa in the vicinity of the vats with the covers described above, and in addition, a mortar at Sigi in the Paloe valley.   In a more recent publication he mentions another image at Gintoe in the district of Bada.   This image, however, is buried up to its neck in the earth.

The only general work, so far as I know, that treats of East Indian archaeology earlier than the Islamic, Buddist and Hindoo cultures, is that of W. J. Perry, 1918, on The Megalithic Culture of Indonesia.   In this book the attempt is made to show that the stone objects of Central Celebes are part of an early culture that was spread from Burma to Nias, Borneo, Celebes, Sumbawa, Flores, Sumba, Timor, Aru, "Seran" (Ceram), and adjacent small islands as well as Formosa, by "stone-using immigrants" who imposed this culture upon the indigenous peoples of "Indonesia"; also that these stone-using immigrants, who were in search of gold and other wealth, introduced many other customs, among them terraced irrigation, metal-working and rice-growing.   He states further: "Finally, it must be remembered that the existence of megalithic monuments, terraced irrigation, mining sites, the sun-cult, 'children of the sun,' and other elements of the culture introduced by stone-using immigrants has been recorded in all inhabited regions of the earth."   Notwithstanding this implication of relationship, the vats and images of Celebes contrast so strikingly in shape and other characters with stone objects in other parts of the Indo-Malayan region that I cannot believe that they belong to the same culture.

· · · · · · · · · ·

A MINOAN PUZZLE
Graham, J. Walter; *Archaeology,* 26:101-105, 1973.

During the past fifty years the French excavators at the Minoan site of Mallia have been turning up a kind of object unmatched anywhere else in Bronze Age Crete.   Found in the ruins of the great palace, and in houses and small shrines as well as other buildings, these enigmatic objects have been noncommittally called auges or "troughs" by their excavators.   But their real significance and function have never been determined despite the fact that, all told, some forty of them have been uncovered to date.

These auges are made from a common local sandstone and are rather roughly finished.   They measure, with few exceptions, from two to three feet in length, from one to one and a half feet in width, and from six inches to a foot and a half in thickness.   Sunk into the upper surface of each is a pair of holes, more or less equal in size and roughly circular or rectangular in form. These depressions are accompanied in seven instances by two smaller holes, square or oblong, one at each end of the auge. The specimen from room xxvi of the great palace is a representative example: the two smaller holes measure about two to three inches in length, a little over one inch wide and some two inches deep; the larger holes measure about six inches square and are two to three inches deep.

A representative auge

Many of these blocks were found in their original position. The one in room xxv 2 of the palace is typically situated: it is built into a curving wall of undressed stones surrounding a closet-like space in the northwest corner of the room and appears to form a kind of threshold to this closet's only entrance. When excavated, the interior of this closet space was literally crammed with pottery---cups, saucers, amphoras and three-legged cooking pots. Contents of this nature are reported for only one other such closet.

Two rooms nearby are likewise constructed of undressed stones and have in or near one corner a closet-like space with an auge forming the threshold. These rooms, xxvi and xxvii 6, together with xxv 2, provide some clue to the use the auges served because the quarter of the palace in which they all occur was most likely a service quarter, where food was prepared for the banquets in a great hall on the second floor, just north of the central court---that is, over rooms ix 1-2.

. . . .

OUT-OF-PLACE METALLIC ARTIFACTS

Almost from the time of the first American settlers, people have been discovering old coins in unlikely places. Roman coins, especially, have turned up in farmers' fields, on beaches, and elsewhere across the country. It seems that the Romans and other pre-Columbian peoples either strayed far beyond the Gates of Hercules or a lot of numismatists had holes in their pockets. The many discoveries of ancient coins are closely related to the many seemingly ancient inscriptions found in the Americas. (See Chapter 3.) Pre-Columbian explorations seem to have ranged far and wide.

Items manufactured from iron have on occasion been dug from American Indian mounds. To most archeologists, these artifacts must be "intrusive;" that is, introduced long after the demise of the Moundbuilders and following the advent of the white man and his blacksmiths. Undoubtedly, some iron artifacts are intrusive, but two other views are possible: (1) iron-using explorers landed in America before or during the hey-day of the Moundbuilders; and (2) some American aborigines were more sophisticated technically than generally allowed. The latter line of thought leads directly to the next subsection: High Technology Artifacts.

• Ancient Coins

AN ANCIENT ROMAN COIN FOUND IN ILLINOIS
Anonymous; *Scientific American,* 46:382, 1882.

A farmer in Cass county, Ill., picked up on his farm a curious bronze coin, which Dr. J. F. Snyder sent to Prof. F. F. Hilder, of St. Louis, who writes about it as follows to the Kansas City Review:

Upon examination I identified it as a coin of Antiochus IV., surnamed Epiphanes, one of the kings of Syria, of the family of the Seleucidae, who reigned from 175 B.C. to 164 B.C., and who is mentioned in the Bible (first book of Maccabees, chapter 1, verse 10) as a cruel persecutor of the Jews.

The coin bears on one side a finely executed head of the King, and on the obverse a sitting figure of Jupiter, bearing in his extended right hand a small figure of Victory, and in his left a wand or scepter, with an inscription in ancient Greek characters---Basileos Antiochou, Epiphanous, and another word, partly defaced, which I believed to be Nikephorou; the translation of which is: King Antiochus, Epiphanes (Illustrious), the Victorious. When found it was very much blackened and corroded from long exposure, but when cleaned it appeared in a fine state of preservation and but little worn.

ROMAN COINS FOUND IN ICELAND
Shetelig, Haakon; *Antiquity,* 23:161-163, 1949.

The State Antiquary of Iceland, Kristjan Eldjarn, M.A., published in January this year a fine volume containing a report of his recent excavations of pagan graves, and other contributions to early Icelandic history, under the title of Gengidh a Reika, Akureyri, 1948 (1). It is very important that we have got here reliable accounts of systematically explored Viking burials, with diagrams and photographs, all very well done, as Iceland had produced, till now, very little of similar publications (2). But really exciting is undeniably the news of the discovery of three Roman coins in Iceland.

The place of discovery was at the farm Bragdhavellir, at the head of Hamarsfjord, in the district of Sudhur Mulasyssel, on the southeast coast of Iceland. In a small valley called Djupibotn the gales had partially denuded the ground leaving only the hard stony gravel subsoil. In this place the remains of two primitive houses came to light, certainly representing an ancient farm which had been deserted for long ages. A peasant of the vicinity Jon Sigfusson started searching the site for antiquities and collected a lot of such poor objects as are generally left in country dwellings of the early Middle-Ages, nails and fragments of iron, broken pots of soapstone, stone whorls, some teeth of horse and cow, bits of charcoal, etc. The only object of a more distinct character was a bead of variegated glass, reddish-brown with black and white, possibly dating from the Viking Period. Subsequently a number of the antiquities were sent to the National Museum in Reykjavik, including two Roman coins said to have been found on the same site and under same conditions as the other articles.

One of the coins is an Antoninianus of Probus, found in 1905, and the other a similar coin of Aurelian found in 1933. The following year, 1934, the State Antiquary, Matthias Thordharson visited the site and explored the ruins of the houses. He found a number of relics of the same description as already mentioned, but could obtain no further precise and definite information about the discovery of the coins. He was convinced, however, that there was no reason to suspect intentional fraud.

In the meantime a third Roman coin had been found in an equally surprising way. An English teacher, Mr. Leonard Hawkes, was in Iceland in 1923, and visited the same neighbourhood in Sudhur Mulasyssel. In passing the Hvalsdal, between Hvalsness and Krossaness, he accidentally discovered a Roman coin in the sand. He searched a little with the fingers, but found nothing more. The coin is an Antoninianus of Diocletian and is now preserved in the National Museum in Reykjavik.

The three coins date from the time of the emperors Aurelian (270-5), Probus (276-82) and Diocletian (284-305)---a period some 600 years before the Norse colonization of Iceland towards the end of the 9th century, and thus is raised a most interesting problem concerning the early navigation of the north Atlantic Ocean.

. . . .

$\overline{1}$ The title means roughly: Go on the shore of drift, i. e. to gather drift timber, or drift wood.
2 Daniel Bruun og Finnar Jonsson, Dalvikfundet, <u>Aarboger for nordisk Oldkyndighed og Historie</u>, Kjobenhavn 1910, p. 62. Daniel Bruun, Udgravninger paa Island, <u>Geografisk Tidsskrift,</u> vol. 17, p. 13, Kjobenhavn. cf. <u>Viking,</u> vol. 1, Oslo 1937, p. 205.

ROMAN COIN FOUND IN OSHKOSH

Butler, J. D.; *American Antiquarian,* 8:372, 1886.

In 1883, A. M. Brainerd of Oshkosh, digging in his garden there, turned up a strange coin. He sent it to me. It was indubitably an issue from the mint of the Emperor Hadrian, in the second century. A copper tool and certain stone implements found in the same locality betokened an Indian or pre-historic grave. It seemed to me unlikely that any man in recent times would have passed that spot with any Hadrianic coin in his pocket. Accordingly I looked on this find as proving pre-historic intercommunication between Wisconsin and Italy. I have now more faith than ever in my conjecture for several reasons. Thus I read in Gibbon that "in the sixth century of our era caravans traversed the whole longitude of Asia in two hundred and forty-three days from the Chinese ocean to the sea-coast of Syria." Proofs are not wanting of such intercourse many centuries earlier. In the present year Roman coins of the times of Tiberius (contemporary with Christ) and Aurelian in considerable quantities have been discovered in an inland province of China. When Hadrian's money had reached China it was already two-thirds of the distance to Wisconsin.

What was easier than for some bits of it to cross the streak of silver sea which separates Asia and America? The passage of coins from Alaska to Oshkosh would have been as natural as that of the obsidian arrows which are picked up on the shore of Lake Winnebago for obsidian cannot be detected <u>in situ</u> nearer than the Pacific slope, ---or at least the Yellowstone National Park which according to aboriginal ideas was still harder of access.

My view that the Oshkosh medal came from the west rather than from the east, is confirmed by evidence that has just come to light. At the last Boston meeting of the American Antiquarian Society, several tools and ornaments brought from Costa Rica, and made of <u>jadeite</u> or chloromelanite, were exhibited. The raw material of these specimens up to this time has never been found <u>in situ</u> in America, nor in any other continent except Asia. The articles, chemically tested in the laboratory of Harvard College by the Professor there, were pronounced by him "unquestionably Chinese jade." Oshkosh is not so far as Costa Rica is from Behrings Straits. I am glad of jude coming to thicken other proofs which did demonstrate thinly that it was not Satan alone who of old went to and fro in the earth and walked up and down in it.

Sketch of a Byzantine coin, circa 921 A.D., found on New Jersey coast

SINGULAR OLD COIN

Anonymous; *Scientific American,* 6:250, 1851.

The editor of the Milford (Del.) Beacon, was shown, a few days ago, a coin---a composition of copper and brass---found on the farm of Mr. Ira Hammond, about two miles from that place. It is over 600 years old, bearing, date 1178; on one side is a crown, and upon the other the words "Josephus, I D J-PO RT-ET-AL G-REX," very legible, and the work well executed. This coin is about two hundred years older than the discovery of America, and the question very naturally arises, where did it come from?

CHINESE COINS IN ALASKAN BURIAL

Anonymous; *Nature,* 46:574-575, 1892.

In the <u>Proceedings</u> of the U. S. National Museum (vol. xv.), Lieut. Dix Bolles calls attention to an interesting object included in a collection of ethnological specimens given by him to the museum in 1883-85. This is a wooden mask, which has for its eyes two large bronze Chinese coins. The grave from which the mask was taken is near the Chilcat village, at the mouth of the Chilcat River, Alaska, where stands a row of six gravehouses on a narrow strip of land close to the river, with a swamp behind them. From this particular grave very little was obtained by the explorers, its contents having nearly all rotted away. Lieut. Bolles was told by the natives that it was the grave of a medicine man who had flourished more than 200 years before, six successors having

filled his office, each one living to a good old age. Careful questioning failed to evoke any other answer. When the coins were shown to
the Chilcats, they could not remember having ever seen such objects.
Lieut. Bolles concludes that the coins probably were derived from a
junk driven on the coast about two centuries ago. "To those," he says,
"who doubt the advent of junks on the west coast at this early date, these
facts will probably not be satisfactory, but it will be necessary for them
to break down by direct evidence such a strong plea."

CHINESE COINS IN BRITISH COLUMBIA
Deans, James; *American Naturalist,* 18:98-99, 1884.

In the summer of 1882 a miner found on De Foe (Deorse?) creek,
Cassiar district, Br. Columbia, thirty Chinese coins in the auriferous
sand, twenty-five feet below the surface. They appeared to have been
strung, but on taking them up the miner let them drop apart. The earth
above and around them was as compact as any in the neighborhood. One
of these coins I examined at the store of Chu Chong in Victoria. Neither
in metal nor markings did it resemble the modern coins, but in its figures looked more like an Aztec calendar. So far as I can make out the
markings, this is a Chinese chronological cycle of sixty years, invented
by the Emperor Huungti, 2637 B.C., and circulated in this form to
make his people remember it.

• Iron from Indian Mounds

IRON FROM NORTH CAROLINA MOUNDS
Thomas, Cyrus; *Science,* 3:308-310, 1884.

In the Proceedings of the American antiquarian society, vol. ii.
p. 349 (1883), Professor Putnam reviews the statements of the old
writers respecting metal found in the western mounds. He comes to the
conclusion that Mr. Atwater's iron-bladed sword or steel-bladed dagger
is to be traced to that gentleman's lively imagination.

Although Professor Putnam may be correct in his conclusion, a discovery made in North Carolina by one of the assistants in the Bureau of

ethnology, during the past season, would seem to render the statement made by Atwater in regard to finding the fragment of an iron sword-blade in an Ohio mound at least probable.

In order that the reader may understand the conditions under which the articles to be mentioned were found, it is necessary to give a description of the burial-place, which I do by copying the report of the assistant.

"This is not a mound, but a burial-pit, in the form of a triangle, the two longest sides each forty-eight feet, and the base, thirty-two feet, in which the bodies and articles were deposited, and then covered over, but not raised above the natural surface. The depth of the original excavation, the lines of which could be distinctly traced, varied from two and a half to three feet.

. . . .

On the north-west side of the triangle, at A, fig. 1, ten or more bodies were found which appeared to have been buried at one time; the old chief (?) with his head north-east, face down. Under his head was the larger seashell with hieroglyphics. Around his neck were the largest-sized beads. At or near each ear were the larger pieces of copper: there was also a piece of copper under his breast. His arms were extended, and his hands rested about one foot from each side of his head. Around each wrist was a bracelet composed of long, cylindrical, copper beads and shell beads alternated. At his right hand were found the implements of iron. Under his left hand was a seashell with hieroglyphics inscribed on the concave surface, and filled with beads of all sizes.

"Around and over him, with their heads resting near his, were placed nine or more bodies. Under the heads of two of these skeletons, resting within a foot of the chief's (?), similarly inscribed shells were found. Scattered over and among these ten or more skeletons were found hatchets (polished axes and celts), rubbing and discoidal stones, copper arrow-points, mica, paint, black lead, etc."

This is sufficient to indicate the conditions under which the iron specimens were found. It is proper to state that every article named was immediately forwarded to the bureau, and is now in the National museum. The celts and axes, which are chiefly of greenish sienite, are highly polished, and equal in finish to the finest hitherto discovered in this country. The pipes are well made, and mostly well polished. The engraved shells are fine, large specimens, the engraved design on each being of the same type as that shown in fig. 3, plate xxx., of Jones's Antiquities of the southern Indians. (Figures omitted.)

The iron specimens alluded to are now before me, and are four in number, much corroded, but still showing the form. Two of them are flat pieces, of uniform thickness, not sharpened at the ends or edges, three to three and a half inches long, one to one and a half inches broad, and about a quarter of an inch thick. Another is five inches long, slightly tapering in width from one and an eighth to seven-eighths of an inch, both edges sharp, and is, without doubt, part of the blade of a long, slender, cutting or thrusting weapon of some kind; as a sword, dagger, or large knife. The other specimen is part of some round, awl-shaped implement; and a small fragment of the bone handle in which it was fixed yet remains attached to it.

The bureau is also in possession of another rudely hammered, small iron chisel or celt, found under somewhat similar conditions in a mound in the same section.

It is evident, from what has been stated, that we cannot ascribe the presence of this metal to an intrusive burial. The people who dug the pit, deposited here their deceased chief, or man of authority, and placed around him, and those buried with him, the pipes, celts, axes, engraved shell-gorgets, and other implements and ornaments, undoubtedly placed here, also, the pieces of iron.

Whether the burials were comparatively modern or pre-Columbian, the evidence furnished by these fortunate finds compels us to conclude that the people who made these polished celts and axes, who carved these pipes, who made or at least used these copper implements, and engraved these shells with the figure of the mystic serpent, so strongly reminding us of Central-American figures, also had in possession these iron implements, and were mound-builders. That this burial-pit was made by the same people who erected the mounds of this region cannot be doubted.

MOUND CONTAINING WROUGHT IRON NAIL AND BRASS BUCKLE

Verwyst, J. Chrysostom; *American Antiquarian,* 9:39–40, 1887.

Monday, Nov. 8th, I made an important archaeological discovery five miles above Washburn, about two miles from the Southwestern end of Chequamegon Bay, near Mr. Wyman's place. He showed me two mounds, one of which we dug up a little and examined. The mound was about eight feet in diameter at the base and two feet high and almost entirely covered with a layer of boulders or stones, taken from the beach near by. After removing some of the boulders and clay we came upon a layer of ashes from four to six inches thick. In the ashes we found a long iron nail of wrought iron, hand made and bent, as if it had been clinched when driven into a board; it resembled somewhat a hook and was about 2-1/2 inches long. It tapered down to a sharp point and the head was hammered rough. It was a regular old fashioned nail and was undoubtedly the work of civilized men, of whites. Besides we found part of brass buckle, very artistically made, perhaps the shoe-buckle of some old French officer. Both objects had suffered from the fire. Besides we find what seemed to be a piece of a clay-pipe stem, and pieces of bones of birds, fishes and animals. What do you think was this mound? It was not an Indian mound, for the objects found were decidedly of European make. It is located not far from the site of the ancient Jesuit Mission at the head of Chequamegon Bay. Near by can be seen three small holes, where the dirt was taken out, that covered the mound. It is at the very edge of a point of land, and in a few years will disappear as the bank will cave in and destroy it. I think it would pay to have it entirely uncovered and examined. Perhaps some other relics of the 17th century might be found there. These relics prove conclusively the existence of white men at our bay long, long ago perhaps two centuries or more. I have kept these objects and will show them to you. There is another mound near Wyman's house, which has not been examined yet, except that he threw away some of the stones and leveled the ground somewhat.

HIGH TECHNOLOGY ARTIFACTS

"High technology" is a recent term indicating a high level of scientific and engineering sophistication, as exemplified by computers, lasers, and associated modern marvels. When applying the term to ancient man, the criteria need not be so demanding. Artifacts exhibiting a knowledge of electrochemistry, metallurgy, analog computing, and similar techniques may be safely labelled "high technology" if they are also thousands years old.

Of course, the truly astounding fact is that anything even resembling such technologies existed at all. The recent discovery of an ancient Greek analog computer was sobering testimony that the ancients knew more about mathematics, mechanics, and machine fabrication than we allowed. This computer and other high technology artifacts assembled here tell us that we have not fully appreciated the technological genius of our forebears. Was their technical precocity self-taught?

THE MYSTERIOUS CEMENT CYLINDERS OF NEW CALEDONIA
Rothovius, Andrew; *INFO Journal,* 1:15-16, 1967.

One of the most intriguing and baffling mysteries to confront archaeologists in recent years, has been the discovery in the Southwest Pacific island of New Caledonia, and the adjoining Isle of Pines, of some remarkable lime-mortar cylinders that do not appear to be of natural origin, and whose indicated age is far earlier than all previously known man-made cements.

Discovered by L. Chevalier of the Museum of New Caledonia in the island's capital, Noumea, these cylinders run from 40 to 75 inches in diameter, and from 40 to 100 inches in height. They are of a very hard, homogeneous lime-mortar, containing bits of shells which yield a radio-carbon dating of from 5,120 to 10,950 B.C.---even the lowest date being some 3,000 years earlier than man is believed to have reached the Southwest Pacific from the area of Indonesia. (Lime-mortars of the ancient Mediterranean civilizations do not date earlier than a few hundred years B.C. at the most.)

On their outside, the cylinders are speckled with silica and iron gravel fragments that seem to have hardened into the mortar as it set. This feature is of interest in connection with the tumuli or sand-and-gravel mounds in which the cylinders were found, and that are as peculiar as the cylinders themselves.

There exist 400 of these tumuli on the Isle of Pines, and 17 so far located on New Caledonia itself, at a locality called Paita. On the Isle of Pines, the tumuli consist of a gravelly sand with high iron oxide content; the Paita tumuli are of a silicaceous sand. In both places, the tumuli are from 8 to 9 feet high, and average 300 feet in diameter---bare and featureless, with little or no vegetation taking root in the sands of which they are composed.

To date, only four of the tumuli have been excavated. No bones, artifacts or charcoal were found despite a thorough search; yet three of the tumuli contained one cylinder each, and the fourth had two of them, side by side. In each case, the cylinders were positioned in the center of the tumuli (which appear to resemble giant ant heaps), set vertically.

The impression that M. Chevalier had, was that the mortar had been poured into narrow pits dug into the tops of the tumuli, and allowed to harden in position. Bits of the sand and gravel composing the tumuli would naturally have worked into the mortar, thereby explaining their presence in the outer surfaces of the cylinders.

But what conceivable reason could there be for their being cast at all, in the first place? Natural origin appears ruled out---yet no evidence has been found of any human association with them, or with the tumuli which are also inexplicable as natural phenomena.

One might speculate that perhaps some vehicle from another realm than our Earth, had hovered overhead...and had sent down several hundred investigators in small separate craft, somewhat akin to the LEM module in our Apollo moonlanding craft. When these scouts needed to return to the mother craft, they required small launching pedestals, for which they mixed and poured the lime-mortar into the tops of the sand-and-gravel tumuli they heaped up for this purpose...

Fanciful? Admittedly yes; for what kind of launching mechanism can it have been that left no visible traces on the cylinder tops? Yet, unless some imaginative solution is sought to the mystery they present, the chances are that science will ignore the New Caledonia tumuli and cement cylinders, when it finds no orthodox explanation for them...and they will run the risk of being destroyed and forgotten, when an airport or other major project comes into the area. (New Caledonia was a highly important staging base for the American forces in World War II, and its strategic location makes it highly likely that additional airport developments, whether civilian or military, can be expected there in the not too distant future.)

A possible parallel to the New Caledonia cylinders may perhaps be cited in the strange capped stone pillars on Tinian Island in the Marianas, several thousand miles northwest of New Caledonia. In April, 1819, the French exploring expedition under Captain Louis-Claude de Freycinet in the frigate "Uranie," visited on Tinian a peculiar spot where, in the midst of lush vegetation on every hand, only a meager growth of grass could be found surrounding a double row of stone pillars, about 15 feet high, each topped by a hemispherically shaped boulder, the rounded side resting on the pillar. While the pillars were still in a good state of preservation, their squared sides and corners only slightly eroded, the boulders were more or less crumbling away; being possibly of a softer stone, though M. de Freycinet's account does not make this point clear.

The French explorers did speculate on whether the pillars had once supported a roof or platform, but they could find no trace of any. What puzzled them most was the aridity and sparseness of the grass around the pillars, though the soil as far as they could determine was just as fertile as that from which the rampant jungle sprouted only a few feet away.

Tinian was successively under Spanish, German, and Japanese occupation until the U. S. Marine landing in 1944---and none of these administrations encouraged foreign scientific research. In any event, no further account of the strange stone pillars has been located by this writer, and it is possible that if they still survived in 1944, they were destroyed in the intense fighting that followed the American landing, before the island was secured as the base from which the B-29's made their devastating strikes against the Japanese homeland.

References and sources

Revue de la Societe d'Etudes Melanesiennes (Noumea, 1964); pp. 24-25.
Radiocarbon (pub. by Yale University), Vol. 8, June, 1966: report on C14 datings by the Centre des Faibles Radioactivites, C. N. R. S., Gif-sur-Yvette, Essonnes, France.
Freycinet, Louis-Claude de. Voyage autour du Monde plus Atlas Historique. Paris, 1825, pp. 279-80.

A GREAT GLASS SLAB FROM ANCIENT GALILEE
Brill, Robert H.; *Archaeology, 20:88-95, 1967.*

Beth She' arim is an ancient site in southwestern Galilee, now verdant and beautifully restored. It lies about twelve miles southeast of Haifa, in what is known to have been a glassmaking region during the Roman period, and probably both before and afterward as well. In ancient times it was a famous center of Jewish learning and included an extensive necropolis, where prominent Jews from all over the East were buried.

. . . .

In 1956 it was decided to clear out an ancient filled-in cistern adjacent to some of the catacombs. This cistern, which had probably been enlarged from a natural cave, was to be converted into a small museum. In the course of clearing it the bulldozer encountered a large buried slab. Since the slab was too large to be moved, it was left where it was, lying flat, and the surrounding debris was leveled even with its base. A modern stone floor was then laid and the rest of the construction completed. Today the cistern is a small museum where finds from the catacombs are displayed. In the middle of the museum lies the slab, just off the central axis of the cistern and parallel to it.

It is not quite clear to the author just who first suggested that the slab might be made of glass but, at any rate, in 1963 both the slab and that suggestion were brought to the attention of members of the Corning Museum of Glass-University of Missouri Expedition. In the summers that followed we undertook three small-scale excavations around the slab, and during the two intervening winters carried out a thorough laboratory study of samples taken from it. The experiments proved beyond question that the slab is made of glass---and furthermore, that it is a man-made glass, produced deliberately. Using the archaeological evidence as well, which is described below, it was established that there is no possibility that the slab is a natural geological material or that it represents the remains of accidental firing, or waste from an industrial operation such as the smelting of some kind of ore.

The slab is 3.40 m. long, 1.95 m. wide and averages about 50 cm. in thickness. It weighs about 8.8 tons (about four metric tons). By comparison, the two largest objects of glass ever made by man are the 200-inch reflecting mirror in the Hale Telescope at Mt. Palomar, and the unsuccessful blank first cast for that mirror, now in The Corning Glass Center. They weigh, respectively, 14.5 and 20 tons.

The slab is essentially one solid mass, although there are incipient fractures running through it. Its upper surface is generally smooth and level. In one part of the upper surface there are small craters which resulted from bursting bubbles, and at one end there are sizable rounded blobs piled up on the top. When clean and wet it has an opaque purple color, but the fractured front corner shows intermingled veins of green and purple. The casual visitor---and indeed even the expert---is not easily convinced that the slab is really made of glass. Its surface is weathered and it is not transparent because the glass is filled with tiny devitrification crystals, which make it opaque. (Of course, many glasses, ancient as well as modern, are not transparent.) It is only by examining the fractured corners of the slab that its glassy appearance can be recognized, and when one observes the blobs toward the rear of the slab its molten history becomes evident.

Four questions immediately come to mind during the first few moments when anyone sees the slab, and they persist even through a prolonged study: what is the slab made of, when was it made, how was it made, and why?
. . . .

ON A ROCK-CRYSTAL LENS AND DECOMPOSED GLASS FOUND IN NINEVEH

Brewster, David; *American Journal of Science*, 2:15:122-123, 1853.

Sir David said that he had to bring before the Section an object of so incredible a nature that only the strongest evidence could render the statement at all probable:---it was no less than the finding of a rock-crystal lens, in the treasure-house at Nineveh, where it had for centuries lain entombed in the ruins of that once magnificent city. It was found in company with several bronzes and other objects of value. He had examined the lens with the greatest care and taken its several measurements. It was not entirely circular in its aperture, being 1-6/10ths inches in its longer diameter and 1-4/10ths inches in its shorter. Its general form was that of a plano-concave lens, the plane side having been formed of one of the original faces of the six-sided crystal of quartz, as he had ascertained by its action on polarized light,---this was badly polished and scratched. The convex fact of the lens had not been

ground in a dish-shaped tool in the manner in which lenses are now formed, but was shaped on a lapidary's wheel, or in some such manner.
Hence it was unequally thick, but its extreme thickness was 2/10ths of
an inch, its focal length being 4-1/2 inches. It had twelve remains of
cavities which had originally contained liquids or condensed gases; but
ten of those had been opened probably in the rough handling which it received in the act of being ground; most of them therefore had discharged
their gaseous contents. Sir David concluded by assigning reasons why
this could not be looked on as an ornament, but as a true optical lens.

Sir David then exhibited specimens of the decomposed glass found in
the same ruins. The surface of this was covered with iridescent spots
more brilliant in their colors than Peacock copper ore. Sir David stated
that he had several years since explained how this process of decomposition proceeded, on the occasion of having found a piece of decomposed
glass at St. Leonard's. It had contained manganese, which had separated from the silex of the glass, at central spots around which circles of
most minute crystals of true quartz had arranged themselves; bounded
by irregular jagged circles of manganese, these being arranged in
several concentric rings. When this process reached a certain depth in
the glass it spread off laterally, dividing the glass into very thin layers,
and new centres seemed to form at certain distances, and thus the process extended.

FIRST MASTERS OF THE AMERICAN DESERT: THE HOHOKAM

Haury, Emil W.; *National Geographic Magazine,* 131:670-695, May
1967.

From other imported shards we were able to estimate that the last
three phases of Hohokam history at Snaketown---beginning about A.D.
500---had lasted around 200 years each. Yet there were four earlier
phases here! Even a conservative estimate pushed the beginnings of the
settlement toward the opening of the Christian Era.

There were strong affinities with Mexico in addition to the ball court.
Aptly enough, one of the enduring favorites of the Hohokam craftsman
was the snake. We found him writhing around the sides of pots, forming
the circlet of a shell bracelet, coiling at the rim of a stone incense burner. Quite often a bird is attacking the snake, a very old motif south of
the Rio Grande---and one that survives to this day on Mexico's flag.

Among the many thousands of artifacts gathered, we found countless
stone tools and arrowheads, but it was a small number of decorated
marine shells, dated to about A.D. 1000, that intrigued us most. We
were baffled by the incredible fineness of the working of horned toads,
snakes, and geometric forms that adorned them. ·

Our study pointed to only one plausible hypothesis: The shells were
etched. We knew full well that this meant crediting the Hohokam with
the first etched artifacts in history---hundreds of years before Renaissance armorers in Europe came upon the technique.

We speculated that an Indian artisan accidentally discovered the corrosive power of fermented cactus juice, which produces a weak acetic acid. Shells soaked in the vinegar would be eaten away unless protected by a resistant substance, such as pitch. Hence the procedure, by simple reasoning: Form a design of pitch on a shell, soak it in acid, scrape off the pitch, and the result is an etched design.

Recently I was able to prove this theory with the finding of a shell prepared for an acid treatment never completed (page 680). The invention of etching enabled the Hohokam to create some remarkable works of art.

A final major surprise of that first dig into the Hohokam past was the excavation of a canal system that implied a long period of technological growth. The canals stretched for miles along the upper terrace of the river valley, safe from sudden floods yet near at hand for maintenance and water control and for directing water to the fields.

A cross section of the prehistoric canals showed one imposed upon another as changes were made over a long period of time. The earliest we had found thus far, dated to A. D. 800, seemed every bit as well planned and executed as the latest, dug about 1200. (pp. 676-679)

MAYAN DENTISTRY
Anonymous; *Science,* 70:sup xiv, July 26, 1929.

Mayan Indians who lived in Central America more than 1, 000 years ago practiced dentistry and knew something about the technique of drilling holes in teeth and filling up the cavity with metal. Two teeth containing circular holes filled with iron pyrites are among the discoveries reported by J. Eric Thompson, leader of the Captain Marshall Field Archeological Expedition to British Honduras, which has recently returned to the Field Museum of Natural History. The teeth were found in a vaulted burial chamber in the ruins of the Mayan city of Tzimin Cax, which means "Mountain Cow." A good collection of Mayan painted pottery was found in the chamber. Other burial chambers yielded skeletons and pottery types hitherto unknown in the Mayan art, also jade ear-plugs and apple-green jade beads. While digging in a large mound in the ruins of the city, the expedition made the first authenticated find of a mirror from a site of the Old Empire of the Mayan tribes, that is from the period between 400 and 800 A. D.

ANCIENT INDIAN IRON
Britton, S. C.; *Nature,* 134:238-240 and 134:277-279, 1934.

It appears certain that iron was known in India at a very early date. Mention of its production in ancient writings puts the earliest time of production earlier than 1,000 B.C. According to Herodotus, the Indian contingent of the army of Xerxes were using iron for military purposes about 500 B.C. The description of iron surgical instruments in an ancient medical work, the excavation of iron weapons from burial sites and the presence to this day of masses of iron like the pillars of Delhi and Dhar all indicate that the production of iron steadily increased as the centuries passed.

The methods of production and qualities of Indian iron and steel seem to have early excited the curiosity of the British conquerors and in 1795, Dr. George Pearson published a paper on a kind of steel named 'wootz', then being manufactured in Bombay. The methods of analysis and examination then available only allowed the vague conclusions that the metal was very hard, had about 0.03 per cent carbon, and was believed to have been produced by direct reduction of the ore. Dr. Buchanan's "Travels in the South of India", published in 1807, describes the native Indian processes for iron and steel production then employed, which were believed to be those handed down from previous ages. Numerous other investigations have been made since that time, which increase in thoroughness as methods of examination have improved.

The Delhi Pillar. The Delhi pillar has constantly aroused interest. Sir Alexander Cunningham, in the "Archaeological Survey of India", published during the years 1862-65, reported the pillar as a solid shaft of wrought iron, upwards of sixteen inches in diameter and twenty-two feet in length; he mentions the curious yellow colour of the upper part of the shaft, which at one time caused the belief that the pillar was of bronze. This appearance has been commented upon by many observers since that time. Inscriptions made on the pillar are said still to be perfectly clear and sharp, and these have allowed the approximate date of its erection to be fixed as A.D. 310.

There seems little doubt that the pillar was built up by welding together discs of iron; it is said that the marks of welding can still plainly be seen. Sir Robert Hadfield examined a small specimen of the pillar in 1911 and afterwards was able to make a fairly detailed investigation of a larger piece. The analysis showed the composition C, 0.08; Si, 0.046; Mn, 0; P, 0.114; N, 0.032; Fe, 99.72; Cu and other elements, 0.034. Hadfield described the iron as an excellent type of wrought iron entirely free from inclusions, being better from the point of view of homogeneity and purity than the best modern Swedish charcoal irons. The structure was found to consist of large grains of ferrite with a very small portion of cementite, sometimes located in the grain boundaries and occasionally in the ground mass. A smaller grain structure, independent of the large one, was faintly visible, and there were also a large number of small lines in a regular formation which appeared to be related to the small grain structure; this was mentioned as possibly due to an aging effect. A specimen of the pillar rusted in a single night when water was placed on it in Hadfield's laboratory, but the fractured surface suffered no change in four days when merely exposed to the laboratory atmosphere. Hadfield mentions that the part of the pillar below the ground had suffered from corrosion.

The Dhar Pillar. The great iron pillar found at Dhar is described in detail by Cousins. The pillar is in three portions, having apparently been fractured during religious disturbances in the fourteenth and fifteenth centuries A. D.   There are no original inscriptions on the pillar itself, or sufficiently definite references elsewhere, to give a basis for any but the vaguest conjecture about the date of manufacture.   Its form suggests that it belongs to the Gupta period (A. D. 320-480), and the general belief is that it is approximately contemporaneous with the Delhi pillar.

The original Dhar pillar appears to have been approximately 50 feet long with an average section of 104 square inches and a weight of about 7 tons, and, like the Delhi pillar, it seems to have been constructed by welding together discs of wrought iron.   There are a number of holes in the pillar of about 1-1/4 in. diameter and varying from 1-3/4 in. to 3 in. in depth, which Cousins suggests were intended to hold tommy-bars for turning the mass whilst it was being forged; the finding of the broken end of a bar jammed into one of the holes lends some support to this idea.   Sir Robert Hadfield has examined a specimen of the pillar, and found it to be wrought iron having C, 0.02; P, 0.28; Fe, 99.6.   The Brinell ball hardness varied considerably and irregularly over the material the limits being 240 and 121; the fracture was brought and crystalline, showing laminations.   Further analyses and micrographical investigation by C. J. Smithells and by Prof. Cobb have shown no new features in the iron; it is found to rust fairly quickly in a laboratory atmosphere.

Ancient Sinhalese Iron.   The first thorough investigation of ancient Indian steel was made by Sir Robert Hadfield in 1911-12.   He was able to examine a number of ancient implements which had been excavated from the buried cities of Ceylon.   Many such implements have been unearthed; they are very heavily rusted and apparently continue to rust in the atmosphere of the Museum of Colombo, unless very carefully protected.   Nevertheless, the presence of a considerable quantity of yet unchanged iron shows a marked resistance to corrosion.   An ancient Sinhalese chisel, dating back to the fifth century, was found to have the percentage composition, iron, 99.3; phosphorus, 0.28; sulphur, 0.003; silicon, 0.12; no manganese and only traces of carbon with about 0.3 per cent of slag and oxide inclusions.   Examination of microsections led Hadfield to believe that the chisel had been carburised, had originally been quenched, but had become partially tempered during the long lapse of time.   A nail and an ancient billhook of similar age and origin showed a similar analysis.   All the specimens contained a large amount of slag in lumpy irregular form.   The low sulphur content was held to indicate that the metal was originally produced by charcoal reduction of the ore.   The microscopical examination suggested that the specimens were rather similar to modern puddled iron, and this was further borne out to some extent by mechanical tests.

The Iron Beams at Konarak.   A number of large iron beams which were apparently used in the construction of the collapsed Black Pagoda at Konarak are still lying amid the ruins of the temple in varying states of preservation.   The date most generally accepted for the building of the temple is about 1240 A. D., and it is presumed that the beams were made at the time.   Their appearance is fully described by Graves.

There are some twenty-nine massive bars, most of them broken in the collapse of the building; the largest two are approximately 35 feet long by about 8 inches square and 25-1/2 feet long by 11 inches square respectively.   They show very definite evidence of having been fabricated by welding up small blooms, commonly 2 inches by 1 inch in section and 6 inches long. Many of the broken ends show the existence of irregular and sometimes uniform cavities from which small pieces of cinder can be raked. Some of the beams are very heavily rusted, but many of them are scarcely affected and have a very thin and closely adherent coating. A specimen taken from one of the beams has been examined by Friend and Thornycroft. The presence of many cracks, containing slag inclusions, rendered micrographical investigation difficult. The cracks were found to be bordered by bands of ferrite, the grain boundaries being faintly discernible. Portions of the specimen more distant from the cracks showed a fairly uniform structure, typical of a mild steel containing rather less than 0.15 per cent carbon. The metal was found to be very soft, having a Brinell hardness number of 72. Analysis of a piece chosen as free from slag showed C, 0.110; Si, 0.100; S, 0.024; P, 0.015; Mn, a trace.

An attempt was made to compare the resistance to corrosion of the metal with that of a modern mild steel of unspecified composition. One weighed specimen of each was exposed to alternate wetting by tap-water and drying for one year; reweighing after removal of rust showed that the ancient iron had suffered a loss amounting to 89 per cent of that of the modern steel. The specimens were then exposed to the action of an artificial sea-water for a year and again the ancient iron lost less weight than the modern steel, losses being in the ratio 75 : 100. However, tests of this kind, made on single specimens, and including only one modern steel, really show very little about the corrosion resistance of the ancient metal.

Miscellaneous Specimens. The so-called Pillar of Heliodorus at Besnagar, which is itself of stone, is supported at its base by iron wedges which are still in a partial state of preservation. It is believed that the pillar was erected about 125 B.C. and that the iron supports were used from the outset. However, there is a possibility that the metal was not native India iron, but was imported from Greece. Hadfield has examined a sample of it and describes it as the only ancient ferrous specimen which can be called steel; he actually demonstrated that it could be hardened by quenching. The structure was pearlitic, having elongated and irregularly disposed crystals of sorbitic pearlite upon a ferrite ground mass; after quenching from $850^{o}C.$ in water, a specimen became martensitic. There were seams of slag in some portions. Analysis showed C, 0.70; Si, 0.04; S, 0.008; P, 0.020; Mn, 0.02; Cr, a trace; Fe, 99. The Brinell hardness number was 146.

W. Rosenhain mentions ancient iron chains which assisted pilgrims to climb Adam's Peak, Ceylon. These have been worn round and smooth, but are apparently uncorroded. Rosenhain suggested that the links have corroded down to apparently only a cinder surface protecting the iron below; specimens cut and brought to London rusted as quickly as any other iron. Graves gives a list of 239 pieces of iron ranging up to 17 feet long and up to 6 inches by 4 inches section used in the construction of the Garden Temple at Puri, which was built not later than the first half of the twelfth century. However, no further information on these is available.

Iron swords and daggers of uncertain date have been unearthed from burial sites in the district of Tinnevelly and specimens of third century iron have been recovered from Buddha Gaya but no examination appears to have been made.

It seems possible that many specimens of iron exist in India of which the date of manufacture cannot be established, but which may well be ancient, and there are no doubt others of ascertainable date yet to be excavated from the earth.

GILDING OF COPPER AMONG THE PRE-COLUMBIAN INDIANS
Bergoe, Paul; *Nature,* 141:829, 1938.

I have already given an account of certain investigations regarding the metallurgical methods employed by the pre-Columbian Indians, especially their methods of procuring platinum in coherent form without fusing it, and I have demonstrated the metallurgical processes adopted by them in soldering by 'sweating', wire-drawing, the plating of gold with platinum, etc. Further investigations have now disclosed the fact that the Indians, at any rate those in the Esmeraldas district, gilded their copper objects in a fashion which appears to have been completely unknown hitherto, both to the ancient world and to us. It was previously supposed that such gilding must have been carried out in America with the help of mercury. Although it has been impossible to demonstrate traces of mercury in any of the gilded objects, no other explanation has been suggested.

After cleansing such objects to remove the products of corrosion and the remnants of gold still adhering to them, I have shown by chemical analysis that the copper contains varying quantities of gold in alloyed form---the largest amount on the surface and decreasing gradually towards the centre. Such unequal gold content might well be imagined to have arisen from the melted gold permeating the copper. Gilding must have been done by dipping the copper into a melted gold-copper eutectic (gold with about 20 per cent copper) the melting point of which is some 200°C. lower than that of copper; or possibly, the gold-copper alloy was applied to the copper and kept at red heat on charcoal by means of a blow-pipe. The alloy will then fuse and run over the copper without the use of flux being necessary, the reducing flame securing a glowing surface free of oxide. Investigations have shown that copper has a tendency to absorb the melted alloy in the same manner as melted tin permeates copper or a zinc rod absorbs mercury. The copper nucleus thus becomes a gold-copper alloy richest in gold at the surface, the amount of gold decreasing gradually. After the gilding process had thus been accomplished, the reddish tinge of the coating was improved by boiling out in pickle---in French, mise en couleur, in German, Abochung---a method with which, we know with certainty, the Indians were acquainted.

I have examined breastplates covered with gold, but only on one side, originating from Ecuador. These plates appear to have been beaten out from thicker plates which had already been gilded. This is quite feasible if care is taken that the gilding is not too thick. Gilding was used by the Esmeraldas Indians for other purposes than decoration. Of the thirty-five fish-hooks found, all were gilded, but not one single specimen of thirty-two sewing needles discovered. The gold which penetrates the copper fish-hooks makes the metal much harder, and hardness is the first consideration in a fish-hook.

Objects gilded in this manner are far more exposed to the attacks of corrosion than copper, and this probably has been a contributory factor to the difficulty which previous investigators have had in discovering the above facts.

Investigations have also shown that it is possible to silver copper in the same way.

ANCIENT ELECTROPLATING

Anonymous; *1933 Annual Log*, Scientific American Publishing Co., New York, 1933, p. 85.

A 5,000-year-old Egyptian secret was recently brought to light in the laboratories of Columbia University through the study of ancient Egyptian vases belonging to the Metropolitan Museum of Art. This was revealed by Dr. Colin G. Fink, head of the division of electro-chemistry at Columbia, in a lecture before the New York chapter of the American Institute of Chemists.

In his work on the restoration of ancient Egyptian metal art objects, corroded almost beyond recognition in the course of five millenniums, Dr. Fink found that the Egyptians knew the secret of coating copper vessels with thin layers of antimony, by means of which they achieved the same results now accomplished by modern electro-plating.

To explain the existence of antimony-coated vessels, we must conclude that the Egyptians knew the secret of electro-chemical exchange, a secret later lost and not rediscovered until the last century by Faraday.

Antimony sulphide was an abundant mineral in ancient Egypt and is mentioned in its hieroglyphics as "kohl," from which our word coal is derived. The substance was used by Egyptian beauties to pencil their eyebrows and eyelashes.

To accomplish their electro-plating, the Egyptians must have dipped their copper vessels in a solution of antimony sulphide, vinegar and salt (sodium chloride). When this is done an electro-chemical exchange takes place---the copper goes into the solution and the antimony becomes deposited on the vessel's surface.

Dr. Fink, who lectured on the electro-chemist in art and archaeology, told of recently developed scientific methods to preserve, restore and to establish the authenticity of ancient works of art. The work is being carried on at the Metropolitan Museum and at the Field Museum in Chicago.

Professor Fink is the inventor of the tungsten filament electric light bulb and the process for electro-plating with chromium.

THE METALLURGY OF GOLD AND PLATINUM IN PRE-COLUMBIAN ECUADOR
Maryon, Herbert; *Man* 41:124-126, 1941.

The territory of Ecuador lies on the equator on the North-Western side of South America. Native gold-seekers, washing the river sands in search of the precious metal, find in their pans, among the gold dust, small objects of wrought gold and of platinum---needles, awls, fish-hooks, forceps, safety-pins, spoons and nails, together with many fragments of jewellery. They were made by the Indians before the era of the Spanish conquests. They exhibit quite unexpected qualities of workmanship. For these natives seem to have been the first people in the world to work platinum. From it they made jewellery, and with it they plated gold. They also showed extraordinary delicacy and technical skill in the production of some of their ornaments.

Mr. Bergsoe's researches enabled him to copy both the materials and the technique of these early goldsmiths. His examination of the material resulted in a number of interesting discoveries. The goldsmiths of Ecuador had no free silver, but they produced a kind of fore-runner of our Sheffield plate by soldering together thin sheets of gold and of platinum, from which to make jewellery. They also joined together pieces of platinum.

What method did the native craftsman employ in order to plate gold with platinum? When the objects were composed of two or more pieces of metal, originally separate but now one, how were they fastened together? Were they soldered, welded, or put together by some other process?

Mr. Bergsoe provides a convincing answer to the first question, and a partial answer to the second. Many of the specimens were made from the natural nuggets of gold, hammered to shape. Others were made from ingots of gold, i.e. from pieces of gold which had been fused together in the charcoal fire with the aid of the blowpipe, or some other means of producing a draught. The wood-grain impression from the charcoal block upon which the ingot was melted may be seen on several specimens. But no objects in silver are known; the goldsmiths did not know how to extract it, even if they had suspected its presence.

Other objects were made of an alloy of gold and platinum, with some copper and silver. These are generally white in colour. Others have a high percentage of copper, so high that the copper must have been added deliberately; no native gold with so high a percentage of copper being available.

To make the white alloy the smith, after removing all the larger nuggets, seems to have taken the minute grains of gold and platinum which were found in the pan of the gold-seeker, and to have heated them together on the charcoal slab. When the temperature reached perhaps 900°C. the grains of gold, i.e. composed of gold with its natural alloys, would melt and flow over the surface of the platinum grains, joining them together. At the same time the gold would become paler in colour, perhaps quite white, for some of the platinum would penetrate and dissolve in the gold. This process of penetration and diffusion, under the influence of heat, is, of course, 'sintering' (cf. Man, 1941, 85). The resulting mass is a true alloy. The temperature of the platinum has never approached melting point, but the two metals, platinum and gold, have mutually dissolved in each other.

Small masses of this sintered gold-and-platinum would be alternately hammered, and again heated, until they were forged into a compact mass. Then several of these small masses were combined to form a larger; the gold in them again acting as the cementing material. In this manner a mass of any required size could be obtained. It could then be beaten out into a thin sheet. Another sheet, this time of gold, would be prepared. The two sheets, one of gold, the other of the platinum-gold alloy, would be laid one upon the other on the charcoal, or possibly on a terracotta slab. Heat would be applied sufficient to cause the gold to run, and the two sheets would become fastened together; the gold again acting as a cement. As a result, a plate, one side of which was of gold, the other of the platinum-gold alloy, white in colour, was obtained. This could ·be worked into any desired form.

Discovery of the method by which objects, originally composed of two or more separate pieces of metal, were joined together provided Mr. Bergsoe with some difficult problems. At first he thought that they might have been put together without any soldering material, and he suggested that 'autogenous welding' was the method employed. But for reasons stated above it is probable that they were soldered. It is clear that the ancient goldsmith, with his primitive appliances, frequently overfired his work, and unwittingly left this difficult problem for his successors to solve.

All the South American objects discussed above, which were found at La Tolita, Atacames, and elsewhere, on the coast of the province of Esmeraldas, Ecuador, are now in the Danish National Museum at Capenhagen.

ANCIENT METALLURGY IN RHODESIA
Rickard, T. A.; *Nature,* 126:758, 1930.

My attention has been directed to an article on "Early Man in N. Rhodesia", by Prof. Raymond Dart, which appeared in the Times of Aug. 22 and was noticed in Nature of Aug. 30. Echoes of the statements made in the article are finding their way into our local Press, and the unprotected public is being told that iron was being fabricated "3000 to 4000 years" ago by a people of Palaeolithic culture dwelling in central Africa.

On the face of it, such an accomplishment is highly improbable, because the oldest man-made iron of known date is that of the discovery made by Sir Flinders Petrie at Gerar, in Palestine, in 1927. The date of this iron, as determined by associated scarabs and amulets, is 1350 B.C. It is probable that the smelting of iron was begun a little earlier, say, 1400 B.C., in the Hittite uplands, between the Taurus and the Caucasus, a region to which classical tradition points as the cradle of metallurgy. All iron earlier than 1400 B.C. is probably of meteoric origin; many older relics have been tested for their nickel content (which is the criterion) and have proved to be of celestial metal. It is unlikely that the smelting of iron was known long before 1350 B. C., because the knowledge of the art would have been of supreme importance, in trade and war, to any primitive people; it would have sufficed to give them instant dominance over their contemporaries.

We must meet Prof. Dart's conclusion, therefore, with justifiable scepticism. He says: "These facts reveal the extreme age (3000 to 4000 years) of the knowledge of smelting and the working of metals in Northern Rhodesia". This dictum is based upon the finding, by an Italian scientific expedition, of a foundry, slag, and ashes at a depth of six feet in a deposit containing implements characteristic of the Stone Age. The deposit lies within a limestone cave at Mumbwa, near the Kafue river, a tributary of the Zambezi. The find is said to prove that "the smelting is coeval with the later phases of the Palaeolithic period in Northern Rhodesia", and shows that "the knowledge of metallurgy was introduced by a superior race into an Africa still in the throes of the Stone Age". This is true enough, but it does not prove an antiquity of 3000 or 4000 years, that is, so long ago as 2070 B. C. What it does prove, I submit, is that foreigners, versed in iron-making, established themselves for a time in the cave, possibly for self-defence, and during their sojourn they made iron weapons for use against the natives, who then were using the "quartz flakes and quartz implements of the Late Stone Age type"---in short, were the savages that Livingstone, Cameron, and Stanley found in that part of the world seventy years ago.

The invaders probably were slave-hunting Arabs, and the date of their incursion may be anything from A. D. 1200 to A. D. 1900, but no B. C. chronology is permissible. The Italian expedition has not finished its exploratory research; perhaps when all the information available is collected we shall be given a more convincing interpretation of the facts.

Apropos of early iron-making, I may mention that sundry writers have imputed the ancient Egyptians' knowledge of the art to a borrowing from their southern neighbours, the Ethiopians, this idea being lent some colour by the fact that the natives in central Africa, more particularly the Kenya and Congo regions, know how to make iron in a crude manner. Crudity of method, however, does not prove antiquity of origin. The denial to any such supposition is found in the description by Herodotus of the weapons used by the Ethiopian contingent in the army of Xerxes. Their armament consisted of "long bows, on which they placed short arrows made of cane, not tipped with iron, but with stone that was made sharp, and of the kind of which we engrave seals. Besides these they had javelins, tipped with antelope's horn that had been made sharp, like a lance. They had also knotted clubs." All of which indicates a complete ignorance of metallurgy.

LODESTONE COMPASS: CHINESE OR OLMEC PRIMACY?

Carlson, John B.; *Science,* 189:760, 1975. (Copyright 1975 by the American Association for the Advancement of Science)

In entering upon this subject [magnetic directivity and the

compass], it may be well to pause for a moment to consider the incalculable importance of the discovery of the magnetic compass, as the first and oldest representative of all those dials and pointer readings which play so great a part in modern scientific observation. ... No apology is needed, therefore, for an attempt as thorough as possible to ascertain what was the oldest form of compass...and when its successive developments were introduced.

This preface to Needham's study of the development of the magnetic compass in his monumental work Science and Civilisation in China expresses the spirit in which I undertook the study of the properties of a unique and curious Olmec artifact in late 1973.

The artifact, henceforth designated M-160 (Michigan sample), was found in situ at the Early Formative Olmec site in San Lorenzo, Veracruz. It was excavated by P. Krotser of the Yale University excavation project headed by archeologist M. D. Coe. According to Coe's analysis the fill in which M-160 was unearthed contained no material later than the San Lorenzo A and B Phases, which have been well dated by radiocarbon methods at 1400 to 1000 B.C.; according to current correlations this unequivocally places the manufacture of M-160 earlier than 1000 B.C. In general appearance, the artifact

.... Immediately suggested to Coe that it might be part of a compass. To test the possibility, he cut a piece from a cork mat, placed the object on it, and floated it in a plastic bowl full of water. It consistently oriented itself to the same direction, which was slightly west of magnetic north. Turned over, the pointer always aligned itself to a consistent orientation slightly east of magnetic north.

After Coe established in 1967 that the fragment M-160 would perform as a lodestone floater compass---a geomagnetically self-orienting device ---no further investigations were carried out until the experiments described in this article were undertaken.

In studying the properties of M-160 and later interpreting them to reconstruct the original function of the artifact, I used an interdisciplinary approach which is of interest in itself as well as in the conclusions reached. Adaptations of Mossbauer spectroscopy, spinner magnetometry, and archeomagnetic dating have been applied here to problems of chronology and cultural interaction. The study thus serves as an example of the application of techniques of physical science to archeological questions.

The analysis of M-160 indicates that the Olmec may have discovered and used the geomagnetic lodestone compass earlier than 1000 B.C.--- predating the Chinese discovery by more than a millennium. Archeologists often find it useful, when material for interpreting the cultural significance of artifacts is sparse, as with the Olmec, to draw analogies between ethnographic reality and archeological materials on both an intracultural and crosscultural basis. There is evidence, for example, for a Mesoamerican as well as a Chinese penchant for the directional orientation of the dwellings of the living and the interments of the dead. Such comparisons shed a revealing light on the interpretation of Olmec practices and the function of M-160.

. . . .

Analysis of M-160. The artifact is a small, carefully shaped, highly polished rectangular bar of hematite with a trapezoidal cross section. It is a fragment of a larger piece, broken off in ancient times. The greater dimensions of M-160 are 34 by 9 by 4 mm, with the trapezoidal cross section measuring approximately 3 by 4 by 8.5 by 9 mm. I estimate that this fragment is about half of the original artifact. Running down the approximate central axis of one of the large flat faces, and approximately but (I think intentionally) not exactly parallel to the edges, is a carefully executed hemicylindrical groove of diameter 2 mm. The groove is flared slightly at the finished end, which suggests that it may have been cut and polished with a cord soaked with water and polishing compound. Except for the broken end, all sides are optically flat and highly polished. Great care and purpose are exhibited in the production of M-160. The mineral is hard and brittle and its finishing and polishing must have required great skill and much time. To my knowledge, M-160 is unique in morphology among all known examples of worked Mesoamerican iron ore.

In December 1973, I received M-160 on request from the University of Michigan, where it was part of the collection of San Lorenzo iron ore artifacts awaiting Mossbauer spectral analysis. I performed several experiments in which M-160 was floated both on liquid mercury and on a cork mat in water. In both cases a covered petri dish (9 cm in diameter) was used to minimize disturbances from air currents in the outdoors. With M-160 floating groove side up, alignments were made by looking down the groove and sighting a stadia rod held more than 30 m away. Bearings and reverse bearings were taken many times at three separate locations; the orientations were checked against measurements with a magnetic sighting compass. The fragment M-160 could be used consistently to align the stadia rod to within half a degree, and the average orientation was found to be 35.5° west of magnetic north. The consistency of the orientations indicated that the internal magnetic field was strong enough and the magnetic moment vector was close enough to the "floating plane" to respond quickly to the geomagnetic field even with vibrations and disturbances of the support on a windy day. (The experiment could also have been performed inside an iron-free building.)

It is apparent that the longer the original artifact (of which M-160 is a fragment), the better pointer it would be. From the maximum size for finds of polished iron ores and the extreme brittleness of the mineral, I estimate that the original bar was probably no longer than 10 cm. Also, the hemicylindrical groove is incised at a slight but noticeable angle--- about 2°---to the axis of the bar. There seems to me no doubt that this was done with purpose. The care with which the bar was fashioned would indicate that a parallel groove was certainly possible if desired. Could this groove have been incised at a slight angle, as the final calibration step, to obtain a desired orientation?

I used liquid mercury to float M-160 for several reasons. Mercury is easily manufactured by heating the common orange mineral cinnabar (HgS) under the proper conditions. Liquid mercury has a density 13.6 times that of water, so virtually anything will float on it. A pool of liquid mercury would be a fascinating mirror, perhaps inducing an Olmec priest to float one of his polished iron ore mirrors. Finally, the Maya possessed liquid mercury. According to Fuson substantial quantities of liquid mercury have been found at Copan, Quirigua, Paraiso, and Kaminaljuyu. The Olmec may also have discovered liquid mercury and one might speculate that it played a role in the discovery and use of a floated lodestone compass.

The artifact and several iron ore mirrors were examined under a microscope with a magnification up to x 400. The high degree of polish and optical flatness is quite amazing. The techniques used to shape and polish the artifact are unknown. Flannery mentions the discovery of quartz and iron ore polishers and traces of hematite rouges or ochre at San Jose Mogote; they were probably used in the manufacture and polishing of the mirrors produced at that site. The only scratches or possible work marks found on M-160 or any of the mirrors examined were randomly oriented straight grooves. No curved work marks and no traces of adhesive, inlay, or paint were found. I have tried to polish magnetite with no outstanding success; obviously, great skill and patience were involved in the manufacturing process. Having examined the external morphology of M-160, I proceeded to investigate its internal properties.

. . . .

Conclusions. Considering the unique morphology (purposefully shaped polished bar with a groove) and composition (magnetic mineral with magnetic moment vector in the floating plane) of M-160, and acknowledging that the Olmec were a sophisticated people who possessed advanced knowledge and skill in working iron ore minerals, I would suggest for consideration that the Early Formative artifact M-160 was probably manufactured and used as what I have called a zeroth-order compass, if not a first-order compass. The data I have presented in this article support this hypothesis, although they are not sufficient to prove it. That M-160 could be used today as a geomagnetically directed pointer is undeniable. The original whole bar may indeed have pointed close to magnetic north-south. The groove functions well as a sighting mark, and the slight angle it makes with the axis of the bar appears to be the result of calibration rather than accident. A negative supporting argument is that M-160 looks utilitarian rather than decorative, and no function for the object other than that of a compass pointer has been suggested by anyone who has examined it critically. Whether such a pointer would have been used to point to something astronomical (zeroth-order compass) or to geomagnetic north-south (first-order compass) is entirely open to speculation.

The observation of the family of Olmec site alignments 8° west of north is a curiosity in its own right, and the possibility that these alignments have an astronomical or geomagnetic origin should be explored.

I also believe that it is constructive to compare the first millennium Chinese, who used the lodestone compass for geomancy, with the Gulf Coast Olmec since both were agrarian-terrestrial societies. The Olmec's apparent concern with orientation and skillful use of magnetic minerals also stimulates one to draw cross-cultural parallels.

The evidence and analysis offered in this article provide a basis for hypotheses of parallel cultural developments in China and the Olmec New World. If the Olmec did discover the geomagnetic orienting properties of lodestone, as did the Han Chinese, it is most reasonable to speculate that they would have used their compass for comparable geomantic purposes. It should, however, be recognized that the Olmec claim, if documented, predates the Chinese discovery of the geomagnetic lodestone compass by more than a millennium.

At present, M-160 is a unique artifact and San Lorenzo a unique site: "The first civilized center of Mesoamerica and probably of the New World." Further documentation of the Olmec claim must await the discovery of similar artifacts in museums, private collections, or as yet undiscovered Olmec sites.

EXPLORATION OF THE ZAPOTECAN TOMBS IN SOUTHERN MEXICO

Saville, Marshall H.; *American Anthropologist,* 1:350–362, 1899.

Mound 7---While this work was progressing, two Indians were digging a large hole at the southwestern end of Mound 7 in order to destroy some nests of ants, which were doing great injury to their crops. They discovered at the base of the mound a low stone wall, running east and west, several feet below the surface of their field. Rising from the wall at an angle of forty-five degrees was a covering of cement, which, at one time, probably enveloped the mound; it was in the form of an irregular dome with four square sides.

The attention of the Indians was called to a terra-cotta tubing or pipe

Terra cotta tubing leading from Mound 7, Xoxo, Mexico

which ran from under the cement covering, coming downward, and ending a few feet away in the field, perhaps three feet from the surface and ten feet beyond the stone wall.   I made an excavation here and followed the tubing upward for thirty-six feet, until it ended near the edge of a cement floor.   The character of this singular tube may be seen in plate XXI.   It was laid in short sections, of varying length, one end being smaller than the other, the small end of one tube being fitted into the large end of the next.   Several of the joints still preserved the cement with which they were made tight. ˙ The explorations did not reveal the use of the pipe.   I learned from an Indian who has a milpa on the summit of Monte Alban, of a single section of tubing which he found in digging in the end of a mound near the eastern part of the ruins, which specimen is now in the collections of the American Museum of Natural History. I was informed by Sr. Don Francisco Leon, Director of the Museum in the city of Oaxaca, that sections have also been found by the Indians at Zachila.   No such terra-cotta tubing has ever been discovered elsewhere in Mexico, and a new problem is therefore presented.   Near one of the sections of the tube was the cover of a beautiful portrait funeral urn, placed with the face upward.   (pp. 354-355)

UNWORLDLY MECHANICS
de Solla Price, Derek J.; *Natural History,* 71:8-17, March 1962.

This evidence was an object brought to the surface in the first and unexpected discovery in underwater archeology, in 1900.   During that year, Greek sponge divers, driven by storm to anchor near the tiny island of Antikythera, below Kythera in the south of the Peloponnesus, came upon the wreck of a treasure ship.   Later research has shown that the ship, loaded with bronze and marble statues and other art objects, must have been wrecked about 65 B. C. (plus or minus ten years), while making a journey from the neighborhood of Rhodes and Cos and on its way, presumably, to Rome.

Among the surviving art objects and the lumps of corroded bronze and pock-marked marble, there was one pitiably formless lump not noticed particularly when it was first hauled from the sea.   Some time later, while drying out, it split into pieces, and the archeologists on the job immediately recognized it as being of the greatest importance.   Within the lump were the remains of bronze plates to which adhered the remnants of many complicated gear wheels and engraved scales.   Some of the plates were marked with barely recognizable inscriptions, written in Greek characters of the first century B. C., and just enough could be made of the sense to tell that the subject matter was undoubtedly astronomical.

. . . .

Little by little, the pieces fitted together until there resulted a fair idea of the nature and purpose of the machine and of the main character of the inscriptions with which it was covered.   The original Antikythera mechanism must have borne a remarkable resemblance to a good modern mechanical clock. It consisted of a wooden frame that supported metal plates, front and back, each plate having quite complicated dials with pointers moving around them. The whole device was about as large as a thick folio encyclopedia volume. Inside the box formed by frame and plates was a mechanism of gear wheels, some twenty of them at least, arranged in a non-obvious way and including differential gears and a crown wheel, the whole lot being mounted on an internal bronze plate. A shaft ran into the box from the side and, when this was turned, all the pointers moved over their dials at various speeds. The dial plates were protected by bronze doors hinged to them, and dials and doors carried the long inscriptions that described how to operate the machine.

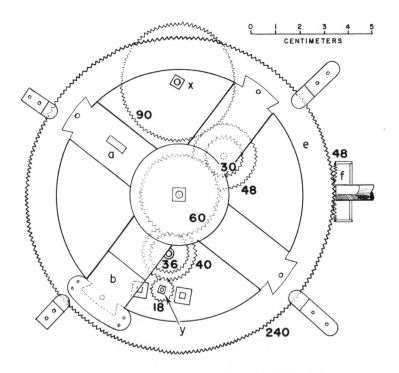

Main mechanism of Greek "computer." Numbers refer to the approximate numbers of teeth in the gears.

It appears that this was, indeed, a computing machine that could work out and exhibit the motions of the sun and moon and probably also the planets. Exactly how it did this is not clear, but the evidence thus far suggests that it was quite different from all other planetary models. It was not like the more familiar planetarium or orrery, which shows the planets moving at their various speeds, but much more like a mechanization of the purely arithmetical Babylonian methods. One just read the dials in accordance with the instructions, and legends on the dials indicated which phenomena would occur at any given time.

ELECTRIC BATTERIES OF 2,000 YEARS AGO
Schwalb, Harry M.; *Science Digest,* 41:17-19, April 1957.

Yet in Cleopatra's day, up-and-coming Baghdad silversmiths were goldplating jewelry---using electric batteries.

It's no myth; young scientist Willard F. M. Gray, of General Electric's High Voltage Laboratory in Pittsfield, Mass., has proved it. He made an exact replica of one of the 2,000-year-old wet cells and connected it to a galvanometer. When he closed the switch---current flowed!

These B.C.-vintage batteries (made by the Parthians, who dominated the Baghdad region between 250 B.C. and 224 A.D.) are quite simple. Thin sheet-copper was soldered into a cylinder less than 4 inches long and about an inch in diameter---roughly the size of two flashlight batteries end to end. The solder was a 60/40 tin-lead alloy .---"one of the best in use today," Gray points out.

The bottom of the cylinder was a crimped-in copper disc insulated with a layer of asphaltum (the "bitumen" that the Bible tells us Noah used to caulk the Ark). The top was closed with an asphalt stopper, through which projected the end of an iron rod. To stand upright, it was cemented into a small vase.

. . . .

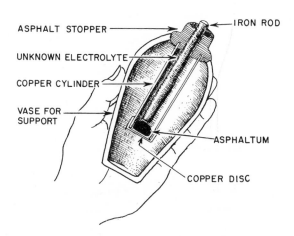

Model of a supposed electric battery from ancient Baghdad, showing iron electrode insulated with asphalt and a copper cylinder filled with an unknown electrolyte.

What electrolyte the Parthian jewelers used is a mystery, but Gray's model works well with copper sulfate. Acetic or citric acid, which the ancient chemists had in plenty, should be even better.

This evidence of man's first industrial use of electricity was discovered 20 years ago by a German archeologist, Wilhelm Konig, at the Iraq Museum. A small hill with the resounding name of Khujut Rabu'a, on the outskirts of Baghdad, was being dug away and the remains of a Parthian town were revealed. The Museum at once began scientific excavations, and in the digging turned up a peculiar object that---to Konig ---looked very much like a present-day dry-cell.

. . . .

THE LITTLE WOODEN AIRPLANE
Anonymous; *Pursuit*, 5:88, 1972.

We mentioned, but just tangentially, in our last issue when speaking of "flight" by the Ancients (p. 68), that the most amazing example yet to come to light was the discovery of a scale model of a very advanced type of cargo-carrying pusher plane or powered glider in an ancient Egyptian tomb at Saqqara, and dated as having been made in or about the year 200 B. C.

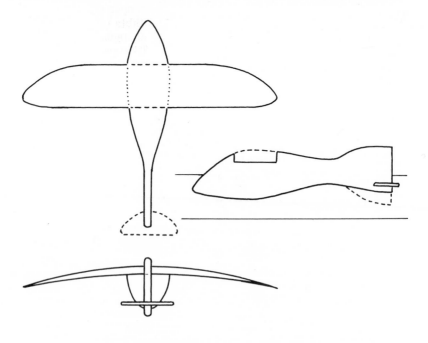

Ancient Egyptian wooden "airplane"

The Ancient Egyptian technologists always made scale models of things they were going to build, all the way from temples to ships. This item was originally discovered in 1898 and, airplanes being unknown in those days, was thrown into a box marked "wooden bird models" and then stored in the basement of the famous museum in Cairo. Here it was rediscovered by one Dr. Khalil Messiha who has made a life study of these models made by the ancients. So important was this "discovery" considered that the Egyptian Ministry of Culture set up a special committee of leading scientists to study it. The result of their findings was that a special exhibit was set up in the central hall of the museum with this little model as its centerpiece. It is even labelled as a model airplane. This is not the kind of behavior one expects of a committee of experts; especially archaeologists and in a museum at that.

To tell the whole story would fill all of this issue, so we will confine ourselves to pointing out a few of the amazing aspects of this story. First of all, this thing has the exact proportions of a very advanced form of what is called a pusher-glider that is still having the "bugs ironed out of it". This device is actually a glider that will almost stay in the air of itself so that even a tiny engine would keep it going at speeds as low as 45 to 65 m.p.h. while it could carry an enormous pay-load. The whole business depends upon the strange shape and proportions of the wings. These, as you will see from the drawing, curve down at the tips. This is called a "reversedihedral wing".

Now comes this startling outline of the controversial European superplane Concorde, the design of every part of which was planned to give this juggernaut the maximum lift without detracting from its speed. And so what do we see?

Precisely the same wing form and proportions. It seems rather incredible to us that anybody, for any reason, should have devised just such a model 2000 years ago. Is this another "left-over" from some greatly advanced prior technological civilization, the more useful techniques of which were carefully preserved by the priesthoods? It looks like it.

PREHISTORIC SALT BOILING
Riehm, Karl; *Antiquity,* 35:181-191, 1961.

The Red Hills of the English Coast. Just over fifty years ago the puzzling Red Hills on the coast of Essex were arousing considerable interest among English prehistorians. Already in the spring of 1906, under the chairmanship of J. Chalkley Gould and supported by the Essex Field Club, the Society of Antiquaries of London had formed a 'Red Hills Exploration Committee', which counted among its members not only archaeologists but also geologists, botanists and chemists, and had ample means at its disposal. Eminent specialists and scholars examined suitable hills with the utmost care and published their findings and conclusions in comprehensive papers.

But in what consists the peculiarity and the riddle of these Red Hills, which obviously date back to prehistoric times and have since time immemorial lain in close proximity to the coast of England? The striking way in which they are built of loose red burnt clay unmistakably points to a human-made origin. As a rule these mounds rise by only as much as 18 in. to 6 ft. above their surroundings, and their extent varies between a few square yards to several hundred. How did these numerous and extensive heaps of burnt clay come about in prehistoric times?

A further riddle about these hills are the peculiar objects of burnt clay, fragments of which are found in varying numbers within them, often embedded in layers of ash and charcoal. Thousands of similar finds have been known from the upper reaches of the Seille valley in Lorraine, which is rich in salt springs, and where, since Keune's diggings, they have been connected with the gaining of salt from salt wells, in prehistory. Of the various unusual objects of this kind, in Essex as well as in Lorraine, particularly striking are bar-like fragments, round, square or rectangular in section, made of a mixture of clay and chaff, while the multiform connecting pieces or lutings do not show this addition of perishable material to the clay at either place of discovery. Among further typical component parts of this group of finds in both places we wish to mention as important variously-shaped porous clay containers, as well as numerous sherds of large cooking pots. According to the linguistic usage of French scholars, who first described these finds on the Seille as early as 1740, the scientific designation of brequetage has become customary for this complex of finds.

'Red Hills' are found very frequently on the coast of Essex, where several hundred of them have been counted. But also in the counties north of Essex these mounds are no rarity---always situated in the vicinity of the sea or of the mouth of a river. There are also sites on the south and west coast of England (Kent, Sussex, Hampshire, Dorset, Somerset), as well as in the Channel Islands, where finds similar to those of the Red Hills are encountered, though fewer in number. In other parts of Europe, too, numerous places containing briquetage have been discovered, as, for example, on the Atlantic coast of France, especially in southern Brittany, on the Dutch-Belgian coast, as well as on the Caucasian Black Sea coast. There are a few sites also in the interior of Germany, where occur great quantities of briquetage or similar shaped strange objects of clay. This is the case especially in central Germany in the region of the ancient salt town Halle on Saale. Other important places of briquetage in Germany are Schwabisch Hall and Bad Nauheim.

. . . .

R. A. Smith submitted a series of reports on briquetage sites on the Continent, which confirmed his view that the Red Hills fragments should be interpreted as the remnants of an extensive salt gaining industry of pre-Roman times. He concluded by offering his very own detailed suggestion of a reconstruction of the forgotten technique of the ancient salt boilers; this interpretation points to new ways, especially in the exact description of prehistoric basins of evaporation; in the end, however, Smith closely approximated his interpretation to that of the Lorraine scholars.

. . . .

Chapter 3
GRAPHIC AND SYMBOLIC ARTIFACTS

INTRODUCTION

A common measure of a culture's development is its use of symbols and writing---the more abstract, the more advanced the civilization. This yardstick may be unfair because ancient man's success at dealing with the cosmos may be unrelated to writing. Indeed, writing is really a crutch for poor memories. Nonetheless, the use of graphics does suggest more than brutish mental processes, so we present a representative collection of anomalous symbols and inscriptions.

Four subclasses of graphic artifacts are recognized here:

1. Pictorial artifacts; particularly pictographs and statues that are anomalous because they suggest men, animals, or things that are out-of-place; viz., elephants in pre-Columbian America.

2. Macroforms; that is, gigantic drawings and symbols that can be fully appreciated only from the air. Since ancient man presumably did not have the ability to fly, the purpose of macroforms is most perplexing.

3. Symbols and notations that either indicate unexpected mathematical and astronomical development or resist interpretation altogether.

4. Writing that is precocious, untranslatable, or found where anthropological theory says it should not exist.

Because we place so much emphasis on the value of words and symbols, many of the artifacts described below have been the subject of bitter controversy. Hoaxes have been frequent, but so has dogmatism.

STRANGE PICTOGRAPHS AND STATUARY

The human propensity for drawing himself, animals, and certain designs is well known and not startling in itself. Sometimes, though, the pictures of ancient man portray things that should not be. These find their ways into this handbook.

The controversial Nampa Image, a statue found far below the surface by well diggers, certainly poses problems of explanation if legitimate. Also out of place are the many ancient accurate representations of elephant-like creatures found in the Americas. Either knowledge of the elephant was brought from Asia or the mammoth lingered later than believed possible. The anthropoid figurines of the American Northwest are in the same category.

Perhaps most curious of all are the odd stripes found in caves, the "fingerprint drawings," and the strangely carved stone spheres. We do not know whether these are simply exhuberant art or symbols carrying arcane messages. Lacking pen and paper, ancient man, we suppose, might have doodled in stone; but that seems like a lot of work for such a trivial urge.

• The Human Form

THE IDAHO FIND
Wright, G. Frederick; *American Antiquarian*, 11:379–381, 1889.

In the latter part of September I received from Charles Francis Adams, president of the Union Pacific Railroad, a letter stating that while at Boise City, Idaho, a short time before, he had heard much about a "clay image," which had been found while boring for artesian water at Nampa, Idaho, a station on the Oregon Short Line railroad, about twenty miles from Boise City, and about half way between Boise river and Smoke river, being seven miles from the former and twelve from the latter. This whole region, like hundreds of thousands of square miles of the Pacific Slope, is covered with deposits of lava rock belonging to late tertiary or quarternary times. Beneath these lava deposits in California occurs much of the gold-bearing gravel; and in this gravel, thus covered with lava, Professor Whitney, some years ago, reported the discovery of many human implements, and the celebrated Calaveras skull. But, because of the advanced stage of culture evinced, and of the high character of the skull, the archaeologists of Europe have been slow to accept the genuineness of Professor Whitney's alleged discoveries; for they do not tally with their preconceived notions respecting the slow and regular evolution of the human race from ape-like progenitors. The present discovery comes, therefore, with great confirmatory power to the support of Professor Whitney, and from its character bears strongly against the extreme views as to the evolution of man. It points rather to a degeneracy of the race in the case of paleolithic man in the Eastern United States and in Europe.

The circumstances under which the Nampa image was found are as follows: Mr. M. A. Kurtz, an educated and competent man, was engaged in boring an artesan (sic) well. After penetrating the surface soil sixty feet, fifteen or twenty feet of lava rock was encountered. Below this for upward of 200 feet there was nothing but alternate beds of quicksand and clay; then coarse sand was struck in which the image came up, then below was vegetable soil and then sand rock. Thus it is evident that the image lay buried to the depth of about 300 feet, beneath deposits which had accumulated in a lake formed by some ancient obstruction of the Snake river valley and that over this accumulation there had been an outflow of lava sufficient to cover the whole and seal it up.

In reply to letters of inquiry as to the possibility that the image had fallen in from the top or been thrown in, Mr. Kurtz says the well is tubed from the top with heavy six-inch wire tubing, section after section having been added as the whole was driven down, so that nothing could have fallen in. As to the theory that the image was thrown in, Mr. Kurtz well says that in that case, falling on the top of the water and sand, it would have been ground to pieces by the sand pump. Furthermore, when subjected to the inspection under a magnifying-glass by Professors Haynes and Putnam it became at once evident that it is not a clay image, as Mr. Adams and Mr. Kurtz supposed, but that it has been carved out of fine and rather soft pumice-stone, and that the reddish coating over it was such a film of oxide of iron as would form only after long exposure in peculiar conditions. In this case also small particles of sand were cemented into the crevice between the arm and the body. All this shows that it is no recent affair, and that it can not be a hoax.

In reference to the age of the stratum where the image lay, Mr.

The Nampa Image (actual size)

Emmons, of the U. S. Geological Survey, who is more familiar than any other geologist with the region, writes me that, in his opinion (subject, however, to correction), they are "probably of far greater antiquity than any deposits in which human implements have hitherto been discovered."

It is difficult to institute any trustworthy comparison between the age of this image and that of the paleolithic implements found in the eastern part of the United States. At Trenton, N. J., Madisonville, O., Medora, Ind., and Little Falls, Minn., rough stone implements, similar in type to the paleolithics discovered in the valley of the Somme in France and at various places in Southern England, have been found in glacial gravels, thus connecting man with the closing scenes of the glacial period. From data connected with the recession of the Falls of Niagara and of St. Anthony, however, it is found that this period may not have been more than eight or ten thousand years ago.

As to the connection of the deposits on the Pacific Slope with the glacial age, we have no very definite data, though it seems altogether probable that there was some connection. During the great ice age glaciers abounded throughout the Sierra Nevada and the Rocky Mountains, and their melting was probably hastened by the vast lava outflows which occurred in the region. The Snake river rises in the mountains surrounding the Yellow Stone park, where glaciers were of great extent. The sudden melting of these may, very likely, be the cause of the rapid accummulation of silt in the temporary lake of Nampa, where the image was found.

The high degree of art displayed in the image is noteworthy. It is not the work of a boy or of a novice. The proportions are perfect, and there is a pose of the body that is remarkable, and which differentiates it from anything that has been found among the relics of the Moundbuilders. Altogether it supports the hypothesis of Professor Putnam, advanced some years ago, that civilization advanced on the Pacific Coast long in advance of that which has anywhere else been discovered. And it is by no means impassible that we have some relics of those catastrophies by floods which are so universal in the traditions of all nations.

THE CRYSTAL SKULL
Willis, R.; *INFO Journal*, 3:1-4, 1973.

If we can believe the stories F. A. Mitchell-Hedges told about himself, which are supported by others, he was truly an interesting character. Born in England, making fortunes at the drop of a hat and losing them as easily, he came to America to make another fortune. He wound up playing poker with J. P. Morgan and his friends, winning $29,000 one night. A little later he was washing dishes for his keep in a New Orleans restaurant, and even was a cowboy for a while. He joined Pancho Villa's army, when Ambrose Bierce was traveling with it, possibly as a secret agent. He roamed through Mexico, apparently was the first to discover and excavate the great Mayan center of Lubaantun, and investigated the islands off British Honduras, which he thought showed signs of a recent cataclysm, considering the area part of lost Atlantis.

He adopted a young girl named Anna Le Guillon. The common story of the appearance of the skull is that in 1927 while excavating at Lubaantun, in the southern part of British Honduras, Anna Mitchell-Hedges found, under an altar that had been covered by a collapsed wall, a skull carved out of quartz crystal. Three months later, the detached lower jaw of quartz was found by Anna 25 feet away. What was this "crystal skull?"

It is, as the illustrations show, one of the most interesting gem stones in existence. The skull is essentially life-size, probably patterned after a female skull. Its carving is basically realistic, with the exception that the sutures of the skull are not shown. Curiously this extremely valuable specimen attracted very little notice, and was put up for sale by a London art dealer who held it as collateral on a loan to Mitchell-Hedges, in 1940---and it could not be sold for 400 pounds ($2,000). Today it is estimated to be worth $250,000 and is probably worth much more.

The skull attracted little notice until the late 1960's. A great deal has been written recently on the skull, primarily on its reputed psychic properties. The skull has never been fully accepted by archeologists as a legitimate artifact. Indeed, its finding is still controversial. There are stories that Mitchell-Hedges bought the object in London, but there is no proof of this. There is also more than one version of the story of Anna finding it at Lubaantun. However, Anna did make a formal affidavit that she <u>did</u> find it there, under the conditions described above. The great argument seems to be whether the skull is ancient or modern.

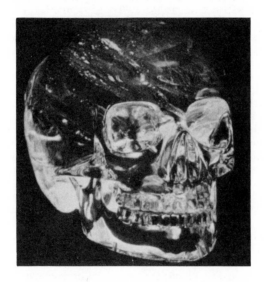

The Mitchell-Hedges crystal skull

The use of the skull in Amerindian art is common, as most of us know. The Museum of the American Indian in New York had a display called "Visions of Mortality, The Skull Motif in Indian Art," from November, 1972 to March 1973, in which the Mitchell-Hedges skull was shown. The guide to the exhibit points out that the skull was an integral part of the concept of life being germinated through death. The Mexican festival of skulls at Halloween is a continuation of these early rituals. The ceramics of pre-Columbian Peru show skeletons engaged in life activities with living people, even erotically.

The production of or at least the finding of small crystal skulls in Mexico is documented. They are usually called Aztec and some of them at least were in their possession when the Spanish came and "liberated" them. Mitchell-Hedges' claim of finding the Crystal Skull in Mayan ruins is plausible considering the background of the motif in Mexico, if not as strong in Mayan country. His claim that it came originally from Atlantis is another matter. At any rate there is a skull of quartz crystal, the same size as the Mitchell-Hedges skull, but more crudely formed, and with the lower jaw attached, in the British museum. There is another skull in the Musee de l'Homme in Paris. There are also other smaller and cruder specimens of such skulls in other museums.

There have been statements that the Crystal Skull could not be made today because it represents such a fine and difficult piece of work to cut such an object from quartz crystal. This is not very defensible since we have more tools and materials today (we presume) than any ancient technician would have had. If it were made in the ancient past, it would have indeed represented a great investment in time and technological knowledge ---but it was probably possible for the Mayans and others. Quartz crystal has a hardness of 7 on the Moh's scale. This means that a standard steel pocket knife blade will not scratch it. Topaz, corundum and diamond are harder and will scratch or cut quartz. Using diamond tools a modern artist could rough out the form in relatively short order. However it should be noted that the Japanese who have long been noted for making crystal balls from quartz crystals, often used the technique of chipping the ball to the rough form merely by striking it with a hammer. The rough grinding of the skull after having been crudely shaped out, would have been the greatest problem. Grinding with sand, which is the same chemical structure, SiO_2, and same hardness, is possible but very time consuming. There is no indication that diamonds were ever used or their hardness appreciated until relatively modern times. Corundum likewise does not seem to have been known or used although there were quantities in North America. The British Museum skull has been noted to have marks separating the teeth indicating that the artisan used a rotating object to cut the line. This skull which is accepted to be at least as old as the Aztecs indicates that the artisans may well have used rotary tools powered by a bow, as in fire-drills, which would have substantially cut the labor of grinding.

A final polish can be given with red rouge which was known to the ancients. Perhaps the high polish on the skull could have been done with this. Or perhaps the final polish was done in the manner used by Indian gem cutters in days past---having a poor Indian working for starvation wages rub the stone all day with a rag for a year or so. This produces the ultimate polish on a gem. At any rate a great deal of labor had to be expended on the skull, especially considering that the lower jaw was formed by cutting it from the main crystal.

Studies of the Crystal Skull have concluded that it is ancient but the grounds for this is not very clear. There is no satisfactory way of using scientific methodology for dating the skull---any such dating would, anyway, be of the crystal---not the carved object. However the fact that the British Museum skull is the same size as the Mitchell-Hedges skull suggests that it might be a sister skull, one that was not finished off to the same extent as the Mitchell-Hedges.

Quartz crystals large enough to be used for such a piece are rare, but are found in Europe, Asia and the U.S. In fact, the Crystal Skull crystal is identical to that found in Calaveras County, Calif. Cut quartz and quartz crystals have been widely considered unusual, and are considered "magical" in many places. Crystal balls have been found in the tombs of the Romans, King Childeric, and several of the French Kings. Interestingly enough, the Mayans even today prize clear crystal stones, their "Zaztun," as magical objects---even in the very areas where Anna was reported to have found the Crystal Skull.

Notable in the skull is the fact that the zygomatic arches are completely and accurately separated from the body of the piece and act as "light pipes" to help carry light towards the orbits. Also under the skull, where the palate would be, the surface areas are actually carved as prisms and a light source from below is refracted throughout the skull in a truly awesome way. There are small holes where it is suggested a mechanism was arranged to hold on the jaws and make them moveable. The skull could have been set up in the black interior of a shrine, perhaps, and with concealed light from below, in conjunction with the movement of the jaws, it would have indeed been an effective oracle or ritual figure.

. . . .

A CRYSTAL MASK FROM TIBET
Anonymous; *Nature*, 119:174, 1927.

Mr. H. C. Beasley has published in Man for January an illustration of a remarkable crystal mask from Tibet. The mask is that of the goddess Palden Lhamo, one of the Eight Terribles, as is shown by a third eye in the middle of the forehead. The body of her face is worked up from a lump of rock crystal, the features are applied in gilt bronze, and the teeth are probably human, while the eyes are of ivory. It is said that the mask was used to attract evil demons, who were then dealt with by the officiating lama. Palden Lhamo corresponds to Kali of Indian mythology, and in Japan appears as a goblin under the name Mitsume. The Chinese god of disease Yu yuen, recognisable by his long teeth, also has a third eye, and is probably derived from Palden Lhamo. She was also believed by the Tibetans to have been reincarnated in Queen Victoria. As one of the Eight Terribles, Palden Lhamo rides a chestnut mule, the offspring of a winged mare, and the gift of the goddess of the sea. She carries a string of skulls, and she feeds on corpses given her by the goblins who haunt graveyards, while her scanty garment is a girdle made of the skin of a recently flayed man. She is often shown drinking blood from a cup formed of a human skull.

EASTER ISLAND
Anonymous; *Nature*, 46:258-260, 1892.

The prehistoric remains of Easter Island make it for archaeologists one of the most interesting islands in the Pacific. They will therefore read with interest an elaborate paper in the Report of the U. S. National Museum for 1888-89, which has just been issued. The paper is entitled

"Te Pito Te Henua, or Easter Island," and is by William J. Thomson, Paymaster, U.S. Navy. It records the results of researches made by Mr. Thomson during a visit paid to Easter Island by the American vessel, the Mohican, towards the end of 1886. The Mohican anchored in the Bay of Hanga Roa on the morning of December 18, 1886, and remained till the evening of the last day of the year, when she sailed for Valparaiso.

. . . .

Mr. Thomson has, of course, much to say about the stone images with the idea of which Easter Island is intimately associated in the minds of all who have devoted any attention to its antiquities. Every image in the island was counted, and the list shows a total of 555 images. Mr. Thomson says:---

"Of this number forty are standing inside of the crater, and nearly as many more on the outside of Rana Roraka, at the foot of the slope where they were placed as finished and ready for removal to the different platforms for which they were designed; some finished statues lie scattered over the plains as though they were being dragged toward a particular locality but were suddenly abandoned. The large majority of the images, however, are lying near platforms all around the coast, all more or less mutilated, and some reduced to a mere shapeless fragment. Not one stands in its original position upon a platform. The largest image is in one of the workshops in an unfinished state, and measures 70 feet in length; the smallest was found in one of the caves, and is a little short of three feet in length. One of the largest images that has been in position lies near the platform which it ornamented, near Ovahe; it is 32 feet long, and weighs 50 tons.

"Images representing females were found. One at Anakena is called 'Viri-viri Moai-a Taka,' and is apparently as perfect as the day it was finished; another, on the plain west of Rana Roraka is called 'Moai Putu, and is in a fair state of preservation. The natives have names for every one of the images. The designation of images and platforms as obtained from the guides during the exploration was afterwards checked off in company with other individuals without confusion in the record. The coarse gray trachytic lava of which the images were made is found only in the vicinity of Rana Roraka, and was selected because the conglomerate character of the material made it easily worked with the rude stone implements that constituted the only tools possessed by the natives. The disintegration of the material when exposed to the action of the elements is about equivalent to that of sandstone under similar conditions, and admits of an estimate in regard to the probable age. The traditions in regard to the images are numerous, but relate principally to impossible occurrences, such as being endowed with power to walk about in the darkness, assisting certain clans by subtle means in contests, and delivering oracular judgments. The legends state that a son of King Mahuta Ariiki, named Tro Kaiho, designed the first image, but it is difficult to arrive at an estimation of the period. The journals of the early navigators throw but little light upon the subject. The workshops must have been in operation at the time of Captain Cook's visit, but unfortunately his exploration of the island was not directed towards the crater of Rana Roraka.

"Although the images range in size from the colossus of 70 feet down to the pigmy of 3 feet, they are clearly all of the same type and general characteristics. The head is long, the eyes close under the heavy brows, the nose long, low-bridged, and expanded at the nostrils, the upper lip short and the lips pouting. The aspect is slightly upwards, and the expression is firm and profoundly solemn. Careful investigation failed to detect the slightest evidence that the sockets had ever been fitted with artificial eyes, made of bone and obsidian, such as are placed in the wooden images.

"The head was in all cases cut flat on top, to accommodate the red tufa crowns with which they were ornamented, but the images standing outside of the crater had flatter heads and bodies than those found around the coast. The images represent the human body only from the head to the hips, where it is cut squarely off to afford a good polygon of support when standing. The artists seem to have exhausted their talents in executing the features, very little work being done below the shoulders, and the arms being merely cut in low relief. The ears are only rectangular projections, but the lobes are represented longer in the older statues than in those of more recent date.

"The images were designed as effigies of distinguished persons, and intended as monuments to perpetuate their memory. They were never regarded as idols, and were not venerated or worshipped in any manner. The natives had their tutelary genii, gods, and goddesses, but they were represented by small wooden or stone idols, which bore no relation to the images that ornamented the burial platforms. The image-makers were a privileged class, and the profession descended from father to son.

Some of the natives still claim a descent from the image-makers, and refer to their ancestors with as much pride as to the royal family.

"The work of carving the image into shape, and detaching it from the rock of which it was a part, did not consume a great deal of time, but the chief difficulty was, in the absence of mechanical contrivances, to launch it safely down the slope of the mountain and transport it to a distant point. It was lowered to the plain by a system of chocks and wedges, and the rest was a dead drag accomplished by main strength. A roadway was constructed, over which the images were dragged by means of ropes made of indigenous hemp, and sea-weed and grass made excellent lubricants. The platforms were all built with sloping terraces in the rear, and up this incline a temporary road-way was constructed of a suitable height, upon which the statue could be rolled until the base was over its proper resting-place. The earth was then dug away to allow the image to settle down into position, the ropes being used to steady it in the meantime."

• Elephants in America?

THE MOAB MASTADON PICTOGRAPH
Anonymous; *Scientific Monthly*, 41:378-379, 1935.

Rock carvings, variously known as pictographs or petroglyphs, are familiar features to persons who have worked in the canyon-cut country of the Southwest.   That they have not excited greater interest is perhaps due to the fact that they commonly portray such things as aboriginal man was doubtless familiar with; goats, serpents, human figures and fowls make up most of those I have personally examined.   In 1924, however, I was informed by John Bristol, of Moab, Utah, that there was what he believed to be a mastodon pictograph some three miles down the Colorado Canyon from that village.   Though this excited my interest, the search had to wait for ten years until I was again in that vicinity last summer. In August of last year, Dennis Baldwin, Fred Strong, Jr., and I, after considerable searching, found the desired pictograph.

That this carving is designed to be an elephant or mastodon is evident.   It represents a good deal of work on the part of the primitive artist, for the figure, from the end of his very "pachydermous" tail to the tip of his trunk, is almost two feet long and appears to have been made by a painstaking method of chipping the whole figure from the solid rock wall with a blunt pick, chisel or similar tool.   It is a recessed or etched figure, composed of closely spaced "pock marks."

. . . .

THE LENAPE STONE

Greene, Richard L.; *NEARA Newsletter*, 7:16–18, 1972.

A century ago in the Spring of 1872, a farm boy plowing in the fields near Doylestown, Pennsylvania, allegedly discovered an unusual stone.   It seemed to be the larger section of a broken "gorget stone" or pendant, with two holes through it for inserting a thong to hang it about one's neck.   The finder, Bernard Hansell, noted that the stone was carved on one side with an assortment of pictographs, and on the other with the form of an animal resembling an elephant.   Hansell kept the stone in his pocket for several days and later stored it with the other artifacts he had found about the farm. He kept in mind the place where he had found the stone and occasionally searched for the missing half.

Nine years later in 1881 Hansell sold his entire collection of artifacts to one Henry Paxton of Doylestown, for $2.50. The sale brought the carved stone to light and it soon became a topic of widening interest. Hansell redoubled efforts to find the missing piece of stone and was, indeed, successful several months after the sale. Hansell then gave the second part of the stone to Paxton free of charge and the combination of the pieces produced a scene which could only be interpreted as a pictographic account of an Indian encounter with a mammoth.

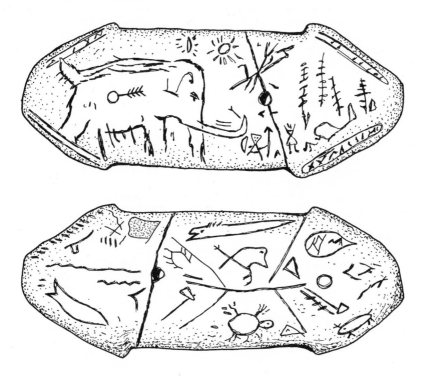

The Lenape Stone

The Lenape stone, as it came to be called, after a local branch of the Delaware Indians, produced a storm of controversy, which was well documented by Henry C. Mercer in his book, The Lenape Stone or Indian and the Mammoth, G. P. Putnam's Sons (1885). Mercer was a local antiquarian and was to become the leading figure in the Buck's County Historical Society. His reputation as a researcher is well established today for his studies on colonial firebacks (The Bible in Iron), on Ancient Carpenter's Tools (the standard work in this field) and various subjects related to early American architecture. Based on interviews with the parties concerned, and additional research. Mercer's conclusion was that the Lenape Stone was authentic.

He felt that a hoax was out of the question for two reasons. First of all, he thought that Bernard Hansell was quite incapable of such a hoax, a point which a reader feels would have been made more strongly had not Mercer been so polite. Reading between the lines, Hansell seems to have been a dolt. He had made no profit from the stone and even suggested that he had been cheated as the stone's notoriety spread. If Hansell were innocent, then who would have contrived a plot that would have been based on chance discovery, and taken nine years in the unfolding?

The Lenape Stone becomes much more interesting in light of related evidence unearthed by Mercer's research. Foremost among this evidence are the Indian traditions of a tremendous animal variously called the "Great Elk" or "Father of Oxen", etc., traditions which are similar and recorded in a number of different tribes. These include such far-flung tribes as the Delawares, Wyandots, Iroquois, and Osage. These traditions tell the story of the Indians' attempt to stop the rampage of a great beast aided by the thunderbolts of the great spirit. The Lenape Stone, with its battle scene and the jagged lightning in the sky, seems to come into sharper focus in light of the "Great Elk" legend.

As his study unfolds, Mercer brings in every possible source to suggest the late survival of the mammoth. First, he exhibits Mayan architectural designs which suggest the trunk and facial features of the animal. He goes on to cite the carved stone "elephant pipes"---two calumets from Louisa County, Iowa; and the Elephant Effigy Mound of Grant County, Wisconsin, as further indications of Indian knowledge of such an animal. (Note: The Elephant Mound is discussed in the Smithsonian Report, 1872, p. 416). These last items, unfortunately, have not themselves been wholly free of controversy.

The Lenape Stone raises questions about the mammoth in America. It does not answer them. While the claims for its authenticity are strong, they are not positive and a reader of Mercer's study is caught between the fear of accepting what might easily be a fake and rejecting that which could possibly be authentic. To take either side is an expression of faith rather than acceptance of absolutely proven fact.

The cloudy circumstances of the Stone's discovery will forever rob the Stone of an importance it might otherwise have had. If it had been found by the careful methods of a critical dig in the context of other datable artifacts, it would be a piece in the archaeological puzzle rather than unfilled space. One wonders if it would not have been better had the Stone remained in the earth in the hope of a discovery under more favorable circumstances. It is easy to see how a different sort of discovery might have changed the Stone's credibility. If nothing else, the Stone, authentic or not, certainly stands as a lesson that an artifact found out of archaeological context is all but meaningless. Looking to the future, one would hope that items of such potential importance as the Lenape Stone will not be unearthed so haphazardly.

EARLY MAN AT HOLLY OAK, DELAWARE
Kraft, John C., and Thomas, Ronald A.; *Science*, 192:756-761, 1976.

A reevaluation of an association of early man in northern Delaware
with the woolly mammoth (Mammuthus or Elephas sp.) suggests a time
from the early to middle Holocene epoch (8000 to 4000 B.C.) or, alternatively, an extremely early association in the early Wisconsin and late
Sangamon ages. Stratigraphic and palynological analyses identify thin
sedimentary layers as representing paleoenvironments of the late
Holocene epoch and early Wisconsin and Sangamon ages in the northern
Delaware region at the boundary between the piedmont and coastal plain
geomorphic provinces. These sediments are closely associated with
occurrences of abundant Archaic and Paleo-Indian artifacts and a carving of the woolly mammoth. Below, we discuss the probability of
association of these artifacts of early American man with the woolly
mammoth as well as with the mastodon in either the early to middle
Holocene epoch (5,000 to 10,000 years ago) and the very latest Wisconsin age or early Wisconsin and late Sangamon ages (60,000 to 100,000
years ago).

The Holly Oak Pendant. An interesting discovery pertaining to
early man in the New World occurred in 1864 when H. T. Cresson and
W. L. deSuralt found a number of artifacts associated with some peats
near the Holly Oak railroad station in northern Delaware. Among the
items found was a pendant carved from a fossil whelk shell, into which
was incised the image of a woolly mammoth (Fig. 1). Needless to say,
great excitement ensued concerning this evidence of early American
man.

Unfortunately, the story of the exact location of discovery of the
pendant is somewhat in doubt. One report states that it was found amidst
some peat being dug from a "deep" hole on the Delaware River plain

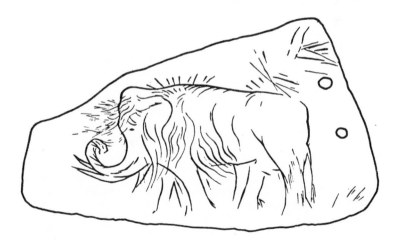

The Holly Oak pendant, carved on the surface of a large whelk

opposite the Holly Oak station of the Pennsylvania Railroad. The farmers are said to have been digging peat for use as fertilizer. Another account, reports that the Holly Oak pendant was found amidst some peat already spread on a farmer's field near the Holly Oak station of the Wilmington and Baltimore Railroad. The peat was said to have been taken from a "fallen forest layer in one of the adjoining estuaries of the Delaware River."

From 1864 until his death in 1894, Cresson pursued a career as an archeologist and continued to search the northern Delaware piedmont and coastal plain area for further evidences of early man in America. By 1880, he and a few associates had found more than 1000 artifacts, including logs with evidence of cutting, stone sinkers, arrowheads, spearheads, stone knives, hammerstones, splinters of bone, potsherds, stone axes, celts, chips of argillite, quartz, quartzite, flint, jasper, shell beads, a mastodon tooth, human teeth, bone implements, and other remains. Many of these artifacts were ultimately deposited in the Peabody Museum, Yale University, and in the National Museum of Natural History, Smithsonian Institution. This conglomeration of tools, carvings, bones, teeth, and beads is indeed puzzling. Much of the association appears to be from the Archaic period (8000 to 2000 B.C.). However, the bone implements and the mammoth carved on the Holly Oak pendant suggest a possible Paleo-Indian origin (before 8000 B.C.). Obviously, a great deal of reevaluation needs to be done with regard to the discoveries of Cresson and his associates in northern Delaware.

Cresson's work ranged along the relatively narrow coastal plain adjacent to the fall zone and piedmont of northern Delaware. Some of the artifacts are reported to have been dug from a rock shelter near the town of Claymont. Many others were found in a layer of peat under the tidal mud that extended under the bed of Naaman's Creek at its confluence with the Delaware River. Unfortunately, detailed records of the stratigraphy of the sites and of precise locations of the discoveries were not maintained. Interestingly, during the same part of the late 19th century, other discoveries were being made in North America of remains of "early man" or "ice age man." These included the discovery of the Lenape stone, bearing the carving of a mammoth pursued by hunters and found in Buckingham Township, Pennsylvania, in 1872. In addition, Charles Abbott, an amateur archeologist, reported a large aboriginal site south of Trenton. Abbott reported finding crude weapons in river gravels that he interpreted to be of "ice age" origin.

During the later years of the 19th century, many amateur and professional archeologists examined the finds of Cresson and others. Some said that the artifacts were up to 50,000 years old and from a glacial epoch. From the turn of the century into the early part of the 20th century, argument continued as to the age and meaning of the tremendous number of artifacts collected by Cresson. In view of the questionable geological relationships, skeptics began to insist that Cresson had not actually discovered some of the objects he claimed or that the discoveries were spurious or, in some cases, modern in origin. A major criticism raised was that Cresson's discovery of the mammoth carved on the shell occurred in the same year as the discovery by Lartet of a similar carving on a mammoth tusk in the cave of La Madeleine in France. The Lenape stone is suspect for the same reason. In addition, from 1936 to 1941 an intensive restudy was made of Abbott's discoveries near Trenton. This study with modern techniques and by trained archeologists and geologists suggested that the Abbott's farm occurrence in New Jersey was not of great antiquity. Continued lack of confirmed evidence of early man in eastern North America led to a general low regard for Cresson's discoveries and to the idea that Paleo-Indian occupancy of eastern North America probably did not begin until the rather late date of 10,000 to 12,000 years ago. A survey of books and publications on ancient man in North America and Paleo-Indian discoveries almost never reveals references to the Holly Oak pendant and its "mammoth."

Recent studies of the geomorphology and geologic history of the Delaware coastal plain where it borders the piedmont (the fall zone) suggest that sedimentary deposits occur in a time span that lends some credence to the occurrence of Paleo-Indian or Archaic man in the Delaware area at the same time as the woolly mammoth occupation. Accordingly, a new evaluation of the Holly Oak pendant was made. Clifford Evans and his colleagues at the Smithsonian Institution reexamined the carving on the surface of the shell and reached the conclusion that the incisions show the same stages of weathering as the shell surface itself. Most who have examined the Holly Oak specimen "indicated that they think this object is legitimate, and do not see any possibility of even suggesting the remote conception that it is a fake." Figure 1 shows a detailed interpretation of the carving on the Holly Oak pendant, constructed by B. J. Meggers of the Smithsonian Institution. It is clear that the Holly Oak pendant is old and bears a carving of a woolly mammoth that was incised at the time of construction of the weathered pendant and near the time of origin of the shell. The question remains: How old is the pendant?

. . . .

Paleo-Indian or Earlier? In view of the poor detail of recorded association of artifact finds with the Holly Oak pendant, there is not enough evidence to determine precisely the age of the Holly Oak pendant. However, a low-lying coastal plain land surface extended along the ancestral Delaware River and adjacent to the piedmont crystalline uplands in Archaic times (4,000 to 10,000 years ago). This land surface included widespread areas of peaty and organic alluvial silts. The silts were deposited as alluvial floodplain deposits at a time more than 40,000 years ago and probably in the early Wisconsin and Sangamon ages (about 60,000 to 100,000 years ago). Possibly the Holly Oak pendant and some of the other artifacts were deposited in this sediment that is more than 40,000 years old and, presumably, of the early Wisconsin and Sangamon ages. Conversely, it is also possible that these artifacts were lost or buried in the land surface of Archaic times as sea level continued to rise and cover the sediment that is more than 40,000 years old. Ultimately, the entire erosional or unconformity surface was covered by the modern late Holocene marsh as the late Holocene rise in relative sea level and coastal transgression continued. In view of this, intrusions through late Holocene sediments (Woodland period) and deposits of the Archaic period could lie in close association along this surface.

A precise timing cannot be set for the carving of the Holly Oak pendant. However, we suggest several possibilities.

1) The Holly Oak mammoth may have been carved by Paleo-Indian

peoples or American Indians of the early Archaic period. It is clearly
indicated by the times of formation of the geologic units that early man
lived in association with the late Pleistocene and early Holocene mastodon and mammoth.

2) It is also possible that the pendant is extremely old and was deposited with the alluvial floodplain sediments more than 40,000 years
ago, probably in early Wisconsin or Sangamon age. If so, the case
might be made for a truly early American man in earliest Wisconsin
or Sangamon times.

3) A third hypothesis could be made, although it is not very tenable.
The Holly Oak pendant might have been found in the sediment layers of
two and a half millennia ago. This would introduce the possibility of a
very late occurrence of the woolly mammoth in eastern North America.

4) It is remotely possible that the pendant was removed from its
original place of deposition by later Indians of the Woodland period.

5) Finally, it is possible that the pendant was skillfully manufactured and dropped at the Holly Oak site by Cresson, de Suralt, or an
unknown person.

The heavily traveled "fall zone corridor" of Delaware is now covered by Governor Printz Boulevard, Interstate 95, the Penn Central Railroad, a power transmission system, and much industry and "fill."
However, a few areas for potential exploration still exist. A renewed
effort might still solve the problems of archeologists, anthropologists,
and geologists faced with much evidence of early man in northern Delaware: thousands of artifacts, an "old" carving of a mammoth on a shell,
early Wisconsin and Sangamon age floodplain deposits; and almost nowhere
to excavate. Reexamination of old discoveries, coupled with the application of new concepts in sedimentology-stratigraphy and palynology, has
led to an exciting new association of early man with the woolly mammoth
in America. Possibly, further work will prove truly ancient (early Wisconsin and Sangamon age) presence of early man. It is probably time to
reexamine many of our legends, historical records, and archeologic discoveries in the light of new geoscience techniques.

THE ELEPHANT PIPE

Farquharson, R. J.; *American Antiquarian*, 2:67-69, 1879.

By a letter from Mr. Peter Mare (the original finder), now living
in Kansas, we learn that he found this elephant pipe six or seven years
ago (1872 or 1873), while planting corn on his farm, where he resided,
in Louisa County, Iowa. (The man from whom we obtained it---the
brother-in-law of Mare---was under the impression that it was found
in Muscatine County, and it was so stated in the first published account.)

Mr. Mare kept the pipe until he moved to Kansas in 1878, and then
gave it to his brother-in-law, from whom we obtained it. The Rev. Mr.
Gass, having indirectly heard last winter of the existence of such a
relic, sought out the owner and endeavored to purchase it, but in vain;

he however succeeded in borrowing it for the purpose of taking casts and photographs.

While being copied in plaster it was accidentally broken, and then by compromising the matter with the owner, and paying him about five dollars, we obtained the ownership. The finder, Mr. Mare, an illiterate German farmer, had no appreciation of any scientific value or special interest attaching to his pipe. He wanted and got nothing for it, regarding it merely as a curiosity. He found various other "Indian stones," as he called them, but all these were lost in moving about.

The ancient mounds are very abundant in that region (Louisa County), and also very rich in relics, and it is a significant fact that, in exploring a considerable number of them, we found that in their construction no excavation had been made, but that the bodies and relics had been deposited on the original surface of the ground, and the mound raised by bringing the earth, apparently, from the immediate vicinity. In such a case it would not be strange if in a mound gradually removed by long cultivation, the relics so deposited should at last be reached and turned up by the plow.

The material of the pipe is a soft, fragile sandstone. This was not detected until the fracture showed its true nature, a dark, external polish, apparently the result of use, misleading us at first. The weight of the pipe is 164 grammes. The accompanying wood cut (3/4 size) gives a tolerably good representation of the figure of the animal, but, unfortunately the engraver has failed to reproduce the pointed, projecting lower lip, an elephantine feature well marked in the original.

Elephant pipe found in an Indian mound

The dimensions of the figure are as follows, viz.: Extreme length (from frontal protuberance to root of tail) 88 millimetres; height (at shoulders), 39 ms.; girth, 85 ms.; thickness (at shoulders), 24 ms.; circumference of trunk (at the extremity of the lower lip), 33 ms.; length of trunk (from the tip to the angle of the mouth), 35 ms; length of tail, 29 ms. The animal is represented as standing with the feet together, and with the trunk coiled and resting on the ground, the tip reaching up to the fore-knee (properly the wrist); this position of the trunk and its comparative length shows that the artist was aware of the greater proportionate height of the animal, but was cramped in the execution of his sculpture by the typical and conventional form of the Mound Builder's pipe, or by some unfitness of the material, or perhaps by both of these causes.

. . . .

However disproportioned the figure may be, there can be no doubt of its representing some one of the elephant family, and as, in this country, the mastodon was the last to survive, and in all probability only disappeared a few centuries ago, we may safely infer that it was the animal represented.

From 1794, when Jefferson published the Indian tradition concerning the recent existence of the "pere aux boeufs" to the discovery of this pipe, in 1879, there has been a steady and gradual, if slow, accumulation of evidence to prove this contemporaneous existence of man and the mastodon.

The artist who made this pipe must have been familiar with the elephant form, either from having seen the living animal or a delineation by a preceding artist, or from oral tradition in his tribe; the alternative idea or other horn of the dilemma being that he "evolved it out of his inner consciousness," in other words, that it was a product of his imagination.

One feature of the delineation remains unaccountable, the omission of the tusks, which were so large and formidable in the mastodon: yet they are omitted here, as also in the elephant mound in Wisconsin. In Materiaux Tom. IV., p. 197, is depicted the head of a mammoth in bronze, found in Siberia, which is also represented without tusks.

THE PLEISTOCENE CARVED BONE FROM TEQUIXQUIAC, MEXICO: A REAPPRAISAL

De Anda, Luis A. A.; *American Antiquity*, 30:261-277, 1965.

Abstract. A carved sacrum from a fossil camelid was found near Tequixquiac in 1870 in Upper Pleistocene deposits of the Valley of Mexico. At that time it was described as one of the first discoveries that proved the co-existence of man with extinct fauna in the New World. The specimen was apparently lost at the end of the 19th century and serious doubts have been expressed about its authenticity. This carved bone was rediscovered in 1956, and recent studies of the specimen tend to demonstrate its authenticity and scientific value. A survey of all known examples of similar finds in North America suggests that the Tequixquiac bone is probably the only example of true art that has yet been found in Paleo-Indian levels in the New World.

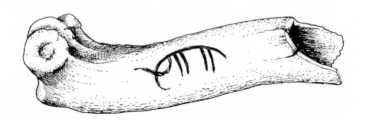

PRE-COLUMBIAN REPRESENTATIONS OF THE ELEPHANT IN AMERICA

Smith, G. Eliot; *Nature*, 96:340-341, 1915.

More than sixty years ago, in his "Incidents of Travel in Central America," Stephens directed attention to an elaborately carved "idol" at Copan, and stated that "the two ornaments at the top look like the trunks of elephants, an animal unknown in that country."

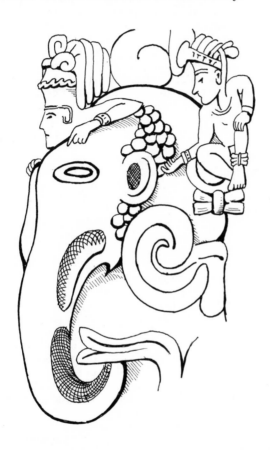

No one who looks at the accompanying tracing, which I have taken from Dr. A. P. Maudslay's magnificent atlas of photographs and drawings of the Central American monuments (Godman and Salvia's "Biologia Centrali-Americana," Archaeology, plate xxxiv.), should have any doubt about the justification for Stephens's comment. Moreover, the outline of the head is so accurately drawn as to enable the zoologist to identify the original model for the design as the Indian species of elephant. It is equally clear that the sculptor of the monument was not familiar with the actual animal, for, according to Drs. Maudslay and Seler, he has mistaken the eye for the nostril, and the auditory meatus for the eye, and represented the tusk (note its relation to the lower lip) and the ventral surface of the trunk in a conventionalised manner, without any adequate realisation of the true nature of the features he was modelling.

Certain early Chinese craftsmen adopted a similar convention in their representation of the elephant's tusk and the ventral aspect of the trunk (see, for example, "Chinese Art," vol. ii., Fig. 55, Victoria and Albert Museum Handbooks).

Having converted the auditory meatus into an eye, the sculptor had to deal with the auditory pinna, the meaning of which no doubt was a puzzle to him. He resolved these difficulties by converting it into a geometrical pattern, which, however, he was careful to restrict to the area occupied by the relatively small pinna that is distinctive of the Indian species of elephant. (In the representation of elephants on a beautiful Chinese vase of the Ming period, now in the Victoria and Albert Museum, the posterior border of the pinna is lobulated, and suggests a transition to the geometrical pattern of the Copan design.)

The designer also lost his bearings when he came to deal with the turbaned rider of the elephant. No doubt in the original model the rider's leg was obscured by the pinna; but in the Copan sculpture he lost his trunk also.

All these features go to prove quite conclusively that the sculpture represents an elephant's head, and that it was not modelled from the real creature. In other words, the craftsman was copying an earlier model (presumably made by some immigrant from Asia) without understanding the "points" of the elephant.

In the introduction to his "Mexican Archaeology" (1914) Mr. T. A. Joyce refers to Dr. A. P. Maudslay and Dr. Seler as leading modern investigators who "have done so much to place the study of American antiquities upon a thoroughly scientific footing." It is interesting to inquire what the voice of modern science has to say with reference to these Copan elephants.

In part ii. (text, p. 43) of his great monograph, to which I have already referred, Dr. Maudslay says, in his description of the figure which I have reproduced here:---"The elephant-like appearance of these heads has been the subject of much discussion, but I fail to see any reason why the form may not have been taken from the tapir, an animal still commonly found in the neighbourhood." But if this is so, it is surely a remarkable coincidence that, when the sculptor set about transforming the tapir into so untapir-like a form, he should have arrived at the precise profile of the Indian elephant. Moreover, if the tapir was so familiar to him, why did he mistake its eye for its nostril and its meatus for its eye? Why also did he add the embellishments exactly corresponding in distribution to the elephant's pinna, tusk, and under surface of the trunk, which become meaningless if the creature is a tapir? The position of the turbaned man on the head, as well as the instrument in his hand, also became unintelligible if the head is that of a tapir.

Dr. Eduard Seler holds very different views, which do more credit to his powers of imagination than to his plausibility. For he regards the objects under discussion as heads of tortoises! It is scarcely necessary to follow the remarkable line of argument which led him to this astounding conclusion (Archiv f. Ethnologie, 1910, pp. 50-53).

Dr. Seler's view is all the more remarkable in view of the fact that in the same journal two years previously (Archiv f. Ethnologie, 1908, p.

716) Dr. W. Stempell (after reviewing the literature concerning these elephant heads from the time of van Humboldt onwards) vigorously protested against the idea that they were intended to be anything else than elephants. He claimed that no one with any zoological knowledge could have any doubt on the matter. But with an amazing disregard for considerations of chronology he suggested that they represent the early Pleistocene <u>Elephas columbi</u>!

If these sculptures, definite as their features are, were the only representations of the elephant in pre-Columbian America, one might perhaps be justified in adopting an attitude of reserve as to their significance. But they do not stand alone. Another most remarkable and unmistakable example appears as a headdress in a bas-relief at Palenque (see Bancroft's "Native Races of the Pacific States of North America," vol iv., p. 305). Another is a highly conventionalised representation of an elephant's trunk, which appears as a projecting ornament on the Casa del Gobenador at Uxmal (Bancroft, <u>op. cit.</u>, p. 163).

Equally remarkable instances of the use of the elephant as a design ---in these cases the whole creature---will be found in the so-called "Elephant Mound" of Wisconsin, and the "Elephant Pipes" of Iowa (see Henshaw, Second Ann. Report of the Bureau of Ethnology, for 1880--- 1, pp. 152 and 155 respectively, and McGuire, "Pipes and Smoking Customs of the American Aborigines," 1898, p. 523).

The use of the elephant design in these different ways becomes more intelligible when it is recalled that in India and eastern Asia the elephant was frequently represented on temples and dagobas, and special sanctity became attached to it in religious architecture. Some of the earliest sculptured representations of the elephant in India, going back to the Asokan period (third century B.C.), are found to have the tusk and the ventral surface of the trunk exposed in precisely the same way as the Copan elephants (see, for example, A. K. Coomaraswamy's "Visvakarma," 1914, plate 91).

Thirty-six years ago Sir Edward Tylor proved that the pre-Columbian Mexicans had acquired the Hindu game called <u>pachisi</u> (Journ. Anthr. Inst., 1879, p. 128). Fifteen years later the same distinguished anthropologist directed attention (British Association Report, 1894, p. 774) to the fact that the Mexican scribes had represented in their Aztec picture-writing (Vatican Codex) a series of scenes taken from Japanese Buddhist temple scrolls. If this is admitted---and the facts are much too definite and precise to be denied---the last reason disappears for refusing to admit the identification of the Copan heads as elephants. For if it has been possible for complicated games and a series of strange beliefs (and elaborate pictorial illustrations of them) to make their way to the other side of the Pacific, the much simpler design of an elephant's head could also have been transferred from India or the Far East to America.

• Anomalous Scenes

REMARKABLE ANCIENT SCULPTURES FROM NORTH-WEST AMERICA
Wallace, Alfred R.; *Nature*, 43:396, 1891.

Mr. James Terry has just published descriptions and photographs of some of the most remarkable works of prehistoric man yet discovered on the American continent. The title of his paper is sufficiently start-ling, but it is fully borne out by the beautiful full-size and half-size photo-graphic prints with which it is illustrated. They represent three rude, yet bold, characteristic, and even life-like sculptures of simian heads, executed in basalt. One of these belongs to the author, one to Mr. T. Condon, and the third to Prof. O. C. Marsh, who referred to it, in his address "On Vertebrate Life in America," in the following terms:---
"On the Columbia River I have found evidence of the former existence of inhabitants much superior to the Indians at present there, and of which no tradition remains. Among many stone carvings which I saw, there were a number of heads which so strongly resembled those of apes that the likeness at once suggests itself. Whence came these sculptures and by whom were they made?" Unfortunately we have no detailed informa-tion as to the conditions under which these specimens were found, except that "they would be classed as 'surface finds,' from the fact that the shifting sand-dunes, which were largely utilized for burial purposes, are continually bringing them to the surface and exposing them." This gives no indication of their antiquity, but is quite compatible with any age which their other characteristics may suggest.
The size of the heads varies from eight to ten inches in total height, and from five and three-quarters to six and a half inches in width. The three are so different from each other that they appear to represent three distinct animals; and, so far as I can judge, they all differ con-siderably from the heads of any known anthropoid apes. In particular, the nostrils are much farther from the eyes and much nearer to the mouth than in any of the apes. In this respect they are more human; yet the general form of the head and face, the low and strongly-ridged fore-head, and the ridges on the head and cheeks seem to point to a very low type of anthropoid. In a letter to Mr. Terry, Mr. Condon suggests "that they were copied from the figure-head of some Malay proa that may have been wrecked on the coast;" but such a supposition is quite inadmissible, since nothing at all resembling these heads is ever carved on Malay proas, and there is no reason to believe that if such a carving did come into the possession of the natives they would ever think of copying it in stone; while these sculptures were found two hundred miles from the coast on the east side of the Cascade Mountains.
Taking into consideration the enormous antiquity of the stone mor-tars and human remains found in the auriferous gravels of California buried under ancient lava streams and associated with a flora and fauna

altogether different from that of any part of America at the present time, Mr. Terry's own conclusion appears the more probable. It is, "either that the animals which these carvings represent once existed in the Columbia valley, or that, in the remote past, a migration of natives from some region containing these monkeys reached this valley, and left one of the vivid impressions of their former surroundings in these imperishable sculptures." The latter alternative appears to me, for many reasons, to be highly improbable; and though the former will seem to many persons to be still more improbable, I am inclined provisionally to accept it.

THE PIASA
Anonymous; *American Antiquarian,* 28:262-265, 1906.

Although the United States has no folk lore of its own, such as is possessed by Germany, Sweden, Denmark and other countries, its primitive history abounds in Indian legends and stories that are full of romance, tragedy and adventure.

The Indians of early days were imbued with a certain kind of religious faith, to which they adhered with all the tenacity of their race, and certain symbols, signs and painted languages were pregnant with sifnificance. The Great Manitou was their god and the happy hunting grounds their heaven, and their teachings were as sacred to them as the Christian religion is to us to-day.

One legend was as follows:

Many thousand moons before the arrival of the paleface there existed a bird of such dimensions that he could easily carry off in his talons a full-grown deer. Having obtained a taste for human flesh, from that time he would prey on nothing else. He was artful as he was powerful, and would dart suddenly and unexpectedly upon an Indian, bear him off into one of the caves of the bluffs and devour him. Hundreds of warriors had attempted for years to destroy him, but without success. Whole villages were nearly depopulated and consternation spread through all the tribes of the Illini.

Such was the state of affairs when Ouatogo, the great chief of the Illini, whose fame extended beyond the great lakes, fasted in solitude, separating himself from the rest of his tribe for the space of a whole moon, and prayed to the Great Spirit, the Master of Life, that He would protect His children from the Piasa.

On the last night of the feast the Great Spirit appeared to Ouatogo in a dream and directed him to select twenty of his bravest warriors, each armed with a bow and poisoned arrows, and conceal them in a designated spot. Near the place of concealment another warrior was to stand in open view as a victim for the Piasa, which they must shoot the instant it pounced upon its prey.

When the chief awoke in the morning he thanked the Great Spirit, and returning to his tribe told them of his vision. The warriors were quickly selected and placed in ambush as directed.

Ouatogo offered himself as the victim. He was willing to die for his people. Placing himself in open view on the bluff he soon saw the Piasa perched on the cliff, eyeing his intended prey. The chief drew up his manly form to its utmost height, and planting his feet firmly upon the earth, he began to chant the death song of an Indian warrior. A moment after the Piasa rose into the air, and, swift as a thunderbolt, darted down upon his victim. But scarcely had the horrid creature reached Ouatogo when every bow was sprung and every arrow was sent quivering to the feather into his body. The Piasa uttered a fearful scream that sounded far over the opposite side of the river, and immediately expired. Ouatogo was unharmed. Not an arrow, not even the talons of the bird touched him. The Master of Life, in admiration of Ouatogo's deed, had held over him an invisible shield.

There was the wildest rejoicing among the Illini, and the brave chief was carried in triumph to the council-house, where it was solemnly agreed that, in memory of the great event in their national history, the image of Piasa should be portrayed upon the bluff.

Such is the Indian tradition. It is a matter of fact that the image of a huge bird was painted on the rock.

It was some twenty or twenty-five feet long and seven or eight feet high. A dark red was used, which was very durable, the outlines and especially the wings, strongly marked with heavy horizontal lines, being plainly visible as long as the rock was left in place, while the other portions in a lighter tint gradually became indistinct.

As long as it remained there, an Indian never passed the place in his canoe without firing his gun or arrow at the figure, and the face of the bluff was covered with the marks of their missiles.

The image of this monstrous being was painted on a rock located near the City of Alton, Ill., on the banks of the Mississippi river. This rock has since been destroyed, and the place where it stood is now occupied by Chautauqua grounds.

. . . .

Pictographs on rock wall near Alton, Illinois

THE CLAY FIGURINES OF ACAMBARO, GUANAJUATO, MEXICO

Di Peso, Charles C.; *American Antiquity,* 18:388-389, 1953.

For the past eight years, stories have appeared concerning a vast collection of animal and human figurines of great antiquity, gathered in the vicinity of Acambaro in the state of Guanajuato, Mexico. Senor Waldemar Julsrud possesses some 32,000 of these artifacts of his private collection. These ceramic figures consist of such forms as Brontosaurus, Tyrannosaurus Rex. Stegosaurus, Trachodon, Dimetrodon and other Mesozoic reptilian life-forms. Also included in the collection are a number of modern life-forms such as cow, horse, hippopotamus, elephant, rabbit, and dog. Even more fabulous is the number of miniature Egyptian sarcophagi found in the collection.

Such popular articles as have appeared in the Los Angeles Times (Mexico Finds Give Hint of Lost World, by Lowell Harmer, Los Angeles Times, March 25, 1951, pt. 2, pp. 1-2), Fortnight (Archaeological Quandary by William N. Russell, Fortnight Nov. 12, 1951, pp. 38-39) and Fate Magazine (Did Man Tame the Dinosaur? by William N. Russell, Fate Magazine Feb.-March, 1952, pp. 20-27.) all emphasize the thought that man possessing the knowledge of ceramics lived contemporaneously with the Mesozoic reptiles. This, if true, would have thrown either the archaeological prehistory time-scale out of line or would have seriously shifted the paleontologists' concept of sequence dating. Senor Julsrud in his paper "Enigmas Del Pasado," (Acambaro, Gto., 1947), indicated that the archaeologists were mistaken in their estimates of time.

The Amerind Foundation, Inc., was prevailed upon to make an investigation of the materials. To imply falsification merely on the strength of the life-forms represented was not sufficient, for there was always the bare possibility that the figurines were chance similarities to Mesozoic forms as defined by modern scientists in the last two hundred years. It was within the realm of chance that they were the work of some imaginative prehistoric artist who may have taken his inspiration from the smaller reptiles still in existence today. A number of sherds were sent to the Amerind Museum and were tested in the laboratory. Chemical tests were made of the soils composing the figurines. Sherds were crushed and the contents were inspected for any inclusions that might give a clue as to the date of manufacture. Laboratory tests proved nothing. It was therefore decided that a representative should be sent into the field to witness the actual excavation of these figurines.

The author arrived in Acambaro in June and examined the collection owned by Senor Julsrud. The examination raised grave doubts as to the antiquity of the materials. Both the great variability of form and the volume of material were disturbing. Further, none of the specimens were marred by patination nor did they possess the surface coating of soluble salts characteristic of objects of more certain antiquity coming from the same area. Upon the word of the owner none of the figures had been washed in acid. Examination showed the edges of the depressions forming eyes, mouths, or scales to be sharp and new. No dirt was packed into any of the crevices.

The figures were broken, in most cases, where the appendages attached themselves to the body of the figurines; it appeared that the manufacturers willfully broke legs, necks, tails, etc., to suggest age.

No parts were missing. Further, none of the broken surfaces were worn smooth. In the entire collection of 32,000 specimens no shovel, mattock, or pick marks were noted. This would indicate that the excavators possessed a digging technique exceeding anything known to professional archaeologists or that they knew precisely where to dig. Their field technique when witnessed on the site, however, indicated that they were neither skillful nor careful nor experienced.

The excavators, consisting of a father and his son, invited the author to their site, an actual prehistoric Tarascan ruin. To make the test-find, they chose the northwest corner of a room approximately nine meters long and four meters wide. The author spent two days watching the excavators burrow and dig; during the course of their search they managed to break a number of authentic prehistoric objects. On the second day the two struck the cache and the author examined the material in situ. The cache had been very recently buried by digging a down sloping tunnel into the black fill dirt of the prehistoric room. This fill ran to a depth of approximately 1.30 m. Within this stratum were authentic Tarascan sherds, obsidian blades, tripod metates, manos, etc., but these objects held no concern for the excavators. In burying the cache of figurines the natives had unwittingly cut some 15 cms. below the black fill into the sterile red earth floor of the prehistoric room. In back-filling the tunnel they mixed this sterile red earth with the black earth; the tracing of their original excavation was, as a result, a simple task.

In their attempt to disguise the figurines they had packed the bowls and crevices with dirt, the same mixed dirt as characterized the backfill of their new-cut tunnel. Not only was the dirt thus mixed but small chips of limestone, chipped from the boulder walls of the prehistoric room during excavation of the tunnel, were also in evidence.

As if to cap the case, finger prints were visible on the freshly packed earth which filled a small bowl. This bit of evidence, plus the presence of some fresh animal manure in the tunnel fill, offered proof enough that the material had been recently planted.

Further investigation revealed that a family living in the vicinity of Acambaro make these figurines during the winter months when their fields lie idle. Their ideas of form could have come from the local cinema in Acambaro as well as from the multitude of comic books and newspapers sold on the streets. Or from the library as well as the school, which are available in the town, which has a population of some 20,000 persons. Three trains a day carry natives to Mexico City where the Museo Nacional, among others, is available and where, incidentally, there is a fine collection of prehistoric Egyptian art. Certain forms in the Julsrud collection strongly suggest that some of the native manufacturers have visited this Egyptian exhibit.

Apparently these objects have been made and sold since 1944, when the first cache was opened for Senor Julsrud's inspection. Intrigued by the wierd forms he began his collecting and paid a peso for each item brought to his home. Since the above mentioned date the material has all come from three small fields in mass concentrations, and Sr. Julsrud has continued to buy.

Thus the investigation ended; it seems almost superfluous to state that Acambaro figurines are not prehistoric nor were they made by a prehistoric race who lived in association with Mesozoic reptiles.

A VIKING SAGA IN TENNESSEE?

Verrill, L. Ruth, and Keeler, Clyde; *Georgia Academy of Sciences, Bulletin*, 19:78-82, 1961.

The so-called Thruston Tablet was found with other relics near stone graves, mounds, and earthworks at Catalian Springs, beside Rocky Creek, Sumner County, Tennessee. Although it was discovered about 1874, it is very little known today. From the time of its presentation to the Tennessee Historical Society twelve years elapsed before it was placed on exhibit at what was then the new Historical Rooms of Watkins' Institute, Nashville, Tennessee. From the first, this tablet has been considered very ancient and a genuine relic, but a truly critical study of it appears never to have been made. The slab is an unevenly surfaced, irregularly-shaped piece of limestone about 19 inches long and 15 inches wide, having all appearances of great age. A photograph of it may have been published first in the <u>Tenth Annual Report</u> of the Smithsonian Institution, Bureau of American Ethnology, 1888-1889 and published in 1893, although it was described in 1890 by Gates P. Thruston in his book, <u>Antiquities of Tennessee</u>.

Sketch of the Thruston Tablet

In 1897 Thruston, in his second edition of <u>Antiquities of Tennessee</u>, pages 88 to 97, tells of its finding and his interpretation of it. He says: It was well and deeply graven, probably with some implement of quartz or flint upon the softer limestone's surface." The engraving depicts in considerable detail what must have been a highly important event. It seems to represent a surprise attack on the temporary camp of the ray-eyed

ones at Rocky Creek by almond-eyed aborigines who came from over a
chain of low hills or mountains (represented by four vertical scallops at
the back of what we take to be a small medicine-lodge). The attackers
are not ray-eyed. Their faces are painted. Their leader has four lines
on his cheek, a custom common to certain tribes of Tennessee and
Arkansas, while the others have one horizontal line with a number of
short vertical lines extending above it. Each native wears a gorget and
sun-disk. Their skirts are of animal skins. One has the fur on the outside and two have the fur inside, the latter type permitting the skin side
to be decorated with circular patterns. The aboriginal leader at the
left has in his right hand an axe like those of copper found in the Spiro
Burial Mound, Spiro, Oklahoma, illustrated and described by the Museum
of the American Indian, Heye Foundation, New York, in Contributions
from the Museum of the American Indian, Heye Foundation, Vol. XIV.
The Spiro Mound Collection in the Museum by E. K. Burnett. Historical
Sketch of the Spiro Mound by Forrest E. Clements, New York, 1945,
Plate LXXI. The head of the axe has the shape of a rabbit's head. The
aboriginals wear ankle and wrist bands but do not have moccasins. Their
headdresses are elaborate. The fourth figure to the right has at his back
the severed head of a ray-eyed person. The eye is closed in death.
Above the head the bleeding heart of the victim can be seen near the
bound ankles; the soles of the feet being upward. The knees of the dead
are also bound. The bleeding torso is probably suspended in the engraving. The mutilation of the dead person indicates the nature of the cult
followed by the natives.

An other head is faintly discernable beneath the engraving thought to
represent a medicine-lodge. A spear, that must have had a metal head
(for it is bent to a forty-five degree angle), lies on the ground above and
to the right of the little medicine lodge. Spearheads of this type were
used by the Vikings, some having unusually long shanks. In The Vikings
by Johannes Bronsfed, published by Cox and Wyman, London, 1960
(Penguin Book), plate 2, spearheads of this type are shown. The bearer
of a huge square object is obviously the leader of the ray-eyed ones.
The position of legs and shod feet indicate that the square object is a
shield, being held in a defensive position. On this individual's head is
a Phrygian or Roman-type helmet with its large crescent-shaped crest.
He wears shoes. The native leader is threatening him with an axe, and
the ray-eyed one fearlessly defends himself with his spear and shield.
The shield is not of an American type in shape or in decoration. It is
possible that the design on the shield is significant, for it could represent a log stockade about a cleared area in which diagonally runs from
corner to a crenulated vallum or earthworks. Perhaps the bearer of the
shield is the Holder-of-the- Fort.

In the book Viking Ships by Broger & Stretetig, Morgensen & Company, Los Angeles, 1960, page 250, it is noted that the Normans had
rectangular shields, and the round ones carried at the ships' rail in
Viking pictures were placed there mainly for show when leaving or
entering port. To the right of the ray-eyed leader is a figure to be that
of an almond-eyed Indian female. The hair is secured in an elongated
bun, a type of hair styling seen on a pottery head from ancient earthworks near Hickman, Tennessee, and engraved on shell gorgets from
stone graves. There are also representations of persons wearing this
type of bun from other parts of Tennessee. See Aboriginal Remains of

Tennessee by Dr. Chas. C. Jones, page 63. She wears no face paint, has a fabric skirt and neat shoes. In her right hand she holds what may be a wampum belt, an offering of peace. However, a sling may be intended because the duplicated arms of her attacker and herself could indicate a struggle. Here we may have a counterpart of Cortes' mistress, Marina.

At the lower end of the engraved scene is shown what we think to be a small, windowless, matting-lined medicine-lodge with one doorway. The frame is of small logs or poles lashed and secured by vines or rope-like roots. The little room is of a size for squatting or kneeling, as the kneeling figure shows. Many Amerindian tribes had such small medicine-lodges or shrines. The sketch of a small medicine-lodge of this sort has been published in the Bulletin of Georgia Academy of Science, 17:139, 1959.

The kneeling figure is a ray-eyed person who may be female because the hair is long and well-kept. The features are soft and there is no headdress. The rayed-eye is looking upward as if appealing in prayer to her deity. She wears no ornaments and her hair is not done up. This could indicate mourning in humility. Do these rayed-eyes denote eyelashes which are more obvious on fairer persons or do they indicate that the eyes are light in color (blue or gray)? We cannot say.

The kneeling figure is wrapped in fabric from the waist to about the knees. The pipe being smoked is common archaeologically to Tennessee. Smoking in early times was a ritual, a ceremony, part of ancient cults among many Amerindian tribes and not the general habit as it now has become. At the upper part of the engraving is carved, in surprising and accurate detail, a Viking-type boat of a style that was in use from around 800 to 1,000 A.D. that seems to have escaped notice up to the present. The figurehead is well drawn. At the base in back is the deep notch where a steering oar was used. The ropes supporting the mast and yard arm run to the figurehead at the bow and are in their proper positions.

The stem of the boat is distinctly European and not Amerindian. It is of correct proportion and shape and is like that of the Nydam boat in Slisvig from the fourth century, A.D. The figurehead is similar to that of the Oseberg boat. The Viking-type single mast and yard arm carry the sail. Their position and the pattern of the boat are features comparable to those of boats used by North European traders, explorers and colonizers up to about 1200 A.D. Such ships are represented on ancient Swedish coins (Fig. 4). The sail is made of six vertical strips of hand-loom material. Each strip would be from about 27 inches to 36 inches wide. This would mean that the sail was about 18 feet wide. This is a normal width for the sail of such a craft. A hauser-hole is discernible just back of the notch for the steering oar. This is comparable with its position on the Oseberg boat.

The boat's commander stands at the prow, wearing a pair of the familiar Viking horns, denoting his leadership. The "Bison," Norway's most famous Viking ship, carried oarsmen who wore Gallic-type helmets. There could have been about 20 oarsmen on a boat such as that shown in the engraving, and here five of them depicted as seated at the rowing level. The paddle ends of their oars are round or oval like those in the supposed iron-age Viking rock carvings of a boat at Brandskog, Uppland, Sweden. In both boats, the oar holes are at floor level as are those of the Oseberg boat.

Midway of the boat in the engraving can be seen a grappling or land-ing hook which would be of hard metal. To the left of this is a diamond-shaped fender of sennett-work, suspended from the boat's rail. It is mirrored in the calm water of the creek. Toward the stern a mooring line extends into the water. At the stern is clearly outlined an anchor of a well-known type that Vikings made out of granite and oak wood, at least in certain instances. See Archaeology, Winter 1960, Vol. 13, No. 4, page 227. New Light on Viking Trade in Norway, by Charlotte Blindheim. The Kaupang boat anchor is of granite and oak, styled like that shown on the boat in the Tennessee engraving. Kaupang farms are near Larvik, County Vestfold, and not far from the famous royal Viking burial ship of Oseberg. The boat burials at Kaupang dated about 800 A. D. to 950, which affords a possible dating for the boat shown on the Thruston Tablet because several features are comparable. The boat's stern is squarred and a tiller appears to be represented. This type of stern re-placed the earlier pointed type at a period shortly after 1180 A. D. There seem to be a few brief inscriptions. That on the ray-eyed leader's shield may be his identification. Just above the medicine-lodge at the right are glyphs that could give the name of the supposed female with the bun-style hair arrangement. Back of the head of the figure in the medi-cine-lodge is a single glyph.

It may be of interest to note that the southern boundry of Sumner County, Tennessee, is formed by the Cumberland River that flows into the Ohio. This, in turn, empties into the Mississippi River at Cairo, Illinois. Thus, such a boat could have entered the Gulf of Mexico and sailed via the Mississippi River, the Ohio River, the Cumberland River, and Rock Creek to Castalian Springs, where the so-called Thruston Tablet was found.

• Stripes, Bands, Fingerprints

THE ANCIENT ARTISTS OF SOUTHWESTERN EUROPE
Haddon, A. C.; *Nature*, 91:560-562, 1913.

At Batuecas, in west-central Spain, enormous panels are covered with dots, rows of lines, branched, scaliform, pectiform, and other signs, circles, and rayed figures, together with very schematic men and animals, which are later then certain more naturalistic drawings. Precisely similar diagrammatic signs occur in profusion in Andalusia, and below a few of them l'Abbe Breuil has found small, poorly executed, but realistic figures of the same kind as those at Batuecas. The signs agree with those that are found superimposed on Magdalenian drawings

in the Franco-Cantabrian area, so there is little doubt that they charac-
terise the Azilian culture. Prof. Breuil has given in <u>Rev. Arch.</u>, XIX.,
1912, p. 193, a large number of sketches from central and south Spain
which are evidently degraded representations of the human form.

Azilian signs at Salamanca resembling colored pebbles and pictographs in Andalusia

    In the same article he points out that, so far as is known, the art
of the Franco-Cantabrian area developed in situ throughout a considerable period during which the climate, vegetation, and fauna were modified several times, while migrations of peoples, all of whom were hunters and collectors, took place in different directions. The realistic
representations of animals by the Aurignacians continued through
Solutrian to the end of Magdalenian times, and until the extinction of
the reindeer in France and central Europe. Human figures, as we have
seen, were rarely portrayed except at the beginning of this series of
cultures. Then an invasion from the Italian and Iberian peninsulas
brought other peoples to north-west Europe, who painted schematic and
geometric forms, often very like those painted on rocks in south and
west Spain. These latter seem attributable for the most part to peoples
who, while in the Palaeolithic stage of evolution, did not progress
through the Aurignacian-Solutrian-Magdalenian line of evolution that
extends from Cantabria to Poland, but advanced in the direction of the
industries termed "Capsian" by de Morgan and "Getulian" by Pallary.
The eastern Spanish art may have been derived from north of the
Pyrenees or influenced by it, at the same time undergoing a local development. On the other hand, Breuil notes that influences of the
schematic art of the south-west were felt in the Magdalenian art of
Cantabria and even of the Pyrenees, and that a cave in Ariege also
shows pictorial influence from the artistic province of east and north-
east Spain.
    "As a result of the arrival of Neolithic man in the south of the
Iberian peninsula, the Capsians flowed over the Magdalenian world,
substituting their schematic art for the realistic art of the Magdalenians; borrowing from them some slightly modified industrial objects,
like the harpoon, they spread not only to Gascony and Aquitaine, but
to Dauphine, Switzerland, Bavaria, and even to Scotland. On the other
hand, some Capsians of Andalusia and Murcia seem to have rallied to
the new state of things, since certain painted rocks represent 'idols'
known only in the ancient Neolithic age in these regions, and certain
Portuguese dolmens preserve a mural decoration conceived in their
style. Perhaps other Capsian groups, driven from Morocco by the new-
comers, migrated into central Sudan, unless the strange analogy of the
paintings found there with those of Andalusia be purely fortuitous."

RED BANDS PAINTED IN CAVES
Anonymous; *Nature*, 90:256-257, 1912.

An account of certain red bands observed by Profs. Breuil and Sollas in Bacon's Hole, on the Gower peninsula, and apparently of prehistoric origin, appeared in <u>Nature</u> of October 17 (p. 195). According to <u>The Cambria Daily Leader</u> of October 18, the markings were made by a Mumbles boatman eighteen years ago, and were produced with a brush having red paint upon it, which was part of the salvage from the wreck of a Norwegian barque. Several other explanations have since been put forward, and are referred to in a short article in Tuesday's <u>Times</u>. Whether the markings are of ancient or modern origin does not appear yet to have been decided definitely, but the position of the question is shown by the following extract from <u>The Times</u> article:---"When they observed the marks the first question which presented itself to Prof. Breuil and Prof. Sollas was: 'Are they ancient or modern?' Prof. Breuil, having wetted the surface, attempted to remove the paint by vigorous rubbing; not succeeding in this, he concluded they were ancient. Prof. Sollas closely examined the wall to see whether the paint was covered by stalactite, and convinced himself that it was. To reassure himself on this point Prof. Sollas has lately revisited the cave. He was able with a hammer and chisel to detach a fragment of the painted surface from a projecting corner. This affords an excellent section through the deposits, revealing a layer of the red paint, which covers an older layer of stalactite, and is itself covered by a later layer, in some places as much as two millimetres thick. There can be no doubt that Prof. Breuil and Prof. Sollas were scrupulously exact in their observations, and as the marks resemble in general character the accepted paintings of Upper Palaeolithic age, and in particular some red bands at the extremity of the great gallery in Foul de Gaume, they were amply justified---whatever the final verdict may be---in assigning the paintings of Bacon Hole to an ancient period."

THE "FINGER-PRINT" CARVINGS OF STONEAGE MEN IN BRITTANY
Cummins, Harold; *Scientific Monthly*, 31:273-279, 1930.

A story partly told suggests diverse settings, and except to him who relates it all may seem equally fitting. Attempts to reconstruct the life and thought of prehistoric man are based necessarily upon uncompleted stories, which are revealed in remains of handiwork, sometimes so piecing together as to give consistence to the whole, yet often being quite fragmentary and tantalizing to the restorer. Occasional fantastic reconstructions of episodes in prehistory are inevitable. Carved on the stones of a Neolithic burial chamber in Brittany there are designs presenting a singular likeness to finger-prints, and these carvings may be said to constitute a passage in the unwritten history of men living several

thousands of years ago. It is an obscure passage, for there are nearly
as many interpretations as commentaries discussing it. One interpretation, backed by an impressive array of evidence showing that counterparts of the figures are to be found in actual finger-prints, holds that
they are copies of these natural designs. The implications of the story
thus rendered are far-reaching, having even a relation to the question
of the origin of decorative design. If it be true that Neolithic men
really noted the cutaneous patterns, and with the attention to minute
detail which is claimed, credit is due them for a spontaneous interest
and keenness in such observation hardly matched by average men of the
present day. Accepting the finger-print source of the designs, the
question naturally arises as to the purpose of the sculpturing. One
(Doctor A. ," writing in <u>La Chronique Medicale</u>, goes so far as to suggest that the designs are registries of the finger-prints of chieftains,
recorded with precisely the object of modern finger-print files, that
is, for the purpose of personal identification. These questions anticipate
the issue, for the first concern should be the merit of the interpretation
of the designs as finger-print motifs.

Neolithic men, in contrast to their Paleolithic forebears, engaged in
building. Their success in handling immense stones evokes a deep respect for the engineering of the Stone Age. A stone weighing forty-four
tons is thought to have been transported over a distance of nearly nineteen miles to the site of a dolmen at La Perotte. In the neighborhood
of the structure which is ornamented with the "finger-print" carvings
there lies a broken monument having a total length of over sixty-seven
feet and an estimated weight of over three hundred and thirty tons, which
is presumed to have been brought to the present site from a point five
eights of a mile distant, then lifted to a vertical position. Neolithic architecture has a definite association with the cult of the dead, many of the
monuments, known as dolmens, serving as actual burial chambers.
Dolmens are to be found in Europe, Asia and Africa; they number nearly
five thousand in France alone. In Brittany there is one which has been
described as the finest megalithic monument in the world, and it is this
dolmen which bears the "finger-print" gravings. The dolmen is situated
on a tiny island, L'Ile de Gavr'inis (Goat Island), in the Gulf of Morbihan,
near Loemariaquer. It exemplifies a form of dolmenic construction
termed the passage grave, allee couverte, characterized by the presence
of an entrance gallery or vestibule leading to a widened compartment.
The Gavr'inis dolmen has an entrance gallery forty-one feet long and
about four and one half feet wide, the terminal chamber enlarging to a
cubicle almost twice the width of the entering passage and having a height
of nearly six feet. The walls are constructed of twenty-nine upright
stones, and the whole is paved and roofed by slabs. The structure is
imbedded, characteristically, within a low broad mound of earth, or
tumulus. When the dolmen was explored in 1832 it was found despoiled
of movable contents. The impressive feature of the interior consists
in the sculpturing of the walls with incised lines, fashioned into designs
of great variety. It is worthy of note that the carvings are confined to
the slabs of granite, two quartz uprights being unmarked. The cutting
could have been accomplished with stone tools, though it is possible that
implements of bronze were employed.

The photographs shown in Figs. 1 and 2 [not reproduced] illustrate
the general appearance of the sculpturings, as well as their size in

Fingerprint carvings on dolmens

relation to the dolmen. Fig. 3 contains several detail drawings of the
designs. Concentric systems of horseshoe form, concentric subcircu-
lar figures, spirals, arching lines, sinuous lines, straight lines and
other markings occur in various combinations.

Stockis, a distinguished authority on finger-prints, is the chief pro-
ponent of the interpretation which identifies the Gavr'inis carvings with
the cutaneous patterns, holding that these natural designs served as
models for the man-made designs on the stones. He points out that more
or less exact counterparts of many features of the carved designs occur
in the finger-prints of modern men. Not only are the patterns of the
finger tips represented, but in two instances the portion of the palm near
the wrist is reproduced. Stockis presents seventy-nine figures to substantiate this statement, illustrating actual prints in parallel with the
carvings which they resemble. He directs notice, further, to the occurrence of interruptions, bifurcations and similar details of the sculptured
lines, in support of the contention that the sculptures are faithful even to
the degree of picturing the finest details of the single skin ridges.

. . . .

LARGE-SCALE DRAWINGS, EFFIGIES, AND MOSAICS

We can understand why ancient man might draw and sculpt for art's sake and his own amusement. However, he also left behind giant pictures and symbols that survived centuries unseen until the modern airplane. The famed Nazca lines, the Blythe Giant, and many other graphic artifacts can be appreciated fully only from the air. Some cannot, in fact, be discerned at all at ground level. Such "macroforms" have helped perpetuate the ancient astronaut theme because other interpretations are so hard to come by.

The boulder mosaics and effigy mounds of North America can be made out to some degree at ground level, and the giant English chalk figures are clear enough. Nevertheless, an aerial perspective really emphasizes their contrast with the natural surroundings. Perhaps, they, too, were directed at some Sky God. Or, they may have had some ritual purpose. All we know is that these immense figures of men and animals have revealed neither purpose or message.

• Large-Scale Drawings

GIANT ETCHINGS ON CALIFORNIA DESERT SANDS
Anonymous; *Literary Digest*, 114:22, November 12, 1932.

Giant drawings etched in the California desert floor east of Los Angeles may be linked to tribal legends that left a deep impress on Indian life.

Army Air Corps flyers have photographed human and other shapes outlined in pebbles in an isolated area near Blythe, California. Says an Associated Press dispatch in the New York <u>Times</u>:

There were hopes that the airmen would take pictures of similar desert etchings of which the scientists have heard, and around which are woven tribal legends that might have inspired the Blythe artists also.

Near the strange figures found by George Palmer while flying from Hoover Dam to Blythe are no hills to give the elevation necessary to distinguish them, and but for his efforts to find an emergency landing-place they might have escaped discovery years longer.

Palmer reported his find to Arthur Woodward, ethnologist of the Los Angeles museum, who drove across several miles of trackless desert to inspect them.

The figures were made by scraping away the thick ground

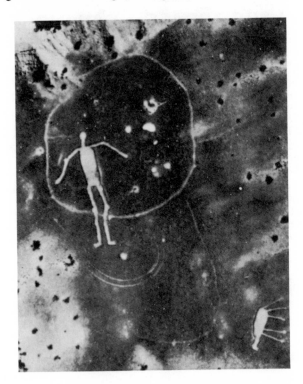

Giant figures drawn in sand north of Blythe, California

covering of brown pebbles to the alkali soil beneath. They range in length from 50 to 167 feet. Near two of the human shapes are figures of serpents and four-legged animals with long tails. One giant, or god, appears just to have stept out of a large dance ring.

Woodward's early efforts to find who made the figures were not productive. The Mohave and Chemehuevi Indians, who once frequented this area, said they had no knowledge of them. But he found new hope upon learning that there was another similar figure near Sacaton, Arizona, on the north branch of the Gila River, which the Pima Indians call Haakvaak, or Hawk-Lying-Down.

A Pima legend says that when the Hohoken (sic) Indians, who perished long ago, inhabited the area, one of their most courageous braves drove out a cannibalistic she-creature which was preying upon them.

In her flight she paused to rest, and when she had gone the Indians scraped away the pebbles where she had lain and so preserved her form. Offerings for years later were made to this figure.

THE MYSTERIOUS MARKINGS OF NAZCA

Kosok, Paul, and Reiche, Maria; *Natural History,* 56:200-207, and 237-238, May 1947. (Reprinted with permission from *Natural History* Magazine, May, 1947. Copyright © The American Museum of Natural History)

Flying over the dramatic desert plains and hills along the lower branches of the Rio Grande River in southern Peru, one sees the strange and unique networks of lines and geometric figures shown in these photographs. They are visible in many places, sometimes lacing back and forth in extremely complex and apparently chaotic ways across an extensive area more than 40 miles long and some 5 to 10 miles wide.

This region is one of the driest deserts in the world. A number of neighboring rivers, running from the Andes westward toward the Pacific and combining near the coast to form the Rio Grande River, provide the water necessary for irrigating the adjoining fields. These fields are not extensive, for the rivers are small and have water only during four to five months of the year. Each valley contains only one or two villages and supports today, as it undoubtedly did in the past, a population of no more than several thousand. The markings are found on the slightly elevated desert plateaus and on near-by ridges between the banks of adjacent rivers.

The lines themselves run straight as an arrow in various directions, sometimes only a few yards, sometimes for many miles. Most of them are actually double parallel lines and look like roads with slightly elevated edges. They all seem to have been made by the simple process of removing the many pebbles that have been darkened by exposure to the air from the lighter colored soil in the center of the "road" and piling them in a uniform way along both sides. The lighter color of the smooth central portion makes the "road" easier to see. Today the elevated sides of the "road" are generally only a few inches high, in some cases so low that they are barely perceptible even in the early morning or late afternoon when the shadows are longest.

The geometric figures---triangles, rectangles, and trapezoids of various sizes---were made in the same way as were the "roads."

The Spanish conquerors, unfortunately, never mentioned these markings in any of their writings; and the present inhabitants of the region, while knowing of them, possess no traditions or legends that might help to explain them. The people sometimes refer to them as "Inca Roads," but their very nature, size and position indicate that they could never have been used for ordinary purposes of transportation. The possibility that they are the remains of ancient irrigation canals must also be ruled out, for they are often found running over hillocks. And where this is not the case, they have no possible physical connection with the river, which would be the primary requisite for irrigation canals.

The Key to the Problem. Some years ago, while studying the extent and nature of the ancient irrigation systems along the coast of Peru, my wife and I decided to see what logical explanation might be given for the markings and whether they might be related to our major study.

Our first clue came one day when we went out on a Peruvian government truck to explore one of the "Inca Roads." Following a wide one that crossed the Pan American Highway to the south of Palpa, we found that after about half a mile it led straight up the steep side of a small mesa, or plateau, and stopped.

On top of this mesa, we saw that this "road" was the largest and

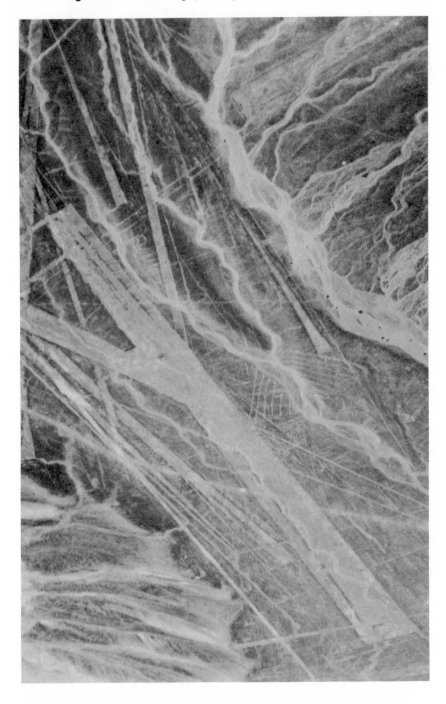

Nazca lines on desert mesa near the Ingenio Valley, Peru

most impressive of several other similar but narrower ones which, together with a number of single lines, radiated from a kind of center near
where we stood.

Roaming around the top of this flat plateau, which extended for several
miles in an easterly direction toward the near-by mountains, we found not
only many more lines but also two huge rectangles or trapezoids. One of
these had rows of pebble-heaps along two sides, the other had a series of
very short parallel lines, both of which looked like recording or counting
devices. Most amazing of all, we found adjacent to one of the rectangles
and close to the original center, the faint remains of a huge, peculiar
pebble and dirt drawing over 150 feet long, which reminded us somewhat
of the designs found on the old Nazca pottery of this region. (See illustrations of some of these large figures on pages 204-5.) (Figures omitted.)

Finally, with our minds whirling with endless questions about these
strange and fantastic remains, we returned to the center of radiation to
view an impressive sunset. Just as we were watching the sun go down behind the horizon, we suddenly noticed that it was setting almost exactly
over the end of one of the long single lines! A moment later we recalled
that it was June 22, the day of the winter solstice in the Southern Hemis-
phere---the shortest day in the year and the day when the sun sets farthest north of due west. With a great thrill we realized at once that we had
apparently found the key to the riddle! For undoubtedly the ancient
Nazcans had constructed this line to mark the winter solstice. And if
this were so, then the other markings might very likely be tied up in
some way with astronomical and related activities. Had we actually
stumbled upon a huge aggregation of historic astronomical formations,
somewhat similar to those found in Great Britain, Northern France,
and other parts of the world?

Even though our theory was a very tenuous one, we nevertheless
realized that we had probably found an entering wedge which would help
to take the problem out of the realm of idle speculation and place it
where it could be subjected to rigid scientific tests.

With what seemed to us "the largest astronomy book in the world"
spread out in front of us, the question immediately arose: How could we
learn to read it? In the few weeks at my disposal, during which I was
forced to continue the investigation alone, I decided to make a general
survey of the whole region and to take directional readings of as many
lines as possible. Through the courtesy of the Faucett Aviation Company,
I was able to make several flights over the area. Ingeneiro Galvez, the
Mayor of Nazca, and others in the region gave me valuable advice and
aid in arranging trips. I was soon able to get a general picture of the
whole layout, with the result that I succeeded in locating at least a dozen
radiating centers in various parts of the pampas.

Then I ascertained the direction of many of the lines radiating from
some of these centers, by means of a good compass, the readings from
which were corrected by data furnished by the Huancayo Magnetic Observatory. A number of the lines and "roads" were found to have a solstitial
direction; a few with equinoctial direction could also be identified. Moreover, various alignments were found to be repeated in many different
places, though I could not identify them in the time at my disposal. After
only a preliminary survey this astronomical approach had produced some
positive results, for some sign of order had been detected in what had
been detected in what had been an apparent chaos.

At this juncture, I was forced to interrupt these observations at Nazca and to return to the north of Peru. But I gave the information to Miss Maria Reiche of Lima, Peru, whose training in astronomy and mathematics enabled her to go ahead with the computations. From the material at hand, she drew up several preliminary work charts. Since then, the work has been carried on jointly by both of us. She visited Nazca during the period of the summer solstice in December, 1941, and confirmed the solstitial nature of some of the lines and roads I had plotted on the basis of my compass readings. She did this by actually watching, as the ancient Peruvians had done, the sunrise and sunset from several centers. Up to the present, twelve solstitial lines have already been confirmed in this manner.

The Progress. Since the end of the war, Miss Maria Reiche has resumed her field work, visiting Nazca during the periods of the September equinox and the June and December solstices of 1946. The extensive observations and new charts prepared have not only confirmed the validity of our whole approach but have raised the results to a new level. In this article it is only possible to give a short summary of our joint findings and theories. For the sake of clarity, they may best be presented in the following order:

1. The apparently chaotic mass of markings possesses a definite element of organization. Many of them radiate from a relatively limited number of centers, which are often located on little hillocks. In some cases the centers are on the flat plain but contain the ruins of small stone structures that probably were once used either as observation posts or "altars," perhaps as both.

Because of the importance and sacredness of such centers, they may contain burials. If this is so, the material from them should enable us to relate them to some specific archaeological period or periods of the region and thus obtain their relative ages.

In certain cases, roads and lines that do not leave from centers are associated with the large rectangles and triangles. No lines or figures have been found that are not associated with others in some organized fashion.

2. The single lines form only a minority of the markings on the pampas. A number of these have been identified as solstitial lines by actual observation in the field. In June, 1946, during the period of the winter solstice, Miss Reiche discovered an unusual variant of a solstitial lines by actual observation in the field. In June, 1946, during the period of the winter solstice, Miss Reiche discovered an unusual variant of a solstitial line. It was not a sight line, but its position marked the movement of the shadow of an important hill across the plain during the course of the day. Since there were several other similar lines near by, she assumed that these probably represented the position of the shadow on other important days of the year.

3. The great majority of lines are really double lines that appear like roads. Possibly they were sacred ceremonial roads as Mejia Xesspe already suggested in 1939. And they may have led to important burial centers as proposed by Professor Hans Horkheimer of Trujillo, Peru, who visited this region last year and who kindly put his findings at my disposal. But the fact that some of the "roads" have now been shown to have a solstitial direction indicates that they were not built in a hit-and-miss fashion but were given definite sacred alignments, determined by the position of heavenly bodies.

The solstitial lines and "roads" are easy to confirm in the field because, unlike the stars, the rising and setting position of the sun on the horizon does not change sufficiently in the course of one or two thousand years to obscure identification. This is why they were the first to be isolated in our work. But this does not mean that the ancient Nazcans were necessarily sun worshippers. It merely means that they already knew and marked the basic sun alignments. Only when the many other lines and "roads" that have a repetitive pattern have been accurately studied to determine any relation they may have to the motions of the other heavenly bodies can we gain some idea of the extent and character of the astronomical knowledge of the ancient Nazcans.

4. The triangular, rectangular, and trapezoidal figures are of various sizes, the largest being over five hundred feet wide and several thousand feet long. Their purpose has not yet been determined. But since hundreds and even thousands of people could easily have gathered within their limits, these figures may well have been used as special ceremonial enclosures or "temples" by the various local kinship groups or other social units from the near-by valleys. They would thus be similar to the more developed ones found in other parts of Peru and among other peoples of the world. If so, their sides, like those of similar enclosures and temples elsewhere in the world, may prove to have definite astronomical alignments and their shapes some sacred significance.

Most of the geometrical figures have a large stone heap near one or both ends. These heaps, like those found at several "centers," may likewise be the remains of some kind of observation posts or altars, or both. They may also be found to have burials beneath them. In many cases it was found that lines outside the enclosed areas pointed directly toward these "altars."

5. The huge "drawings," which were made in the same way as the lines, are often several hundred feet long. They remind one somewhat of the animal mounds in northern United States and of sand and dirt drawings in other parts of the world. I found one near Palpa in 1940, but Miss Reiche has recently located eighteen additional ones in the Nazca region. She writes that "they have the shapes of plants, many-headed serpents, and other animals, while some consist of geometric designs, including spirals. Their general appearance is similar to the various Nazca pottery and textile designs." Since the chronological sequence of the different types of these designs is known, it should help to determine the relative dates of the dirt figures and their related markings. One peculiarity about them is that most of them seem to have been drawn to means of one uninterrupted line or narrow path. The line or path begins at one side of the figure and turns and twists in various directions until it runs out near the original starting place. Since the path does not cross itself, it could have been used as a procession path during ceremonies.

In one case, at least, it has been found that the line forming one of these drawings is a continuation of a long, straight solstice line, thus linking these figures with astronomical observations.

The figures are always found closely associated with a large enclosure or a wide road. A possible explanation is that these figures were totem-like symbols belonging to the various kinship groups or other organizations that used the ceremonial enclosures. This explanation is probably not too far-fetched, for it is doubtful whether the social and political organization of the people in these small valleys ever developed much beyond federations of kinship units. And if it did, these people, like most others, undoubtedly retained many of their kinship social forms and traditions. This would not prevent the figures from also having become symbols of various heavenly bodies, for elsewhere in the world at a certain transitional stage of social development, the old totem figures have sometimes become identified with certain heavenly bodies or constellations. In fact, the names of some of our present-day constellations are undoubtedly of totemic origin.

6. Series of pebble-piles and short parallel lines found in conjunction with the geometric figures may have been recording devices for heavenly or earthly events. But these require further study.

What Remains to be Done. Our general results thus far directly support our original hypothesis of the astronomical nature of these markings ---in any case they are not at variance with it. Whatever may have been the social purposes of these various kinds of markings, the astronomical orientation or relationship serves as an integrating factor whose solution will help us to acquire a better understanding of the Nazcan culture and that of Peru as a whole.

The most difficult part of our problem, however, still remains: namely, to identify the large number of lines and "roads" that are not directly related to the solstices or equinoxes. Five additional possibilities present themselves in connection with these---possibilities dictated by the facts of astronomy and supported by the astronomical knowledge that other peoples are known to have possessed in similar stages of cultural development.

1. Risings or settings of the sun on other days than the equinoxes and solstices. In England, for instance, the ancients had sight posts or lines dividing the year into eight parts. And in Yucatan, still other days of the year were apparently used in recording the movements of the sun.

2. Risings and settings of the moon throughout the years. These have generally occupied the interest of both primitive and civilized peoples, for lunations and the 19-year moon cycles were used widely in reckoning time sequences. Spanish records mention the importance of moon worship along the coast of Peru.

3. Risings and settings of the various planets. These presented a more complex problem to the early astronomers; but we know that many peoples of the world, including the Mayans of Yucatan, had gained an accurate knowledge of the movements of planets even in early times, and that the planets were often an important part of the religious cult. That this was likewise true among the ancient Peruvians is indicated by a few remarks on the subject by the early Spanish chroniclers. The periodicity of Venus, and possibly Jupiter and Mercury, were apparently used by the priesthood for calculations.

4. Risings and settings of important stars. Various studies have shown what weight certain early peoples attached to the heliacal risings and settings of a particular star or star group that might be connected with important economic or religious activities. We know that in Peru the Pleiades provided a common time marker; in fact, among the Chimus this constellation was supposed to have been the dominant star group. Since in the Nazca region the Pleiades in the course of the centuries rose and set near the solstices, some of the observed solstice lines may have also been Pleiades lines.

5. Derivative directions. Some of the lines and "roads" may not have been sight lines but may have been made to connect important lines

and points or to construct related figures.

Because of the complex nature of the problem, it may at first seem well-nigh hopeless to identify the various lines and "roads" in the Nazca region. However, a further analysis shows that we can concentrate on one aspect of the problem at first. If we were to stand at a point in the desert and watch all the risings of the sun, moon, and planets in the course of the years, we would find that they would all occur within a relatively narrow arc of about 33 to 34 degrees north of east and the same distance south of east---that is, a total angular range of about 67 degrees on the horizon. The same holds true of the settings in the west. (See shaded areas in diagram.) Of course, the very richness of this field makes it difficult to work with, especially since within these two arcs we also find the rising and setting points of certain stars. However, the much larger arcs to the north and south along the horizon (the unshaded areas of the diagram) would give us sight lines that refer only to stars. This simplifies the problem considerably and indicates where a systematic study may well begin. In fact, the groundwork for this has already been laid.

One difficulty still remains. The point at which each star rises or sets shifts noticeably in the course of the centuries. This obviously makes identification of a star with its corresponding line difficult. However, since the number of bright stars that would have been used for sighting purposes is limited, the association of certain recurrent lines with important stars becomes possible.

This difficulty is really a blessing in disguise. Since the annual shift of each star is now known with great accuracy, we can, by working backward, determine the approximate date when the corresponding sight line was made. Such a procedure must, of course, be carried out with great care and skill in order to avoid the errors that have sometimes been made in studies of this sort in Egypt and elsewhere. Even an approximate dating of these remains would be of great importance to Peruvian archaeology.

It can be noticed that some of the lines of one center or figure are often built over the lines and markings of other centers, indicating different periods of construction. This indicates chronological sequence. If we can correlate such sequence with the culture sequence of the region and perhaps even with rough datings, new vistas in archaeology may be opened.

A solid year of fieldwork would no doubt yield the answers to certain basic questions. Aerial surveys of this region now in progress will be most useful in getting the overall picture and in locating certain details. However, the basic work lies in determining accurately by means of a theodolite the orientation of all the lines, "roads," and figures, together with the angles of elevation of the rather irregular horizon. Actual observations of the risings and settings of the various heavenly bodies while in the field would act as a valuable check on the results.

During this time the most important pyramids, walls, and other structures along the northern coast of Peru should also be surveyed. In that section the social and political organization reached a considerably higher stage than in the Nazca area and with it probably certain aspects of astronomy. This would be the first attempt to open up the whole problem in the North, and the results would almost certainly throw light on the development in the Nazca region. In 1941, while in the North, I measured with a compass the alignments of various pyramids and found somewhat similar evidence of solstitial and equinoctial alignments as well as the repeated pattern of several other alignments that have not yet been identified.

The fieldwork must be done soon, however, because plans are already under way to irrigate some of the most valuable areas within a few years. This will destroy at a stroke what has come down to us unharmed as a priceless heritage from the distant past.

The Significance of the Nazca Lines. It might at first seem astonishing that the Nazcans and other people in the early stages of civilization should have taken such an intense interest in astronomical observations and have developed elaborate astrological cults. On closer analysis, however, it seems less surprising. The rise of a more developed agriculture and transformation of tribal society into the early period of civilization brought about the growth of a more complex and organized social life. This resulted in an increasing realization that there was likewise an extremely complex organization among the heavenly bodies above. When they learned that the annual movements of most of the heavenly bodies could be correlated with the progress of the seasons, around which the whole productive and social process revolved, a fuller understanding of astronomy became imperative. Increasingly systematic attempts were therefore made to understand, predict, and control the various fluctuating social and natural events of earth. With this purpose, a rising priesthood built up an extensive system of observations and calculations and established involved rituals of supplication addressed to the heavenly bodies, which, with their relentless and unfluctuating periodicity, seemed completely to dominate life on earth. Thus the first science, astronomy, was born.

The control that the heavenly bodies apparently exercised over earthly affairs led to the development of an accurate and well-organized calendar for determining "holy" and "lucky" dates for planting and harvesting crops and for a host of other events both practical and ceremonial. In an irrigated economy the rise and fall of the life-giving water in the rivers, around which the whole productive and ceremonial processes revolve, becomes one of the chief problems around which astronomical predictions and activities are centered.

Moreover, as the development of an agricultural economy led to a growth of social differentiations, the astronomer-priests probably found that the more complex were their astronomical knowledge and ceremonial forms, the more they could impress the populace with their mysterious supernatural powers. Thereby they strengthened their privileged position. Thus, a whole system of interacting forces evolved which, once established, developed through its own internal momentum and probably went far beyond the actual practical needs.

Our lack of knowledge of this development is due partly to the absence of native records and partly to the fact that the Spanish chroniclers were not especially interested in recording the astronomical or astrological knowledge of the "heathen" priests. And even if the interest had been present, it is doubtful that these priests would have yielded the most sacred secrets of their profession to the foreign conquerors. When the Nazca markings have been deciphered, an effort should be made to correlate the findings with Baron Erland Nordenskiold's tentative analysis of the ancient Peruvian analysis of the ancient Peruvian knotted cords, or quipus, as well as with the more elaborate calendrical studies of Fritz Buck and with similar work of Stansbury Hagar and Zelia Nuttall.

When that is done, we should have new insight into a phase of ancient Peruvian culture that still rests in obscurity. We will then be able to understand concretely what underlies a statement of one of the old chroniclers, Cieza de Leon, who wrote: "These Indians watched the heavens and the signs very constantly, which made them such great soothsayers."

But the question remains: Why should such a poor region as Nazca have produced such elaborate and peculiar forms? A general explanation may lie in the fact that in Nazca, as among the Mayans of Yucatan, the early appearance and continued existence of a certain level of culture, together with the absence of restraining influences of a centralized secular state, permitted the powerful priesthood to develop its astronomical investigations and practices to the fullest extent possible.

At the same time, we must not exaggerate the complexity of observations made by the ancients and the labor required in the construction of the markings. Actually, building slightly elevated structures of this sort is one of the simplest and cheapest ways of creating sight lines, ceremonial "roads" and enclosures. The still poorer valleys between Nazca and the Chilean border also contain similar markings, though naturally they are smaller in size and number. Furthermore, the valleys of the region have been inhabited for a long time, and each generation and century was forced to carry on its activities in the same place ---with the resulting chaotic maze of superimposed lines, figures, and centers. Add to this the fact that this region is practically a perfect desert with no further economic value, and the persistence of these complex markings down to the present becomes less surprising.

In the richer regions of the northwest coast of Peru, as well as in other more advanced parts of the rest of the world, these simpler forms apparently also once existed. Remains of "roads" and rectangles have been reported from the Lurin and Viru valleys in Peru. In the Zana and Lambayeque valleys I found "roads" similar to those of Nazca. But gradually, with the accumulation of greater wealth, it was possible to build much more elaborate and expensive roads, walls, pyramids, and temples for similar astronomical-religious purposes. It is true that in these more advanced areas as the secular power grew at the expense of the priesthood and the people, only such forms of astronomy came to be supported as were concerned with the interests of the state. Nevertheless, the attempt to obtain the aid of the heavenly bodies to rule the world continued as an important endeavor of the state-directed priesthood.

Thus as we pursue our study, we must bear in mind the close and continuous relationship between ancient Peruvian astronomy and the whole life of the people. Only then can we obtain results that will be a step forward in understanding both. At the same time, by correlating our results with what we know of the astronomy and culture of other prehistoric peoples, we should be able to broaden our knowledge of this early stage of human development, the remains of which now present us with such a host of perplexing questions.

AUSTRALIAN GROUND AND TREE DRAWINGS
Mathews, R. H.; *American Anthropologist*, 9:33-49, 1896.

Drawings on the Ground. These drawings consist of several kinds.
(1) Some are outlined by laying down logs, bark, or bushes to a certain
height and then covering them with earth. This was no doubt done because the natives had very primitive tools for digging; in large figures
raising a considerable quantity of earth would require much time and labor, especially if the ground were hard or clayey. (2) Others are formed entirely of loose earth heaped up into the required shape. A modification of this form of drawing was observable on the Bora ground at
Gundabloui, described by me, where there were two human figures,
a man and a woman, roughly modeled in raised earth; then a sheet of
bark was cut into human outline, showing the arms, legs, etc., and this
was laid on top of the raised earth. (3) Another kind of drawing consists of figures of men, animals, and devices in various patterns* cut
into the surface of the ground, a nick or groove from two to three inches
wide and about two inches deep being cut in the turf along the outline of
each. These grooves were cut with tomahawks or with flat pieces of
wood on which an edge had been formed. (4) Others again are merely
drawn upon the sand with a stick.

The earliest authentic account of native drawings on the turf with
which I am acquainted is that contained in Mr. J. Henderson's work. In
describing a Bora ground near Wellington, New South Wales, he says:
"A long straight avenue of trees extended for about a mile.... On one
extremity of this, the earth had been heaped up, so as to resemble the
gigantic figure of a human being extended on his breast, while through
the whole length of this sylvan temple a variety of other characters were
observed rudely imprinted on the turf." Mr. Henderson states also that
"the devices on the turf bore a strong similitude to the lingen of the
Hindoos, and that he "recognized several hieroglyphics which seemed
also to represent under different forms the same symbol which the Hindoos have selected in order to indicate the creative attributes of the
divinity." In a plate at the end of his work he gives copies of a few of
these characters.

The Rev. William Ridley describes a Bora ground on which "there
was the horizontal figure of a man roughly modeled by laying down sticks
and covering them with earth, so as to raise it from four to seven inches
above the level of the ground. It was 22 feet long, 12 feet from hand to
hand, and the width of the body four feet." He gives an illustration of
this figure on the same page.

While exploring in Cape York peninsula, Queensland, Mr. Norman
Taylor found on the hardened earth flats at the back of a beach some
regularly drawn turtles cut out in outline.

At a corroboree witnessed by Mr. W. T. Wyndham near either Barwan or Condamine river, Queensland, he saw an image made of earth
and logs on the surface of the ground, which the blacks told him represented the bunyip, warway, or polgun, a water monster.

---

* These drawings on the turf are sometimes very numerous and cover a
considerable area. At Gundabloui a space 320 yards long by 40 feet wide
was covered with a great variety of such drawings.

Mr. E. M. Curr thus refers to a raised earthen figured formed by the aborigines in the county of Karkarooc, Victoria: "The work was described to me as a mound about 100 feet or yards long, I forget which, made to resemble a huge snake. Its locality was close to the Murray river, some twenty miles below Euston, but on the other side. It was said by the blacks to have been made to charm away the smallpox which raged in those parts probably about 1820 or 1830.

Mr. A. W. Howitt in speaking of the initiation ceremonies of the blacks about Bega, New South Wales, says: "The old men having carefully cleared a piece of ground proceed to mold in earth in high relief the life-sized figure of a naked man in the attitude of the dance.... This is Daramulun."

Mr. J. K. McKay informs me that upward of 30 years ago he saw a figure made by the aborigines on the right bank of Moonie river, near a large water hole in that stream, about 30 miles above Nindigully. It was apparently intended to represent a swan of enormous proportions. The body was about 15 feet long, about 6 feet wide, and 4 feet high; it was formed of brushes and leaves pressed closely together and covered with a thick coating of mud; the head and neck consisted of a bent log of the required shape about 10 feet long, one extremity of which was fixed into the ground at one end of the heap of bushes, the other extremity being cut to represent the head, which was elevated several feet above the surface; the whole figure was then ornamented with daubs of white and red, the head being painted red. This figure was at a deserted camp of the natives, and before going away they had taken all the sheets of bark which they had been using for their own shelters or gunyahs and laid them over the monster to protect it from rain. There was a cleared space about 20 or 30 feet wide all round this animal, where the natives had apparently been dancing corroborees while remaining in the camp adjacent.

In my paper on "The Bora or Initiation Ceremonies of the Kamilaroi Tribe" I gave a full and detailed description of a variety of figures drawn upon the soil in various ways. In plate XXI of that paper, figure 3 represents a horizontal image of Baiamai 15 feet long and formed of logs covered with earth and raised 2 feet 6 inches above the ground. Figures 2, 4, and 16 represent two snakes, a woman, and an emu respectively, all composed of raised earth. Figures 5, 6, 7, and 8 were formed by cutting grooves into the surface of the soil along the outlines of the objects to be drawn. Figure 5 of the plate referred to is especially interesting, representing a group of twelve persons life size, their hands and feet joining the hands and feet of others.

Beside the figures just referred to, other objects were formed on the ground in a similar manner. Some of the drawings displayed the inventive, humorous, and imitative faculties of the natives. As an example, I may refer to the group representing a stump, a broken cart, a horse, and the driver, illustrating the adventures of an old king dressed in his regalia, on his way to the Bora. The raised earthen figure of a bullock, on one end of which was fixed the skeleton of a bullock's head, a crooked stick stuck in the other end for a tail, is also deserving of attention.

In my paper on an "Aboriginal Bora held at Gundabloui in 1894" is described a gigantic figure of an iguana, about 20 feet long, composed of pieces of bark covered with earth. The pieces of bark were about 2 feet 6 inches long, chopped in the middle sufficiently to admit of their being bent at an acute angle. The two ends were then placed on the ground about 18 inches apart and about a foot high, forming a figure like the gable end of a house. A sufficient number of these were used in continuation to make up the required length of the body, and the whole was then covered over with earth. The head, tail, and legs were made of earth alone.

A gentleman who has been engaged on stations in northern Queensland informs me that on the Lower Gilbert river, which flows into the gulf of Carpentaria, he saw the representation of an alligator formed by heaping up the loose earth into the required shape. It was about 25 feet long, 2 feet wide across the body, and 1 foot high. He also told me that he had occasionally seen similar figures formed on the ground on other rivers in that part of the country.

Mr. J. W. Fawcett informs me that at Townsville, Queensland, between 1870 and 1875, he saw the figure of a man formed on the ground by means of raised earth, the head pointing toward the north. There were other figures contiguous, but their outline was broken and partially leveled by stock. The same correspondent also mentions having seen other earth-molded figures about a mile northerly from Charters Towers, Queensland. Some of these figures appeared to have been intended for emus and kangaroos, but were much trodden down by cattle and sheep.

The same correspondent, writing from Dungeness, near the mouth of Herbert river, Queensland, states that the aborigines of that place and also those of Hinchinbrook island adjacent, sometimes amused themselves by drawing figures on the beach with sticks. Some of the figures mentioned represented men, birds, lizards, turtles, canoes, etc.

Mr. S. Gason, of Beltana, South Australia, states that he has seen the aborigines, old and young, amuse themselves by portraying various objects on the sand by means of a piece of stick. These drawings consisted chiefly of kangaroos, dogs, snakes, fish, and emus and other birds.

Mr. C. Winnecke informs me that it is a frequent pastime of the natives in several places in South Australia, as well as in the northern territory, to select a clay-pan and on its flat surface to outline circles, squares, and other figures by means of small stones placed in a single row along the outlines of the figures to be delineated. The stones are sometimes carried to the clay-pans from long distances, none being obtainable in the immediate vicinity.

I will now proceed to give a detailed description, from personal observation, of all the drawings on the ground, which are shown in accompanying figures 18 to 36.

Figure 18---This is a huge representation of Baiamai, and was formed entirely of loose earth, heaped to the height of two feet. The length of the figure was 15 feet, the width from hand to hand 12 feet 3 inches, and the body was built in proportion. This raised earthen drawing was on a Bora ground of one of the Kamilaroi tribes and was situated close to the left bank of Gnoura Gnoura creek, about two miles northerly from the town of Kunopia, parish of Boonanga, county of Benarba, New South Wales.

Figure 19---This drawing, which represents Gunnanbeely, the wife of Baiamai, was also composed of the earth, heaped so as to resemble a gigantic human being extended on the ground. The length of the body was 10 feet, the width from hand to hand 8 feet, and the height above the

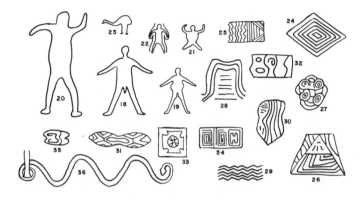

Australian ground drawings

surface of the ground 1 foot 6 inches. This figure was close to the image of Baiamai described in the last paragraph.

Figure 20---This colossal horizontal representation of Baiamai was formed on a Burbung ground of one of the Wiradthuri tribes and is situated near the left bank of Bulgeraga creek, an Ana branch of Macquarie river, in the parish of Wullamgambone, county of Gregory, New South Wales. It was composed entirely of raised earth, and was 21 feet 8 inches long, 5 feet 6 inches across the body, and the arms were each 7 feet 3 inches long. The height of the breast above the level of the ground was about 1 foot 6 inches.

Figure 21---On the same Burbung ground as figure 20 was a life-sized representation of a woman, outlined by means of a nick or groove cut in the ground about 2 inches deep and from 2 to 3 inches wide, cut out with tomahawks and sharpened sticks.

Figure 22---Not far from figure 20 was a drawing which the blacks informed me was intended for one of Baiamai's sons, executed in the same manner as figure 21. The length was 6 feet 6 inches and the width from hand to hand four feet. A grooved line, apparently for ornamentation, was cut along the outside of each arm and along the body down to the foot on each side of this figure, as shown in the figure.

Figure 23---About a chain from the feet of Baiamai, figure 20, was the representation of an emu, delineated by means of a groove cut in the soil; its length from the point of the bill to the end of the tail was 6 feet 7 inches, and from the feet to the curve of the back four feet.

Figures 24 to 30---These represent some of the devices cut upon the turf on the Kamilaroi Bora ground at Gundabloui, near Moonie river, parish of Gundabloui, county of Finch, New South Wales. There were about 40 of these designs cut in the ground in various places and at irregular intervals along the track connecting the two circles. They consisted chiefly of straight, wavy, and zigzag lines, forming imperfect rectangles, ovals, and different indefinite patterns, no two of which are alike, although there is a general similarity in their construction. Three of these carvings in the soil are shown in figures 6, 7, 8, plate

XXI, of my paper on "The Bora or Initiation Ceremonies of the Kamilaroi Tribe."

Figures 31 to 35---These designs were cut in the soil on the Wiradthuri Burbung ground referred to in describing figure 20, and have a general resemblance to figures 24 to 30 just described. There were a considerable number of these devices cut upon the ground in all the clear spaces between the trees and saplings throughout a distance of about 140 yards. Designs such as these, whether cut upon the ground or upon trees, are called <u>yammun-yamun</u> by the natives of the Kamilaroi and Wiradthuri tribes.

Figure 36---This drawing, which occurs on the Burbung ground previously mentioned, represents a legendary monster called <u>Wahwee</u> by the natives of the Castlereagh, Macquarie, and Barwan rivers. It is supposed to have its abode in very deep water holes and devours human beings. The figure here shown measures 59 feet in length and a foot across the body at the widest part; it is formed by a nick or groove about three inches wide and two inches deep cut in the turf along its outline; it has a head and neck like a large snake, and it is here delineated with its tail coiled round the butt of a belar sapling. This is probably the mythical animal Mr. Wyndham calls <u>warway</u> and which was composed of earth and logs in the case mentioned by him. (See my quotation at page 35 of this paper.) (pp. 34-40)

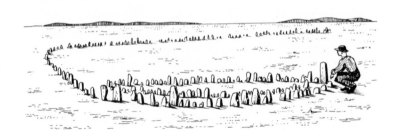

Australian rock alignment. It is regarded as a snake by aborigines.

THE LONG DIVINITY OF SUSSEX

Massingham, H. J.; *Contemporary Review*, 129:351-356, 1926.

If then the figure on Windover Hill was the Long Divinity I take him to be, he, like the Cerne giant, has been engraved more or less where we should expect him to have been, and serves the office of a kind of anthropomorphic shrine for all the busy workers in the neighbourhood. Very little has ever been written about him, and the only detailed account I have been able to find occurs in the 20th volume of the Sussex Archaeological Collections (1875). The writer dismisses the theory that the Long Man was carved upon a hill-side, so steep that after rain you go one step up for two steps down, by the "idle monks" of the old Priory. To incise so colossal an effigy into the turf of so precipitous a hill is certainly not my notion of paying suit to Comus, and the very last thing that monks were likely to do was to devote themselves to so obviously heathenish a naked figure. The venerable prior would never have re-covered from the shock, and there is, in fact, every evidence of an attempt to fill in and to obscure the figure. Nor is the giant much more likely to have been of Celtic than monkish workmanship. The Celts, as the study of their remains clearly reveals, were not in the habit of con-structing the toilsome and ambitious works of the civilisation that pre-ceded them. The Celts, again, were a warlike people, and the imple-ments unearthed near Windover Hill are purely industrial. Moreover, the giants of the chronicles and romances were a legacy to the Celts from the archaic civilisation; all their affinities were to it and, if there is any truth in the chroniclers' descriptions of the early Celtic fear of and hostility to giants, the Long Man is hardly likely to have been a Celtic idol, even in their heathen days. The foreign giants, too, can be "equated" to the deified kings of this civilisation that the Celts destroyed both in England and in Western Europe, and it is probable that we have an account of that destruction in England in the chroniclers' records of the wars against the giants. Lastly, the anthropomorphic representa-tions of the gods certainly belong to an earlier period of prehistory than the Celtic.

Long Man of Wilmington, East Sussex (Janet & Colin Bord)

Hand of Cerne Abbas Giant cut in chalk, Dorset (Janet & Colin Bord)

But what of the clues to the identity of the Long Man of Windover Hill? In his hands he carries two staffs.

Now I do not wish to lay too much stress upon this twinning of the staffs of the Long Man upon the northern slope of Windover Hill. If it were not for supporting data I would not even mention it, for to do so necessarily exposes me to the charge of seeing double in order to buttress a case for the existence of the "dual organisation" (reproduced all over the East) in England. But there is just sufficient testimony bearing from other quarters upon this duality to warrant me in the bare suggestion that it may not be accidental. There is first of all the pairing of the giants in their boulder contests, of which there are dozens of examples in folklore. These "singles" of prehistoric tennis may be due, of course, simply to the putting up one champion against another. But that does not explain the dualistic survival of the names Gog and Magog for two more of the Gargantuans. Secondly, there were a pair of Saxon gods (and the Saxons certainly inherited many elements of the archaic civilisation) worshipped in this particular quarter of the old Andredsweald, and called Andras and Andred. And why two staffs? The Long Man may or may not be a god of travellers (as the article mentioned above suggests), but though the steepness of the ascent gave me every justification, I did not set out to climb his "vast bodily composure" from

the fairy vale of Cuckmere, like a Lilliputian up Gulliver, with two
walking-sticks. What does so valiant a god want with two staffs?

A still more pertinent question, and one capable, I think, of a less
dubious answer is, What does he want with one, what is he doing with a
staff at all? The article in the Sussex Archaeological Collections calls
him the "god of travellers" on the ground that he is a Celtic representation of Mercury, and Dr. Phene and others of the older archaeologists
are inclined to the same view. Now when these older prehistorians
spoke of the Celtic period they meant the Bronze Age, and it is probable
that the first wave of the Celts broke upon England before the Bronze Age
had run its course. We may take it, therefore, that the Long Man is of
the Bronze Age, though precedent to the first invasion of the Celts, who
doubtless adopted him, as they did the dragon, as a blend of idol and
demon. (pp. 354-355)

• Effigy Mounds

ABORIGINAL STRUCTURES IN GEORGIA
Jones, Charles C., Jr.; *Smithsonian Annual Report, 1877,* pp. 278-282.

The existence of curious effigy-mounds in the southern counties of
Wisconsin was noted by Mr. Lapham in 1836. Subsequently, Mr. Taylor,
Professor Locke, and Messrs. Squier and Davis furnished additional information in regard to the distinctive characteristics of these unusual
structures. It was reserved, however, for the Smithsonian Institution,
in the seventh volume of its "Contributions," to furnish, from the pen of
Mr. Lapham, the most complete account of these interesting remains.
They were quite numerous along the great Indian trail or war-path from
Lake Michigan, near Milwaukee, to the Mississippi above the Prairie
du Chien. Generally representing men, buffaloes, elks, bears, otters,
wolves, raccoons, birds, serpents, lizards, turtles, and frogs, in
some instances they were supposed to typify inanimate objects, such
as bows and arrows, crosses, and tobacco-pipes. While the outlines
of not a few had been seriously impaired, others in a spirited and correct manner declared the objects of their imitation. Constructed of
earth, they varied in height from 6 inches to 7 feet. In certain localities
the animals were delineated not in relief but in intaglio, by excavations
and not by elevations.

Two animal mounds have been observed in Ohio. On an elevated spur
of land near Granville is an earthwork known in the neighborhood as the
Alligator. Its total length is 250 feet. The head and body, four sprawl-

ing legs and a curled tail, were all clearly defined. Across the body it was 40 feet broad, and the length of the legs was 36 feet. Four feet expressed the average height, while at the shoulders the mound attained an elevation of 6 feet. It was manifestly the effort of the primitive workmen to preserve the proportions of the reptile.

Situated on a ridge rising 150 feet above Brush Creek, in Adams County, is a still more remarkable structure, which, from its configuration, has received the appellation of the <u>Great Serpent</u>. "Conforming to the curve of the hill, and occupying its very summit, is the serpent, its head resting near the point and its body winding back for 700 feet in graceful undulations, terminating in a triple coil at the tail." If extended, its entire length would be not less than 1,000 feet. The embankment is upward of 5 feet high, with a base diameter of 30 feet at the center of the body, whence it diminishes somewhat toward the head and tail. "The neck of the serpent is stretched out and slightly curved, and its mouth is opened wide, as if in the act of swallowing or ejecting an oval figure, which rests partially within the distended jaws."

When and by whom these remarkable tumuli were built is not known. The object of their construction is equally a matter of conjecture.

It has been supposed that these animal-shaped mounds existed only in Wisconsin and a few other localities in the West. Our recent observations prove, however, that the primitive dwellers in the South have left similar traces of their constructive skill.

Six miles and a half north of Eatonton, in Putnam County, Georgia, on a plantation owned by the heirs of the late Mr. I. H. Scott, may now be seen a bird-shaped mound of definite configuration. Located in the midst of a beautiful wood, and crowning a high ridge near the headwaters of Little Glady Creek, it is composed entirely of bowlders of

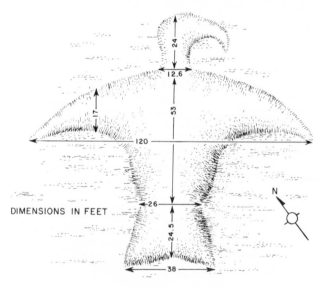

Bird-shaped mound, Putnam County, Georgia

white quartz rock, gathered from the adjacent territory. Most of these bowlders are of such size that they could have been transported by a single individual. For the removal of others two or three persons would have been requisite. These bowlders were carefully piled one above another, the interstices being filled with smaller fragments of milky quartz. Into the composition of the structure enters neither earth nor clay.

This stone mound represents an eagle lying upon its back, with extended wings. The head is turned toward the east. In the construction of this tumulus respect was had to the object imitated; the height of the tumulus at the breast of the bird being between 7 and 8 feet, its altitude thence decreasing toward the head and beak, where it is not more than 2-1/2 feet high, and also toward the extremity of the wings and tail, where it has an elevation of scarcely 2 feet. The beak is decidedly aquiline, and the tail is indented. Measured from the top of the head to the extremity of the tail this structure is 102 feet long. From tip to tip of the wings, measured across the body, we have a distance of 120 feet. The greatest expanse of tail is 38 feet, the same as the lateral diameter of the body. The proportions of the head, neck, wings, and tail are cleverly preserved. That this tumulus was designed to typify an eagle, we think may be affirmed with some degree of confidence, and that it possesses unusual attractions will not be denied. Surrounded by primitive forest and composed of most durable material, its antiquity is evidently very considerable. If undisturbed, it will preserve its integrity for an indefinite period.

By some curious persons an attempt was made, years ago, to pry into its secrets. A partial opening was effected in the breast, but with what results we could not learn. It excites no surprise that the eagle should have been selected in ancient times as a symbol of all that was swift, powerful, watchful, daring, and noble. Of its feathers was the battleflag of the Creeks made. Their council-lodges were surmounted with carved images or stuffed skins of this regal bird. None among the Cherokees, save approved warriors, were permitted to wear its plumes. To this king of the feathered tribe were religious honors paid by the Natchez, who regarded its feathers not simply as ornaments and trophies, but as marks of dignity and insignia of no common import.

About a mile and a half from Lawrence's Ferry, on the Oconee River, and situated on a stony ridge near the main road, on the plantation of Mr. Kinchen D. Little, in Putnam County, is another of these bird-shaped mounds. Like the former, it is composed wholly of bowlders of white quartz rock, collected from the hill on which it stands.

Its dimensions do not materially differ from those of the tumulus on the Scott place. The tail, however, is bifurcated. The head of the bird lies to the southeast, and its wings are extended in the direction of northeast and southwest. The entire length of the structure, from the crown of the head to the end of the tail, is 102 feet and 3 inches. For a distance of twelve feet the tail is bifurcated, and just above the point of bifurcation it is 12 feet wide. Across the body, and from tip to tip of the wings, the tape gave us a measurement of 132 feet. The body of this bird, which is evidently lying upon its back, is stouter than that of the eagle, being 76 feet in diameter. Its wings are relatively shorter. The proportions of the head, neck, and tail are tolerably well observed. What particular bird this tumulus is designed to typify, we are at a loss to suggest. The altitude at the breast is about 5 feet, and from that point the structure tapers to the head and tail, which are some two-feet high. At the tips of the wings, which are short and curved, the height is not more than a foot and a half. The ridge upon which this mound rests has never been cleared.

Surrounding this bird-shaped tumulus is an inclosure of rocks similar to those of which the mound is built. This stone-circle is symmetrical in outline, and at its nearest approach passes within a few feet of the tips of the wings.

. . . .

THE GREAT SERPENT AND OTHER EFFIGIES

Peet, Stephen D.; *American Antiquarian*, 12:211-228, 1890.

One of the most remarkable prehistoric monuments in America is the great serpent mound in Ohio. This mound was surveyed and described by the authors of "Ancient Monuments" as early as 1845. It has been frequently visited and described since then. The last survey was that made by Prof. Putnam in the year 1889. His description was published in The Century magazine for that year. Prof. Putnam, it would seem, has taken the same position as did Squier and Davis, and advocates the theory of an European or Asiatic origin. The following is his description: "Approaching the serpent cliff by fording Brush Creek, our attention was suddenly arrested by the rugged overhanging rocks above our heads, and we knew that we were near the object of our search. Leaving the wagon we scrambled up the steep hill, and pushing on through brush and briar, were soon following the folds of the great serpent along the hilltop. The most singular sensation of awe and admiration overwhelmed me, for here before me was the mysterious work of an unknown people, whose seemingly most sacred place we had invaded. Was this a symbol of the old serpent faith here on the western continent, which from the earliest time in the religions of the East, held so many people enthralled? Following the ridge of the hill northerly one is forced again to pause and admire the scene---the beautiful hill-girt valley, the silvery line of the river, the vistas opening here and there, where are the broader and deeper portions of the river, etc. Turning from this view, and ascending the knoll, one sees before him, eighty feet from the edge of the cliff, the western end of the oval figure in front of the serpent's jaws.

The oval is one hundred and twenty feet long and sixty feet in breadth. Near the center is a small mound of stone, which was formerly much larger. Many of the stones show signs of fire. Prof. Putnam says: "A careful examination of sections through the oval shows that both parts of the earth-work were outlined upon a smooth surface, clay mixed with ashes being used in some places, but a pavement of stone to prevent washing used in other places. The whole structure was carefully planned and thoroughly built. " Prof. Putnam speaks also of the crescent shaped bank between the jaws of the serpent, the extremities being seventy-five feet apart, but the bank being seventeen feet wide. This crescent is worthy of notice. The head of the serpent is thirty feet wide and five feet high. The serpent itself is 1,254 feet in length, measured from the tip of the jaw to the end of the tail. The average width is twenty feet, and the height from four to five feet. The tail decreases where it begins to coil, and is at the end about a foot high and two feet wide. "The graceful curves throughout the whole length of this singular effigy give it a strange lifelike appearance, as if a huge serpent slowly uncoiling itself and creeping silently and stealthily along the crest of the hill, was about to seize the oval within its extended jaws. In the oval embankment, with its central pile of burnt stones in combination with the serpent, we have the three symbols everywhere regarded in the old world as emblems of primitive faith. Here we find the Linga in Yoni of India, or the reciprocal principle of nature guarded by the serpent, or life, power, knowledge and eternity. Moreover its position---east and west---indicates the nourishing source of

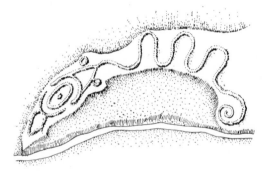

Early sketch of Ohio's Great Serpent Mound showing head details not in later drawings

fertility, the great sun god whose first rays fall upon the altar of stones in the centre of the oval."

Prof. Putnam also refers to the remarkable serpent effigy which was discovered by Dr. J. W. Phene in Argyleshire, Scotland, and quotes a description of this, written by Miss Gordon-Cummings. The following is the quotation:

"The tail of the serpent rests near the shore of Loch Nell, and the ground gradually rises seventeen to twenty feet in height, and is continued for three hundred feet, forming a double curve, like a huge letter S, and wonderfully perfect in outline. The head formed a circular cairn, on which there still remains some trace of an altar. Dr. Phene excavated the circular cairn, or circle of stones, and found three large stones, forming a megalithic chamber. From the ridge of the serpent's back, it was found that the whole length of the spine was constructed with stones, regularly and systematically placed at such an angle as to throw off the rain. The spine is, in fact, a long narrow causeway, made of large stones, set like the vertebrae of some huge animal, the ridge slop-

ing off at each side is continued downward with an arrangement of smaller stones, suggestive of ribs. The mound has been formed in such a
position that the worshipers, standing at the altar, would naturally look
eastward, directly along the whole length of the great reptile, and across
the dark lane, to the tripple peaks of Ben Cruachan." Prof. Putnam
says: "Is there not something more than a mere coincidence in the resemblances between the Loch Nell and the Ohio serpent. Each has the
head pointing west, each terminates with a circular enclosure containing
an altar, from each, looking along the most prominent portion of the serpent, the rising sun may be seen. If the serpent of Scotland is a symbol
of an ancient faith, surely that of Ohio is the same." Here then we have
the full committal of the professor of archaeology in Harvard College to
this theory of the foreign origin of the great serpent. (pp. 213-215)

THE CAMEL AND ELEPHANT MOUNDS AT PRAIRIE DU CHIEN

Lewis, T. H.; *American Antiquarian,* 6:348–349, 1884.

While prosecuting archaeological researches in Vernon and Crawford
counties, Wisconsin, lately, my attention was especially called to that
part of your article on "Effigy Mounds, published in Vol. 9, of the Wisconsin Historical Society Collection, which treats of certain earthworks
of that class, situated in Campbell's Coolie, not far from Prairie du
Chien. The style in which your informant, Dr. Phene, treated them
naturally created a curiosity which only actual examination could satisfy.
I therefore visited this locality and made an instrumental survey of the
best preserved of these remains---two so-called elephants. This place
is two miles north of the center of Prairie du Chien and two and one-
half miles east of the Mississippi river. There are three groups of
effigies in the coolie proper; one at the mouth, one about one-quarter
mile from Dousman's house (surveyed) and one near the spring, one-
half mile off. I found the elephants to be the only figures with perfect

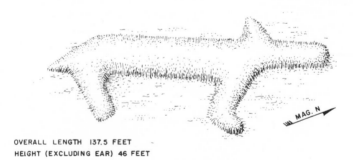

OVERALL LENGTH 137.5 FEET
HEIGHT (EXCLUDING EAR) 46 FEET

Elephant effigy mound in Wisconsin

outlines. In connection with them were one cross, three birds and twelve other mounds and embankments, but not worth surveying.

A camel at Campbell's Coolie might be somewhere on the surrounding bluff, for I do not believe that these "elephants" were the effigies Dr. Phene saw, but I rather think the "camel" was in some other coolie, as no one at Campbell's knew of any person having been there to see the groups I have just described. There are some mounds and embankments on the bluffs, but I could not find or hear of any effigy with them. People living a few miles further up, however, said that visitors in carriages had been seen one time in their neighborhood looking for such things. Nearly one mile west of these "elephants" is another ruined one, in a field near the Catholic burial ground.

It occurred to me that perhaps you might think drawings of these "elephants," plotted from my field-notes, worthy of the attention of your readers, and I therefore send you three diagrams herewith. Two are large scale plans (1:400) of the animal figures separately, the third is a little outline map, one-fifth the scale of the others (or, 1:2,000), showing the two creatures in their relative positions to each other, and to the slope of the contiguous hill.

These pictured outlines may be considered, I think, in the light of a trustworthy contribution to the material needed in the discussion of the subject of the co-existence of <u>man and mammoth</u> in this northwestern region; at any rate they are interesting subjects for speculation.

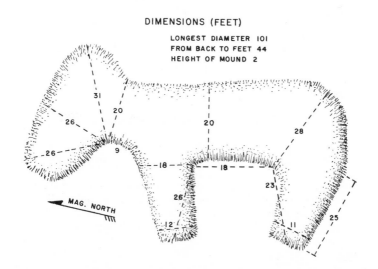

DIMENSIONS (FEET)

LONGEST DIAMETER 101
FROM BACK TO FEET 44
HEIGHT OF MOUND 2

MAG. NORTH

Another Wisconsin elephant mound

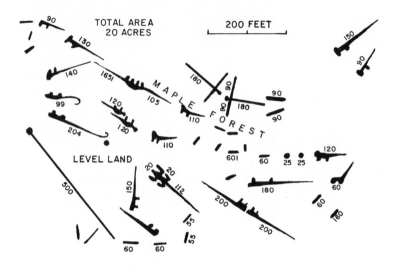

Map of a group of Wisconsin effigy mounds

• Boulder Mosaics

STONE MONUMENTS IN SOUTHERN DAKOTA
Lewis, T. H.; *American Anthropologist,* 2:159–167, 1889.

There is a class of antiquities in the Northwest which have not as yet received the attention to which their importance entitles them. They consist of outline figures made by placing bowlders upon the ground in the shape of circles and squares, but occasionally they constitute other forms. Scarcely any of the bowlders used exceed a foot in diameter.

These outline figures are found over a large territory, extending from Southern Iowa and Nebraska to Manitoba, on the north, and from the Mississippi river through Dakota into Montana.

The Man and Woman. Punished Woman's Hill, on which are located two of the best-known works of this class, is situated about three miles south of Punished Woman's Lakes, in the northeastern corner of Coding-ton County, Dakota. The hill is a high "hog-back," with spurs, rather than a rounded, symmetrical elevation, and the country in its vicinity is somewhat rolling and broken, lying as it does on the eastern part of the Plateau du Coteau des Prairies, which divides the waters of the Minne-sota river from those of the Big Sioux.

I visited this section in September, 1883, and found the outlines so interesting that I made a complete survey of what remained in good condition. They represented a man and a woman.

The male figure is near the end of a spur which runs northward from a knoll several feet higher. The length from the top of the head to the heels is 13-1/2 feet. It is the representation of a man lying upon his back, with uplifted arms. The number of bowlders used in making this figure is one hundred and four.

The female figure, or woman, is on the same spur, 42 feet distant from the man, to the southeast. She is also represented as lying upon her back, with outstretched arms. Her length from the top of the head to the heels is 8 feet, and the number of bowlders used in the figure is ninety-two. Her outline is much ruder than that of the man.

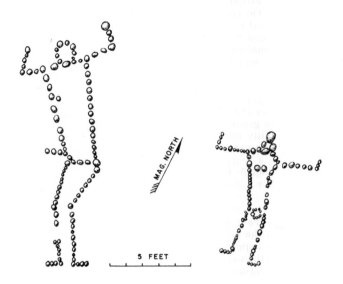

The Man and Woman; Dakota boulder mosaics

Commencing at the feet of the man and running in a southerly direction past the woman is a trail, 102 feet long, formed by placing bowlders at irregular intervals. It ends at the foot of a slope, 31 feet from a cairn, which is some four feet in height. On this knoll with the cairn there are two small shallow excavations---one four feet in diameter and the other four by six feet. Nearly south of this knoll, at the end of a small spur, there is another small cairn. Seventy feet to the west of the first cairn begins another trail of bowlders running nearly west along a hog-back for 285 feet, to within 15 feet of a third cairn. This is on a knoll of about the same height as that of the first knoll, the hog-back being somewhat lower. There are two cairns on this. One of them, composed of large, heavy bowlders, is nearly six feet high; the other is nearly as massive, but is only about five feet high. Near the smaller cairn there is an excavation which has the appearance of a sunken grave. On the south side of the trail, along the hog-back, there is another figure, which apparently represented a person, but vandals have defaced it by carrying away the stones.

The Dakotas have a tradition in regard to Punished Woman's Hill, which runs as follows: A chief of that nation had a very beautiful daughter, whom he forced to marry against her will. She soon, however, ran away with the brave of her own choice, and they camped on a hill overlooking the lake. The lawful husband followed their trail, and when he discovered them he killed the lover and savagely wounded the woman, leaving her to die. On returning to the village he boasted of what he had done. The chief loved his daughter, and so, taking the people of his village, he went to see if what had been said was true. Finding that it was, he killed the husband. The Indians marked the places where the lover and wife were found, and also the spot where the husband was killed. The trails, with the bowlders strewn along at intervals, are said to mark the ground over which the woman crawled towards the lake in search of water. The cairns are reported to be monuments to mark the hill upon which the tragedy occurred.

The tradition as given above was related to me by a Dakota chief, but the story was probably invented by the Indians to account for these monuments, for the hill is not even in sight of the lake, and the trail runs from or to the man's feet, leaving the woman to one side.

The Snake. About 3-1/2 miles to the southwest of the village of Blunt, Hughes county, and 11 miles in a straight line from the Missouri river, is a high, irregular table-land, called "Medicine Butte," the top of which is some 400 feet above Medicine creek, distant about 2 miles to the east. At different points on this table grand views of the country may be had. From the point where the figure next to be described is situated the view is especially fine, a grand panorama being spread out to the north and northwest. The sides of the butte are very steep in some places, but in others there are long spurs extending out from its sides.

The figure in question is built upon the north end of this Paha Wakan (Medicine Knoll) of the Dakotas, and represents a snake. Its head is 10 feet in length and nearly 7 feet wide at the broadest point. Two oblong stones represent the eyes. The body varies in width from 3 to 10 feet. The stones composing the outline of the tail are much smaller than those used for the body, many of them being no larger than an egg. There are said to have been several large bowlders extending out from the end of the tail, representing rattles, but on September 7, 1884, when this survey was made, there was no indication that there ever had been any bowlders at that point. The total length of the snake, following the curves, is 360 feet, and the total number of stones and bowlders used in the outline and including the two for the eyes is 825, of which at least ten occupied their present positions previous to the construction of the snake, as shown on the diagram.

About midway and to its right there is a small stone heap or cairn, which some barbarian has partially demolished, that must have been from three to four feet in height.

I was told by the Indians that the snake was built in commemoration of a great war speech made by a Dakota chief at a time when that tribe had just returned from a grand hunt in which they had been very successful. But from the apparent age of these monuments this story is extremely doubtful.

The snake is not the only bowlder-outline figure on top of this butte, for there are many circles, a few squares, and some other shapes. There are also several cairns in addition to that already mentioned as lying near the main figure. The Indians claim that the stone circles mark the places where in former times the tepees of their people were located, and that the bowlders held down the edges of the skin tents in place. This explanation, however, is unsatisfactory, for if the bowlders had been used for that purpose they would have been scattered round more or less, and it would not have required so many of them, and besides many of the circles are rather small to be accounted for in that way, some being only eight feet in diameter.

The "Turtle." The bowlder-outline figure locally known as the "Turtle" is located on the north side of "Snake Butte," a hill situated some six miles north of Pierre, in Hughes county. It is near the edge of the bluff and within a mile of the Missouri river. It may have been built to represent a tortoise, but is is just as likely that some sort of beetle was meant.

There is a line of small stones which divides the head from the body. Near the center of this line a similar one runs back to the center of the body and ends in a small circle. From the end of the nose to the tip of the tail it is 15 feet, and the width of the body is about 8 feet. The distance between the ends of the fore feet is 13 feet, and between the hind feet 17 feet. The legs are from 5-1/2 to 7 feet in length, and the tail is 4-1/2 feet long.

Running in a northerly direction along the edge of the bluff for from 500 to 800 yards there is a row of bowlders, placed at irregular intervals. According to Indian tradition these bowlders are said to mark the places where blood dripped from an Arikara chief as he fled from the Dakotas, who had mortally wounded him.

Strung along the bluff, near its edge, there are many squares, circles, some parallelograms, and other figures, which it is impossible to describe or to determine what they were intended to represent.

On the top of Snake Butte proper there are a few circles and other figures.

When I surveyed the "Turtle," September 15, 1884, the butte and the land immediately surrounding it were almost undisturbed prairie, there being but a few acres under cultivation.

Conclusion. --- The localities treated of mostly lie to one side of the routes of explorers and travelers prior to the era of railroad building in the farther Northwest, and I can find no account of them, or any other places similarly distinguished, in their books, nor any narrations of traditions connected with them.

Although the Indians have a way of accounting for these outline figures, as they have for everything else that is peculiar or wonderful, it is evident that they are very ancient. In every instance I have found the bowlders composing them imbedded in the ground to a greater or less depth, and occasionally they are imbedded to such an extent that only small portions of them are visible, and might easily be taken for stones deposited there by nature, as seen so plentifully at various places. I think there can be little room to doubt that the construction of these figures must have antedated the residence in that region of any of the

Dakota tribes.

It is prudent to dismiss any ideas of a community of origin between the ancient stone monuments of North America and those of other continents derived merely from resemblances of shape, and yet it may not be out of place to point out that the bowlder-outline figures of our Northwestern regions are not without parallel in the eastern hemisphere---at least so far as the circles, squares, and other forms not imitative of animals are concerned. Those who are interested enough to make research will find proof of the statement in J. W. Waring's "Stone monuments, tumuli, and ornaments of remote ages" (London, 1870), where they will see specimens of similar circular and other arrangements of stone---"ancient cemeteries"---situated in Sweden, North Germany, the Italian Alps, Algeria, and India.

BOWLDER OUTLINE FIGURES IN THE DAKOTAS.....
Lewis, T. H.; *American Anthropologist*, 4:19-24, 1891.

The American Anthropologist for April, 1889, and July, 1890, contains articles describing certain "Stone Monuments" in southern Dakota, northwestern Iowa, and southwestern Minnesota. The present paper refers to the same class of works, which are now termed bowlder outline figures, because the words "stone monuments" are apt to convey to most minds the idea of solid work and vertical extension, rather than that of a simple placing of one layer of bowlders or large pebbles on the surface of the ground. In the months of July and August last I noted many fine specimens of works of this kind in the Dakotas, lying to the west of those previously described, but yet east of the Missouri river, and here furnish a concise account of such of them as I made measurements of.

In Stutsman County, N. D. On the bluffs bordering the valley of James river, in the southeastern part of the county, bowlder outlines are very numerous, especially on the west side of the river. This region is particularly interesting, for, in addition to the ordinary circles, several new forms or elaborations of that simple figure were met with.

On the N. W. 1/4 of section 13, township 138, range 63, on the west side of the river, there are two circles, the centers of which are 27-1/2 feet apart. Each circular area is surrounded by three rows of bowlders laid close together, after the fashion of bowlder pavements. In each one there are openings, which are three feet in width and are exactly opposite each other. Nearly half-way between the two openings there are two small clusters of bowlders which are two feet apart, and each one is about two feet in diameter.

The northern circle is 16 feet in diameter, from center to center of the pavement, and opposite to the opening, on the northern side, there is a circular attachment which is four feet in diameter, inside measurement, with a small opening, one foot wide, facing the north. This attachment is formed by a single row of bowlders, and is connected with

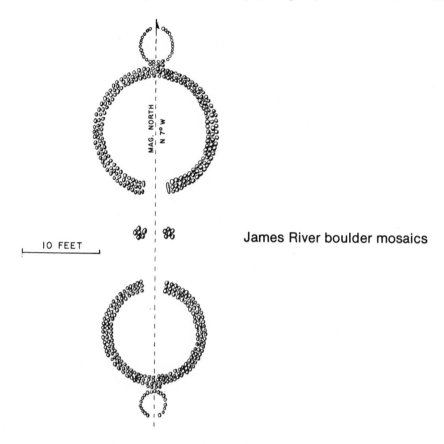

MAG. NORTH
N 7° W

10 FEET

James River boulder mosaics

the pavement by a row of four other bowlders.

The southern circle is similar in form and mode of construction, but it is only thirteen feet in diameter, and the attachment is but three feet wide, with an opening of one foot.

In the same group there is a circle seventeen feet in diameter, with an opening on the northern side which is two and a half feet in width. On the opposite side from the opening, but on the outside of the circle, there is an attachment consisting of twelve bowlders, laid in three rows of five, four, and three bowlders each respectively. On each side, half-way to the opening, there are two other attachments, consisting of three rows of four bowlders each, laid close together.

About one-fourth of a mile distant, on the southwest quarter of the same section, there are two other interesting circles. One of them is divided into two equal parts, and the other into four equal parts. Such divided circles exist at several other points along the valley. Some of them have small openings, while in others there are none whatever.

On the northwest quarter of section 31, township 138, range 62, on the east side of the river and about four miles below the preceding locality, there are two parallelograms which have rounded ends, but are without openings. They are about three hundred feet apart, on a

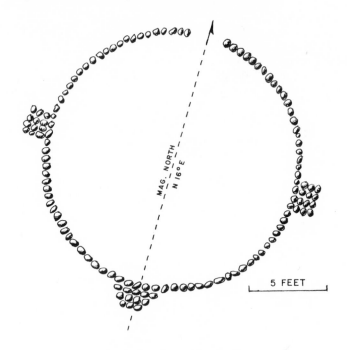

MAG. NORTH
N 16° E

5 FEET

James River boulder mosaic

magnetic bearing of S. 32-1/2° W., which would also nearly coincide with their axes, but that seems to come mostly from the contour of the ground they lie on. The northern parallelogram is 57-1/2 feet in length and 6 feet wide, inside measurement. The southern one is 75 feet in length and 4-1/2 feet wide inside. Attached to the northern end of the latter there is a semi-circle of bowlders extending outward like a pair of horns, the points of which are 4-1/2 feet apart; also, about 100 feet to the northwest of this southern parallelogram, is found one of the circles already described as divided into four parts, like a wheel with four spokes only.

In Jerauld County, S. D. About four miles north and a little west of Wessington Springs there is a high knob, which is locally known as "Turtle Peak." It is located on the N. W. 1/4 of section 35, township 108, range 65, and is on the eastern border of the said hills, a low range running nearly north and south. Its top is elevated some 450 feet above Firesteel creek, which is a branch of James river. East of the creek there is a dividing ridge, which rises, perhaps 150 feet above the river, and separates the two valleys. From the top of the peak a grand view may be had of the adjacent country to the north, south, and east; and on a clear day several towns and villages are within view, including Huron, which is located more than 25 miles to the northeast, in an air line.

On the highest point of the peak there is an ancient mound 45 feet in diameter, which averages 3 feet in height. On the top of the mound there was an intrusive grave, covered over with bowlders, which has been excavated. On the southwest side of the mound, and partially over-lapping its base, are two noteworthy bowlder outlines, one representing a woman and the other a tortoise or other quadruped.

The woman is rather rude in outline, and some of the bowlders have been removed. The length of the figure, in an air line, is about 15 feet, and there are 111 bowlders still remaining in place. Near the woman is the other figure, representing, apparently, a tortoise. Its length, in an air line, from the end of the tail to terminus of the head, is 18-3/4 feet, or along the centre 20-3/4 feet. Some of the bowlders have evidently been removed, but there are 125 still remaining in place.

The stones and bowlders forming these two figures are of various sizes and shapes, the largest being some six inches in diameter. The bowlders forming the tortoise are imbedded somewhat deeper than those of the other figure, but this fact would hardly imply that it was the oldest; for, its position being somewhat lower down than that of the other figure, it is quite evident that there would be a greater accumulation of soil on its site in a given period than on that of the woman.

It has been asserted by some persons residing in the vicinity, and still seems to be the impression of some of them, that these figures were constructed in very recent years; but this theory is evidently erroneous, for their existence has been known since the country was first settled---at least, such is the statement of the oldest citizens, and I see no reason for doubting them.

To the south and southwest there are several stone heaps, large and small, which probably mark graves. A short distance to the southwest of the mound there is a circular bowlder pavement, which is fourteen feet in diameter, and slopes slightly in all directions from its center. The bowlders forming it are nearly equal in size, and the surface is as nearly even as it is possible to lay them.

On a knob about two miles south and east from the Turtle Peak, on the N. W. 1/4 of section 12, township 107, range 65, there is an odd form of bowlder-work, but in a general way it is similar to some found on the west side of the James river, in North Dakota. A circular area 17-1/2 feet in diameter, inside measurement, is surrounded by a pavement, which has no opening. On the northern side there is an attachment ex-tending outward.

On the hills adjacent to the two localities described above, and also on the lower plateaus bordering the bottom lands, there are many circles, small stone heaps, and other figures.

From the best sources of information accessible it is evident that the bowlder outlines are very numerous in the Ree and Wessington Hills, and also in the intermediate country.

The bowlders in most of the figures described in this paper are very numerous, and were therefore not counted. Wherever bowlders were counted their number is given.

UNUSUAL SYMBOLS AND NOTATION

One of the most curious global motifs is the "cup and ring." This symbol, if that is what it is, seems to have originated in the megalithic culture. Cups and rings are most common in Great Britain, Ireland, and the Scandanavian countries, but they have also been found in the Americas and Asia, although in lesser profusion. These symbols are peculiar and undecipherable, hinting vaguely at some strange theme or natural phenomenon. And who carried them to all continents 4,000 years ago?

Equally puzzling are the painted pebbles found in Europe. In the Americas, we have painted beans. Are these objects merely decorative or are they some form of three-dimensional writing? We have no definite answers.

In our current attempts to understand the jottings and structures of ancient man, it is fashionable to wring astronomical significance out of artifacts. Some supposed calendric notations are included here to illustrate the genre.

In a final category, we place those symbols that seem to convey some message but which do not seem like conventional writing with its repeating characters. The figures engraved on the Great Idol of Tiahuanaco, for example, seem more than decorative. Although astronomical interpretations exist here, they are not well accepted.

Symbols form an important part of human communication, but most of the symbols of ancient cultures are about as meaningful to us as Morse Code would be to megalithic man.

• Painted Pebbles

THE PROBLEM OF THE PAINTED PEBBLES OF MAS D'AZIL
Lang, Andrew; *Man*, 4:37–39, 1904.

In L'Anthropologie for November there appears an interesting article by Mr. Arthur Bernard Cook on the painted pebbles of Mas d'Azil. As is well known, these relics of early neolithic or mesolithic culture are painted, some with dots, varying in number; some with transverse strokes; some with very conventionalised designs (perhaps) of trees, serpents, or plants; and some with about fourteen arbitrary characters resembling letters, or the signs of the prehistoric Mediterranean Signary, familiar from the recent discoveries of Mr. Arthur Evans and Mr. Flinders Petrie. M. Piette, the discoverer of the pebbles, argues that some of them with dots were used in calculations, and that even if they were markers in a game they still imply calculation, scoring in each case so many points. In the same number of L'Anthropologie he reinforces this theory, and, as is well known, he regards the pebbles with alphabetiform marks as in some way connected with the very early Cretan, AEgean, and other Mediterranean characters on ancient seals,

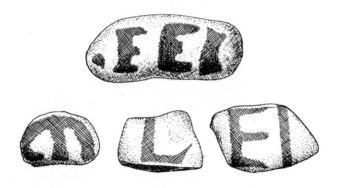

Painted pebbles from the cavern of Mas d'Azil

pots, and other objects.

Mr. Cook replies that "we cannot compare two sets of simple combinations of lines "without observing many cases of purely accidental coincidence," and alphabets are simple combinations of lines. It seems to me that many marks in Mr. Petrie's "Mediterranean Signary" may be found almost anywhere in the pictographs and petroglyphs inscribed by savage or barbaric races. For example, in the Report of the Bureau of Ethnology for 1888-89 is Colonel Mallery's valuable work on such inscriptions. Whoever looks at the plates illustrating the petroglyphs in Owen's Valley, California (pages 56-61), will see much to remind him of Mr. Petrie's signs on Egyptian pottery of circa 5000 B.C. onwards, in Volume I. of Royal Tombs. Mingled with obvious conventionalisings of animal and human figures, in the American rock graffiti, are signs, apparently arbitrary, which have their representatives in archaic Greek, Iberian, Phoenician, and Runic alphabets, and also among the painted pebbles of Mas d'Azil. Anyone who knows the archaic alphabets and the Signary can pick out at least thirteen signs common to these and to the Californian petroglyphs. The signs in these Californian cases cannot, as a rule, be certainly recognised as conventional debasements of representations of objects, but they are isolated in each case, and do not, as in Crete, Egypt, and elsewhere, recur in fixed combinations. They are, therefore, not early letters or elements in an early syllabary, though, to judge from the case of the inscriptions of Oakley Wells (Report, page 329), they may be totem marks inscribed by Indians. These marks at Oakley Wells occasionally represent merely a part of, or the track of, the totem animals, and are in three or four cases at Oakley Wells accidentally alphabetic in form. In other cases also where the form is alphabetic the origin may be totemistic, though the meaning cannot be interpreted, as it was at Oakley Wells, by an Oraibe chief, the last of the Raincloud totems. It is not inconceivable that some signs in the Mediterranean Signary may once have been totem marks; the three-pronged may have represented the track of a bird (as in American and Australian rock paintings or petroglyphs); but all this is mere conjecture in the case of the Mediterranean signs, which clearly had some meaning as characters, perhaps syllabic.

Mr. Cook's suggestion is that the painted pebbles of Mas d'Azil may have corresponded to the painted or incised stones of the Arunta, called Churinga, or "sacred things," and interpreted in accordance with the peculiar totemistic and animistic ideas of the Central Australians. He shows that there is an example of a French palaeolithic pendeloque in bone or ivory, which in shape, serrated edges, and decoration (concentric circles) is exactly akin to some Australian bullroarers.

Another, from a Moravian site, is figured in Hoernes's Der Diluviale Mensch, p. 138 (1903). Dr. Hoernes does not remark on the thoroughly Australian appearance of this object. It may be inferred from these examples and from other in amber from the Baltic coasts, published by Klebs, that palaeolithic and neolithic men had bullroarers, and probably had such religious ideas as among savages are attached to bullroarers, as uttering the Voice (or "Word") of some supernormal being.

But when Mr. Cook argues that the site of Mas d'Azil may have been a kind of storehouse of "sacred things" (Churinga) like the Ertnatulunga of the Arunta, it seems to me that difficulties arise.

To take but a small objection, perhaps, three of the brochs on Sir J. Barry's estate, in Sutherland, yielded a store of painted pebbles curiously analogous to those of Mas d'Azil. A description, with photographs, is in Dr. Joseph Anderson's article on Brocks (Proceedings of the Society of Scottish Antiquaries, 1900-1901). It can hardly be denied I think, that, taken as a whole, the broch-painted pebbles are much more akin to those of Mas d'Azil than are the Arunta churinga as far as we know them at present. Yet the brochs---ingenious, concentric towers built of stone without mortar---represent a stage of culture infinitely above that of Mas d'Azil, which again is far above that of the Arunta. Religious or quasi-religious ideas and customs may survive indefinitely, but it is not very probable that the broch folk of 200 A.D. at earliest kept sacred storehouses of churinga. To all appearance the brochs may have been built first in the third or fourth centuries of our era, in a late chalkosideric age. Yet they show Asylian painted pebbles, whereas Arunta churinga seem, as a rule, to be fashioned stones with incised--- not painted---decorations, and the pebbles of Mas d'Azil are all painted, as are those of the brochs. The patterns on the broch pebbles are usually dots of colour, though lineal designs do occur. The inference, roughly speaking, appears to be that as painted pebbles occur in three very different stages of culture--- Arunta, Mas d'Azil, and early Scotch (or Pictish)---they may in each case have had three very different purposes, and it would be indiscreet to argue from the Arunta purpose, which is known, to the unknown purposes of Mas d'Azil and Caithness.

It is next to be observed that neither the site of Mas d'Azil nor the brochs of Caithness, which yield painted pebbles, answers to the Ertnatulunga, or sacred storehouses of the Australians. In these Ertnatulunga they keep their sacred things, which sometimes (apparently but seldom) are small painted stones, of which only one figured by Messrs.

Spencer and Gillen resembles the pebble of Mas d'Azil. It is a churinga of the Hakea tree totem of the Arunta (Spencer and Gillen, Figure 21, page 5). The resemblance in this case is very close, but the Australian painted stone is of a kind apparently rare among churinga. Most churinga bear concentric circles and half circles, horseshoes, and interconnecing lines incised on stone or wood. The sacred storehouse in Australia is "a small cave or crevice;" the entrance is "carefully blocked up with stones;" the surrounding region is holy, and a sanctuary for wild animals. On the other hand, the shelter of Mas d'Azil was a place of human habitation, as is proved by the remains of food, bones, plumstones, and other objects, while the brochs which yield painted pebbles were mere normal dwelling-places. It seems to follow that Mas d'Azil was no sacred storehouse of mesolithic churinga any more than the brochs were, and when this is recognised we seem to see little reason for supposing that the painted pebbles of Mas d'Azil were religious objects. In Australia a few painted stones and many incised fashioned stones are sacred things, or churinga, and are kept in bundles in sacred caves and crevices. It obviously does not follow that the painted stones so numerous and so variously marked in a mesolithic or early neolithic place of habitation were sacred things or totemistic things. As good a guess as any is that some, at least, of the Mas d'Azil pebbles, and perhaps of the broch pebbles, were used, like the coloured stones in the Mexican game of patolli, "to decide the values in a game by the several "designs, and by the pebbles falling on the coloured or unmarked side" (Report, ut supra, page 550). Pebbles with stripes or spots might be, like cards dice, of various values; pebbles with other designs might answer to "court cards." Savages are no less addicted to gambling than to superstition. But the cards with spots may also have been used in calculations; the "court cards" may have represented conventionalised totemistic designs or other designs. In fact, all is matter of conjecture, and though it would be most interesting to find churinga of the Arunta sort at Mas d'Azil, as it is interesting to find palaeolithic pendeloques of the bullroarer pattern, the evidence rather makes against the sacred and in favour of the sportive character of the Mas d'Azil painted pebbles.

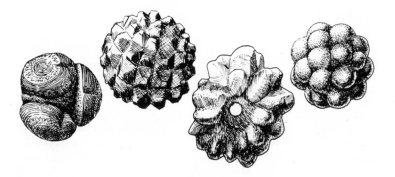

Curious carved stone spheres found in eastern Scotland dated about 1,000 B.C. (Adapted from Evan Hadingham, *Circles and Standing Stones,* 1975.)

WHO'D WRITE ON LIMA BEANS? ANCIENT INDIANS, APPARENTLY

Anonymous; *Science News Letter*, 36:21, 1939.

Who'd ever think of writing on lima beans?

Ancient Americans apparently did, is the conclusion of a noted Peruvian, Senor Rafael Larco Hoyle. He has a theory that clever Chimu Indians of the sandy north coast of Peru actually invented a lima bean writing system by marking the beans with signs that could be recognized.

If Senor Larco's detective reasoning is correct, then it means that ancient American civilization in Peru, which ultimately was welded into the Incan Empire, was not entirely dependent on memory and knot-tying for its important communications. It means that these Indians, like the Mayas and Aztecs of Mexico, were literate in their own fashion. They could read and write.

. . . .

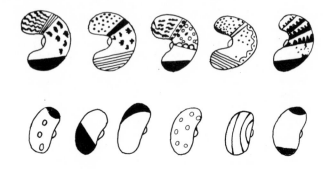

Bean messages from ancient Peru?

The first American telegraph system, you might call this way of speeding correspondence by fast runners carrying a briefed message.

What makes him think beans were in the bag in this: He finds lima beans conspicuous in Chimu art, and the curving bean shape was usually decorated with lines, dots, or colors. Pictures of Indian runners particularly were accompanied by these decorated beans in odd spaces. Even the messagers were sometimes drawn as bean-men with human faces and legs and lima-bean bodies. Putting two and two together, the Peruvian archaeologist deduces that these Indians probably did mark or inscribe real garden beans and gave them to messengers as memorandums to be relayed to a distant receiver.

• Cups and Rings

CUP SCULPTURES
Mallery, Garrick; *Picture-Writing of the American Indians,* vol. 1, New York, 1972, pp. 189-194.

The simplest form of rock inscription is almost ubiquitous. In Europe, Asia, Africa, America, and Oceanica, shallow, round, cup-like depressions are found, sometimes in rows, sometimes singly, sometimes surrounded by a ring or rings, but often quite plain. The cup-markers often arranged their sculpturings in regularly spaced rows, not infrequently surrounding them with one or more clearly cut rings; sometimes, again, they associated them with concentric circles or spirals. Occasionally the sculptors demonstrated the artificial characters of their work by carving it in spots beyond the reach of atmospheric influences, such as the interiors of stone cists or of dwellings. It must, however, be noted that, although there is thus established a distinction between those markings which are natural and those which are artificial, it is possible that there may have been some distant connection between the two, and that the depressions worn by wind and rain may have suggested the idea of the devices, now called cup-markings, to those who first sculptured them.

Vast numbers of these cup stones are found in the British islands, often connected with other petroglyphs. In the county of Northumberland alone there are 53 stones charged with 350 sculptures, among which are many cup depressions. So also in Germany, France, Denmark, and indeed everywhere in Europe, but these forms took their greatest development in India.

The leading work relating to this kind of sculpture is that of Prof. J. Y. Simpson (a), afterward known as Sir James Simpson, who reduces the forms of the cup sculptures to seven elementary types, here reproduced in Fig. 147. His classification is as follows: (Figures omitted.)

First type. Single cups.---They are the simplest type of these ancient stone-cuttings. Their diameter varies from 1 inch to 3 inches and more, while they are often only half an inch deep, but rarely deeper than an inch or an inch and a half. They commonly appear in different sizes on the same stone or rock, and although they sometimes form the only sculptures on a surface they are more frequently associated with figures of a different character. They are in general scattered without order over the surface, but occasionally four or five or more of them are placed in more or less regular groups, exhibiting a constellation-like arrangement.

Second type. Cups surrounded by a single ring.---The incised rings are usually much shallower than the cups and mostly surround cups of comparatively large size. The ring is either complete or broken, and in the latter case it is often traversed by a radial groove which runs from the central cup through and even beyond the ring.

Third type. Cups surrounded by a series of concentric complete rings. ---In this complete annular form the central cup is generally more deeply cut than the surrounding rings, but not always.

Fourth type. Cups surrounded by a series of concentric, but incomplete rings having a straight radial groove. ---This type constitutes perhaps the most common form of the circular carvings. The rings generally touch the radial line at both extremities, but

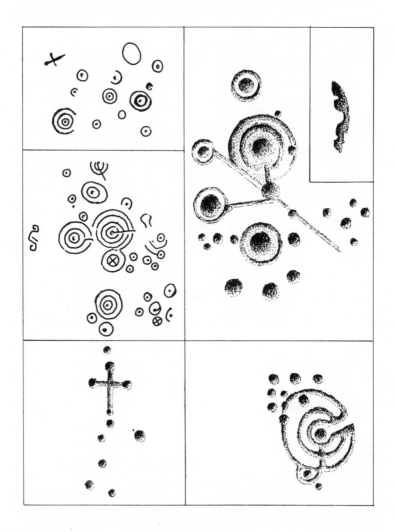

Irish cups and rings, representing most of the types discussed by Mallery

sometimes they terminate on each side of it without touching it.
The radial groove occasionally extends considerably beyond the
outer circle, and in most cases it runs in a more or less downward direction on the stone or rock. Sometimes it runs on and
unites into a common line with other ducts or grooves coming from
other circles, till thus several series of concentric rings are con-
joined into a larger or smaller cluster, united together by the extension of their radial branch-like grooves.

Fifth type. Cups surrounded by concentric rings and flexed
lines. ---The number of inclosing or concentric rings is generally fewer in this type than in the two last preceding types, and
seldom exceeds two or three in number.

Sixth type. Concentric rings without a central cup. ---In many
cases the concentric rings of the types already described appear
without a central cup or depression, which is most frequently
wanting in the complete concentric circles of the third type.

Seventh type. Concentric circular lines of the form of a spiral
or volute. ---The central beginning of the spiral line is usually,
but not always, marked by a cup-like excavation.

It often occurs that two, three, or more of these various types are
found on the same stone or rock, a fact indicating that they are intimately allied to each other.

Prof. Simpson presents what he calls "the chief deviations from the
principal types" reproduced here as Fig. 148.

The first four designs represent cups connected by grooves, which
is a noticeable and frequently occurring feature. In Fig. 149 views of
sculptured rock surfaces at Auchnabreach, Argyleshire, Scotland, are
given. Simple cups, cups surrounded by one ring or by concentric rings,
with radial grooves and spirals, appear here promiscuously mingled.
Fig. 150 exhibits isolated as well as connected cups, a cup surrounded
by a ring, and concentric rings with radial grooves, on a standing stone
(menhir), belonging to a group of seven at Ballymenach, in the parish of
Kilmichael-Glassary, in Argyleshire, Scotland.

Dr. Berthold Seeman remarks concerning the characters in Fig. 105,
supra, copied from a rock in Chiriqui, Panama, that he discovers in it
a great resemblance to those of Northumberland, Scotland, and other
parts of Great Britain. He says, as quoted by Dr. Rau (d):

It is singular that, thousands of miles away, in a remote corner
of tropical America, we should find the concentric rings and several
other characters typically identical with those engraved on the British
rocks.

The characters in Chiriqui are, like those of Great Britain,
incised on large stones, the surface of which has not previously
undergone any smoothing process. The incised stones occur in
a district of Veraguas (Chiriqui or Alanje), which is now thinly
inhabited, but which, judging from the numerous tombs, was once
densely peopled.

From information received during my two visits to Chiriqui
and from what has been published since I first drew attention to
this subject, I am led to believe that there are a great many inscribed rocks in that district. But I myself have seen only one,
the now famous piedra pintal (i. e. , painted stone), which is
found on a plain at Caldera, a few leagues from the town of David.
It is 15 feet high, nearly 50 feet in circumference, and rather

flat on the top. Every part, especially the eastern side, is covered with incised characters about an inch or half an inch deep. The first figure on the left hand side represents a radiant sun, followed by a series of heads or what appear to be heads, all with some variation. It is these heads, particularly the appendages (perhaps intended for hair?), which show a certain resemblance to one of the most curious characters found on the British rocks, and calling to mind the so-called "Ogham characters." These "heads" are succeeded by scorpion-like or branched and other fantastic figures. The top of the stone and the other sides are covered with a great number of concentric rings and ovals, crossed by lines. It is especially these which bear so striking a resemblance to the Northumbrian characters.

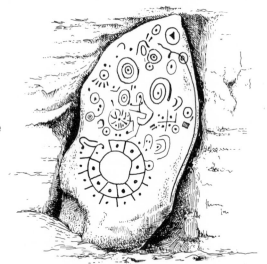

Lough Craw cairnstone

CUPSTONES NEAR OLD FT. RANSOM, N.D.

Lewis, T, H.; *American Naturalist*, 25:455–461, 1891.

Apparently the earliest mention of cup-stones, in print, was in 1751, in a historical work on the Province of Brandenburg, by J. C. Bekmann. The author speaks of certain boulders there which have on them napf-chensteine, or little-bowl-stones, as he terms them. Next, in 1773, there was found at Lynsfort, in North Britain, a druidical altar full of "rock basons," which was pictured in Camden's Brittannia, 1789. From that time on, at intervals, first incidentally, then by purposed search, interesting discoveries were made until, so far as the rings were concerned, almost every country on the earth was represented. As regards the cups, their distribution has not yet proved to be nearly so widespread.

Still they have been found in the British Isles, France, Switzerland, Bohemia, Austria, Northern Germany, the Danish Islands, and Sweden; but these are all the European countries known to possess them, apparently, according to the authorities. Flitting now eastward over vast kingdoms we meet with them again in far-off India. Here, in 1867, Mr. Rivett-Carnac found cup-cuttings upon the stones of the cycloliths of Nagpoor, and, shortly after, upon rocks in situ of the mountains of mountains of Kumaon, where, in one place, he found them to the number of more than two hundred, arranged in groups of apparently parallel rows. In the Kumaon region he also found ring sculpturing, which very much resembled that which is seen in Europe. Outside of these named countries, and North America to be mentioned further on, the world is a blank as regards cup-cuttings on rocks, so far as our present knowledge goes, or at least to the extent that I have been able to find recorded information of the same.

Although met with and described nearly a century and a half ago, as hereinbefore related, it is only within the last forty-five years that incised cups on rocks and stones have been particularly written about, either in Europe or in the United States, and speculative theories advanced concerning their origin and uses.

It was in 1847 that Messrs. Squier and Davis, partners in original research in the state of Ohio, brought their operations to a close by the production of the "Ancient Monuments of the Mississippi Valley," the comprehensive work which methodically displayed all that was then known of the antiquities of the great region implied by that geographical expression. In this book (on page 206) there is a description, with woodcut illustration, of a block of sandstone which had been found in some unnamed Ohio mound. The stone weighed between thirty and forty pounds, and showed several circular depressions, evidently artificial, which our authors thought were used as moulds for the purpose of hammering thin plates of copper into small bosses of convavo-convex shape, such as had been often found. This is the prototype of the cup-stones of the western hemisphere. [1]

Professor Daniel Wilson, of Toronto, in his "Prehistoric Man," (third edition, 1876, Vol. I.), also devotes several pages to the subject, and gives drawings of two cup-stones found, too, in Ohio. Of the first he speaks thus: "A cupped sandstone block on the banks of the Ohio, a little below Cincinnati. Others much larger were described to me by Dr. Hill," etc. The second one he describes as a "cupped sandstone boulder," found near Tronton [Ironton] in 1874. The author, in this work, considers that the use of these cups---everywhere, all the world over--- was to grind the ends of stone implements, and that where they were accompanied by concentric circles and other devices the latter were no more than additions of idle fancy.

The late Professor Charles Rau, of Washington, D. C., seems, however, to be the first writer in the United States to bring forward and collate comprehensively in a special treatise the data relating to cup-stones on this side of the Atlantic, and to treat of their resemblance to those found in the eastern hemisphere. In his "Observations on Cup-Shaped and Other Lapidarian Sculptures in the Old World and America" (1881) he[2] describes a few specimens whose characteristics are undoubted. The best of these are the "incised rock" in Forsyth County, Georgia; the sandstone block with cup-cavities discovered by Dr. H. H. Hill in

Cups and rings on Roughting Linn inscribed stone, Northumberland
(Janet & Colin Bord)

Lawrence county, Ohio;[3] and the sculptures on Bald Friar Rock in the
usquehanna [sic] River, Cecil county, Maryland.   Toward the end of the
work Professor Rau gives the various speculations which have been published as to the purpose for which cup-and-ring-cuttings were made,
but states that after all that has been said concerning their significance
in the Old World, he hardly ventures to offer an opinion of his own.   Still
he thinks that both kinds of sculpture belong to one primitive system, of
which the former seems to be the earlier expression.   Turning to
America, he considers that here, as yet, the number of discovered cup-
stones is by far too small to permit the merest attempt at generalization.
     The author just referred to has shown in his book that true cup-
stones have been found in the United States as far east as Connecticut
and as far west as Illinois, but the fact that rocks having such incised
work exist also far beyond the Mississippi valley has not yet, apparently, become known to the antiquarian world.   It is therefore for the purpose of describing one so located that this paper is written.
     The rock in question is situated in Ransom county, North Dakota,
and, with others, it came under my observation in the middle of last
August, at which time full notes were taken, and the pictographs to be
described further on carefully copied.
     Ransom county derives its name from a post of the United States

army which was formerly maintained on the west side of the Shyenne
River, in that part of its course known as the Great Bend. The top of
the bluff on which the ruined fort stands is about two-hundred-and-fifty
feet above the river. About one-quarter of a mile to the westward, on
the north half of the southwest quarter of section II, town 135, range 58,
there is a large spring known as the "Fort Springs," situated in the
bottom of a deep ravine, which is about ninety feet below the fort site.
It is probably formed by a seepage from "Big Slough," which starts
about one mile south and extends some fifteen or twenty miles in a
southerly direction. The bluff immediately to the west of the ravine
rises to the height of about one-hundred-and-sixty feet, and on the top,
over a quarter of a mile away in a northwesterly direction, there is a
small knoll which was called "Bear's-Den Hill" by the Indians. On the
steep slope of the bluff, about one hundred yards north of west from the
spring and fifty-three feet above it, there is a large light-colored granite boulder, on which there are a number of incised lines, cups, and
other figures. The base of the boulder, which is firmly imbedded in
the side-hill, is eight-and-a-half feet in length and four-and-a-half feet
in width, and on the side next to the spring extends out of the ground about
three feet. The top surface on which the carvings occur is irregular in
outline, and is seven feet two inches in length, and from two feet six
inches to three feet ten inches in width, sloping slightly towards the east.
The particular figures seen upon it, and reproduced here in fac-simile
as regards their forms, are explainable somewhat as follows, viz.:

Fig. 1.---Apparently the horns of some animal.

Fig. 2.---A nondescript. There is a similar figure on the quartzite
ledge near Little Cottonwood Falls, in Cottonwood county, Minn.

Fig. 3.---A crescent. This figure is often found along the Mississippi River in Minnesota, Wisconsin, and Iowa.

Fig. 4.---A nondescript animal.

Fig. 5.---A peculiar-shaped cross. There is one similar in form
on the face of a cliff a few miles above Stillwater, Minn.

Figs. 6, 6.---"Pins," so-called. There are two of the same shape
on the quartzite lege, among other figures, near the "Three Maidens,"
at Pipestone, Minn.

Figs. 7, 7, 7.---Three pairs of cups, one set being joined by a
straight groove, and the other two by curved grooves.[4]

Figs. 8, 8, 8, 8.---Are four long grooves with odd-shaped ends.
These grooves are only about one-eighth of an inch in depth, while the
ends are from one to one-and-a-half inches in depth.

Cups (not numbered).---The cups or circular depressions are from
about one-half-inch to nearly two inches in diameter, and one inch to
one-quarter of an inch in depth. Some are perfect circles, while others
are oblong in outline. There are thirty-four single cups and twenty-five
cups that are connected with or intersected by grooves, making a total
of fifty-nine positive cups, without considering the terminals of the four
long grooves and others that are more doubtful. Where grooves intersect the cups an arbitrary line has been drawn on the illustration, in
order to separate them and to more fully demonstrate the character of
the designs. In every instance where this has been done the cups are
well defined, but yet they cannot otherwise be fully shown on a tracing
giving only surface outlines.

Within a radius of four hundred feet from the spring there are thir-

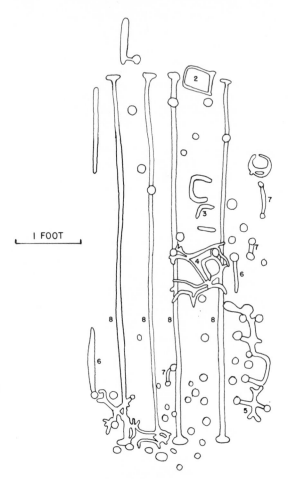

I FOOT

North Dakota cupstones

teen incised boulders of various sizes and shapes, the one here described being the largest and finest of the group. The pictures, etc., on
five of the best ones were copied; the others having only slight grooves
and a few cups were not.

On the bluffs on both sides of the ravine there are a number of
ancient mounds of the mound-building period, one of which is located
on the west side immediately above the spring.

There are other boulders at various places in the northwest on which
these cup-like depressions occur, and they are also occasionally found
on the face of perpendicular ledges and on the walls of caves, but in
nearly every instance there are other incised figures on the same surface. It may be further stated that the cup-cavities as shown at the
terminals of Fig. 5 of the illustration now given are also seen in connection with incised figures on rocks at these other localities referred to.

The cup-stones (large boulders or rocks) are not to be confounded
with the smaller stones called "nut-holders" or "anvils," which are from
two to twenty inches in diameter, one to four inches in thickness, and

which have one or more slight cavities or pits on each face. These cavities average about one inch in diameter, and very rarely exceed one-half inch in depth, the average being one-fourth of an inch. These relics are found throughout the west and south along the streams and lakes, and the prairies are no exception to the rule. Still less should cup-stones proper be confounded with the large circular excavations in rocks found in various regions which have been used as mortars. Mortars are found in fields. The rocks may be ten inches square and upwards, and the cavities range from six to fifteen inches in diameter and from one to five inches in depth. They are also found on the upper surface of ledgesand on the tops of very large boulders. In one place in this vicinity there are at least twenty-five mortars on two acres of land.

While the American cup-stones are similar in nearly every respect to those found in Europe and other portions of the globe, it would be the best policy to study them as an entirely separate class of antiquities, for in all probability there is not even a remote connection between the two hemispheres in this respect. After a thorough comparison has been made and the necessary links have been found, there will then be ample time in which to bring forward the facts to prove relationship. In the meanwhile, awaiting thorough exploration of the field, all such attempts, though interesting in a literary point of view, may be considered somewhat premature in a scientific one.

Since the above was written I have examined a book, just published, which treats of the same kind of ancient work. It appears nine or ten years after Rau's, and, so far as known to me, is the only general handling of the subject within that period. Its title is "Archaic Rock Inscriptions; an Account of the Cup and Ring Markings on the Sculptured Stones of the Old and New Worlds." It is of anonymous authorship, but bears the imprint of A. Reader, London, 1891, and is a 12mo of only 99 pages. The writer is evidently one of the mystical antiquarians who, to speak figuratively, have their eyes continually turned to those igncs fatui the elusive and ever unapproachable ancient faiths---the Tree, Serpent, Phallic, Fire, Sun, and Ancestor worships---and delight in the search for analogies concerning them. As regards the cup- and ring-markings, he himself adopts the phallic theory for their origin. His little book, however, admirably fulfills the promise of its title, for it not only includes most that prior writers collected, but gives interesting facts not accessible or not discovered when Professor Rau wrote. The most striking piece of new information is concerning the cup- and ring-markings on the rocks in the environs of Ilkley, Yorkshire,---a new locality. Here the cups have been counted into the hundreds in all; many of them are connected by grooves.

As regards America, all that this new author finds---and probably all there is to find---are two articles in the American Naturalist. The first one is contained in the number for December, 1884, and is entitled "Rock Inscriptions in Brazil, " by J. C. Branner. The author does not use the word cups at all, nor do his diagrams show any; he only mentions in his text certain "points or indentations, " often arranged in parallel vertical lines, and portrays them in the drawings, where also single circles are shown---mostly provided with a central point. He found, however, "Mortars" scooped out on the rocks by the river. The other article appears in the number for July, 1885, under the heading of "Ancient Rock Inscriptions on the Lake of the Woods, " by A. C. Lawson.

Neither does this writer mention <u>cups</u>, but his illustrations show concentric circles which have the usual central dot.

---

[1] Were the facts concerning the <u>Teololinga</u> rock, situated sixteen leagues southeast of Orizaba, Mexico, exactly known, it might with propriety take precedence here in the text of the Squier and Davis stone; for it was discovered in 1805 by Captain Dupaix, who said that on its surface were some circular holes of little depth. By reason of the dissimilarity of the published representations of it, however, Professor Rau (1881) thought that a proper doubt remained, not to be removed until the stone had again been examined and reported upon.

[2] In "Contributions to North American Ethnology," Vol. V., Washington, 1882.

[3] This is the same as the "cupped sandstone boulder" already illustrated in Professor Wilson's "Prehistoric Man" (1876).

[4] Sir James Simpson describes and figures an isolated stone near Balvraid, in Invernessshire, Scotland, which has five pairs of cups that are joined by straight or curved grooves. See Plate xiv., 2 of his "Archaic Sculpturings upon Stones in Scotland," etc., Edinburgh, 1867. The same type occurs on boulders and slabs found in France, Switzerland, and Sweden. Similar figures also appear on early British coins prior to Cunobeline's time (A. D. 40), and on the French-Keltic coins of moulded bronze. See Plates liii. and lv. of Waring's "Stone Monuments," etc., London, 1870.

Cupules on a megalith near Xochipala, Guerrero, Mexico

CUP-MARKS IN THE SHORAPUR DOAB (SOUTH INDIA)
Paddayya, K.; *Man*, 11:35-38, 1976.

In several of the previous issues of Man and South African Archaeological Bulletin, M. D. W. Jeffreys, K. R. Robinson, B. E. B. Fagg, E. C. Lanning, A. J. H. Goodwin and others published a series of accounts reporting the discovery of rock gongs producing musical sounds. These ringing or sounding rocks, as they are sometimes also called, are found at several places in Nigeria, Uganda, Sudan and Rhodesia. Some of these consist of boulders, slabs and spalls, while others are in the form of cup-shaped depressions made on solid stone blocks of different sizes and shapes. They all yield clear metallic or ringing sounds on being struck with a fist-sized piece of stone. At some places, pottery, stone artefacts and rock paintings are found in association with them, so that the suggestion has been put forward that these gongs date back to the Iron Age. But some of these are clearly modern because they are still being used by the aboriginal groups. From the published accounts it is clear that these musical devices cannot be invested with any functional uniformity; rather, they serve a variety of functions--- rain-making, merry-making, warding off evil spirits, fertility rites, communication with spirits, harvest ceremonies, etc.

The present note brings to the notice of scholars a similar phenomenon from an area called the Shorapur Doab, lying in the Gulbarga District of Mysore State (South India). The finds here consist exclusively of cup-marks. The credit for their discovery goes to the late C. Mahadevan; in the course of his geological investigations, he found these at three places, viz., the Vitragal hillock near Mallur, Devapur and Kupgal.

. . . .

THE GEOMETRY OF CUP-AND-RING MARKS
Thom, A.; *Ancient Monument Society, Transactions*, 16:77-82, 1969.

This paper is based entirely on a set of rubbings kindly made available to the author by R. W. B. Morris. A knowledge that the unit of length used in setting out these marks is exactly one-fortieth of the Megalithic yard enables the geometry to be unravelled. This geometry and that which we find in the Megalithic stone circles are both controlled by the same rules and conventions.

It has been shown in Thom (1968) that a definite unit of length appears in the diameters of the rings associated with cup-and-ring marks when these rings are intended to be true circles. This unit will here be called the Megalithic inch "(mi.)". Its value is 0.816 British Standard inches (20.73 mm.) or exactly one-fortieth of the Megalithic yard (2.720 0.003 ft.). It has also been shown that when the marks are not pure circles the geometry follows generally the same rules as apply for the stone rings (Thom, 1967). These rules are:

1. Any length used in the construction is to be an integral multiple of the unit.
2. The perimeter of any ring used is to be as near as possible an integral multiple of 2-1/2 primary units.

The second rule may have arisen from the fact that the circumference of a circle of diameter 8 is very nearly 25.

It has been shown (Thom, 1967) that the primary unit may be sub-divided into halves or quarters but never into thirds. For longer distances 2-1/2, 5 or 10 primary units were frequently used.

There is evidence that sometimes the rock surface was prepared by being rubbed and polished to a smooth if not always a plane surface. It has become evident from the geometry that the designs must have been set out originally with a precision approaching that attained today by a mechanic using a finely-divided scale, a scriber and dividers. Unless archaeologists produce evidence to the contrary we can rule out dividers and assume that beam compasses or trammels were used and that these would not be adjustable. The megalithic draughtsman would use a set of trammels with the distances between the scribing points (flint or quartz?) advancing by Megalithic inches or perhaps half and quarter inches. Thus no divided scale such as we use today would be necessary. The trammels for 1, 2, 5 and 8 mi were easily checked by stepping 40, 20, 8 and 5 times along the standard yard of 40 mi. The other sizes would follow by addition or subtraction. An accuracy of a few thousandths of an inch is possible and if anyone cares to reconstruct the figures shown here he will find that unless this kind of accuracy is maintained the design will get out of hand.

This use of standard trammels was undoubtedly the reason for rule (1) above. Special trammels were precluded or perhaps forbidden and so all construction lengths and the radii of all arcs had to be integral.

An elementary example is found in the spiral at Hawthornden which is built up from semi-circles of radii 4, 3-1/4, 2-1/2, 1-3/4 and 1 mi., the common interval in the radii being 3/4 mi. But we must face up to the fact that in the rock markings as in the stone circles (Thom, 1967) ellipses are frequently found. Perhaps the most interesting and beautiful example is that found at Knock, near Whithorn, Wigtonshire (see Vol. 14, p. 100 (no. 518) of these <u>Transactions</u>). This example consists of a spiral built up from 6 half-ellipses and a semi-circle. To understand how remarkable this design really is we must recall the following theorem: Let $\underline{a}$ be the major axis of an ellipse, $\underline{b}$ the minor axis and $\underline{c}$ the distance between the foci. Then always

$$a^2 = b^2 + c^2$$

This is the Pythagorean relation between the hypotenuse and the sides of a right-angled triangle. It follows that if the Megalithic draughtsman followed the first rule when drawing ellipses he had to find for each ellipse a triangle that was the correct size and would at the same time satisfy the Pythagorean relation in integers. Let us see how neatly he succeeded in this apparently impossible task.

In Table 1 the first three columns contain the nominal values of $\underline{a}$, $\underline{b}$ and $\underline{c}$ for the six ellipses. The next column is the calculated value of $\underline{a}$ assuming that $\underline{b}$ and $\underline{c}$ retain their nominal values. The last two columns give the discrepancy in Megalithic inches and in British Standard inches.

Table 1

a mi.	b mi.	c mi.	a cal.	Discrepancy mi.	Discrepancy inches
7-1/2	6-1/2	3-3/4	7.504	0.004	0.003
6-1/2	6	2-1/2	6.500	0.000	0.000
5-1/2	4-3/4	2-3/4	5.489	0.011	0.009
4-1/2	4-1/4	1-1/2	4.507	0.007	0.006
3-1/2	3	1-3/4	3.473	0.027	0.022
1-3/4	1-1/2	7/8	1.737	0.013	0.011

Another remarkable feature of the resulting design is that the spacing of the large whorls on the major axis is everywhere exactly one unit and on the minor axes 7/8 unit and yet every one of the ellipses is based on an almost perfect triangle.

It is almost inconceivable that the accuracy shown in Table 1 could have been obtained graphically while working on a rock surface. How then were these triangles discovered? It seems almost certain that the designer knew the Pythagorean Theorem and could use it to check any assumed triangle. How else did he know that the 12, 35, 37 triangle was exact? He certainly used the theorem at his obviously important site at Woodhenge, and elsewhere (Thom, 1967). The calculations would have been done in units or in quarter-units. It would be convenient if today we had names for his quarter-yard (0.68 ft.), and for his quarter-inch (0.204 in.).

• String Figures

CODE OF ANCIENT PERUVIAN KNOTTED CORDS (QUIPUS)
Ascher, Marcia, and Ascher, Robert; *Nature,* 222:529–533, 1969.

A quipu is an arrangement of coloured wool or cotton cords with clusters of knots tied in the cords. As artefacts of ancient Peru, quipus are coded in the sense that we do not know their grammar, however clear it may have been to some long-dead Peruvians. We also do not know what quipus mean. Of obvious interest to archaeologists, quipus are also important in the history of mathematics and are alleged to be important for the history of astronomical observation. Mathematical interest comes from the notion that the quipu has a numerical solution. Astronomy enters when, for example, a quipu is said to signify the number of days in the solar year. The numerical solution was provided by Locke in 1912; in the ensuing half century there have been no advances in this area. The notion of astronomical significance was published by Nordenskiold in 1925. Today, the astronomical hypothesis remains the only attempt to assign meaning to a large number of specimens. Under the impetus of the work on Stonehenge by Hawkins, Hoyle and others, the astronomical hypothesis has recently reappeared in much the same form as when it was first published. Here we are primarily concerned with the code of the quipu---we also examine the astronomical hypothesis. (Figures and references omitted.)

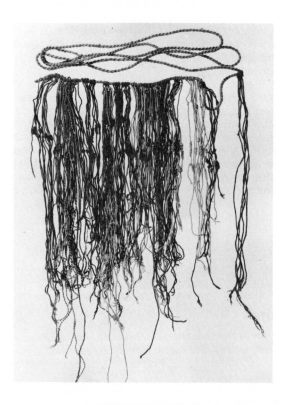

A Peruvian quipu. A message is incorporated in the complex of knotted, colored strings. (Smithsonian Institution)

Physical Properties. Let us begin with a description of the chief physical properties. For illustration, here and throughout the article, we use Locke's classic quipa, L-1. (Locke and Nordenskiold published 17 and 14 quipu respectively. These 31 quipu are the data used by us. Both Locke and Nordenskiold identified their specimens by number, for example, Quipu 6. Here we retain the original numbers. To distinguish between the authors, the specimens published by Locke are preceded by an L, and those by Nordenskiold are preceded by an N. L-1 is published in refs. 1, 2 and 5; L-2 is published in ref. 5. L-3 to L-29 are pub-

lished in ref. 6. N-1 to N-14 are published in ref. 2. One quipu, unnumbered by Locke, we designate L-46; this specimen is published in
refs. 7 and 4.) All quipus have two kinds of cords, a main cord and
pendant cords. Some specimens have top cords and several have subsidiary cords. Of the four kinds of cord, three are found on L-1. If
the fourth kind were present, they would be attached at about the middle
of one or more pendant cords. To complete the physical description,
we need only consider two properties of the cords: their colours and
knots. A cord is usually woven from several strands dyed in one or
more colours. In Fig. 2, the main cord is white and dark brown, the
top cord in A is light brown, and so on for each cord. A cord is generally tied with clusters of knots and individual knots. For example, the
second pendant cord in B of Fig. 2 contains, from the bottom up, an
individual knot followed by a space, a cluster of four knots followed by a
space, and finally a cluster of six knots followed by a space. Other
physical properties are found on one or a few quipus; for example, subsidiaries of subsidiaries occur. We introduce special properties only
where they contribute to understanding the code or the meaning of the
quipu.

The Numerical Solution. Several years after proposing his numerical solution, Locke recorded the circumstances surrounding his work
with these words: "In a study of the large collection [of quipus] in the
American Museum of Natural History made during 1910-1911, one specimen was found which, by the peculiar arrangement of strands, provided
an indisputable key to the significance of the quipu knots." This was the
quipu L-1.

From the writings of the sixteenth century chroniclers of ancient
Peruvian civilization, Locke gleaned these notions: a cluster of knots
can stand for a digit; one cord can represent one number; the base of the
number system is ten. To illustrate how one might read values using
these notions, look once again at the arrangement of knots on the second
pendant cord in B, Fig. 2. If one assumes that the highest valued position is that closest to the main cord, the number is 6 (knots in the
hundreds place), 4 (knots in the tens place), 1 (knot in the units place);
that is, 641. Reading in a similar manner, the top cord of B is 1,417.
Locke read every cord this way. In six instances on L-1, four pendant
cords are tied to a top cord. Locke added the values on the four pendant
cords in each of the six instances and found, with two exceptions, that
the sum of the values on the pendant cords equalled the value on the associated top cord. The instances where the equality did not hold could be
accounted for by a fragmentary cord and an apparent error. (The fragment is shown in group E, third pendant cord from the left. Fig. 2. The
error is in one knot in group B. Due to several possible sources of
error introduced in making the quipu, in differential archaeological preservation, in counting knots on quipus, and in publishing results, an
error of 1 is admissible. In this case, we assume the error is in the
third pendant cord from the left in the cluster closest to the main cord.
That is, this cord should read 536 rather than 636.) At first, Locke believed that L-1 alone had top cords and thought of it as unique, but he
soon examined other similarly constructed specimens. After some years
he published readings of 15 quipus constructed in various ways, believing them all to be soluble in the sense that each knotted cord on a quipu
could be assigned a specific number. In the end, he and his colleagues

felt that the solution was total and the issue closed.

In reopening the issue of the code, we first ask if it is justifiable to interpret every cord as a number. Where internal corroboration exists, such as a cord that sums other cords, few doubts need be raised. Elsewhere, one must proceed with caution. Locke's reading of one specimen (L-27), for example, yields 157 non-zero digits among which there are no 7s, 8s or 9s, while 93 per cent are 1s, 2s or 3s. What can be made of this unlikely distribution? Lacking internal corroboration when the numbers are read in the base 10---and conversion to the base 7 offers no clues---Locke's solution is questionable. In another instance (L-4), 36 of 154 cords (96 pendants; 58 subsidiaries), as read by Locke, have "digits" of 10 to 15 that occur in positions representing units, tens, hundreds and thousands. Whether read in the base 10, or read by us in the base 16, there is no internal corroboration for the association of digits with clusters of knots. Surely in many cases it is justifiable to associate numbers with cords, but the association is not universal. The additions to the quipu code that we propose are not universal either. Indeed, it is the permutation of the elements of the code that lend interest to working with it.

Further Aspects of the Code. In the quipu code it is necessary to distinguish two kinds of arrangements. The first consists of clusters of knots and their positions on cords. The second is that of cords, and we now consider questions such as the placement of cords. To clarify the distinction, one might formulate the kinds of arrangements this way: in the first, the largest unit is the cord and the smallest the knot; in the second, the largest unit is the quipu, and the smallest is the cord of specified colour and knot clusters. In moving from cord to quipu, we reconsider one set of elements and recognize a new one. After an example of a combination of elements, we show, by analysis, that relations as well as numbers must be a part of the solution to the code.

The Entire Quipu. All one really needs for a quipu is a long cord with other shorter cords hung from it. Tie together some of the hung cords, but not all of them, with another cord, or attach some cords to those already hung, and you have a more complex artefact. Evidently, to make a quipu is to put material into a particular spatial array. Earlier workers must have seen this, for the names they gave to the cords of the quipu suggest spatial relevance. We say that this particular array is itself a part of the quipu grammar. The largest unit that concerns us, the entire quipu, is constructed in space out of cords such that the cords act differently in accordance with their positions relative to other cords. Every cord, in fact, can be specified as belonging to one of four subdivisions depending on its position in the quipu. For example, the 37 read from a top cord is not the same (that is, not playing the same part) as the same number read from a subsidiary cord because the two cords are in different positions on the quipu. Where knots appear on main cords they summarize the cords hung from them by recording either a count of the pendant cords or a sum of the values on them (for example, L-4, 9, 27); if top cords appear, the numbers on them sum the values of the pendants they unite (for example, L-1, 2, 46). Subsidiary cords relate to the cords they are attached to by, for example, being an addition, or subtraction, or a part of the whole (for example, L-6, 46; N-12).

The Cord Group. Larger than the building block of the whole cord, but smaller than the quipu with its subdivisions, is the cord group. By a cord group we mean an association of adjacent pendant cords. A cord group is indicated in one or more ways. A top cord may unite two or more pendant cords, intervening space may separate a number of cords from other cords, or a number of cords may be one colour followed by a number of differently coloured cords, and so on. In the trivial case, the entire quipu is composed of one cord group. Interesting instances chosen from colour include one specimen where 6 brown cords alternate with 6 white for 108 cords (N–10), and another (L–6) where a mixed brown and white cord is at the centre of a quipu, while 15 white cords are to one side and 15 brown cords are on the other side. The cord group is an element which is focal to an understanding of the quipu code. The association is strong. One is no freer to reassociate individual pendant cords than one is free to associate 3 knots from one cluster of 6, with another cluster of 2, and call the "digit" 5.

The code elements discussed so far are variously combined on particular specimens. Just as a sentence gives reality to a grammar, so an example of a combination may lend reality to the code. One such combination (L–2), unusual in the number of elements that appear simultaneously, is a cord group from a quipu containing 11 such groups. The 6 cords forming the group are united by a top cord and separated from other groups. Note that three adjacent pendants are red and three that follow are green. Calling a group contained by a group a subgroup, we have here two subgroups, one red and the other green. The attachment of subsidiaries to a top cord is rare and calls for further attention. As expected, if the values of the pendants are summed, they are found to equal 50, the value of the top cord. Because the top cord plays a summation part, one would anticipate a similar role for the subsidiaries attached to it. The value of the green subsidiary on the top cord is 14 and the sum of the green subgroup is also 14. The sum of the pendant cord subsidiaries is 14 which equals, with an error of one, the sum of the two remaining top cord subsidiaries. Alternative readings are possible and the reader is invited to try his hand. In any case, it seems that the value of at least one of the subsidiaries on the top cord is a part of the 50 on that cord.

. . . .

Meaning. We now turn to the suggested meaning of the quipus: the astronomical hypothesis. It is in a discussion of a particular specimen (N–1) that Nordenskiold expressed the hypothesis directly. He wrote: "In this quipu we find the principle underlying most of the quipus: (1) That all numbers express days. (2) That in one way or another astronomical numbers enter into the quipu. (3) That in one way or another the number 7 plays a predominant part." The first and second part are closely related; the third is tangential. The hypothesis is best understood and evaluated by seeing how the astronomical numbers are determined.

Nordenskiold found astronomical meaning in fourteen quipus. Two of these fourteen were first described by Locke, and one of them is L–1. Again, for convenience of illustration we can make use of this specimen. According to Nordenskiold, the following is significant about L–1. The sums of the groups are 17, 41 x 37, 5 x 23 x 7, 4 x 3 x 3 x 17, 5 x 27, 2 x 7 x 47, and hence display multiples of 7, 17, 27, 37 and 47. This refers to the third part of the hypothesis cited here. Now, assuming that the numbers represent days---part one of the hypothesis---part two, the astronomical significance, enters in three ways: (1) The sum of the pendants in groups $\underline{C}$ and $\underline{F}$ is 1,463; 1,463 = 7 x 209 = 4 x 365 + 3. Note the 365. (2) The sum of all top cords is 3,644; 3,644 10 x 364 4. Of the discrepancy in group $\underline{B}$ (that is, sum of pendants 1,517. top cord

1,417). Nordenskiold writes: "It may, after all, have been intentionally that 1,417 was knotted instead of 1,517. 364 has the quality of being nearly 365, while being divisible by 7." (3) The sum of the pendants in groups $\underline{A}$, $\underline{B}$, $\underline{C}$ and $\underline{F}$ is 2,997. The next calculation we cite in full. It reads:

$$"2,997 = 2,920 + 77$$
$$2,920 = 8 \text{ x } 365 \text{ or } 5 \text{ x } 584$$
$$2,997 = 8 \text{ x } 365 + 77 \text{ or } 5 \text{ x } 584 + 77"$$

The 584 is considered close enough to the revolution of Venus to be so interpreted. In sum, Nordenskiold finds the number of days of the year and the revolution of Venus in L-1.

Astronomical numbers on specimens other than L-1 are determined in the same way. In general, the procedure is to sum the values of two or more cords and then factor this sum, trying to exhibit an astronomical number as one of the factors. If this factoring does not produce a wanted number, the factors are sought in values that differ from the sum by at most 9 or by some number containing 7. This selective summing and forced factoring is seen in the illustration. In the illustration the pendant and top cords are summed independently but, often as not, values of pendant, top cords and subsidiaries are combined. If it were conceded that a quipu is a mere collection of numbers, it would still be difficult to accept this demonstration that they are astronomical. The "important" numbers appear nowhere on the quipu but are obtained by far-fetched computation. But, of course, a quipu is more than a collection of numbers as we have shown here.

We are as far now from knowledge of the meaning of specific quipus as we have ever been. With a newly appreciated richness of the quipu code, there is need for a fresh approach to the question of meaning. The approach is to seek meaning that corresponds to particular adaptations of the code.

ABORIGINAL AUSTRALIAN STRING FIGURES
Rishbeth, K.; *Nature*, 148:701, 1941.

As time goes on, more and more attention is given to primitive man in his physical, mental and cultural aspects, and among the last-named may be classed that singularly fascinating and complicated pursuit known to us as string figures. It is now nearly forty years since the first collection of string figures was made and described from Torres Straits by Rivers and Haddon, and since then there has been a steady interest in the subject and a mounting number of collections made in different parts of the world. The latest is embodied in an article by D. S. Davidson (Proc. Amer. Phil. Soc. , 84, No. 6; Aug. 1941) in which he sums up our present knowledge of the subject and adds a most interesting collection made by him from the Australian aborigines.

That a goodly store was to be collected there was evident from Roth's illustrations of numerous Queensland figures, unfortunately without directions for their making, published in 1902; from some collected by myself from a few restricted areas in 1914, and from Stanley's collections, again from north Queensland, in 1926. Mr. Davidson's studies form a much-needed addition to our knowledge of the subject and are the more valuable in that he traces the possible connexions of these Australian figures with those occurring in other parts of Oceania. According to his conclusions, string figures are of comparatively recent introduction into Australia from Melanesia, as they are found in greatest numbers in north-west Queensland, whereas in Western Australia they are almost lacking and what exist are of recent introduction.

Mr. Davidson considers that Australia, Melanesia, Micronesia and Polynesia comprise a major string-figure area, and from the evidence of the string figures themselves suggests the possibility that they were brought into the Pacific by the Polynesians or Micronesians, and spread from the west into New Guinea and western Melanesia late in the pre-Polynesian period. He suggests also that the diffusion of string figures into the New World and Africa from some Asiatic point of origin might have taken several thousands of years, but he does not appear to consider their possible spontaneous generation in unrelated areas. This is known to have occurred recently among the Brahmins in India and seems likely to be an explanation of their world-wide distribution, seeing that string---or its equivalent---is co-existent with man.

. . . .

• Supposed Calendars

STONE FOUND WITH POSSIBLE CALENDRIC NOTATION
Anonymous; *American Antiquity*, 32:564, 1967.

Connecticut. Investigations by Bernard W. Powell have resulted in recovery of a lightly incised tabular piece of rock, said to have come from a Nova Scotia coastal midden. This stone appears to bear a series of concentric circles and straight-line ticks that are reminiscent of another stone earlier recovered and reported by Powel near Norwalk, in Fairfield County (American Antiquity, Vol. 30, No. 1). Both stones are ocherous in composition, roughly the same size, have extremely light, fine incising best seen under magnification, and were found in shell-middens along the coast. An additional element of interest is added by A. Marshack, who is currently studying calendric evidences on Upper Paleolithic Euro-Asian artifacts and has examined the stones with Powell. It is Marshack's feeling that at least one of the stones suggests a sequential notation system---possibly not unlike the lunar calendric notation system he has postulated for Europe. Both researchers are continuing their study and would welcome notice of other such stones from anyone having knowledge of them.

"LUNAR CALENDAR" FROM THE HUNGARIAN UPPER PALEOLITHIC
Vertes, Laszlo; *Science*, 149:855-856, 1965.

In 1963, loess excavated near Bodrogkeresztur in northern Hungary uncovered the remains of an occupied site belonging to the older level of the East Gravettian group. Among the finds was an object, carved from limestone, that was shaped like a halfmoon or horseshoe; it measured 56 by 56 by 17 mm. If the object were oriented, the top is "north" left is "west," and right is "east"; the base of the halfmoon is "south." Near the center of the northern edge are two near-vertical carved lines, 6 to 7 mm long, that slightly converge to the north. Eastward and westward from the lines, the sharp edges of the object are notched almost symmetrically. There are 11 notches on the eastern side and 12 on the western; all notches extend to the reverse side. Parallel with and near the southern edge is a carved line 12 mm long.

I do not propose to list all possible interpretations of the object.

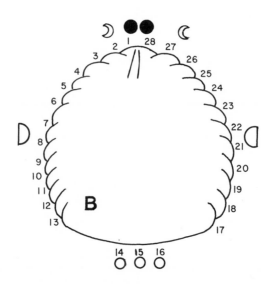

Because of its positive-negative conformity with other objects that were found at Kostienki I, I chose to regard the Bodrogkeresztur object as a uterus symbol, although its lunar or solar shape was noted. However, on the basis of Marshack's paper I have considered the following possible interpretation.

The western of the pair of converging lines (northern edge) may be regarded as the symbol of the new moon. The 12 notches to the west of this line symbolize the crescent moon (13 days, including the new moon). The unnotched southern side may represent the 3 days of the full moon: days 14 through 16. The 11 notches on the east side may represent the days of the waning moon: days 17 through 27. Finally, the eastern of the pair of lines may symbolize the vanished moon on the 28th day (or 29th day, if we allocate 4 days to the unnotched southern edge: the 28.5 days of the lunar cycle may have led primitive man to reckon either 28 or 29 days).

. . . .

SUPPOSED DISCOVERY OF THE CALENDAR OF THE MOUND BUILDERS
Anonymous; *Popular Astronomy*, 2:429, 1895

In a number of the Lyons Republican, published Feb. 22, 1895, Mr. Veeder of Lyons, N. Y., has an article entitled "Pre-historic Man," which calls attention to a curiously engraved stone that has marked upon it the supposed calendar of the ancient Mound Builders. The stone was found in a large mound in Cincinnati with other relics of interest. Its size is reported to be 5 inches long, 2.6 inches across the middle and 3 inches at the ends and can be easily held in the hand. A cut and a description of it will be found in Wilson's Pre-historic Man. Mr. Veeder thinks that this stone has engraved upon it a method of keeping time as it was recorded by the Mound Builders. His reasons are fully given in the paper above referred to.

After some correspondence with able scientists in Ohio about this matter, it seems to us that Mr. Veeder's reasons are not sufficient to raise a probability that his theory is correct.

1. Because the stone has no authentic history.

2. Because frauds of the same kind have been committed in Ohio before. More than 30 years ago, a regularly marked stone was professedly found in large ancient works at Newark, 35 miles east of Columbus. Its markings caused it to be sent from city to city, from one learned society to another,---it was read as Phenecian, Chaldean, Coptie, Hebrew and some other languages---proved this, that and the other, and excited this whole side of the continent. It turned out to be a fraud, manufactured and duly stamped so as to deceive the "very elect." When the fraud was known it caused a great deal of merriment.

3. Persons who have followed the work that has been done in trying to decipher hieroglyphic records know something of the extreme difficulty of such a task. Such knowledge makes interpreters exceedingly cautious in assigning meaning to forms they know so little about.

• Abstruse Notation

AN UNUSUAL DECORATED STEATITE SLAB FROM NORTH-WESTERN CALIFORNIA

Heizer, Robert F.; *American Antiquity*, 15:252–254, 1950.

The prehistory of northwestern California is yet largely unknown. Any information on archaeological types is therefore of interest. The following note constitutes the description of a unique flat steatite slab upon one of whose surfaces drilled conical pits and holes, together with some incised lines, occur.

. . . .

The specimen described here is in the private collection of Dr. H. H. Stuart of Eureka, and was recovered by him many years ago from the surface of the site of the village of Tsapekw which lies toward the northern end of Stone Lagoon on the ocean shore of Humboldt County.

The slab, of pale green color, is 29 inches log, 12 inches wide at one end, and 7. 5 inches wide at the other. The thickness is 1. 75 inches. The piece weighs 44. 8 pounds. The under side shows tool marks resulting from the maker's efforts to smooth the surface. The tool used was probably of hard stone, and appears to have had a sharpened point about 1/4 inch wide. Stone-pecking was usually employed in this region for fashioning stone objects of all sorts. The tool-marked, slightly convex under side has been slightly smoothed, but the gouge marks are plainly visible.

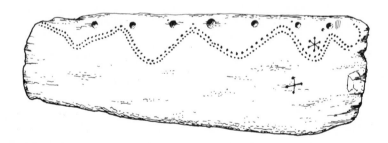

California steatite stone showing possible astronomical notation

The top surface is smooth and highly polished. A few very shallow concavities modify its otherwise absolutely level surface. Whether these irregularities had any purpose, or are simply worn spots which have degraded in softer areas is difficult to tell, but the latter seems more probable.

Along one edge are seven conical holes or deep pits about 1/4 inch in diameter. Whether these were drilled with a rotating shaft drill, or with a hand drill held between the thumb and forefingers is impossible to say, though they look like the result of the first-named process. The center hole is not man-made, but is a hole made by a piddock clam, and would indicate that the stone had at one time lain in salt water. If this slab had been picked up on a beach near a steatite outcrop with the piddock clam hole in its edge, the additional six holes may have been made in imitation of the natural hole. The second hole from the left is a pit which was not drilled sufficiently deep to pierce the bottom surface as shown in the section view.

The flat surface of the slab bears a double wavy or zigzag line of conically drilled pits each about 1 inch in diameter and 1 inch deep. Lightly incised zigzag lines are inscribed along the lower edge to the left of the center hole. At two points a constellation of drilled pits have been connected with incised lines to form a four and six spoked "wheel."

The function of the slab is unknown, but A. L. Kroeber has suggested to me that it may have been a device for keeping account of time. The Hupa "calendar stone" described by Goldschmidt shows that inscribed rocks were so employed in northwestern California.

ROCK INSCRIPTIONS IN BRAZIL
Branner, John C.; *American Naturalist,* 18:1187–1192, 1884.

In 1876 I visited Aguas Bellas, a small town in the interior of the province of Pernambuco, and about a hundred miles from the coast, for the purpose of examining localities said to contain the remains of extinct mammals.

The fossils were found at and in the vicinity of a cattle ranch known as Lagoa da Lagea, eight leagues east of Aguas Bellas. During the time spent at this place I learned of several rocks in the vicinity bearing inscriptions which, it was said, no man could read. I took time to visit the most convenient of these localities and to make careful drawings of the markings, the characteristic ones of which are here represented.

The first place visited for this purpose was a small farm about a league from Lagoa da Lagea, known as Cacimba Circada. The rock found at this place, together with its inscription, is shown at k. This rock is a gneiss boulder of decomposition, about 10' x 6' x 6', lying upon the bed rock near the Rio Garanhunzinho. On the right, as one faces the inscription, is an asterisk a foot in diameter, made by four lines crossing each other at equal angles, while the remainder of the inscription on the left consists of three rows of marks or indentations that run down from near the top of the rock about two and one-half feet to where a portion of the block has split off from the lower left corner, probably carrying away part of the inscription. It is impossible to determine the exact number of these points, for some of them, especially those next the top, have become very indistinct through the weathering of the face of the rock. The inscriptions appear to have been made by pecking with stone implements, and in the case of the asterisk the stone was rubbed up and down the line until the furrows were well polished. After being ground out these points and lines were painted, the color now having a dull red or brown appearance.

The next place visited was Pedra Pintada (painted stone) which is located upon a stream (during the rainy season) taking its name from the marked stones---Rio da Pedra Pintada. It is said to be ten leagues from Aguas Bellas, twelve from Garanhuns and nine from Papacaca. There are here about forty designs engraved, and part of them both en-graved and painted upon the large blocks of gneiss on the banks, and upon the flat smooth rock in the dry bed of the stream. There is a cas-cade about twenty-five feet high just here, and at the foot of it a pot-hole, now filled up, which is about fifteen feet wide by as many deep, and to the presence of which these inscriptions are possibly due, as I shall show. The forms of the inscriptions are shown in the figures, which are drawn to scale, and I need not describe them in detail. Figs. a, b, c, d, e, f, r and s are engraved on the bed rock of the stream above the cascade. These are not painted, and if they ever were, the paint has been washed off by the stream charged with sand and gravel. Many of these are becoming indistinct, some of them have almost entirely dis-appeared, while others have doubtless disappeared altogether. The con-centric chipping of the rock, so common in the tropics, has also remov-ed some of the inscriptions both in the bed of the stream and upon the banks.

The engraving appears to have been done like that at Cacimba Circada, by pecking and grinding with stones having thin rounded edges. After be-ing thus polished these marks were painted, the color now showing as a dull red or brown. In some cases the points and lines are combined as is shown in e and f. The arrangement of points in parallel vertical lines is rather frequent, occurring several times here, as well as at Cacimba Circada, and at Sant' Anna. There are several such rings as that shown at e, one of them having thirty-four points instead of thirty-six, while others are broken, or the points are too indistinct to be determined. There are two asterisks of eight rays, one associated with other mark-ings and another one independent, while still another asterisk has twenty rays. The only figure that seems to be intended to represent anything is Fig. r, which appears to be a rude representation of a spear-head. Part of Fig. d might be supposed to represent a fish, but I fancy that whatever resemblance there may be is accidental. The resemblance be-tween some of these designs and some given by Professor Hartt from the Amazon region is noteworthy, especially that of the spiral shown in h and that of the circle with the point at the center, such as are shown at j.

Returning from Aguas Bellas to the Rio Sao Francisco by way of the village of Sant' Anna, in the province of Alagoas, at half a league from this latter place I found the figures shown at x inscribed upon the side of a large gneiss boulder of decomposition. These figures are both cut and painted, and have the same dull red color as those at Pedra Pintada. There are other marks upon the vertical faces of this and of the other boulders of the group, evidently made by the same hands. These are simply polished spots varying in size from one to two feet in diameter. They are, for the most part, nearly round, but some of them are ob-

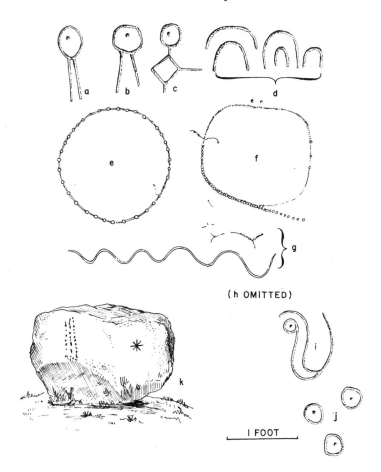

Brazilian rock inscription

long, and none of them are more than about a quarter of an inch in depth---most of them not so deep, and are all painted. The stones upon which these inscriptions are made, as has already been stated, are gneiss boulders of decomposition, about a dozen in number, from six to twelve feet in height, and are grouped together upon the summit of a little hill of solid gneiss, as shown in the accompanying sketch.

The inscription x is upon the largest and most prominent of these boulders, while many, though not all the others, have polished places upon their sides such as I have described. During dry weather there is no water in the immediate vicinity. though the Ipanema is only about a mile distant. (Some figures omitted.)

It should be noted that these inscriptions, as well as many others which I heard of through this part of the country, are all upon these large stones, and generally in some such prominent place. One inscription in particular was mentioned to me by several persons, all of whom gave substantially the same account of it. This inscribed rock is near Agua Branca, twelve leagues above Piranhas and ten leagues from the falls of Paulo Affonso, on the Fazenda da Caisara, and is known as the pedra navio, or ship stone. It is said to be a large and nearly round boulder, standing upon a very narrow base upon the solid rock, and to have all its sides covered with Indian inscriptions.

Through this part of the country, where the archaean rocks form a wide belt between the plateaus of the interior and the Cretaceous and Tertiary beds near the coast, these boulders of decomposition are not uncommon, and almost every one that I have seen has had some sort of artificial marks upon it, generally too badly eroded to be defined, but sufficiently distinct to leave no doubt concerning their origin.

· · · · · · · · · ·

POSSIBLE ASTONOMICAL NOTATION ON THE GREAT IDOL OF TIAHUANACO

Bellamy, H. S., and Allan, P.; *The Great Idol of Tiahuanaco*, London, 1959, pp. 16–18.

In 1932, Wendell Bennett and John Phillips, under the patronage of Mr. Frank Phillips, went to Tiahuanaco for the American Museum of Natural History, New York City. Having obtained permission from the Bolivian Government to sink a few pits with a surface area of not over ten square metres each, Professor Posnansky advised Bennett to sink also one pit within the area of the Old Temple. Accordingly a pit was sunk in the northern half of the Temple. When less than two feet of soil had been removed the huge head of a gigantic monolithic statue was encountered by the astounded archaeologists. The pit was not widened, very careful digging followed, and finally the whole amazing statue was revealed: The Great Idol of Tiahuanaco.

This statue, the largest and, next to the Calendar Gate, by far the most important object yet found in Tiahuanaco, is of the shape of a monolithic pillar; it is cut from a single block of red sandstone, has a length of 24 ft. 4 in., and weighs about 20 tons. About one quarter of the monolith consists of a plain base. Its head, which takes up about a third of the figure, measures 6 ft. 3 in., its width and thickness at the headband is about 3 ft. 5 in.; the shoulders have a width of about 4 ft. 2 in.; at the waistband the width is about 3 ft. 9 in.; and the plain base also has a width and thickness of about 3 ft. 9 in., tapering towards its bottom end to about 3 ft. 3 in.

· · · · · · · · · ·

Bennett, however, was a very careful and methodical archaeologist and, besides, there was Posnansky always near to see that things were done right; also, the Bolivian Authorities were by now aware of the immense importance of all that the Tiahuanaco site yielded. In spite of all that, however, some damage was done to the front of the statue by careless people treading about on it during the process of its being unearthed: for the rather porous red sandstone of which it is made was sodden and brittle. But let Posnansky tell the story of the finding of the Great Idol in his own words:

'After the superficial excavation carried out by Bennett this magnificent

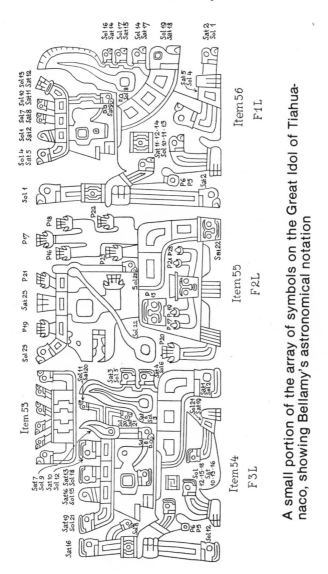

A small portion of the array of symbols on the Great Idol of Tiahuanaco, showing Bellamy's astronomical notation

sculptural work was... lying in an undrained ditch. The... boots of the tourists, and other visitors, had already begun to destroy the surface of the piece... The author suspecting... that the back of the piece probably contained something very magnificent, and to put a stop to the... regrettable destruction of one of the most sacred pieces of Tiahuanaco... then began to effect an excavation beneath the idol... The massive piece was put on a scaffold of wooden crossties... on which rested the head and the feet of the Idol. Then was begun an excavation... below the body so that the block might be exposed to the open air and dry out. This arduous labour in water and mud was generously rewarded... The author on his back in the semi-liquid mud under the Idol, holding in one hand...a candle and with the nails of the other removing from the back of the Idol the last bits of sticky clay, finally saw appear something which had been hidden from the eyes of man for thousands of years:...A large collection of figures which had been preserved perfectly, due to that reddish and impermeable clay on which the age-old image had rested, as on a bed...Then it was necessary to do everything possible to preserve forever this relic of inestimable value for the study of the prehistory and religion of American Man.

INSCRIBED TABLET FOUND IN IOWA
Hoover, J. T. A.; *American Antiquarian,* 2:69–70, 1879.

I find on my premises traces of former civilization, in pottery and other relics which are not used by the present Indians. In 1873 I broke a piece of land on the S. E. 1/4 Sec. 27, T. 12, R. 11 E. S. M. In so doing I opened a place where there was once, no doubt, a Pottery. There was a circle 40 feet in diameter in which I found hard burned clay and fragments of pottery in considerable quantity. This pottery and clay was both of a white and a dark color. Forty rods north of this place is an extensive bank of white kaolin, the clay from which is used for modern pottery in Louisville. In 1874 I broke another piece of land on the southwest quarter of the same section, which is one of the highest points of land, situated a mile from the Platte River. The plow struck a sand-

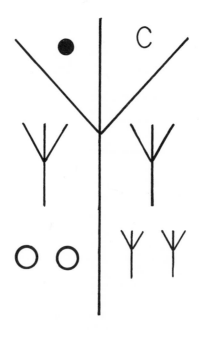

stone one foot long, a cut of which I send you. It is one foot long, eight inches broad, and six inches thick. It was in the ground ten inches below the surface. The stone is hollowed out about an inch from all sides, and has the impression found in the cut. I also plowed out pottery on the creek near this, and among the fragments one whole vessel with handles, black in color, but not glazed, and showing traces of sand as mixed with the clay. I found one broken stone axe, of green granite. No granite is found in this State. Stone here is sand or lime. It is evident that one part of this country was inhabited before the present race of Indians.

PREHISTORIC ASTRONOMY
Schoemfeld, M.; *Scientific American Monthly*, 3:301–303, 1921.

The province of Bohuslan which was originally in Norway, but now belongs to Sweden, contains the most abundant collection of the Scandinavian engravings on rocks known in the language of the country as "Helleristninger."

. . . .

Rock carvings in Bohuslan Province, Norway

Men of learning have long debated concerning these mysterious inscriptions seeking terms of comparison for them in the well-known legends of Nordic mythology, but the results of their discussions have been meager enough.

While examining Plate 49-50 of Series 1 in Balzer's works I was suddenly struck by the idea that it evidently contained a representation of the Great Bear and of the Milky Way in their exact relative positions. Upon making a search farther down beneath a crevice in the rock I was rewarded by finding a series of signs which recalled for the most part the classical signs of the Zodiac in their regular succession: Cancer the crab, near Canis Minor, the little dog, Equuleus, the foal behind Pegasus and then Capricorn, the goat.

Since there seems to be no possible mistake about the matter, it only remained to interpret the figures situated between these two groups upon Baltzer's plate.

To begin with I observe two pairs of animals facing each other. Just Bing has compared these to the general type of the conventionalized pigeons found upon many Scandinavian monuments. But when we attempt to interpret the ingraving in the sense of an astronomical chart we are obliged to reject this interpretation, and to identify these two pairs of animals respectively with the two hunting dogs, Canes Venatici and the two lions. While the two lower animals resemble dogs rather than lions, there is nothing to surprise us in this since the lion is an animal which is foreign to Scandinavia.

A third pair situated beneath and representing two human beings almost identical in form is readily identified with the heavenly twins Castor and Pollux. A third person who is turning his back upon the supposed figure of Pollux suggests the idea that it is meant to represent Auriga. A giant brandishing his hatchet and situated a little farther to the right may be meant for the giant Orion, while the two individuals to the left of Gemini may be Hercules and Bootes. The elongated animal to the right of the lions seems to be meant for the Lynx. A stag beneath Gemini may be meant for Draco and another lower down for the Monoceros; since these two animals are not found among the fauna of Scandinavia their transformation into stags would be only natural. Finally, the Cross placed above the Lynx probably corresponds to the <u>Mouche</u>. (<u>The author evidently refers to Musca---not the constellation in the southern hemisphere but a group north of Aries that formerly went by this name.</u> ---Editor.)

Thus, according to this interpretation the constellations comprised between the Great Bear and the Zodiac are all represented in a succession which is partially irregular. If our interpretation appears to be debatable in certain points its general correctness is supported, nevertheless, by the fact that all of these astronomical figures are visible in the sky of the Bohuslan from September 23 to October 21 during the autumnal Equinox (Fig. 2).

Moreover, Baltzer's works contain other maps of the sky which are quite interesting. Fig. 3 represents Plates 3 and 4, No. 13 of Series II. In these we behold a long series of astronomical signs in perfectly correct order and without any accessory figures intermingled among them. In the middle is a really perfect representation of the Great Bear with the North Star directly above; to the right there follow in order the Lynx, Castor and Pollux, and Orion; to the left is Bootes the Herdsman; below are Cancer the Crab, and Leo the Lion, the latter extending along the image of a boat. If the reader is still capable of feeling any doubt with regard to the correctness of our interpretation, he will surely be convinced that we are right if he will cast a glance at the three symbolic figures at the left of the engraving; the Serpent with its head turned to the left imitating almost exactly the position of the stars in this constellation: the two hounds, one of them standing and the other lying down (while the latter is less easily recognized his curling tail is unmistakable). This chart corresponds to the constellations visible in the sky from the 17th to the 21st of January; the choice among the signs is in large part identical with that of the picture previously examined, only the signs of the Zodiac being lacking.

. . . .

IS THE HOUSE OF TCUHU THE MINOAN LABYRINTH?
Colton, Harold Sellers; *Science*, 45:667-668, 1917.

While going through a back number of the American Anthropologist the writer's attention was attracted by the figure illustrated in Fig. 1. This was in a short paper by Dr. J. Walter Fewkes entitled "A Fictitious Ruin in the Gila Valley, Arizona." In this he showed that this symbol which was first observed by an eighteenth-century Spaniard scratched in the sand by a Pima Indian did not represent the plan of a ruin as previously interpreted, but was used in some way in a game "the house of Tcuhu" (Tcuhiki).

It was curious but this diagram was familiar to the writer and his familiarity came from a distant part of the world. As shown in Fig. 2 this diagram appears on the reverse of a silver coin of Cnossus in Crete of the Greek Period (B.C. 200-67). In this case the figure represents the Minoan Labyrinth. On other coins from Cnossus it sometimes appears in a square form, but even then it has the same ramifications. A comparison of this Greek coin, with House of Tchuhu when inverted, shows that the two are identical in every respect.

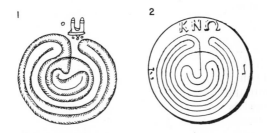

Arizona Indian House of Tcuhu compared with Minoan labyrinth on Greek coin

There are three possible explanations for the coincidence. First, these symbols may have arisen independently in the new and the old world. Secondly, the symbol may have originated in the old world and have been transported to the new in pre-Columbian times. Thirdly, that the symbol was introduced into America with the Spanish conquest.

On the one hand, it has been pointed out by Fewkes that the symbol or something like it was early known to the Pima Indians, as the diagram in slightly modified form appears scratched on the adobe wall of the Casa Grande ruin among obviously Indian pictographs. On the other hand, it is possible that this diagram may have had a Spanish origin.

While it is quite generally accepted by American ethnologists that such simple forms as the cross, the swastika, the wall of Troy, etc., arose in the new world as well as in the old; yet it is hard to believe that such complicated labyrinths similar in every detail could have had separate origins. Similar environments often call forth similar responses in different organisms. In such cases the similarities when carefully analyzed are found to be superficial. The details will not agree. In this case, however, the agreement is exact.

Again there is a possible question that the figure from Fewkes is not of genuine Pima origin. A brief history of this symbol will make this clear. It seems that an unknown Spanish traveler visited the Pima country in the year 1761 or 1762. An account of this visit exists in the form of a manuscript. On the margin of one of the pages of this manuscript appears the figure which I have reprinted from Fewkes. According to the unknown Spaniard the Pimas draw the symbol on the sand. He stated that it represents "a house of amusement rather than that of a magnate." As no ruin has ever been discovered with such a ground plan, Dr. Fewkes was led to question an old Pima concerning it.

When Higgins (the name of the Indian) was shown the figure and told the opening lines of the quotation (from the Spanish narrative), the last clause being withheld, he responded that he knew of no ancient house in that region which had a ground plan like that indicated in the figure. He was acquainted with a children's game that employed a similar figure traced in the sand. The Pimas, he said, call the figure Tcuhuki, the house of Tcuhu, a cultus hero sometimes identified with Moctezuma.

A search in Russell's work on the Pima Indian and Culin's "Games of the North American Indians" failed to discover a description of such a game. However, Russell did describe a game called Tculikwikut, a dart and ring game in which count is kept by means of little stones. These are moved on a diagram made up of a series of small holes in the sand arranged in the form of a whorl arising from a center called Tcunni Ki (the council house).

According to Russell Tcuhu in the mythology of the Pima is Gopher, who dug the spiral hole through which the Pima clans came up from the underworld. From this it seems possible that both Russell and Fewkes were dealing with the same game. Strength is given to this idea by the fact that Dr. Fewkes showed "Higgins" the diagram and the Indian said that it was the House of Tcuhu. The Indian did not draw the diagram. He may have simply recognized the spiral character of the labyrinth and not have considered the details.

With such fragments of evidence and with so many gaps to be filled it would be premature to draw any conclusion as to how this complicated symbol happens to be found in both the old world and the new. The writer publishes this in hopes that some reader will also be familiar with the symbol and can aid in its interpretation.

SOME ENIGMAS OF ANCIENT WRITING

Ancient writing is found on all continents. In some cases, such as the Easter Island "talking boards, " acceptable translation has been impossible, making the inscriptions candidates for this book. The great majority of anomalous writings are "out-of-place;" that is, they should not be where they are found. Phoenician inscriptions in the Americas are anomalies, as are Viking runes in Oklahoma. Many are the exhumed tablets and many are the exothermic controversies. Also, many are the hoaxes.

Rather than introduce each discovery separately, it is perhaps better to generalize on the nature of the arguments each find stirs up. It is all too tempting to label each out-of-place written artifact a hoax because it contradicts current dogma. Fraud is sometimes charged too quickly, as seems to have been the case with the infamous Glozel Tablets. The American Davenport and Bat Creek tablets have been called hoaxes for years, but more recently some doubts about this categorization have arisen. On the other side of the coin, it is equally easy to read Phoenician, Iberian, or Hebrew messages in every group of scratches and symbols. We have again the classic case of a conservative scientific establishment ranged against peripheral (usually amateur) groups. Was that light in the sky Venus or an extraterrestrial UFO? Is this inscription fakery or evidence of pre-Columbian contact?

THE DAVENPORT TABLETS
Anonymous; *American Antiquarian,* 1:167-168, 1879.

Mr. Lucien Adam presented to the Congress an extract from the Proceedings of the Academy of Natural Sciences of Davenport, Iowa, in which is given an account of a discovery of the highest importance made recently by the Rev. J. Gass.

Mr. Adam said: "The 10th of January, 1877, Mr. Gass had the good fortune to find at the base of a conical mound, situated on the farm of Conk, not far from Davenport, two tablets of bituminous clay, upon one of which are engraved: upon one side, a funeral scene accompanied by an inscription; and upon the reverse, a hunting scene. "

"It appears to result from underground proof regularly given (des constatations reoulierement faites par l'Academie) to the Academy of

Natural Sciences of Davenport, that this time the find is authentic.

"In fact, Mr. Gass exhumed the tablets propia manu, and under the eyes of several gentlemen who assisted him in the digging, which was conducted without any interruption."

"The scene represented on the face of one of the tablets makes us present at an inhumation which is collective, and precedes a crema- tion: a big fire is kindled on the summit of a slightly elevated mound. Three dead bodies are deposited on the ground, and thirteen Indians, joined hand in hand, dance around the funeral pile. This rude work of a pre-Columbian artist confirms in all points archaeological inductions. But the importance of this discovery consists much more again in the unexpected fact, that the funeral scene is accompanied by an inscription consisting of 98 signs, of which 74 are different, while 24 are simply repetitions. This circumstance that a certain number of signs (eight) are repeated, six and four, three times, justifies the expression," inscription" which I make use of."

"I propose to the assembly to decide that the study of this precious monument be placed on the order of the day for the next session."

The Count de Marsy said: "The discovery of a Mound-builders' inscription presents such an interest, that it would be proper, if never- theless the thing is possible: that the plate which we have before us, be reproduced in the proceedings of the session."

The President, de Rosny, said: "The idea is an excellent one."

Mr. Adam said: "The committee of publication will certainly gratify the wish expressed by Messrs. de Marsy and de Rosny. But, as the dis- covery of Mr. Gass contains besides this, a hunting scene, on which a supposed elephant is recognized, and also a second tablet called a "calendar stone," I ask the archaeologists present to make a note of the exact like of the pamphlet sent us by our friends in North America."

THE DAVENPORT TABLET
Thomas, Cyrus; *Science*, 6:564, 1885.

As there appears to be a doubt in the minds of many archeologists as to whether these relics should be considered genuine specimens of mound-builders' art, a discussion of their claims to this distinction seems to be demanded.

To do this satisfactorily, a personal inspection of the relics, and a thorough investigation of all the circumstances attending their discovery, should be made. I do not claim to be thus prepared, nor is it my inten- tion to enter at this time upon such discussion; my only object in view in this communication being to call attention to some items in reference to the 'limestone tablet' represented on plate vii., vol. ii., of the Pro- ceedings of the Davenport academy of sciences. The unique and extra- ordinary character of these relics is calculated, of itself, to raise a doubt in the minds of antiquarians which requires more than ordinary proof of genuineness to render their acceptance as such universal. Ex-

amining the excellent albertype of the limestone tablet given on plate
vii., vol. ii., of the Proceedings, we are somewhat surprised to see
the sun represented with a face; nor is this surprise lessened by finding
to the left of the 'hatchet' a regularly formed Arabic 8, made as is customary with writers of the present day, and near the upper right-hand
corner the Roman numeral viii. These are not museum marks, as some
might suppose, but parts of the original inscription on the stone when
found.

The facts regarding the finding, as published by the academy and
given by its members, are not calculated to strengthen belief in its genuineness. According to the account given in the Proceedings, (vol. ii.
pp. 221-224), the exploration of the mound in which it was found was
made by Mr. Gass, assisted by Mr. C. E. Harrison and Mr. John Hume.
The account is by Mr. Harrison. The annexed cut is an exact copy of the
figure of the mound as given in this account. There was an excavation
in the original earth in which was built a pile of stones (x in the figure),
over which the mound of earth was thrown. This earth was comparatively loose, "easy to handle, being composed of dark soil with some admixture of clay," and there appeared to have been no indications of
stratification. At the bottom of the stone pile was a miniature vault
covered by a single flat stone. Lying on the clay bottom of this vault
was the tablet, as indicated in the figure. This vault was about thirteen or fourteen inches square, five inches deep, and, with the exception
of the tablet (an inch and a half thick), four arrow-points, a little quartz
crystal, and a Unio shell, was empty, as appears from this published
account; for it is stated, that, "on raising the flat stone, an irregularly
rectangular, engraved tablet was suddenly exposed to view as it lay face
up on a walled vault, evidently built for its reception" (A in the figure).
But in order to be certain as to this inference, I addressed the following
inquiry to Mr. W. H. Pratt, the curator of the museum of the academy:
"Was the cavity A (fig. 17, Proc. Dav. acad. sc., p. 222, vol. ii) filled
with dirt when first observed?" to which he kindly returned this answer:
"Mr. C. E. Harrison, who assisted in the work, states that the cavity
in which the limestone tablet was found contained scarcely any dirt when
the flat stone with which it was covered was raised, exposing it to view."

That there should have been an unfilled space in a pile of loose stone
in an excavation, beneath a heap of comparatively loose dirt which had
stood there for centuries, is certainly most extraordinary.

In a letter now in my possession, written by Mr. A. S. Tiffany in
1882, I find the following statement: "The limestone tablet I am certain
is a fraud. Mr. Gass was assisted in digging it out by Mr. Harrison
and Mr. Hume. Mr. Hume informs me that there was a wall of small
bowlders around the tablet. On the tablet there were some arrow-points,
a quartz crystal, and a Unio shell filled with red paint, the whole being
covered with a rough limestone slab, the space between it and the tablet
not filled with earth, and the paint bright and clean." Mr. Tiffany was
one of the founders of the academy, and, as appears from the Proceedings, was long one of its most prominent, active, and trusted local
members, and is still a member.

If these statements in regard to the conditions under which this tablet was found be correct,---which we have no reason to doubt, as they
appear to agree in all essential particulars,---there are strong reasons
for suspecting that it was a plant made by some unknown person to de-

ceive the members of the academy. The simple fact that the little
vault under the pile of loose stones was empty, save the presence of the
relics, appears to absolutely forbid the idea of age. It is well known to
all who have taken any part in excavating, that the water, running down
through earth and a pile of stones beneath, will at length fill all the
crevices with earth, and in fact all places not hermetically sealed.

It is proper to add here that Mr. Tiffany, in the same letter, vouch-
es for the honesty of Mr. Gass (the finder), who, he believes, was deceived. Speaking of the elephant pipe found by Mr. Gass, which he also
thinks was a plant, he says, "It bears the same finger-marks as the
first one [first pipe], and Mr. Gass could be deceived with that plant as
he was with the tablet. Mr. Gass is honest." I have Mr. Tuffany's
acknowledgement that this letter, which has been in my possession since
1882, is authentic.

THE DAVENPORT FORGERIES PROBLEM
Kling, Marjorie; *NEARA Newsletter*, 5:29–33, 1970.

Ever since the winters of 1877 and '78, when the Reverend Jacob Gass,
an amateur archaeologist, came upon them in his excavations of the Cook
Farm mounds, now considered to be of Hopewellian culture (1), the three
Davenport, Iowa, tablets have been the center of a controversy.

Are they the authentic works of those who had built the mounds? Or are
they simply the product of a practical joke played by members of the then
Davenport Academy of Natural Sciences? (2)

To answer this question, Dr. Marshall McKusick, Iowa State Archaeologist, has been gathering pertinent information not only from formal sources,
but also from the private, previously uncited, documents of those involved in
the affair. And in The Davenport Conspiracy, just published by the University
of Iowa, he reports his findings: the Davenport tablets are frauds. He presents his evidence of the hoax in concise, table form, together with numerous
photographs, in the final section of the book and provides a detailed description in the preceding chapters.

Using the state of American archaeology in the late 19th century as his
point of departure, Dr. McKusick first traces the history of the two protagon-
ists involved in the discovery of the tablets and other relics---the Davenport
Academy of Natural Sciences and the Rev. Jacob Gass. He then proceeds to
the discovery itself and the subsequent reaction, both favorable and critical,
that developed into bitter controversy.

Characters were assailed, and the Davenport Academy expelled two of
its members---one of its founders, A. S. Tiffany, who claimed fraud in the
case of the limestone tablet and elephant pipe, and a member who rose to his
defense, Dr. Clarence T. Lindley. (At the May, 1885, hearing conducted by
the Academy's investigation committee, Dr. Lindley declared he had seen
curved base pipes being manufactured in the basement of the Academy and
called the janitor, John Graham, to testify. The latter admitted he had made

effigy pipes, including an elephant specimen (3), at home but had done some of the work at the Academy.)

For the authorship of the tablets, Dr. McKusick relates an account of the fraud by Judge James Wills Bollinger, who claimed to have participated in the manufacture of the tablets and who, prior to his death in 1951, had passed on the story to Irving Hurlbut, a former volunteer worker for the Davenport Public Museum.

Judge Bollinger declared that he had removed slate shingles from a building in Davenport known as the Old Slate House. And he and some Academy members, using old German and Hebrew almanacs together with their imaginations, produced the inscription and other items appearing on the tablets. (The inscription occurs on the tablet containing the "Cremation Scene" (4), on the reverse of which is the "Hunting Scene". The zodiac for the "Calendar Stone" tablet was copied either from old almanacs or Webster's Dictionary and its rings inscribed with a steel compass)

The limestone for the third tablet, according to Bollinger, was obtained from Schmidt's Quarry nearby, while the objects found with it---the quartz crystal, shell and red ochre---were acquired from Mr. Tiffany's mineral collection and the Academy, respectively.

Although many portions of this account have been corroborated by documents and manuscripts, Dr. McKusick notes that Judge Bollinger was only a nine-year-old boy in the fall of 1876 when the slate tablets were placed in the Cook mounds for the unsuspecting Gass to find. Thus, he feels the narrative has been marred by exaggeration.

But one fact remains agreed upon: the object of the hoax was the Rev. Jacob Gass, who had incurred the disfavor of his fellow Academy members and who later was to remark he had been "the victim of all." Begun as an attempt to discredit one man, the hoax, however, became a conspiracy that Dr. McKusick concludes "is an almost unbelievable degradation of scientific research."

Notes
(1) Robert Silverberg, Mound Builders of Ancient America, N. Y. Graphic Society, 1968.
(2) Mrs. Carol Hunt, Registrar, Davenport Public Museum, letter dated 5/21/69 to this writer.
(3) It is interesting to note that an elephant or mastodon headed pipe was found by Eber Russell (NEARA Newsletter, Dec., 1968) in a plowed-up Indian grave, dated to the 2nd Algonkian Occupation c. 1500 B. C., on Cattaraugus Reservation, N. Y., near Lake Erie. According to William A. Ritchie, the Hopewell culture had its origin in a proto-culture of an Algonkian people inhabiting the eastern end of Lake Ontario. (1) (Fig. 1)
(4) Fig. 2. Of the 72 different symbols appearing in the inscription, 25, we have found, occur elsewhere on the continent. Nothing on this subject is mentioned in the book.

DECIPHERING THE DAVENPORT TABLETS
Fell, Barry; *America B.C.*; New York, 1976, pp. 265–268.

In the middle of the stele is an engraved scene, and around it are inscriptions in three languages, namely Egyptian, Iberian Punic, and Libyan, each in its appropriate alphabet or hieroglyphic character. The Iberian and Libyan texts, written on engraved scrolls, each report that the stone carries an inscription that gives the secret of regulating the calendar. These parts of the inscription and their alphabets are shown on pages 262 and 263. The remainder of the inscription is in Egyptian hieratic hieroglyphs, and the details of the decipherment are shown here and on the opposite page. The Egyptian text, given literally in the captions, may be rendered into English as follows:

"To a pillar attach a mirror in such manner that when the sun rises on New Year's day it will cast a reflection on to the stone called "The

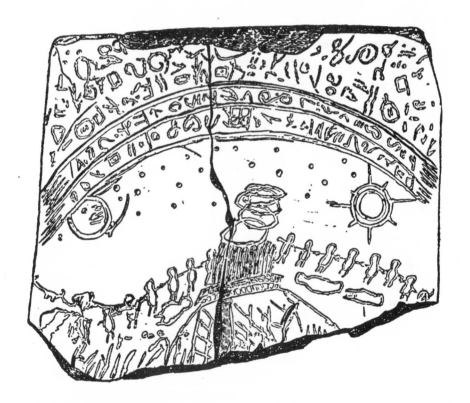

Portion of the Davenport Tablet. Fell believes that the inscription is written in three languages; Egyptian hieroglyphs at the top, Iberian-Punic along the upper arc, and Libyan along the lower arc.

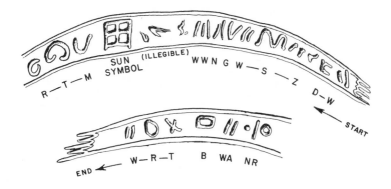

Libyan text of the Davenport Tablet according to Fell.

Watcher." New Year's day occurs when the sun is in conjunction with the zodiacal constellation Aries, in the House of the Ram, the balance of night and day being about to reverse. At this time (the spring equinox) hold the Festival of the New Year, and the Religious Rite of the New Year."

The tablet carries an engraving which depicts the Egyptian celebration of the New Year on the morning of the March equinox (corresponding to the modern date March 21, but later in March in ancient times). This festival consists in the ceremonial erection, by parties of worshippers pulling on ropes, of a special New Year Pillar called the Djed. It is made of bundles of reeds, surmounted by four or five rings. It represents the backbone of the god Osiris.

To the left is seen a carving of the mirror, and beside it are hieroglyphs that read "Mirror of the Egyptians." On the mirror are hieroglyphs that read "reflecting metal." To the right is the rising sun, with the hieroglyph Ra (Sun god or Sun) written on the disk of the sun. Stars as seen in the morning sky are above. As the caption on the illustration shows, the Iowa stele confirms what we already know from evidence yielded by a tomb in Thebes, about the ceremony of the Djed column on New Year's day. The Egyptian record tells us that the ceremony occurred in Koiakh, a word meaning the month of March, again confirming the statements on the Iowa stele. The Egyptian text of the Davenport stele goes on to say that it is the work of Wnty (Star-watcher), a priest of Osiris in the Libyan regions.

How did this extraordinary document come to be in a mound burial in Iowa? Is it genuine? Certainly it is genuine, for neither the Libyan nor the Iberian scripts had been deciphered at the time Gass found the stone. The Libyan and Iberian texts are consistent with each other and with the hieroglyphic text. As to how it came to be in Iowa, some speculations may be made.

The stele appears to be of local American manufacture. Perhaps made by a Libyan or an Iberian astronomer who copied an older model brought from Egypt or more likely from Libya, hence probably brought on a Libyan ship. The Priest of Osiris may have issued the stone originally as a means of regulating the calendar in far distant lands. The date is unlikely to be earlier than about 800 B. C., for we do not know of Iberian or Libyan inscriptions earlier than that date. The Egyptian text, as stated above, may merely be a local American copy of some original. That original could be as old as about 1400 B. C., to judge by the writing style.

INSCRIBED STONE OF GRAVE CREEK MOUND
Reid, M. C.; *American Antiquarian*, 1:139-149, 1879.

In studying this supposed relic of the past we are to search for all available evidence to enable us to answer the following questions:

1st: Is the inscription on the stone alphabetical? For if not, the question when and by whom it was made is of no practical importance.

2nd: If alphabetical does it represent any of the known alphabets of the world?

3rd: Is it an authentic find? That was, is it found in the mound in such a position, that we can safely say it is as old as the mound, and was buried in it at the time of its construction.

4th: If alphabetical and authentic what does its burial and character indicate?

Under the latter head the following facts should be considered. It is not a costly or elaborate piece of work. It could easily be made by any one with or without the use of iron. It is a thin piece of sandstone, unpolished, of the form accident has given it, the edges only wrought, with an inscription which required only a few minutes to make. If alphabetical and deposited in the tomb of one of the mound builders, it indicates a knowledge of the use of letters so common that the art of writing was not confined to a special class. Its simplicity indicates that it was written hastily for some special purpose and if intentionally deposited in the tomb that it was written as a charm, or to designate the name or rank of the person buried, or to render him some imagined assistance.

If a writing, it is a piece of carnal ordinary work to be used and thrown away as an unimportant note that has been read, or written at the time of burial to be buried with the dead. In either case it indicates the common use of writing and makes it appear very strange that in all the mounds carefully examined no other similar inscriptions have been found.

. . . .

But is it alphabetical? Schoolcraft, who had no doubt as to its alphabetical character, after correspondence with noted antiquarians, finds in the inscription four characters corresponding to the ancient Greek; four Etruscan; five Runic; six ancient Gallic; seven old Erse; ten Phoenician; fourteen old British; sixteen Celtiberic, with some resemblance to the Hebrew, but is inclined to regard the whole inscription as Celtiberic. Now in the old alphabets of the world which took their form before the local invention of paper, when writing was not writing but engraving, the ingenuity of man was substantially exhausted in the formation of letters by a combination of straight lines, so that now it is very difficult, if not wholly impossible to engrave on a stone twenty arbitrary characters of which a large number will not be simply reproductions of ancient letters. I have asked several different persons, who had never seen the inscriptions in Cesnola's Cyprus, to write down for me twenty or more arbitrary characters not resembling any figures or alphabetical characters known to them, and composed of straight lines or combinations of straight lines. In every case an inscription was produced presenting as many indications of being alphabetical as the one under discussion, and on comparing them with Cesnolas' inscriptions alone---of one, five would be pronounced Cypriotic and three Phoenician; of another, eleven Cypriotic and two Phoenician; of another, eight Cypriotic and three Phoenician; and of the other, ten Cypriotic and

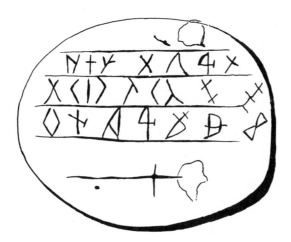

The Grave Greek inscription

eleven Phoenician; while the tendency to reproduce familiar forms was shown in the fact that in every case one or more of the characters would, in inscriptions, be pronounced English.

In this inscription a similar tendency is apparent. The familiar forms are a cross, found twice; an X; a diamond; an hour-glass; the capital D with a line which makes it represent a bow and arrow; and the figure 4, the latter exactly representing our printed figure. This much is evident, that the inscription is not necessarily alphabetic. It is just such a medley of characters as any one would produce who undertook to invent an inscription to puzzle the curious. It might be objected that in such an attempt, care would be taken not to produce any modern forms. But these fabricated inscriptions were made by those who were especially cautioned to make their characters unlike any letter or figure with which they were familiar, and were limited to the use of straight lines and combinations of straight lines. None of them in a first attempt were able to observe the condition imposed, and they were not permitted to improve upon their first attempt.

. . . .

All the evidence it seems to me compels the following conclusions:

1st.   The inscription is not necessarily to be regarded as alphabetical.

2d.   If it is assumed to be alphabetical it cannot be referred to any known language.

3d.   It is precisely of such a character as would be the result of an ordinary attempt to manufacture an inscription.

4th.   Its manufacture is within the capacity of any laborer of ordinary intelligence who may have been employed in the work of exploring the mound.

5th.   At the time of its discovery there was no proper scrutiny of the inscription to determine whether it was of recent manufacture or not.

6th.   The evidence that it came from the mound is by no means conclusive.

7th.   Its history is such that the subsequent discovery of unquestioned ancient inscriptions with similar characters would warrant us in concluding that this also is ancient.

8th.   Until its authenticity is thus fully established it ought not to be regarded as <u>any</u> evidence of the character, ethnical relationship or intellectual culture of the builders of the mounds.

PRINTER'S KNOWLEDGE OF DICKENS SOLVES SCIENTIFIC HOAX

Davis, Emily C.; *Science News Letter*, 17:324–325, 1930.

"Bil Stumps Stone Oct 14 1838"

This inscription in cabalistic writing, cut into a little piece of stone, has baffled scientists both in America and abroad ever since it was dug out of an Indian mound in West Virginia almost a century ago.

Many experts on the world's languages tried in all seriousness to translate the cryptic writing, believing it to be written by ancient man in Canaanite, Celtic, Runic, or what not. Some of the scholars announced success, and strange and weird were their translations.

It has finally taken a West Virginia printer, who knows his Dickens and who has a keen sense of humor, to succeed where the scholars failed. His reading of the inscription "in good old West Virginian" clears up one of the greatest hoaxes in the record of American science. That hoax, perpetrated by some unknown practical jokesmith, has stood triumphantly undetected for ninety odd years.

The printer, Andrew Price, is an historian by hobby. He is President of the West Virginia Historical Society and a member of the West Virginia Academy of Science. He has been intrigued by the inscription for a long time, but never tried his hand at deciphering it until recently.

In a statement explaining how he came to solve the riddle, Mr. Price

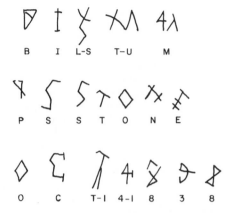

One interpretation of the Grave Greek inscription. The characters should be compared with those in the preceding illustration.

reminds us of the delightful bit of satire in a novel by Charles Dickens which gave the American joker his idea. Poking fun at British scientists of a century ago, Dickens had concocted the following inscription:

X
BILST
U M
PSHI
S. M.
ARK

Dickens had his famous character, Mr. Pickwick, discover this strange inscription on a small broken stone, lying partly buried by an ancient cottage. Mr. Pickwick, very much excited, asked the cottage owner about the age of the stone and was told that "It was here long before I war born, or any on us." Whereupon Mr. Pickwick bought the stone and returned in haste to London feeling that he had attained a great ambition. He, the Chairman of the Pickwick Club, had unearthed a curious inscription of unquestionable antiquity.

THE MILL RIVER INSCRIPTION

Whittall, James P., II; *Early Sites Research Society, Bulletin*, 4:8-10, 1976.

In April 1975 Gertrude Johnson, researcher for Early Sites, brought to my attention an inscription shown to her many years earlier by member Sinclair Bowman. She felt the inscription was somewhat similar to the

Bourne inscription (Early Sites Bulletin, 1975, Vol. 3, No. 2) and there-fore, might be Iberian. I contacted Scotty Bowman and we made a trip to South Weymouth to relocate the inscribed stone. Scotty hadn't been there for seven years, but after a short search we located the inscription. Fortunately, no damage had been inflicted on the stone since his last trip.

The inscribed stone is located on a knoll that projects out into the sur-rounding marshy area just east of where the Mill River flows from a large pond down to the sea. It is probable that the area around the knoll was once covered by water. The stone was set originally on two large stones nearby and anyone travelling on foot to the point or by water would have noticed the inscription.

The markings are carved into a slab of granite 6 feet long by 18 inches wide by 9 inches deep. Some of the markings are quite deep; whereas

others are eroded to a point of being barely visible. It looked like someone recently had "freshened" the first four characters in the first line, The rock had been quarried from a larger boulder nearby, and though there were no signs of drill marks the stone had been neatly dressed.

During the summer I took Dr. Barry Fell, President of the Epigraphic Society, and Peter Farfall to examine the inscription. Dr. Fell agreed with Gertrude's opinion that the inscription was Iberian and he felt that with some study he could give a translation. We then photographed the inscription and made latex peels to be studied later.

In the fall, Dr. Fell gave me a suggested translation of the inscription, but he felt it needed more attention. This past winter he made a more ex-tensive study and presented me with the following information. The inscrip-tion is in the Iberian-Punic, and translates into the following message in contemporary English:

CEASE TRESPASSING

ANYONE TREADING (HERE) IS DESECRATING A BURIAL PLACE

A more detailed analysis of the translation is shown below:

WORD

IBERIC   s-s-g / t-y / y-b-d / l-b / d-t-r / h-a-q

ARABIC   sazaga tayah iabd laba datara naq

ENGLISH	cease trespassing anyone	treading	desecrate		burial cist
		loitering	destroy		

Deciphered: Prof. Barry Fell - March 27, 1976

The time frame for this inscription is considered to be around the 3rd or 4th century B. C.

Comparison:

The phraseology of the Mill River stele is reminiscent of the similar inscription of a grave stele from Herdade do Pego, Portugal, illustrated by Luis Coelho (Arqueologo Portuques, III ser., IV, p. 168, 1970). The letter styles, however, differ in the two steles. The peculiar B of the Mill River stele points to Arabian influence.

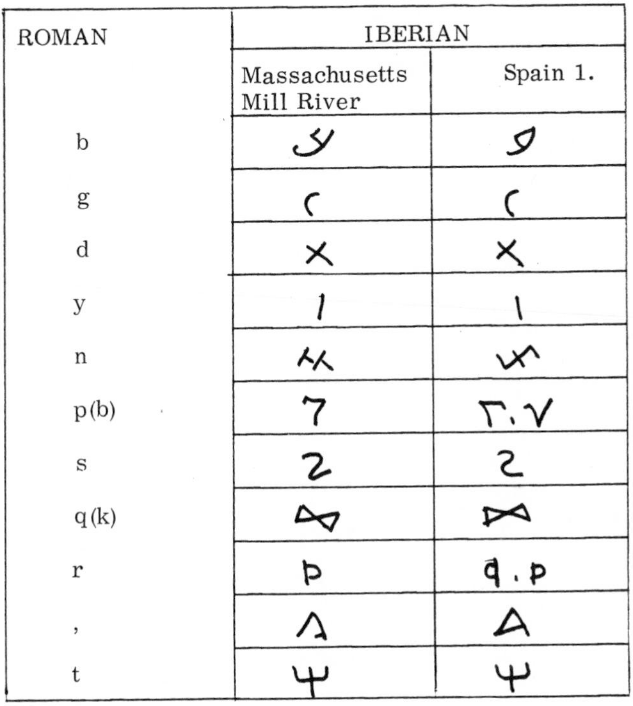

ROMAN	IBERIAN	
	Massachusetts Mill River	Spain 1.
b	ᶴᵞ	ᵞ
g	(	(
d	✕	✕
y	1	\
n	⋏⋏	⋏
p (b)	7	Γ.ᵞ
s	2	ᒿ
q (k)	⋈	⋈
r	Þ	�𐌒 . Þ
'	⋀	△
t	Ѱ	Ѱ

Mill River and Iberian alphabets compared

AN ANCIENT JUDEAN INSCRIPTION FROM TENNESSEE

Stieglitz, Robert R.; *Epigraphic Society, Occasional Publications,* vol. 3, no. 65, 1976.

In 1885 an inscribed stone was discovered in an excavation conducted by the Smithsonian Institution, in Loudon County, Tennessee. The Bat Creek stone, as it is known, is a slate-like ironstone, 11.5 cm. long and 5.1 cm. wide. It was found in a sealed archaeological context: a Burial mound which contained nine skeletons. Various grave goods were interned under the head of one of the skeletons, as was the stone itself. Presently, the stone is kept at the Smithsonian Institution (U.S.N.M. Archive No. 134902). In the original excavation report, Professor Cyrus Thomas identified the inscription as "beyond question letters of the Cherokee alphabet, said to have been invented by George Guess (or Sequoyah), a half-breed Cherokee, about 1821."

Since the original publication, it had been noted that the letters of the inscription- when viewed in a position upside-down from that in which it was originally published- show a remarkably close resemblance to the ancient Phoenician-Hebrew alphabet. An investigation and interpretation of the inscription was carried out by Professor Cyrus H. Gordon in 1971, in which he confirmed the nature of the script as ancient Hebrew. He also produced a reading of the inscription and a historical interpretation. In light of the extraordinary implications involved in this interpretation, especially as far as the history of seafaring and interconnections between the Old and New World are concerned, it seems important to review the historical background which could help explain how a Judean inscription from the Roman period could turn up in an archaeological context in America.

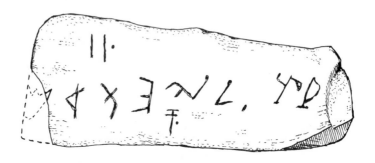

Bat Creek Stone from Tennessee

Epigraphic analysis of the inscription enables us to obtain an approximate date on the basis of the letter-forms. The characters on this stone have their closest parallels in the ancient Hebrew script utilized on the Jewish coins which were minted during the rebellions against the Romans: The Jewish War (66-73 A.D.), the Bar-Kokhba's Revolt (132-135 A.D.). On strictly palaeographic grounds, the script of the stone is closer to the letter forms utilized on the coins of the Jewish War. This, of course, does not preclude a later date. Still, a more precise dating is at present not possible on palaeographic grounds, and must be left at ca. 100 A.D.

The inscription consists of two words, separated by a word-divider, and of two signs: one above and one below the line of the inscription. The left end of the stone is broken and at the edge traces of another letter are visible. I attempt here a reconstruction of the missing letter:

The line reads from right to left, and the second word is easily read in comparison with the difficult signs of the first word. I have suggested that the reading should be: (Gordon, 1971:185)

ziq . layyehudi(m)

A Comet for the Jew(s)

The supralinear sign, a dot plus two vertical lines is probably a sign for the numeral "2" (Gordon, 1972:18 n. 13). If this is correct, it most likely stands for the two skeletons buried separately from the other seven bodies in the grave. The nine skeletons were arranged in two groups: seven at the north of the circular burial lie with their heads towards North. The two remaining skeletons, to the south of this group, lie in tete-beche position (North-South). The grave goods and stone were located under the head of the skeleton with its head to the south. This was, therefore, the most important person in the grave. The horizontal section of the burial may be found in Thomas, 1894:393, Fig. 272; and Gordon, 1971:181. The infralinear sign consists of a dot and the letter ✕ aleph. Letters were used on the ancient Jewish coins to indicate dates, most commonly the minting date. The aleph sign hete, then, may also have this meaning, in which case we can translate the entire inscription as follows:

2 .

A Comet . for the Jew(s)

(Year) 1 . (of the Messianic Era)

The significance of this short message is enormous. It evidently refers to a Judean leader designated as "Comet," for this is what ziq means in Late Hebrew. The Babylonian Talmud (Berachoth 58b) defines the term ziq as: ט ׳ב ש ד ✕ ׏ ׏ ׏ ׀ ׏   kokeba desabit 'comet, bright star'. In Biblical Hebrew this term meant 'firebrand, spark' (Isaiah 50:11). The term is derived from the root z-q-q which means 'to smelt, cause to sparkle, purify'. Such an inscription is indeed most appropriate to the times in which a leader of the Jewish Revolt against Rome, who was held by some noted Rabbinic authorities to be The Messiah, was given the epithet Bar Kokhba "Son of the Star'.

The historical background, especially its naval aspects, must now be reviewed if we are to propose an explanation for this Roman era inscription in America. We may begin by noting that this is not the first evidence for the presence of Mediterranean people in the New World before Columbus. What is unique about this inscription is its sealed archaeological context. There is much evidence both in historical sources and from modern investigations which indicates that Phoenicians and other Mediterranean peoples reached the shores of the New World in the centuries before the Roman era.

THE WILSON-BRAXTON TABLET
Keeler, Clyde; *NEARA Newsletter*, 8:56, 1973.

The tablet was found by a rural schoolboy, Blaine Wilson in Braxton County along Triplett Creek 8 miles west of Gossaway, West Virginia, in 1931.

The Wilson-Braxton stone is about 4-3/16" x 3-5/16" and it is about 1" thick. It is a well-prepared tablet of fine sandstone showing considerable weathering, in that the matrix between surface sand grains has disappeared, giving it a finely pebbled appearance.

It bears three rows of runes that are deeply incised. These are placed on horizontal lines and below the inscription is a Christian Cross symbol such as was commonly placed on Viking Inscriptions between 1000 and 1050 AD.

The Wilson-Braxton Tablet

Curiously enough, on the reverse side the corners of the stone had been rounded off as though the tablet was intended to be cemented into a shallow pocket in some stone marker. This suggestion of a marker or stone tumulus has already been offered as an explanation of why several small flat rune-stones were found near each other at Popham Beach, Maine.

Olaf Strandwold who described and translated the Wilson-Braxton tablet in 1948, worked from a photo of the obverse side of the stone taken by A. L. Kenna. Strandwold recognized the runerow employed as Helsinge, the second R in RIKAR as Swedish-Norwegian. The last rune in the first line is a stung O, also found in the third line. The first symbol in the second line is a bind-rune for KU. The fifth symbol in the second line (+) is a stung I which gives the sound of soft E. The fourth symbol in the third line is a bindrune for NU, meaning NOW in English.

The Inscription is easily read: "Richard owns the island. Gudrid had a husband in Erik, now Ole", as Strandwold pointed out.

But because Strandwold examined only a photo, he fell into one error. He reported that there is a faint Hammer of Thor on the right hand end of the cross symbol, like the one on the Grave Creek tablet. However, this is a discoloration on the Wilson tablet that Strandwold mistook for a Thor Hammer.

I have examined the stone carefully with dissecting goggles and there are absolutely no incisions in the place where the Thor Hammer was said to be.

This tablet has been considered by professionals as a fake with symbols copied from the Grave Creek Tablet, which was the original fake.

But the maker of the Grave Creek Tablet must have been an expert on Helsinge runes and also on the old Norse language, and must have inserted his "fake" into the upper burial in the Great Moundville Mound roughly 900 years ago. The inscription makes sense.

The "faker" of the Wilson-Braxton Tablet must also have been an expert on old Norse because the inscription makes sense. He must also have been an expert on Helsinge runes because he has added runes not on the Grave Creek Tablet. For example, he has added the bindrune KU, used a different form for E, and has simplified Ø. He used a different R.

An examination of the facts supports the authenticity of both the Grave Creek Tablet and the Wilson-Braxton Tablet.

THE MONHEGAN INSCRIPTION

Whittall, James P., II; *Early Sites Research Society, Bulletin,* 4:1-7, 1976.

In 1855 while roaming about the island of Manana, Dr. Augustus E. Hamlin noticed some markings on an outcrop of ledge which he felt certain was an inscription. (It is likely that someone had mentioned the markings to him at an earlier date.) Dr. Hamlin exhibited a cast of the inscription at the Albany meeting of the American Association for the Advancement of Science in 1856, suggesting that it was the work of "some illiterate Scandinavian, whose knowledge of the runic form was very imperfect." At this time there was great interest in Norse exploration of America and every new carving that showed up was eagerly studied and declared Norse. Samuel Adams Drake, in his Pine Tree State said, "it was generally attributed to the Northmen or the devil." Others of the period such as Mallery, Daniel Wilson, and De Costa expressed the opinions that the markings were only freaks of surface erosion. These opinions were based for the most part on a report made by G. O. Stone in Science in 1885 after a personal examination.

. . . .

After researching the Bourne inscription, I decided to take another look at known inscribed stones along the New England coast. During the summer of 1975 with a fellow member of Early Sites, William Nisbet, we travelled out to Monhegan and Manana islands to examine the inscribed ledge in detail. At that time we made a latex cast of the markings and photographed the inscription as it appears today.

. . . .

In September 1975, I gave the latex peel to Dr. Barry Fell, president of the Epigraphic Society to cast and study. His research on the inscription and in ancient text from Europe brought to light a new and interesting translation. Dr. Fell, researching other inscriptions in America, had been working with the ogam script and all its 71 known variations when he noticed the similarities between the markings on the Manana cast and an ogam script known as Annso (Book of Ballymote, #3) which had been recorded in the 14th century. Working with this script he came up with the following, Reading right to left:

"L-NG-BH-T BH F-N-C C-HD L-BH-(R-G)

Then applying Celtic language, Goidelic group, vowels omitted, to the script he uncovered the following message:

Long-bhata bho Finici; cuidhe labhraig

Or clearly stated in English, <u>Long ships from Phoenicia: Cargo-lots landing-quay</u>

From previous work by Dr. Fell, (<u>Occ. Publ</u>, Vol. 3, No. 50) we now know that ogam was used by the Celts in the Iberian Peninsula at a time when they would have had contact with the Phoenicians. This message implies that both Punic seafarers and Celtic explorers had been at Monhegan. From research work we would suggest a time frame of about 400 B.C.

Why a message of that nature? The Phoenician, beyond their well known ability as navigators, were also the merchants of the world in 400 B.C. They dealt in any commodity which would return a profit. As in the 17th century A.D., I think Monhegan was used as a fishing station for export back to the Iberian markets. However, this time the control was by Phoenicians not British colonists. Ancient Phoenician fishing stations were known on the Iberian peninsula from Cadiz up the Atlantic coast to Figueira de Foz, an area where extensive salt works were developed by the Phoenicians. As fishing was depleted along the Iberian coast, fishermen looked to new areas. It seems that fishing off the New England coast might have taken place as early as 2000 B.C. In this case the fishermen were probably Iberian-celts who left their cargo for the Phoenician traders at Monhegan. It is possible that they also included furs, which were in high demand in Europe, at the cargo platform. The message near a high point on Manana would be spotted by mariners visiting the island and they would know that they had a trade contact.

AN AEGEAN SCRIPT STONE FROM GEORGIA?
Rothovius, Andrew E.; *NEARA Newsletter*, 5:27-28, 1970.

One of the most interesting recent discoveries of an apparently pre-Columbian inscription indicative of European contact was that made in the fall of 1966 by Manfred Metcalf of Ft. Benning, Ga. His find, of a stone inscribed with symbols resembling the early Aegean scripts of the Minoan and Mycenean cultures, has not been properly presented in the few press accounts that have appeared of it, except in the journal, <u>Manuscripts</u>, which in its Summer, 1969, issue carried an article by NEARA consultant Dr. Cyrus H. Gordon of Brandeis University, describing the stone and its implications.

. . . .

Mr. Metcalf came across the stone while seeking flat rocks suitable for constructing a barbecue pit. In the ruinous foundation courses of a vanished 19th century mill, he found a brownish-yellow, flat sandstone, which upon being cleaned of a ferrous crust, proved to have on one side several inscribed symbols as shown on the opposite page. As Mr. Metcalf had for several

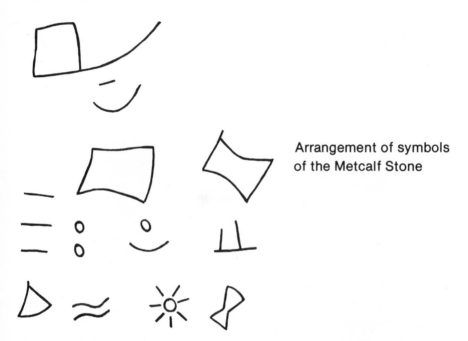

Arrangement of symbols
of the Metcalf Stone

years been engaged in a study of the Mediterranean affinities of the Yuchi Indians of southwestern Georgia, who were forcibly removed to Oklahoma in 1836, he was intrigued by the resemblance of these symbols to those of the Aegean scripts of the 2nd millenium B. C. In May, 1968, he contacted Dr. Gordon, who provided the following evaluation of the inscription.

As can easily be seen in the table, practically every symbol on the Metcalf stone is to be found in the syllabaries of the Minoan Linear A and Mycenean Linear B scripts. The character of the symbols indicates that the Metcalf tablet is an inventory of goods---Dr. Gordon suggests a conjectural reading of "one double-axe weighing one mina, made of copper" for the last line.

This is not to be understood as an assertion that the tablet is written in an Aegean language; the syllabaries are known to have been used for two entirely different languages, Minoan and Mycenean, and it is entirely possible that their symbols could have been used for representation of other languages as well. In this connection, no resemblance has been found between any words in the Yuchi language and those in the Aegean languages of antiquity;

and even if the Yuchi did actually---as their tribal legends and rituals hint---reach America from the Mediterranean some three or four millennia ago, bringing a knowledge of Aegean script symbols with them, they may well have been a people completely unrelated to the Minoans and Myceneans, and speaking a totally different tongue. The script may have been widely distributed in the Mediterranean area---if its use was limited, as appears probable from the Cretan examples so far found, to inventories and records of mercantile transactions, tablets bearing it may yet be found in other Mediterranean areas far removed from Crete.

    Dr. Gordon further suggests that it will be profitable to study Mayan and Aztec glyphs with a view to finding correspondences with the Aegean script, from which some of them may have derived. (A preliminary study along this line has already been undertaken by Pierre Honore in his In Quest of the White God, Putnam, N. Y. , 1964; and in a more comprehensive German edition, 1965.) The German scholar, Alexander von Wuthenau, has pointed out (Altmerikanische Tonplastic, 1965) that until about 300 A. D. , the Mesoamerican sculpture figurines seem to show no Amerindian facial types but rather Oriental, Semitic and Negroid, suggesting a very substantial ratio of trans-Oceanic contact.

An inscribed stone found near Hawley, Pennsylvania, in 1970. The symbols resemble runes.

THE RIDDLE OF AMERICA'S ELEPHANT SLABS
Harris, Neill J.; *Science Digest,* 69:74-77, March 1971.

Commonly known as the Elephant Slabs, the carved rocks were found in 800-year-old Indian ruins located on the south side of the Animas River just opposite Flora Vista. According to a famous archaeologist, the late Earl Halstead Morris, the small boy sold the carvings to arch- aeologist Charles Avery Amsden, who reportedly took Morris to where the boy had found the slabs. Morris, an expert on primitive Southwest- ern artifacts, dated these Indian ruins at about A. D. 1200, based on potsherds found lying on the surface of the Flora Vista site.

"I can see no reason to doubt the authenticity of these specimens, " wrote Morris concerning the Elephant Slabs, "but how to explain them I would not say. In all my experience I have seen nothing similar. "

. . . .

The principal slab measures six inches wide, six inches long; a deep groove on the left-hand side shows where it was probably broken off from a larger stone. The unknown petroglypher meticulously chisel- ed 55 signs and pictures into exceedingly hard stone and left no obvious traces of tool slippage or overcrossing lines.

The second slab measures six inches wide, 14 inches long and bears only 10 faintly incised signs including outlines of an elephant---the sur- prising fact that gave the slabs their name---a bird, and what looks like a mountain lion. Both slabs, particularly the longer one, closely re- semble the stone hoes or knives of the Southwest.

DETAIL OF SLAB B

If genuine, the Elephant Slabs preserve the only written examples found north of Mexico of an ancient language, ranking them high among our most important historical relics. The slabs may truly record an Indian's written account of elephants. (pp. 74-75)

THE ANCIENT INSCRIPTION AT CHATATA, TENNESSEE
Rawson, A. L.; *American Antiquarian,* 14:221-223, 1892.

In March, 1891, the Cleveland (Tennessee) <u>Express</u> printed a short account of a discovery of a supposed ancient wall near that place. Mr. Carson, who wrote the article, had seen the stones and felt sure the marks on them are artificial.

I visited the place in May of that year, and made drawings, some of which are reproduced here, as also one from transcript made by Dr. J. Hampden Porter, of the Smithsonian Institute, Washington, D. C., who was there in the October following.

A cousin of Mr. Hooper carried me in a buffy from Cleveland, thirteen miles to Chatata, where Mr. J. H. Hooper, who found the wall on his farm, resides. We arrived late at his house and were entertained all night. After supper the stones were mentioned, and one they had at the house was shown me, and I transcribed the marks. In the morning six or eight more stones, about sixteen or eighteen inches across, and irregular in fracture and about ten inches thick, were shown, as they lay under a rude shed where the children at play could injure them.

Later we drove to the place, about a mile from the house, on a sandstone ridge that is at least twenty miles long, north to south, flanked by limestone east and west, ending at the south near the Tennessee river at Chattanooga.

As we neared the place we saw several places where a single stone had been dug out of the clay soil, and those stones occurred at intervals of twenty-five or thirty feet for nearly one thousand feet. At the north end of the ridge the inscribed wall was found.

Mr. Hooper noticed first stone Fig. 1, which stood exposed a few inches above the ground and saw, what seemed to him, a figure 8, which he supposed was on a stone placed at the head of some soldier's grave. After digging it out in the hope of learning the name he was surprised to find some unreadable marks. Further exploration exposed a formation of brown or red sandstone in three thicknesses, upright, about ten inches each, and apparently cemented together, forming what seemed to be a wall, with an inscription on the middle course on its west side. The lines run diagonally, ascending towards the right, and one cut on the raised surface of narrow ridges or flutings, parallel but not exactly straight. The works are from one and a half to two and a half inches across, and are cut into the surface of the rock a quarter or an eighth of an inch, varying, not uniform in depth. These incisions are filled with cement, perhaps by natural deposit from the soil above. A few groups are of figures of birds, or of animals, three to six inches across.

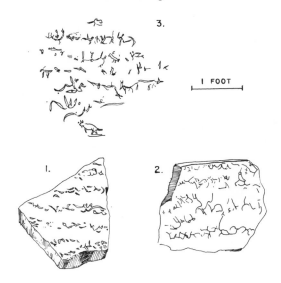

Inscription discovered at Chatata, Tennessee

Mr. J. Hampden Porter wrote me from Chatata, October 21: "This formation is not a wall, but a red sandstone ridge and faced with clay, red, slaty and yellow also, to an unknown depth. In uncovering the rock for a space of twelve by sixteen feet, no implements and no traces of previous excavation have been found. Supposing the works were made there by some prehistoric people, five, ten, or more thousand years ago, all traces of former disturbance would have disappeared, unless some stone implements had been left; and such would have been too valuable to leave there. With regard to the characters themselves, it appears to me that they cannot be otherwise than artificial. On the basis of eight hundred and twenty-five signs I have found that by bringing together those that were alike, and in numerous instances identical, there is a recurrence of essential forms and fac similes which would show the chances in favor of their accidental origin to be almost infinitely small. If they be a true script it is in a transition phase, and nearer the ideographic than the pictorial stage of writing. Still the representations of animal forms and emblems belonging to peoples widely separated, geographically, certainly present themselves here."

He recognizes the figure of the old and of the new moon, and of the "destroying quoit," the thunder bird, serpent, etc., etc., "united in lines on the stones, with letter-like markings" in great variety. Mr. Porter also thinks there are forms like many Old World alphabets, which of course are accidental, for these marks may antedate the oldest---the Moabite, or even the Egyptian sacred text, or the Demotic script. I engrave here a copy of a line of the marks from his letter. Of them he says: "The figurings are more regular than the originals, but the forms are given truly." Good photographs of the whole face of the tablet and of sections of it have been taken, which Mr. Duncan, of Chatata, can supply.

This inscription, whether it is on a wall or a ridge, is one of many evidences of a prehistoric people who were highly civilized on this continent. Not far from this wall, on Jolly Island, at the confluence of the Hiawassee with the Tennessee river, is a temple mound, which, Dr. Porter says, is built with mathematical precision. Another cyclopean wall is on Fort Mountain, in Murray county, Georgia, in the Appalachian chain. A spur juts out very precipitously on three sides, and has about one hundred acres on its top, cut off from the mountain by a wall fifteen hundred feet long, five feet thick and six feet high, with many angles and curves, as if to command approaches. One opening is guarded by three towers.

Scholars will delight to compare the Chatata writings with those at Dighton, Mass., and also with some altaic characters in the old world, such as the Hamath Inscriptions.

The skeletons with copper masks, found in mounds near Chillicothe, Ohio, were evidently those of well-to-do people, for with them were found hundreds of thousands of pearls, some an inch or more in size.

THE CHEROKEES IN PRE-COLUMBIAN TIMES
Thomas, Cyrus; *Science*, 15:328, 1890.

"The Tipton group [of mounds] is situated on the north side of the Little Tennessee, about two miles from Morganton. No. 3 of this group, which stands about one hundred feet from No. 2, is of small size, measuring twenty eight feet in diameter and about five feet in height. Some large trees," says Mr. Emmert, the Bureau agent, "were standing on the mound, and Mr. Tipton informed me that he had cut other trees off of it forty years ago, and that it had been a cluster of trees and grape-vines as far back as the oldest settler could recollect. There was an old stump yet in the centre, the roots of which ran down in the mound almost or quite to where the skeletons were found.... Having worked to the bottom, I found here nine skeletons lying at full length on the natural surface, with faces up, and surrounded by dark-colored earth. No. 1 (as shown in the diagram which accompanies his report) was lying with head to the south; while No. 2, close by the side of it, had the head to the north, and feet almost touching the head of the other. On the same level, but apart from the preceding, were seven other skeletons lying closely side by side, heads all to the north, and all in a line. No relics of any kind were found with any of the skeletons except No. 1. Immediately under the skull and jaw-bones were two copper bracelets, an engraved stone, a small drilled stone, a single copper bead, a bone instrument, and some small pieces of polished wood. The earth about the skeletons was wet, and the pieces of wood were soft and colored green by contact with the copper bracelets. These bracelets had been rolled up in something which crumbled off when they were taken out, but whether buckskin or bark I was unable to decide. The engraved stone was lying partially under the skull. I punched it with my steel prod on

the rough side in probing, before I reached the skeletons. "

As soon as the collections made by Mr. Emmert during this exploration were received at the office in Washington, a member of the Bureau
was sent to the field where Mr. Emmert was at work, to learn the whole
history of the find. This course was taken by the Bureau merely as a
means of being fortified with all possible evidence as to the facts of the
find being as stated. The examination by the person sent confirmed the
statement by Mr. Emmert in every particular. This, therefore, neces-
sitates one of two conclusions,---that the mound was thrown up since
1820, or that some one was at work on the Cherokee alphabet before Mr.
Guess's time.

. . . .

A DESCRIPTION OF PREHISTORIC RELICS FOUND NEAR WILMINGTON, OHIO

Welch, L. B., and Richardson, J. M.; *American Antiquarian*, 4:40–48, 1881.

The mound in question is situated upon the road leading from Wilmington to Harveysburg, and known as the Wilmington and Waynesville Pike,
and about three and a half miles from the former place, due west, upon
the Sparks farm, and has long been known as the Sparks Mound. It is on
the north side, and perhaps two hundred yards from the pike. In shape,
the mound is almost round, being forty feet north and south by forty-five
east and west, and in height six and a half feet. As the timber was removed but about four years ago, and the ground has never been plowed
but once, the mound is perhaps near its original height. The earth of
which the mound is composed is of the same character as that found in
the fields adjacent, being the yellowish clay of the glacial period. Upon
the summit of the mound and about the center stood a large sugar tree
(Acer saccharinum) stump; about fifteen or sixteen feet north of the
center, stood another of same kind and size. There is nothing remarkable in the surroundings of the mound, save the evidence of an ancient
roadway or approach leading up from the valley of Todd's Fork, which
by a gradual rise brings one to the mound, which, after being reached,
is found to occupy a position from where a wide and extended view of the
creek bottoms and the hills beyond can be had. Included in the landscape
are other mounds.

The opening was made from east to west. After reaching a depth of three feet, a layer of charcoal and ashes from four to six inches in depth, and which covered the entire surface of the mound, that is, what was the surface at the time the deposit was made, was struck, amidst which were found skeletons. The bodies had been buried in regular order, each having the head to the center and the feet toward the outer edge of the mound, radiating from the center as the spokes in a wheel radiate from the hub. Here reposed, side by side, infancy, manhood and old age, as evidenced by the fact that here was found that least perishable part of all the human anatomy, that portion upon which the ravages of time make slowest inroads---the teeth. Side by side with the nearly crownless teeth of old age we find the undeveloped teeth of youth and the fully developed teeth of middle age.

After penetrating the layer last described, the same characteristics marked the next three feet as did the first three. When the original surface of the ground was reached, and within eight feet of the center of the mound, two square holes were found, one south east and the other north east of the center. These holes were near eighteen inches deep and twelve by twenty inches, and were filled with charcoal and ashes with many bits of bone. At an elevation of about six inches above the original surface, and four or five feet from the center, embedded in charcoal and ashes, was found a piece of mica three eights of an inch thick and ten by thirteen inches in width.

When the center of the mound was reached a truncated cone shaped mass, about two feet high and four feet in diameter, composed of clay that had evidently been mixed and burned until it assumed the color of a salmon brick, was found. Directly west, and one foot from the base of the cone was discovered a vault nine feet long and three feet wide, the head and foot of which were plainly marked by a wall of round, smooth boulders. The vault was filled with charcoal and ashes, which, after being removed to a depth of nearly two feet, disclosed the skeleton of a man who had been buried face downward and in a horizontal position. The body had been buried two feet below the original surface or level of the ground. The walls of boulders extended no farther than to the shoulders on either side of the head, and those at the feet no farther than to the ankles. Upon a removal of the bones of the skeleton, within those of the left hand was found clasped the tablet marked Figure 1. This tablet is of Waverly sandstone, three and seven eights inches wide, four and seven-eights long, and five eights of an inch thick; the obverse being shown in Plate No. 1, it is only necessary here to speak of the reverse, which is unmarked save by five deep and three shallow grooves, and of these markings we have but this to offer as to their significance or meaning: Those acquainted with the character of the Waverly sandstone know that it possesses a fine sharp grit, and is well calculated for polishing purposes, and therefore we have no hesitancy in saying that so much of this stone as is missing was removed to be used in polishing the surface, or drilling holes in some object of interest to the people or person to whom they belonged.

This relic was found by Mr. J. M. Richardson on the 31st day of January, 1879, and is named the "Richardson Tablet," in honor of the discoverer. He was assisted in his labors by John W. Jones.

After a thorough investigation of the vault was made, nothing farther of interest being found, the opening was filled up. Extremely cold wea-

Wilmington, Ohio, Tablet (Plate 1)

ther setting in nothing more could be done at the time, but on the 12th day of the month following another excavation was commenced and continued in a southwesterly direction from the vault. Scarcely two feet from the edge of the vault, and about the same distance from the base of the cone-like center of the mound, was encountered a circle of round stones similar to those forming the extremities of the vault. This circle was upon the original surface of the ground, and in diameter was about thirty inches and was built up to a height of twenty inches. The space enclosed by these stones was filled with charcoal and ashes, and during their removal the piece shown in Plate No. 3 was found standing upon edge near the center of the pit, the bottom of which was formed of two stones, lying in a trough-like shape.

By reference to the engravings, Nos. 3 and 4, the reader will no doubt admit that this last piece found is perhaps the most interesting relic of that age about which so little is known and so much is speculatory---the Mound Builder's Period---that has ever yet been found. Probably the most notable object in plate No. 3 is the figure of a man, large, well formed, and of excellent proportions. The features are bold, massive, and of such a character as a student of ethnology would expect to find in a man of the race that constructed such almost imperishable monuments as the Mound Builders have left throughout the Middle and Western States. The head is of the brachycephalic, or short-headed type; it is squarely set on a neck and shoulders that are indicative of strength. These facts are all apparent, however, and need no farther explanation from us. In connection therewith we find an illustration of the use that was made of a certain half-moon shaped stone implement that is frequently met with in archaeological collections, viz: an ornament, hand hold or finish to the spear and axe handle. Another

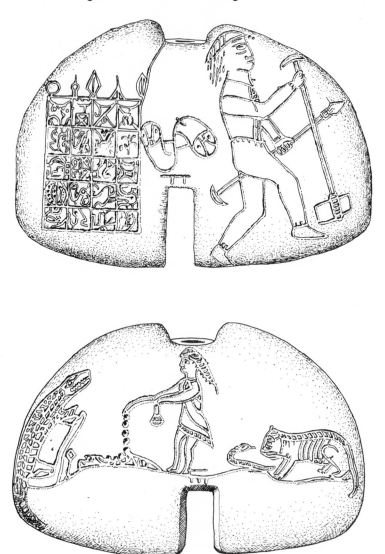

Wilmington, Ohio Tablet (Nos. 3 and 4)

mooted question is also settled, that of the manner of fastening the spear and axe upon their handles; and another important matter is set at rest certainly beyond all doubt, and that is that the so called Indian–battle axe is not of Indian origin, but belongs to a people who evinced a skill in the formation of implements devoted to warfare or the chase, far in advance of the red man, who only made use of the labor of other hands. The next thing in order is the costume, of which but little need be said, for all can see it and study it; but we are greatly of the opinion that it is conclusive evidence that the wearer thereof was an inhabitant of a warm climate. As to the central figure, we can say but little; but as it suggests to us the union of two bodies might it not be typical of marriage?

In the square or tablet upon the left wing of the butterfly is the center of interest, to us at least. And of this what can we say? What mean those mysterious angles, curves, circles and squares? How much of history is hidden in these strangely wrought figures; how much that science has sought for, and how much of the origin, the habits, the life, language, and possibly the destiny of the people who are only known to us as the Mound Builders.

In Plate No. 4 we have a representation of the reverse of Plate No. 3, and in it we find the most difficult part of our task. So much is suggested by the figures here represented. Of what is the scene here given emblematic? Does it represent an act of worship, propitiation, or is it sepulchral in its significance? The animals here represented have all been, at some time, objects of worship to a people that have not yet entirely passed away. As slabs of mica are almost invariably found in connection with human remains in ancient mounds, may not the object in front of the recumbent figure be a mica mirror? As to the reptile in the rear of the female figure we need say but little. It is plainly a rattlesnake, one of the species now known as the Crotalus horridus, and

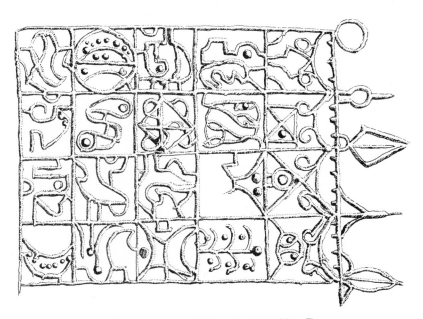

Wilmington, Ohio, Tablet (No. 5)

is in an attitude of antagonism to the animal upon the extremity of the
Plate. Here, again, we are presented with good evidence that the person represented is an inhabitant of a warm climate, as shown by the
costume, which, in ornamentation, at least, resembles the one worn by
the male figure on the obverse of the stone.

The last described relic has been named by Mr. Richardson the
"Welch Butterfly," in honor of Dr. L. B. Welch, of Wilmington, O.

Plate No. 5 is a reproduction of the tablet on the left of Plate No. 3,
enlarged two and a half diameters, for the purpose, if possible, of rendering it more legible.

We well recollect the cry of fraud that was raised against the Cincinnati Tablet when it was found, and that the circumstances connected with
the discovery of it was of such a character as to possibly throw some
discredit upon its genuineness, we do not dispute; but as to the circumstances attending the discovery of the relics herein described, we are
free to say that no chance for doubt exists, and having enjoyed a privilege no others ever have, that of seeing the Richardson Tablet and the
Cincinnati Tablet (through the kindness of Dr. H. H. Hill, of Cincinnati)
placed side by side, we do most unequivocally pronounce the Cincinnati
Tablet genuine. Farther: we do unhesitatingly say that in these tablets
we have the fact well established that pre-historic man, upon this continent, possessed a written language; not a pictorial language, but a
language composed of different and distinct characters, well and plainly
written.

. . . .

NEW JERSEY ALPHABETICAL STONES
Anonymous; *American Antiquarian*, 1:178, 1879.

In the last number of the Antiquarian (page 107) the editor has alluded
to a recent find of alphabetical stones. In digging a post-hole near Woods-
town, N.J., forty-six flat, elliptical or circular, water-worn pebbles,

Some of the characters on the
New Jersey alphabetical stones

about the size of a silver half-dollar, were unearthed some twenty inches
below the surface. On each side, near the center, is a small circular depression or ring which resembles the commencement of a perforation,
and seems to have been made with a hollow reed. On one side of each
pebble a character has been scratched or "pecked," which bears a greater resemblance to an alphabetical symbol than anything of the kind yet
discovered in the U.S. Of the forty-six characters, but three are duplicated. Whether these stones are authentic aboriginal productions, can
only be determined by a careful investigation, although the large number
would seem to point to their genuineness. The annexed cut will convey
some idea of nine of the most characteristic. In a future number of the
magazine, their authenticity will be discussed. Mr. Wm. S. Vaux, of
Philadelphia, who is in possession of them, believes them to be of Indian
workmanship, and, indeed, they have every appearance of considerable
antiquity; but, if such is the case, it is impossible, at present, to decide whether the characters possess any significance or whether they
are simply unmeaning devices. Collectively they resemble no known alphabet, though some few of them are almost identical with ancient Greek,
Phoenician and Cypriote characters.

ENIGMAS IN LEAD
Burridge, Gaston; *Pursuit,* 4:17-18, 1971.

One of the fascinating riddles of our great Southwest has several names---
"The Tucson Artefacts", "Lead Crosses", "Arizona Romans". It all began
along the Silverbell Road northwest of Tucson, Arizona, on the 13th September,
1924, when Mr. Charles E. Manier discovered the first relic by accident.
The mystery of their origin continues to patina these items with ever increasingly colorful words---from plain "hoax" to romantic "adventures of 800 A.D."
---and little has been done to scrape away this patina and learn the truth.
Could a band of late Roman adventurers possibly have managed to get into
Arizona so early? Present academicians in archaeology look askance at the
entire idea, while laymen tend to emphasize the positive and neglect the negative, both of which exist.

More than 30 relics have been unearthed, and there may well be others
still buried. One large cross weighed 62 pounds.* There were other crosses,
spears, spearhead, batons, daggers, sword-like weapons---and a "something" which looked rather like a giant pancake turner but is far too thick.
Other objects bear serpent-like appendages wound around them. Many items
are inscribed with letters, words, and graphic symbols. These words and
symbols have been deciphered and yield comprehensible messages. It is
from these that the dates 560 A.D. to 800 A.D. are derived.

---

*The crosses vary in size: the largest is 18 inches long, its cross arms 12
inches overall. The face is 4 inches wide and 2 inches thick; the smallest
8-5/8 inches long, its cross arm 8-1/4 inches, its face width 2-1/4 inches,
but only 7/16 inch thick (this was very poorly cast).

One 'item' proves intriguing and seems important. It rests with the word caliche (ka-le-cha). What is caliche and why is it important here?

Caliche exists in most desert soils. It "grows" as a result of water action and reaction with certain chemicals in the soil---calcium carbonate in particular. Caliche gathers as a hard, crust-like sheet or layer at varying depths in desert soils, generally at that place where surface water stops descending for lack of reinforcement from above. In dry years a layer of caliche builds close to the surface. In wet years the stratum forms much lower. There are often several layers, one above the other. Caliche also accumulates around buried metal objects and builds a tough, hard deposit of uneven thickness around them. Photographs taken immediately after some of these artefacts were exhumed show heavy deposits of caliche. Others of the relics were recovered from between layers of caliche. Photographs of the site itself indicate several strata were below the five-foot surface level. This seems to indicate a wide range of rainfall and the passage of a great deal of time, and thus suggests that the artefacts are very old indeed.

The first Tucson Artefact was discovered by accident on land belonging to Mr. Thomas Bent, an attorney of Tucson, but not by him. He retains the entire collection of artefacts, and has also kept careful records of each "dig", recording the date, who was present, what conditions were encountered while the digging took place. Further, Mr. Bent had made a careful photographic record of each item as it was dug out. The negatives are still in his possession. Bent has never tried to commercialize any of the finds. He has sought only to further a scientific investigation of these pieces. Now 73 years old and in ill health, Bent is no longer actively attempting to foster general interest in and investigation of the riddle.

Some prominent archaeologists and mine engineers were present at the site during several digs. They included Drs. Frank Fowler, Byron Cummings Andrew E. Douglass, Neil Judd, and Charles Vorhies.

The artefacts themselves are case of lead---some of the crosses in two halves riveted together. This metal resembles that which is present in ores found in the area now. The relics showed no radioactivity when unearthed, indicating that they had been buried for a considerable time; but no really accurate method of determining age was known in 1924-25. The objects were not found in a cache but well distributed over an area of 80 by 100 feet. They were located from three to six feet below the surface. This would seem to rule out the possibility that they had been "planted". It has been pointed out that the inscriptions incised upon some of the relics contain words and idioms which did not come into general Latin usage until much later than the indicated 800 A.D. This is one of the factors some authorities cite as a basis for the claim that this is a hoax.

In 1964 Mr. Bent published a 400-page monograph covering all the then known facts about the relics. It is detailed and complete but was published in a very limited edition, and all copies have been distributed, being given to those institutions and individuals Mr. Bent felt would be most likely to further genuine scientific study to determine the true nature of the entire matter.

INTERESTING HEBREW RELIC

Anonymous; *Scientific American*, 7:131, 1852.

By the politeness of Col. Lea, Commissioner of Indian affairs, we have seen a curiosity of great rarity and interest, left for a few days at the Bureau. It was brought from the Pottawatomie Reservation, on the Kansas river, by Dr. Lykins, who has been residing there nearly twenty years of the thirty he has spent on the frontier. It consists of four small rolls or strips of parchment, closely packed in the small compartments of a little box or locket of about an inch cubical content. On these parchments are written in a style of unsurpassed excellence, and far more beautiful than print, portions of the Pentateuch, to be worn as frontlets, and intended as stimulants to the memory and moral sense.

Dr. Lykins obtained it from Pategwe, a Pottawatomie, who got it from his grandmother, a very old woman. It has been in this particular family about fifty years. They had originally two of them, but on one occasion, as the party in possession were crossing a rapid in some river in the lake country of the North, the other was irrecoverably lost. The one lost was believed by the Indians to contain an account of the creation of the world. That brought by Dr. Lykins has been kept for a very long period in the medicine bag of the tribe, used as a charm, and never allowed to suffer any exposure, until, by strong entreaty and the great influence he had with Topinepee, the principal Pottawatomie chief, he was permitted to bring it on to Washington, but under a firm pledge to restore it on his return.

It has hitherto been most carefully kept from the rapacious vision of the white man. Pategwe had it in his possession many years before his curiosity prompted him to cut the stitches of the cover and disclose the contents. But this coming to the knowledge of old Billy Caldwell, chief of the Council Bluff branch of the tribe, he strenuously advised Pategwe to shut it up and keep it close, and say nothing about having it. Dr. Lykins came to a knowledge of the circumstance of its possession from a half breed.

The wonder is how this singular article came into their possession. When asked how long they can trace back its history, they reply they cannot tell the time when they had it not. The question occurs here, does not this circumstance give some color to the idea, long and extensively entertained, that the Indians of our continent are more or less Jewish in their origin?

[There is some hocus-pocus about this piece of parchment which has apparently a near relationship to the woolly horse---at least that is our view of the subject. The Indians have not a single Jewish trait about them.]

THE KEKIP-SESOATORS, OR ANCIENT SACRIFICIAL STONE, OF THE NORTH-WEST TRIBES OF CANADA

L'Heureux, Jean; *Anthropological Institute, Journal*, 15:161-165, 1885.

Ethnological studies, tradition, language, and architectural remains furnish data by which to trace the migration of ancient peoples. It is now an established fact, admitted by the most eminent ethnologists of America, that the Hue-hue Tlapalan, or the primitive habitation of the ancient Toltecs, was situated in the Far West, and that the whole of the Nahua tribes were one of the primitive races that peopled the north-west at a remote period.

It is not improbable that the Nahuas of old, while few in number, arrived at our north-western coast, where they found a home until they became a tribe of considerable proportion. Thousands of their newly explored tumuli in Oregon and British Columbia speak more of permanent sojourn than of a migratory residence. Crossing the watershed between the sources of the Columbia and Missouri rivers, a large portion of the tribe found its way to the Mississippi and Ohio valleys, where, under the name of Mound-building people, they laid the foundation of a widespread empire. The remainder of the Nahuas, instead of crossing the mountains, migrated southward into Utah, establishing a civilisation, the remains of which are seen all over the San Juan valley in the cliff-dwellers which abound in that region.

An ancient site of the western branch of the Mound-builders appears to have been the head-waters of Missouri river, whence they spread themselves north as far as the South Saskatchewan and its tributaries, establishing numerous colonies all alont the eastern base of the mountains and away south to the headwaters of Rio Grande, by the south pass of the Rockies.

The scattered remains of Mound-builders' works in the north-west territory are connected by a similar chain of works at James river, in Northern Dakota, with the great artery of the Missouri mounds, and show more of a migratory movement than of a fixed residence.

The most important of these ancient relics of the past are principally found in the Alberta district, close to the international boundaries, amongst which the more northern works are the defence works of Blackfoot Crossing, the ruins at the Canantzi vollage, the Onacina pictured rocks, the graded mound of the third Napa on Bow river, the tumuli of Red-Deer river, the walled city of the dead in the inland Lake of Big Sandy Hill on the South Saskatchewan, and the Sesoators or sacrificial stones of the country, to describe one of which is the object of the present paper.

The recorded traditions of the ancient civilised nations of the Pacific States corroborated to some extent the tradition of the Indian tribes of the north-west. The Kamuco of the Quiche mourn over a portion of their people whom they left in Northern Tullan. The Papol-Vuh, speaking of the cultus of the morning star amongst the ancient Toltecs or Nahuas, states that they were drawing blood from their own bodies and offering it to their stone god Tohil, whose worship they first receive when inhabiting the north. The Napas tradition says that, "In the third sun (Natose) of the age of the earth, in the days of the Bull of the Nile, the third Napa of the Chokitapia, or the plain people, when returning from the great river of the south, caused to be erected in the sacred land of the Napas (Alberta district), upon certain high hills of the country, seven sesoators or sacrificial stones for religious services amongst his people."

The religious idea in man, whether observed in the darkest heathenism or partially enlightened civilisation, has always associated a place of worship with condition of elevation and isolation. These high places of worship of the Napa's tradition were the ever-open sanctuaries of a migratory people, at whose shrines the worshipper was himself first victim and sacrifice in the rites, and point to the belief of an early age, not entirely forgotten by the remnant of the race whose remains of ancient works seem to sustain the claim of our Indian traditional lore.

A constant tradition of the Chokitapia or Blackfeet Indians, a powerful tribe of remote Nahua parentage, inhabiting at the present day the southern part of the north-west territory of the Dominion of Canada, has always pointed to a high hill situated on the south side of Red-Deer river, opposite to Hand Hill, two miles east of the Broken-knife ridge, as the site of one of those ancient cities of the bygone days of the primitive race.

Elevated 200 feet above the level of the surrounding plain, Kekip-kip Sesoators, "the hill of the Blood Sacrifice," stands like a huge pyramidal mound commanding an extensive view of both Red-Deer and Bow river valleys. A natural platform of about 100 feet crowns its lofty conical summit. At the north end of this platform, resting upon the soil, is the Sesoators, a rough boulder of fine grained quartzose rock, hemispherical in form, and hewn horizontally at the bottom, measuring 15 inches high and about 14 in diameter. Upon its surface is sculptured, half-an-inch deep, the crescent figure of the moon, with a shining star over it. Two small concave basins about 2 inches in diameter are hollowed into the stone, one in the centre of the star-like figure, the other about 7 inches farther in a straight line with the star figure. Around them are traced strange hieroglyphic signs, bearing some likeness to the hieroglyphs of the Davenport tablet and the Copan altar. Interwoven all over are numerous small circlets, which remind one of the sacrificial stone of Mexico.

. . . .

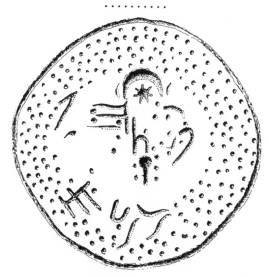

The Kekip-Sesoators, or ancient sacrifical stone of the Northwest tribes

RUNIC PARK IN OKLAHOMA!!!!!

Anonymous; *INFO Journal*, 2:34, 1969.

On Poteau Mountain, near Heavener, Okla., stands a 12 foot high stone with a runic inscription:

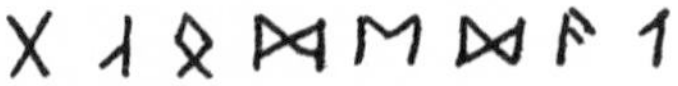

This appears to be read as "Gnomedal." A gnome is of course a goblin or diminutive earth-dweller, and dal means valley. The inscription may mean valley of the gnomes.

The story goes that there were many other runestones formerly, but they were dynamited by treasure hunters in the 1920s. It is interesting to note that "poteau" in French means "post" or "stake."

The Oklahoma legislature has now voted money to make the area with the Heavener rune stone a state park.

NO STONES UNTURNED: DIFFERING VIEWS OF OKLAHOMA'S RUNESTONES

Wyckoff, Don G.; *Popular Archaeology*, 2:16-31, no. 12, 1973.

Persons touring eastern Oklahoma sooner or later have their attention drawn to visiting the Clem Hamilton State Park in the scenic northern fringe of the Ouachita Mountains. A drive to this location rewards the visitor with picturesque views of lush, green valleys and forested mountains. However, the park's main focus of attention is a large, upturned slab of sandstone. On this slab are pecked eight symbols. A pamphlet available from the visitor's center proclaims, "The Vikings were here....It could have happened like this...." Perusal of the pamphlet reveals that the symbols are from runic alphabets commonly associated with northern Europe some 700 to 1600 years ago. Further reading indicates the belief that the runic letters were pecked by Viking explorers some 900 years ago. Given this intriguing, historical background, the park visitor views the upright stone and idyllic setting with more than casual appreciation. In fact, it is possible to leave this scene believing that one has learned a very important bit of information: namely that this country was visited and explored by Europeans almost 500 years before the well-publicized, Columbus discovery.

Viewers of the upright stone and peaceful park surroundings are generally lulled into accepting the presentation as substantiated fact. After all, doesn't the pamphlet mention other runestones for eastern Oklahoma? Isn't there a great deal of local interest and pride in the park? Hasn't the state spent considerable sums of money developing the park? The answers to these questions are yes. However, it is unfortunate that most park visitors are not made aware of the serious controversy regarding the authenticity and origins of this and other comparably marked stones reported in Oklahoma.

Both sides of the runestone controversy have not been, nor are being, presented to the public at the Hamilton State Park. Consequently, there is a deep concern that a potentially distorted image of Oklahoma's history and prehistory is being fostered and perpetuated. With regard to interpreting a Viking incursion into Oklahoma the image may not only be distorted; it may be entirely a mirage. There are serious questions regarding the validity of attributing the runic markings to pre-Columbian, Viking explorers. Such questions involve the basic data, the interpretive logic, and the resulting interpretations of those propounding an 11th century, Viking origin for the runic markings. The questioning and concern is being expressed by both professional archaeologists and historians who have dedicated their careers to studying, teaching, and writing about man's past and accomplishments in Oklahoma.

Viking Explorations of North America. There is no doubt that there were Viking explorations of North America some 450 years before the Columbus voyage. Such explorations were a part of, and cannot be divorced from, the general westward settlement of Iceland and Greenland between A. D. 800 and 1000. For those desiring detailed accounts of Viking history, these excellent summaries can be recommended: A History of the Vikings, by Gwyn Jones (Oxford University Press, 1968); The Norsemen, by Eric Oxenstierna (Studio Vista, 1965); and The Viking Achievement, by P. G. Foote and D. M. Wilson (Praeger, 1970).

As a brief background, Norse people seeking land for farms and pastures explored the Iceland coast and settled the favorable areas before A. D. 900. By the late 900's, all of Iceland's arable coastlands were claimed, subdivided, and settled. In about A. D. 982, a Norseman, Eirik the Red, was banished from Iceland for manslaughter. Eirik set sail west to eventually find and explore what is now southern and western Greenland. Finding habitable coastal regions abounding with game and no people, Eirik returned to Iceland just at a time when that island's settlements were experiencing a drastic famine. Without much trouble Eirik was able to get a following of people desiring land and better conditions to go with him and colonize Greenland. He left Iceland in A. D. 986 with some 25 ships; it is believed some 14 ships arrived safely. Jones estimates the initial Greenland colony to have consisted of some 450 people. Eventually two areas of western and southern Greenland were settled. As its florescence the Greenland colony had some 3,000 people. The settlements existed between A. D. 1000 and 1400, and, though viable, they depended greatly on trade with Norway for such basics as timber, iron, and barley.

Between A. D. 1200 and 1400, all northern land masses began experiencing increasingly cooler climates. Greenland began having trouble with ice blocking the shore and potential ports. As a result, contact with Norway became increasingly difficult and irregular. During this same time, the Greenland settlements began having trouble with Eskimo people, resulting in some abandoning their farmsteads and leaving for Iceland when possible. People continued to live in Greenland after 1400, but the colony died out, apparently tragically, by 1500.

The Viking exploration of North America was actually undertaken by people from Greenland. There was even a brief colonization attempt by some of these Greenlanders. Our knowledge of these trips and the respective leaders stems primarily from studies of several Icelandic sagas, roughly contemporary literary accounts written in a rather romantic and poetic style.

Knowledge of land lying west of Greenland came about through accident. In A.D. 986, a ship, blown off course, sighted but did not land at a forested coast west of Greenland. It was not until around A.D. 1000 that Leif, son of Eirik, embarked northward and then westward and recorded landings at what are believed to be locales in southern Baffin Island and coasts of Labrador and Newfoundland. A few years later, Leif's brother, Thornvald, also tried to explore portions of the coastal land to the west of Greenland. Thornvald's party encountered Indians, and in the resulting skirmish Thornvald was killed by an arrow.

The single colonization effort in Vinland (as the land west of Greenland was sometimes called) was undertaken around A.D. 1020. Thorfinn Karlsefni and a group of Greenland colonists attempted to settle a coastal region. Most scholars believe this settlement took place somewhere in the Labrador-Newfoundland region. However, Frederick Pohl has continually argued the settlement to be much further south, perhaps as ar south as Virginia. Wherever situated these Greenland colonists stuck it out for three winters. But dissension within the group; inadequate support from Greenland, Iceland, and Norway; and increasing difficulties with Indian peoples caused Karlsefni and the survivors to abandon the location and return to Greenland.

After the Karlsefni colony, Vinland was a land visited only occasionally. There is, however, some data indicating ships from Greenland sporadically came for timber and furs. The last recorded visit was in A.D. 1347 when the Icelandic Annals report that a Greenland vessel returning from the western land was blown off its Greenland course and forced to land in Iceland (Jones, p. 306).

There is much supportive evidence for the above historical sketch. Extensive archaeological work has been undertaken at the early settlements in both Iceland and Greenland. Fortunately, the excavators did not have to rely solely on the testimony of the spade. Scholars of many aspects of Scandinavian history were able to study sagas, other historical documents, and even maps and thus provide a framework of knowledge to which the archaeological pieces might be compared and fitted. This has been done with considerable success.

Undoubtedly of utmost significance to the question of Vikings and North America are the findings of a pre-Columbian, Norse settlement on the north coast of Newfoundland. The field work of H. Ingstad and his teams of specialists has provided exciting evidence for what is probably the location where Leif, son of Eirik, established a temporary camp and where, later, Karlsefni and the Greenland colonists settled for three years (see Westward to Vinland, by H. Ingstad; St. Martin's Press, 1969). It should be noted, however, that Ingstad's findings did not result from chance. Years were spent accumulating pertinent data from original Icelandic and Norse accounts. They then applied this knowledge by personally examining mile after mile of coastline settings from Rhode Island north to Labrador. In essence, they continually used pertinent data from the historical background of Norse westward expansion to define and delimit the possibilities.

Runestones, Vikings, and Oklahoma. Against the historical backdrop of Norse westward explorations and settlement have been placed many claims for Viking incursions into the interior of Canada and the United States. From Maine to Tennessee to Minnesota have been reported finds of metal objects or stones with runic markings. Such finds have usually consisted of single objects for which the contexts and authenticity were questionable at best. When such objects have been analyzed by those trained in Scandinavian history, runic translation, and archaeology, the consistent conclusions have been that the objects were "plants", recently made copies, or not of Norse origin. In spite of these studied conclusions, certain such finds have always had a few staunch and vocal supporters (typically of Scandinavian descent) who beat the drums and claim these finds as evidence for Norse exploring parties ranging throughout the continental United States. By and large, many people grow to like these claims. There is a lure about the stories of stalwart Viking men coasting along the Mississippi in their sturdy dragon ships. Also, such claims and stories are a lot more interesting and fulfilling than the qualified answers and scoffing remarks given by scholars.

The proponents for Vikings exploring the interior of this continent content the Norse groups travelled south along the Atlantic coast, west along the Gulf coast, and up the Mississippi and its several tributaries. In support of this contention, these proponents refer to runic inscriptions and to scenes found on stones in Maine, Massachusetts, Rhode Island, Texas, Arkansas, and Oklahoma. The inscriptions are generally being attributed to Viking visits dating between A. D. 1000 and 1400.

The immediate concern of this paper is the series of runestones reported for Oklahoma. As a professional archaeologist hired by the state, I do have an obvious and direct interest in any material evidence pertaining to man's past (prehistoric and historic) activities in Oklahoma. After all, this is the subject matter of my profession (at least as it's defined in Webster's Dictionary). This point bears some emphasis, particularly since some concerned individuals have reportedly mentioned that the runestones were not really within the realm of archaeological study. The runestones are the material evidence of past human activity, and that is archaeology's field.

At this point it should be noted that no archaeological excavations have yet been conducted at or near the locations where any of the runestones are situated. Oklahoma has had an infant, state-supported program of archaeology. For five years this state program has had sufficient funds to conduct only limited salvage work at key sites threatened with imminent destruction. A properly planned, field program has not been financially possible at any of the reported runestone sites.

Basic Data About Oklahoma's Runestones. Controversies typically involve differing interpretations of some form of basic, observable data. Oklahoma's runestone controversy is no exception. In this instance, the basic data consists of seven stones which bear inscriptions in runic or runic-like symbols. The reported seven stones include three near Heavener, one from Poteau, one near Tulsa, one near Shawnee, and one near Krebs. These locations are shown on page 21. One of those near Heavener is the upright stone previously mentioned in the Hamilton State Park. The stones from Poteau and Shawnee have been donated to the Eastern Oklahoma Historical Society and are currently on display at the Kerr Foundation Museum near Poteau. The Tulsa, Krebs, and one of the Heavener stones are on private property and are not generally available for public viewing. The remaining Heavener stone has been moved for safekeeping.

All of the inscribed stones are of lithic materials common to the locales in which each stone was found. There is no evidence that the

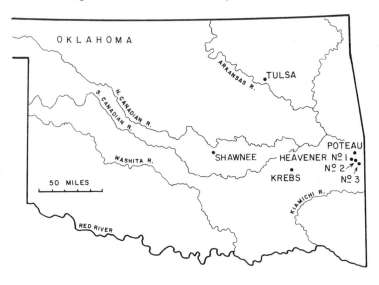

Locations of some Oklahoma "runestones"

stones have been transported from some geologically different region. Generally, various formations of sandstone are represented, each having different physical properties regarding composition, hardness, color, weathering characteristics, etc.

The runic and runic-like inscriptions on these seven stones do vary in number and arrangement of characters, sizes of characters, and in the methods by which the characters were produced. The number and general arrangement of characters has been reproduced above. Other pertinent details (gathered from personal inspection, from Survey photographs, and from publications of G. Farley and O. G. Landsverk) are tabulated below:

Stone	No. of Char.	Approx. Ht. of Char.	Method of Inscribing
Heavener No. 1	8	6-7 inches	Pecking
Heavener No. 2	2	2 and 12 inches	Pecking
Heavener No. 3	3	6-9 inches	Chiseled (abraded?)
Poteau	8	2 inches	Chiseled
Tulsa	7	6 inches	Abraded
Shawnee	5	2 inches	Abraded
Krebs	Data not yet made public		

The above noted, observable details about Oklahoma's runestones cannot be dismissed. The stones and inscriptions can be seen and touched. They constitute the "cold, hard facts." Any further statements about the stones and their inscriptions represent interpretation, and interpretation consists of judging and explaining physical evidence on the basis of previously gained and currently available knowledge. Thus, interpretation is always a very personal action which involves the individual's background (training in that particular study), motivation, and interests.

It is at the interpretive level that the Oklahoma runestones achieve the status of a controversy. The main disagreements involve the ages and origins of the inscriptions. One group of persons interprets the inscriptions to have been carved by members of a Norse exploration party some 900 years ago. With a drastically different interpretation are those persons who believe the runic inscriptions to have been made within the past 100 years, some within the past 10 years, and thus none provide acceptable evidence for Viking explorations in Oklahoma. Given these two positions, there is no room for compromise.

One Archaeologist's Evaluation of Oklahoma's Runestones. In the remaining paragraphs, I should like to present my evaluation of Oklahoma's runestones. I have personally viewed and inspected the Heavener No. 1, Heavener No. 2, Poteau, and Shawnee stones and have had conversations with those familiar with the other stones and their settings. To supplement this personal gathering of data, I have read nearly all the voluminous literature, pro and con, written about Oklahoma's runestones and their interpretation. Such reading has also necessitated becoming familiar with presentations and evaluations of runestone findings from other states as well. Finally, I have discussed at length my impressions and questions about the inscriptions with the proponents of a pre-Columbian, Viking origin for the Oklahoma inscriptions.

Inspection and study of the Oklahoma runestones has led the proponents of their Viking origin to these deductions (see: <u>Norse Medieval Cryptography in Runic Carvings</u>, by A. Monge, and O. G. Landsverk, Norseman Press, 1969; <u>The Vikings Were Here</u>, by G. Farley, private printing, 1970):

1. The inscriptions are carved into hard sandstone rocks and are old. The earliest living viewer of the Heavener No. 1 inscription reported seeing it in 1898, but there are traditions among descendants of Choctaw settlers that it was present in the 1830's. The Heavener No. 2 and No. 3 stones were viewed as early as 1904 and 1914, respectively. On the basis of these reported sightings, the inscriptions cannot be considered of recent manufacture.

2. The inscriptions are in runic alphabets and were made by persons familiar with such alphabets.

3. The inscriptions contain symbols from two different runic alphabets: a) an "Old Norse" alphabet of 24 runes generally in use from A. D. 500 to about A. D. 1000; b) an alphabet of 16 runes in use in Norway and Sweden after A. D. 900.

4. When translated into English letters and letter sequence, the inscriptions made little to no sense.

5. Through use of cryptography, the study of writing in secret characters, it was claimed the inscriptions were actually dates given in a code based on a perpetual calendar used by early Norse churches.

6. The dates interpreted through code for the Oklahoma inscriptions are:

a.	Heavener No. 1	November 11, 1012
b.	Heavener No. 2	December 25, 1015
c.	Heavener No. 3	December 30, 1022
d.	Poteau	November 11, 1017

e. Tulsa	December 22, 1022
f. Shawnee	November 24, 1024
g. Krebs	No date derived as yet

On the basis of the above series of inductions and deductions, the Viking proponents summarize the Oklahoma inscriptions as authentic runes made during the early 11th century. Moreover, they are convinced the inscriptions were made by a single monk or priestly member of a Norse expedition which reached Oklahoma by sailing up the Mississippi and Arkansas rivers.

Are All the Inscriptions Runic? I question the claim that all seven inscriptions are in runic characters. The Heavener No. 2 and No. 3 inscriptions occur in arrangement and format completely different from the five inscriptions which are in runic symbols. If all seven inscriptions were the work of one runemaster, as is claimed, it is rather strange that he would so drastically alter his usual format.

My main objection to considering the Heavener No. 2 and No. 3 inscriptions as runic is because all the characters on these two stones have long been demonstrated to be part of prehistoric and early historic Indian symbolism. I believe the symbols and their arrangement to be directly comparable to practices of Indian people. The symbols and their arrangement to be directly comparable to practices of Indian people. The symbols found on these two stones include the turkey-track, two intersecting lines (×), and a stylized arrow. Generally, such symbols are associated with indigenous Indian cultures dating from around 500 B.C. to the A.D. 1800's (see: Sun Circles and Human Hands, by E. Fundabark and M. Formen, Paragon Press, 1957). Thus these symbols are a part of several regional, native art traditions that well predate the Viking era. Could it be that the Vikings borrowed some of their runic symbols from North American Indian cultures?

Monge and Landsverk (in Norse Medieval Cryptography in Runic Carvings) assert these two inscriptions contain hidden calendrical dates. For this reason, they believe the stones should be considered as authen-

STONE	CHARACTERS AND ARRANGEMENT
HEAVENER Nº 1	X ⌐ ⋛ ⋈ M ⋈ ⊦ 1
HEAVENER Nº 2	Y +
HEAVENER Nº 3	⋎ ⤳ ×
POTEAU	X ⌐ ⋚ I M ⊦ ⊦ ⧝
TULSA	X ⊥ ⊤ Y ⟨ ⊦ ⊥
SHAWNEE	⋈ ⋀ ⋈ ⋛ ⟨
KREBS	NO PUBLISHED DATA AVAILABLE

tic runestones. Their assertions and belief stems from results they obtained when they applied cryptologic studies to the inscriptions. Their cryptological approach and its results will be discussed further below.

Are All the Inscriptions Old? The Viking proponents claim that all the inscriptions are old and date to the 11th century. In support of this claim they cite early views reported for some of the stones, geological knowledge (hardness, weathering, etc.) about the stones, and the cryptologically derived calendrical dates hidden within the inscriptions. But is the evidence sufficient to substantiate the ages being attributed to each inscription? I contend it is not and that, in fact, several of the inscriptions are of very recent manufacture.

Geology is not able to tell us exactly when the inscriptions were cut. But certain geological principles can add a perspective about relative ages for the inscriptions. For instance, the Heavener No. 2 and No. 3 inscriptions are on stones of comparable composition and hardness, and the inscriptions appear equally weathered. On the basis of these observations a justifiable deduction is that the inscriptions are of comparable age. That they relate to prehistoric times seems quite acceptable, particularly since the motifs relate to a context of prehistoric Indian symbolism found in this region and elsewhere.

In direct contrast is the situation regarding the Heavener No. 1 and Poteau stones and their respective inscriptions. Both stones are of the same lithic formation, a very hard (7 on Mohs scale) cemented sandstone. If we accept the cryptologically derived dates for these two inscriptions, we must recognize they were cut five years apart in a period over 950 years ago. If the two inscriptions were cut in the same stone material some 950 years ago, then the two inscriptions should be comparably worn and discolored whether buried in the ground or exposed to the elements. My study of these two stones clearly indicates their inscriptions are not comparably weathered. The Heavener No. 1 characters are discolored and somewhat worn. The characters on the Poteau stone are remarkably fresh. The inscriptions on both stones have been thoroughly cleaned, and the observed differences do not result from such cleaning.

The runes of the Poteau inscription show sharp lateral edges while their bottoms display sharp, high ridges resulting from each jump the metal tool (slightly larger diameter than a nail punch) made while being hammered. Some of the runic characters also exhibit scars where the cutting accidentally broke away areas of the natural surface; these accidental scars are sharp and unworn. Finally, the surfaces within the characters show the tan-brown color of the stone's interior and have not discolored, due to weathering, to the stone's exterior surface color. All of the above physical attributes are evident on the Poteau inscription and not on the Heavener No. 1 inscription. The two inscriptions cannot be even roughly contemporary. The attributes of the Poteau inscription indicate to me that it was cut very recently, probably within the past ten years and probably by someone who had seen the Heavener No. 1 inscription.

The Shawnee inscription is also of undoubted recent origin. This inscription occurs on a small tabular block of the red, Permian sandstone which is so sommon to central and western Oklahoma. Such sandstone is relatively soft (from 2 to 4 on Mohs scale), and some varieties can be inscribed with sharpened sticks while others require a pocketknife.

This sandstone is not well cemented and weathers very easily. The

Shawnee stone was purportedly found eroding out near a stream in 1967. The Shawnee inscription is supposed to date, through cryptology, to almost 950 years ago. However, the inscription is, again, remarkably fresh and certainly not as worn or weathered as the stone's natural surface. The Survey staff has viewed other exposures of this Permian sandstone which have carved dates of as late as 1957 that are more worn and weathered than the Shawnee inscription. It has been stated that the fresh appearance of this inscription is due to the characters having been cleaned out with a metal tool when found. However, I fail to see potentially recent striations that overlie the original cutting of the characters. From my perspective the Shawnee inscription appears fresh enough to have been cut within the past ten years.

The Tulsa stone has an inscription which appears fairly weathered. There is little way to establish a relative or exact age however. The Viking proponents have been informed by a Tulsa man, who grew up in the immediate vicinity, that the inscription was not present in the late 1920's when he was a boy. His observation has been disregarded on the grounds that the inscription contains good runic symbols and because the cryptologist has been able to derive a hidden date comparable to those of the other inscriptions.

In summary, physical evidence exhibited by the Poteau and Shawnee inscriptions is inconsistent with claims that these two runestones are over 950 years old. These two stones are also divergent from Heavener No. 1 and Tulsa in that the stones themselves are small and portable and the characters are considerably smaller. All in all, the internal inconsistencies indicate the Poteau and Shawnee inscriptions are not a part of the inscription series represented by the relatively older Heavener No. 1 and Tulsa inscriptions. In stating that the Poteau and Shawnee inscriptions are undoubtedly of very recent origin, there is no intent to condemn the stones' finders. There is no reason to doubt statements by the finders regarding circumstances of the finds. These people are simply the innocent individuals who happen to find what others, intent on fooling the experts, had left to be found.

· · · · · · · · · ·

Supportive Evidence for Viking Incursions into North America. Individuals claiming authenticity for Oklahoma's runestones have continually referred to Norse finds made elsewhere in the United States. The Kensington runestone in Minnesota is held in special reverence; it, too, holds crypto-puzzles and dates that prove its antiquity. Also of some importance are runestones reported for Massachusetts, Rhode Island, and, most recently, Maine. Other finds cited for their significance are series of mooring stones in Minnesota and various Norse artifacts reported from such varied areas as Minnesota, Wisconsin, Michigan, North Dakota, and Tennessee.

None of the above finds have yet been validated as authentic by persons trained in pertinent areas of historical or archaeological research. In general, research on these finds has consistently concluded that they fall in one of the following categories: 1) a mistaken identification; 2) an authentic artifact but recently introduced or, "planted", in a contrived context; or 3) outright hoaxes. Yet, it never ceases to amaze how such things as the Kensington stone and the Newport Tower got resurrected as hard evidence about Vikings in North America. The extensive, thorough studies by E. Wahlgren (The Kensington Stone, A Mystery Solved; University of Wisconsin Press; 1958) and T. C. Blegan (The Kensington Stone, New Light on an Old Riddle; Minnesota Historical Society; 1968) performed the final rites for the late 19th century construction, the Kensington runestone. Likewise, the Newport Tower, a rock structure with a runic marking in Rhode Island, was found through archaeological investigation to have been built in the 17th century (W. S. Godfrey, American Antiquity, Vol. 17, 1951). And now, the widely acclaimed runestones from Popham Beach, Maine, have been thoroughly studied by the respected Harvard scholar, Dr. E. Haugen, who concludes the stones are a recent forgery ("The Rune Stones of Spirit Pond, Maine", Man in the Northeast; Vol. 4; 1972).

In summary, the so-called Viking finds from elsewhere in the United States are anything but authenticated. None have been verified by persons recognized for their training in pertinent areas of study. That such finds should be claimed as supportive evidence for Viking incursions into Oklahoma is baseless and irresponsible.

Archaeological Studies in Oklahoma and Arkansas. Since the 1930's, both Oklahoma and Arkansas have been the scenes of numerous archaeological surveys, test programs, and site excavations. If 11th century Norsemen were in this region for 12 years it seems odd that 35 years of archaeological research has failed to find any signs of their presence. In Oklahoma alone, there are over 1,000 reported archaeological sites within 100 miles north, south, and west of the Heavener No. 1 runestone. There are almost 200 sites known along the Arkansas and Poteau rivers and along Fourche Maline Creek. Of these 200 locations, excavations have been conducted at nearly 25 sites which were occupied from roughly A.D. 1000 to A.D. 1400. As of yet, there has been no evidence recovered that could be construed as Viking relics or as Viking influences on the native Indian cultures of eastern Oklahoma.

Whether it is believed or not, it is true that archaeologists are very human, and all the professionals that I know like to receive some recognition for their research. Rest assured, if an archaeologist would uncover any reliable evidence pointing to Norse contact with native Indian peoples, he or she would see that the evidence was published and available for evaluation by all. Archaeologists have not been prone to hide or disregard evidence out of fear of being criticised.

Final Glances at the Other Sides of Oklahoma's Runestones. Certainly the occurrence in Oklahoma of stones with runic and runic-like inscriptions is sufficient to catch one's interest and attention. However, is it necessary to invoke pre-Columbian, Viking visitors as the creative source for these inscriptions? I think not.

As has been indicated, the Heavener No. 2 and No. 3 stones contain only motifs long associated with symbolism of America's native people. Three other inscriptions are certainly of recent origin: Tulsa being apparently cut in the 1930's; the Poteau and Shawnee stones appear to have been carved in the past 10 years or so.

At this point, we are left with the Heavener No. 1 stone and inscription. It is somewhat of an enigma. The symbols are discolored and relatively weathered, though perhaps not as much as one would expect given the proposed 900 years of exposure. The inscription is definitely the oldest one of the series; it was reported in a letter to Smithsonian Institution in 1923. But to whom do we attribute the inscription and when?

The Heavener No. 1 inscription contains characters from two runic alphabets. The usage of this alphabet mixture is known to have been practiced in Europe as late as the 19th century. There is no reason why the inscription could not have been cut in the 1800's by European visitors to this region. One need only recall that Ft. Smith, Arkansas, was the key military post and westernmost point of American expansion for much of the era from 1820 to 1890. Ft. Smith was visited by both European scholars and military men, people with an European educational background that would have included the study of runic alphabets. It would have been no trouble for such visitors to travel the 35 miles from Ft. Smith to the outlook at the southern end of the Poteau River valley, the site of the Heavener No. 1 stone. Even more recently, a resort operated during the 1890's just 20 miles east-southeast of Heavener and was visited by affluent, educated families from Germany and Holland, countries where runic alphabets were known. It would have made a lovely outing to ride the train, or a wagon, to Heavener and climb the prominent hill at the south end of the Poteau valley.

All in all, Oklahoma's runestones have a lure of mystery and intrigue. As a consequence much has been claimed for them and more will, undoubtedly, be forthcoming. However, as viewed by one concerned about Oklahoma's cultural heritage, prehistoric and historic, I believe our limited funds and energies would be best spent on sites and situations for which we have evidence about their significance to the state, region, and nation. In this regard, pre-Columbian Vikings had no verified role.

THE KENSINGTON STONE
Moltke, Erik; *Antiquity*, 25:87-93, 1951.

In 1898 a Swedish-American farmer, Olaf Ohman, cut down an aspen tree on his farm. He found enveloped in its roots a large flat stone which he only just managed to get out without ruining his axe. When his ten year old son had brushed some of the dirt from the stone, Ohman discovered that one of the faces and one of the edges were covered with strange engraved figures. It was soon decided that these had something to do with runes. This is where the saga of the Kensington stone begins: from Ohman's farm to a shop window in Kensington, to Prof. O. J. Breda in Minneapolis, to Prof. George O. Curme, back to Ohman's farm condemned as a blatant forgery. Here it lay despised as 'a stepping stone near his granary for eight years, without further notice'. It was 'rediscovered' by Hjalmar Holand, bought by him, and he devoted his life (three large books and innumerable articles) to attempting to prove that the inscription was genuine. Finally in its Jubilee year 1948 it was given the place of honour in the National Museum at the Smithsonian Institute in Washington as one of the finest pre-Columbian monuments of America.

American and European newspapers during the Jubilee year were full of articles about the stone, partly because two leading Scandinavian scientists had been called to America to give an opinion. They were the Swedish runologist Sven B. F. Jansson, who declared subsequently in a talk on the American radio that the stone was false, and the Danish professor of Archaeology Johs. Brondsted, who brought back an excellent copy of the inscription but otherwise left the conclusive word to the students of runes and language.

In 1910 a little book was published:---The Kensington Rune Stone: Preliminary Report to the Minnesota Historical Society by its Museum Committee. The result of the investigations by the committee was that the inscription was genuine, pre-Columbian. Nevertheless the report ends with a letter from Prof. N. H. Winchell, the philological expert on the committee. In it he is sorry that he is going away, but he says: 'I have examined your report carefully, have visited Kensington and neighbourhood, and have read most of the papers and articles relating to the rune stone. I have always agreed with the great authorities of Norway and Sweden, Magnus Olsen, Moltke, Moe, M. Hogstad (i.e. Haegstad), Bugge, Noreen, Schrick (i.e. Schuck), Montelius, in thinking that the language is too modern, besides being faulty; and a more careful study of the words has not changed my opinion'. To these outstanding names, and especially the runologists and philologists Sophus Bugge, Magnus Olsen and Adolf Noreen, may be added the names of the greatest runologists of Sweden and Denmark, Otto v. Friesen, Elias Wessen and Ludvig F. A. Wimmer. Now two younger runologists have severely questioned the authenticity of the stone, namely the present writer, and also Sven B. F. Jansson in <u>Nordisk Tidskrift</u> 1949. A couple of years before the appearance of these articles the above-mentioned journal <u>Danske Studier</u> for 1946-47 published an article on the inscription by the Danish Emeritus Prof. in the Eskimo Language, William Thalbitzer, who upholds the authenticity of the inscription. Recently a paper by S. N. Hagen has appeared in the American Journal <u>Speculum</u> (July 1950). Hagen says; 'As far as I know, no linguist or runologist has come forward with the reconsideration suggested by Einarsson [disagreeing with Holand who is deficient in certain elementary fundamentals]. While we are awaiting a study of the inscription by a competent scholar, I offer a few observations...' Hagen supports the authenticity of the inscription, for example in the following words: 'This inscription should be a perfect joy to the linguist because it is such a delightfully honest and unsophisticated record of its author's own speech. A forger would have tried to imitate a language other than his own. It is clear that this author tried to imitate no language but his own. In branding this beautiful inscription as a forgery, scholars have thrown away not only an important historical document but also a faithful record of medieval Scandinavian speech'. Finally I am acquainted with an article in the Swiss Journal <u>Atlantis</u> (Sept. 1950). It is written by one of the former supporters of the inscription, Prof. Richard Hennig, Dusseldorf, and although he knows both Jansson's and my article, he concludes his statement with the following pompous words, reminiscent of the runologists of the Hitler period: 'The authenticity of the Kensington Stone has been proved and thereby the presence of Scandinavians in America fully 130 years before Columbus is no longer in doubt.'

As far as the most recent authors are concerned, one may well say that Thalbitzer's philological arguments have been so hard hit by the specialised criticism of Jansson and Harry Andersen that they have no leg to stand on. In spite of Hennig's determined judgment he produces no new argument, but confines himself to an enumeration of all Holand's old chestnuts. As for Hagen, his article shows that he is a scholarly Scandinavist---from time to time he puts his comrade in arms, Holand, gently and kindly on the right road, when the latter displays his ignorance of the elementary rules of Old Nordic grammar. He makes a really honest attempt to confute the philological arguments against its authenticity, but his deep attachment to 'this beautiful inscription' gives its peculiar forms of speech such a wide margin as to leave the thinking reader with the impression that had the inscription been in Chinese, Hagen would have let it pass as good Latin! But more of this below.

It is striking not only to the Scandinavian scholar, but to any ordinary reader of the Kensington inscription that this living document can be very easily read when transcribed in the Latin alphabet. But this is not the impression one gets from the language of the 14th century which is somewhat incomprehensible for the ordinary Scandinavian reader. That is why Hagen looks in vain for writings by Scandinavian specialists about this stone. They do not merely believe and feel that this inscription is impossible, but know it for certain in the same way as an Englishman would know at once that an inscription in modern English with a few old-fashioned forms added (which moreover combine words of different gender and case) could not belong to the 14th century. To show how <u>every</u> Scandinavian scholar regards the inscription I will quote what Professor Jon Helgason, professor in Icelandic at the University of Copenhagen, said to me when he read my first article on the Kensington Stone: 'In my opinion the inscription on the Kensington Stone is such that no philologist with any self-respect could in any decency write about it; any more than an archaeologist would trouble to publish a grave-find of the Iron Age if he found a telephone book under the urn'. In my heart of hearts I agree with Jon Helgason. On the other hand there has been so much fuss made about this inscription that a stop must be put to it.

. . . .

> (We were) 8 Goths and 22 Norwegians on a journey of exploration from Vinland to the west. We had (our) camp by two skerries one day's journey from this stone. We were out to fish (fishing) one day. Arrived home we found 10 men red with blood and dead. A V M (A Ve Maria), free (us) from evil. (We) have ten men by the sea to look after our ship(s) 14 days' journey from this island. (In the) year 1362.
>
> ### One translation of the Kensington runestone

We could keep on like this; but we will spare the now impatient reader further philological explanations. Let us pretend that the language is in order; without a qualm we will take it for granted that the inscriber, who, as the diagrams show, knew both the runic alphabet and the Latin alphabet (to some extent), has forgotten everything he learned at his monastic school about the rules of spelling which he must have known at one time, and that he wrote as he spoke. This is what the supporters of the inscription would have us do, and we will forget that this supposition is not able to explain the linguistic anomalies either, even if we are willing to admit that our knowledge of the spoken language of the 14th century is very slight. We admit that language is a strangely lively fish which it is given to few armchair philologists to grasp. We will for the time being turn our backs on the language and consider the runes, to see if the solution to the problem may not lie with them.

Runes ceased to be used in Denmark and Norway about 1300, but they survived in Sweden on grave-stones and on household goods, not to mention the runic calendars which continued up to the 1700's. But it is actually true of all medieval runic inscriptions whether of Denmark, Norway or Sweden, that there is an even development to be traced from the earliest Viking times right up to the latest runic inscription, not only in the forms of the runes themselves but also in the language. The Kensington inscription does not fit into the unbroken chain of Scandinavian runic inscriptions. Look at the alphabets and see for yourself that almost half the stone's runes have shapes which are not to be found in the runic alphabet of the Middle Ages.

It is however a fact that runes, as mentioned above, were retained right down to the 18th century in the Swedish runic calendars in the possession of the common man in many Swedish districts. And if we examine these we find that those of the 16th and 17th centuries employ very degenerate forms of the runic alphabet---forms which are not unlike those on the Kensington Stone. Therefore there can be no doubt that the person who engraved the Kensington Stone constructed his alphabet on the basis of the alphabet of such a Swedish runic calendar, and this is completely corroborated by the symbols which he used for numbers. They are those usual in runic calendars (known since the 14th century) but completely unknown in the general run of runic inscriptions. The engraver has not slavishly followed the alphabet of his runic calendar but has invented new symbols. In the formation of these new symbols he has offended against the system of the runic alphabet in ways we shall not go into here. The patient reader interested in the Kensington Stone will have already noticed that it is now in rather a precarious position. But it has not received the coup de grace. Here it comes. In his eagerness to have as complete an alphabet as possible the engraver of the Kensington Stone has invented a j-rune. He ought not to have gone as far as that. The fact is that the letter 'j' is a development within the Latin alphabet (like v). Both these letters were invented by the French philosopher Petrus Ramus in the 16th century. He took the letters jod and vau from the Hebrew alphabet and supplied the Latin alphabet with these two sadly needed consonants. In Scandinavian and German jod kept its name, while vau became vee in Scandinavian and English. Only the Germans have kept the old Hebraic name vau (fau). Just as striking is the letter o, with the two dots above it, on the stone. This trick was introduced into Sweden about the time of the Reformation. In other words we have before us a rune-stone which used symbols---j and o---which were not invented until c. 1550, and the stone is dated 1366!

Now all the linguistic objections are on a firm footing; now we really understand the forms like vi hade instead of wi hafdum; now we realise how a word like opdagelsesfaerd', impossible in the 14th century, can be found in the inscription (opdage, discover, meant oplyse, enlighten). With our eye on the American language we nod in recognition to words like <u>ded</u> (dead) and <u>from</u>.

But it is possible that there may be still a sceptic maintaining that Petrus Ramus---by thought transference---got the idea for the letter j from the author of the Kensington Stone inscription. Leading mineralogists have really accounted for the weathering and patina of the stone. But Professor Brondsted's examination has a crushing reply to this. He has proved that an h carved in the stone by Holand about 40 years ago has already taken on a certain patina. And that in spite of the fact that in these 40 years the stone has not been acted upon by the wind and weather but has been kept in a sheltered room. Farewell, Kensington Stone of 1362, farewell Paul Knutsson expedition, which perhaps never even started and which very likely never got to America; at any rate farewell to all the fruitless labour of scholars of nearly every branch of learning.

Apart from the battering Sven B. F. Jansson gave the Kensington Stone inscription both in general and in detail in his above-mentioned article, it is interesting to note that he shows how Holand in his massive books seems to have suppressed important material which argues against the authenticity of the stone.

From information I have received from Prof. J. A. Holvik, Moorhead, Minnesota, it appears that not a single archive of the Minnesota Society was properly examined by Holand. Prof. Holvik here discovered a document which must be considered as no less than sensational in this connection. It concerns a sheet of paper covered with runes and is apparently the <u>engraver's rough draft for the inscription on the Kensington Stone</u>. Holvik, who published it in the paper <u>The Concordian</u>, no. 10, Nov. 18, 1949, accompanies it with the following words: 'This sketch of the Runestone inscription was sent in a letter by J. P. Hedberg of Kensington, to Swan (Swen?) J. Turnblad of Minneapolis. The letter is dated January 1, 1899. Mr. Hedberg calls the sketch an exact copy of writing on a stone brought to him by Olof Ohman. Both the letter and the sketch were filed in the archives of the Minnesota Historical Society in August 1925. (Holand's first book on the inscription was published 1932). I found it there last month. A detailed comparison of the individual characters and spelling of each word with those on the Kensington stone shows that this sketch is not a copy of the inscription on the stone. <u>It is an original preliminary draft of the story later inscribed on the stone</u>'. With reference to Plate V, which is a reproduction of a photostat copy sent to me by Holvik, I emphasize in agreement with him that (1) in Plate V the word 'from' is written <u>fro</u> in the first line and <u>from</u> in the fourth; the stone has here only <u>fro</u>. (2) Plate V has the word 'red' written with h-rune (<u>rehde</u>). The stone has <u>rode</u>. (3) Plate V spells the word 'blood' as <u>blod</u>, the stone has correctly <u>blod</u>.

The sketch is older than 1899; at some time before this year (and no doubt in the autumn of 1898, when the stone was found), it was given to a man (Hedberg) by the finder of the rune stone (Ohman), who publicly had declared that he knew nothing about runes. Nothing is intimated of how far the sketch was undertaken by Ohman. But the spelling of <u>rohde</u> compared with <u>rode</u> (on the stone) cannot have been a transcriber's error by a man who knew nothing about runes, and that is evidence that the sketch is not a copy of the stone's inscription. This is stressed and strengthened by the two other examples. Notice also that <u>pep</u> (dead) was first written <u>pop</u>, but corrected to <u>pep</u>. No reader, whether layman or not, could transcribe the stone's regular and correct o-rune in blod by the complicated o-rune. But if the paper is not the copy, then it must be the original!

In this connection I must draw attention to a book, some of whose pages have been copied photostatically and the copies sent to me by Prof. Holvik. These are extremely interesting. The Book is called: Den kunskapsrike Skolmastaren eller Hufvedgrunderna uti de for ett borgerligt samfundsliv nodigaste Vetenskapen, by Carl Rosander (The well-informed Schoolmaster or the Fundamentals of popular Science), 1883, new edition 1893. On the title page is Ohman's signature and 'Kensington 2.3.91'. On pages 63 ff is to be found an account of the Swedish language and its development. An example of the Lord's Prayer of c. 1300 ends with the words: froelsae os af illu; here can be found the spelling ok and og (and), here even can be found h to lengthen vowels, and remarkably enough the spelling rohd (red).

How these remarkable coincidences are to be explained is naturally difficult to say. But it must be admitted that the consensus of opinion among Scandinavian scientists is that if there was in America at the end of the last century a Scandinavian with no training in philology but who had dabbled a little in books on popular science, and if he had had the idea of making a runic inscription, then that inscription would take on the same appearance as the one on the Kensington Stone.

THE AUTHENTICITY OF THE PHOENICIAN TEXT FROM PARAHYBA

Gordon, Cyrus; *Orientalia*; 37:75-80, 1968.

Professor Jules Piccus of the University of Massachusetts acquired a scrap-book containing a letter from Ladislau Netto to Wilberforce Eames about the Phoenician inscription from Parahyba, Brazil. Netto made a copy in his own hand and enclosed it with the letter he wrote on January 31, 1874. The envelope has three postmarks: Rio de Janeiro on that date; Liverpool on February 27, 1874; and finally New York on March 12 when it was delivered to Eames.

On November 22, 1967, Piccus sent me a xeroxed copy of the scrap-book with a request for my opinion on the authenticity of the text.

I was already acquainted with the Parahyba inscription but the only facsimile I had seen was the garbled copy of F. Calleja in the Bulletin de la Societe de Geographie d' Alger 4 (1899) 214. Mark Lidzbarski had declared the text a forgery in 1898 (Handbuch der Nordsemitischen Epigraphik I, 132) but when I compared his Hebrew transcription with Netto's clear copy I was surprised to find so many misreadings. Worse yet, Lidzbarski condemns Konst. Schlottmann for being open-minded and treating the text as though it might possibly be genuine ("als konnte sie auch echt sein").

The script is Sidonian, close to the letter-forms of the Eshmunazar inscription of the early fifty century B.C. However the ז and ר are more archaic and suggest a sixth-century date.

The linguistic oddities that have cast suspicion on the text actually support its genuineness. No forger who knew enough Semitics to compose such a document would have committed so many apparent errors. Now that nearly a century has passed, it is obvious that the text is genuine, because subsequently discovered Phoenician, Ugaritic, and other Northwest Semitic inscriptions confront us with the same "errors".

. . . .

The foregoing demonstration of the authenticity of the Parahyba inscription does not mean that all the problems have been solved and that every word and construction have been finally and perfectly interpreted. However, the text is not more difficult or anomalous than the rest of the Phoenician corpus.

. . . .

[Translation] We are Sons of Canaan from Sidon, the city of the king. Commerce has cast us on this distant shore, a land of mountains. We set (= sacrificed) a youth for the exalted gods and goddesses in the nineteenth year of Hiram, our mighty king. We embarked from Ezion-Geber into the Red Sea and voyaged with ten ships. We were at sea together for two years around the land belonging to Ham (= Africa) but were separated by a storm (lit., 'from the hand of Baal') and we were no longer with our companions. So we have come here, twelve men and three women, on a. . . . shore which I, The Admiral, control. But auspiciously may the exalted gods and goddesses favor us!

. . . .

The importance of this inscription lies in its historical significance. A distinguished Pre-Columbian Americanist stated at the turn of the century: "...the role of the Phoenicians, as intermediaries of ancient civilization, was greater than has been supposed, and....America must have been intermittently colonized by the intermediation of Mediterranean seafarers" (Zelia Nuttall, The Fundamental Principles of Old and New World Civilizations [Peabody Museum, Cambridge, Mass. 1901] 6). In her book of over 600 pages she did not even mention the Parahyba text, which had been condemned as spurious. But the growing mass of evidence confirming her ostracized thesis leaves no doubt as to the correctness of her conclusion that we have just quoted. Its establishment among Americanists and historians must be preceded by the recognition of the authenticity of the Parahyba inscription by Semitists. The rest will then fall into place. That the crucial step can now be taken we owe to the perspicacity and initiative of Jules Piccus.

UNDECIPHERED SCRIPTS
Anonymous; *Nature*, 130:502, 1932.

According to a letter from Sir Denison Ross in the Times of Sept. 21, M. Guillaume Hevesy, a Hungarian resident in Paris, has discovered that a number of the signs of the prehistoric Indian script on seals from Mohenjo-daro also appear in the script of the Easter Island inscribed wooden tablets, while some of the Easter Island signs, not present on the Indian seals, are to be found in the proto-Elamic of Susa. It would now be interesting to hear whether there is any coincidence in the interpretation of the prehistoric Indian signs suggested by Sir Flinders Petrie (see <u>Nature</u>, Sept. 17, p. 429) and those suggested for the Easter Island script in the Report of the Committee of the Royal Anthropological Institute of which Mr. Sidney Ray was chairman. The suggestion of a connexion between the two scripts is not the only attempt to find an affinity between Easter Island and this part of Asia. M. J. Hackin, of the Musee Guimet, has recently directed attention to the resemblance which has been noted between the wooden statues, probably ancestral, which were objects of reverence among the Kafirs of Afghanistan before they were overwhelmed by Islam, of which examples are now preserved in the Kabul Museum, and the well-known statues of Easter Island. The resemblances certainly are strong, although it might be argued that they do not go beyond what may be due to the limitations of an undeveloped technique. It must also be admitted that when the material which it is sought to bring into relation is so widely separated in date as in these instances, the comparison, in default of intervening links, carries more interest than conviction.

SOUTH ASIA'S EARLIEST WRITING STILL UNDECIPHERED
Dales, George F.; *Expedition*, 9:34-39, Summer 1967.

Just think how rich is our knowledge and understanding of ancient Egypt, Mesopotamia, and the Classical World because of the preservation of both archaeological and written records. But there are other early societies, equally as impressive archaeologically, which stand as mute and unintelligible giants before our curious eyes. In some instances the ancient populations were apparently non-literate, but in others the fault rests with us in our inability to decipher the records left to us.

So it is in South Asia where the earliest deciphered records date merely to the third century B.C. And yet archaeology has revealed the presence of a vast ancient literate civilization centered along the basin of the Indus River in what is now West Pakistan and western India. This Indus---or Harappan---civilization was thriving from at least 2400 to 1900 B.C. There are strong indications that it was in contact with the Persian Gulf region and the Sumero-Akkadian cultures of southern Mesopotamia.

There is no doubt that the Harappans were literate, or had at least a literate social class. There are abundant examples of their script to verify this but as yet not a single word can be read. We know virtually nothing of the structure of the language nor do we even know to which linguistic family it belongs. This is not to say that valiant attempts have

not been made to decipher it. Since the initial discovery of Harapan
writing some ninety years ago, scholars and dilettantes alike have produced "decipherments" and "translations" which have associated the
Harappan language with practically everything from Cretan, Egyptian,
and Sumerian in the west, to Chinese in the north, to Sanskrit and Dravid-
ian languages in South Asia, to Easter Island in the South Pacific. The
story of these many "decipherments" is a fascinating one---both amusing at times and maddening at others. We find, for example, such puzzling "translations" as:

> "This is the eight (formed) God one of whose sides
> (forms) (is) the sprinkled great fish"

or a "translation" of what is called the longest known Harappan inscription (although it may in fact be three short separate inscriptions!):

> "The great god, who has the two sides (forms) of the
> high Sun of the eight (parts) or Orur, (which is) outside
> the land of the rain clouds of the (constellation or month of
> the) Scale, which approaches with peals of thunder, of the
> united lands of Minad (the country of the Fish), (is) the
> rain of the year of a house of brushes."

These and other claimed decipherments are not accepted save by a
few dedicated "believers," and for good reasons. The primary problem
is that all of the surviving inscriptions are too short to allow any analysis of the structure of the script and the language it represents. Most
of the inscriptions consist of from two to five symbols, with a few having as many as ten. These curt notations give no hint as to their contents.
Are they personal or place names, titles, or complete phrases or sentences?

. . . .

There is yet another problem hampering any decipherment of the
Indus writings and it is one that has unfortunately been created largely
by the archaeologists themselves. Although there are hundreds of known
inscriptions on seals, pottery, and small objects there is no clear chronological sequence of them to demonstrate a development in the script.
We see it mainly in its mature stage. Only very recently have Indian
archaeologists uncovered evidence for a late simplified stage of Harappan writing but the details are as yet unavailable. As for the early
stages and the origin of the script, we have no positive evidence at all.

. . . .

In the meantime, all we can meaningfully do is to continue the study
of the Harappan script, as a script alone, and refrain from overzealous
efforts to "decipher" it. There is still need for more detailed analysis
of the groupings and arrangements of the symbols and of the possible
connections between the inscriptions and the types of objects on which
they are found. As a start in that direction it may be helpful to describe
the material evidence available for any study of the Indus script. There
are at least ten different types of objects upon which are found examples
of the script.

Most numerous are the stamp seals which apparently served the
same basic function as the well known cylinder seals of Mesopotamia---
that of personal identification of ownership. These Harappan stamp
seals, made of steatite, are one of the hallmarks of Harappan civilization. The most common variety is square in shape and depicts an

animal in relief above which is an inscription. A second variety is rectangular or square in shape and contains only script.

Logically we should expect to find impressions of such seals. And indeed there are lumps of clay, stamped with seal impressions, which were originally sealings around the mouths of jars or on bundles of goods wrapped for shipment. Impressions of seals are also seen on certain types of pottery goblets. As far as I know, such impressions on pottery display only script, and none of the animal representations.

Next we find numerous examples of Indus script scratched into the surface of pottery. Such scratchings are usually crudely done on the body of vessels or more carefully executed on the rims. The significance of these incised inscriptions escapes us.

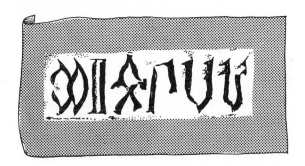

Stamp seal from Mohenjo-daro

More suggestive, however, are examples of script on the bottom halves of large storage jars. The bottoms of these jars were apparently formed in an open mold. The script on the jars is seen in raised relief. This can only mean that the original inscription was incised into the mold and that every vessel made in such a mold would bear the same inscription. Indeed, several sherds displaying identical raised script were found during the 1964-65 University Museum excavations at Mohenjo-daro.

Inscriptions are also found on metal objects. Copper or bronze blades, axeheads, and small flat plates sometimes have several signs scratched on them. There are not enough examples unfortunately to allow conclusions as to the relationship between the inscriptions and the types of objects.

Another class of objects does, on the other hand, have potential significance for the use and early development of the script. There is a relatively large collection of tiny steatite seals or amulets of various shapes found only in the lower and earliest levels of Harappa. The signs seen on these objects are quite limited in number but those that do appear seem to have the same form as the signs on the later stamp seals.

There is a very interesting class of baked clay objects which must have been amulets or some such thing rather than seals. These objects are in the shape of short rods or sticks having either a triangular or round cross section and carrying script and pictures in raised relief. One fine example of a triangular sectioned object was discovered during the Museum's excavations at Mohenjo-daro. One side depicts an Indian crocodile (gawnai or gnamul) with a fish in its jaws, the second side depicts a rare example of a boat and the third side has script.

Harappan sites contain hundreds of ivory and bone objects. Among these are rods or sticks decorated with incised geometric patterns. A few examples have beautifully engraved script. The interesting fact about these inscribed sticks is the striking similarity among their inscriptions. In the majority of examples, the last two symbols at the left ends of the sticks are identical. One is tempted to see here some definite correlation between the inscriptions and the objects---either the type of object, the material of which they are made, or the use of them.

Lastly, Harappan script is sometimes found scratched into the sides of baked clay cones. These cones are themselves especially intriguing. Averaging about two and a half inches in length, they often resemble stylized shells. In fact, several cones actually made of shell have been found. These cones are ubiquitous and very numerous at Harappan sites but their purpose has never been explained. Only one suggestion might be made here. The tips of the cones are characteristically worn flat on one or more sides, indicating that they did have a functional purpose. Now one of the most enigmatic questions concerning the Harappans is what did they write on in everyday life and what did they write with. After all, the inscriptions we study today represent only a fraction of the original written records of the Harappans. There must be lost a vast collection of writing on less durable materials than stone and baked clay---such as perhaps palm leaves, bark, wood, cloth, leather, or wax tablets. Is it unreasonable to suggest that these clay cones with their worn tips might have been the instruments with which the writing was executed? It is always dangerous and presumptuous to bring in parallels from places and times far removed from the subject, but here a most tempting parallel can be suggested from later Indian sculpture. A provocative sculpture from 10th-11th century A. D. Khajuraho in northern India depicts a woman writing on what may have been a wax tablet with a cone-shaped stylus. Could this late sculpture equally as well have portrayed an inhabitant of Mohenjo-daro or Harappa three thousand years earlier writing a text which is now eternally lost?

TWO EASTER ISLAND TABLETS IN BERNICE PAULAHI BISHOP MUSEUM, HONOLULU

Metraux, A., *Man*, 38:1-4, 1938.

Since the time when Easter Island tablets were first discovered by Bishop Tepano Jaussen of Tahiti, they have been regarded as highly valuable objects. With few exceptions, the early missionaries and visitors to the island made every attempt to secure these rare and precious documents. In the beginning the natives apparently showed no reluctance to part with the tablets, but Father Zumbohn, a missionary on the island in 1866-1870, tells that a beautiful tablet 135 cm. long, which he had purchased from a native, was lost or destroyed 'out of jealousy.' Possibly many tablets were burned by the natives. It is sheer calumny to state that they were destroyed by order of the missionaries, who, on the contrary, tried their utmost to save them.

We know of the existence of sixteen authentic tablets in several institutions. To these may be added a few objects bearing tablet signs for ornamental or other purposes. Most of these tablets have been mentioned or described in scientific papers. The Bernice Pauahi Bishop Museum, in Honolulu, owns two tablets and a fragment of a third. These have never been described and have passed unnoticed by those who have studied the subject. The fragment of tablet was acquired on Easter Island, in 1886, by Lieutenant Symonds of the U.S.S. Mohican and was later presented to the Museum.

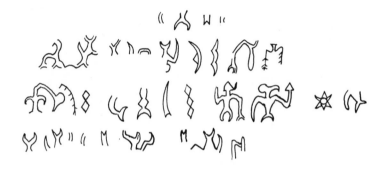

Representative symbols from Easter Island "talking boards"

The Bernice Bishop Museum also has a piece of wood (B. 3622) bearing twenty-two tablet signs. This specimen is not described here, as its authenticity is doubtful. The signs appear to have been incised with a steel implement, and do not show the regularity and beauty of outline which characterize the original tablets. Modern natives of Easter Island are fully aware of the great value of the tablets. Many of them have specialized in the manufacture of imitations. Several faked tablets, purchased on the island in recent times, have reached private or public collections, where they are held as genuine specimens. Among these modern tablets is one in the Lateran Museum in Rome (Cat. 6442).

The tablet in the British Museum was acquired by that institution not long ago (1903). Judging from photographs, this tablet does not appear to me to be a relic of the ancient culture of Easter Island. The signs are poorly engraved and suggest the style of modern artists. Faked tablets had been made on the island prior to 1882, as evidenced by a wooden gorget acquired by a German officer of the Hyena in that year. This gorget bears signs unmistakably of recent origin. It is preserved in the Australian Museum.

. . . .

Interest in the tablets was revived a few years ago when an Hungarian linguist, Mr. de Hevezy, pointed out striking and 'incontrovertible parallels' between the pictographic script discovered in the ruins of Mohenjo-daro and Harappa, in the Indus Valley, and certain signs of Easter Island tablets. The examples shown by Mr. de Hevezy were so striking and so perfect that no doubt could be entertained about the relationship between the two writings. Though Easter Island is almost at the antipodes of the Indus and its culture is separated from that of India by 5,000 years, the similarity of the two 'writings' was too great to be attributed to chance. Scientific authorities took a definite stand in the

	INDUS SCRIPT	HEVEZY'S VERSION	EASTER ISLAND TABLETS
1			
2			
3			
4			
5			
6			

question and considered the parallels as evident. I happened to compare the examples chosen by Mr. de Hevezy with the original photographs of the Mohenjo-daro seals published by Sir John Marshall and with the catalogue of the Indus signs prepared by Dr. G. H. Hunter. To my surprise, I discovered that most of the Indus or Easter Island signs presented by Mr. de Hevezy lacked the accuracy desirable in such work. He has taken regrettable liberties with the signs. When restored to their original proportions or outlines, identical signs in his list ceased to show any similarity. For instance, he compares to an Easter Island sign a symbol of the Mohenjo-daro script which, as reproduced by him, represents a man wearing a sort of kilt. The Indus seal on which this figure appears is broken, and half of the image is missing. In the catalogue, the missing part has been indicated as usual by shading. Mr. de Hevezy makes a kilt of this conventional marking and compares the sign thus reconstructed to an Easter Island figure whose lower part is hatched.

The sign which Mr. de Hevezy compares to an Easter Island symbol representing a wooden breastplate (rei-miro) has been inaccurately reproduced. The small strokes at the ends of the curve have been fused with the curved line so as to make the sign resemble more or less the outline of the Easter Island design. Most of the signs have been submitted to similar adjustments.

If we discard these inaccuracies, the resemblances between Mohenjo-daro script and Easter Island 'writing' become extremely few and are reduced to simple geometrical signs. Mr. de Hevezy contends that his drawings prove his discovery more eloquently than words. I shall follow his example and show that figures are more persuasive than comments. In figure 4 the column to the left has the Mohenjo-daro signs copied from photographs of the seal, in the central column are parallels presented by Mr. de Hevezy, and in the third column are the Easter Island symbols as they usually appear on the tablets. I may mention the fact that among hundreds of variants of the different signs which appear on the tablets, Mr. de Hevezy has picked out variants or isolated cases without paying any attention to the series of deformations and shapes a single sign is bound to take. In his comparisons he has applied the method of certain linguists who compare at random words from two languages without considering roots or derived forms.

The Indus script compared with almost any primitive pictography shows a wider range of parallels than those it exhibits with Easter Island symbol.

We do not know the age of the tablets. Mr. de Hevezy thinks that they may be thousands of years old. On this question one fact is certain: the largest tablet in existence (the Tahua tablet ('The Oar') in the Museum of Braine-Lecomte) has been carved on a European oar. The signs on this tablet are perfect and the authenticity of this tablet has never been questioned, not even by Mr. de Hevezy.

. . . .

NOTE ON PHOENICIAN CHARACTERS FROM SUMATRA

Harrison, J. P.; *Anthropological Institute, Journal*, 4:387-389, 1875.

These characters are said to be still in use in the districts of Rejang, Lemba, and Passummah, in Sumatra. Manuscripts on thirty-one tablets formed of split bamboos were, it appears, acquired many years ago by the old East India Company, and are now in the library of the India Office. Nearly the whole of the letters inscribed on the convex surfaces of the bamboos are identical in form with Phoenician characters mostly of a pure period, and afford a very remarkable instance of the survival of an early form of writing adopted by a non-literary race.

Marsden states that the letters of the Rejang alphabet consist of twenty-three characters. Corrected forms are given in his "History of Sumatra," third edition, and letters of the same form and number are found upon the margins of twenty-three of the bamboo tablets. This confirms Marsden's statement regarding the numbers of the characters, and shows that there is an unbroken set of tablets. Eight others have two letters each on the margins of the tablets---duplicates of the first eight letters of the Rejang alphabet.

In the fac-simile, which is derived from a photograph of the first tablet, it will be noticed that there are several forms which are not found in the Rejang alphabet. They are letters with occasional affixes or signs attached to them on the left side, which serve, according to Marsden, to alter the terminal sounds. There are eight of these signs (see plate). Examples of their use occur in the eighth and eleventh characters (from the commencement) of the first line of the manuscript,

REJANG ALPHABET

1 2 3 4 5 6 7 8 9 10 11 12 13 14 15 16 17 18 19 20 21 22 23

(VARIANTS)

PHOENICIAN CHARACTERS

PART OF A REJANG M.S. ON BAMBOO
(FROM SUMATRA)

SIGNS = " „ V ∧ / \ ) c , o.   (DIMENSIONS = 13 x 1.25 INCHES)

where the seventh and fourteenth letters of the alphabet appear with the fourth sign attached to them. Also, in the second line, the sixth and fourteenth characters have the same sign attached to the fifteenth letter of the alphabet. Two letters, viz. Nos. 11 and 22 are distinguished from No. 4 by slight additions. It really seems as if Nos. 11 and 22 were originally of the same form as No. 4 (the three thus answering to the Phoenician characters B, D, and R), but that the difficulty of distinguishing letters so much alike led to the addition of permanent suffixes.---The twentieth letter of the Rejang alphabet is the only one that has not been identified.

It should be mentioned that the order of the letters is not the same as in Phoenician, and the letters themselves are generally reversed; their values, also, are different.

Both in Java and Sumatra written traditions, mixed with fable, refer to the arrival of ships in remote times, and at two different epochs, from the Red Sea and the Persian Gulf---in the one case at a time when vessels still coasted round the Bay of Bengal; in the other, in the age of Alexander, who is said to have built a bridge "in the sea," which may mean that ships commanded by some of his officers arrived direct from India. Three of his descendants are also said to have become kings of Palinbang, &c. The ships would have been manned principally by Phoenician sailors. Stript of legendary matter, there seems nothing contrary to, or inconsistent with, history in these traditions, which consequently possess a certain value apart from the evidence afforded by the manuscripts. The importance attending the identification of these characters is principally ethnographical.

EGYPTIAN RELICS UNEARTHED IN NEW SOUTH WALES, AUSTRALIA
Anonymous; *INFO Journal*, 2:30, 1969.

Sydney---Archaeologists will begin digging soon in Wollongong, on the south coast, for Egyptian carvings. Relics, carved during Cleopatra's reign, about 30 BC, were recently unearthed about two miles from the city, 50 miles south of Sydney.

Diagrams of the hieroglyphics were sent to Egypt for identification. The carvings were found by Prof. R. Gilroy, director of the Mt. York History Museum at Mt. Victoria in the Blue Mountains. Most of the carvings were excavated near a beach though the actual spot has been kept secret to prevent vandalism.

In recent weeks archaeologists have uncovered 12 footprints dating back more than one million years in the area between Wollongong and nearby Gerringong.

Prof. Gilroy says he has also unearthed a block of stone used as a navagation tablet by the ancient Spanish. He claims the ancient Egyptians may have visited the south coast accidently. A ship sailing to South-East Asia may have blown off course and landed on the Australian coastline, he said. (Daily News, Sydney, July 22, 1969)

ODD OLD STONES
Pindar Pete; *Producers' Review*, 66:47, October 1976.

Canegrowers in the Kamma-Green Hills region of the Hambledon area have unearthed some interesting and puzzling stones in the last seventy years.

There have been the usual aboriginal axes, grinding stones and grinding plates but one recent item thrown up by a plough would quicken the pulse of any archaeologist.

It's a small, but perfectly shaped stone heart and it is certainly not a natural piece of gibber. Which raises the question of what the crafts- man who shaped it had in mind when he whittled it into size a few cen- turies ago. Maybe he was an early day medical lecturer and needed the piece to demonstrate heart transplants to a gathering of which doctors sitting amongst their boomerangs. Or are we looking at the very first homegrown Australian Valentine Day Card?

Another piece of gravel which really raises a question came out of the ground a couple of metres down in the early 1900's.

It's a sculptured stone Egyptian sacred scarab beetle, worshipped in temples around 700 B.C. in the land of the Nile. This smaller ver- sion had another function. They were issued to generals and admirals for use in sealing dispatches so that the boss king knew he was reading an authentic account of a brawl or expedition.

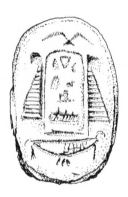

Underside of a stone scarab dug up in an Australian cane field

That's why the beetle was carved with a flat belly and had indented hieroglyphics to push into sealing wax and then on to the grass paper.

Odd sort of thing to find a north Queensland canefarm but just to make things a bit more confusing, there existed until a few years ago (when it was bulldozed to bits) a carved rock high up above the head- waters of the Mulgrave River. This carving took the form of symbols something like shorthand. Experts who saw copies didn't reckon it looked like shorthand at all however---they said it was Chaldean writing. Which, for the record, went out of fashion around 4000 B.C.

Then, of course, there was the coin found in the bottom of a hole being dug for a fence post in the mountains west of Cairns in 1908. That coin was minted in the reign of Ptolemy X, who was Cleopatra's grand- daddy. Sounds like there must have been a practical joker around in the 1880's who had a good knowledge of very ancient history. Or was Captain Cook a lot later than he thought?

AN EGYPTIAN SHIPWRECK AT PITCAIRN ISLAND

Fell, Barry; *Epigraphic Society, Occasional Publications*, vol. 1, no. 1, 1974.

I am indebted to Ruth K. Hanner of Kauai, Hawai'i, for a copy of a Pitcairn rock inscription originally reported by Taylor (1870). Attempts at decipherment were made at the time of the discovery, but no significant result then emerged, owing to the then lack of knowledge of hieroglyphics. It is understood that the inscription was subsequently severely damaged by the islanders in attempts to remove the letters for the purpose of sale to visitors. Since Taylor's time the inscription, as he reported it, seems to have been overlooked.

Inspection of Taylor's rendering of the inscription (Figure 1) shows that the language is Egyptian, the dialect Libyan, and the reading flow runs from the top left hand corner in a clockwise spiral to the lower left corner, than obliquely to the centre along an underscored section.

Pitcairn inscription (to be read in a clockwise spiral from top left)

Spirally coiled inscriptions occur in Mediterranean islands adjacent to Libya. The letters are of two kinds. (1), standard monumental hieroglyphs of the Egyptian series, here used in the abbreviated system, such as occurs for example on steles of Rameses III, where the determinative stands for the entire word. Thus the first letter, the bow, pedet, signifies a crew, generally of foreign mercenaries. (2) Libyan syllabic signs of the so-called Numidian inscriptions of the 2nd and 1st centuries B.C. The underlined section is, as the preceding hieroglyphs indicate, a quotation from scripture; this section appears in Libyan letters to which have been added vowel points similar to those found in Java in Polynesian inscriptions, and apparently corresponding to those used in India during the third century B.C., as in the inscriptions of Ashoka. As Ashoka records that he corresponded with Ptolemy III, and it is known that Egyptian ships were sailing to India at that time, it seems likely that the Pitcairn inscription is coeval, dating perhaps to ca 250 B.C. If this inference is correct, then the visit occurred some six hundred years before the main migration of Maori colonists from Java

Pedeta	peno	shenyta	tā	dwā,	ta – pa – nu	mānwa	niwt

dwān	Rā,	menwe	dwā:	"Mi – ro – ne	rā	kāi'.'

Rectified text of Pitcairn inscription in standard hieroglyphs and Libyan symbolic signs, according to Fell

at the end of the fourth century A. D.

Read as Egyptian, the translation is:

> Our crew, wrecked in a storm, made land, thank God! We are people from the Manu region. We worship Ra in accordance with the scripture: "We behold the sun and give voice."

Read as Maori, the translation is:

> Our craft got into difficulties in a fierce gale, we landed and offered oblations. Our forebears are from Manu. We sacrifice to Ra in accordance with the inscribed chant: "Honor the sun and cry aloud."

Spiral inscriptions characterize the early documents of the Sea Peoples; from Egyptian records we know that the Sea Peoples colonized Libya.

This is the only inscription known thus far from Polynesia in which monumental hieroglyphs are combined with the more usual Libyan (or Maurian) syllabic signs, and the only inscription in which vowel points are found in association with monumental hieroglyphs.

The phrase "Ta-pa-nu M3nw" (We are people from Manu) occurs, in Libyo-Punic letters on a carved wooden bird from Easter Island, now in the American Museum of Natural History (S 5309). Manu signifies the highlands of eastern Libya, the hieroglyph pigeon (M3nw in Ancient Egyptian, modern Maori manu, bird) serving thus.

A phrase similar to the scriptural citation, but substituting da-ra (rays of the sun) for Ra (sun), occurs on an inscription at the Suku pyramid in Java, as I shall shortly be reporting. The Suku inscription is in Libyan syllabics.

We appear, therefore, to be encountering some formalized language, connected with sun worship, and persisting in Polynesia from classical Egyptian times until the religious revolution of the 12th or 13th century.

It would also appear likely that early settlers from Manu are the same "Menehune" who, tradition states, built the large temples in

Hawai'i. The term Manu-hunu would mean "pioneer Manu" in modern Maori.
Reference.
Taylor, Rev. Richard (1870). New Zealand and its Inhabitants.

GLOZEL, A MYSTERY
Riesman, David; *Science*, 72:127-131, 1930.

Those who have read something about Glozel may wonder why I speak of it here. Is it not a dead issue? No, for as a study of human credulity and as a commentary on the hot-headedness or should I say pig-headedness of many men of science, it will always occupy a prominent place in the history of civilization.

Although many of the audience are probably familiar with the main facts, I want to give a brief synopsis of the involved story. I say "story" advisedly, for from the very outset the mystery of Glozel has formed a fascinating tale, very much in the genre of our best thrillers, with plot and counter-plot, gum-shoe detectives and all the pertinent paraphernalia.

Glozel is a small hamlet of four farmhouses, about fifteen miles from the famous spa of Vichy. Emile Fradin, then a youth of eighteen and belonging to an old local family, was one day working in his grandfather's field when a cow suddenly slipped into an unsuspected hole. Fradin went to investigate and found that the hole led into an oval pit containing a variety of remarkable objects---bricks, tablets, vases--- which he gathered and as soon as possible showed to the village schoolmistress, Mlle. Picandet. The latter in turn showed some of the tablets to M. Clement, a school teacher in la Guillermie. Eventually the news of the discoveries came to the ears of Dr. Albert Morlet, a surgeon of Vichy and an amateur archeologist. Thereafter Dr. Morlet and Emile Fradin together began to excavate at Glozel and brought to light more and more buried objects which they collected in grandfather Fradin's house and which Dr. Morlet described in detail in an endless series of articles in a literary journal, the Mercure de France. It was through this magazine---the Atlantic Monthly of France in more senses than one---that I became interested in the Glozelian discoveries. My interest was especially aroused by the claim of Morlet and others that an alphabet had been discovered at Glozel which antedated every other alphabet then known. I therefore decided while spending a vacation in the Auvergne to see Glozel for myself, but before doing so I determined to interview Dr. Morlet in Vichy. At first he suspected me of being an archeologist, but when in answer to a direct question I denied the soft impeachment and proclaimed myself merely a doctor, he became cordiality itself and showed me his collection of Gallo-Roman and Glozel antiquities. He told me that he as well as others had been inclined to consider Glozel as belonging to the Magdalenian age because of the presence of harpoons and of stones engraved with reindeer and other animals long extinct in France, but further studies had led to the conclusion that Glozel was Neolithic. Dr. Morlet kindly asked me to stay over until the following day and dig with him and Professor Bjorn, of Sweden, but I was unable to do so.

After leaving Morlet I motored, together with two American friends, to Glozel. Emile Fradin received us and at once offered to take us to the field of excavation. It was at the bottom of a deep ravine and was surrounded by a barbed-wire fence and scarred by trenches and holes. He showed us the original oval pit and the two tombs subsequently discovered. As it was raining hard and as the clayey ground was slippery, I declined his invitation to crawl into one of the tombs but asked instead to see the museum. After paying two francs each we entered through a low door above which was a crude sign with the pretentious words, Musee de Glozel, and found ourselves in a square low-ceilinged room with shelves on the walls and very primitive glass cases standing on the floor. The objects exhibited on shelves and in cases were astounding in number and variety---vases, tablets, engraved stones, ornaments especially pendants, some pieces of glass and harpoons, the last not nearly as artistic as those of Magdalenian age I had seen at Les Eyzies and at Laugerie-Basse. Three articles attracted my special attention ---vases or vase-like pottery-ware having eyes, nose and ears but no mouth, which Morlet has called death masks, explaining the absence of the mouth by assuming that the primitive makers wanted to express the silence of the grave. Secondly, a squarish object suggesting the female figure with a cylindrical projection from the forehead interpreted as the phallus---this Fradin told me was a bisexual idol; and most striking of all, clay tablets with graven signs looking in every way like alphabetical characters. I was struck by the clean red color of these tablets. When I spoke of this to Fradin, he explained it by saying that the soil in which the tablets had been found was such that it did not readily fuse with the clay and hence was easily brushed off. There were also some large casts of the human hand which differed from the imprints of the hands in the Spanish and French caves in having all the fingers present.

I offered to buy some of the articles, especially a tablet, but Fradin resolutely refused to sell. During the whole of our stay in the museum, the grandfather stood silent and motionless in a doorway leading to an inner room.

The reputed discoveries of an alphabet dating back to Neolithic times of which I had now seen the alleged evidence in abundance created a tremendous sensation in informed circles. Altogether about 136 characters had been distinguished, representing every letter of the alphabet except the letter B.

Hitherto the credit for creating an alphabet had been given to the Phoenicians, but the oldest known Phoenician record found at Byblos a few years previously dated back only to about 1300 B.C.; Sir Arthur Evans's baffling Cretan inscriptions of ninety characters, to ca 300 B.C. If Morlet and those who agreed with him were right, then Glozel was truly what M. Reinach called it---one of the greatest archeological discoveries of all time.[2]

Almost immediately after the first appearance of Morlet's reports, doubts began to be voiced about the authenticity of Glozel, though in the early period of the controversy there were perhaps as many scientists who accepted the discoveries in good faith as there were doubters. Soon the pro- and anti-Glozelians became personal and attacked each other with a vituperative vehemence and a destructive sarcasm for which the French language appears to be the ideal medium. Reputations were shattered, old friendships broken, and---as one of the French dailies remarked---even butcher boys came to blows on the streets of Paris.[3] In fact Mrs. O'Leary's cow did no greater damage to Chicago than Fradin's to the reputation of some French savants.

Before long the leading French prehistorians with only an occasional exception began to deny altogether the authenticity of Glozel and to declare the excavated articles to be forgeries. A number of Englishmen were likewise unconvinced. However, Dr. Foat, a London scientist, makes the categorical statement that "if the finds of Glozel are not authentic, it is equally necessary to consider as false all that I have seen in museums between London and Constantinople." Several Scandinavian, Belgian and Portuguese scientists also supported Dr. Morlet, and a German, Dr. Wilke, in a recent article enthusiastically upholds the standard of Glozel.

Are Dr. Morlet's supporters right or is Glozel but one more of the long series of frauds that history recounts since Jacob imposed upon his father Isaac? Many will come to your minds---Thomas Chatterton, our own Dr. Cook, Constantine Simonides, the pretended author of the Codex Sinaiticus, the forger of the Mecklenburg Declaration, the Lincoln love letters in the Atlantic Monthly, the Tiara of Saitapharnes, Ferrante Stocco, the Calabrian priest who created a saint, Giovanni Cala, and invented a life for him, and countless others. Two perhaps are germane and worth recounting. In the early eighteenth century George Psalmanazar, born in the south of France, came to England and with the connivance of a rascally clergyman, Alexander Innes, proclaimed himself a native of the Island of Formosa. He was lionized in London, wrote a description of the island which he had never seen and included in the book an alphabet and grammar of the Formosan language. Though many doubted his veracity, the book passed through two editions and was translated into French. Toward the end of his life he revealed himself in his own memoirs as a colossal faker and declared that all he had published including the language and the grammar was a hoax.

One of the most interesting cases and the one having the greatest analogy to Glozel, if Glozel be a fake, is that of the so-called "Figured Stones of Wurzburg."

In the first half of the eighteenth century there lived in Wurzburg, in Bavaria, an ultra-pious physician named Johann Bartholomaeus Adam Beringer. He is not remembered for any great discovery or contribution to science, but for his share in a remarkable scientific hoax. At the time in which Beringer flourished an active discussion was going on as to the source and meaning of fossils. Although Leonardo da Vinci had understood their true nature---even Herodotus, 400 B.C., had a correct idea---the scientists of two hundred years ago accounted for them as the result of "stone-making forces" of "formative qualities" or as growths from seeds. We may be inclined to smile, but with Dayton in Tennessee to chasten us, we can not throw stones at the Wurzburg of two centuries ago or at the Sorbonne which a hundred years later deprived the great Buffon of his chair because of his heterodox views.

Beringer had committed himself publicly to the belief that fossils were the capricious fabrication of God, hidden by Him in the earth for some inscrutable purpose. His zealous maintenance of this fundamentalist position led some of the students together with members of the faculty and wags of the town to make numerous fossils of clay which they buried in the side of a hill where they knew the professor was wont to search for specimens. Beringer chancing upon these objects was completely deceived. The jokers then became bolder and buried the most extraordinary and extravagant figures their whimsical imagination could suggest. They fashioned tablets bearing inscriptions in Hebrew, Babylonian, Syriac and Arabic and buried them not far from the original spot. Beringer was overjoyed to find such abundant confirmation of his doctrines, and forthwith in true German fashion proceeded to write an exhaustive treatise. The wags now began to realize that they had gone too far. They expostulated with him and revealed to him the whole truth. Instead of believing them Beringer became more than ever convinced that the story his frightened colleagues told was a ruse to rob him of the honor of his discoveries. No one could stop him. At great expense he published in 1728 the "Lithographiae Wirceburgenses."

Only too soon the shout of laughter with which the book was greeted brought the truth home to him. In chagrin and despair he exhausted nearly his entire fortune in a fruitless endeavor to suppress the edition and to buy up the copies already issued. He died soon afterwards, it is said, of a broken heart.

Is Dr. Morlet like Johann Beringer the victim of deception? Upon me personally he made the impression of an honest man. In certain quarters he was accused of fraud, for example, by the <u>Journal des Debats</u> and by the French Society of Prehistory. He promptly brought suit against these and won a verdict of 1,000 francs damages. The defendants carried the case to the Court of Appeals at Riom, the native town of Willa Cather's lovable archbishop. In confirming the verdict, the court gave expression to an amusing quibble. It held that Morlet, being a surgeon by profession and only by avocation a prehistorian, was not injured in the eyes of his real colleagues but only as an amateur archeologist. But as the defendants had not actually proved fraud, they were declared guilty of libel though the fine was reduced to one franc and costs.

Another humorous episode might be mentioned. Regnault, president of the French Society of Prehistory, sued a M. X___ because he, Regnault, had been compelled to pay the sum of four francs to see a collection of fake objects. As part of this legal action, the police of Moulins broke into Fradin's premises and took away a number of objects which were afterwards submitted to the public expert, M. Bayle. The latter reported that the tablets were of recent manufacture. Pieces of clay from a tablet crumbled readily in water; hence it was not conceivable that the tablets could have resisted the moisture in the ground had they been there for many years. Furthermore, a bit of grass picked out of a piece of earthenware showed under the microscope vegetable cells and chlorophyl,[4] and some of the bone instruments still contained marrow. Bayle was soon afterward shot to death by one Philopponet against whom he had testified in court.[5]

The Fradins themselves brought suit against M. Dussaud, member of the Institut, who in a trenchant brochure had called them fakers.

Let us now delve a little more deeply into this mystery so that we may understand better the basis of the whole controversy. The first serious doubt as to the authenticity of Glozel was based on the heterogeneity of the articles in Fradin's museum. How could one explain the presence of so many dissimilar and unrelated objects in one small field of excavation---the two or three thousand at the time of my visit have now grown to five thousand? No other archeologic site offers a parallel. Morlet answered this by saying that Glozel was a champ des morts, a cemetery, and that, as among many primitive peoples of later times, everything belonging to the dead had been buried with him. C. Jullian, who considers Glozel a Gallo-Roman station, accounts for the multiplicity of objects on the assumption that Glozel was a sorcerer's sanctuary. He was added greatly to the gaiety of nations by attempting a full translation of the inscribed tablets from the published illustrations. Dr. Morlet showed me with much amusement a crack in one of the tablets which Jullian had translated as a character.

Aside from the puzzling complexity of the collection, it has been pointed out that the tablets first exhumed bore fewer and less perfect characters than the later ones. Further, as soon as some one had made a criticism, the objects next exhumed would often be free from the criticized defect. Quite frequently certain features appeared that could be traced directly to scientific articles published shortly before. These facts seem of course very significant. Moreover, the scratches on stones whether representing animal figures or alphabetic characters were without the patina covering other parts of the stones, suggesting a recent production. Much was made of the penetration of roots into vases or tablets; but upon examination these roots were not found to be properly fossilized, which would have to be the case had the objects been in the ground for long ages. The utensils---harpoons, hand-axes, scrapers---are far less artistic than those in other Neolithic stations. Vayson de Pradenne and Abbe Breuil indeed contend that none of them could ever have been used.

Dr. Morlet and his chief supporter Van Gennep did their best to answer all these objections. The former at the height of the verbal battle-royal made a request for a governmental commission which was speedily granted, but when he found that a bitter anti-Glozelian, the well-known archeologist Capitan, was a member, he objected and the commission was never sent. Eventually, at the International Anthropological Congress at Amsterdam an International Commission was formally appointed to investigate Glozel. The commission consisted of Absolon, director of the Archeological Museum of the State of Moravia; Bosch Gimpera, professor in the university and director of the archeological work of Barcelona; the Abbe Favret; Forrer, director of the Prehistoric and of the Gallo-Roman Museum at Strasbourg; Miss Dorothy Garrod, member of the Royal Anthropological Institute and of the French Prehistoric Society; Hamal-Nandrin, lecturer on prehistory in the Museum of Liege; Peyrony, director of the Museum of Les Eyzies, and Pittard, professor of anthropology in the University of Geneva. Absolon was prevented from taking part in the work of the commission.

After spending three days at the site the commission issued a unanimous report which was kindly sent to me by Miss Dorothy Garrod. This report states unequivocally that the articles are for the most part of recent manufacture and have undoubtedly been planted in the ground by some one whom the commission does not name, and that Glozel is neither prehistoric nor authentic. Vayson de Pradenne, in a devastating brochure in which he declared the Glozel finds fakes, also accused no one by name but put the blame upon the esprit de Glozel---in other words, upon a fairy.

One might think with the leading French, English and American scientists---Peyrony, Pradenne, Abbe Breuil, Sir Arthur Evans, [6] Dussaud and, I believe, Professor MacCurdy---arrayed against Glozel, and will the destructive judgment of the international commission, that Glozel would cease from troubling the scientific and the lay mind. Though all due obsequies have been performed, Glozel refuses to remain in its sepulcher, and the literary battle continues. Dr. Morlet very kindly sends me newspapers and pamphlets, and a distinguished pro-Glozelian of Belgium, Professor Tricot-Royer, has just supplied me with his defense of Glozel which is particularly interesting because Professor Tricot-Royer was present during the visit of the international commission.

What keeps Glozel alive? First, we have the fact that when men take sides in print they are loath to recant, fearing ridicule---the more untenable their position, the more stubborn their resistance.

Secondly, six months after the international commission's visit Dr. Morlet called together a comite d'etudes of twelve men, consisting of Dr. Foat, Bayet and Tricot-Royer, of Belgium; Reinach, J. Loth, W. Loth, Van Gennep, Deperet, Ajcelin, Roman and Audollent, of France, and Soderman, of Sweden. At their meeting they pronounced unanimously in favor of the genuineness of Glozel.

Another reason is found in the attitude of a group of French and German scientists who are opposed to the traditional belief that ex oriente lux---that civilization is of oriental origin. The alleged Neolithic alphabet of Glozel and similar finds at Alvao in Portugal are grist to their mill.

In addition quasi-political factors have entered into the controversy ---Fradin an obscure peasant, Morlet a provincial doctor without much influence have a definite appeal for the proletariat and for a large section of the press.

And finally, it must be remembered that the Academicians are not always right---that they ridiculed Pasteur and Boucher des Perthes, and that even Koch and Lister met a similar fate in the beginning. [7]

All these elements cooperate to keep the spark of life in Glozel. Within the past few weeks the publication of an exhaustive treatise by Dr. Morlet has been announced. This, however, I fear, can throw no new light upon the subject.

As a detective tale the story of Glozel remains unfinished and will remain so until a Sherlock Holmes discovers the supposed person or persons who manufactured the articles and put them in the ground. What was the motive? How are we to explain the extraordinary industry that has fashioned five thousand or more articles, and how is it that he, the esprit de Glozel, escaped detection in a community of twenty-nine souls where every one knows every one else's business? Or how, if there are witnesses to the dark deed, can we explain an unbroken neighborly silence extending over a period of six exciting years?

---

[1] Read by invitation before the American Philosophical Society on April 24, 1930.

[2] Dr. Hackh in an exhaustive essay on the "History of the Alphabet" makes no reference to Glozel; if true, Glozel belongs at the very bottom of the

linguistic tree.

3 The Glozel affair has been made the subject of bitting burlesque per-
formances in Paris theaters and is the theme of a sarcastic novel by Rene
Benjamin.

4 A report has just been made to the Academie des Sciences (Mercure de
France, May 1, 1930; La Depeche de Vichy, April 12, 1930) of the finding in Russia of chlorophyl in fossil plants of the Tertiary epoch, millions of years old.

5 Bayle's reputation has been seriously tarnished through recent post-
humous revelations. He suffered, as one writer puts it, from "mercan-
tilitis," a post-war malady. A number of years ago he divorced his wife
so as to consecrate himself solely and wholly to science. "I shall not
remarry," he exclaimed. Nevertheless he took another wife soon afterwards. The first wife was unaware of this, for he continued to visit her
every evening during a period of seven years.

6 Personal communication.

7 Recently the Geological Society of Normandy (Mercure de France,
April 15, 1930) has formally proffered "ses plus vives felicitations" to
Dr. Morlet for his science, his tenacity and above all for the magnificent energy with which he has faced the attacks and unjust calumnies to
which he has been subjected and which the Court of Appeals at Riom has
definitely condemned.

THE GLOZEL AFFAIR
Hall, E. T.; *Nature*, 257:355, 1975.

In the world of professional archaeology of the 1920s and early 30s,
the fact that you were a 'Glozelian' or 'Anti-Glozelian' determined who
were your friends; this was particularly significant in an academic dis-
cipline not unknown for acrimonious controversies. The reason for
this in-fighting was based on a reported discovery of artefacts which to
most archaeologists were---and to many still are---unacceptable and
were therefore labelled as fakes. The first pieces were reported in
1924 by a local farmer, Emile Fradin, who is still very much alive
living in the same farmhouse at Glozel, an isolated village south of
Vichy in France; these discoveries were quickly followed by many more
undertaken by a M. Morlet, a doctor from Vichy. What caused the furore was the fact that these objects were like nothing seen before anywhere in the world and covered an amazing spectrum of different types.
There were clay tablets with mysterious incised inscriptions in an unknown language, jars and other ceramics with and without inscriptions,
pottery phallic symbols, animals inscribed on bone and pebbles. None
of these objects was recognisable archaeologically and even if accepted
as something new, many found it impossible to reconcile the different
periods represented apparently cheek by jowl; for instance what might
conceivably be Neolithic incised stones were apparently found in the
same context as clay tablets with inscriptions, which, some said, rep-

resented early Iberian scripts.

The controversy raged more or less continuously until the War in 1939. During this time two international commissions of inquiry sat and pronounced exactly opposite decisions and some five law suits were fought with varying results. In Britain the balance against the Glozelians was heavy although on the continent such eminent archaeologists as Professor Reinach were strongly opposed to the notion that deliberate forgery had taken place.

There the matter rested until 1974 when Glyn Daniel, Professor of Archaeology at Cambridge University, decided to dot the i's and cross the t's in his lecture on archaeological fakes and forgeries; he would have a few pottery samples from Glozel tested using the thermoluminescent (TL) technique in order to illustrate their modern date. Exactly the opposite result transpired---the TL measurements clearly indicated that the ceramics were not modern, but seemed to have been manufactured in the Gallo-Roman period (Antiquity, December, 1974).

These results, which were later more thoroughly confirmed by further measurements, have again divided the archaeologists. To some the antiquity of the ceramics in particular is no great surprise, although the admixture of these ceramics in the same context as other less acceptable material, such as engraved bone and pebbles of apparently Neolithic date (which are less amenable to dating techniques), makes the unravelling of the whole story very difficult. To other archaeologists the affair is still a distasteful hoax and TL dating must be in error; for them it is similar to telling a physicist that the laws of thermodynamics are no longer valid and, not surprisingly, they find it difficult even to listen.

Where then can the explanation lie? At the symposium on Archaeometry at Oxford University in March, details of the work undertaken by McKerrell at Edinburgh and Mejdahl in Denmark were given, and discussed at length by both physicists and archaeologists. There can now be little doubt that the ceramic material is not modern; preliminary dating results on the bone using the ^{14}C technique tend to support the TL measurements. It has been suggested by some that the ceramics, which were low-fired, could be ancient material such as tiles which had been reshaped and inscribed recently. Though this is a possibility with some tablets, with others it is ruled out because on close examination small bubbles of vitrification can be seen in the grooves of some of the inscriptions. Others have suggested recent deliberate irradiation by X rays or Y rays to give the correct TL dates; such possibilities are ruled out by comparatively simple tests which have indeed been carried out. However it is generally agreed that the archaeology associated with the digging is most unsatisfactory. No properly controlled digging took place except for attempts by both commissions of inquiry of a very limited kind and when 'planting' of finds seemed a distinct possibility. There is, therefore, no scientific evidence that all of the objects were in fact from the same stratigraphical context or even from Glozel itself.

It is important in these discussions to differentiate between authentication and dating by TL measurements. When a ceramic object has been removed from its immediate surroundings and has been kept in a museum for some years the extent of the radioactive bombardment from the surrounding soil (as opposed to the internal contribution) becomes a matter of conjecture. Dating by TL measurements of such an object must then have much wider limits than when the precise environment is known and an accuracy of 10% or better can be expected; when the burial environment is unknown the dating accuracy must be subject to greater errors, although in the instance under discussion the approximate level of soil radioactivity would be known provided, of course, that the objects were in fact excavated from the Glozel area. In the case of authentication however we are dealing with a different order of magnitude; in this case we are deciding between an age of 50 and at least 500 years: an error of 1,000% or more. The Glozel measurements would seem to show without doubt that the ceramics are not modern fakes, but it might be a little rash to differentiate with any complete confidence between, say, a Gallo-Roman and a mediaeval provenance. The idea of a mediaeval date becomes a clear possibility after the work of Huxtable and Aitken reported in the latest issue of <u>Antiquity</u> (September 1975), albeit on a single specimen. Such a date is perhaps more likely since an archaeologically acceptable mediaeval kiln was discovered on the site. They also point out that McKerrell and Mejdahl's results are based on only five dates and it will be interesting to see, when full publication is made, whether all the objects sampled fall into a coherently dated group, taking into account the wide range inherent in this type of TL measurement.

How does TL dating come out of the controversy? There have during the past four years been some dramatic exposes of modern fakes which had been unsuspected until the advent of TL dating; many Tang wares from Hong Kong. Hacilar from Turkey, Amlash from Tehran and massive Etruscan terracottas from Italy have all been shown to have been manufactured during the past few years on a large scale and are (or were) decorating shelves in private collections or public museums around the world. These results are now accepted almost unanimously by the relevant authorities and there have been no obvious instances where results undertaken by a reputable laboratory have been shown to be in error as far as authentication is concerned; in other words, so far TL authentication has been shown over many hundreds of samples to be reliable. It would seem unlikely that the Glozel ceramics should be an extraordinary exception to this story of reliability particularly since they do not exhibit any anomalous behaviour during measurement and give entirely normal TL glow curves.

A number of the archaeological objections to the authenticity of the site would be removed if it were found that certain of the objects were genuine and some false. For instance; one might postulate that the higher fired tablets were genuine, but the weird face urns, phallic symbols, bone and pebble carvings were not, if the ceramics in the latter category had been fabricated from tiles or bricks fired in antiquity and reconstituted, this could give an explanation of their apparent ancient TL date. Measurements being undertaken at Oxford using archaeomagnetic techniques may give some clues as to whether this is a possibility.

It is to be hoped that the projected scientific re-excavation of the site by French archaeologists will proceed apace---a preliminary magnetometer survey has already been undertaken. Although the site has been extensively and randomly dug by many different excavators, if the site is genuine, some objects must remain and their archaeological contexts may help to explain this perplexing problem.

RECENT DISCOVERIES BEARING ON THE ANTIQUITY OF MAN IN EUROPE

MacCurdy, G. G.; *Smithsonian Institution Annual Report, 1909*, pp. 531-583.

From the beginning of the Magdalenian epoch, symbolism began to play an important role in paleolithic art. According to Piette, symbols are figures or images employed as signs of objects; therefore they represent words. In the process of time the words were divided into syllables, the syllables into letters; the same signs have designated successively words, syllables, and letters. Among the earliest paleolithic symbols are the dotted circle, the lozenge and the spiral or sigmoid scroll. The first is supposed to be a sun symbol. It reappears as an Egyptian hieroglyph, also on dolmens and menhirs, on bronze age funerary urns and ornaments of the first iron age. The circle without the dot passed into the ancient alphabets and from them into modern alphabets. The lozenge was employed as an artist's signature. The spiral has flourished in all succeeding ages and like some other symbols may have developed independently in various ages and lands.

Piette distinguishes two successive systems of writing in the Magdalenian---the first hieroglyphic and the second cursive. He believes the latter was derived from the former, but admits that since symbols are creatures of convention they may have been from the beginning figures formed by geometric lines instead of being simplified images. An example of cursive writing dating from the Magdalenian epoch is given in figure 17. It is from the classic station of La Madaleine (Dordorgne). The inscription is composed of eight signs, some of which resemble certain letters of the Phenician and ancient Greek alphabet, as well as Cypriote signs. While these may not have been real letters to the Magdalenians, they did become so in passing from a symbolic and phonetic stage combined to one purely phonetic.

The first sign resembles the Phenician guimel, the gamma of ancient and modern Greek and a sign in Asylian writing which dates from the epoch of transition between the paleolithic and neolithic. Allowing for some negligence in execution, the second sign is comparable to the Phenician alef, the alpha of ancient and classic Greek, and A of our own alphabet. The third character is the Phenician guimel, the gamma of primitive and classic Greek. The fourth sign is the same as the third, only reversed. This is also found in the Asylian. The fifth and sixth signs are alike; they are comparable to the letter 1 of the Lycian alphabet and of the classic Greek---the equivalent of the Cypriote sign go. The seventh sign, which is also found on one of the painted pebbles of Mas d'Azil, resembles the character ti, di, thi of the Cypriote alphabet. The eighth character bears some analogy to the Cypriote vi or yi.

Cursive writing was developed still further during the Asylian epoch (Fig. 18), which is the connecting link between the paleolithic and neolithic periods. The transitional character of this epoch is revealed in both faunal and industrial remains. The fauna is composed entirely of species still living in temperate regions. Asylian culture is a heritage from the Magdalenian. It is characterized by the appearance of flat, perforated harpoons (fig. 18) made of staghorn, that replaced two successive types of Magdalenian harpoons---the older with a single row of lateral barbs and the younger with two rows of lateral barbs. The stratigraphic position of the Asylian, reposing on the upper Magdalenian, is in harmony with the cultural and faunal elements.   This is the horizon of the remarkable painted pebbles (fig. 18) found in the cavern of Mas l'Azil (Ariege), that have thrown so much light on paleolithic systems of writing and their connection with subsequent systems.   According to Piette we are indebted to the Asylian for at least a dozen symbols that have come down from the close of the Quatenary through the Phenician, Archaic and classic Greek, Latin and Lydian. (Original spelling retained.)

Inscription from the Upper Magdalenian

Chapter 4
GEOLOGICAL EVIDENCE

INTRODUCTION

Most of ancient man's artifacts reside on the earth's surface or slightly below it, in geological situations suggesting acceptably recent origins. Down the years, though, a few apparently human traces have been discovered deeper, in rocks millions of years old---far older than current anthropological theory allows. All such finds are hotly contested and frequently rejected out of hand. Many such "wild points" never see print. Those that do are relatively rare and often have doubtful pedigrees. Who, for example, will believe the story of an exquisitely wrought metal bell found in solid rock? Would a collection of one hundred similar tales be believed? Probably not, because they cannot be assimilated into any reasonable theory of man.

The second type of geological evidence recorded here involves human skeletons that are anomalous either in biological make-up, geographical distribution, or geological age. Some human or near-human skeletons have, for example, been found in coal beds and other strata that are manifestly "too old." Neanderthal man's remains have been found essentially everywhere. Then, there are skeletons with too many teeth or of giant or pigmy stature. Unfortunately, the accepted temporal and geographical corridors of human evolution are very narrow, and such observations are also rejected as "background noise."

In sum, the data of this chapter are not really so much controversial as they are inadmissible to the court of science.

FOSSIL HUMAN FOOTPRINTS

Geologists have no problem visualizing dinosaurs treading ponderously over a sandbar, leaving in their wakes footprints that are ultimately silted in, petrified, and preserved for men-yet-to-evolve to wonder at. But human footprints in rocks many millions of years old? Impossible!

The word "impossible" is apt because if human footprints in ancient rocks are genuine, either men existed long before evolution stipulated they should or our geological dating schemes are seriously in error. There are two ways out when fossil human footprints are discovered: (1) declare them to be the distorted tracks of animals; or (2) claim that the tracks were engraved by Indians of yore. Unquestionably, the Indians sculptured many footprints and handprints in rock, but the Indian theory collapses when footprints are found only after the removal of overlying rock strata.

In the accounts that follow, a few recognized Indian petroglyphs are included along with footprints that demand an alternative explanation. In addition, there are some footprints from Central America that have recently been legitimatized because the strata seem young enough to allow for human perambulation. Less than a century ago, though, these same and similar footprints were denied and ridicule heaped upon their defenders.

REMARKS ON THE PRINTS OF HUMAN FEET, OBSERVED IN THE SECONDARY LIMESTONE OF THE MISSISSIPPI VALLEY

Schoolcraft, Henry R.; *American Journal of Science,* 1:5:223-230, 1822.

I now send you a drawing of two curious prints of the human foot in limestone rock, observed by me last summer, in a detached slab of secondary formation, at Harmony, on the Wabash; together with a letter of Col. Thos. H. Benton, a senator in Congress from Missouri, on the same subject. The slab of stone containing these impressions, was originally quarried on the west bank of the Mississippi river, at St. Louis, and belongs to the elder floetz range of limestone, which pervades that country to a very great extent.

These prints appear to have been noticed by the French soon after they penetrated into that country from the Canadas, and during the progress of settlement at St. Louis, were frequently resorted to as a phenomenon in the works of nature. But no person appears to have entertained the idea of raising them from the quarry with a view to preservation, until Mr. Rappe visited that place five or six years ago. He immediately determined to remove the stone containing them to his village of Harmony, then recently transferred from Butler county in Pennsylvania, to the banks of the Wabash; but this determination was no sooner known than popular sentiment began to arraign his motives, and people were ready to attribute to religious fanaticism or arch deception, what was, more probably, a mere act of momentary caprice, or settled taste. His followers, it was said, were to regard these prints as the sacred impress of the feet of our Saviour. Few persons thought of interposing a charitable remark in favour of religious tenets, of which we can judge only by the peaceful, industrious, and devotional lives; the neat and cleanly appearance; and the inoffensive manners of those who profess them. Still less could be conceded in favour of a personal taste for objects of natural history or curiosity, of which this act is, at least, a proof. Be this as it may, Mr. Rappe contracted with a stone mason to cut out the block with the impressions, paying him at the same time a liberal price for his labour, and ordered it to be transported by water to his residence in Posy county, Indiana. Visiting this place during the last summer, in the suite of Governor Cass, Mr. Rappe conducted us to see this curiosity, which has been placed upon mason work in a paved area between his dwelling house and garden, in the manner represented in figure II. of the drawing. The slab of stone thus preserved, forms a parallelogram of eight feet in length, by three and a half in breadth, and has a thickness of eight inches, which appears to be the natural thickness of eight inches, which appears to be the natural thickness of the stratum of limestone rock, of which it is a part. This limestone possesses a firm and compact structure, of the peculiar greyish blue tint common to the calcareous rocks of the Mississippi valley, and contains fossil encrinites, and some analagous remains, very plentifully imbedded. It is quarried at St. Louis, both for the purposes of building stone, and for quicklime. It becomes beautifully white on parting with its carbonic acid and water, and those who have used it, observe, that it makes a good cement, with the usual proportion of sand.

The prints are those of a man standing erect, with his heels drawn in, and his toes turned outward, which is the most natural position. The distance between the heels, by accurate measurement, is 6-1/4 inches,

Human footprints in limestone near St. Louis

and between the toes, 13-1/2 inches; but it will be perceived, that these are not the impressions of feet accustomed to a close shoe, the toes being very much spread, and the foot flattened in a manner that happens to those who have been habituated to go a great length of time without shoes. Notwithstanding this circumstance, the prints are strikingly natural, exhibiting every muscular impression, and swell of the heel and toes, with a precision and faithfulness to nature, which I have not been able to copy, with perfect exactness, in the present drawing. The length of each foot, as indicated by the prints, is 10-1/2 inches, and the width across the spread of the toes, 4 inches, which diminishes to 2-1/2 inches, at the swell of the heels, indicating, as it is thought, a stature of the common size.

This rock presents a plain and smooth surface, having acquired a polish from the sand and water, to which its original position periodically subjected it. Upon this smooth surface, commencing in front of the tracks, there is a kind of scroll, which is two feet and a half in length. The shape of this is very irregular, and not equally plain and perfect in all parts, and would convey to the observer the idea of a man idly marking with his fingers, or with a smooth stick, fanciful figures upon a soft surface. Some pretend to observe in this scroll, the figure of an Indian bow, but this inference did not appear, to any of our party, to be justified.

Every appearance will warrant the conclusion that these impressions were made at a time when the rock was soft enough to receive them by pressure, and that the marks of feet are natural and genuine. Such was the opinion of Gov. Cass and myself, formed upon the spot, and there is nothing that I have subsequently seen to alter this view: on the contrary, there are some corroborating facts calculated to strengthen and confirm it. But it will be observed by a letter which is transmitted with these remarks, that Col. Benton entertains a different opinion, and supposes them to be the result of human labour, at the same period of time when those enigmatical mounds upon the American Bottom, and above the town of St. Louis, were constructed. The reasons which have induced him to reject the opinion of their being organic impressions are these:

"1. The hardness of the rock.

"2. The want of tracks leading to and from them.

"3. The difficulty of supposing a change so instantaneous and apropos, as must have taken place in the formation of the rock, if impressed when soft enough to receive such deep and distinct tracks."

To those who are familiar with the facts of the existence of sea and fresh water shells, ferns, madrepores, and other fossil organic remains, in the hardest sandstones and limestone of our continent, the hardness of the rock, and the supposed rapidity of its consolidation, will not present objections of that force, which the writer supposes. But the want of tracks leading to and from them, presents a difficulty, which cannot, perhaps, be so readily obviated. We should certainly suppose such tracks to exist, unless it could be ascertained that the toes of the prints, when in situ, pointed inland, in which case we should be at liberty to conjecture, that the person making them, had landed from the Mississippi, and proceeded no further into the interior. But no enquiry has enabled me to ascertain this fact, the circumstance not being recollected by Col. Benton, and others, who have often visited this curiosity while it remained in its natural position at St. Louis.

The following considerations, it will be seen, are stated by Col. Benton, as capable of being urged in opposition to his theory of their being of factitious origin.

"1. The exquisiteness of the workmanship.

"2. The difficulty of working such hard material without steel or iron."

The strikingly natural appearance of these prints, has always appeared to me, to be one of the best evidences of their being genuine; for I cannot suppose that there is any artist <u>now</u> in America possessed of the skill necessary to produce such perfect and masterly pieces of sculpture: yet, what are we to say of the skill of that people, who are supposed to have been capable of producing such finished pieces of art, without the aid of iron tools? For, let it constantly be borne in mind, that the antiquity of these prints can be traced back to the earliest discovery of the country, and consequently to the introduction of iron tools and weapons among the aborigines. There are none of our Indian tribes who have made any proficiency in sculpture, even since the iron hatchet and knife, have been exchanged for those of flint, and of obsidian. All their attempts in this way are grotesque, and exhibit a lamentable want of proportions, the same which was seen in the paintings, and in the figured vases and pottery of the Asteecks of Mexico, when their towns and temples were first visited by the Spanish conqueror.

HUMAN FOOTPRINTS IN NICARAGUA
Flint, Earl; *American Antiquarian,* 6:112–112, 1884.

In a recent trip to Managua for the Peabody Museum, to examine the human footprints found there in one of the quarries, now being worked for building purposes, I uncovered six rows of impressions, breaking through a layer of rock seven inches thick, over a space of six yards by two. Under this was a layer of black sand with an average thickness of one inch, resting on a layer of friable rock from one and one-half to two inches thick, covering the surface of the lowest layer of rock found in the quarry. Below this thin layer was a thin deposit of volcanic sand and gravel, filling up the inequalities caused by the impressions, with an average of one inch in thickness, as seen in the side cuttings.

The rock seems to owe its formation to a volcanic detritus, and ash brought down after the first volcanic eruption. I cannot account in any other way, for its original plasticity, as but little clay could reach the surface, if the eruption covered the neighborhood with rock and ash--- evidenced in many places of a large district where this kind of rock occurs. Impressions of leaves and stems occur on the under surface, denoting an absence of forest at the point worked. The upper surface is nearly level, with a barely perceptible dip toward the lake shore---distant some 300 yards, and whose waters must have formerly occupied--- or overflowed at times of high water, as some of the aquatic plants, common in the marshy districts, are among the impressions preserved.

The footprints are from one-half to three inches in depth, consequently not made, as some had judged, by a people, fleeing from an inundation. In those exposed there is no length of stride to indicate it, and in the many removed by the owner of the quarry, none exceeded eighteen inches. Some of the impressions are nearly closed, the soft surface falling back into the impression, and a crevice about two inches in width is all one sees, and my first glance at some parallel to one less deep, gave me an idea that the owner of the latter was using a stave to assist him in walk-

ing. In some the substance flowed outward, leaving a ridge around it---
seen in one secured for the museum; the stride is variable, owing to
size of person, and the changing nature of surface passed over. The
longest one uncovered was seventeen inches, length of foot ten inches,
and width four inches, feet arched, steps in a right line, measured from
center of heel to center of great toe over three steps. The people making them were going both ways in a direction consonant to that of the
present lake shore E. and W. more or less. The nearly level surface
extending around the neighborhood of the quarry prevented me from
judging as to the nature of or mode of arrival other than that mentioned.
As far as worked out, the thickness varied but little from twenty-eight
to thirty inches. Following the inequalities of the primitive soil, the
perpendicular cuttings on the southern and eastern faces of the quarry
above the layers mentioned, show in only one place a barely perceptible
dip to the east. The layer removed was covered by one of hard clay,
with streaks of white pumice stone beneath and mingled with its lower
surface---thickness seen in the cutting twelve inches; above this was a
layer of ash, slate colored, very hard, seen in the cuttings along the
Masaya road, and also between Granada and Jinotepe---west of latter
place, 15 feet in thickness, under 15 feet of loam. In the location worked was only 14 inches, mixed with stems of plants and leaves on and near
its under surface. Above this ashy formation are four successive layers
of rock, similar to the lower one and are being used for building. The
lowest averages 28 inches; the others from 17 to 20 inches. The detritus
separating the layers is insignificant. Saw many blocks, and found cavities formerly occupied by stems of plants, but none have leaves like the
lowest layer. I think these layers were the results of different eruptions.
The clay deposit one of repose.

The depth from the surface of the impressions was 14 feet 10 inches
---not counting the surface soil, the strides from 11 to 17 inches. I
would mention that later, the purchaser of those remaining uncovered,
intends removing them to Europe and will be able to give a correct estimate of each. He kindly gave me permission to remove two. Had he
not purchased the site, only the story of their occurrence could be relied
on to prove man's antiquity here.

It is useless to speculate on the lapse of time that has passed since
their occurrence. Experts in geology may give approximate dates.

Before examining them I was inclined to believe they were coevil
with those at San Rafael, but am now convinced that they are in an entirely different formation. The former occurs on sedimentary rock of
that locality. One human footprint associated with those of a tiger on
hard volcanic rock, on the banks of Grand river, at Pinon, west of
Jinotepe is now easily explained. I went in May to cut it out and found
the place covered by water, but intend visiting San Rafael to procure
specimens from them. Unlike those at Nevada the people of this region
needed no covering to protect their feet from a vigorous climate. The
discovery is unique and worth recording.

NEW LIGHT ON ANCIENT NICARAGUAN FOOTPRINTS
Bryan, Alan L.; *Archaeology,* 26:146–147, 1973.

In 1878 Dr. Earl Flint was in Central America collecting antiquities for the Peabody Museum of Harvard University. During his travels he learned that quarrymen near Managua, Nicaragua, had been uncovering fossilized human footprints in a mudstone layer; after visiting the quarries and seeing the well-preserved footprints, which were buried from 16 to 24 feet beneath the ground, he was convinced that they belonged to very early man. Between 1884 and 1889 Flint argued in the American Antiquarian that the footprints dated to at least 50,000 years and possibly as far back as 200,000 years, a dating which would have placed their owners in the Tertiary Period.

. . . .

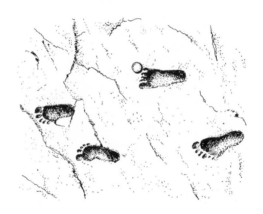

Some of the Nicaraguan human footprints

Soon after the excavations began in 1941, Dr. Howell Williams, a geologist at the University of California, arrived and began studying the history of volcanic action in the area. His aim was to understand the stratigraphic section which Richardson had unearthed and to establish the exact nature of the depositional sequence. He concluded in his report to the Carnegie Institution in 1952 that the El Cauce footprints were not extremely old; volcanic ash and mudflow deposits of the kind that covered the site are caused by torrential rains that re-deposit fresh, unconsolidated ash in low-lying areas. Deposits of this sort can accumulate rapidly and in the case of mudflows, harden soon after deposition. Williams had discovered remnants of two soil layers above the mudflow, and an eroded soil beneath that represented the original land surface on which the inhabitants had lived. The sum of the evidence suggested to him that the footprints were made between two and five thousand years ago and should not be older than that.

Today's refined techniques of radiocarbon dating substantiate Williams' surmise. In 1969 I visited Managua and collected a sample of soil from the layer below the mudflow; when tested at the Saskatchewan laboratory, it revealed a radiocarbon age of 5945 ± 145 years, which means we can now be reasonably certain of the era during which these people left their footprints. Allowing a thousand years for soil development on the original land surface, the footprints should date around 3000 B.C., a time by which central Mexican man was already domesticating beans, corn and squash. Very likely such agrarian developments---which eventually led to the rise of the Mesoamerican civilizations---had spread as far as Lake Managua, although it is also probable that the people of the area still largely depended on game as their primary source of food. Someday, perhaps, someone will uncover the settlement these people once inhabited; so fortunate a find would tell us whether they actually were involved in plant domestication and help explain why Mesoamerican urbanization left this area so largely untouched.

PREHISTORIC FOOTPRINTS FROM EL SALVADOR

Haberland, Wolfgang, and Grebe, Willi-Herbert; *American Antiquity,* 22:282–285, 1957.

During 1955, while working on geological and archaeological reconnaissance, the writers learned incidentally about the discovery of some "footprints in stone" on the hacienda La Carrera. They were found during the construction of a farm road in a territory locally called "La Rama," 10 km. southwest of the town Usulutan, 4 km. northeast of the little harbor Puerto El Triunfo on the Bahia de Jiquilisco, and 2 to 3 km. north of the coastal mangrove swamps. Some of the slabs were saved out of curiosity by local workmen and brought to the hacienda while the rest were destroyed by tractors using the road. At the time of our visit to the hacienda the slabs deposited there were mostly heavily weathered, but the imprints were still distinguishable. One of them was quite perfect and showed a human right foot 26 cm. long. Besides these human signs there were 2 different animal tracks, the larger one, measuring 10 cm. in diameter, certainly belonging to the cat family.

After locating one of the workmen who originally found the tracks, we went with him to the spot and made cuts in the steep banks of the road. On the north side only one very poor imprint, indicating a southeasterly direction could be found, while on the southern side eight of them were revealed, with certainly more to the north. These imprints, showing 4 right and 4 left feet, belong at least to 5 persons walking in a northwesterly direction. They were deeper (up to 5 cm.) and not as clear as the ones seen at the hacienda, certainly due to softer soil. The largest of them had a length of 32 cm., the smallest, perhaps of a child, of 21 cm.

As regards the determination of age of the tracks, geological and archaeological considerations have to be combined. The footprints are

1.50 m. under the surface. The profile shows in the upper parts a darkish brown soil; 1.20 m. beneath the surface a layer 30 cm. thick consists of dark brown, partly consolidated sand, which is separated from
the tracks by a layer of fine-grained sand only a few centimeters thick.
The imprints themselves are embedded in a light brown, partly greenish
sandstone of unequally-grained consistency. Remains of plants and an
imprint of an unidentifiable bone farther down than the tracks were found
in it. This layer was examined to a depth of 30 cm.

. . . .

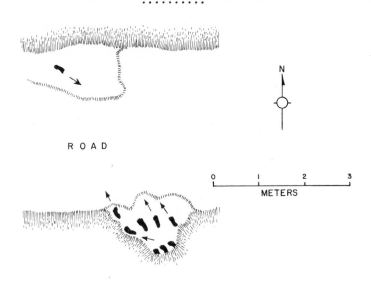

Fossil footprints uncovered during road construction in El Salvador

Therefore, we are inclined to date these footprints between A. D. 200
and 800. With this dating they are very much younger than the only known
other example of fossil footprints in Central America, those of Acahua-
linca near Managua, Nicaragua, excellently described and discussed by
Howel Williams in 1953.

ALLEGED HUMAN FOOTPRINTS IN TENNESSEE ROCKS
Anonymous; *Scientific American,* 47:388, 1882.

A correspondent of the Nashville <u>American</u> tells of some curious
footprints in sandrock at a place about twenty miles west of Nashville.

"At this point Harpeth River forms a horseshoe bend, making a circuit of six miles, and doubling back on itself to within 80 or 90 yards. In the heel of the shoe rises a ridge, forming almost a perpendicular bluff on both sides, extending about half a mile south in the direction of the toe of the shoe. It rises to the height of about 400 feet, and at the highest point is not more than eight feet wide on the top, with a perpendicular face on the east side for 100 feet or more---that is, a plumb line suspended from the edge of the precipice at the top would hang clear for 100 feet or more before it would encounter any obstruction. The ridge at the bed of the river is some 90 yards wide, but the slope which brings it to that width at the bottom is mostly on the western side.

"At the highest point on the crest of this ridge is a flat surface rock, and on that rock are imprinted six and a half tracks of human feet. These tracks are indented into the rock as much as a quarter of an inch, or in some places more. The tracks are of bare feet, toes all pointing in the same north. They are less than the average size man's foot, and larger than the average size woman's foot, one a little in advance of the other. The next pair is on the south side, but near to the first. In size and appearance they represent the tracks of a child fifteen or eighteen months old. The track of the right foot of this pair is turned in a little at the toes, and the toes of that foot are turned down, as we often see children, when first learning to walk, seem to endeavor to clutch the floor with their toes, as if to avoid falling or slipping. The topographical relation of these tracks to the large ones indicates that the child might have been holding to the finger or hand of the larger person.

"South of these little tracks, but near to them, is the third pair, indicating a child some four to six years old. These last were made by a beautiful pair of feet, and are as pretty tracks as a child ever made in the dust or soft earth. All of these tracks are within three or four feet of the edge of the precipice on the eastern side, as already described. But I have said there was a half track, which is the most interesting feature on the tablet. This half track is printed on the very edge of the precipice, and represents the heel and hinder half of the foot from the middle of the instep back, and would indicate that the toes and front part of the foot projected over the precipice, or that the rock had broken off at that point. This half track is of the large size foot, or foot of the adult person, and is immediately in front of the large pair of tracks already mentioned. "

THE NEVADA BIPED TRACKS

Cope, E.D.; *American Naturalist,* 17:69-71, 1883.

The discovery that the tracks of several species of Pliocene Mammalia in the argillaceous sandstones of the quarry of the Nevada State Prison at Carson, are accompanied by those of a biped resembling man, is a further confirmation of these views. The tracks are clearly those of a biped, and are not those of a member of the Simiidae, but must be referred to the Hominidae. Whether they belong to a species of the genus Homo or not, cannot be ascertained from the tracks alone, but can be determined on the discovery of the bones and teeth. In any case the animal was probably the ancestor of existing man, and was a contemporary of the Elephas primigenius and a species of Equus.

Human footprints in sandstone quarry, Carson, Nevada

ON THE SUPPOSED HUMAN FOOTPRINTS RECENTLY FOUND IN NEVADA
Anonymous; *Nature*, 28:370-371, 1883.

During the past summer various accounts have been published of the discovery of human footprints in sandstone near Carson, Nevada. The locality is in the yard of the State prison, and the tracks were uncovered in quarrying stone for building purposes. Many different kinds of tracks were found, some of which were made by an animal allied to the elephant; some resembled those of the horse and the deer; others were apparently made by a wolf. There were also tracks made by large birds.

The footprints occur in series, and are all nearly in the same horizon. Some of the smaller tracks are sharp and distinct, but most of the impressions are indefinite in outline, owing apparently to the fact that the exact surface on which they were made is not usually exposed.

The supposed human footprints are in six series, each with alternate right and left tracks. The stride is from two and a half to over three feet in extent. The individual footprints are from eighteen to twenty inches in length, and about eight inches wide. The distance between the line of right-hand and left-hand tracks, or the straddle, is eighteen to nineteen inches.

The form and general appearance of the supposed human tracks is shown in Fig. 2, which is a reduced copy of one of the impressions represented by Dr. W. H. Harkness, in his paper before the California Academy of Sciences, August 7, 1882. The shaded portion was restored by him from other footprints of the series. A copy of this impression was given also by Prof. Joseph LeConte, in his paper before the same Society, August 27, 1882.

The size of these footprints, and especially the width between the right and left series, are strong evidence that they were not made by men, as has been so generally supposed.

A more probable explanation is that the impressions are the tracks of a large sloth, either <u>Mylodon</u> or <u>Morotherium</u>, remains of which have been found in essentially the same horizon. In support of this view it may be said that the footprints are almost exactly what these animals would make if the hind feet covered the impressions of those in front. In size, in stride, and in width between the right and left series of impressions, the footprints agree closely with what we should expect <u>Mylodon</u> or <u>Morotherium</u> to make. In Fig. 1 the bones of the left hind foot of a species of Mylodon are represented, the figure being reduced to the same scale as the accompanying cut, Fig. 2, of one of the supposed human footprints.

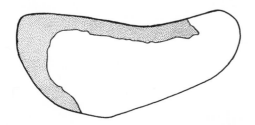

The geological horizon of these interesting footprints is near the junction of the Pliocene and Quaternary. The evidence, at present, appears to point to the Equus beds of the upper Pliocene as the nearest equivalent.

Since the above communication was read, the writer has had an opportunity of examining photographs and casts of the Carson footprints, and is confirmed in his opinion that the supposed human tracks were made by large Edentates. The important fact has recently been determined that some of these tracks show impressions of the fore feet. The latter are somewhat outside of the large footprints, as would naturally be the case if the animal changed its course.

AN ANCIENT GRAVE

Anonymous; *American Antiquarian,* 13:179-180, 1891.

These remains of an unknown race that once inhabited this country recall other very interesting remains found on the farm of William D. Huff, near Irondale, Mo., and about twelve miles from Bonne Terre. These latter are found in a rocky glade, covered with a soft, yellowish bastard limestone, in which, many years ago, there were hundreds of tracks of human feet and of almost every animal formerly inhabiting the country. Years ago, however, the locality became known to curiosity hunters, and all the best specimens have been carried away. Among the foot-prints were those of bears, deer, turkeys, etc., as well as human feet, most of which were as perfect as if they had been made by the impression of the foot in soft mud which dried into stone; and, indeed, there are some who believe this to have been the case. Notwithstanding the great number of specimens that have been carried away, there are still many left; and to those who take an interest in such matters the locality is a highly interesting one.

IMPRESSIONS (CHIEFLY TRACKS) ON ALLUVIAL CLAY, IN HADLEY, MASS.

Hitchcock, Charles H.; *American Journal of Science,* 2:19:391-396. 1855.

In the summer of 1852, in company with Mr. E. C. Bolles of Hartford, I accidentally discovered various impressions on a clay bed situated upon the east bank of the Connecticut river directly south of Hadley Centre, and a short distance north of Shepard's Island. The bed lies beneath about twenty feet of alluvial sand, which abounds in ferruginous tubular concretions. By the action of freshets, a large amount of the sand lying upon the clay has been removed, leaving about two or three acres of level surface exposed. The bed itself is close by the place described in my father's (Pres. Hitchcock's) Final Report on the Geology of Massachusetts, as abounding in claystones of remarkable forms.

The impressions are principally found upon muddy deposits made by rains in the irregularities of the surface. The circumstances in which these impressions occur, afford an admirable illustration of the manner in which similar appearances were produced upon what is now solid rock. It is to be lamented that recent tracks were not more studied at the time when it was doubted by men of science whether ichnolites were originally made by animals. In those days of discussion at least one of such doubters was convinced that the impressions were foot-marks, by noticing a piece of clay in the cabinet having on it a few tracks of a snipe. Though skeptics are now few on this subject, additional confirmation of the facts and deductions of Ichnolithology may still be of value.

Impressions of thirteen different kinds of animals have been noticed at this locality: viz., of man, four species of birds, two of quadrupeds, one batrachian, snails and annelids, besides two or three of a doubtful character.

The human imprint is one of the most interesting. It is a single impression of a boy's foot, and occurs with two of a crow. Raindrop impressions had been made on the spot before the others had been formed, and were not entirely obliterated by the foot of the boy. All the striae and lines upon the sole of the foot appear distinctly on the specimens, particularly the fine striae and ridges. The phalangeal impressions and papillae of the crow's foot are also strongly marked. The difference between the integuments of the foot of man and birds is finely exhibited: in the former the lines are much finer, and parallel to one another, running mostly across the foot; while in the latter the papillae cover the whole phalanx with dots, scattered irregularly.

. . . .

HUMAN FOOT-PRINTS IN THE STRATIFIED ROCK

Hubbell, Herbert P.; *Popular Science Monthly,* 22:262, 1882.

Near the mouth of the Little Cheyenne River, in Dakota Territory, there is a rock on which are some curious indentations. The rock lies on the north slope of a bowlder-covered hill, and is itself an erratic. It is about twelve feet long by seven or eight feet wide, and rises above the surface of the ground about eighteen inches. Its edges are angular, its surface flat, and it shows but little, if any, effect of ice-action. It appears to be magnesian limestone, and its size and whiteness make it a conspicuous object.

On the surface, near the southeast corner of it, is a perfect foot-print as though made by the left, moccasined foot of a woman, or boy of, say, fourteen years. The toes are toward the north. The indentation is about half an inch deep. About four and a half feet in front of it and in line with it, near the middle of the rock, is a deeper indentation made with the <u>right</u> foot, the heel being deeper than the rest of the foot. And again, about five and a half feet in front of this, and in line with both the others, is a third foot-print, this time with the <u>left</u> foot.

The three foot-prints are of the same size, and are such as would apparently be made by a person running rapidly. The foot-print of the right foot is an inch deep at the heel, and three quarters of an inch at the ball. The third foot-print is about three quarters of an inch in depth. In all three the arch of the instep is well defined, and the toes faintly indicated. The rock is hard, and not of uniform texture, having vein-like markings about a quarter of an inch wide running through it, which, weathering harder than the body of the rock, present slightly raised surfaces. <u>This difference in the weathering of the rock is the same in the bottom of the foot-prints as on the surface of the rock.</u>

From Mr. LeBeau, a "squaw-man," who has lived in that region for twenty-six years, I learned that it is known to the Indians as a "medicine" rock, and that they worship it. He says that none of the present Indians know anything of the origin of the foot-prints. A town has been recently started within half a mile of it, called Waneta, and white children playing about it have found numerous beads and other trinkets, probably placed there as offerings.

I had heard of the rock several weeks previous to my visit, and expected to find either the work of nature with only a fancied resemblance, or the rude sculpturing of the Indians. The uniformity in size and direction discredits the former view, as the difference between the foot-prints seem to make the latter doubtful; and the <u>possibility</u> of the foot-prints having been made when the material of which the rock is composed was in a soft state presents itself as the best solution of the problem.

ANCIENT HUMAN FOOTPRINTS

Barnaby, Wendy; *Nature,* 254:553, 1975.

This footprint may be 250,000 years old: one of the oldest recorded prints of man.   Pressed into volcanic ash, it was uncovered with some others in 1970 during the construction of a dam near Demirkopru in Turkey.   It is now on display at the Museum of National history in Stockholm, as part of an exhibition about the origins and future of man.

The Museum acquired the print from Mr. Thomas Barton, one of the engineers working on the project in Turkey when the print was uncovered. He did not, however, actually see it extracted as he was working some miles away at the time.   He was given it later by men at the discovery site, who told him of its possible interest, and when he returned to Stockholm he brought it with him.

The placard explaining the exhibit states that the Turkish Metal Research Institute in Ankara determined the age of the ash and that the National Laboratory of Forensic Science in Stockholm has examined the print and agrees with the Turkish institute's findings.   The forensic laboratory however, denies having tested the ash.   According to a spokesman there, two members of staff were only asked to determine whether the imprint was actually of a foot or not.   In their opinion it was.   Neither has the Natural History Museum itself carried out any tests on the ash, as the equipment at its disposal cannot cope with the supposed youth of the sample.   In the opinion of Professor Welin, of the museum's research department, any tests he could do would yield only a very approximate indication of the age of the ash.   And there is no equipment elsewhere in Stockholm which could make a more accurate determination.

Apart from the Turkish test, then, where has the 250,000 year old estimate come from?

The impression of the heel is deeper than that of the instep and the whole print is slightly blurred, suggesting it was made by someone running in the ash.   The foot was pointing in the direction of the River Gediz. The theory advanced to fit these facts is that a man was caught in the midst of a volcanic eruption and ran for his life towards the river, imprinting the ash which, because of rain and heat, was baked into that form and shortly afterwards covered with lava.   And Mr. Barton says that there was volcanic activity in Turkey 250,000 years ago.

If this theory is correct, the print would belong to the Quaternary period.   The Museum states that the print predates Cro-Magnon man, who came to Europe at the end of the last ice age.   If this is true the runner would have lived during the Pleistocene period---possibly at the same time as Neanderthal man.

. . . .

FOSSIL FOOTPRINTS
Armstrong, H. L.; *Nature,* 255:668, 1975.

The account of the finding of a fossilised human footprint in Turkey (Nature, April 17) would seem to indicate that fossil human footprints are now becoming scientifically respectable.

If this is so, readers might be interested in comparing those found in and around the Paluxy River, near Glen Rose, Texas, in rock usually identified as Cretaceous. The unusual thing there is that dinosaur footprints are found in the same strata.

These footprints have been shown in a well known film <u>Footprints in Stone</u>. Also, descriptions and comments have been given from time to time in the <u>Creation Research Society Quarterly</u>.

I have seen neither the prints themselves from Texas nor, of course, those from Turkey. On the basis of photographs, however, I can only say that the prints from Texas appear to be much better ones.

FOSSILIZED TECHNOLOGY

In examining our vast scientific heritage, one stumbles with surprising frequency across accounts of blocks of coal that yield items of obvious human manufacture. Some of these stories are doubtless hoaxes, but are they all? All <u>should</u> be, because coal and most rocks are supposed to be considerably more ancient than the human species. Still, many such stories exist. Creationists have been most diligent in collecting accounts of young things in old rocks, for they wish to show that the rocks and the earth are really young, as their literal interpretation of the Bible requires. An alternative view, assuming these stories are true, is that man is actually much older than prevailing theories predict.

This rather bizarre line of investigation is closely linked to the <u>much more frequent</u> reports of living animals, especially toads, found in solid rock and other incredible geological situations. (See the <u>Strange Planet</u> series of sourcebooks.) Entombed toads and man-made spoons found in coal must all be rejected to avoid time paradoxes. Like UFOs and sea monsters, these contrary, seemingly trivial observations keep recurring. The incredible number of such incredibilities make one wonder if we are not missing something.

QUERIES AND STATEMENTS CONCERNING A NAIL FOUND IMBEDDED IN A BLOCK OF SANDSTONE. . . . .
Brewster, David; *Report of the British Association*, pt. 2, 51, 1844.

This communication, drawn up by Mr. Buist, consisted of a series of queries, with the answers that had been returned by different persons connected with the quarry, the inquiry being set on foot by persons present on the discovery of the nail or immediately afterwards. The following is the substance of the investigation.

1. The circumstance of the discovery of the nail in the block of stone.
The stone in Kingoodie quarry consists of alternate layers of hard
stone and a soft clayey substance called "till;" the courses of stone varying from six inches to upwards of six feet in thickness. The particular
block in which the nail was found, was nine inches thick, and in proceed-
ing to clear the rough block for dressing, the point of the nail was found
projecting about half an inch (quite eaten with rust) into the "till," the
rest of the nail laying along the surface of the stone to within an inch of
the head, which went right down into the body of the stone. The nail was
not discovered while the stone remained in the quarry, but when the rough
block (measuring two feet in length, one in breadth, and nine inches in
thickness) was being cleared of the superficial "till." There is no evidence beyond the condition of the stone to prove what part of the quarry
this block may have come from.
    2. The condition of the quarry from which the block of stone was
obtained.
The quarry itself (called the east quarry) has only been worked for
about twenty years, but an adjoining one (the west quarry) has been formerly very much worked, and has given employment at one time to as
many as 500 men. Very large blocks of stone have at intervals been
obtained from both. It is observed that the rough block in which the nail
was found must have been turned over and handled at least four or five
times in its journey to Inchyra, at which place it was put before masons
for working, and where the nail was discovered.

COIN IN LUMP OF COAL
Anonymous; *Strand Magazine,* 21:477, 1901.

Mr. R. C. Hardman, of Meadhurst, Uppingham, has been the fortunate finder of a coin dated 1397 embedded in a lump of coal, which
formed part and parcel of a ton of that useful commodity bought at
current prices.

MOLDED METALLIC OBJECTS FOUND IN CHALK BED
Anonymous; *INFO Journal,* 1:22-23, 1969.

Translation of a letter to Mssrs. Pauwels and Bergier, Editions
Planete, Paris.

Caen, France 30, Sept. 1968
We would like to bring to your attention the following facts, and hope
you will give our discovery some consideration. As speleologists and in-

vestigators, we have studied for several years the Pays d'Auge region of Calvados. During the year 1968 we discovered some metallic nodules in a hollow in an Aptian chalk bed in a quarry being worked in Saint-Jean de Livet. These metallic nodules have a reddish brown color, a form absolutely identical (semi-ovoid, but are of different size. A central section had a form corresponding with the exterior form.

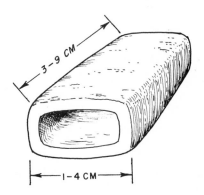

These nodules at first seemed to be fossils, but having examined them carefully we became conscious of their entirely metallic nature. Experiments at the forge showed that the carbon content was higher than castings of today. We were lead to consider the hypothesis that they were meteorites, but five pieces were found all of the same nature, which lead us to reject this hypothesis. There remains only an intelligent intervention in the Secondary Era (the end of the Cretaceous) of beings who could cast such objects. These objects, then, prove the presence of intelligent life on earth long before the limits given today by prehistoric archeology. (Y. Druet and H. Salfati)

P. S.: The Geomorphology Laboratory of the University of Caen is now studying these objects which we have sent them (without great hopes.)

EVE'S THIMBLE

Adams, J. Q.; *American Antiquarian*, 5:331-332, 1883.

Such is the name given to a thimble owned by a well known "ranchman" of this state. I have recently seen the thimble and give you a description of it, and of the circumstances of finding it. The thimble appears to be of iron, moulded, and when first found was a whole top thimble. By much handling since some of it has crumbled away. What is left is "flaky" and could be easily picked to pieces. It is marked something as thimbles are now, and has a slight shoulder at the base.

Some years ago when Colorado coal was first burned, the present owner of the thimble drove some 14 or 15 miles to what is now known as the Marshal coal bed to get a load of coal. One old man was the owner and miner of the coal. A "drift" had been run 150 ft. into the side of the bluff, the farther end being about 300 feet from the surface. From this point the coal was taken. Upon my friends return home he placed some large chunks of the coal in the stove, but upon its not burning well, he broke them and in the midst of one, imbedded in a hollow place, but completely surrounded by the coal, the thimble was found. These coal beds are classed by Prof. Hayden as l ignitic and lying between the Tertiary and the Cretaceous. Much of the coal is "fresh", some of it too "green" to burn well. My informant says the chunk in which the thimble was found "showed the grain of the wood." For sometime he kept it, but it is now lost. The thimble was full of coal and sand and retained its shape well.

Where did the thimble come from? How did it get there? Were there any of these western tribes who possessed such a thing before the coming of the white man? Who can answer?

A CURIOSITY FROM COAL
Wiant, Harry V., Jr.; *Creation Research Society Quarterly,* 13:74, 1976.

I recently published a photograph of a stone carving at the Copan Mayan Indian ruins in Honduras which appeared to represent gears with spoked wheels and housing. In response, Mrs. Myrna R. Burdick wrote to me and mentioned a spoon she and her mother found in soft Pennsylvania coal in 1937. Through further correspondence I obtained a photograph and details of the find.

The spoon was found in a mass of off-brown colored ash which remained after burning a large piece of coal. The ashes, when disturbed, fell apart, revealing the spoon.

It was intact when first found, but was broken later, perhaps while being examined at the Smithsonian Institute. The Institute personnel, of course, rejected the idea that such an item could be found in coal.

This might well be a relic from the antediluvian world.

NOT THE SALZBURG STEEL CUBE, BUT AN IRON OBJECT FROM WOLFSEGG
Malthaner, Hubert; *Pursuit,* 6:90–93, 1973.

In the autumn of 1885 in the iron foundry of Isidor Braun's sons at Schondorf near Vocklabruck in Upper Austria a workman was smashing big

blocks of coal which had arrived from the coal pit at Wolfsegg as fuel for
heating a smelter. During the course of this work he found the now famous
object, a find that was then widely noticed because of its form and circumstance of discovery. In 1886 a mining engineer, Dr. Adolf Gurlt, gave a
lecture for the Naturhistorischer Verein (Natural History Society) at Bonn
concerning his investigations of the object. He told the audience that some
specialists felt that, because of its roughly square form, the metal object
might have been worked on, but that in his opinion it was a fossil iron
meteorite because of a thin film of oxide on the surfaces and the strange,
hollow marks thereon. The report was printed in Verhandlungen des Natur-
historischen Vereins der preussischen Rheinlande, Verlag Max Cohen &
Sohn, Bonn, 1886, page 188. This was the first report on the object and the
source of all later reports. Translated into English, the most pertinent
section reads as follows:

"Dr. Gurlt submitted a strange iron meteorite, so-called Holosiderite
...which was found in tertiary brown coal. It is in the possession of the
municipal Carolino-Augusteum Museum at Salzburg and was presented to it
by Messrs. Isidor Braun Sons at Schondorf near Vocklabruck in Upper
Austria. The object was discovered at the steel and file factory of this firm,
accidentally...in 1885 by a workman when he smashed a block of brown coal
...". The essential contents of this report were those included in Nature
and L'Astronomie. Dr. Gurlt further told his audience that a polished and
etched surface showed no Widmanstatten pattern. He thought that the shape
of the iron object was caused by the strong heat plus the rotation of the
"meteorite" during its flight through the atmosphere. Dr. Gurlt also stated,
erroneously, that the object was kept in the Carolino-Augusteum Museum at
Salzburg, but the object was in fact never at Salzburg. In my opinion, Dr.
Gurlt was confused by the similar-sounding names of two museums, one at
Salzburg and the other at Linz. The Francisco-Carolinum Museum at Linz
had the object from 1950 to 1958 and I suppose that it had been presented to
this museum by its finders. This museum, which is today the Oberoster-
reichisches Landesmuseum, has in its possession a plaster copy of the
"Wolfsegg Iron". Photographs 1 and 2 are of this plaster copy because they
show the uninjured outline of the object.

The original "cube" was in the possession of the Braun family at Vocklabruck but in 1958 the Wolfsegg Iron was presented to a local museum, the
Heimathaus at Vocklabruck, where it is in the loving custody of Herrn Ober-
schulrat Robert Bernhart, retired. I was able to inspect it personally this
year. Photographs 3 and 4 show the original object in its present form. In
my opinion these photographs will eliminate all speculation about a "cube".
The only smooth surface occurs where a sample was taken for analysis in
Vienna in 1966 (A). One can see there also an older cut and polished surface
where, in Dr. Gurlt's time, an unidentified scientific institution (alledgedly
in Paris) had tried in vain to find Widmanstatten figures (B in photo).

In 1966/67 the object was subjected to the most modern electron-beam
microanalysis at the Vienna Naturhistorisches Museum and it was found that
the "Wolfsegg Iron" contained no traces of nickel, chromium, or cobalt and
that, therefore, it could not be a meteorite. Because the object contains
very little manganese, the final opinion of Dr. Kurat of the Naturhistorisches
Museum and Dr. R. Grill of the Geologische Bundesanstalt in Vienna is that
the object is cast-iron. Dr. Grill believes that such iron objects were used
as ballast with primitive mining machinery.

Thus far in examining the iron find from Wolfsegg we have approached truth through several statements in the negative: it is not steel, it is not a cube, and it is not a meteorite. And, though Dr. Gurlt told his audience that the object was found enclosed in tertiary brown coal, there seems at the moment to be no way positively to ascertain such an alleged age for it. And as we have seen, there are several errors in his report. Apparently Dr. Gurlt had neither visited the correct museum nor had he examined the block of brown coal with the intention of finding the cavity or part of a cavity which might have contained the iron object. The man who is today the owner of I. Braun's Sons file factory, Herr Diplomingenieur Martin Braun, does not exclude the possibility that the object was simply found between the coal fragments and might perhaps not have been actually enclosed in any of them. If the object is cast iron and was found in an iron foundry, it might very well have originated there, and in fact even have been cast there.

It seems to me that this strange object could well have been made in the following way: to cast any object one needs a pattern to make a mould. The rows of hollow marks on the surface of the object show us a possible way in which it might have been manufactured. The pattern was kneaded from some soft material (clay or wax); and the marks are imprints of fingertips. When the periphery of the two opposite faces being rounded was pressed down, the four edges were pressed outward. In this way the "deep incision round the four sides of the cube" could have originated. The pattern was moulded in sand and then the "Iron of Wolfsegg" was cast.

This ends my report on the strange find which has become known around the globe and has posed an enigma to several generations. In my opinion the facts are now clear, though an intriguing residue of unsolved problems still plagues my mind.

A RELIC OF A BY-GONE AGE

Anonymous; *Scientific American,* 7:298, 1852.

A few days ago a powerful blast was made in the rock at Meeting House Hill, in Dorchester, a few rods south of Rev. Mr. Hall's meeting house. The blast threw out an immense mass of rock, some of the pieces weighing several tons and scattered small fragments in all directions. Among them was picked up a metallic vessel in two parts, rent assunder by the explosion. On putting the two parts together it formed a bell-shaped vessel, 4-1/2 inches high, 6-1/2 inches at the base 2-1/2 inches at the top, and about an eighth of an inch in thickness. The body of this vessel resembles zinc in color, or a composition metal, in which there is a considerable portion of silver. On the sides there are six figures of a flower, or bouquet, beautifully inlaid with pure silver, and around the lower part of the vessel a vine, or wreath, inlaid also with silver. The chasing, carving, and inlaying are exquisitely done by the art of some cunning workman. This curious and unknown vessel was blown out of the solid pudding stone, fifteen feet below the surface. It is now in the possession of Mr. John Kettell. Dr. J. V. C. Smith, who has recently travelled in the East, and examined hundreds of curious domestic utensils, and has drawings of them, has never seen anything resembling this. He has taken a drawing and accurate dimensions of it, to be submitted to the scientific. There is no doubt but that this curiosity was blown out of the rock, as above stated; but will Professor Agassiz, or some other scientific man please to tell us how it came there? The matter is worthy of investigation, as there is no deception in the case.

SINGULAR IMPRESSION IN MARBLE

Browne, J. B.; *American Journal of Science,* 1:19:361, 1831.

About twelve miles N. W. of this city, is a marble quarry owned by Mr. Henderson. It belongs to the primitive lime formation, and in this district forms the last of that series. The order in which the rocks repose are, commencing at Philadelphia, as follows; gneiss, mica slate, hornblende, talcose slate, primitive clay slate, a very narrow strip of eurite, and then the primitive lime rock, to which this belongs. The quarry has been worked for many years, in some places to the depths of sixty, seventy, and eighty feet. In the month of November last, a block of marble measuring upwards of thirty cubic feet, was taken out from the depth of between sixty and seventy feet, and sent to Mr. Savage's marble saw mill in Norristown to be cut into slabs. One was taken off about three feet wide and about six feet long, and in the body of the marble, exposed by the cutting, was immediately discovered an indentation, about one and a half inches long and about five eighths of an inch wide, in which were the two raised characters. Fortunately, several of the most respectable gentlemen residing in Norristown were called upon to witness this remarkable phenomenon, without whose testimony it might have been difficult, if not impossible, to have satisfied the public, that an imposition had not been practised by cutting the indentation and carving the letters after the slab was cut off.

I send you a cast of the impressions by the bearer of this letter. I am Sir very sincerely, your obt. servt.

PREHISTORIC SURGERY—A NEOLITHIC SURVIVAL

MacCurdy, George G.; *American Anthropologist,* 7:17, 1905.

Our knowledge of prehistoric surgery is limited to operations that affected the bony tissue. One of the best known and most remarkable operations performed by our neolithic ancestors is without question that of trepanation, the evidence of their skill and success in the use of rude instruments being nothing short of marvelous.

The object of this paper is to call attention to a peculiar type of prehistoric surgery having certain points in common with trepanning, and which have been brought to light during the last decade. So far as at present known, this type occurs in France over a limited area lying to the north of Paris, between the Seine and the Oise. The history of the series of discoveries, as well as of Prof. L. Manouvrier's successive observations and attempts at an explanation until finally the correct solution was reached, forms an interesting chapter in methods of arriving at scientific facts.

The crania bearing marks of the operation in question are not only from a limited area, but are also from dolmens belonging to the neolithic period. The Dolmen de la Justice at Epone, near Mantes (Seine-et-Oise), had been known since 1833---in fact so long that, owing to its dilapidated condition, it was supposed to have been already robbed of its contents. However, M. Perrier du Carne, of Mantes, thought it worth while, in 1881, to obtain from the owner, Madame Piot, a permit to excavate, and was very much surprised to find the sepulture intact. In addition to pottery, stone implements, and ornaments, he obtained portions of about sixty skeletons, including twelve crania. Professor Manouvrier, to whom the human bones were referred for examination, observed that three of the female crania were marked by curious and similar mutilations in the region of the vertex. In every case the cicatrice is T-shaped. The antero-posterior branch begins just above the anterior curve of the frontal, extends along the sagittal suture, and terminates near the obelion where the transverse branch is encountered. The latter descends on either side to a point back of the parietal protuberances. The scars are evidently the result of lesions of the scalp made during life, and deep enough to affect, directly or indirectly, the periosteum.

Searching through the Broca collection, Manouvrier found three other examples of the cicatrice in T, and all three on feminine subjects. They came from three dolmens in the neighborhood of the dolmen of Epone, namely, Vaureal, Conflans-Sainte-Honorine, and Feigneux, all in the department of Seine-et-Oise. In one of these three cases the cicatrice was very slight, in another the diploe was uncovered by either the wound or the suppuration.

In every instance the lines forming the T were broken at intervals, giving the appearance of successive operations. The operation on the scalp, however, may have been performed at one time and in a continuous line without affecting the skull at all points. None of the crania presents pathological characters. As to the meaning of these marks, Manouvrier suggested that an explanation might be found in practices connected with religion, war, penal justice, mourning, therapeutics, or coiffure. While admitting that the peculiar shape of the scar might be due to the hieratic value attributed to T, he expresses preference for a simpler and more rational explanation. What could be more simple, for instance, than to suppose that a surgical operation on the scalp should follow the natural partings of the hair. One of these is the median line from the forehead to the whorl at the crown; the other descends laterally from the crown on either side, and they account for a feminine fashion of combining the hair which is still in use.

Dolmens to the north of Paris and within a radius of 50 kilometers were searched for further examples, and they were soon forthcoming. Of eighteen crania found by M. Fouju in the dolmen of Menouville, near l'Isle d'Adam (Seine-et-Oise), one bore the antero-posterior branch of the lesion in question, one was marked by an enigmatical oval scar in the region of the bregma (evidently to be classed as a variation of the same general type of operation), and three were unquestioned cases of trepanation---a large percentage for a sepulture containing not more than forty skeletons. The reduction of the so-called "sincipital T" to a line in the one instance and to an oval in the other led Manouvrier to substitute for the name first chosen that of "sincipital marks"; and the presence in the same dolmen of crania thus scarred, in juxtaposition with trepanned crania, supported his favorite hypothesis that the sincipital marks were, like trepanation, the result of therapeutic treatment.

. . . .

The oval scar in the region of the bregma cited above recalls precisely similar ones observed by von Luschan, of Berlin, on ancient Guanche crania from the island of Teneriffe. Of the 210 Teneriffe crania in the museums of Berlin, Leipzig, and Braunschweig, 25 have suffered scarification in the region of the grand fontanelle, two of these being completely perforated by the operation or as a result of it. Von Luschan regarded the operation as surgical and related to trepanning proper. In his opinion the bone was removed by scraping. To show that similar results could be obtained by the use of a counter-irritant, Virchow produced the skull of a patient who was treated about the year 1846 at the Charity Hospital (insane ward), Berlin. When, as a young man, Virchow was assistant at the Hospital, Professor Ideler, the physician in charge, often applied tartar-emetic ointment (Brechweinstein-Salbe) to the scalp of demented patients in order to drive out supposed inflammation. The unguent caused suppuration that occasionally attacked the skull even to the extent of producing a perforation.

Von Luschan was the first to point out the analogy between the oval lesions of the crania from the Canary islands and the T-shaped lesions on neolithic crania. This analogy became all the more evident with Manouvrier's description of the two Menouville crania, called forth a timely article by Lehmann-Nitsche in which he quotes from the ancient chroniclers of the Canaries as cited by Chil y Naranjo. The passage describing the operation is as follows:

"They made large scarifications with their stone knives on the skin of the part affected, and then cauterized the wound with roots of Malacca cane (jonc) dipped in boiling grease; preference being given to the use of goat's grease."

Almost coincident with the appearance of Lehmann-Nitsche's paper, Manouvrier had the good fortune to find in a recent work by M. Auguste Brachet, quotations from ancient books on surgery that not only serve as an explanation of the sincipital marks on neolithic crania, but also prove that similar operations were performed during the Dark Ages by the successors of Galen.

. . . .

That these oval lesions are the result of cauterization would be evident even without the support of the ancient authors whose documentary evidence must have come as an agreeable surprise to the finder---all the more so because it was unexpected. It would seem incredible were it not for the fact that any primitive art is apt to remain unchanged until transformed by the growth of its complementary science. When we consider what scientific limitations are imposed on the twentieth century art of healing nervous and mental diseases, there is little wonder that Avicenna, Albucasis, et al. should have made so little progress over the neolithic surgeons. Rather do the latter command anew our admiration because of their skill and courage. Their success, too, may be measured by the number that survived treatment, even if they were not cured. That they had courage in daring to operate on cases that would now be regarded as hopeless seems to be abundantly attested by the Champignolles example, where the hardihood of the surgeon was certainly equaled by the fortitude of the patient.

What could better explain the marks on these skulls, especially the one from Champignolles, than Avicenna's prescription for melancholia: "When nothing else avails, the head is to be cauterized in the form of a cross"; or that of Albucasis for the same disease, which is even more explicit: "When there is a tendency toward hypochondria, the cautery is to be applied lightly but at numerous points.... This kind of cauterization restores to the brain its normal humidity." For epilepsy, the same authority says to "cauterize on the vertex, on the occiput, and on the frontal protuberances" (forehead). Cephalalgia being caused, as he thought, by an excess of cold and humidity in the brain, the proper corrective would be found in heat, and the resulting noisome vapors would pass by exhalation through the points cauterized. Such was the doctrine of Albucasis, and it tallies perfectly with neolithic practice.

CURIOUS HUMAN SKELETONS

Archeologists dote on fragments of human bones, pottery, and stone tools found in the top-most film of dirt and rock covering the earth. Just as geologists construct time-ordered sequences of strata showing terrestrial evolution, archeologists build models of cultural succession that demonstrate ever-upward biological and cultural evolution. All of these statements of evolution represent prevailing dogmas that are continually challenged by discoveries of anomalies. Human skeletons "should not" be too old, in the wrong places, or stray too far from the acceptable human model. Exceptions abound; and we have had no difficulty in assembling a curious collection of osseous anomalies.

First, there are skeletons that have been found in rocks far too ancient; second, many human remains found in North America belie the prevailing view than man is a relative newcomer to the continent. Finally, some ancient skeletons are too big, too small, or are constructed with the wrong numbers of parts. A few biological sports are acceptable, but graves of giants and extensive pigmy cemeteries in the United States must be disbelieved.

• Fossil Man

A NEW OREOPITHECUS SKELETON
Straus, William L., Jr.; *Science,* 128:523, 1958.

On the morning of 2 August 1958 a presumably complete skeleton of what is apparently an Oreopithecus bambolii, was discovered by a coal-miner at Baccinello, Italy, some 200 meters below the surface. All previous Oreopithecus specimens have been fragmentary. This discovery therefore is particularly noteworthy, since it may provide the evidence needed to settle definitely the controversy about the taxonomic position of Oreopithecus, a matter of prime importance [see Science 126, 345 (23 August 1957)].

The block of lignite containing the skeleton will eventually be studied at the Natural History Museum, Basel, Switzerland, by Johannes Hurzeler, who, supported by the Wenner-Gren Foundation for Anthropological Research of New York City and some Swiss friends, has collected many specimens of Oreopithecus at Baccinello. Hurzeler was in Baccinello at the time of this latest discovery and personally supervised the difficult removal of the fossil from the mine.

. . . .

ON THE PROBABLE EXISTENCE OF MAN DURING THE MIOCENE PERIOD
Calvert, Frank; *Anthropological Institute, Journal,* 3:127–129, 1873.

I have had the good fortune to discover, in the vicinity of the Dardanelles, conclusive proofs of the existence of man during the Miocene period of the tertiary age. From the face of a cliff composed of strata

of that period, at a geological depth of eight hundred feet, I have myself
extracted a fragment of the joint of a bone of either a dinotherium or a
mastodon, on the convex side of which is deeply incised the unmistake-
able figure of a horned quadruped, with arched neck, lozenge-shaped
chest, long body, straight fore-legs, and broad feet. There are also
traces of seven or eight other figures which, together with the hind quarters of the first, are nearly obliterated. The whole design encircles the
exterior portion of the fragment, which measures nine inches in diameter
and five in thickness. I have also found in different parts of the same
cliff, not far from the site of the engraved bone, a flint flake and some
bones of animals, fractured longitudinally, obviously by the hand of man
for the purpose of extracting the marrow, according to the practice of
all primitive races.

There can be no doubt as to the geological character of the formation
from which I disinterred these interesting relics. The well-known writer
on the geology of Asia Minor, M. de Tchihatcheff, who visited this region,
determined it to be of the miocene period; and the fact is further confirmed by the fossil bones, teeth, and shells of the epoch found there.
I sent drawings of some of these fossils to Sir John Lubbock, who oblig-
ingly informs me that having submitted them to Messrs. G. Busk and
Jeffreys, those eminent authorities have identified amongst them the remains of dinotherium, and the shell of a species of melania, both of
which strictly appertain to the miocene epoch.

In addition to these discoveries, and at about ten miles distance from
the above locality, I have lately come upon other traces of man's existence in drift two or three hundred feet thick, underlying four or five
hundred feet of stratified rocks. I cannot positively affirm that this
formation is likewise miocene, the fossil shells it contains not having
yet been examined scientifically; but in all probability such will prove
to be the case. Throughout this drift, I have found numerous stone implements, much worn. Flint is comparatively rare, but other hard
stones have been adopted, jasper, of red and other colours, being predominant. Some of the implements are of large size, and weigh upwards
of nine pounds.

It is not more than forty or fifty years since the possibility of man's
having come into being at an earlier period than the received term of
six thousand years was first discussed; and it is only quite recently that
geologists, upon the evidence furnished by the quaternary drift, are
agreed to assign him an antiquity of about one hundred thousand years.
Some suspected traces of his existence have indeed been noticed in the
pliocene and miocene formations, but not sufficiently marked to be conclusive.

. . . .

THE CASE OF THE BONES IN STONE

Barnes, F. A.; *Desert Magazine,* 38:36–39, February 1975.

The mini-bus pulled off of the road into an area where bulldozers had removed tons of vegetation, sand and rock to leave a fairly flat, open area in the broken pinion-juniper desertland.

As the vehicle pulled to a stop in the dozed area, several passengers stepped out eagerly. This was a special rock-hounding tour, and this was prime rock-hounding country.

Within seconds after he had stepped out, too, Lin Ottinger, the tour guide, stooped to pick up something, then called out to the others.

"Hey! This is what you're looking for here."

He held a marble-sized sandy sphere in his hand. But the tiny ball was not sandy colored, it was a bright azure blue.

"Azurite balls! Here's another one!"

The hunt was on. The group scattered out across the flat area of almost colorless, decomposing sandstone, looking for little spheres of blue azurite, happy as kids at a picnic. The bulldozed land belonged to a mining company that had operations nearby, but Ottinger had obtained permission to bring rockhound tours to this special place where azurite balls were plentiful.

The search went on, and the curious blue spheres were found by the handful. Other bits of unusual rock were occasionally brought to the guide for identification. He quickly identified most specimens as fairly common local minerals. Then a collector, a woman, handed Lin a different type of specimen, a brown-stained tooth, asking him what animal it came from. He felt he knew at a glance but pulled out a magnifying lens to make sure.

Yes, it was a human tooth!

With a shout, Lin called his group of scattered rockhounds together, told them what to look for, then joined them as they set about a careful, coordinated search of the bulldozed area, watching this time for more human teeth, bits of bone fragments and, maybe, the brownish stains that decaying organic matter leaves in sand.

Within minutes, several more teeth and a number of pieces of bone were found. Some of the bone was obviously from a human skull or jawbone.

Then someone found a trace of telltale brown in the white semi-rock sand. Lin quickly went to the spot and started carefully removing the decomposing sandstone from around the dark stain. After a few minutes of careful, almost surgical excavating with his knifeblade, Lin paused. A smoothly rounded object was appearing in the center of the discolored area.

Bone! Yes, there was still whole bone left in the semi-rock, bone that had acquired a greenish tinge from the copper minerals in the sandstone. Azurite balls are a blue "cupric" form of copper compound, but the mild, complex acids released by organic decay can produce "cuprous" copper compounds. These are green.

Lin stopped digging. If this was what he suspected, it could have considerable scientific value. Bones, apparently in place, "in situ," in ancient rock strata could mean a new species of prehistoric animal. Lin had found such before. But human bones in place within rock would be even more unusual, a seeming contradiction of all currently held scientific theories about the age of mankind. Human bones 'in situ' in a rock formation had to be as old as the rock they were in, yet even the "newest" rock is far older than scientists thought the human race could possibly be.

Knowing full well the possible value of the find, Lin carefully covered

the exposed bone end with wetted paper to protect it from exposure to the
desert air and sun, then covered the paper with loose sand.

Then he explained the situation to the puzzled group. He ended his
explanation by pointing out that only an accredited scientist could establish that the bones were, indeed, human and that they were "in situ"
within the rock. And if the answers to both of these questions were
affirmative, then only the scientific community had a chance of finding
an explanation for human bones within rock strata millions of years old.

This was the beginning of a mystery story, one more of the countless
mysteries that have come to light within the great Southwestern deserts
of North America. And one whose solution, like so many others, may
never be found.

The next chapter of this story occurred about a week later, when a
scientist from the University of Utah arrived in Moab to visit the discovery site. Lin Ottinger had notified Dr. W. Lee Stokes, with whom he
had worked on previous paleontological finds, and Dr. Stokes had referred the matter to Dr. J. P. Marwitt, a professor of anthropology
at the University of Utah in Salt Lake City.

A natural history television photography team, a local news reporter
and several other interested people accompanied Lin and Dr. Marwitt
to the site, which was located in a remote desert valley some 35 miles
to the southeast of the remote Utah community of Moab.

Once there, Dr. Marwitt immediately set to work on Lin's concealed
find, carefully scraping the surrounding material from the discolored
bone! The material was neither hard sandstone nor loose sand, but
somewhere in between, a kind of semi-rock that forms when loose sand
bonds together in the presence of moisture over a long period of time.
The resulting "semi-rock" was too hard to penetrate with bare fingers,
yet scraped away readily enough with the knife blades and pointed trowels
being used for the delicate excavation.

The small group watched intently as the excavation progressed.
Movies and still photographs were taken for the record at various stages
and excitement grew as more and more bones were uncovered, bones
that were obviously still articulated, or joined together in a natural configuration.

After several hours of painstaking work, Dr. Marwitt stopped his
meticulous efforts and settled back to study what he had uncovered. By
then, officials of the nearby copper mine were on hand. Dr. Marwitt
questioned them closely about the nature of the terrain that had been
'dozed away from above the partial human skeletons now exposed.

Then the anthropologist summarized the clues to the mystery that
had come to light in this desolate desert valley.

The bones were obviously human and "in situ," that is, in place and
not washed or fallen into the stratum where they rested from higher,
younger strata. The portions of the two skeletons that were exposed
were still articulated, indicating that the bodies were still intact when
buried or covered.

Further, the bones were stained a bright green by the copper salts
that occur in the vicinity, and some of the bright blue azurite balls that
were found in and around the bones were partially turned green by reaction with the organic material of the bodies. In addition, the dark organic
stains found around the bones indicated that the bones had been complete
bodies when deposited in the ancient sandstone.

There was some question as to the exact geological formation in which the bones were found. Mine metallurgist Keith Barrett, of the Big Indian Copper Mine that owned the discovery site, recalled that the rock and sandy soil that had been removed by 'dozer from above the bones had been solid, with no visible caves or crevices. He also remembered that at least 15 feet of material had been removed, including five or six feet of solid rock. This provided strong, but not conclusive, evidence that the remains were as old as the stratum in which they were found.

And that stratum was at least 100 million years old. Due to considerable local faulting and shifting, the site could either be in the lower Dakota or the still older upper Morrison formation.

Dr. Marwitt pointed out several curious aspects of the discovery. While one body seemed to be in the doubled-up position sometimes used by ancient Indian tribes for formal burials, the other was not. Both upper bodies were missing, most probably carried away by the bulldozer that had removed the overburden during earlier routine mine development work.

This conjecture was verified by the many scattered teeth, skull fragments and other pieces of bone found lying around loose in the vicinity. Some of these had been picked up on the day of the discovery. Others had been just found, by the process of screening much of the loose sand near the undisturbed parts of the skeletons.

But, even though the bones were in place in rock over 100 million years old, they appeared to be relatively modern in configuration, that is, Homo sapiens rather than one of his ancient, half-animal predecessors.

This was not the only contradiction in the find. Even though the rock and soil layers originally above the bones were continuous and unbroken as claimed by the mine officials, there was still the possibility that there once may have been some kind of a natural or excavated opening that allowed the original owners of the mystery bones to go deep below the surface.

Further, the greenish tinge to the azurite balls next to the bones indicated that they, and the sand in which they formed, were much older than the bones. The anthropologist found this, and copper-green hue of the bones, to be most unusual. He had never seen this phenomenon before.

There seemed to be only one way to resolve the mystery posed by the green human bones in rock over 100 megayears old. Present scientific theories hold that the human race is no more than two or three million years old, and even this depends upon defining "human" in a rather loose manner.

But laboratory age-dating could determine the true age of the bones with fair accuracy. Therefore, once the bones had been thoroughly photographed and studied in their original position, Dr. Marwitt carefully removed them for transport to the university laboratories. He also took with him the loose bone fragments and teeth found in the vicinity.

There the matter rested for some time. And there the matter still rests. Somehow, the university scientists never got around to age-dating the mystery bones. Dr. Marwitt seemed to lose interest in the matter, then transferred to an eastern university. No one else took over the investigation. Lin Ottinger, growing tired of waiting after more than a year, reclaimed his box of bones.

We may never know exactly how human bones came to be in place in rock formations more than 100 million years old. It is highly probable that the bones are, indeed, this old. Yet, who knows? Without the vital age-dating, no one can say positively that they are not. Every year, new and startling finds are being made at archeological sites in Africa and each one pushes the origin of mankind back still further by another half million years or more.

Part of the mystery, of course, is why the University of Utah scientists chose not to age-date the mystery bones and clear up at least the question of their actual age.

And so the mystery remains, perhaps never to be solved.

FOSSIL MAN IN MEXICO
Anonymous; *American Naturalist,* 18:920, 1884.

Dr. Mariano Barcena, director of the department of Geology and Palaeontology of the National Museum of Mexico, recently discovered the facial and mandibular parts of a human skull in a hard rock not far from the city of Mexico. The specimen was found in a hard siliceous limestone near the border of Lake Texcoco, at some elevation above the level of the water of the lake. Overlying the bed of limestone, is a lacustrine deposit, which is similar to that made by the present lake, and contains the same mollusca, etc. Whether the limestone be a still more ancient deposit of the lake, has not yet been determined by Dr. Barcena, but the overlying deposit indicates the former wider extension of its waters. It is also evident that since the entombment of the human skull, both deposits have been elevated several feet, and separated from the part now under the lake by a fault. This was probably accomplished at the time of the projection of an eruptive hill near the locality. Dr. Barcena, from whom the above statements are derived, will shortly describe the characters of this interesting specimen.

• Antiquity of American Man

EARLY MAN IN THE NEW WORLD
Kennedy, G. E.; *Nature,* 255:274-275, 1975.

The question of man's antiquity in the New World has been the source of long and often acrimonious debate. The matter has polarised around two widely differing points of view. An ultra-conservative approach, first developed by Holmes in the 1890s and brought to full culmination by Hrdlicka in this century, was based on two premises: that man was a relatively recent immigrant to the New World and that all Amerindians were of Mongoloid racial type. Hrdlicka was especially effective in destroying any claim to an early arrival of man in the New World and the vigour of his opposition had an almost paralytic effect on the early development of Palaeoindian studies. The conservative viewpoint, scepticism now tempered with careful scholarship, has continued in the work of Haynes, Irwin and others who maintain that empirical evidence of man in the New World prior to about 12,000 BP is very tenuous. The alternate viewpoint accepts considerable antiquity for man in the Western Hemisphere. Workers such as Wormington, MacNeish and Krieger, for example, while properly maintaining that many claims of great antiquity are spurious, have pointed to some early dates which are, in fact, very difficult to dispute.

The evidence of man's occupation of the New World prior to about 12,000 BP falls neatly into two categories: archaeological evidence and human skeletal evidence. Unfortunately, the association of tools and human remains occurs at very few early sites. The Yuha site in southern California, dated at 21,500 BP ± 2,000 (Childers, Anthrop. J. Can. 12, 2; 1974) and the Marmes Rock Shelter, in Washington state, dated to about 13,000 BP (Fryxell et al., Am. Ant., 33, 511; 1968) are two of the very few early sites where such associations occur.

George Carter, whose archaeological work has centered mainly in southern California, is one of the leading proponents of great antiquity for man in the New World; he has suggested that stone tools from the Texas Street site, in San Diego, for example, possibly date to the last interglacial (Pleistocene Man at San Diego, Baltimore, 1957). His claims have been widely disputed and most archaeologists consider that the Texas Street 'tools' were formed by natural rather than human processes. The Calico archaeological site, in the desert east of Los Angeles, has been claimed to demonstrate evidence of human occupation at about 50,000 to 80,000 years ago and dates of 120,000 years ago, based on geological evidence, have also been suggested (Leakey, Simpson and Clements, Science, 160, 1022; 1968). Evidence has been put forward at Calico to support the existence of one and perhaps several hearths deeply buried in an alluvial fan. Though the human origin of the 'hearths' has been questioned the interpretation, as tools, of flaked and chipped lithic material from the site is very difficult to dispute. Conclusions

regarding the Calico site should await a more comprehensive study of the lithic materials than has been undertaken so far.   Other early sites, from Canada to South America, show artefacts of unquestioned human design in firmly dated contexts.   The Lewisville site, in eastern Texas, comprises more than 21 hearths which, in many cases, contain the burnt remains of now-extinct Upper Pleistocene fauna; charcoal from two of these hearths has been dated to more than 37,000 years (Crook and Harris, Am. Ant., 23, 233; 1958).   On Santa Rosa Island, off the southern California coast, burnt mammoth bone has been dated to 29,700
3,000 (L290R, Broecker and Kulp, Science, 126, 1324; 1957).   Other material, obtained from a fire area on the island was reportedly beyond the range of radiocarbon dating (UCLA 749, Berger and Libby, Proc. natn. Acad. Sci. USA, 56, 1678; 1966).   A recently reported site from the Old Crow River basin in north-eastern Canada has yielded a worked caribou tibia dated to 27,000 ± 3,000 -2,000 (Irving and Harington, Science, 179, 335; 1973).   One of the most indisputable of the palaeo-indian tool sites is in the Ayacucho Valley of Peru; here, in a deposit underlying a level with a radiocarbon date of 19,600 BP ± 3,000, Mac Neish has found stone tools in association with the bones of Pleistocene fauna (Scient. Am., 224, 36; 1971).   On the basis of the early occurence of this "core tool tradition" in South America, Mac Neish has suggested that man may have entered the New World as early as 100,000 years ago.

In the analysis of human skeletal material, the field of Amerindian palacontology is still in its infancy, in spite of nineteenth century origins.   Very little early human material is known and of that material provenance and associations are sometimes unsure.   With a few notable exceptions none of the very early material has been completely described and without exception none of this early material has been analysed within the statistical framework of population theory.   Such treatment, in a comparative context, is vital if we are to gain objective insight into the origins and relationships of the earliest Amerindians.

Of the human material that is available, the child's remains from Taber, Alberta may have present claim to the greatest antiquity; stratigraphical evidence suggests that the site is more than 37,000 years old and may be as much as 60,000 years old (A. Stalker, Am. Ant. 34, 425; 1969).   The racemisation dating technique has been of considerable importance in placing many specimens, long undated, in a chronological framework.   The earliest of the racemisation dates has been obtained from the 'Del Mar' skull; this nearly complete cranium from southern California has been dated to 48,000 BP (Bada et al., Science, 184, 791; 1974).   A frontal fragment from the same area has been dated to 44,000 BP and a potentially important group of post-dranial material has been dated at 28,000 BP (ibid.).   This latter material, however, recovered 49 years ago, has not yet been cleared from its matrix.   The 'Los Angeles Man' cranium has been dated with both radiocarbon and racemisation and these dates are in close agreement: 23,600 in the first case (Berger et al., Contr. Arch. Res Fac., No. 12, University of California at Berkeley, 1971) and 26,000 in the latter (Bada et al., ibid.).   The clear antiquity of Los Angeles Man makes the unaccountable loss of the associated post-cranial material very regrettable.   The Laguna skull, also from the southern California coastal region, has been dated to 17,150 ± 1,470 (Berger et al., ibid.).

Although there is no question of the Mongoloid affinities of the modern

Amerindians the origins of the earliest groups are not as clear. Some
anthropologists consider that the Mongoloid populations of Asia are
among the most recently developed of the major human racial groups.
Coon and Birdsell, for example, would argue that the Mongoloids developed, as a population, not more than 10,000 years ago. If this is true,
then obviously the earlier New World immigrants must have had non-
Mongoloid affinities. Birdsell, Hooton, Howells and others have, in fact,
detected possible Caucasoid elements in the remains of some early Amerindians and have linked these with Upper Pleistocene populations in eastern Asia; Birdsell has used the term 'Amurian' for these Asian groups.
The question of the population affinities of the earliest Amerindians is a
complex one and the answer must await further data from both Asia and
the New World.

ALLEGED DISCOVERY OF AN ANCIENT HUMAN SKULL IN CALIFORNIA

B., W. H.; *American Journal of Science,* 2:42:424, 1866.

Accounts have recently been going the rounds of the press of the discovery of a human skull in or beneath certain volcanic deposits in California, which has attracted much attention from the various ages that
have been assigned to it. The facts of the case, so far as they have
reached us from authentic sources, are as follows. The skull in question is alleged to have been found at a depth of 153 feet, in a shaft sunk
in the consolidated volcanic ash, known locally as "lava," near Angel's
Camp, in Calavaras county. Five beds of this consolidated ash were
passed through, separated by beds of gravel.
    The skull was found by a miner, and it soon came into the hands of
Prof. J. D. Whitney, state geologist of California, who visited the locality and investigated the matter as far as was then possible, but owing to
the presence of water and the stoppage of work in the shaft, the examination was not fully satisfactory. He has made a preliminary statement
before the California Academy of Natural Sciences, but defers any extended notice until the subject can be investigated with more completeness and accuracy. He thinks the skull was found in the position claimed,
and will investigate the subject when the water is pumped out of the shaft
and work resumed, which is expected to be done soon.
    The precise age of the beds in question is as yet uncertain. In the
geology of California, Prof. W. considers that the eruption of the great
mass of volcanic materials on the western slope of the Sierra Nevada
began in the Pliocene age, and that it continued into the Post-pliocene,
and possibly to comparatively modern times. The alleged position of
the skull is a lower one than any in which the remains of the mastodon
have there been found, and therefore the question of its authenticity becomes a very important one; and when the more complete examination
has been made, we will lay the results before the readers of the Journal.

REVIEW OF THE EVIDENCE RELATING TO AURIFEROUS GRAVEL MAN IN CALIFORNIA

Holmes, William H.; *Smithsonian Institution Annual Report, 1899,* pp. 419-472.

A brief summary of the arguments for and against the great antiquity of man in the gold belt of California may well be presented here for convenience of reference. The principal considerations arrayed in support of the affirmative are as follows:

(1) During the three or four decades succeeding the discovery of gold in California the miners of the auriferous belt reported many finds of implements and human remains from the mines. The formations most prominently involved are of Neocene age; that is to say, the middle and later portions of the Tertiary.

(2) Most of the objects came from surface mines, but some were apparently derived from tunnels entering horizontally or obliquely and to great depths and distances beneath mountain summits capped with Tertiary lavas, leading to a belief in their great age.

(3) The finds were very numerous and were reported by many persons, at various times, and from sites distributed over a vast area of country. They were made, with one exception, by inexpert observers---by miners in pursuit of their ordinary calling---but the statements made by the finders are reasonably lucid and show no indications of intentional exaggeration or attempted deception.

(4) The stories as recorded are uniform and consistent in character, and the objects preserved are, it is claimed, of a few simple types, such as might be expected of a very ancient and primitive people. The evidence, coming from apparently unrelated sources, is described as remarkable for its coherency.

(5) The reported finding of an implement in place in the late Tertiary strata of Table Mountain by Mr. Clarence King is especially important and gives countenance to the reports of inexpert observers.

(6) The osseous remains recovered are, in some cases, said to be fossilized, having lost nearly all their animal matter, and some are coated with firmly adhering gravels resembling those of the ancient deposits. These conditions give rise to the impression of great age.

(7) The flora and fauna with which the human remains and relics appear to be associated indicate climatic conditions and food supply favorable to the existence of the human species. It is a noteworthy fact that in many cases the intimate association of the human remains with those of extinct animal forms is noted.

(8) The evidence as presented by Whitney and others seem abundant and convincing, and many scientific men have accepted it as satisfactory proof of a Tertiary man in America. It is clearly the strongest body of evidence yet brought together tending to connect man with any geologic formation earlier than post-Glacial.

On the other hand, numerous considerations are urged against great antiquity, as follows:

(1) It is held that the strength of testimony should be proportioned directly to the magnitude of the propositions to be supported and that this case requires proofs of a higher order than have as yet been presented.

(2) The existence of a Tertiary man, even of the lowest grade, has not yet been fully established in any country, and this California evi-

dence, therefore, stands absolutely alone. It implies a human race
older by at least one-half than Pithecanthropus erectus of Dubois, which
may be regarded as an incipient form of human creature only. The finds
reported indicate a Middle Tertiary people well advanced in the elements
of culture; and culture, especially in the earlier stages, is necessarily
of exceedingly slow growth. The Pithecanthropus of California would
have to be looked for somewhere in the early Tertiary if not in a preceding period. The burdens thus thrown upon the auriferous gravel evidence
are enormous.

(3) The presumption that a Tertiary man could have survived to the
present time in California may well be held in abeyance. The physical
and biological changes in the region have been profound and far-reaching.
The western half of the continent has been twice or thrice remodeled
since Middle Tertiary times, and every known species of plant and all
species of the higher forms of animal life have been obliterated. Evidence based on random and inexpert observations is not sufficient to establish such a proposition.

(4) If it could be admitted that man did survive throughout the ages
and continental transformations, it appears quite improbable that his
physical characters and his culture should have remained unchanged.
It seems equally unlikely that a modern race could have sprung up dup-
licating the man of a million years before in every essential particular.

(5) Examination of the human relics reported from the gravels fails
to give support to the claim of antiquity. Fossilization of the osseous
remains, upon which so much stress has been laid, may have taken place
in comparatively recent times. The chemical changes noted are such as
might be expected to characterize remains buried for a few hundred years
in the deep pits and caverns of the region. The crania recovered are
identical in character with recent crania.

(6) Objects of art from the auriferous gravels are said to be of the
most primitive character, and, in large measure, peculiar to the gravels.
When critically examined, however, they are found to belong to the pol-
ished-stone stage and to duplicate modern implements in every essential
respect. They are such as may have fallen in from Indian camp sites
or been carried in by the Indians themselves. They are made from varieties of stone belonging to formations ranging from the oldest to the
youngest found in the district, and have been shaped by the ordinary
processes employed by our aborigines. They evidently served purposes
identical with the corresponding implements of our Indian tribes.

(7) None of these objects show evidence of unusual age, and none
bear traces of the wear and tear that would come from transportation
in Tertiary torrents. These striking facts relating to the condition of
the human and cultural remains confirm and enforce the impressions
received from a study of the geological and biological history of the
region.

(8) The case against antiquity is strengthened again by a study of the
recent history of California. All, or nearly all, of the phenomena relied
upon to prove antiquity can readily be accounted for without assuming a
Tertiary man. Indian tribes have occupied the region for centuries.
They buried their dead in pits, caves, and deep ravines, where the remains were readily covered by accumulations of debris or of calcareous
matter deposited by water. As soon as mining operations began, the
region became noted as a place of skulls.

(9) Coupled with the above is the fact that no other country in the world has been so extensively and profoundly dug over as this same auriferous gravel region. The miners worked out the ossuaries and, at the same time, undermined the village sites, and thousands of the native implements and utensils were introduced into the mines and became intermingled with the gravels. Implements and utensils may also have been introduced into the deep mines by their owners who were helpers in the mining work.

(10) When these objects began to be observed by the miners, individuals interested in relics commenced making collections, but neither miners nor collectors understood the need of discrimination, the fact that the objects came from the mines being to them satisfactory evidence that they belonged originally in the gravels.

(11) Again, it is possible that deception was often practiced. A mining camp is the natural home of practical joking, and the notion that finds of human relics in the gravels tended to excite heated discussion would spread quickly from camp to camp until the whole region would be affected.

(12) The testimony for antiquity is greatly weakened by the facts (1) that the finds on which it is based were made almost wholly by inexpert observers, and (2) that all observations were recorded at second hand. Affidavits can not redeem it. Nothing short of abundant expert testimony will convince the critical mind that a Tertiary race of men using symmetrically shaped and beautiful implements, wearing necklaces of wampum and polished beads of marble or travertine bored accurately with revolving drills, and having a religious system so highly developed that at least two forms of ceremonial stones were specialized, could have occupied the American continent long enough to develop this marked degree of culture without leaving some really distinctive traces of its existence, something different from the ordinary belongings of our present Indian tribes. (pp. 469-472)

ANCIENT SKULLS DISCOVERED NEAR SANTA BARBARA
Anonymous; *Nature,* 112:699, 1923.

According to a telegram from New York which appeared in the Times of October 31, an expedition of the Smithsonian Institution, of which Dr. J. P. Harrington is the head, has discovered, at Santa Barbara, in California, two human skulls for which a very high antiquity is claimed. They are said to belong to an era far earlier than that of Neanderthal man. The evidence upon which this claim is based would appear to be a low forehead and very pronounced eyebrow ridges. The mouth cavity is extremely large and the walls of the skull very thick. They are said to be twice the thickness of ancient Indians' skulls. Until more detailed evidence is available, judgment must be suspended as to the likelihood of this claim to a high antiquity being substantiated; but it may be pointed out that skulls exhibiting Neanderthaloid characteristics, especially in the pronounced eyebrow ridges, have been found on more than one occasion in the United States. Although a great age has been attributed to them, upon further examination they have been pronounced to be merely a relatively modern variety of the Indian type. It is significant that the new Santa Barbara skulls were associated with a material culture, implements, fish-hooks, etc., which is said to show a great advance upon any culture that can be associated with Neanderthal man.

HUMAN SKULL FOUND DEEP UNDER STANFORD CAMPUS
Anonymous; *Science*, 69:sup lii, February 1, 1929.

The molar teeth of a mastodon, together with fragments of a tusk and pieces of ribs and other bones, have been found 22 feet beneath the ground level, near Menlo Park, California, about 28 miles southeast of San Francisco. Dr. Eliot Blackwelder, geologist of Stanford University, has reported the find to the Journal of the Washington Academy of Sciences. With the exception of one of the teeth, the bones have all been placed in the university museum. Because a human skull was found buried under the Stanford campus some years ago, at about the same depth, Dr. Blackwelder hints at a possible great age for this relic, saying, "The suggestion of contemporaneity is not to be lightly dismissed." However, Dr. J. W. Gidley, of the U. S. National Museum, is inclined to look somewhat askance on a human skull claiming to be so old. "If this mastodon is of late Miocene or early Pliocene age, as Dr. Blackwelder says it is, that sets it back some two or three million years. And we have as yet no evidence that man has been on earth that long."

GLACIAL MAN IN KANSAS
Upham, Warren; *American Anthropologist,* 4:566-568, 1902.

Two miles southeast of Lansing, Kansas, and about twenty miles northwest of Kansas City, a human skeleton was found last spring by farmers in digging a long tunnel excavation for us as a dairy cellar. Soon after the discovery, the place was visited by M. C. Long and Edwin Butts, of Kansas City, the former being curator of the public museum there, for which they obtained the skeleton. Mr. Butts, a civil engineer, made measurements of the excavation, which extends 72 feet into the bluff. Its floor is a nearly level stratum of carboniferous limestone; and its lower part consists of debris of limestone and earth, while its upper part is the fine calcareous silt called loess. The skeleton was found mostly in a disjointed and partly broken and decayed condition, at the distance of 68 to 70 feet from the entrance of the tunnel, about two feet above its floor, and 20 feet below the surface of the ground exactly above it. Half of the lower jaw was found ten feet nearer the entrance, and a foot lower, than the principal parts of the skeleton, including the other half of the lower jaw.

About a month ago this locality was carefully examined again by Mr. Long and Prof. S. W. Williston, of the Kansas State University, and the latter wrote a short article, "A Fossil Man in Kansas," which was published in Science, August 1. Before this article appeared, newspaper accounts had been seen by Prof. N. H. Winchell, of Minneapolis, and by myself in St. Paul, which had led us to plan a journey to Kansas, partly for the purpose of examining the Lansing skeleton and the drift section in which it was discovered. We accordingly visited this tunnel excavation, at the house of Martin Concannon, on Saturday, August 9. Professors S. W. Williston and Erasmus Haworth, of the Kansas State University, and M. C. Long, Sidney J. Hare, and P. A. Sutermeister, of Kansas City, accompanied us. Mr. Concannon, owner of the farm, and his sons, who dug the tunnel and found the skeleton, were also present and explained again all the circumstances of their discovery.

The entire section of the tunnel, which is about 10 feet wide, 7 feet high with arched top, and 72 feet long, was examined; additional bones, as of the hands and feet, were found in the dump outside; and the skeleton, in Kansas City, was inspected. According to Professor Williston's measurements of the bones, the fossil man was about five feet eight inches in stature, and was probably more than fifty years of age, as estimated from the worn condition of the teeth. The skull is dolichocephalic, with receding forehead, strongly developed supraciliary ridges, and a markedly prognathous face and chin. Most of the vertebrae and ribs are wanting, probably because of their decay previous to the deep inhumation by the overlying loess.

The skeleton lay in the upper part of the earthy debris, which included many small limestone fragments and some as large as two or three feet in length. Just above it, at an irregular line a few inches to a foot higher, a horizontally stratified water deposit of fine loess begins, forms the upper two thirds of the tunnel, and extends up to the surface 20 feet above the place of the skeleton. The loess continues up to Mr. Concannon's house, which is about 100 feet distant, on a slight terrace, about 35 feet above the horizon of the skeleton, and 47 feet above the level reached by the adjoining Missouri river at its highest flood since Mr. Concannon's settlement here thirty-five years ago. This flood, in 1881, was 25 feet above the lowest stage of the river, which is 735 feet above the sea. The carboniferous limestone outcrops about 50 feet southeast of the house, and rises gradually in a spur ridge southeastward to a height of 150 feet or more above the river.

Within a quarter of a mile southward, and also within half a mile to the west and northwest, the loess forms uplands about 200 feet above the Missouri; and at the end of the loess deposition it doubtless stretched as a broad floodplain, 200 or 250 feet above the present river level, across the Missouri valley, which has been subsequently reexcavated. The skeleton appeared to all our party to have been entombed at the beginning of the loess deposition, which would refer it to the Iowan stage of the Glacial period, long after the ice-sheet had receded from Missouri and Kansas, but while it still enveloped northern Iowa and nearly all of Wisconsin and Minnesota. In other words, it belonged to a time before the prominent moraines of these last-named states were formed on the borders of the waning ice-sheet. The very old Kansas glacial drift, including many bowlders of the red Sioux quartzite, is very thinly spread on this northeastern part of Kansas, under the loess, and reaches about thirty miles south of Lansing, terminating along an east to west boundary 12 to 15 miles south of the Kansas or Kaw river.

The loess and the Lansing skeleton are of Lake Glacial age, but are probably twice or perhaps three times as ancient as the traces of man in his stone implements and quartz chips occurring in glacial gravel and sand beds at Trenton, N. J., and Little Falls, Minn. In the Somme valley and other parts of France, as also in southern England, stone implements in river drift prove that man existed there before the Ice age, that is, probably 100,000 years ago, or doubtless four or five times longer ago than the date of the skeleton at Lansing, Kansas.

PREHISTORIC REMAINS IN FLORIDA
Anonymous; *Science*, 92:sup x, August 28, 1925.

That prehistoric man lived in America at the same time as did the mammoths and mastodons, and that those now extinct elephants survived in the South 10,000 to 50,000 years later than in other parts of the continent, is indicated by remains discovered by a joint expedition of the Smithsonian Institution and Amherst College near the towns of Melbourne and Vero, Florida. These preliminary results of the expedition were tentatively announced by Dr. J. W. Gidley, of the Smithsonian Institution, who has returned from Florida. Dr. Gidley, in cooperation with Professor F. B. Loomis, of Amherst, directed the excavations which revealed a crushed human skull, together with stone arrow heads, ten feet below the surface in close association with prehistoric animal remains.

Similar deposits were found in three different places near Melbourne and at Vero showing that the remains are typical of a wide extent of country. In the more recent accumulations of limestone shells, lying above the mammoth and human bones, were found fragments of pottery, while in the sands below the elephant layer were discovered the teeth of horses, camels and saber-tooth tigers typical of the pleistocene period of 50,000 or more years ago.

Dr. Gidley states that there is every evidence that the human remains were not buried in the mammoth strata at some more recent time, but that they were deposited during the same period and in a similar way to the animal bones.

The discovery of the existence of this distinct layer of ancient elephant and human relics not only shows that man was a contemporary of the mammoth on this continent as in Europe, but reveals for the first time that the big elephants probably survived for thousands of years later than has hitherto been thought. Dr. Gidley estimates that these American elephants lived in Florida perhaps 10,000 years after those whose remains were recently discovered in the former swamps of Indiana, and which have been assigned to the late pleistocene or Ice Age.

The crushed skull found at Melbourne will be pieced together in an effort to determine whether this human contemporary of the mastodon had the same type of head as modern Indians or whether he shows the characteristics of the more primitive cave man.

. . . .

NEW EVIDENCE FOR THE ANTIQUITY OF MAN IN NORTH AMERICA DEDUCED FROM ASPARTIC ACID RACEMIZATION
Bada, Jeffrey L., et al; *Science*, 179:792–794, 1973.

The antiquity of man in the New World is still a subject which is debated by paleoanthropologists. In general, most evidence to date is interpreted as indicating that man has only recently populated the New World. This expansion is thought to have occurred within the last 20,000 years, by migration across the Bering Sea land bridge at a time during the last Ice Age when the sea level was lower. There are opinions, however, that man 100,000 years B. P. (before the present) or perhaps even earlier. The evidence for the latter case consists of artifacts and other indications of the presence of man, but no actual hominid fossils that support this proposition have been found and dated.

One of the difficulties is the scarcity of well-dated New World hominid fossils. Although there have been a fairly large number of fragmentary hominid fossils found in North America, most of these are available in insufficient amounts for radiocarbon analysis and therefore have never been directly dated.

Recent evidence has shown that the anuno acid racemization reaction can be used, with certain limitations, to estimate the age of fossil bones. Only L-amino acide are usually found in the proteins of living organisms, but over long periods of geological time these L-amino acids undergo slow racemization, producing the nonprotein D-amino acids. The proportion of D- to L-amino acids in a fossil steadily increases with time. Thus, by determining the extent of racemization in a fossil bone, its age can be estimated. Each amino acid, with the exception of glycine, undergoes racemization. However, some amino acids racemize much faster than others. In the age range of ~ 5,000 to ~ 100,000 years, the racemization of aspartic acid is the most useful reaction. Relative to radiocarbon dating, much smaller quantities are required in the racemization dating method, and, moreover, the range of applicability exceeds that of radiocarbon dating. We report here ages deduced for several California hominid fossils by using the aspartic acid racemization reaction. These ages suggest that man was present in the New World earlier than was previously estimated.

. . . .

• The Ubiquitous Neanderthals

DISCOVERY OF AN EARLY TYPE OF MAN IN NEBRASKA
Barbour, E. H., and Ward, H. B.; *Science*, 24:628-629, 1906.

In a circular mound recently opened on a Loess hill north of Florence, near Omaha, Nebraska, various skeletal parts, and eight human skulls of a primitive type were exposed. The credit of the discovery belongs to Mr. Robert F. Gilder, of Omaha, who described and figured the skulls in the World-Herald, October 21.

That there was intrusive burial in this mound is apparent from the fact that the skulls found below a layer of burned clay are of a much more primitive type than those found above it. Already five skulls have been taken from the lower level, and three from the upper, and others are in evidence and will be dug out later. Those of the upper layer probably belonged to Indians of a later period, and may be left out of account for the present. The skulls of the lower layer are low-browed and inferior, the superciliary ridges being thick and protruding, the distance through the temples narrow, and the frontal eminences being as feebly developed as in Neanderthal man. The low arch of the skull is not the result of head-binding, but is normal and characteristic as is evidenced by five crania, two of which are fairly complete. Unfortunately the occiput is fragmentary or wanting in the specimens now at hand.

The skulls are brachycephalic, and extremely narrow in transverse diameter through the temples, expanding rapidly at the parietals. Length of skull 182 mm.; minimum breadth 93 mm.; maximum breadth 160 mm.

In shape and size the mandible agrees well with that of modern man, although the following marked differences are to be noted; the bone, particularly in the region of the symphysis, is far heavier, the muscular scars more prominent, and the third molar in each case is ground to the very gum, while the second and third are ground in a diminishing ratio. The canines are weak and scarcely distinguishable from the incisors, and the space between the molars and the base of the coronoid is wide.

The limb bones indicate a stature of six feet, the femora being somewhat stronger, and the humeri being somewhat weaker than might be expected. The femora, which are massive, manifest an interior curvature more pronounced than ordinary, and in cross section they appear triangular through the great development of the linea aspera, all muscular scars and tuberosities are noticeably prominent, the scar for ligamentum teres being elliptical in outline, deep and nearly twice as long as broad.

The skulls of the Nebraska man seem to be inferior to those of the mound builder, but for the present at least will be viewed as early representatives of that tribe.

In corroboration are the flint implements or chips found associated with the skulls and bones, and the mode of burial. As work progresses a detailed illustrated report will be made.

NEANDERTHAL MAN IN CENTRAL ASIA
Anonymous; *Nature,* 145:63, 1940.

A preliminary account of the discovery of skeletal remains of
Neanderthal man in Central Asia is given by Dr. Ales Hrdlicka through
the Smithsonian Institution of Washington. The remains---the skull of
a child, with the lower jaw and all the teeth, and some of the bones of
the skeleton in a fragmentary state---were found by Dr. A. Nokladni-
kov in a cave of the Gissar Mountains of Siberia. The discovery is of
special importance, as not only is this the first example of Neanderthal
man to be recorded from Central Asia, but it is also the farthest extension of the type eastward hitherto known. With the exception of the
finds in Palestine, all previous specimens have been found in Europe.
Dr. Hrdlicka, who has had an opportunity of examining the material
while on a visit to Siberia recently, regards it as one of the most important discoveries in anthropology of the last two decades, and further
as lending support to his view that there is an overlap in skull pattern
between Sinanthropus and Neanderthal man.

In an account of the find which Dr. Hrdlicka received at first hand
from those who were responsible for the discovery, it was stated that
the cave deposits contained many splintered bones of deer, leopards,
wild horses, goats, boars, marmots and birds. Many of these showed
evidence of having been used in the manufacture of stone implements.
Most of these implements were made of local limestone, but the finest
were of jasper. Good material for implement-making, however, was
scarce. Typical Mousterian scrapers and small pointed implements,
chipped on one side, were associated with the animal bones, and both
were in relation to fire-places. The human skeletal remains were imbedded in a sterile underlying stratum. An interesting feature of their
disposal was that they were encircled by five pairs of goat horns, of
which three were still united.

CRIMEAN NEANDERTHAL REMAINS
Anonymous; *Science*, 61:sup x, March 13, 1925.

Professor Bontisch-Osmolovsky in an interview with a Science
Service representative has stated the details of his recent find of two
primitive human Neanderthaloid skulls near Simferopol, in the Crimea,
hundreds of miles to the eastward of any previous discoveries of that
race of cavemen.

"I had an idea that when the last glacial period began, something
less than fifty thousand years ago, the men then living retreated before
the oncoming cold into the country now known as the Crimea," said Prof.
fessor Bontisch-Osmolovsky. "In 1923 I began systematic explorations
to test this theory, twenty-five miles from Simferopol, near the village
of Kipchak. In a cave known as Koush Kbat I came upon my first evi-

dences. I found here skeletal remains of the mammoth, Siberian rhinoc-
eros, cave hyena, cave bear, wild horse, wild ass, deer and other animals, together with a number of small primitive tools and the remains
of a hearth, which indicated that the cave had once been a dwelling place
of human beings.

"In 1924 I made my first find of actual human remains in a neighboring cave called Kiik Koba, in geological strata of the quaternary period.
Here were two fragmentary hearths, with layers of ashes and coals and
here, in regularly made graves, were two human skeletons. In this
cave also were remains of the same animals I had found in my first explorations, together with many flint implements, typical of the Middle
Paleolithic period. This is the first find of its kind ever made in
Russia, and is in my opinion a discovery of great scientific importance.

"The bones are very different from those of modern man. Their
measurements have not yet been completed, but those so far made suggest that they are representative specimens of the Neanderthaloid race.
Some pieces, including a part of one of the skulls, are still missing, and
I hope to find these by further search. Investigation of all the material
in the Kiik Koba cave can not be completed in Russia, since there is no
comparative material in this country for a study of Middle Paleolithic
Quaternary man. "

Professor Joukoff of the Anthropological Research Institution states
that statistical analysis of the bones of the Kiik Koba skeleton gives data
approaching the Neanderthaloid type, with even a partial inclination
toward the conformation of the anthropoid apes. A final decision will
be pronounced when the data can be compared with figures for Neanderthal remains from older finds in western Europe.

. . . .

NEANDERTHAL MAN IN PALESTINE
Anonymous; *Nature*, 129:712-713, 1932.

A cablegram has been received from Mr. Theodore McCown, who,
in the temporary absence of Miss Dorothy Garrod, is directing the exploration of caves in Mount Carmel, announcing the discovery of fossil
remains of three individuals of the Neanderthal species of mankind. The
discovery thus announced is of more than usual importance; it brings to
a successful issue a search which has been conducted in Palestine since
1925, first by the British School of Archaeology and latterly by a combined expedition fitted out by that School in conjunction with the American School of Prehistoric Research. Miss Garrod is in charge of the
combined expedition, and to her must go the chief credit.

. . . .

LATE SURVIVAL OF NEANDERTHAL TYPE
Anonymous; *Nature*, 77:587, 1908.

In the February issue of the Bulletin international of the Academy of Sciences of Cracow, Mr. K. Stolyhwo describes a human skull dating from the historic period which presents strong indications of close affinity with the Spy-Neanderthal type, the so-called Homo primigenius, of the Palaeolithic epoch. The skull, it appears, formed part of a skeleton from a tomb in which was also buried a suit of chain-armour, together with iron spear-heads, &c. In the great development of the supra-orbital ridges and of the notch at the root of the nasals, the skull, which was found at Nowosiolka, closely approximates to the Neanderthal type. It may be added that, in view of Prof. Sollas's recent reference of the latter to the Australian stock, the occurrence in eastern Europe of a late survival of the same type is a matter of profound interest.

LIVING NEANDERTHAL MAN
Anonymous; *Nature*, 85:176, 1910.

In the Philippine Journal of Science for June Dr. R. B. Bean, of the Anatomical Laboratory, Manila, reports the discovery of a living specimen in the island of Luzon which he believes to bear close relationship to the Palaeolithic type represented by the Neanderthal skull. The massive lower jaw with its square ramus and receding chin, the low cephalic index (73.68), heavy brow ridges, rounded orbits, large nasal apertures and high nasal index (102.2), combined with small stature (156.8 cm.), muscular frame and short femur, all approximate to a form similar to that of the antediluvian man of Europe, Homo heidelbergensis. Dr. Bean in the same issue of the Journal continues his study of the racial anatomy of the people of Taytay, dealing here with the women, whom he finds to be more primitive than the men, and closely resembling the women of Siberia. The Blend type is largely primitive in character, and the Austroloid variety comes between the Iberian and the primitive.

• Pigmies and Giants

PIGMIES
Anonymous; *Gentlemen's Magazine*, 3:8:182, 1837.

A short distance from Cochocton, Ohio, U.S., a singular ancient burying-ground has lately been discovered. "It is situated," says a writer in Silliman's Journal, "on one of those elevated, gravelly alluvions, so common on the rivers of the West. From some remains of wood, still apparent in the earth around the bones, the bodies seem all to have been deposited in coffins; and what is still more curious, is the fact that the bodies buried here were generally not more than from three to four and a half feet in length. They are very numerous, and must have been tenants of a considerable city, or their numbers could not have been so great. A large number of graves have been opened, the inmates of which are all of this pigmy race. No metallic articles or utensils have yet been found to throw light on the period or the nation to which they belonged."

A PIGMY GRAVEYARD IN TENNESSEE
Anonymous; *Anthropological Institute, Journal*, 6:100, 1876.

An ancient graveyard of vast proportions has been found in Coffee county. It is similar to those found in White county and other places in Middle Tennessee, but is vastly more extensive, and shows that the race of pigmies who once inhabited this country were very numerous. The same peculiarities of position observed in the White county graves are found in these. The writer of the letter says:---"Some considerable excitement and curiosity took place a few days since, near Hillsboro, Coffee county, on James Brown's farm. A man was ploughing in a field which had been cultivated many years, and ploughed up a man's skull and other bones. After making further examination they found that there were about six acres in the graveyard. They were buried in a sitting or standing position. The bones show that they were a dwarf tribe of people, about three feet high. It is estimated that there were about 75,000 to 100,000 buried there. This shows that this country was inhabited hundreds of years ago."

A PREHISTORIC CEMETERY
Anonymous; *Scientific American,* 48:296, 1883.

Two miles from Mandan, on the bluffs near the junction of the Hart and Missouri Rivers, says the local newspaper, the Pioneer, is an old cemetery of fully 100 acres in extent filled with bones of a giant race. This vast city of the dead lies just east of the Fort Lincoln road. The ground has the appearance of having been filled with trenches piled full of dead bodies, both man and beast, and covered with several feet of earth. In many places mounds from 8 to 10 feet high, and some of them 100 feet or more in length, have been thrown up and are filled with bones, broken pottery, vases of various bright colored flint, and agates. The pottery is of a dark material, beautifully decorated, delicate in finish, and as light as wood, showing the work of a people skilled in the arts and possessed of a high state of civilization. This has evidently been a grand battlefield, where thousands of men and horses have fallen. Nothing like a systematic or intelligent exploration has been made, as only little holes two or three feet in depth have been dug in some of the mounds, but many parts of the anatomy of man and beast, and beautiful specimens of broken pottery and other curiosities, have been found in these feeble efforts at excavation. Five miles above Mandan, on the opposite side of the Missouri, is another vast cemetery, as yet unexplored. We asked an aged Indian what his people knew of these ancient graveyards. He answered: "Me know nothing about them. They were here before the red man."

A LARGE SKULL FROM THE ALEUTIAN ISLANDS
Anonymous; *Science,* 84:sup 6, October 9, 1936.

Dr. Ales Hrdlicka, of the Smithsonian Institution, reports the discovery by his expedition to Alaska, of a large skull belonging to a man who lived hundreds of years ago. The skull, belonging to a man of the Aleutian Islands, is shaped to hold a brain of fully 2,005 cubic centimeters. The average man has a brain of 1,450 cubic centimeters. A woman averages about 1,250 to 1,300.

Dr. Hrdlicka makes a comparison of this with other brains on record. Daniel Webster is credited with having the largest head of any American within historic times. But his massive brain was smaller than the Aleut's, being about 2,000 cubic centimeters. Bismarck's brain is estimated to have been about 1,965; Beethoven's, 1,750. The Russian author, Turgeniev, with a brain of 2,030 cubic centimeters, still holds the world record in this respect.

The newly found American skull, only a trifle smaller than Turgeniev's, is pronounced entirely normal by Dr. Hrdlicka. Examination showed that the man who carried the massive head on his shoulders was no sufferer from any such head-deforming malady as water on the brain, or the thickened bones of gigantism. He was not a person of great size or strength, judging by the moderate size of the bones for muscle attachments. It is believed probable that he was a man of intelligence as well as in quantity of brain matter.

. . . .

GIANT SKELETON IN PENNSYLVANIA MOUND
Anonymous; *American Antiquarian,* 7:52, 1885.

A large Indian mound near the town of Gastersville, Pa. , has recently been opened and examined by a committee of scientists sent out from the Smithsonian Institute. At some depth from the surface a kind of vault was found in which was discovered the skeleton of a giant measuring seven feet two inches. His hair was coarse and jet black, and hung to the waist, the brow being ornamented with a copper crown. The skeleton was remarkably well preserved. Near it were also found the bodies of several children of various sizes, the remains being covered with beads made of bone of some kind. Upon removing these, the bodies were seen to be enclosed in a net-work of straw or reeds, and beneath this was a covering of the skin of some animal. On the stones which covered the vault were carved inscriptions, and these when deciphered, will doubtless lift the veil that now shrouds the history of the race of people that at one time inhabited this part of the American continent. The relics have been carefully packed and forwarded to the Smithsonian Institute, and they are said to be the most interesting collection ever found in the United States. The explorers are now at work on another mound in Barton county, Pa.

"GIANT" FOSSIL MAN
S., W. L., Jr.; *Science,* 129:455, 1959.

During the past quarter of a century there have been repeated discoveries in Southeast Asia of very large fossil primate teeth of the Pleistocene epoch. There have been attributed to truly gigantic animals by some students. Von Koenigswald thought the huge teeth which he discovered in Hong Kong "drugstores" (Gigantopithecus), Kwangsi Province being their probable provenance, belonged to a giant ape, whereas he regarded the two jaw fragments with teeth which he discovered at Sangiran, Java (Meganthropus), as those of a giant protohominid. Weidenreich went even further concluding that both Gigantopithecus and Meganthropus were not only giants but actually hominids on the line leading to true man. On the basis of tooth size, he estimated that the Javanese "giant" was much bigger than any living gorilla and that the Chinese "giant" was correspondingly bigger---one-and-one-half times as large as the gargantuan Javanese, and twice as large as a male gorilla. In this connection, it may be noted that adult male gorillas are known to attain a weight of 600 or more pounds. Weidenreich postulated, therefore, that the ancestors of man were giants---this standing in contrast to the general paleontological rule that ancestral forms tend to be smaller than their descendants. Pei, referring to a recently discovered jaw with teeth from Luntsai Mountain in Kwangsi, South China, which is almost certainly a specimen of Gigantopithecus, reverted to von Koenigswald's idea of a giant ape which he estimated as having had a stature of "some 12 feet." Large-toothed forms, notably Paranthropus crassidens, also occur among the australopithecines; but no serious claims of gigantic body size have at yet been made for these South African hominids.

The crux of the problem involves the question of whether tooth-size is in any way indicative of body-size. Von Koenigswald, Weidenreich, and Pei have all assumed that there is a positive correlation; but of this they have had no proof. With this in mind, S. M. Garn and A. B. Lewis [Am. Anthropologist, 60, 874 (Oct. 1958)] compared tooth size with stature among several groups of living men and between living men and certain other, fossil hominids (Pithecanthropus; Sinanthropus; and three australopithecines---Paranthropus robustus, P. crassidens, and Plesianthropus). They found little indication of a marked positive correlation between tooth size and body size in living men, even when allowance is made for nutritional differences. Evidently, therefore, these dimensions are effectively independent in various human races, as they are in pigs and in various breeds of dogs. Moreover, it was found within a population that tooth size is unrelated to body size and therefore again nonpredictive. The tallest human populations actually possess teeth that are among the smallest. Similarly, the available data for the fossil hominid forms---for which stature was estimated from limb-bone fragments---fail to support the concept of a simple proportionality between size of teeth and size of body; instead, they reveal a negative relationship.

Thus, there is no indication that tooth size is a clue to body size in either Homo sapiens or nonsapient hominids and, consequently, no evidence to support the notion that the Chinese and Javanese megadonts were giants. Indeed, the authors conclude that if the australopithecines are any guide the ape from Luntsai Mountain had a stature of scarcely more than 5 feet. Garn and Lewis suggest that "it may well be that the forms with giant teeth, both from Africa and Asia, had the task of grinding nutrients and calories from tough and bulky vegetable material, but without the gastro-intestinal adaptations of herbivores." This might account for a disproportionately large dentition.

• Anomalous Skeletons

HUMAN SKELETONS WITH 36 TEETH
Anonymous; *Nature*, 93:90, 1914.

The discovery of ancient human remains in German East Africa by Dr. Hans Reck, of the Geological Institute of Berlin University, may prove to be an event of some importance to anthropologists. The report of the discovery, published in the Times of March 19, leaves us in some doubt as to the antiquity and racial characters to be assigned to these East African human remains, but apparently they are of mid-Pleistocene date, and show the distinctive features of the negro. If such prove to be the case, we must conclude that the negro race was already evolved in Africa at an earlier date than is now generally supposed. The Times report also informs us that the man thus discovered had thirty-six teeth---four more than is given to human and anthropoid races. The teeth are also said to show marks of filing; it would indeed be a remarkable fact if the habit of filing the teeth, so common in modern African races, should have been in use at the early date assigned to these prehistoric remains.

DESCRIPTION OF AN ANCIENT ANOMALOUS SKELETON FROM THE VALLEY OF MEXICO
Hrdlicka, Ales; *American Museum of Natural History, Bulletin*, 12:81-107, 1899.

The skeleton described in this paper was exhumed at the adobe-works at St. Simon Tonaguae, a small suburb of the City of Mexico. The same place has yielded from time to time human bones and various objects of archaeological interest. The bones were procured directly from the workmen by Dr. Carl Lumholtz during his explorations for the American Museum of Natural History, and are now in the Anthropological Department of the Museum.

The skeleton was discovered about three metres below the surface. The workmen were unable to give definite information regarding the surroundings of the bones. The importance of the skeleton induced me to make, on my recent visit to Mexico, a special examination of the adobe-works about St. Simon.

. . . .

The constituents of the thorax of this skeleton are very remarkable.

There are 26 ribs present, instead of 24, the usual number. By careful and repeated examinations, the characteristics of these ribs have been found entirely homogeneous, so that it is impossible to eliminate any pair as extraneous. Of these ribs 13 are right, and 13 left. They agree in color, form, and size. The skeleton, so far as we know, was found isolated, was kept together, and in the Museum it has since been kept separate. No question as to the identity of all the ribs with the skeleton has been raised by any one of the numerous scientists who have examined it.

We have here a pair of supernumerary ribs. The question is, Which of the thirteen pairs is the supernumerary one? Examination of the ribs alone does not satisfy us on this point. There are two pairs of floating ribs, as usual; and none of the remaining pairs can be distinguished from the regular ribs. On examining the vertebrae, however, we find an articular facet on each side of the seventh cervical; and a reconstruction of the upper part of the thorax demonstrates that the ribs begin at this vertebra, not at the first dorsal. There is no rudimentary or floating cervical rib. The first pair of ribs, although presenting an anomaly on one side, which will be described later on, has otherwise all the characteristics of the regular first dorsal ribs; and in the same way all the following pairs of ribs resemble the corresponding regular pairs of the normal thorax. Granted that the two uppermost ribs are cervical, the condition is really then that of an extension of the thorax upward, which is much more interesting than the existence of a rudimentary pair of cervical or other ribs. Sir William Turner, who on his last visit to the United States examined the skeleton, particularly the ribs, expressed the opinion that we have here a pair of cervical ribs articulating with the seventh cervical vertebra, and that all the thoracic structures, the blood-vessels included, were elevated, the extra cervical ribs assuming the anatomical relations which ordinarily belong to the first dorsal pair.

The greater number of ribs, however, is not the only peculiarity in the case. Examination of the ribs of the left side shows the first and second ribs partly blended together. The spinal articular parts of both ribs are normal, though much closer together than they would be ordinarily; and the bones continue independent for about 2 cm., at which point they gradually blend and form one rib. This shows no further marks of union, and is much broader and stronger than the first rib of the right side, which has a large single articular surface on the sternum, situated lower than the corresponding one of the other side. The third ribs are normal, and equal on both sides; and none of the remaining pairs show any thing unusual. The maximum breadth of the conjoint rib on the left is 2.2 cm.: that of the first right rib, 1.3 cm.

The anomaly just described is rare in the human species. It has received the name of 'bicipital rib.' It was first described by M. Hunauld, and was given considerable attention by Sir William Turner. The anomaly occurs invariably at the apex of the thorax (Turner), and consists mostly of a union of a cervical rib with the first thoracic. The anatomical peculiarity, according to Sir William Turner. "is not due to a bifurcation of the shaft of a single rib at its vertebral end into two heads, but to the fusion of what ought to have been the shafts of two distinct ribs into a common body." The significance of the anomaly, when due to a union of a cervical with the first thoracic rib, must be about the same as that of a free cervical rib, the causes of which are not yet fully established.

Supernumerary ribs occur both in man and in lower animals, and signify in all probability a recurrence of lower forms. Cuvier found supernumerary ribs in the bison; Turner says the condition is quite common in the Cetaceae; and I have been told by naturalists of examples of this kind in other mammals. Dr. F. Boas informs me that he found supernumerary ribs and vertebrae in quite a high percentage of human skeletons from northwest Vancouver Islands, and reference to such phenomena are found in medical literature. In the majority of cases, the supernumerary ribs are cervical. Single supernumerary ribs are not so infrequent as the bicipital ribs, though I have lately seen in Professor Dwight's collection in the Anatomical Museum of the Harvard Medical School, Boston, Mass., a specimen of bicipital rib, much like that here described.

The union of two ribs in the manner here observed, in whatever portion of the thorax it may occur, implies a deficient evolution of one of the ribs concerned, and a fusion of the two bones along more or less of their course during the early stages of ossification of the parts. If the supernumerary rib is so deficient, as it is in this case, it shows that its cause, be it a reversion or any thing else, was less complete in this than in other instances where a similar rib is free.

. . . .

THE OLECRANON PERFORATION
Lamb, D. S.; *American Anthropologist*, 3:159–174, 1890.

In a collection of sixty-nine skeletons and parts of skeletons of prehistoric Arizona Indians from the valley of the Salado I found that 54 per cent. of the eighty-nine humeri showed the olecranon perforation; forty-three of the right side, with nineteen foramina, or 44 per cent., and forty-six of the left side, with twenty-nine foramina, or 63 per cent.

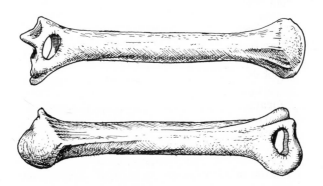

The olecranon perforation

In another collection from ruins of the ancient Seven Cities of Cibola, near Zuni, New Mexico, were sixty-one humeri, with twelve foramina, or 20 per cent.; thirty right humeri showed two foramina, or 7 per cent.; thirty-one left, ten foramina, or 32 per cent.

In a third collection of Indian bones from mounds in different parts of the United States, including New York, Maryland, Illinois, Wisconsin, and Dakota, there are sixty-two humeri, with seventeen foramina, or 20 per cent.; thirty-five right, with seven foramina, or 20 per cent., and twenty-seven left, with ten foramina, or 37 per cent.

The Army Medical Museum also contains forty-eight skeletons from nineteen of the existing tribes of Indians. Of these ninety-six humeri the foramen is present in but five, or 5 per cent., a remarkable contrast with the prehistoric races. One of these skeletons showing the foramen is of a Sioux only about twenty years old.

There are eight skeletons of negroes and mulattoes with but one olecranon foramen, or 6 per cent. Standing alone, this would seem to favor the statement of Pruner-Bey and others that the foramen is not present in the negro race. There is a skeleton of a Chinese woman showing the foramen present on both sides, and one of a Frenchman showing it on one side.

In the pathological series of the Museum are 298 humeri, with twenty-two foramina, or 7.5 per cent. Of these humeri 160 are of the right side, with six foramina, or nearly 4 per cent., and 138 left, with sixteen foramina, or nearly 12 per cent. These bones are nearly all from soldiers in the military service, and principally white, thus disposing of the suggestion that the foramina are found only in the female sex. One of the injured bones is from a Mexican boy.

With few exceptions the skeletons in the Museum are either infantile or adult. It is the more interesting, therefore, to know that of the adolescents two show the foramen.

In my own private collection of humeri, twenty in number, there are six foramina, or 30 per cent.; eleven are of the right side, with two foramina, or 18 per cent., and nine of the left, with four foramina, or 44 per cent. These humeri were obtained from cadavers used in dissection, and as most cadavers in this locality are of negroes or mulattoes it is reasonable to suppose that most of these humeri are from the negro race.

A review of the humeri in the above collections shows that the foramen was found in the proportion of 13 on the right side to 27.5 on the left, or more than twice as often on the left side.

The examination covered nearly 650 humeri and seemed to establish---

1st. The greater frequency of the foramen in the ancient peoples.

2d. Its greater frequency on the left side.

3rd. Its occurence in adolescents, as well as mature individuals, in both sexes, and not confined to any one race.

The most important question which arises is as to the use and significance of the foramen. It is obvious that the more the coronoid or olecranon fossae are deepened the thinner becomes the partition, and a step further produces a perforation. This deepening and perforation increase the extent of flexion and extension of the forearm. What was there in the habits of the prehistoric and ancient peoples which needed this increased flexion or extension and resulted in the foramen? and why should this be more frequent on one side, and that side the left?

....

THE GUANCHES: THE ANCIENT INHABITANTS OF CANARY

Gambier, J. W.; *Smithsonian Institution Annual Report, 1894*, pp. 541–553.

As regards this structural alteration, it may be briefly said that a certain peculiarity in the elbow joint---which doubtless served some purpose to our aboreal progenitors, but which in parts of Europe where races have been more rapidly mixed, or where civilization has made more rapid strides, and consequently the process of evolution become more determined, has ceased to exist---existed among the Guanches, and is still found among their descendants to this day in a proportion far exceeding that in any other known race. In England, in our days, this peculiarity is practically extinct---in some parts of the world it reaches 2 per cent of the population---but here, among the Guanches, it has been ascertained by actual observation to reach to the astonishing number of 20 per cent, showing a race who have been so little intermixed and so direct in descent from the Stone age as it would be difficult to find except in the most isolated parts of the world, among races such as the Aztecs, or the inhabitants of some of the Pacific Ocean islands, or among the natives of Australia. This is one of the peculiar interests of the Guanche race. (p. 542)

ELEPHANT REMAINS IN MEXICO

Anonymous; *American Antiquarian*, 25:395–397, 1903.

From the City of Mexico comes a statement bearing the signature of Dr. Nicholas Leon, archaeologist of the National Museum of Mexico. The signature would justify the belief that proper investigation of the facts related has been made.

The one great fact is that an ancient city, which was located near the present town of Paredon, in the state of Coahuila, some 500 miles north of the City of Mexico, was suddenly destroyed in some past age by an overflow of water and mud, and that its remains are still existent on the spot. Many massive walls have been found, but they are covered with a mass of deposited earth, sixty feet in thickness. And mingled in this earth are human skeletons, the tusks of elephants, etc., distributed in a way which indicates that the overflow of water and mud was sudden, giving no time for escape.

The account which has fallen under our notice is somewhat brief. We cannot vouch for its accuracy, and simply present the report:

"Portions of buildings, so far unearthed, show that the city---at least the largest of the cities were covered by the debris of the flood, there being at least three cities destroyed---was very extensive. The indications are that there were many massive structures in the fallen city, and that they were of a class of architecture not to be found elsewhere in Mexico. According to the estimates of the scientists under whose directions the excavations are now being made, the city in question had a population of at least 50,000.

"The destruction which was brought by the flood was complete. All the inhabitants of the cities were killed, as well as all the animals. Skeletons of the human inhabitants of the cities and of the animals are strewn all through the debris, from a depth of three feet from the surface to a depth of sixty feet, showing that all the debris was deposited almost at once. Measurements show that the debris is on an average, sixty feet deep where the largest of the cities stood.

"Most remarkable of the minor finds that have been made at Paredon is that of the remains of elephants. Never before in the history of Mexico has it been ascertained positively that elephants were ever in the service of the ancient inhabitants. The remains of the elephants that have been found. Paredon show plainly that the inhabitants of the buried cities made elephants work for them. Elephants were as much in evidence in the cities as horses. Upon many of the tusks that have been found were rings of silver. Most of the tusks encountered so far have an average length, for grown elephants, of three feet, and an average diameter at the roots of six inches. Judging from the remains of the elephants so far unearthed, the animals were about ten feet in height and sixteen to eighteen feet in length, differing very little from those at present in existence."

[Now, these statements in reference to the elephants' bones found among the ruined cities need confirmation, before they are accepted by the majority of archaeologists. It is true that the tusks and bones of mastodons are frequently found in the swamps of Michigan, Ohio, and Indiana, but they are supposed to belong to the same species which are found in the frozen mud of Siberia and the gravels of the Northwest coast. A species covered with hair and adapted to the cold climate, and quite different from any that would be found as far south as Mexico. The circumpolar regions are full of these creatures, which have perished, but their bodies have been preserved in the ice-beds. Other animals, such as the buffalo and bison, have over run portions of this continent, since the days of the mastodon, but none of them reached as far south as Mexico.

The cities of Mexico are supposed to have been built not earlier than 1500 A.D.---about 500 years ago. If any were built earlier, they are in ruins, but no remains of elephants have been discovered among the ruins, in fact no semblance of the elephant has been recognized in the sculpture, except in a few cases, where what resembles an elephant's trunk, or the trunk of a tapir, is found on the sculptured columns at Copan. The discovery of elephant bones would be too important a matter to be ignored, but the article seems sensational and has been sent to the newspapers as a sensational item, and not to the scientific societies, so far as we have learned.

The whole subject of the presence of the mastodon on the American continent is discussed in the August and September numbers of The Records of the Past. The arguments which favor a recent date are: first, the presence of the bones in the peat swamps of Ohio and Michigan; second, the drawing on the Mercer tablet of an elephant attacked by Indians; third, the figure of an elephant on a pottery pitcher from the cliff-dwellings. All these are, however, outside of Mexico, and so prove nothing in reference to this sensational report.---Ed.]

Chapter 5
ANTHROPOLOGICAL EVIDENCE

INTRODUCTION

Did the ships of ancient man sail the oceans of the world, leaving in their wakes genes, languages, and cultures? Diffusionists point to hundreds, possibly thousands, of anthropological similarities and echoes. Resemblances in blood types, in skin colorings, in physical character-istics, and so on; all are grist for the diffusionist's mill. Word congru-ences, too, are often taken as proof that Chinese, Hebrews, or others passed through a region centuries ago.

When considering the validity of such associations, the factor of independent invention always arises. Men's minds, after all, are con-structed from roughly the same molds; and it is not surprising that many words, customs, inventions, and sports are similar among peoples separated even by oceanic and mountain barriers. For those who believe that the New World was isolated save for Bering Strait crossings at the end of the last Ice Age, anthropological links indicating earlier contacts with the Americas are highly suspect. On the other hand, the committed diffusionist often seizes upon every vague similar-ity as proof of his belief. Since prevailing anthropological dogma seems overly conservative regarding cultural isolation, most data presented in this chapter support the idea that ancient man wandered far and wide and early.

• Skin Color

WHITE RACE OF THE ATLAS
Anonymous; *American Journal of Science,* 1:32:400, 1837.

M. Guyon, chief surgeon to the African army, writes to M. Dureau de la Malle, that at Bourgia there is now living, a woman originally from the interior, supposed to be descended from the white tribe of

Mount Aureps. She is at most twenty six or twenty-eight years of age, of very agreeable physiognomy, blue eyes, fair hair, beautiful teeth, and has a very delicate white skin. She is married to the Imaun of the mosques, Sidi Hamed, by whom she has three children, bearing a strong resemblance to herself. M. Arago observes, that these white people are not so rare in that part of the world as might be supposed, for when he was going from Bougia to Algiers, in 1808, by land, he saw women of all ages in the different villages, who were quite white, had blue eyes and fair hair, but that the nature of his journey did not permit him to stop and ask if they came from any peculiar tribe.

A SKETCH OF THE MANDAN INDIANS

Hayden, F. V.; *American Journal of Science,* 2:34:57–66, 1862.

In the year 1833 the Mandans were in their most prosperous state, well armed, good hunters, good warriors, with herds of buffalo within sight of their village---large cornfields and a trading post from which they could at all times obtain needed supplies. In their personal appearance prior to the ravages of small-pox, they were not surpassed by any nation in the Northwest. The men were tall and well made, with regular features and a mild expression of countenance not usually seen among Indians. Their complexion also was a shade lighter than that of other tribes, often approaching very near to that of some European nations. Another peculiarity, which has often been observed by travellers, was that some of them had fair hair, and gray or blue eyes, which are very rarely met with among other tribes. A majority of the women, particularly the young, were quite handsome, with fair complexions and modest in their deportment. They were also noted for their virtue. This was regarded as an honorable and most valuable quality amongst the young women, and each year a ceremony was performed in the presence of the whole village, at which time all females who had preserved their virginity, came forward, struck a post, and challenged the world to say ought derogatory of their character. As this was a religious ceremony, any persons present, who could with truth contradict the statement, felt bound to do so, and if detected in a false statement, the female lost her standing forever afterward among the young of both sexes. In ordeals of this kind it was remarked that more than two thirds of the Mandan females came off victorious which is regarded as a great proportion, when the early training and the influences that surround them are taken into consideration. The fact that a ceremony of this kind exists among savages, tending to promote virtue and discourage vice, is, of itself, sufficient evidence of their mental as well as moral superiority.

THE BLOND MANDAN: A CRITICAL REVIEW OF AN OLD PROBLEM

Newman, Marshall T.; *Southwestern Journal of Anthropology,* 6:255-272, 1950.

Introduction. Some of the 18th and 19th century explorers and traders visiting the Mandan Indians on the upper Missouri River were struck by physical and cultural features that seemed out of place to them in the northern Plains. Their reports of blondism and other non-Indian physical traits, an unusual language and mythology, fortified villages and a developed horticulture provided the evidence for two theories of Mandan origin through pre-Columbian contact with Europeans. One of these theories, widely held in the latter part of the 18th century, and revived in 1841 by the artist George Catlin, was that the Mandan were the descendants of a legendary 12th century expedition of Welsh led by Madoc. The other theory claimed the Mandan to be the mixed descendants of Scandinavian explorers. The most recent version of this theory identifies the Scandinavians as members of a 14th century expedition led by Paul Knutson. These theories stimulated me to look into the question of blondism and other non-Indian physical traits attributed to the Mandan of one to two centuries ago.

The information bearing upon this question lies almost wholly in the explorers' and traders' reports. The few Mandan living today are too mixed with other tribes and with recent Whites to give any clear picture of what the pre-contact Mandan were like. There are, however, a few early portraits and photographs. Only a few identifiably Mandan skeletons have been recovered, not enough to provide representative data. Therefore I have had to be content with an analysis of the eye-witness reports. The areas of agreement in these reports have provided several points of high probable validity which I have interpreted in the light of modern knowledge.

Reports of White Indians. The earliest reports of White Indians that I have located were those told to La Verendrye in the 1720's before he made the first recorded visit to the Mandan. His informants were the Cree and Assiniboine around the Lake of the Woods. According to La Verendrye, they

> .... took the Ouachipounnes [Mandan] for Frenchmen, they talk and sing like us, their forts and houses are very much like ours, except that the roofs are flat and covered with earth and stones, and their houses have cellars in which they store their Indian corn in great wicker baskets....
>
> They are very tall of stature, white in colour, with hair light, chestnut, and red, and in a few cases black; they have beards which they either cut or pull out, though a few allow it to grow; they walk with their feet turned out....

This description continued for several pages, giving quite complete treatment to the actual manners and customs of the Mandan, embroidered, however, with strange figments of Cree-Assiniboine imagination.

In 1738, however, La Verendrye was able to lead a party to the Mandan villages. After his first meeting with the Mandan, when thirty of them were present, his reaction was strong:

I confess I was greatly surprised, as I expected to see people
quite different from the other savages according to the stories
that had been told us. They [the Mandan] do not differ from the
Assiniboin, being naked except for a garment of buffalo skin carelessly worn without any breechcloth. I knew then that there was
a large discount to be taken off all that had been told me.

. . . .

Eye-Witness Reports. La Verendrye's bare report of the physical
characteristics of the Mandan as he saw them in 1738 is in apparent
contradiction to his denial of Mandan distinctiveness from other tribes.
He stated,

This tribe is of mixed blood, black and white. The women
are rather handsome, particularly the light-colored ones; they
have an abundance of fair hair.

There are certain ambiguities in this statement that are hard to resolve. For example, the phrase ". . . of mixed blood, black and white"
suggests that he was only describing the range of hair color, since
Indian skin color in the northern Plains could hardly be described as
black.

The next account is that of d'Eglise, who pioneered the upstream
route from St. Louis to the Mandan villages in 1790. He remarked to
Trudeau that the Mandan ". . . are white like Europeans, much more
civilized than any other Indians. "

In 1796-97, John Evans, in the employ of the Missouri Fur Company,
spent over six months with the Mandan. He was thoroughly familiar
with the story of the 12th century expedition of Welsh led by Madoc; in
fact, Thomas Jefferson himself believed that Evans' ". . . original object
. . . had been to go in search of the Welsh Indians said to be up the Missouri. " Although Evans did not comment on the physical characteristics
of the Mandan, his observations forced him to deny the existence of
Welsh Indians along the Missouri.

According to David Thompson, who saw the Mandan in 1797,

Both men and women are of a stature fully equal to Europeans; and as fair as our french canadians; their eyes of a
dark hazel, their hair of dark brown or black, but not coarse;
prominent nose, cheek bones moderate.

Lewis and Clark, who wintered with the Mandan in 1804-05, made
general comment on their light pigmentation, and remarked upon a half-
breed boy among them. Sgt. Gass, in the same party, stated, "These
Indians have better [lighter ?] complexions than most other Indians, and
many of the children have fair hair. "

Alexander Henry, who visited the Mandan during the summer of 1806,
had this to say:

What struck me as extraordinary among these people was
several children about 10 years old, whose hair was perfectly
grey, and who thus resembled aged persons; those I saw were
all girls. The people in general have not such strong coarse
hair as other natives of North America; they have it much
finer, rather inclining to dark brown, and I observed some whose
hair was almost fair. . . . Their eyes are not of that jet black
which is common to other Indians, but, like their hair, inclined
to a dark brown; some few are dark grey.

Bradbury, who passed through the Mandan villages in 1811, indicated his surprise that the wife and child of one of the chiefs had brown hair, although "...their skins did not appear to be lighter coloured than the rest of the tribe." The wife was said to be over forty years of age, and therefore not as likely as a younger person to have been a mixed-breed.

The fullest description of the Mandan comes from the artist Catlin who visited their villages in 1832. The following statements seem to have been slanted in support of his Welsh Indian theory.

A stranger in the Mandan village is first struck with the different shades of complexion and various colours of hair which he sees in a crowd about him; and is at once almost disposed to exclaim that "these are not Indians."

There are a great many of these people whose complexions appear as light as half-breeds; and amongst the women particularly, there are many whose skins are almost white, with the most pleasing symmetry and proportion of the features; with hazel, with grey, and with blue eyes....

The diversity in the colour of the hair is almost equally as great as that in the complexion; for in a numerous group of these people (and more particularly amongst the females, who never take pains to change its natural colour, as the men often do), there may be seen every shade and colour of hair that can be seen in our own country [England], with the exception of red or auburn, which is not to be found.... There are very many, of both sexes and of every age, from infancy to manhood to old age, with hair of a bright silvery grey, and in some instances almost perfectly white....I have ascertained, on a careful enquiry, that about 1 in 10 or 12 of the whole tribe are what the French call "cheveux gris" ... and that this strange and unaccountable phenomenon is not the result of disease or habit, but that it is unquestionably a hereditary character which runs in families.... And by passing this hair through my hands,...I have found it uniformly to be as coarse and harsh as a horse's mane; differing materially from the hair of other colours, which amongst the Mandans, is generally as fine and as soft as silk.

In a later publication, Catlin gave a rather different version of the Mandan appearance.

In complexion, colour of hair, and eyes, they generally bore a family resemblance to the rest of the American tribes, but there were exceptions, constituting perhaps one-fifth or one-sixth part of the tribe, whose complexions were nearly white, with hair of a silvery-grey from childhood to old age, their eyes light blue, their faces oval, devoid of the salient angles so strongly characterizing all other American tribes and owing, unquestionably, to the infusion of some foreign stock.

The differences between the two statements suggest that in his later writings Catlin decided that because of recent White admixture only the strange combination of grey hair, light skin and eyes, and oval faces constituted good evidence of Welsh influence. Unfortunately for his argument, his portrait of a Mandan girl with grey hair fails to show light skin and eye color.

Maximilian, the first trained scientist to see the Mandan, reached

their villages in the early summer of 1833, and returned to them that
autumn. He held a very low opinion of Catlin's Welsh Indian theory, and
stated that there was no evidence of White influence in the Mandan
villages prior to the 18th Century. Of the physical appearance of the
Mandan he stated,

> Their physiognomy is, in general, the same as that of most
> of the Missouri Indians, but their noses are not so long and arched
> as those of the Sioux, nor have they such high cheekbones. The
> nose of the Mandans and Manitares [Hidatsa] is not as broad---
> sometimes aquiline or slightly curved, and often quite straight.
> The eyes are, in general, long and narrow, of a dark brown
> colour. The mouth is broad, large, rather prominent, and the
> lower jaw broad and angular....Their hair is long, thick, lank
> and black....That of the children is often only dark brown, espe-
> cially at the tips....There are whole families among them, as
> well as among the Blackfeet, whose hair is grey, or black mixed
> with white, so that the whole head appears grey.

Maximilian also spoke of a Mandan man between twenty and thirty
years old, who had "distinct locks of brown, black, silvery grey [hair],
but mostly white, and his eyebrows perfectly white."

Of skin color he stated,

> The colour of these Indians is a fine brown, sometimes reddish,
> more or less dark, which might, sometimes, come under the de-
> nomination of copper colour. In some it is more of a greyish-
> brown, in others yellowish; after a thorough ablution the skin of
> some of them appears almost white, and even some colour in
> their cheeks.

He also indicated that the notion that the Mandan had "fairer complexions" than other Indians was as unfounded as the assertion that they
spoke Gaelic.

....

Summary. At the present time, the racially mixed status of the few
living Mandan and the paucity of identifiably Mandan skeletal material
preclude a first-hand investigation of the blondism and other European
characters attributed to them. And the 18th and 19th century eye-witness
reports on this subject lack detail and sometimes accuracy. Some of
them may have been colored by the exaggerated stories of White civilized
Indians that were then current, or biased by romantic appeal of Welsh
Indian and other theories. In addition, the results of the White admixture
which probably began before 1850 have been interpreted in several reports as aboriginal peculiarities. Finally, the unusual amount of premature greying of the hair was confused with blondism on more than one
occasion.

An analysis of these 18th and 19th century reports indicates that
some of the presumptively unmixed Mandan were at least as light-skinned
as darker Europeans; dark brown rather than black hair and eyes, and
fine rather than coarse hair texture, were frequent. Light skin color
was reported among other northern tribes as well. Careful modern
studies indicate that dark brown hair and eyes, and fine hair texture
are indeed most characteristic of North American Indians. Indeed,
Mandan life in earth lodges north of 45°N would not only tend to reduce
selection against light skin color, but would also result in less weather-

ing of the skin than among nomadic tribes. This difference would be especially noticeable in the winter, which was the season of extended observation by Whites in the Mandan villages.

The alternative explanation involving the pre-Columbian introduction and subsequent persistence of European genes for blondism is hardly tenable. It must assume, first of all, extraordinary procreative abilities for a handful of Europeans, and over 400 years of inbreeding on the part of the mixed European-Mandan group. Difficult as it may be to explain the light pigmentation of some of the Mandan by old admixture with Europeans, it seems impossible to use the same explanation for the other allegedly light-skinned Indian tribes of North America. In addition, the whereabouts of the Mandan prior to the late 15th century are not definitely known, so that the chances of contact between them and any wandering Europeans cannot be adequately appraised. Also, enough is known about Plains Indians so that the high cultural development of the Mandan need not be explained as a grafting from European technology of the Middle Ages.

In conclusion, this review indicates that the blondism and other non-Indian characteristics reported for the Mandan of the 18th and early 19th centuries are much more plausibly explained by intertribal and individual variability in pigmentation and facial features, augmented by recent White admixture, than by pre-Columbian miscegenation with European exploring parties.

A TRIBE OF WHITE ESKIMOS
MacRitchie, David; *Nature,* 90:133, 1912.

Considerable interest has been aroused by the announcement made by M. Vilhjalmar Stefansson (in Nature of August 22, p. 644), communicated to the Press through Reuter on September 10, that he had discovered a tribe---or, to be more accurate, thirteen tribes---of white Eskimos living in the neighborhood of Coronation Gulf and Victoria Island. He stated that ten of these tribes had never heard of white people---other than themselves. Consequently, it cannot be assumed that this fair complexion is derived from the intercourse, so frequent in recent times, between Eskimos and the men of whaling ships. The telegraphed account states that M. Stefansson believes the white Eskimos are descendants of the colony which set out from Norway to Greenland some time after the discovery of that island. Ethnologically, the white Eskimos bear not a single trace of the Mongolian type, differing in the shape of the skull and general features, colour of eyes, and texture of hair, which in many cases is red. They spoke Eskimo, though the explorer thought he detected some Norse words. They probably numbered two thousand. Many of them had perfectly blue eyes and blonde eyebrows."

It is, of course, quite possible that a newspaper correspondent may have given a very free rendering of the statements made to him by M. Stefansson: But, in any case, it is important to bear in mind that a description of a race of fair-complexioned Eskimos, living on the shores of Davis Straits, was printed in Europe in 1658. This account occurs in De Poincy's "Histoire Naturelle & Morale des Iles Antilles de l'Amerique," which was published at Rotterdam in that year, and contains a chapter (xviii.) incorporating the narrative of Nicolas Tunes, captain of a Flushing vessel, just returned from Davis Straits at the time when De Poincy was occupied with a description of the narwhal---a subject which led him into a long digression on the hunters of the northern narwhal. De Poincy indicates the locality in question in the following terms, here translated from his somewhat archaic French:---"The captain, from whom we have received this narrative, having set out from Zealand at the end of the spring of 1656, with the intention of discovering some new source of trade in those northern lands, arrived at the end of June in Davis Straits, whence, having entered a river which begins at 64° 10' N. lat., he sailed to the seventy-second degree, where the land about to be described is situated."

A very full description is given of the natives, but only the following sentences need be quoted here:---"As regards the inhabitants, our travellers report having seen two kinds, who live together on the most friendly terms. Of these, one kind is described as very tall, well-built, of rather fair complexion, and very swift of foot. The others are very much smaller, of an olive complexion, and tolerably well-proportioned, except that their legs are short and thick. The former kind delight in hunting, for which they are suited by their agility and natural disposition, whereas the latter occupy themselves in fishing. All of them have very white, compact teeth, black hair, animated eyes, and the features of the face so well made that they present no notable deformity. Moreover, they are all so vigorous and of such a strong constitution that several of them who have passed their hundredth year are still lively and robust."

In the small, olive-complexioned, short-legged people here described, there is no difficulty in recognising true Eskimos. Those of the tall, comparatively fair type may easily have been the descendants of the Norse colonists, intermingled, it may be, with Eskimos. It is believed by many---for example, by Dr. Nansen ("In Northern Mists," London, 1911, vol. ii., p. 103)---that the early Norsemen in Greenland were not exterminated by the Eskimos, but were gradually absorbed by them through successive intermarriages. Admitting this, it would seem that the fusion of the two races was still only partial in 1656. Tunes and his comrades speak of black hair as common to both types, but that need not mean much. If black hair was not common among tenth-century Norsemen, there would have been no distinction in Harald's designation of haar-fager.

However, the point is that an expedition of the year 1656 reported a tall, light-complexioned caste of natives living on the shores of Davis Straits at the same time as others of genuine Eskimo type. It is quite possible that the former, still retaining their individuality, may have migrated westward to Victoria Land.

WHITE IMMIGRANTS IN POLYNESIAN TRADITION
Anonymous; *Nature*, 125:614, 1930.

Mr. W. Ivens, in <u>Man</u> for March, discusses a number of traditions relating to white beings which occur in various parts of the Pacific. Malekula, New Hebrides, is said once to have been inhabited by a race called Ambat, who were white, and when Europeans first arrived on the island, they were believed to belong to that race and called by the same name. The Maoris believed in the existence of a white race of <u>atua</u>, and on Motu Island, Banks group, Bishop Selwyn and Bishop Patteson were taken for Kwat, the legendary hero, the origin of the association possibly being that he may have been supposed to be white. On North Mala, Solomon Islands, immigrants, white in colour, are said to have arrived in outrigger canoes at a place called Suuna Rii. They wore clothes and coverings to conceal their hair. Their hair was red, but for anyone to see it meant death at their hands. No name is given them, but they are accredited with the introduction of fighting, of magic, and of food plants, including the areca nut. They are worshipped on North Mala as <u>agalo i mae</u>, ghosts of war. The head covering of the <u>agalo i mae</u> survives in the pigtail of the statues of south-east Solomons, and the carved figures on Vanua Leva, Banks Islands, have a decided pigtail. In the Paumotus and Tahiti there are traditions of red-headed women who rose up from the floor of the lagoon. If, as seems possible, any connexion is to be seen between all these legends, the people to whom they relate may represent a movement into the Pacific at a very early date.

A NEW TRIBE OF LIGHT-SKINNED NATIVES IN NEW GUINEA
Anonymous; *Science,* 85:sup 16-18, March 6, 1937.

Discovery of a new tribe of light-skinned natives, in the treacherous depths of New Guinea, is stirring anthropologists to ask if roving sea-farers, some primitive branch of the white race, found their way to New Guinea in the South Pacific, there to lose themselves in the heart of an island jungle? That this did happen long ago, giving pale-face ancestry to a tribe that now numbers some 50,000 people, is the conviction of Jack Hides, discoverer of the tribe. Mr. Hides is a resident magistrate of New Guinea. His discovery has awakened much interest among anthropologists. It suggests that New Guinea was settled by both whites and blacks---some branch of the Indo-European race, as well as the negroid people from Asia.

Mr. Hides gave the following description of these unknown people to Science Service:

"These people were short in stature. They were light-skinned, something similar to the Malays. They had large mops of brown-tinged hair, high cheek bones, and yet rather good features. They were bow and arrow people and made beautiful axes of stone. They call themselves the Tarifuroro.

"Their methods of agriculture were the best I had ever seen. Their terraced gardens of an unusual squareness, marked off by pretty hedges of croton and hibiscus, were not unlike the Chinese market gardens we see in Australia. They grow sugar cane, ginger, bananas, sweet potatoes, spinach, mimica and native asparagus. There were no taro or yams. They often brought us pretty baskets of brown salt, which they obtained by burning logs of certain wood.

"I believe that further to the westward of these people in the adjoining valley, which is even larger than the Tarifuroro, we will find an even larger population and a more clearly defined Asiatic type. My reason for stating this is, as I traveled eastward across the Tari and Purari tableland, I found the light-skinned people merging into the darker-skinned Papuans, until just before I crossed the limestone barrier again, I found the real black Papuan men using the same methods of agriculture as the light-skinned Tarifuroro. It rather suggested to me that, at one time, these light-skinned people inhabited the whole of this tableland and were driven back westwards by the more virile Papuans."

Mr. Hides found the light-skinned tribe when he made an exploring journey, accompanied by a patrol officer, nine native policemen and 28 native carriers. Traveling up the Strickland River in a schooner, and thence up an unknown river to its source in dugout canoes, the party then climbed a difficult limestone barrier and found themselves on a high plateau inhabited by unknown thousands of New Guineans.

. . . .

THE KOREANS
Anonymous; *Science,* 95:sup 10, June 26, 1942.

Koreans have certain physical resemblances to white men, according to Dr. Ales Hrdlicka, of the Smithsonian Institution.

There are three distinguishable racial strains among Koreans. One group, living in territory nearest China, resemble the Chinese. Another, short, stocky and dark, are more like aboriginal inhabitants of Siberia. The third group, comprising the great majority of Koreans, are somewhat taller and have lighter skins. Young people of this type frequently have ruddy cheeks, a rarity among Mongolians. Some of the men have heads shaped very nearly like those of the Alpine racial type in Europe. These resemblances to white men, Dr. Hrdlicka suggests, point to a white group of Asiatic origin somewhere in the Korean ancestry.

Where Koreans originally came from is a foggy mystery. They may have migrated to their peninsula from somewhere in northern India, during prehistoric times. But as long as their own and Chinese history tells anything, they have always been there.

. . . .

WHITE INDIANS OF DARIEN

Fairchild, H. L.; *Science,* 60:235-237, 1924.

The Indian people of the Atlantic coast of Darien, generally known as the San Blas, are a superior group in an advanced stage of culture, and must not be called "savages." They are threatened by the white man's diseases, by encroachment of the negroids and by what they claim to be unjust treatment by the authorities. When Mr. Marsh had crossed the Cordillera and reached Caledonia Bay with his reduced party he found the Indians in danger from smallpox. Going down to the coast to a navy wireless station on the coast of Colombia he obtained doctors and vaccine from Colon and checked the epidemic. This, along with extended conferences with the chiefs, won the confidence and friendship of the Indians. The chiefs, in assembly, agreed to follow his advice and accept his help in safeguarding their people. Then Mr. Marsh said that he wished to see their white people. They replied that there were no white Indians. Marsh told them that he knew there were, for he had proofs and had seen several. He also said that their white Indians would interest the people of the United States and form a bond of sympathy which would aid in securing their safety and protecting their rights. Then they called in the white Indians from their seclusion in the hills, and they appeared in great numbers. The moving and still pictures taken by Charlton will be evidence. About 400 blondes were seen and information given that they have villages in the hills of the Cordillera. Such a village had been seen by an army aviator.

Mr. Marsh was told that their legends were to the effect that white members had existed in the tribes from ancient times, but that their hatred of white Europeans, on account of the Spanish cruelty, had resulted in dislike of their own white people, and that they had tried to suppress them. The effect was their seclusion and segregation in less accessible districts.

Three white children were selected by Mr. Marsh from among many that were offered to him, and with five dark adults they were brought to New York on July 6. One of the blonde children is a robust girl of 14 years, the father and mother being among the five dark adults. These parents have had seven children, five being white and two dark. The mother's mother was a white Indian. The two other children are boys, one 14 and one 10 years, the latter selected as the best example seen of the dark blotching of the white skin. These children have golden hair, hazel or hazel-blue eyes and pink gums. Mr. Marsh says that he did not see a typical albino among the hundreds of blondes. He believes, from his observations on the San Blas, that there are at least three types of Indians, possibly due to the commingling on the isthmus of migrations from the northern and southern continents. He thinks that the white girl and her parents represent a type of larger frame, larger heads and generally a more lusty physique than the ordinary San Blas. He feels sure that the blonde strain will be found limited to this type.

We find here an interesting ethnologic problem. The evening of July 8 the Pathe News gave a dinner at the Waldorf-Astoria to Mr. Marsh and his Indians and members of his expedition, to which were invited a number of anthropologists. The white children were examined at this conference, and it was the unanimous opinion that the phenomenon was not albinism. Major Cuthbert Christy, of England, a specialist

in tropical diseases, thought it was pathologic, due to some physiologic
condition inhibiting pigmentation.

The anthropologists of the American Museum of Natural History examined the Indians and attributed the whiteness to albinism. Their report, given currency in the daily press and in the Literary Digest of
August 9, contains, as stated by Mr. Marsh, an unfortunate error, that
the smaller size of the heads of the dark Indians is due to massaging in
infancy. This statement was based on reply by the Indians to questions
which they misunderstood. When subsequently questioned by Mr. Marsh
they repudiated with scorn and amusement the idea of any manipulation
of the heads of the children.

In connection with the recent meeting at Toronto of the British
Association three members of the Section of Anthropology visited the
Indians at their camp on the St. Lawrence, in the absence of Mr. Marsh,
and concluded that the white characters were a form of albinism, and
'that ostracism had encouraged its propagation, as summarized by the
chairman, Dr. F. C. Shrubsall, in a short presentation at the close of
the meeting. Following this paper, Mr. Marsh made the following
statement:

(1) The difference in size and shape between the skulls of the
blonde Indians and those of the standard San Blas has been attributed to artificial deformation of those of the dark infants, while
those of the white infants are natural. This is wholly untrue.
The San Blas Indians do not massage nor in any way alter the
heads of their children. The rounder, broader and higher crania
of the whites can not be explained in that way.

(2) The timid demeanor of the children and the behavior of
their eyes when under inspection by strangers is misleading.
They are not mentally deficient nor abnormal in any way. On the
contrary, they are unusually alert and keen, with excellent memory. They are rapidly learning English.

(3) That the blonde Indians do not spring from the normal
San Blas Indians but from the larger and more robust type,
which occupy the hills back from the coast.

It is evident that the great number of these blonde Indians and their
birth from both white and dark parents present an interesting and important problem, either ethnologic or medical. Thus far we have the
following tentative explanations:

(1) A peculiar form of transmissible and stabilized albinism. This
names but does not explain. The blonde complexion, the procreation
and the large number rule out ordinary albinism.

(2) Some disease or pathologic condition preventing pigmentation.
It appears that the physiologic defect is transmissible as an acquired
character.

(3) That the blondes are biologic "sports." This argues for a new
variety or race of the human species.

(4) That the phenomenon is atavism, the effect of a long-ago infusion of white or Nordic blood. The anthropologists are inclined to discredit the many legends of ancient or Pre-Columbian immigration from
Europe. But it may be wise to critically review the historic narratives.

One important matter is not yet determined, that is, if the white
parents ever have dark children.

Summarizing, it would seem that we may be limited to two views.

The first three of the above explanations suggest the initiation of a new white race, and fortifies the belief of many anthropologists that our own white race sprang from dark ancestry.   Either this explanation or the ancient introduction of Nordic blood.

THE RED RACE OF MADAGASCAR
Anonymous; *Science,* 5:266, 1897.

It is a curious fact that the older navigators who visited Madagascar describe a red race there, which now seems to be extinct.   In the 'Bull. de la Soc. d'Anthropologie,' of Paris (Tome VII., fasc. 5), Dr. Block collects a number of extracts bearing upon this.   The red people are described as tall, without beards, nose prominent, hair straight and long, the features of the European rather than Mongolian type, and the color of the skin red or reddish.   This race, the description of which corresponds singularly with that of the North American Indian of the Algonquian or Iroquoian stock, appears to have passed out of existence about the middle of the last century.   It is to be hoped that at least some ancient cemeteries may supply their osseous remains.   One writer, Flacourt, believes them to have been the ancestors of the Hovas, but the physical traits do not correspond.

THE YELLOW MEN OF CENTRAL AFRICA
Verner, Samuel P.; *American Anthropologist,* 5:539-544, 1903.

The fact that there are large numbers of indigenes in the remote parts of the African continent whose skin is of bright copper color and whose physiognomy is quite different from that of the typical negro, is one comparatively little known to men of science, and is a source of surprise to the general public, although students of African anthropology and explorers of the interior of the continent are well aware of its occurrence.   In my journeyings in the great Congo–Zambezi region I found many of these yellow people and became interested in their character and history.   I have already described the appearance and character of my friend Ndombe, "king" of the Baschilange, who was one of the finest types of these light-colored men; but I have not yet recorded the facts connected with this phenomenon nor discussed the possible reasons for it.

These yellow people of Central Africa are not detached tribes, but are families scattered throughout many different tribes.   It is safe to say that at least fifteen percent of the entire population of Central Africa (which perhaps numbers 65,000,000) are light colored. To put it comparatively, there are as many yellow Africans in Central Africa as there are negroes in the United States. I did not find a single tribe without some of these yellow individuals, or, most frequently, families, included in its membership.

One noteworthy feature of these people is the extent of their geographical distribution. They are found all over Central and South Africa from the central Soudan to the Cape. They are found in relatively larger numbers in the more elevated parts of the country, especially in the headlands about the sources of the Nile, the Congo, and the Zambesi. So far as my observation went, these copper-colored people are confined to the Bantu division of the African race, but I do not think that this is exclusively the rule. They live in the villages with the blacks, and in nowise seem to separate themselves into distinct political or social groups. For example, the uncle, and highly respected prime minister of the yellow king Ndombe, was Joka, whose skin was of a veritable ebon hue. The color did not seem to be a cause of geographical segregation at all.

....

Of one thing I became thoroughly convinced---the color of these Africans is not the result of any recent admixture of white blood. The yellow men are descendants of other yellow men for many generations, probably for many centuries. This is supported by several points of evidence. The traditions of the colored men indicate no white ancestry; and owing to their remarkable powers of memory, the careful preservation of tradition, its transmission as a sacred possession to posterity, and the pride with which the Afro-Caucasian of mixed blood always refers to any known white ancestry, this traditionary testimony of an unmixed descent for hundreds of years is of considerable value. Moreover, the history of African exploration, which is full and accurate, clearly shows no white residents for centuries in many parts of the continent where these yellow people have long resided. Again, there are no ethnic residua of white influence save of the most remote character, which will be discussed presently. A peculiar fact in this connection is that the color of the copper-hued Africans is not at all that of the mulatto or other degree of Caucasian mixture; their color is quite sui generis---of a curiously reddish tinge, somewhat like that of the American Indian, which the careful observer can readily distinguish from the other. For example, there were in my employ two copper-colored lads, one of whom was partly Portuguese, the other wholly African; yet the only external difference, so far as the skin was concerned, was this peculiar reddish tinge.

The question naturally arises, Whence the color of these millions of light Africans in the depths of the Dark Continent? This is one of the most difficult problems in the entire field of African anthropology. Like the question of the origin of their remarkable neighbors, the pygmies, the mystery of the development of these yellow men is both ancient and profound. Some light may be thrown on the problem, however, as the result of special research.

....

• Miscellaneous Evidence of Diffusion

ORIGIN OF THE INDIANS—THE POLYNESIAN ROUTE
Wickersham, James; *American Antiquarian,* 16:323-335, 1894.

The first fact, and the important one, too, is the existence of the northern equatorial current forever bathing the shores of the islands of Oceanica with its westward flow. This and the "Kuro-shiwo," or "black stream" of the Japanese, make a great wheel current in the North Pacific ocean, upon the outer circumference of which are scattered the wrecks of eastern Asia and western America. This endless ocean river bathes the shores of Asia, America and the Polynesian islands with its warm waters; it carries the drift of Asia to America, and the accumulation of Asia and America to the islands of the mid-Pacific. This unique current of the world's greatest ocean is the explanation of the similarity between the people of Asia, America and Oceanica; it has for countless centuries cast the drifting east-Asian not only on the coasts of America, but, missing that, upon the islands of the Pacific. On the outer rim of this great circling current is found the same type of man, inhabiting the far distant regions of Japan, Southern Alaska to Oregon, Hawaii, New Zealand and the many small islands of Polynesia. This wide distribution of the same type of man was accomplished by this never-ending, ever-flowing, revolving ocean current.

Of the possible thousands of wrecks cast upon the shores of America and the islands of the equatorial Pacific prior to 1492 we can know nothing; but since that date, and especially since the beginning of the seventeenth century, sufficient evidence has been preserved upon which to base an estimate of what must have happened ever since Asia has been inhabited by a seafaring people.

Seven castaway Japanese vessels have been thrown upon the Aleutian islands since the beginning of the seventeenth century. "In July, 1871, the old chief at Atter Island, aged 70 years, reported that three Japanese junks had been lost upon the surrounding islets during his recollection, besides one stranded not far from the harbor of that island in 1862." In 1782 a Japanese junk was wrecked upon the Aleutian islands, from which the survivors were taken in one of the Russian-American company's vessels to Kamtschatka and thence returned to their native island. In 1805 a junk was wrecked upon the coast of Alaska, near Sitka, and the crew was quartered on Japonski Island, and afterwards returned by the Russians to Japan. Another of these wrecks was cast upon Queen Charlotte's Island, and two upon Vancouver's Island. In 1833 another was thrown ashore at Cape Flattery, and the crew was rescued from slavery among the Makahs and returned to Japan by the Hudson Bay Company. Another vessel loaded with beeswax was thrown ashore near the mouth of the Columbia river, where the crew was captured by and amalgamated with the Indians. Several floating but abandoned wrecks have been sighted off the coasts of California, while three were thrown ashore on Lower

California and two in Mexico. "In 1845 the United States frigate St. Louis took from Mexico to Ningpo, in China, three ship-wrecked Japanese, being survivors of the crew of a junk which had drifted from the coast of Japan, entirely across the Pacific ocean and finally stranded on the coast of Mexico, where they remained two years." For ages last past the shores of America, from the Aleutian islands to Mexico, as well as the Pacific islands, have been strewn with wrecks from Asia carrying human freight. "In 23 cases where the actual number on board was named, they aggregated 293 persons, an average of 12-3/4 persons to a junk---ranging from 3 to 35 in individual cases. Where definite statistics of the saved are given, we find 222 persons saved in 33 cases; an average of 6-3/4 persons in each disaster. On eight occasions three persons were rescued; in four cases, one person; and on four other cases, four persons; three times, eleven were saved; and twice each, 5, 12, 15, 17; and once each, 2, 6, 7, 9, 10, 13 were saved. * * Fifteen vessels mention having drifted helplessly at sea an aggregate of 106-1/2 months, averaging a little over seven months each."---"Japanese Wrecks," Brooks, 1876.

The above facts sufficiently prove the probability of peopling America from Asia via the "Kuro-shiwo," or "black stream," of Japan, yet singularly enough the author of the above paper, which was read before the California Academy of Science in March, 1875, in a later paper read before the same society in May, 1876, used these and additional facts to prove that Asia (and incidentally Polynesia, too,) was peopled from America, via the equatorial current of the Pacific.---"Origin of the Chinese Race," Brooks, 1876.

In this last paper Mr. Brooks shows how easy it would be for vessels leaving the coast of Peru, or even Central America, taking advantage of both wind and current, to reach the continent of Asia, and says: "While we have cited facts showing it reasonable to suppose that early Peruvians or Central Americans may have come to China by the aid of continual fair winds, it is no less necessary to show the almost insurmountable difficulties which exist during a greater part of the year to impede their return by sea. To beat back against strong trade winds and the long regular seas of the Pacific would be a task in which they would surpass our best modern clippers, which now can only make the voyage by running far north and crossing from Japan to the coast of California, upon the arc of a great circle, and sailing thence southerly, close hauled on the wind, to the neighborhood of Tahiti in the South Pacific, which must then be crossed in an easterly direction, south of the trade winds, which in turn enable them to make northing and reach the coast of Peru. Such a return voyage would require the most skillful knowledge of winds, coasts and scientific navigation, such as we have possessed in comparatively recent times, and would also require exceeding strong and weatherly vessels. There seems, therefore, less likelihood that any Chinese ever reached Peru in pre-historic times by such a route."

***

Sir Edward Belcher gives a very full record of the landing of a castaway Japanese junk on the Sandwich Islands, in his "Voyage Round the World," pp. 304-5. He says: "About the same time another Japanese junk was wrecked on the island of Oahu, Sandwich Islands." From the Hawaiian Spectator, Vol. I, p. 296, I have the details: "A junk laden

with fish, and having nine hands on board, left one of the northern
islands of the Japanese group for Jeddo, but, encountering a typhoon,
was driven to sea. After wandering about the ocean for ten or eleven
months, they anchored on the last Sunday of December, 1832, near the
harbor of Waialea, Oahu. Their supply of water during the voyage had
been obtained from casual showers. On being visited four persons
were found on board; three of these were severely afflicted with scurvy,
two being unable to walk and the third nearly so. The fourth was in
good health, and had the sole management of the vessel. After remaining at Waialea for five or six days, an attempt was made to bring the
vessel to Honolulu, when she was wrecked off Barber's Point, on the
evening of January 1, 1833. Everything but the crew was lost, with the
exception of a few trifling articles. The men remained at Honolulu
eighteen months, when they were forwarded to Kamtschatka, from
whence they hoped, eventually, to work their way, by stealth, into their
own country, approaching by way of the most northerly island of the
group. When the people (Hawaiians) saw the junk, and learned from
whence it came, they said it was plain, now, whence they themselves
originated. They had supposed, before, that they could not have come
from either of the continents; but now they saw a people much resembling themselves in person and in many of their habits; a people, too,
who came to these islands without designing to come; they said, 'It is
plain, now, we came from Asia. '''

Belcher records the fact that a similar circumstance happened in
the same bay on the Hawaiian Islands long before the whites came there.
In 1854 the American ship <u>Lady Pierce</u> returned to Japan the sole survivor of a crew of fifteen; who was taken from a floating junk near the
Hawaiian Islands; the vessel had been drifting seven months from the
coast of Japan. A junk was cast upon the windward side of Kauaii, one
of the Hawaiian Islands, and the survivors landed at Hanalie harbor.
Ocean and Brooks' Islands are the most western of the Sandwich Island
system; in 1859 the bark <u>Gambia</u>, Captain Brooks found the remains of
a Japanese junk on Ocean Island, and in the same year, on July 4, the
remains of two stranded junks with lower masts high on the beach,
were found on the east, or lagoon side of Brooks' Island. Hawaiian
traditions maintain that <u>many</u> castaways were thrown on these islands
in times past.

Drift-wood from the northwest coast is cast upon these islands.
"The winds and ocean currents set directly from the northwest coast
of America to the Hawaiian Islands; logs and skiffs are constantly being borne from California and Oregon to their shores; none is borne or
could be borne from any other direction, except by the way of the Japan
current, which unites with the California current a little north of the
latitude of these islands. And it is supposed that some of an anterior
race, as the Toltec race, were out of their canoes on a sailing or fishing excursion and got blown off from the shore, got into the current and
were carried to the islands. And that the Hawaiians came from the
northwest coast of America is supported by such an array of probabilities and possibilities that they exclude any other hypothesis. When I was
in Hilo, in 1880, a log drifted into Hilo bay that we know grows in no
part of the world except the northwest coast, and the bark on the log was
still green, and the scar where it was cut off was still white, so anything
getting into the current, it takes but a short time to be carried to the

island. "---" Life in the Sandwich Islands, " Bennett, p. 3.

On September 10, 1862, an enormous Oregon tree, about 150 feet in length and fully six feet in diameter above the butt, drifted past the island of Mauii, Hawaiian Islands. Many saw-logs and pieces of drift-wood were thrown ashore at this time, and the windward shores of the Hawaiian Islands are literally lined with this material, as well as red-wood logs from California.

Baker's Island lies on the equator, in the very center of Polynesia: "A Japanese junk drifted past Baker's Island, latitude 0^0 52' north, longitude 176^0 22' west, some time in 1863; boats were sent out and towed it to the beach; there were four Japanese bodies on board; all were dead. " "In 1864, February 4, on Providence Island, latitude 9^0 52' north, longitude 160^0 65' east, on the lagoon side of the island, was seen the portions of a vessel which had been many years a wreck. Scattered along the outer shore were many red-wood logs, some of them of great size. "---"Japanese Wrecks, " Brooks, 1875.

Many more instances could be cited if necessary, but I think suffi-cient has been shown to make out a case. One well attested fact is worth unnumbered theories. The facts show that Polynesia may have received her inhabitants from Asia; there is no reason to doubt that canoes of Indians from the northwest coast of America may not have also been carried to these Polynesian islands with the masses of drift cer-tainly going from the same region. But I believe the source of popula-tion for the northwest coast of America, as well as for Polynesia, was Japan and Eastern Asia. From the east coast of Japan the Mongolian of Asia passed over the "Kuro-shiwo" to both America and Polynesia. The Sandwich Islands stretching from Hawaii to Ocean Island presented a barrier full across the southern and return flow of the Japan current, and probably the whole of Polynesia was peopled from their shores. "According to native tradition, frequent intercourse existed between the various groups of islands, and the canoes then used were larger and of better construction. In the Hawaiian meles, or songs, the names of Nuuhioa and Tahuata, two of the Marquesan Islands; Opolu and Savaii, belonging to the Samoan group; and Tahiti, with others in that neighbor-hood, frequently occur, besides the names of headlands and towns in these islands. These songs also make allusions to voyages from Oahu and Kauai to islands far west. "---"Hawaii, " Hopkins, p. 81.

We know that the Hawaiians went to Tahiti; the New Zealanders were emigrants from Tahiti; the conclusion seems to be fair that far-distant New Zealand was peopled by castaways from Asia, via. the "Kuro-shiwo" and Hawaii.

While the records, traditions, songs and history give many instances of migrations westward, in Polynesia none are mentioned toward the rising sun. Every tradition goes with the ocean drift---westward; the migrations go west and south, but never to the east. There is not a single known exception to this rule.

"If the march of mankind was towards the east, and they had already swarmed downwards and peopled the upper continent of America, there would indeed be no difficulty in the supposition that from the western shores men had taken another departure and reached the nearest of the islands of the Pacific. For the trade winds blow steadily from the north-east during nine months of the year, and cattle have been conveyed in an open boat from the Californian coast to the Hawaiian islands, which can be reached in a few days. So that either accident or a desire to make maritime discoveries, might have thrown upon the shores of Hawaii the crew of a lost canoe or a more organized band of emigrants. "

CHINA AND THE MAYA
Anonymous; *Nature,* 133:68, 1934.

A communication from Dr. Kiang Kang-Hu on the resemblances between the Maya civilisation of Central America and that of the Chinese, accompanied by an introductory note, dealing broadly with the question of cultural diffusion across the Pacific, by Dr. W. D. Lighthall, has appeared (Trans. Roy. Soc. Canada, Ser. 3, 27, Section 2). Dr. Kiang from his familiarity with the cultures of his own and kindred peoples is able to bring forward a number of instances, in which he sees resemblances between the two civilisations, for the further scrutiny of specialists. Among these are the physical characters and the mental outlook of the two peoples, the Maya more nearly resembling the Chinese physically than any other of the aboriginal tribes of Central and North America. He also points to similarities in language, in the complicated and elaborate calendrical system, both peoples using the 'large' and 'small' month count. Their religion and deities, sacrifice and worship are also alike, especially in regard to the use of idols of wood and clay to which human blood was applied. China, however, does not appear to have practised human sacrifice, although there are traditions of it in ancient days and remote parts. The astronomical and astrological system are strikingly similar; and the creation legends of the two peoples have many common features, as also have the story of the deluge and of the creation of the first men out of mud. Art, dress and ornament are reviewed with the same result. Setting aside the elements which are common to many primitive peoples, many resemblances remain which cannot be dismissed lightly. If the Mayas were of Chinese origin, they must have crossed to America more than six thousand years ago, otherwise their culture would be more specifically Chinese. Alternatively, they may have been derived from other adjacent races, different from, but culturally related to, the Chinese.

THE SACRAL SPOT IN MAYA INDIANS
Starr, Frederick; *Science,* 17:432-433, 1903.

In 1901, while at Tekax, Yucatan, making measurement of the Mayas of that district, the parish priest told me that it was commonly believed that every pure-blood Maya Indian had a blue or purple spot upon his back, in the sacral region. He said that this spot was called <u>uits</u>, 'bread, ' and that it was an insult to a Maya to make reference to his <u>uits</u>. To satisfy the curiosity of the priest, and my own, I examined a boy of ten years and two men, all of pure Maya blood. No one of the three presented any trace of a sacral spot, and I concluded that the common belief, if it had any basis, must relate to an infantile spot such as had long been known to occur in the Japanese, Eskimo, etc. Having no opportunity then to examine Maya babies, I determined to watch for the sacral spot among the infants of such tribes as I might later visit.

In my last journey to Mexico, just ended, I expected to see babies among six Indian populations---Aztecs, Zapotecs, Tzotzils, Tzendals, Chols and Mayas. From changes in my plan I really came into contact with the Aztecs and Mayas only. Aztec friends in whom I have confidence, in the states of Pueblo, Mexico and Tlaxcala, agreed that Aztec babies do <u>not</u> have a sacral spot; I made no personal examination.

In the town of Palenque, Chiapas, I examined all the <u>little</u> babies of the town---not a heavy labor, as the town is small. The people here call themselves Mayas, but claim to be closely related to the Chols. Probably the population is a mixture of the two peoples, who are closely related in language, and probably in blood. To my surprise, I found the spot in every one of the seven babies of pure Indian blood. It seems, however, to be far more evanescent among the Mayas than among the Japanese and other populations, being rarely found in individuals of more than ten months of age. Three babies, less than ten months in age, but of mestizo (mixed-blood) parentage, showed no trace of the spot. The spot is variable in size, shape and position, but it is always in the sacral region; in color it is blue or a bluish-purple; it gradually disappears and two or three of the cases seem to show an original single spot broken up into separate blotches which lose distinctness.

The sizes and shapes of the spots observed are accurately shown in the accompanying cut, reduced to one half the diameter. The notes made regarding each are here presented:

1. Boy; eight months. Spot well marked; dark purple; median, three inches above the anal fold. An older brother, two years old, showed no sign of the spot, but his mother says he was equally well marked at birth.

2. Girl; one year. Spot well defined; just to the right of the upper end of the fold.

3. Girl; three months. Two faint and badly defined spots just to the left of the upper end of the anal fold; a darker and better defined spot above.

4. Boy; two months. Two faint and badly defined spots, one on either side of the anal fold; a third, darker and better defined, above.

5. Boy; ten months. Only the lower of three spots is fairly defined, and it is faint, like a disappearing bruise; the other two are fainter. The three look like the separated parts of a spot which is disappearing. The group is median and located a little above the anal fold.

6, 7. Boys; twins of two months. Spots are pale blue but well defined; they are almost identical in form, size, color and position. They just overlap the upper end of the anal fold.

WAS MIDDLE AMERICA PEOPLED FROM ASIA?
Morse, Edward S.; *Popular Science Monthly*, 54:1-15, November 1898.

It may be of interest to remind those who have only a vague idea of
the contention that there are many earnest scholars who insist that the
wonderful architectural remains in Mexico, Yucatan, and other regions
of the west coast are due to Asiatic contact in the past. As proofs of
this contact are cited similarities as seen in the monuments, the facial
characteristics of certain tribes, ancient customs, astronomical ideas,
serpent worship, certain games, etc. Particularly is it believed by the
scholars that the "land of Fusang" mentioned in early Chinese historical
records is no other than Mexico or some contiguous country.

....

To the French Orientalist, M. de Guines, we are indebted for our
first knowledge of certain ancient records of the Chinese, which briefly
record the visit of Chinese Buddhist monks to the land of Fusang in the
year 458 of our era, and the return of a single Buddhist monk from this
land in 499. De Guines's memoir appeared in 1761, and for forty years
but little attention was drawn to it. Humboldt says that, according to
the learned researches of Father Gaubil, it appears doubtful whether the
Chinese ever visited the western coast of America at the time stated by
De Guines. In 1831, Klaproth, the eminent German Orientalist, combated the idea that Fusang was Mexico, and insisted that it was Japan.
In 1844 the Chevalier de Paravey argued that Fusang should be looked
for in America. Prof. Karl Friedrich Neumann also defended this idea.
In magazine articles in 1850-1862, and finally in book form in 1875,
Mr. C. G. Leland supported with great ingenuity the idea of Chinese
contact based on the Fusang account. In 1862 M. Jose Perez also defended the idea. In 1865 M. Gustave d'Eichthal published his memoir
on the Buddhistic origin of American civilization, and in the same year
M. Vivien de Saint-Martin combated the theory, and since that time
many others have written upon the subject in favor or in opposition to
the idea of Asiatic contact.

....

If we now turn to China as a possible region from which migrations
may have come in the past, we have only to study the historical records
of that ancient people to realize how hopeless it is to establish any relationship. Let one study the Ceremonial Usages of the Chinese (1121
B. C.---translated by Gingell), and he will then appreciate the wonderful
advancement of the Chinese at that early date---the organized government, the arts, customs, manufacturers, and the minute observances
and regulations concerning every detail of life. With these records before him he may search in vain for the direct introduction of any art or
device described in this old Chinese work. A few similarities are certainly found between the East and the West, but these arise from the
identity in man's mental and physical structure. With two legs only,
for example, it is found difficult to sit on a seat comfortably in more
than a few ways. One may sit with both legs down, with one leg under,
with legs crossed a la Turk, or the unconventional way throughout the
world with one leg over the other at various angles. It would seem with
this limited number of adjustments that any similarities in the attitude
of certain stone statues in America and Asia could have but little weight.

Prof. F. W. Putnam believes that he has established an Asiatic origin
of certain jade ornaments found in Central America. If this conclusion
could be sustained, we should then have evidences of contact with an
Asiatic people in the stone age, which in itself was one of great antiquity
for the Chinese, and one long antedating the origin of Buddhism. In the
Chinese work above alluded to the whetstone is mentioned for sharpening
swords, and the craft employed in polishing the musical stone. Con-
fucius also refers to the musical stone in his Analects. This is as near
as we get to the use of stone eleven hundred years before Christ. It is
to the merit of Putnam to have first called attention to the fact that many
of the jade ornaments, amulets, etc., of Central America had originally
been portions of jade celts. The discovery is one of importance, whatever explanation may be reached as to the origin of the stone. In Costa
Rica these celt-derived ornaments have been cut from celts composed of
the native rock, and it would seem that these old implements handed
down in the family led to their being preserved in the form of beads,
amulets, etc., much in the same spirit that animates us to-day in making paper-cutters, penholders, and the like from wood of the Charter
Oak, frigate Constitution, and other venerated relics. Among other evidences of contact the existence of the Chinese calendar in Mexico is cited.
Dr. Brinton shows, however, that the Mexican calendar is an indigenous
production, and has no relation to the calendar of the Chinese. In a similar way the Mexican game of patolli is correlated with the East Indian
game of parchesi by Dr. E. B. Tylor. Dr. Stewart Culin, who has made
a profound study of the games of the world, and Mr. Frank Hamilton
Cushing, the distinguished student of the ethnology of southern North
America, are both convinced that this game had an independent origin in
various parts of the world. Mexican divisions of time marked by five
colors are recognized as being allied to a similar device in China. The
application of colors to the meaning of certain ideographs is common in
other parts of the world as well. It is important to remark that the colors
named include nearly the whole category as selected by barbarous people,
and in the use of colors in this way it would be difficult to avoid similarities.

The evidences of contact in early times must be settled by the comparison of early relics of the two shores of the Pacific. Resemblances
there are, and none will dispute them, but that they are fortuitous and
have no value in the discussion is unquestionable. As illustrations of
these fortuitous resemblances may be cited a tazza from the United States
of Colombia having a high support with triangular perforations identical in
form with that of a similar object found among the mortuary vessels of
Korea, and Greece as well. A curious, three-lobed knob of a pot rim,
so common in the shell mounds of Omori, Japan, has its exact counterpart in the shell mounds of the upper Amazon. In the Omori pottery a
peculiar curtain-shaped decoration on a special form of jar has its exact parallel in the ancient pottery of Porto Rico. These instances might
be mutiplied, but such coincidences as are often seen in the identity of
certain words are familiar to all students. The account of the land of
Fusang appears in the records of the Liang dynasty contained in the
Nanshi, or History of the South, written by Li Yen-Shau, who lived in
the beginning of the seventh century. It purports to have been told by
a monk who returned from the land of Fusang in 499 of our era. This
hypothetical region has been believed to be Japan, Saghalin, and Mexico.
The record is filled with fabulous statements of impossible animals,

trees of impossible dimensions, and is so utterly beyond credence in many ways that it should have no weight as evidence. If it had any foundation in fact, then one might infer that some traveler had entered Saghalin from the north, had crossed to Yeso and Japan, and found his way back to China. His own recollections, supplemented by stories told him by others, would form the substance of his account. The record is brief, but any one familiar with Japan as Klaproth was is persuaded with him that the account refers to Japan and adjacent regions. The twenty thousand li the monk is said to have traveled may parallel his mulberry trees several thousand feet high and his silkworms seven feet long. In a more remote Chinese record, as mentioned by Dr. Gustave Schlegel, the statement is made that the inhabitants had to dig down ten thousand feet to obtain blue tenacious clay for roofing tiles! A number of ardent writers convinced that signs of Chinese contact are seen in the relics of middle America have seized upon this account of Fusang in support of this belief. These convictions have arisen by finding it difficult to believe that the ancient civilizations of Mexico and Peru could have been indigenous. In seeking for an exterior origin in the Fusang account overweight has been credited to every possible resemblance, and all discrepancies have been ignored.

The fabulous account of the land of Fusang evidently supplied documentary evidence, and Mexico was conceived to be the mythical Fusang. Mr. Vining goes so far as to declare that "some time in the past the nations of Mexico, Yucatan, and Central America were powerfully affected by the introduction of Asiatic arts, customs, and religious belief." To establish the details in the Chinese account the entire western hemisphere is laid under contribution: now it is the buffalo of North America, then the llama of Peru, the reindeer of the arctic, or some native word. These writers do not hesitate to bring to life animals that became extinct in the upper Tertiaries, and to account for the absence of others by supposing them to have become extinct. Literal statements of horses dragging wheeled vehicles are interpreted as an allusion in Buddhist cult which refers by metaphor to attributes and not to actual objects. As an illustration of the wild way in which some of these resemblances are established, Mr. Vining quotes the account of M. Jose Perez (Revue Orientale et Americaine, vol. viii). Perez reminds us that the inhabitants of the New World gave Old World names to places in the new continent, citing New York, New Orleans, and New Brunswick as examples, and then says that at some remote epoch the Asiatics had given to the cities of the New World the same names as the cities of their mother country; so the name of the famous Japanese city Ohosaka (Osaka), to the west of the Pacific, became Oaxaca in Mexico on the eastern side. Now it is well known that the ancient name of Osaka was Namihawa; this became corrupted into Naniwa, and not till 1492 does the name Osaka appear. Rev. J. Summers gives a full account of these successive names with their meanings (Transactions of the Asiatic Society of Japan, vol. vii, part iv). The real question to be answered is not what might have been accomplished by ancient explorers from Asia, but what was accomplished. It is shown that Chinese Buddhist priests went to India in the years 388, 399, 629, and so on, and the question is asked, Why may they not have reached Mexico on the east? Migration on parallels of latitude with no intervening ocean is one matter; to go from latitude 30° on one side of the Pacific almost to the Arctic Ocean, and down on the other side nearly to the equator, is quite another exploit. It is assumed that five priests had gone to Mexico in 468 A. D. , and there in-grafted Buddhistic cult on the races with whom they came in contact. It is simply beyond reason to believe that the introduction of Buddhism into Mexico antedated by half a century its introduction into Japan. Communication between Korea and Japan has been from the earliest times one without effort or peril: in the one case a trip of a day or more, in the other case a journey of unnumbered thousands of miles through perilous seas, across stormy fiords and raging waters, including arctic and tropical climates and contact with multitudinous savage hordes. Those who hold that Mexico and Central America were powerfully affected by Asiatic contact must be called upon to explain the absence of certain Asiatic arts and customs which would have been introduced by any contact of sufficient magnitude to leave its impress so strongly in other directions. A savage people takes but little from a civilized people save its diseases, gunpowder, and rum. The contact of barbarous with civilized people results in an interchange of many useful objects and ideas, but these introductions must be through repeated invasions and by considerable numbers. Peschel, while believing in the Asiatic origin of the American race, would place the time far back in the savage state. He repudiates the Fusang idea, and expresses his belief that "a high state of civilization can not be transmitted by a few individuals, and that the progress in culture takes place in dense populations and by means of a division of labor which fits each individual into a highly complex but most effective organization, " and then insists that "the phenomena of American civilization originated independently and spontaneously"; and Keane shows how interesting the social, religious, and political institutions of America become when "once severed from the fictitious Asiatic connection and influences. " That the savage derives little or derives slowly from contact with a superior race is seen in the fact that he still remains savage. Thus the Ainu, a low, savage people, though they have been in contact with the Japanese for nearly two thousand years, have never acquired the more powerful Mongolian arrow release, while the Persians, though Aryan, yet early acquired this release from their Mongolian neighbors. The Scandinavians, who in prehistoric times practiced the primary release, yet later acquired the more efficient Mediterranean method. Let us for a moment consider what would have occurred as a result of an Asiatic contact with a people advanced enough to have been powerfully affected in their "arts, customs, and religious belief. " It seems reasonable to believe that traces of a Mongolian release would be found in Central America, the more so as a warlike people would eagerly seize upon a more powerful method of pulling the bow, yet no trace of a stone or metal thumb ring has ever been found in the western hemisphere. Ancient Mexican codices, while depicting the archer, reveal no trace of the Mongolian method. In the Old World this release crept westward as a result of the migration of, or contact with, Asiatic tribes, and metal thumb rings are dug up on the Mediterranean littoral. While the arrow release of China might not have effected a lodgment in America, the terra-cotta roofing tile certainly would. This important device, according to Schlegel, was probably known in China 2200 B. C. , in Korea 500 B. C. , and in Japan in the early years of our era. In the ancient records of Japan reference is made to "breaking a hole in the roof tiles of the hall, " etc. , and green-glazed tiles are dug up on the sites of ancient temples in Japan. The fragments are not only unmistakable but indestructible. I have shown elsewhere that the primi-

tive roofing tile crept into Europe from the East, distributing itself
along both shores of the Mediterranean, and extending north to latitude
44°. Graeber finds its earliest use in the temple of Hira in Olympia,
1000 B. C. The ancient Greeks had no knowledge of the roofing tile.
Among the thousands of fragments and multitudinous articles of pottery
found by Schliemann in the ruins of Ilios, not a trace of the roofing tile
was discovered. One is forced to believe that so useful an object, and
one so easily made, would have been immediately adopted by a people
so skillful in the making of pottery as the ancient Mexicans. Certainly
these people and those of contiguous countries were equal to the ancient
Greeks in the variety of their fictile products. Huge jars, whistles,
masks, men in armor, curious pots of an infinite variety attest to their
skill as potters, yet the western hemisphere has not revealed a single
fragment of a pre-Columbian roofing tile. Vining, in his work, cites
an observation of the Rev. W. Lobscheid, the author of a Chinese grammar. In crossing the Isthmus of Panama this writer was much struck
with the similarities to China; "the principal edifices on elevated ground
and the roofing tiles identical to those of China." The roofing tile is
indeed identical with that of China. It is the form that I have elsewhere
defined as the normal or Asiatic tile, but it reached America for the
first time by way of the Mediterranean and Spain, and thence with the
Spaniards across the Atlantic, where it immediately gained a footing,
and rapidly spread through South America and along the west coast north,
as may be seen in the old mission buildings in California.

In China, Korea, and Japan the sandal has a bifureated toe cord, the
base of which, springing from the front of the sandal, passes between
the first and second toes. It belongs to the Old World through its entire
extent. It is the only form represented in ancient Egyptian, Assyrian,
and Greek sculpture. One would have expected that with any close contact with Asian people this method of holding the sandal to the foot
have been established in Central America, yet one may seek in vain for
the evidences of even a sporadic introduction of this method. Where
representations are given in the sculptured stone pottery, or codex, the
sandal is represented with two cords, one passing between the first and
second and the other between the third and fourth toes. Dr. Otis T.
Mason, who has given us an exhaustive monograph of the foot gear of
the world, says that every authority on Mexico and Central America
pictures the sandal with two cords, and he further says, in a general
article on the same subject, "An examination of any collection of pottery
of middle America reveals the fact at once, if the human foot is portrayed, that the single toe string was not anciently known."

The Thibetans, Chinese, Koreans, and Japanese have used the serviceable carrying stick from time immemorial. The nearest approach
to this method in this country is seen in Guadalajara, where a shoulder
piece is used to carry jars. The representation of this method shows
that the pole rests across the back in such a manner that the load is
steadied by both the right and left hand simultaneously---identical, in
fact, with methods in vogue to-day through western Europe. We find,
however, the northern races, as the Ainu and Kamchadels, use the head
band in carrying loads, and this method has been depicted in ancient
American sculpture. The carrying stick, so peculiarly Asiatic, according to Dr. Mason, is not met with on this continent.

With the evidences of Asiatic contact supposed to be so strong in

Central America, one might have imagined that so useful a device as
the simple chopsticks would have secured a footing. These two sticks,
held in one hand and known in China as "hasteners or nimble lads," are
certainly the most useful, the most economical, and the most efficient
device for their purposes ever invented by man. Throughout that vast
Asian region, embracing a population of five hundred million, the chopstick is used as a substitute for fork, tongs, and certain forms of
tweezers. Even fish, omelet, and cake are separated with the chopsticks, and the cook, the street scavenger, and the watch repairer use
this device in the form of iron, long bamboo, and delicate ivory. The
bamboo chopstick was known in China 1000 B. C., and shortly after this
date the ivory form was devised. Their use is one of great antiquity
in Japan, as attested by references to it in the ancient records of that
country. One may search in vain for the trace of any object in the nature
of a chopstick in Central or South America. Knitting needles of wood are
found in the work baskets associated with ancient Peruvian mummies,
but the chopstick has not been found. Curious pottery rests for the
chopsticks are exhumed in Japan, but even this enduring testimony of
its early use is yet to be revealed in this country.

The plow in all its varieties has existed in China for countless centuries. Its ideograph is written in a score of ways. It was early introduced into Korea and Japan, and spread westward through the Old World
to Scandinavia. There it has been found in the peat bogs. It is figured
on ancient Egyptian monuments, yet it made its appearance in the New
World only with the advent of the Spaniards. This indispensable implement of agriculture when once introduced was instantly adopted by the
races who came in contact with the Spaniards. Even in Peru, with its
wonderful agricultural development and irrigating canals, no trace of
this device is anciently known, and to-day the tribes of Central and South
America still follow the rude and primitive model first introduced by
their conquerors.

If we study the musical instruments of the New World races we find
various forms of whistles, flutes, rattles, split bells, and drums, but
seek in vain for a stringed instrument of any kind. This is all the more
surprising when we find evidences of the ancient use of the bow. If Dr.
Tylor is right, we may well imagine that the lute of ancient Egypt was
evolved from the musical bow with its gourd resonator (so common in
various parts of Africa), and this in turn an outgrowth of the archer's
bow, or, what at the moment seems quite as probable, the musical bow
might have been the primitive form from which was evolved the archer's
bow on the one hand and the lute on the other. Dr. Mason, in a brief
study of the musical bow, finds it in various forms in Africa and sporadic cases of it in this country, and expresses the conviction that stringed
musical instruments were not known to any of the aborigines of the western hemisphere before Columbus. Dr. Brinton is inclined to dispute
this conclusion, though I am led to believe that Dr. Mason is right; for
had this simple musical device been known anciently in this country, it
would have spread so widely that its pre-Columbian use would have been
beyond any contention. In Japan evidences of a stringed instrument run
back to the third or fourth century of our era, and in China the <u>kin</u> (five
strings) and <u>seih</u> (thirteen strings) were known a thousand years before
Christ. These were played in temples of worship, at religious rites,
times of offering, etc. It seems incredible that any contact sufficient

to affect the religious customs of Mexico or Central America could have occurred without the introduction of a stringed instrument of some kind.

In the Ceremonial Usages of the Chinese (1100 B. C.), a work already referred to, one may find allusions to a number of forms of wheeled carriages, with directions for their construction. Minute details even are given as to material and dimensions, such as measuring the spoke holes in the rim with millet seed (reminding one of the modern method of ascertaining the cubic contents of crania), all indicating the advanced development of wheeled vehicles. If from this early date in China up to the fifth century A. D., any people had found their way from China to middle America, one wonders why the wheel was not introduced. Its absence must be accounted for. It was certainly not for lack of good roads or constructive skill. Its appearance in this hemisphere was synchronous with the Spanish invasion, and when once introduced spread rapidly north and south. Like the plow, it still remains to-day the clumsy and primitive model of its Spanish prototype.

The potter's wheel is known to have existed in Asia from the earliest times; the evidence is not only historical, but is attested by the occurrence of lathe-turned pottery in ancient graves. We look in vain for a trace of a potter's wheel in America previous to the sixteenth century. Mr. Henry C. Mercer regards a potter's device used in Yucatan as a potter's wheel, and believes it to have been pre-Columbian. This device, known as the kabal, consists of a thick disk of wood which rests on a slippery board, the potter turning the disk with his feet. The primitive workman uses his feet to turn, hold, and move objects in many operations. The primitive potter has always turned his jar in manipulation rather than move himself about it. Resting the vessel on a block and revolving it with his feet is certainly the initial step toward the potter's wheel, but so simple an expedient must not be regarded as having any relation to the true potter's wheel, which originated in regions where other kinds of wheels revolving on pivots were known.

It seems reasonable to believe that had the Chinese, Japanese, or Koreans visited the Mexican coast in such numbers as is believed they did, we ought certainly to find some influence, some faint strain, at least, of the Chinese method of writing in the hitherto unfathomable inscriptions of Maya and Aztec. Until recently it was not known whether they were phonetic or ideographic; indeed, Dr. Brinton has devised a new word to express their character, which he calls ikonomatic. This distinguished philologist of the American languages confesses that not even the threshold of investigation in the solution of these enigmatical puzzles has been passed. Had the Chinese introduced or modified or even influenced in any way the method of writing as seen on the rock inscriptions of Central America, one familiar with Chinese might have found some clew, as was the case in deciphering the ancient writings of Assyria and Egypt. Grotefend's work on cuneiform inscriptions and Champollion's interpretation of Egyptian came about by the assumption of certain inclosures representing historic characters, which were revealed in one case by an inference and in another by an accompanying Greek inscription. If we examine the early Chinese characters as shown on ancient coins of the Hea dynasty (1756 to 2142 B. C.), or the characters on ancient bronze vases of the Shang dynasty 1113 to 1755 B. C.), we find most of them readily deciphered by sinologists, and coming down a few centuries later the characters are quite like those as written to-day.

On some of the many inscribed stone monuments of Central America one might expect to find some traces of Chinese characters if any intercourse had taken place, whereas the Maya glypts are remotely unlike either Chinese or Egyptian writing. Some acute students of this subject are inclined to believe that these undecipherable characters have been evolved from pictographs which were primarily derived from the simple picture writing so common among the races of the New World.

It seems clearly impossible that any intercourse could have taken place between Asia and America without an interchange of certain social commodities. The "divine weed," tobacco, has been the comfort of the races of the western hemisphere north and south for unnumbered centuries: stone tobacco pipes are exhumed in various parts of the continent; cigarettes made of corn husks are found in ancient graves and caves; the metatarsals of a deer, doubly perforated, through which to inhale tobacco or its smoke in some form, are dug up on the shores of Lake Titicaca.

The question naturally arises why tobacco was not carried back to Asia by some of the returning emigrants, or why tea was not introduced into this country by those early invaders. A Buddhist priest without tea or tobacco would be an anomaly. There are many other herbs, food plants, etc., that should not have waited for the Spanish invasion on the one hand, or the Dutch and Portuguese navigator along the Chinese coast on the other.

Finally, if evidences of Asiatic contact exist, they should certainly be found in those matters most closely connected with man, such as his weapons, clothing, sandals, methods of conveyance, pottery making and devices thereon, musical instruments, and above all house structure and modes of burial. More remote perhaps would be survivals of language, and if the invaders had a written one, the characters, whether phonetic or ideographic, would have been left in the enduring rock inscriptions. If now a study of the aborigines of the western hemisphere from Hudson Bay to Tierra del Fuego fails to reveal even a remote suggestion of resemblance to any of these various matters above enumerated, their absence must in some way be accounted for by Asiaticists.

THE SIMILARITY OF CHINESE AND INDIAN LANGUAGES
Anonymous; *Science,* 62: sup xii, October 9, 1925.

New light has been thrown on the ancestry of the American Indian by Dr. Edward Sapir, the Canadian anthropologist now on the faculty of the University of Chicago. Dr. Sapir said that his research work on Indian linguistics has convinced him of the identity of the language of certain Indian tribes with that of the primitive Chinese.

The similarity of the two tongues and the linguistic distribution of tribes scattered at random over the Americas have convinced Dr. Sapir that these groups must have entered this continent as a wedge from Asia. By a close comparison of the primitive Chinese, Siamese and

Tibetian, all in the same language category, with the language of the "Nadine group" of North America, Dr. Sapir has found the same peculiarities of phonetics, vocabulary and grammatical structure on both sides of the Pacific Ocean.

The American Indian groups speaking the language of the Nadine group are found in all parts of the North American continent from northern Mexico to the southern boundary of Alaska, widely distributed among other Indian tribes whose language and customs are entirely different.

With minor changes the Navajo of New Mexico speaks the language of the Sarcee in Alberta, and the linguistic stock of the Tlingit, just south of the Eskimos in Alaska, is much the same as that of the Hupa in California.

It is probable, according to Dr. Sapir, that the migration of Asiatics speaking primitive Chinese or Tibetian took place at some time in the past, and that these immigrants settled or moved over the mountains and plains, some remaining in northwestern Canada to become the Tlingits, and others moving out to the Queen Charlotte Islands off the west coast to form the Haida group, and still others penetrating to the deserts of the Southwest.

From the modern Chinese, which in academic circles is considered relatively simple, students of linguistics can reconstruct primitive Chinese which is far more complex than any of the dialects known to the Mongolian layman of to-day. Dr. Sapir has discovered not only that the Indians of the Nadine groups speak with a tonal accent, raising or lowering of the voice to give certain meaning to words, in a manner similar to the tonal peculiarities of the early Chinese, but also that the meanings of certain words are identical. Further, he has disclosed the fact that the Indians have retained certain prefixes and suffixes that long ago have disappeared from the Chinese speech, but which are clearly discernible in the early forms.

MUSICAL INSTRUMENTS OF MALAYSIA AND THE WEST COAST OF SOUTH AMERICA

Hawley, E. H.; *Science,* 22:597, 1905.

To the Editor of Science: A short time ago the National Museum received from Mr. C. Boden Kloss, curator of the Johore Museum, No. 40 of the Journal of the Straits Branch of the Royal Asiatic Society, for June, 1904, containing an illustrated catalogue of the ethnographical collection of the Sarawak Museum, Part I., Musical Instruments, by R. Shelford.

On page 29, Mr. Shelford thus describes a flageolet of the tribe called Murut, in Borneo:

    a. Murut---Flageolet. (Plate VIII., figs. 7 and 8.)

Distal end open and cut square, proximal end closed by the natural septum, the bamboo has not been cut flush with this but projects con-

siderably beyond it; in the wall of this projecting part a small hole is
bored quite close to the septum, and a groove runs on the outside of the
flute from this hole to the sound-hole, the groove being covered by a
slip of bamboo luted on with dammar.   The edge of the sound-hole is
sharpened by a piece of palm-leaf stuck on.   The sound-hole is 5 centim.
from the proximal end; there are two stops 8.5 centim. apart, bored
with a red-hot iron in a flattened strip on the same side as the sound-
hole, the upper one is 32 centim. from the sound-hole.   Total length
52.5 cm.; diam. 2.5 cm.

Catalogue No. 1291.   F. J. D. Cox, Esq. (P. vii 03).   From the
Trusan river.

This is precisely similar to the mystery flute of some of the early
writings about the North American Indians.   The Museum has just received an additional example from Arizona, through E. H. Nelson.
They are usually made of cane, having a closed joint at or near the
middle.   A hole is pierced on either side of the septum of the joint
through the walls of the cane and an air channel cut on the outside from
one hole to the other.   If the upper hole and the channel are covered by
a bandage or the finger as far as the lower face of the septum and the
upper tube blown into, it gives a whistling sound.   In the lower section
three or four finger holes are made.   If more than that number, it shows
a European influence.   If an instrument of this kind that has no bandage
is handed to one ignorant of its characteristics, he would not be apt to
place a finger in the precise spot required to make a sound, and how to
sound it would be a mystery to him.   Some of the North American
Indians construct bone whistles in the same manner.   For the reason
that this method of construction is seldom seen elsewhere, the instrument is supposed to have been original with the Indians of North
America.

This is another interesting connecting link between Malaysia and the
west coast of America, because of these two identical instruments in
regions far apart.   A search for the cause of this identity will be interesting to ethnologists.

THE TRANSPACIFIC ORIGIN OF MESOAMERICAN CIVILI-
ZATION....

Meggers, Betty J.; *American Anthropologist,* 77:1-27, 1975.

Summary of Shang-Olmec Resemblances.   The traits and complexes
just reviewed vary greatly in magnitude and degree of specificity.   At
one extreme is a distinctive kind of skull deformation; at the opposite extreme is a settlement pattern embracing a number of characteristics
(earth platform) north-south orientation, wattle-and-daub buildings,
ceremonial-administrative centers, etc. each of which might have been
listed separately.   Expression ranges from material objects such as
jade celts, to abstract concepts, such as the religious significance of
felines and mountains.   Some elements are well documented archaeologically or historically in both areas, the long-range acquisition of pro-

ducts being an example. Others are inferences, among them the suggestion that batons were symbols of rank among the Olmec as they were among the Shang. Another variable is the disparate stylistic expression of traits that seem comparable in general conception, obvious in the representations of felines. Considered as a whole, however, there are a remarkable number of striking resemblances between the inception and content of the earliest civilizations of China and Mesoamerica. They can be summarized as follows:

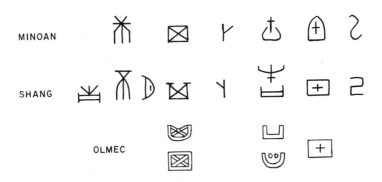

Comparison of Minoan Linear A script (1700-1600 B.C.) with inscription on Shang oracle bones and Olmec rock carvings

(1) At about 1200 B.C., there was a quantum change in Mesoamerica from a village farming way of life to Olmec civilization; a similarly abrupt transformation took place about 500 years earlier in China, when the Shang Dynasty was imposed on a pre-existing Neolithic population.

(2) The Shang and the Olmec are credited with the possession of writing, a reliable calendar, a social structure capable of procuring and directing labor for large-scale construction, an organized religion administered by a priesthood, and a trade or acquisition network that channeled materials from distant sources to the administrative or ceremonial centers; both treated jade as a material of exceptional value.

(3) The settlement pattern of both cultures consisted of small, scattered villages, the inhabitants of which contributed labor, luxury goods, food, and other commodities and services to centers occupied by an aristocracy. Among the Olmec, the nature and composition of the latter is unknown; among the Shang, the documents describe a hierarchy composed of a sovereign, administrators of differing rank, and feudal lords.

(4) The principal structures in Olmec centers and Shang capitals were rectangular earth platforms surmounted by perishable wattle-and-daub buildings; the main axis of the components and the site as a whole was north-south. Underground drains, dedicatory caches, and tombs are among the associated features.

(5) Shang documents indicate that the emperor and the subordinate lords employed specific types of jade batons as symbols of authority and

rank; Olmec bas-reliefs depict elaborately attired men, some of whom hold a staff or plaque of similar shape in one or both hands.

(6) The feline was a major focus of religious expression among both Shang and Olmec, and was associated with the earth. Depiction ranges from realistic to highly stylized and from fanged and snarling to gentle and placid. Frequently, the lower jaw was omitted. Serpents and birds were also emphasized and features of these animals were sometimes combined in the iconography of both cultures to produce a dragon.

What is the significance of these resemblances? Are they evidence of the arrival in Mesoamerica about 1200 B.C. of immigrants of Shang origin or are they independent duplications explainable by the operation of general laws of cultural evolution? (pp. 16-17)

THE LANGUAGE AND ORIGIN OF THE BASQUES
H. A. C.; *Nature*, 64:90-91, 1901.

The Basques or Euskaldunak (i. e. "the Men"), as they call themselves, are a most remarkable people who have long been an interesting problem to ethnologists. The most anomalous point about the Basques is their language, which is as typically agglutinative as any Asiatic or American tongue. Ripley, in his fine book "The Races of Europe," points out that the verb habitually includes all pronouns, adverbs and other allied parts of speech; as an example of the appalling complexity possible as a result, Blade gives fifty forms in the third person singular of the present indicative of the regular verb "to give" alone. Another often quoted example of the effect of such agglutination occurs in a reputed Basque word meaning "the lower field of the high hill of Azpicuelta," which runs,

Azpilcuelagarayeosaroyarenberecolarrea.

No wonder that the French peasants state that the devil studied the Basque language for seven years and learned only two words. Like many other undeveloped languages, the principle of abstraction or generalisation is but slightly developed; for example, as there is no general word for "sister" the Basques have to say "sister of the man" or "sister of the woman," &c. Owing to their isolation on both flanks of the Pyrenees, many primitive institutions persist among the Basques. In some places the eldest daughter takes precedence over all the sons in inheritance, which may be a relic of a former matriarcal family; communal ownership within the family is frequently practised. The remarkable custom now known as the couvade, in which the father takes to his bed on the birth of a child, was attributed to these people by Strabo, and it is believed by some not to have completely died out at the present day though there is great difficulty in proving its existence, as G. Buschan points out in Globus (Bd. lxxix. p. 117). H. Schuchardt has recently (Globus, Bd. lxxix. p. 208) expressed his wonder that this statement has again been dragged from the realm of fable. The same writer makes some remarks on misapprehensions respecting the Basque language.

Many wild theories have been promulgated as to the origin of the Basques, one of the most absurd being an attempt to relate them with a certain tribe in Central America. Several scholars have sought to affiliate the people with Lapps and Finns, and they have been supposed to be related to the ancient Egyptians, the ancient Phoenicians, the extinct Etruscans and to the Picts. The Basque language appears to be absolutely without connection with any of the so-called Turanian (Ural-Altaic) languages, since, as Keane shows in his "Man Past and Present" (p. 460), there is no longer any doubt as to the relationship of the Basque with the Berber language.

The anthropometrical evidence has given rise to much controversy. The French Basques have an average cephalic index (on the living) of 83, while the Spanish Basques average 78, according to Collignon, and 79 according to de Aranzadi in the graphic curve published by the latter anthropologist, who, by the bye, is himself a Basque; there are two distinct maxima, one at 76 and the other at 80, indicating, probably, that there are at least two elements in the group. The French Basques are on an average three-quarters of an inch shorter than their Spanish brethren, 1657 mm. (5ft. 5-1/4ins.) and 1638 mm. (5ft. 4-1/2ins.) respectively. Both branches of the stock have a similar very characteristic head; the cranium is distinctly long even in the most brachycephalic subjects, and is enormously swollen in the temporal region, a character which is absolutely peculiar to this people, the forehead is high and straight and narrow below, the face is very elongated and has the shape of an inverted triangle, the chin being thin and pointed; the nose is correspondingly long and narrow.

Certain anthropologists have claimed that those Basques who live north of the Pyrenees more nearly represent the primitive stock, while the same has been asserted for those south of that range. De Aranzadi thinks that those Spanish Basques with dark hair and eyes and a rather narrow head and of middle stature are of true Iberian origin and are related to the Berbers. Those with darkish brown hair and greenish hazel eyes, a broad head and low stature are, according to him, of Ugrian or Finnish descent. G. Buschan, in a recent number of Globus (Bd. lxxix. p. 123), regards it as highly probable that the Basque race resulted from a crossing of the short-heads of the earliest prehistoric time, who probably wandered from Asia into Europe, with the long-headed indigenous Mediterranean race. The first of these two constituents he recognises as the race of Grenelle (French authors) or as the type of Sion or Disentis (His-Rutimeyer) or as the celts of Broca. Buschan has overlooked the fact that Canon Isaac Taylor, in his "Origin of the Aryans," had suggested this same explanation in 1890 and Beddoe had alluded to it in his "Anthropological History of Europe" in 1893. De Aranzadi recognises a third element with light hair, blue eyes, narrow head and tall stature, which is a later addition of Kymric or Germanic origin, and he suggests that this element is related to the accursed race of the Cagots who were isolated from their neighbours and had a separate church door for themselves.

Collignon, who has made many brilliant studies in the anthropology of France, draws attention to the very anomalous relation that exists between a cephalic index of 82.5, which is clearly brachycephalic, and a cranial length as great as 191 mm. He is of opinion that this permits us to look for the affinities of the Basque race more in the direction of the long-headed races; the Nordic, or Eutonic, being clearly out of the question, relationship must be sought among the Mediterranean group of peoples rather than in the direction of the brachycephals of France and of Central Europe. Collignon's view is that the Basque type is a variety of the Mediterranean race that has for a long period of time been geographically isolated, and the retention of a difficult and uncouth language has formed an equally efficient linguistic barrier. These factors induced in- and in-breeding, and a well marked human variety has resulted. Collignon's contention that the French Basques more nearly represent the primitive stock is now generally admitted; the head of the Spanish Basques has been narrowed and their stature diminished by mixture with Spaniards who had been driven into the mountains by the Moorish invasion. Those who desire to learn more about this paradoxical people will find numerous references to the literature in the valuable appendix to Ripley's "Races of Europe," and additional titles are given by Buschan in Globus (Bd, lxxix. February 28, 1901).

JEWISH AND ZULU CUSTOMS

Anonymous; *American Antiquarian,* 7:52, 1885.

A paper received from Natal Africa, contains an article by Rev. Josiah Tyler on the similarity of Jewish and Zulu customs. Among them we mention several: The feast of first fruits, rejection of swine's flesh, right of circumcision, the slayer of the king not allowed to live, Zulu girls go upon the mountains and mourn days and nights, saying, "Hoi! Hoi!" like Jepthah's daughter, traditions of the universal deluge, and of the passage of Red Sea; great men have servants to pour water on their hands; and throwing stones into a pile; blood sprinkled on houses. The authors' belief is that the Zulus were cradled in the land of the Bible. Certain customs are mentioned which may be ascribed to the primitive tribal organism. These are as follows: Marriages commonly among their own tribe; uncle called father, nephew a son, niece a daughter; inheritance descends from father to eldest son. If there are no sons it goes to the paternal uncle. A surmise has been advanced by some that the relics of the Queen of Sheba's palace may be found in certain ancient ruins described by Peterman, Baines and others, and the Ophir of scripture has been located at Sofala, an African port.

Chapter 6
BIOLOGICAL EVIDENCE

INTRODUCTION

This chapter is a brief introduction to the concept that the travels of ancient man can be discerned in part by analyzing the global distribution of plants and animals important to human culture. One danger in such research, of course, is that plants and animals have ways of leapfrogging oceans and other natural barriers by nonhuman means, such as the winds and ocean currents. Indeed, this is another one of those branches of science where the evidence is interpreted more in terms of what the analyst thinks should have happened rather than what might have happened. The evidence presented here must also be considered in the context of other hints that ancient man was an ambitious traveller; viz., anomalous inscriptions, similar customs, blood-type distributions, and coincident technical capabilities.

BABIRUSSA TUSKS FROM AN INDIAN GRAVE IN BRITISH COLUMBIA
True, F. W.; *Science,* 4:34, 1884.

Many curious and unlooked-for objects are frequently found in Indian graves, and not least among these is a pair of the tusks of the Babirussa. They were extracted in August of last year by Mr. James S. Swan from the grave of an old Indian doctor at Kah-te-lay-juk-te-wos Point, near the north-western end of Graham Island, one of the Queen Charlotte Islands, off the coast of British Columbia. The Babirussa, as every one knows, is an animal of the hog tribe, inhabiting only Celebes and the adjacent islands. The question then arises, How did these teeth come into the possession of the Indian doctor, who died some fifty years since at an advanced age?

Mr. Swan suggests an ingenious and plausible solution of the problem. In his letter of the 4th of January to Professor Baird, he writes as follows: "Lieut. Bolles, of the U. S. surveying schooner Ernest, tells me that the Siamese junks make regular trading-voyages to the coast of Africa, even as far as the Cape of Good Hope, running down with the north-east monsoons, and returning when the favorable monsoon blows. They bring products of every kind, and trade with Japan and China. He thinks that some of these junks may have been wrecked, and carried by the Japanese current to the American side, and perhaps cast ashore on the west coast of the Queen Charlotte Islands, where quantities of drift-stuff of every kind is to be found.

"Charles Solcott Brooks, in his able report on Japanese vessels wrecked in the North Pacific Ocean, read before the Californian academy of sciences, March 1, 1876, says, 'Every junk found adrift or stranded on the coast of North America, or on the Hawaiian or adjacent islands, has, on examination, proved to be Japanese, and no single instance of any Chinese vessel has ever been reported.'

"One of these junks was wrecked on the Queen Charlotte Islands in 1831, and numerous others have been wrecked on other parts of the north-west coast. The tusks of the Babirussa were undoubtedly an article of commerce among a people who would be likely to use them for carving or for manufacturing into fancy articles, and it is not improbable that the tusks in question were procured from some one of these old Japanese wrecks."

It is difficult to conceive of another origin for these tusks. The commerce of California fifty years ago was of a very limited character, and Babirussa tusks are among the objects least likely to have been sent there through any regular channel.

A POSSIBLE HINDU INFLUENCE AT TEOTIHUACAN

Voke, Emily H.; *American Antiquity,* 29:94-95, 1963.

Abstract. The conch shell figured on the Temple of Quetzalcoatl at Teotihuacan, is Turbinella angulata, the West Indian Chank. This species is closely related to the "Sacred Chank" of India, a shell which figures prominently in Hindu mythology, religion, and art. This finding may be interpreted as one more bit of evidence for transpacific influences on prehistoric Mesoamerican culture.

PLANT EVIDENCE FOR EARLY CONTACTS WITH AMERICA

Carter, George F.; *Southwestern Journal of Anthropology,* 6:161-182, 1950.

Introduction. The question of direct contacts between American centers of high culture and those of the Old World has been a vexing problem. Extremists on one side have claimed Egyptian influence in America and extremists on the opposite side have denied any contact with America by anyone at any time. We need to review the evidence. In such a review, the plant evidence suggesting contacts with Old World agriculture peoples offers certain unique advantages. Plants are not constructs of the mind. They are less subject than most data to appeals to the psychic unity of mankind, parallelisms, independent inventions, limitations of techniques, and so forth.

But even plants do not supply us with absolute answers. The possible transfer of plants across oceans by some most unusual means; the remote chance that man on both sides of the ocean might then domesticate the plant or use it for identical purposes, and even give the plant a similar name, can not be dismissed. The possibility always exists. On the other hand we can show that such things probably did not happen. The whole evolution of the plant world indicates that the oceans have served as highly efficient barriers to plant movement. The history of plant domestication, while it suggests plural origins of agriculture, shows that it has been quite rare for man to domesticate the same or closely related plants in areas not in contact with each other.

When we deal with more than one plant which can be shown probably to have been transferred by man across the ocean, the "probables" have a cumulative effect. The cumulative nature of the evidence is important. Neither the individual plants, nor the plant evidence as a whole, stands alone. Rather, the plant evidence is part of a complex whole, and the coherency of the whole can legitimately be used in defense of the validity of the parts.

Some domestic plants reproduce vegetatively only and only through the intervention of man can they cross such water barriers as the oceans. We have in them unique markers. As O. F. Cook remarked nearly fifty years ago,

the same plant does not originate twice, and [that] varieties dependent everywhere for their very existence on human care must also have been distributed by human agency.
[And again:] For the present purposes it suffices to remember that the actual introduction of plants by human agency discounts in advance all objections on the ground of distances and difficulties of communication, and justifies the fullest use of biological or other data in tracing the origin and dissemination of agricultural civilization in the Tropics of both hemispheres.

The Evidence of Cultivated Plants. The sweet potato (Ipomea batatas) is an American plant. Yet before 1864 it was noted that in Polynesia it was known to the natives by the Quechua name of kumar. In 1888 Hillebrand, writing with the background of long residence in the Hawaiian Islands and acquainted with their legends and history, wrote:

The Sweet Potato, of aboriginal cultivation, was, next to the taro, the principal article of food to the natives at the time of discovery. They enumerate about twenty varieties which differ as much in shape, color, and quality of the tuber as in the shape of the leaves. The vernacular name "Uala" corresponds well with the Tahitian "Umara" and the New Zealand "Kumara," and it is interesting to note that B. Seeman has met with the same verbal root "Cumar" for this esculent among the Quichuas of Ecuador.

These data, and they could be multiplied, seem not to have impressed Americanists.

In 1932 Dixon, who was no protagonist for trans-Pacific influences, reported on the question of the sweet potato in the Pacific. From an

examination of the historical accounts of the voyages of discovery he
concluded that the sweet potato was pre-Spanish in both Polynesia and
Melanesia. Dixon noted that the Maori legends state that the sweet
potato had been carried to New Zealand both by the migrants of the fourteenth century and those of an earlier migration. The retention of the
name for the sweet potato by the Chatham Islanders suggested to Dixon
the likelihood of the validity of the earlier introduction.

That the plant had been in Polynesia for a considerable length of
time is indicated by the linguistic changes that the name kumar under-
went in the various islands. Since the sweet potato is vegetatively reproduced, variation would expectably be quite slow. Yet Hawaii had
many varieties and this, also, must mean either considerable antiquity
or importation of a considerable range of varieties. In Hawaii also Dixon
noted that the plant is referred to in the most archaic cosmogonic chants
and myths and is associated with the major gods. It has elaborate rituals
associated with its planting, cultivation, and storage. Evidence from
traditions, botany, language, and ritual all suggest antiquity for the crop.

There is also physical evidence. At the time of discovery New Zealand had extensive areas of land in sweet potatoes. Pits from which
gravel was dug for hilling the potatoes covered many acres and some had
been excavated to depths of five or six feet. In some of these pits trees
of great age were growing. Excavation of an acre of ground to a depth
of five feet involves the removal of approximately twenty million pounds
of gravel. The loads may have been basket loads of perhaps five pounds
each. That suggests four million loads of gravel carried for each acre
of ground so excavated. When it is remembered that there were many
acres, and that the work would have been done intermittently, then an
impression of a considerable elapse of time is gained.

Dixon failed to find any account of contacts with America in the Polynesian traditions. He thought that had such a contact been made in the
period of long voyages between the tenth and fourteenth centuries, the
account would be preserved. He suggested, therefore, that the contact
may have been made in the initial period of voyaging, centuries before
1000 AD. This would be in agreement with his suggestion that the importance of the plant in marginal, and its unimportance in central, Polynesia may be related to diffusion prior to the influences on central Polynesia in medieval times.

The several lines of arguments are mutually supporting and indicate
an importation from the area where kumara was the name for the sweet
potato at a period long preceding 1000 AD. There can be no question
that man carried the plant. The fact of vegetative reproduction and the
Quechua name establish proof beyond all reasonable doubt. Only the absolute date remains in doubt.

Hibiscus Tiliaceous: It would be strange if there were contacts between the New World and Polynesians of such intimacy that they led to the
exchange of a plant together with its name, if the contacts were limited
to one plant. Cook long ago pointed out that this was not the case. He
noted that Hibiscus tiliaceous grew wild in America and was used in the
same way as in Polynesia. Oviedo, Dampier, Sloane, Barrerre were
cited by Cook as describing the plant and its uses. Cook found the plant
to be widely distributed in tropical America and to be known under the
name of maho or mahagua, or some variant of this name. In Polynesia
he noted the plant is also widespread, wild, widely used and known as

<u>mao</u>, <u>mau</u>, <u>au</u>, <u>hau</u>, <u>fau</u>, <u>vau</u>; <u>moanua</u>, the closest approach to <u>mahagua</u>, being found on Easter Island. In America he found the name also to be applied locally to many other fiber-bearing plants such as <u>Thespesia</u>, <u>Ficus</u>, <u>Agave</u>, and so forth. Cook was wedded to the idea that agriculture began in America and spread thence across the Pacific to Asia. Quite naturally, therefore, he concluded that man had carried the <u>Hibiscus</u>, also. The identity of names and usages in parallel to the sweet potato were convincing to him, and, one would think, to anyone.

However, the mental climate was then even less receptive to ideas of early trans-Pacific contacts with America than it is now. A challenge to Cook's ideas was bound to be made. Merrill took up the cudgels almost at once. He noted that the plant had a pan-tropic strand distribution; that it was never cultivated in the tropics of the Old World or New World outside Polynesia because better fiber sources existed in those areas. Its seeds are perfectly adapted to float for months, hence its presence on two sides of an ocean can not be evidence that man carried it. He argued that the fact that the word for this hibiscus in Polynesia was applied to many bast fiber plants and could be traced back into Malaya showed that the word was a general one for bast in Indo-Malaya and only had its specific meaning of hibiscus in Polynesia. He concluded therefore:

> The probabilities are very great that all of the Polynesian <u>mao</u> series are merely modifications of the Indo-Malayan <u>bago</u> series; and that the Polynesians in their migration, having adopted the name while in the Indo-Malayan region, merely applied it to the wild plant which they found all over Polynesia. It would seem, therefore, that this root has nothing to do with the tropical American <u>maho</u> series, the resemblances being merely accidental.

These arguments seem to me to be excellent specimens of the result of fixed ideas. Cook was so intent on proving the American origin of agriculture that he was incautious, if not unwise, in using a halophytic plant with a seed well adapted to water transportation as <u>proof</u> of man's carrying plants across the ocean. Merrill on the other hand was either so incensed by Cook's special pleading or so allergic to trans-Pacific contacts (or both) that the violence of his reaction blinded him to the virtues of Cook's arguments.

Cook pointed to a plant common to America and Polynesia, used in identical ways, and known by names of near identity. He made two further important points. There was an exact parallel to this plant in the case of the sweet potato; and the plant name in America was applied not only to hibiscus but to other fiber bearing plants. Merrill pointed to seed qualities as invalidating the argument for the <u>necessity</u> of man carrying the plant, but did not realize that this did not amount to showing that man did <u>not</u> carry the plant. Winds and currents suggest that if the plant was carried across the Pacific by natural means it must have been from America to Polynesia. But natural carriage would leave the problem of usages and name to be solved. To argue, as Merrill did, that the name in Polynesia was derivable from a generic term for bast while ignoring evidence suggesting the same thing in America is weak indeed. To ignore the parallel of hibiscus to the sweet potato is only understandable from a history of ideas standpoint. The identity of names and uses in Polynesia and America, when coupled with the positive evidence from the sweet potato, makes it certain that whether or not the plant crossed the seas by natural means, man carried the name for the plant and quite possibly the usages across the same seas. It even seems probable that he carried the plant also.

The yam: The yam (Dioscorea alata) presents an equally interesting problem. It probably was domesticated in Java and spread from that center into Polynesia, perhaps with the original migrants. The yam is a plant widespread in Melanesia and Polynesia and is mentioned in China in the second or third century AD according to Laufer. Yet it seems to have been present in the Caribbean when Columbus reached there. This evidence has been canvassed by competent scholars.

Asa Gray and J. Hammond Trumbull reviewed De Condolle's Origin of Cultivated Plants and dealt at length with some of the plants described by the early chroniclers of the Caribbean. They found that three root crops---sweet potatoes, yams, and manioc---were described from the time of earliest contact with the Caribbean. Although there was occasional confusion between all three, the identity of each is clearly established. Oviedo's account of 1535 contains a passage describing the shape, venation, stem, and the hanging habit of the leaf of the yam, differentiating this plant from the sweet potato, and giving the native name as ajes. Ajes are described in Navarette's account of Columbus' voyage. Gray and Trumbull noted that Alexander von Humboldt had reached the same conclusion, as early as 1811.

Here then is another plant which, like the sweet potato, is propagated vegetatively and hence most unlikely to cross wide seas by wind, drift, birds, or other non-human agencies, but which crossed the ocean in pre-Columbian times. The Caribbean location might suggest an African source for this plant, though there is little evidence that the yam was known in Africa at this time. The recording of the yam in the Caribbean, rather than on the Pacific coast of Central America may be but an accident of history. At the moment we have no insight into the time when the yam was carried into America. It could have been brought by those who carried the sweet potato back into the Pacific.

The bottle gourd (Lagenaria siceraria): The bottle gourd is probably a native of India according to De Candolle, who also notes Sanskrit names for it and quote Bretschneider as his authority for its fifth or sixth century appearance in China. The bottle gourd is, however, archaeologically well documented in America. In Peru it has long been known to be at least as early as Nasca.

Recent work has produced a pre-Chavin agriculture containing the bottle gourd but lacking corn. Guesses at the age of this material suggest something earlier than 1000 BC and possibly as old as 3000 BC. These are guesses, but highly interesting ones in view of the probable Asiatic origin of the bottle gourd and the implied arrival of Old World agricultural peoples in Peru at this early date. If the bottle gourd was brought from Polynesia, where it is a very important plant, this date would be in interesting agreement with Dixon's suggestion that the sweet potato evidence suggested that contact with America may have been made long prior to 1000 AD, though Dixon was not thinking of 1000 BC or earlier.

It is inevitable that some one should appeal to winds and currents to bring the bottle gourd to America. Its shell is thick and hard. Perhaps then it could float here. Botanists have long discussed the possibilities of plants being drifted across the seas. Few plant seeds or fruits are given any chance of surviving such lengthy soaking and just as little chance of successfully competing on a foreign shore. Those for which there is such evidence are shore dwelling plants adapted to saline conditions, possessed of highly resistant seeds, and able to root and flourish in strand locations. Lagenaria possesses none of these quanlities and the occurrence of the same genus and species in both the Old World and the New is probably man's work. We need to know more about the history of Lagenaria. We need particularly in inquire into its African distribution. The evidence already at hand, however, is in agreement with that presented for sweet potatoes and yams. If man carried them across the sea, then it seems probable that he also carried the bottle gourd. It remains possible that the gourd floated across and was independently seized upon by man in America. But that is a remote possibility as opposed to the very probable human carriage. Hence I would conclude that Lagenaria probably was carried by man across the oceans, probably across the Pacific, at a time well before 1000 AD, and if the Peruvian guess-dates are valid, well before 1000 BC.

Cotton (Gossypium sp.): Cotton has recently had extensive genetic study. It has been found that the cottons of the world can be placed in three groups: Old World with 13 large chromosomes, whether wild or domesticated; American wild with 13 small chromosomes; and American cultivated and Hawaiian wild with 26 chromosomes, of which 13 are large and 13 are small.

Genetic study shows that the 26-chromosomed cottons contain both the Asiatic and American set of chromosomes. This indicates that at some time after the differentiation of the cotton genera the Asiatic and American cottons have been grown alongside each other and a crossing accompanied by a doubling of chromosome numbers has occurred. One must assume a common center of origin for all cottons. Their separation for a lengthy period of time is necessary to allow the development of the Old World and the New World genom types. Thereafter, the American and Asiatic types must be brought into proximity to each other in order that the 26-chromosomed American domestic type (and Hawaiian wild) be created.

Originally the crossing of the two 13-chromosomed species was thought to have occurred in the geologic past. Appeals were made to land bridges across the Pacific as a means of bringing these separate species together. More recently numerous difficulties with this argument have been pointed out, not the least of these being that not one but two linkings of the Old World and New World land masses would be called for and that there is no geological support for any such trans-Pacific land bridge at any time. To account for the distribution of the two sets of wild cottons (Afro-Asian and American) one must accept some form of Wegener's hypothesis of drifting continents. But not even the followers of Wegener claim the facile union-separation, union-separation of continents seemingly required to develop the present cotton picture.

Other postulates can be made to defend an ancient origin of 26-chromosomed cottons. Perhaps the Asiatic genom was anciently present in America, crossed with the American genom, and thereafter died out in America though surviving in Asia. This, however, is contrary to the outstanding feature of the taxonomy of Gossypium---that is the way in which diversification has accompanied geographical distribution. To quote Hutchinson, Silow, and Stephens,

> Evidently the continental groups which carry these widely dis-
> tinct genoms must have been isolated from each other for a very
> long period, and in view of the fact that they are inhabitants of
> arid regions, and bear seeds that are not adapted to distribution
> over long distances by water, it can only be supposed that they
> reached their present areas by dispersal across land masses
> with a dry climate.

To accomplish this they appeal to Wegener's theory of drifting continents
and point to Wulf's utilization of this theory to explain similar phenomena.

Much of the tendency to appeal to an ancient crossing of the Asiatic
and American cottons and to land bridges stems from two factors. First,
26-chromosomed cottons found wild in the Pacific Islands (Fiji, Marquesas, Hawaii, Galapagos) were thought to be remnants of an ancient
distribution. In addition to other evidence to be presented below, the
ecological niche occupied by the cottons in these islands suggests that
they are introduced plants, possibly escapes from cultivation. Secondly,
it was believed that man could not have been instrumental in bringing
the two forms together. Sweet potatoes, yams, and bottle gourds alone
---and they do not stand alone---show that man could have brought the
Old World and New World cottons together in recent times, perhaps as
early as 3000 BC.

Genetic study of cotton also has changed our understanding of the
cottons of the Pacific Islands. All but the Hawaiian cotton have now been
shown to be but derivatives of American domestic forms and not to be
early or ancestral forms. Indeed, they can be shown to be derived
from specialized forms of relatively late origin---late origin in a
botanical sense, for Captain Cook collected cotton in Polynesia. That
on the Galapagos islands is a little differentiated form of Gossypium
barbadense, the South American cotton. Those in Fiji and Marquesas
are G. hirsutum punctatum and are similar to a Caribbean variety of
punctatum. This indicates that the hybrid cottons of America had already
differentiated before they were carried back into the Pacific. The genetics of cotton suggests that the barbadense cottons are the basic type
from which hirsutum can be derived, just as punctatum must in turn be
derived from hirsutum. This is not, however, a reversible sequence.
Punctatum in Polynesia is a late development, not an early, basic, or
primitive form.

This has important cultural meaning also. It suggests an early introduction of Asiatic cotton into America and the creation by hybridization
of new types of cotton in South America. After these new cottons had
diffused to Mexico and after the passage of sufficient centuries to allow
the differentiation of new species and beyond that of a variety of that new
species, this variety was carried back into the Pacific at least as far as
Fiji. This was accomplished so early that the plant was later abandoned
and apparently all memory of its introduction and use lost. This suggests, then, an early voyage by Asiatics to America, and many centuries later another voyage from America to Polynesia.

Still another pertinent bit of information is that of all the American
wild cottons only Gossypium raimondi of Peru seems likely, when combined with Asiatic cotton, to give rise to cotton of the American 26-
chromosomed types. It is probably no accident that the earliest cotton
growing known in the New World is in Peru, that the bottle gourd---an

Old World plant---is found right with it, and that when the sweet potato was carried from America into Polynesia, it was carried from the same area.

Even the endemic cotton of Hawaii is suspect. Its 26 chromosomes and its possession of spinnable lint suggest American origin and a history as a fiber plant. The presence of sweet potatoes shows that plants of American origin were carried that far. The bigger mystery concerns why it was carried. Was cotton originally carried as a source of oil seeds, as suggested by Hutchinson, Silow, and Stephens? Or was weaving later given up in the Pacific area for bark cloth? Is part of the answer to the latter to be found in Bird's finding that the weaving in his early Peruvian site was done without the use of the heddle? Would bark cloth be able to replace such primitive weaving, though it would probably not replace true loom weaving? Or, was cotton weaving little understood and unable to replace an established bark cloth industry in Polynesia?

There is probably no such thing as absolute proof of anything. Land bridges can not account for the plant picture. Man did cross the Pacific bearing domestic plants. Genetics suggest cotton was carried by man to America. That man carried Asiatic domestic cotton to the New World at an early date is the simplest reasonable explanation. Other explanations are more complicated and improbable. I am inclined, therefore, to accept cotton as another of the plants carried across the Pacific and use it to explore the possible time that man may have accomplished this crossing.

Cotton appears with the bottle gourd (which is clearly Asiatic in origin) in Peru at the site previously mentioned, which is guess-dated between 1000 BC and 3000 BC. These guess-dates can be checked in two ways.

An original domestication of cotton for its oily seeds in southern Arabia or northeastern Africa has been suggested. From there it was carried into the Sind. By the time of Mohenjo Daro (1500 BC) cotton of modern Indian type was being expertly woven, suggesting that linted cottons had been developed well before this date. It seems likely that by this time the plant was being diffused eastward toward Bengal and Java and beginning its differentiation into Gossypium arboreum, the type which would have been available to man sailing from this area out into the Pacific. One must also envision the possibility of direct sailing from some part of India. Here we stop on the Asiatic side. By 1500 BC linted cottons existed for diffusion eastward. How long prior to 1500 BC, how long they took to diffuse eastward, and when they may have been carried to Peru, we do not know.

On the American side we have absolute dating only in the southwestern United States. Cotton appears here by 700 AD. It has diffused nearly three thousand miles through varied climates and cultures. Only Gossypium hirsutum punctatum is known in the Southwest. This is a species differentiation from the original American cotton Gossypium barbadense and a subspecies differentiation beyond that. This speciation may have taken only a number of centuries, but it could as well have taken several millenia. Should we be ultra conservative and allow only three hundred years for the differentiation of punctatum from hirsutum, only seven hundred years for the differentiation of hirsutum from barbadense, and consider diffusion to have been instantaneous, we would have a date for the origin of Gossypium barbadense in Peru at 300 BC.

Prior to that date, if Hutchinson, Silow, and Stephens are right, Asiatic cotton must have been introduced into Peru and grown for some indeterminate period in the proximity of the wild cotton of Peru (Gossypium raimondi). An unusual crossing of these plants gave rise to new types of cotton which were seized upon by man and formed the basis for Gossypium barbadense.

The assumptions of instantaneous diffusion and improbably short periods of differentiation of species makes such a date as 300 BC rather meaningless. If we compare the rate of diffusion of traits from the Near East to Europe in early times, we find that useful traits often took a thousand years to go a lesser distance through fewer climates and cultures. Botanists seem to think of speciation as a matter of thousands if not millions of years. Bird's guess-date of 3000 BC is then not at all impossible. Neither, of course, is it proven.

Man and Cosmopolitan Weeds. Some plants have a nearly world wide distribution. They appear on both sides of the Pacific as soon as botanical records begin. They have been labelled as cosmopolitan weeds and generally attributed to accidental distribution by man in the post-Columbian period. Some of them are of interest to this problem of trans-Pacific movements.

Argemone mexicana, the Mexican poppy, is a good example. All of the Argemones are American. The homeland of mexicana is Central America and the West Indies. From there it has spread through the warm tropics of the world. A glance at Fedde's monograph on the Papaveracea, where the uses of this family of plants get a cursory examination, shows that Argemone mexicana is used medicinally in many areas. Is it not strange that a mere weed accidentally carried should come to enter so many primitive pharmacopoeias? One finds in Fedde's very brief list through a process involving hybridization with Tripsacum seems indicated. Evidence for great antiquity of corn in any culture in America has yet to be demonstrated.

A peculiar parallel can be drawn between maize and cotton. Hybridization in the New World has been postulated for both to have given rise to a new set of characters and led to the development of more useful plants than would otherwise have been possible. For cotton this hybridization was probably the result of introducing an Old World plant into the New World. It is possible that maize presents the same picture.

On Localization of Traits and Direction of Origin. It seems important to note that the presence of a center of diversity of maize in Columbia and Peru can not be used against the possibility of African origin of the original maize plant. Neither for that matter can the presence of the yam in the Caribbean be used to argue against a possible Pacific derivation of that plant. Arguments have been leveled in the past against many traits for which possible transoceanic origins, usually Asian, have been advanced, on the basis that said traits were on the wrong side of the continent. It is interesting in attempting to see what might have happened in a remote and unknown past, to consider what we know to have occurred in the recent well known past.

The Spanish actions in America are probably the best illustrations that we possess of what could have happened in earlier times. There were relatively few Spanish. Yet in the period 1520 to 1540 they explored virtually the entire New World from Kansas to Argentina. Nor can all this be laid to force of arms. Cabeza de Vaca, shipwrecked and barely clad, was able to walk from somewhere on the Gulf Coast of the United States across the continent through all the intervening tribes, to the Gulf of California and thence down to the Spanish holdings in Mexico.

Of great interest is the location of the seats of Spanish settlement and power. They established themselves on the Mexican and Central American plateaus, in the irrigated valleys of Peru, the Mediterranean-type lands of Chile, and in the high plateaus of the Andes. They controlled the Argentine not from nearby Spain but from remote Lima. All foods and officers for Argentina came by way of Panama and were hauled over the Andes!

The Spaniards valued gold and silver and desired a large dependable labor supply. They went where these things were to be found. They also tended to avoid the wet and humid forested areas and settled on arid uplands or irrigated valleys more like their own Spanish homeland. The presence of silver in the uplands reinforced this choice: probably the malaria and yellow fever that they introduced into the lowlands did likewise.

We can not then argue from the location of the center of dispersal of a trait, possibly introduced in the past, to the direction from which the introducers may have come. Invaders of the past might, as the Spaniards did, go great distances to settle in the area that provided them what they sought for or that most suited to their way of life.

Had peoples from southeast Asia ever reached Middle America, they might well have gone to considerable effort to find areas suitable to their cultural outlook. Their choice of location would depend almost entirely on who they were and their particular outlook toward their environment. Unless we know their culture, we cannot predict their choice of site. How then can we deny that peoples coming to America from some southeast Asian home might not go to the Caribbean islands or the Amazon basin to settle? How then can traits be denied as of possible Asiatic origin because they are on the wrong side of the American continents?

Plant Evidence on the Nature of Asiatic-American Contacts. The plants tell us something of the nature of the contacts that must have been made. It can not have been a fleeting contact. The exchange of crop plants involves reciprocal learning. Plants must be used to be appreciated. Methods of use, including cooking, planting, harvesting, and storage, are peculiar to each plant. Such learning involves intimate association and exchange of knowledge lasting at least through a growing season. Argemone suggests that the exchange of knowledge went beyond food plants into medicine and its associated magic and ritual. Another example is to be found in fish poisons. The Lonchocarpus of tropical America is not only used in identical fashion to the Derris of tropical Asia but appears botanically to be the same plant. Here, too, the evidence from names of plants is significant. That the sweet potato and the hibiscus were known in Polynesia and America by the same names speaks of intimate contacts.

Further, carrying plants across an ocean is not an easy undertaking. Vegetatively reproduced plants present special difficulties, but even seeds can stand only moderate amounts of moisture, heat, drought, or salinity. The seeds of cotton, for instance, rapidly lose their power to germinate when exposed to moist air. Quite expectably then, one finds suggestions in Polynesian accounts that in most cases plants were only carried by colonizing expeditions and usually when setting out for known lands. Thus we hear of canoes reaching New Zealand sending back for useful plants. The sweet potato tubers brought by one boat, tradition says, were carried by a woman in a belt next to her body to keep them warm, protected, and viable.

One of the legends concerning the coconut's introduction to Hawaii also suggests the purposefulness of introductions and the failure to carry plants without definite planning. Here is a paraphrase of the account: The coconut was brought by Apua and his elder brother Aukalenuiaku. When they came to Hawaii the first time they did not bring any plants, for they thought all the plants of their country would be found in Hawaii. They went back to Kahiki and returned bringing various plants such as bananas and taro, and coconut, though only for the coconut is it specified that this was their introduction into Hawaii. Because of the greater distance and consequent difficulties it seems probable that only deliberately would plants be borne to or from America also. Only after careful preparation and planning could plants be carried so great a distance. This would be undertaken only if the presence of a land lacking the useful plants of the homeland of the explorers was known. This suggests purposeful, repeated voyages, not accidental, short-lived single contacts.

The plant evidence, then, is in total disagreement with the conclusion that, although contacts with America were made rarely and at long intervals, the net result was negligible. Considering the time involved, the absence of written records, and the fact that only a few of the plants that suggest Asiatic-American contacts have been discussed here, the existence of this much evidence is striking. It is suggestive of long continued and important contacts of which we have in the plant evidence only a most incomplete and fortuitous record. Further, cultural items reinforce the judgment from plant evidence that the exchange of knowledge was no hurried and limited affair. Quipus common to Polynesia and Peru, the abacus in Peru and China, pachisi in Mexico and India are highly specific and very complex traits. The concepts surrounding their use, the understanding of their utility, and the fitting of them into an alien culture would not be easily and quickly done. A claim that such a cluster of complex cultural traits as these should be independently invented is not only mathematically and logically improbable, but indefensible in view of the demonstrable contacts of the people of America with peoples from the Pacific either possessing these traits or in contact with people who did.

To those who would object that the islands of the Pacific were not populated until late, it must be said that the plant evidence is against them. Further the possibility exists that voyages were made to America from the Asiatic mainland with stopovers on the Pacific islands but without a colonization of the islands. That a very early peopling of the islands did occur is, however, indicated. The Polynesians themselves state that they found some of the islands inhabited. In Hawaii there is geological evidence suggesting respectable evidence for man.

History is against those who would object that boat culture was not sufficiently developed as early as the plant and cultural evidence suggests to be necessary. Developed navigation is indicated for the Aegean civilization before 3000 BC. About the same time people were apparently sailing from India to Arabia. Shortly thereafter people from the Mediterranean were sailing at least as far as Ireland and England. Pythias has left us a clear account of sailing so far north as to approach the arctic circle. The Norse and, even more strikingly, the Irish and the later Polynesian voyages show that oceanic voyages are entirely within the means of peoples equipped with boats of the type known to have existed by 3000 BC.

Clearer proof for contact between peoples from the Pacific with the peoples of Middle America could hardly be asked than that supplied by the sweet potato and by the hibiscus known as maho. Yams, Argemone, cotton, some of the so-called cosmopolitan weeds, and corn all suggest further such contacts, though with the weight of the evidence leading to a varying conclusion from highly probable to merely suggestive. The cumulative effect of the evidence in combination with the other lines of evidence indicate that the parallel origin of civilization in the Old World and the New must be seriously questioned. Surely our picture of the origin and growth of the Middle American high cultures can no longer rest on the easy assumption of absence of extensive and ancient Old World contacts.

Chapter 7
MYTHS AND LEGENDS

INTRODUCTION

When myths and legends are persistent and nearly universal, they may have some factual substance. True, one has no stone artifact in hand or ancient skull in a museum tray to study, but myths may contain intentional messages propagated through the ages by word of mouth. Distortion, exaggeration, and outright fabrication are hazards to be expected, as is the possibility of independent invention of similar stories. But all sciences have their pitfalls; and stones and bones are not free of contention .

Two basic themes are obvious in our heritage of ancient tales: (1) the existence of "little men" and giants in the old days; and (2) the possession by the ancients of extraordinary technical capabilities and precocious insights into the workings of nature.

Before dismissing these possibilities out of hand, read the following sampling and note its compatibility with the more conventional evidence in the other chapters.

• Little Men and Giants

THE HISTORICAL EXISTENCE OF FAIRIES
Thorstenberg, Edward; *Yale Review*, 1:286-301, 1912.

In the oldest legendary and romantic literature of Ireland, the very earliest inhabitants mentioned are known by the name of the Tuatha De Dannan, and are described as a celebrated race of magicians. This primitive race is said to have been defeated in battle and dispossessed by the Gaelic and Celtic invaders, whom Celtic tradition calls the Milesians. The reputation which the Tuatha people had as magicians or wizards and their obscure and mysterious manner of living seem to have impressed the minds of their conquerors with the belief that they were supernatural beings. Accordingly, one early belief of the Milesians was that, after the Tuatha hordes had been defeated by them, they entered the underground as gods, each taking possession of his or her particular domain; and there, from particular centres, generally places where tumuli existed, they ruled and marshalled their invisible hosts, much as the chieftains of the upper world ruled theirs.

The earth houses or barrows into which the defeated Tuatha or De Dannan people are said to have taken refuge before the warlike Celts, are known in tradition by the name of <u>sidhe</u> (now pronounced "shee"). In course of time these sidhe-mounds came to be regarded as entrances to an underground realm of inexhaustible splendor and delight. After a further lapse of time the belief in the sidhe-mounds as underground homes of a deified race seems to have widened until every hillock was conceived of as occupied by fairy people; and the fabled occupants themselves were thought to lead a life of freedom from care, sickness, and death, and "to spend the smiling hours in simple, sensuous pleasures."

In some of these earliest legendary accounts the memory of the sidhe-people as a deified race appears in the form of a cult in which ancestor worship figures as one of two dominant elements. This form of worship is known to have been current at the time of the druids and to have continued, along with druidism, until after the introduction of Christianity. But except for their existing thus side by side, the two forms of belief seem to have had no real connection with one another. On the contrary, the worshippers of the sidhe or sidhe-people appear in direct antagonism with the druids, as in the story of "Connla of the Golden Hair."

In this ancient story the kind calls his druid to his assistance to prevent a <u>ben-sidhe</u>, or fairy woman, from bewitching and carrying away his son to the "Land of the Living." Between the two the following conversation takes place:---"Whence hast thou come, O Lady?" said the druid. "I have come," said she, "from the lands of the living in which there is neither death, nor sin, nor strife; we enjoy perpetual feasts without anxiety, and benevolence without contention. A large sidhe is where we dwell, so that it is hence we are called the sidhe-people." From what follows in the narration, it is evident that the sympathies of the listeners are all enlisted on the side of the fairy as against the druid, whose incantations are finally of no avail against her powers.

From a single account like the one just cited it appears, then, that the writers of early Irish fiction remembered the dwellers of the sidhe not altogether as mythical beings, but rather as real people who were thought to be endowed with supernatural powers. There is also evidence to show that the memory of their existence as a real race of men had not entirely disappeared at the time of the first Christian missionaries. Thus, in describing the strange medley of druidism and fairyism as it existed at this time, one authority quotes from an old manuscript that "the demoniac power was great before the introduction of the Christian faith, and so great was it that the <u>aes-sidhe</u>, or dwellers in the hills, used to tempt people in human bodies, and that they used to show them secrets, and places of happiness where they should be immortal; and it was in that way they were believed; and it was these phantoms that the unlearned people called sidhe, or fairies, and aes-sidhe, or fairy people." In a mediaeval "Life of Saint Patrick" it is further narrated that, at one time in his travels, the national saint repaired to a fountain, to which place came also two daughters of the king. Encountering the assembly of the clergy at the well, in their white vestments, with their books, the two maidens wondered much at their appearance, and thought that they were fairies or phantoms. They questioned Saint Patrick on the subject, and asked, "Whence have ye come? Whither do ye go? Are ye men of the sidhe or are ye gods?" Thus it appears again that when this story was composed, the sidhe-people were, in popular imagination, ordinary human beings.

There are then, as we see, various distinct though fragmentary traces of ethnological characteristics attaching to the sidhe or fairy folk, as we find them mentioned in the oldest Celtic myths and legends. But fragmentary as this earliest form of ethnological evidence is, it is, nevertheless, important, for it is confirmed throughout by the fairy accounts of those popular tales which oral tradition has preserved to our own times.

In the tales of the latter class the fairies are always represented as living in green mounds. They pop up their heads when disturbed by people treading on their houses. They seem to live on familiar terms with people about them when they treat them well, to punish them when they treat them ill. Instances are mentioned of alliances having been formed between fairies and men, and the former are even said to have hired themselves as servants to the latter. The fairies are generally described as a small race, the men about four feet in height, the women in many cases considerably less. Both sexes are commonly dressed in green, though in some places the men, on account of the conical red hats worn by them, are now and then referred to as "the little red men." As a general thing, the little fabled beings love showy splendor, and mortal man has often been impressed with the gorgeousness of their apparel in their pageants. According to current popular belief, they formerly used stone arrows. They worked at trades, especially smith work and weaving. They had hammers and anvils, and excelled in their use; but though good weavers, they had to steal wool and borrow looms. In fact, stealing or pilfering is a very common trait of fairies, as is also their propensity for various other forms of petty mischief; and their fondness for hoarding treasures is proverbial.

The characteristic uniformity of this kind of ethnological evidence, its seeming tangibility and matter-of-fact directness,---these and similar qualities that might be mentioned conspire to make an almost irresistible appeal of reality to the mind of the student and investigator of folklore. One eminent English scholar expresses himself as "thoroughly persuaded of the former existence, all over the United Kingdom, of a race of men who were smaller in stature than the Celts," and whose other marks of identification agree in all essential features with those of the fairies. Another has pointed out that Irish fairy superstitions are so well localized that a map of fairy Ireland could be easily drawn showing, with almost political exactness, the various kingdoms of the sidhe. "But far less easy," he adds, "would be the task of ascertaining the origin and lineage of these fabled beings."

In reality, the remark just made suggests the crucial point of our whole problem, for unless the available evidence warrants a reasonably close identification of our fairies with some distinct ethnological race, the question of their existence as creatures of flesh and blood must remain as before, largely a matter of conjecture. What really tangible evidence is there, then, of the prehistoric existence of a race of men whose geographical distribution, physical characteristics, and probable occupations and habits of life justify a direct comparison between them and the sidhe-people of the British Isles? Or, putting the question more concisely, in how far does the ethnological testimony of tradition agree with the facts disclosed by scientific research? Any attempt to answer this question in detail would carry the discussion far beyond the limits of a brief essay. For the purposes of the present inquiry it may be well, therefore, to focus our attention on one or two phases of that particular science which has yielded the most positive results and thus become the most reliable source of information, ---the science of archaeology.

Modern archaeology has established beyond all reasonable doubt the prehistoric existence in Europe of one or two non-Aryan races comprising two, possibly three, fairly distinct types. The first in the series are the Iberians, a dark short race with long skulls. Their territory extended over large sections of France and Spain, as well as most of the British Isles, including the Hebrides. This pygmy race are thought to have survived in the short, dark haired Welshmen and in the Basques of the Pyrenees. The representatives of the second type, distinguished from the Iberians by the round shape of skull, but like them very dark and very short, are the so-called Ligurians. They are known to have occupied certain sections of France, Belgium, and Switzerland, and are believed to have been the original Celts of ethnology; they are commonly identified with the Auvergnats of France and the Lapps of the extreme northern regions of Norway, Sweden, and Russia. To these two types of prehistoric races is sometimes added a third, namely, a type of men who were characterized by round skulls, as the Ligurians, but who differed from both of the other two in being comparatively tall in stature and of a fair complexion. The time of their appearance in western Europe is set at a much later date than that of the other two. The representatives of this group, probably of Celto-Slavic stock, are classed with the tall, fair-haired Irishmen and Danes. Their remains have been found chiefly in the round barrows of Britain.

Most of the British barrows, however, indicate by their construction, as well as by the bones found in them, that they were inhabited in primitive times by people belonging to the dark Neolithic race of Iberians already mentioned. These Neoliths were so small in stature that a man five feet and a half in height was a giant among them, and one just five feet was not accounted short; while some of them reached only to four feet and ten inches. The same barrows or mounds have also been found to contain a sufficiently large number of hand-made articles to prove that the people who built them, or those, at any rate, whose bones were finally interred there, knew the art of weaving and were skilled in the manufacture of various implements, utensils, and ornaments of stone, bone, and clay, such as hatchets, combs, cups, bowls, urns, and necklaces. There is also every indication that the ultimate purpose of the tomb was to serve as the home of the dead chieftain. "The tomb," says Professor Dawkins, "was, to the Neolithic mind, as truly the habitation of the spirits of the dead as the hut was that of the living. It was the home of the dead chieftain and the centre into which the members of the family or clan were gradually gathered, and where they led a joyous and happy life similar to that which they enjoyed on the earth." Hence when the Neolithic chieftain died, he was buried with all his belongings; and in his tomb were placed the bones of wild boar, deer, pigs, and oxen, so that his ghost might hunt their ghosts in the other world.

These outline references to the results of archaeological investigation afford some illustration of the character of the evidence upon which "the realistic theory" of fairy origins mainly rests. It is, in other words, on such evidence as this that modern scholars have sought to establish for the sidhe-folk of Britain a truly human descent.

In support of certain arguments that have been advanced in favor of identifying the sidhe-people with the Iberian aborigines of Britain, it has been urged as a most significant fact that the belief in fairies is most rife in those particular parts of the islands (Ireland, Wales, and the Highlands of Scotland) in which the Iberian population has most largely survived. It is in these districts also that the fairies most retain their primitive characteristic as mischievous people, injuring cattle and causing sickness among children. Here, too, the use of fairy charms to counteract such mischief is said to be general, as is also the hoarding of elfin shots and thunderbolts, and the employment of euphemistic or conciliatory language about "the good people." Beyond this, present conditions hardly warrant immediate comparison between the sidhe-people and the Iberian aborigines; any attempt looking to direct identification between them would, at all events, be futile,---partly on account of the complete extinction of the Iberians as an unmixed race, partly also because of the absence of all information regarding their presence in Britain, except such information as may be obtained by inference from archaeological remains.

This being the case, it may be well to inquire into the possibility of establishing some satisfactory connection between our fairies and that other pygmy race of non-Aryan aborigines already mentioned above. I refer to the Ligurians and their descendants, the Lapps. This is by no means a novel suggestion; in fact, it has been known to scholars for fully fifty years, or since the publication of J. F. Campbell's collection of "Popular Tales of the West Highlands."

In the introduction to this collection, Campbell showed that there is a remarkably close agreement between the current fairy descriptions of the Scotch Highlanders and certain observations which he himself had made of the Lapps during a sojourn among them. He had found that, on the basis of fairy descriptions as he knew them, some of the very closest parallels could be drawn between the fairies and the Lapps, not from one but from several points of view: for example, their characteristic dwarfish stature; the nature of their habitations; the cut and color of their dress; their mode of living, including industries and occupations, ---even to such a detail as that of milking deer; their shyness in the presence of ordinary mortals; and, lastly, their widespread reputation as wizards. Having discussed these points of similarity at length, the author summarized his conclusions as follows:---"There is much more reason to believe that fairies were a real people, like the Lapps, who are still remembered, than that they are 'creatures of imagination,' or 'spirits in prison,' or 'fallen angels'; and the evidence of their actual existence is very much more direct and substantial than that which has driven people to the verge of insanity in the matter of those palpable-impalpable, visible-invisible spirits who rap double knocks upon dancing deal boards."

More recently, one of the contributors to the "Archaeological Review" has sought to identify the Lapps with a race of quasi-mythical beings who are variously mentioned in Highland tradition as the Cruithne or the Pechts (Picts), but who are colloquially called fairies. In support of his contention this writer shows that the heathen religion of the Cruithne strongly resembles that of the Lapps and Finns, especially as regards their supposed power of bringing on snowstorms, darkness, and unfavorable winds. The same writer has also pointed out that Gaelic and Highland tradition bears testimony to the former existence in Scotland of a special race or caste of people who are known by a name (<u>Feinn</u>, <u>Feinne</u>) which resembles that of <u>Finn</u> so closely that it may reasonably be regarded as only a variant of the same, ---a comparison which can be rightly understood, only if we bear in mind that the Lapps were, until the late Middle Ages, commonly called Finns. Yet these are not the only grounds for comparison, as the following paragraphs purpose to show.

In discussing the general contents of the old Irish story of Cuchulainn, the author of "Celtic Folklore," after referring to the hero of the story as an incarnation of Lug, emphasizes the fact that the circumstances which relate to his incarnation or rebirth are strikingly similar to certain notions formerly held by the Lapps; and that the whole idea is entirely unlike anything known to have been Aryan. But strange to say, this author seems to have completely overlooked the remarkable resemblance of the Irish name <u>Lug</u> to the Lappish word <u>Laugo,</u> a term which was used by the Lapps to denote a special form of baptism administered by them at the time of the supposed incarnation itself. However, the author returns to the subject again when he remarks, near the end of his work, that some of the birth stories of Cuchulainn and Etain seem to have passed through the hands of the sidhe or mound folk, and that they bear a striking resemblance to certain notions of the Lapps. "In fact," he says, "the nature of the habitations of our little people, together with other points which might be mentioned, would seem at first sight to betoken affinity with the Lapps."

Fortunately, our line of evidence tending to establish actual affinity between the sidhe-folk and the ancient Lapps does not necessarily end here. There still remains to be considered---since it has entirely escaped the attention of scholars heretofore---at least one form of testimony which can hardly fail to carry conviction with it, provided that we are willing to admit its having any bearing whatsoever upon the subject. And our position in this respect will depend in turn upon the attitude we may choose to take regarding the question of etymological kinship between the Celtic word <u>sidhe</u> itself and the very similar Lappish form <u>Sieide</u> or Seite (plur. <u>Sieideh</u> or <u>Seiteh</u>).

As to the meaning of the Lappish word, there is but one source from which any first hand information may be obtained, ---the accounts of a few missionaries who were sent to preach the Gospel among the heathen Lapps during the seventeenth and eighteenth centuries. Unfortunately, these missionaries do not fully agree as to what the specific definition of the word should be, some having translated it by "idol," others by "shrine"; one has taken it to be equivalent to "oracle," while another has given it the meaning of "manes." They all agree, however, in connecting it very closely with a particular form of idolatry practised by the Lapps at the time.

Since ages past the Lapps believed that in certain mountains or hills, which they called <u>Saivo-vare</u> or <u>Passe-vare</u>, there dwelt a race of men much like their own, carrying on the same occupations and owning the same kind of animals as theirs, but differing from them otherwise in having reached a higher state of perfection and in leading a life of more perfect bliss. This Saivo-race were thought to be a people of great wealth and splendor, well versed in witchcraft and in the use of the magic drum, while, in comparison, the Lapps on earth regarded themselves as poor, miserable creatures constantly in need of the protection, instruction, and aid of the others. Some Lapps claimed to have visited Saivo in person and to have drunk, danced, sung, and beat the drum with its inhabitants, whom they had seen in person and whose names they had heard; they had spent several weeks with them at a time, they said; they had been feasted by them, and had received instructions and admonitions from them. As soon as a Lapp attained the age of manhood, therefore, he was exceedingly anxious to become the owner of such Saivo-hills, as many as a dozen or more, whose inhabitants from then on became his protectors and assistants in the pursuit of witchcraft.

To mark such places where the Saivo-people were supposed to dwell, the Lapps of certain localities put up crude images of stone or wood which they called Sieide (plur. Sieideh), and around them whole communities often assembled for worship or adoration. To these shrines or consecrated centres of worship they would go on holidays, or when some misfortune had befallen them, decking themselves in their best attire, offering their devotions and prayers and making sacrifices of large heaps of reindeer horns.

The Lapps also had a number of Sieide-images which were carried from place to place and worshipped independently of the Saivo-hills. Owing to this circumstance, it has been thought by some that the real gods, to whom these heathen people looked for protection of person, as well as for success in the ordinary pursuits of life, were not the Saivo-olmak or Saivo-people but the Sieide-images themselves. Others have maintained, after careful examination of various references to each of the two, that the latter were in reality looked upon as the visible representatives of the former; and this, view seems to be the right one to take. At any rate, this much appears to be certain, that to the mind of the heathen Lapp the Sieideh and the Saivo-people were essentially one and the same thing; that both represented his own beatified ancestors, who were thought to dwell in the vicinity of their earthly habitations, to protect their descendants, and to wield a personal influence over them.

If this identification is correct, it is easy to see, in turn, the reasonableness of the assumption that Celtic sidhe and Lappish Sieide (Seite) are cognate forms, for it is evident from previous considerations that the Celtic conception of the sidhe-mounds and the Lappish conception of the Sieide (Saivo)-hills were synonymous, the notion in both cases being that of an underground realm of inexhaustible delight, inhabited by a happy race of wizards. One important distinction should, however, be carefully borne in mind, namely, that while the Lapps regarded the fabled dwellers of the hills as people of their own kind, the Celts believed them to be of a race entirely foreign to themselves.

Other things being equal, the natural inference from all this would be, that the sidhe-folk of Celtic tradition and the deified ancestors of the ancient Lapps were in reality one and the same people; in other words, that the fairies of Britain are of Lappish descent. Further comparison shows, however, that a general or sweeping inference like this would be open to serious objections on craniological grounds; for while the crania of the Lapps are of a uniformly broad or round type, there is conclusive evidence that the population of the British Isles was characterized throughout the whole of the Neolithic age by the long or oval type of skull. In view of this disparity of type, there can be but one satisfactory conclu-

sion regarding the ethnological position of the ancient sidhe-dwellers of
Britain: that they belonged to that group of non-Aryan aborigines known
as the Iberians, but that they brought with them those religious beliefs
and practices which they had in common with the Ligurian ancestors of
the Lapps from a time when these two branches of the Mongolian family
lived as neighbors on the Continent.

But while the facts at hand thus definitely tend to disprove the notion
of racial identity between the British fairies and the ancient Lapps, they
do not on this account preclude, nor even lessen the probability of
Lappish descent for the very largest part of that motley train of dwarfs,
trolls, elves, and goblins so constantly met with in the folklore of the
Scandinavian North. As in the case of the fairies of Highland tradition,
the dwarfs of the Sagas have been found to resemble the Lapps so closely
that a person who is familiar with the facts will with difficulty be able to
think of the one class of beings without bringing them into mental association with the other. In addition to their diminutive stature, clumsy
looking bodies, and gay-colored dress, the two resemble each other also
to a remarkably high degree in a number of other respects: for example,
their cowardly, cunning, and deceitful ways, their skill as craftsmen,
their delight in glittering metals, and lastly their reputation for wizard-
ry or sorcery, especially as regards their supposed ability to render
themselves invisible at will and to transport themselves with instantaneous swiftness from one place to another. "Everybody who wishes to do
so," says Professor Sven Nilsson, "can easily convince himself that
stories similar to those which are told in the old Sagas about Finns,
dwarfs, and goblins, and which are still told by the country people in
the south of Sweden, of pygmies and goblins who formerly dwelt in such
and such a mountain-district, are related even to this day by the peasants
in the northern parts of Norway of the Finn Laplanders. The locality has
been changed, but the scene is the same, with the difference only which
a different degree of civilization must create."

If we then admit the theory as well founded that the fairy superstitions
of Britain and Scandinavia for the most part go back ultimately to the
subtle and mysterious influence which a pygmy race exercised over the
minds of a simple people, we are forced by the very nature of things to
make a similar concession in regard to European fairy lore in general.
We have already seen how the non-Aryan burial mound in early times
became the centre of Celtic fairydom. If we now pause to reflect, we
realize at once that there is no essential difference between the Celtic
conception of the sidhe-mound and the Germanic conception of the subterranean dwarf palace where Alberich, Elbegast, Laurin, Oberon, or
some other little dwarf king rules; with certain modifications the same
idea appears again in the case of the German Horselberg or Venusberg,
where the hero of the Tannhauser legend fell a victim to Frau Holda's
magic charms. Further comparison shows, in turn, that Tannhauser's
enchantment by Holda is in substance the same as that which Ulysses is
said to have experienced at the hands of queen Calypso on the mythical
island of Ogygia.

In the manner here indicated, series upon series of parallels might
be easily drawn, each of them representing some particular type of myth
or fairy tale whose characteristic feature is always the same---always
a clash or conflict between a weird race of wizards on the one hand and
some branch or member of the Aryan family on the other. Taken singly,

the various types also betray remarkable uniformity as regards those
supernatural elements which enter most prominently into their fabric;
for example, animal metamorphosis, the magic ring, the cap of invisi-
bility, or the girdle of strength. These facts, when regarded in the
light of what has already been said, are not without significance; they
confirm throughout the position taken at the outset, that, mythical as
the fairies have now become, they represent the last traditional memories of an historical race.

FAIRIES
Gatschet, Albert S.; *Journal of American Folk-Lore,* 1:237, 1888.

The fairies who figure in the folk-lore of every European nation
also exist in the mythologies of the American Indians, but have not
been studied there to any extent. When we know more about them we
can decide whether "fairies" is the right name for these products of
Indian imagination. Some of them inspire terror, while others are
innocuous or beneficial to mankind. The Creek Indians, once in Ala-
bama and Georgia, now in the Indian Territory, call them i'sti lupu'tski,
or "little people," but distinguish two sorts, the one being longer, the
others shorter, in stature. The taller ones are called, from this very
peculiarity, i' sti tsa'ptsagi; the shorter, or dwarfish ones, subdivide
themselves again into (a) itu'-uf-asa'ki and (b) i'sti tsa'htsa'na. Both
are archaic terms, no longer understood by the present generation,
but itu'-uf means "in the woods," and the whole designation of (a)
probably signifies "found in the deep forest." The i'sti tsa'htsa'na are
the cause of a crazed condition of mind, which makes Indians run away
from their lodges. No others can see these last-mentioned little folks
except the Indians who are seized in this manner by a sudden craze.
The Klamath Indians of Oregon know of a dwarf, na'hni'as, whose tracks
are sometimes seen in the snow. Only those initiated into conjurer's
mysteries can see him. His footprints are not larger than those of a
babe, and the name points to a being which swings the body from one
side to the other when walking. It is doubtful if this genius can be
brought under the category of the fairies.

MYTHICAL DWARF PEOPLE IN POLYNESIAN LEGEND
Anonymous; *Nature,* 168:639, 1951.

The existence of 'little people' is a belief that is of world-wide,
though sporadic, occurrence. For the most part, they are dwarfish,

more-or-less benevolent, hard-working in spite of their small stature, nocturnal and dwelling underground or in woods or forests. Such being their attributes, they are very difficult to pin down, as their habits make observation extremely difficult, and accounts of them vary with almost every supposed observer. In the Hawaiian Islands these nocturnal pygmies are known as 'Menehune', and Katherine Luomala, whose researches into Polynesian folk-lore are well known, gives an extensive and fascinating investigation of this subject in a booklet entitled "The Menehune of Polynesia and other Mythical Little People of Oceania" (Bernice P. Bishop Museum, Honolulu; Bull. 203; pp. 95; 1951). Her account of these tiny folk is gathered from many sources and includes their physical and cultural characteristics, their housing and social structure, their relations with other little peoples and their possible origin. All this gives them such a corporal existence that it is quite difficult to believe that they are mythical. They originate, apparently, from the old semi-slave common class of people who did all the hard work and were presumably stunted by toil and privation. The buildings they erected seemed worthy of a tradition, and so by the usual process of exaggerating the size of the subjects of the tradition both down and up (the clever little man and the stupid giant) these Menehune became smaller and smaller as time went on in order that their works might be more glorified. Other Polynesian islands also have their legends of Menehune or similar little peoples, and an account is given of the various myths connected with them.

PREHISTORIC PEOPLES OF JAPAN
Hitchcock, Romyn; *American Antiquarian,* 16:209–211, 1894.

The origin of the Japanese people is an unsolved problem in ethnography. They are distinct from the peoples on the adjacent coast of Asia, and also entirely different from the original inhabitants of the land. That they are somewhat related to the early peoples of Corea is not improbable. There are ancient graves in Corea from which have been dug up vessels of crude pottery, that cannot be distinguished from those found in the old tombs or rock-built dolmens of Japan. These are all prehistoric remains, dating back into the period of myth and tradition, to the time of the reputed first emperor, the famous Jimmu Tenno, whose descent is traced directly from the Sun-goddess, the highest deity of the Shinto faith. The advent of Jimmu Tenno, according to the accepted chronology, was in the seventh century, B.C. The testimony of tradition clearly proves that he and his followers were invaders of a land whose inhabitants were of a different race and strange. Moreover, it tells of two distinct peoples who lived in the country, one a race of dwarfs, who had tails and lived in underground burrows or caves, the other a race of hairy savages whom they designated Ebisu.

Archaeological research has confirmed these traditions in a remarkable manner. The existence of a race of dwarfs with tails has not indeed been confirmed. Even if we attribute the tails to the too vivid imagination of the early Japanese observer, himself no doubt something of a tale-bearer, we are still at a loss to know who were the dwarfs. We have evidence that there was a people once inhabiting northern Japan at least, who lived in half-underground earth-dwellings; but there are no indications that those people were small of stature, except that there are numerous allusions in old books to the people of northern Yezo, describing them as pit-dwelling dwarfs. Anutschin estimated their height at four and one-half feet, but upon what evidence I do not know. I shall show you some photographs of dwellings on the Island of Shikotan, off the eastern coast of Yezo, which, perhaps, represent a later form of the ancient pit-dwellings. In many parts of Yezo there may be seen large pits or depressions in the earth, usually circular or oval in shape, and ten to twenty feet across. The depressions are usually bordered by heaped up earth, so that the bottom is not much, if at all, lower than the general surface of the ground. Capt. T. W. Blakiston, well known as a traveler in Yezo and in China, first drew particular attention to these, and suggested that they were the remains of human habitations. This view is reasonable, and my own observations tend to confirm it, although the evidence is mostly of a negative character. I have found such pits in many parts of the island, and hundreds of them in most excellent preservation on the Island of Yeterof, beyond the town of Shyana, on the north coast, where Capt. Blakiston reported having secured some fragments of pottery, but where my own digging yielded no results.

If these pits are the remains of earth-dwellings, they must certainly have belonged to a race that has passed away. We naturally associate them with the "dwellers under ground," the "dwarfs" or Tsuchi-gumo of Japanese tradition. The absence of such remains on the larger island of Japan, in the localities where Jimmu Tenno first encountered them, is, perhaps, only a natural consequence of the activity of a large agricultural population. In Yezo and the Kuriles but few people live, and they do not till the soil.

Tradition of another kind is confirmatory of this view. The Ainos tell of a race of Koro-pok-guru, who inhabited Yezo before themselves, and who were exterminated by them. These were likewise dwellers under ground, and it is reasonable to suppose that the predecessors of the Ainos, and the Tsuchi-gumo of Japan tradition, were, therefore, the same people; and that, as we follow the remains of their dwellings northward into Yezo, and on through the bleak and barren Kuriles, we trace the remnants of an aboriginal race, along the course of its last migration, to extinction and oblivion.

Still, around those early peoples there remains a halo of mystery too deep for speculation to solve. Were they an hirsute people? Were they dwarfs? Did they make the decorated pottery which is found now and then around the pits, the same as is found in the pre-Japanese shell heaps?

. . . .

PRE-BANTU OCCUPANTS OF EAST AFRICA
Beech, M. W. H.; *Man,* 15:40–41, 1915.

Apropos of Sir Harvy Johnston's most interesting survey of the Ethnology of Africa and Mr. Emil Torday's remarks thereon in Vol. XLIII
(1913) of the Journal, the following note, which I took a year or two ago,
just before leaving the Kikuyu country, may perhaps be of interest as
showing a Kikuyu tradition concerning the occupation of their country
by two pre-Bantu peoples. During a conversation with some A-Kikuyu
elders I was informed that in the land they now occupy in the Dagoneta
district, which was until quite recently covered with dense forests but
is now cleared and cultivated, if they dug down low enough (which they
seldom do) they not unfrequently came across pieces of ancient pottery
of a workmanship entirely different from their own.

Although I left the district before succeeding in obtaining a piece,
all the elders agreed that this pottery was the work of the "Gumba,"
a people who inhabited the Kikuyu country after displacing a race of
cannibal dwarfs called Maithoachiana, and that further information
could doubtless be obtained from the elders of the Fort Hall district,
whence the present occupiers of Kikuyu had come less (probably) than
100 years ago.

Mr. Northcote, the District Commissioner of Fort Hall, kindly
questioned his elders, and sent me the following:---

"The Maithoachiana appear to be a variety of earth-gnomes with
many of the usual attributes: they are rich, very fierce, very touchy,
e.g., if you meet one and ask him who his father is he will spear you;
or if he asks you where you caught sight of him first, unless you say
that you had seen him from afar, he will kill you, the inference being,
I suppose, that you have seen what he was doing, burying treasure, &c.
This is only a guess on my part.

"Like earth-gnomes in most folklore, they are skilled in the art of
iron-working. They originally lived round this part (i.e., south of
Mount Kenia), but they were driven out by another legendary people
called the 'Gumba,' who dwelt in caves dug in the earth, and who disappeared one night after teaching the Kikuyu the art of smelting.
Another account says that they lived in the earth themselves. It is a
Kikuyu insult to say 'You are the son of a Maithoachiana.'"

The references might well be to Bushmen, Pygmies, or both, and
it is, perhaps, not unreasonable to suppose that the Maithoachiana
were an indigenous pigmy or bushman race of the Stone Age who made
and used the many stone implements which are to be found everywhere
in the Kikuyu district. In this case Mr. Northcote's informant may have
erroneously attributed to them the skill in iron work which was in reality only possessed by their successors, the Gumba.

The Gumba are said to have made pottery and to have "taught the
Kikuyu "the art of smelting," which is equivalent to the A-Kikuyu admitting that they did not bring a knowledge of iron with them or find it
out for themselves.

Assuming the tradition to be substantially true, and unless the
Gumba who, be it noted, are not described as dwarfs, were pre-Bantu
Harnite invaders (a supposition for which, as far as I know, there is
absolutely no warrant) the legend would appear to be in favour of the
first discovery of iron having been in Africa.

THE ASAMANUKPAI OF THE GOLD COAST
Field, M. J.; _Man,_ 34:186–189, 1934.

Behind the Ga village of Bawyi rises a forested hill marked on the map Aboaso, but known to the Gas as Adzanote. Monkeys and wild pigs live there, but no hunter will venture on the hill by himself for fear of Asamanukpai.

These Asamanukpai (also called Asamanua, Adope, Abodo) seem to be identical with the Mmoetia described by Rattray. They are dwarf-men, with feet turned back to front, 'a little bigger than a monkey,' and either black, white, or 'red.' Red (tfuru) is the only Ga word available for describing all shades of buff and brown, besides scarlet, crimson and pink, and here it undoubtedly means 'mulatto colour.' The old dwarfs are the biggest and are bearded. They all eat and dance on out-crops of smooth stone which they themselves polish.

The disc-shaped quartz thunderstones, holed through the middle, of unknown origin, which are plentiful in the district, and are said to have fallen from heaven, are also said to have had their holes made by being caught, on falling, between the finger and thumb of an asamanukpa.

Hunters obliged to invade the haunts of asamanukpai propitiate them with offerings of rum, placed against their dancing-stones, and with the pans of clean water in which they like to bathe and splash. If disturbed or angered they stone the offender, lead him into the depths of the forest and there lose him.

Occasionally they lead a man away in order to befriend him, and during his stay with them they teach him all they know, and squeeze into his eyes, ears and mouth the juice of a plant which enables him thereafter to see and hear all men's thoughts, to foresee all events, and also to sing and talk with the Asamanukpa people. On returning to his home after a sojourn of a week or two, he is known as an Abodowonnu (or Abodowonyo if a woman) and becomes a much revered fortune-teller (gbalo), and gives of advice on medical and other matters.

Not only do these dwarfs haunt the forest, they are known by the sea. A story is told in Osu of the days before the lagoon was drained. The Asamanukpa people were then so plentiful that Friday was set aside as theirs, and nobody would visit their seashore haunts on that day. A man named Dzani had an unreasonable wife who on a Friday asked him to fetch her from the beach a flat stone for grinding corn. He refused, whereupon she wept and nagged so persistently that he consented. On the shore he found the rocks spread with pieces of drying cloth. He started to collect these and at once was set upon by a mob of enraged Asamanukpai, who stoned him, especially about the head. He returned to the town crying and raving, ran about, demented, for several days and then died.

....

Rattray describes his mmoetia in the same section as he describes the pirafo, who are a few flesh and blood dwarfs, probably cretins, met with here and there in Ashanti. He seems to be hinting that the mmoetia lore is the remnant of recollections of a real pygmy tribe, a suggestion which has been made also about the fairies of Europe. If this is the origin of asamanukpai there may be a real basis for their association with quartz discs, polished stone and stone missiles.

There is another possibility which, if accepted, would explain the origin, not only of mmoetia and asamanukpai, but of all the various fairies, elves, pixies, gnomes and other 'little people' of Europe.

One of the recognized 'types' in European lunatic asylums is the patient who sees 'little people. ' I believe such cases are usually tidied up, medically, into the category of 'frustrated maternal instinct, ' though the 'little people' are not necessarily children. In the Gold Coast this category would not take in every seer of asamanukpai, though there does seem to be a case for regarding normal wedded life as a bar to fairy friendship.

It will have been noted that the man Dzani died raving mad and the two fishermen of melancholia. The old man, Danloh, is obviously not normal, the old woman Koko had been feted with rum. Concerning people lost for a week on Adzanote it is more than likely that they are lost before they see the dwarfs. I have myself been on this hill, guided by two hunters cutting their way with cutlasses and now and then having to climb a tree to take bearings. It would be easy to get lost there and it would be very terrifying. It is an established fact that people lost in the Australian bush go mad, and to the effects of being lost must be added the effects of fasting and thirst. That fasting is often used to produce visions is well known to anthropologists. Rattray himself says somewhere that his Ashanti medicine men say they cannot hear the voice of their god except when fasting.

It is certain that asamanukpai are seen only by people in abnormal states, and that the form of the hallucination is fixed by tradition---as is so often the case with visions. But it still remains to find out whether the form of the tradition has a real basis in the remote past or whether it is itself to be referred back to a common type of hallucination.

GIANTS AND DWARFS

Seaver, W. A.; *Harper's New Monthly Magazine,* 39:202-210, 1869.

From the days of Adam down to the days of Grant and Seymour, there have been giants. We first read of them in Genesis, vi. 4: "There were giants in the earth in those days; and also after that, when the sons of God came in unto the daughters of men, and they bare children to them, the same became mighty men which were of old, men of renown. " After these were the Rephaim, who were defeated by Chedorlaomer. After them the Emims, alluded to in the second chapter of Deuteronomy, and the Anakims, and the Zamzummims; all of whom in time disappeared, leaving only Og, the King of Bashan, a rather lengthy monarch, "whose bedstead was a bedstead of iron; nine cubits was the length thereof, and four cubits the breadth of it, after the cubit of a man. " The cubit of a man is the space from the tip of the finger to the elbow, that is, half a yard; therefore Og's bedstead was 13-1/2 feet long. Reckoning the size of men to their bedsteads, Og was probably about 9 feet high. He has furnished material for many Eastern legends, in one of which he is said to have escaped the Flood by wading only knee-deep beside the ark, and to have lived 3000 years. One of his bones is reputed to have long served for a bridge over a river; and he is credited with having "roasted at the sun a freshly-caught fish," Goliath, the famous Gath man, who had a difficulty with David, was in height "six cubits and a span," which would make him 9 feet 9 inches high. His coat of mail weighed 5000 shekels of brass, which is about 208 pounds, and his spear, "like a weaver's beam," about 25 pounds.

In 1718 a French academician named Henrion endeavored to show a great decrease in the height of men between the periods of the Creation and the Christian Era. Adam, he says, was 123 feet 9 inches high; Eve, 118 feet 9 inches; Noah, 27 feet; Abraham, 20 feet; Moses, 13 feet. The allegation about Adam is moderate compared with that made by early Rabbinical writers, who affirm that his head overtopped the atmosphere, and that he touched the Arctic Pole with one hand and the Antarctic with the other. Traditionary memorials of the primeval giants still exist in Palestine in the form of graves of enormous dimensions; as the grave of Abel near Damascus, which is 30 feet long; that of Seth about the same size; and that of Noah, in Lebanon, which is 70 yards in length!

The monkish historians promulgated the idea that the earliest possessors of Great Britain were men of immense stature. John de Warrin, in the "Chronicles of Great Britain," written in 1445, relates that in the time of Jahir, the third Judge of Israel after Joshua, Lady Albine and her sisters came to and settled in an island which they named Albien after her, afterward called Britain. While they were living there the devil assumed the shape of a man, and dwelt among the wicked women, and by them had issue great and terrible, giants and giantesses, who occupied the land until Brutus came and conquered them. At the time of his visit there were two giants more wonderful than all the rest, Gogmagog and Lancorigan. It is the former, it is said, whom Milton had in mind when he wrote:

> "His spear---to equal which the tallest pine
> Hewn on Norwegian hills, to be the mast
> Of some great amiral, was but a wand."

The ancient people of most countries seem to have possessed in the strongest degree a faith in giantology, as evidenced by the vast images of their gods and their colossal monuments of architecture. In front of the portals of the palace of Carnac, in Egypt, are gigantic human statues; and in one of the courts are twelve immense stone figures 52 feet high, which impress upon the beholder that he is entering a home of departed giants. The adjacent palace of Luxor has two granite statues, each 38 feet high, at the entrance. In the ruins near Thebes are three huge figures, now thrown down, one being 64 feet long. In the Parthenon of Athens, many years before Christ, was a statue of Minerva 36 feet high. The temple of Jupiter at Olympia, before Christ, contained a seated statue of a god which rose almost to the ceiling of the building, and that was 68 feet high.

Pliny says that by an earthquake in Crete a mountain was opened, and in it was discovered a skeleton standing upright, 46 cubits long, which was supposed to be that of Orion or Otus. The same author relates that in the time of Claudius Caesar there was a man, named

Gabbaras, brought by that Emperor from Arabia to Rome, who was
9 feet 4 inches high, "the tallest man that has been seen in our times."
But this giant was not so tall as Posio and Secundilla, in the reign of
Augustus Caesar, whose bodies were preserved as curiosities in a
museum in the Sallustian Gardens, and each of whom measured in
length 10 feet 3 inches.

During the Cretan war there was discovered a body of prodigious
size. The rivers rose to an unusual height, and when the floods were
gone, in a great cleft of the earth there was found the carcass of a
man of the length of 33 cubits, or near 42 feet. Lucius Flaccus, the
then legate, allured with the novelty of the report, went with a party
of friends to the place to take a view of it; and they there saw what
upon hearsay they had imagined to be a fable.

The Emperor Maximus (very much of a man) was 9 feet high, and
was in the habit of using his wife's bracelet for a thumb-ring. His
shoe was a foot longer than that of any other man, and his strength so
great that he could draw a carriage which two oxen could not move.
He generally ate forty pounds' weight of flesh and drank six gallons of
wine every day. Not at all a desirable or profitable guest for the "St.
Nicholas," even at the current price of board; though not so tall as one
of whom Josephus tells, viz.: Eleazar, a Jew, who was one of the
hostages whom the King of Persia sent to Rome after a peace. This
giant was over 10 feet high. But these are pigmies compared with him
of whom Kircher writes (though this is what a Yankee philosopher would
denominate a whopper!). The skeleton of this giant was dug out of a
stone sepulchre near Rome in the reign of the Emperor Henry II., and
which, by an inscription attached to it, was known to be that of Pallas,
who was slain by Turnus, and was higher than the walls of the city!
The same author tells us that another skeleton was found near Palermo
that must have belonged to a man 400 feet high; and who, therefore,
could have been no other than one of the Cyclops, most probably Poly-
phemus himself, who might

> "Easily have overstepped
> Goliah's helmed head, or that huge King
> Of Basan, hugest of the Anakim."

To come down one or two hundred feet. Father Jerome de Monceaux
writes of the skeleton of a giant 96 feet long, found in a wall in Mace-
donia. This fact was communicated to him by Father Jerome de Rhetel,
a missionary in the Levant, who, in a letter written from Scio, stated
that this giant's skull was found entire, and could contain 210 pounds
of corn; that a tooth of the under-jaw weighed fifteen pounds, and was
seven inches two lines in length! There was a man! Was there a Bar-
num then extant?

In times more modern (1613), some masons digging near the ruins
of a castle in Dauphine, in a field which by tradition had long been
called "The Giant's Field," at the depth of 18 feet discovered a brick
tomb 30 feet long, 12 feet wide, and 8 feet high, on which was a gray
stone with the words "Theutobochus Rex" cut thereon. When the tomb
was opened they found a human skeleton entire, 25-1/2 feet long, 10
feet wide across the shoulders, and 5 feet deep from the breast to the
back. His teeth were about the size of an ox's foot, and his shin-bone
measured 4 feet in length.

Plot, in his "Oxfordshire," 1676, says that a skeleton 17 feet high was then to be seen in the town-hall in Lucerne. It had been found under an old oak in Willisau, near the village of Reyden. He instances numerous gigantic bones which had been dug up in England, and adds: "It remains that (notwithstanding their extravagant magnitude) they must have been the bones of men or women; nor does any thing hinder but they may have been so, provided it be clearly made out that there have been men and women of proportionable stature in all ages of the world, down even to our own days."

Old Cotton Mather held the belief that there had been in the antediluvian world men of very prodigious stature, in consequence of the finding of bones and teeth of great size, which he judged to be human, in Albany. He describes one particular grinder weighing 4-3/4 pounds, and a broad, flat, fore-tooth four fingers in breadth; also a bone, supposed to be a thigh-bone, 17 feet long, which, with the others, crumbled to pieces as soon as it was exposed to the air.

Giants have always been great favorites with fiction-writers, and they live in the folk-lore of every country. Some of the most popular works in modern literature have had for their heroes these fabulous creations. Spenser, in his "Faery Queene," tells us of

> "An hideous giant, horrible and hie,
> That with his talnesse seem'd to threat the skie."

Rabelais invented Gargantua. Bunyan found the Giant Despair very useful in his story. Gulliver would not be Gulliver without the giants and dwarfs. And the world of romance would be dull without Blunderbuss, Cormoran, King Arthur, Fingal, and such.

. . . .

Come we now to the Pigmies:

It is curious that the Bible, which contains so many allusions to giants, contains but one mention of a dwarf, and that is in Leviticus, xxi. 20, where it is commanded that no man who was a dwarf should make the offerings at the altar. This, however, is scarcely true, if taken in a jocular sense. The writer, in conversation with a Doctor of Divinity concerning brief people---it was at the time of Tom Thumb's nuptials---said Ne-hi-miah (Knee-high-miah) was shorter than Mr. Thumb, as was also Bildad, the Shu-hite (Shoe-height); but neither of the Old Testament little ones was as "short" as the one in the New Testament, who said: "Silver and gold have I none;" for the man who was minus both those commodities was probably as "short" a person as was ever known.

The first record we have of the assumption of the name of Tom Thumb, by a dwarf, was in 1597. In 1630 was printed a poem entitled "Tom Thumbe, his Life and Death," which says, of a later Thumb:

> "In Arthur's court Tom Thumbe did live,
>   A man of mickle might,
> The best of all the table round,
>   And eke a doughty knight:
> His stature but an inch in height,
>   Or quarter of a span:
> Then thinke you not this little knight
>   Was prov'd a valiant man."

Sir John Mandeville, who traveled in Asia and Africa between 1322 and 1356, tells us of a land of pigmies, where there were men only three spans long. Both men and women were fair and gentle, and were married when they were half a year old. They generally lived only six or seven years, and at eight were considered to be old. They were the best workmen of silk and cotton, and of all manner of other things that were in the world. They scorned great men as we do giants, and had them to travel for them and to till the land.

In a rare book by Laurens Andrewes, entitled "Noble Lyfe and Nature of Man," is the following curious description of pigmies:

"Pigmies be men & women, and but one cubite longe, dwellinge in the mountaines of Yude; they be full growen at their third yere, & at their seven yere they be olde; & they gader them in May a grete company togeder, & arme them in theyr best maner; and than go they to the water syde, & where-so-ever they fynd any cranes nestis, they breake all the egges, & kyll all the yonges that they fynde; and this they do because the cranes do them many displeasures, & fight with them often tymes, & do them great scathe; but these folke cover their houses with the cranes feders & egshels."

One of the Hebrides is called the "Isle of Pigmies," where it is reputed that several miniature bones of the human species have been dug up in the ruins of a chapel there. William Collins, in his "Ode on the Popular Superstitions of the Highlands of Scotland," refers

"To that hoar pile which still its ruins shows;
    In whose small vaults a pigmy folk is found,
Whose bones the delver with his spade upthrows,
    And culls them, wondering, from the hallow'd ground."

Tennessee newspapers, of the year 1828, stated that in that year several burying-grounds, from a half acre to an acre in extent, were discovered in Sparta, White County, Tennessee, wherein very small people had been deposited in tombs or coffins of stone. The greatest length of the skeletons was 19 inches. The bones were strong and well set, and the whole frames were well formed. The graves were about 2 feet deep. The dead were all buried with their heads to the east and in regular order, laid on their backs, and with their hands on their breasts. In the bend of the left arm was found a cruse or vessel that would hold nearly a pint, made of ground stone or shell of a gray color, in which was found two or three shells. One of these skeletons had about its neck ninety-four pearl beads. Webber, in his "Romance of Nature History," 1853, refers to the diminutive sarcophagi found in Kentucky and Tennessee, and he describes these receptacles to be about 3 feet in length by 18 inches deep, and constructed, bottom, sides, and top, of flat, unhewn stones.

. . . .

TRADITIONS OF PRECOLUMBIAN LANDINGS ON THE WEST-ERN COAST OF SOUTH AMERICA

Bandelier, Adolph F.; *American Anthropologist,* 7:250-270, 1905.

Among Indian myths that appear to touch on an extra-American descent of the natives in the western parts of South America, we must discriminate between (1) allusions to the appearance of strange individuals or groups of individuals, long before the epoch of Columbus but while the land was already peopled; (2) tales mentioning a primitive settlement of parts of South America from other parts of the globe; and (3) stories of landings on the western coast of the southern continent.

The tale of Tonapa (sometimes identified with Viracocha), in the interior of Peru and Bolivia, has already been discussed by me, so far as the scanty material and its nature permitted. The Tonapa story, in its later version by Calancha, begins in Brazil. It tells of the wanderings of two white men, at a time quite remote, but still after the beginning of our era. These white travelers are reputed to have landed on the Brazilian shore, whence they pushed inland, preaching to and teaching the natives after the manner of Christian apostles or missionaries. They are accredited with accomplishing the portentous journey through southern Brazil, Paraguay, and northern Argentina into western Bolivia, where, near the shores of Lake Titicaca, one of them suffered death at the hands of the natives, while the other pursued his way to the Pacific and there disappeared. This version, however, dates from the middle of the seventeenth century, and extends the scope of the original Tonapa or Viracocha lore obtained in southern Peru and in Bolivia. It bears the stamp not merely of confirmation, but of explanation and adaptation to Christian legends about apostolic labors in remote corners of the earth. The early, hence more authentic, versions of the Tonapa and Viracocha story, heard not later than sixteen years after the arrival of Pizarro, and probably even within a decade of that event, either represent the origin of that mysterious individual from Lake Titicaca (not necessarily from the island of that name) or make him appear on the Bolivian plateau from the south and to direct his steps toward the north where, on the shores of Ecuador, he disappears, together with his companions, on the waters of the ocean. In the heart of Peru a similar tradition was found among the Indians at an early date, and while these tales must be accepted cum grano salis, they may have had their nucleus in original recollections that already had become veiled and distorted prior to the sixteenth century.

The traditions of central western Peru differ partly from the tales of Tonapa-Viracocha in that they also mention a settlement of strangers. The report of the Augustines on their investigations among the Indians of Huamachuco between 1552 and 1561, states that most of the settlers perished and that the few survivors were driven out of the country. But this part of the story appears to be distinct from the tale of white "teachers" of the Tonapa legend, and to refer to another set of individuals. The term "culture-heroes" has been introduced into American ethnology for such personages. In this case their labors would have left few, if any, cultural traces.

Almost parallel with the Tonapa and Viracocha lore is the myth of Bochica or Nemquetheba (Nemtherequeteba), also called Zuhe, among the Muysca or Chibcha Indians of Colombia. The four names apply,

according to Piedrahita, to one individual. Fray Pedro Simon, who
wrote somewhat earlier, discriminates between Bochica and Nemtherequeteba. Piedrahita asserts that, according to Chibcha tradition,
Bochica "came" to the plateau of Bogota---whence, he does not state.
He describes him as with a long beard and wearing long garments, as
having walked with bare feet and gone about preaching and teaching the
Indians a better mode of life. At Sogamoso, in the Colombian highlands,
Bochica lived two thousand years, and died there after performing many
miracles, among which the opening of the cleft at Tequendama is most
conspicuous. There is a certain analogy between this personage and
Tonapa or Viracocha. In Peru, as is well known, the Indians called and
still call the whites <u>Viracochas</u>. Piedrahita asserts that the surname
Zuhe, given to Bochica, was used by the Chibcha to designate the first
Europeans they saw.

Simon has Nemtherequeteba (whom he also calls Zuhe) reside east
of the Bogota plateau, in the Orinoco region of Venezuela, for fourteen
hundred years. Thence he went to the Columbian tableland, disappearing about Sogamoso. His personal appearance is described in the same
manner as by Piedrahita, but the miracle at Tequendama Simon ascribes
to Bochica. The former remarks: "And some say that there was not
one stranger alone, but three, who at distinct times entered preaching,
but the most common and usually believed is that there was but one with
the three surnames mentioned."

Elsewhere I have called attention to the possibility of these traditions
not being fully primitive.

The Jesuit missionary Father Anello Oliva was a contemporary of
both Simon and Piedrahita. He spent forty-five years of his life in Peru
and in what is now Bolivia, the latter being the scene of his apostolic
labors for many years. It is not known that he ever paid attention to
Colombian topics. It is strange, therefore, that Oliva represents the
peopling of South America as having taken place from the side whence
the mysterious white men are said to have reached the Bogota plateau,
namely, from the east. The chief sources of his work were, according
to his own statements, some writings of Father Blas Valera from the
second half of the fifteenth century, and especially stories related to
him by an Indian from Cochabamba in central Bolivia. This Indian,
whose name was Catari (an Aymara word signifying "snake," "viper,"
a venomous serpent in general, distinguished from the innocuous kinds
which the Aymara call <u>aseru</u>), was particularly well versed in ancient
lore of the Inca tribe; hence it appears unlikely that Oliva should have
gathered information, at least directly, from Colombian sources.

According to Oliva the first settlers of South America landed on the
coast of Venezuela near where the city of Craacas now stands, whence
they gradually spread over the continent, reaching, among other places,
Santa Elena in Ecuador, where they settled. Of these settlers some
bands in course of time traversed the coast southward, occupying Tum-
bez and Lima. While these immigrants from eastern South America
were establishing themselves on the coast of Ecuador and Peru, there
took place at Santa Elena a landing of "giants." What Oliva says of the
fate of these giants appears to have been taken almost literally from
Cieza and Zarate. To this I shall refer later. After the reputed
destruction of the intruders by fire from heaven, the settlers on the
coast continued to extend their excursions with more or less success:

some went in the direction of Chile and the straits of Magellan, and were not heard of again; others settled at various points on the Peruvian shore; still others penetrated inland and reached Lake Titicaca and the Cuzco region. It is noteworthy that these reputed settlers from the coast found the interior already inhabited and the shrine on Titicaca island in full operation.

Assuming, for the present, that Oliva reported primitive, hence genuine, Indian lore, the following appear to be the essential points of his tales:

(1) The earliest landing in Venezuela, therefore in northeastern South America.

(2) A gradual spread over the northern sections to the westward as far as the coast of Ecuador.

(3) Coast voyages thence to the south as far as the southern extremity of the continent.

(4) After the settlement on the western coast had been effected and some of these voyages were in progress, there took place a landing, from parts unknown, of strange people who were destroyed by some cataclysm and left no impression beyond some remains and recollections of their appearance.

(5) A gradual spread from the coast to the eastward into sections that were already peopled.

The first part of this story recalls <u>Colombian</u> traditions, while the landing of the so-called giants is a <u>local</u> tale heard by the Spaniards on the shores of Ecuador at a very early day. The coast voyages also, as I shall show, were mentioned by Spanish sources half a century prior to Oliva's time.

Oliva acknowledges another source of information---"original papers" given to him by a Dr. Bartolome Cervantes, of Charcas, Bolivia. Under any circumstance all his knowledge is derived at second hand. It bears the stamp of compilation from various sides, as well as the impress of <u>adaptation</u> to the favorite belief in the peopling of America from the old world. Parts of his material, so far as based on local tales, may contain a nucleus of primitive Indian recollection, but it is manifestly woven into a general story highly colored by European ideas.

Among Indian lore collected soon after the conquest, and therefore presumably genuine, there are traces of the drifting of tribes into the interior of Peru from the western coast. On this point Cieza states:

They also relate what I have written in my first part, that on the Island of Titicaca, in former centuries, there were white men, bearded like ourselves, and that, sallying from the valley of Coquimbo, a captain whose name was Cari, he came to where now is Chucuito, whence, after making a few more settlements, he passed with his people over to the island and made such war on the people of which I speak that he killed all of them.

If the word "Coquimbo" is correctly rendered from the original text, and not one of the clerical mistakes that so frequently crept into copies of old manuscripts, then Cari and his men came from the coast of northern Chile. But, as in the case of those who, according to Oliva, would have reached Lake Titicaca from the Peruvian coast, they found the shores and islands of that lake already inhabited. Concerning the white men exterminated by Cari, Cieza fails to state whence they came, but he assures us that he heard the tale from an Indian who may have been well versed in ancient lore.

Montesinos, a contemporary of Simon, Oliva, Calancha, and Piedrahita, treats of the peopling of America in a general way, making the earliest settlers appear from every quarter of the globe, hence also from the South sea. In his own words:

At that time, which as far as I have been able to ascertain was six hundred years after the deluge, all these provinces filled up with people. Many people came from the direction of Chile, others by the Andes, others by the mainland and the South sea, so that its coasts became settled from the island of Santa Elena and Puerto Viejo to Chile; this can be gathered from the poetry and ancient songs of the Indians,

Salcamayhua, an Indian writer of the same period, bases, as he claims, on original lore preserved by the Indians of "Orcasuyo, between Canas and Canchis of Collasuyo," the traditions which he says he heard from his father and other old men. He relates:

They say that, in the time of Purunpacha, all the nations of Tahuantinsuyo came from the direction of above Potossi in three or four armies ready for war, and so they came settling, occupying the places, every band remaining on unoccupied lands.

This hints at a movement of tribes from south to north, in upper Peru and Bolivia. How far the tales are genuine, that is, wholly precolumbian, is not yet easy to ascertain. Salcamayhua makes most fervent protestations of Christianity, so fervent, indeed, that there arises a suspicion of the infiltration of many European elements in his version of native lore. It is particularly marked in what he relates of the person, travels, and deeds of Tonapa. And he merely mentions some migrations to the interior of the continent, without stating whence the settlers originally came.

Pedro de Cieza remarks in a general way: "In Peru the Indians speak of nothing else than that the ones came from one part [direction] and the others from another."

Similar to the stories preserved by the Augustine missionaries, in the sixteenth century, are tales recorded by Miguel Cabello Balboa in his "Antarctic Miscellany" concluded in 1586. But he also furnishes a long story to the effect that South America, or at least the coast of Chile, was peopled originally by pirates from the East Indies. To Balboa I shall return later, having yet to refer to some traditions found in the interior of Peru, likewise in the second half of the sixteenth century and recorded in the year that Balboa finished his work, hence they are either a coincidence or Balboa obtained them from the same source or was told of them by the authorities of Guamanga, who wrote the report on the "Repartimiento de los Rucanas Antamarcas," dated January 27, 1586. This report contains the following statement:

The old Indians say that they have notice from their forefathers, by hearsay, that in very remote times, before the Incas ruled them, there came to this country people whom they called Viracochas, not many of them; and that the Indians followed them, listening to their speech, and now the Indians say they were Saints.

I call attention to the last phrase---that now the Indians call these people "Saints."

Returning to Miguel Cabello Balboa, it is noted, as before stated, that he attributes the settlement of southern Chile to pirates from the East Indies, whom he calls <u>Nayres</u>. He traces the career of these people over nearly the whole eastern world, making a part of them finally land near the southern extremity of America. According to Balboa they were "the origin and trunk of the Indians of Chile, from whom also descend the Chiriguanaes, or (rather) Chiliganaes. By these were made those strange fortifications that in Ayavira and Tiahuanaco (and in other parts of this section of the world) are seen," etc. After the "Nayres" had "conquered the austral regions, they penetrated inland and were never afterward heard from. Their intrusion in these our Indies is conjecture, for the reason that old Indians state they have it from ancient traditions of their forefathers, who told them that from that part of the world there came these pestiferous tyrants [the Nayres], and those of Chile say the same, pointing out that they came from this side of the straits which we call of Magellan."

While the eagerness displayed by Balboa to defend a favorite theory renders his statements liable to suspicion, it is worthy of investigation whether the tales are genuine or not, but I have not at my command the material necessary. While in Peru Balboa joined the order of the Jesuits and was a contemporary of Acosta and of the Dominican Fray Gregorio Garcia. Neither of these, in their classical works on America, makes any mention of his story, a lack manifestly due to their due unacquainted with the "Miscellany," only a part of which, to this time, has appeared in print as a French translation by Henri Ternaux-Compans.

But Cabello Balboa does not confine himself to ancient lore of a <u>general</u> character; he also has preserved what bears every mark of being a genuine local tradition of Indians from the northern Peruvian coast. According to him, the aborigines of the villages of Motupe and Lambayeque said that "in times very remote, so remote that they cannot count them, there came from the upper parts of this Piru, with a great fleet of rafts, a mighty warrior, of great valor and many qualities, called Naymlap, and he had with him a number of concubines, the principal of whom they say was called Ceterni; and with him and in his company he brought many followers whom he led as captain and leader. This chief Naymlap, with his entire retinue, landed and disembarked at the mouth of a river (now called Faquisllanga, where they abandoned their rafts and penetrated inland."

This indicates a coastwise expedition, possibly from some point on the shores of Ecuador, as far as the vicinity of Cichlayo and Lambayeque. It recalls the coast voyages told of by Oliva, and seems to confirm them. There is no apparent connection, however, between the sources of Balboa (who alludes to direct Indian information from tradition) and those mentioned by Oliva; nor is it said that the people led by Naymlap were of extra-American issue.

. . . .

The only traditional record of a <u>landing</u> on the western coast of South America is that of the "giants," near Punta Santa Elena in Ecuador. According to Zarate, it was known to the Spaniards prior to 1543, but not credited until the discovery of large fossil bones in that year furnished, in the light of knowledge of the times, an apparent confirmation. The finding of fossil remains of unusual size was not altogether accidental. The captain Juan de Olmost, lieutenant governor at Puerto Viejo in the year aforesaid, hearing of "all these things, caused excavations to be made in that valley, where they found such large ribs and other bones that, if the skulls had not appeared at the same time, it would not have been credible they were of human persons.... Teeth then found were sent to different parts of Peru; they were three fingers broad and four in length." Although these remains were found beneath the surface, it is possible that some skull had previously been seen by the Indians who founded thereon an "observation myth". On the other hand, the tale may probably be a distorted reminiscence of some precolumbian occurrence on the coast of Ecquador.

It is not likely that the earliest Spanish discoverers of Peru had already heard of the tradition. Oviedo surely would have mentioned it, as he carefully recorded everything that came to his notice at the time. He conversed with Diego de Almagro on the return of the latter to Panama from the first expedition in 1527; in 1534 he questioned several of the returning members of Pizarro's corps, on the island of Santa Domingo, and in 1536 conversed with Pedro de Alvarado. Had any of these mentioned the "giants," Oviedo would not have failed to note it in his voluminous work. It is therefore likely that the Spaniards first heard of the tradition between 1536 and 1543.

The earliest reports on the "giants" are by Cieza and Zarate, printed in 1553 and 1555, respectively. The former says:

The natives tell, from what they heard through their forefathers, who heard and had it from far back, that there came by sea in rafts of reeds after the manner of large boats, some men who were so tall that from the knee down they were as big as the full length of an ordinary fair-sized man, and the limbs were in proportion to their bodies, so misshapen that it was monstrous to look at their heads, as large as they were, and with the hair that came down to the shoulders. The eyes they give to understand were of the size of small plates. They affirm that they had no beards and that some were clad in skins of animals, while others came as nature made them, and there were no women along. Arriving at this point, and after making on it their settlement in the form of a village (even at the present day the sites of the houses are known), they did not find water, and in order to supply the need thereof, made some deep wells, a work that is certainly worthy of remembrance, performed by as strong men as it is presumed they were, judging from their size. And they dug these wells in the live rock until they found water, and afterward lined them with stone to the mouth, in such manner that they will last for many ages, in which [wells] there is always good and savory water, and always so cold that it is a great pleasure to drink it. Having thus established themselves, these tall men or giants, and having these wells or cisterns out of which they drank, they ate and wasted all the food they could find in the land, for each one of them consumed more than fifty of the natives of the country, and as the supply was not sufficient for them, they killed much fish in the sea by means of their nets and contrivances which, it stands to reason, they must have had. The natives abhorred them, for they killed their women in making use of them, and the men they killed for other reasons. The Indians did not feel strong enough to kill these new people that had come to take their country and domain, although great meetings were held to confer about it; but they dare not attack them. After a few years, the giants being still in the country, and having no women, and those of the Indians not suiting their great size, or because it may have been by advice and inducement of the demon, they resorted to the unnatural vice of sodomy, which they committed openly in public, with no fear of God and little shame of themselves.

Then followed the punishment of which I shall treat at length in a subsequent paper---an angel appeared in a mass of fire from heaven and killed them all. Cieza is fully convinced of the truth of the story and refers to the large fossil bones in evidence, showing that he obtained his data after 1543.

Agustin de Zarate differs but little from Cieza in his main statements, except that he does not mention their landing on the coast.

After these two primitive sources, the tale was often repeated, with slight variations. I shall refer to only a part of one of the later versions, contained in an anonymous description of the "government" of Guayaquil, dating from about the year 1605, apparently an official document by one who was intimately acquainted with the district. It says:

They drink water out of wells, especially of one they call of the Giants which, according to the sayings of the ancient Indians, lived in that country, not as original inhabitants, but from other parts.

The fossil remains of large size are also alluded to: "They are chiefly preserved in the deposits of pitch, of which there are few."

It thus seems that the tale of the landing of so-called giants on the coast of southern Ecuador is a genuine Indian tradition from a period antedating the sixteenth century. It appears also that it refers to people entirely distinct from the American natives; but we are at a loss to find even an inkling as to whence these people may have come.

Under these circumstances it is at least premature to attempt conjectures as to the part of the globe whence the so-called giants came. If their original home lay beyond the American continent, some of the island groups of the South sea might be considered as affording the answer. How far the craft in use by the islanders might have enabled such long voyages, and in what manner oceanic currents and winds might have favored or impeded them, are subjects for investigation on the islands themselves.

It is possible that the strange beings came from some point on the western coast of America, although the marked difference in appearance between them and the coast Indians of Ecuador would rather indicate an extra-American origin.

The large stature attributed to the intruders should not be taken too literally. During the course of many ages traditional personages easily assume exaggerated proportions. The Indians of Ecuador and Peru are of low stature, comparatively speaking, and anyone above their average height becomes, in their eyes, first a tall, later a very tall man. If to unusual size, hostile demeanor is added, after a lapse of time aboriginal lore converts him into a monster morally and physically, and it is in some such sense that the term "giant" should be understood---a being with superior physical power and destructive tendencies. As for the manner in which the "giants" came to be exterminated, it may be said that, while the natural phenomenon described in connection with

their destruction seems to indicate the fall of a meteorite of unusual
size, the possibility of some volcanic disturbance should not be excluded.

THE MEXICAN MESSIAH
Daly, Dominick; *American Antiquarian,* 11:14-30, 1889.

There are few more puzzling characters to be found in the pages
of history than Quetzatcoatl, the wandering stranger whom the early
Mexicans adopted as the Air-God of their mythology. That he was a
real personage; that he was a white man from this side of the Atlantic,
who lived and taught in Mexico centuries before Columbus; that what he
taught was Christianity and Christian manners and morals---all these
are plausible inferences from facts and circumstances so peculiar as
to render other conclusion well-nigh impossible.
When, in 1519, Cortez and his 600 companions landed in Mexico
they were astonished at their coming being hailed as the realization of
an ancient native tradition, which ran in this wise: Many centuries
previously a white man had come to Mexico from across the sea (the
Atlantic) in a boat with wings (sails) like those of the Spanish vessels.
He stayed many years in the country and taught the people a system of
religion, instructed them in principles of government, and imparted
to them a knowledge of many industrial arts. He won their esteem
and veneration by his piety, his many virtues, his great wisdom and
his knowledge of divine things. His stay was a kind of golden age for
Mexico. The seasons were uniformly favorable and the earth gave forth
its produce almost spontaneously and in miraculous abundance and
variety. In those days a single head of maize was a load for a man,
the cotton trees produced quantities of cotton already tinted in many
brilliant hues; flowers filled the air with delicious perfumes; birds of
magnificent plumage incessantly poured forth the most exquisite melody.
Under the auspices of this good white man, or god, peace, plenty and
happiness prevailed throughout the land. The Mexicans knew him as
Quetzatcoatl, or the green serpent, the word green in this language
being a term for a rare and precious thing. Through some malign in-
fluence---brought about by the enmity of a rival deity---Quetzatcoatl
was induced or obliged to quit the country. On his way to the coast he
stayed for a time at the city of Cholula, where subsequently a great
pyramidal mound surmounted by a temple was erected in his honor. On
the shores of the gulf of Mexico he took leave of his followers, soothing
their sorrow at his departure with the assurance that he would not forget them, and that he himself or some one sent by him would return at
some future time to visit them. He had made for himself a vessel of
serpents' skins, and in this strange contrivance he sailed away in a
northeasterly direction for his own country, the holy island of Hapallan,
lying beyond the great ocean.
Such in outline was the strange tradition which Cortez found prevalent

in Mexico on his arrival there, and powerfully influencing every inhabitant of the country from the great Montezuma, who ruled as king paramount in the city of Mexico, to the humblest serf who tilled the fields of his lord.   Equally to their surprise and advantage the Spaniards found that their advent was hailed as the fulfilment of the promise of Quetzatcoatl to return.   The natives saw that they were white men and bearded like him, they had come in sailing vessels such as the one he had used across the sea; they had clearly come from the mysterious Hapallan; they were undoubtedly Quetzatcoatl and his brethren come, in fulfilment of ancient prophecy, to restore and permanently re-establish in Mexico the reign of peace and happiness of which the country had had a brief experience many centuries before.

The Spaniards made no scruple of encouraging and confirming a belief so highly favorable to their designs and it is conceded by their writers that this belief to a large extent accounts for the comparative ease and marvelous rapidity with which a mere handful of men made themselves masters of a great and civilized empire and subjugated a warlike population of millions.   To the last the unfortunate emperor Montezuma, in spite of much evidence of the ungodlike character of the Spaniards held to the belief that the king of Spain was Quetzatcoatl and Cortez his lieutenant and emissary under a sort of divine commission.

The Mexicans had preserved a minute and apparently an accurate description of the personal appearance and habits of Quetzatcoatl.   He was a white man, advanced in years and tall in stature.   His forehead was broad; he had a large beard and black hair.   He is described as dressing in a long garment, over which there was a mantle marked with crosses.   He was chaste and austere, temperate and abstemious, fasting frequently and sometimes inflicting severe penances on himself, even to the drawing of blood.   This is a description which was preserved for centuries in the traditions of a people who had no intercourse with or knowledge of Europe, who had never seen a white man, and who were themselves dark skinned with but few scanty hairs on the skin to represent a beard.

It is therefore difficult to suppose that this curiously accurate portraiture of Quetzatcoatl as an early European ecclesiastic was a mere invention in all its parts---a mere fable which happened to hit on every particular and characteristic of such an individual.   Nor is it easier to understand why the early Mexicans should have been at pains to invent a messiah so different from themselves, and with such peculiar attributes.   Yet in spite of destructive wars, revolutions and invasions--- in spite of the breaking up and dispersal of tribes and nations once settled in the vast region now passing under the name of Mexico---the tradition of Quetzatcoatl and the account of his personal peculiarities survived among the people to the days of the Spanish invasion.   Everything therefore tends to show that Quetzatcoatl was an European who by some strange adventure was thrown amongst the Mexican people and left with them recollections of his beneficent influence which time and change did not obliterate.   But time and change must have done much in the course of centuries to confuse the teachings of Quetzatcoatl.   These would naturally be more susceptible of mutation than the few striking items of his personal appearance which (if only on account of their singularity) must have deeply impressed the Mexicans, generation after

generation. Notwithstanding such mutation enough remained of the
teachings of Quetzatcoatl to impress the Spaniards of the sixteenth
century with the belief that he must have been an early Christian missionary as well as a native of Europe. They found that many of the
religious beliefs of the Mexicans bore an unaccountable resemblance
to those of Christians. The Spanish ecclesiastics, in particular, were
astounded at what they saw and knew not what to make of it. Some of
them supposed that St. Thomas, "the apostle of India," had been in the
country and imparted a knowledge of Christianity to the people; others
with pious horror and in mental bewilderment declared that the Evil
One himself had set up a travesty of the religion of Christ for the more
effectual damning of the souls of the pagan Mexicans.

The religion of the Mexicans as the Spaniards found it was in truth
an amazing and most unnatural combination of what appeared to be
Christian beliefs and Christian virtues and morality with the bloody
rites and idolatrous practices of pagan barbarians. The mystery was
soon explained to the Spaniards by the Mexicans themselves. The milder
part of the Mexican religion was that which Quetzatcoatl had taught them.
He had taught it to the Toltecs, a people who had ruled in Mexico some
centuries before the arrival of the Spaniards. The Aztecs were in poses-
sion of power when the Spaniards came and it was they who had introduced
that part of the Mexican religion which was in such strong contrast to
the religion established by Quetzatcoatl. It appeared further that the
Toltec rule in the land had ceased about the middle of the eleventh century. They were a people remarkably advanced in civilization and mental
and moral development. Somewhere between the latter part of the fourth
century and the middle of the seventh century they were supposed to have
come into Mexico from the Northeast---possibly from the Ohio valley,
where vast remains of a strange character have been found. They were
versed in the arts and sciences, and their astronomical knowledge was
in many respects in advance of that of Europe. They established laws
and regular government in Mexico during their stay in the country, but
about the year 1050 A. D. they disappeared south by a voluntary migration, the cause of which remains a mystery. They are supposed to have
been, subsequently, the builders of the great cities the marvelous remains of which are found in the wilds of Central America. In the migration of the Toltecs some remained behind from choice or necessity,
but no attempt appears to have been made at reestablishing a Toltec
empire and government in Mexico.

After the lapse of a century or more from the era of the great Toltec
migration the first bands of Aztecs began to appear. They were wanderers from the Northwest, the Pacific slopes of North America, and were
a fierce and warlike people, possessing little capacity for the mental
and moral refinement and high civilization of their Toltec predecessors.
It was not until the middle of the fourteenth century that the Aztecs
acquired sufficient settled habits to enable them to found states and cities,
and by that time they seem to have adopted so much of what had been left
of Toltec civilization and Toltec religion as they were capable of absorb-
ing, without, however, abandoning their own ruder ideas and propensities.
Hence the incongruous mixture of civilization and barbarism, mildness
and ferocity, gentleness and cruelty, refinement and brutality, presented
by Mexican civilization and religion to the astonished contemplation of the
Spaniards when they entered the city two centuries later. "Aztec civili-

zation was made up" (as Prescott, the author of the History of Mexico, says), "of incongruities apparently irreconcilable. It blended into one the marked peculiarities of different nations, not only of the same phase of civilization, but as far removed from each other as the extremes of barbarism and refinement."

. . . .

• Legends of Technology

THE EXISTENCE OF AMERICA KNOWN EARLY IN THE CHRISTIAN ERA

F., A. L., Jr.; *American Journal of Archaeology,* 4:456, 1888.

In 708 A.D., Jacob of Edessa, the famous Syrian ecclesiastic, encyclopaedist, and writer, wrote his work entitled Hexameron. Attention has been called to its importance by the Abbe Martin in two papers published in the Journal Asiatique (1888). One point is of especial interest. He remarks (p. 455): "I have already said that this learned Syrian had some idea of the existence of a vast continent between Spain and Tingitana, on one side, and China. This appears from his remark concerning an unknown land situated to the East of China, but he speaks of it still more clearly in treating another subject, that of the dimensions of the earth. Jacob says: The length (of the earth) is measured beginning at the Western Ocean; at the gulf placed outside Gadira (Gades?), an island placed in the 5th degree of longitude, at the Western extremity of the inhabited earth. It is said (lit. written) that in front of Spain and the columns of Herakles, between them and the country of the Chinese, which is to the East of India, there is an unknown and uninhabited land."

It is evident, then, that rumors of the existence of America had reached the Syrians, before the time of Jacob of Edessa. Whence could these rumors have come? Possibly from China. It is well known that the Syrian missionaries, especially those belonging to the Nestorian sect, spread over the Far-East and had numerous settlements in India and in China, along the seacoast. This had been an accomplished fact for over two centuries before Jacob of Edessa; and, even at the present day, memorials of their presence are found in China. Communications between the Far-East and Syria were therefore likely to be not infrequent; and these countries seem to have been better known at that time, than they were later, to Arabian travellers and geographers. These facts suggest the interesting enquiries, whether this rumor of an unknown continent reached Syria from China; whether, at this early time, the Chinese were acquainted with the coast of Alaska; and whether their knowledge of America went any further.

THE LAND OF FU-SANG
Anonymous; *Science,* 20:148, 1892.

Now that the discussion of the various discoveries of America is in
order, that which is referred to in Chinese annals as far back as the
seventh century, in connection with the name Fu-Sang, should receive
attention. It was first brought to the notice of scholars in 1761 by the
French orientalist, De Guignes, and of course created some sensation.
Various writers since then have warmly espoused his views, among
whom may be mentioned in our own country Charles G. Leland and E. P.
Vining, both of whom have issued volumes in proof of De Guignes's
identification.

The coup de grace seems to have been dealt the theory by Gustave
Schiegel in his book published in Leyden this year entitled "Fou-Sang
Kouo; le Pays de Fou-Sang." He is a Chinese scholar of acknowledged
competence, and takes up the story as receited in the original, with as
many side-lights as he can bring to bear upon it.

The result of his researches is to knock every pin from under the
notion that any part of America could have been intended in the description of Fu-Sang. As far as any real land can be discerned through the
fog of exaggeration and fable which encircles the whole account, it is
that of the island Krafto or Saghalien, and the people described resembled the Ainos more than any others. A variety of arguments are
adduced to show that Mexico is out of all question; and therefore those
fanciful archaeologists who have been ready to find Buddhistic elements
in American religions will have to look for them elsewhere than in the
legend of Fu-Sang.

DID THE VIKINGS REACH THE PACIFIC COAST?
Rothovius, Andrew E.; *INFO Journal,* 2:1-4, 1969.

In the midst of all the upsurge of interest in recent years over the Viking
voyages to the Atlantic coast of North America---interest sparked by Yale's
discovery of the Vinland Map and the finding of actual remains of Norse
settlements in Newfoundland and northern Labrador---it is somewhat curious
that little or no attention has been drawn to the evidence suggesting that at
least one Viking voyage, and perhaps several, made it all the way around the
top of North America and through the Bering Strait to the Pacific Coast.

Actually, when we consider that at the time of Eric the Red and Leif
Ericson---the 10th and 11th Centuries A. D. ---the Northern Hemisphere was
enjoying the second warmest period since the last Ice Age, and the Arctic ice
was so greatly diminished that sailing vessels would probably have had no
difficulty threading their way through the maze of islands and passages that
form the Northwest Passage north of Canada, there is nothing so very surprising in the idea of the Vikings seeking to find what lay beyond those
passages. Because, however, the prevailing winds in those high latitudes

are from the east, it would have been more difficult for them to make their way back; and the indications are that none who set out on this adventure ever returned.

The first piece of evidence for a Viking voyage to the Pacific comes from the tribal traditions of the Seri Indians on the island of Tiburon in the Gulf of California. Now reduced to only a couple of hundred souls, the Seris were once a much more numerous tribe who were dominant over all the other Indians on the eastern (Mexican mainland) coast of the Gulf. They still tell the tale of the "Come-From-Afar-Men" who, "a long time ago when God was a little boy," landed on Tiburon from a "long boat with a head like a snake."

These strangers, the Seri legends aver, were white-bearded and white-haired, and their womenfolk were red-haired. They hunted the whales that abounded in the Gulf (it was a favorite hunting ground of the Yankee whalers in the 19th Century), cut up their huge carcasses and packed the meat--- which they cooked on shore---in baskets that they wove from the reeds that grew on Tiburon. Then, having thus provisioned themselves, the strangers sailed away down the coast to the south, but had gone only a short distance when their ship ran aground and was ripped apart by the breakers.

The survivors of the wreck swam ashore and were well treated by the Mayo tribe, with whom they intermarried. To this day, the Mayos produce in each generation a few individuals with blonde hair, blue eyes, or both, which they say were characteristics of the "Come-From-Afar-Men"; and until the 1920's they expelled from the tribe all who married outside of it, in order to preserve this heritage.

At the Toronto Meteorological Conference, held Sept. 9 to 15, 1953, Ronald L. Ives of the Cornell Aeronautical Laboratory, Buffalo, N.Y., read a paper on "Climatological Studies in Western North America" in which he cited the above legends, which are given more at length in D. and M. R. Coolidge's "Last of the Seris" (E. P. Dutton, New York, 1939), as supporting evidence for the Secondary Thermal Maximum as the Viking-era warm spell is technically known. Archaeologists, however, took no note of this report; and it has remained unknown to the general public until the recent publication by the World Publishing Co., Cleveland, of "The Mysterious West" by Brad Williams and Choral Pepper.

In this book, the authors refer not only to the Seri legends, but provide additional evidence for Viking ships having reached the Gulf of California area. The still living widow of a Baja California bushwhacker, Santiago Socio, claims that he told her of finding the hull of an ancient ship, with round shields on the gunwales, on the floor of a canyon some 40 kilometers northeast of Tecate on the U. S.-Mexican border east of Tijuana. And in March 1933, Louis and Myrtle Botts of Julian, Calif., well-known as qualified antiquarian researchers, found the dragon prow of a Viking-like ship projecting from a canyon wall near Ague Caliente Springs, just on the U. S. side of the border. The great Long Beach earthquake of that month triggered a rockslide that sealed the canyon before they could further investigate their find.

A further case is adduced, of a settler named Nils Jacobsen finding the remains of a wooden ship in the desert near Imperial City, Calif., in 1907, and using them to build a pig pen. It is possible that this could have been one of the ships of Juan de Iturbe, who in 1615 found his fleet trapped in a now vanished bay at the head of the Gulf of California, and had to abandon them and hike back to Mexico. The reason he gave was that the water level dropped suddenly in the channel leading out of the bay and prevented his ships from sailing out.

Iturbe's story has always been treated skeptically, most authorities believing he lost his ships to pirates and made up the yarn about their being embayed, to escape prosecution for not effectively resisting the buccaneers. Yet it may be he was telling the truth, and that the sudden alterations of sea level to which the head of the Gulf of California appears to be indeed subject, both because of seismic activity and the periodic overflows of the Colorado such as that which created the Salton Sea in the desert sixty years ago, may also have trapped Viking ships that once sailed up narrow inlets into what are now arid canyons. Certainly it would seem that a thorough investigation of this area is in order, to determine whether any Viking artifacts may yet be recoverable that would compel a vast new rethinking of our ideas of the range of these intrepid sea rovers.

THE BUDDHIST DISCOVERY OF AMERICA A THOUSAND YEARS BEFORE COLUMBUS

Fryer, John; *Harper's Monthly Magazine,* 103:251-258, 1901.

The ease of making a trip from Asia to America along the Kurile and Aleutian islands to Alaska strikes one at the first glance. Starting from Kamtchatka, which was early known to the Chinese, and to a certain extent under their control, the voyage in an open boat or canoe, following the great thermal ocean current, could at most times of the year be undertaken without the least danger or difficulty, it being unnecessary to be more than a short time out of sight of land. From Alaska down the American coast the journey would be still easier. Such a trip, compared with some of the well-authenticated wanderings of Buddhist priests, especially of those who travelled overland between China and India, is a mere trifle. Each part of the journey from Asia to America would be as well known to the natives of the various chains of islands in the fifth century as it is now. Hence the zealous missionary, determined to fulfil the commands of Buddha and carry his gospel to all lands, would merely have to press on from one island to another. The natives of each island would tell him of the large continent farther east; and thus he would ultimately find himself in America.

The direct evidence of this early Buddhist mission, though chiefly based on Chinese historical documents, covers also the traditions, histories, religious beliefs, and antiquities to be found in America, extending all the way down the Pacific coast from Alaska to Mexico, as well as to many localities lying at a considerable distance inland.

From early times the Chinese classics, as well as the historical, geographical, and poetical works, allude to a country or continent at a great distance to the east of China, under the name of Fusang or Fusu. Its approximate distance is given as twenty thousand li, or above six thousand five hundred miles. Its breadth is stated to be ten thousand li, or about three thousand two hundred and fifty miles. A wide sea is said to lie beyond it, which would seem like a reference to the Atlantic

Ocean. It grew a wonderful kind of tree called the "fusang," from which
the name of the continent is derived. The name would seem to imply
that this is a species of mulberry, but every part of the description is
utterly unlike any known species of that tree. What answers most nearly to the description is the Mexican agave or maguey. In ancient poetry
the name of this land is used as a synonym for the extreme East, and
many fabulous or fantastic accounts are given of its marvels. No doubt
during the many catastrophes that overtook Chinese literature, whatever
knowledge existed of this distant land became distorted, vague, and even
contradictory. Yet enough was known with certainty to fire the enthu-
siasm of any itinerant Buddhist priest who wanted to spread his religion
to the utmost bounds of the world. He would know of those who had gone
to preach the Buddhist faith in the extreme West, and would naturally
ask why he should not go to the extreme East.

The narrative of only one visit to the land of Fusang is on record in
Chinese history, namely, that of Hui Shen, a native of Cophene, or
Cabul, which was the great centre of Buddhist missionary exertions in
early times. Since this account was considered of sufficient importance to deserve a place in the imperial archives of the Liang dynasty,
and is handed down with the full authority of the great Chinese historian
Ma Tuan-Lin, there should be no doubt as to its authenticity. Any
attempt at fraud or misrepresentation would have been easily detected
at the time, or before very long, and would have been of no advantage
to the narrator, who certainly had nothing to gain but everything to lose
by deception. His short story contains nothing marvellous or unnatural,
and the internal evidence of truthfulness is such that only a foreign
critic would ever suppose it might be a figment of the imagination.

The narrative states that there was a Buddhist priest named Hui
Shen, originally a native of Cabul, who in the year 499 A. D. , during
the reign of the emperor Yung Yuan, came from the country of Fusang
to King-chow, the capital of the dynasty of Tsi, situated on the river
Yang-tse. The country being in a state of revolution, it was not till the
year 502 that he had an opportunity of going to the court of the emperor
Wu Ti, of the new Liang dynasty. He gave presents to the emperor of
curious articles brought from Fusang, among which was a material
looking like silk, but the threads of which could support a great weight
without breaking. This was evidently the fibre of the Mexican agave.
He also presented a mirror of a foot in diameter, possessing wonderful properties, and resembling those in use in Mexico and other localities in America at that time. The emperor treated him as an envoy
from Fusang, and deputed one of the four principal feudal lords, named
Yu Kie, to interrogate him respecting the country, and to take down his
story in writing. This was accordingly done, and we have what is undoubtedly the original text, with only perhaps here and there a typogra-
phical error which can be easily explained.

Among other things, Hui Shen said that the people of Fusang were
formerly in ignorance of the doctrines of Buddha, but during the reign
of the Chinese emperor Ta Ming, of the Sung dynasty, or A. D. 458,
there were five bikshus, or Buddhist monks, from Cabul, who travelled
there and promulgated the knowledge of the doctrines, books, and images
of Buddhism. Their labors were successful, so that they ordained
monks from among the natives; and thus the customs and manners of
the people were soon reformed. He gave particulars of the journey

through the Aleutian Islands, and Alaska, with the length of the route, and a description of the inhabitants. He described the country of Fusang as twenty thousand li, or six thousand five hundred miles, to the east of Kamtchatka, and also due east from China. It grows great numbers of fusang-trees, which when they first appear aboveground are like bamboo shoots, and the people eat them. Threads are spun from the skin of the plant, which are woven into cloth from which clothing is made, or else it is made into embroidery. They also use the fibrous material of the fusang for making paper. These and many other features seem to point unmistakably to the Mexican agave. Red pears are mentioned which agree in description with the fruit of the prickly-pear, while grapes are represented as plentiful. There is plenty of copper, but no iron; and no money value is put on gold or silver. Their markets are free, and there are no fixed prices.

The manners and customs of the people, their forms of government, their marriage and funeral ceremonies, their food and clothing, the method of constructing their houses, the absence of soldiers and military weapons, cities and fortresses, are all particularly noted, and agree with what is found in no countries bordering on the Pacific, except on the continent of America in general, and in Mexico in particular. To suppose that Hui Shen could have invented all these statements, and that his story can be satisfactorily explained upon any other theory than that he had actually made the journey which he so truthfully and soberly describes, is to say the least of it absurd.

But it is time to take another view of the subject, and search for proofs of Hui Shen's visit among the early inhabitants of the American continent. There exists in Mexico a tradition of the visit of an extraordinary personage having a white complexion, and clothed in a long robe and mantle, who taught the people to abstain from evil and to live righteously, soberly, and peacefully. At last he met with severe persecutions, and his life being threatened, he suddenly disappeared, but left the imprint of his foot on a rock. A statue erected to his memory still stands upon a high rock at the village of Magdalena. He bore the name of Wi-shi-pecocha, which is probably a transliteration of Hui Shen bikshu. Another foreign teacher is described as coming with his followers to Mexico, named Quetzalcoatl. He landed on the Pacific coast, coming from the north by way of Panuco, and was most probably the leader of the party of five Buddhist priests that are already referred to. Hui Shen may have been one of the five, from the rest of whom he may afterwards have become separated, and then returned to China alone. The teachings ascribed to these visitors closely resemble those of Buddhism.

The religious customs and beliefs of the nations of Mexico, Yucatan, and Central America, their architecture, their calendar, their arts, and many other things which were found by the Spaniards when they conquered America, exhibit the most surprising coincidences with the details of Asiatic beliefs and Asiatic civilization. So much is this the case that those independent observers who have known nothing of the story of Hui Shen have been convinced that there must have been some kind of communication between America and Asia since the beginning of the Christian era. Thirty-five of these coincidences are given by Mr. Edward P. Vining, of San Francisco, in his exhaustive study of the subject, contained in his work entitled, An Inglorious Columbus. He says: "Almost any one of these coincidences might be fortuitous, but it seems impossible that so many coincidences could have existed unless the civilization of one continent was to some extent borrowed from the other." It may be added that the majority of these coincidences point most unmistakably to Buddhism, and if not actually introduced by Hui Shen and the party of Buddhist priests which he mentions, they must have been introduced in some similar way.

Searching for traces of Buddhist origin among the old names of persons, places, and things in America brings to light some curious facts. The name "Buddha" is not in general use in Asia, but instead is used his patronymic, "Gautama," or the name of his race, "Sakhya." Hence we may expect to find these names constantly recurring in America. In the places Guatemala, Huatamo, etc., in the high-priest Guatemotzin, etc., we find echoes of the first of these names. In Oaxaca, Zacatecas, Sacatepec. Zacatlan, Sacapulas, etc., we find more than a hint of the second. In fact, the high-priest of Mixteca had the title "Taysacca," or the man of Sacca. On an image representing Buddha at Palenque there is the name "Chaac-mol," which might have been derived from Sakhyamuni, the full rendering of one of Buddha's names. The Buddhist priests in Tibet and North China are called "lamas," and the Mexican priest is known as the "tlama." A deified priest or lama, who is said to have lived on a small island near the Colorado River, had the name of Quatu Sacca, which seems to combine the two names Gautama and Sakhya. No very great value, however, is due to any single case of these resemblances to Buddhist names, but there being so many makes it highly probable that they are not all accidental. Again, it is worthy of notice that if "fusang" was used by Hui Shen to represent the maguey or agave plant, then as Mexico signifies "the place or region of the agave," it follows naturally that if Mexico was the country he visited, he would call it the country of the "fusang."

When we come to look for visible traces of Buddhism among the antiquities of Mexico, we are soon amply rewarded. Images and sculptured tablets, ornaments, temples, pyramids, etc., abound that cannot well be ascribed to any other source with the show of reason. Among these may be mentioned the following: A large image found in Campeachy representing accurately a Buddhist priest in his robes.---An image of Buddha at Palenque, sitting cross-legged on a seat formed of two lions placed back to back, closely representing images found in India and China.---An elaborate elephant-faced god found among the Aztecs, which is evidently an imitation of the Indian image of Ganesha.---A Buddhist altar or table of stone found at Palenque.---Figures of Buddha sitting cross-legged with an aureola around his head, and placed in niches in the walls of the temples at Uxmal, Palenque, etc., being the exact counterparts of the images found in niches both inside and outside of Buddhist temples in China, Japan, and India.---A perfect elephant's head sculptured on the walls at Palenque, the elephant being the usual symbol of Buddha in Asia, and no elephants being found in America.--- An old Mexican image now in the Ethnographical Societies' museum at Paris, and depicting Buddha sitting in the usual cross-legged attitude, with an inscription on either side, one of the characters being evidently intended for the Chinese character for Buddha, but engraved by a sculptor who did not know the Chinese written language.---On the walls of the temple of Uxmal there are astronomical diagrams and images, representing among other things the dragon which causes eclipses by

swallowing the sun---a thoroughly Chinese notion---but instead of
scales it is covered with feathers, showing the idea that it can fly.---
The enormous temples or palaces at Palenque and Mitla are almost the
counterparts of Buddhist temples that are found in Asia, particularly
in Java, North China, and Mongolia, the large pyramidal base and the
mode of construction all seeming to point to Buddhist origin.---The
ornaments in the walls of the temples in different parts of Mexico are
similar in design to those of many buildings in China and India; particularly the pattern known as the "Greek fret" or "Greek key" pattern,
which is found in an almost endless variety of diamond fret, labyrinth
fret, meander fret, double fret---having the fillets interlacing at right
angles---and others for which we have no names. These may be seen
to advantage in pictures of the walls of the "Room of Mosaics," of
Mitla, at Uxmal, and elsewhere.---There is a Buddhist cross, or symbol of Buddha, carved on a pillar at Palenque.

It must be acknowledged that there are many difficulties and inconsistencies in Hui Shen's account of the introduction of Buddhism into
Fusang, or America. These, however, are easily accounted for when
it is remembered he was a native of Cabul, speaking Chinese imperfectly, while Yu Kie, who had never travelled, must have failed to understand some of his statements. The account was written before printing
was in use, and hence in the copying many errors may have crept in.
Furthermore, the Chinese characters are subject to changes, in the
lapse of time, both in sound and meaning. Again, when the Spanish
overran America they soon abolished all the features of the indigenous
civilization, which they supplanted by their own. Hence proofs which
may then have remained of the introduction of Buddhism in the fifth
century may have been soon swept out of existence.

. . . .

SIRIUS—A CONJECTURE AND AN APPEAL

McCrea, W. H.; *British Astronomical Association, Journal,* 84:63-64,
1973.

The beliefs of the Dogon about Sirius are fully documented. They
hold that Sirius has a dark companion star in orbit about it, that the
companion becomes visible once a year, that Sirius, and this companion
when seen, are white but may seem to be red. The companion when
seen is said to have curious shapes and behaviour. It is said also to be
exceedingly dense. The Dogon say that it goes round Sirius in a period
counted twice to be a hundred years. They say that there is a third member of the system that also goes round Sirius in the same sense, with
the same period, but much further out. All this is said to be a well-
guarded tribal mystery which has been handed down since the forgotten
origins of the Dogon; it seems clear that it depends upon no observations
known to the Dogon themselves.

It is well known that the ancient Egyptians attached great significance to the heliacal rising (and setting) or Sirius, and that they watched for it and observed it with much assiduity. Looking east or west from any-where near the Nile Valley to see the rising or setting Sun, the Egyptian observers would have had to look across a desert. This is the usual sit-uation for the occurrence of a mirage over land. Normally a mirage provides one or more images in addition to the observed object itself and in general all are seen in line one above the other. One would sup-pose the conditions to be more favourable for producing a mirage at sun-set (rather than at sunrise) when the hot sand is cooling rapidly so that there could be a temperature inversion quite close to the ground. This would give an "inferior mirage", with the image well below the object itself. Were the object Sirius, the appearance would be of Sirius sinking to the horizon preceded by an apparent companion. This would give the impression that the 'companion' is heavier than the brightest star in the sky, and so presumably much more dense. Obviously this observation would be possible only once a year, at the time of the heliacal setting of Sirius. At any other time when Sirius is visible, no 'companion' would be seen, and so the supposed companion would have to be considered dark. Also, seen close to the horizon at sunset, Sirius would be apt to appear redder than at other times; any mirage image would have closely the same colour as the object itself. Under certain conditions, there could be a second image further from the object; were the atmosphere rather unsteady, an image could be distorted into some of the fantastic shapes that are seen in mirages; all this would agree with some of the Dogon descriptions.

Nearly all the Dogon effects could thus be accounted for in a very simple manner. These effects would, of course, have nothing whatever to do with the actual companion Sirius B, about which they and their predecessors could have discovered nothing by any known means. The one effect that might seem to be exceptional is the alleged period. A mirage image would not show any periodicity; on the other hand the alleged period seems to be about 50 years, and the period of the actual binary Sirius A, B is 49.9 years! Incredible as the coincidence may seem, it is even more incredible that it could be anything but fortuitous. In any case the time mentioned is 100 years and, even if this is meant to be the period counted twice, the coincidence is less startling than it would be were 50 years explicitly quoted in the first place. However, one surmises that the original observers detected no period so that, if they felt there had to be a period, it would be natural to give a figure longer than anyone could well observe. Also the fact that they gave the same 'period' also for the supposed second companion is further indica-tion that they were simply guessing.

Thus the people that we do know to have observed Sirius under appro-priate conditions could apparently have found all, or almost all, the re-ported phenomena. Were this idea valid so far as it goes, it would still be a fascinating problem to discover how the Dogon people acquired their beliefs in these phenomena (and to discover whether any other cultures included similar beliefs).

SUBJECT INDEX

81819